Library of
Davidson College

*The*

*Making of the*

*American*

*Republic*

# IN CONGRESS, JULY 4, 1776.

## The unanimous Declaration of the thirteen united States of America.

When in the Course of human events, it becomes necessary for one people to dissolve the political bands which have connected them with another, and to assume among the powers of the earth, the separate and equal station to which the Laws of Nature and of Nature's God entitle them, a decent respect to the opinions of mankind requires that they should declare the causes which impel them to the separation.

We hold these truths to be self-evident, that all men are created equal, that they are endowed by their Creator with certain unalienable Rights, that among these are Life, Liberty and the pursuit of Happiness.—That to secure these rights, Governments are instituted among Men, deriving their just powers from the consent of the governed,—That whenever any Form of Government becomes destructive of these ends, it is the Right of the People to alter or to abolish it, and to institute new Government, laying its foundation on such principles and organizing its powers in such form, as to them shall seem most likely to effect their Safety and Happiness. Prudence, indeed, will dictate that Governments long established should not be changed for light and transient causes; and accordingly all experience hath shewn, that mankind are more disposed to suffer, while evils are sufferable, than to right themselves by abolishing the forms to which they are accustomed. But when a long train of abuses and usurpations, pursuing invariably the same Object evinces a design to reduce them under absolute Despotism, it is their right, it is their duty, to throw off such Government, and to provide new Guards for their future security.—Such has been the patient sufferance of these Colonies; and such is now the necessity which constrains them to alter their former Systems of Government. The history of the present King of Great Britain is a history of repeated injuries and usurpations, all having in direct object the establishment of an absolute Tyranny over these States. To prove this, let Facts be submitted to a candid world.

He has refused his Assent to Laws, the most wholesome and necessary for the public good.
He has forbidden his Governors to pass Laws of immediate and pressing importance, unless suspended in their operation till his Assent should be obtained; and when so suspended, he has utterly neglected to attend to them.
He has refused to pass other Laws for the accommodation of large districts of people, unless those people would relinquish the right of Representation in the Legislature, a right inestimable to them and formidable to tyrants only.
He has called together legislative bodies at places unusual, uncomfortable, and distant from the depository of their public Records, for the sole purpose of fatiguing them into compliance with his measures.
He has dissolved Representative Houses repeatedly, for opposing with manly firmness his invasions on the rights of the people.
He has refused for a long time, after such dissolutions, to cause others to be elected; whereby the Legislative powers, incapable of Annihilation, have returned to the People at large for their exercise; the State remaining in the mean time exposed to all the dangers of invasion from without, and convulsions within.
He has endeavoured to prevent the population of these States; for that purpose obstructing the Laws for Naturalization of Foreigners; refusing to pass others to encourage their migrations hither, and raising the conditions of new Appropriations of Lands.
He has obstructed the Administration of Justice, by refusing his Assent to Laws for establishing Judiciary powers.
He has made Judges dependent on his Will alone, for the tenure of their offices, and the amount and payment of their salaries.
He has erected a multitude of New Offices, and sent hither swarms of Officers to harrass our people, and eat out their substance.
He has kept among us, in times of peace, Standing Armies without the Consent of our legislatures.
He has affected to render the Military independent of and superior to the Civil power.
He has combined with others to subject us to a jurisdiction foreign to our constitution, and unacknowledged by our laws; giving his Assent to their Acts of pretended Legislation:—For Quartering large bodies of armed troops among us:—For protecting them, by a mock Trial, from punishment for any Murders which they should commit on the Inhabitants of these States:—For cutting off our Trade with all parts of the world:—For imposing Taxes on us without our Consent:—For depriving us in many cases, of the benefits of Trial by Jury:—For transporting us beyond Seas to be tried for pretended offences:—For abolishing the free System of English Laws in a neighbouring Province, establishing therein an Arbitrary government, and enlarging its Boundaries so as to render it at once an example and fit instrument for introducing the same absolute rule into these Colonies:—For taking away our Charters, abolishing our most valuable Laws, and altering fundamentally the Forms of our Governments:—For suspending our own Legislatures, and declaring themselves invested with power to legislate for us in all cases whatsoever.
He has abdicated Government here, by declaring us out of his Protection and waging War against us.
He has plundered our seas, ravaged our Coasts, burnt our towns, and destroyed the lives of our people.
He is at this time transporting large Armies of foreign Mercenaries to compleat the works of death, desolation and tyranny, already begun with circumstances of Cruelty & perfidy scarcely paralleled in the most barbarous ages, and totally unworthy the Head of a civilized nation.
He has constrained our fellow Citizens taken Captive on the high Seas to bear Arms against their Country, to become the executioners of their friends and Brethren, or to fall themselves by their Hands.
He has excited domestic insurrections amongst us, and has endeavoured to bring on the inhabitants of our frontiers, the merciless Indian Savages, whose known rule of warfare, is an undistinguished destruction of all ages, sexes and conditions.

In every stage of these Oppressions We have Petitioned for Redress in the most humble terms: Our repeated Petitions have been answered only by repeated injury. A Prince, whose character is thus marked by every act which may define a Tyrant, is unfit to be the ruler of a free people. Nor have We been wanting in attentions to our British brethren. We have warned them from time to time of attempts by their legislature to extend an unwarrantable jurisdiction over us. We have reminded them of the circumstances of our emigration and settlement here. We have appealed to their native justice and magnanimity, and we have conjured them by the ties of our common kindred to disavow these usurpations, which, would inevitably interrupt our connections and correspondence. They too have been deaf to the voice of justice and of consanguinity. We must, therefore, acquiesce in the necessity, which denounces our Separation, and hold them, as we hold the rest of mankind, Enemies in War, in Peace Friends.

We, therefore, the Representatives of the united States of America, in General Congress, Assembled, appealing to the Supreme Judge of the world for the rectitude of our intentions, do, in the Name, and by Authority of the good People of these Colonies, solemnly publish and declare, That these United Colonies are, and of Right ought to be Free and Independent States; that they are Absolved from all Allegiance to the British Crown, and that all political connection between them and the State of Great Britain, is and ought to be totally dissolved; and that as Free and Independent States, they have full Power to levy War, conclude Peace, contract Alliances, establish Commerce, and to do all other Acts and Things which Independent States may of right do. And for the support of this Declaration, with a firm reliance on the protection of divine Providence, we mutually pledge to each other our Lives, our Fortunes and our sacred Honor.

# The Making of the American Republic

## THE GREAT DOCUMENTS, 1774-1789

EDITED BY

CHARLES CALLAN TANSILL

Arlington House   New Rochelle, New York

Prepared Under the General Supervision of
H. H. B. Meyer
Former Director, Legislative Reference Service
Library of Congress

Library of Congress Catalog Card Number: 72–78484

ISBN 0–87000–181–7

MANUFACTURED IN THE UNITED STATES OF AMERICA

# CONTENTS

| | Page |
|---|---|
| Declaration and resolves of the First Continental Congress, October 14, 1774.. | 1–5 |
| Resolves adopted in Charlotte Town, Mecklenburg County, N. C., May 31, 1775. | 6–9 |
| Declaration of the causes and necessity of taking up arms, July 6, 1775........ | 10–17 |
| Resolution of secrecy adopted by the Continental Congress, November 9, 1775.. | 18 |
| Preamble and resolution of the Virginia Convention, May 15, 1776, instructing the Virginia Delegates in the Continental Congress to "propose to that respectable body to declare the United Colonies free and independent States".. | 19–20 |
| Resolution introduced in the Continental Congress by Richard Henry Lee (Virginia) proposing a Declaration of Independence, June 7, 1776........... | 21 |
| Declaration of Independence, July 4, 1776................................. | 22–26 |
| Articles of Confederation, March 1, 1781.................................... | 27–37 |
| Resolution of the General Assembly of Virginia, January 21, 1786, proposing a joint meeting of commissioners from the States to consider and recommend a Federal plan for regulating commerce..................................... | 38 |
| Proceedings of commissioners to remedy defects of the Federal Government, Annapolis, Md., 1786................................................. | 39–43 |
| Report of proceedings in Congress, Wednesday, February 21, 1787............ | 44–46 |
| Ordinance of 1787, July 13, 1787.......................................... | 47–54 |
| Credentials of the members of the Federal Convention...................... | 55–84 |
| List of delegates appointed by the States represented in the Federal Convention. | 85–86 |
| Notes of Major William Pierce (Georgia) in the Federal Convention of 1787: | |
|    *a.* Loose sketches and notes taken in the convention, May, 1787.......... | 87–95 |
|    *b.* Characters in the convention of the States held at Philadelphia, May, 1787................................................................ | 96–108 |
| Debates in the Federal Convention of 1787 as reported by James Madison.... | 109–745 |
| Secret proceedings and debates of the convention assembled at Philadelphia, in the year 1787, for the purpose of forming the Constitution of the United States of America. (From the notes taken by the late Robert Yates, Esq., Chief Justice of New York (Albany, 1821))..................................... | 746–843 |
| Notes of Rufus King in the Federal Convention of 1787.................... | 844–878 |
| Notes of William Paterson in the Federal Convention of 1787............... | 879–912 |
| Notes of Alexander Hamilton in the Federal Convention of 1787............ | 913–922 |
| Papers of Dr. James McHenry on the Federal Convention of 1787............ | 923–952 |
| Variant texts of the Virginia plan presented by Edmund Randolph to the Federal Convention, May 29, 1787: | |
|    Text A...................................................... | 953–956 |
|    Text B...................................................... | 957–959 |
|    Text C...................................................... | 960–963 |
| The plan of Charles Pinckney (South Carolina), presented to the Federal Convention, May 29, 1787................................................. | 964–966 |

## Contents

Page

Variant texts of the plan presented by William Paterson (New Jersey), to the Federal Convention, June 15, 1787:

    Text A............................................................ 967–970
    Text B............................................................ 971–974
    Text C............................................................ 975–978

Variant texts of the plan presented by Alexander Hamilton to the Federal Convention, June 18, 1787:

    Text A............................................................ 979–980
    Text B............................................................ 981–982
    Text C............................................................ 983–984
    Text D............................................................ 985–986
    Text E............................................................ 987–988

The Constitution of the United States................................ 989–1002

Letter of the president of the Federal Convention, September 17, 1787, to the President of Congress, transmitting the Constitution................... 1003–1004

Resolution of the Federal Convention submitting the Constitution to Congress, September 17, 1787............................................... 1005–1006

Resolution of Congress, September 28, 1787, submitting the Constitution to the several States...................................................... 1007

Circular letter of the Secretary of Congress, September 28, 1787, transmitting copy of the Constitution to the several governors........................ 1008

Ratification of the Constitution by the several States, arranged in the order of their ratification................................................. 1009–1059

Resolution of Congress, July 2, 1788, submitting ratifications of the Constitution to a committee.................................................. 1060–1061

Resolution of the Congress, September 13, 1788, fixing date for the election of a President, and the organization of the Government under the Constitution.. 1062

Resolution of the First Congress submitting 12 amendments to the Constitution............................................................... 1063–1065

The first 10 amendments to the Constitution............................ 1066–1067

Subsequent amendments to the Constitution.............................. 1068–1072

# DECLARATION AND RESOLVES OF THE FIRST CONTINENTAL CONGRESS OCTOBER 14, 1774

Whereas, since the close of the last war, the British parliament, claiming a power, of right, to bind the people of America by statutes in all cases whatsoever, hath, in some acts, expressly imposed taxes on them, and in others, under various pretences, but in fact for the purpose of raising a revenue, hath imposed rates and duties payable in these colonies, established a board of commissioners, with unconstitutional powers, and extended the jurisdiction of courts of admiralty, not only for collecting the said duties, but for the trial of causes merely arising within the body of a county.

And whereas, in consequence of other statutes, judges, who before held only estates at will in their offices, have been made dependant on the crown alone for their salaries, and standing armies kept in times of peace: And whereas it has lately been resolved in parliament, that by force of a statute, made in the thirty-fifth year of the reign of King Henry the Eighth, colonists may be transported to England, and tried there upon accusations for treasons and misprisions, or concealments of treasons committed in the colonies, and by a late statute, such trials have been directed in cases therein mentioned:

And whereas, in the last session of parliament, three statutes were made; one entitled, "An act to discontinue, in such manner and for such time as are therein mentioned, the landing and discharging, lading, or shipping of goods, wares and merchandise, at the town, and within the harbour of Boston, in the province of Massachusetts-Bay in North-America;" another entitled, "An act for the better regulating the government of the province of Massachusetts-Bay in New England;" and another entitled, "An act for the impartial administration of justice, in the cases of persons questioned for any act done by them in the execution of the law, or for the suppression of riots and tumults, in the province of the Massachusetts-Bay in New England;" and another statute was then made, "for making more effectual provision for the government of the province of Quebec, etc." All which statutes are impolitic, unjust, and cruel, as well as unconstitutional, and most dangerous and destructive of American rights:

And whereas, assemblies have been frequently dissolved, contrary to the rights of the people, when they attempted to deliberate on grievances; and their dutiful, humble, loyal, and reasonable petitions to the crown for redress, have been repeatedly treated with contempt, by his Majesty's ministers of state:

The good people of the several colonies of New-Hampshire, Massachusetts-Bay, Rhode-Island and Providence Plantations, Connecticut, New-York, New-Jersey, Pennsylvania, Newcastle, Kent, and Sussex on Delaware, Maryland, Virginia, North-Carolina, and South-Carolina, justly alarmed at these arbitrary proceedings of parliament and administration, have severally elected, constituted, and appointed deputies to meet, and sit in general Congress, in the city of Philadelphia, in order to obtain such establishment, as that their religion, laws, and liberties, may not be subverted: Whereupon the deputies so appointed being now assembled, in a full and free representation of these colonies, taking into their most serious consideration, the best means of attaining the ends aforesaid, do, in the first place, as Englishmen, their ancestors in like cases have usually done, for asserting and vindicating their rights and liberties, DECLARE,

That the inhabitants of the English colonies in North-America, by the immutable laws of nature, the principles of the English constitution, and the several charters or compacts, have the following RIGHTS:

*Resolved, N. C. D.* 1. That they are entitled to life, liberty and property: and they have never ceded to any foreign power whatever, a right to dispose of either without their consent.

*Resolved, N. C. D.* 2. That our ancestors, who first settled these colonies, were at the time of their emigration from the mother country, entitled to all the rights, liberties, and immunities of free and natural-born subjects, within the realm of England.

*Resolved, N. C. D.* 3. That by such emigration they by no means forfeited, surrendered, or lost any of those rights, but that they were, and their descendants now are, entitled to the exercise and enjoyment of all such of them, as their local and other circumstances enable them to exercise and enjoy.

*Resolved,* 4. That the foundation of English liberty, and of all free government, is a right in the people to participate in their legislative council: and as the English colonists are not represented, and from their local and other circumstances, cannot properly be represented in the British parliament, they are entitled to a free and exclusive power of legislation in their several provincial legislatures, where their right of representation can alone be preserved, in all cases of taxation and internal polity, subject only to the negative of their sovereign, in such manner as has been heretofore used and accustomed: But, from the necessity of the case, and a regard to the mutual interest of both countries, we cheerfully consent to the operation of such acts of the British parliament, as are bona fide, restrained to the regulation of our external commerce, for the purpose of securing the commercial advantages of the whole empire to the mother country, and the commercial benefits of its respective members; excluding every idea of taxation internal or external, for raising a revenue on the subjects, in America, without their consent.

*Resolved, N. C. D.* 5. That the respective colonies are entitled to the common law of England, and more especially to the great and inestimable privilege of being tried by their peers of the vicinage, according to the course of that law.

*Resolved,* 6. That they are entitled to the benefit of such of the English statutes, as existed at the time of their colonization; and which they have, by experience, respectively found to be applicable to their several local and other circumstances.

*Resolved, N. C. D.* 7. That these, his majesty's colonies, are likewise entitled to all the immunities and privileges granted and confirmed to them by royal charters, or secured by their several codes of provincial laws.

*Resolved, N. C. D.* 8. That they have a right peaceably to assemble, consider of their grievances, and petition the king; and that all prosecutions, prohibitory proclamations, and commitments for the same, are illegal.

*Resolved, N. C. D.* 9. That the keeping a standing army in these colonies, in times of peace, without the consent of the legislature of that colony, in which such army is kept, is against law.

*Resolved, N. C. D.* 10. It is indispensably necessary to good government, and rendered essential by the English constitution, that the constituent branches of the legislature be independent of each other; that, therefore, the exercise of legislative power in several colonies, by a council appointed, during pleasure, by the crown, is unconstitutional, dangerous and destructive to the freedom of American legislation.

All and each of which the aforesaid deputies, in behalf of themselves, and their constituents, do claim, demand, and insist on, as their indubitable rights and liberties; which cannot be legally taken from them, altered or abridged by any power whatever, without their own consent, by their representatives in their several provincial legislatures.

In the course of our inquiry, we find many infringements and violations of the foregoing rights, which, from an ardent desire, that harmony and mutual intercourse of affection and interest may be restored, we pass over for the present, and proceed to state such acts and measures as have been adopted since the last war, which demonstrate a system formed to enslave America.

*Resolved, N. C. D.* That the following acts of parliament are infringements and violations of the rights of the colonists; and that the repeal of them is essentially necessary, in order to restore harmony between Great-Britain and the American colonies, viz.

The several acts of 4 Geo. III. ch. 15, and ch. 34.—5 Geo. III. ch. 25.—6 Geo. III. ch. 52.—7 Geo. III. ch. 41. and ch. 46.—8 Geo. III. ch. 22. which impose duties for the purpose of raising a revenue in America, extend the power of the admiralty courts beyond their ancient limits, deprive the American subject of trial by jury, authorise the judges certificate to indemnify the prosecutor from damages, that he might otherwise be liable to, requiring oppressive security from a claimant of ships and goods seized, before he shall be allowed to defend his property, and are subversive of American rights.

Also 12 Geo. III. ch. 24. intituled, "An act for the better securing his majesty's dockyards, magazines, ships, ammunition, and stores," which declares a new offence in America, and deprives the American subject of a constitutional trial by jury of the vicinage, by authorising the trial of any person, charged with the committing any offence described in the said act, out of the realm, to be indicted and tried for the same in any shire or county within the realm.

Also the three acts passed in the last session of parliament, for stopping the port and blocking up the harbour of Boston, for altering the charter and government of Massachusetts-Bay, and that which is entitled, "An act for the better administration of justice, etc."

Also the act passed in the same session for establishing the Roman Catholic religion, in the province of Quebec, abolishing the equitable system of English laws, and erecting a tyranny there, to the great danger (from so total a dissimilarity of religion, law and government) of the neighbouring British colonies, by the assistance of whose blood and treasure the said country was conquered from France.

Also the act passed in the same session, for the better providing suitable quarters for officers and soldiers in his majesty's service, in North-America.

Also, that the keeping a standing army in several of these colonies, in time of peace, without the consent of the legislature of that colony, in which such army is kept, is against law.

To these grievous acts and measures, Americans cannot submit, but in hopes their fellow subjects in Great-Britain will, on a revision of them, restore us to that state, in which both countries found happiness and prosperity, we have for the present, only resolved to pursue the following peaceable measures: 1. To enter into a non-importation, non-consumption, and non-exportation agreement or association. 2. To prepare an address to the people of Great-Britain, and a memorial to the inhabitants of British America: and 3. To prepare a loyal address to his majesty, agreeable to resolutions already entered into.[1]

---
[1] Journals of Congress (ed. 1800), I., pp. 26-30.

# RESOLVES ADOPTED IN CHARLOTTE TOWN, MECKLENBURG COUNTY, NORTH CAROLINA, MAY 31, 1775

Charlotte *Town*, Mecklenburg *County*, May 31.
*This Day the* Committee *met, and passed the following*

RESOLVES:

Whereas by an Address presented to his Majesty by both Houses of Parliament in *February* last, the *American* Colonies are declared to be in a State of actual Rebellion, we conceive that all Laws and Commissions confirmed by, or derived from the Authority of the King or Parliament, are annulled and vacated, and the former civil Constitution of these Colonies for the present wholly suspended. To provide in some Degree for the Exigencies of the County in the present alarming Period, we deem it proper and necessary to pass the following Resolves, *viz.*

1. That all Commissions, civil and military, heretofore granted by the Crown, to be exercised in these Colonies, are null and void, and the Constitution of each particular Colony wholly suspended.

2. That the Provincial Congress of each Province, under the Direction of the Great Continental Congress, is invested with all legislative and executive Powers within their respective Provinces; and that no other Legislative or Executive does or can exist, at this Time, in any of these Colonies.

3. As all former Laws are now suspended in this Province, and the Congress have not yet provided others, we judge it necessary, for the better Preservation of good Order, to form certain Rules and Regulations for the internal Government of this County, until Laws shall be provided for us by the Congress.

4. That the Inhabitants of this County do meet on a certain Day appointed by this Committee, and having formed themselves into nine Companies, to *wit*, eight for the County, and one for the Town of *Charlotte*, do choose a Colonel and other military Officers, who shall hold and exercise their several Powers by Virtue of this Choice, and independent of *Great-Britain*, and former Constitution of this Province.

5. That for the better Preservation of the Peace, and Administration of Justice, each of these Companies do choose from their own Body two discreet Freeholders, who shall be impowered each by himself, and singly, to decide and determine all Matters of Controversy arising within the said Company under the Sum of Twenty Shillings, and jointly and together all Controversies under the Sum of Forty Shillings, yet so as their Decisions may admit of Appeals to the Convention of the Select Men of the whole County; and also, that any one of these shall have Power to examine, and commit to Confinement, Persons accused of Petit Larceny.

6. That those two Select Men, thus chosen, do, jointly and together, choose from the Body of their particular Company two Persons, properly qualified to serve as Constables, who may assist them in the Execution of their Office.

7. That upon the Complaint of any Person to either of these Select Men, he do issue his Warrant, directed to the Constable, commanding him to bring the Aggressor before him or them to answer the said Complaint.

8. That these eighteen Select Men, thus appointed, do meet every third *Tuesday* in *January*, *April*, *July*, and *October*, at the Court-House, in *Charlotte*, to hear and determine all Matters of Controversy for Sums exceeding Forty Shillings; also Appeals: And in Cases of Felony, to commit the Person or Persons convicted thereof to close Confinement, until the Provincial Congress shall provide and establish Laws and Modes of Proceeding in all such Cases.

9. That these Eighteen Select Men, thus convened, do choose a Clerk to record the Transactions of said Convention; and that the said Clerk, upon the Application of any Person or Persons aggrieved, do issue his Warrant to one of the Constables, to summons and warn said Offender to appear before the Convention at their next sitting, to answer the aforesaid Complaint.

10. That any Person making complaint upon Oath to the Clerk, or any Member of the Convention, that he has Reason to suspect that any Person or Persons indebted to him in a Sum above Forty Shillings, do intend clandestinely to withdraw from the County

without paying such Debt; the Clerk, or such Member, shall issue his Warrant to the Constable, commanding him to take the said Person or Persons into safe Custody, until the next sitting of the Convention.

11. That when a Debtor for a Sum below Forty Shillings shall abscond and leave the County, the Warrant granted as aforesaid shall extend to any Goods or Chattels of the said Debtor as may be found, and such Goods or Chattels be seized and held in Custody by the Constable for the Space of Thirty Days; in which Term if the Debtor fails to return and discharge the Debt, the Constable shall return the Warrant to one of the Select Men of the Company where the Goods and Chattels are found, who shall issue Orders to the Constable to sell such a Part of the said Goods as shall amount to the Sum due; that when the Debt exceeds Forty Shillings, the Return shall be made to the Convention, who shall issue the Orders for Sale.

12. That all Receivers and Collectors of Quitrents, Public and County Taxes, do pay the same into the Hands of the Chairman of this Committee, to be by them disbursed as the public Exigencies may require. And that such Receivers and Collectors proceed no farther in their Office until they be approved of by, and have given to this Committee good and sufficient Security for a faithful Return of such Monies when collected.

13. That the Committee be accountable to the County for the Application of all Monies received from such public Officers.

14. That all these Officers hold their Commissions during the Pleasure of their respective Constituents.

15. That this Committee will sustain all Damages that may ever hereafter accrue to all or any of these Officers thus appointed, and thus acting, on Account of their Obedience and Conformity to these Resolves.

16. That whatever Person shall hereafter receive a Commission from the Crown, or attempt to exercise any such Commission heretofore received, shall be deemed an Enemy to his Country; and upon Information being made to the Captain of the Company where he resides, the said Captain shall cause him to be apprehended, and conveyed before the two Select Men of the said Company, who,

upon Proof of the Fact, shall commit him the said Offender, into safe Custody, until the next setting of the Convention, who shall deal with him as Prudence may direct.

17. That any Person refusing to yield Obedience to the above Resolves shall be deemed equally criminal, and liable to the same Punishments as the Offenders above last mentioned.

18. That these Resolves be in full Force and Virtue, until Instructions from the General Congress of this Province, regulating the Jurisprudence of this Province, shall provide otherwise, or the legislative Body of *Great-Britain* resign its unjust and arbitrary Pretentions with Respect to *America*.

19. That the several Militia Companies in this county do provide themselves with proper Arms and Accoutrements, and hold themselves in Readiness to execute the commands and Directions of the Provincial Congress, and of this committee.

20. That this committee do appoint Colonel *Thomas Polk*, and Doctor *Joseph Kennedy*, to purchase 300 lb. of Powder, 600 lb. of Lead, and 1000 Flints, and deposit the same in some safe Place, hereafter to be appointed by the committee.

*Signed by Order of the Committee.*
EPH. BREVARD, *Clerk of the Committee.*[1]

---

[1] Quoted from American Historical Review, vol. 13, pp. 16–19.

# DECLARATION OF THE CAUSES AND NECESSITY OF TAKING UP ARMS, JULY 6, 1775

A DECLARATION BY THE REPRESENTATIVES OF THE UNITED COLONIES OF NORTH-AMERICA, NOW MET IN CONGRESS AT PHILADELPHIA, SETTING FORTH THE CAUSES AND NECESSITY OF THEIR TAKING UP ARMS

If it was possible for men, who exercise their reason to believe, that the divine Author of our existence intended a part of the human race to hold an absolute property in, and an unbounded power over others, marked out by his infinite goodness and wisdom, as the objects of a legal domination never rightfully resistible, however severe and oppressive, the inhabitants of these colonies might at least require from the parliament of Great-Britain some evidence, that this dreadful authority over them, has been granted to that body. But a reverence for our great Creator, principles of humanity, and the dictates of common sense, must convince all those who reflect upon the subject, that government was instituted to promote the welfare of mankind, and ought to be administered for the attainment of that end. The legislature of Great-Britain, however, stimulated by an inordinate passion for a power not only unjustifiable, but which they know to be peculiarly reprobated by the very constitution of that kingdom, and desparate of success in any mode of contest, where regard should be had to truth, law, or right, have at length, deserting those, attempted to effect their cruel and impolitic purpose of enslaving these colonies by violence, and have thereby rendered it necessary for us to close with their last appeal from reason to arms.—Yet, however blinded that assembly may be, by their intemperate rage for unlimited domination, so to slight justice and the opinion of mankind, we esteem ourselves bound by obligations of respect to the rest of the world, to make known the justice of our cause.

Our forefathers, inhabitants of the island of Great-Britain, left their native land, to seek on these shores a residence for civil and religious freedom. At the expense of their blood, at the hazard of their fortunes, without the least charge to the country from which they removed, by unceasing labour, and an unconquerable spirit, they effected settlements in the distant and inhospitable wilds of America, then filled with numerous and warlike nations of barbarians.—Societies or governments, vested with perfect legislatures, were formed under charters from the crown, and an harmonious intercourse was established between the colonies and the kingdom from which they derived their origin. The mutual benefits of this union became in a short time so extraordinary, as to excite astonishment. It is universally confessed, that the amazing increase of the wealth, strength, and navigation of the realm, arose from this source; and the minister, who so wisely and successfully directed the measures of Great-Britain in the late war, publicly declared, that these colonies enabled her to triumph over her enemies.—Towards the conclusion of that war, it pleased our sovereign to make a change in his counsels.—From that fatal moment, the affairs of the British empire began to fall into confusion, and gradually sliding from the summit of glorious prosperity, to which they had been advanced by the virtues and abilities of one man, are at length distracted by the convulsions, that now shake it to its deepest foundations.—The new ministry finding the brave foes of Britain, though frequently defeated, yet still contending, took up the unfortunate idea of granting them a hasty peace, and of then subduing her faithful friends.

These devoted colonies were judged to be in such a state, as to present victories without bloodshed, and all the easy emoluments of statuteable plunder.—The uninterrupted tenor of their peaceable and respectful behaviour from the beginning of colonization, their dutiful, zealous, and useful services during the war, though so recently and amply acknowledged in the most honourable manner by his majesty, by the late king, and by parliament, could not save them from the meditated innovations.—Parliament was influenced to adopt the pernicious project, and assuming a new power over them, have in the course of eleven years, given such decisive specimens of the spirit and consequences attending this power, as to leave no doubt concerning the effects of acquiescence under it. They have undertaken to give and grant our money without our consent, though we have ever exercised an exclusive right to dispose of our own property; statutes have been passed for extending the jurisdiction of courts of admiralty and vice-admiralty beyond their ancient limits; for depriving us of the accustomed and inestimable privilege of trial by jury, in cases affecting both life and property; for suspending the legislature of one of the colonies; for interdicting all commerce to the capital of another; and for altering fundamentally the form of government established by charter, and secured by acts of its own legislature solemnly confirmed by the crown; for exempting the "murderers" of colonists from legal trial, and in effect, from punishment; for erecting in a neighbouring province, acquired by the joint arms of Great-Britain and America, a despotism dangerous to our very existence; and for quartering soldiers upon the colonists in time of profound peace. It has also been resolved in parliament, that colonists charged with committing certain offences, shall be transported to England to be tried.

But why should we enumerate our injuries in detail? By one statute it is declared, that parliament can "of right make laws to bind us in all cases whatsoever." What is to defend us against so enormous, so unlimited a power? Not a single man of those who assume it, is chosen by us; or is subject to our controul or influence; but, on the contrary, they are all of them exempt from the operation of such laws, and an American revenue, if not diverted from the ostensible purposes for which it is raised, would actually lighten their own burdens in proportion, as they increase ours. We saw the misery to which such despotism would reduce us. We for ten years incessantly and ineffectually besieged the throne as supplicants; we reasoned, we remonstrated with parliament, in the most mild and decent language.

Administration sensible that we should regard these oppressive measures as freemen ought to do, sent over fleets and armies to enforce them. The indignation of the Americans was roused, it is true; but it was the indignation of a virtuous, loyal, and affectionate people. A Congress of delegates from the United Colonies was assembled at Philadelphia, on the fifth day of last September. We resolved again to offer an humble and dutiful petition to the

King, and also addressed our fellow-subjects of Great-Britain. We have pursued every temperate, every respectful measure: we have even proceeded to break off our commercial intercourse with our fellow-subjects, as the last peaceable admonition, that our attachment to no nation upon earth should supplant our attachment to liberty.—This, we flattered ourselves, was the ultimate step of the controversy: but subsequent events have shewn, how vain was this hope of finding moderation in our enemies.

Several threatening expressions against the colonies were inserted in his majesty's speech; our petition, tho' we were told it was a decent one, and that his majesty had been pleased to receive it graciously, and to promise laying it before his parliament, was huddled into both houses among a bundle of American papers, and there neglected. The lords and commons in their address, in the month of February, said, that "a rebellion at that time actually existed within the province of Massachusetts-Bay; and that those concerned in it, had been countenanced and encouraged by unlawful combinations and engagements, entered into by his majesty's subjects in several of the other colonies; and therefore they besought his majesty, that he would take the most effectual measures to inforce due obedience to the laws and authority of the supreme legislature."—Soon after, the commercial intercourse of whole colonies, with foreign countries, and with each other, was cut off by an act of parliament; by another several of them were intirely prohibited from the fisheries in the seas near their co[a]sts, on which they always depended for their sustenance; and large reinforcements of ships and troops were immediately sent over to general Gage.

Fruitless were all the entreaties, arguments, and eloquence of an illustrious band of the most distinguished peers, and commoners, who nobly and stren[u]ously asserted the justice of our cause, to stay, or even to mitigate the heedless fury with which these accumulated and unexampled outrages were hurried on.— Equally fruitless was the interference of the city of London, of Bristol, and many other respectable towns in our favour. Parliament adopted an insidious manoeuvre calculated to divide us, to establish a perpetual auction of taxations where colony should bid against colony, all of them uninformed what ransom would redeem their lives; and thus to extort from us, at the point of the bayonet, the unknown sums that should be sufficient to gratify, if possible to gratify, ministerial rapacity, with the miserable indulgence left to us of raising, in our own mode, the prescribed tribute. What terms more rigid and humiliating could have been dictated by remorseless victors to conquered enemies? in our circumstances to accept them, would be to deserve them.

Soon after the intelligence of these proceedings arrived on this continent, general Gage, who in the course of the last year had taken possession of the town of Boston, in the province of Massachusetts-Bay, and still occupied it is [as] a garrison, on the 19th day of April, sent out from that place a large detachment of his army, who made an unprovoked assault on the inhabitants of the said province, at the town of Lexington, as appears by the affidavits of a great number of persons, some of whom were officers and soldiers of that detachment, murdered eight of the inhabitants, and wounded many others. From thence the troops proceeded in warlike array to the town of Concord, where they set upon another party of the inhabitants of the same province, killing several and wounding more, until compelled to retreat by the country people suddenly assembled to repel this cruel aggression. Hostilities, thus commenced by the British troops, have been since prosecuted by them without regard to faith or reputation.—The inhabitants of Boston being confined within that town by the general their governor, and having, in order to procure their dismission, entered into a treaty with him, it was stipulated that the said inhabitants having deposited their arms with their own magistrates, should have liberty to depart, taking with them their other effects. They accordingly delivered up their arms, but in open violation of honour, in defiance of the obligation of treaties, which even savage nations esteemed sacred, the governor ordered the arms deposited as aforesaid, that they might be preserved for their owners, to be seized by a body of soldiers; detained the greatest part of the inhabitants in the town, and compelled the few who were permitted to retire, to leave their most valuable effects behind.

By this perfidy wives are separated from their husbands, children from their parents, the aged and the sick from their relations and friends, who wish to attend and comfort them; and those who have been used to live in plenty and even elegance, are reduced to deplorable distress.

The general, further emulating his ministerial masters, by a proclamation bearing date on the 12th day of June, after venting the grossest falsehoods and calumnies against the good people of these colonies, proceeds to "declare them all, either by name or description, to be rebels and traitors, to supersede the course of the common law, and instead thereof to publish and order the use and exercise of the law martial."—His troops have butchered our countrymen, have wantonly burnt Charlestown, besides a considerable number of houses in other places; our ships and vessels are seized; the necessary supplies of provisions are intercepted, and he is exerting his utmost power to spread destruction and devastation around him.

We have received certain intelligence, that general Carelton *Carleton*], the governor of Canada, is instigating the people of that province and the Indians to fall upon us; and we have but too much reason to apprehend, that schemes have been formed to excite domestic enemies against us. In brief, a part of these colonies now feel, and all of them are sure of feeling, as far as the vengeance of administration can inflict them, the complicated calamities of fire, sword, and famine. We* are reduced to the alternative of chusing an unconditional submission to the tyranny of irritated ministers, or resistance by force.—The latter is our choice.—We have counted the cost of this contest, and find nothing so dreadful as voluntary slavery.—Honour, justice, and humanity, forbid us tamely to surrender that freedom which we received from our gallant ancestors, and which our innocent posterity have a right to receive from us. We cannot endure the infamy and guilt of resigning succeeding generations to that wretchedness which inevitably awaits them, if we basely entail hereditary bondage upon them.

---

\* From this point the declaration follows Jefferson's draft.

Our cause is just. Our union is perfect. Our internal resources are great, and, if necessary, foreign assistance is undoubtedly attainable.—We gratefully acknowledge, as signal instances of the Divine favour towards us, that his Providence would not permit us to be called into this severe controversy, until we were grown up to our present strength, had been previously exercised in warlike operation, and possessed of the means of defending ourselves. With hearts fortified with these animating reflections, we most solemnly, before God and the world, *declare*, that, exerting the utmost energy of those powers, which our beneficent Creator hath graciously bestowed upon us, the arms we have been compelled by our enemies to assume, we will, in defiance of every hazard, with unabating firmness and perseverence, employ for the preservation of our liberties; being with one mind resolved to die freemen rather than to live slaves.

Lest this declaration should disquiet the minds of our friends and fellow-subjects in any part of the empire, we assure them that we mean not to dissolve that union which has so long and so happily subsisted between us, and which we sincerely wish to see restored.—Necessity has not yet driven us into that desperate measure, or induced us to excite any other nation to war against them.—We have not raised armies with ambitious designs of separating from Great-Britain, and establishing independent states. We fight not for glory or for conquest. We exhibit to mankind the remarkable spectacle of a people attacked by unprovoked enemies, without any imputation or even suspicion of offence. They boast of their privileges and civilization, and yet proffer no milder conditions than servitude or death.

In our own native land, in defence of the freedom that is our birthright, and which we ever enjoyed till the late violation of it—for the protection of our property, acquired solely by the honest industry of our fore-fathers and ourselves, against violence actually offered, we have taken up arms. We shall lay them down when hostilities shall cease on the part of the aggressors, and all danger of their being renewed shall be removed, and not before.

With an humble confidence in the mercies of the supreme and impartial Judge and Ruler of the Universe, we most devoutly implore his divine goodness to protect us happily through this great conflict, to dispose our adversaries to reconciliation on reasonable terms, and thereby to relieve the empire from the calamities of civil war.[1]

---

[1] Journal of Congress (ed. 1800), I., pp. 134–139.

# RESOLUTION OF SECRECY ADOPTED BY THE CONTINENTAL CONGRESS, NOVEMBER 9, 1775

*Resolved*, That every member of this Congress considers himself under the ties of virtue, honour, and love of his country, not to divulge, directly or indirectly, any matter or thing agitated or debated in Congress, before the same shall have been determined, without leave of the Congress; nor any matter or thing determined in Congress, which a majority of the Congress shall order to be kept secret. And that if any member shall violate this agreement, he shall be expelled this Congress, and deemed an enemy to the liberties of America, and liable to be treated as such; and that every member signify his consent to this agreement by signing the same.[1]

---

[1] Quoted from *Secret Journals of the Acts and Proceedings of U. S. Congress*, Vol. I, p. 34.

PREAMBLE AND RESOLUTION OF THE VIRGINIA CONVENTION, MAY 15, 1776, INSTRUCTING THE VIRGINIA DELEGATES IN THE CONTINENTAL CONGRESS TO "PROPOSE TO THAT RESPECTABLE BODY TO DECLARE THE UNITED COLONIES FREE AND INDEPENDENT STATES"

Forasmuch as all the endeavours of the United Colonies, by the most decent representations and petitions to the King and Parliament of *Great Britain*, to restore peace and security to *America* under the *British* Government, and a reunion with that people upon just and liberal terms, instead of a redress of grievances, have produced, from an imperious and vindictive Administration, increased insult, oppression, and a vigorous attempt to effect our total destruction:—By a late act all these Colonies are declared to be in rebellion, and out of the protection of the *British* Crown, our properties subjected to confiscation, our people, when captivated, compelled to join in the murder and plunder of their relations and countrymen, and all former rapine and oppression of *Americans* declared legal and just; fleets and armies are raised, and the aid of foreign troops engaged to assist these destructive purposes; the King's representative in this Colony hath not only withheld all the powers of Government from operating for our safety, but, having retired on board an armed ship, is carrying on a piratical and savage war against us, tempting our slaves by every artifice to resort to him, and training and employing them against their masters. In this state of extreme danger, we have no alternative left but an abject submission to the will of those overbearing tyrants, or a total separation from the Crown and Government of *Great Britain*, uniting and exerting the strength of all *America* for defence, and forming alliances with foreign Powers for commerce and aid in war:—Wherefore, appealing to the Searcher of hearts for the sincerity of former declarations expressing our desire to preserve the connection with that nation, and that we are driven from that inclination by their wicked councils, and the eternal law of self-preservation:

*Resolved, unanimously,* That the Delegates appointed to represent this Colony in General Congress be instructed to propose to that respectable body to declare the United Colonies free and independent States, absolved from all allegiance to, or dependance upon, the Crown or Parliament of *Great Britain;* and that they give the assent of this Colony to such declaration, and to whatever measures may be thought proper and necessary by the Congress for forming foreign alliances, and a Confederation of the Colonies, at such time and in the manner as to them shall seem best: *Provided,* That the power of forming Government for, and the regulations of the internal concerns of each Colony, be left to the respective Colonial Legislatures.

*Resolved, unanimously,* That a Committee be appointed to prepare a Declaration of Rights, and such a plan of Government as will be most likely to maintain peace and order in this Colony, and secure substantial and equal liberty to the people.

And a Committee was appointed of the following gentlemen: Mr. Archibald Cary, Mr. Meriwether Smith, Mr. Mercer, Mr. Henry Lee, Mr. Treasurer, Mr. Henry, Mr. Dandridge, Mr. Edmund Randolph, Mr. Gilmer, Mr. Bland, Mr. Digges, Mr. Carrington, Mr. Thomas Ludwell Lee, Mr. Cabell, Mr. Jones, Mr. Blair, Mr. Fleming, Mr. Tazewell, Mr. Richard Cary, Mr. Bullitt, Mr. Watts, Mr. Banister, Mr. Page, Mr. Starke, Mr. David Mason, Mr. Adams, Mr. Read, and Mr. Thomas Lewis.[1]

---

[1] Quoted from Force, Peter. *American Archives*, 4th series, Vol. VI, p. 1523.

## RESOLUTION INTRODUCED IN THE CONTINENTAL CONGRESS BY RICHARD HENRY LEE (VA.) PROPOSING A DECLARATION OF INDEPENDENCE, JUNE 7, 1776 [1]

*Resolved*, That these United Colonies are, and of right ought to be, free and independent States, that they are absolved from all allegiance to the British Crown, and that all political connection between them and the State of Great Britain is, and ought to be, totally dissolved.

That it is expedient forthwith to take the most effectual measures for forming foreign Alliances.

That a plan of confederation be prepared and transmitted to the respective Colonies for their consideration and approbation.[2]

---

[1] Quoted from *Journals of the Continental Congress*, Library of Congress edition, Vol. V, p. 425.

[2] This resolution, in the writing of Richard Henry Lee, is in the *Papers of the Continental Congress* No. 23, folio 11. It has the following endorsement in three writings: "Resolved that it is the Opinion of this Com. that the first Resolution [Benjamin Harrison] be postponed to this day three weeks, and that in the mean time [Charles Thomson], least any time sh$^d$ be lost in case the Congress agree to this resolution [Robert R. Livingston], a committee be appointed to prepare a Declaration to the effect of the said first resolution [Charles Thomson]." The postponement was made to give an opportunity to the Delegates from those Colonies which had not as yet given authority to adopt this decisive measure, to consult their constituents. The motion was seconded by John Adams.

# THE DECLARATION OF INDEPENDENCE—1776 [1]

IN CONGRESS, JULY 4, 1776

THE UNANIMOUS DECLARATION OF THE THIRTEEN UNITED STATES OF AMERICA

WHEN in the Course of human events, it becomes necessary for one people to dissolve the political bands which have connected them with another, and to assume among the powers of the earth, the separate and equal station to which the Laws of Nature and of Nature's God entitle them, a decent respect to the opinions of mankind requires that they should declare the causes which impel them to the separation.—We hold these truths to be self-evident, that all men are created equal, that they are endowed by their Creator with certain unalienable Rights, that among these are Life, Liberty and the pursuit of Happiness.—That to secure these rights, Governments are instituted among Men, deriving their just powers from the consent of the governed,—That whenever any Form of Government becomes destructive of these ends, it is the Right of the People to alter or to abolish it, and to institute new Government, laying its foundation on such principles and organizing its powers in such form, as to them shall seem most likely to effect their Safety and Happiness. Prudence, indeed, will dictate that Governments long established should not be changed for light and transient causes; and accordingly all experience hath shown, that mankind are more disposed to suffer, while evils are sufferable, than to right themselves by abolishing the forms to which they are accustomed. But when a long train of abuses and usurpations, pursuing invariably the same Object evinces a design to reduce them under absolute Despotism, it is their right, it is their duty, to throw off such Government, and to provide new Guards for their future security.—Such has been the patient sufferance of these Colonies; and such is now the necessity which constrains them to alter their former Systems of Government. The history of the present King of Great Britain

---

[1] Printed from the facsimile of the engrossed copy of the original manuscript in the Library of Congress.

is a history of repeated injuries and usurpations, all having in direct object the establishment of an absolute Tyranny over these States. To prove this, let Facts be submitted to a candid world.—He has refused his Assent to Laws, the most wholesome and necessary for the public good.—He has forbidden his Governors to pass Laws of immediate and pressing importance, unless suspended in their operation till his Assent should be obtained; and when so suspended, he has utterly neglected to attend to them.—He has refused to pass other Laws for the accommodation of large districts of people, unless those people would relinquish the right of Representation in the Legislature, a right inestimable to them and formidable to tyrants only.—He has called together legislative bodies at places unusual, uncomfortable, and distant from the depository of their public Records, for the sole purpose of fatiguing them into compliance with his measures.—He has dissolved Representative Houses repeatedly, for opposing with manly firmness his invasions on the rights of the people.—He has refused for a long time, after such dissolutions, to cause others to be elected; whereby the Legislative powers, incapable of Annihilation, have returned to the People at large for their exercise; the State remaining in the mean time exposed to all the dangers of invasion from without, and convulsions within.—He has endeavoured to prevent the population of these States; for that purpose obstructing the Laws for Naturalization of Foreigners; refusing to pass others to encourage their migration hither, and raising the conditions of new Appropriations of Lands.—He has obstructed the Administration of Justice, by refusing his Assent to Laws for establishing Judiciary powers.—He has made Judges dependent on his Will alone, for the tenure of their offices, and the amount and payment of their salaries.—He has erected a multitude of New Offices, and sent hither swarms of Officers to harrass our people, and eat out their substance.—He has kept among us, in times of peace, Standing Armies, without the Consent of our legislatures.—He has affected to render the Military independent of and superior to the Civil power.—He has combined with others to subject us to a jurisdiction foreign to our constitution, and unacknowledged by our laws; giving his Assent to their Acts of pretended Legislation:—For quartering large bodies of armed troops among us:—For protecting them, by a mock Trial, from punishment for any Murders which they should commit on the Inhabitants of these States:—For cutting off our Trade with all parts of the world:—For imposing Taxes on us without our Consent:—For depriving us in many cases, of the benefits of Trial by Jury:—For transporting us beyond Seas to be tried for pretended offences:—For abolishing the free System of English Laws in a neighbouring Province, establishing therein an Arbitrary government, and enlarging its Boundaries so as to render it at once an example and fit instrument for introducing the same absolute rule into these Colonies:—For taking away our Charters, abolishing our most valuable Laws, and altering fundamentally the Forms of our Governments:—For suspending our own Legislatures, and declaring themselves invested with power to legislate for us in all cases whatsoever.—He has abdicated Government here, by declaring us out of his Protection and waging War against us.—He has plundered our seas, ravaged our Coasts, burnt our towns, and destroyed the lives of our people.—He is at this time transporting large Armies of foreign Mercenaries to compleat the works of death, desolation and tyranny, already begun with circumstances of Cruelty & perfidy scarcely paralleled in the most barbarous ages, and totally unworthy the Head of a civilized nation.—He has constrained our fellow Citizens taken Captive on the high Seas to bear Arms against their Country, to become the executioners of their friends and Brethren, or to fall themselves by their Hands.— He has excited domestic insurrections amongst us, and has endeavoured to bring on the inhabitants of our frontiers, the merciless Indian Savages, whose known rule of warfare, is an undistinguished destruction of all ages, sexes and conditions. In every stage of these Oppressions We have Petitioned for Redress in the most humble terms: Our repeated Petitions have been answered only by repeated injury. A Prince, whose character is thus marked by every act which may define a Tyrant, is unfit to be the ruler of a free people. Nor have We been wanting in attentions to our Brittish brethren. We have warned them from time to time of attempts by their legislature to extend an unwarrantable jurisdiction over us. We have reminded them of the circumstances of our emigration and settlement here. We have appealed to their native justice and magnanimity, and we have conjured them by the ties of our common kindred to disavow these usurpations, which, would inevitably interrupt our connections and correspondence. They too have been deaf to the voice of justice and of consanguinity. We must, therefore, acquiesce in the necessity, which denounces our Separation, and hold them, as we hold the rest of mankind, Enemies in War, in Peace Friends.—

WE, THEREFORE, the REPRESENTATIVES of the UNITED STATES OF AMERICA, in General Congress, Assembled, appealing to the Supreme Judge of the world for the rectitude of our intentions, do, in the Name, and by Authority of the good People of these Colonies, solemnly publish and declare, That these United Colonies are, and of Right ought to be FREE AND INDEPENDENT STATES; that they are Absolved from all Allegiance to the British Crown, and that all political connection between them and the State of Great Britain, is and ought to be totally dissolved; and that as Free and Independent States, they have full Power to levy War, conclude Peace, contract Alliances, establish Commerce, and to do all other Acts and Things which Independent States may of right do.—And for the support of this Declaration, with a firm reliance on the protection of Divine Providence, we mutually pledge to each other our Lives, our Fortunes and our sacred Honor.

JOHN HANCOCK.

*New Hampshire*
  JOSIAH BARTLETT,
  WM. WHIPPLE,
  MATTHEW THORNTON.

*Massachusetts Bay*
  SAML. ADAMS,
  JOHN ADAMS,
  ROBT. TREAT PAINE,
  ELBRIDGE GERRY

*Rhode Island*
  STEP. HOPKINS,
  WILLIAM ELLERY.

*Connecticut*
  ROGER SHERMAN,
  SAM'EL HUNTINGTON,
  WM. WILLIAMS,
  OLIVER WOLCOTT.

*New York*
  WM. FLOYD,
  PHIL. LIVINGSTON,
  FRANS. LEWIS,
  LEWIS MORRIS.

*New Jersey*
  RICHD. STOCKTON,
  JNO. WITHERSPOON,
  FRAS. HOPKINSON,
  JOHN HART,
  ABRA. CLARK.

*Pennsylvania*
  ROBT. MORRIS,
  BENJAMIN RUSH,
  BENJA. FRANKLIN,
  JOHN MORTON,
  GEO. CLYMER,
  JAS. SMITH,
  GEO. TAYLOR,
  JAMES WILSON,
  GEO. ROSS.

*Delaware*
  CAESAR RODNEY,
  GEO. READ,
  THO. M'KEAN.

*Maryland*
  SAMUEL CHASE,
  WM. PACA,
  THOS. STONE,
  CHARLES CARROLL of Carrollton.

*Virginia*
  GEORGE WYTHE,
  RICHARD HENRY LEE,
  TH. JEFFERSON,
  BENJA. HARRISON,
  THS. NELSON, JR.,
  FRANCIS LIGHTFOOT LEE,
  CARTER BRAXTON.

*North Carolina*
  WM. HOOPER,
  JOSEPH HEWES,
  JOHN PENN.

*South Carolina*
  EDWARD RUTLEDGE,
  THOS. HEYWARD, JUNR.,
  THOMAS LYNCH, JUNR.,
  ARTHUR MIDDLETON.

*Georgia*
  BUTTON GWINNETT,
  LYMAN HALL,
  GEO. WALTON.

NOTE.—Mr. Ferdinand Jefferson, Keeper of the Rolls in the Department of State, at Washington, says: "The names of the signers are spelt above as in the facsimile of the original, but the punctuation of them is not always the same; neither do the names of the States appear in the facsimile of the original. The names of the signers of each State are grouped together in the facsimile of the original, except the name of Matthew Thornton, which follows that of Oliver Wolcott."—*Revised Statutes of the United States*, 2d edition, 1878, p. 6.

# ARTICLES OF CONFEDERATION,[1] MARCH 1, 1781

*To all to whom these Presents shall come, we the under signed Delegates of the States affixed to our Names, send greeting.*

Whereas the Delegates of the United States of America, in Congress assembled, did, on the 15th day of November, in the Year of Our Lord One thousand Seven Hundred and Seventy seven, and in the Second Year of the Independence of America, agree to certain articles of Confederation and perpetual Union between the States of Newhampshire, Massachusetts-bay, Rhodeisland and Providence Plantations, Connecticut, New York, New Jersey, Pennsylvania, Delaware, Maryland, Virginia, North-Carolina, South-Carolina, and Georgia in the words following, viz. "Articles of Confederation and perpetual Union between the states of Newhampshire, Massachusetts-bay, Rhodeisland and Providence Plantations, Connecticut, New-York, New-Jersey, Pennsylvania, Delaware, Maryland, Virginia, North-Carolina, South-Carolina and Georgia.

Article I. The Stile of this confederacy shall be "The United States of America."

Article II. Each state retains its sovereignty, freedom, and independence, and every Power, Jurisdiction and right, which is not by this confederation expressly delegated to the United States, in Congress assembled.

Article III. The said states hereby severally enter into a firm league of friendship with each other, for their common defence, the security of their Liberties, and their mutual and general welfare, binding themselves to assist each other, against all force offered to, or attacks made upon them, or any of them, on account of religion, sovereignty, trade, or any other pretence whatever.

---

[1] *Journals of the Cotinnental Congress*, Library of Congress edition, Vol. XIX (1912), p. 214.

The Articles of Confederation were agreed to by the Congress, November 15, 1777. They were, as appears from the list of signatures affixed to these Articles, signed at different times by the delegates of the different American States. On March 1, 1781, the delegates from Maryland, the last of the States to take action, "did, in behalf of the said State of Maryland, sign and ratify the said articles, by which act the Confederation of the United States of America was completed, each and every of the Thirteen United States, from New Hampshire to Georgia, both included, having adopted and confirmed, and by their delegates in Congress, ratified the same." *Ibid.*, p. 214.

Article IV. The better to secure and perpetuate mutual friendship and intercourse among the people of the different states in this union, the free inhabitants of each of these states, paupers, vagabonds and fugitives from justice excepted, shall be entitled to all privileges and immunities of free citizens in the several states; and the people of each state shall have free ingress and regress to and from any other state, and shall enjoy therein all the privileges of trade and commerce, subject to the same duties, impositions and restrictions as the inhabitants thereof respectively, provided that such restriction shall not extend so far as to prevent the removal of property imported into any state, to any other state, of which the Owner is an inhabitant; provided also that no imposition, duties or restriction shall be laid by any state, on the property of the united states, or either of them.

If any Person guilty of, or charged with treason, felony, or other high misdemeanor in any state, shall flee from Justice, and be found in any of the united states, he shall, upon demand of the Governor or executive power, of the state from which he fled, be delivered up and removed to the state having jurisdiction of his offence.

Full faith and credit shall be given in each of these states to the records, acts and judicial proceedings of the courts and magistrates of every other state.

Article V. For the more convenient management of the general interests of the united states, delegates shall be annually appointed in such manner as the legislature of each state shall direct, to meet in Congress on the first Monday in November, in every year, with a power reserved to each state, to recal its delegates, or any of them, at any time within the year, and to send others in their stead, for the remainder of the Year.

No state shall be represented in Congress by less than two, nor by more than seven Members; and no person shall be capable of being a delegate for more than three years in any term of six years; nor shall any person, being a delegate, be capable of holding any office under the united states, for which he, or another for his benefit receives any salary, fees or emolument of any kind.

Each state shall maintain its own delegates in a meeting of the states, and while they act as members of the committee of the states.

In determining questons in the united states in Congress assembled, each state shall have one vote.

Freedom of speech and debate in Congress shall not be impeached or questioned in any Court, or place out of Congress, and the members of congress shall be protected in their persons from arrests and imprisonments, during the time of their going to and from, and attendance on congress, except for treason, felony, or breach of the peace.

Article VI. No state, without the Consent of the united states in congress assembled, shall send any embassy to, or receive any embassy from, or enter into any conference, agreement, alliance or treaty with any King prince or state; nor shall any person holding any office of profit or trust under the united states, or any of them, accept of any present, emolument, office or title of any kind whatever from any king, prince or foreign state; nor shall the united states in congress assembled, or any of them, grant any title of nobility.

No two or more states shall enter into any treaty, confederation or alliance whatever between them, without the consent of the united states in congress assembled, specifying accurately the purposes for which the same is to be entered into, and how long it shall continue.

No state shall lay any imposts or duties, which may interfere with any stipulations in treaties, entered into by the united states in congress assembled, with any king, prince or state, in pursuance of any treaties already proposed by congress, to the courts of France and Spain.

No vessels of war shall be kept up in time of peace by any state, except such number only, as shall be deemed necessary by the united states in congress assembled, for the defence of such state, or its trade; nor shall any body of forces be kept up by any state, in time of peace, except such number only, as in the judgment of the united states, in congress assembled, shall be deemed requisite to garrison the forts necessary for the defence of such state; but every state shall always keep up a well regulated and disciplined militia, sufficiently armed and accoutred, and shall provide and constantly have ready for use, in public stores, a due number of field pieces and tents, and a proper quantity of arms, ammunition and camp equipage.

No state shall engage in any war without the consent of the united states in congress assembled, unless such state be actually invaded by enemies, or shall have received certain advice of a resolution being formed by some nation of Indians to invade such state, and the danger is so imminent as not to admit of a delay till the united states in congress assembled can be consulted: nor shall any state grant commissions to any ships or vessels of war, nor letters of marque or reprisal, except it be after a declaration of war by the united states in congress assembled, and then only against the kingdom or state and the subjects thereof, against which war has been so declared, and under such regulations as shall be established by the united states in congress assembled, unless such state be infested by pirates, in which case vessels of war may be fitted out for that occasion, and kept so long as the danger shall continue, or until the united states in congress assembled, shall determine otherwise.

Article VII. When land-forces are raised by any state for the common defence, all officers of or under the rank of colonel, shall be appointed by the legislature of each state respectively, by whom such forces shall be raised, or in such manner as such state shall direct, and all vacancies shall be filled up by the State which first made the appointment.

Article VIII. All charges of war, and all other expences that shall be incurred for the common defence or general welfare, and allowed by the united states in congress assembled, shall be defrayed out of a common treasury, which shall be supplied by the several states in proportion to the value of all land within each state, granted to or surveyed for any Person, as such land and the buildings and improvements thereon shall be estimated according to such mode as the united states in congress assembled, shall from time to time direct and appoint.

The taxes for paying that proportion shall be laid and levied by the authority and direction of the legislatures of the several states within the time agreed upon by the united states in congress assembled.

Article IX. The united states in congress assembled, shall have the sole and exclusive right and power of determining on peace and war, except in the cases mentioned in the sixth article—of sending and receiving ambassadors—entering into treaties and alliances, provided that no treaty of commerce shall be made whereby the legislative power of the respective states shall be restrained from imposing such imposts and duties on foreigners as their own people are subjected to, or from prohibiting the exportation or importation of any species of goods or commodities, whatsoever—of establishing rules for deciding in all cases, what captures on land or water shall be legal, and in what manner prizes taken by land or naval forces in the service of the united states shall be divided or appropriated—of granting letters of marque and reprisal in times of peace—appointing courts for the trial of piracies and felonies committed on the high seas and establishing courts for receiving and determining finally appeals in all cases of captures, provided that no member of congress shall be appointed a judge of any of the said courts.

The united states in congress assembled shall also be the last resort on appeal in all disputes and differences now subsisting or that hereafter may arise between two or more states concerning boundary, jurisdiction or any other cause whatever; which authority shall always be exercised in the manner following. Whenever the legislative or executive authority or lawful agent of any state in controversy with another shall present a petition to congress stating the matter in question and praying for a hearing, notice thereof shall be given by order of congress to the legislative or executive authority of the other state in controversy, and a day assigned for the appearance of the parties by their lawful agents, who shall then be directed to appoint by joint consent, commissioners or judges to constitute a court for hearing and determining the matter in question: but if they cannot agree, congress shall name three persons out of each of the united states, and from the list of such persons each party shall alternately strike out one, the petitioners beginning, until the number shall be reduced to thirteen; and from that number not less than seven, nor more than nine names as congress shall direct, shall in the presence of congress be drawn out by lot, and the persons whose names shall be so drawn or any five of them, shall be commissioners or judges, to hear and finally determine the controversy, so always as a major part of the judges who shall hear the cause shall agree in the determination: and if either party shall neglect to attend at the day appointed, without showing reasons, which congress shall judge sufficient, or being present shall refuse to strike, the congress shall proceed to nominate three persons out of each state, and the secretary of congress shall strike in behalf of such party absent or refusing; and the judgment and sentence of the court to be appointed, in the manner before prescribed, shall be final and conclusive; and if any of the parties shall refuse to submit to the authority of such court, or to appear or defend their claim or cause, the court shall nevertheless proceed to pronounce sentence, or judgment, which shall in like manner be final and decisive, the judgment or sentence and other proceedings being in either case transmitted to congress, and lodged among the acts of congress for the security of the parties concerned: provided that every commissioner, before he sits in judgment, shall take an oath to be administered by one of the judges of the supreme or superior court of the state, where the cause shall be tried, "well and truly to hear and determine the matter in question, according to the best of his judgment, without favour, affection or hope of reward:" provided also, that no state shall be deprived of territory for the benefit of the united states.

All controversies concerning the private right of soil claimed under different grants of two or more states, whose jurisdictions as they may respect such lands, and the states which passed such grants are adjusted, the said grants or either of them being at the same time claimed to have originated antecedent to such settlement of jurisdiction, shall on the petition of either party to the congress of the united states, be finally determined as near as may be in the same manner as is before prescribed for deciding disputes respecting territorial jurisdiction between different states.

The united states in congress assembled shall also have the sole and exclusive right and power of regulating the alloy and value of coin struck by their own authority, or by that of the respective states—fixing the standard of weights and measures throughout the united states—regulating the trade and managing all affairs with the Indians, not members of any of the states, provided that the legislative right of any state within its own limits be not infringed or violated—establishing or regulating post-offices from one state to another, throughout all the united states, and exacting such postage on the papers passing thro' the same as may be requisite to defray the expences of the said office—appointing all officers of the land forces, in the service of the united states, excepting regimental officers—appointing all the officers of the naval forces, and commissioning all officers whatever in the service of the united states—making rules for the government and regulation of the said land and naval forces, and directing their operations.

The united states in congress assembled shall have authority to appoint a committee, to sit in the recess of congress, to be denominated "A Committee of the States," and to consist of one delegate from each state; and to appoint such other committees and civil officers as may be necessary for managing the general affairs of the united states under their direction—to appoint one of their number to preside, provided that no person be allowed to serve in the office of president more than one year in any term of three years; to ascertain the necessary sums of money to be raised for the service of the united states, and to appropriate and apply the same for defraying the public expences—to borrow money, or emit bills on the credit of the united states, transmitting every half year to the respective states an account of the sums of money so borrowed or emitted,—to build and equip a navy—to agree upon the number of land forces, and to make requisitions from each state for its quota, in proportion to the number of white inhabitants in such state; which requisition shall be binding, and thereupon the legislature of each state shall appoint the regimental officers, raise the men and cloath, arm and equip them in a soldier like manner, at the expence of the united states; and the officers and men so cloathed, armed and equipped shall march to the place appointed, and within the time agreed on by the united states in congress assembled: But if the united states in congress assembled shall, on consideration of circumstances judge proper that any state should not raise men, or should raise a smaller number than its quota, and that any other state should raise a greater number of men than the quota thereof, such extra number shall be raised, officered, cloathed, armed and equipped in the same manner as the quota of such state, unless the legislature of such state shall judge that such extra number cannot be safely spared out of the same, in which case they shall raise officer, cloath, arm and equip as many of such extra number as they judge can be safely spared. And the officers and men so cloathed, armed and equipped, shall march to the place appointed, and within the time agreed on by the united states in congress assembled.

The united states in congress assembled shall never engage in a war, nor grant letters of marque and reprisal in time of peace, nor enter into any treaties or alliances, nor coin money, nor regulate the value thereof, nor ascertain the sums and expences necessary for the defence and welfare of the united states, or any of them, nor emit bills, nor borrow money on the credit of the united states, nor appropriate money, nor agree upon the number of vessels of war, to be built or purchased, or the number of land or sea forces to be raised, nor appoint a commander in chief of the army or navy, unless nine states assent to the same: nor shall a question on any other point, except for adjourning from day to day be determined, unless by the votes of a majority of the united states in congress assembled.

The congress of the united states shall have power to adjourn to any time within the year, and to any place within the united states, so that no period of adjournment be for a longer duration than the space of six Months, and shall publish the Journal of their proceedings monthly, except such parts thereof relating to treaties, alliances or military operations, as in their judgment require secrecy; and the yeas and nays of the delegates of each state on any question shall be entered on the Journal, when it is desired by any delegate; and the delegates of a state, or any of them, at his or their request shall be furnished with a transcript of the said Journal, except such parts as are above excepted, to lay before the legislatures of the several states.

Article X. The committee of the states, or any nine of them, shall be authorized to execute, in the recess of congress, such of the powers of congress as the united states in congress assembled, by the consent of nine states, shall from time to time think expedient to vest them with; provided that no power be delegated to the said committee, for the exercise of which, by the articles of confederation, the voice of nine states in the congress of the united states assembled is requisite.

Article XI. Canada acceding to this confederation, and joining in the measures of the united states, shall be admitted into, and entitled to all the advantages of this union: but no other colony shall be admitted into the same, unless such admission be agreed to by nine states.

Article XII. All bills of credit emitted, monies borrowed and debts contracted by, or under the authority of congress, before the assembling of the united states, in pursuance of the present confederation, shall be deemed and considered as a charge against the united states, for payment and satisfaction whereof the said united states, and the public faith are hereby solemnly pledged.

Article XIII. Every state shall abide by the determinations of the united states in congress assembled, on all questions which by this confederation are submitted to them. And the Articles of this confederation shall be inviolably observed by every state, and the union shall be perpetual; nor shall any alteration at any time hereafter be made in any of them; unless such alteration be agreed to in a congress of the united states, and be afterwards confirmed by the legislatures of every state.

And Whereas it hath pleased the Great Governor of the World to incline the hearts of the legislatures we respectively represent in congress, to approve of, and to authorize us to ratify the said articles of confederation and perpetual union. Know Ye that we the undersigned delegates, by virtue of the power and authority to us given for that purpose, do by these presents, in the name and in behalf of our respective constituents, fully and entirely ratify and confirm each and every of the said articles of confederation and perpetual union, and all and singular the matters and things therein contained: And we do further solemnly plight and engage the faith of our respective constituents, that they shall abide by the determinations of the united states in congress assembled, on all questions, which by the said confederation are submitted to them. And that the articles thereof shall be inviolably observed by the states we respectively represent, and that the union shall be perpetual. In Witness whereof we have hereunto set our hands in Congress. Done at Philadelphia in the state of Pennsylvania the ninth day of July, in the Year of our Lord one Thousand seven Hundred and Seventy-eight, and in the third year of the independence of America.

Josiah Bartlett,
John Wentworth, jun$^r$
    August 8th, 1778,
} On the part & behalf of the State of New Hampshire.

John Hancock,
Samuel Adams,
Elbridge Gerry,
Francis Dana,
James Lovell,
Samuel Holten,
} On the part and behalf of the State of Massachusetts Bay.

William Ellery,
Henry Marchant,
John Collins,
} On the part and behalf of the State of Rhode-Island and Providence Plantations.

Roger Sherman,
Samuel Huntington,
Oliver Wolcott,
Titus Hosmer,
Andrew Adams,
} On the part and behalf of the State of Connecticut.

Ja$^s$ Duane,
Fra: Lewis,
W$^m$ Duer,
Gouv$^r$ Morris,
} On the part and behalf of the State of New York.

Jn$^o$ Witherspoon,
Nath$^l$ Scudder,
} On the Part and in Behalf of the State of New Jersey, November 26th, 1778.

Robert Morris,
Daniel Roberdeau,
Jon. Bayard Smith,
William Clingar,
Joseph Reed,
    22d July, 1778,
} On the part and behalf of the State of Pennsylvania.

Thos McKean,
    Feby 22d, 1779,
John Dickinson,        } On the part & behalf of the State of Delaware.
    May 5th, 1779,
Nicholas Van Dyke,

John Hanson,
    March 1, 1781,      } On the part and behalf of the State of Maryland.
Daniel Carroll, do

Richard Henry Lee,
John Banister,
Thomas Adams,        } On the Part and Behalf of the State of Virginia.
Jno Harvie,
Francis Lightfoot Lee,

John Penn,
    July 21st, 1778,     } On the part and behalf of the State of North Carolina.
Corns Harnett,
Jno Williams,

Henry Laurens,
William Henry Drayton,
Jno Mathews,         } On the part and on behalf of the State of South Carolina.
Richd Hutson,
Thos Heyward, junr.

Jno Walton,
    24th July, 1778,    } On the part and behalf of the State of Georgia.[1]
Edwd Telfair,
Edwd Langworthy,

---

[1] The proceedings of this day with respect to the signing of the Articles of Confederation, the Articles themselves and the signers are entered in the *Papers of the Continental Congress*, No. 9 (History of the Confederation), but not in the Journal itself. The Articles are printed here from the original roll in the Bureau of Rolls and Library, Department of State.

RESOLUTION OF THE GENERAL ASSEMBLY OF VIRGINIA, JANUARY 21, 1786, PROPOSING A JOINT MEETING OF COMMISSIONERS FROM THE STATES TO CONSIDER AND RECOMMEND A FEDERAL PLAN FOR REGULATING COMMERCE [1]

A motion was made, that the House do come to the following resolution:

*Resolved*, That Edmund Randolph, James Madison, jun. Walter Jones, Saint George Tucker and Meriwether Smith, Esquires, be appointed commissioners, who, or any three of whom, shall meet such commissioners as may be appointed by the other States in the Union, at a time and place to be agreed on, to take into consideration the trade of the United States; to examine the relative situations and trade of the said States; to consider how far a uniform system in their commercial regulations may be necessary to their common interest and their permanent harmony; and to report to the several States, such an act relative to this great object, as, when unanimously ratified by them, will enable the United States in Congress, effectually to provide for the same.

---

[1] Journal of the House of Delegates of the Commonwealth of Virginia, January 21, 1786, p. 153; Richmond, 1828. Journal of the Senate, January 21, 1786, p. 102; Richmond, 1827.

"In the Senate a further addition was made of Col. Mason, Mr. D. Ross and Mr. Ronald. The name of the latter was struck out at his desire." James Madison to James Monroe, January 22, 1786. *Writings of James Madison*, Hunt, Editor, Vol. II (1901), p. 223.

# PROCEEDINGS OF COMMISSIONERS TO REMEDY DEFECTS OF THE FEDERAL GOVERNMENT [1]

### ANNAPOLIS IN THE STATE OF MARYLAND

### SEPTEMBER 11th 1786

At a meeting of Commissioners, from the States of New York, New Jersey, Pennsylvania, Delaware and Virginia—

### Present

| | |
|---|---|
| ALEXANDER HAMILTON<br>EGBERT BENSON | New York |
| ABRAHAM CLARKE<br>WILLIAM C. HOUSTON<br>JAMES SCHUARMAN | New Jersey |
| TENCH COXE | Pennsylvania |
| GEORGE READ<br>JOHN DICKINSON<br>RICHARD BASSETT | Delaware |
| EDMUND RANDOLPH<br>JAMES MADISON, Junior<br>SAINT GEORGE TUCKER | Virginia |

M: Dickinson was unanimously elected Chairman.

The Commissioners produced their Credentials from their respective States; which were read.

After a full communication of Sentiments, and deliberate consideration of what would be proper to be done by the Commissioners now assembled, it was unanimously agreed: that a Committee be appointed to prepare a draft of a Report to be made to the States having Commissioners attending at this meeting—Adjourned 'till Wednesday Morning.

---

[1] From the original in the Library of Congress.
Notwithstanding the order to the chairman to sign the address it was signed by all the members of the Convention.

## Wednesday September 13th 1786

Met agreeable to Adjournment.

The Committee, appointed for that purpose, reported the draft of the report; which being read, the meeting proceeded to the consideration thereof, and after some time spent therein, Adjourned 'till tomorrow Morning.

## Thursday Sept: 14th 1786

Met agreeable to Adjournment.

The meeting resumed the consideration of the draft of the Report, and after some time spent therein, and amendments made, the same was unanimously agreed to, and is as follows, to wit.

*To the Honorable, the Legislatures of Virginia, Delaware, Pennsylvania, New Jersey, and New York—*

The Commissioners from the said States, respectively assembled at Annapolis, humbly beg leave to report.

That, pursuant to their several appointments, they met, at Annapolis in the State of Maryland, on the eleventh day of September Instant, and having proceeded to a Communication of their powers; they found that the States of New York, Pennsylvania, and Virginia, had, in substance, and nearly in the same terms, authorised their respective Commissioners "to meet such Commissioners as were, or might be, appointed by the other States in the Union, at such time and place, as should be agreed upon by the said Commissioners to take into consideration the trade and Commerce of the United States, to consider how far an uniform system in their commercial intercourse and regulations might be necessary to their common interest and permanent harmony, and to report to the several States such an Act, relative to this great object, as when unanimously ratified by them would enable the United States in Congress assembled effectually to provide for the same."

That the State of Delaware, had given similar powers to their Commissioners, with this difference only, that the Act to be framed in virtue of those powers, is required to be reported "to the United

States in Congress assembled, to be agreed to by them, and confirmed by the Legislatures of every State."

That the State of New Jersey had enlarged the object of their appointment, empowering their Commissioners, "to consider how far an uniform system in their commercial regulations and *other important matters*, might be necessary to the common interest and permanent harmony of the several States," and to report such an Act on the subject, as when ratified by them "would enable the United States in Congress assembled, effectually to provide for the exigencies of the Union."

That appointments of Commissioners have also been made by the States of New Hampshire, Massachusetts, Rhode Island, and North Carolina, none of whom however have attended; but that no information has been received by your Commissioners, of any appointment having been made by the States of Connecticut, Maryland, South Carolina or Georgia.

That the express terms of the powers to your Commissioners supposing a deputation from all the States, and having for object the Trade and Commerce of the United States, Your Commissioners did not conceive it advisable to proceed on the business of their mission, under the Circumstance of so partial and defective a representation.

Deeply impressed however with the magnitude and importance of the object confided to them on this occasion, your Commissioners cannot forbear to indulge an expression of their earnest and unanimous wish, that speedy measures may be taken, to effect a general meeting, of the States, in a future Convention, for the same, and such other purposes, as the situation of public affairs, may be found to require.

If in expressing this wish, or in intimating any other sentiment, your Commissioners should seem to exceed the strict bounds of their appointment, they entertain a full confidence, that a conduct, dictated by an anxiety for the welfare, of the United States, will not fail to receive an indulgent construction.

In this persuasion, your Commissioners submit an opinion, that the Idea of extending the powers of their Deputies, to other objects, than those of Commerce, which has been adopted by the State of

New Jersey, was an improvement on the original plan, and will deserve to be incorporated into that of a future Convention; they are the more naturally led to this conclusion, as in the course of their reflections on the subject, they have been induced to think, that the power of regulating trade is of such comprehensive extent, and will enter so far into the general System of the fœderal government, that to give it efficacy, and to obviate questions and doubts concerning its precise nature and limits, may require a correspondent adjustment of other parts of the Fœderal System.

That there are important defects in the system of the Fœderal Government is acknowledged by the Acts of all those States, which have concurred in the present Meeting; That the defects, upon a closer examination, may be found greater and more numerous, than even these acts imply, is at least so far probable, from the embarrassments which characterise the present State of our national affairs, foreign and domestic, as may reasonably be supposed to merit a deliberate and candid discussion, in some mode, which will unite the Sentiments and Councils of all the States. In the choice of the mode, your Commissioners are of opinion, that a Convention of Deputies from the different States, for the special and sole purpose of entering into this investigation, and digesting a plan for supplying such defects as may be discovered to exist, will be entitled to a preference from considerations, which will occur, without being particularised.

Your Commissioners decline an enumeration of those national circumstances on which their opinion respecting the propriety of a future Convention, with more enlarged powers, is founded; as it would be an useless intrusion of facts and observations, most of which have been frequently the subject of public discussion, and none of which can have escaped the penetration of those to whom they would in this instance be addressed. They are however of a nature so serious, as, in the view of your Commissioners to render the situation of the United States delicate and critical, calling for an exertion of the united virtue and wisdom of all the members of the Confederacy.

Under this impression, Your Commissioners, with the most respectful deference, beg leave to suggest their unanimous conviction, that it may essentially tend to advance the interests of the union, if the States, by whom they have been respectively delegated, would themselves concur, and use their endeavours to procure the concurrence of the other States, in the appointment of Commissioners, to meet at Philadelphia on the second Monday in May next, to take into consideration the situation of the United States, to devise such further provisions as shall appear to them necessary to render the constitution of the Fœderal Government adequate to the exigencies of the Union; and to report such an Act for that purpose to the United States in Congress assembled, as when agreed to, by them, and afterwards confirmed by the Legislatures of every State, will effectually provide for the same.

Though your Commissioners could not with propriety address these observations and sentiments to any but the States they have the honor to Represent, they have nevertheless concluded from motives of respect, to transmit Copies of this Report to the United States in Congress assembled, and to the executives of the other States.

By order of the Commissioners.

Dated at Annapolis
September 14th, 1786

Resolved, that the Chairman sign the aforegoing Report in behalf of the Commissioners.

Then adjourned without day—

Egb: Benson
Alexander Hamilton } New York

Abra: Clark
W<sup>m</sup> Ch.<sup>n</sup> Houston
J<sup>s</sup> Schureman } New Jersey

Tench Coxe   Pennsylvania

Geo: Read
John Dickinson
Richard Bassett } Delaware

Edmund Randolph
J<sup>s</sup> Madison J<sup>r</sup>
S<sup>t</sup> George Tucker } Virginia

# REPORT OF PROCEEDINGS IN CONGRESS,[1]
## WEDNESDAY FEB? 21, 1787

Congress assembled as before.

The report of a grand com.ᵉᵉ consisting of M.ʳ Dane M.ʳ Varnum M.ʳ S. M. Mitchell M.ʳ Smith M.ʳ Cadwallader M.ʳ Irwine M.ʳ N. Mitchell M.ʳ Forrest M.ʳ Grayson M.ʳ Blount M.ʳ Bull & M.ʳ Few, to whom was referred a letter of 14 Sept.ʳ 1786 from J. Dickinson written at the request of Commissioners from the States of Virginia Delaware Pensylvania New Jersey & New York assembled at the City of Annapolis together with a copy of the report of the said commissioners to the legislatures of the States by whom they were appointed, being an order of the day was called up & which is contained in the following resolution viz

"Congress having had under consideration the letter of John Dickinson esq.ʳ chairman of the Commissioners who assembled at Annapolis during the last year also the proceedings of the said commissioners and entirely coinciding with them as to the inefficiency of the federal government and the necessity of devising such farther provisions as shall render the same adequate to the exigencies of the Union do strongly recommend to the different legislatures to send forward delegates to meet the proposed convention on the second Monday in May next at the city of Philadelphia"

The delegates for the state of New York thereupon laid before Congress Instructions which they had received from their constituents, & in pursuance of the said instructions moved to postpone the farther consideration of the report in order to take up the following proposition to wit

"That it be recommended to the States composing the Union that a convention of representatives from the said States respectively be held at ——— on ——— for the purpose of revising the Articles of Confederation and perpetual Union between the United

---

[1] *Journals of the Continental Congress*, vol. 38 (manuscript), Library of Congress.

States of America and reporting to the United States in Congress assembled and to the States respectively such alterations and amendments of the said Articles of Confederation as the representatives met in such convention shall judge proper and necessary to render them adequate to the preservation and support of the Union"

On the question to postpone for the purpose above mentioned the yeas & nays being required by the delegates for New York.

| | | | |
|---|---|---|---|
| Massachusetts | Mr. King | ay | ay |
| | Mr. Dane | ay | |
| Connecticut | Mr. Johnson | ay | d |
| | Mr. S. M. Mitchell | no | |
| New York | Mr. Smith | ay | ay |
| | Mr. Benson | ay | |
| New Jersey | Mr. Cadwallader | ay | |
| | Mr. Clarke | no | no |
| | Mr. Schurman | no | |
| Pensylvania | Mr. Irwine | no | |
| | Mr. Meredith | ay | no |
| | Mr. Bingham | no | |
| Delaware | Mr. N. Mitchell | no x | |
| Maryland | Mr. Forest | no x | |
| Virginia | Mr. Grayson | ay | ay |
| | Mr. Madison | ay | |
| North Carolina | Mr. Blount | no | no |
| | Mr. Hawkins | no | |
| South Carolina | Mr. Bull | no | |
| | Mr. Kean | no | no |
| | Mr. Huger | no | |
| | Mr. Parker | no | |
| Georgia | Mr. Few | ay | d |
| | Mr. Pierce | no | |

So the question was lost.

A motion was then made by the delegates for Massachusetts to postpone the farther consideration of the report in order to take into consideration a motion which they read in their place, this being agreed to, the motion of the delegates for Massachusetts was taken up and being amended was agreed to as follows

Whereas there is provision in the Articles of Confederation & perpetual Union for making alterations therein by the assent of a Congress of the United States and of the legislatures of the several

States; And whereas experience hath evinced that there are defects in the present Confederation, as a mean to remedy which several of the States and particularly the State of New York by express instructions to their delegates in Congress have suggested a convention for the purposes expressed in the following resolution and such convention appearing to be the most probable mean of establishing in these states a firm national government.

Resolved that in the opinion of Congress it is expedient that on the second Monday in May next a Convention of delegates who shall have been appointed by the several states be held at Philadelphia for the sole and express purpose of revising the Articles of Confederation and reporting to Congress and the several legislatures such alterations and provisions therein as shall when agreed to in Congress and confirmed by the states render the federal constitution adequate to the exigencies of Government & the preservation of the Union.

# ORDINANCE OF 1787, JULY 13, 1787.

An Ordinance for the government of the territory of the United States northwest of the river Ohio

Section 1. *Be it ordained by the United States in Congress assembled,* That the said Territory, for the purpose of temporary government, be one district, subject, however, to be divided into two districts, as future circumstances may, in the opinion of Congress, make it expedient.

Sec. 2. *Be it ordained by the authority aforesaid,* That the estates both of resident and non-resident proprietors in the said territory, dying intestate, shall descend to, and be distributed among, their children and the descendants of a deceased child in equal parts, the descendants of a deceased child or grandchild to take the share of their deceased parent in equal parts among them; and where there shall be no children or descendants, then in equal parts to the next of kin, in equal degree; and among collaterals, the children of a deceased brother or sister of the intestate shall have, in equal parts among them, their deceased parent's share; and there shall, in no case, be a distinction between kindred of the whole and half blood; saving in all cases to the widow of the intestate, her third part of the real estate for life, and one-third part of the personal estate; and this law relative to descents and dower, shall remain in full force until altered by the legislature of the district. And until the governor and judges shall adopt laws as hereinafter mentioned, estates in the said territory may be devised or bequeathed by wills in writing, signed and sealed by him or her in whom the estate may be, (being of full age,) and attested by three witnesses; and real estates may be conveyed by lease and release, or bargain and sale, signed, sealed, and delivered by the person, being of full age, in whom the estate may be, and attested by two witnesses, provided such wills be duly proved, and such conveyances be acknowledged, or the execution thereof duly proved, and be recorded within one year after proper magistrates, courts, and registers, shall be appointed for that purpose; and personal property may be transferred by delivery, saving, however, to the French and Canadian inhabitants, and other settlers of the Kaskaskies, Saint Vincents, and the neighboring villages, who have heretofore professed themselves citizens of Virginia, their laws and customs now in force among them, relative to the descent and conveyance of property.

Sec. 3. *Be it ordained by the authority aforesaid,* That there shall be appointed, from time to time, by Congress, a governor, whose commission shall continue in force for the term of three years, unless sooner revoked by Congress; he shall reside in the district, and have a freehold estate therein, in one thousand acres of land, while in the exercise of his office.

Sec. 4. There shall be appointed from time to time, by Congress, a secretary, whose commission shall continue in force for four years, unless sooner revoked; he shall reside in the district, and have a freehold estate therein, in five hundred acres of land, while in the exercise of his office. It shall be his duty to keep and preserve the acts and laws passed by the legislature, and the public records of the district, and the proceedings of the governor in his executive department, and transmit authentic copies of such acts and proceedings every six months to the Secretary of Congress. There shall also be appointed a court, to consist of three judges, any two of whom to form a court, who shall have a common-law jurisdiction and reside in the district, and have each therein a freehold estate, in five hundred acres of land, while in the exercise of their offices; and their commissions shall continue in force during good behavior.

Sec. 5. The governor and judges, or a majority of them, shall adopt and publish in the district such laws of the original States, criminal and civil, as may be necessary, and best suited to the circumstances of the district, and report them to Congress from time to time, which laws shall be in force in the district until the organization of the general assembly therein, unless disapproved of by Congress; but afterwards the legislature shall have authority to alter them as they shall think fit.

Sec. 6. The governor, for the time being, shall be commander-in-chief of the militia, appoint and commission all officers in the same below the rank of general officers; all general officers shall be appointed and commissioned by Congress.

Sec. 7. Previous to the organization of the general assembly the governor shall appoint such magistrates, and other civil officers, in each county or township, as he shall find necessary for the preservation of the peace and good order in the same. After the general assembly shall be organized the powers and duties of magistrates and other civil officers shall be regulated and defined by the said assembly; but all magistrates and other civil officers, not herein otherwise directed, shall, during the continuance of this temporary government, be appointed by the governor.

Sec. 8. For the preveniton of crimes, and injuries, the laws to be adopted or made shall have force in all parts of the district, and for the execution of process, criminal and civil, the governor shall make proper divisions thereof; and he shall proceed, from time to time, as circumstances may require, to lay out the parts of the district in which the Indian titles shall have been extinguished, into counties and townships, subject, however, to such alterations as may thereafter be made by the legislature.

Sec. 9. So soon as there shall be five thousand free male inhabitants, of full age, in the district, upon giving proof thereof to the governor, they shall receive authority, with time and place, to elect representatives from their counties or townships, to represent them in the general assembly: *Provided*, That for every five hundred free male inhabitants there shall be one representative, and so on, progressively, with the number of free male inhabitants, shall the right of representation increase, until the number of representatives shall amount to twenty-five; after which the number and proportion of representatives shall be regulated by the legislature: *Provided*, That no person be eligible or qualified to act as a representative, unless he shall have been a citizen of one of the United States three years, and be a resident in the district, or unless he shall have resided in the district three years; and, in either case, shall likewise hold in his own right, in fee-simple, two hundred acres of land within the same: *Provided also*, That a freehold in fifty acres of land in the district, having been a citizen of one of the States, and being resident in the district, or the like freehold and two years' residence in the district, shall be necessary to qualify a man as an elector of a representative.

Sec. 10. The representatives thus elected shall serve for the term of two years; and in case of the death of a representative, or removal from office, the governor shall issue a writ to the county or township, for which he was a member, to elect another in his stead, to serve for the residue of the term.

Sec. 11. The general assembly, or legislature, shall consist of the governor, legislative council, and a house of representatives. The legislative council shall consist of five members, to continue in office five years, unless sooner removed by Congress; any three of whom to be a quorum; and the members of the council shall be nominated and appointed in the following manner, to wit: As soon as representatives shall be elected the governor shall appoint a time and place for them to meet together, and when met they shall nominate ten persons, resident in the district, and each possessed of a freehold in five hundred acres of land, and return their names to Congress, five of whom Congress shall appoint and commission to serve as aforesaid; and whenever a vacancy shall happen in the Council, by death or removal from office, the house of representatives shall nominate two persons, qualified as aforesaid, for each vacancy, and return their names to Congress, one of whom Congress shall appoint and commission for the residue of the term; and every five years, four months at least before the expiration of the time of service of the members of the council, the said house shall nominate ten persons, qualified as aforesaid, and return their names to Congress, five of whom Congress shall appoint and commission to serve as members of the council five years, unless sooner removed. And the governor, legislative council, and house of representatives shall have authority to make laws in all cases for the good government of the district, not repugnant to the principles and articles in this ordinance established and declared. And all bills, having passed by a majority in the house, and by a majority in the council, shall be referred to the governor for his assent; but no bill, or legislative act whatever, shall be of any force without his assent. The governor shall have power to convene, prorogue, and dissolve the general assembly when, in his opinion, it shall be expedient.

Sec. 12. The governor, judges, legislative council, secretary, and such other officers as Congress shall appoint in the district, shall take an oath or affirmation of fidelity, and of office; the governor before the President of Congress, and all other officers before the governor. As soon as a legislature shall be formed in the district, the council and house assembled, in one room, shall have authority, by joint ballot, to elect a delegate to Congress, who shall have a seat in Congress, with a right of debating, but not of voting, during this temporary government.

Sec. 13. And for extending the fundamental principles of civil and religious liberty, which form the basis whereon these republics, their laws and constitutions, are erected; to fix and establish those principles as the basis of all laws, constitutions, and governments, which forever hereafter shall be formed in the said territory; to provide, also, for the establishment of States, and permanent government therein, and for their admission to a share in the Federal councils on an equal footing with the original States, at as early periods as may be consistent with the general interest:

Sec. 14. It is hereby ordained and declared, by the authority aforesaid, that the following articles shall be considered as articles of compact, between the original States and the people and States in the said territory, and forever remain unalterable, unless by common consent, to wit:

## Article I

No person, demeaning himself in a peaceable and orderly manner, shall ever be molested on account of his mode of worship, or religious sentiments, in the said territory.

## Article II

The inhabitants of the said territory shall always be entitled to the benefits of the writs of *habeas corpus*, and of the trial by jury; of a proportionate representation of the people in the legislature, and of judicial proceedings according to the course of the common law. All persons shall be bailable, unless for capital offences, where the proof shall be evident, or the presumption great All fines shall be moderate; and no cruel or unusual punishment shall be inflicted. No man shall be deprived of his liberty or property, but by the judgment of his peers, or the law of the land, and should the public exigencies make it necessary, for the common preservation, to take any person's property, or to demand his particular services, full compensation shall be made for the same. And, in the just preservation of rights and property, it is understood and declared, that no law ought ever to be made or have force in the said territory, that shall, in any manner whatever, interfere with or affect private contracts, or engagements, *bona fide*, and without fraud previously formed.

## Article III

Religion, morality, and knowledge being necessary to good government and the happiness of mankind, schools and the means of education shall forever be encouraged. The utmost good faith shall always be observed towards the Indians; their lands and property shall never be taken from them without their consent; and in their property, rights, and liberty they never shall be invaded or disturbed unless in just and lawful wars authorized by Congress; but laws founded in justice and humanity shall, from time to time, be made, for preventing wrongs being done to them, and for preserving peace and friendship with them.

## Article IV

The said territory, and the States which may be formed therein, shall forever remain a part of this confederacy of the United States of America, subject to the articles of Confederation, and to such alterations therein as shall be constitutionally made; and to all the acts and ordinances of the United States in Congress assembled, conformable thereto. The inhabitants and settlers in the said territory shall be subject to pay a part of the Federal debts, contracted, or to be contracted, and a proportional part of the expenses of government to be apportioned on them by Congress, according to the same common rule and measure by which apportionments thereof shall be made on the other States; and the taxes for paying their proportion shall be laid and levied by the authority and direction of the legislatures of the district, or districts, or new States, as in the original States, within the time agreed upon by the United States in Congress assembled. The legislatures of those districts, or new States, shall never interfere with the primary disposal of the soil by the United States in Congress assembled, nor with any regulations Congress may find necessary for securing the title in such soil to the *bona-fide* purchasers. No tax shall be imposed on lands the property of the United States; and in no case shall non-resident proprietors be taxed higher than residents. The navigable waters leading into the Mississippi and Saint Lawrence, and the carrying places between the same, shall be common highways, and forever free, as well to the inhabitants of the said territory as to the citizens of the United States, and those of any other States that may be admitted into the confederacy, without any tax, impost, or duty therefor.

## Article V

There shall be formed in the said territory not less than three nor more than five States; and the boundaries of the States, as soon as Virginia shall alter her act of cession and consent to the same, shall become fixed and established as follows, to wit: The western State, in the said territory, shall be bounded by the Mississippi, the Ohio, and the Wabash Rivers; a direct line drawn from the Wabash and Post Vincents, due north, to the territorial line between the United States and Canada; and by the said territorial line to the Lake of the Woods and Mississippi. The middle State shall be bounded by the said direct line, the Wabash from Post Vincents to the Ohio, by the Ohio, by a direct line drawn due north from the mouth of the Great Miami to the said territorial line, and by the said territorial line. The eastern State shall be bounded by the last-mentioned direct line, the Ohio, Pennsylvania, and the said territorial line: *Provided, however*, And it is further understood and declared, that the boundaries of these three States shall be subject so far to be altered, that, if Congress shall hereafter find it expedient, they shall have authority to form one or two States in that part of the said territory which lies north of an east and west line drawn through the southerly bend or extreme of Lake Michigan. And whenever any of the said States shall have sixty thousand free inhabitants therein, such State shall be admitted by its delegates, into the Congress of the United States, on an equal footing with the original States, in all respects whatever; and shall be at liberty to form a permanent constitution and State government: *Provided*, The constitution and government, so to be formed, shall be republican, and in conformity to the principles contained in these articles, and, so far as it can be consistent with the general interest of the confederacy, such admission shall be allowed at an earlier period, and when there may be a less number of free inhabitants in the State than sixty thousand.

## Article VI

There shall be neither slavery nor involuntary servitude in the said territory, otherwise than in the punishment of crimes, whereof the party shall have been duly convicted: *Provided always*, That any person escaping into the same, from whom labor or service is lawfully claimed in any one of the original States, such fugitive may be lawfully reclaimed, and conveyed to the person claiming his or her labor or service as aforesaid.

*Be it ordained by the authority aforesaid*, That the resolutions of the 23d of April, 1784, relative to the subject of this ordinance, be, and the same are hereby, repealed, and declared null and void.

Done by the United States, in Congress assembled, the 13th day of July, in the year of our Lord 1787, and of their sovereignty and independence the twelfth.[1]

---

[1] *Journals of Congress* (ed. 1823), IV., pp. 752-54.

# CREDENTIALS OF THE MEMBERS OF THE FEDERAL CONVENTION [1]

### STATE OF NEW HAMPSHIRE [2]

In the Year of our Lord One thousand seven hundred and Eighty seven.

An Act for appointing Deputies from this State to the Convention, proposed to be holden in the City of Philadelphia in May 1787 for the purpose of revising the federal Constitution.

Whereas in the formation of the federal Compact, which frames the bond of Union of the American States, it was not possible in the infant state of our Republic to devise a system which in the course of time and experience, would not manifest imperfections that it would be necessary to reform.

And Whereas the limited powers, which by the Articles of Confederation, are vested in the Congress of the United States, have been found far inadequate, to the enlarged purposes which they were intended to produce. And Whereas Congress hath, by repeated and most urgent representations, endeavoured to awaken this, and other States of the Union, to a sense of the truly critical and alarming situation in which they may inevitably be involved, unless timely measures be taken to enlarge the powers of Congress, that they may be thereby enabled to avert the dangers which threaten our existence as a free and independent People. And Whereas this State hath been ever desirous to act upon the liberal system of the general good of the United States, without circumscribing its views, to the narrow and selfish objects of partial convenience; and has been at all times ready to make every concession to the safety and happiness of the whole, which justice and sound policy could vindicate.

---

[1] The States of Virginia, New Jersey, Pennsylvania, North Carolina, New Hampshire, Delaware, and Georgia took legislative action, and in the order named, before the resolution of Congress of February 21, 1787, formally authorizing the Convention.

Thereafter, and in the order named, the States of New York, South Carolina, Massachusetts, Connecticut, and Maryland took legislative actions to be represented in the Federal Convention.

Rhode Island took no action and was not represented in the Federal Convention.

[2] Reprinted from *Documentary History of the Constitution*, Vol. I (1894), pp. 9, 10.

BE IT THEREFORE ENACTED, by the Senate and House of Representatives in General Court convened that JOHN LANGDON, JOHN PICKERING, NICHOLAS GILMAN & BENJAMIN WEST ESQUIRES be and hereby are appointed Commissioners, they or any two of them, are hereby authorized, and empowered, as Deputies from this State to meet at Philadelphia said Convention or any other place, to which the Convention may be adjourned, for the purposes aforesaid, there to confer with such Deputies, as are, or may be appointed by the other States for similar purposes; and with them to discuss and decide upon the most effectual means to remedy the defects of our federal Union; and to procure, and secure, the enlarged purposes which it was intended to effect, and to report such an Act, to the United States in Congress, as when agreed to by them, and duly confirmed by the several States, will effectually provide for the same.

State of New Hampshire } In the House of Representatives June 27$^{th}$ 1787.

The foregoing Bill having been read a third time, Voted that it pass to be enacted.

Sent up for Concurrence

JOHN SPARHAWK Speaker

In Senate, the same day—This Bill having been read a third time,—Voted that the same be enacted.

J$^{no}$ SULLIVAN President.

Copy Examined.

P$^r$ JOSEPH PEARSON Sec$^y$. (Seal append$^t$.)

COMMONWEALTH OF MASSACHUSETTS [3]

(Seal Append$^t$.) By His Excellency James Bowdoin Esquire Governor of the Commonwealth of Massachusetts.

To the Honorable Francis Dana, Elbridge Gerry, Nathaniel Gorham, Rufus King and Caleb Strong Esquires. Greeting.

Whereas Congress did on the twenty first day of February A° D$^i$ 1787, Resolve "that in the opinion of Congress it is expedient that on the second Monday in May next a Convention of Delegates who

---

[3] Reprinted from *Documentary History of the Constitution*, Vol. I (1894), pp. 11, 12.

shall have been appointed by the several States to be held at Philadelphia for the sole and express purpose of revising the Articles of Confederation and reporting to Congress and the several Legislatures, such alterations and provisions therein as shall when agreed to in Congress, and confirmed by the States render the federal Constitution adequate to the exigencies of government and the preservation of the Union." And Whereas the General Court have constituted and appointed you their Delegates to attend and represent this Commonwealth in the said proposed Convention; and have by Resolution of theirs of the tenth of March last, requested me to Commission you for that purpose.

Now therefore Know Ye, that in pursuance of the resolutions aforesaid, I do by these presents, commission you the said Francis Dana, Elbridge Gerry Nathaniel Gorham, Rufus King & Caleb Strong Esquires or any three of you to meet such Delegates as may be appointed by the other or any of the other States in the Union to meet in Convention at Philadelphia at the time and for the purposes aforesaid.

In Testimony whereof I have caused the Public Seal of the Commonwealth aforesaid to be hereunto affixed.

> Given at the Council Chamber in Boston the Ninth day of April A° D?ᵐ 1787 and in the Eleventh Year of the Independence of the United States of America.
>
> JAMES BOWDOIN

By His Excellency's Command.

JOHN AVERY JUNʳ, Secretary

### STATE OF CONNECTICUT[4]

(Seal.) At a General Assembly of the State of Connecticut in America, holden at Hartford on the second Thursday of May, Anno Domini 1787.

An Act for appointing Delegates to meet in a Convention of the States to be held at the City of Philadelphia on the second Monday of May instant.

Whereas the Congress of the United States by their Act of the twenty first of February 1787 have recommended that on the

---

[4] Reprinted from *Documentary History of the Constitution*, Vol. I (1894), pp. 12, 13.

second Monday of May instant, a Convention of Delegates, who shall have been appointed by the several States, be held at Philadelphia for the sole and express purpose of revising the Articles of Confederation.

Be it enacted by the Governor, Council and Representatives in General Court Assembled and by the Authority of the same.

That the Honorable William Samuel Johnson, Roger Sherman, and Oliver Ellsworth Esquires, be and they hereby are appointed Delegates to attend the said Convention, and are requested to proceed to the City of Philadelphia for that purpose without delay; And the said Delegates, and in case of sickness or accident, such one or more of them as shall actually attend the said Convention, is and are hereby authorized and empowered to Represent this State therein, and to confer with such Delegates appointed by the several States, for the purposes mentioned in the said Act of Congress that may be present and duly empowered to act in said Convention, and to discuss upon such Alterations and Provisions agreeable to the general Principles of Republican Government as they shall think proper to render the federal Constitution adequate to the exigencies of Government and, the preservation of the Union; And they are further directed, pursuant to the said Act of Congress to report such alterations and provisions as may be agreed to by a majority of the United States represented in Convention to the Congress of the United States, and to the General Assembly of this State.

       A true Copy of Record
       Exam$^d$
        By GEORGE WYLLYS Sec$^y$.

NEW-YORK [5]

(Seal)  By His Excellency George Clinton Esquire Governor of the State of New York General and Commander in Chief of all the Militia and Admiral of the Navy of the same.

---

[5] Reprinted from *Documentary History of the Constitution*, Vol. I (1894), pp. 13-16.

To all to whom these Presents shall come

It is by these Presents certified that John M$^c$Kesson who has subscribed the annexed Copies of Resolutions is Clerk of the Assembly of this State.

> In Testimony whereof I have caused the Privy Seal of the said State to be hereunto affixed this Ninth day of May in the Eleventh Year of the Independence of the said State.

GEO: CLINTON.

State of New York

In Assembly February 28<sup>th</sup> 1787.

A Copy of a Resolution of the honorable the Senate, delivered by M$^r$ Williams, was read, and is in the Words following, viz$^t$.

Resolved, if the honorable the Assembly concur herein, that three Delegates be appointed on the part of this State, to meet such Delegates as may be appointed on the part of the other States respectively, on the second Monday in may next, at Philadelphia, for the sole and express purpose of revising the Articles of Confederation, and reporting to Congress, and to the several Legislatures, such alterations and Provisions therein, as shall, when agreed to in Congress, and confirmed by the several States, render the federal Constitution adequate to the Exigencies of Government, and the preservation of the Union; and that in case of such concurrence, the two Houses of the Legislature, will, on Tuesday next, proceed to nominate and appoint the said Delegates, in like manner as is directed by the Constitution of this State, for nominating and appointing Delegates to Congress.

Resolved, that this House do concur with the honorable the Senate, in the said Resolution.

In Assembly March 6<sup>th</sup> 1787.

Resolved, that the Honorable Robert Yates Esquire, and Alexander Hamilton and John Lansing, Junior Esquires, be, and they are hereby nominated by this House, Delegates on the part of this State, to meet such Delegates as may be appointed on the part of the other States respectively, on the second Monday in May next, at Philadelphia, pursuant to concurrent Resolutions of both Houses of the Legislature, on the 28<sup>th</sup> Ultimo.

Resolved, that this House will meet the Honorable the Senate, immediately, at such place as they shall appoint, to compare the Lists of Persons nominated by the Senate and Assembly respectively, as Delegates on the part of this State, to meet such Delegates as may be appointed on the part of the other States respectively, on the second Monday in May next, at Philadelphia, pursuant to concurrent Resolutions, of both Houses of the Legislature, on the 28$^t$ Ultimo.

Ordered That M$^r$ N. Smith deliver a Copy of the last preceding Resolution, to the Honorable the Senate.

A Copy of a Resolution of the Honorable the Senate, was delivered by M$^r$ Vanderbilt, that the Senate will immediately meet this House in the Assembly Chamber, to compare the Lists of Persons nominated by the Senate and Assembly respectively, as Delegates, pursuant to the Resolutions before mentioned.

The Honorable the Senate accordingly attended in the Assembly Chamber, to compare the Lists of Persons nominated for Delegates, as above mentioned.

The list of Persons nominated by the Honorable the Senate were the Honorable Robert Yates Esquire, and John Lansing Junior, and Alexander Hamilton Esquires; and on comparing the Lists of the Persons nominated by the Senate and Assembly respectively, it appeared that the same Persons were nominated in both Lists. Thereupon, Resolved that the Honorable Robert Yates, John Lansing Junior and Alexander Hamilton Esquires, be, and they are hereby declared duly nominated and appointed Delegates, on the part of this State, to meet such Delegates as may be appointed on the part of the other States respectively, on the second Monday in May next, at Philadelphia, for the sole and express purpose of revising the Articles of Confederation, and reporting to Congress, and to the several Legislatures, such alterations and provisions therein, as shall, when agreed to in Congress, and confirmed by the several States, render the federal Constitution adequate to the exigencies of Government, and the preservation of the Union.

True Extracts from the Journals of the Assembly

JOHN M$^c$KESSON Clk.

THE STATE OF NEW JERSEY [6]

(Seal) To the Honorable David Brearly, William Churchill Houston, William Patterson and John Neilson Esquires. Greeting.

The Council and Assembly reposing especial trust and confidence in your integrity, prudence and ability, have at a joint meeting appointed you the said David Brearly, William Churchill Houston, William Patterson and John Neilson Esquires, or any three of you, Commissioners to meet such Commissioners, as have been or may be appointed by the other States in the Union, at the City of Philadelphia in the Commonwealth of Pensylvania, on the second Monday in May next for the purpose of taking into Consideration the state of the Union, as to trade and other important objects, and of devising such other Provisions as shall appear to be necessary to render the Constitution of the Federal Government adequate to the exigencies thereof.

> In testimony whereof the Great Seal of the State is hereunto affixed. Witness William Livingston Esquire, Governor, Captain General and Commander in Chief in and over the State of New Jersey and Territories thereunto belonging Chancellor and Ordinary in the same, at Trenton the Twenty third day of November in the Year of our Lord One thousand seven hundred and Eighty six and of our Sovereignty and Independence the Eleventh.
>
> WIL: LIVINGSTON.

By His Excellency's Command
    BOWES REED Sec<sup>y</sup>.

The STATE OF NEW JERSEY.

(Seal) To His Excellency William Livingston and the Honorable Abraham Clark Esquires Greeting.

The Council and Assembly reposing especial trust and Confidence in your integrity, prudence and ability have at a joint Meeting appointed You the said William Livingston and Abraham Clark Esquires, in conjunction with the Honorable David Brearley, William Churchill Houston & William Patterson Esquires, or any three of

---

[6] Reprinted from *Documentary History of the Constitution*, Vol. I (1894), pp. 16-19.

you, Commissioners to meet such Commissioners as have been appointed by the other States in the Union at the City of Philadelphia in the Commonwealth of Pensylvania on the second Monday of this present Month for the purpose of taking into consideration the state of the Union as to trade and other important Objects, and of devising such other Provisions as shall appear to be necessary to render the Constitution of the federal Government adequate to the exigencies thereof.

> In Testimony whereof the Great Seal of the State is hereunto affixed. Witness William Livingston Esquire, Governor, Captain General and Commander in Chief in and over the State of New Jersey and Territories thereunto belonging Chancellor and Ordinary in the same at Burlington the Eighteenth day of May in the Year of our Lord One thousand seven hundred and Eighty seven and of our Sovereignty and Independence the Eleventh.

WIL: LIVINGSTON

By His Excellency's Command
BOWES REED Sec<sup>y</sup>.

The STATE OF NEW JERSEY.
To the Honorable Jonathan Dayton Esquire

The Council and Assembly reposing especial trust and confidence in your integrity, prudence and ability have at a joint Meeting appointed You the said Jonathan Dayton Esquire, in conjunction with His Excellency William Livingston, the Honorable David Brearley, William Churchill Houston, William Patterson and Abraham Clark Esquires, or any three of you, Commissioners to meet such Commissioners as have been appointed by the other States in the Union at the City of Philadelphia in the Commonwealth of Pensylvania, for the purposes of taking into consideration the state of the Union as to trade and other important objects, and of devising such other Provision as shall appear to be necessary to render the Constitution of the federal Government adequate to the exigencies thereof.

> In Testimony whereof the Great Seal of the State is hereunto affixed:—Witness Robert Lettis Hooper Esquire, Vice-President, Captain General and Commander in Chief

in and over the State of New Jersey and Territories thereunto belonging, Chancellor and Ordinary in the same at Burlington this fifth day of June in the Year of our Lord One thousand seven hundred and Eighty seven and of our Sovereignty and Independence the Eleventh.

ROB<sup>T</sup> L. HOOPER

By his Honor's Command
        BOWES REED Sec<sup>y</sup>.

### PENSYLVANIA [7]

An Act appointing Deputies to the Convention intended to be held in the City of Philadelphia for the purpose of revising the fœderal Constitution.

Section 1<sup>st</sup> Whereas the General Assembly of this Commonwealth taking into their serious Consideration the Representations heretofore made to the Legislatures of the several States in the Union by the United States in Congress Assembled, and also weighing the difficulties under which the Confederated States now labour, are fully convinced of the necessity of revising the federal Constitution for the purpose of making such Alterations and amendments as the exigencies of our Public Affairs require. And Whereas the Legislature of the State of Virginia have already passed an Act of that Commonwealth empowering certain Commissioners to meet at the City of Philadelphia in May next, a Convention of Commissioners or Deputies from the different States; And the Legislature of this State are fully sensible of the important advantages which may be derived to the United States, and every of them from co-operating with the Commonwealth of Virginia, and the other States of the Confederation in the said Design.

Section 2<sup>nd</sup> Be it enacted, and it is hereby enacted by the Representatives of the Freemen of the Commonwealth of Pensylvia in General Assembly met, and by the Authority of the same, That Thomas Mifflin, Robert Morris, George Clymer, Jared Ingersoll, Thomas Fitzsimmons, James Wilson and Governeur Morris Esquires, are hereby appointed Deputies from this State to meet in the Convention of the Deputies of the respective States of North

---

[7] Reprinted from *Documentary History of the Constitution*, Vol. I (1894), pp. 19-23.

America to be held at the City of Philadelphia on the second day of the Month of May next; And the said Thomas Mifflin, Robert Morris, George Clymer, Jared Ingersoll, Thomas Fitzsimmons, James Wilson and Governeur Morris Esquires, or any four of them, are hereby constituted and appointed Deputies from this State, with Powers to meet such Deputies as may be appointed and authorized by the other States, to assemble in the said Convention at the City aforesaid, and to join with them in devising, deliberating on, and discussing, all such alterations and further Provisions, as may be necessary to render the fœderal Constitution fully adequate to the exigencies of the Union, and in reporting such Act or Acts for that purpose to the United States in Congress Assembled, as when agreed to by them and duly confirmed by the several States, will effectually provide for the same.

Section $3^d$ And be it further enacted by the Authority aforesaid, That in case any of the $s^d$ Deputies hereby nominated, shall happen to die, or to resign his or their said Appointment or Appointments, the Supreme Executive Council shall be and hereby are empowered and required, to nominate and appoint other Persons or Persons in lieu of him or them so deceased, or who has or have so resigned, which Person or Persons, from and after such Nomination and Appointment, shall be and hereby are declared to be vested with the same Powers respectively, as any of the Deputies Nominated and Appointed by this Act, is vested with by the same: Provided Always, that the Council are not hereby authorised, nor shall they make any such Nomination or Appointment, except in Vacation and during the Recess of the General Assembly of this State.

Signed by Order of the House

{Seal of the Laws of Pensylvania}   THOMAS MIFFLIN Speaker

Enacted into a Law at Philadelphia on Saturday December the thirtieth in the Year of our Lord one thousand seven hundred and Eighty six.

PETER ZACHARY LLOYD
Clerk of the General Assembly.

I Mathew Irwin Esquire Master of the Rolls for the State of Pensylvania Do Certify the Preceding Writing to be a true Copy (or Exemplification) of a certain Act of Assembly lodged in my Office.

(Seal.) In Witness whereof I have hereunto set my Hand and Seal of Office the 15 May A. D. 1787.

MATH$^w$. IRWINE
M. R.

(Seal) A Supplement to the Act entitled "An Act appointing Deputies to the Convention intended to be held in the City of Philadelphia for the purpose of revising the Federal Constitution.

Section 1$^{st}$ Whereas by the Act to which this Act is a Supplement, certain Persons were appointed as Deputies from this State to sit in the said Convention: And Whereas it is the desire of the General Assembly that His Excellency Benjamin Franklin Esquire, President of this State should also sit in the said Convention as a Deputy from this State—therefore

Section 2$^d$ Be it enacted and it is hereby enacted by the Representatives of the Freemen of the Commonwealth of Pensylvania, in General Assembly met, and by the Authority of the same, that His Excellency Benjamin Franklin Esquire, be, and he is hereby, appointed and authorised to sit in the said Convention as a Deputy from this State in addition to the Persons heretofore appointed; And that he be, and he hereby is invested with like Powers and authorities as are invested in the said Deputies or any of them.

Signed by Order of the House

THOMAS MIFFLIN Speaker.

Enacted into a Law at Philadelphia on Wednesday the twenty eighth day of March, in the Year of our Lord one thousand seven hundred & eighty seven.  PETER ZACHARY LLOYD
Clerk of the General Assembly.

I Mathew Irwine Esquire, Master of the Rolls for the State of Pensylvania Do Certify the above to be a true Copy (or Exemplification) of a Supplement to a certain Act of Assembly which Supplement is lodged in my Office

(Seal) In Witness whereof I have hereunto set my Hand and Seal of Office the 15 May A$^o$ D. 1787.

MATH$^w$ IRWINE
M. R.

## DELAWARE [8]

(Seal) His Excellency Thomas Collins, Esquire, President, Captain General, and Commander in Chief of the Delaware State; To all to whom these Presents shall come, Greeting. Know Ye, that among the Laws of the said State, passed by the General Assembly of the same, on the third day of February, in the Year of our Lord One thousand seven hundred and Eighty seven, it is thus inrolled.

In the Eleventh Year of the Independence of the Delaware State

An Act appointing Deputies from this State to the Convention proposed to be held in the City of Philadelphia for the Purpose of revising the Federal Constitution.

Whereas the General Assembly of this State are fully convinced of the Necessity of revising the Federal Constitution, and adding thereto such further Provisions, as may render the same more adequate to the Exigencies of the Union; And Whereas the Legislature of Virginia have already passed an Act of that Commonwealth, appointing and authorizing certain Commissioners to meet, at the City of Philadelphia, in May next, a Convention of Commissioners or Deputies from the different States: And this State being willing and desirous of co-operating with the Commonwealth of Virginia, and the other States in the Confederation, in so useful a design.

Be it therefore enacted by the General Assembly of Delaware, that George Read, Gunning Bedford, John Dickinson, Richard Bassett and Jacob Broom, Esquires, are hereby appointed Deputies from this State to meet in the Convention of the Deputies of other States, to be held at the City of Philadelphia on the Second day of May next: And the said George Read, Gunning Bedford, John Dickinson, Richard Bassett and Jacob Broom, Esquires, or any three of them, are hereby constituted and appointed Deputies from this State, with Powers to meet such Deputies as may be appointed and authorized by the other States to assemble in the said Convention at the City aforesaid, and to join with them in devising, deliberating on, and discussing, such Alterations and further

---

[8] Reprinted from *Documentary History of the Constitution*, Vol. I (1894), pp. 23-25.

Provisions as may be necessary to render the Fœderal Constitution adequate to the Exigencies of the Union; and in reporting such Act or Acts for that purpose to the United States in Congress Assembled, as when agreed to by them, and duly confirmed by the several States, may effectually provide for the same: So always and Provided, that such Alterations or further Provisions, or any of them, do not extend to that part of the Fifth Article of the Confederation of the said States, finally ratified on the first day of March, in the Year One thousand seven hundred and eighty one, which declares that "in determining Questions in the United States in Congress Assembled each State shall have one Vote."

And be it enacted, that in Case any of the said Deputies hereby nominated, shall happen to die, or to resign his or their Appointment, the President or Commander in Chief with the Advice of the Privy Council, in the Recess of the General Assembly, is hereby authorized to supply such Vacancies

Passed at Dover, February 3ᵈ 1787.

Signed by Order of the House of Assembly
JOHN COOK, Speaker
Signed by Order of the Council
GEO CRAGHEAD, Speaker.

All and singular which Premises by the Tenor of these Presents, I have caused to be Exemplified. In Testimony whereof I have hereunto subscribed my Name, and caused the Great-Seal of the said State to be affixed to these Presents, at New Castle the Second day of April in the Year of our Lord One thousand seven hundred and eighty seven, and in the Eleventh Year of the Independence of the United States of America

Attest                                           THOˢ COLLINS
JA BOOTH Secʸ.

## MARYLAND [9]

An Act for the Appointment of, and conferring Powers in Deputies from this State to the fœderal Convention.

Be it enacted by the General Assembly of Maryland, That the Honorable James MᶜHenry Daniel, of Saint Thomas Jenifer,

---
[⁶] Reprinted from *Documentary History of the Constitution*, Vol. I (1894), pp. 25-26.

Daniel Carroll, John Francis Mercer and Luther Martin Esquires, be appointed and authorised on behalf of this State, to meet such Deputies as may be appointed and authorised by any other of the United States to assemble in Convention at Philadelphia for the purpose of revising the Fœderal System, and to join with them in considering such Alterations and further Provisions as may be necessary to render the Fœderal Constitution adequate to the Exigencies of the Union and in reporting such an Act for that purpose to the United States in Congress Assembled as when agreed to by them, and duly confirmed by the several States will effectually provide for the same, and the said Deputies or such of them as shall attend the said Convention shall have full Power to represent this State for the Purposes aforesaid, and the said Deputies are hereby directed to report the Proceedings of the said Convention, and any Act agreed to therein, to the next session of the General Assembly of this State.

By the Senate May 26. 1787.  By the House of Delegates May
    Read and Assented to    26ᵈ 1787.
By Order J. Dorsey Clk.     Read and Asented to
True Copy from the Original   By Order Wᵐ Harwood Clk.
    J. DORSEY Clk. Senate.   True Copy from the Original
                                  Wᴹ HARWOOD Clk Ho Del.

W. SMALLWOOD.

VIRGINIA [10]

GENERAL ASSEMBLY begun and held at the Public Buildings in the City of Richmond on Monday the sixteenth day of October in the Year of our Lord one thousand seven hundred and Eighty six

AN ACT for appointing Deputies from this Commonwealth to a Convention proposed to be held in the City of Philadelphia in May next for the purpose of revising the federal Constitution.

WHEREAS the Commissioners who assembled at Annapolis on the fourteenth day of September last for the purpose of devising and reporting the means of enabling Congress to provide effectually for the Commercial Interests of the United States have represented

---

[10] Reprinted from *Documentary History of the Constitution*, Vol. I (1894), pp. 26-31.

the necessity of extending the revision of the fœderal System to all it's defects and have recommended that Deputies for that purpose be appointed by the several Legislatures to meet in Convention in the City of Philadelphia on the second [Mon]day of May next a provision which was preferable [11] to a discussion of the subject in Congress where it might be too much interrupted by the ordinary business before them and where it would besides be deprived of the valuable Counsels of sundry Individuals who are disqualified by the Constitution or Laws of particular States or restrained by peculiar circumstances from a Seat in that Assembly: AND WHEREAS the General Assembly of this Commonwealth taking into view the actual situation of the Confederacy as well as reflecting on the alarming representations made from time to time by the United States in Congress particularly in their Act of the fifteenth day of February last can no longer doubt that the Crisis is arrived at which the good People of America are to decide the solemn question whether they will by wise and magnanimous Efforts reap the just fruits of that Independence which they have so gloriously acquired and of that Union which they have cemented with so much of their common Blood, or whether by giving way to unmanly Jealousies and Prejudices or to partial and transitory Interests they will renounce the auspicious blessings prepared for them by the Revolution, and furnish to its Enemies an eventual Triumph over those by whose virtue and valor it has been accomplished: AND WHEREAS the same noble and extended policy and the same fraternal and affectionate Sentiments which originally determined the Citizens of this Commonwealth to unite with their Brethren of the other States in establishing a Fœderal Government cannot but be Felt with equal force now as motives to lay aside every inferior consideration and to concur in such farther concessions and Provisions as may be necessary to secure the great Objects for which that Government was instituted and to render the *United States* as happy in peace as they have been glorious in War BE IT THEREFORE ENACTED by the General Assembly of the Commonwealth of Virginia that seven Commissioners be appointed by joint Ballot of both Houses of Assembly

---

[11] The original law reads "which seems preferable."

who or any three of them are hereby authorized as Deputies from this Commonwealth to meet such Deputies as may be appointed and authorized by other States to assemble in Convention at Philadelphia as above recommended and to join with them in devising and discussing all such Alterations and farther Provisions as may be necessary to render the Fœderal Constitution adequate to the Exigencies of the Union and in reporting such an Act for that purpose to the United States in Congress as when agreed to by them and duly confirmed by the several States will effectually provide for the same. AND BE IT FURTHER ENACTED that in case of the death of any of the said Deputies or of their declining their appointments the Executive are hereby authorized to supply such Vacancies. AND the Governor is requested to transmit forthwith a Copy of this Act to the United States in Congress and to the Executives of each of the States in the Union.

Signed   JOHN JONES Speaker of the Senate
     JOSEPH PRENTIS, Speaker of the
            House of Delegates.

A true Copy from the Inrollment
  JOHN BECKLEY Clk House Del<sup>s</sup>

In the House of Delegates

Monday the 4<sup>th</sup> of December 1786.

THE HOUSE according to the Order of the Day proceeded by joint Ballot with the Senate to the appointment of Seven Deputies from this Commonwealth to a Convention proposed to be held in the City of Philadelphia in May next for the purpose of revising the Fœderal Constitution, and the Members having prepared Tickets with the names of the Persons to be appointed, and deposited the same in the Ballot-boxes, M<sup>r</sup> Corbin, M<sup>r</sup> Matthews, M<sup>r</sup> David Stuart, M<sup>r</sup> George Nicholas, M<sup>r</sup> Richard Lee, M<sup>r</sup> Wills, M<sup>r</sup> Thomas Smith, M<sup>r</sup> Goodall and M<sup>r</sup> Turberville were nominated a Committee to meet a Committee from the Senate in the Conference-Chamber and jointly with them to examine the Ballot-boxes and report to the House on whom the Majority of Votes should fall. The Committee then withdrew and after some time returned into the House and reported that the Committee had, according to order, met a Committee from the Senate in the Conference-Chamber, and jointly with them examined the Ballot-boxes and found a majority of Votes in favor of George Washington, Patrick Henry, Edmund Randolph, John Blair, James Madison, George Mason and George Wythe Esquires.

    Extract from the Journal,
          JOHN BECKLEY Clk House Del$^s$

{ Attest JOHN BECKLEY }
{   Clk. H. Del$^s$    }

    In the House of Senators
     Monday the 4$^{th}$ of December 1786.

THE SENATE according to the Order of the Day proceeded by joint Ballot with the House of Delegates to the Appointment of Seven Deputies from this Commonwealth to a Convention proposed to be held in the City of Philadelphia in May next for the purpose of revising the Fœderal Constitution, and the Members having prepared Tickets with the names of the Persons to be appointed, and deposited the same in the Ballot-boxes, M$^r$ Anderson, M$^r$ Nelson and M$^r$ Lee were nominated a Committee to meet a Committee from the House of Delegates in the Conference-Chamber and joinly with them to examine the Ballot-boxes and report to the House on whom the Majority of Votes should fall. The Committee then withdrew and after some time returned into the House and reported that the Committee had, according to order, met a Committee from the House of Delegates in the Conference-Chamber, and jointly with them examined the Ballot-boxes and found a Majority of Votes in favor of George Washington, Patrick Henry Edmund Randolph, John Blair, James Madison George Mason and George Wythe Esquires.

    Extract from the Journal
Attest,           JOHN BECKLEY Clk, H. D$^s$
 H. BROOK Clk S.

VIRGINIA TO WIT

  (Seal)  I do Certify and make known, to all whom it may Concern, that John Beckley Esquire, is Clerk of the House of Delegates for this Commonwealth, and the proper

Officer for attesting the proceedings of the General Assembly of the said Commonwealth, And that full Faith and Credit ought to be given to all things attested by the said John Beckley Esquire, by Virtue of his Office aforesaid.

> Given under my hand as Governor of the Commonwealth of Virginia and under the Seal thereof, at Richmond this fourth day of May, one thousand seven hundred and Eighty seven.
>
> EDM: RANDOLPH

VIRGINIA TO WIT.

(Seal) I do hereby Certify, that Patrick Henry, Esquire, one of the seven Commissioners appointed by joint ballot of both Houses of Assembly of the Commonwealth of Virginia, authorized as a Deputy therefrom, to meet such Deputies as might be appointed and authorized by other States to assemble in Philadelphia and to join with them in devising and discussing all such Alterations and further Provisions, as might be necessary to render the Fœderal Constitution adequate to the exigencies of the Union; and in reporting such an Act for that purpose to the United States in Congress, as when agreed to by them and duly confirmed by the several States, might effectually provide for the same, did decline his appointment aforesaid; and thereupon in pursuance of an Act of the General Assembly of the said Commonwealth intituled "An Act for appointing Deputies from this Commonwealth to a Convention proposed to be held in the City of Philadelphia in May next, for the purpose of revising the Fœderal Constitution" I do hereby with the advice of the Council of State, supply the said Vacancy by nominating James McClurg, Esquire, a Deputy for the Purposes aforesaid.

> Given under my Hand as Governor of the said Commonwealth and under the Seal thereof this second day of May in the Year of our Lord One thousand seven hundred and eighty seven.
>
> EDM: RANDOLPH

STATE OF NORTH CAROLINA [12]

To the Honorable Alexander Martin Esquire, Greeting.

WHEREAS our General Assembly, in their late session holden at Fayette-ville, by adjournment, in the Month of January last, did by joint ballot of the Senate and House of Commons, elect Richard Caswell, Alexander Martin, William Richardson Davie, Richard Dobbs Spaight, and Willie Jones, Esquires, Deputies to attend a Convention of Delegates from the several United States of America, proposed to be held at the City of Philadelphia in May next for the purpose of revising the Fœderal Constitution.

We do therefore by these Presents, nominate, Commissionate and appoint you the said ALEXANDER MARTIN, one of the Deputies for and in our behalf to meet with our other Deputies at Philadelphia on the first day of May next and with them or any two of them to confer with such Deputies as may have been or shall be appointed by the other States, for the purpose aforesaid: *To hold*, exercise and enjoy the appointment aforesaid, with all Powers, Authorities and Emoluments to the same belonging or in any wise appertaining, You conforming, in every instance, to the Act of our said Assembly under which you are appointed.

> WITNESS Richard Caswell Esquire, our Governor, Captain-General and Commander in Chief, under his Hand and our Great Seal at Kinston the 24th day of February in the XI Year of our Independence

$\qquad$ RIC$^D$ (Seal) CASWELL.

A° D¹ 1787.

By His Excellency's
Command.

$\qquad$ WINSTON CASWELL P. Sec$^y$

The State of NORTH-CAROLINA

To the Honorable WILLIAM RICHARDSON DAVIE Esquire Greeting.

Whereas our General Assembly in their late session holden at Fayette-ville, by adjournment, in the Month of January last, did by joint-ballot of the Senate and House of Commons, elect Richard Caswell, Alexander Martin, William Richardson Davie, Richard

---

[12] Reprinted from *Documentary History of the Constitution*, Vol. I (1894), pp. 32-38.

Dobbs Spaight & Willie Jones Esquires, Deputies to attend a Convention of Delegates from the several United States of America proposed to be held in the City of Philadelphia in May next for the purpose of revising the Fœderal Constitution.

We do therefore, by these Presents, nominate Commissionate and appoint you the said WILLIAM RICHARDSON DAVIE one of the Deputies for and in our behalf to meet with our other Deputies at Philadelphia on the first day of May next and with them or any two of them to confer with such Deputies as may have been or shall be appointed by the other States for the Purposes aforesaid *To hold*, exercise and enjoy the said appointment with all Powers authorities and emoluments to the same belonging or in any wise appertaining, You conforming, in every instance, to the Act of our said Assembly under which you are appointed.

WITNESS Richard Caswell Esquire, our Governor, Captain-General and Commander in Chief under his Hand and our Great Seal at Kinston the 24th day of February in the XI. Year of our Independence, Anno. Dom. 1787:

R? (Seal) CASWELL

By His Excellency's Command

WINSTON CASWELL P. Secy

The State of NORTH CAROLINA

To the Honorable *Richard Dobbs Spaight* Esquire, Greeting.

WHEREAS our General Assembly in their late session holden at Fayette-ville, by adjournment, in the month of January last, did elect you the said Richard Dobbs Spaight with Richard Caswell, Alexander Martin, William Richardson Davie, and Willie Jones Esquires, Deputies to attend a Convention of Delegates from the several United States of America proposed to be held in the City of Philadelphia in May next, for the purpose of revising the Fœderal Constitution.

We do therefore, by these Presents nominate, Commissionate and appoint you the said RICHARD DOBBS SPAIGHT one of the Deputies for and in behalf of us to meet with our other Deputies at Philadelphia on the first day of May next and with them or any two of them to confer with such Deputies as may have been or shall be appointed by the other States for the purpose aforesaid. *To hold*, exercise and enjoy the said Appointment with all Powers, Authorities and Emoluments to the same incident and belonging or in any wise appertaining. You conforming in every instance, to the Act of our said Assembly under which you are appointed.

WITNESS Richard Caswell Esquire, our Governor Captain-General and Commander in Chief under his Hand and our Great Seal at Kinston the 14$^{th}$ day of April in the XI$^{th}$ Year of our Independence Anno. Dom. 1787.

R$^D$ (Seal) CASWELL

By His Excellency's Command
    WINSTON CASWELL P. Sec$^y$

State of NORTH-CAROLINA

His Excellency Richard Caswell Esquire Governor, Captain General and Commander in Chief in and over the State aforesaid.

To all to whom these Presents shall come

Greeting

WHEREAS by an Act of the General Assembly of the said State passed the sixth day of January last, entitled "An Act for appointing Deputies from this State, to a Convention proposed to be held in the City of Philadelphia in May next, for the purpose of Revising the Fœderal Constitution" among other things it is Enacted "That five Commissioners be appointed by joint-ballot of both Houses of Assembly who, or any three of them, are hereby authorized as Deputies from this State to meet at Philadelphia on the first day of May next, then and there to meet and confer with such Deputies as may be appointed by the other States for similar purposes, and with them to discuss and decide upon the most effectual means to remove the defects of our Fœderal Union, and to procure the enlarged Purposes which it was intended to effect, and that they report such an Act to the General Assembly of this State as when agreed to by them, will effectually provide for the same." And it is by the said Act, further Enacted, "That in case of the death or resignation of any of the Deputies or of their declining their Appointments, His Excellency the Governor for the Time being, is hereby authorized to supply such Vacancies." And Whereas, in consequence of the said Act, Richard Caswell, Alexander Martin, William Richardson Davie, Richard Dobbs Spaight and Willie Jones Esquires, were by joint-ballot of the two Houses of Assembly, elected Deputies for the purposes aforesaid: And Whereas the said Richard Caswell hath resigned his said Appointment as one of the Deputies aforesaid.

Now know Ye that I have appointed and by these Presents do appoint the Honorable WILLIAM BLOUNT Esquire, one of the Deputies to represent this State in the Convention aforesaid, in the room and stead of the aforesaid Richard Caswell, hereby giving and granting to the said WILLIAM BLOUNT the same Powers, Privileges and Emoluments which the said Richard Caswell would have been vested with or entitled to, had he continued in the Appointment aforesaid.

>Given under my Hand and the Great Seal of the State, at Kinston, the 23$^d$ day of April Anno Dom 1787. And in the Eleventh Year of American Independence.

>Ri$^D$. (Seal) CASWELL

By His Excellency's Command
>WINSTON CASWELL P. Sec$^y$

State of NORTH-CAROLINA

>His Excellency Richard Caswell Esquire, Governor, Captain-General and Commander in Chief, in and over the State aforesaid.

To all to whom these Presents shall come
>Greeting

Whereas by an Act of the General Assembly of the said State, passed the sixth day of January last, entitled "An Act for appointing Deputies from this State, to a Convention proposed to be held in the City of Philadelphia in May next for the purpose of revising the Fœderal Constitution" among other things it is enacted "That five Commissioners be appointed by joint-ballot of both Houses of Assembly, who, or any three of them, are hereby authorized as

Deputies from this State, to meet at Philadelphia on the first day of May next, then and there to meet and confer with such Deputies as may be appointed by the other States for similar purposes and with them to discuss and decide upon the most effectual means to remove the defects of our Fœderal Union, and to procure the enlarged purposes, which it was intended to effect, and that they report such an Act to the General Assembly of this State, as when agreed to by them, will effectually provide for the same." And it is by the said Act, further enacted "That in case of the death or resignation of any of the Deputies, or their declining their Appointments His Excellency the Governor for the Time being is hereby authorized to supply such vacancies."

AND WHEREAS in consequence of the said Act Richard Caswell, Alexander Martin, William Richardson Davie, Richard Dobbs Spaight and Willie Jones Esquires, were by joint-ballot of y$^e$ two Houses of Assembly elected Deputies for the purposes aforesaid. And Whereas the said Willie Jones hath declined his Appointment as one of the Deputies aforesaid

NOW KNOW YE that I have appointed and by these Presents do appoint the Honorable HUGH WILLIAMSON Esquire, one of the Deputies to represent this State in the Convention aforesaid in the room and stead of the aforesaid Willie Jones, hereby giving and granting to the said HUGH WILLIAMSON the same Powers, Privileges and emoluments which the said Willie Jones would have been vested with and entitled to had he acted under the Appointment aforesaid.

>Given under my Hand and the Great Seal of the State at Kinston the third day of April Anno Dom. 1787. and in the Eleventh Year of American Independence
>
>R$^D$ (Seal) CASWELL

By His Excellency's Command
>DALLAM CASWELL Pro
>>Secretary

### State of South Carolina [13]

By His Excellency Thomas Pinckney Esquire, Governor and Commander in Chief in and over the State aforesaid.

To the Honorable John Rutledge Esquire

Greeting.

By Virtue of the Power and Authority in me vested by the Legislature of this State in their Act passed the eighth day of March last I do hereby Commission You the said John Rutledge as one of the Deputies appointed from this State to meet such Deputies or Commissioners as may be appointed and authorized by other of the United States to assemble in Convention at the City of Philadelphia in the Month of May next, or as soon thereafter as may be, and to join with such Deputies or Commissioners (they being duly authorized and empowered) in devising and discussing all such Alterations, Clauses, Articles and Provisions, as may be thought necessary to render the Fœderal Constitution entirely adequate to the actual Situation and future good Government of the confederated States, and that you together with the said Deputies or Commissioners or a Majority of them who shall be present (provided the State be not represented by less than two) do join in reporting such an Act, to the United States in Congress Assembled as when approved and agreed to by them, and duly ratified and confirmed by the several States will effectually provide for the Exigencies of the Union.

> Given under my hand and the Great Seal of the State in the City of Charleston, this tenth day of April in the Year of our Lord, One thousand seven hundred and eighty seven and of the Sovereignty and Independence of the United States of America the Eleventh.
>
> THOMAS (Seal.) PINCKNEY.

By his Excellency's Command

PETER FRENEAU Secretary.

---

[13] Reprinted from *Documentary History of the Constitution*, Vol. I (1894), pp. 38-42.

State of SOUTH CAROLINA

 By His Excellency Thomas Pinckney Esquire, Governor and Commander in Chief in and over the State aforesaid.

To the Honorable Charles Pinckney Esquire.

      Greeting.

By Virtue of the Power and Authority in me vested by the Legislature of this State in their Act passed the eighth day of March last, I do hereby Commission you the said Charles Pinckney, as one of the Deputies appointed from this State to meet such Deputies or Commissioners as may be appointed and authorized by other of the United States to assemble in Convention at the City of Philadelphia in the Month of May next, or as soon thereafter as may be, and to join with such Deputies or Commissioners (they being duly authorized and empowered) in devising and discussing all such Alterations, Clauses, Articles and Provisions, as may be thought necessary to render the Fœderal Constitution entirely adequate to the actual Situation and future good Government of the confederated States, and that you together with the said Deputies or Commissioners or a Majority of them who shall be present (provided the State be not represented by less than two) do join in reporting such an Act, to the United States in Congress Assembled as when approved and agreed to by them and duly ratified and confirmed by the several States will effectually provide for the Exigencies of the Union.

 Given under my hand and the Great Seal of the State in the City of Charleston this Tenth day of April in the Year of our Lord One thousand seven hundred and Eighty Seven and of the Sovereignty and Independence of the United States of America the Eleventh.

      THOMAS (Seal.) PINCKNEY.

By His Excellency's Command

 PETER FRENEAU Secretary.

State of SOUTH-CAROLINA.

By His Excellency Thomas Pinckney Esquire, Governor and Commander in Chief in and over the State aforesaid.

To the Honorable Charles Cotesworth Pinckney Esquire,

Greeting.

By Virtue of the Power and Authority in me vested by the Legislature of this State in their Act passed the eighth day of March last, I do hereby Commission you the said Charles Cotesworth Pinckney as one of the Deputies appointed from this State to meet such Deputies or Commissioners as may be appointed and authorized by other of the United States to assemble in Convention at the City of Philadelphia in the Month of May next or as soon thereafter as may be, and to join with such Deputies or Commissioners (they being duly authorized and empowered) in devising and discussing all such Alterations, Clauses, Articles and Provisions as may be thought necessary to render the Fœderal Constitution entirely adequate to the actual Situation and future good Government of the Confederated States, and that you together with the said Deputies or Commissioners, or a Majority of them, who shall be present (provided the State be not represented by less than two) do join in reporting such an Act to the United States in Congress Assembled as when approved and agreed to by them and duly ratified and confirmed by the several States will effectually provide for the Exigencies of the Union.

Given under my hand and the Great Seal of the State in the City of Charleston this tenth day of April in the Year of our Lord one thousand seven hundred and eighty seven and of the Sovereignty and Independence of the United States of America the Eleventh.

THOMAS (Seal.) PINCKNEY.

By His Excellency's Command

PETER FRENEAU Secretary.

State of SOUTH-CAROLINA.

By His Excellency Thomas Pinckney Esquire, Governor and Commander in Chief in and over the State aforesaid.

To the Honorable Pierce Butler Esquire

Greeting

By Virtue of the Power and authority in me vested by the Legislature of this State in their Act passed the eighth day of March last, I do hereby Commission you the said Pierce Butler, as one of the Deputies appointed from this State to meet such Deputies or Commissioners as may be appointed and authorized by other of the United States to assemble in Convention at the City of Philadelphia in the Month of May next, or as soon thereafter as may be and to join with such Deputies or Commissioners (they being duly authorised and empowered) in devising and discussing, all such Alterations, Clauses, Articles and Provisions as may be thought necessary to render the Fœderal Constitution entirely adequate to the actual Situation and future good government of the confederated States, and that you together with the said Deputies or Commissioners or a Majority of them who shall be present (provided the State be not represented by less than two) do join in reporting such an Act, to the United States in Congress Assembled as when approved and agreed to by them and duly ratified and confirmed by the several States will effectually provide for the Exigencies of the Union.

Given under my hand and the Great Seal of the State in the City of Charleston this Tenth day of April in the Year of our Lord one thousand seven hundred and Eighty seven, and of the Sovereignty and Independence of the United States of America the Eleventh.

THOMAS (Seal.) PINCKNEY.

By His Excellency's Command

PETER FRENEAU Secretary.

## STATE OF GEORGIA [14]

The State of Georgia by the grace of God, free, Sovereign and Independent.

To the Honorable WILLIAM PIERCE Esquire.

WHEREAS you the said William Pierce, are in and by an Ordinance of the General Assembly of our said State Nominated and Appointed a Deputy to represent the same in a Convention of the United States to be assembled at Philadelphia, for the Purposes of revising and discussing all such Alterations and farther Provisions as may be necessary to render the Fœderal Constitution adequate to the Exigencies of the Union.

You are therefore hereby Commissioned to proceed on the duties required of you in virtue of the said Ordinance

WITNESS our trusty and well beloved *George Mathews* Esquire, our Captain General, Governor and Commander in Chief, under his hand and our Great Seal at Augusta this Seventeenth day of April in the Year of our Lord one thousand seven hundred and eighty seven and of our Sovereignty and Independence the Eleventh.

(GEO: MATHEWS (Seal.))

By His Honor's Command.

J. MILTON. Sec<sup>y</sup>.

The State of Georgia by the grace of God free, Sovereign and Independent.

To the Honorable WILLIAM FEW Esquire.

WHEREAS you the said William Few, are in and by an Ordinance of the General Assembly of our said State Nominated and appointed a Deputy to represent the same in a Convention of the United States to be assembled at Philadelphia, for the Purposes of devising and discussing all such Alterations and farther Provisions as may be necessary to render the Fœderal Constitution adequate to the Exigencies of the Union.

You are therefore hereby Commissioned to proceed on the duties required of you in virtue of the said Ordinance.

---

[14] Reprinted from *Documentary History of the Constitution*, Vol. I (1894), pp. 43–46.

GEO (Seal.) MATHEWS
WITNESS our trusty and well-beloved GEORGE MATHEWS Esquire our Captain-General, Governor and Commander in Chief, under his hand and our Great Seal at Augusta, this seventeenth day of April in the Year of our Lord One thousand seven hundred and eighty Seven, and of our Sovereignty and Independence the Eleventh.

By His Honor's Command

J. MILTON Sec$^y$.

The State of Georgia by the grace of God, free; Sovereign and Independent.

To the Honorable WILLIAM HOUSTOUN Esquire

WHEREAS you the said *William Houstoun*, are in and by an Ordinance of the General Assembly of our said State nominated and appointed a Deputy to represent the same in a Convention of the United States to be assembled at Philadelphia, for the purposes of devising and discussing all such Alterations and farther Provisions as may be necessary to render the Fœderal Constitution adequate to the Exigencies of the Union.

You are therefore hereby Commissioned to proceed on the Duties required of you in virtue of the said Ordinance.

GEO: (Seal.) MATHEWS
WITNESS our trusty and well-beloved GEORGE MATHEWS Esquire, our Captain-General, Governor and Commander in Chief, under his hand and our Great Seal at Augusta, this seventeenth day of April in the Year of our Lord One thousand seven hundred and eighty seven, and of our Sovereignty and Independence the Eleventh.

By his Honor's Command

J. MILTON. Sec$^y$.

GEORGIA.

By the Honorable GEORGE MATHEWS Esquire, Captain General, Governor and Commander in Chief, in and over the said State aforesaid.

To all to whom these Presents shall come Greeting.

KNOW YE that JOHN MILTON Esquire, who hath Certified the annexed Copy of an Ordinance intitled "An Ordinance for the appointment of Deputies from this State for the purpose of revising the Fœderal Constitution"—is Secretary of the said State in whose Office the Archives of the same are deposited. Therefore all due faith, Credit and Authority are and ought to be had and given the same.

GEO: (Seal) MATHEWS.

IN TESTIMONY whereof I have hereunto set my hand and caused the Great Seal of the said State to be put and affixed at *Augusta*, this Twenty fourth day of April in the Year of our Lord One thousand seven hundred and eighty Seven and of our Sovereignty and Independence the Eleventh.

By his Honor's Command

J. MILTON Sec$^y$

AN ORDINANCE for the appointment of Deputies from this State for the purpose of revising the Fœderal Constitution.

BE IT ORDAINED by the Representatives of the Freemen of the State of Georgia in General Assembly met and by the Authority of the same, that WILLIAM FEW, ABRAHAM BALDWIN, WILLIAM PIERCE, GEORGE WALTON WILLIAM HOUSTOUN AND NATHANIEL PENDLETON ESQUIRES, Be, and they are hereby appointed Commissioners, who, or any two or more of them are hereby authorized as Deputies from this State to meet such deputies as may be appointed and authorized by other States to assemble in *Convention* at *Philadelphia* and to join with them in devising and discussing all such Alterations and farther Provisions as may be necessary to render the *Fœderal Constitution* adequate to the exigencies of the Union, and in reporting such an Act for that purpose to the United States in Congress Assembled as when agreed to by them, and duly confirmed by the several States, will effectually provide for the same. In case of the death of any of the said Deputies, or of their declining their appointments, the Executive are hereby authorized to supply such Vacancies.

By Order of the House

(signed) W$^M$ GIBBONS Speaker.

Augusta the 10 February 1787.

Georgia.

Secretary's Office

The above is a true Copy from the Original Ordinance deposited in my Office.

J: MILTON Sec$^y$.

Augusta }
24 April 1787 }

# LIST OF DELEGATES APPOINTED BY THE STATES REPRESENTED IN THE FEDERAL CONVENTION.[1]

| From | | Attended |
|---|---|---|
| New Hampshire. | 1. John Langdon, | July 23, 1787 |
| | *John Pickering,* | |
| | 2. Nicholas Gilman, | July 23, |
| | *Benjamin West.* | |
| Massachusetts. | *Francis Dana,* | |
| | Elbridge Gerry, | May 29, |
| | 3. Nathaniel Gorham, | May 28, |
| | 4. Rufus King, | May 25, |
| | Caleb Strong, | May 28, |
| Rhode Island. | [No appointment.] | |
| Connecticut. | 5. Wm. Sam. Johnson, | June 2, |
| | 6. Roger Sherman, | May 30, |
| | Oliver Elsworth, | May 29, |
| New York. | Robert Yates, | May 25, |
| | 7. Alexander Hamilton, | do. |
| | John Lansing, | June 2, |
| New Jersey. | 8. William Livingston, | June 5, |
| | 9. David Brearley, | May 25, |
| | William C. Houston, | do. |
| | 10. William Patterson, | do. |
| | *John Neilson.* | |
| | *Abraham Clark.* | |
| | 11. Jonathan Dayton, | June 21, |
| Pennsylvania. | 12. Benjamin Franklin, | May 28, |
| | 13. Thomas Mifflin, | do. |
| | 14. Robert Morris, | May 25, |
| | 15. George Clymer, | May 28, |
| | 16. Thomas Fitzsimons, | May 25, |
| | 17. Jared Ingersoll, | May 28, |
| | 18. James Wilson, | May 25, |
| | 19. Gouverneur Morris, | do. |
| Delaware. | 20. George Read, | do. |
| | 21. Gunning Bedford, jr. | May 28, |

---

[1] Reprinted from *Journal, Acts and Proceedings of the Convention which formed the Constitution of the United States,* John Quincy Adams, Editor (1819), pp. 13-15.
For a more elaborate list including the names of delegates who were elected but declined, and fuller and revised details of attendance, see *The Records of the Federal Convention of 1787,* Max Farrand, Editor, Vol. III (1901) pp. 557-559, 586-590.

|  |  | *From* | *Attended* |
|---|---|---|---|
| Delaware. | 22. | John Dickinson, | May 28, |
|  | 23. | Richard Basset, | May 25, |
|  | 24. | Jacob Broom, | do |
| Maryland. | 25. | James M'Henry, | May 29, |
|  | 26. | Daniel of St. Thomas Jenifer, | June 2, |
|  | 27. | Daniel Carroll, | July 9, |
|  |  | John Francis Mercer, | Aug. 6, |
|  |  | Luther Martin, | June 9, |
| Virginia. | 28. | George Washington, | May 25, |
|  |  | *Patrick Henry*, | (declined.) |
|  |  | Edmund Randolph, | May 25, |
|  | 29. | John Blair, | do. |
|  | 30. | James Madison, jr | do. |
|  |  | George Mason, | do. |
|  |  | George Wythe, | do. |
|  |  | James M'Clurg, (in the room of P. Henry) | do. |
| North Carolina. |  | *Richard Caswell*, | (resigned.) |
|  |  | Alexander Martin, | May 25, |
|  |  | William R. Davie, | do. |
|  | 31. | William Blount, (in the room of R. Caswell) | June 20, |
|  |  | *Willie Jones*, | (declined.) |
|  | 32. | Richard D. Spaight, | May 25, |
|  | 33. | Hugh Williamson (in the room of W. Jones) | May 25, |
| South Carolina. | 34. | John Rutledge, | do. |
|  | 35. | Charles C. Pinckney, | do. |
|  | 36. | Charles Pinckney, | do. |
|  | 37. | Pierce Butler, | do. |
| Georgia. | 38. | William Few. | do. |
|  | 39. | Abraham Baldwin, | June 11, |
|  |  | William Pierce, | May 31, |
|  |  | *George Walton.* |  |
|  |  | William Houstoun, | June 1, |
|  |  | *Nathaniel Pendleton.* |  |

Those with numbers before their names, signed the Constitution.................................................. 39
Those in Italicks, never attended........................ 10
Members who attended, but did not sign the Constitution.... 16

65

# NOTES OF MAJOR WILLIAM PIERCE (GA.)[1] IN THE FEDERAL CONVENTION OF 1787

## a. LOOSE SKETCHES AND NOTES TAKEN IN THE CONVENTION, MAY, 1787

On the 30th May Gov[r] Randolph brought forward the principles of a federal Government. The idea suggested was, a national Government to consist of three branches. Agreed.[2] The Legislature to consist of two branches.

Resolved that the first branch of the Legislature ought to be elected by the People of the several States.[3]

A debate arose on this point.

M[r] Sherman thought the State Legislatures were better qualified to elect the Members than the people were.

M[r] Gerry was of the same opinion.

M[r] Mason was of the opinion that the appointment of the Legislature coming from the people would make the representation actual, but if it came from the State Legislatures it will be only virtual.

M[r] Wilson thought that one branch of the Legislature ought to be drawn from the people, because on the great foundation of the people all Government ought to rest. He would wish to see the new Constitution established on a broad basis, and rise like a pyramid to a respectable point.

M[r] Maddison was of the opinion that the appointment of the Members to the first branch of the national Legislature ought to be made by the people for two reasons,—one was that it would inspire confidence, and the other that it would induce the Government to sympathize with the people.

---

[1] Text and footnotes reprinted from *The American Historical Review*, vol. III., (1898), pp. 317-334. Governor Randolph brought forward the principles suggested by the Virginia delegation, on May 29; *Documentary History*, I. 55, *Madison Papers* (Gilpin) 728-735; Yates, in Elliot 1836, I. 390, 391. Major Pierce took his seat on May 31; *Doc. Hist.* I. 56.

[2] May 30. *Doc. Hist.*, I. 200; *Madison Papers*, 749; Yates in Elliot, I. 392.

[3] May 31. *Doc. Hist.*, I. 201, 202; Elliot, I. 392, 393. The debate which here follows is reported in the *Madison Papers*, 753-759, in which however the remarks of Strong, the first and second speeches of King, the third and fourth of Butler, and the final remarks of Mason, are omitted. The final remarks of Sherman are here given at greater length.

Mr Gerry was of opinion that the representation would not be equally good if the people chose them, as if the appointment was made by the State Legislatures. He also touched on the principles of liberal support, and reprobated that idea of œconomy in the different States that has been so injuriously practised.

Mr Strong would agree to the principle, provided it would undergo a certain modification, but pointed out nothing.

Mr Butler was opposed to the appointment by the people, because the State Legislatures he thought better calculated to make choice of such Members as would best answer the purpose.

Mr Spaight thought it necessary previous to the decision on this point that the mode of appointing the Senate should be pointed out. He therefore moved that the second branch of the Legislature should be appointed by the State Legislatures.

Mr King observed that the Question called for was premature, and out of order,—that unless we go on regularly from one principle to the other we shall draw out our proceedings to an endless length.

Mr Butler called on Govr Randolph to point out the number of Men necessary for the Senate, for on a knowledge of that will depend his opinion of the style and manner of appointing the first branch.

Mr Randolph said he could not then point out the exact number of Members for the Senate, but he would observe that they ought to be less than the House of Commons. He was for offering such a check as to keep up the balance, and to restrain, if possible, the fury of democracy. He thought it would be impossible for the State Legislatures to appoint the Senators, because it would not produce the check intended. The first branch of the fœderal Legislature should have the appointment of the Senators, and then the check would be compleat.

Butler said that until the number of the Senate could be known it would be impossible for him to give a vote on it.

Mr Wilson was of opinion that the appointment of the 2d branch ought to be made by the people provided the mode of election is as he would have it, and that is to divide the union into districts from which the Senators should be chosen. He hopes that a fœderal Government may be established that will insure freedom and yet be vigorous.

Mr Maddison thinks the mode pointed out in the original propositions the best.

Mr Butler moved to have the proposition relating to the first branch postponed, in order to take up another,—which was that the second branch of the Legislature consist of blank.

Mr King objected to the postponement for the reasons which he had offered before.

Mr Sherman was of opinion that if the Senate was to be appointed by the first branch and out of that Body that it would make them too dependent, and thereby destroy the end for which the Senate ought to be appointed.

Mr Mason was of opinion that it would be highly improper to draw the Senate out of the first branch; that it would occasion vacancies which would cost much time, trouble, and expence to have filled up,—besides which it would make the Members too dependent on the first branch.

Mr Ch⁹ Pinckney said he meant to propose to divide the Continent into four Divisions, out of which a certain number of persons shd be nominated, and out of that nomination to appoint a Senate.

I was myself of opinion that it would be right first to know how the Senate should be appointed, because it would determine many Gentlemen how to vote for the choice of Members for the first branch,—it appeared clear to me that unless we established a Government that should carry at least some of its principles into the mass of the people, we might as well depend upon the present confederation. If the influence of the States is not lost in some part of the new Government we never shall have any thing like a national institution. But in my opinion it will be right to shew the sovereignty of the State in one branch of the Legislature, and that should be in the Senate.

On the proposition in the words following—"to legislate in all cases where the different States shall prove incompetent." [4]

---
[4] *Doc. Hist.*, I. 202. The debate on this question is presented in the *Madison Papers*, 760–761, but none of the remarks here reported are to be found there, save the second speech of Madison.

Mr Sherman was of opinion that it would be too indifinitely expressed,—and yet it would be hard to define all the powers by detail. It appeared to him that it would be improper for the national Legislature to negative all the Laws that were connected with the States themselves.

Mr Maddison said it was necessary to adopt some general principles on which we should act,—that we were wandering from one thing to another without seeming to be settled in any one principle.

Mr Wythe observed that it would be right to establish general principles before we go into detail, or very shortly Gentlemen would find themselves in confusion, and would be obliged to have recurrence to the point from whence they sat out.

Mr King was of opinion that the principles ought first to be established before we proceed to the framing of the Act. He apprehends that the principles only go so far as to embrace all the power that is given up by the people to the Legislature, and to the fœderal Government, but no farther.

Mr Randolph was of opinion that it would be impossible to define the powers and the length to which the federal Legislature ought to extend just at this time.

Mr Wilson observed that it would be impossible to enumerate the powers which the federal Legislature ought to have.

Mr Maddison said he had brought with him a strong prepossession for the defining of the limits and powers of the federal Legislature, but he brought with him some doubts about the practicability of doing it :—at present he was convinced it could not be done.

## ON THE EXECUTIVE POWER [5]

Mr Wilson said the great qualities in the several parts of the Executive are vigor and dispatch. Making peace and war are generally determined by Writers on the Laws of Nations to be legislative powers.

---

[5] June 1. *Doc. Hist.* I, 203, 204. An ampler report of this debate is given in the *Madison Papers*, 762–764 where however the first remarks of Madison here given and those of Dickinson are omitted; but they are summarized in King's notes, *Life and Correspondence*, I, 588, 589.

Mr Maddison was of opinion that an Executive formed of one Man would answer the purpose when aided by a Council, who should have the right to advise and record their proceedings, but not to control his authority.

Mr Gerry was of opinion that a Council ought to be the medium through which the feelings of the people ought to be communicated to the Executive.

Mr Randolph advanced a variety of arguments opposed to a unity of the Executive, and doubted whether even a Council would be sufficient to check the improper views of an ambitious Man. A unity of the Executive he observed would savor too much of a monarchy.

Mr Wilson said that in his opinion so far from a unity of the Executive tending to progress towards a monarchy it would be the circumstance to prevent it. A plurality in the Executive of Government would probably produce a tyranny as bad as the thirty Tyrants of Athens, or as the Decemvirs of Rome.

A confederated republic joins the happiest kind of Government with the most certain security to liberty.

(A consideration)

Every Government has certain moral and physical qualities engrafted in their very nature,—one operates on the sentiments of men, the other on their fears.

Mr Dickinson was of opinion that the powers of the Executive ought to be defined before we say in whom the power shall vest.

Mr Bedford [6] said he was for appointing the Executive Officer for three years, and that he should be eligible for nine years only.

Mr Maddison observed that to prevent a Man from holding an Office longer than he ought, he may for mal-practice be impeached and removed;—he is not for any ineligibility.

Mr Charles Pinckney was of opinion [7] that the election of the Executive ought to be by the national Legislature, that then respect will be paid to that character best qualified to fill the Executive department of Government.

---

[6] The question was now on the duration of the term of the executive. *Doc. Hist.*, I. 204; *Madison Papers* 766, 767, with omission of the remarks of Madison here reported.

[7] June 2. The question was now on the mode of appointing the executive; *Doc. Hist.* I. 205. The following debate, except the remarks of Charles Pinckney, is to be found in the *Madison Papers*, 768–770.

Mr Wilson proposed that the U. States should be divided into districts, each of which should elect a certain number of persons, who should have the appointment of the Executive.

Mr Gerry observed that if the appointment of the Executive should be made by the national Legislature, it would be done in such a way as to prevent intrigue. If the States are divided into districts, there will be too much inconvenience in nominating the Electors.

Mr Wm'son[8] observed that if the Electors were to chuse the Executive it would be attended with considerable expence and trouble; whereas the appointment made by the Legislature would be easy, and in his opinion, the least liable to objection.

On the subject of salary to the Executive Dr Franklin arose and produced a written Speech.[9] It was, on account of his age, read by Mr Wilson, in which was advanced an opinion that no salaries should be allowed the public Officers, but that their necessary expences should be defrayed. This would make Men, he said, more desirous of obtaining the Esteem of their Country-men,— than avaricious or eager, in the pursuit of wealth.

Mr Dickinson moved[10] that the Executive should be removed at the request of a majority of the State Legislatures.

No Government can produce such good consequences as a limitted monarchy, especially such as the English Constitution.

The application of the several Legislatures brings with it no force to the national Legislature.

Mr Maddison said it was far from being his wish that every executive Officer should remain in Office, without being amenable to some Body for his conduct.

Mr Randolph[11] was for appointing three Persons, from three districts of the Union, to compose the Executive. A single Person may be considered the fœtus of a Monarchy.

Mr Butler was of opinion that a unity of the Executive would be necessary in order to promote dispatch;—that a plurality of

---

[8] Hugh Williamson of North Carolina.
[9] *Doc. Hist.*, I. 206. The text of Dr. Franklin's speech is given in the *Madison Papers*, 771-775.
[10] *Doc. Hist.*, I. 206, 207. Excepting Madison's own remarks, the ensuing debate reported in the *Madison Papers*, 776-778.
[11] The question was now on the motion that the executive consist of a single person. *Doc. Hist.*, I, 207, 208; *Madison Papers*, 779-782.

Persons would never do. When he was in Holland the States general were obliged to give up their power to a French Man to direct their military operations.

Mʳ Wilson [12] said that all the Constitutions of America from New Hampshire to Georgia have their Executive in a single Person. A single Person will produce vigor and activity. Suppose the Executive to be in the hands of a number they will probably be divided in opinion.

It was proposed that the Judicial should be joined with the Executive to revise the Laws.[13]

Mʳ King was of opinion that the Judicial ought not to join in the negative of a Law, because the Judges will have the expounding of those Laws when they come before them; and they will no doubt stop the operation of such as shall appear repugnant to the constitution.

Dʳ Franklin thinks it would be improper to put it in the power of any Man to negative a Law passed by the Legislature because it would give him the controul of the Legislature; and mentioned the influence of the British King, and the influence which a Governor of Pennsylvania once had in arresting (for the consideration of an encrease of salary) the power out of the hands of the Legislature.

Mʳ Maddison was of opinion [14] that no Man would be so daring as to place a veto on a Law that that had passed with the assent of the Legislature.

Mʳ Butler observed that power was always encreasing on the part of the Executive. When he voted for a single Person to hold the Executive power he did it that Government be expeditiously executed, and not that it should be clogged.

---

[12] June 4.

[13] *Doc. Hist.*, I, 208, 209. The notes which follow relate to the debate on this proposition and on that for a veto by the executive; *Madison Papers*, 784-789, where, however, King's interesting remark about the judiciary holding statutes void does not appear.

[14] It appears that this passage was animadverted upon when these notes were printed in the *Savannah Georgian* in 1828. In Madison's letter to Tefft, cited above, p. 310, speaking of the numbers of that news paper which he had once received, he says, "They were probably sent on account of a marginal suggestion of inconsistency between language held by me in the Convention with regard to the Executive veto, and the use made of the power by myself, when in the Executive Administration. The inconsistency is done away by the distinction, not adverted to, between an *absolute* veto, to which the language was applied, and the *qualified* veto which was exercised" (*Writings*, IV. 139). The marginal note in the newspaper reads: "This same Mr. Madison did so when President. Eds. Geo."

Mr Bedford was of opinion that no check was necessary on a Legislature composed as the national Legislature would be, with two branches,—an upper and a lower House.

Mr Mason was of opinion that it would be so dangerous for the Executive in a single Person to negative a Law that the People will not accept of it. He asked if Gentlemen had ever reflected on that awful period of time between the passing and final adoption of this constitution;—what alarm might possibly take place in the public mind.

Mr Maddison in a very able and ingenious Speech,[15] ran through the whole Scheme of the Government,—pointed out all the beauties and defects of ancient Republics; compared their situation with ours wherever it appeared to bear any anology, and proved that the only way to make a Government answer all the end of its institution was to collect the wisdom of its several parts in aid of each other whenever it was necessary. Hence the propriety of incorporating the Judicial with the Executive in the revision of the Laws. He was of opinion that by joining the Judges with the Supreme Executive Magistrate would be strictly proper, and would by no means interfere with that indepence so much to be approved and distinguished in the several departments.

Mr Dickinson could not agree with Gentlemen in blending the national Judicial with the Executive, because the one is the expounder, and the other the Executor of the Laws.

Mr Rutledge was of opinion that it would be right to make the adjudications of the State Judges, appealable to the national Judicial.

Mr Maddison was for appointing the Judges by the Senate.

Mr Hamilton suggested the idea of the Executive's appointing or nominating the Judges to the Senate which should have the right of rejecting or approving.

---

[15] June 6. If Madison's report is right, it would appear that Pierce has here fused two speeches made by Madison on that day, one on the election of the first branch by the legislatures, the other on the association of the judiciary in the revisal of the laws, a question postponed from June 4. *Doc. Hist.*, I. 214; *Madison Papers*, 804–806, 809–811. Dickinson's remarks, which here follow, relate to this latter question; King, I. 592. But those of Rutledge and Madison which succeed were, according to the *Madison Papers*, 792, 793, made on June 5 in the debate on the election of the judiciary. Hamilton's remarks are not given there.

M! Butler was of opinion [16] that the alteration of the confederation ought not to be confirmed by the different Legislatures because they have sworne to support the Government under which they act, and therefore that Deputies should be chosen by the People for the purpose of ratifying it.

M! King thought that the Convention would be under the necessity of referring the amendments to the different Legislatures, because one of the Articles of the confederation expressly make it necessary.

As the word perpetual in the Articles of confederation gave occasion for several Members to insist upon the main principles of the confederacy, i e that the several States should meet in the general Council on a footing of compleat equality each claiming the right of sovereignty, M! Butler observed that the word perpetual in the confederation meant only the constant existence of our Union, and not the particular words which compose the Articles of the union.

Some general discussions came on.—M! Charles Pinckney said [17] he was for appointing the first branch of the Legislature by the State Legislatures, and that the rule for appointing it ought to be by the contributions made by the different States.

M! Wilson was of opinion that the Judicial, Legislative and Executive departments ought to be commensurate.

M! Cotesworth Pinckney was of opinion that the State Legislatures ought to appoint the 1st branch of the national Legislature;—that the election cannot be made from the People in South Carolina. If the people choose it will have a tendency to destroy the foundation of the State Governments.

M! Maddison observed that Gentlemen reasoned very clear on most points under discussion, but they drew different conclusions. What is the reason? Because they reason from different principles. The primary objects of civil society are the security of property and public safety.

---

[16] The following remarks were apparently made in the debate of June 5 on the fifteenth Virginia resolution, that relating to ratification. *Doc. Hist.*, I. 212; *Madison Papers*, 797, 798 (Butler's second speech being omitted).

[17] June 6. *Doc. Hist.*, I. 213; *Madison Papers*, 800. Wilson, ibid., 801, 802 C. C. Pinckney, ibid., 808. The concluding remarks of Madison I do not identify.

*b.* CHARACTERS IN THE CONVENTION OF THE STATES HELD AT PHILADELPHIA; MAY 1787.

From New Hampshire.

Jn? Langdon Esq<sup>r</sup> and Nich<sup>s</sup> Gilman Esquire.

M<sup>r</sup> Langdon is a Man of considerable fortune, possesses a liberal mind, and a good plain understanding.—about 40 years old.[18]

M<sup>r</sup> Gilman is modest, genteel, and sensible. There is nothing brilliant or striking in his character, but there is something respectable and worthy in the Man.—about 30 years of age.

From Massachusetts.

Rufus King, Nat<sup>l</sup> Gorham, Gerry and Jn? Strong [19] Esquires.

M<sup>r</sup> King is a Man much distinguished for his eloquence and great parliamentary talents. He was educated in Massachusetts, and is said to have good classical as well as legal knowledge. He has served for three years in the Congress of the United States with great and deserved applause, and is at this time high in the confidence and approbation of his Country-men. This Gentleman is about thirty three years of age, about five feet ten Inches high, well formed, an handsome face, with a strong expressive Eye, and a sweet high toned voice. In his public speaking there is something peculiarly strong and rich in his expression, clear, and convincing in his arguments, rapid and irresistible at times in his eloquence but he is not always equal. His action is natural, swimming, and graceful, but there is a rudeness of manner sometimes accompanying it. But take him *tout en semble*, he may with propriety be ranked among the Luminaries of the present Age.

M<sup>r</sup> Gorham is a Merchant in Boston, high in reputation, and much in the esteem of his Country-men. He is a Man of very good sense, but not much improved in his education. He is eloquent and easy in public debate, but has nothing fashionable or elegant in his style;—all he aims at is to convince, and where he fails it never is from his auditory not understanding him, for no Man is more perspicuous and full. He has been President of Congress, and three years a Member of that Body. M<sup>r</sup> Gorham is about 46 years of age, rather lusty, and has an agreable and pleasing manner.

---

[18] Pierce's statements of age, throughout the paper, are only approximately correct.
[19] *Caleb* Strong.

Mʳ Gerry's character is marked for integrity and perseverance. He is a hesitating and laborious speaker;—possesses a great degree of confidence and goes extensively into all subjects that he speaks on, without respect to elegance or flower of diction. He is connected and sometimes clear in his arguments, conceives well, and cherishes as his first virtue, a love for his Country. Mʳ Gerry is very much of a Gentleman in his principles and manners;—he has been engaged in the mercantile line and is a Man of property. He is about 37 years of age.

Mʳ Strong is a Lawyer of some eminence,—he has received a liberal education, and has good connections to recommend him. As a Speaker he is feeble, and without confidence. This Gentⁿ is about thirty five years of age, and greatly in the esteem of his Colleagues.

From Connecticut.

Samˡ Johnson, Roger Sherman, and W. Elsworth [20] Esquires.

Dʳ Johnson is a character much celebrated for his legal knowledge; he is said to be one of the first classics in America, and certainly possesses a very strong and enlightened understanding.

As an Orator in my opinion, there is nothing in him that warrants the high reputation which he has for public speaking. There is something in the tone of his voice not pleasing to the Ear,—but he is eloquent and clear,—always abounding with information and instruction. He was once employed as an Agent for the State of Connecticut to state her claims to certain landed territory before the British House of Commons; this Office he discharged with so much dignity, and made such an ingenious display of his powers, that he laid the foundation of a reputation which will probably last much longer than his own life. Dʳ Johnson is about sixty years of age, possesses the manners of a Gentleman, and engages the Hearts of Men by the sweetness of his temper, and that affectionate style of address with which he accosts his acquaintance.

Mʳ Sherman exhibits the oddest shaped character I ever remember to have met with. He is awkward, un-meaning, and unaccountably strange in his manner. But in his train of thinking there is something regular, deep, and comprehensive; yet the

---

[20] *Oliver* Ellsworth.

oddity of his address, the vulgarisms that accompany his public speaking, and that strange new England cant which runs through his public as well as his private speaking make everything that is connected with him grotesque and laughable;—and yet he deserves infinite praise,—no Man has a better Heart or a clearer Head. If he cannot embellish he can furnish thoughts that are wise and useful. He is an able politician, and extremely artful in accomplishing any particular object;—it is remarked that he seldom fails. I am told he sits on the Bench in Connecticut, and is very correct in the discharge of his Judicial functions. In the early part of his life he was a Shoe-maker;—but despising the lowness of his condition, he turned Almanack maker, and so progressed upwards to a Judge. He has been several years a Member of Congress, and discharged the duties of his Office with honor and credit to himself, and advantage to the State he represented. He is about 60.

Mr Elsworth is a Judge of the Supreme Court in Connecticut;—he is a Gentleman of a clear, deep, and copious understanding; eloquent, and connected in public debate; and always attentive to his duty. He is very happy in a reply, and choice in selecting such parts of his adversary's arguments as he finds make the strongest impressions,—in order to take off the force of them, so as to admit the power of his own. Mr Elsworth is about 37 years of age, a Man much respected for his integrity, and venerated for his abilities.

From New York.
    Alexander Hamilton,     Yates, and W. Lansing [21] Esquires.

Col? Hamilton is deservedly celebrated for his talents. He is a practitioner of the Law, and reputed to be a finished Scholar. To a clear and strong judgment he unites the ornaments of fancy, and whilst he is able, convincing, and engaging in his eloquence the Heart and Head sympathize in approving him. Yet there is something too feeble in his voice to be equal to the strains of oratory;—it is my opinion that he is rather a convincing Speaker, that [than] a blazing Orator. Col? Hamilton requires time to think,—he enquires into every part of his subject with the search-

---
[21] *John* Lansing.

ings of phylosophy, and when he comes forward he comes highly charged with interesting matter, there is no skimming over the surface of a subject with him, he must sink to the bottom to see what foundation it rests on.—His language is not always equal, sometimes didactic like Bolingbroke's, at others light and tripping like Stern's. His eloquence is not so defusive as to trifle with the senses, but he rambles just enough to strike and keep up the attention. He is about 33 years old, of small stature, and lean. His manners are tinctured with stiffness, and sometimes with a degree of vanity that is highly disagreable.

M$^r$ Yates is said to be an able Judge. He is a Man of great legal abilities, but not distinguished as an Orator. Some of his Enemies say he is an anti-federal Man, but I discovered no such disposition in him. He is about 45 years old, and enjoys a great share of health.

M$^r$ Lansing is a practicing Attorney at Albany, and Mayor of that Corporation. He has a hisitation in his speech, that will prevent his being an Orator of any eminence;—his legal knowledge I am told is not extensive, nor his education a good one. He is however a Man of good sense, plain in his manners, and sincere in his friendships. He is about 32 years of age.

From New Jersey.

W$^m$ Livingston, David Brearly, W$^m$ Patterson, and Jon$^a$ Dayton, Esquires.[22]

Governor Livingston is confessedly a Man of the first rate talents, but he appears to me rather to indulge a sportiveness of wit, than a strength of thinking. He is however equal to anything, from the extensiveness of his education and genius. His writings teem with satyr and a neatness of style. But he is no Orator, and seems little acquainted with the guiles of policy. He is about 60 years old, and remarkably healthy.

M$^r$ Brearly is a man of good, rather than of brilliant parts. He is a Judge of the Supreme Court of New Jersey, and is very much in the esteem of the people. As an Orator he has little to boast of, but as a Man he has every virtue to recommend him. M$^r$ Brearly is about 40 years of age.

---

[22] W. C. Houstoun omitted.

Mʳ Patterson is one of those kind of Men whose powers break in upon you, and create wonder and astonishment. He is a Man of great modesty, with looks that bespeak talents of no great extent,—but he is a Classic, a Lawyer, and an Orator;—and of a disposition so favorable to his advancement that every one seemed ready to exalt him with their praises. He is very happy in the choice of time and manner of engaging in a debate, and never speaks but when he understands his subject well. This Gentleman is about 34 yˢ of age, of a very low stature.

Capᵗ Dayton is a young Gentleman of talents, with ambition to exert them. He possesses a good education and some reading; he speaks well, and seems desirous of improving himself in Oratory. There is an impetuosity in his temper that is injurious to him; but there is an honest rectitude about him that makes him a valuable Member of Society, and secures to him the esteem of all good Men. He is about 30 years old, served with me as a Brother Aid to General Sullivan in the Western expedition of '79.

From Pennsylvania.

 Benjᵃ Franklin, Thoˢ Mifflin, Robᵗ Morris, Geo. Clymer, Thomas Fitzsimons, Jared Ingersol, James Wilson, Governeur Morris.

Dʳ Franklin is well known to be the greatest phylosopher of the present age;—all the operations of nature he seems to understand,—the very heavens obey him, and the Clouds yield up their Lightning to be imprisoned in his rod. But what claim he has to the politician, posterity must determine. It is certain that he does not shine much in public Council,—he is no Speaker, nor does he seem to let politics engage his attention. He is, however, a most extraordinary Man, and tells a story in a style more engaging than anything I ever heard. Let his Biographer finish his character. He is 82 years old, and possesses an activity of mind equal to a youth of 25 years of age.

General Mifflin is well known for the activity of his mind, and the brilliancy of his parts. He is well informed and a graceful Speaker. The General is about 40 years of age, and a very handsome man.

Robert Morris is a merchant of great eminence and wealth; an able Financier, and a worthy Patriot. He has an understanding equal to any public object, and possesses an energy of mind that few Men can boast of. Although he is not learned, yet he is as great as those who are. I am told that when he speaks in the Assembly of Pennsylvania, that he bears down all before him. What could have been his reason for not Speaking in the Convention I know not,—but he never once spoke on any point. This Gentleman is about 50 years old.

Mr Clymer is a lawyer of some abilities;—he is a respectable Man, and much esteemed. Mr Clymer is about 40 years old.

Mr Fitzsimons is a Merchant of considerable talents, and speaks very well I am told, in the Legislature of Pennsylvania. He is about 40 years old.

Mr Ingersol is a very able Attorney, and possesses a clear legal understanding. He is well aducated in the Classic's, and is a Man of very extensive reading. Mr Ingersol speaks well, and comprehends his subject fully. There is a modesty in his character that keeps him back. He is about 36 years old.

Mr Wilson ranks among the foremost in legal and political knowledge. He has joined to a fine genius all that can set him off and show him to advantage. He is well acquainted with Man, and understands all the passions that influence him. Government seems to have been his peculiar Study, all the political institutions of the World he knows in detail, and can trace the causes and effects of every revolution from the earliest stages of the Grecian commonwealth down to the present time. No man is more clear, copious, and comprehensive than Mr Wilson, yet he is no great Orator. He draws the attention not by the charm of his eloquence, but by the force of his reasoning. He is about 45 years old.

Mr Governeur Morris is one of those Genius's in whom every species of talents combine to render him conspicuous and flourishing in public debate:—He winds through all the mazes of rhetoric, and throws around him such a glare that he charms, captivates, and leads away the senses of all who hear him. With an infinite streach of fancy he brings to view things when he is engaged in deep argumentation, that render all the labor of reasoning easy and pleasing. But with all these powers he is fickle and inconstant,—never pursuing one train of thinking,—nor ever regular. He has gone through a very extensive course of reading, and is acquainted with all the sciences. No Man has more wit,—nor can any one engage the attention more than Mr Morris. He was bred to the Law, but I am told he disliked the profession, and turned Merchant. He is engaged in some great mercantile matters with his namesake Mr Robt Morris. This Gentleman is about 38 years old, he has been unfortunate in losing one of his Legs, and getting all the flesh taken off his right arm by a scald, when a youth.

From Delaware.

 Jno Dickinson, Gunning Bedford, Geo: Read, Richd Bassett, and Jacob Broom Esquires.

Mr Dickinson has been famed through all America, for his Farmers Letters; he is a Scholar, and said to be a Man of very extensive information. When I saw him in the Convention I was induced to pay the greatest attention to him whenever he spoke. I had often heard that he was a great Orator, but I found him an indifferent Speaker. With an affected air of wisdom he labors to produce a trifle,—his language is irregular and incorrect,—his flourishes, (for he sometimes attempts them), are like expiring flames, they just shew themselves and go out;—no traces of them are left on the mind to chear or animate it. He is, however, a good writer and will be ever considered one of the most important characters in the United States. He is about 55 years old, and was bred a Quaker.

Mr Bedford was educated for the Bar, and in his profession I am told, has merit. He is a bold and nervous Speaker, and has a very commanding and striking manner;—but he is warm and impetuous in his temper, and precipitate in his judgment. Mr Bedford is about 32 years old, and very corpulent.

Mr Read is a Lawyer and a Judge;—his legal abilities are said to be very great, but his powers of Oratory are fatiguing and tiresome to the last degree;—his voice is feeble, and his articulation so bad that few can have patience to attend to him. He is a very good Man, and bears an amiable character with those who know him. Mr Read is about 50, of a low stature, and a weak constitution.

Mr Bassett is a religious enthusiast, lately turned Methodist, and serves his Country because it is the will of the people that he should do so. He is a Man of plain sense, and has modesty enough to hold his Tongue. He is a Gentlemanly Man, and is in high estimation among the Methodists. Mr Bassett is about 36 years old.

Mr Broom is a plain good Man, with some abilities, but nothing to render him conspicuous. He is silent in public, but chearful and conversable in private. He is about 35 years old.

From Maryland.

    Luther Martin, Jas McHenry, Daniel of St Thomas Jenifer, and Daniel Carrol Esquires.[23]

Mr Martin was educated for the Bar, and is Attorney general for the State of Maryland. This Gentleman possesses a good deal of information, but he has a very bad delivery, and so extremely prolix, that he never speaks without tiring the patience of all who hear him. He is about 34 years of age.

Mr McHenry was bred a physician, but he afterwards turned Soldier and acted as Aid to Genl Washington and the Marquis de la Fayette. He is a Man of specious talents, with nothing of genious to improve them. As a politician there is nothing remarkable in him, nor has he any of the graces of the Orator. He is however, a very respectable young Gentleman, and deserves the honor which his Country has bestowed on him. Mr McHenry is about 32 years of age.

Mr Jenifer is a Gentleman of fortune in Maryland;—he is always in good humour, and never fails to make his company pleased with him. He sits silent in the Senate, and seems to be conscious that he is no politician. From his long continuance in single life, no doubt but he has made the vow of celibacy. He speaks warmly of the Ladies notwithstanding. Mr Jenifer is about 55 years of Age, and once served as an Aid de Camp to Major Genl Lee.

---

[23] James Francis Mercer omitted.

Mr Carrol is a Man of large fortune, and influence in his State. He possesses plain good sense, and is in the full confidence of his Countrymen. This Gentleman is about   years of age.

From Virginia.

Genl Geo: Washington, Geo: Wythe, Geo: Mason, Jas Maddison junr Jno Blair, Edmd Randolph, and James McLurg.

Genl Washington is well known as the Commander in chief of the late American Army. Having conducted these States to independence and peace, he now appears to assist in framing a Government to make the People happy. Like Gustavus Vasa, he may be said to be the deliverer of his Country;—like Peter the great he appears as the politician and the States-man; and like Cincinnatus he returned to his farm perfectly contented with being only a plain Citizen, after enjoying the highest honor of the Confederacy,—and now only seeks for the approbation of his Countrymen by being virtuous and useful. The General was conducted to the Chair as President of the Convention by the unanimous voice of its Members. He is in the 52d year of his age.

Mr Wythe is the famous Professor of Law at the University of William and Mary. He is confessedly one of the most learned legal Characters of the present age. From his close attention to the study of general learning he has acquired a compleat knowledge of the dead languages and all the sciences. He is remarked for his examplary life, and universally esteemed for his good principles. No Man it is said understands the history of Government better than Mr Wythe,—nor any one who understands the fluctuating condition to which all societies are liable better than he does, yet from his too favorable opinion of Men, he is no great politician. He is a neat and pleasing Speaker, and a most correct and able Writer. Mr Wythe is about 55 years of age.

Mr Mason is a Gentleman of remarkable strong powers, and possesses a clear and copious understanding. He is able and convincing in debate, steady and firm in his principles, and undoubtedly one of the best politicians in America. Mr Mason is about 60 years old, with a fine strong constitution.

Mʳ Maddison is a character who has long been in public life; and what is very remarkable every Person seems to acknowledge his greatness. He blends together the profound politician, with the Scholar. In the management of every great question he evidently took the lead in the Convention, and tho' he cannot be called an Orator, he is a most agreable, eloquent, and convincing Speaker. From a spirit of industry and application which he possesses in a most eminent degree, he always comes forward the best informed Man of any point in debate. The affairs of the United States, he perhaps, has the most correct knowledge of, of any Man in the Union. He has been twice a Member of Congress, and was always thought one of the ablest Members that ever sat in that Council. Mʳ Maddison is about 37 years of age, a Gentleman of great modesty,—with a remarkable sweet temper. He is easy and unreserved among his acquaintance, and has a most agreable style of conversation.

Mʳ Blair is one of the most respectable Men in Virginia, both on account of his Family as well as fortune. He is one of the Judges of the Supreme Court in Virginia, and acknowledged to have a very extensive knowledge of the Laws. Mʳ Blair is however, no Orator, but his good sense, and most excellent principles, compensate for other deficiencies. He is about 50 years of age.

Mʳ Randolph is Governor of Virginia,—a young Gentleman in whom unite all the accomplishments of the Scholar, and the Statesman. He came forward with the postulata, or first principles, on which the Convention acted, and he supported them with a force of eloquence and reasoning that did him great honor. He has a most harmonious voice, a fine person and striking manners. Mʳ Randolph is about 32 years of age.

Mʳ McLurg is a learned physician, but having never appeared before in public life his character as a politician is not sufficiently known. He attempted once or twice to speak, but with no great success. It is certain that he has a foundation of learning, on which, if he pleases, he may erect a character of high renown. The Doctor is about 38 years of age, a Gentleman of great respectability, and of a fair and unblemished character.

North Carolina.

W$^m$ Blount, Rich$^d$ Dobbs Spaight, Hugh Williamson, W$^m$ Davey, and Jn$^o$ Martin [24] Esquires.

M$^r$ Blount is a character strongly marked for integrity and honor. He has been twice a Member of Congress, and in that office discharged his duty with ability and faithfulness. He is no Speaker, nor does he possess any of those talents that make Men shine;—he is plain, honest, and sincere. M$^r$ Blount is about 36 years of age.

M$^r$ Spaight is a worthy Man, of some abilities, and fortune. Without possessing a Genius to render him briliant, he is able to discharge any public trust that his Country may repose in him. He is about 31 years of age.

M$^r$ Williamson is a Gentleman of education and talents. He enters freely into public debate from his close attention to most subjects, but he is no Orator. There is a great degree of good humour and pleasantry in his character; and in his manners there is a strong trait of the Gentleman. He is about 48 years of age.

M$^r$ Davey is a Lawyer of some eminence in his State. He is said to have a good classical education, and is a Gentleman of considerable literary talents. He was silent in the Convention,[25] but his opinion was always respected. M$^r$ Davy is about 30 years of age.

M$^r$ Martin was lately Governor of North Carolina, which office he filled with credit. He is a Man of sense, and undoubtedly is a good politician, but he is not formed to shine in public debate, being no Speaker. M$^r$ Martin was once a Colonel in the American Army, but proved unfit for the field. He is about 40 years of age.

South Carolina.

Jn$^o$ Rutledge, Ch$^s$ Cotesworth Pinckney, Charles Pinckney, and Pierce Butler Esquires.

M$^r$ Rutledge is one of those characters who was highly mounted at the commencement of the late revolution;—his reputation in the first Congress gave him a distinguished rank among the American Worthies. He was bred to the Law, and now acts as

---

[24] *Alexander* Martin.
[25] Not absolutely; see *Madison Papers*, 1007, 1039, 1081, 1154, 1191.

one of the Chancellors of South Carolina. This Gentleman is much famed in his own State as an Orator, but in my opinion he is too rapid in his public speaking to be denominated an agreeable Orator. He is undoubtedly a man of abilities, and a Gentleman of distinction and fortune. Mr Rutledge was once Governor of South Carolina. He is about 48 years of age.

Mr Chs Cotesworth Pinckney is a Gentleman of Family and fortune in his own State. He has received the advantage of a liberal education, and possesses a very extensive degree of legal knowledge. When warm in a debate he sometimes speaks well,— but he is generally considered an indifferent Orator. Mr Pinckney was an Officer of high rank in the American Army, and served with great reputation through the War. He is now about 40 years of age.

Mr Charles Pinckney is a young Gentleman of the most promising talents. He is, altho' only 24 ys of age, in possession of a very great variety of knowledge. Government, Law, History and Phylosophy are his favorite studies, but he is intimately acquainted with every species of polite learning, and has a spirit of application and industry beyond most men. He speaks with great neatness and perspicuity, and treats every subject as fully, without running into prolixity, as it requires. He has been a member of Congress, and served in that Body with ability and eclat.

Mr Butler is a character much respected for the many excellent virtues which he possesses. But as a politician or an Orator, he has no pretentions to either. He is a Gentleman of fortune, and takes rank among the first in South Carolina. He has been appointed to Congress, and is now a Member of the Legislature of South Carolina. Mr Butler is about 40 years of age; an Irishman by birth.

For Georgia.
    Wm Few, Abraham Baldwin, Wm Pierce, and Wm Houstoun Esqrs

Mr Few possesses a strong natural Genius, and from application has acquired some knowledge of legal matters;—he practises at the bar of Georgia, and speaks tolerably well in the Legislature. He has been twice a Member of Congress, and served in that capacity with fidelity to his State, and honor to himself. M.^r Few is about 35 years of age.

M.^r Baldwin is a Gentleman of superior abilities, and joins in a public debate with great art and eloquence. Having laid the foundation of a compleat classical education at Harvard College, he pursues every other study with ease. He is well acquainted with Books and Characters, and has an accomodating turn of mind, which enables him to gain the confidence of Men, and to understand them. He is a practising Attorney in Georgia, and has been twice a Member of Congress. M.^r Baldwin is about 38 years of age.

M.^r Houstoun is an Attorney at Law, and has been Member of Congress for the State of Georgia. He is a Gentleman of Family, and was educated in England. As to his legal or political knowledge he has very little to boast of. Nature seems to have done more for his corporeal than mental powers. His Person is striking, but his mind very little improved with useful or elegant knowledge. He has none of the talents requisite for the Orator, but in public debate is confused and irregular. M.^r Houstoun is about 30 years of age of an amiable and sweet temper, and of good and honorable principles.

My own character I shall not attempt to draw, but leave those who may choose to speculate on it, to consider it in any light that their fancy or imagination may depict. I am conscious of having discharged my duty as a Soldier through the course of the late revolution with honor and propriety; and my services in Congress and the Convention were bestowed with the best intention towards the interest of Georgia, and towards the general welfare of the Confederacy. I possess ambition, and it was that, and the flattering opinion which some of my Friends had of me, that gave me a seat in the wisest Council in the World, and furnished me with an opportunity of giving these short Sketches of the Characters who composed it.

M 1787

Monday May 14. was the day fixed for the meeting of the deputies in Convention for revising the federal ~~institution~~ system of Government. On that day a small number only ~~met~~ ~~seven~~ States were not convened till,

*see note A.*  Friday 25 of May when the following members appeared

Mr. Robert Morris informed the members assembled that by the instruction in behalf of the deputation of Pen^a. he proposed the George Washington Esq^r. ~~~~ late ~~~~ in chief ~~~~ for president of the Convention. M^r Jn^o Rutledge seconded the ~~~~ expressing his confidence that the choice would be unanimous, and observing that the ~~~~ of Gen^l. Washington forbade any observations on the occasion which might otherwise have been proper.

Washington
~~The General~~ was accordingly unanimously elected by ballot, and conducted to the chair by M^r. R. Morris and M^r. Rutledge; from which ~~he returned his~~ in a very emphatic manner, ~~he thanked~~ the Convention for the honor they had conferred on him, ~~reminded~~ them of the novel ~~~~ better ~~~~ the scene of business in which he was to act, lamented his want of ~~~~ and claimed the indulgence of the House towards the involuntary errors which his inexperience might occasion.

[ The ~~nomination~~ came with particular grace from Penn^a, as D^r as a competitor. Franklin alone would have been thought of ~~~~. The Doct^r. was himself to have made the nomination of General Washington, but the state of the weather and ~~~~ of his health confined him to ~~~~ his house.]

M^r Wilson moved that a Secretary ~~should~~ be appointed, and nominated M^r. Temple Franklin.
Col Hamilton nominated Major Jackson.
On the ballot Maj^r. Jackson had 5 votes & M^r. Franklin 2 votes

FACSIMILE FROM THE ORIGINAL NOTES OF DEBATES IN THE HANDWRITING OF JAMES MADISON

# DEBATES IN THE FEDERAL CONVENTION OF 1787 AS REPORTED BY JAMES MADISON.

[1] Monday May 14th 1787 was the day fixed for the meeting of the deputies in Convention for revising the federal system of Government. On that day a small number only had assembled. Seven States were not convened till,

Friday 25 of May, when the following members [2] appeared to wit: see Note A.[3]

viz,[3] From *Massachusetts* Rufus King. *N. York* Robert Yates,[4] Alexr Hamilton. *N. Jersey*, David Brearly, William Churchill Houston,[4] William Patterson. *Pennsylvania*, Robert Morris, Thomas Fitzsimmons, James Wilson,[4] Govurneur Morris. *Delaware*, George Read, Richard Basset,[4] Jacob Broome. *Virginia*, George Washington, Edmund Randolph, John Blair, James Madison, George Mason, George Wythe,[4] James McClurg. *N. Carolina*, Alexander Martin, William Richardson Davie, Richard Dobbs Spaight,[4] Hugh Williamson. *S. Carolina*, John Rutlidge, Charles Cotesworth Pinckney, Charles Pinckney,[4] Pierce Butler. *Georgia*, William Few.

Mr ROBERT MORRIS informed the members assembled that by the instruction & in behalf, of the deputation of Pena he proposed George Washington Esqr late Commander in chief for president of the Convention.[5] Mr JNo RUTLIDGE seconded the motion; expressing his confidence that the choice would be unanimous, and observing that the presence of Genl Washington forbade any observations on the occasion which might otherwise be proper.

---
[1] Text and footnotes reprinted from *The Debates in the Federal Convention of 1787*, edited by Gaillard Hunt and James Brown Scott (Wash., 1920). The text of the present edition of Madison's Debates has been read against the manuscript of the transcript in the Library of Congress, and every difference between Madison's original manuscript and the transcript has been noted except typographical differences, such as capitalization, spelling (including abbreviation of words and figures), punctuation and paragraphing.
The word "Debates" is used as a heading in the transcript.

[2] Madison is not uniform in the spelling of proper names, but the correct form in each instance is to be found in the credentials of the delegates.

[3] The words "to wit: see Note A. viz," are omitted in the transcript.

[4] The word "and" is here inserted in the transcript.

[5] The paragraph in brackets beginning with the words "The nomination" and ending with the word "house" is printed as a footnote in the transcript with reference mark after the word "Convention."

General WASHINGTON was accordingly unanimously elected by ballot, and conducted to the Chair by Mr R. Morris and Mr Rutlidge; from which in a very emphatic manner he thanked the Convention for the honor they had conferred on him, reminded them of the novelty of the scene of business in which he was to act, lamented his want of better qualifications, and claimed the indulgence of the House towards the involuntary errors which his inexperience might occasion.

[6][The nomination came with particular grace from Penna. as Docr Franklin alone could have been thought of as a competitor. The Docr was himself to have made the nomination of General Washington, but the state of the weather and of his health confined him to his house.]

Mr WILSON moved that a Secretary be appointed, and nominated Mr Temple Franklin.

Col HAMILTON nominated Major Jackson.

On the ballot Majr Jackson had 5 votes & Mr Franklin 2 votes.

On reading the credentials of the deputies it was noticed that those from Delaware were prohibited from changing the article in the Confederation establishing an equality of votes among the States.

The appointment of a Committee, consisting of Messrs Wythe, Hamilton & C. Pinckney, on the motion of Mr C. PINCKNEY,[7] to prepare standing rules & orders was the only remaining step taken on this day.

---

## MONDAY MAY 28 [8]

[9] From Massts Nat: Gorham & Caleb Strong. From Connecticut Oliver Elseworth. From Delaware, Gunning Bedford. From Maryland James McHenry. From Penna B. Franklin, George Clymer, Ths Mifflin & Jared Ingersol took their seats.

Mr WYTHE from the Committee for preparing rules made a report which employed the deliberations of this day.

---

[6] See footnote.[5]
[7] The phrase "on the motion of Mr. C. Pinckney" is transposed in the transcript so that it reads: "The appointment of a Committee, on the motion of Mr. C. Pinckney, consisting," etc.
[8] The year "1787" is here inserted in the transcript.
[9] The words "In Convention" are here inserted in the transcript.

M![r] KING objected to one of the rules in the Report authorising any member to call for the yeas & nays and have them entered on the minutes. He urged that as the acts of the Convention were not to bind the Constituents, it was unnecessary to exhibit this evidence of the votes; and improper as changes of opinion would be frequent in the course of the business & would fill the minutes with contradictions.

Col. MASON seconded the objection; adding that such a record of the opinions of members would be an obstacle to a change of them on conviction; and in case of its being hereafter promulged must furnish handles to the adversaries of the Result of the Meeting.

The proposed rule was rejected nem. contradicente. The standing rules *[10] agreed to were as follow: [see the Journal & copy here the printed rules][11]

[viz. [12] A House to do business shall consist of the Deputies of not less than seven States; and all questions shall be decided by the greater number of these which shall be fully represented: but a less number than seven may adjourn from day to day.

Immediately after the President shall have taken the chair, and the members their seats, the minutes of the preceding day shall be read by the Secretary.

Every member, rising to speak, shall address the President; and whilst he shall be speaking, none shall pass between them, or hold discourse with another, or read a book, pamphlet or paper, printed or manuscript—and of two members rising [13] at the same time, the President shall name him who shall be first heard.

---

*Previous to the arrival of a majority of the States, the rule by which they ought to vote in the Convention had been made a subject of conversation among the members present. It was pressed by Governeur Morris and favored by Robert Morris and others from Pennsylvania, that the large States should unite in firmly refusing to the small states an equal vote, as unreasonable, and as enabling the small States to negative every good system of Government, which must in the nature of things, be founded on a violation of that equality. The members from Virginia, conceiving that such an attempt might beget fatal altercations between the large & small States, and that it would be easier to prevail on the latter, in the course of the deliberations, to give up their equality for the sake of an effective Government, than on taking the field of discussion to disarm themselves of the right & thereby throw themselves on the mercy of the large States, discountenanced & stifled the project.

[10] Madison's reference mark after the word "rules" is placed in the transcript after the word "him" (page 20) thus placing the footnote at the end of the rules instead of at the beginning.

[11] Madison's direction is omitted from the transcript and the word "Rules" is inserted.

[12] The word "viz." is omitted in the transcript.

[13] The words "to speak" are inserted in the transcript after "rising."

A member shall not speak oftener than twice, without special leave, upon the same question; and not the second time, before every other, who had been silent, shall have been heard, if he choose to speak upon the subject.

A motion made and seconded, shall be repeated, and if written, as it shall be when any member shall so require, read aloud by the Secretary, before it shall be debated; and may be withdrawn at any time, before the vote upon it shall have been declared.

Orders of the day shall be read next after the minutes, and either discussed or postponed, before any other business shall be introduced.

When a debate shall arise upon a question, no motion, other than to amend the question, to commit it, or to postpone the debate shall be received.]

[A question which is complicated, shall, at the request of any member, be divided, and put separately on [14] the propositions, of which it is compounded.

The determination of a question, altho' fully debated, shall be postponed, if the deputies of any State desire it until the next day.

A writing which contains any matter brought on to be considered, shall be read once throughout for information, then by paragraphs to be debated, and again, with the amendments, if any, made on the second reading; and afterwards, the question shall be put on [14] the whole, amended, or approved in its original form, as the case shall be.

[15] Committees shall be appointed by ballot; and [15] the members who have the greatest number of ballots, altho' not a majority of the votes present, shall [16] be the Committee— When two or more members have an equal number of votes, the member standing first on the list in the order of taking down the ballots, shall be preferred.

A member may be called to order by any other member, as well as by the President; and may be allowed to explain his conduct or expressions supposed to be reprehensible.— And all questions of order shall be decided by the President without appeal or debate.

---

[14] The word "upon" is substituted for "on" in the transcript.
[15] The word "that" is here inserted in the transcript.
[16] The word "shall" is omitted in the transcript.

Upon a question to adjourn for the day, which may be made at any time, if it be seconded, the question shall be put without a debate.

When the House shall adjourn, every member shall stand in his place, until the President pass him.][17]

A letter from sundry persons of the State of Rho. Island addressed to the Honorable [18] The Chairman of the General Convention was presented to the Chair by M![r] Gov![r] MORRIS, and being read, was ordered to lie on the table for further consideration. [For the letter see Note in the Appendix] [19]

M![r] BUTLER moved that the House provide ag![st] interruption of business by absence of members, and against licentious publications of their proceedings—to which was added by—M![r] SPAIGHT—a motion to provide that on the one hand the House might not be precluded by a vote upon any question, from revising the subject matter of it when they see cause, nor, on the other hand, be led too hastily to rescind a decision, which was the result of mature discussion.—Whereupon it was ordered that these motions be referred to [20] the consideration of the Committee appointed to draw up the standing rules and that the Committee make report thereon.

Adj![d] till tomorrow [21] 10. OClock.

---

## TUESDAY MAY 29 [22]

John Dickenson, and Elbridge Gerry, the former from Delaware, the latter from Mass![ts] took their seats. The following rules were added, on the report of M![r] Wythe from the Committee [see the Journal]—[23]

Additional rules. [see preceding page][23]

That no member be absent from the House, so as to interrupt the representation of the State, without leave.

That Committees do not sit whilst the House shall be or ought to be, sitting.

---

[17] See footnote [10].
[18] The words "the Honorable" are omitted in the transcript.
[19] The footnote in the transcript reads as follows: "For the letter, see Appendix No. blank."
[20] The word "for" is substituted in the transcript for the word "to."
[21] The word "at" is here inserted in the transcript.
[22] The words "In convention" are here inserted in the transcript.
[23] Madison's directions "[see the Journal]—" and "[see preceding page]" are omitted in the transcript as are also the words "Additional rules."

That no copy be taken of any entry on the journal during the sitting of the House without leave of the House.

That members only be permitted to inspect the journal.

That nothing spoken in the House be printed, or otherwise published or communicated without leave.

That a motion to reconsider a matter which had [24] been determined by a majority, may be made, with leave unanimously given, on the same day on which the vote passed; but otherwise not without one day's previous notice: in which last case, if the House agree to the reconsideration, some future day shall be assigned for the [25] purpose.

M.\ C. PINKNEY moved that a Committee be appointed to superintend the Minutes.

M.\ GOV.\ MORRIS objected to it. The entry of the proceedings of the Convention belonged to the Secretary as their impartial officer. A committee might have an interest & bias in moulding the entry according to their opinions and wishes.

The motion was negatived, 5 noes, 4 ays.

M.\ RANDOLPH then opened the main business.

[Here insert his speech [26] including his resolutions.] [27]

(M.\ R. Speech A. to be inserted Tuesday May 29) [27]

He expressed his regret, that it should fall to him, rather than those, who were of longer standing in life and political experience, to open the great subject of their mission. But, as the convention had originated from Virginia, and his colleagues supposed that some proposition was expected from them, they had imposed this task on him.

He then commented on the difficulty of the crisis, and the necessity of preventing the fulfilment of the prophecies of the American downfal.

He observed that in revising the fœderal system we ought to inquire 1.[28] into the properties, which such a government ought to possess, 2.[28] the defects of the confederation, 3.[28] the danger of our situation & 4.[28] the remedy.

---

[24] The word "has" is substituted in the transcript for "had."

[25] The word "that" is substituted in the transcript for "the."

[26] The speech is in Randolph's handwriting.

[27] Madison's direction is omitted in the transcript.

[28] The figures indicated by the reference mark [28] are changed in the transcript to "first," "secondly," "thirdly," etc.

1. The Character of such a government ought to secure 1.[28] against foreign invasion: 2.[28] against dissentions between members of the Union, or seditions in particular states: 3.[28] to procure to the several States, various blessings, of which an isolated situation was incapable: 4.[28,29] to be able to defend itself against incroachment: & 5.[28] to be paramount to the state constitutions.

2. In speaking of the defects of the confederation he professed a high respect for its authors, and considered them, as having done all that patriots could do, in the then infancy of the science, of constitutions, & of confederacies,—when the inefficiency of requisitions was unknown—no commercial discord had arisen among any states—no rebellion had appeared as in Mass$^{ts}$—foreign debts had not become urgent—the havoc of paper money had not been foreseen—treaties had not been violated—and perhaps nothing better could be obtained from the jealousy of the states with regard to their sovereignty.

He then proceeded to enumerate the defects: 1.[30] that the confederation produced no security against foreign invasion; congress not being permitted to prevent a war nor to support it by their own authority—Of this he cited many examples; most of which tended to shew, that they could not cause infractions of treaties or of the law of nations, to be punished: that particular states might by their conduct provoke war without controul; and that neither militia nor draughts being fit for defence on such occasions, inlistments only could be successful, and these could not be executed without money.

2.[30] that the fœderal government could not check the quarrels between states, nor a rebellion in any, not having constitutional power nor means to interpose according to the exigency:

3.[30] that there were many advantages, which the U. S. might acquire, which were not attainable under the confederation—such as a productive impost—counteraction of the commercial regulations of other nations—pushing of commerce ad libitum—&c &c.

---

[28] The figures indicated by the reference mark [28] are changed in the transcript to "first," "secondly," "thirdly," etc.

[29] The words "it should" are here inserted in the transcript.

[30] The figures indicated by the reference mark [30] are changed in the transcript to "First," "Secondly," etc.

4.[30] that the fœderal government could not defend itself against the [31] incroachments from the states.

5.[30] that it was not even paramount to the state constitutions, ratified, as it was in may of the states.

3. He next reviewed the danger of our situation,[32] appealed to the sense of the best friends of the U. S.—the prospect of anarchy from the laxity of government every where; and to other considerations.

4. He then proceeded to the remedy; the basis of which he said must be the republican principle

He proposed as conformable to his ideas the following resolutions, which he explained one by one [Here insert ye Resolutions annexed.][33]

## Resolutions proposed by M$^r$ Randolph in Convention May 29, 1787 [33]

1. Resolved that the Articles of Confederation ought to be so corrected & enlarged as to accomplish the objects proposed by their institution; namely, "common defence, security of liberty and general welfare."

2. Res$^d$ therefore that the rights of suffrage in the National Legislature ought to be proportioned to the Quotas of contribution, or to the number of free inhabitants, as the one or the other rule may seem best in different cases.

3. Res$^d$ that the National Legislature ought to consist of two branches.

4. Res$^d$ that the members of the first branch of the National Legislature ought to be elected by the people of the several States every          for the term of          ; to be of the age of          years at least, to receive liberal stipends by which they may be compensated for the devotion of their time to [1] public service; to be ineligible to any office established by a particular State, or under the authority of the United States, except those peculiarly

---

[30] The figures indicated by the reference mark [30] are changed in the transcript to "First," "Secondly," etc.

[31] The word "the" is crossed out in the transcript.

[32] The word "and" is here inserted in the transcript.

[33] This direction and the heading are omitted in the transcript.

[1] The word "the" is here inserted in the transcript.

belonging to the functions of the first branch, during the term of service, and for the space of       after its expiration; to be incapable of reelection for the space of       after the expiration of their term of service, and to be subject to recall.

5. Resol{d} that the members of the second branch of the National Legislature ought to be elected by those of the first, out of a proper number of persons nominated by the individual Legislatures, to be of the age of       years at least; to hold their offices for a term sufficient to ensure their independency;[2] to receive liberal stipends, by which they may be compensated for the devotion of their time to [3] public service; and to be ineligible to any office established by a particular State, or under the authority of the United States, except those peculiarly belonging to the functions of the second branch, during the term of service, and for the space of       after the expiration thereof.

6. Resolved that each branch ought to possess the right of originating Acts; that the National Legislature ought to be impowered to enjoy the Legislative Rights vested in Congress by the Confederation & moreover to legislate in all cases to which the separate States are incompetent, or in which the harmony of the United States may be interrupted by the exercise of individual Legislation; to negative all laws passed by the several States, contravening in the opinion of the National Legislature the articles of Union;[4] and to call forth the force of the Union ag{st} any member of the Union failing to fulfill its duty under the articles thereof.

7. Res{d} that a National Executive be instituted; to be chosen by the National Legislature for the term of       years,[5] to receive punctually at stated times, a fixed compensation for the services rendered, in which no increase or [6] diminution shall be made so as to affect the Magistracy, existing at the time of increase or diminution, and to be ineligible a second time; and that besides a general authority to execute the National laws, it ought to enjoy the Executive rights vested in Congress by the Confederation.

---

[2] The word "independency" is changed to "independence" in the transcript.
[3] The word "the" is here inserted in the transcript.
[4] The phrase "of any treaty subsisting under the authority of the Union" is here added in the transcript.
[5] The word "years" is omitted in the transcript.
[6] The word "or" is changed to "nor" in the transcript.

8. Res.d that the Executive and a convenient number of the National Judiciary, ought to compose a Council of revision with authority to examine every act of the National Legislature before it shall operate, & every act of a particular Legislature before a Negative thereon shall be final; and that the dissent of the said Council shall amount to a rejection, unless the Act of the National Legislature be again passed, or that of a particular Legislature be again negatived by      of the members of each branch.

9. Res.d that a National Judiciary be established to consist of one or more supreme tribunals, and of inferior tribunals to be chosen by the National Legislature, to hold their offices during good behaviour; and to receive punctually at stated times fixed compensation for their services, in which no increase or diminution shall be made so as to affect the persons actually in office at the time of such increase or diminution. that the jurisdiction of the inferior tribunals shall be to hear & determine in the first instance, and of the supreme tribunal to hear and determine in the dernier resort, all piracies & felonies on the high seas, captures from an enemy; cases in which foreigners or citizens of other States applying to such jurisdictions may be interested, or which respect the collection of the National revenue; impeachments of any National officers, and questions which may involve the national peace and harmony.

10. Resolv.d that provision ought to be made for the admission of States lawfully arising within the limits of the United States, whether from a voluntary junction of Government & Territory or otherwise, with the consent of a number of voices in the National legislature less than the whole.

11. Res.d that a Republican Government & the territory of each State, except in the instance of a voluntary junction of Government & territory, ought to be guarantied by the United States to each State

12. Res.d that provision ought to be made for the continuance of Congress and their authorities and privileges, until a given day after the reform of the articles of Union shall be adopted, and for the completion of all their engagements.

13. Res.d that provision ought to be made for the amendment of the Articles of Union whensoever it shall seem necessary, and that the assent of the National Legislature ought not to be required thereto.

14. Res.d that the Legislative Executive & Judiciary powers within the several States ought to be bound by oath to support the articles of Union

15. Res.d that the amendments which shall be offered to the Confederation, by the Convention ought at a proper time, or times, after the approbation of Congress to be submitted to an assembly or assemblies of Representatives, recommended by the several Legislatures to be expressly chosen by the people, to consider & decide thereon.[7]

He concluded with an exhortation, not to suffer the present opportunity of establishing general peace, harmony, happiness and liberty in the U. S. to pass away unimproved.*

It was then Resolved—That the House will tomorrow resolve itself into a Committee of the Whole House to consider of the state of the American Union.—and that the propositions moved by M.r Randolph be referred to the said Committee.

M.r CHARLES PINKNEY laid before the house the draught of a federal Government which he had prepared, to be agreed upon between the free and independent States of America.[35]—M.r P. plan [36] ordered that the same be referred to the Committee of the Whole appointed to consider the state of the American Union.

adjourned.

---

[7] The fifteen resolutions, constituting the "Virginia Plan," are in Madison's handwriting.

* This Abstract of the speech was furnished to J. M. by M.r Randolph and is in his handwriting. [34] As a report of it from him had been relied on, it was omitted by J. M.

[34] This sentence is omitted in the transcript.

[35] Robert Yates, a delegate from New York, gives the following account of Pinckney's motion: "Mr. C. Pinkney, a member from South-Carolina, then added, that he had reduced his ideas of a new government to a system, which he read, and confessed that it was grounded on the same principle as of the above resolutions." (*Secret Proceedings of the Federal Convention* (1821), p. 97.)

[36] The words, "Mr. P. plan," are omitted in the transcript, and what purports to be the plan itself is here inserted.

Madison himself did not take a copy of the draft nor did Pinckney furnish him one, as he did a copy of his speech which he later delivered in the Convention and which is printed as a part of the debates (session of Monday, June 25). Many years later, in 1818, when John Quincy Adams, then Secretary of State, was preparing the Journal of the Convention for publication, he wrote to Pinckney, requesting a copy of his plan, and, in compliance with this request, Pinckney sent him what purported to be the draft, but which appears to have been a copy of the report of the Committee of Detail of August 6, 1787, with certain alterations and additions. The alleged draft and Pinckney's letter transmitting it were written upon paper bearing the water-mark, "Russell & Co. 1797."

The Pinckney draft was not debated; it was neither used in the Committee of the Whole nor in the Convention. It was however referred to the Committee of Detail, which appears to have made some use of it, as extracts from it have been identified by J. Franklin Jameson and an outline of it discovered by Andrew C. McLaughlin, among the papers and in the handwriting of James Wilson, a delegate from Pennsylvania, deposited with the Pennsylvania Historical Society.

## Wednesday May 30

Roger Sherman (from Connecticut) took his seat.

The House went into Committee of the Whole on the State of the Union. M̃ʳ Gorham was elected to the Chair by Ballot.

The propositions of Mʳ RANDOLPH which had been referred to the Committee being taken up. He moved on the suggestion of Mʳ G. Morris, that the first of his propositions to wit "Resolved that the articles of Confederation ought to be so corrected & enlarged, as to accomplish the objects proposed by their institution; namely, common defence, security of liberty & general welfare:[37]—should be postponed, in order to consider the 3 following:

1. that a Union of the States merely federal will not accomplish the objects proposed by the articles of Confederation, namely common defence, security of liberty, & genˡ welfare.

2. that no treaty or treaties among the whole or part of the States, as individual Sovereignties, would be sufficient.

3. that a *national* Government ought to be established consisting of a *supreme* Legislative, Executive & Judiciary.

The motion for postponing was seconded by Mʳ Govʳ MORRIS and unanimously agreed to.

Some verbal criticisms were raised agˢᵗ the first proposition, and it was agreed on motion of Mʳ BUTLER seconded by Mʳ RANDOLPH, to pass on to the third, which underwent a discussion, less however on its general merits than on the force and extent of the particular terms *national* & *supreme*.

Mʳ CHARLES PINKNEY wished to know of Mʳ Randolph whether he meant to abolish the State Governtˢ altogether. Mʳ R. replied that he meant by these general propositions merely to introduce the particular ones which explained the outlines of the system he had in view.

Mʳ BUTLER said he had not made up his mind on the subject, and was open to the light which discussion might throw on it. After some general observations he concluded with saying that he had opposed the grant of powers to Congˢ heretofore, because the whole power was vested in one body. The proposed dis-

---

[37] The resolution is italicized in the transcript.

JOHN RUTLEDGE

tribution of the powers into [38] different bodies changed the case, and would induce him to go great lengths.

Gen! PINKNEY expressed a doubt whether the act of Cong? recommending the Convention, or the Commissions of the Deputies to it, could [39] authorise a discussion of a System founded on different principles from the federal Constitution.

M! GERRY seemed to entertain the same doubt.

M! Gov! MORRIS explained the distinction between a *federal* and *national, supreme*, Gov!; the former being a mere compact resting on the good faith of the parties; the latter having a compleat and *compulsive* operation. He contended that in all Communities there must be one supreme power, and one only.

M! MASON observed that the present confederation was not only [40] deficient in not providing for coercion & punishment ag!t delinquent States; but argued very cogently that punishment could not in the nature of things be executed on the States collectively, and therefore that such a Gov! was necessary as could directly operate on individuals, and would punish those only whose guilt required it.

M! SHERMAN who took his seat today,[41] admitted that the Confederation had not given sufficient power to Cong? and that additional powers were necessary; particularly that of raising money which he said would involve many other powers. He admitted also that the General & particular jurisdictions ought in no case to be concurrent. He seemed however not [42] be disposed to make too great inroads on the existing system; intimating as one reason that it would be wrong to lose every amendment, by inserting such as would not be agreed to by the States.

It was moved by M! READ [43] 2ded by M! Ch? COTESWORTH PINKNEY, to postpone the 3d proposition last offered by M! Randolph viz that a national Government ought to be established consisting of a supreme Legislative Executive and Judiciary,"

---

[38] The word "with" is substituted in the transcript for "into."
[39] The word "would" is substituted in the transcript for "could."
[40] The words "not only" are transposed in the transcript, which reads as follows: "Mr. Mason observed, not only that the present Confederation was deficient," . . .
[41] The phrase "who took his seat today" is omitted in the transcript.
[42] The word "to" is here inserted in the transcript.
[43] The word "and" is here inserted in the transcript.

in order to take up the following—viz. "Resolved that in order to carry into execution the Design of the States in forming this Convention, and to accomplish the objects proposed by the Confederation a more effective Government consisting of a Legislative, Executive and Judiciary ought to be established." The motion to postpone for this purpose was lost:

Yeas [44] Massachusetts, Connecticut, Delaware, S. Carolina—[44] 4
Nays.[45] N. Y. Pennsylvania, Virginia, North Carolina—[45] 4.

On the question as moved by M: Butler, on the third proposition it was resolved in Committee of the whole that a national govern! ought to be established consisting of a supreme Legislative Executive & Judiciary." Mass!ˢ being ay—Connect.—no. N. York divided [Col. Hamilton ay M: Yates no] Penᵃ ay. Delaware ay. Virgᵃ ay. N. C. ay. S. C. ay.[46]

Resol: 2. of M: R's proposition towit—see May 29.[47]

The following Resolution being the 2ᵈ of those proposed by M: Randolph was taken up, viz—"that the rights of suffrage in the National Legislature ought to be proportioned to the quotas of contribution, or to the number of free inhabitants, as the one or the other rule may seem best in different cases." [48]

M: MADISON observing that the words *"or to the number of free inhabitants,"* might occasion debates which would divert the Committee from the general question whether the principle of representation should be changed, moved that they might be struck out.

M: KING observed that the quotas of contribution which would alone remain as the measure of representation, would not answer, because waving every other view of the matter, the revenue might hereafter be so collected by the general Gov! that the sums respectively drawn from the States would not appear; and would besides be continually varying.

M: MADISON admitted the propriety of the observation, and that some better rule ought to be found.

---

[44] The word "Yeas" is omitted in the transcript and the word "aye" inserted before the figure "4."
[45] The word "Nays" is omitted in the transcript and the word "no" inserted before the figure "4."
[46] In the transcript the vote reads: Massachusetts, Pennsylvania, Delaware, Virginia, North Carolina, South Carolina, aye—6; Connecticut, no—1; New York, divided (Colonel Hamilton, aye, Mr. Yates, no)." [Note E][47]
[47] Madison's direction is omitted in the transcript.
[48] The resolution is italicized in the transcript.

Col. HAMILTON moved to alter the resolution so as to read "that the rights of suffrage in the national Legislature ought to be proportioned to the number of free inhabitants. Mʳ SPAIGHT 2ded the motion.

It was then moved that the Resolution be postponed, which was agreed to.

Mʳ RANDOLPH and Mʳ MADISON then moved the following resolution—"that the rights of suffrage in the national Legislature ought to be proportioned."

It was moved and 2ded to amend it by adding "and not according to the present system"—which was agreed to.

It was then moved and 2ded to alter the resolution so as to read "that the rights of suffrage in the national Legislature ought not to be according to the present system."

It was then moved & 2ded to postpone the Resolution moved by Mʳ Randolph & Mʳ Madison, which being agreed to:

Mʳ MADISON, moved, in order to get over the difficulties, the following resolution—"that the equality of suffrage established by the articles of Confederation ought not to prevail in the national Legislature, and that an equitable ratio of representation ought to be substituted." This was 2ded by Mʳ Govʳ MORRIS, and being generally relished, would have been agreed to; when,

Mʳ REED moved that the whole clause relating to the point of Representation be postponed; reminding the Comᵉ that the deputies from Delaware were restrained by their commission from assenting to any change of the rule of suffrage, and in case such a change should be fixed on, it might become their duty to retire from the Convention.

Mʳ Govʳ MORRIS observed that the valuable assistance of those members could not be lost without real concern, and that so early a proof of discord in the Convention as a secession of a State, would add much to the regret; that the change proposed was however so fundamental an article in a national Govᵗ that it could not be dispensed with.

Mʳ MADISON observed that whatever reason might have existed for the equality of suffrage when the Union was a federal one among sovereign States, it must cease when a national Goverm.t should be put into the place. In the former case, the acts of Cong.s depended so much for their efficacy on the cooperation of the States, that these had a weight both within & without Congress, nearly in proportion to their extent and importance. In the latter case, as the acts of the Gen.l Gov.t would take effect without the intervention of the State legislatures, a vote from a small State w.d have the same efficacy & importance as a vote from a large one, and there was the same reason for different numbers of representatives from different States, as from Counties of different extents within particular States. He suggested as an expedient for at once taking the sense of the members on this point and saving the Delaware deputies from embarrassment, that the question should be taken in Committee, and the clause on report to the House be postponed without a question there. This however did not appear to satisfy M.r Read.

By several it was observed that no just construction of the Act of Delaware, could require or justify a secession of her deputies, even if the resolution were to be carried thro' the House as well as the Committee. It was finally agreed however that the clause should be postponed: it being understood that in the event the proposed change of representation would certainly be agreed to, no objection or difficulty being started from any other quarter than from Delaware.

The motion of M.r Read to postpone being agreed to,

The Committee then rose. The Chairman reported progress, and the House having resolved to resume the subject in Committee tomorrow,

Adjourned to 10 OClock.

THURSDAY MAY 31 [49]

William Pierce from Georgia took his seat.

In Committee of the whole on M.r Randolph's propositions.

The 3.d Resolution "that the national Legislature ought to consist of two branches" was agreed to without debate or dissent,

---

[49] The year "1787" is here inserted in the transcript.

except that of Pennsylvania, given probably from complaisance to Doc.<sup>r</sup> Franklin who was understood to be partial to a single House of Legislation.

Resol: 4.[50] first clause "that the members of the first branch of the National Legislature ought to be elected by the people of the several States" being taken up,

M.<sup>r</sup> SHERMAN opposed the election by the people, insisting that it ought to be by the State Legislatures. The people he said, immediately should have as little to do as may be about the Government. They want information and are constantly liable to be misled.

M.<sup>r</sup> GERRY. The evils we experience flow from the excess of democracy. The people do not want virtue, but are the dupes of pretended patriots. In Mass.<sup>ts</sup> it had been fully confirmed by experience that they are daily misled into the most baneful measures and opinions by the false reports circulated by designing men, and which no one on the spot can refute. One principal evil arises from the want of due provision for those employed in the administration of Governm.<sup>t</sup> It would seem to be a maxim of democracy to starve the public servants. He mentioned the popular clamour in Mass.<sup>ts</sup> for the reduction of salaries and the attack made on that of the Gov.<sup>r</sup> though secured by the spirit of the Constitution itself. He had he said been too republican heretofore: he was still however republican, but had been taught by experience the danger of the levelling spirit.

M.<sup>r</sup> MASON, argued strongly for an election of the larger branch by the people. It was to be the grand depository of the democratic principle of the Govt.<sup>t</sup> It was, so to speak, to be our House of Commons—It ought to know & sympathise with every part of the community; and ought therefore to be taken not only from different parts of the whole republic, but also from different districts of the larger members of it, which had in several instances particularly in Virg.<sup>a</sup>, different interests and views arising from difference of produce, of habits &c &c. He admitted that we had been too democratic but was afraid we s.<sup>d</sup> incautiously run into the opposite extreme. We ought to attend to the rights of

---

[50] The transcript changes "Resol: 4." to "The fourth Resolution."

every class of the people. He had often wondered at the indifference of the superior classes of society to this dictate of humanity & policy; considering that however affluent their circumstances, or elevated their situations, might be, the course of a few years, not only might but certainly would, distribute their posterity throughout the lowest classes of Society. Every selfish motive therefore, every family attachment, ought to recommend such a system of policy as would provide no less carefully for the rights and happiness of the lowest than of the highest orders of Citizens.

M!̣ WILSON contended strenuously for drawing the most numerous branch of the Legislature immediately from the people. He was for raising the federal pyramid to a considerable altitude, and for that reason wished to give it as broad a basis as possible. No government could long subsist without the confidence of the people. In a republican Government this confidence was peculiarly essential. He also thought it wrong to increase the weight of the State Legislatures by making them the electors of the national Legislature. All interference between the general and local Governm!ṣ should be obviated as much as possible. On examination it would be found that the opposition of States to federal measures had proceded much more from the officers of the States, than from the people at large.

M!̣ MADISON considered the popular election of one branch of the National Legislature as essential to every plan of free Government. He observed that in some of the States one branch of the Legislature was composed of men already removed from the people by an intervening body of electors. That if the first branch of the general legislature should be elected by the State Legislatures, the second branch elected by the first—the Executive by the second together with the first; and other appointments again made for subordinate purposes by the Executive, the people would be lost sight of altogether; and the necessary sympathy between them and their rulers and officers, too little felt. He was an advocate for the policy of refining the popular appointments by successive filtrations, but thought it might be pushed too far. He wished the expedient to be resorted to only in the appointment of the second branch of the Legislature, and in the Executive & judiciary branches of the Government. He thought too that the great fabric to be raised would be more stable and durable, if it should rest on the solid foundation of the people themselves, than if it should stand merely on the pillars of the Legislatures.

Mr GERRY did not like the election by the people. The maxims taken from the British constitution were often fallacious when applied to our situation which was extremely different. Experience he said had shewn that the State legislatures drawn immediately from the people did not always possess their confidence. He had no objection however to an election by the people if it were so qualified that men of honor & character might not be unwilling to be joined in the appointments. He seemed to think the people might nominate a certain number out of which the State legislatures should be bound to choose.

Mr BUTLER thought an election by the people an impracticable mode.

On the question for an election of the first branch of the national Legislature by the people.

Mass<sup>ts</sup> ay. Connec<sup>t</sup> div<sup>d</sup> N. York ay. N. Jersey no. Pen<sup>a</sup> ay. Delaw<sup>e</sup> div<sup>d</sup> V<sup>a</sup> ay. N. C. ay. S. C. no. Georg<sup>a</sup> ay.

The remaining Clauses of Resolution 4<sup>th</sup> [51] relating to the qualifications of members of the National Legislature,[51] being posp<sup>d</sup> nem. con., as entering too much into detail for general propositions:

The Committee proceeded to Resolution 5.[52] "that the second, [or senatorial] branch of the National Legislature ought to be chosen by the first branch out of persons nominated by the State Legislatures."

Mr SPAIGHT contended that the 2<sup>d</sup> branch ought to be chosen by the State Legislatures and moved an amendment to that effect.

Mr BUTLER apprehended that the taking so many powers out of the hands of the States as was proposed, tended to destroy all that balance and security of interests among the States which it was necessary to preserve; and called on Mr Randolph the mover

---

[51] In the transcript the words "Resolution 4<sup>th</sup>" are changed to "the fourth Resolution" and the phrase "the qualifications of members of the National Legislature" is italicized.

[52] In the transcript the words "Resolution 5," are changed to "the fifth Resolution" and the words of the resolution are italicized.

of the propositions, to explain the extent of his ideas, and particularly the number of members he meant to assign to this second branch.

Mr RAND⁕ observed that he had at the time of offering his propositions stated his ideas as far as the nature of general propositions required; that details made no part of the plan, and could not perhaps with propriety have been introduced. If he was to give an opinion as to the number of the second branch, he should say that it ought to be much smaller than that of the first; so small as to be exempt from the passionate proceedings to which numerous assemblies are liable. He observed that the general object was to provide a cure for the evils under which the U. S. laboured; that in tracing these evils to their origin every man had found it in the turbulence and follies of democracy: that some check therefore was to be sought for agst this tendency of our Governments: and that a good Senate seemed most likely to answer the purpose.

Mr KING reminded the Committee that the choice of the second branch as proposed (by Mr Spaight) viz. by the State Legislatures would be impracticable, unless it was to be very numerous, or *the idea of proportion* among the States was to be disregarded. According to this *idea*, there must be 80 or 100 members to entitle Delaware to the choice of one of them.—Mr SPAIGHT withdrew his motion.

Mr WILSON opposed both a nomination by the State Legislatures, and an election by the first branch of the national Legislature, because the second branch of the latter, ought to be independent of both. He thought both branches of the National Legislature ought to be chosen by the people, but was not prepared with a specific proposition. He suggested the mode of chusing the Senate of N. York to wit of uniting several election districts, for one branch, in chusing members for the other branch, as a good model.

Mr MADISON observed that such a mode would destroy the influence of the smaller States associated with larger ones in the same district; as the latter would chuse from within themselves, altho' better men might be found in the former. The election of Senators in Virga where large & small counties were often formed into one district for the purpose, had illustrated this consequence Local partiality, would often prefer a resident within the County or State, to a candidate of superior merit residing out of it. Less merit also in a resident would be more known throughout his own State.

Mr SHERMAN favored an election of one member by each of the State Legislatures.

Mr PINKNEY moved to strike out the "nomination by the State Legislatures." On this question.

*Massts no. Cont no. N. Y. no. N. J. no. Pena no. Del divd Va no. N. C. no. S. C. no. Georg no.[53]

On the whole question for electing by the first branch out of nominations by the State Legislatures, Mass. ay. Cont. no. N Y. no. N. Jersey. no. Pena no. Del. no. Virga ay. N. C. no. S. C. ay. Ga no.[54]

So the clause was disagreed to & a chasm left in this part of the plan.

[55] The sixth Resolution stating the cases in which the national Legislature ought to legislate was next taken into discussion: On the question whether each branch shd originate laws, there was an unanimous affirmative without debate. On the question for transferring all the Legislative powers of the existing Congs to this Assembly, there was also a silent affirmative nem. con.

On the proposition for giving "Legislative power in all cases to which the State Legislatures were individually incompetent."

Mr PINKNEY & Mr RUTLEDGE objected to the vagueness of the term *incompetent*, and said they could not well decide how to vote until they should see an exact enumeration of the powers comprehended by this definition.

---

*This question[53] omitted in the printed Journal, & the votes applied to the succeeding one, instead of the votes as here stated [this note to be in the bottom margin].[53]

[53] In the transcript the vote reads: "*Massachusetts, Connecticut, New York, New Jersey, Pennsylvania, Virginia, North Carolina, South Carolina, Georgia, no—9; Delaware divided"; and Madison's direction concerning the footnote is omitted. The word "is" is inserted after the word "question."

[54] In the transcript the vote reads: "Massachusetts, Virginia, South Carolina, aye—3; Connecticut, New York, New Jersey, Pennsylvania, Delaware, North Carolina, Georgia, no—7."

[55] In this paragraph the transcript italicizes the following phrases: "the cases in which the national Legislature ought to legislate," "whether each branch shd originate laws," "for transferring all the Legislative powers of the existing Cong. to this Assembly"; and the phrase "a silent affirmative nem. con." is changed to "an unanimous affirmative, without debate."

M: BUTLER repeated his fears that we were running into an extreme in taking away the powers of the States, and called on M: Randolp for the extent of his meaning.

M: RANDOLPH disclaimed any intention to give indefinite powers to the national Legislature, declaring that he was entirely opposed to such an inroad on the State jurisdictions, and that he did not think any considerations whatever could ever change his determination. His opinion was fixed on this point.

M: MADISON said that he had brought with him into the Convention a strong bias in favor of an enumeration and definition of the powers necessary to be exercised by the national Legislature; but had also brought doubts concerning its practicability. His wishes remained unaltered; but his doubts had become stronger. What his opinion might ultimately be he could not yet tell. But he should shrink from nothing which should be found essential to such a form of Gov! as would provide for the safety, liberty and happiness of the community. This being the end of all our deliberations, all the necessary means for attaining it must, however reluctantly, be submitted to.

On the question for giving powers, in cases to which the States are not competent, Mass!: ay. Con: div? [Sharman no Elseworth ay] N. Y. ay. N. J. ay. P: ay. Del. ay. V: ay. N. C. ay. S. Carolina ay. Georg: ay. [56]

The other clauses [57] giving powers necessary to preserve harmony among the States to negative all State laws contravening in the opinion of the Nat. Leg. the articles of union, down to the last clause, (the words "or any treaties subsisting under the authority of the Union," being added after the words "contravening &c. the articles of the Union," on motion of D: FRANKLIN) were agreed to with! debate or dissent.

The last clause of Resolution 6.[58] authorizing an exertion of the force of the whole ag:t a delinquent State came next into consideration.

---

[56] In the transcript the vote reads: "Massachusetts, New York, New Jersey, Pennsylvania, Delaware, Virginia, North Carolina, South Carolina, Georgia, aye—9; Connecticut divided (Sherman, no, Ellsworth, aye)."

[57] The phrase, "giving powers necessary to preserve harmony among the States to negative all State laws contravening in the opinion of the Nat. Leg. the articles of union" is italicized in the transcript.

[58] The words "the sixth Resolution" are substituted in the transcript for "Resolution 6" and the phrase "authorizing and exertion of the force of the whole ag:t a delinquent State" is italicized.

The last of ~~proposition~~ Resolution 6. authorizing

The clause ~~proposing~~ an exertion of the force of the 'state of its delinquent

State came next into consideration.

Mr. Madison, observed that the more he reflected on the use of
force, the more he doubted the practicability, the justice and the efficacy of it
when applied to people collectively and not individually. — A union of
the States ~~found~~ containing such an ingredient seemed to provide for its own destruction. The
use of force of a State, would look more like a declaration of war. Then an infliction of punishment, and would probably be considered by the party attacked as a
dissolution of all previous compacts by which it might be bound. He hoped that such
a system would be framed as might render this resource unnecessary, and moved that
the clause ~~ought~~ be postponed. ~~This motion~~ ~~~~~

— This motion was agreed to nem. con.

The Committee then rose & the House

Adjourned

Mr Madison, observed that the more he reflected on the use of force, the more he doubted the practicability, the justice and the efficacy of it when applied to people collectively and not individually.—A union of the States containing such an ingredient seemed to provide for its own destruction. The use of force agst a State, would look more like a declaration of war, than an infliction of punishment, and would probably be considered by the party attacked as a dissolution of all previous compacts by which it might be bound. He hoped that such a system would be framed as might render this recourse [59] unnecessary, and moved that the clause be postponed. This motion was agreed to nem. con.

The Committee then rose & the House

Adjourned

---

Friday June 1st 1787

William Houston from Georgia took his seat.

The Committee of the whole proceeded to Resolution 7.[60] "that a national Executive be instituted, to be chosen by the national Legislature—for the term of years &c to be ineligible thereafter, to possess the executive powers of Congress &c."

Mr Pinkney was for a vigorous Executive but was afraid the Executive powers of the existing Congress might extend to peace & war &c., which would render the Executive a monarchy, of the worst kind, to wit an elective one.

Mr Wilson moved that the Executive consist of a single person. Mr C Pinkney seconded the motion, so as to read "that a National Ex. to consist of a single person, be instituted.

A considerable pause ensuing and the Chairman asking if he should put the question, Docr Franklin observed that it was a point of great importance and wished that the gentlemen would deliver their sentiments on it before the question was put.

Mr Rutlidge animadverted on the shyness of gentlemen on this and other subjects. He said it looked as if they supposed themselves precluded by having frankly disclosed their opinions from afterwards changing them, which he did not take to be at all

---

59 The word "resource" is substituted in the transcript for "recourse."

60 The words "the seventh Resolution" are substituted in the transcript for "Resolution 7" and the words of the resolution are italicized.

the case. He said he was for vesting the Executive power in a single person, tho' he was not for giving him the power of war and peace. A single man would feel the greatest responsibility and administer the public affairs best.

Mr SHERMAN said he considered the Executive magistracy as nothing more than an institution for carrying the will of the Legislature into effect, that the person or persons ought to be appointed by and accountable to the Legislature only, which was the depositary of the supreme will of the Society. As they were the best judges of the business which ought to be done by the Executive department, and consequently of the number necessary from time to time for doing it, he wished the number might not be fixed but that the legislature should be at liberty to appoint one or more as experience might dictate.

Mr WILSON preferred a single magistrate, as giving most energy dispatch and responsibility to the office. He did not consider the Prerogatives of the British Monarch as a proper guide in defining the Executive powers. Some of these prerogatives were of Legislative nature. Among others that of war & peace &c. The only powers he conceived[61] strictly Executive were those of executing the laws, and appointing officers, not appertaining to and appointed by the Legislature.

Mr GERRY favored the policy of annexing a Council to the Executive in order to give weight & inspire confidence.

Mr RANDOLPH strenuously opposed a unity in the Executive magistracy. He regarded it as the fœtus of monarchy. We had he said no motive to be governed by the British Governmᵗ as our prototype. He did not mean however to throw censure on that Excellent fabric. If we were in a situation to copy it he did not know that he should be opposed to it; but the fixt genius of the people of America required a different form of Government. He could not see why the great requisites for the Executive department, vigor, despatch & responsibility could not be found in three men, as well as in one man. The Executive ought to be independent. It ought therefore in order to support its independence to consist of more than one.

---

[61] The transcript here substitutes the word "considered" for "conceived."

Mr WILSON said that unity in the Executive instead of being the fetus of monarchy would be the best safeguard against tyranny. He repeated that he was not governed by the British Model which was inapplicable to the situation of this Country; the extent of which was so great, and the manners so republican, that nothing but a great confederated Republic would do for it.

Mr Wilson's motion for a single magistrate was postponed by common consent, the Committee seeming unprepared for any decision on it; and the first part of the clause agreed to, viz—"that a National Executive be instituted."

Mr MADISON thought it would be proper, before a choice sh$^d$ be made between a unity and a plurality in the Executive, to fix the extent of the Executive authority; that as certain powers were in their nature Executive, and must be given to that departm$^t$ whether administered by one or more persons, a definition of their extent would assist the judgment in determining how far they might be safely entrusted to a single officer. He accordingly moved that so much of the clause before the Committee as related to the powers of the Executive sh$^d$ be struck out & that after the words "that a national Executive ought to be instituted" there be inserted the words following viz. "with power to carry into effect the national laws, to appoint to offices in cases not otherwise provided for, and to execute such other powers "not Legislative nor Judiciary in their nature," as may from time to time be delegated by the national Legislature." The words "not legislative nor judiciary in their nature" were added to the proposed amendment in consequence of a suggestion by Gen$^l$ Pinkney that improper powers might otherwise be delegated.

Mr WILSON seconded this motion—

Mr PINKNEY moved to amend the amendment by striking out the last member of it; viz: "and to execute such other powers not Legislative nor Judiciary in their nature as may from time to time be delegated." He said they were unnecessary, the object of them being included in the "power [62] to carry into effect the national laws."

Mr RANDOLPH seconded the motion.

---
[62] The transcript uses the word "power" in the plural.

Mr MADISON did not know that the words were absolutely necessary, or even the preceding words—"to appoint to offices &c. the whole being perhaps included in the first member of the proposition. He did not however see any inconveniency [63] in retaining them, and cases might happen in which they might serve to prevent doubts and misconstructions.

In consequence of the motion of Mr Pinkney, the question on Mr Madison's motion was divided; and the words objected to by Mr Pinkney struck out; by the votes of Connecticut, N. Y. N. J. Pena. Del. N. C. & Geo.[64] agst Mass. Virga & S. Carolina [64] the preceding part of the motion being first agreed to; Connecticut divided, all the other States in the affirmative.

The next clause in Resolution 7,[65] relating to the mode of appointing, & the duration of, the Executive being under consideration,

Mr WILSON said he was almost unwilling to declare the mode which he wished to take place, being apprehensive that it might appear chimerical. He would say however at least that in theory he was for an election by the people. Experience, particularly in N. York & Massts, shewed that an election of the first magistrate by the people at large, was both a convenient & successful mode. The objects of choice in such cases must be persons whose merits have general notoriety.

Mr SHERMAN was for the appointment by the Legislature, and for making him absolutely dependent on that body, as it was the will of that which was to be executed. An independence of the Executive on the supreme Legislature, was in his opinion the very essence of tyranny if there was any such thing.

Mr WILSON moves that the blank for the term of duration should be filled with three years, observing at the same time that he preferred this short period, on the supposition that a re-eligibility would be provided for.

Mr PINKNEY moves for seven years.

---

[63] The transcript changes the word "inconveniency" to "inconvenience."
[64] In the transcript the figures "7" and "3" are inserted after the States Georgia and South Carolina respectively.
[65] The words "the seventh Resolution" are substituted in the transcript for "Resolution 7."

M:͟ SHERMAN was for three years, and ag:͟t the doctrine of rotation as throwing out of office the men best qualifyed to execute its duties.

M:͟ MASON was for seven years at least, and for prohibiting a re-eligibility as the best expedient both for preventing the effect of a false complaisance on the side of the Legislature towards unfit characters; and a temptation on the side of the Executive to intrigue with the Legislature for a re-appointment.

M:͟ BEDFORD was strongly opposed to so long a term as seven years. He begged the committee to consider what the situation of the Country would be, in case the first magistrate should be saddled on it for such a period and it should be found on trial that he did not possess the qualifications ascribed to him, or should lose them after his appointment. An impeachment he said would be no cure for this evil, as an impeachment would reach misfeasance only, not incapacity. He was for a triennial election, and for an ineligibility after a period of nine years.

On the question for seven years,[66]

Mass:͟t:͟ divid:͟d Con:͟t no. N. Y. ay. N. J. ay. Pen:͟a ay. Del. ay. Virg:͟a ay. N. C. no. S. C. no. Geor. no.[67] There being 5ays, 4 noes, 1 div:͟d, a question was asked whether a majority had voted in the affirmative? The President decided that it was an affirmative vote.

The *mode of appointing* the Executive was the next question.

M:͟ WILSON renewed his declarations in favor of an appointment by the people. He wished to derive not only both branches of the Legislature from the people, without the intervention of the State Legislatures but the Executive also; in order to make them as independent as possible of each other, as well as of the States;

Col. MASON favors the idea, but thinks it impracticable. He wishes however that M:͟ Wilson might have time to digest it into his own form.—the clause "to be chosen by the National Legislature"—was accordingly postponed.—

---

[66] The transcript italicizes the phrase "for seven years."
[67] In the transcript the vote reads: "New York, New Jersey, Pennsylvania, Delaware, Virginia, aye—5; Connecticut, North Carolina, South Carolina, Georgia, no—4; Massachusetts, divided."

Mr RUTLIDGE suggests an election of the Executive by the second branch only of the national Legislature.

The Committee then rose and the House
> Adjourned.

---

SATURDAY JUNE 2ᴅ [68] IN COMMITTEE OF WHOLE

*[Insert the words noted here][69]   * William Saml Johnson from Connecticut, Daniel of St. Thomas Jennifer, from Maryd & John Lansing Jr from N. York, took their seats.

It was movd & 2ded to postpone ye Resol: of Mr Randolph respecting the Executive, in order to take up the 2d branch of the Legislature; which being negatived by Mas: Con: Del: Virg: N. C. S. C. Geo:[70] agst. N. Y. Pena Maryd [70]   The mode of appointg ye Executive was resumed.

Mr WILSON made the following motion, to be substituted for the mode proposed by Mr Randolph's resolution, "that the Executive Magistracy shall be elected in the following manner: That the States be divided into       districts: & that the persons qualified to vote in each district for members of the first branch of the national Legislature elect       members for their respective districts to be electors of the Executive magistracy, that the said Electors of the Executive magistracy meet at       and they or any       of them so met shall proceed to elect by ballot, but not out of their own body       person   in whom the Executive authority of the national Government shall be vested."

Mr WILSON repeated his arguments in favor of an election without the intervention of the States. He supposed too that this mode would produce more confidence among the people in the first magistrate, than an election by the national Legislature.

Mr GERRY, opposed the election by the national legislature. There would be a constant intrigue kept up for the appointment. The Legislature & the candidates wd bargain & play into one another's hands, votes would be given by the former under

---

[68] The year "1787" is here inserted in the transcript.
[69] Madison's direction is omitted in the transcript.
[70] In the transcript the figures "7" and "3" are inserted after the States Georgia and Maryland, respectively.

promises or expectations from the latter, of recompensing them by services to members of the Legislature or to [71] their friends. He liked the principle of M.<sup>r</sup> Wilson's motion, but fears it would alarm & give a handle to the State partisans, as tending to supersede altogether the State authorities. He thought the Community not yet ripe for stripping the States of their powers, even such as might not be requisite for local purposes. He was for waiting till people should feel more the necessity of it. He seemed to prefer the taking the suffrages of the States instead of Electors, or letting the Legislatures nominate, and the electors appoint. He was not clear that the people ought to act directly even in the choice of electors, being too little informed of personal characters in large districts, and liable to deceptions.

M.<sup>r</sup> WILLIAMSON could see no advantage in the introduction of Electors chosen by the people who would stand in the same relation to them as the State Legislatures, whilst the expedient would be attended with great trouble and expence.

On the question for agreeing to M.<sup>r</sup> Wilson's substitute, it was negatived: Mass.<sup>ts</sup> no. Con.<sup>t</sup> no. N. Y. no.* P.<sup>a</sup> ay. Del. no. Mar.<sup>d</sup> ay. Virg.<sup>a</sup> no. N. C. no. S. C. no. Geo.<sup>a</sup> no.[72]

On the question for electing the Executive by the national Legislature for the term of seven years, it was agreed to Mass.<sup>ts</sup> ay. Con.<sup>t</sup> ay. N. Y. ay. Pen.<sup>a</sup> no. Del. ay. Mary.<sup>d</sup> no. V.<sup>a</sup> ay. N. C. ay. S. C. ay. Geo. ay.[73]

Doc.<sup>r</sup> FRANKLIN moved that what related to the compensation for the services of the Executive be postponed, in order to substitute—"whose necessary expences shall be defrayed, but who shall receive no salary, stipend fee or reward whatsoever for their services"—He said that being very sensible of the effect of age on his memory, he had been unwilling to trust to that for the observations which seemed to support his motion, and had reduced them to writing, that he might with the permission of the Committee read instead of speaking them. M.<sup>r</sup> WILSON made an offer to

---

\* N. Y. in the printed Journal—'divided.'

[71] The word "to" is omitted in the transcript.

[72] In the transcript the vote reads: "Pennsylvania, Maryland, aye—2; Massachusetts, Connecticut, New York,* Delaware, Virginia, North Carolina, South Carolina, Georgia, no—8."

[73] In the transcript the vote reads: "Massachusetts, Connecticut, New York, Delaware, Virginia, North Carolina, South Carolina, Georgia, aye—8; Pennsylvania, Maryland, no—2."

read the paper, which was accepted—The following is a literal copy of the paper.

Sir.

It is with reluctance that I rise to express a disapprobation of any one article of the plan for which we are so much obliged to the honorable gentleman who laid it before us. From its first reading I have borne a good will to it, and in general wished it success. In this particular of salaries to the Executive branch I happen to differ; and as my opinion may appear new and chimerical, it is only from a persuasion that it is right, and from a sense of duty that I hazard it. The Committee will judge of my reasons when they have heard them, and their judgment may possibly change mine.—I think I see inconveniences in the appointment of salaries; I see none in refusing them, but on the contrary, great advantages.

Sir, there are two passions which have a powerful influence on the affairs of men. These are ambition and avarice; the love of power, and the love of money. Separately each of these has great force in prompting men to action; but when united in view of the same object, they have in many minds the most violent effects. Place before the eyes of such men, a post of *honour* that shall be at the same time a place of *profit*, and they will move heaven and earth to obtain it. The vast number of such places it is that renders the British Government so tempestuous. The struggles for them are the true sources of all those factions which are perpetually dividing the Nation, distracting its Councils, hurrying sometimes into fruitless & mischievous wars, and often compelling a submission to dishonorable terms of peace.

And of what kind are the men that will strive for this profitable pre-eminence, through all the bustle of cabal, the heat of contention, the infinite mutual abuse of parties, tearing to pieces the best of characters? It will not be the wise and moderate; the lovers of peace and good order, the men fittest for the trust. It will be the bold and the violent, the men of strong passions and indefatigable activity in their selfish pursuits. These will thrust themselves into your Government and be your rulers.—And these too will be mistaken in the expected happiness of their situation: For their vanquished competitors of the same spirit, and from the same motives will perpetually be endeavouring to distress their administration, thwart their measures, and render them odious to the people.

Besides these evils, Sir, tho' we may set out in the beginning with moderate salaries, we shall find that such will not be of long continuance. Reasons will never be wanting for proposed augmentations. And there will always be a party for giving more to the rulers, that the rulers may be able in return to give more to them.— Hence as all history informs us, there has been in every State & Kingdom a constant kind of warfare between the governing & governed: the one striving to obtain more for its support, and the other to pay less. And this has alone occasioned great convulsions, actual civil wars, ending either in dethroning of the Princes, or enslaving of the people. Generally indeed the ruling power carries its point, the revenues of princes constantly increasing, and we see that they are never satisfied, but always in want of more. The more the people are discontented with the oppression of taxes; the greater need the prince has of money to distribute among his partizans and pay the troops that are to suppress all resistance, and enable him to plunder at pleasure. There is scarce a king in a hundred who would not, if he could, follow the example of Pharoah, get first all the peoples money, then all their lands, and then make them and their children servants for ever. It will be said, that we don't propose to establish Kings. I know it. But there is a natural inclination in mankind to Kingly Government. It sometimes relieves them from Aristocratic domination. They had rather have one tyrant than five hundred. It gives more of the appearance of equality among Citizens, and that they like. I am apprehensive therefore, perhaps too apprehensive, that the Government of these States, may in future times, end in a Monarchy. But this Catastrophe I think may be long delayed, if in our proposed System we do not sow the seeds of contention, faction & tumult, by making our posts of honor, places of profit. If we do, I fear that tho' we do employ at first a number, and not a single person, the number will in time be set aside, it will only nourish the fœtus of a King, as the honorable gentleman from Virginia very aptly expressed it, and a King will the sooner be set over us.

It may be imagined by some that this is an Utopian Idea, and that we can never find men to serve us in the Executive department, without paying them well for their services. I conceive this to be a mistake. Some existing facts present themselves to me, which incline me to a contrary opinion. The high Sheriff of a County in England is an honorable office, but it is not a profitable one. It is rather expensive and therefore not sought for. But yet, it is executed and well executed, and usually by some of the principal Gentlemen of the County. In France, the office of Counsellor or Member of their Judiciary Parliaments is more honorable. It is therefore purchased at a high price: There are indeed fees on the law proceedings, which are divided among them, but these fees do not amount to more than three per Cent on the sum paid for the place. Therefore as legal interest is there at five per C$^t$ they in fact pay two per C$^t$ for being allowed to do the Judiciary business of the Nation, which is at the same time entirely exempt from the burden of paying them any salaries for their services. I do not however mean to recommend this as an eligible mode for our Judiciary department. I only bring the instance to shew that the pleasure of doing good & serving their Country and the respect such conduct entitles them to, are sufficient motives with some minds to give up a great portion of their time to the public, without the mean inducement of pecuniary satisfaction.

Another instance is that of a respectable Society who have made the experiment, and practised it with success more than an [74] hundred years. I mean the Quakers. It is an established rule with them, that they are not to go to law; but in their controversies they must apply to their monthly, quarterly and yearly meetings. Committees of these sit with patience to hear the parties, and spend much time in composing their differences. In doing this, they are supported by a sense of duty, and the respect paid to usefulness. It is honorable to be so employed, but it was [75] never made profitable by salaries, fees, or perquisites. And indeed in all cases of public service the less the profit the greater the honor.

---

[74] The word "one" is substituted in the transcript for "an."

[75] The word "is" is substituted in the transcript for "was."

OLIVER ELLSWORTH

To bring the matter nearer home, have we not seen, the great and most important of our offices, that of General of our armies executed for eight years together without the smallest salary, by a Patriot whom I will not now offend by any other praise; and this through fatigues and distresses in common with the other brave men his military friends & Companions, and the constant anxieties peculiar to his station? And shall we doubt finding three or four men in all the U. States, with public spirit enough to bear sitting in peaceful Council for perhaps an equal term, merely to preside over our civil concerns, and see that our laws are duly executed. Sir, I have a better opinion of our Country. I think we shall never be without a sufficient number of wise and good men to undertake and execute well and faithfully the office in question.

Sir, The saving of the salaries that may at first be proposed is not an object with me. The subsequent mischiefs of proposing them are what I apprehend. And therefore it is, that I move the amendment. If it is not seconded or accepted I must be contented with the satisfaction of having delivered my opinion frankly and done my duty.

The motion was seconded by Col. HAMILTON with the view he said merely of bringing so respectable a proposition before the Committee, and which was besides enforced by arguments that had a certain degree of weight. No debate ensued, and the proposition was postponed for the consideration of the members. It was treated with great respect, but rather for the author of it, than from any apparent conviction of its expediency or practicability.

M⸢r⸣ DICKENSON moved "that the Executive be made removeable by the National Legislature on the request of a majority of the Legislatures of individual States." It was necessary he said to place the power of removing somewhere. He did not like the plan of impeaching the Great officers of State. He did not know how provision could be made for removal of them in a better mode than that which he had proposed. He had no idea of abolishing the State Governments as some gentlemen seemed inclined to do. The happiness of this Country in his opinion required considerable powers to be left in the hands of the States.

Mr BEDFORD seconded the motion.

Mr SHERMAN contended that the National Legislature should have power to remove the Executive at pleasure.

Mr MASON. Some mode of displacing an unfit magistrate is rendered indispensable by the fallibility of those who choose, as well as by the corruptibility of the man chosen. He opposed decidedly the making the Executive the mere creature of the Legislature as a violation of the fundamental principle of good Government.

Mr MADISON & Mr WILSON observed that it would leave an equality of agency in the small with the great States; that it would enable a minority of the people to prevent ye removal of an officer who had rendered himself justly criminal in the eyes of a majority; that it would open a door for intrigues agst him in States where his administration tho' just might be unpopular, and might tempt him to pay court to particular States whose leading partizans he might fear, or wish to engage as his partizans. They both thought it bad policy to introduce such a mixture of the State authorities, where their agency could be otherwise supplied.

Mr DICKENSON considered the business as so important that no man ought to be silent or reserved. He went into a discourse of some length, the sum of which was, that the Legislative, Executive, & Judiciary departments ought to be made as independent as possible; but that such an Executive as some seemed to have in contemplation was not consistent with a republic: that a firm Executive could only exist in a limited monarchy. In the British Govt itself the weight of the Executive arises from the attachments which the Crown draws to itself, & not merely from the force of its prerogatives. In place of these attachments we must look out for something else. One source of stability is the double branch of the Legislature. The division of the Country into distinct States formed the other principal source of stability. This division ought therefore to be maintained, and considerable powers to be left with the States. This was the ground of his consolation for the future fate of his Country. Without this, and in case of a consolidation of the States into one great Republic, we might read its fate in the history of smaller ones. A limited

Monarchy he considered as *one* of the best Governments in the world. It was not *certain* that the same blessings were derivable from any other form. It was certain that equal blessings had never yet been derived from any of the republican form. A limited Monarchy however was out of the question. The spirit of the times—the state of our affairs, forbade the experiment, if it were desireable. Was it possible moreover in the nature of things to introduce it even if these obstacles were less insuperable. A House of Nobles was essential to such a Gov.t could these be created by a breath, or by a stroke of the pen? No. They were the growth of ages, and could only arise under a complication of circumstances none of which existed in this Country. But though a form the most perfect *perhaps* in itself be unattainable, we must not despair. If antient republics have been found to flourish for a moment only & then vanish for ever, it only proves that they were badly constituted; and that we ought to seek for every remedy for their diseases. One of these remedies he conceived to be the accidental lucky division of this Country into distinct States; a division which some seemed desirous to abolish altogether. As to the point of representation in the national Legislature as it might affect States of different sizes, he said it must probably end in mutual concession. He hoped that each State would retain an equal voice at least in one branch of the National Legislature, and supposed the sums paid within each State would form a better ratio for the other branch than either the number of inhabitants or the quantum of property.

A motion being made to strike out "on request by a majority of the Legislatures of the individual States" and rejected, Connecticut, S. Carol: & Geo. being ay, the rest no: the question was taken—

On M.r DICKENSON's motion for making [76] Executive removeable by [76] Nat.l; Legislature at [76] request of [77] majority of State Legislatures [78] was also rejected—all the States being in the negative Except Delaware which gave an affirmative vote.

---

[76] The word "the" is here inserted in the transcript.
[77] The word "a" is here inserted in the transcript.
[78] The word "which" is here inserted in the transcript.

The Question for making y.̣ Executive ineligible after seven years,[79] was next taken, and agreed to:

Mass.̣ts; ay. Con.̣t; no. N. Y. ay. P.̣a div.̣d Del. ay. Mary.̣d ay. V.̣a ay. N. C. ay. S. C. ay. Geo. no:* [80]

M.̣r WILLIAMSON 2.̣ded by M.̣r DAVIE moved to add to the last Clause, the words—"and to be removeable on impeachment & conviction of mal-practice or neglect of duty"—which was agreed to.

M.̣r RUTLIDGE & M.̣r C. PINKNEY moved that the blank for the n.̣o of persons in the Executive be filled with the words "one person." He supposed the reasons to be so obvious & conclusive in favor of one that no member would oppose the motion.

M.̣r RANDOLPH opposed it with great earnestness, declaring that he should not do justice to the Country which sent him if he were silently to suffer the establishm.̣t of a Unity in the Executive department. He felt an opposition to it which he believed he should continue to feel as long as he lived. He urged 1. that the permanent temper of the people was adverse to the very semblance of Monarchy. 2.[82] that a unity was unnecessary a plurality being equally competent to all the objects of the department. 3.[82] that the necessary confidence would never be reposed in a single Magistrate. 4.[82] that the appointments would generally be in favor of some inhabitant near the center of the Community, and consequently the remote parts would not be on an equal footing. He was in favor of three members of the Executive to be drawn from different portions of the Country.

M.̣r BUTLER contended strongly for a single magistrate as most likely to answer the purpose of the remote parts. If one man should be appointed he would be responsible to the whole, and would be impartial to its interests. If three or more should be taken from as many districts, there would be a constant struggle for local advantages. In Military matters this would be particularly mischievous. He said his opinion on this point had been

---

* In [81] printed Journal Geo. ay.
[79] The phrase "ineligible after seven years" is italicized in the transcript.
[80] In the transcript the vote reads: "Massachusetts, New York, Delaware, Maryland, Virginia, North Carolina, South Carolina, aye—7; Connecticut, Georgia,* no—2; Pennsylvania, divided."
[81] The word "the" is here inserted in the transcript.
[82] The figures "1," "2," "3" and "4" are changed to "first," "secondly," "thirdly" and "fourthly."

formed under the opportunity he had had of seeing the manner in which a plurality of military heads [83] distracted Holland when threatened with invasion by the imperial troops. One man was for directing the force to the defence of this part, another to that part of the Country, just as he happened to be swayed by prejudice or interest.

The motion was then postp<sup>d</sup> the Committee rose & the House Adj<sup>d</sup>

MONDAY JUNE 4.[84] IN COMMITTEE OF THE WHOLE

The Question was resumed on motion of M<sup>r</sup> PINKNEY 2<sup>ded</sup> by [85] WILSON, "shall the blank for the number of the Executive be filled with a single person?"

M<sup>r</sup> WILSON was in favor of the motion. It had been opposed by the gentleman from Virg<sup>a</sup> [M<sup>r</sup> Randolph] but the arguments used had not convinced him. He observed that the objections of M<sup>r</sup> R. were levelled not so much ag<sup>st</sup> the measure itself, as ag<sup>st</sup> its unpopularity. If he could suppose that it would occasion a rejection of the plan of which it should form a part, though the part was [86] an important one, yet he would give it up rather than lose the whole. On examination he could see no evidence of the alledged antipathy of the people. On the contrary he was persuaded that it does not exist. All know that a single magistrate is not a King. One fact has great weight with him. All the 13 States tho agreeing in scarce any other instance, agree in placing a single magistrate at the head of the Govern<sup>t</sup> The idea of three heads has taken place in none. The degree of power is indeed different; but there are no co-ordinate heads. In addition to his former reasons for preferring a unity, he would mention another. The *tranquility* not less than the vigor of the Gov<sup>t</sup> he thought would be favored by it. Among three equal members, he foresaw nothing but uncontrouled, continued, & violent animosities; which would not only interrupt the public administration; but diffuse their poison thro' the other

---

[83] The transcript italicizes the phrase "plurality of military heads."
[84] The year "1787" is here inserted in the transcript.
[85] The transcript inserts the word "Mr." before "Wilson."
[86] The word "was" is changed to "were" in the transcript.

branches of Gov$^t$, thro' the States, and at length thro' the people at large. If the members were to be unequal in power the principle of the [87] opposition to the unity was given up. If equal, the making them an odd number would not be a remedy. In Courts of Justice there are two sides only to a question. In the Legislative & Executive departm$^{ts}$ questions have commonly many sides. Each member therefore might espouse a separate one & no two agree.

M$^r$ SHERMAN. This matter is of great importance and ought to be well considered before it is determined. M$^r$ Wilson he said had observed that in each State a single magistrate was placed at the head of the Gov$^t$ It was so he admitted, and properly so, and he wished the same policy to prevail in the federal Gov$^t$ But then it should be also remarked that in all the States there was a Council of advice, without which the first magistrate could not act. A council he thought necessary to make the establishment acceptable to the people. Even in G. B. the King has a Council; and though he appoints it himself, its advice has its weight with him, and attracts the Confidence of the people.

M$^r$ WILLIAMSON asks M$^r$ WILSON whether he means to annex a Council.

M$^r$ WILSON means to have no Council, which oftener serves to cover, than prevent malpractices.

M$^r$ GERRY was at a loss to discover the policy of three members for the Executive. It w$^d$ be extremely inconvenient in many instances, particularly in military matters, whether relating to the militia, an army, or a navy. It would be a general with three heads.

On the question for a single Executive it was agreed to Mass$^{ts}$ ay. Con$^t$ ay. N. Y. no. Pen$^a$ ay. Del. no. Mary$^d$ no. Virg. ay. [M$^r$ R. & M$^r$ Blair no—Doc$^r$ M$^c$C$^g$ M$^r$ M. & Gen W. ay. Col. Mason being no, but not in house, M$^r$ Wythe ay but gone home]. N. C. ay. S. C. ay. Georg$^a$ ay.[88]

---

[87] The word "the" is omitted in the transcript.

[88] In the transcript the vote reads: "Massachusetts, Connecticut, Pennsylvania, Virginia, (Mr. Randolph and Mr. Blair, no; Doctor McClurg, Mr. Madison, and General Washington, aye; Colonel Mason being no, but not in the House, Mr. Wythe, aye, but gone home), North Carolina, South Carolina, Georgia, aye ; New York, Delaware, Maryland, no—3."

First Clause of Proposition 8th [89] relating *to a Council of Revision* taken into consideration.

Mr GERRY doubts whether the Judiciary ought to form a part of it, as they will have a sufficient check agst encroachments on their own department by their exposition of the laws, which involved a power of deciding on their Constitutionality. In some States the Judges had actually set aside laws as being agst the Constitution. This was done too with general approbation. It was quite foreign from the nature of ye office to make them judges of the policy of public measures. He moves to postpone the clause in order to propose "that the National Executive shall have a right to negative any Legislative act which shall not be afterwards passed by       parts of each branch of the national Legislature."

Mr KING seconds the motion, observing that the Judges ought to be able to expound the law as it should come before them, free from the bias of having participated in its formation.

Mr WILSON thinks neither the original proposition nor the amendment go far enough. If the Legislative Exetv & Judiciary ought to be distinct & independent. The Executive ought to have an absolute negative. Without such a self-defense the Legislature can at any moment sink it into non-existence. He was for varying the proposition in such a manner as to give the Executive & Judiciary jointly an absolute negative.

On the question to postpone in order to take Mr Gerry's proposition into consideration it was agreed to, Masss ay. Cont no. N. Y. ay. Pa ay. Del. no. Maryd no. Virga no. N. C. ay. S. C. ay. Ga ay.[90]

Mr GERRY'S proposition being now before [91] Committee, Mr WILSON & Mr HAMILTON move that the last part of it [viz. "wch sd not be afterwds passed unless [92] by       parts of each branch of the National legislature] be struck out, so as to give the Executive an absolute negative on the laws. There was no danger

---

[89] The phrase "the eighth Resolution" is substituted in the transcript for "Proposition 8th."
[90] In the transcript the vote reads: "Massachusetts, New York, Pennsylvania, North Carolina, South Carolina, Georgia, aye—6; Connecticut, Delaware, Maryland, Virginia, no—4."
[91] The word "the" is here inserted in the transcript.
[92] The word "unless" is crossed out in the transcript.

they thought of such a power being too much exercised. It was mentioned by Col: HAMILTON that the King of G. B. had not exerted his negative since the Revolution.

Mr GERRY sees no necessity for so great a controul over the legislature as the best men in the Community would be comprised in the two branches of it.

Docr FRANKLIN, said he was sorry to differ from his colleague for whom he had a very great respect, on any occasion, but he could not help it on this. He had had some experience of this check in the Executive on the Legislature, under the proprietary Government of Pena. The negative of the Governor was constantly made use of to extort money. No good law whatever could be passed without a private bargain with him. An increase of his salary, or some donation, was always made a condition; till at last it became the regular practice, to have orders in his favor on the Treasury, presented along with the bills to be signed, so that he might actually receive the former before he should sign the latter. When the Indians were scalping the western people, and notice of it arrived, the concurrence of the Governor in the means of self-defence could not'be got, till it was agreed that his Estate should be exempted from taxation: so that the people were to fight for the security of his property, whilst he was to bear no share of the burden. This was a mischievous sort of check. If the Executive was to have a Council, such a power would be less objectionable. It was true, the King of G. B. had not, as was said, exerted his negative since the Revolution; but that matter was easily explained. The bribes and emoluments now given to the members of parliament rendered it unnecessary, every thing being done according to the will of the Ministers. He was afraid, if a negative should be given as proposed, that more power and money would be demanded, till at last eno' would be gotten [93] to influence & bribe the Legislature into a compleat subjection to the will of the Executive.

Mr SHERMAN was agst enabling any one man to stop the will of the whole. No one man could be found so far above all the rest in wisdom. He thought we ought to avail ourselves of his wisdom in

---

[93] In the transcript the syllable "ten" is stricken from the word "gotten."

revising the laws, but not permit him to overule the decided and cool opinions of the Legislature.

M! MADISON supposed that if a proper proportion of each branch should be required to overrule the objections of the Executive, it would answer the same purpose as an absolute negative. It would rarely if ever happen that the Executive constituted as ours is proposed to be would, have firmness eno' to resist the legislature, unless backed by a certain part of the body itself. The King of G. B. with all his splendid attributes would not be able to withstand y? unanimous and eager wishes of both houses of Parliament. To give such a prerogative would certainly be obnoxious to the temper of this Country; its present temper at least.

M! WILSON believed as others did that this power would seldom be used. The Legislature would know that such a power existed, and would refrain from such laws, as it would be sure to defeat. Its silent operation would therefore preserve harmony and prevent mischief. The case of Pen? formerly was very different from its present case. The Executive was not then as now to be appointed by the people. It will not in this case as in the one cited be supported by the head of a Great Empire, actuated by a different & sometimes opposite interest. The salary too is now proposed to be fixed by the Constitution, or if D! F.'s idea should be adopted all salary whatever interdicted. The requiring a large proportion of each House to overrule the Executive check might do in peaceable times; but there might be tempestuous moments in which animosities may run high between the Executive and Legislative branches, and in which the former ought to be able to defend itself.

M! BUTLER had been in favor of a single Executive Magistrate; but could he have entertained an idea that a compleat negative on the laws was to be given him he certainly should have acted very differently. It had been observed that in all countries the Executive power is in a constant course of increase. This was certainly the case in G. B. Gentlemen seemed to think that we had nothing to apprehend from an abuse of the Executive power. But why might not a Cataline or a Cromwell arise in this Country as well as in others.

M.<sup>r</sup> BEDFORD was opposed to every check on the Legislative,[94] even the Council of Revision first proposed. He thought it would be sufficient to mark out in the Constitution the boundaries to the Legislative Authority, which would give all the requisite security to the rights of the other departments. The Representatives of the people were the best Judges of what was for their interest, and ought to be under no external controul whatever. The two branches would produce a sufficient controul within the Legislature itself.

Col. MASON observed that a vote had already passed he found [he was out at the time] for vesting the executive powers in a single person. Among these powers was that of appointing to offices in certain cases. The probable abuses of a negative had been well explained by D.<sup>r</sup> F. as proved by experience, the best of all tests. Will not the same door be opened here. The Executive may refuse its assent to necessary measures till new appointments shall be referred to him; and having by degrees engrossed all these into his own hands, the American Executive, like the British, will by bribery & influence, save himself the trouble & odium of exerting his negative afterwards. We are M.<sup>r</sup> Chairman going very far in this business. We are not indeed constituting a British Government, but a more dangerous monarchy, an elective one. We are introducing a new principle into our system, and not necessary as in the British Gov.<sup>t</sup> where the Executive has greater rights to defend. Do gentlemen mean to pave the way to hereditary Monarchy? Do they flatter themselves that the people will ever consent to such an innovation? If they do I venture to tell them, they are mistaken. The people never will consent. And do gentlemen consider the danger of delay, and the still greater danger of a a rejection, not for a moment but forever, of the plan which shall be proposed to them. Notwithstanding the oppressions & injustice experienced among us from democracy; the genius of the people is in favor of it, and the genius of the people must be consulted. He could not but consider the federal system as in effect dissolved by the appointment of this

---

[94] In the transcript the syllable ".tive" is stricken from the word "Legislative" and "ture" is written above it.

Convention to devise a better one. And do gentlemen look forward to the dangerous interval between the extinction of an old, and the establishment of a new Governm<sup>t</sup> and to the scenes of confusion which may ensue. He hoped that nothing like a Monarchy would ever be attempted in this Country. A hatred to its oppressions had carried the people through the late Revolution. Will it not be eno' to enable the Executive to suspend offensive laws, till they shall be coolly revised, and the objections to them overruled by a greater majority than was required in the first instance. He never could agree to give up all the rights of the people to a single Magistrate. If more than one had been fixed on, greater powers might have been entrusted to the Executive. He hoped this attempt to give such powers would have its weight hereafter as an argument for increasing the number of the Executive.

Doc<sup>r</sup> FRANKLIN. A Gentleman from S. C. [M<sup>r</sup> Butler] a day or two ago called our attention to the case of the U. Netherlands. He wished the gentleman had been a little fuller, and had gone back to the original of that Gov<sup>t</sup> The people being under great obligations to the Prince of Orange whose wisdom and bravery had saved them, chose him for the Stadtholder. He did very well. Inconveniences however were felt from his powers; which growing more & more oppressive, they were at length set aside. Still however there was a party for the P. of Orange, which descended to his son who excited insurrections, spilt a great deal of blood, murdered the de Witts, and got the powers revested in the Stadtholder. Afterwards another Prince had power to excite insurrections & to [95] make the Stadtholdership hereditary. And the present Stadth<sup>der</sup> is ready to wade thro a bloody civil war to the establishment of a monarchy. Col. Mason had mentioned the circumstance of appointing officers. He knew how that point would be managed. No new appointment would be suffered as heretofore in Pens<sup>a</sup> unless it be referred to the Executive; so that all profitable offices will be at his disposal. The first man put at the helm will be a good one. No body knows what sort may

---

[95] The word "to" is omitted in the transcript.

come afterwards. The Executive will be always increasing here, as elsewhere, till it ends in a Monarchy

On the question for striking out so as to give [96] Executive an absolute negative—Mass^ts no. Con^t no. N. Y. no. P^a no. Dl. no. M^d no. V^a no. N. C. no. S. C. no. Georg^a no.[97]

M^r BUTLER moved that the Resol^n be altered so as to read—"Resolved that the National Executive have a power to suspend any Legislative act for the term of    ."

Doct^r FRANKLIN seconds the motion.

M^r GERRY observed that a [98] power of suspending might do all the mischief dreaded from the negative of useful laws; without answering the salutary purpose of checking unjust or unwise ones.

On [96] question for giving this suspending power" all the States, to wit Mass^ts Con^t N. Y. P^a Del. Mary^d Virg^a N. C. S. C. Georgia were *No*.

On a question for enabling *two thirds* of each branch of the Legislature to overrule the revisionary [99] check: it passed in the affirmative sub silentio; and was inserted in the blank of M^r Gerry's motion.

On the question on M^r Gerry's motion which gave the Executive alone without the Judiciary the revisionary controul on the laws unless overruled by ⅔ of each branch; Mass^ts ay. Con^t no. N. Y. ay. P^a ay. Del. ay. Mary^d no. V^a ay. N. C. ay. S. C. ay. Geo. ay.[1]

It was moved by M^r WILSON 2^ded by M^r MADISON—that the following amendment be made to the last resolution—after the words "National Ex." to add "& a convenient number of the National Judiciary."

An objection of order being taken by M^r HAMILTON to the introduction of the last amendment at this time, notice was given by M^r W. & M^r M.—that the same w^d be moved tomorrow,—where-

---

[96] The word "the" is here inserted in the transcript.
[97] In the transcript the vote reads "Masssachuetts, Connecticut, New York, Pennsylvania, Delaware, Maryland, Virginia, North Carolina, South Carolina, Georgia, no—10."
[98] The word "the" is substituted in the transcript for "a."
[99] In the transcript the word "provisionary" was erroneously used in place of "revisionary."
[1] In the transcript this vote reads: "Massachusetts, New York, Pennsylvania, Delaware, Virginia, North Carolina, South Carolina, Georgia, aye—8; Connecticut, Maryland, no—2."

upon Wednesday (the day after)[2] was assigned to reconsider the amendment of M! Gerry.

It was then moved & 2ded to proceed to the consideration of the 9th resolution submitted by M! Randolph—when on motion to agree to the first clause namely "Resolved that a National Judiciary be established"[3] It passed in the affirmative nem. con.

It was then moved & 2ded to add these words to the first clause of the ninth resolution namely—"to consist of one supreme tribunal, and of one or more inferior tribunals," which passed in the affirmative—

The Comm? then rose and the House
Adjourned

TEUSDAY JUNE 5.  IN COMMITTEE OF THE WHOLE

Governor Livingston from [4] New Jersey, took his seat.

The words, "one or more" were struck out before "inferior tribunals" as an amendment to the last clause of Resoln 9th [5] The Clause—"that the National Judiciary be chosen by the National Legislature," being under consideration.

M! WILSON opposed the appointmt of Judges by the National Legisl: Experience shewed the impropriety of such appointmts by numerous bodies. Intrigue, partiality, and concealment were the necessary consequences. A principal reason for unity in the Executive was that officers might be appointed by a single, responsible person.

M! RUTLIDGE was by no means disposed to grant so great a power to any single person. The people will think we are leaning too much towards Monarchy. He was against establishing any national tribunal except a single supreme one. The State tribunals are most proper to decide in all cases in the first instance.

Doc! FRANKLIN observed that two modes of chusing the Judges had been mentioned, to wit, by the Legislature and by the Executive. He wished such other modes to be suggested as might occur

---

[2] The phrase "(the day after)" is crossed out in the transcript.
[3] The phrase "Resolved that a National Judiciary be established" is italicized in the transcript.
[4] The word "of" is substituted in the transcript for "from."
[5] The phrase "the ninth Resolution" is used in the transcript in place of "Resoln 9th"

to other gentlemen; it being a point of great moment. He would mention one which he had understood was practiced in Scotland. He then in a brief and entertaining manner related a Scotch mode, in which the nomination proceeded from the Lawyers, who always selected the ablest of the profession in order to get rid of him, and share his practice among themselves. It was here he said the interest of the electors to make the best choice, which should always be made the case if possible.

M!͟ MADISON disliked the election of the Judges by the Legislature or any numerous body. Besides, the danger of intrigue and partiality, many of the members were not judges of the requisite qualifications. The Legislative talents which were very different from those of a Judge, commonly recommended men to the favor of Legislative Assemblies. It was known too that the accidental circumstances of presence and absence, of being a member or not a member, had a very undue influence on the appointment. On the other hand he was not satisfied with referring the appointment to the Executive. He rather inclined to give it to the Senatorial branch, as numerous eno' to be confided in—as not so numerous as to be governed by the motives of the other branch; and as being sufficiently stable and independent to follow their deliberate judgments. He hinted this only and moved that the *appointment by the Legislature* might be struck out, & a blank left to be hereafter filled on maturer reflection. M!͟ WILSON seconds it. On the question for striking out. Mass!͟s ay. Con!͟ no. N. Y. ay. N. J. ay. Pen!͟a ay. Del. ay. M!͟d ay. V!͟a ay. N. C. ay. S. C. no. Geo. ay.[6]

M!͟ WILSON gave notice that he should at a future day move for a reconsideration of that clause which respects "inferior tribunals."

M!͟ PINKNEY gave notice that when the clause respecting the appointment of the Judiciary should again come before the Committee he should move to restore the "appointment by the national Legislature."

The following clauses of Resol: 9.[7] were agreed to viz "to hold their offices during good behaviour, and to receive punctually at

---

[6] In the transcript the vote reads: "Massachusetts, New York, New Jersey, Pennsylvania, Delaware, Maryland, Virginia, North Carolina, South Carolina, no, Georgia, aye—9; Connecticut, South Carolina,—2."

[7] The transcript uses the phrase "the ninth Resolution" in place of "Resol: 9," and italicizes the resolution.

stated times, a fixed compensation for their services, in which no increase or diminution shall be made so as to affect the persons actually in office at the time of such increase or diminution."

The remaining clause of Resolution 9.[8] was posponed.

Resolution 10 [9] was agreed to—viz—that provision ought to be made for the admission of States lawfully arising within the limits of the U. States, whether from a voluntary junction of Government & territory, or otherwise, with the consent of a number of voices in the National Legislature less than the whole.

The 11. propos:[10] "*for guarantying to States Republican* Gov[t] & territory &c., being read, M[r] PATTERSON wished the point of representation could be decided before this clause should be considered, and moved to postpone it: which was not opposed, and agreed to: Connecticut & S. Carolina only voting ag[st] it.

Propos. 12 [11] "*for continuing Cong[s] till a given day and for fulfilling their engagements,*" produced no debate.

On the question, Mass. ay. Con[t] no. N. Y. ay. N. J.* ay. P[a] ay. Del. no. M[d] ay. V[a] ay. N. C. ay. S. C. ay. G. ay.

Propos: 13.[12] "that *provision ought to be made for hereafter amending the system now to be established, without requiring the assent of the Nat[l] Legislature,*" being taken up,

M[r] PINKNEY doubted the propriety or necessity of it.

M[r] GERRY favored it. The novelty & difficulty of the experiment requires periodical revision. The prospect of such a revision would also give intermediate stability to the Gov[t] Nothing had yet happened in the States where this provision existed to prove its impropriety. The proposition was postponed for further consideration: the votes being, Mas: Con. N. Y. P[a] Del. Ma. N. C.— ay   Virg[a] S. C. Geo: no

Propos. 14.[13] "*requiring oath from the State officers to support National Gov[t]*" was postponed after a short uninteresting conversa-

---

[8] The transcript here uses the phrase "the ninth Resolution."
*New Jersey omitted in the printed Journal.
[9] The phrase " The tenth Resolution " is here used in the transcript.
[10] In place of the words " The 11. propos:" the transcript reads: " The eleventh Resolution."
[11] The transcript changes "Propos. 12" to " The twelfth Resolution."
[12] The transcript changes "Propos: 13" to read as follows: " The thirteenth Resolution, to the effect."
[13] The transcript changes "Propos. 14" to " The fourteenth Resolution."

tion: the votes, Con. N. Jersey. M^d Virg^a: S. C. Geo. ay N. Y. P^a Del. N. C. – – – no Massachusetts – – – divided.

Propos. 15 [14] for "*recommending Conventions under appointment of the people to ratify the new Constitution*" &c. being taken up.

M^r SHARMAN thought such a popular ratification unnecessary: the articles of Confederation providing for changes and alterations with the assent of Cong^s and ratification of State Legislatures.

M^r MADISON thought this provision essential. The articles of Confed^n themselves were defective in this respect, resting in many of the States on the Legislative sanction only. Hence in conflicts between acts of the States, and of Cong^s especially where the former are of posterior date, and the decision is to be made by State tribunals, an uncertainty must necessarily prevail, or rather perhaps a certain decision in favor of the State authority. He suggested also that as far as the articles of Union were to be considered as a Treaty only of a particular sort, among the Governments of Independent States, the doctrine might be set up that a breach of any one article, by any of the parties, absolved the other parties from the whole obligation. For these reasons as well as others he thought it indispensable that the new Constitution should be ratified in the most unexceptionable form, and by the supreme authority of the people themselves.

M^r GERRY observed that in the Eastern States the Confed^n had been sanctioned by the people themselves. He seemed afraid of referring the new system to them. The people in that quarter have at this time the wildest ideas of Government in the world. They were for abolishing the Senate in Mass^ts and giving all the other powers of Gov^t to the other branch of the Legislature.

M^r KING supposed that the last article of y^e Confed^n rendered the legislature competent to the ratification. The people of the Southern States where the federal articles had been ratified by the Legislatures only, had since *impliedly* given their sanction to it. He thought notwithstanding that there might be policy in varying the mode. A Convention being a single house, the adoption may more easily be carried thro' it, than thro' the Legislatures where

---

[14] The transcript changes "Propos. 15" to "The fifteenth Resolution."

there are several branches. The Legislatures also being to lose power, will be most likely to raise objections. The people having already parted with the necessary powers it is immaterial to them, by which Government they are possessed, provided they be well employed.

M̃ WILSON took this occasion to lead the Committee by a train of observations to the idea of not suffering a disposition in the plurality of States to confederate anew on better principles, to be defeated by the inconsiderate or selfish opposition of a few States. He hoped the provision for ratifying would be put on such a footing as to admit of such a partial union, with a door open for the acession of the rest.*

M̃ PINKNEY hoped that in case the experiment should not unanimously take place, nine States might be authorized to unite under the same Govern̤

The propos. 15.¹⁶ was postponed nem. con̤

M̃ PINKNEY & M̃ RUTLIDGE moved that tomorrow be assigned to reconsider that clause of Propos. 4: ¹⁷ which respects the election of the first branch of the National Legislature—which passed in ¹⁸ affirmative: Con: N. Y. P̲ª Del: ᵈ V̲ª—ay—6 Mas. N. J. N. C. S. C. Geo. no. 5.

M̃ RUTLIDGE havᵍ obtained a rule for reconsideration of the clause for establishing *inferior* tribunals under the national authority, now moved that that part of the clause in propos. 9.¹⁹ should be expunged: arguing that the State Tribunals might and ought to be left in all cases to decide in the first instance the right of appeal to the supreme national tribunal being sufficient to secure the national rights & uniformity of Judgm̃ᵗˢ: that it was making an unnecessary encroachment on the jurisdiction of the States and creating unnecessary obstacles to their adoption of the new system.—M̃ SHERMAN 2ᵈᵉᵈ the motion.

---

*The note in brackets to be transferred to bottom margin. ¹⁵
[This hint was probably meant in terrorem to the smaller States of N. Jersey & Delaware. Nothing was said in reply to it.]

¹⁵ Madison's direction is omitted in the transcript.
¹⁶ The transcript changes " The propos. 15 " to " The fifteenth Resolution."
¹⁷ The transcript changes " Propos. 4 " to " the fourth Resolution."
¹⁸ The word "the" is here inserted in the transcript.
¹⁹ The transcript changes " propos. 9 " to " the ninth Resolution."

M<sup>r</sup> MADISON observed that unless inferior tribunals were dispersed throughout the Republic with *final* jurisdiction in *many* cases, appeals would be multiplied to a most oppressive degree; that besides, an appeal would not in many cases be a remedy. What was to be done after improper Verdicts in State tribunals obtained under the biassed directions of a dependent Judge, or the local prejudices of an undirected jury? To remand the cause for a new trial would answer no purpose. To order a new trial at the Supreme bar would oblige the parties to bring up their witnesses, tho' ever so distant from the seat of the Court. An effective Judiciary establishment commensurate to the legislative authority, was essential. A Government without a proper Executive & Judiciary would be the mere trunk of a body, without arms or legs to act or move.

M<sup>r</sup> WILSON opposed the motion on like grounds. he said the admiralty jurisdiction ought to be given wholly to the national Government, as it related to cases not within the jurisdiction of particular states, & to a scene in which controversies with foreigners would be most likely to happen.

M<sup>r</sup> SHERMAN was in favor of the motion. He dwelt chiefly on the supposed expensiveness of having a new set of Courts, when the existing State Courts would answer the same purpose.

M<sup>r</sup> DICKINSON contended strongly that if there was to be a National Legislature, there ought to be a national Judiciary, and that the former ought to have authority to institute the latter.

On the question for M<sup>r</sup> Rutlidge's motion to strike out "inferior tribunals" [20]

Mass<sup>ts</sup> divided. Con<sup>t</sup> ay. N. Y. div<sup>d</sup> N. J. ay. P<sup>a</sup> no. Del. no. M<sup>d</sup> no. V<sup>a</sup> no. N. C. ay. S. C. ay. Geo. ay.[21]

M<sup>r</sup> WILSON & M<sup>r</sup> MADISON then moved, in pursuance of the idea expressed above by M<sup>r</sup> Dickinson, to add to Resol: 9.[22] the words following "that the National Legislature be empowered to institute inferior tribunals." They observed that there was a dis-

---

[20] The phrase "it passed in the affirmative" is here inserted in the transcript.

[21] In the transcript the vote reads: "Connecticut, New York, New Jersey, North Carolina, South Carolina, Georgia, aye—5; Pennsylvania, Delaware, Maryland, Virginia, no—4; Massachusetts, divided." New York which was "divided" was erroneously placed among the "ayes" in copying, although the number was correctly given as "5."

[22] The transcript changes "Resol: 9" to "the ninth Resolution."

tinction between establishing such tribunals absolutely, and giving a discretion to the Legislature to establish or not establish them. They repeated the necessity of some such provision.

Mʳ BUTLER. The people will not bear such innovations. The States will revolt at such encroachments. Supposing such an establishment to be useful, we must not venture on it. We must follow the example of Solon who gave the Athenians not the best Govᵗ he could devise; but the best they wᵈ receive.

Mʳ KING remarked as to the comparative expence that the establishment of inferior tribunals wᵈ cost infinitely less than the appeals that would be prevented by them.

On this question as moved by Mʳ W. & Mʳ M.

Mass. ay. Cᵗ no. N. Y. divᵈ N. J.* ay. Pᵃ ay. Del. ay. Mᵈ ay. Vᵃ ay. N. C. ay. S. C. no. Geo. ay.

The Committee then rose & the House adjourned to 11 OC tomʷ ²³

---

WEDNESDAY JUNE 6ᵀᴴ IN COMMITTEE OF THE WHOLE

Mʳ PINKNEY according to previous notice & rule obtained, moved "that the first branch of the national Legislature be elected by the State Legislatures, and not by the people." contending that the people were less fit Judges in such a case, and that the Legislatures would be less likely to promote the adoption of the new Government, if they were to be excluded from all share in it.

Mʳ RUTLIDGE 2ᵈᵉᵈ the motion.

Mʳ GERRY. Much depends on the mode of election. In England, the people will probably lose their liberty from the smallness of the proportion having a right of suffrage. Our danger arises from the opposite extreme: hence in Massᵗˢ the worst men get into the Legislature. Several members of that Body had lately been convicted of infamous crimes. Men of indigence, ignorance & baseness, spare no pains, however dirty to carry their point agˢᵗ men who are superior to the artifices practised. He was not disposed to run into extremes. He was as much principled as ever agˢᵗ aristocracy and monarchy. It was necessary on the one hand

---

* In the printed Journal N. Jersey—no. ²³ The transcript omits the phrase "to 11 OC tomʷ"

that the people should appoint one branch of the Gov.<sup>t</sup> in order to inspire them with the necessary confidence. But he wished the election on the other to be so modified as to secure more effectually a just preference of merit. His idea was that the people should nominate certain persons in certain districts, out of whom the State Legislatures sh.<sup>d</sup> make the appointment.

M.<sup>r</sup> WILSON. He wished for vigor in the Gov.<sup>t</sup>, but he wished that vigorous authority to flow immediately from the legitimate source of all authority. The Gov.<sup>t</sup> ought to possess not only 1.<sup>st</sup> the *force*, but 2.<sup>dly</sup> the *mind or sense* of the people at large. The Legislature ought to be the most exact transcript of the whole Society. Representation is made necessary only because it is impossible for the people to act collectively. The opposition was to be expected he said from the *Governments*, not from the Citizens of the States. The latter had parted as was observed [by M.<sup>r</sup> King] with all the necessary powers;[24] and it was immaterial to them, by whom they were exercised, if well exercised. The State officers were to be the losers of power. The people he supposed would be rather more attached to the national Gov.<sup>t</sup> than to the State Gov.<sup>ts</sup> as being more important in itself, and more flattering to their pride. There is no danger of improper elections if made by *large* districts. Bad elections proceed from the smallness of the districts which give an opportunity to bad men to intrigue themselves into office.

M.<sup>r</sup> SHERMAN. If it were in view to abolish the State Gov.<sup>ts</sup> the elections ought to be by the people. If the State Gov.<sup>ts</sup> are to be continued, it is necessary in order to preserve harmony between the National & State Gov.<sup>ts</sup> that the elections to the former sh.<sup>d</sup> be made by the latter. The right of participating in the National Gov.<sup>t</sup> would be sufficiently secured to the people by their election of the State Legislatures. The objects of the Union, he thought were few. 1.[25] defence ag.<sup>st</sup> foreign danger. 2.[25] ag.<sup>st</sup> internal disputes & a resort to force. 3.[25] Treaties with foreign nations. 4.[25] regulating foreign commerce, & drawing revenue from it. These & perhaps a few lesser objects alone rendered a Con-

---

[24] The phrase "with all the necessary powers" is italicized in the transcript.
[25] The figures "1," "2," "3" and "4" are changed to "first," "secondly," etc. in the transcript.

federation of the States necessary. All other matters civil & criminal would be much better in the hands of the States. The people are more happy in small than [26] large States. States may indeed be too small as Rhode Island, & thereby be too subject to faction. Some others were perhaps too large, the powers of Govt not being able to pervade them. He was for giving the General Govt power to legislate and execute within a defined province.

COL. MASON. Under the existing Confederacy, Congs represent the *States* [27] not the *people* of the States: their acts operate on the *States*, not on the individuals.[28] The case will be changed in the new plan of Govt The people will be represented; they ought therefore to choose the Representatives. The requisites in actual representation are that the Reps should sympathize with their constituents; shd think as they think, & feel as they feel; and that for these purposes shd even be residents among them. Much he sd had been alledged agst democratic elections. He admitted that much might be said; but it was to be considered that no Govt was free from imperfections & evils; and that improper elections in many instances, were inseparable from Republican Govts But compare these with the advantage of this Form in favor of the rights of the people, in favor of human nature. He was persuaded there was a better chance for proper elections by the people, if divided into large districts, than by the State Legislatures. Paper money had been issued by the latter when the former were against it. Was it to be supposed that the State Legislatures then wd not send to the Natl legislature patrons of such projects, if the choice depended on them.

Mr MADISON considered an election of one branch at least of the Legislature by the people immediately, as a clear principle of free Govt and that this mode under proper regulations had the additional advantage of securing better representatives, as well as of avoiding too great an agency of the State Governments in the General one.—He differed from the member from Connecticut [Mr Sharman] in thinking the objects mentioned to be all the principal ones that required a National Govt Those were certainly impor-

---

[26] The word "in" is here inserted in the transcript.
[27] The word "and" is here inserted in the transcript.
[28] The transcript italicizes the word "individuals."

tant and necessary objects; but he combined with them the necessity of providing more effectually for the security of private rights, and the steady dispensation of Justice. Interferences with these were evils which had more perhaps than any thing else, produced this convention. Was it to be supposed that republican liberty could long exist under the abuses of it practised in some of the States. The gentleman [M$^r$ Sharman] had admitted that in a very small State, faction & oppression w$^d$ prevail. It was to be inferred then that wherever these prevailed the State was too small. Had they not prevailed in the largest as well as the smallest tho' less than in the smallest; and were we not thence admonished to enlarge the sphere as far as the nature of the Gov$^t$ would admit. This was the only defence ag$^{st}$ the inconveniencies of democracy consistent with the democratic form of Gov$^t$ All civilized Societies would be divided into different Sects, Factions, & interests, as they happened to consist of rich & poor, debtors & creditors, the landed, the manufacturing, the commercial interests, the inhabitants of this district or that district, the followers of this political leader or that political leader, the disciples of this religious Sect or that religious Sect. In all cases where a majority are united by a common interest or passion, the rights of the minority are in danger. What motives are to restrain them? A prudent regard to the maxim that honesty is the best policy is found by experience to be as little regarded by bodies of men as by individuals. Respect for character is always diminished in proportion to the number among whom the blame or praise is to be divided. Conscience, the only remaining tie, is known to be inadequate in individuals: In large numbers, little is to be expected from it. Besides, Religion itself may become a motive to persecution & oppression.—These observations are verified by the Histories of every Country antient & modern. In Greece & Rome the rich & poor, the creditors & debtors, as well as the patricians & plebians alternately oppressed each other with equal unmercifulness. What a source of oppression was the relation between the parent cities of Rome, Athens & Carthage, & their respective provinces: the former possessing the power, & the latter being sufficiently distinguished to be separate objects of it? Why was America so justly apprehensive of Parliamentary injustice? Because G. Britain had a separate interest real or supposed, & if her authority had been admitted, could have pursued that interest at our expence. We have seen the mere distinction of colour made in the most enlightened period of time, a ground of the most oppressive dominion ever exercised by man over man. What has been the source of those unjust laws complained of among ourselves? Has it not been the real or supposed interest of the major number? Debtors have defrauded their creditors. The landed interest has borne hard on the mercantile interest. The Holders of one species of property have thrown a disproportion of taxes on the holders of another species. The lesson we are to draw from the whole is that where a majority are united by a common sentiment, and have an opportunity, the rights of the minor party become insecure. In a Republican Gov$^t$ the Majority if united have always an opportunity. The only remedy is to enlarge the sphere, & thereby divide the community into so great a number of interests & parties, that in the 1$^{st}$ place a majority will not be likely at the same moment to have a common interest separate from that of the whole or of the minority; and in the 2$^d$ place, that in case they sh$^d$ have such an interest, they may not be [29] apt to unite in the pursuit of it. It was incumbent on us then to try this remedy, and with that view to frame a republican system on such a scale & in such a form as will controul all the evils w$^{ch}$ have been experienced.

M$^r$ DICKENSON considered it as [30] essential that one branch of the Legislature sh$^d$ be drawn immediately from the people; and as expedient that the other sh$^d$ be chosen by the Legislatures of the States. This combination of the State Gov$^{ts}$ with the national Gov$^t$ was as politic as it was unavoidable. In the formation of the Senate we ought to carry it through such a refining process as will assimilate it as near as may be to the House of Lords in England. He repeated his warm eulogiums on the British Constitution. He was for a strong National Gov$^t$ but for leaving the States a considerable agency in the System. The objection ag$^{st}$ making the former dependent on the latter might be obviated by giving to the

---

[29] The word "so" is here inserted in the transcript.
[30] The word "as" is omitted in the transcript.

Senate an authority permanent & irrevocable for three, five or seven years. Being thus independent they will speak [31] & decide with becoming freedom.

M! READ. Too much attachment is betrayed to the State Govern!! We must look beyond their continuance. A national Gov! must soon of necessity swallow all of them [32] up. They will soon be reduced to the mere office of electing the National Senate. He was ag!t patching up the old federal System: he hoped the idea w! be dismissed. It would be like putting new cloth on an old garment. The confederation was founded on temporary principles. It cannot last: it cannot be amended. If we do not establish a good Gov! on new principles, we must either go to ruin, or have the work to do over again. The people at large are wrongly suspected of being averse to a Gen! Gov! The aversion lies among interested men who possess their confidence.

M! PIERCE was for an election by the people as to the 1st branch & by the States as to the 2d branch; by which means the Citizens of the States w! be represented both *individually* & *collectively*.

General PINKNEY wished to have a good National Gov! & at the same time to leave a considerable share of power in the States. An election of either branch by the people scattered as they are in many States, particularly in S. Carolina was totally impracticable. He differed from gentlemen who thought that a choice by the people w! be a better guard ag!t bad measures, than by the Legislatures. A majority of the people in S. Carolina were notoriously for paper money as a legal tender; the Legislature had refused to make it a legal tender. The reason was that the latter had some sense of character and were restrained by that consideration. The State Legislatures also he said would be more jealous, & more ready to thwart the National Gov!, if excluded from a participation in it. The Idea of abolishing these Legislatures w! never go down.

M! WILSON, would not have spoken again, but for what had fallen from M! Read; namely, that the idea of preserving the State Gov!! ought to be abandoned. He saw no incompatibility between

---

[31] The word "check" is substituted in the transcript for "speak."
[32] The words "them all" are substituted in the transcript for "all of them."

the National & State Gov$^{ts}$ provided the latter were restrained to certain local purposes; nor any probability of their being devoured by the former. In all confederated Systems antient & modern the reverse had happened; the Generality being destroyed gradually by the usurpations of the parts composing it.

On the question for electing the 1$^{st}$ branch by the State Legislatures as moved by M$^r$ Pinkney: it was negatived:

Mass. no. C$^t$ ay. N. Y. no. N. J. ay. P$^a$ no. Del. no. M$^d$ no. V$^a$ no. N. C. no. S. C. ay. Geo. no.[33]

M$^r$ WILSON moved to reconsider the vote excluding the Judiciary from a share in the revision of the laws, and to add after " National Executive" the words " with a convenient number of the national Judiciary"; remarking the expediency of reinforcing the Executive with the influence of that Department.

M$^r$ MADISON 2$^{ded}$ the motion. He observed that the great difficulty in rendering the Executive competent to its own defence arose from the nature of Republican Gov$^t$ which could not give to an individual citizen that settled pre-eminence in the eyes of the rest, that weight of property, that personal interest ag$^{st}$ betraying the national interest, which appertain to an hereditary magistrate. In a Republic personal merit alone could be the ground of political exaltation, but it would rarely happen that this merit would be so pre-eminent as to produce universal acquiescence. The Executive Magistrate would be envied & assailed by disappointed competitors: His firmness therefore w$^d$ need support. He would not possess those great emoluments from his station, nor that permanent stake in the public interest which w$^d$ place him out of the reach of foreign corruption: He would stand in need therefore of being controuled as well as supported. An association of the Judges in his revisionary function w$^d$ both double the advantage and diminish the danger. It w$^d$ also enable the Judiciary Department the better to defend itself ag$^{st}$ Legislative encroachments. Two objections had been made 1$^{st}$ that the Judges ought not to be subject to the bias which a participation in the making of laws might give in the exposition of them. 2$^{dly}$ that the Judiciary

---

[33] In the transcript the vote reads "Connecticut, New Jersey, South Carolina, aye—3; Massachusetts, New York, Pennsylvania, Delaware, Maryland, Virginia, North Carolina, Georgia, no—8."

Departm! ought to be separate & distinct from the other great Departments. The 1st objection had some weight; but it was much diminished by reflecting that a small proportion of the laws coming in question before a Judge w? be such wherein he had been consulted; that a small part of this proportion w? be so ambiguous as to leave room for his prepossessions; and that but a few cases w? probably arise in the life of a Judge under such ambiguous passages. How much good on the other hand w? proceed from the perspicuity, the conciseness, and the systematic character w<sup>ch</sup> the Code of laws w? receive from the Judiciary talents. As to the 2<sup>d</sup> objection, it either had no weight, or it applied with equal weight to the Executive & to the Judiciary revision of the laws. The maxim on which the objection was founded required a separation of the Executive as well as of [34] the Judiciary from the Legislature & from each other. There w? in truth however be no improper mixture of these distinct powers in the present case. In England, whence the maxim itself had been drawn, the Executive had an absolute negative on the laws; and the supreme tribunal of Justice [the House of Lords] formed one of the other branches of the Legislature. In short whether the object of the revisionary power was to restrain the Legislature from encroaching on the other co-ordinate Departments, or on the rights of the people at large; or from passing laws unwise in their principle, or incorrect in their form, the utility of annexing the wisdom and weight of the Judiciary to the Executive seemed incontestable.

M! GERRY thought the Executive, whilst standing alone w? be more impartial than when he c? be covered by the sanction & seduced by the sophistry of the Judges.

M! KING. If the Unity of the Executive was preferred for the sake of responsibility, the policy of it is as applicable to the revisionary as to the Executive power.

M! PINKNEY had been at first in favor of joining the heads of the principal departm<sup>ts</sup> the Secretary of War, of foreign affairs &— in the council of revision. He had however relinquished the idea from a consideration that these could be called in [35] by the Execu-

---

[34] The word "of" is omitted in the transcript.
[35] The word "on" is substituted in the transcript for "in."

tive Magistrate whenever he pleased to consult them. He was opposed to an [36] introduction of the Judges into the business.

Col. MASON was for giving all possible weight to the revisionary institution. The Executive power ought to be well secured ag$^{st}$ Legislative usurpations on it. The purse & the sword ought never to get into the same hands whether Legislative or Executive.

M$^r$ DICKENSON. Secrecy, vigor & despatch are not the principal properties req$^d$ in the Executive. Important as these are, that of responsibility is more so, which can only be preserved; by leaving it singly to dicharge its functions. He thought too a junction of the Judiciary to it, involved an improper mixture of powers.

M$^r$ WILSON remarked, that the responsibility required belonged to his Executive duties. The revisionary duty was an extraneous one, calculated for collateral purposes.

M$^r$ WILLIAMSON, was for substituting a clause requiring ⅔ for every effective act of the Legislature, in place of the revisionary provision.

On the question for joining the Judges to the Executive in the revisionary business, Mass. no. Con$^t$ ay. N. Y. ay. N. J. no. P$^a$ no. Del. no. M$^d$ no. V$^a$ ay. N. C. no. S. C. No. Geo. no.[37]

M$^r$ PINKNEY gave notice that tomorrow he should move for the reconsideration of that clause in the sixth Resolution adopted by the Comm$^e$ which vests a negative in the National Legislature on the laws of the several States.

The Com$^e$ rose & the House adj$^d$ to 11 OC.[38]

---

THURSDAY JUNE 7$^{th}$ 1787 [39]—IN COMMITTEE OF THE WHOLE

M$^r$ PINKNEY according to notice moved to reconsider the clause respecting the negative on State laws, which was agreed to and tomorrow for fixed [40] the purpose.

---

[36] The word "the" is substituted in the transcript for "an."
[37] In the transcript the vote reads: "Connecticut, New York, Virginia, aye—3; Massachusetts, New Jersey, Pennsylvania, Delaware, Maryland, North Carolina, South Carolina, Georgia, no—8."
[38] The expression "to 11 OC" is omitted in the transcript.
[39] The year "1787" is omitted in the transcript.
[40] The words "for fixed" are corrected in the transcript to "fixed for."

The Clause providing for y̌e appointment of the 2ᵈ branch of the national Legislature, having lain blank since the last vote on the mode of electing it, to wit, by the 1ˢᵗ branch, Mʳ DICKENSON now moved "that the members of the 2ᵈ branch ought to be chosen by the individual Legislatures."

Mʳ SHARMAN seconded the motion; observing that the particular States would thus become interested in supporting the national Governmᵗ and that a due harmony between the two Governments would be maintained. He admitted that the two ought to have separate and distinct jurisdictions, but that they ought to have a mutual interest in supporting each other.

Mʳ PINKNEY. If the small States should be allowed one Senator only, the number will be too great, there will be 80 at least.

Mʳ DICKENSON had two reasons for his motion. 1.[41] because the sense of the States would be better collected through their Governments; than immediately from the people at large; 2.[41] because he wished the Senate to consist of the most distinguished characters, distinguished for their rank in life and their weight of property, and bearing as strong a likeness to the British House of Lords as possible; and he thought such characters more likely to be selected by the State Legislatures, than in any other mode. The greatness of the number was no objection with him. He hoped there would be 80 and twice 80. of them. If their number should be small, the popular branch could not be balanced by them. The legislature of a numerous people ought to be a numerous body.

Mʳ WILLIAMSON, preferred a small number of Senators, but wished that each State should have at least one. He suggested 25 as a convenient number. The different modes of representation in the different branches, will serve as a mutual check.

Mʳ BUTLER was anxious to know the ratio of representation before he gave any opinion.

Mʳ WILSON. If we are to establish a national Government, that Government ought to flow from the people at large. If one branch of it should be chosen by the Legislatures, and the other by the people, the two branches will rest on different foundations, and dissensions will naturally arise between them. He wished the Senate

---

[41] The figures "1" and "2" are changed to "First" and "secondly" in the transcript.

to be elected by the people as well as the other branch, and the people might be divided into proper districts for the purpose &[42] moved to postpone the motion of M! Dickenson, in order to take up one of that import.

M! MORRIS 2^{ded} him.

M! READ proposed "that the Senate should be appointed by the Executive Magistrate out of a proper number of persons to be nominated by the individual legislatures." He said he thought it his duty, to speak his mind frankly. Gentlemen he hoped would not be alarmed at the idea. Nothing short of this approach towards a proper model of Government would answer the purpose, and he thought it best to come directly to the point at once.— His proposition was not seconded nor supported.

M! MADISON, if the motion [of Mr. Dickenson] should be agreed to, we must either depart from the doctrine of proportional representation; or admit into the Senate a very large number of members. The first is inadmissible, being evidently unjust. The second is inexpedient. The use of the Senate is to consist in its proceeding with more coolness, with more system, & with more wisdom, than the popular branch. Enlarge their number and you communicate to them the vices which they are meant to correct. He differed from M! D. who thought that the additional number would give additional weight to the body. On the contrary it appeared to him that their weight would be in an inverse ratio to their number.[43] The example of the Roman Tribunes was applicable. They lost their influence and power, in proportion as their number was augmented. The reason seemed to be obvious: They were appointed to take care of the popular interests & pretensions at Rome, because the people by reason of their numbers could not act in concert;[44] were liable to fall into factions among themselves, and to become a prey to their aristocratic adversaries. The more the representatives of the people therefore were multiplied, the more they partook of the infirmities of their constituents, the more liable they became to be divided among themselves either from their own indiscretions or the

---

[42] The word "he" is here inserted in the transcript.
[43] The transcript uses the word "number" in the plural.
[44] The word "and" is here inserted in the transcript.

artifices of the opposite faction, and of course the less capable of fulfilling their trust. When the weight of a set of men depends merely on their personal characters; the greater the number the greater the weight. When it depends on the degree of political authority lodged in them the smaller the number the greater the weight. These considerations might perhaps be combined in the intended Senate; but the latter was the material one.

M$^r$ GERRY. 4 modes of appointing the Senate have been mentioned. 1.[45] by the 1$^{st}$ branch of the National Legislature. This would create a dependence contrary to the end proposed. 2.[45] by the National Executive. This is a stride towards monarchy that few will think of. 3.[45] by the people. The people have two great interests, the landed interest, and the commercial including the stockholders. To draw both branches from the people will leave no security to the latter interest; the people being chiefly composed of the landed interest, and erroneously supposing, that the other interests are adverse to it. 4[45] by the Individual Legislatures. The elections being carried thro' this refinement, will be most likely to provide some check in favor of the commercial interest ag$^{st}$ the landed; without which oppression will take place, and no free Gov$^t$ can last long where that is the case. He was therefore in favor of this last.

M$^r$ DICKENSON.* The preservation of the States in a certain degree of agency is indispensable. It will produce that collision between the different authorities which should be wished for in order to check each other. To attempt to abolish the States altogether, would degrade the Councils of our Country, would be impracticable, would be ruinous. He compared the proposed National System to the Solar System, in which the States were the planets, and ought to be left to move freely in their proper orbits. The Gentleman from P$^a$ [M$^r$ Wilson] wished he said to extinguish these planets. If the State Governments were excluded from all agency in the national one, and all power drawn from the people

---

\* It will throw light on this discussion to remark that an election by the State Legislatures involved a surrender of the principle insisted on by the large States & dreaded by the small ones, namely that of a proportional representation in the Senate. Such a rule w$^d$ make the body too numerous, as the smallest State must elect one member at least.

[45] The figures "1," "2," "3" and "4" are changed to "First," "Secondly," etc., in the transcript.

at large, the consequence would be that the national Govt would move in the same direction as the State Govts now do, and would run into all the same mischiefs. The reform would only unite the 13 small streams into one great current pursuing the same course without any opposition whatever. He adhered to the opinion that the Senate ought to be composed of a large number, and that their influence from family weight & other causes would be increased thereby. He did not admit that the Tribunes lost their weight in proportion as their no was augmented and gave a historical sketch of this institution. If the reasoning of [Mr Madison] was good it would prove that the number of the Senate ought to be reduced below ten, the highest no of the Tribunitial corps.

Mr WILSON. The subject it must be owned is surrounded with doubts and difficulties. But we must surmount them. The British Governmt cannot be our model. We have no materials for a similar one. Our manners, our laws, the abolition of entails and of primogeniture, the whole genius of the people, are opposed to it. He did not see the danger of the States being devoured by the Natiol Govt On the contrary, he wished to keep them from devouring the national Govt He was not however for extinguishing these planets as was supposed by Mr D.—neither did he on the other hand, believe that they would warm or enlighten the Sun. Within their proper orbits they must still be suffered to act for subordinate purposes for which their existence is made essential by the great extent of our Country. He could not comprehend in what manner the landed interest wd be rendered less predominant in the Senate, by an election through the medium of the Legislatures then by the people themselves. If the Legislatures, as was now complained, sacrificed the commercial to the landed interest, what reason was there to expect such a choice from them as would defeat their own views. He was for an election by the people in large districts which wd be most likely to obtain men of intelligence & uprightness; subdividing the districts only for the accomodation of voters.

Mr MADISON could as little comprehend in what manner family weight, as desired by Mr D. would be more certainly conveyed into the Senate through elections by the State Legislatures, than in some other modes. The true question was in what mode the best choice wᵈ be made? If an election by the people, or thro' any other channel than the State Legislatures promised as uncorrupt & impartial a preference of merit, there could surely be no necessity for an appointment by those Legislatures. Nor was it apparent that a more useful check would be derived thro' that channel than from the people thro' some other. The great evils complained of were that the State Legislatures run into schemes of paper money &c. whenever solicited by the people, & sometimes without even the sanction of the people. Their influence then, instead of checking a like propensity in the National Legislature, may be expected to promote it. Nothing can be more contradictory than to say that the Natˡ Legislature withᵗ a proper check, will follow the example of the State Legislatures, & in the same breath, that the State Legislatures are the only proper check.

Mʳ SHARMAN opposed elections by the people in districts, as not likely to produce such fit men as elections by the State Legislatures.

Mʳ GERRY insisted that the commercial & monied interest wᵈ be more secure in the hands of the State Legislatures, than of the people at large. The former have more sense of character, and will be restrained by that from injustice. The people are for paper money when the Legislatures are agˢᵗ it. In Massᵗˢ the County Conventions had declared a wish for a *depreciating* paper that wᵈ sink itself. Besides, in some States there are two Branches in the Legislature, one of which is somewhat aristocratic. There wᵈ therefore be so far a better chance of refinement in the choice. There seemed, he thought to be three powerful objections agˢᵗ elections by districts. 1.[46] it is impracticable; the people cannot be brought to one place for the purpose; and whether brought to the same place or not, numberless frauds wᵈ be unavoidable. 2.[46] small States forming part of the same district with a large one, or [47] large part of a large one, wᵈ have no chance of gaining an appointment for its citizens

---

[46] The figures "1," "2" and "3" are changed to "First," "Secondly," and "Thirdly" in the transcript.
[47] The word "a" is here inserted in the transcript.

of merit. 3 [46] a new source of discord w.d be opened between different parts of the same district.

M.r PINKNEY thought the 2.d branch ought to be permanent & independent, & that the members of it w.d be rendered more so by receiving their appointment [48] from the State Legislatures. This mode w.d avoid the rivalships & discontents incident to the election by districts. He was for dividing the States into three classes according to their respective sizes, & for allowing to the 1.st class three members—to the 2.d two, & to the 3.d one.

On the question for postponing M.r Dickinson's motion referring the appointment of the Senate to the State Legislatures, in order to consider M.r Wilson's for referring it to the people

Mass. no. Con.t no. N. Y. no. N. J. no. P.a ay Del. no. M.d no. V.a no. N. C. no. S. C. no. Geo. no.[49]

Col. MASON. whatever power may be necessary for the Nat.l Gov.t a certain portion must necessarily be left in [50] the States. It is impossible for one power to pervade the extreme parts of the U. S. so as to carry equal justice to them. The State Legislatures also ought to have some means of defending themselves ag.st encroachments of the Nat.l Gov.t In every other department we have studiously endeavored to provide for its self-defence. Shall we leave the States alone unprovided with the means for this purpose? And what better means can we provide than the giving them some share in, or rather to make them a constituent part of, the Nat.l Establishment. There is danger on both sides no doubt; but we have only seen the evils arising on the side of the State Gov.ts Those on the other side remain to be displayed. The example of Cong.s does not apply. Cong.s had no power to carry their acts into execution as the Nat.l Gov.t will have.

On M.r DICKINSON's motion for an appointment of the Senate by the State-Legislatures.

Mass. ay. C.t ay. N. Y. ay. P.a ay Del. ay. M.d ay. V.a ay N. C. ay. S. C. ay. Geo. ay.[51]

---

[46] The figures "1," "2" and "3" are changed to "First," "Secondly," and "Thirdly" in the transcript.
[48] The word "appointment" is used in the plural in the transcript.
[49] In the transcript the vote reads: "Pennsylvania, aye—1; Massachusetts, Connecticut, New York, New Jersey, Delaware, Maryland, Virginia, North Carolina, South Carolina, Georgia, no—10."
[50] The word "with" is substituted in the transcript for "in."
[51] In the transcript the vote reads: "Massachusetts, Connecticut, New York, Pennsylvania, Delaware, Maryland, Virginia, North Carolina, South Carolina, Georgia, aye—10."

Mʳ GERRY gave notice that he wᵈ tomorrow move for a reconsideration of the mode of appointing the Natˡ Executive in order to substitute an appointmᵗ by the State Executives

The Committee rose & The House adjᵈ

---

FRIDAY JUNE 8ᵀᴴ  IN COMMITTEE OF THE WHOLE

On a reconsideration of the clause giving the Natˡ Legislature a negative on such laws of the States as might be contrary to the articles of Union, or Treaties with foreign nations,

Mʳ PINKNEY moved "that the National Legislature shᵈ have authority to negative all laws which they shᵈ judge to be improper." He urged that such a universality of the power was indispensably necessary to render it effectual; that the States must be kept in due subordination to the nation; that if the States were left to act of themselves in any case, it wᵈ be impossible to defend the national prerogatives, however extensive they might be on paper; that the acts of Congress had been defeated by this means; nor had foreign treaties escaped repeated violations; that this universal negative was in fact the corner stone of an efficient national Govᵗ; that under the British Govᵗ the negative of the Crown had been found beneficial, and the *States* are more one nation now, than the *Colonies* were then.

Mʳ MADISON seconded the motion. He could not but regard an indefinite power to negative legislative acts of the States as absolutely necessary to a perfect system. Experience had evinced a constant tendency in the States to encroach on the federal authority; to violate national Treaties; to infringe the rights & interests of each other; to oppress the weaker party within their respective jurisdictions. A negative was the mildest expedient that could be devised for preventing these mischiefs. The existence of such a check would prevent attempts to commit them. Should no such precaution be engrafted, the only remedy wᵈ lie [52] in an appeal to coercion. Was such a remedy eligible? was it practicable? Could the national resources, if exerted to the utmost enforce a national decree agˢᵗ

---

[52] The word "be" is substituted in the transcript for "lie."

Mass^ts abetted perhaps by several of her neighbours? It w^d not be possible. A small proportion of the Community, in a compact situation, acting on the defensive, and at one of its extremities might at any time bid defiance to the National authority. Any Gov^t for the U. States formed on the supposed practicability of using force ag^st the unconstitutional proceedings of the States, w^d prove as visionary & fallacious as the Gov^t of Cong^s The negative w^d render the use of force unnecessary. The States c^d of themselves then [53] pass no operative act, any more than one branch of a Legislature where there are two branches, can proceed without the other. But in order to give the negative this efficacy, it must extend to all cases. A discrimination w^d only be a fresh source of contention between the two authorities. In a word, to recur to the illustrations borrowed from the planetary system. This prerogative of the General Gov^t is the great pervading principle that must controul the centrifugal tendency of the States; which, without it, will continually fly out of their proper orbits and destroy the order & harmony of the political System.

M^r WILLIAMSON was ag^st giving a power that might restrain the States from regulating their internal police.

M^r GERRY c^d not see the extent of such a power, and was ag^st every power that was not necessary. He thought a remonstrance ag^st unreasonable acts of the States w^d reclaim [54] them If it sh^d not force might be resorted to. He had no objection to authorize a negative to paper money and similar measures. When the confederation was depending before Congress, Massachussetts was then for inserting the power of emitting paper money am^g the exclusive powers of Congress. He observed that the proposed negative w^d extend to the regulations of the Militia, a matter on which the existence of a [55] State might depend. The Nat^l Legislature with such a power may enslave the States. Such an idea as this will never be acceded to. It has never been suggested or conceived among the people. No speculative projector, and there are eno' of that character among us, in politics

---

[53] The word "then" is omitted in the transcript.
[54] The word "restrain" is substituted in the transcript for "reclaim."
[55] The word "the" is substituted in the trmscript for "a."

as well as in other things, has in any pamphlet or newspaper thrown out the idea. The States too have different interests and are ignorant of each other's interests. The negative therefore will be abused. New States too having separate views from the old States will never come into the Union. They may even be under some foreign influence; are they in such case to participate in the negative on the will of the other States?

Mʳ SHERMAN thought the cases in which the negative ought to be exercised, might be defined. He wished the point might not be decided till a trial at least shᵈ be made for that purpose.

Mʳ WILSON would not say what modifications of the proposed power might be practicable or expedient. But however novel it might appear the principle of it when viewed with a close & steady eye, is right. There is no instance in which the laws say that the individual shᵈ be bound in one case, & at liberty to judge whether he will obey or disobey in another. The cases are parallel. Abuses of the power over the individual person may happen as well as over the individual States. Federal liberty is to [56] States, what civil liberty, is to private individuals. And States are not more unwilling to purchase it, by the necessary concession of their political sovereignty, that [57] the savage is to purchase civil liberty by the surrender of his [58] personal sovereignty, which he enjoys in a State of nature. A definition of the cases in which the Negative should be exercised, is impracticable. A discretion must be left on one side or the other? will it not be most safely lodged on the side of the Natˡ Govᵗ? Among the first sentiments expressed in the first Congˢ one was that Virgᵃ is no more, that Masᵗˢ is no [59], that Pᵃ is no more &c. We are now one nation of brethren. We must bury all local interests & distinctions. This language continued for some time. The tables at length began to turn. No sooner were the State Govᵗˢ formed than their jealousy & ambition began to display themselves. Each endeavoured to cut a slice from the common loaf, to add to its own morsel, till at length the confederation became frittered down to the impotent condi-

---

[56] The word "the" is here inserted in the transcript.
[57] The word "that" is changed to "than" in the transcript.
[58] The word "the" is substituted in the transcript for "his."
[59] The word "more" is here inserted in the transcript.

tion in which it now stands. Review the progress of the articles of Confederation thro' Congress & compare the first & last draught of it. To correct its vices is the business of this convention. One of its vices is the want of an effectual controul in the whole over its parts. What danger is there that the whole will unnecessarily sacrifice a part? But reverse the case, and leave the whole at the mercy of each part, and will not the general interest be continually sacrificed to local interests?

M! DICKENSON deemed it impossible to draw a line between the cases proper & improper for the exercise of the negative. We must take our choice of two things. We must either subject the States to the danger of being injured by the power of the Nat! Gov! or the latter to the danger of being injured by that of the States. He thought the danger greater from the States. To leave the power doubtful, would be opening another spring of discord, and he was for shutting as many of them as possible.

M! BEDFORD. In answer to his colleague's question where w! be the danger to the States from this power, would refer him to the smallness of his own State which may be injured at pleasure without redress. It was meant he found to strip the small States of their equal right of suffrage. In this case Delaware would have about $\frac{1}{90}$ for its share in the General Councils, whilst P! & V! would possess $\frac{1}{3}$ of the whole. Is there no difference of interests, no rivalship of commerce, of manufactures? Will not these large States crush the small ones whenever they stand in the way of their ambitious or interested views. This shews the impossibility of adopting such a system as that on the table, or any other founded on a change in the principle of representation. And after all, if a State does not obey the law of the new System, must not force be resorted to as the only ultimate remedy, in this as in any other system. It seems as if P! & V! by the conduct of their deputies wished to provide a system in which they would have an enormous & monstrous influence. Besides, How can it be thought that the proposed negative can be exercised? are the laws of the States to be suspended in the most urgent cases until they can be sent seven or eight hundred miles, and undergo the deliberations [60] of a body who may be incapable of Judging of them? Is the National Legislature too to sit continually in order to revise the laws of the States?

Mr. MADISON observed that the difficulties which had been started were worthy of attention and ought to be answered before the question was put. The case of laws of urgent necessity must be provided for by some emanation of the power from the Natl. Govt. into each State so far as to give a temporary assent at least. This was the practice in Royal Colonies before the Revolution and would not have been inconvenient, if the supreme power of negativing had been faithful to the American interest, and had possessed the necessary information. He supposed that the negative might be very properly lodged in the senate alone, and that the more numerous & expensive branch therefore might not be obliged to sit constantly.—He asked Mr. B. what would be the consequence to the small States of a dissolution of the Union wch. seemed likely to happen if no effectual substitute was made for the defective System existing, and he did not conceive any effectual system could be substituted on any other basis than that of a proportional suffrage? If the large States possessed the avarice & ambition with which they were charged, would the small ones in their neighbourhood, be more secure when all controul of a Genl. Govt. was withdrawn.

Mr. BUTLER was vehement agst. the Negative in the proposed extent, as cutting off all hope of equal justice to the distant States. The people there would not he was sure give it a hearing.

On the question for extending the negative power to all cases as propos d. by [Mr. P. & Mr. M—] Mass. ay. Cont. no. N. Y. no. N. J. no. Pa. ay. Del. divd. Mr. Read & Mr. Dickenson ay. Mr. Bedford & Mr. Basset no. Maryd. no. Va. ay. Mr. R. Mr. Mason no. Mr. Blair, Docr. Mc. & Mr. M. ay. Genl. W. not consulted. N. C. no. S. C. no. Geo. no.[61]

On motion of Mr. GERRY and Mr. KING tomorrow was assigned for reconsidering the mode of appointing the National Executive: the

---

[60] The transcript uses the word "deliberations" in the singular.

[61] In the transcript the vote reads: "Massachusetts, Pennsylvania, Virginia, [Mr. Randolph and Mr. Mason, no; Mr. Blair, Doctor McClurg and Mr. Madison, aye; General Washington not consulted,] aye—3; Connecticut, New York, New Jersey, Maryland, North Carolina, South Carolina, Georgia, no—7; Delaware, divided, [Mr. Read and Mr. Dickinson, aye; Mr. Bedford and Mr. Basset, no]."

reconsideration being voted for by all the States except Connecticut & N. Carolina.

M! PINKNEY and M! RUTLIDGE moved to add to Resol? 4.⁶² agreed to by the Com? the following, viz. "that the States be divided into three classes, the 1ˢᵗ class to have 3 members, the 2ᵈ two. & the 3ᵈ one member each; that an estimate be taken of the comparative importance of each State at fixed periods, so as to ascertain the number of members they may from time to time be entitled to" The Committee then rose and the House adjourned.

---

SATURDAY JUNE 9ᵀᴴ M^R LUTHER MARTIN FROM MARYLAND TOOK HIS SEAT IN COMMITTEE OF THE WHOLE

M! GERRY, according to previous notice given by him, moved "that the National Executive should be elected by the Executives of the States whose proportion of votes should be the same with that allowed to the States in the election of the Senate." If the appointm! should be made by the Nat! Legislature, it would lessen that independence of the Executive which ought to prevail, would give birth to intrigue and corruption between the Executive & Legislature previous to the election, and to partiality in the Executive afterwards to the friends who promoted him. Some other mode therefore appeared to him necessary. He proposed that of appointing by the State Executives as most analogous to the principle observed in electing the other branches of the Nat! Gov!; the first branch being chosen by the *people* of the States, & the 2ᵈ by the Legislatures of the States; he did not see any objection ag?ᵗ letting the Executive be appointed by the Executives of the States. He supposed the Executives would be most likely to select the fittest men, and that it would be their interest to support the man of their own choice.

M! RANDOLPH, urged strongly the inexpediency of M! Gerry's mode of appointing the Nat! Executive. The confidence of the people would not be secured by it to the Nat! magistrate. The small States would lose all chance of an appointm! from within themselves. Bad appointments would be made; the Executives

---

⁶² The words "the fourth Resolution" are substituted in the transcript for "Resol? 4."

of the States being little conversant with characters not within their own small spheres. The State Executives too notwithstanding their constitutional independence, being in fact dependent on the State Legislatures will generally be guided by the views of the latter, and prefer either favorites within the States, or such as it may be expected will be most partial to the interests of the State. A Nat! Executive thus chosen will not be likely to defend with becoming vigilance & firmness the National rights ag$^{st}$ State encroachments. Vacancies also must happen. How can these be filled? He could not suppose either that the Executives would feel the interest in supporting the Nat! Executive which had been imagined. They will not cherish the great Oak which is to reduce them to paltry shrubs.

On the question for referring the appointment of the Nat! Exexecutive to the State Executives as prop$^d$ by M$^r$ Gerry Mass$^{ts}$ no. Con$^t$ no. N. Y. no. N. J. no. P$^a$ no. Del. div$^d$ M$^d$ no. V$^a$ no. S. C. no. Geo. no.[63]

M$^r$ PATTERSON moves that the Committee resume the clause relating to the rule of suffrage in the Nat! Legislature.

M$^r$ BREARLY seconds him. He was sorry he said that any question on this point was brought into view. It had been much agitated in Cong$^s$ at the time of forming the Confederation, and was then rightly settled by allowing to each sovereign State an equal vote. Otherwise the smaller States must have been destroyed instead of being saved. The substitution of a ratio, he admitted carried fairness on the face of it; but on a deeper examination was unfair and unjust. Judging of the disparity of the States by the quota of Cong$^s$ Virg$^a$ would have 16 votes, and Georgia but one. A like proportion to the others will make the whole number ninity. There will be 3. large states, and 10 small ones. The large States by which he meant Mass$^{ts}$ Pen$^a$ & Virg$^a$ will carry every thing before them. It had been admitted, and was known to him from facts within N. Jersey that where large & small counties were united into a district for electing representatives for the district, the large counties always carried their

---

[63] In the transcript the vote reads: "Massachusetts, Connecticut, New York, New Jersey, Pennsylvania, Maryland, Virginia, South Carolina, Georgia, no; Delaware divided."

A Adams

point, and Consequently that [64] the large States would do so. Virga with her sixteen votes will be a solid column indeed, a formidable phalanx. While Georgie with her Solitary vote, and the other little States will be obliged to throw themselves constantly into the scale of some large one, in order to have any weight at all. He had come to the convention with a view of being as useful as he could in giving energy and stability to the federal Government. When the proposition for destroying the equality of votes came forward, he was astonished, he was alarmed. Is it fair then it will be asked that Georgia should have an equal vote with Virga? He would not say it was. What remedy then? One only, that a map of the U. S. be spread out, that all the existing boundaries be erased, and that a new partition of the whole be made into 13 equal parts.

Mr PATTERSON considered the proposition for a proportional representation as striking at the existence of the lesser States. He wd premise however to an investigation of this question some remarks on the nature structure and powers of the Convention. The Convention he said was formed in pursuance of an Act of Congs that this act was recited in several of the Commissions, particularly that of Massts which he required to be read: that the amendment of the confederacy was the object of all the laws and commissions on the subject; that the articles of the Confederation were therefore the proper basis of all the proceedings of the Convention.[65] We ought to keep within its limits, or we should be charged by our Constituents with usurpation, that the people of America were sharp-sighted and not to be deceived. But the Commissions under which we acted were not only the measure of our power, they denoted also the sentiments of the States on the subject of our deliberation. The idea of a national Govt as contradistinguished from a federal one, never entered into the mind of any of them, and to the public mind we must accomodate ourselves. We have no power to go beyond the federal scheme, and if we had the people are not ripe for any other. We must follow the people;

---

[64] The word "that" is omitted in the transcript.
[65] The word "that" is here inserted in the transcript.

the people will not follow us.—The *proposition* could not be maintained whether considered in reference to us as a nation, or as a confederacy. A confederacy supposes sovereignty in the members composing it & sovereignty supposes equality. If we are to be considered as a nation, all State distinctions must be abolished, the whole must be thrown into hotchpot, and when an equal division is made, then there may be fairly an equality of representation. He held up Virg$^a$ Mass$^{ts}$ & P$^a$ as the three large States, and the other ten as small ones; repeating the calculations of M$^r$ Brearly as to the disparity of votes which w$^d$ take place, and affirming that the small States would never agree to it. He said there was no more reason that a great individual State contributing much, should have more votes than a small one contributing little, than that a rich individual citizen should have more votes than an indigent one. If the rateable property of A was to that of B as 40 to 1, ought A for that reason to have 40 times as many votes as B. Such a principle would never be admitted, and if it were admitted would put B entirely at the mercy of A. As A. has more to be protected than B so he ought to contribute more for the common protection. The same may be said of a large State w$^{ch}$ has more to be protected than a small one. Give the large States an influence in proportion to their magnitude, and what will be the consequence? Their ambition will be proportionally increased, and the small States will have every thing to fear. It was once proposed by Galloway & some others that America should be represented in the British Parl$^t$ and then be bound by its laws. America could not have been entitled to more than $\frac{1}{3}$ of the n$^o$ of [66] Representatives which would fall to the share of G. B. Would American rights & interests have been safe under an authority thus constituted? It has been said that if a Nat$^l$ Gov$^t$ is to be formed so as to operate on the people and not on the States, the representatives ought to be drawn from the people. But why so? May not a Legislature filled by the State Legislatures operate on the people who chuse the State Legislatures? or may not a practicable coercion be found. He admitted that there was none such in the existing System.—He was attached strongly to the

---

[66] The words "n$^o$ of" are omitted in the transcript.

plan of the existing confederacy, in which the people chuse their Legislative representatives; and the Legislatures their federal representatives. No other amendments were wanting than to mark the orbits of the States with due precision, and provide for the use of coercion, which was the great point. He alluded to the hint thrown out heretofore by Mr Wilson of the necessity to which the large States might be reduced of confederating among themselves, by a refusal of the others to concur. Let them unite if they please, but let them remember that they have no authority to compel the others to unite. N. Jersey will never confederate on the plan before the Committee. She would be swallowed up. He had rather submit to a monarch, to a despot, than to such a fate. He would not only oppose the plan here but on his return home do every thing in his power to defeat it there.

Mr WILSON hoped if the Confederacy should be dissolved, that a *majority*, that a *minority* of the States would unite for their safety. He entered elaborately into the defence of a proportional representation, stating for his first position that as all authority was derived from the people, equal numbers of people ought to have an equal n° of representatives, and different numbers of people different numbers of representatives. This principle had been improperly violated in the Confederation, owing to the urgent circumstances of the time. As to the case of A. & B, stated by Mr Patterson, he observed that in districts as large as the States, the number of people was the best measure of their comparative wealth. Whether therefore wealth or numbers were [67] to form the ratio it would be the same. Mr P. admitted persons, not property to be the measure of suffrage. Are not the Citizens of Pena equal to those of N. Jersey? does it require 150 of the former to balance 50 of the latter? Representatives of different districts ought clearly to hold the same proportion to each other, as their respective Constituents hold to each other. If the small States will not confederate on this plan, Pena & he presumed some other States, would not confederate on any other. We have been told that each State being sovereign, all are equal. So each man is naturally a sovereign over himself, and all men are therefore nat-

---

[67] The word "was" is substituted in the transcript for "were."

urally equal. Can he retain this equality when he becomes a member of Civil Government? He can not. As little can a Sovereign State, when it becomes a member of a federal Gov:nt If N. J. will not part with her Sovereignty it is in vain to talk of Gov:t A new partition of the States is desireable, but evidently & totally impracticable.

M: WILLIAMSON, illustrated the cases by a comparison of the different States, to Counties of different sizes within the same State; observing that proportional representation was admitted to be just in the latter case, and could not therefore be fairly contested in the former.

The Question being about to be put M: PATTERSON hoped that as so much depended on it, it might be thought best to postpone the decision till tomorrow, which was done nem. con.

The Com:e rose & the House adjourned.

MONDAY. JUNE 11TH M:R ABRAHAM BALDWIN FROM GEORGIA TOOK HIS SEAT. IN COMMITTEE OF THE WHOLE

The clause concerning the rule of suffrage in the nat:l Legislature postponed on Saturday was resumed.

M: SHARMAN proposed that the proportion of suffrage in the 1:st branch should be according to the respective numbers of free inhabitants; and that in the second branch or Senate, each State should have one vote and no more. He said as the States would remain possessed of certain individual rights, each State ought to be able to protect itself: otherwise a few large States will rule the rest. The House of Lords in England he observed had certain particular rights under the Constitution, and hence they have an equal vote with the House of Commons that they may be able to defend their rights.

M: RUTLIDGE proposed that the proportion of suffrage in the 1:st branch should be according to the quotas of contribution. The justice of this rule he said could not be contested. M: BUTLER urged the same idea: adding that money was power; and that the States ought to have weight in the Gov:t in proportion to their wealth.

M͟ʳ KING & M͟ʳ WILSON,* in order to bring the question to a point moved "that the right of suffrage in the first branch of the national Legislature ought not to be according [68] the rule established in the articles of Confederation, but according to some equitable ratio of representation." The clause so far as it related to suffrage in the first branch was postponed in order to consider this motion.

M͟ʳ DICKENSON contended for the *actual* contributions of the States as the rule of their representation & suffrage in the first branch. By thus connecting the interest [69] of the States with their duty, the latter would be sure to be performed.

M͟ʳ KING remarked that it was uncertain what mode might be used in levying a national revenue; but that it was probable, imposts would be one source of it. If the *actual* contributions were to be the rule the non-importing States, as Con͟t & N. Jersey, w͟d be in a bad situation indeed. It might so happen that they w͟d have no representation. This situation of particular States had been always one powerful argument in favor of the 5 Per C͟t impost.

The question being ab͟t to be put Doc͟r FRANKLIN s͟d he had thrown his ideas of the matter on a paper w͟ch M͟ʳ Wilson read to the Committee in the words following—

M͟ʳ CHAIRMAN

It has given me great pleasure to observe that till this point, the proportion of representation, came before us, our debates were carried on with great coolness & temper. If any thing of a contrary kind, has on this occasion appeared, I hope it will not be repeated; for we are sent here to *consult*, not to *contend*, with each other; and declarations of a fixed opinion, and of determined resolution, never to change it, neither enlighten nor convince us. Positiveness and warmth on one side, naturally beget their like on the other; and tend to create and augment discord & division in a great concern, wherein harmony & Union are extremely necessary to give weight to our Councils, and render them effectual in promoting & securing the common good.

---

* In the printed Journal Mr. Rutlidge is named as the seconder of the motion.
[68] The word "to" is here inserted in the transcript.
[69] The transcript uses the word "interest" in the plural.

I must own that I was originally of opinion it would be better if every member of Congress, or our national Council, were to consider himself rather as a representative of the whole, than as an Agent for the interests of a particular State; in which case the proportion of members for each State would be of less consequence, & it would not be very material whether they voted by States or individually. But as I find this is not to be expected, I now think the number of Representatives should bear some proportion to the number of the Represented; and that the decisions sh$^d$ be by the majority of members, not by the majority of [70] States. This is objected to from an apprehension that the greater States would then swallow up the smaller. I do not at present clearly see what advantage the greater States could propose to themselves by swallowing [71] the smaller, and therefore do not apprehend they would attempt it. I recollect that in the beginning of this Century, when the Union was proposed of the two Kingdoms, England & Scotland, the Scotch Patriots were full of fears, that unless they had an equal number of Representatives in Parliament, they should be ruined by the superiority of the English. They finally agreed however that the different proportions of importance in the Union, of the two Nations should be attended to, whereby they were to have only forty members in the House of Commons, and only sixteen in the House of Lords; A very great inferiority of numbers! And yet to this day I do not recollect that any thing has been done in the Parliament of Great Britain to the prejudice of Scotland; and whoever looks over the lists of public officers, Civil & military of that nation will find I believe that the North Britons enjoy at least their full proportion of emolument.

But, Sir, in the present mode of voting by States, it is equally in the power of the lesser States to swallow up the greater; and this is mathematically demonstrable. Suppose for example, that 7 smaller States had each 3 members in the House, and the 6 larger to have one with another 6 members; and that upon a question, two members of each smaller State should be in the affirmative and one in the Negative; they will [72] make

---

[70] The word "the" is here inserted in the transcript.
[71] The word "up" is here inserted in the transcript.
[72] The word "will" is changed to "would" in the transcript.

| | | | |
|---|---|---|---|
| Affirmatives............ | 14 ...... | Negatives | 7 |
| And that all the larger States should be unanimously in the Negative, they would make........... | | Negatives | 36 |
| In all............................... | | | 43 |

It is then apparent that the 14 carry the question against the 43, and the minority overpowers the majority, contrary to the common practice of Assemblies in all Countries and Ages.

The greater States Sir are naturally as unwilling to have their property left in the disposition of the smaller, as the smaller are to have theirs in the disposition of the greater. An honorable gentleman has, to avoid this difficulty, hinted a proposition of equalizing the States. It appears to me an equitable one, and I should, for my own part, not be against such a measure, if it might be found practicable. Formerly, indeed, when almost every province had a different Constitution, some with greater others with fewer privileges, it was of importance to the borderers when their boundaries were contested, whether by running the division lines, they were placed on one side or the other. At present when such differences are done away, it is less material. The Interest of a State is made up of the interests of its individual members. If they are not injured, the State is not injured. Small States are more easily well & happily governed than large ones. If therefore in such an equal division, it should be found necessary to diminish Pennsylvania, I should not be averse to the giving a part of it to N. Jersey, and another to Delaware. But as there would probably be considerable difficulties in adjusting such a division; and however equally made at first, it would be continually varying by the augmentation of inhabitants in some States, and their [73] fixed proportion in others; and thence frequent occasion for new divisions, I beg leave to propose for the consideration of the Committee another mode, which appears to me, to be as equitable, more easily carried into practice, and more permanent in its nature.

---

[73] The word "more" is in the Franklin manuscript.

Let the weakest State say what proportion of money or force it is able and willing to furnish for the general purposes of the Union.

Let all the others oblige themselves to furnish each an equal proportion.

The whole of these joint supplies to be absolutely in the disposition of Congress.

The Congress in this case to be composed of an equal number of Delegates from each State.

And their decisions to be by the Majority of individual members voting.

If these joint and equal supplies should on particular occasions not be sufficient, Let Congress make requisitions on the richer and more powerful States for farther aids, to be voluntarily afforded, leaving to each State the right of considering the necessity and utility of the aid desired, and of giving more or less as it should be found proper.

This mode is not new, it was formerly practised with success by the British Government with respect to Ireland and the Colonies. We sometimes gave even more than they expected, or thought just to accept; and in the last war carried on while we were united, they gave us back in 5 years a million Sterling. We should probably have continued such voluntary contributions, whenever the occasions appeared to require them for the common good of the Empire. It was not till they chose to force us, and to deprive us of the merit and pleasure of voluntary contributions that we refused & resisted. Those [74] contributions however were to be disposed of at the pleasure of a Government in which we had no representative. I am therefore persuaded, that they will not be refused to one in which the Representation shall be equal

My learned Colleague [M$^r$ Wilson] has already mentioned that the present method of voting by States, was submitted to originally by Congress, under a conviction of its impropriety, inequality, and injustice. This appears in the words of their Resolution. It is of Sep$^r$ 6. 1774. The words are

---

[47] The word "These" is substituted in the transcript for "Those."

"Resolved that in determining questions in this Cong? each Colony or province shall have one vote: The Cong? not being possessed of or at present able to procure materials for ascertaining the importance of each Colony."

On the question for agreeing to M? Kings and M? Wilsons motion it passed in the affirmative

Massts ay. Ct ay. N. Y. no. N. J. no. Pa ay. Del. no. Md divd. Va ay. N. C. ay. S. C. ay. Geo. ay.[75]

It was then moved by M? RUTLIDGE 2ded by M? BUTLER to add to the words "equitable ratio of representation" at the end of the motion just agreed to, the words "according to the quotas of contribution." On motion of M? WILSON seconded by M? C. PINCKNEY, this was postponed; in order to add, after, after the words "equitable ratio of representation" the words following "in proportion to the whole number of white & other free Citizens & inhabitants of every age sex & condition including those bound to servitude for a term of years and three fifths of all other persons not comprehended in the foregoing description, except Indians not paying taxes, in each State," this being the rule in the Act of Congress agreed to by eleven States, for apportioning quotas of revenue on the States, and requiring a Census only every 5–7, or 10 years.

M? GERRY thought property not the rule of representation. Why then shd the blacks, who were property in the South, be in the rule of representation more than the Cattle & horses of the North.

On the question,—Mass: Con: N. Y. Pen: Maryd Virga N. C. S. C. & Geo: were in the affirmative:[76] N. J. & Del.: in the negative.[76]

M? SHARMAN moved that a question be taken whether each State shall have one vote in the 2d branch. Every thing he said depended on this. The smaller States would never agree to the plan on any other principle than an equality of suffrage in this branch. M? ELSWORTH seconded the motion. On the question for allowing each State one vote in the 2d branch.

---

[75] In the transcript the vote reads: "Massachusetts, Connecticut, Pennsylvania, Virginia, North Carolina, South Carolina, Georgia, aye—7; New York, New Jersey, Delaware, no—3; Maryland divided."

[76] In place of the phrase "were in the affirmative" the transcript substitutes "aye—9;" and instead of "in the negative" the expression "no—2" is used.

Mass^ts no. Con^t ay. N. Y. ay. N. J. ay. P^a no. Del. ay. M^d ay. V^a no. N. C. no. S. C. no. Geo. no.[77]

M^r WILSON & M^r HAMILTON moved that the right of suffrage in the 2^d branch ought to be according to the same rule as in the 1^st branch. On this question for making the ratio of representation the same in the 2^d as in the 1^st branch it passed in the affirmative:

Mass^ts ay. Con^t no. N. Y. no. N. J. no. P^a ay. Del. no. M^d no. V^a ay. N. C. ay. S. C. ay. Geo. ay.[78]

Resol: 11,[79] for guarantying Republican Gov^t & territory to each State being considered: the words "or partition" were, on motion of M^r MADISON, added, after the words "voluntary junction:"

Mas. N. Y. P. V^a N. C. S. C. G. ay [80] Con: N. J. Del. M^d no.[80]

M^r READ disliked the idea of guarantying territory. It abetted the idea of distinct States w^ch would be a perpetual source of discord. There can be no cure for this evil but in doing away States altogether and uniting them all into one great Society.

Alterations having been made in the Resolution, making it read "that a republican Constitution & its existing laws ought to be guaranteed to each State by the U. States" the whole was agreed to nem. con.

Resolution 13,[81] for amending the national Constitution hereafter without consent of [82] Nat^l Legislature being considered, several members did not see the necessity of the Resolution at all, nor the propriety of making the consent of the Nat^l Legisl. unnecessary.

Col. MASON urged the necessity of such a provision. The plan now to be formed will certainly be defective, as the Confederation has been found on trial to be. Amendments therefore will be necessary, and it will be better to provide for them, in an easy, regular and Constitutional way than to trust to chance and violence. It would be improper to require the consent of the Nat^l Legislature, because they may abuse their power, and refuse their

---

[77] In the transcript the vote reads: "Connecticut, New York, New Jersey, Delaware, Maryland, aye—5; Massachusetts, Pennsylvania, Virginia, North Carolina, South Carolina, Georgia, no—6."

[78] In the transcript the vote reads: "Massachusetts, Pennsylvania, Virginia, North Carolina, South Carolina, Georgia, aye; Connecticut, New York, New Jersey, Delaware, Maryland, no."

[79] The words "The eleventh Resolution" are substituted in the transcript for "Resol: 11."

[80] The figures "7" and "4" are inserted in the transcript after "ay" and "no," respectively.

[81] The words "The thirteenth Resolution" are substituted in the transcript for "Resolution 13."

[82] The word "the" is here inserted in the transcript.

consent [83] on that very account. The opportunity for such an abuse, may be the fault of the Constitution calling for amendm:

M: RANDOLPH enforced these arguments.

The words, "without requiring the consent of the Nat! Legislature" were postponed. The other provision in the clause passed nem. con.

Resolution 14,[84] requiring oaths from the members of the State Gov:ts to observe the Nat! Constitution & laws, being considered.

M: SHARMAN opposed it as unnecessarily intruding into the State jurisdictions.

M: RANDOLPH considered it as [85] necessary to prevent that competition between the National Constitution & laws & those of the particular States, which had already been felt. The officers of the States are already under oath to the States. To preserve a due impartiality they ought to be equally bound to the Nat! Gov: The Nat! authority needs every support we can give it. The Executive & Judiciary of the States, notwithstanding their nominal independence on the State Legislatures are in fact, so dependent on them, that unless they be brought under some tie to the Nat! System, they will always lean too much to the State systems, whenever a contest arises between the two.

M: GERRY did not like the clause. He thought there was as much reason for requiring an oath of fidelity to the States, from Nat! officers, as vice. versa.

M: LUTHER MARTIN moved to strike out the words requiring such an oath from the State officers, viz "within the several States" observing that if the new oath should be contrary to that already taken by them it would be improper; if coincident the oaths already taken will be sufficient.

On the question for striking out as proposed by M: L. Martin

Mass:ts no. Con: ay. N. Y. no. N. J. ay. P:a no. Del. ay. M:d ay. V:a no. N. C. no. S. C. no. Geo. no.[86]

Question on [87] whole Resolution as proposed by M: Randolph;

---

[83] The word "assent" is substituted in the transcript for "consent."
[84] The words "The fourteenth Resolution" are substituted in the transcript for "Resolution 14."
[85] The word "as" is crossed out in the transcript.
[86] In the transcript the vote reads: "Connecticut, New Jersey, Delaware, Maryland, aye—4; Massachusetts, New York, Pennsylvania, Virginia, North Carolina, South Carolina, Georgia, no—7."
[87] The word "the" is here inserted in the transcript.

Mass.<sup>ts</sup> ay.   Con.<sup>t</sup> no.   N. Y. no.   N. J. no.   P.<sup>a</sup> ay.   Del. no. M.<sup>d</sup> no.   V.<sup>a</sup> ay.   N. C. ay.   S. C. ay.   Geo. ay.[88]

[89] Com.<sup>e</sup> rose & [89] House adj.<sup>d</sup>

---

### Teusday June 12<sup>th</sup> in Committee of [89] Whole

The Question [90] taken on Resolution 15,[91] to wit, referring the new system to the people of the [92] States for ratification it passed in the affirmative: Mass.<sup>ts</sup> ay.   Con.<sup>t</sup> no.   N. Y. no.   N. J. no.   P.<sup>a</sup>* ay.   Del. div.<sup>d</sup>   M.<sup>d</sup> div.<sup>d</sup>   V.<sup>a</sup> ay.   N. C. ay.   S. C. ay.   Geo. ay.[93]

M.<sup>r</sup> Sharman & M.<sup>r</sup> Elseworth moved to fill the blank left in the 4<sup>th</sup> Resolution for the periods of electing the members of the first branch with the words, "every year." M.<sup>r</sup> Sharman observing that he did it in order to bring on some question.

M.<sup>r</sup> Rutlidge proposed "every two years."

M.<sup>r</sup> Jennifer prop.<sup>d</sup> "every three years," observing that the too great frequency of elections rendered the people indifferent to them, and made the best men unwilling to engage in so precarious a service.

M.<sup>r</sup> Madison seconded the motion for three years. Instability is one of the great vices of our republics, to be remedied. Three years will be necessary, in a Government so extensive, for members to form any knowledge of the various interests of the States to which they do not belong, and of which they can know but little from the situation and affairs of their own. One year will be almost consumed in preparing for and travelling to & from the seat of national business.

M.<sup>r</sup> Gerry. The people of New England will never give up the point of annual elections, they know of the transition made in England from triennial to septennial elections, and will consider such an innovation here as the prelude to a like usurpation. He considered

---

\* Pennsylvani omitted in the printed Journal. The vote is there entered as of June 11th.

[88] In the transcript the vote reads: "Massachusetts, Pennsylvania, Virginia, North Carolina, South Carolina, Georgia, aye—6; Connecticut, New York, New Jersey, Delaware, Maryland, no—5."

[89] The word "the" is here inserted in the transcript.

[90] The word "was" is here inserted in the transcript.

[91] The words "the fifteenth Resolution" are substituted in the transcript for "Resolution 15."

[92] The word "United" is here inserted in the transcript.

[93] In the transcript the vote reads: "Massachusetts, Pennsylvania,* Virginia, North Carolina, South Carolina, Georgia, aye—6; Connecticut, New York, New Jersey, no—3; Delaware, Maryland, divided."

annual elections as the only defence of the people ag:st tyranny. He was as much ag:st a triennial House as ag:st a hereditary Executive.

M: MADISON, observed that if the opinions of the people were to be our guide, it w:d be difficult to say what course we ought to take. No member of the Convention could say what the opinions of his Constituents were at this time; much less could he say what they would think if possessed of the information & lights possessed by the members here; & still less what would be their way of thinking 6 or 12 months hence. We ought to consider what was right & necessary in itself for the attainment of a proper Governm:t A plan adjusted to this idea will recommend itself—The respectability of this convention will give weight to their recommendation of it. Experience will be constantly urging the adoption of it, and all the most enlightened & respectable citizens will be its advocates. Should we fall short of the necessary & proper point, this influential class of Citizens will be turned against the plan, and little support in opposition to them can be gained to it from the unreflecting multitude.

M: GERRY repeated his opinion that it was necessary to consider what the people would approve. This had been the policy of all Legislators. If the reasoning of M: Madison were just, and we supposed a limited Monarchy the best form in itself, we ought to recommend it, tho' the genius of the people was decidedly adverse to it, and having no hereditary distinctions among us, we were destitute of the essential materials for such an innovation.

On the question for [94] triennial election of the 1:st branch

Mass. no. [M: King ay.] M: Ghorum wavering. Con:t no. N. Y. ay. N. J. ay. P:a ay. Del. ay. M:d ay. V:a ay. N. C. no. S. C. no. Geo. ay.[95]

The words requiring members of y:e 1:st branch to be of the age of _____ years were struck out Maryland alone, no. The words "*liberal compensation for members*" being consid:d M: MADISON moves to insert the words, " *& fixt*." He observed that it would be improper to leave the members of the Nat:l legislature to be

---

[94] The word "the" is here inserted in the transcript.
[95] In the transcript the vote reads: "New York, New Jersey, Pennsylvania, Delaware, Maryland, Virginia, Georgia, aye—7; Massachusetts [Mr. King, aye, Mr. Gorham, wavering] Connecticut, North Carolina, South Carolina, no—4."

provided for by the State Legisl: because it would create an improper dependence; and to leave them to regulate their own wages, was an indecent thing, and might in time prove a dangerous one. He thought wheat or some other article of which the average price throughout a reasonable period preceding might be settled in some convenient mode, would form a proper standard.

Col. MASON seconded the motion; adding that it would be improper for other reasons to leave the wages to be regulated by the States. 1.[96] the different States would make different provision for their representatives, and an inequality would be felt among them, whereas he thought they ought to be in all respects equal. 2.[96] the parsimony of the States might reduce the provision so low that as had already happened in choosing delegates to Congress, the question would be not who were most fit to be chosen, but who were most willing to serve.

On the question for inserting the words "and fixt."

Mass:ts no. Con:t no. N. Y. ay. N. J. ay. P:a ay. Del. ay. M:d ay. V:a ay. N. C. ay. S. C. no. Geo. ay.[97]

Doct:r FRANKLYN said he approved of the amendment just made for rendering the salaries as fixed as possible; but disliked the word "*liberal*." he would prefer the word moderate if it was necessary to substitute any other. He remarked the tendency of abuses in every case, to grow of themselves when once begun, and related very pleasantly the progression in ecclesiastical benefices, from the first departure from the gratuitous provision for the Apostles, to the establishment of the papal system. The word "liberal" was struck out nem. con.

On the motion of M:r PIERCE, that the wages should be paid out of the National Treasury, Mass:ts ay. C:t no. N. Y. no. N. J. ay. P:a ay. Del. ay. M:d ay. V:a ay. N. C. ay. S. C. no. G. ay.[98]

Question on the clause relating to term of service & compensation of [99] 1:st branch

---

[96] The figures "1" and "2" are changed to "First" and "Secondly" in the transcript.

[97] In the transcript the vote reads: "New York, New Jersey, Pennsylvania, Delaware, Maryland, Virginia, North Carolina, Georgia, aye—8; Massachusetts, Connecticut, South Carolina, no—3."

[98] In the transcript the vote reads: "Massachusetts, New Jersey, Pennsylvania, Dalaware, Maryland, Virginia, North Carolina, Georgia, aye—8; Connecticut, New York, South Carolina, no—3."

[99] The word "the" is here inserted in the transcript.

Mass.ᵗˢ ay.. Cᵗ no. N. Y. no. N. J. ay. Pᵃ ay. Del. ay. Mᵈ ay. Vᵃ ay. N. C. ay. S. C. no. Geo. ay.¹

On a question for striking out the "*ineligibility* of members of ⁹⁹ Natˡ Legis: to *State offices.*"

Mass.ᵗˢ divᵈ Conᵗ ay. N. Y. ay. N. J. no. Pᵃ no. Del. no. Mᵈ divᵈ Vᵃ no. N. C. ay. S. C. ay. Geo. no ²

On the question for agreeing to the clause as amended

Mass.ᵗˢ ay. Conᵗ no. N. Y. ay. N. J. ay. Pᵃ ay. Del. ay. Mᵈ ay. Vᵃ ay. N. C. ay. S. C. ay. Geo. ay.³

On a question for making Members of ⁴ Natˡ legislature *ineligible* to any office under the Natˡ Govᵗ for the term of 3 years after ceasing to be members.

Mass.ᵗˢ no. Conᵗ no. N. Y. no. N. J. no. Pᵃ no. Del. no. Mᵈ ay. Vᵃ no. N. C. no. S. C. no. Geo. no.⁵

On the question for such ineligibility for one year

Mass.ᵗˢ ay. Cᵗ ay. N. Y. no. N. J. ay. Pᵃ ay. Del. ay. Mᵈ divᵈ Vᵃ ay. N. C. ay. S. C. ay. Geo. no.⁶

On ⁴ question moved by Mʳ PINCKNEY for striking out "incapable of re-election into ⁴ 1ˢᵗ branch of ⁴ Natˡ Legisl. for years, and subject to recall" agᵈ to nem. con.

On ⁴ question for striking out from Resol: 5 ⁷ the words requiring members of the senatorial branch to be of the age of years at least

Mass.ᵗˢ no. Conᵗ ay. N. Y. no. N. J. ay. Pᵃ ay. Del. no. Mᵈ no. Vᵃ no. N. C. divᵈ. S. C. no. Geo. divᵈ ⁸

On the question for filling the blank with 30 years as the qualification; it was agreed to.

---

⁹⁹ The word "the" is here inserted in the transcript.

¹ In the transcript the vote reads: "Massachusetts, New Jersey, Pennsylvania, Delaware, Maryland, Virginia, North Carolina, Georgia, aye—8; Connecticut, New York, South Carolina, no—3."

² In the transcript the vote reads: "Connecticut, New York, North Carolina, South Carolina, aye—4; New Jersey, Pennsylvania, Delaware, Virginia, Georgia, no—5; Massachusetts, Maryland, divided."

³ In the transcript the vote reads: "Massachusetts, New York, New Jersey, Pennsylvania, Delaware, Maryland, Virginia, North Carolina, South Carolina, Georgia, aye—10; Connecticut, no—1."

⁴ The word "the" is here inserted in the transcript.

⁵ In the transcript the vote reads: "Maryland, aye—1; Massachusetts, Connecticut, New York, New Jersey, Pennsylvania, Delaware, Virginia, North Carolina, South Carolina, Georgia, no—10."

⁶ In the transcript the vote reads: "Massachusetts, Connecticut, New Jersey, Pennsylvania, Delaware, Virginia, North Carolina, South Carolina, aye—8; New York, Georgia, no—2; Maryland, divided."

⁷ The words "the fifth Resolution" are substituted in the transcript for "Resol: 5."

⁸ In the transcript the vote reads: "Connecticut, New Jersey, Pennsylvania, aye—3; Massachusetts, New York, Delaware, Maryland, Virginia, South Carolina, no—6; North Carolina, Georgia, divided."

Massts ay. Cont no. N. Y. ay N. J. no. Pa ay Del. no Md ay Va ay N. C. ay S. C ay Geo. no [9]

Mr SPAIGHT moved to fill the blank for the duration of the appointmts to the 2d branch of the National Legislature with the words "7 years.

Mr SHERMAN, thought 7 years too long. He grounded his opposition he said on the principle that if they did their duty well, they would be reelected. And if they acted amiss, an earlier opportunity should be allowed for getting rid of them. He preferred 5 years which wd be between the terms of [10] 1st branch & of the executive

Mr PIERCE proposed 3 years. 7 years would raise an alarm. Great mischiefs had [11] arisen in England from their septennial act which was reprobated by most of their patriotic Statesmen.

Mr RANDOLPH was for the term of 7 years. The democratic licentiousness of the State Legislatures proved the necessity of a firm Senate. The object of this 2d branch is to controul the democratic branch of the Natl Legislature. If it be not a firm body, the other branch being more numerous, and coming immediately from the people, will overwhelm it. The Senate of Maryland constituted on like principles had been scarcely able to stem the popular torrent. No mischief can be apprehended, as the concurrence of the other branch, and in some measure, of the Executive, will in all cases be necessary. A firmness & independence may be the more necessary also in this branch, as it ought to guard the Constitution agst encroachments of the Executive who will be apt to form combinations with the demagogues of the popular branch.

Mr MADISON, considered 7 years as a term by no means too long. What we wished was to give to the Govt that stability which was every where called for, and which the Enemies of the Republican form alledged to be inconsistent with its nature. He was not afraid of giving too much stability by the term of Seven years. His fear was that the popular branch would still

---

[9] In the transcript the vote reads: "Massachusetts, New York, Pennsylvania, Maryland, Virginia, North Carolina, South Carolina, aye—7; Connecticut, New Jersey, Delaware, Georgia, no—4."
[10] The word "the" is here inserted in the transcript.
[11] The word "have" is substituted in the transcript for "had."

be too great an overmatch for it. It was to be much lamented that we had so little direct experience to guide us. The Constitution of Maryland was the only one that bore any analogy to this part of the plan. In no instance had the Senate of Mary.ᵈ created just suspicions of danger from it. In some instances perhaps it may have erred by yielding to the H. of Delegates. In every instance of their opposition to the measures of the H. of D. they had had with them the suffrages of the most enlightened and impartial people of the other States as well as of their own. In the States where the Senates were chosen in the same manner as the other branches, of the Legislature, and held their seats for 4 years, the institution was found to be no check whatever ag.ˢᵗ the instabilities of the other branches. He conceived it to be of great importance that a stable & firm Gov.ᵗ organized in the republican form should be held out to the people. If this be not done, and the people be left to judge of this species of Gov.ᵗ by y.ᵉ operations of the defective systems under which they now live, it is much to be feared the time is not distant when, in universal disgust, they will renounce the blessing which they have purchased at so dear a rate, and be ready for any change that may be proposed to them.

On the question for "seven years" as the term for the 2.ᵈ branch Mass.ᵗˢ divided (M.ʳ King, M.ʳ Ghorum ay—M.ʳ Gerry, M.ʳ Strong, no) Con.ᵗ no. N. Y. div.ᵈ N. J. ay. P.ᵃ ay. Del. ay. M.ᵈ ay. V.ᵗ ay. N. C. ay. S. C. ay. Geo. ay.¹²

M.ʳ BUTLER & M.ʳ RUTLIDGE proposed that the members of the 2.ᵈ branch should be entitled to no salary or compensation for their services  On the question,*

Mass.ᵗˢ div.ᵈ Con.ᵗ ay. N. Y. no. N. J. no. P. no. Del. ay. M.ᵈ no. V.ᵃ no. N. C. no. S. C. ay. Geo. no.¹⁴

---

* [It is probable y.ᵉ votes here turned chiefly on the idea that if the salaries were not here provided for the members would be paid by their respective States]
  This note for the bottom margin.¹³

[12] In the transcript the vote reads: "New Jersey, Pennsylvania, Delaware, Maryland, Virginia, North Carolina, South Carolina, Georgia, aye—8; Connecticut, no—1; Massachusetts [Mr. Gorham and Mr. King, aye; Mr. Gerry and Mr. Strong, no] New York, divided."

[13] Madison's direction is omitted in the transcript.

[14] In the transcript the vote reads: "Connecticut, Delaware, South Carolina, aye—3; New York, New Jersey, Pennsylvania, Maryland, Virginia, North Carolina, Georgia, no—7; Massachusetts, divided."

It was then moved & agreed that the clauses respecting the stipends & ineligibility of the 2ᵈ branch be the same as, of the 1ˢᵗ branch: Con: disagreeing to the ineligibility.

It was moved & 2ᵈᵉᵈ to alter Resol: 9.[15] so as to read "that the jurisdiction of the supreme tribunal shall be to hear & determine in the dernier resort, all piracies, felonies &c."

It was moved & 2ᵈᵉᵈ to strike out "all piracies & felonies on the high seas," which was agreed to.

It was moved & agreed to strike out "all captures from an enemy."

It was moved & agreed to strike out "other States" and insert "two distinct States of the Union"

It was moved & agreed to postpone the consideration of Resolution 9,[15] relating to the Judiciary:

The Comᵉ then rose & the House adjourned

WEDNESDAY JUNE 13. IN COMMITTEE OF THE WHOLE

Resol: 9 [15] being resumed

The latter parts of the clause relating to the jurisdiction of the Natiˡ tribunals, was struck out nem. con in order to leave full room for their organization.

Mr RANDOLPH & Mr MADISON, then moved the following resolution respecting a National Judiciary, viz "that the jurisdiction of the National Judiciary shall extend to cases, which respect the collection of the national revenue, impeachments of any national officers, and questions which involve the national peace and harmony" which was agreed to.

Mr PINKNEY & Mr SHERMAN moved to insert after the words "one supreme tribunal" the words "the Judges of which to be appointed by the national Legislature."

Mr MADISON, objected to an appᵗ by the whole Legislature. Many of them were [16] incompetent Judges of the requisite qualifications. They were too much influenced by their partialities. The candidate who was present, who had displayed a talent for

---

[15] The words "the ninth Resolution" are substituted in the transcript for "Resol: 9."
[16] The word "are" is substituted in the transcript for "were."

business in the legislative field, who had perhaps assisted ignorant members in business of their own, or of their Constituents, or used other winning means, would without any of the essential qualifications for an expositor of the laws prevail over a competitor not having these recommendations, but possessed of every necessary accomplishment. He proposed that the appointment should be made by the Senate, which as a less numerous & more select body, would be more competent judges, and which was sufficiently numerous to justify such a confidence in them.

M$^r$ SHARMAN & M$^r$ PINKNEY withdrew their motion, and the app$^t$ by the Senate was ag$^d$ to nem. con.

M$^r$ GERRY. moved to restrain the Senatorial branch from originating money bills. The other branch was more immediately the representatives of the people, and it was a maxim that the people ought to hold the purse-strings. If the Senate should be allowed to originate such bills, they w$^d$ repeat the experiment, till chance should furnish a sett of representatives in the other branch who will fall into their snares.

M$^r$ BUTLER saw no reason for such a discrimination. We were always following the British Constitution when the reason of it did not apply. There was no analogy between the H. of Lords and the body proposed to be established. If the Senate should be degraded by any such discriminations, the best men would be apt to decline serving in it in favor of the other branch. And it will lead the latter into the practice of tacking other clauses to money bills.

M$^r$ MADISON observed that the Commentators on the Brit: Const: had not yet agreed on the reason of the restriction on the H. of L. in money bills. Certain it was there could be no similar reason in the case before us. The Senate would be the representatives of the people as well as the 1$^{st}$ branch. If they s$^d$ have any dangerous influence over it, they would easily prevail on some member of the latter to originate the bill they wished to be passed. As the Senate would be generally a more capable sett of men, it w$^d$ be wrong to disable them from any preparation of the business, especially of that which was most important, and in our republics, worse prepared than any other. The Gentleman in pursuance of his principle ought to carry the restraint to the *amendment*, as well as the originating of money bills, since, an addition of a given sum w:d be equivalent to a distinct proposition of it.

M:r KING differed from M:r GERRY, and concurred in the objections to the proposition.

M:r READ favored the proposition, but would not extend the restraint to the case of amendments.

M:r PINKNEY thinks the question premature. If the Senate sh:d be formed on the *same* proportional representation as it stands at present, they s:d have equal power, otherwise if a different principle s:d be introduced.

M:r SHERMAN. As both branches must concur, there can be no danger whichever way the Senate [17] be formed. We establish two branches in order to get more wisdom, which is particularly needed in the finance business—The Senate bear their share of the taxes, and are also the representatives of the people. What a man does by another, he does by himself is a maxim. In Con:t both branches can originate in all cases, and it has been found safe & convenient. Whatever might have been the reason of the rule as to The H. of Lords, it is clear that no good arises from it now even there.

Gen:l PINKNEY. This distinction prevails in S. C. & has been a source of pernicious disputes between y:e 2 branches. The Constitution is now evaded, by informal schedules of amendments handed from y:e Senate to the other House.

M:r WILLIAMSON wishes for a question chiefly to prevent re-discussion. The restriction will have one advantage, it will oblige some member in [18] lower branch to move, & people can then mark him.

On the question for excepting money bills as prop:d by M:r Gerry, Mass. no. Con:t no. N. Y. ay. N. J. no. Del. ay. M:d no. V:a ay. N. C. no. S. C. no. Geo. no.[19]

[20] Committee rose & M:r GHORUM made report, which was postponed till tomorrow, to give an opportunity for other plans to be proposed. The report was in the words following:

---

[17] The word "may" is here inserted in the transcript.
[18] The word "the" is here inserted in the transcript.
[19] In the transcript the vote reads: "New York, Delaware, Virginia, aye—3; Massachusetts, Connecticut, New Jersey, Maryland, North Carolina, South Carolina, Georgia no—7."
[20] The word "the" is here inserted in the transcript.

The Home of John Adams.

### REPORT OF THE COMMITTEE OF WHOLE ON M.ʳ RANDOLPH'S PROPOSITIONS [21]

1. Res.ᵈ that it is the opinion of this Committee that a National Governm.ᵗ ought to be established, consisting of a supreme Legislative, Executive & Judiciary.

2. Resol.ᵈ that the National Legislature ought to consist of two branches.

3. Res.ᵈ that the members of the first branch of the National Legislature ought to be elected by the people of the several States for the term of three years, to receive fixed Stipends by which they may be compensated for the devotion of their time to [20] public service, to be paid out of the National Treasury: to be ineligible to any office established by a particular State, or under the authority of the U. States, (except those peculiarly belonging to the functions of the first branch), during the term of service, and under the national Government for the space of one year after its expiration.

4. Res.ᵈ that the members of the second branch of the Nat.ˡ Legislature ought to be chosen by the individual Legislatures, to be of the age of 30 years at least, to hold their offices for a term sufficient to ensure their independency,[22] namely, seven years, to receive fixed stipends by which they may be compensated for the devotion of their time to [20] public service to be paid out of the National Treasury; to be ineligible to any office established by a particular State, or under the authority of the U. States, (except those peculiarly belonging to the functions of the second branch) during the term of service, and under the Nat.ˡ Gov.ᵗ for the space of one year after its expiration.

5. Res.ᵈ that each branch ought to possess the right of originating Acts

6. Res.ᵈ that the Nat.ˡ Legislature ought to be empowered to enjoy the Legislative rights vested in Cong.ˢ by the Confederation, and moreover to legislate in all cases to which the separate States are incompetent; or in which the harmony of the U. S. may be interrupted by the exercise of individual legislation; to negative all laws passed by the several States contravening in the opinion of the National Legislature the articles of Union, or any treaties subsisting under the authority of the Union.

---

[21] This heading is omitted in the transcript.
[22] The word "independency" is changed to "independence" in the transcript.

7. Resᵈ that the rights of suffrage in the 1ˢᵗ branch of the National Legislature, ought not to be according to the rule established in the articles of confederation but according to some equitable ratio of representation, namely, in proportion to the whole number of white & other free citizens & inhabitants, of every age sex and condition, including those bound to servitude for a term of years, & three fifths of all other persons, not comprehended in the foregoing description, except Indians not paying taxes in each State:

8. Resolved that the right of suffrage in the 2ᵈ branch of the National Legislature ought to be according to the rule established for the first.

9. Resolved that a National Executive be instituted to consist of a single person, to be chosen by the Natⁱˡ Legislature for the term of seven years, with power to carry into execution the national laws, to appoint to offices in cases not otherwise provided for—to be ineligible a second time, & to be removeable on impeachment and conviction of malpractices or neglect of duty—to receive a fixed stipend by which he may be compensated for the devotion of his time to [23] public service to be paid out of the national Treasury.

10. Resolᵈ that the Natˡ Executive shall have a right to negative any Legislative Act, which shall not be afterwards passed unless [24] by two thirds of each branch of the National Legislature.

11. Resolᵈ that a Natˡ Judiciary be established, to consist of one supreme tribunal, the Judges of which to [25] be appointed by the 2ᵈ branch of the Natˡ Legislature, to hold their offices during good behaviour, & to receive punctually at stated times a fixed compensation for their services, in which no increase or diminution shall be made, so as to affect the persons actually in office at the time of such increase or diminution.

12. Resolᵈ that the Natˡ Legislature be empowered to appoint inferior Tribunals.

13. Resᵈ that the jurisdiction of the Natˡ Judiciary shall extend to all cases which respect the collection of the Natˡ revenue, im-

---

[23] The word "the" is here inserted in the transcript.
[24] The word "unless" is omitted in the transcript.
[25] The word "shall" is substituted in the transcript for "to."

peachments of any Nat! Officers, and questions which involve the national peace & harmony.

14. Res? that provision ought to be made for the admission of States lawfully arising within the limits of the U. States, whether from a voluntary junction of Government & territory or otherwise, with the consent of a number of voices in the Nat! Legislature less than the whole.

15. Res? that provision ought to be made for the continuance of Congress and their authorities and privileges untill a given day after the reform of the articles of Union shall be adopted and for the completion of all their engagements.

16. Res? that a Republican Constitution & its existing laws ought to be guaranteed to each State by the U. States.

17. Res? that provision ought to be made for the amendment of the Articles of Union whensoever it shall seem necessary.

18. Res? that the Legislative, Executive & Judiciary powers within the several States ought to be bound by oath to support the articles of Union.

19. Res? that the amendments which shall be offered to the confederation by the Convention ought at a proper time or times after the approbation of Cong? to be submitted to an Assembly or Assemblies recommended by the several Legislatures to be expressly chosen by the people to consider and decide thereon.

---

THURSDAY JUNE 14. IN CONVENTION [26]

M? PATTERSON, observed to the Convention that it was the wish of several deputations, particularly that of N. Jersey, that further time might be allowed them to contemplate the plan reported from the Committee of the Whole, and to digest one purely federal, and contradistinguished from the reported plan. He said they hoped to have such an one ready by tomorrow to be laid before the Convention: And the Convention adjourned that leisure might be given for the purpose.

---

[26] The words "In Convention" are crossed out in the transcript.

## Friday June 15th 1787 [27]

[28] Mr PATTERSON, laid before the Convention the plan which he said several of the deputations wished to be substituted in place of that proposed by Mr Randolph. After some little discussion of the most proper mode of giving it a fair deliberation it was agreed that it should be referred to a Committee of the whole, and that in order to place the two plans in due comparison, the other should be recommitted. At the earnest desire [29] of Mr Lansing & some other gentlemen, it was also agreed that the Convention should not go into Committee of the whole on the subject till tomorrow, by which delay the friends of the plan proposed by Mr Patterson wd be better prepared to explain & support it, and all would have an opportuy of taking copies.*

The propositions from N. Jersey moved by Mr Patterson were in the words following.

1. Resd that the articles of Confederation ought to be so revised, corrected & enlarged, as to render the federal Constitution adequate to the exigencies of Government, & the preservation of the Union.

2. Resd that in addition to the powers vested in the U. States in Congress, by the present existing articles of Confederation, they be authorized to pass acts for raising a revenue, by levying a duty or duties on all goods or merchandizes of foreign growth or manufacture, imported into any part of the U. States, by Stamps on paper, vellum or parchment, and by a postage on all letters or packages passing through the general post-office, to be applied

---

[* this plan had been concerted among the deputations or members thereof, from Cont N. Y. N. J Del. and perhaps Mr Martin from Maryd who made with them a common cause [30] on different principles Cont & N. Y. were agst a departure from the principle of the Confederation, wishing rather to add a few new powers to Congs than to substitute a National Govt. The States of N. J. & Del. were opposed to a National Govt because its patrons considered a proportional representation of the States as the basis of it. The eagourness displayed by the members opposed to a Natl Govt from these different motives began now to produce serious anxiety for the result of the Convention. Mr Dickenson said to Mr Madison—You see the consequence of pushing things too far. Some of the members from the small States wish for two branches in the General Legislature, and are friends to a good National Government; but we would sooner submit to a foreign power than submit to be deprived of an equality of suffrage,[31] in both branches of the legislature, and thereby be thrown under the domination of the large States ]
* The note in brackets for the margin.[32]
[27] The year "1787" is omitted in the transcript.
[28] The words "In Convention" are here inserted in the transcript.
[29] The word "request" is substituted in the transcript for "desire."
[30] The word "though" is here inserted in the transcript.
[31] The phrase "of an equality of suffrage" is transposed so that the transcript reads "deprived, in both branches of the legislature of an equality of suffrage, and thereby" . . .
[32] Madison's direction is omitted in the transcript.

to such federal purposes as they shall deem proper & expedient; to make rules & regulations for the collection thereof; and the same from time to time, to alter & amend in such manner as they shall think proper: to pass Acts for the regulation of trade & commerce as well with foreign nations as with each other: provided that all punishments, fines, forfeitures & penalties to be incurred for contravening such acts rules and regulations shall be adjudged by the Common law Judiciaries of the State in which any offence contrary to the true intent & meaning of such Acts rules & regulations shall have been committed or perpetrated, with liberty of commencing in the first instance all suits & prosecutions for that purpose in the superior common law Judiciary in such State, subject nevertheless, for the correction of all errors, both in law & fact in rendering Judgment, to an appeal to the Judiciary of the U. States.

3. Res$^d$ that whenever requisitions shall be necessary, instead of the rule for making requisitions mentioned in the articles of Confederation, the United States in Cong$^s$ be authorized to make such requisitions in proportion to the whole number of white & other free citizens & inhabitants of every age sex and condition including those bound to servitude for a term of years & three fifths of all other persons not comprehended in the foregoing description, except Indians not paying taxes; that if such requisitions be not complied with, in the time specified therein, to direct the collection thereof in the non complying States & for that purpose to devise and pass acts directing & authorizing the same; provided that none of the powers hereby vested in the U. States in Cong$^s$ shall be exercised without the consent of at least         States, and in that proportion if the number of Confederated States should hereafter be increased or diminished.

4. Res$^d$ that the U. States in Cong$^s$ be authorized to elect a federal Executive to consist of         persons, to continue in office for the term of         years, to receive punctually at stated times a fixed compensation for their services, in which no increase or diminution shall be made so as to affect the persons composing the Executive at the time of such increase or diminution, to be

paid out of the federal treasury; to be incapable of holding any other office or appointment during their time of service and for    years thereafter; to be ineligible a second time, & removeable by Congˢ on application by a majority of the Executives of the several States; that the Executives *a* besides their general authority to execute the federal acts ought to appoint all federal officers not otherwise provided for, & to direct all military operations; provided that none of the persons composing the federal Executive shall on any occasion take command of any troops, so as personally to conduct any *b* enterprise as General or in other capacity.

5. Resᵈ that a federal Judiciary be established to consist of a supreme Tribunal the Judges of which to be appointed by the Executive, & to hold their offices during good behaviour, to receive punctually at stated times a fixed compensation for their services in which no increase or diminution shall be made, so as to affect the persons actually in office at the time of such increase or diminution; that the Judiciary so established shall have authority to hear & determine in the first instance on all impeachments of federal officers, & by way of appeal in the dernier resort in all cases touching the rights of Ambassadors, in all cases of captures from an enemy, in all cases of piracies & felonies on the high Seas, in all cases in which foreigners may be interested, in the construction of any treaty or treaties, or which may arise on any of the Acts for *c* regulation of trade, or the collection of the federal Revenue: that none of the Judiciary shall during the time they remain in office be capable of receiving or holding any other office or appointment during their time *d* of service, or for    thereafter.

6. Resᵈ that all Acts of the U. States in Congˢ made by virtue & in pursuance of the powers hereby & by the articles of Confederation vested in them, and all Treaties made & ratified under the authority of the U. States shall be the supreme law of the respective States so far forth as those Acts or Treaties shall relate to the

---

*a* The transcript uses the word "Executives" in the singular.
*b* The word "military" is here inserted in the transcript.
*c* The word "the" is here inserted in the transcript.
*d* The word "term" is substituted in the transcript for "time."

said States or their Citizens, and that the Judiciary of the several States shall be bound thereby in their decisions, any thing in the respective laws of the Individual States to the contrary notwithstanding; and that if any State, or any body of men in any State shall oppose or prevent y:d carrying into execution such acts or treaties, the federal Executive shall be authorized to call forth y:e power of the Confederated States, or so much thereof as may be necessary to enforce and compel an obedience to such Acts, or an observance of such Treaties.

7. Res:d that provision be made for the admission of new States into the Union.

8. Res:d the rule for naturalization ought to be the same in every State.

9. Res:d 5 that a Citizen of one State committing an offense in another State of the Union, shall be deemed guilty of the same offense as if it had been committed by a Citizen of the State in which the offense was committed.*

Adjourned.

SATURDAY JUNE 16. IN COMMITTEE OF THE WHOLE ON [33] RESOLUTIONS PROPOS:D BY M:R P. & M:R R

M:r LANSING called for the reading of the 1:st resolution of each plan, which he considered as involving principles directly in contrast; that of M:r Patterson says he sustains the sovereignty of the respective States, that of M:r Randolph distroys it: the latter requires a negative on all the laws of the particular States; the former, only certain general powers for the general good. The plan of M:r R. in short absorbs all power except what may be exercised in the little local matters of the States which are not objects worthy of the supreme cognizance. He grounded his preference of M:r P.'s plan, chiefly on two objections ag:st [34] that of M:r R.

---

* This copy of M:r Patterson's propositions varies in a few clauses from that in the printed Journal furnished from the papers of M:r Brearley a Colleague of M:r Patterson. A confidence is felt, notwithstanding, in its accuracy. That the copy in the Journal is not entirely correct is shewn by the ensuing speech of M:r Wilson [June 16] in which he refers to the mode of removing the Executive by impeachment & conviction as a feature in the Virg:a plan forming one of its contrasts to that of M:r Patterson, which proposed a removal on the application of a majority of the Executives of the States. In the copy printed in the Journal, the two modes are combined in the same clause; whether through inadvertence, or as a contemplated amendment does not appear.

[5] The word "that" is here inserted in the transcript.
[33] The word "the" is here inserted in the transcript.
[34] The word "to" is substituted in the transcript for "ag:st"

1.³⁵ want of power in the Convention to discuss & propose it. 2³⁵ the improbability of its being adopted. 1. He was decidedly of opinion that the power of the Convention was restrained to amendments of a federal nature, and having for their basis the Confederacy in being. The Act of Congress The tenor of the Acts of the States, the Commissions produced by the several deputations all proved this. And this limitation of the power to an amendment of the Confederacy, marked the opinion of the States, that it was unnecessary & improper to go farther. He was sure that this was the case with his State. N. York would never have concurred in sending deputies to the convention, if she had supposed the deliberations were to turn on a consolidation of the States, and a National Government.

2. was it probable that the States would adopt & ratify a scheme, which they had never authorized us to propose? and which so far exceeded what they regarded as sufficient? We see by their several Acts particularly in relation to the plan of revenue proposed by Cong. in 1783, not authorized by the Articles of Confederation, what were the ideas they then entertained. Can so great a change be supposed to have already taken place. To rely on any change which is hereafter to take place in the sentiments of the people would be trusting to too great an uncertainty. We know only what their present sentiments are. And it is in vain to propose what will not accord with these. The States will never feel a sufficient confidence in a general Government to give it a negative on their laws. The Scheme is itself totally novel. There is no parallel to it to be found. The authority of Congress is familiar to the people, and an augmentation of the powers of Congress will be readily approved by them.

Mʳ PATTERSON, said as he had on a former occasion given his sentiments on the plan proposed by Mʳ R. he would now avoiding repetition as much as possible give his reasons in favor of that proposed by himself. He preferred it because it accorded 1.³⁶ with the powers of the Convention, 2³⁶ with the sentiments of the people. If the confederacy was radically wrong, let us return

---

³⁵ The figures "1" and "2" are changed to "first" and "secondly" in the transcript.
³⁶ The figures "1" and "2" are changed to "first" and "secondly" in the transcript.

to our States, and obtain larger powers, not assume them of ourselves. I came here not to speak my own sentiments, but the sentiments of those who sent me. Our object is not such a Governm.<sup>t</sup> as may be best in itself, but such a one as our Constituents have authorized us to prepare, and as they will approve. If we argue the matter on the supposition that no Confederacy at present exists, it can not be denied that all the States stand on the footing of equal sovereignty. All therefore must concur before any can be bound. If a proportional representation be right, why do we not vote so here? If we argue on the fact that a federal compact actually exists, and consult the articles of it we still find an equal Sovereignty to be the basis of it. He reads the 5<sup>th</sup> art: of [37] Confederation giving each State a vote— & the 13<sup>th</sup> declaring that no alteration shall be made without unanimous consent. This is the nature of all treaties. What is unanimously done, must be unanimously undone. It was observed [by M.<sup>r</sup> Wilson] that the larger States gave up the point, not because it was right, but because the circumstances of the moment urged the concession. Be it so. Are they for that reason at liberty to take it back. Can the donor resume his gift without the consent of the donee. This doctrine may be convenient, but it is a doctrine that will sacrifice the lesser States. The large States acceded readily to the confederacy. It was the small ones that came in reluctantly and slowly. N. Jersey & Maryland were the two last, the former objecting to the want of power in Congress over trade: both of them to the want of power to appropriate the vacant territory to the benefit of the whole.—If the sovereignty of the States is to be maintained, the Representatives must be drawn immediately from the States, not from the people: and we have no power to vary the idea of equal sovereignty. The only expedient that will cure the difficulty, is that of throwing the States into Hotchpot. To say that this is impracticable, will not make it so. Let it be tried, and we shall see whether the Citizens of Mass.<sup>ts</sup> Pen.<sup>a</sup> & V.<sup>a</sup> accede to it. It will be objected that Coercion will be impracticable. But will it be more so in one plan than the other? Its efficacy will

---

[37] The word "the" is here inserted in the transcript.

depend on the quantum of power collected, not on its being drawn from the States, or from the individuals; and according to his plan it may be exerted on individuals as well as according [38] that of Mʳ R. A distinct executive & Judiciary also were equally provided by his plan. It is urged that two branches in the Legislature are necessary. Why? for the purpose of a check. But the reason of [39] the precaution is not applicable to this case. Within a particular State, where party heats prevail, such a check may be necessary. In such a body as Congress it is less necessary, and besides, the delegations of the different States are checks on each other. Do the people at large complain of Congˢ? No, what they wish is that Congˢ may have more power. If the power now proposed be not eno', the people hereafter will make additions to it. With proper powers Congˢ will act with more energy & wisdom than the proposed Natˡ Legislature; being fewer in number, and more secreted & refined by the mode of election. The plan of Mʳ R. will also be enormously expensive. Allowing Georgia & Del. two representatives each in the popular branch the aggregate number of that branch will be 180. Add to it half as many for the other branch and you have 270. members coming once at least a year from the most distant as well as the most central parts of the republic. In the present deranged state of our finances can so expensive a system be seriously thought of? By enlarging the powers of Congˢ the greatest part of this expence will be saved, and all purposes will be answered. At least a trial ought to be made.

Mʳ WILSON entered into a contrast of the principal points of the two plans so far he said as there had been time to examine the one last proposed. These points were 1. in the Virgᵃ plan there are *2* & in some degree 3 branches in the Legislature: in the plan from N. J. there is to be a *single* legislature only—2. Representation of the people at large is the basis of the [40] one:—the State Legislatures, the pillars of the other—3. proportional representation prevails in one:—equality of suffrage in the other—4. A single Exec-

---
[38] The word "to" is here inserted in the transcript.
[39] The word "for" is substituted in the transcript for "of."
[40] The word "the" is omitted in the transcript.

utive Magistrate is at the head of the one:—a plurality is held out in the other.—5. in the one the [41] majority of the people of the U. S. must prevail:—in the other a minority may prevail. 6. the Natl Legislature is to make laws in all cases to which the separate States are incompetent &—:—in place of this Congs are to have additional power in a few cases only—7. A negative on the laws of the States:—in place of this coertion to be substituted —8. The Executive to be removeable on impeachment & conviction;—in one plan: in the other to be removeable at the instance of [42] majority of the Executives of the States—9. Revision of the laws provided for in one:—no such check in the other—10. inferior national tribunals in one:—none such in the other. 11. In ye one jurisdiction of Natl tribunals to extend &c—; an appellate jurisdiction only allowed in the other. 12. Here the jurisdiction is to extend to all cases affecting the Nationl peace & harmony: there, a few cases only are marked out. 13. finally ye ratification is in this to be by the people themselves:—in that by the legislative authorities according to the 13 art: of [43] Confederation.

With regard to the *power of the Convention*, he conceived himself authorized to *conclude nothing*, but to be at liberty to *propose any thing*. In this particular he felt himself perfectly indifferent to the two plans.

With *regard to the sentiments of the people*, he conceived it difficult to know precisely what they are. Those of the particular circle in which one moved, were commonly mistaken for the general voice. He could not persuade himself that the State Govts & Sovereignties were so much the idols of the people, nor a Natl Govt so obnoxious to them, as some supposed. Why sd a Natl Govt be unpopular? Has it less dignity? will each Citizen enjoy under it less liberty or protection? Will a Citizen of *Delaware* be degraded by becoming a Citizen of the *United States*?[44] Where do the people look at present for relief from the evils of which they complain? Is it from an internal reform of their Govts? no, Sir. It is from the Natl Councils that relief is expected. For

---

[41] The word "a" is substituted in the transcript for "the."
[42] The word "a" is here inserted in the transcript.
[43] The word "the" is here inserted in the transcript.
[44] The transcript does not italicize the word "States."

these reasons he did not fear, that the people would not follow us into a national Gov! and it will be a further recommendation of Mr R.'s plan that it is to be submitted to *them*, and not to the *Legislatures*, for ratification.

proceeding now to the 1st point on which he had contrasted the two plans, he observed that anxious as he was for some augmentation of the federal powers, it would be with extreme reluctance indeed that he could ever consent to give powers to Cong! he had two reasons either of wch was sufficient. 1.[45] Cong! as a Legislative body does not stand on the people. 2.[45] it is a *single* body. 1. He would not repeat the remarks he had formerly made on the principles of Representation. he would only say that an inequality in it, has ever been a poison contaminating every branch of Gov! In G. Britain where this poison has had a full operation, the security of private rights is owing entirely to the purity of Her tribunals of Justice, the Judges of which are neither appointed nor paid, by a venal Parliament. The political liberty of that Nation, owing to the inequality of representation is at the mercy of its rulers. He means not to insinuate that there is any parallel between the situation of that Country & ours at present. But it is a lesson we ought not to disregard, that the smallest bodies in G. B. are notoriously the most corrupt. Every other source of influence must also be stronger in small than [46] large bodies of men. When Lord Chesterfield had told us that one of the Dutch provinces had been seduced into the views of France, he need not have added, that it was not Holland, but one of the *smallest* of them. There are facts among ourselves which are known to all. Passing over others, he [47] will only remark that the *Impost*, so anxiously wished for by the public was defeated not by any of the *larger* States in the Union. 2. *Congress is a single Legislature.* Despotism comes on Mankind in different Shapes, sometimes in an Executive, sometimes in a Military, one. Is there no danger of a Legislative despotism? Theory & practice both proclaim it. If the Legislative authority be not restrained, there can be neither liberty nor stability; and it can only be restrained by dividing it within

---

[45] The figures "1" and "2" are changed to "first" and "secondly" in the transcript.
[46] The word "in" is here inserted in the transcript.
[47] The word "we" is substituted in the transcript for "he."

itself, into distinct and independent branches. In a single House there is no check, but the inadequate one, of the virtue & good sense of those who compose it.

On another great point, the contrast was equally favorable to the plan reported by the Committee of the whole. It vested the Executive powers in a single Magistrate. The plan of N. Jersey, vested them in a plurality. In order to controul the Legislative authority, you must divide it. In order to controul the Executive you must unite it. One man will be more responsible than three. Three will contend among themselves till one becomes the master of his colleagues. In the triumvirates of Rome first Cæsar, then Augustus, are witnesses of this truth. The Kings of Sparta, & the Consuls of Rome prove also the factious consequences of dividing the Executive Magistracy. Having already taken up so much time he w$^d$ not he s$^d$ proceed to any of the other points. Those on which he had dwelt, are sufficient of themselves: and on a decision of them, the fate of the others will depend.

M$^r$ PINKNEY, the whole comes to this, as he conceived. Give N. Jersey an equal vote, and she will dismiss her scruples, and concur in the Nati$^l$ system. He thought the Convention authorized to go any length in recommending, which they found necessary to remedy the evils which produced this Convention.

M$^r$ ELSEWORTH proposed as a more distinctive form of collecting the mind of the Committee on the subject, "that the Legislative power of the U. S. should remain in Cong$^s$" This was not seconded though it seemed better calculated for the purpose than the 1$^{st}$ proposition of M$^r$ Patterson in place of which M$^r$ E. wished to substitute it.

M$^r$ RANDOLPH, was not scrupulous on the point of power. When the salvation of the Republic was at stake, it would be treason to our trust, not to propose what we found necessary. He painted in strong colours, the imbecility of the existing Confederacy, & the danger of delaying a substantial reform. In answer to the objection drawn from the sense of our Constituents as denoted by their acts relating to the Convention and the objects of their deliberation, he observed that as each State acted separately in the case, it would have been indecent for it to have charged the existing Constitution with all the vices which it might have perceived in it. The first State that set on foot this experiment would not have been justified in going so far, ignorant as it was of the opinion of others, and sensible as it must have been of the uncertainty of a successful issue to the experiment. There are certainly seasons [48] of a peculiar nature where the ordinary cautions must be dispensed with; and this is certainly one of them. He w$^d$ not as far as depended on him leave any thing that seemed necessary, undone. The present moment is favorable, and is probably the last that will offer.

The true question is whether we shall adhere to the federal plan, or introduce the national plan. The insufficiency of the former has been fully displayed by the trial already made. There are but two modes, by which the end of a Gen$^l$ Gov$^t$ can be attained: the 1$^{st}$ is [49] by coercion as proposed by M$^r$ P.s plan 2.[50] by real legislation as prop$^d$ by the other plan. Coercion he pronounced to be *impracticable, expensive, cruel to individuals.* It tended also to habituate the instruments of it to shed the blood & riot in the spoils of their fellow Citizens, and consequently trained them up for the service of ambition. We must resort therefor to a National [51] *Legislation over individuals,* for which Cong$^s$ are unfit. To vest such power in them, would be blending the Legislative with the Executive, contrary to the rec$^d$ maxim on this subject: If the Union of these powers heretofore in Cong$^s$ has been safe, it has been owing to the general impotency of that body. Cong$^s$ are moreover not elected by the people, but by the Legislatures who retain even a power of recall. They have therefore no will of their own, they are a mere diplomatic body, and are always obsequious to the views of the States, who are always encroaching on the authority of the U. States. A provision for harmony among the States, as in trade, naturalization &c.—for crushing rebellion whenever it may rear its crest—and for certain other general benefits, must be made. The powers for these purposes, can never be given to a body,

---

[48] The words "certainly seasons" are transposed to read "seasons certainly" in the transcript; but the word "seasons" was erroneously printed "reasons," which error has been followed in other editions of Madison's notes.
[49] The word "is" is omitted in the transcript.
[50] The figure "2" is changed to "the second" in the transcript.
[51] The transcript italicizes the word "National."

inadequate as Congress are in point of representation, elected in the mode in which they are, and possessing no more confidence than they do: for notwithstanding what has been said to the contrary, his own experience satisfied him that a rooted distrust of Congress pretty generally prevailed. A Nat! Gov! alone, properly constituted, will answer the purpose; and he begged it to be considered that the present is the last moment for establishing one. After this select experiment, the people will yield to despair.

The Committee rose & the House adjourned.

MONDAY JUNE 18. IN COMMITTEE OF THE WHOLE ON THE PROPOSITIONS OF M? PATTERSON & M? RANDOLPH

On motion of M? DICKINSON to postpone the 1?ˢᵗ Resolution in M? Patterson's plan, in order to take up the following viz—"that the Articles of Confederation ought to be revised and amended, so as to render the Government of the U. S. adequate to the exigences, the preservation and the prosperity of the Union" the postponement was agreed to by 10 States, Pen: divided.

M? HAMILTON, had been hitherto silent on the business before the Convention, partly from respect to others whose superior abilities age & experience rendered him unwilling to bring forward ideas dissimilar to theirs, and partly from his delicate situation with respect to his own State, to whose sentiments as expressed by his Colleagues, he could by no means accede. The crisis however which now marked our affairs, was too serious to permit any scruples whatever to prevail over the duty imposed on every man to contribute his efforts for the public safety & happiness. He was obliged therefore to declare himself unfriendly to both plans. He was particularly opposed to that from N. Jersey, being fully convinced, that no amendment of the Confederation, leaving the States in possession of their Sovereignty could possibly answer the purpose. On the other hand he confessed he was much discouraged by the amazing extent of Country in expecting the desired blessings from any general sovereignty that could be substituted.—As to the powers of the Convention, he thought the doubts started on that subject had arisen from distinctions &

reasonings too subtle. A *federal* Gov.<sup>t</sup> he conceived to mean an association of independent Communities into one. Different Confederacies have different powers, and exercise them in different ways. In some instances the powers are exercised over collective bodies; in others over individuals, as in the German Diet—& among ourselves in cases of piracy. Great latitude therefore must be given to the signification of the term. The plan last proposed departs itself from the *federal* idea, as understood by some, since it is to operate eventually on individuals. He agreed moreover with the Honble gentleman from V.<sup>a</sup> [M.<sup>r</sup> R.] that we owed it to our Country, to do on this emergency whatever we should deem essential to its happiness. The States sent us here to provide for the exigences of the Union. To rely on & propose any plan not adequate to these exigences, merely because it was not [52] clearly within our powers, would be to sacrifice the means to the end. It may be said that the *States* can not *ratify* a plan not within the purview of the article of [53] Confederation providing for alterations & amendments. But may not the States themselves in which no constitutional authority equal to this purpose exists in the Legislatures, have had in view a reference to the people at large. In the Senate of N. York, a proviso was moved, that no act of the Convention should be binding untill it should be referred to the people & ratified; and the motion was lost by a single voice only, the reason assigned ag.<sup>st</sup> it being, that it might possibly be found an inconvenient shackle.

The great question is what provision shall we make for the happiness of our Country? He would first make a comparative examination of the two plans—prove that there were essential defects in both—and point out such changes as might render a *national one*, efficacious.—The great & essential principles necessary for the support of Government are 1. an active & constant interest in supporting it. This principle does not exist in the States in favor of the federal Gov.<sup>t</sup> They have evidently in a high degree, the esprit de corps. They constantly pursue internal interests adverse to those of the whole. They have their particu-

---

[52] The word "not" is blotted in the notes but is retained because it is in the transcript.
[53] The word "the" is here inserted in the transcript.

lar debts—their particular plans of finance &c. All these when opposed to, invariably prevail over the requisitions & plans of Congress. 2. The love of power. Men love power. The same remarks are applicable to this principle. The States have constantly shewn a disposition rather to regain the powers delegated by them than to part with more, or to give effect to what they had parted with. The ambition of their demagogues is known to hate the controul of the Gen! Government. It may be remarked too that the Citizens have not that anxiety to prevent a dissolution of the Gen! Gov! as of the particular Gov't: A dissolution of the latter would be fatal; of the former would still leave the purposes of Gov! attainable to a considerable degree. Consider what such a State as Virg? will be in a few years, a few compared with the life of nations. How strongly will it feel its importance & self-sufficiency? 3. An habitual attachment of the people. The whole force of this tie is on the side of the State Gov! Its sovereignty is immediately before the eyes of the people: its protection is immediately enjoyed by them. From its hand distributive justice, and all those acts which familiarize & endear [54] Gov! to a people, are dispensed to them. 4. *Force* by which may be understood a *coertion of laws* or *coertion of arms*. Cong? have not the former except in few cases. In particular States, this coercion is nearly sufficient; tho' he held it in most cases, not entirely so. A certain portion of military force is absolutely necessary in large communities. Mass? is now feeling this necessity & making provision for it. But how can this force be exerted on the States collectively. It is impossible. It amounts to a war between the parties. Foreign powers also will not be idle spectators. They will interpose, the confusion will increase, and a dissolution of the Union ensue. 5. *influence*. he did not mean corruption, but a dispensation of those regular honors & emoluments, which produce an attachment to the Gov! Almost all the weight of these is on the side of the States; and must continue so as long as the States continue to exist. All the passions then we see, of avarice, ambition, interest, which govern most individuals, and all public bodies, fall into the current of the States, and do not flow in the

---

[54] The word "a" is here inserted in the transcript.

stream of the Gen! Gov! The former therefore will generally be an overmatch for the Gen! Gov! and render any confederacy, in its very nature precarious. Theory is in this case fully confirmed by experience. The Amphyctionic Council had it would seem ample powers for general purposes. It had in particular the power of fining and using force ag$^{st}$ delinquent members. What was the consequence. Their decrees were mere signals of war. The Phocian war is a striking example of it. Philip at length taking advantage of their disunion, and insinuating himself into their Councils, made himself master of their fortunes. The German Confederacy affords another lesson. The authority of Charlemagne seemed to be as great as could be necessary. The great feudal chiefs however, exercising their local sovereignties, soon felt the spirit & found the means of, encroachments, which reduced the imperial authority to a nominal sovereignty. The Diet has succeeded, which tho' aided by a Prince at its head, of great authority independently of his imperial attributes, is a striking illustration of the weakness of Confederated Governments. Other examples instruct us in the same truth. The Swiss cantons have scarce any Union at all, and have been more than once at war with one another—How then are all these evils to be avoided? only by such a compleat sovereignty in the general Governm$^t$ as will turn all the strong principles & passions above mentioned on its side. Does the scheme of N. Jersey produce this effect? does it afford any substantial remedy whatever? On the contrary it labors under great defects, and the defect of some of its provisions will destroy the efficacy of others. It gives a direct revenue to Cong$^s$ but this will not be sufficient. The balance can only be supplied by requisitions: which experience proves can not be relied on. If States are to deliberate on the mode, they will also deliberate on the object of the supplies, and will grant or not grant as they approve or disapprove of it. The delinquency of one will invite and countenance it in others. Quotas too must in the nature of things be so unequal as to produce the same evil. To what standard will you resort? Land is a fallacious one. Compare Holland with Russia: France or Eng$^d$ with other countries of Europe. Pen$^a$ with N. Carol$^a$ will the relative pecuniary abilities in those instances, correspond with the relative value of land. Take numbers of inhabitants for the rule and make like comparison of different countries, and you will find it to be equally unjust. The different degrees of industry and improvement in different Countries render the first object a precarious measure of wealth. Much depends too on *situation*. Con: N. Jersey & N. Carolina, not being commercial States & contributing to the wealth of the commercial ones, can never bear quotas assessed by the ordinary rules of proportion. They will & must fail in their duty, their example will be followed, and the Union itself be dissolved. Whence then is the national revenue to be drawn? from Commerce? even from exports which notwithstanding the common opinion are fit objects of moderate taxation, from excise, &c &c. These tho' not equal, are less unequal than quotas. Another destructive ingredient in the plan, is that equality of suffrage which is so much desired by the small States. It is not in human nature that V: & the large States should consent to it, or if they did that they sh: long abide by it. It shocks too much the [55] ideas of Justice, and every human feeling. Bad principles in a Gov: tho slow are sure in their operation and will gradually destroy it. A doubt has been raised whether Cong: at present have a right to keep Ships or troops in time of peace. He leans to the negative. M: P: plan provides no remedy.—If the powers proposed were adequate, the organization of Cong: is such that they could never be properly & effectually exercised. The members of Cong: being chosen by the States & subject to recall, represent all the local prejudices. Should the powers be found effectual, they will from time to time be heaped on them, till a tyrannic sway shall be established. The general power whatever be its form if it preserves itself, must swallow up the State powers. Otherwise it will be swallowed up by them. It is ag:t all the principles of a good Government to vest the requisite powers in such a body as Cong: Two Sovereignties can not co-exist within the same limits. Giving powers to Cong: must eventuate in a bad Gov: or in no Gov: The plan of N. Jersey therefore will not do. What then is to be done? Here he was embarrassed. The extent of the Country to be

---

[55] The word "all" is substituted in the transcript for "the."

governed, discouraged him. The expence of a general Gov.^t was also formidable; unless there were such a diminution of expence on the side of the State Gov^ts as the case would admit. If they were extinguished, he was persuaded that great œconomy might be obtained by substituting a general Gov.^t He did not mean however to shock the public opinion by proposing such a measure. On the other hand he saw no *other* necessity for declining it. They are not necessary for any of the great purposes of commerce, revenue, or agriculture. Subordinate authorities he was aware would be necessary. There must be district tribunals: corporations for local purposes. But cui bono, the vast & expensive apparatus now appertaining to the States. The only difficulty of a serious nature which occurred to him, was that of drawing representatives from the extremes to the center of the Community. What inducements can be offered that will suffice? The moderate wages for the 1.^st branch would [56] only be a bait to little demagogues. Three dollars or thereabouts he supposed would be the utmost. The Senate he feared from a similar cause, would be filled by certain undertakers who wish for particular offices under the Gov.^t This view of the subject almost led to him despair that a Republican Gov.^t could be established over so great an extent. He was sensible at the same time that it would be unwise to propose one of any other form. In his private opinion he had no scruple in declaring, supported as he was by the opinions of so many of the wise & good, that the British Gov.^t was the best in the world: and that he doubted much whether any thing short of it would do in America. He hoped Gentlemen of different opinions would bear with him in this, and begged them to recollect the change of opinion on this subject which had taken place and was still going on. It was once thought that the power of Cong.^s was amply sufficient to secure the end of their institution. The error was now seen by every one. The members most tenacious of republicanism, he observed, were as loud as any in declaiming ag.^st the vices of democracy. This progress of the public mind led him to anticipate the time, when others as well as himself

---

[56] The word "could" is substituted in the transcript for "would."

would join in the praise bestowed by M！ Neckar on the British Constitution, namely, that it is the only Gov！ in the world "which unites public strength with individual security."—In every community where industry is encouraged, there will be a division of it into the few & the many. Hence separate interests will arise. There will be debtors & creditors &c. Give all power to the many, they will oppress the few. Give all power to the few, they will oppress the many. Both therefore ought to have [57] power, that each may defend itself ag！ the other. To the want of this check we owe our paper money, instalment laws &c. To the proper adjustment of it the British owe the excellence of their Constitution. Their house of Lords is a most noble institution. Having nothing to hope for by a change, and a sufficient interest by means of their property, in being faithful to the national interest, they form a permanent barrier ag！ every pernicious innovation, whether attempted on the part of the Crown or of the Commons. No temporary Senate will have firmness eno' to answer the purpose. The Senate [of Maryland] which seems to be so much appealed to, has not yet been sufficiently tried. Had the people been unanimous & eager, in the late appeal to them on the subject of a paper emission they would would have yielded to the torrent. Their acquiescing in such an appeal is a proof of it.—Gentlemen differ in their opinions concerning the necessary checks, from the different estimates they form of the human passions. They suppose seven years a sufficient period to give the senate an adequate firmness, from not duly considering the amazing violence & turbulence of the democratic spirit. When a great object of Gov！ is pursued, which seizes the popular passions, they spread like wild fire, and become irresistable. He appealed to the gentlemen from the N. England States whether experience had not there verified the remark.—As to the Executive, it seemed to be admitted that no good one could be established on Republican principles. Was not this giving up the merits of the question: for can there be a good Gov！ without a good Executive. The English model was the only good one on this subject. The Hereditary interest of the King was so interwoven with that of

---

[57] The word "the" is here inserted in the transcript.

the Nation, and his personal emoluments so great, that he was placed above the danger of being corrupted from abroad—and at the same time was both sufficiently independent and sufficiently controuled, to answer the purpose of the institution at home. one of the weak sides of Republics was their being liable to foreign influence & corruption. Men of little character, acquiring great power become easily the tools of intermedling Neibours. Sweeden was a striking instance. The French & English had each their parties during the late Revolution which was effected by the predominant influence of the former.—What is the inference from all these observations? That we ought to go as far in order to attain stability and permanency, as republican principles will admit. Let one branch of the Legislature hold their places for life or at least during good behaviour. Let the Executive also be for life. He appealed to the feelings of the members present whether a term of seven years, would induce the sacrifices of private affairs which an acceptance of public trust would require, so so as to ensure the services of the best Citizens. On this plan we should have in the Senate a permanent will, a weighty interest, which would answer essential purposes. But is this a Republican Gov$^t$, it will be asked? Yes if all the Magistrates are appointed, and vacancies are filled, by the people, or a process of election originating with the people. He was sensible that an Executive constituted as he proposed would have in fact but little of the power and independence that might be necessary. On the other plan of appointing him for 7 years, he thought the Executive ought to have but little power. He would be ambitious, with the means of making creatures; and as the object of his ambition w$^d$ be to *prolong* his power, it is probable that in case of a [58] war, he would avail himself of the emergence,[59] to evade or refuse a degradation from his place. An Executive for life has not this motive for forgetting his fidelity, and will therefore be a safer depository of power. It will be objected probably, that such an Executive will be an *elective Monarch*, and will give birth to the tumults which characterize that form of Gov$^t$ He w$^d$ reply that

---

[58] The word "a" is omitted in the transcript.
[59] The word "emergence" is changed to "emergency" in the transcript.

*Monarch* is an indefinite term. It marks not either the degree or duration of power. If this Executive Magistrate w.d be a monarch for life—the other prop.d by the Report from the Comtte of the whole, w.d be a monarch for seven years. The circumstance of being elective was also applicable to both. It had been observed by judicious writers that elective monarchies w.d be the best if they could be guarded ag.st the *tumults* excited by the ambition and intrigues of competitors. He was not sure that tumults were an inseparable evil. He rather thought this character of Elective Monarchies had been taken rather from particular cases than from general principles. The election of Roman Emperors was made by the *Army*. In *Poland* the election is made by great rival *princes* with independent power, and ample means, of raising commotions. In the German Empire, the appointment is made by the Electors & Princes, who have equal motives & means, for exciting cabals & parties. Might not such a mode of election be devised among ourselves as will defend the community ag.st these effects in any dangerous degree? Having made these observations he would read to the Committee a sketch of a plan which he sh.d prefer to either of those under consideration. He was aware that it went beyond the ideas of most members. But will such a plan be adopted out of doors? In return he would ask will the people adopt the other plan? At present they will adopt neither. But he sees the Union dissolving or already dissolved— he sees evils operating in the States which must soon cure the people of their fondness for democracies—he sees that a great progress has been already made & is still going on in the public mind. He thinks therefore that the people will in time be unshackled from their prejudices; and whenever that happens, they will themselves not be satisfied at stopping where the plan of M.r R. w.d place them, but be ready to go as far at least as he proposes. He did not mean to offer the paper he had sketched as a proposition to the Committee. It was meant only to give a more correct view of his ideas, and to suggest the amendments which he should probably propose to the plan of M.r R. in the proper stages of its future discussion. He read [60] his sketch in the words following: towit

---

[60] The word "reads" is substituted in the transcript for "read."

I. "The Supreme Legislative power of the United States of America to be vested in two different bodies of men; the one to be called the Assembly, the other the Senate who together shall form the Legislature of the United States with power to pass all laws whatsoever subject to the Negative hereafter mentioned.

II. The Assembly to consist of persons elected by the people to serve for three years.

III. The Senate to consist of persons elected to serve during good behaviour; their election to be made by electors chosen for that purpose by the people: in order to this the States to be divided into election districts. On the death, removal or resignation of any Senator his place to be filled out of the district from which he came.

IV. The supreme Executive authority of the United States to be vested in a Governour to be elected to serve during good behaviour—the election to be made by Electors chosen by the people in the Election Districts aforesaid—The authorities & functions of the Executive to be as follows: to have a negative on all laws about to be passed, and the execution of all laws passed, to have the direction of war when authorized or begun; to have with the advice and approbation of the Senate the power of making all treaties; to have the sole appointment of the heads or chief officers of the departments of Finance, War and Foreign Affairs; to have the nomination of all other officers (Ambassadors to foreign Nations included) subject to the approbation or rejection of the Senate; to have the power of pardoning all offences except Treason; which he shall not pardon without the approbation of the Senate.

V. On the death, resignation or removal of the Governour his authorities to be exercised by the President of the Senate till a Successor be appointed.

VI. The Senate to have the sole power of declaring war, the power of advising and approving all Treaties, the power of approving or rejecting all appointments of officers except the heads or chiefs of the departments of Finance War and foreign affairs.

VII. The supreme Judicial authority to be vested in Judges to hold their offices during good behaviour with adequate and permanent salaries. This Court to have original jurisdiction in all causes of capture, and an appellative jurisdiction in all causes in which the revenues of the general Government or the Citizens of foreign Nations are concerned.

VIII. The Legislature of the United States to have power to institute Courts in each State for the determination of all matters of general concern.

IX. The Governour Senators and all officers of the United States to be liable to impeachment for mal- and corrupt conduct; and upon conviction to be removed from office, & disqualified for holding any place of trust or profit—All impeachments to be tried by a Court to consist of the Chief      or Judge of the superior Court of Law of each State, provided such Judge shall hold his place during good behavior, and have a permanent salary.

X. All laws of the particular States contrary to the Constitution or laws of the United States to be utterly void; and the better to prevent such laws being passed, the Governour or president of each State shall be appointed by the General Government and shall have a negative upon the laws about to be passed in the State of which he is *a* Governour or President.

XI. No State to have any forces land or Naval; and the Militia cf all the States to be under the sole and exclusive direction of the United States, the officers of which to be appointed and commissioned by them.

On these several articles he entered into explanatory observations [61] corresponding with the principles of his introductory reasoning.

[63] Committee rose & the House Adjourned.

---

*a* The word "the" is here inserted in the transcript.

[61] In the transcript the following footnote was inserted with reference mark after "observations":

"The speech introducing the plan, as above taken down & written out was seen by Mr. Hamilton, who approved its correctness, with one or two verbal changes, which were made as he suggested. The explanatory observations which did not immediately follow, were to have been furnished by Mr. H. who did not find leisure at the time to write them out, and they were not obtained.

"Judge Yates, in his notes, appears to have consolidated the explanatory with the introductory observations of Mr. Hamilton (under date of June 19th, a typographical error). It was in the former, Mr. Madison observed, that Mr. Hamilton, in speaking of popular governments, however modified, made the remark attributed to him by Judge Yates, that they were '*but pork still with a little change of sauce.*'"

[63] The word "the" is here inserted in the transcript.

TEUSDAY JUNE 19TH IN COMMITTEE OF [63] WHOLE ON THE PROPOSITIONS OF MR PATTERSON

The substitute offered yesterday by Mr Dickenson being rejected by a vote now taken on it; Con. N. Y. N. J. Del. ay.[64] Mas. Pa. V. N. C. S. C. Geo. no.[65] Mayd divided. Mr Patterson's plan was again at large before the Committee.

Mr MADISON. Much stress had [66] been laid by some gentlemen on the want of power in the Convention to propose any other than a *federal* plan. To what had been answered by others, he would only add, that neither of the characteristics attached to a *federal* plan would support this objection. One characteristic, was that in a *federal* Government, the power was exercised not on the people individually; [67] but on the people *collectively*, on the *States*. Yet in some instances as in piracies, captures &c. the existing Confederacy, and in many instances, the amendments to it proposed by Mr Patterson, must operate immediately on individuals. The other characteristic was that a *federal* Govt derived its appointments not immediately from the people, but from the States which they respectively composed. Here too were facts on the other side. In two of the States, Connect and Rh. Island, the delegates to Congs were chosen, not by the Legislatures, but by the people at large; and the plan of Mr P. intended no change in this particular.

It had been alledged [by Mr Patterson], that the Confederation having been formed by unanimous consent, could be dissolved by unanimous Consent only. Does this doctrine result from the nature of compacts? does it arise from any particular stipulation in the articles of Confederation? If we consider the federal union as analogous to the fundamental compact by which individuals compose one Society, and which must in its theoretic origin at least, have been the unanimous act of the component members, it can not be said that no dissolution of the compact can be effected without unanimous consent. A breach of the fundamental prin-

---

[63] The word "The" is here inserted in the transcript.
[64] The figure "4" is here inserted in the transcript.
[65] The figure "6" is here inserted in the transcript.
[66] The word "has" is substituted in the transcript for "had."
[67] The transcript italicizes the word "individually."

ciples of the compact by a part of the Society would certainly absolve the other part from their obligations to it. If the breach of *any* article by *any* of the parties, does not set the others at liberty, it is because, the contrary is *implied* in the compact itself, and particularly by that law of it, which gives an indifinite authority to the majority to bind the whole in all cases. This latter circumstance shews that we are not to consider the federal Union as analogous to the social compact of individuals: for if it were so, a Majority would have a right to bind the rest, and even to form a new Constitution for the whole, which the Gent? from N. Jersey would be among the last to admit. If we consider the federal Union as analogous not to the social compacts among individual men: but to the conventions among individual States. What is the doctrine resulting from these conventions? Clearly, according to the Expositors of the law of Nations, that a breach of any one article, by any one party, leaves all the other parties at liberty, to consider the whole convention as dissolved, unless they choose rather to compel the delinquent party to repair the breach. In some treaties indeed it is expressly stipulated that a violation of particular articles shall not have this consequence, and even that particular articles shall remain in force during war, which in general is [68] understood to dissolve all subsisting Treaties. But are there any exceptions of this sort to the Articles of confederation? So far from it that there is not even an express stipulation that force shall be used to compel an offending member of the Union to discharge its duty. He observed that the violations of the federal articles had been numerous & notorious. Among the most notorious was an act of N. Jersey herself; by which she *expressly refused* to comply with a constitutional requisition of Cong? and yielded no farther to the expostulations of their deputies, than barely to rescind her vote of refusal without passing any positive act of compliance. He did not wish to draw any rigid inferences from these observations. He thought it proper however that the true nature of the existing confederacy should be investigated, and he was not anxious to strengthen the foundations on which it now stands.

---

[68] The words "in general is" are transposed to read "is in general" in the transcript.

Proceeding to the consideration of Mr Patterson's plan, he stated the object of a proper plan to be twofold. 1.[69] to preserve the Union. 2.[69] to provide a Governmt that will remedy the evils felt by the States both in their united and individual capacities. Examine Mr P.s plan, & say whether it promises satisfaction in these respects.

1. Will it prevent those violations of the law of nations & of Treaties which if not prevented must involve us in the calamities of foreign wars? The tendency of the States to these violations has been manifested in sundry instances. The files of Congs contain complaints already, from almost every nation with which treaties have been formed. Hitherto indulgence has been shewn to us. This can not be the permanent disposition of foreign nations. A rupture with other powers is among the greatest of national calamities. It ought therefore to be effectually provided that no part of a nation shall have it in its power to bring them on the whole. The existing Confederacy does not sufficiently provide against this evil. The proposed amendment to it does not supply the omission. It leaves the will of the States as uncontrouled as ever.

2. Will it prevent encroachments on the federal authority? A tendency to such encroachments has been sufficiently exemplified, among ourselves, as well [70] in every other confederated republic antient and Modern. By the federal articles, transactions with the Indians appertain to Congs Yet in several instances, the States have entered into treaties & wars with them. In like manner no two or more States can form among themselves any treaties &c. without the consent of Congs Yet Virga & Maryd in one instance—Pena & N. Jersey in another, have entered into compacts, without previous application or subsequent apology. No State again can of right raise troops in time of peace without the like consent. Of all cases of the league, this seems to require the most scrupulous observance. Has not Massts, notwithstanding, the most powerful member of the Union, already raised a body of troops? Is she not now aug-

---

[69] The figures "1" and "2" are changed to "first" and "secondly" in the transcript.
[70] The word "as" is here inserted in the transcript.

menting them, without having even deigned to apprise Congˢ of Her intention? In fine—Have we not seen the public land dealt out to Conᵗ to bribe her acquiescence in the decree constitutionally awarded agˢᵗ her claim on the territory of Penᵃ? for no other possible motive can account for the policy of Congˢ in that measure?—If we recur to the examples of other confederacies, we shall find in all of them the same tendency of the parts to encroach on the authority of the whole. He then reviewed the Amphyctionic & Achæan confederacies among the antients, and the Helvetic, Germanic & Belgic among the moderns, tracing their analogy to the U. States—in the constitution and extent of their federal authorities—in the tendency of the particular members to usurp on these authorities; and to bring confusion & ruin on the whole.—He observed that the plan of Mr. Pat-son besides omitting a controul over the States as a general defence of the federal prerogatives was particularly defective in two of its provisions. 1.[71] Its ratification was not to be by the people at large, but by the *legislatures*. It could not therefore render the Acts of Congˢ in pursuance of their powers, even legally *paramount* to the Acts of the States. 2.[72] It gave to the federal Tribunal an appellate jurisdiction only—even in the criminal cases enumerated, The necessity of any such provision supposed a danger of undue acquittals[73] in the State tribunals. Of what avail cᵈ [74] an appellate tribunal be, after an acquittal? Besides in most if not all of the States, the Executives have by their respective *Constitutions* the right of pardˢ How could this be taken from them by a *legislative*[75] ratification only?

3. Will it prevent trespasses of the States on each other? Of these enough has been already seen. He instanced Acts of Virgˢ & Maryland which give[76] a preference to their own Citizens in cases where the Citizens of other States are entitled to equality of privileges by the Articles of Confederation. He considered

---

[71] The figure "1" is changed to "In the first place" in the transcript.
[72] The figure "2" is changed to "and in the second place" in the transcript.
[73] The transcript uses the word "acquittals" in the singular.
[74] The word "would" is substituted in the transcript for "cᵈ"
[75] The word "*legislative*" is not italicized in the transcript.
[76] The word "gave" is substituted in the transcript for "give."

the emissions of paper money & other kindred measures as also aggressions. The States relatively to one an other being each of them either Debtor or Creditor; The creditor States must suffer unjustly from every emission by the debtor States. We have seen retaliating acts on this subject which threatened danger not to the harmony only, but the tranquility of the Union. The plan of M! Paterson, not giving even a negative on the acts of the States, left them as much at liberty as ever to execute their unrighteous projects ag:st each other.

4. Will it secure the internal tranquility of the States themselves? The insurrections in Mass:ts admonished all the States of the danger to which they were exposed. Yet the plan of M! P. contained no provisions for supplying the defect of the Confederation on this point. According to the Republican theory indeed, Right & power being both vested in the majority, are held to be synonimous. According to fact & experience, a minority may in an appeal to force be an overmatch for the majority. 1.[77] If the minority happen to include all such as possess the skill & habits of military life, with such as possess the great pecuniary resources, one third may conquer the remaining two thirds. 2.[78] one third of those who participate in the choice of rulers may be rendered a majority by the accession of those whose poverty disqualifies them from a suffrage, & who for obvious reasons may [79] be more ready to join the standard of sedition than that of the [80] established Government. 3.[81] where slavery exists, the Republican Theory becomes still more fallacious.

5. Will it secure a good internal legislation & administration to the particular States? In developing the evils which vitiate the political system of the U. S. it is proper to take into view those which prevail within the States individually as well as those which affect them collectively: Since the former indirectly affect the whole; and there is great reason to believe that the pressure of them had a full share in the motives which produced the present

---

[77] The figure "1" is changed to "in the first place" in the transcript.
[78] The figure "2" is changed to "in the second place" in the transcript.
[79] The word "must" is substituted in the transcript for "may".
[80] The word "the" is omitted in the transcript.
[81] The gure "3" is changed to "and in the third place."

Convention. Under this head he enumerated and animadverted on 1.[82] the multiplicity of the laws passed by the several States. 2.[82] the mutability of their laws. 3.[82] the injustice of them. 4.[83] the impotence of them: observing that M<sup>r</sup> Patterson's plan contained no remedy for this dreadful class of evils, and could not therefore be received as an adequate provision for the exigences of the Community.

6. Will it secure the Union ag<sup>st</sup> the influence of foreign powers over its members. He pretended not to say that any such influence had yet been tried: but it was naturally to be expected that occasions would produce it. As lessons which claimed particular attention, he cited the intrigues practised among the Amphyctionic Confederates first by the Kings of Persia, and afterwards fatally by Philip of Macedon: among the Achæans, first by Macedon & afterwards no less fatally by Rome: among the Swiss by Austria, France & the lesser neighbouring powers: among the members of the Germanic Body by France, England, Spain & Russia—: and in the Belgic Republic, by all the great neighbouring powers. The plan of M<sup>r</sup> Patterson, not giving to the general Councils any negative on the will of the particular States, left the door open for the like pernicious machinations among ourselves.

7. He begged the smaller States which were most attached to M<sup>r</sup> Pattersons plan to consider the situation in which it would leave them. In the first place they would continue to bear the whole expence of maintaining their Delegates in Congress. It ought not to be said that if they were willing to bear this burden, no others had a right to complain. As far as it led the small States to forbear keeping up a representation, by which the public business was delayed, it was evidently a matter of common concern. An examination of the minutes of Congress would satisfy every one that the public business had been frequently delayed by this cause; and that the States most frequently unrepresented in Cong<sup>s</sup> were not the larger States. He reminded the convention of another consequence of leaving on a small State the burden of maintaining

---

[82] The figures "1," "2" and "3" are changed to "first," "secondly," and "thirdly" in the transcript.
[83] The figure "4" is changed to "and fourthly" in the transcript.

a Representation in Cong$^s$ During a considerable period of the War, one of the Representatives of Delaware, in whom alone before the signing of the Confederation the entire vote of that State and after that event one half of its vote, frequently resided, was a Citizen & Resident of Pen$^a$ and held an office in his own State incompatible with an appointment from it to Cong$^s$ During another period, the same State was represented by three delegates two of whom were citizens of Penn$^a$ and the third a Citizen of New Jersey. These expedients must have been intended to avoid the burden of supporting delegates from their own State. But whatever might have been y$^e$ cause, was not in effect the vote of one State doubled, and the influence of another increased by it? In the 2$^d$ place The coercion, on which the efficacy of the plan depends, can never be exerted but on themselves. The larger States will be impregnable, the smaller only can feel the vengeance of it. He illustrated the position by the history of the Amphyctionic Confederates: and the ban of the German Empire. It was the cobweb w$^ch$ could entangle the weak, but would be the sport of the strong.

8. He begged them to consider the situation in which they would remain in case their pertinacious adherence to an inadmissible plan, should prevent the adoption of any plan. The contemplation of such an event was painful; but it woud be prudent to submit to the task of examining it at a distance, that the means of escaping it might be the more readily embraced. Let the Union of the States be dissolved, and one of two consequences must happen. Either the States must remain individually independent & sovereign; or two or more Confederacies must be formed among them. In the first event would the small States be more secure ag$^st$ the ambition & power of their larger neighbours, than they would be under a general Government pervading with equal energy every part of the Empire, and having an equal interest in protecting every part ag$^st$ every other part? In the second, can the smaller expect that their larger neighbours would confederate with them on the principle of the present confederacy, which gives to each member, an equal suffrage; or that they would exact less severe concessions

from the smaller States, than are proposed in the scheme of M!̣ Randolph?

The great difficulty lies in the affair of Representation; and if this could be adjusted, all others would be surmountable. It was admitted by both the gentlemen from N. Jersey [M!̣ Brearly and M!̣ Patterson] that it would not be *just to allow Virg?* which was 16 times as large as Delaware an equal vote only. Their language was that it would not be *safe for Delaware* to allow Virg?̣ 16 times as many votes. The expedient proposed by them was that all the States should be thrown into one mass and a new partition be made into 13 equal parts. Would such a scheme be practicable? The dissimilarities existing in the rules of property, as well as in the manners, habits and prejudices of the [84] different States, amounted to a prohibition of the attempt. It had been found impossible for the power of one of the most absolute princes in Europe [K. of France] directed by the wisdom of one of the most enlightened and patriotic Ministers [M!̣ Neckar] that any age has produced to equalize in some points only the different usages & regulations of the different provinces. But admitting a general amalgamation and repartition of the States to be practicable, and the danger apprehended by the smaller States from a proportional representation to be real; would not a particular and voluntary coalition of these with their neighbours, be less inconvenient to the whole community, and equally effectual for their own safety. If N. Jersey or Delaware conceived that an advantage would accrue to them from an equalization of the States, in which case they would necessaryly form a junction with their neighbours, why might not this end be attained by leaving them at liberty by the Constitution to form such a junction whenever they pleased? And why should they wish to obtrude a like arrangement on all the States, when it was, to say the least, extremely difficult, would be obnoxious to many of the States, and when neither the inconveniency,[85] nor the benefit of the expedient to themselves, would be lessened, by confining it to themselves.—The prospect of many new States to the Westward was

---

[84] The word "the" is crossed out in the transcript.
[85] The word "inconveniency" is changed to "inconvenience" in the transcript.

another consideration of importance. If they should come into the Union at all, they would come when they contained but few inhabitants. If they sh? be entitled to vote according to their proportions of inhabitants, all would be right & safe. Let them have an equal vote, and a more objectionable minority than ever might give law to the whole.

On a question for postponing generally the 1$^{st}$ proposition of M$^r$ Patterson's plan, it was agreed to: N. Y. & N J. only being no—

On the question moved by M$^r$ King whether the Committee should rise & M$^r$ Randolphs propositions be re-reported without alteration, which was in fact a question whether M$^r$ R's should be adhered to as preferable to those of M$^r$ Patterson:

Mass$^{ts}$ ay. Con$^t$ ay. N. Y. no. N. J. no. P$^a$ ay. Del. no. M$^d$ div$^d$ V$^a$ ay. N. C. ay. S. C. ay. Geo. ay.[86]

Insert here from Printed Journal p. 13[87] copy of the Resol$^{ns}$ of M$^r$ R. as altered in the Com$^e$ and reported to the House[88]

[State of the resolutions submitted to the consideration of the House by the honorable Mr. Randolph, as altered, amended, and agreed to, in a Committee of the whole House.

1. Resolved    that it is the opinion of this Committee that a national government ought to be established consisting of a Supreme Legislative, Judiciary, and Executive.
2. Resolved.   that the national Legislature ought to consist of Two Branches.
3  Resolved    that the members of the first branch of the national Legislature ought to be elected by the People of the several States for the term of Three years. to receive fixed stipends, by which they may be compensated for the devotion of their time to public service to be paid out of the National-Treasury. to be ineligible to any Office established by a particular State or under the authority of the United-States

---

[86] In the transcript the vote reads: "Massachusetts, Connecticut, Pennsylvania, Virginia, North Carolina, South Carolina, Georgia, aye—7; New York, New Jersey, Delaware, no—3; Maryland divided."

[87] Found at page 134 instead of page 13, and here printed from the original manuscript deposited in the Department of State by President Washington.

[88] Madison's direction concerning Mr. Randolph's Resolutions and the Resolutions themselves are omitted in the transcript.

(except those peculiarly belonging to the functions of the first branch) during the term of service, and under the national government for the space of one year after it's expiration.

4  Resolved. that the members of the second Branch of the national Legislature ought to be chosen by the individual Legislatures. to be of the age of thirty years at least. to hold their offices for a term sufficient to ensure their independency, namely seven years. to receive fixed stipends, by which they may be compensated for the devotion of their time to public service—to be paid out of the National Treasury to be ineligible to any office established by a particular State, or under the authority of the United States (except those peculiarly belonging to the functions of the second branch) during the term of service, and under the national government, for the space of one year after it's expiration.

5. Resolved that each branch ought to possess the right of originating acts.

6. Resolved. that the national Legislature ought to be empowered to enjoy the legislative rights vested in Congress by the confederation—and moreover to legislate in all cases to which the separate States are incompetent: or in which the harmony of the United States may be interrupted by the exercise of individual legislation. to negative all laws passed by the several States contravening, in the opinion of the national Legislature, the articles of union, or any treaties subsisting under the authority of the union.

7. Resolved. that the right of suffrage in the first branch of the national Legislature ought not to be according to the rule established in the articles of confederation: but according to some equitable ratio of representation—namely, in proportion to the whole number of white and other free citizens and inhabitants of every

age, sex, and condition including those bound to servitude for a term of years, and three fifths of all other persons not comprehended in the foregoing description, except Indians, not paying taxes in each State.

8 Resolved. that the right of suffrage in the second branch of the national Legislature ought to be according to the rule established for the first.

9 Resolved. that a national Executive be instituted to consist of a single person. to be chosen by the National Legislature. for the term of seven years. with power to carry into execution the national Laws, to appoint to Offices in cases not otherwise provided for to be ineligible a second time, and to be removable on impeachment and conviction of mal practice or neglect of duty. to receive a fixed stipend, by which he may be compensated for the devotion of his time to public service to be paid out of the national Treasury.

10 Resolved. that the national executive shall have a right to negative any legislative act: which shall not be afterwards passed unless by two third parts of each branch of the national Legislature.

11 Resolved. that a national Judiciary be established to consist of One Supreme Tribunal. The Judges of which to be appointed by the second Branch of the National Legislature. to hold their offices during good behaviour to receive, punctually, at stated times, a fixed compensation for their services: in which no encrease or diminution shall be made so as to affect the persons actually in office at the time of such encrease or diminution

12 Resolved. That the national Legislature be empowered to appoint inferior Tribunals.

13 Resolved. that the jurisdiction of the national Judiciary shall extend to cases which respect the collection of the national revenue: impeachments of any national officers: and questions which involve the national peace and harmony.

14. Resolved. that provision ought to be made for the admission of States, lawfully arising within the

|     |           | limits of the United States, whether from a voluntary junction of government and territory, or otherwise, with the consent of a number of voices in the national Legislature less than the whole. |
| --- | --- | --- |
| 15. | Resolved. | that provision ought to be made for the continuance of Congress and their authorities until a given day after the reform of the articles of Union shall be adopted; and for the completion of all their engagements. |
| 16. | Resolved | that a republican constitution, and its existing laws, ought to be guaranteed to each State by the United States. |
| 17. | Resolved. | that provision ought to be made for the amendment of the articles of Union, whensoever it shall seem necessary. |
| 18 | Resolved. | that the Legislative, Executive, and Judiciary powers within the several States ought to be bound by oath to support the articles of Union. |
| 19 | Resolved. | that the amendments which shall be offered to the confederation by the Convention, ought at a proper time or times, after the approbation of Congress to be submitted to an assembly or assemblies of representatives, recommended by the several Legislatures, to be expressly chosen by the People to consider and decide thereon. |

(Of [89] M! Randolph's plan as reported from the Committee)[90]. the 1. propos: "that a Nat! Gov! ought to be established consisting &c." being taken up in the House.[91]

M! WILSON observed that by a Nat! Gov! he did not mean one that would swallow up the State Gov!s as seemed to be wished by some gentlemen. He was tenacious of the idea of preserving the latter. He thought, contrary to the opinion of [Col. Hamilton] that they might not only subsist but subsist on friendly terms with the former. They were absolutely necessary for certain purposes which the former could not reach. All large Governments must

---

[89] The word "of" is omitted in the transcript.
[90] The words "June 13 being before the house" are here inserted in the transcript.
[91] The words "in the House" are omitted in the transcript.

be subdivided into lesser jurisdictions. As Examples he mentioned Persia, Rome, and particularly the divisions & subdivisions of England by Alfred.

Col. HAMILTON coincided with the proposition as it stood in the Report. He had not been understood yesterday. By an abolition of the States, he meant that no boundary could be drawn between the National & State Legislatures; that the former must therefore have indefinite authority. If it were limited at all, the rivalship of the States would gradually subvert it. Even as Corporations the extent of some of them as Vª Massts &c. would be formidable. As *States*, he thought they ought to be abolished. But he admitted the necessity of leaving in them, subordinate jurisdictions. The examples of Persia & the Roman Empire, cited by [Mr Wilson] were he thought in favor of his doctrine: the great powers delegated to the Satraps & proconsuls, having frequently produced revolts, and schemes of independence.

Mr KING, wished as every thing depended on this proposition, that no objections might be improperly indulged agst the phraseology of it. He conceived that the import of the terms "States" "Sovereignty" "*national*" "federal," had been often used & applied in the discussions inaccurately & delusively. The States were not "Sovereigns" in the sense contended for by some. They did not possess the peculiar features of sovereignty, they could not make war, nor peace, nor alliances nor treaties. Considering them as political Beings, they were dumb, for they could not speak to any foreign Sovereign whatever. They were deaf, for they could not hear any propositions from such Sovereign. They had not even the organs or faculties of defence or offence, for they could not of themselves raise troops, or equip vessels, for war. On the other side, if the Union of the States comprizes the idea of a confederation, it comprizes that also of consolidation. A Union of the States is a Union of the men composing them, from whence a *national* character results to the whole. Congs can act alone without the States—they can act & their acts will be binding agst the Instructions of the States. If they declare war: war is de jure declared—captures made in pursuance of it are lawful—No acts of the States can vary the situation, or prevent the judicial consequences. If the States therefore retained some portion of their sovereignty, they had certainly divested themselves of essential portions of it. If they formed a confederacy in some respects— they formed a Nation in others—The Convention could clearly deliberate on & propose any alterations that Congs could have done under ye federal articles, and could not Congs propose by virtue of the last article, a change in any article whatever: and as well that relating to the equality of suffrage, as any other. He made these remarks to obviate some scruples which had been expressed. He doubted much the practicability of annihilating the States; but thought that much of their power ought to be taken from them.

Mr MARTIN, said he considered that the separation from G. B. placed the 13 States in a state of Nature towards each other; that they would have remained in that state till this time, but for the confederation; that they entered into the confederation on the footing of equality; that they met now to to amend it on the same footing; and that he could never accede to a plan that would introduce an inequality and lay 10 States at the mercy of Va Massts and Penna

Mr WILSON, could not admit the doctrine that when the Colonies became independent of G. Britain, they became independent also of each other. He read the declaration of Independence, observing thereon that the *United Colonies* were declared to be free & independent States; and inferring that they were independent, not *individually* but *Unitedly* and that they were confederated as they were independent, States.

Col. HAMILTON, assented to the doctrine of Mr Wilson. He denied the doctrine that the States were thrown into a State of Nature He was not yet prepared to admit the doctrine that the Confederacy, could be dissolved by partial infractions of it. He admitted that the States met now on an equal footing but could see no inference from that against concerting a change of the system in this particular. He took this occasion of observing for the purpose of appeasing the fears of the small States, that two circumstances would render them secure under a National Govt in which they might lose the equality of rank they now held: one was the local situation of the 3 largest States Virgª Masᵗˢ & Pª They were separated from each other by distance of place, and equally so, by all the pecularities which distinguish the interests of one State from those of another. No combination therefore could be dreaded. In the second place, as there was a gradation in the States from Vª the largest down to Delaware the smallest, it would always happen that ambitious combinations among a few States might & wᵈ be counteracted by defensive combinations of greater extent among the rest. No combination has been seen among [92] large Counties merely as such, agˢᵗ lesser Counties. The more close the Union of the States, and the more compleat the authority of the whole: the less opportunity will be allowed [93] the stronger States to injure the weaker.

Adjᵈ

---

WEDNESDAY JUNE 20. 1787.[94] IN CONVENTION

Mʳ William Blount from N. Carolina took his seat.

1ˢᵗ propos:[95] of the Report of Comᵉ of the whole [96] before the House.

Mʳ ELSEWORTH 2ᵈᵉᵈ by Mʳ GORHAM, moves to alter it so as to run "that the Government of the United States ought to consist of a supreme legislative, Executive and Judiciary." This alteration he said would drop the word *national*, and retain the proper title "the United States." He could not admit the doctrine that a breach of any of the federal articles could dissolve the whole. It would be highly dangerous not to consider the Confederation as still subsisting. He wished also the plan of the Convention to go forth as an amendment to [97] the articles of [98] Confederation, since under this idea the authority of the Legislatures could ratify it. If they are unwilling, the people will be so too. If the plan goes forth to the people for ratification several succeeding Conventions within the States would be unavoidable. He did

---

[92] The word "the" is here inserted in the transcript.
[93] The word "to" is here inserted in the transcript.
[94] The year "1787" is omitted in the transcript.
[95] The words "The first Resolution" are substituted in the transcript for "1ˢᵗ propos."
[96] The word "being" is here inserted in the transcript.
[97] The word "of" is substituted in the transcript for "to."
[98] The word "the" is here inserted in the transcript.

not like these conventions. They were better fitted to pull down than to build up Constitutions.

M.<sup>r</sup> RANDOLPH, did not object to the change of expression, but apprised the gentlemen [99] who wished for it that he did not admit it for the reasons assigned; particularly that of getting rid of a reference to the people for ratification. The motion of M.<sup>r</sup> Ellsew.<sup>th</sup> was acquiesced in nem: con:

The 2.<sup>d</sup> Resol: "that the national Legislature ought to consist of two branches"[1] taken up, the word "national" struck out as of course.

M.<sup>r</sup>. LANSING, observed that the true question here was, whether the Convention would adhere to or depart from the foundation of the present Confederacy; and moved instead of the 2.<sup>d</sup> Resolution, "that the powers of Legislation be vested in the U. States in Congress." He had already assigned two reasons ag.<sup>st</sup> such an innovation as was proposed: 1[2] the want of competent powers in the Convention.—2.[2] the state of the public mind. It had been observed by [M.<sup>r</sup> Madison] in discussing the first point, that in two States the Delegates to Cong.<sup>s</sup> were chosen by the people. Notwithstanding the first appearance of this remark, it had in fact no weight, as the Delegates however chosen, did not represent the people merely as so many individuals; but as forming a Sovereign State. [M.<sup>r</sup> Randolph] put it, he said, on its true footing namely that the public safety superseded the scruple arising from the review of our powers. But in order to feel the force of this consideration, the same impression must be had of the public danger. He had not himself the same impression, and could not therefore dismiss his scruple. [M.<sup>r</sup> Wilson] contended that as the Convention were only to recommend, they might recommend what they pleased. He differed much from him. Any act whatever of so respectable a body must have a great effect, and if it does not succeed, will be a source of great dissentions. He admitted that there was no certain criterion of the public mind on the subject. He therefore recurred to the evidence of it given by the opposition in the States to the scheme of an Impost. It could not be expected that those

---

[99] The word "gentlemen" is used in the singular in the transcript.
[1] The word "being" is here inserted in the transcript.
[2] The figures "1" and "2" are changed to "first" and "secondly" in the transcript.

possessing Sovereignty could ever voluntarily part with it. It was not to be expected from any one State, much less from thirteen. He proceeded to make some observations on the plan itself and the argum$^{ts}$ urged in support of it. The point of Representation could receive no elucidation from the case of England. The corruption of the boroughs did not proceed from their comparative smallness: but from the actual fewness of the inhabitants, some of them not having more than one or two. A great inequality existed in the Counties of England. Yet the like complaint of peculiar corruption in the small ones had not been made. It had been said that Congress represent the State prejudices: will not any other body whether chosen by the Legislatures or people of the States, also represent their prejudices? It had been asserted by his colleague [Col. Hamilton] that there was no coincidence of interests among the large States that ought to excite fears of oppression in the smaller. If it were true that such a uniformity of interests existed among the States, there was equal safety for all of them, whether the representation remained as heretofore, or were proportioned as now proposed. It is proposed that the Gen$^l$ Legislature shall have a negative on the laws of the States. Is it conceivable that there will be leisure for such a task? there will on the most moderate calculation, be as many Acts sent up from the States as there are days in the year. Will the members of the general Legislature be competent Judges? Will a gentleman from Georgia be a Judge of the expediency of a law which is to operate in N. Hamshire. Such a Negative would be more injurious than that of Great Britain heretofore was. It is said that the National Gov$^t$ must have the influence arising from the grant of offices and honors. In order to render such a Government effectual be believed such an influence to be necessary. But if the States will not agree to it, it is in vain, worse than in vain to make the proposition. If this influence is to be attained, the States must be entirely abolished. Will any one say this would ever be agreed to? He doubted whether any Gen$^l$ Government equally beneficial to all can be attained. That now under consideration he is sure, must be utterly unattainable. He had another objection. The system was too novel & complex. No man could foresee what its operation will be either with respect to the Genl Govt or the State Govts One or other it has been surmised must absorb the whole.

Col. MASON, did not expect this point would have been reagitated. The essential differences between the two plans, had been clearly stated. The principal objections agst that of Mr R. were the *want of power* & the *want of practicability*. There can be no weight in the first as the fiat is not to be *here*, but in the people. He thought with his colleague Mr R. that there were besides certain crisises, in which all the ordinary cautions yielded to public necessity. He gave as an example, the eventual Treaty with G. B. in forming which the Comrs. of the U. S. had boldly disregarded the improvident shackles of Congs had given to their Country an honorable & happy peace, and instead of being censured for the transgression of their powers, had raised to themselves a monument more durable than brass. The *impracticability* of gaining the public concurrence he thought was still more groundless. [Mr Lansing] had cited the attempts of Congress to gain an enlargement of their powers, and had inferred from the miscarriage of these attempts, the hopelessness of the plan which he [Mr L] opposed. He thought a very different inference ought to have been drawn; viz that the plan which [Mr L] espoused, and which proposed to augment the powers of Congress, never could be expected to succeed. He meant not to throw any reflections on Congs as a body, much less on any particular members of it. He meant however to speak his sentiments without reserve on this subject; it was a privilege of Age, and perhaps the only compensation which nature had given for the privation of so many other enjoyments: and he should not scruple to exercise it freely. Is it to be thought that the people of America, so watchful over their interests; so jealous of their liberties, will give up their all, will surrender both the sword and the purse, to the same body, and that too not chosen immediately by themselves? They never will. They never ought. Will they trust such a body, with the regulation of their trade, with the regulation of their taxes; with all the other great powers, which are in contemplation? Will they give unbounded confidence to a secret Journal—to the intrigues—to the factions which in the nature of things appertain to such an Assembly? If any man doubts the existence of these characters of Congress, let him consult their Journals for the years 78, 79, & 80.—It will be said, that if the people are averse to parting with power, why is it hoped that they will part with it to a National Legislature. The proper answer is that in this case they do not part with power: they only transfer it from one sett of immediate Representatives to another sett.— Much has been said of the unsettled state of the mind of the people, he believed the mind of the people of America, as elsewhere, was unsettled as to some points; but settled as to others. In two points he was sure it was well settled. 1.[3] in an attachment to Republican Government. 2.[3] in an attachment to more than one branch in the Legislature. Their constitutions accord so generally in both these circumstances, that they seem almost to have been preconcerted. This must either have been a miracle, or have resulted from the genius of the people. The only exceptions to the establishm.[t] of two branches in the Legislatures are the State of P.[a] & Cong.[s] and the latter the only single one not chosen by the people themselves. What has been the consequence? The people have been constantly averse to giving that Body further powers—It was acknowledged by [M.[r] Patterson] that his plan could not be enforced without military coertion. Does he consider the force of this concession. The most jarring elements of Nature; fire & water themselves are not more incompatible that [4] such a mixture of civil liberty and military execution. Will the militia march from one State to [5] another, in order to collect the arrears of taxes from the delinquent members of the Republic? Will they maintain an army for this purpose? Will not the Citizens of the invaded State assist one another till they rise as one Man, and shake off the Union altogether. Rebellion is the only case, in which the military force of the State can be properly exerted ag.[st] its Citizens. In one point of view he was struck with horror at the prospect of recurring to this expedient. To punish the non-payment of taxes with death, was a severity not yet adopted by despotism itself: yet this unexampled cruelty would be mercy compared to a military collection of revenue, in which the bayonet could make no dis-

---

[3] The figures "1" and "2" are changed to "first" and "secondly" in the transcript.
[4] The word "than" is substituted in the transcript for "that."
[5] The word "into" is substituted in the transcript for "in."

crimination between the innocent and the guilty. He took this occasion to repeat, that notwithstanding his solicitude to establish a national Government, he never would agree to abolish the State Gov^ts or render them absolutely insignificant. They were as necessary as the Gen! Gov? and he would be equally careful to preserve them. He was aware of the difficulty of drawing the line between them, but hoped it was not insurmountable. The Convention, tho' comprising so many distinguished characters, could not be expected to make a faultless Gov? And he would prefer trusting to posterity the amendment of its defects, rather than to push the experiment too far.

M^r LUTHER MARTIN agreed with [Col Mason] as to the importance of the State Gov^ts he would support them at the expence of the Gen! Gov? which was instituted for the purpose of that support. He saw no necessity for two branches, and if it existed Congress might be organized into two. He considered Cong^s as representing the people, being chosen by the Legislatures who were chosen by the people. At any rate, Congress represented the Legislatures; and it was the Legislatures not the people who refused to enlarge their powers. Nor could the rule of voting have been the ground of objection, otherwise ten of the States must always have been ready, to place further confidence in Cong? The causes of repugnance must therefore be looked for elsewhere.—At the separation from the British Empire, the people of America preferred the establishment of themselves into thirteen separate sovereignties instead of incorporating themselves into one: to these they look up for the security of their lives, liberties & properties: to these they must look up. The federal Gov? they formed, to defend the whole ag^st foreign nations, in case of war, and to defend the lesser States ag^st the ambition of the larger: they are afraid of granting powers [6] unnecessarily, lest they should defeat the original end of the Union; lest the powers should prove dangerous to the sovereignties of the particular States which the Union was meant to support; and expose the lesser to being swallowed up by the larger. He conceived also that the people of the States having already vested their powers in their respective Legis-

---

[6] The transcript uses the word "powers" in the singular.

latures, could not resume them without a dissolution of their Governments. He was ag$^{st}$ Conventions in the States: was not ag$^{st}$ assisting States ag$^{st}$ rebellious subjects; thought the *federal* plan of M$^r$ Patterson did not require coercion more than the *National one*, as the latter must depend for the deficiency of its revenues on requisitions & quotas, and that a national Judiciary extended into the States would be ineffectual, and would be viewed with a jealousy inconsistent with its usefulness.

M$^r$ SHERMAN 2$^{ded}$ & supported M$^r$ Lansings motion. He admitted two branches to be necessary in the State Legislatures, but saw no necessity for them in a Confederacy of States. The examples were all, of a single Council. Cong$^s$ carried us thro' the war, and perhaps as well as any Gov$^t$ could have done. The complaints at present are not that the views of Cong$^s$ are unwise or unfaithful; but that their powers are insufficient for the execution of their views. The national debt & the want of power somewhere to draw forth the National resources, are the great matters that press. All the States were sensible of the defect of power in Cong$^s$ He thought much might be said in apology for the failure of the State Legislatures to comply with the confederation. They were afraid of bearing too hard on the people, by accumulating taxes; no *constitutional* rule had been or could be observed in the quotas—the accounts also were unsettled & every State supposed itself in advance, rather than in arrears. For want of a general system, taxes to a due amount had not been drawn from trade which was the most convenient resource. As almost all the States had agreed to the recommendation of Cong$^s$ on the subject of an impost, it appeared clearly that they were willing to trust Cong$^s$ with power to draw revenue from Trade. There is no weight therefore in the argument drawn from a distrust of Cong$^s$ for money matters being the most important of all, if the people will trust them with power as to them, they will trust them with any other necessary powers. Cong$^s$ indeed by the confederation have in fact the right of saying how much the people shall pay, and to what purpose it shall be applied: and this right was granted to them in the expectation that it would in all cases have its effect. If another branch were to be added to Cong$^s$ to be chosen by the people, it would serve to embarrass. The people would not much interest themselves in the elections, a few designing men in the large districts would carry their points, and the people would have no more confidence in their new representatives than in Cong$^s$ He saw no reason why the State Legislatures should be unfriendly as had been suggested, to Cong$^s$ If they appoint Cong$^s$ and approve of their measures, they would be rather favorable and partial to them. The disparity of the States in point of size he perceived was the main difficulty. But the large States had not yet suffered from the equality of votes enjoyed by the small ones. In all great and general points, the interests of all the States were the same. The State of Virg$^a$ notwithstanding the equality of votes, ratified the Confederation without, or [7] even proposing, any alteration. Mass$^{ts}$ also ratified without any material difficulty &c. In none of the ratifications is the want of two branches noticed or complained of. To consolidate the States as some had proposed would dissolve our Treaties with foreign Nations, which had been formed with us, as *confederated* States. He did not however suppose that the creation of two branches in the Legislature would have such an effect. If the difficulty on the subject of representation can not be otherwise got over, he would agree to have two branches, and a proportional representation in one of them; provided each State had an equal voice in the other. This was necessary to secure the rights of the lesser States; otherwise three or four of the large States would rule the others as they please. Each State like each individual had its peculiar habits usages and manners, which constituted its happiness. It would not therefore give to others a power over this happiness, any more than an individual would do, when he could avoid it.

M$^r$ WILSON, urged the necessity of two branches; observed that if a proper model were [8] not to be found in other Confederacies it was not to be wondered at. The number of them was small & the duration of some at least short. The Amphyctionic & Achæan were formed in the infancy of political Science; and appear by their History & fate, to have contained radical defects. The Swiss & Belgic Confederacies were held together not by any vital principle

---

[7] The word "or" is stricken out in the transcript.
[8] The word "was" is substituted in the transcript for "were."

of energy but by the incumbent pressure of formidable neighbouring nations: The German owed its continuance to the influence of the H. of Austria. He appealed to our own experience for the defects of our Confederacy. He had been 6 years in [9] the 12 since the commencement of the Revolution, a member of Congress, and had felt all its weaknesses. He appealed to the recollection of others whether on many important occasions, the public interest had not been obstructed by the small members of the Union. The success of the Revolution was owing to other causes, than the Constitution of Congress. In many instances it went on even ag:t the difficulties arising from Cong: themselves. He admitted that the large States did accede as had been stated, to the Confederation in its present form. But it was the effect of necessity not of choice. There are other instances of their yielding from the same motive to the unreasonable measures of the small States. The situation of things is now a little altered. He insisted that a jealousy would exist between the State Legislatures & the General Legislature: observing that the members of the former would have views & feelings very distinct in this respect from their constituents. A private Citizen of a State is indifferent whether power be exercised by the Gen: or State Legislatures, provided it be exercised most for his happiness. His representative has an interest in its being exercised by the body to which he belongs. He will therefore view the National Legisl: with the eye of a jealous rival. He observed that the addresses of Cong: to the people at large, had always been better received & produced greater effect, than those made to the Legislatures.

On the question for postponing in order to take up M: Lansings proposition "to vest the powers of Legislation in Cong:"

Mass: no. Con: ay. N. Y. ay. N. J. ay. P:a no. Del. ay. M:d div:d V:a no. N. C. no. S. C. no. Geo. no.[10]

On motion of the Deputies from Delaware, the question on the 2:d Resolution in the Report from the Committee of the whole was postponed till tomorrow.

Adj:d

---

[9] The word "of" is substituted in the transcript for "in."
[10] In the transcript the vote reads: "Connecticut, New York, New Jersey, Delaware, aye—4; Massachusetts, Pennsylvania, Virginia, North Carolina, South Carolina, Georgia, no—6; Maryland divided."

## Thursday June 21. in Convention

Mr Jonathan Dayton from N. Jersey took his seat.*

[12] Docr JOHNSON. On a comparison of the two plans which had been proposed from Virginia & N. Jersey, it appeared that the peculiarity which characterized the latter was its being calculated to preserve the individuality of the States. The plan from Va did not profess to destroy this individuality altogether, but was charged with such a tendency. One Gentleman alone (Col. Hamilton) in his animadversions on the plan of N. Jersey, boldly and decisively contended for an abolition of the State Govts. Mr Wilson & the gentlemen from Virga who also were adversaries of the plan of N. Jersey held a different language. They wished to leave the States in possession of a considerable, tho' a subordinate jurisdiction. They had not yet however shewn how this cd consist with, or be secured agst the general sovereignty & jurisdiction, which they proposed to give to the national Government. If this could be shewn in such a manner as to satisfy the patrons of the N. Jersey propositions, that the individuality of the States would not be endangered, many of their objections would no doubt be removed. If this could not be shewn their objections would have their full force. He wished it therefore to be well considered whether in case the States, as was proposed, shd retain some portion of sovereignty at least, this portion could be preserved, without allowing them to participate effectually in the Genl Govt, without giving them each a distinct and equal vote for the purpose of defending themselves in the general Councils.

Mr WILSON's respect for Docr Johnson, added to the importance of the subject led him to attempt, unprepared as he was, to solve the difficulty which had been started. It was asked how the Genl Govt and individuality of the particular States could be reconciled to each other; and how the latter could be secured agst the former? Might it not, on the other side be asked how the former was to be

---

*From June 21 to July 18 inclusive not copied by Mr Eppes.[11]

[11] This footnote is omitted in the transcript. It refers to a copy of Madison's journal made by John W. Eppes, Jefferson's son-in-law, for Jefferson's use some time between 1799 and 1810. "*The Writings of James Madison*, Hunt, Editor, Vol. VI (1906), 329, n; *Documentary History of the Constitution*, Vol. V (1905), 294–296.

[12] The transcript here inserts the following: "The second Resolution in the Report from the Committee of the Whole, being under consideration."

secured ag:t the latter? It was generally admitted that a jealousy & rivalship would be felt between the Gen! & particular Gov:ts As the plan now stood, tho' indeed contrary to his opinion, one branch of the Gen! Gov: (the Senate or second branch) was to be appointed by the State Legislatures. The State Legislatures, therefore, by this participation in the Gen! Gov: would have an opportunity of defending their rights. Ought not a reciprocal opportunity to be given to the Gen! Gov: of defending itself by having an appointment of some one constituent branch of the State Gov:ts If a security be necessary on one side, it w:d seem reasonable to demand it on the other. But taking the matter in a more general view, he saw no danger to the States from the Gen! Gov: In case a combination should be made by the large ones it w:d produce a general alarm among the rest; and the project w:d be frustrated. But there was no temptation to such a project. The States having in general a similar interest, in case of any proposition [13] in the National Legislature to encroach on the State Legislatures, he conceived a general alarm w:d take place in the National Legislature itself, that it would communicate itself to the State Legislatures, and w:d finally spread among the people at large. The Gen! Gov: will be as ready to preserve the rights of the States as the latter are to preserve the rights of individuals; all the members of the former, having a common interest, as representatives of all the people of the latter, to leave the State Gov:ts in possession of what the people wish them to retain. He could not discover, therefore any danger whatever on the side from which it had been [14] apprehended. On the contrary, he conceived that in spite of every precaution the general Gov: would be in perpetual danger of encroachments from the State Gov:ts

M: MADISON was of the opinion [15] that there was 1. less danger of encroachment from the Gen! Gov: than from the State Gov:ts 2.[16] that the mischief from encroachments would be less fatal if made by the former, than if made by the latter. 1. All the examples

---

[13] The transcript uses the word "proposition" in the plural.
[14] The word "was" is substituted in the transcript for "had been."
[15] The phrase "in the first place" is here inserted in the transcript and the figure "1" is omitted.
[16] The figure "2" is changed to "and in the second place" in the transcript.

of other confederacies prove the greater tendency in such systems to anarchy than to tyranny; to a disobedience of the members than to [17] usurpations of the federal head. Our own experience had fully illustrated this tendency.—But it will be said that the proposed change in the principles & form of the Union will vary the tendency; that the Genl Govt will have real & greater powers, and will be derived in one branch at least from the people, not from the Govts of the States. To give full force to this objection, let it be supposed for a moment that indefinite power should be given to the Genl Legislature, and the States reduced to corporations dependent on the Genl Legislature; Why shd it follow that the Genl Govt wd take from the States any branch of their power as far as its operation was beneficial, and its continuance desireable to the people? In some of the States, particularly in Connecticut, all the Townships are incorporated, and have a certain limited jurisdiction. Have the Representatives of the people of the Townships in the Legislature of the State ever endeavored to despoil the Townships of any part of their local authority? As far as this local authority is convenient to the people they are attached to it; and their representatives chosen by & amenable to them naturally respect their attachment to this, as much as their attachment to any other right or interest. The relation of a General Govt to State Govts is parallel. 2. Guards were more necessary agst encroachments of the State Govts on the Genl Govt than of the latter on the former. The great objection made agst an abolition of the State Govts was that the Genl Govt could not extend its care to all the minute objects which fall under the cognizance of the local jurisdictions. The objection as stated lay not agst the probable abuse of the general power, but agst the imperfect use that could be made of it throughout so great an extent of country, and over so great a variety of objects. As far as as its operation would be practicable it could not in this view be improper; as far as it would be impracticable, the conveniency[18] of the Genl Govt itself would concur with that of the people in the maintenance of subordinate Governments. Were it practica-

---

[17] The word "to" is omitted in the transcript.
[18] The word "conveniency" is changed to "convenience" in the transcript.

ble for the Genl Govt to extend its care to every requisite object without the cooperation of the State Govts the people would not be less free as members of one great Republic than as members of thirteen small ones. A Citizen of Delaware was not more free than a Citizen of Virginia: nor would either be more free than a Citizen of America. Supposing therefore a tendency in the Genl Government to absorb the State Govts no fatal [19] consequence could result. Taking the reverse of [20] the supposition, that a tendency should be left in the State Govts towards an independence on the General Govt and the gloomy consequences need not be pointed out. The imagination of them, must have suggested to the States the experiment we are now making to prevent the calamity, and must have formed the chief motive with those present to undertake the arduous task.

On the question for resolving "that the Legislature ought to consist of two Branches"

Mass. ay. Cont ay. N. Y. no. N. Jersey no Pa ay. Del. no. Md divd Va ay. N. C. ay. S. C. ay. Geo. ay.[21]

The *third* resolution of the Report [22] taken into consideration.

Genl PINKNEY moved "that the 1st branch, instead of being elected by the people, shd be elected in such manner as the Legislature of each State should direct." He urged 1.[23] that this liberty would give more satisfaction, as the Legislatures could then accomodate the mode to the conveniency [24] & opinions of the people. 2.[23] that it would avoid the undue influence of large Counties which would prevail if the elections were to be made in districts as must be the mode intended by the Report of the Committee. 3.[23] that otherwise disputed elections must be referred to the General Legislature which would be attended with intolerable expence and trouble to the distant parts of the republic.

Mr L. MARTIN seconded the Motion.

Col. HAMILTON considered the motion as intended manifestly to transfer the election from the people to the State Legislatures,

---

[19] The transcript italicizes the word "fatal."

[20] The word "as" is substituted in the transcript for "of"

[21] In the transcript the vote reads: "Massachusetts, Connecticut, Pennsylvania, Virginia, North Carolina, South Carolina, Georgia, aye—7; New York, New Jersey, Delaware, no—3; Maryland, divided."

[22] The word "being" is here inserted in the transcript.

[23] The figures "1," "2" and "3" are changed to "first," "secondly" and "thirdly" in the transcript.

[24] The word "conveniency" is changed to "convenience" in the transcript.

which would essentially vitiate the plan. It would increase that State influence which could not be too watchfully guarded ag$^{st}$ All too must admit the possibility, in case the Gen$^l$ Gov$^t$ sh$^d$ maintain itself, that the State Gov$^{ts}$ might gradually dwindle into nothing. The system therefore sh$^d$ not be engrafted on what might possibly fail.

M$^r$ MASON urged the necessity of retaining the election by the people. Whatever inconveniency [25] may attend the democratic principle, it must actuate one part of the Gov$^t$ It is the only security for the rights of the people.

M$^r$ SHERMAN, would like an election by the Legislatures best, but is content with [26] plan as it stands.

M$^r$ RUTLIDGE could not admit the solidity of the distinction between a mediate & immediate election by the people. It was the same thing to act by oneself, and to act by another. An election by the Legislature would be more refined than an election immediately by the people: and would be more likely to correspond with the sense of the whole community. If this Convention had been chosen by the people in districts it is not to be supposed that such proper characters would have been preferred. The Delegates to Cong$^s$ he thought had also been fitter men than would have been appointed by the people at large.

M$^r$ WILSON considered the election of the 1$^{st}$ branch by the people not only as the corner Stone, but as the foundation of the fabric: and that the difference between a mediate & immediate election was immense. The difference was particularly worthy of notice in this respect: that the Legislatures are actuated not merely by the sentiment of the people; but have an official sentiment opposed to that of the Gen$^l$ Gov$^t$ and perhaps to that of the people themselves.

M$^r$ KING enlarged on the same distinction. He supposed the Legislatures w$^d$ constantly choose men subservient to their own views as contrasted to the general interest; and that they might even devise modes of election that w$^d$ be subversive of the end in view. He remarked several instances in which the views of a

---

[25] The word "inconveniency" is changed to "inconvenience" in the transcript.
[26] The word "the" is here inserted in the transcript.

State might be at variance with those of the Gen! Gov!: and mentioned particularly a competition between the National & State debts, for the most certain & productive funds.

Gen! PINKNEY was for making the State Gov!s a part of the General System. If they were to be abolished, or lose their agency, S. Carolina & other States would have but a small share of the benefits of Gov!

On the question for Gen! Pinkney motion to substitute election of [27] 1st branch in such mode as the Legislatures should appoint, in stead of its being elected by the people."

Mass!s no. Con! ay. N. Y. no. N. J. ay. P? no. Del. ay. M? div? V? no. N. C. no. S. C. ay Geo. no.[28]

General PINKNEY then moved that the 1st branch be elected *by the people* in such mode as the Legislatures should direct; but waved it on its being hinted that such a provision might be more properly tried in the detail of the plan.

On the question for y? election of the 1st branch by the *people*."

Mass!s ay. Con! ay. N. Y. ay. N. J. no. P? ay. Del. ay. M? div? V? ay. N. C. ay. S. C. ay Geo. ay.[29]

[27] Election of the 1st branch "for the term of three years,"[30] considered

M! RANDOLPH moved to strike out, "three years" and insert "two years"—he was sensible that annual elections were a source of great mischiefs in the States, yet it was the want of such checks ag!t the popular intemperence as were now proposed, that rendered them so mischievous. He would have preferred annual to biennial, but for the extent of the U. S. and the inconveniency [31] which would result from them to the representatives of the extreme parts of the Empire. The people were attached to frequency of elections. All the Constitutions of the States except that of S. Carolina, had established annual elections.

M! DICKENSON. The idea of annual elections was borrowed from the antient usage of England, a country much less extensive than

---

[27] The word "the" is here inserted in the transcript.

[28] In the transcript the vote reads: "Connecticut, New Jersey, Delaware, South Carolina, aye—4; Massachusetts, New York, Pennsylvania, Virginia, North Carolina, Georgia, no—6; Maryland, divided."

[29] In the transcript the vote reads: "Massachusetts, Connecticut, New York, Pennsylvania, Delaware, Virginia, North Carolina, South Carolina, Georgia, aye—9; New Jersey, no—1; Maryland, divided."

[30] The word "being" is here inserted in the transcript.

[31] The word "inconveniency" is changed to "inconvenience" in the transcript.

ours. He supposed biennial would be inconvenient. He preferred triennial: and in order to prevent the inconveniency [31] of an entire change of the whole number at the same moment, suggested a rotation, by an annual election of one third.

M! ELSEWORTH was opposed to three years, supposing that even one year was preferable to two years. The people were fond of frequent elections and might be safely indulged in one branch of the Legislature. He moved for 1 year.

M! STRONG seconded & supported the motion.

M! WILSON being for making the 1st branch an effectual representation of the people at large, preferred an annual election of it. This frequency was most familiar & pleasing to the people. It would be not [32] more inconvenient to them, than triennial elections, as the people in all the States have annual meetings with which the election of the National representatives might be made to co-incide. He did not conceive that it would be necessary for the Nat! Legisl: to sit constantly; perhaps not half—perhaps not one fourth of the year.

M! MADISON was persuaded that annual elections would be extremely inconvenient and apprehensive that biennial would be too much so: he did not mean inconvenient to the electors; but to the representatives. They would have to travel seven or eight hundred miles from the distant parts of the Union; and would probably not be allowed even a reimbursement of their expences. Besides, none of those who wished to be re-elected would remain at the seat of Governm!; confiding that their absence would not affect them. The members of Cong⁹ had done this with few instances of disappointment. But as the choice was here to be made by the people themselves who would be much less complaisant to individuals, and much more susceptible of impressions from the presence of a Rival candidate, it must be supposed that the members from the most distant States would travel backwards & forwards at least as often as the elections should be repeated. Much was to be said also on the time requisite for new members who would always form a large proportion, to acquire that knowledge of the affairs of the States in general without which their trust could not be usefully discharged.

---

[32] The words "be not" are transposed to read "not be" in the transcript.
[31] The word "inconveniency" is changed to "inconvenience" in the transcript.

Mr SHERMAN preferred annual elections, but would be content with biennial. He thought the Representatives ought to return home and mix with the people. By remaining at the seat of Govt they would acquire the habits of the place which might differ from those of their Constituents.

Col. MASON observed that the States being differently situated such a rule ought to be formed as would put them as nearly as possible on a level. If elections were annual the middle States would have a great advantage over the extreme ones. He wished them to be biennial; and the rather as in that case they would coincide with the periodical elections of S. Carolina as well of the other States.

Col. HAMILTON urged the necessity of 3 years. There ought to be neither too much nor too little dependence, on the popular sentiments. The checks in the other branches of Governt would be but feeble, and would need every auxiliary principle that could be interwoven. The British House of Commons were elected septennially, yet the democratic spirit of ye Constitution had not ceased. Frequency of elections tended to make the people listless to them; and to facilitate the success of little cabals. This evil was complained of in all the States. In Virga it had been lately found necessary to force the attendance & voting of the people by severe regulations.

On the question for striking out "three years"

Massts ay. Cont ay. N. Y. no. N. J. divd Pa ay. Del. no. Md no. Va ay. N. C. ay. S. C. ay. Geo. ay.[33]

The motion for "two years" was then inserted nem. con.

Adjd

---

FRIDAY JUNE 22. IN CONVENTION

The clause in Resol. 3.[34] "to receive fixed stipends to be paid out of the Nationl Treasury"[35] considered.

Mr ELSEWORTH, moved to substitute payment by the States out of their own Treasurys: observing that the manners of differ-

---

[33] In the transcript the vote reads: "Massachusetts, Connecticut, Pennsylvania, Virginia, North Carolina, South Carolina, Georgia, aye—7; New York, Delaware, Maryland, no—3; New Jersey, divided."
[34] The words "the third Resolution" are substituted in the transcript for "Resol. 3."
[35] The word "being" is here inserted in the transcript.

ent States were very different in the Stile of living and in the profits accruing from the exercise of like talents. What would be deemed therefore a reasonable compensation in some States, in others would be very unpopular, and might impede the system of which it made a part.

Mʳ WILLIAMSON favored the idea. He reminded the House of the prospect of new States to the Westward. They would be [36] poor—would pay little into the common Treasury—and would have a different interest from the old States. He did not think therefore that the latter ought to pay the expences of men who would be employed in thwarting their measures & interests.

Mʳ GHORUM, wished not to refer the matter to the State Legislatures who were always paring down salaries in such a manner as to keep out of offices men most capable of executing the functions of them. He thought also it would be wrong to fix the compensations [37] by the constitutions,[37] because we could not venture to make it as liberal as it ought to be without exciting an enmity agˢᵗ the whole plan. Let the Natiˡ Legisl: provide for their own wages from time to time; as the State Legislatures do. He had not seen this part of their power abused, nor did he apprehend an abuse of it.

Mʳ RANDOLPH [38] feared we were going too far, in consulting popular prejudices. Whatever respect might be due to them, in lesser matters, or in cases where they formed the permanent character of the people, he thought it neither incumbent on nor honorable for the Convention, to sacrifice right & justice to that consideration. If the States were to pay the members of the Natˡ Legislature, a dependence would be created that would vitiate the whole System. The whole nation has an interest in the attendance & services of the members. The Nationˡ Treasury therefore is the proper fund for supporting them.

Mʳ KING, urged the danger of creating a dependence on the States by leavᵍ to them the payment of the members of the Natˡ Legislature. He supposed it wᵈ be best to be explicit as to the compensation to be allowed. A reserve on that point, or a reference to

---

[6] The word "too" is here inserted in the transcript.
[37] The transcript uses the words "conpensations" and "constitutions" in the singular
[38] The words "said he" are here inserted in the transcript.

the Nat! Legislature of the quantum, would excite greater opposition than any sum that would be actually necessary or proper.

M! SHERMAN contended for referring both the quantum and the payment of it to the State Legislatures.

M! WILSON was ag!ᵗ *fixing* the compensation as circumstances would change and call for a change of the amount. He thought it of great moment that the members of the Nat! Gov! should be left as independent as possible of the State Gov!ˢ in all respects.

M! MADISON concurred in the necessity of preserving the compensations for the Nat! Gov! independent on the State Gov!ˢ but at the same time approved of *fixing* them by the Constitution, which might be done by taking a standard which w! not vary with circumstances. He disliked particularly the policy suggested by M! Wiliamson of leaving the members from the poor States beyond the Mountains, to the precarious & parsimonious support of their constituents. If the Western States hereafter arising should be admitted into the Union, they ought to be considered as equals & as brethren. If their representatives were to be associated in the Common Councils, it was of common concern that such provisions should be made as would invite the most capable and respectable characters into the service.

M! HAMILTON apprehended inconveniency [39] from *fixing* the wages. He was strenuous ag!ᵗ making the National Council dependent on the Legislative rewards of the States. Those who pay are the masters of those who are paid. Payment by the States would be unequal as the distant States would have to pay for the same term of attendance and more days in travelling to & from the seat of the [40] Gov! He expatiated emphatically on the difference between the feelings & views of the *people*—& the *Governments* of the States arising from the personal interest & official inducements which must render the latter unfriendly to the Gen! Gov!

M! WILSON moved that the Salaries of the 1!ᵗ branch "*be ascertained by the National Legislature,*" [41] and be paid out of the Nat! Treasury.

---

[39] The word "inconveniency" is changed to "inconvenience" in the transcript.
[40] The word "the" is omitted in the transcript.
[41] The transcript does not italicize the phrase "*be ascertained by the National Legislature.*"

Mr MADISON, thought the members of the Legisl. too much interested to ascertain their own compensation. It wd be indecent to put their hands into the public purse for the sake of their own pockets.

On this question [42] Mas. no. Cont. no. N. Y. divd. N. J. ay. Pa. ay. Del. no. Md. no. Va. no. N. C. no. S. C. no. Geo. divd. [43]

On the question for striking out "Natl. Treasury" as moved by Mr. Elseworth.

Mr HAMILTON renewed his opposition to it. He pressed the distinction between [44] State Govts. & the people. The former wd. be the rivals of the Genl. Govt. The State legislatures ought not therefore to be the paymasters of the latter.

Mr ELSEWORTH. If we are jealous of the State Govts. they will be so of us. If on going home I tell them we gave the Gen: Govt. such powers because we cd. not trust you, will they adopt it, and witht. yr. approbation it is a nullity.

[45] Massts. ay. Cont. ay. N. Y. divd.; N. J. no Pena. no. Del. no. Md. no. Va. no. N. C. ay. S. C. ay. Geo. divd.* [46]

On a question for substituting "adequate compensation" in place of "fixt stipends" it was agreed to nem. con. the friends of the latter being willing that the practicability of *fixing* the compensation should be considered hereafter in forming the details.

It was then moved by Mr BUTLER that a question be taken on both points jointly; to wit "adequate compensation to be paid out of the Natl. Treasury." It was objected to as out of order, the parts having been separately decided on. The Presidt. referd. the question of order to the House, and it was determined to be in order. Con. N. J. Del. Md. N. C. S. C.—ay— [47] N. Y. Pa. Va. Geo.

---

* Note. [It appeared that Massts. concurred, not because they thought the State Treasy. ought to be substituted; but because they thought nothing should be said on the subject, in which case it wd. silently devolve on the Natl. Treasury to support the National Legislature.]

[42] The transcript here inserts the following: "shall the salaries of the first branch be ascertained by the National Legislature?"

[43] In the transcript the vote reads: "New Jersey, Pennsylvania, aye—2; Massachusetts, Connecticut, Delaware, Maryland, Virginia, North Carolina, South Carolina, no—7; New York, Georgia, divided."

[44] The word "the" is here inserted in the transcript.

[45] The words "On the question" are here inserted in the transcript.

[46] In the transcript the vote reads: 'Massachusetts,* Connecticut, North Carolina, South Carolina, aye—4; New Jersey, Pennsylvania, Delaware, Maryland, Virginia, no—5; New York, Georgia, divided, so it passed in the negative."

no—⁴⁷ Mass: divided. The question on the sentence was then postponed by S. Carolina in right of the State.

Col. MASON moved to insert " twenty-five years of age as a qualification for the members of the 1ˢᵗ branch." He thought it absurd that a man to day should not be permitted by the law to make a bargain for himself, and tomorrow should be authorized to manage the affairs of a great nation. It was the more extraordinary as every man carried with him in his own experience a scale for measuring the deficiency of young politicians; since he would if interrogated be obliged to declare that his political opinions at the age of 21. were too crude & erroneous to merit an influence on public measures. It had been said that Congˢ had proved a good school for our young men. It might be so for any thing he knew but if it were, he chose that they should bear the expence of their own education.

Mʳ WILSON was agˢᵗ abridging the rights of election in any shape. It was the same thing whether this were done by disqualifying the objects of choice, or the persons chusing. The motion tended to damp the efforts of genius, and of laudable ambition. There was no more reason for incapacitating *youth* than *age*, where the requisite qualifications were found. Many instances might be mentioned of signal services rendered in high stations to the public before the age of 25: The present Mʳ Pitt and Lord Bolingbroke were striking instances.

On the question for inserting " 25 years of age "

Massᵗˢ no. Conᵗ ay. N. Y. divᵈ N. J. ay. Pᵃ no. Del. ay. Mᵈ ay. Vᵃ ay. N. C. ay. S. C. ay. Geo. no.⁴⁸

Mʳ GHORUM moved to strike out the last member of 3 Resol:⁴⁹ concerning ineligibility of members of the 1ˢᵗ branch to offices ⁵⁰ buring the term of their membership & for one year after. He considered it as ⁵¹ unnecessary & injurious. It was true abuses had been displayed in G. B. but no one cᵈ say how far they might have contributed to preserve the due influence of the Govᵗ nor what might have ensued in case the contrary theory had been tried.

---

⁴⁷ In the transcript the figures "6" and "4" are inserted after "ay" and "no" respectively.

⁴⁸ In the transcript the vote reads: "Connecticut, New Jersey, Delaware, Maryland, Virginia, North Carolina, South Carolina, aye—7; Massachusetts, Pennsylvania, Georgia, no—3; New York, divided."

⁴⁹ The words "the third Resolution" are substituted in the transcript for "3 Resol:"

⁵⁰ The letter "s" is stricken out of the word "offices" in the transcript.

⁵¹ The word "as" is stricken out in the transcript.

*The Home of Alexander Hamilton.*

M.^r BUTLER opposed it. This precaution ag.^st intrigue was necessary. He appealed to the example of G. B. where men got [52] into Parl.^t that they might get offices for themselves or their friends. This was the source of the corruption that ruined their Gov.^t

M.^r KING, thought we were refining too much. Such a restriction on the members would discourage merit. It would also give a pretext to the Executive for bad appointments, as he might always plead this as a bar to the choice he wished to have made.

M.^r WILSON was ag.^st fettering elections, and discouraging merit. He suggested also the fatal consequence in time of war, of rendering perhaps the best Commanders ineligible: appealing [53] to our situation during the late war, and indirectly leading to a recollection of the appointment of the Commander in Chief out of Congress.

Col. MASON was for shutting the door at all events ag.^st corruption. He enlarged on the venality and abuses in this particular in G. Britain: and alluded to the multiplicity of foreign Embassies by Cong.^s The disqualification he regarded as a corner stone in the fabric.

Col. HAMILTON. There are inconveniences on both sides. We must take man as we find him, and if we expect him to serve the public must interest his passions in doing so. A reliance on pure patriotism had been the source of many of our errors. He thought the remark of M.^r Ghorum a just one. It was impossible to say what w.^d be [54] effect in G. B. of such a reform as had been urged. It was known that one of the ablest politicians [M.^r Hume,] had pronounced all that influence on the side of the crown, which went under the name of corruption,[55] an essential part of the weight which maintained the equilibrium of the Constitution.

On M.^r Ghorum's Motion for striking out "ineligibility,"[56]

Mas.^ts ay. Con.^t no. N. Y. div.^d N. J. ay. P.^a div.^d Del. div.^d Mar.^d no. V.^a no. N. C. ay. S. C. no. Geo. ay.[57]

Adj.^d

---

[52] The word "get" is substituted in the transcript for "got."
[53] The word "appealed" is substituted in the transcript for "appealing."
[54] The word "the" is here inserted in the transcript.
[55] The transcript italicizes the word "corruption."
[56] The transcript here inserts the following: "it was lost by an equal division of the votes."
[57] In the transcript the vote reads: "Massachusetts, New Jersey, North Carolina, Georgia, aye—4; Connecticut, Maryland, Virginia, South Carolina, no—4; New York, Pennsylvania, Delaware, divided."

SATURDAY JUNE 23.   IN CONVENTION

The 3. Resol: resumed.⁵⁸

On ⁵⁹ Question yesterday postponed by S. Carol: for agreeing to the whole sentence "for allowing an adequate compensation to be paid out of the *Treasury of the U. States*"

Mas$^{ts}$ ay. Con$^t$ no. N. Y. no. N. J. ay. Pen$^a$ ay Del. no. M$^d$ ay. V$^a$ ay. N. C. no. S. C. no. Geo divided.⁶⁰ So the question was lost, & the sentence not inserted:

Gen! PINKNEY moves to strike out the ineligibility of members of the 1$^{st}$ branch to offices established "by a particular State." He argued from the inconveniency ⁶¹ to which such a restriction would expose both the members of the 1$^{st}$ branch, and the States wishing for their services;⁶² from the smallness of the object to be attained by the restriction.

It w$^d$ seem from the ideas of some that we are erecting a Kingdom to be divided ag$^{st}$ itself, he disapproved such a fetter on the Legislature.

M$^r$ SHERMAN seconds the motion. It w$^d$ seem that we are erecting a Kingdom at war with itself. The Legislature ought not to ⁶³ fettered in such a case. on the question

Mas$^{ts}$ no. Con$^t$ ay. N. Y. ay. N. J. ay. P$^a$ no. Del. no. M$^d$ ay. V$^a$ ay. N. C. ay. S. C. ay. Geo. ay.⁶⁴

M$^r$ MADISON renewed his motion yesterday made & waved to render the members of the 1$^{st}$ branch "ineligible during their term of service, & for one year after—to such offices only as should be established, or the emoluments thereof, augmented by the Legislature of the U. States during the time of their being members." He supposed that the unnecessary creation of offices, and increase of salaries, were the evils most experienced, & that if the door was shut ag$^{st}$ them: it might properly be left open for the appoint$^t$ of members to other offices as an encouragem$^t$ to the Legislative service.

---

⁵⁸ In the transcript this sentence reads: "The third Resolution being resumed."
⁵⁹ The word "the" is here inserted in the transcript.
⁶⁰ In the transcript the vote reads: "Massachusetts, New Jersey, Pennsylvania, Maryland, Virginia, aye—5; Connecticut, New York, Delware, North Carolina, South Carolina, no—5; Georgia, divided."
⁶¹ The word "inconveniency" is changed to "inconvenience" in the transcript.
⁶² The word "and" is here inserted in the transcript.
⁶³ The word "be" is here inserted in the transcript.
⁶⁴ In the transcript the vote reads: "Connecticut, New York, New Jersey, Maryland, Virginia, North Carolina, South Carolina, Georgia, aye—8; Massachusetts, Pennsylvania, Delaware, no—3."

Mʳ Alex: MARTIN seconded the motion.

Mʳ BUTLER. The amendᵗ does not go far eno' & wᵈ be easily evaded

Mʳ RUTLIDGE, was for preserving the Legislature as pure as possible, by shutting the door against appointments of its own members to offices,[65] which was one source of its corruption.

Mʳ MASON. The motion of my colleague is but a partial remedy for the evil. He appealed to him as a witness of the shameful partiality of the Legislature of Virginia to its own members. He enlarged on the abuses & corruption in the British Parliament, connected with the appointment of its members. He cᵈ not suppose that a sufficient number of Citizens could not be found who would be ready, without the inducement of eligibility to offices, to undertake the Legislative service. Genius & virtue it may be said, ought to be encouraged. Genius, for aught he knew, might, but that virtue should be encouraged by such a species of venality, was an idea, that at least had the merit of being new.

Mʳ KING remarked that we were refining too much in this business; and that the idea of preventing intrigue and solicitation of offices was chimerical. You say that no member shall himself be eligible to any office. Will this restrain him from from availing himself of the same means which would gain appointments for himself, to gain them for his son, his brother, or any other object of his partiality. We were losing therefore the advantages on one side, without avoiding the evils on the other.

Mʳ WILSON supported the motion. The proper cure he said for corruption in the Legislature was to take from it the power of appointing to offices. One branch of corruption would indeed remain, that of creating unnecessary offices, or granting unnecessary salaries, and for that the amendment would be a proper remedy. He animadverted on the impropriety of stigmatizing with the name of venality the laudable ambition of rising into the honorable offices of the Government; an ambition most likely to be felt in the early & most incorrupt period of life, & which all wise & free Govᵗˢ had deemed it sound policy, to cherish, not to check. The members of the Legislature have perhaps the hardest

---

[65] The transcript uses the word "offices" in the singular.

& least profitable task of any who engage in the service of the state. Ought this merit to be made a disqualification?

M: SHERMAN, observed that the motion did not go far enough. It might be evaded by the creation of a new office, the translation to it of a person from another office, and the appointment of a member of the Legislature to the latter. A new Embassy might be established to a new Court, & an ambassador taken from another, in order to *create* a vacancy for a favorite member. He admitted that inconveniencies lay on both sides. He hoped there wd be sufficient inducements to the public service without resorting to the prospect of desireable offices, and on the whole was rather agst the motion of M: Madison.

M: GERRY thought there was great weight in the objection of M: Sherman. He added as another objection agst admitting the eligibility of members in any case that it would produce intrigues of ambitious men for displacing proper officers, in order to create vacancies for themselves. In answer to M: King he observed that although members, if disqualified themselves might still intrigue & cabal for their sons, brothers &c, yet as their own interest would be dearer to them, than those of their nearest connections, it might be expected they would go greater lengths to promote it.

M: MADISON had been led to this motion as a middle ground beween an eligibility in all cases, and an absolute disqualification. He admitted the probable abuses of an eligibility of the members, to offices, particularly within the gift of the Legislature He had witnessed the partiality of such bodies to their own members, as had been remarked of the Virginia assembly by his colleague [Col. Mason]. He appealed however to him, in turn to vouch another fact not less notorious in Virginia, that the backwardness of the best citizens to engage in the Legislative service gave but too great success to unfit characters. The question was not to be viewed on one side only. The advantages & disadvantages on both ought to be fairly compared. The objects to be aimed at were to fill all offices with the fittest characters, & to draw the wisest & most worthy citizens into the Legislative service. If on one hand, public bodies were partial to their own members; on the other they were as apt to be misled by taking characters on report, or the authority of patrons and dependents. All who had been concerned in the appointment of strangers on those recommendations must be sensible of this truth. Nor w^d the partialities of such Bodies be obviated by disqualifying their own members. Candidates for office would hover round the seat of Gov^t or be found among the residents there, and practise all the means of courting the favor of the members. A great proportion of the appointments made by the States were evidently brought about in this way. In the general Gov^t the evil must be still greater, the characters of distant states, being much less known throughout the U. States than those of the distant parts of the same State. The elections by Congress had generally turned on men living at the seat of the fed^l Gov^t or in its neighbourhood.—As to the next object, the impulse to the Legislative service, was evinced by experience to be in general too feeble with those best qualified for it. This inconveniency [66] w^d also be more felt in the Nat^l Gov^t than in the State Gov^ts as the sacrifices req^d from the distant members, w^d be much greater, and the pecuniary provisions, probably, more disproportiate. It w^d therefore be impolitic to add fresh objections to the Legislative service by an absolute disqualification of its members. The point in question was whether this would be an objection with the most capable citizens. Arguing from experience he concluded that it would. The Legislature of Virg^a would probably have been without many of its best members, if in that situation, they had been ineligible to Cong^s to the Gov^t & other honorable offices of the State.

M^r BUTLER thought Characters fit for office w^d never be unknown.

Col. MASON. If the members of the Legislature are disqualified, still the honors of the State will induce those who aspire to them to enter that service, as the field in which they can best display & improve their talents, & lay the train for their subsequent advancement.

M^r JENIFER remarked that in Maryland, the Senators chosen for five years, c^d hold no other office & that this circumstance gained them the greatest confidence of the people.

---
[66] The word "inconveniency" is changed to "inconvenience" in the transcript.

On the question for agreeing to the motion of M! Madison.

Mass⁹⁸ div⁴ C⁸ ay. N. Y. no. N. J. ay. P⁴ no. Del. no. M⁴ no. V⁴ no. N. C. no. S. C. no. Geo. no.⁶⁷

M⁸ SHERMAN mov⁴ to insert the words "and incapable of holding" after the words "eligible to offices"⁶⁸ wᶜʰ was agreed to without opposition.

The word "established" & the words "⁶⁹ Nat! Gov!" were struck out of Resolution 3ᵈ: ⁷⁰

M⁸ SPAIGHT called for a division of the question, in consequence of which it was so put, as that it turned in ⁷¹ the first member of it, "on the ineligibility of the ⁷² members *during the term for which they were elected*"—whereon the States were,

Mass⁹⁸ div⁴ C⁸ ay. N. Y. ay. N. J. ay. P⁴ no. Del. ay. M⁴ ay. V⁴ ay. N. C. ay. S. C. ay. Geo. no.⁷³

On the 2ᵈ member of the sentence extending ineligibility of members to one year after the term for which they were elected Col MASON thought this essential to guard ag⁹ᵗ evasions by resignations, and stipulations for office to be fulfilled at the expiration of the legislative term. M⁸ GERRY, had known such a case. M⁸ HAMILTON. Evasions c⁴ not be prevented—as by proxies—by friends holding for a year, & them ⁷⁴ opening the way &c. M⁸ RUTLIDGE admitted the possibility of evasions but was for controuling them as possible.⁷⁵ ⁷⁶ Mass. no. C⁸ no. N. Y. ay. N. J. no. P⁴ div⁴ Del. ay. Mar⁴ ay V⁴ no. N. C. no. S. C. ay. Geo. no ⁷⁷

Adjᵈ

---

⁶⁷ In the transcript the vote reads: "Connecticut, New Jersey, aye—2; New York, Pennsylvania, Delaware, Maryland, Virginia, North Carolina, South Carolina, Georgia, no—8; Massachusetts, divided."

⁶⁸ The words "ineligible to any office" are substituted in the transcript for "eligible to offices."

⁶⁹ The words "under the" are here inserted in the transcript.

⁷⁰ The words "the third Resolution" are substituted in the transcript for "Resolution 3ᵈ"

⁷¹ The word "on" is substituted in the transcript for "in."

⁷² The word "the" is omitted in the transcript.

⁷³ In the transcript the vote reads: "Connecticut, New York, New Jersey, Delaware, Maryland, Virginia, North Carolina, South Carolina, aye—8; Pensylvania, Georgia, no—2; Massachusetts, divided."

⁷⁴ The word "then" is substituted in the transcript for "them."

⁷⁵ The phrase "contracting them as far as possible" is substituted in the transcript for "controuling them as possible."

⁷⁶ The words "On the question" are here inserted in the transcript.

⁷⁷ In the transcript the vote reads: "New York, Delaware, Maryland, South Carolina, aye—4; Massachusetts, Connecticut, New Jersey, Virginia, North Carolina, Georgia, no—6; Pennsylvania, divided."

## Monday. June 25. in Convention

Resolution 4.[78] being taken up.

M! PINKNEY [79] spoke as follows— The efficacy of the System will depend on this article. In order to form a right judgm! in the case, it will be proper to examine the situation of this Country more accurately than it has yet been done. The people of the U. States are perhaps the most singular of any we are acquainted with. Among them there are fewer distinctions of fortune & less of rank, than among the inhabitants of any other nation. Every freeman has a right to the same protection & security; and a very moderate share of property entitles them to the possession of all the honors and privileges the public can bestow: hence arises a greater equality, than is to be found among the people of any other country, and an equality which is more likely to continue— I say this equality is likely to continue, because in a new Country, possessing immense tracts of uncultivated lands, where every temptation is offered to emigration & where industry must be rewarded with competency, there will be few poor, and few dependent—Every member of the Society almost, will enjoy an equal power of arriving at the supreme offices & consequently of directing the strength & sentiments of the whole Community. None will be excluded by birth, & few by fortune, from voting for proper persons to fill the offices of Government—the whole community will enjoy in the fullest sense that kind of political liberty which consists in the power the members of the State reserve to themselves, of arriving at the public offices, or at least, of having votes in the nomination of those who fill them.

If this State of things is true & the prospect of its continuing [80] probable, it is perhaps not politic to endeavour too close an imitation of a Government calculated for a people whose situation is, & whose views ought to be extremely different

---

[78] The words "The fourth Resolution" are substituted in the transcript for "Resolution 4."

[79] Pinckney furnished Madison with a copy of this speech which he transcribed, but apparently not with the whole of it, as Madison's note at the end indicates. The original Pinckney draft is among the Madison papers, and shows Madison's copying to have been accurate.

[80] The word "continuance" is substituted in the transcript for "continuing."

Much has been said of the Constitution of G. Britain. I will confess that I believe it to be the best Constitution in existence; but at the same time I am confident it is one that will not or can not be introduced into this Country, for many centuries.—If it were proper to go here into a historical dissertation on the British Constitution, it might easily be shewn that the peculiar excellence, the distinguishing feature of that Governm$^t$ can not possibly be introduced into our System—that its balance between the Crown & the people can not be made a part of our Constitution.—that we neither have or can have the members to compose it, nor the rights, privileges & properties of so distinct a class of Citizens to guard.—that the materials for forming this balance or check do not exist, nor is there a necessity for having so permanent a part of our Legislative, until the Executive power is so constituted as to have something fixed & dangerous in its principle—By this I mean a sole, hereditary, though limited Executive.

That we cannot have a proper body for forming a Legislative balance between the inordinate power of the Executive and the people, is evident from a review of the accidents & circumstances which gave rise to the peerage of Great Britain—I believe it is well ascertained that the parts which compose the British Constitution arose immediately from the forests of Germany; but the antiquity of the establishment of nobility is by no means clearly defined. Some authors are of opinion that the dignity denoted by the titles of dux et [81] comes, was derived from the old Roman to the German Empire; while others are of opinion that they existed among the Germans long before the Romans were acquainted with them. The institution however of nobility is immemorial among the nations who may probably be termed the ancestors of [82] Britain.—At the time they were summoned in England to become a part of the National Council, and [83] the circumstances which have [83] contributed to make them a constituent part of that constitution, must be well known to all gentlemen who have had industry & curiosity enough to investigate

---
[81] The word "and" is substituted in the transcript for "et."
[82] The word "Great" is here inserted in the transcript.
[83] The words "and" and "have" are crossed out in the transcript.

the subject—The nobles with their possessions & and dependents composed a body permanent in their nature and formidable in point of power. They had a distinct interest both from the King and the people; an interest which could only be represented by themselves, and the guardianship [84] could not be safely intrusted to others.—At the time they were originally called to form a part of the National Council, necessity perhaps as much as other cause, induced the Monarch to look up to them. It was necessary to demand the aid of his subjects in personal & pecuniary services. The power and possessions of the Nobility would not permit taxation from any assembly of which they were not a part: & the blending [85] the deputies of the Commons with them, & thus forming what they called their parler-ment [86] was perhaps as much the effect of chance as of any thing else. The Commons were at that time compleatly subordinate to the nobles, whose consequence & influence seem to have been the only reasons for their superiority; a superiority so degrading to the Commons that in the first Summons we find the peers are called upon to consult,[87] the commons to consent.[87] From this time the peers have composed a part of the British Legislature, and notwithstanding their power and influence have diminished & those of the Commons have increased, yet still they have always formed an excellent balance ag$^{st}$ either the encroachments of the Crown or the people.

I have said that such a body cannot exist in this Country for ages, and that untill the situation of our people is exceedingly changed no necessity will exist for so permanent a part of the Legislature. To illustrate this I have remarked that the people of the United States are more equal in their circumstances than the people of any other Country—that they have very few rich men among them,—by rich men I mean those whose riches may have a dangerous influence, or such as are esteemed rich in Europe—perhaps there are not one hundred such on the Continent; that it is not probable this number will be greatly increased: that the genius of the people, their mediocrity of situation & the prospects which

---

[84] The words "of which" are here inserted in the transcript.
[85] The word "of" is here inserted in the transcript.
[86] The transcript italicizes the word "parler-ment."
[87] The transcript italicizes the words "consult" and "consent."

are afforded their industry in a Country which must be a new one for centuries are unfavorable to the rapid distinction of ranks. The destruction of the right of primogeniture & the equal division of the property of Intestates will also have an effect to preserve this mediocrity; for laws invariably affect the manners of a people. On the other hand that vast extent of unpeopled territory which opens to the frugal & industrious a sure road to competency & independence will effectually prevent for a considerable time the increase of the poor or discontented, and be the means of preserving that equality of condition which so eminently distinguishes us.

If equality is as I contend the leading feature of the U. States, where then are the riches & wealth whose representation & protection is the peculiar province of this permanent body. Are they in the hands of the few who may be called rich; in the possession of less than a hundred citizens? certainly not. They are in the great body of the people, among whom there are no men of wealth, and very few of real poverty.—Is it probable that a change will be created, and that a new order of men will arise? If under the British Government, for a century no such change was probable,[88] I think it may be fairly concluded it will not take place while even the semblance of Republicanism remains.—How is this change to be effected? Where are the sources from whence it is to flow? From the landed interest? No. That is too unproductive & too much divided in most of the States. From the Monied interest? If such exists at present, little is to be apprehended from that source. Is it to spring from commerce? I believe it would be the first instance in which a nobility sprang from merchants. Besides, Sir, I apprehend that on this point the policy of the U. States has been much mistaken. We have unwisely considered ourselves as the inhabitants of an old instead of a new country. We have adopted the maxims of a State full of people & manufactures & established in credit. We have deserted our true interest, and instead of applying closely to those improvements in domestic policy which would have ensured the future importance of our commerce, we have rashly & prematurely engaged in schemes as extensive as they are imprudent. This

---

[88] The word "produced" is substituted for the word "probable" in the transcript.

however is an error which daily corrects itself & I have no doubt that a few more severe trials will convince us, that very different commercial principles ought to govern the conduct of these States.

The people of this country are not only very different from the inhabitants of any State we are acquainted with in the modern world; but I assert that their situation is distinct from either the people of Greece or Rome, or of any State we are acquainted with among the antients.—Can the orders introduced by the institution of Solon, can they be found in the United States? Can the military habits & manners of Sparta be resembled to our habits & manners? Are the distinctions of Patrician & Plebeian known among us? Can the Helvetic or Belgic confederacies, or can the unwieldy, unmeaning body called the Germanic Empire, can they be said to possess either the same or a situation like ours? I apprehend not.—They are perfectly different, in their distinctions of rank, their Constitutions, their manners & their policy.

Our true situation appears to me to be this.—a new extensive Country containing within itself the materials for forming a Government capable of extending to its citizens all the blessings of civil & religious liberty—capable of making them happy at home. This is the great end of Republican Establishments. We mistake the object of our Government, if we hope or wish that it is to make us respectable abroad. Conquest or superiority among other powers is not or ought not ever to be the object of republican systems. If they are sufficiently active & energetic to rescue us from contempt & preserve our domestic happiness & security, it is all we can expect from them,—it is more than almost any other Government ensures to its citizens.

I believe this observation will be found generally true:—that no two people are so exactly alike in their situation or circumstances as to admit the exercise of the same Government with equal benefit: that a system must be suited to the habits & genius of the people it is to govern, and must grow out of them.

The people of the U. S. may be divided into three classes— *Professional men* who must from their particular pursuits always have a considerable weight in the Government while it remains popular—*Commercial men*, who may or may not have weight as a wise or injudicious commercial policy is pursued.—If that commercial policy is pursued which I conceive to be the true one, the merchants of this Country will not or ought not for a considerable time to have much weight in the political scale.—The third is the *landed interest*, the owners and cultivators of the soil, who are and ought ever to be the governing spring in the system.—These three classes, however distinct in their pursuits are individually equal in the political scale, and may be easily proved to have but one interest. The dependence of each on the other is mutual. The merchant depends on the planter. Both must in private as well as public affairs be connected with the professional men; who in their turn must in some measure depend upon [89] them. Hence it is clear from this manifest connection, & the equality which I before stated exists, & must for the reasons then assigned, continue, that after all there is one, but one great & equal body of citizens composing the inhabitants of this Country among whom there are no distinctions of rank, and very few or none of fortune.

For a people thus circumstanced are we then to form a government & the question is what kind [90] of Government is best suited to them.

Will it be the British Gov!? No. Why? Because G. Britain contains three orders of people distinct in their situation, their possessions & their principles.—These orders combined form the great body of the Nation, and as in national expences the wealth of the whole community must contribute, so ought each component part to be properly & duly [91] represented—No other combination of power could form this due representation, but the one that exists.—Neither the peers or the people could represent the royalty, nor could the Royalty & the people form a proper representation for the Peers.—Each therefore must of necessity be represented by itself, or the sign of itself; and this accidental mixture has certainly formed a Government admirably well balanced.

---

[89] The word "on" is substituted in the transcript for "upon."
[90] The word "sort" is substituted in the transcript for "kind."
[91] The words "properly & duly" are transposed in the transcript to read "duly and properly."

But the U. States contain but one order that can be assimilated to the British Nation,—this is the order of Commons. They will not surely then attempt to form a Government consisting of three branches, two of which shall have nothing to represent. They will not have an Executive & Senate [hereditary] because the King & Lords of England are so. The same reasons do not exist and therefore the same provisions are not necessary.

We must as has been observed suit our Governm<sup>t</sup> to the people it is to direct. These are I believe as active, intelligent & susceptible of good Governm<sup>t</sup> as any people in the world. The Confusion which has produced the present relaxed State is not owing to them. It is owing to the weakness & [defects] of a Gov<sup>t</sup> incapable of combining the various interests it is intended to unite, and destitute of energy.—All that we have to do then is to distribute the powers of Gov<sup>t</sup> in such a manner, and for such limited periods, as while it gives a proper degree of permanency to the Magistrate, will reserve to the people, the right of election they will not or ought not frequently to part with.—I am of opinion that this may be easily[92] done; and that with some amendments the propositions before the Committee will fully answer this end.

No position appears to me more true than this; that the General Gov<sup>t</sup> can not effectually exist without reserving to the States the possession of their local rights. They are the instruments upon which the Union must frequently depend for the support & execution of their powers, however immediately operating upon the people, and not upon the States.

Much has been said about the propriety of abolishing the distinction of State Governments, & having but one general System. Suffer me for a moment to examine this question.*

---

\* The residue of this speech was not furnished like the above by M<sup>r</sup> Pinckney.[93]

[92] The words "be easily" are transposed in the transcript to "easily be."

[93] "The residue" of Pinckney's speech, according to Robert Yates was as follows:

"The United States include a territory of about 1500 miles in length, and in breadth about 400; the whole of which is divided into states and districts. While we were dependent on the crown of Great Britain, it was in contemplation to have formed the whole into one—but it was found impracticable. No legislature could make good laws for the whole, nor can it now be done. It would necessarily place the power in the hands of the few, nearest the seat of government. State governments must therefore remain, if you mean to prevent confusion. The general negative powers will support the general government. Upon these considerations I am led to form the second branch differently from the report. Their powers are important and the number not too large, upon the principle of proportion. I have considered the subject with great attention; and I propose this plan (reads it) and if no better plan is proposed, I will then move its adoption." *Secret Proceedings and Debates of the Convention Assembled at Philadelphia, in the year 1787, for the purpose of forming the Constitution of the United States of America,* by Robert Yates (1821), p. 163.

The mode of constituting the 2ᵈ branch being under consideration.

The word "national" was struck out and "United States" inserted.

Mʳ GHORUM, inclined to a compromise as to the rule of proportion. He thought there was some weight in the objections of the small States. If Vᵃ should have 16. votes & Delʳᵉ with several other States together 16. those from Virgᵃ would be more likely to unite than the others, and would therefore have an undue influence. This remark was applicable not only to States, but to Counties or other districts of the same State. Accordingly the Constitution of Massᵗˢ had provided that the representatives of the larger districts should not be in an exact ratio to their numbers. And experience he thought had shewn the provision to be expedient.

Mʳ READ. The States have heretofore been in a sort of partnership. They ought to adjust their old affairs before they open[94] a new account. He brought into view the appropriation of the common interest in the Western lands, to the use of particular States. Let justice be done on this head; let the fund be applied fairly & equally to the discharge of the general debt, and the smaller States who had been injured; would listen then perhaps to those ideas of just representation which had been held out.

Mʳ GHORUM. did[95] not see how the Convention could interpose in the case. Errors he allowed had been committed on the subject. But Congˢ were now using their endeavors to rectify them. The best remedy would be such a Government as would have vigor enough to do justice throughout. This was certainly the best chance that could be afforded to the smaller States.

Mʳ WILSON. the question is shall the members of the 2ᵈ branch be chosen by the Legislatures of the States? When he considered the amazing extent of Country—the immense population which is to fill it, the influence which[96] the Govᵗ we are to form will have, not only on the present generation of our people & their multiplied posterity, but on the whole Globe, he was lost in the magnitude of the object. The project of Henry the 4ᵗʰ & his Statesmen was

---

[94] The word "opened" is substituted in the transcript for "open."

[95] The word "could" is substituted in the transcript for "did."

[96] The word "of" is substituted in the transcript for "which."

but the picture in miniature of the great portrait to be exhibited. He was opposed to an election by the State Legislatures. In explaining his reasons it was necessary to observe the twofold relation in which the people would stand. 1.[97] as Citizens of the Genl. Govt. 2.[97] as Citizens of their particular State. The Genl. Govt. was meant for them in the first capacity: the State Govts. in the second. Both Govts. were derived from the people—both meant for the people—both therefore ought to be regulated on the same principles. The same train of ideas which belonged to the relation of the Citizens to their State Govts. were applicable to their relation to the Genl. Govt. and in forming the latter, we ought to proceed, by abstracting as much as possible from the idea of [98] State Govts. With respect to the province & objects [99] of the Genl. Govt. they should be considered as having no existence. The election of the 2d. branch by the Legislatures, will introduce & cherish local interests & local prejudices. The Genl. Govt. is not an assemblage of States, but of individuals for certain political purposes—it is not meant for the States, but for the individuals composing them; the *individuals* therefore not the *States*, ought to be represented in it: A proportion in this representation can be preserved in the 2d. as well as in the 1st. branch; and the election can be made by electors chosen by the people for that purpose. He moved an amendment to that effect which was not seconded.

Mr. ELSEWORTH saw no reason for departing from the mode contained in the Report. Whoever chooses the member, he will be a Citizen of the State he is to represent & will feel the same spirit & act the same part whether he be appointed by the people or the Legislature. Every State has its particular views & prejudices, which will find their way into the general councils, through whatever channel they may flow. Wisdom was one of the characteristics which it was in contemplation to give the second branch. Would not more of it issue from the Legislatures; than from an immediate election by the people. He urged the necessity of maintaining the existence & agency of the States. Without their co-operation it would be impossible to support a Republican Govt.

---

[97] The figure "1" is changed in the transcript to "first," and the figure "2" to "and secondly."
[98] The word "the" is here inserted in the transcript.
[99] The word "objects" is used in the singular in the transcript.

over so great an extent of Country. An army could scarcely render it practicable. The largest States are the worst Governed. Virg: is obliged to acknowledge her incapacity to extend her Gov! to Kentucky. Mas!: can not keep the peace one hundred miles from her capitol and is now forming an army for its support. How long Pen: may be free from a like situation can not be foreseen. If the principles & materials of our Gov! are not adequate to the extent of these single States; how can it be imagined that they can support a single Gov! throughout the U. States. The only chance of supporting a Gen! Gov! lies in engrafting[1] it on that[2] of the individual States.

Doc: JOHNSON urged the necessity of preserving the State Gov!: which would be at the mercy of the Gen! Gov! on M: Wilson's plan.

M: MADISON thought it w? obviate difficulty if the present resol: were postponed. & the 8!ʰ taken up, which is to fix the right of suffrage in the 2? branch.

Doc:[3] WILLIAMSON professed himself a friend to such a system as would secure the existence of the State Gov!: The happiness of the people depended on it. He was at a loss to give his vote as to the Senate untill he knew the number of its members. In order to ascertain this, he moved to insert these words[4] after "2? branch of the Nat! Legislature"—[5] "who shall bear such proportion to the n? of the 1!ᵗ branch as 1 to    ." He was not seconded.

M: MASON. It has been agreed on all hands that an efficient Gov! is necessary that to render it such it ought to have the facuity of self-defence, that to render its different branches effectual each of them ought to have the same power of self defence. He did not wonder that such an agreement should have prevailed in[6] these points. He only wondered that there should be any disagreement about the necessity of allowing the State Gov!: the same self-defence. If they are to be preserved as he conceived

---

[1] The word "grafting" is substituted in the transcript for "engrafting."
[2] The word "those" is substituted in the transcript for "that."
[3] The word "Mr." is substituted in the transcript for "Doc?"
[4] The words "these words" are omitted in the transcript.
[5] The words "the words" are here inserted in the transcript.
[6] The word "on" is substituted in the transcript for "in."

to be essential, they certainly ought to have this power, and the only mode left of giving it to them, was by allowing them to appoint the 2ᵈ branch of the Natˡ Legislature.

Mʳ BUTLER observing that we were put to difficulties at every step by the uncertainty whether an equality or a ratio of representation wᵈ prevail finally in the 2ᵈ branch, moved to postpone the 4ᵗʰ Resol: & to proceed to the ⁷ Resol: on that point. Mʳ MADISON seconded him.

On the question

Massᵗˢ no. Conᵗ no. N. Y. ay. N. J. no. Pᵃ. no. Del. no. Mᵈ no. Vᵃ ay. N. C. no. S. C. ay. Geo. ay.⁸

On a question to postpone the 4 and take up the 7. Resol: ays ⁹— Marᵈ Vᵃ N. C. S. C. Geo:—Noes ¹⁰ Mas. Cᵗ N. Y. N. J. Pᵃ Del: ¹⁰

On the question to agree "that the members of the 2ᵈ branch be chosen by the indivˡ Legislatures" Massᵗˢ ay. Conᵗ ay. N. Y. ay. N. J. ay. Pᵃ no. Del. ay. Mᵈ ay. Vᵃ no. N. C. ay. S. C. ay. Geo. ay.* ¹¹

On a question on the clause requiring the age of 30 years at least—" it was agreed to unanimously: ¹²

On a question to strike out—the words "sufficient to ensure their independency ¹³" after the word "term" it was agreed to.

¹⁴ That the 2ᵈ branch hold their offices for ¹⁵ term of seven years,¹⁶ considered

Mʳ GHORUM suggests a term of "4 years," ¼ to be elected every year.

---

\* It must be kept in view that the largest States particularly Pennsylvania & Virginia always considered the choice of the 2ᵈ Branch by the State Legislatures as opposed to a proportional Representation to which they were attached as a fundamental principle of just Government. The smaller States who had opposite views, were reinforced by the members from the large States most anxious to secure the importance of the State Governments.

⁷ The word "eighth" is here inserted in the transcript.

⁸ In the transcript the vote reads: "New York, Virginia, South Carolina, Georgia, aye—4; Massachusetts, Connecticut, New Jersey, Pennsylvania, Delaware, Maryland, North Carolina, no—7."

⁹ The word "ays" is omitted in the transcript.

¹⁰ The word "noes" is omitted in the transcript; "aye—5" being inserted after "Georgia" and "no—6" after "Delaware."

¹¹ In the transcript this vote reads: "Massachusetts, Connecticut, New York, New Jersey, Delaware, Maryland, North Carolina, South Carolina, Georgia, aye—9; Pennsylvania, Virginia, no—2."

¹² The words "agreed to unanimously" are transposed in the transcript to read "unanimously agreed to."

¹³ The word "independency" is changed to "independence" in the transcript.

¹⁴ The words "The clause" are here inserted in the transcript.

¹⁵ The word "a" is here inserted in the transcript.

¹⁶ The word "being" is here inserted in the transcript.

M.̲ RANDOLPH. supported the idea of rotation, as favorable to the wisdom & stability of the Corps, which might possibly be always sitting, and aiding the Executive. And moves after "7 years" to add, "to go out in fixt proportion" which was agreed to.

M.̲ WILLIAMSON. suggests "6 years," as more convenient for Rotation than 7 years.

M.̲ SHERMAN seconds him.

M.̲ REED proposed that they s.̲d hold their offices "during good" behaviour. M.̲ R. MORRIS seconds him.

Gen.̲l PINKNEY proposed "4 years." A longer term [17] w.̲d fix them at the seat of Gov.̲t They w.̲d acquire an interest there, perhaps transfer their property & lose sight of the States they represent. Under these circumstances the distant States w.̲d labour under great disadvantages.

M.̲ SHERMAN moved to strike out "7 years" in order to take questions on the several propositions.

On the question to strike out "seven"

Mas.̲ts ay. Con.̲t ay. N. Y. ay. N. J. ay. P.̲a no. Del no. M.̲d div.̲d V.̲a no. N. C. ay. S. C. ay. Geo. ay.[18]

On the question to insert "6 years, which failed 5 St.̲s being ay. 5 no. & 1 divided

Mas.̲ts no. Con.̲t ay. N. Y. no. N. J. no. P.̲a ay. Del ay. M.̲d div.̲d V.̲a ay. N. C. ay. S. C. no. Geo. no.[19]

On a motion to adjourn, the votes were 5 for 5 ag.̲st it & 1 divided,—Con. N. J. P.̲a Del. V.̲a —ay.[20] Mass.̲ts N. Y. N. C. S. C. Geo: no.[20] Mary.̲d divided.

On the question for "5 years" it was lost.

Mas.̲ts no. Con.̲t ay. N. Y. no. N. J. no. P.̲a ay. Del. ay. M.̲d div.̲d V.̲a ay. N. C. ay. S. C. no. Geo no.[21]

Adj.̲d

---

[17] The word "time" is substituted in the transcript for "term."

[18] In the transcript the vote reads: "Massachusetts, Connecticut, New York, New Jersey, North Carolina, South Carolina, Georgia, aye—7; Pennsylvania, Delaware, Virginia, no—3; Maryland, divided."

[19] In the transcript the vote reads: "Connecticut, Pennsylvania, Delaware, Virginia, North Carolina, aye—5; Massachusetts, New York, New Jersey, South Carolina, Georgia, no—5; Maryland, divided."

[20] The figure "5" is here inserted in the transcript.

[21] In the transcript the vote reads: "Connecticut, Pennsylvania, Delaware, Virginia, North Carolina, aye—5; Massachusetts, New York, New Jersey, South Carolina, Georgia, no—5; Maryland, divided."

## Tuesday. June 26. In Convention

The duration of the 2ḍ branch [22] under consideration.

Mr GHORUM moved to fill the blank with "six years," one third of the members to go out every second year.

Mr WILSON 2ḍeḍ the motion.

Genḷ PINKNEY opposed six years in favor of four years. The States he said had different interests. Those of the Southern, and of S. Carolina in particular were different from the Northern. If the Senators should be appointed for a long term, they wḍ settle in the State where they exercised their functions; and would in a little time be rather the representatives of that than of the State appointṣ them.

Mr READ movḍ that the term be nine years. This wḍ admit of a very convenient rotation, one third going out triennially. He wḍ still prefer "during good behaviour," but being little supported in that idea, he was willing to take the longest term that could be obtained.

Mr BROOME 2ḍeḍ the motion.

Mr MADISON. In order to judge of the form to be given to this institution, it will be proper to take a view of the ends to be served by it. These were first to protect the people agṣt their rulers: secondly to protect the people agṣt the transient impressions into which they themselves might be led. A people deliberating in a temperate moment, and with the experience of other nations before them, on the plan of Govṭ most likely to secure their happiness, would first be aware, that those chargḍ with the public happiness, might betray their trust. An obvious precaution agṣt this danger wḍ be to divide the trust between different bodies of men, who might watch & check each other. In this they wḍ be governed by the same prudence which has prevailed in organizing the subordinate departments of Govṭ, where all business liable to abuses is made to pass thro' separate hands, the one being a check on the other. It wḍ next occur to such a people, that they themselves were liable to temporary errors, thro' want of information as to their true interest, and that men chosen for a short term, & em-

---

[22] The word "being" is here inserted in the transcript.

ployed but a small portion of that in public affairs, might err from the same cause. This reflection wd naturally suggest that the Govt be so constituted, as that one of its branches might have an oppy of acquiring a competent knowledge of the public interests. Another reflection equally becoming a people on such an occasion, wd be that they themselves, as well as a numerous body of Representatives, were liable to err also, from fickleness and passion. A necessary fence agst this danger would be to select a portion of enlightened citizens, whose limited number, and firmness might seasonably interpose agst impetuous councils. It ought finally to occur to a people deliberating on a Govt for themselves, that as different interests necessarily result from the liberty meant to be secured, the major interest might under sudden impulses be tempted to commit injustice on the minority. In all civilized Countries the people fall into different classes havg a real or supposed difference of interests. There will be creditors & debtors, farmers, merchts & manufacturers. There will be particularly the distinction of rich & poor. It was true as had been observd [by Mr Pinkney] we had not among us those hereditary distinctions, of rank which were a great source of the contests in the ancient Govts as well as the modern States of Europe, nor those extremes of wealth or poverty which characterize the latter. We cannot however be regarded even at this time, as one homogeneous mass, in which every thing that affects a part will affect in the same manner the whole. In framing a system which we wish to last for ages, we shd not lose sight of the changes which ages will produce. An increase of population will of necessity increase the proportion of those who will labour under all the hardships of life, & secretly sigh for a more equal distribution of its blessings. These may in time outnumber those who are placed above the feelings of indigence. According to the equal laws of suffrage, the power will slide into the hands of the former. No agrarian attempts have yet been made in in this Country, but symtoms, of a leveling spirit, as we have understood, have sufficiently appeared in a certain quarters to give notice of the future danger. How is this danger to be guarded agst on republican principles? How is the danger in all cases of interested coalitions to oppress the minority to be

THE DECLARATION OF INDEPENDENCE
*From a painting by Trumbull*

guarded ag$^{st}$? Among other means by the establishment of a body in the Gov$^t$ sufficiently respectable for its wisdom & virtue, to aid on such emergences, the preponderance of justice by throwing its weight into that scale. Such being the objects of the second branch in the proposed Gov$^t$ he thought a considerable duration ought to be given to it. He did not conceive that the term of nine years could threaten any real danger; but in pursuing his particular ideas on the subject, he should require that the long term allowed to the 2$^d$ branch should not commence till such a period of life, as would render a perpetual disqualification to be re-elected little inconvenient either in a public or private view. He observed that as it was more than probable we were now digesting a plan which in its operation w$^d$ decide for ever the fate of Republican Gov$^t$ we ought not only to provide every guard to liberty that its preservation c$^d$ require, but be equally careful to supply the defects which our own experience had particularly pointed out.

M$^r$ SHERMAN. Gov$^t$ is instituted for those who live under it. It ought therefore to be so constituted as not to be dangerous to their liberties. The more permanency it has the worse if it be a bad Gov$^t$. Frequent elections are necessary to preserve the good behavior of rulers. They also tend to give permanency to the Government, by preserving that good behavior, because it ensures their re-election. In Connecticut elections have been very frequent, yet great stability & uniformity both as to persons & measures have been experienced from its original establishm$^t$ to the present time; a period of more than 130 years. He wished to have provision made for steadiness & wisdom in the system to be adopted; but he thought six or four years would be sufficient. He sh$^d$ be content with either.

M$^r$ READ wished it to be considered by the small States that it was their interest that we should become one people as much as possible; that State attachments sh$^d$ be extinguished as much as possible; that the Senate sh$^d$ be so constituted as to have the feelings of Citizens of the whole.

M$^r$ HAMILTON. He did not mean to enter particularly into the subject. He concurred with M$^r$ Madison in thinking we were now to decide for ever the fate of Republican Government; and that if we did not give to that form due stability and wisdom, it would be disgraced & lost among ourselves, disgraced & lost to mankind for ever. He acknowledged himself not to think favorably of Republican Government; but addressed his remarks to those who did think favorably of it, in order to prevail on them to tone their Government as high as possible. He professed himself to be as zealous an advocate for liberty as any man whatever, and trusted he should be as willing a martyr to it though he differed as to the form in which it was most eligible.—He concurred also in the general observations of [M. Madison] on the subject, which might be supported by others if it were necessary. It was certainly true: that nothing like an equality of property existed: that an inequality would exist as long as liberty existed, and that it would unavoidably result from that very liberty itself. This inequality of property constituted the great & fundamental distinction in Society. When the Tribunitial power had levelled the boundary between the *patricians* & *plebeians*, what followed? The distinction between rich & poor was substituted. He meant not however to enlarge on the subject. He rose principally to remark that [M. Sherman] seemed not to recollect that one branch of the proposed Gov.ᵗ was so formed, as to render it particularly the guardians of the poorer orders of Citizens; nor to have adverted to the true causes of the stability which had been exemplified in Con.ᵗ Under the British system as well as the federal, many of the great powers appertaining to Gov.ᵗ particularly all those relating to foreign Nations were not in the hands of the Gov.ᵗ there. Their internal affairs also were extremely simple, owing to sundry causes many of which were peculiar to that Country. Of late the Goverm.ᵗ had entirely given way to the people, and had in fact suspended many of its ordinary functions in order to prevent those turbulent scenes which had appeared elsewhere. He asks M. S. whether the State at this time, dare impose & collect a tax on yᵉ people? To these causes & not to the frequency of elections, the effect, as far as it existed ought to be chiefly ascribed.

M. GERRY. wished we could be united in our ideas concerning a permanent Gov.ᵗ All aim at the same end, but there are great differences as to the means. One circumstance He thought should be carefully attended to. There were not 1/1000 part of our fellow citizens who were not ag:st every approach towards Monarchy. Will they ever agree to a plan which seems to make such an approach. The Convention ought to be extremely cautious in what they hold out to the people. Whatever plan may be proposed will be espoused with warmth by many out of respect to the quarter it proceeds from as well as from an approbation of the plan itself. And if the plan should be of such a nature as to rouse a violent opposition, it is easy to foresee that discord & confusion will ensue, and it is even possible that we may become a prey to foreign powers. He did not deny the position of M.r Madison, that the majority will generally violate justice when they have an interest in so doing; But did not think there was any such temptation in this Country. Our situation was different from that of G. Britain: and the great body of lands yet to be parcelled out & settled would very much prolong the difference. Notwithstanding the symtoms of injustice which had marked many of our public Councils, they had not proceeded so far as not to leave hopes, that there would be a sufficient sense of justice & virtue for the purpose of Gov:t He admitted the evils arising from a frequency of elections: and would agree to give the Senate a duration of four or five years. A longer term would defeat itself. It never would be adopted by the people.

M.r WILSON did not mean to repeat what had fallen from others, but w.d add an observation or two which he believed had not yet been suggested. Every nation may be regarded in two relations 1.[23] to its own citizens. 2 [23] to foreign nations. It is therefore not only liable to anarchy & tyranny within, but has wars to avoid & treaties to obtain from abroad. The Senate will probably be the depositary of the powers concerning the latter objects. It ought therefore to be made respectable in the eyes of foreign Nations. The true reason why G. Britain has not yet listened to a commercial treaty with us has been, because she had no confidence in the stability or efficacy of our Government. 9 years with a rotation, will provide these desirable qualities; and

---

[23] The figures "1" and "2" are changed to "first" and "secondly" in the transcript.

give our Gov.<sup>t</sup> an advantage in this respect over Monarchy itself. In a monarchy much must always depend on the temper of the man. In such a body, the personal character will be lost in the political. He w<sup>d</sup> add another observation. The popular objection ag<sup>st</sup> appointing any public body for a long term was that it might by gradual encroachments prolong itself first into a body for life, and finally become a hereditary one. It would be a satisfactory answer to this objection that as $\frac{1}{3}$ would go out triennially, there would be always three divisions holding their places for unequal terms,[24] and consequently acting under the influence of different views, and different impulses—On the question for 9 years, $\frac{1}{3}$ to go out triennially

Mass.<sup>ts</sup> no. Con.<sup>t</sup> no. N. Y. no. N. J. no. P.<sup>a</sup> ay. Del. ay. M.<sup>d</sup> no. V.<sup>a</sup> ay. N. C. no. S. C. no. Geo. no.[25]

On the question for 6 years $\frac{1}{3}$ to go out biennially

Mass.<sup>ts</sup> ay. Con.<sup>t</sup> ay. N. Y. no. N. J. no. P.<sup>a</sup> ay. Del. ay. M.<sup>d</sup> ay. V.<sup>a</sup> ay. N. C. ay. S. C. no. Geo. no.[26]

[27] "To receive fixt stipends by which they may be compensated for their services." [28] considered

General PINKNEY proposed "that no Salary should be allowed." As this [the Senatorial] branch was meant to represent the wealth of the Country, it ought to be composed of persons of wealth; and if no allowance was to be made the wealthy alone would undertake the service. He moved to strike out the clause.

Doct.<sup>r</sup> FRANKLIN seconded the motion. He wished the Convention to stand fair with the people. There were in it a number of young men who would probably be of the Senate. If lucrative appointments should be recommended we might be chargeable with having carved out places for ourselves. On the question, Mas.<sup>ts</sup> Connecticut* P.<sup>a</sup> M.<sup>d</sup> S. Carolina ay.[30] N. Y. N. J. Del. Virg.<sup>a</sup> N. C. Geo. no.[31]

---

[24] The word "times" is substituted in the transcript for "terms."
[25] In the transcript the vote reads: "Pennsylvania, Delaware, Virginia, aye—3; Massachusetts, Connecticut, New York, New Jersey, Maryland, North Carolina, South Carolina, Georgia, no—8."
[26] In the transcript the vote reads: "Massachusetts, Connecticut, Pennsylvania, Delaware, Maryland, Virginia, North Carolina, aye—7; New York, New Jersey, South Carolina, Georgia, no—4."
[27] The words "The clause of the fourth Resolution" are here inserted in the transcript.
[28] The word "being" is here inserted in the transcript.
* Quer. whether Connecticut should not be—no, & Delaware, ay.[29]
[29] An interrogation mark and the initials "J. M." are here inserted in the transcript. According to the Journal, Connecticut was "ay" and Delaware "no."
[30] The figure "5" is here inserted in the transcript.
[31] The figure "6" is here inserted in the transcript.

Mʳ WILLIAMSON moved to change the expression into these words towit "to receive a compensation for the devotion of their time to the public Service." The motion was seconded by Mʳ Elseworth. And was ³² agreed to by all the States except S. Carolᵃ It seemed to be meant only to get rid of the word "fixt" and leave greater room for modifying the provision on this point.

Mʳ ELSEWORTH moved to strike out "to be paid out of the natᶦ Treasury" and insert "to be paid by their respective States." If the Senate was meant to strengthen the Govᵗ it ought to have the confidence of the States. The States will have an interest in keeping up a representation, and will make such provision for supporting the members as will ensure their attendance.

Mʳ MADISON considered this ³³ a departure from a fundamental principle, and subverting the end intended by allowing the Senate a duration of 6 years. They would if this motion should be agreed to, hold their places during pleasure; during the pleasure of the State Legislatures. One great end of the institution was, that being a firm, wise and impartial body, it might not only give stability to the Genᶦ Govᵗ in its operations on individuals, but hold an even balance among different States. The motion would make the Senate like Congress, the mere Agents & Advocates of State interests & views, instead of being the impartial umpires & Guardians of justice and ³⁴ general Good. Congˢ had lately by the establishment of a board with full powers to decide on the mutual claims be- between the U. States & the individual States, fairly acknowledged themselves to be unfit for discharging this part of the business referred to them by the Confederation.

Mʳ DAYTON considered the payment of the Senate by the States as fatal to their independence. he was decided for paying them out of the Natᶦ Treasury.

On the question for payment of the Senate to be left to the States as moved by Mʳ Elseworth.³⁵

Massᵗˢ no. Conᵗ ay. N. Y. ay. N. J. ay. Pᵃ no. Del. no. Mᵈ no. Vᵃ no. N. C. no. S. C. ay. Geo. ay. ³⁶

---

³² The word "was" is omitted in the transcript.
³³ The word "as" is here inserted in the transcript.
³⁴ The word "the" is here inserted in the transcript.
³⁵ The phrase "it passed in the negative" is here inserted in the transcript.
³⁶ In the transcript the vote reads: "Connecticut, New York, New Jersey, South Carolina, Georgia, aye—5; Massachusetts, Pennsylvania, Delaware, Maryland, Virginia, North Carolina, no—6."

Col. MASON. He did not rise to make any motion, but to hint an idea which seemed to be proper for consideration. One important object in constituting the Senate was to secure the rights of property. To give them weight & firmness for this purpose, a considerable duration in office was thought necessary. But a longer term than 6 years, would be of no avail in this respect, if needy persons should be appointed. He suggested therefore the propriety of annexing to the office a qualification of property. He thought this would be very practicable; as the rules of taxation would supply a scale for measuring the degree of wealth possessed by every man.

A question was then taken whether the words "to be paid out of the public [37] treasury," should stand."

Mass$^{ts}$ ay. Con$^t$ no. N. Y. no. N. J. no. P$^a$ ay. Del. ay. M$^d$ ay. V$^a$ ay. N. C. no. S. C. no. Geo. no.[38]

M$^r$ BUTLER moved to strike out the ineligibility of Senators to *State offices.*

M$^r$ WILLIAMSON seconded the motion.

M$^r$ WILSON remarked the additional dependence this w$^d$ create in the Senators on the States. The longer the time he observed allotted to the officer, the more compleat will be the dependance, if it exists at all.

Gen$^l$ PINKNEY was for making the States as much as could be conveniently done, a part of the Gen$^l$ Gov$^t$: If the Senate was to be appointed by the States, it ought in pursuance of the same idea to be paid by the States: and the States ought not to be barred from the opportunity of calling members of it into offices at home. Such a restriction would also discourage the ablest men from going into the Senate.

M$^r$ WILLIAMSON moved a resolution so penned as to admit of the two following questions. 1.[39] whether the members of the Senate should be ineligible to & incapable of holding offices *under the U. States*

2.[39] Whether &c. under the *particular States.*

---

[37] The word "public" is changed to "national" in the transcript.

[38] In the transcript the vote reads: "Massachusetts, Pennsylvania, Delaware, Maryland, Virginia, aye—5; Connecticut, New York, New Jersey, North Carolina, South Carolina, Georgia, no—6."

[39] The figures "1" and "2" are changed to "first" and "secondly" in the transcript.

287

On the Question to postpone in order to consider [40] Williamson's Resol<sup>n</sup> Mas<sup>ts</sup> no. Con<sup>t</sup> ay. N. Y. no. N. J. no. P<sup>a</sup> ay. Del. ay. M<sup>d</sup> ay. V<sup>a</sup> ay. N. C. ay. S. C. ay. Geo. ay.[41]

M<sup>r</sup> GERRY & M<sup>r</sup> MADISON—move to add to M<sup>r</sup> Williamsons 1,[39] Quest: "and for 1 year thereafter." On this amend<sup>t</sup> Mas<sup>ts</sup> no. Con<sup>t</sup> ay. N. Y. ay. N. J. no. P. no. Del. ay. M<sup>d</sup> ay. V<sup>a</sup> ay. N. C. ay. S. C. ay. Geo. no.[42]

On M<sup>r</sup> Will–son's 1 Question as amend<sup>ed</sup> vz. inelig: & incapable &c. &c for 1 year &c. ag<sup>d</sup> [43] unanimously.

On the 2.[44] question as to ineligibility &c. to State offices.[45] Mas. ay. C<sup>t</sup> no. N. Y. no. N. J. no. P. ay. Del. no. M<sup>d</sup> no. V<sup>a</sup> ay. N. C. no. S. C. no. Geo. no.[46]

The 5.[47] Resol: "that each branch have the right of originating acts" was agreed to nem: con:

Adj<sup>d</sup>

---

## WEDNESDAY JUNE 27. IN CONVENTION

M<sup>r</sup> RUTLIDGE moved to postone the 6<sup>th</sup> Resolution, defining the powers of Cong<sup>s</sup> in order to take up the 7 & 8 which involved the most fundamental points; the rules of suffrage in the 2 branches which was agreed to nem. con.

A question being proposed on Resol: 7 [48]: declaring that the suffrage in the first branch s<sup>d</sup> be according to an equitable ratio.

M<sup>r</sup> L. MARTIN contended at great length and with great eagerness that the General Gov<sup>t</sup> was meant merely to preserve the State Govern<sup>ts</sup>: not to govern individuals: that its powers ought to be kept within narrow limits; that if too little power was given to it, more might be added; but that if too much, it could never be resumed: that individuals as such have little to do but with their

---

[39] The figures "1" and "2" are changed to "first" and "secondly" in the transcript.
[40] The word "Mr." is here inserted in the transcript.
[41] In the transcript the vote reads: "Connecticut, Pennsylvania, Delaware, Maryland, Virginia, North Carolina, South Carolina, Georgia, aye—8; Massachusetts, New York, New Jersey, no—3."
[42] In the transcript the vote reads: "Connecticut, New York, Delaware, Maryland, Virginia, North Carolina, South Carolina, aye—7; Massachusetts, New Jersey, Pennsylvania, Georgia, no—4."
[43] The word "to" is here inserted in the transcript.
[44] The figure "2" is changed to "second" in the transcript.
[45] The transcript italicizes the words "State offices."
[46] In the transcript the vote reads: "Massachusetts, Pennsylvania, Virginia, aye—3; Connecticut, New York, New Jersey, Delaware, Maryland, North Carolina, South Carolina, Georgia, no—8."
[47] The figure "5" is changed to "fifth" in the transcript.
[48] The words "the seventh Resolution" are substituted in the transcript for "Resol: 7."

own States; that the Gen! Gov! has no more to apprehend from the States composing the Union, while it pursues proper measures, that [49] a Gov! over individuals has to apprehend from its subjects: that to resort to the Citizens at large for their sanction to a new Govern! will be throwing them back into a State of Nature: that the dissolution of the State Gov!ᵗˢ is involved in the nature of the process: that the people have no right to do this without the consent of those to whom they have delegated their power for State purposes: through their tongue only they can speak, through their ears, only, can hear: that the States have shewn a good disposition to comply with the Acts, of Cong! weak, contemptibly weak as that body has been; and have failed through inability alone to comply: that the heaviness of the private debts, and the waste of property during the war, were the chief causes of this inability: that he did not conceive the instances mentioned by Mr Madison of compacts between Vᵃ & Mᵈ between Pᵃ & N. J. or of troops raised by Massᵗˢ for defence against the Rebels, to be violations of the articles of confederation—that an equal vote in each State was essential to the federal idea, and was founded in justice & freedom, not merely in policy: that tho' the States may give up this right of sovereignty, yet they had not, and ought not: that the States like individuals were in a State of nature equally sovereign & free. In order to prove that individuals in a State of nature are equally free & independent he read passages from Locke, Vattel, Lord Summers—Priestly. To prove that the case is the same with States till they surrender their equal sovereignty, he read other passages in Locke & Vattel, and also Rutherford: that the States being equal cannot treat or confederate so as to give up an equality of votes without giving up their liberty: that the propositions on the table were a system of slavery for 10 States: that as Vᵃ Masᵗˢ & Pᵃ have $^{42}/_{90}$ of the votes they can do as they please without a miraculous Union of the other ten: that they will have nothing to do, but to gain over one of the ten to make them compleat masters of the rest: that they can then appoint an Execut! & Judiciary & legislate [50]

---

[49] The word "than" is substituted in the transcript for "that."
[50] The word "legislature" is substituted in the transcript for "legislate."

for them as they please: that there was & would continue a natural predilection & partiality in men for their own States; that the States, particularly the smaller, would never allow a negative to be exercised over their laws: that no State in ratifying the Confederation had objected to the equality of votes; that the complaints at present run not ag$^{st}$ this equality but the want of power; that 16 members from V$^a$ would be more likely to act in concert than a like number formed of members from different States; that instead of a junction of the small States as a remedy, he thought a division of the large States would be more eligible.—This was the substance of a speech which was continued more than three hours. He was too much exhausted he said to finish his remarks, and reminded the House that he should to-morrow, resume them.

Adj$^d$

THURSDAY JUNE 28$^{TH}$ IN CONVENTION

M$^r$ L. MARTIN resumed his discourse, contending that the Gen$^l$ Gov$^t$ ought to be formed for the States, not for individuals: that if the States were to have votes in proportion to their numbers of people, it would be the same thing whether their representatives were chosen by the Legislatures or the people; the smaller States would be equally enslaved; that if the large States have the same interest with the smaller as was urged, there could be no danger in giving them an equal vote; they would not injure themselves, and they could not injure the large ones on that supposition without injuring themselves and if the interests, were not the same, the inequality of suffrage w$^d$ be dangerous to the smaller States: that it will be in vain to propose any plan offensive to the rulers of the States, whose influence over the people will certainly prevent their adopting it: that the large States were weak at present in proportion to their extent: & could only be made formidable to the small ones, by the weight of their votes; that in case a dissolution of the Union should take place, the small States would have nothing to fear from their power; that if in such a case the three great States should league themselves together, the other ten could do so too: & that he had rather see partial confederacies take place, than the plan on the table.

This was the substance of the residue of his discourse which was delivered with much diffuseness & considerable vehemence.

M: LANSING & M: DAYTON moved to strike out "not." so that the 7 art: might read that the rights [51] of suffrage in the 1st branch ought to be according to the rule established by the Confederation."

M: DAYTON expressed great anxiety that the question might not be put till tomorrow; Govern: Livingston being kept away by indisposition, and the representation of N. Jersey thereby suspended.

M: WILLIAMSON. thought that if any political truth could be grounded on mathematical demonstration, it was that if the States were equally sovereign now, and parted with equal proportions of sovereignty, that they would remain equally sovereign. He could not comprehend how the smaller States would be injured in the case, and wished some Gentleman would vouchsafe a solution of it. He observed that the small States, if they had a plurality of votes would have an interest in throwing the burdens off their own shoulders on those of the large ones. He begged that the expected addition of new States from the Westward might be kept in [52] view. They would be small States, they would be poor States, they would be unable to pay in proportion to their numbers; their distance from market rendering the produce of their labour less valuable; they would consequently be tempted to combine for the purpose of laying burdens on commerce & consumption which would fall with greatest [53] weight on the old States.

M: MADISON, s.d he was much disposed to concur in any expedient not inconsistent with fundamental principles, that could remove the difficulty concerning the rule of representation. But he could neither be convinced that the rule contended for was just, nor [54] necessary for the safety of the small States ag:st the large States. That it was not just, had been conceded by M: Breerly & M: Patterson themselves. The expedient proposed by them was a new partition of the territory of the U. States. The fallacy of the reasoning drawn from the equality of Sovereign States in the

---

[51] The transcript uses the word "rights" in the singular.
[52] The words "taken into" are substituted in the transcript for "kept in."
[53] The word "greater" is substituted in the transcript for "greatest."
[54] The words "that it was" are here inserted in the transcript.

formation of compacts, lay in confounding mere Treaties, in which were specified certain duties to which the parties were to be bound, and certain rules by which their subjects were to be reciprocally governed in their intercourse, with a compact by which an authority was created paramount to the parties, & making laws for the government of them. If France, England & Spain were to enter into a Treaty for the regulation of commerce &c with the Prince of Monacho & 4 or 5 other of the smallest sovereigns of Europe, they would not hesitate to treat as equals, and to make the regulations perfectly reciprocal. W.d the case be the same, if a Council were to be formed of deputies from each with authority and discretion, to raise money, levy troops, determine the value of coin &c? Would 30 or 40. million [55] of people submit their fortunes into the hands, of a few thousands? If they did it would only prove that they expected more from the terror of their superior force, than they feared from the selfishness of their feeble associates. Why are Counties of the same states represented in proportion to their numbers? Is it because the representatives are chosen by the people themselves? So will be the representatives in the Nation! Legislature. Is it because, the larger have more at stake than the smaller? The case will be the same with the larger & smaller States. Is it because the laws are to operate immediately on their persons & properties? The same is the case in some degree as the articles of confederation stand; the same will be the case in a far greater degree under the plan proposed to be substituted. In the cases of captures, of piracies, and of offences in a federal army; the property & persons of individuals depend on the laws of Cong.s By the plan proposed a compleat power of taxation, the highest prerogative of supremacy is proposed to be vested in the National Gov.t Many other powers are added which assimilate it to the Gov.t of individual States. The negative proposed on the State laws, will make it an essential branch of the State Legislatures & of course will require that it should be exercised by a body established on like principles with the other [56] branches of those Legislatures.— That it is not necessary to secure the small States ag.st the large ones

---

[55] The transcript uses the word "million" in the plural.
[56] The word "other" is omitted in the transcript.

he conceived to be equally obvious: Was a combination of the large ones dreaded? this must arise either from some interest common to V: Mas: & P: & distinguishing them from the other States or from the mere circumstance of similarity of size. Did any such common interest exist? In point of situation they could not have been more effectually separated from each other by the most jealous citizen of the most jealous State. In point of manners, Religion, and the other circumstances which sometimes beget affection between different communities, they were not more assimilated than the other States.—In point of the staple productions they were as dissimilar as any three other States in the Union. The Staple of Mas:ᵗˢ was *fish*, of P: *flower*, of V: *Tob*: Was a combination to be apprehended from the mere circumstance of equality of size? Experience suggested no such danger. The journals of Cong: did not present any peculiar association of these States in the votes recorded. It had never been seen that different Counties in the same State, conformable in extent, but disagreeing in other circumstances, betrayed a propensity to such combinations. Experience rather taught a contrary lesson. Among individuals of superior eminence & weight in Society, rivalships were much more frequent than coalitions. Among independent nations, pre-eminent over their neighbours, the same remark was verified. Carthage & Rome tore one another to pieces instead of uniting their forces to devour the weaker nations of the Earth. The Houses of Austria & France were hostile as long as they remained the greatest powers of Europe. England & France have succeeded to the pre-eminence & to the enmity. To this principle we owe perhaps our liberty. A coalition between those powers would have been fatal to us. Among the principal members of antient & Modern confederacies, we find the same effect from the same cause. The contintions, not the Coalitions of Sparta, Athens & Thebes, proved fatal to the smaller members of the Amphyctionic Confederacy. The contentions, not the combinations of Prussia & Austria, have distracted & oppressed the Germanic [57] empire. Were the large States formidable *singly* to their smaller neighbours? On this supposition the latter ought

---

[57] The word "German" is substituted in the transcript for "Germanic."

to wish for such a general Gov! as will operate with equal energy on the former as on themselves. The more lax the band, the more liberty the larger will have to avail themselves of their superior force. Here again Experience was an instructive monitor. What is yᵉ situation of the weak compared with the strong in those stages of civilization in which the violence of individuals is least controuled by an efficient Government? The Heroic period of Antient Greece the feudal licentiousness of the middle ages of Europe, the existing condition of the American Savages, answer this question. What is the situation of the minor sovereigns in the great society of independent nations, in which the more powerful are under no controul but the nominal authority of the law of Nations? Is not the danger to the former exactly in proportion to their weakness. But there are cases still more in point. What was the condition of the weaker members of the Amphyctionic Confederacy. Plutarch [⁵⁸ life of Themistocles] will inform us that it happened but too often that the strongest cities corrupted & awed the weaker, and that Judgment went in favor of the more powerful party. What is the condition of the lesser states in the German Confederacy? We all know that they are exceedingly trampled upon; and that they owe their safety as far as they enjoy it, partly to their enlisting themselves, under the rival banners of the pre-eminent members, partly to alliances with neighbouring Princes which the Constitution of the Empire does not prohibit. What is the state of things in the lax system of the Dutch Confederacy? Holland contains about ½ the people, supplies about ½ of ⁵⁹ the money, and by her influence, silently & indirectly governs the whole republic. In a word; the two extremes before us are a perfect separation & a perfect incorporation, of the 13 States. In the first case they would be independent nations subject to no law, but the law of nations. In the last, they would be mere counties of one entire republic, subject to one common law. In the first case the smaller States would have every thing to fear from the larger. In the last they would have nothing to fear. The true policy of the small States

---

⁵⁸ The word "see" is here inserted in the transcript.
⁵⁹ The word "of" is omitted in the transcript.

therefore lies in promoting those principles & that form of Gov$^t$ which will most approximate the States to the condition of counties. Another consideration may be added. If the Gen! Gov$^t$ be feeble, the large States distrusting its continuance, and foreseeing that their importance & security may depend on their own size & strength, will never submit to a partition. Give to the Gen! Gov$^t$ sufficient energy & permanency, & you remove the objection. Gradual partitions of the large, & junctions of the small States will be facilitated, and time may effect that equalization, which is wished for by the small States now, but can never be accomplished at once.

M$^r$ WILSON. The leading argument of those who contend for equality of votes among the States is that the States as such being equal, and being represented not as districts of individuals, but in their political & corporate capacities, are entitled to an equality of suffrage. According to this mode of reasoning the representation of the boroughs in Eng$^{ld}$ which has been allowed on all hands to be the rotten part of the Constitution, is perfectly right & proper. They are like the States represented in their corporate capacity like the States therefore they are entitled to equal voices, old Sarum to as many as London. And instead of the injury supposed hitherto to be done to London, the true ground of complaint lies with old Sarum: for London instead of two which is her proper share, sends four representatives to Parliament.

M$^r$ SHERMAN. The question is not what rights naturally belong to men [60]; but how they may be most equally & effectually guarded in Society. And if some give up more than others in order to attain [61] this end, there can be no room for complaint. To do otherwise, to require an equal concession from all, if it would create danger to the rights of some, would be sacrificing the end to the means. The rich man who enters into Society along with the poor man, gives up more than the poor man, yet with an equal vote he is equally safe. Were he to have more votes than the poor man in proportion to his superior stake, the rights of the

---

[60] The word "men" is used in the singular in the transcript.
[61] The word "obtain" is substituted in the transcript for "attain."

poor man would immediately cease to be secure. This consideration prevailed when the articles of Confederation were formed.

The determination of the question from [62] striking out the word "not" was put off till tomorrow at the request of the Deputies of N. York. See opposite page & insert the Speech of Doct: F in this place.[63]

Mr President

The small progress we have made after 4 or five weeks close attendance & continual reasonings with each other—our different sentiments on almost every question, several of the last producing as many noes as ays, is methinks a melancholy proof of the imperfection of the Human Understanding. We indeed seem to feel our own want of political wisdom, since we have been running about in search of it. We have gone back to ancient history for models of Government, and examined the different forms of those Republics which having been formed with the seeds of their own dissolution now no longer exist. And we have viewed Modern States all round Europe, but find none of their Constitutions suitable to our circumstances.

In this situation of this Assembly, groping as it were in the dark to find political truth, and scarce able to distinguish it when presented to us, how has it happened, Sir, that we have not hitherto once thought of humbly applying to the Father of lights to illuminate our understandings? In the beginning of the Contest with G. Britain, when we were sensible of danger we had daily prayer in this room for the divine protection.—Our prayers, Sir, were heard, & they were graciously answered. All of us who were engaged in the struggle must have observed frequent instances of a superintending providence in our favor. To that kind providence we owe this happy opportunity of consulting in peace on the means of establishing our future national felicity. And have we now forgotten that powerful friend? or do we imagine that we no longer need his assistance? I have lived, Sir, a long time, and the longer I live, the more convincing proofs I see of this truth—*that God Governs in the affairs of men.* And if a sparrow cannot

---

[62] The word "from" is changed to "for" in the transcript.
[63] Madison's direction is omitted in the transcript and the words ": Doctor Franklin" are inserted.

fall to the ground without his notice, is it probable that an empire can rise without his aid? We have been assured, Sir, in the sacred writings, that "except the Lord build the House they labour in vain that build it." I firmly believe this; and I also believe that without his concurring aid we shall succeed in this political building no better, than the Builders of Babel: We shall be divided by our little partial local interests; our projects will be confounded, and we ourselves shall become a reproach and bye word down to future ages. And what is worse, mankind may hereafter from this unfortunate instance, despair of establishing Governments by Human wisdom and leave it to chance, war and conquest.

I therefore beg leave to move—that henceforth prayers imploring the assistance of Heaven, and its blessings on our deliberations, be held in this Assembly every morning before we proceed to business, and that one or more of the Clergy of this City be requested to officiate in that Service—

M[r] SHARMAN seconded the motion.

M[r] HAMILTON & several others expressed their apprehensions that however proper such a resolution might have been at the beginning of the convention, it might at this late day, 1.[64] bring on it some disagreeable animadversions. & 2.[65] lead the public to believe that the embarrassments and dissensions within the Convention, had suggested this measure. It was answered by Doc[r] F. M[r] SHERMAN & others, that the past omission of a duty could not justify a further omission—that the rejection of such a proposition would expose the Convention to more unpleasant animadversions than the adoption of it: and that the alarm out of doors that might be excited for the state of things within, would at least be as likely to do good as ill.

M[r] WILLIAMSON, observed that the true cause of the omission could not be mistaken. The Convention had no funds.

M[r] RANDOLPH proposed in order to give a favorable aspect to y[e] measure, that a sermon be preached at the request of the convention on [66] 4[th] of July, the anniversary of Independence; &

---

[64] The figure "1" is changed to "in the first place" in the transcript.
[65] The figure "2" is changed to "in the second place" in the transcript.
[66] The word "the" is here inserted in the transcript.

thenceforward prayers be used [67] in y̆ Convention every morning. D̃ʳ Franḵⁿ 2ᵈᵉᵈ this motion  After several unsuccessful attempts for silently postponing the [68] matter by adjournᵍ the adjournment was at length carried, without any vote on the motion.

## Friday June 29ᵀᴴ  in Convention

Doctʳ Johnson.  The controversy must be endless whilst Gentlemen differ in the grounds of their arguments; Those on one side considering the States as districts of people composing one political Society; those on the other considering them as so many political societies.  The fact is that the States do exist as political Societies, and a Govᵗ is to be formed for them in their political capacity, as well as for the individuals composing them.  Does it not seem to follow, that if the States as such are to exist they must be armed with some power of self-defence.  This is the idea of [Col. Mason] who appears to have looked to the bottom of this matter.  Besides the Aristocratic and other interests, which ought to have the means of defending themselves, the States have their interests as such, and are equally entitled to likes means.  On the whole he thought that as in some respects the States are to be considered in their political capacity, and in others as districts of individual citizens, the two ideas embraced on different sides, instead of being opposed to each other, ought to be combined; that in *one* branch the *people*, ought to be represented; in the *other* the *States*.

Mʳ Ghorum.  The States as now confederated have no doubt a right to refuse to be consolidated, or to be formed into any new system.  But he wished the small States which seemed most ready to object, to consider which are to give up most, they or the larger ones.  He conceived that a rupture of the Union wᵈ be an event unhappy for all, but surely the large States would be least unable to take care of themselves, and to make connections with one another.  The weak therefore were most interested in establishing some general system for maintaining order.  If among individuals, composed partly of weak, and partly of strong, the former most

---
[67] The words "&c to be read" are substituted in the transcript for "be used."
[68] The word "this" is substituted in the transcript for "the."

need the protection of law & Government, the case is exactly the same with weak & powerful States. What would be the situation of Delaware (for these things he found must be spoken out, & it might as well be done [69] first as last) what wᵈ be the situation of Delaware in case of a separation of the States? Would she not lie [70] at themercy of Pennsylvania? would not her true interest lie in being consolidated with her, and ought she not now to wish for such a union with Pᵃ under one Govᵗ as will put it out of the power of Penᵃ to oppress her? Nothing can be more ideal than the danger apprehended by the States, from their being formed into one nation. Massᵗˢ was originally three colonies, viz old Massᵗˢ Plymouth—& the province of Mayne. These apprehensions existed then. An incorporation took place; all parties were safe & satisfied; and every distinction is now forgotten. The case was similar with Connecticut & Newhaven. The dread of union was reciprocal; the consequence of it equally salutary and satisfactory. In like manner N. Jersey has been made one society out of two parts. Should a separation of the States take place, the fate of N. Jersey wᵈ be worst of all. She has no foreign commerce & can have but little. Pᵃ & N. York will continue to levy taxes on her consumption. If she consults her interest she wᵈ beg of all things to be annihilated. The apprehensions of the small States ought to be appeased by another reflection. Massᵗˢ will be divided. The province of Maine is already considered as approaching the term of its annexation to it; and Pᵃ will probably not increase, considering the present state of her population, & other events that may happen. On the whole he considered a Union of the States as necessary to their happiness, & a firm Genˡ Govᵗ as necessary to their Union. He shᵈ consider it as [71] his duty if his colleagues viewed the matter in the same light he did to stay here as long as any other State would remain with them, in order to agree on some plan that could with propriety be recommended to the people.

Mʳ Elsworth, did not despair. He still trusted that some good plan of Govᵗ wᵈ be divised & adopted.

---

[69] The word "at" is here inserted in the transcript.

[70] The word "be" is substituted in the transcript for "lie."

[71] The word "as" is omitted in the transcript.

Mr. READ. He shd have no objection to the system if it were truly national, but it has too much of a federal mixture in it. The little States he thought had not much to fear. He suspected that the large States felt their want of energy, & wished for a Genl Govt to supply the defect. Massts was evidently labouring under her weakness and he believed Delaware wd not be in much danger if in her neighbourhood. Delaware had enjoyed tranquility & he flattered himself wd continue to do so. He was not however so selfish as not to wish for a good Genl Govt. In order to obtain one the whole States must be incorporated. If the States remain, the representatives of the large ones will stick together, and carry every thing before them. The Executive also will be chosen under the influence of this partiality, and will betray it in his administration. These jealousies are inseparable from the scheme of leaving the States in existence. They must be done away. The ungranted lands also which have been assumed by particular States must also [72] be given up. He repeated his approbation of the plan of Mr Hamilton, & wished it to be substituted in place of [73] that on the table.

Mr. MADISON agreed with Docr Johnson, that the mixed nature of the Govt ought to be kept in view; but thought too much stress was laid on the rank of the States as political societies. There was a gradation, he observed from the smallest corporation, with the most limited powers, to the largest empire with the most perfect sovereignty. He pointed out the limitations on the sovereignty of the States, as now confederated their laws in relation to the paramount law of the Confederacy were analogous to that of bye laws to the supreme law within a State. Under the proposed Govt the powers of the States will be much farther reduced. According to the views of every member, the Genl Govt will have powers far beyond those exercised by the British Parliament, when the States were part of the British Empire. It will in particular have the power, without the consent of the State Legislatures, to levy money directly on [74] the people themselves; and therefore not to divest such *unequal*

---

[72] The word "also" is stricken out in the transcript.
[73] The word "for" is substituted in the transcript for "in place of."
[74] The word "from" is substituted in the transcript for "on."

portions of the people as composed the several States, of an *equal* voice, would subject the system to the reproaches & evils which have resulted from the vicious representation in G. B.

He entreated the gentlemen representing the small States to renounce a principle w<sup>ch</sup> was confessedly unjust, which c<sup>d</sup> never be admitted, & [75] if admitted must infuse mortality into a Constitution which we wished to last forever. He prayed them to ponder well the consequences of suffering the Confederacy to go to pieces. It had been s<sup>d</sup> that the want of energy in the large states w<sup>d</sup> be a security to the small. It was forgotten that this want of energy proceeded from the supposed security of the States ag<sup>st</sup> all external danger. Let each state depend on itself for its security, & let apprehensions arise arise of danger, from distant powers or from neighbouring States, & the languishing condition of all the States, large as well as small, w<sup>d</sup> soon be transformed into vigorous & high toned Gov<sup>ts</sup> His great fear was that their Gov<sup>ts</sup> w<sup>d</sup> then have too much energy, that these [76] might not only be formidable in the large to the small States, but fatal to the internal liberty of all. The same causes which have rendered the old world the Theatre of incessant wars, & have banished liberty from the face of it, w<sup>d</sup> soon produce the same effects here. The weakness & jealousy of the small States w<sup>d</sup> quickly introduce some regular military force ag<sup>st</sup> sudden danger from their powerful neighbours. The example w<sup>d</sup> be followed by others, and w<sup>d</sup> soon become universal. In time of actual war, great discretionary powers are constantly given to the Executive Magistrate. Constant apprehension of war, has the same tendency to render the head too large for the body. A standing military force, with an overgrown Executive will not long be safe companions to liberty. The means of defence ag<sup>st</sup> foreign danger, have been always the instruments of tyranny at home. Among the Romans it was a standing maxim to excite a war, whenever a revolt was apprehended. Throughout all Europe, the armies kept up under the pretext of defending, have enslaved the people. It is perhaps questionable, whether the

---

[75] The word "which" is here inserted in the transcript.
[76] The word "these" is stricken out in the transcript and "this" is written above it.

THOMAS JEFFERSON

best concerted system of absolute power in Europe c.d maintain itself, in a situation, where no alarms of external danger c.d tame the people to the domestic yoke. The insular situation of G. Britain was the principal cause of her being an exception to the general fate of Europe. It has rendered less defence necessary, and admitted a kind of defence w.ch c.d not be used for the purpose of oppression.—These consequences he conceived ought to be apprehended whether the States should run into a total separation from each other, or sh.d enter into partial confederacies. Either event w.d be truly deplorable; & those who might be accessary to either, could never be forgiven by their Country, nor by themselves.

\*M.r HAMILTON observed that individuals forming political Societies modify their rights differently, with regard to suffrage. Examples of it are found in all the States. In all of them some individuals are deprived of the right altogether, not having the requisite qualification of property. In some of the States the right of suffrage is allowed in some cases and refused in others. To vote for a member in one branch, a certain quantum of property, to vote for a member in another branch of the Legislature, a higher quantum of property is required. In like manner States may modify their right of suffrage differently, the larger exercising a larger, the smaller a smaller share of it. But as States are a collection of individual men which ought we to respect most, the rights of the people composing them, or of the artificial beings resulting from the composition. Nothing could be more preposterous or absurd than to sacrifice the former to the latter. It has been s.d that if the smaller States renounce their *equality*, they renounce at the same time their *liberty*. The truth is it is a contest for power, not for liberty. Will the men composing the small States be less free than those composing the larger. The State of Delaware having 40,000 souls will *lose* [78] *power*, if she has $\frac{1}{10}$ only of the votes allowed to P.a having 400,000: but will the people of Del: *be less free*, if each citizen has an equal vote with each citizen of P.a He admitted that common residence within the same

---

\*From this date he was absent till the    of [77]

[77] The date, "13th of August," is supplied in the transcript.

[78] The transcript does not italicize the word "*lose*."

302

State would produce a certain degree of attachment; and that this principle might have a certain influence in [79] public affairs. He thought however that this might by some precautions be in a great measure excluded: and that no material inconvenience could result from it, as there could not be any ground for combination among the States whose influence was most dreaded. The only considerable distinction of interests, lay between the carrying & non-carrying States, which divide [80] instead of uniting the largest States. No considerable inconvenience had been found from the division of the State of N. York into different districts of different sizes.

Some of the consequences of a dissolution of the Union, and the establishment of partial confederacies, had been pointed out. He would add another of a most serious nature. Alliances will immediately be formed with different rival & hostile nations of Europes, who will foment disturbances among ourselves, and make us parties to all their own quarrels. Foreign Nations having American dominions [81] are & must be jealous of us. Their representatives betray the utmost anxiety for our fate, & for the result of this meeting, which must have an essential influence on it.—It had been said that respectability in the eyes of foreign Nations was not the object at which we aimed; that the proper object of republican Government was domestic tranquility & happiness. This was an ideal distinction. No Governm.<sup>t</sup> could give us tranquility & happiness at home, which did not possess sufficient stability and strength to make us respectable abroad. This was the critical moment for forming such a Government. We should run every risk in trusting to future amendments. As yet we retain the habits of union. We are weak & sensible of our weakness. Henceforward the motives will become feebler, and the difficulties greater. It is a miracle that we were [82] now here exercising our tranquil & free deliberations on the subject. It would be madness to trust to future miracles. A thousand causes must obstruct a reproduction of them.

---

[79] The word "on" is substituted in the transcript for "in."
[80] The word "divides" is substituted in the transcript for "divide,"
[81] The transcript uses the word "dominions" in the singular.
[82] The word "are" is substituted in the transcript for "were."

Mr PIERCE considered the equality of votes under the Confederation as the great source of the public difficulties. The members of Congs were advocates for local advantages. State distinctions must be sacrificed as far as the general good required, but without destroying the States. Tho' from a small State he felt himself a Citizen of the U. S.

Mr GERRY urged that we never were independent States, were not such now, & never could be even on the principles of the Confederation. The States & the advocates for them were intoxicated with the idea of their *sovereignty*. He was a member of Congress at the time the federal articles were formed. The injustice of allowing each State an equal vote was long insisted on. He voted for it, but it was agst his Judgment, and under the pressure of public danger, and the obstinacy of the lesser States. The present confederation he considered as dissolving. The fate of the Union will be decided by the Convention. If they do not agree on something, few delegates will probably be appointed to Congs If they do Congs will probably be kept up till the new System should be adopted. He lamented that instead of coming here like a band of brothers, belonging to the same family, we seemed to have brought with us the spirit of political negociators.

Mr L. MARTIN. remarked that the language of the States being *sovereign* & *independent*, was once familiar & understood; though it seemed now so strange & obscure. He read those passages in the articles of Confederation, which describe them in that language.

On the question as moved by Mr Lansing. Shall the word "not" be struck out.

Massts no. Cont ay. N. Y. ay. N. J. ay. Pa no. Del. ay. Md divd Va no. N. C. no. S. C. no. Geo. no.[83]

On the motion to agree to the clause as reported, "that the rule of suffrage in the 1st branch ought not to be according to that established by the articles of [84] Confederation.

Mass. ay. Cont no. N. Y. no. N. J. no. Pa ay. Del. no. Md divd Va ay. N. C. ay. S. C. ay. Geo. ay.[85]

---

[83] In the transcript the vote reads: "Connecticut, New York, New Jersey, Delaware, aye—4; Massachusetts, Pennsylvania, Virginia, North Carolina, South Carolina, Georgia, no—6; Maryland, divided."
[84] The word "the" is here inserted in the transcript.
[85] In the transcript the vote reads: "Massachusetts, Pennsylvania, Virginia, North Carolina, South Carolina, Georgia, aye—6; Connecticut, New York, New Jersey, Delaware, no—4; Maryland, divided."

Doc: JOHNSON & M: ELSEWORTH moved to postpone the residue of the clause, & take up—y: 8—Resol:

On [84] question.

Mas. no. Con: ay. N. Y. ay. N. J. ay. P: ay. Del. no. M: ay. V: ay. N. C. ay. S. C. ay. Geo. ay.[86]

M: ELSEWORTH moved that the rule of suffrage in the 2: branch be the same with that established by the articles of confederation." He was not sorry on the whole he said that the vote just passed, had determined against this rule in the first branch. He hoped it would become a ground of compromise with regard to the 2: branch. We were partly national; partly federal. The proportional representation in the first branch was conformable to the national principle & would secure the large States ag:t the small. An equality of voices was conformable to the federal principle and was necessary to secure the Small States ag:t the large. He trusted that on this middle ground a compromise would take place. He did not see that it could on any other. And if no compromise should take place, our meeting would not only be in vain but worse than in vain. To the Eastward he was sure Mass:ts was the only State that would listen to a proposition for excluding the States as equal political Societies, from an equal voice in both branches. The others would risk every consequence rather than part with so dear a right. An attempt to deprive them of it, was at once cutting the body of America in two, and as he supposed would be the case, somewhere about this part of it. The large States he conceived would notwithstanding the equality of votes, have an influence that would maintain their superiority. Holland, as had been admitted [by M: Madison] had, notwithstanding a like equality in the Dutch Confederacy, a prevailing influence in the public measures. The power of self-defence was essential to the small States. Nature had given it to the smallest insect of the creation. He could never admit that there was no danger of combinations among the large States. They will like individuals find out and avail themselves of the advantage to be gained by it. It was true the danger would be greater, if they were contiguous

---

[86] In the transcript the vote reads: "Connecticut, New York, New Jersey, Pennsylvania, Maryland, Virginia, North Carolina, South Carolina, Georgia, aye—9; Massachusetts, Delaware, no—2."

305

and had a more immediate [87] common interest. A defensive combination of the small States was rendered more difficult by their greater number. He would mention another consideration of great weight. The existing confederation was founded on the equality of the States in the article of suffrage: was it meant to pay no regard to this antecedent plighted faith. Let a strong Executive, a Judiciary & Legislative power be created; but Let not too much be attempted; by which all may be lost. He was not in general a half-way man, yet he preferred doing half the good we could, rather than do nothing at all. The other half may be added, when the necessity shall be more fully experienced.

Mr BALDWIN could have wished that the powers of the General Legislature had been defined, before the mode of constituting it had been agitated. He should vote against the motion of Mr Elseworth, tho' he did not like the Resolution as it stood in the Report of the Committee of the whole. He thought the second branch ought to be the representation of property, and that in forming it therefore some reference ought to be had to the relative wealth of their Constituents, and to the principles on which the Senate of Massts was constituted. He concurred with those who thought it wd be impossible for the Genl Legislature to extend its cares to the local matters of the States.

Adjd

---

SATURDAY JUNE 30. 1787.[88] IN CONVENTION

Mr BREARLY moved that the Presidt write to the Executive of N. Hamshire, informing it that the business depending before the Convention was of such a nature as to require the immediate attendance of the deputies of that State. In support of his motion he observed that the difficulties of the subject and the diversity of opinions called for all the assistance we could possibly obtain. [it was well understood that the object was to add N. Hamshire to the no of States opposed to the doctrine of proportional representation, which it was presumed from her relative size she must be adverse to].

---

[87] The word "and" is here inserted in the transcript.
[88] The year "1787" is omitted in the transcript.

M.^r PATTERSON seconded the motion

M.^r RUTLIDGE could see neither the necessity nor propriety of such a measure. They are not unapprized of the meeting, and can attend if they choose. Rho. Island might as well be urged to appoint & send deputies. Are we to suspend the business until the deputies arrive? if we proceed he hoped all the great points would be adjusted before the letter could produce its effect.

M.^r KING. said he had written more than once as a private correspondent, & the answers [89] gave him every reason to expect that State would be represented very shortly, if it sh.^d be so at all. Circumstances of a personal nature had hitherto prevented it. A letter c.^d have no effect.

M.^r WILSON wished to know whether it would be consistent with the rule or reason of secresy, to communicate to N. Hamshire that the business was of such a nature as the motion described. It w.^d spread a great alarm. Besides he doubted the propriety of soliciting any State on the subject; the meeting being merely voluntary—on the [90] motion of M.^r Brearly Mas.^{ts} no. Con.^t no. N. Y. ay. N. J. ay P.^a not on y.^e floor. Del. not on floor. M.^d div.^d V.^a no. N. C . no. S. C. no. Geo. not on floor.[91]

The motion of M.^r Elseworth [92] resumed for allowing each State an equal vote in y.^e 2.^d branch.

M.^r WILSON did not expect such a motion after the establishment of y.^e contrary principle in the 1.^{st} branch; and considering the reasons which would oppose it, even if an equal vote had been allowed in the 1.^{st} branch. The Gentleman from Connecticut [M.^r Elseworth] had pronounced that if the motion should not be acceded to, of all the States North of Pen.^a one only would agree to any Gen.^l Government. He entertained more favorable hopes of Conn.^t and of the other Northern States. He hoped the alarms exceeded their cause, and that they would not abandon a Country to which they were bound by so many strong and endearing ties. But should the deplored event happen, it would neither stagger his

---
[89] The transcript uses the word "answers" in the singular.
[90] The word "the" is omitted in the transcript.
[91] In the transcript the vote reads: "New York, New Jersey, aye—2; Massachusetts, Connecticut, Virginia, North Carolina, South Carolina, no—5; Maryland, divided; Pennsylvania, Delaware, Georgia, no.^t on the floor."
[92] The word "being" is here inserted in the transcript.

sentiments nor his duty. If the minority of the people of America refuse to coalesce with the majority on just and proper principles, if a separation must take place, it could never happen on better grounds. The votes of yesterday ag$^{st}$ the just principle of representation, were as 22 to 90 of the people of America. Taking the opinions to be the same on this point, and he was sure if there was any room for change, it could not be on the side of the majority, the question will be shall less than $\frac{1}{4}$ of the U. States withdraw themselves from the Union; or shall more than $\frac{3}{4}$. renounce the inherent, indisputable, and unalienable rights of men, in favor of the artificial systems of States. If issue must be joined, it was on this point he would chuse to join it. The gentlemen from Connecticut in supposing that the prepondenancy [93] secured to the majority in the 1$^{st}$ branch had removed the objections to an equality of votes in the 2$^d$ branch for the security of the minority, narrowed the case extremely. Such an equality will enable the minority to controul in all cases whatsoever, the sentiments and interests of the majority. Seven States will controul six: Seven States, according to the estimates that had been used, composed $\frac{24}{90}$. of the whole people. It would be in the power then of less than $\frac{1}{3}$ to overrule $\frac{2}{3}$ whenever a question should happen to divide the States in that manner. Can we forget for whom we are forming a Government? Is it for *men*, or for the imaginary beings called *States?* Will our honest Constituents be satisfied with metaphysical distinctions? Will they, ought they to be satisfied with being told that the one third compose the greater number of States? The rule of suffrage ought on every principle to be the same in the 2$^d$ as in the 1$^{st}$ branch. If the Government be not laid on this foundation, it can be neither solid nor lasting. Any other principle will be local, confined & temporary. This will expand with the expansion, and grow with the growth of the U. States.—Much has been said of an imaginary combination of three States. Sometimes a danger of monarchy, sometimes of aristocracy, has been charged on it. No explanation however of the danger has been vouchsafed. It would be easy to prove both from reason & history that rivalships would be more probable than coalitions; and that there are no coinciding

---

[93] The word "prepondenancy" is changed to "preponderance" in the transcript.

interests that could produce the latter. No answer has yet been given to the observations of [M![Madison] on this subject. Should the Executive Magistrate be taken from one of the large States would not the other two be thereby thrown into the scale with the other States? Whence then the danger of monarchy? Are the people of the three large States more aristocratic than those of the small ones? Whence then the danger of aristocracy from their influence? It is all a mere illusion of names. We talk of States, till we forget what they are composed of. Is a real & fair majority, the natural hot-bed of aristocracy? It is a part of the definition of this species of Gov! or rather of tyranny, that the smaller number governs the greater. It is true that a majority of States in the 2ᵈ branch can not carry a law ag:ˢᵗ a majority of the people in the 1ˢᵗ But this removes half only of the objection. Bad Govern:ᵗˢ are of two sorts. 1.⁹⁴ that which does too little. 2.⁹⁴ that which does too much: that which fails thro' weakness; and that which destroys thro' oppression. Under which of these evils do the U. States at present groan? under the weakness and inefficiency of its Govern! To remedy this weakness we have been sent to this Convention. If the motion should be agreed to, we shall leave the U. S. fettered precisely as heretofore; with the additional mortification of seeing the good purposes of y: fair represention of the people in the 1ˢᵗ branch, defeated in ⁹⁵ 2ᵈ Twenty four will still controul sixty six. He lamented that such a disagreement should prevail on the point of representation, as he did not forsee that it would happen on the other point most contested, the boundary between the Gen! & the local authorities. He thought the States necessary & valuable parts of a good system.

M! ELSEWORTH. The capital objection of M! Wilson "that the minority will rule the majority" is not true. The power is given to the few to save them from being destroyed by the many. If an equality of votes had been given to them in both branches, the objection might have had weight. Is it a novel thing that the few should have a check on the many? Is it not the case in the British Constitution the wisdom of which so many gentlemen have

---

⁹⁴ The figures "1" and "2" are changed to "first" and "secondly" in the transcript.
⁹⁵ The word "the" is here inserted in the transcript.

united in applauding? Have not the House of Lords, who form so small a proportion of the nation a negative on the laws, as a necessary defence of their peculiar rights ag$^{st}$ the encroachm$^{ts}$ of the Commons. No instance of a Confederacy has existed in which an equality of voices has not been exercised by the members of it. We are running from one extreme to another. We are razing the foundations of the building, when we need only repair the roof. No salutary measure has been lost for want of *a majority of the States*, to favor it. If security be all that the great States wish for the 1$^{st}$ branch secures them. The danger of combinations among them is not imaginary. Altho' no particular abuses could be foreseen by him, the possibility of them would be sufficient to alarm him. But he could easily conceive cases in which they might result from such combinations. Suppose that in pursuance of some commercial treaty or arrangement, three or four free ports & no more were to be established would not combinations be formed in favor of Boston—Philad$^a$ & & some port in [96] Chesapeak? A like concert might be formed in the appointment of the great officers. He appealed again to the obligations of the federal pact which was still in force, and which had been entered into with so much solemnity; persuading himself that some regard would still be paid to the plighed faith under which each State small as well as great, held an equal right of suffrage in the general Councils. His remarks were not the result of partial or local views. The State he represented [Connecticut] held a middle rank.

M$^r$ MADISON did justice to the able & close reasoning of M$^r$ E. but must observe that it did not always accord with itself. On another occasion, the large States were described by him as the Aristocratic States, ready to oppress the small. Now the small are the House of Lords requiring a negative to defend them ag$^{st}$ the more numerous commons. M$^r$ E. had also erred in saying that no instance had existed in which confederated States had not retained to themselves a perfect equality of suffrage. Passing over the German system in which the K. of Prussia has nine voices, he reminded M$^r$ E. of the Lycian confederacy, in which the component members had votes proportioned to their importance, and which

---

[96] The words "of the" are substituted in the transcript for "in."

Montesquieu recommends as the fittest model for that form of Government. Had the fact been as stated by M.<sup>r</sup> E. it would have been of little avail to him, or rather would have strengthened the arguments ag.<sup>st</sup> him; the History & fate of the several confederacies modern as well as Antient, demonstrating some radical vice in their structure. In reply to the appeal of M.<sup>r</sup> E. to the faith plighted in the existing federal compact, he remarked that the party claiming from others an adherence to a common engagement ought at least to be guiltless itself of a violation. Of all the States however Connecticut was perhaps least able to urge this plea. Besides the various omissions to perform the stipulated acts from which no State was free, the Legislature of that State had by a pretty recent vote, *positively, refused* to pass a law for complying with the Requisitions of Cong.<sup>s</sup> and had transmitted a copy of the vote to Cong.<sup>s</sup> It was urged, he said, continually that an equality of votes in the 2.<sup>d</sup> branch was not only necessary to secure the small, but would be perfectly safe to the large ones whose majority in the 1.<sup>st</sup> branch was an effectual bulwark. But notwithstanding this apparent defence, the majority of States might still injure the majority of [97] people. 1.[98] they could *obstruct* the wishes and interests of the majority. 2.[98] they could *extort* measures repugnant to the wishes & interest of the Majority. 3.[98] they could *impose* measures adverse thereto; as the 2.<sup>d</sup> branch will probly exercise some great powers, in which the 1.<sup>st</sup> will not participate. He admitted that every peculiar interest whether in any class of citizens, or any description of States, ought to be secured as far as possible. Wherever there is danger of attack there ought [99] be given a constitutional power of defence. But he contended that the States were divided into different interests not by their difference of size, but by other circumstances; the most material of which resulted partly from climate, but principally from the effects of their having or not having slaves. These two causes concurred in forming the great division of interests in the U. States. It did not lie between the large & small States: It lay between the Northern & Southern, and if any defensive

---

[97] The word "the" is here inserted in the transcript.
[98] The figures "1," "2" and "3" are changed to "In the first place," "Secondly" and "Thirdly."
[99] The word "to" is here inserted in the transcript.

power were necessary, it ought to be mutually given to these two interests. He was so strongly impressed with this important truth that he had been casting about in his mind for some expedient that would answer the purpose. The one which had occurred was that instead of proportioning the votes of the States in both branches, to their respective numbers of inhabitants computing the slaves in the ratio of 5 to 3, they should be represented in one branch according to the number of free inhabitants only; and in the other according to the whole n? counting the slaves as if [1] free. By this arrangement the Southern Scale would have the advantage in one House, and the Northern in the other. He had been restrained from proposing this expedient by two considerations: one was his unwillingness to urge any diversity of interests on an occasion where it is but too apt to arise of itself—the other was, the inequality of powers that must be vested in the two branches, and which w<sup>d</sup> destroy the equilibrium of interests.

M<sup>r</sup> ELSEWORTH assured the House that whatever might be thought of the Representatives of Connecticut the State was entirely federal in her disposition. He appealed to her great exertions during the war, in supplying both men & money. The muster rolls would show she had more troops in the field than Virg<sup>a</sup> If she had been Delinquent, it had been from inability, and not more so than other States.

M<sup>r</sup> SHERMAN. M<sup>r</sup> Madison has [2] animadverted on the delinquency of the States, when his object required him to prove that the Constitution of Cong<sup>s</sup> was faulty. Cong<sup>s</sup> is not to blame for the faults of the States. Their measures have been right, and the only thing wanting has been, a further power in Cong<sup>s</sup> to render them effectual.

M<sup>r</sup> DAVY was much embarrassed and wished for explanations. The Report of the Committee allowing the Legislatures to choose the Senate, and establishing a proportional representation in it, seemed to be impracticable. There will according to this rule be ninety members in the outset, and the number will increase as new States are added. It was impossible that so numerous a

---
[1] The word "if" is omitted in the transcript.  [2] The word "has" is omitted in the transcript.

body could possess the activity and other qualities required in it. Were he to vote on the comparative merits of the report as it stood, and the amendment, he should be constrained to prefer the latter. The appointment of the Senate by electors chosen by the people for that purpose was he conceived liable to an insuperable difficulty. The larger Counties or districts thrown into a general district, would certainly prevail over the smaller Counties or districts, and merit in the latter would be excluded altogether. The report therefore seemed to be right in referring the appointment to the Legislatures, whose agency in the general System did not appear to him objectionable as it did to some others. The fact was that the local prejudices & interests which could not be denied to exist, would find their way into the national councils whether the Representatives should be chosen by the Legislatures or by the people themselves. On the other hand, if a proportional representation was attended with insuperable difficulties, the making the Senate the Representative of the States, looked like bringing us back to Cong$^s$ again, and shutting out all the advantages expected from it. Under this view of the subject he could not vote for any plan for the Senate yet proposed. He though that in general there were extremes on both sides. We were partly federal, partly national in our Union, and he did not see why the Gov$^t$ might not in some respects operate on the States, in others on the people.

M$^r$ WILSON admitted the question concerning the number of Senators, to be embarrassing. If the smallest States be allowed one, and the others in proportion, the Senate will certainly be too numerous. He looked forward to the time when the smallest States will contain 100,000 souls at least. Let there be then one Senator in each for every 100,000 souls and let the States not having that n$^o$ of inhabitants be allowed one. He was willing himself to submit to this temporary concession to the small States; and threw out the idea as a ground of compromise.

Doc$^r$ FRANKLIN. The diversity of opinions turns on two points. If a proportional representation takes place, the small States contend that their liberties will be in danger. If an equality of votes is to be put in its place, the large States say their money will be in danger. When a broad table is to be made, and the edges of planks do not fit, the artist takes a little from both, and makes a good joint. In like manner here both sides must part with some of their demands, in order that they may join in some accomodating proposition. He had prepared one which he would read, that it might lie on the table for consideration. The proposition was in the words following"

"That the Legislatures of the several States shall choose & send an equal number of Delegates, namely     who are to compose the 2ᵈ branch of the General Legislature—

"That in all cases or questions wherein the Sovereignty of individual States may be affected, or whereby their authority over their own Citizens may be diminished, or the authority of the General Government within the several States augmented, each State shall have equal suffrage.

"That in the appointment of all Civil officers of yᵉ Genˡ Govᵗ in the election of whom the 2ᵈ branch may by the Constitution have part, each State shall have equal suffrage.

"That in fixing the Salaries of such officers, and in all allowances for public services, and generally in all appropriations & dispositions of money to be drawn out of the General Treasury; and in all laws for supplying that Treasury, the Delegates of the several States shall have suffrage in proportion to the Sums which their respective States do actually contribute to the Treasury." Where a Ship had many owners this was the rule of deciding on her expedition. He had been one of the Ministers from this Country to France during the joint war and wᵈ have been very glad if allowed a vote in distributing the money to carry it on.

Mʳ KING observed that the simple question was whether each State should have an equal vote in the 2ᵈ branch; that it must be apparent to those gentlemen who liked neither the motion for this equality, nor the report as it stood, that the report was as susceptible of melioration as the motion; that a reform would be nugatory & nominal only if we should make another Congress of the proposed Senate: that if the adherence to an equality of votes was fixed & unalterable, there could not be less obstinacy on the other side, & that we were in fact cut insunder [3] already, and it was in vain to shut our eyes against it: that he was however filled with

---

[3] The word "asunder" is substituted in the transcript for "insunder."

astonishment that if we were convinced that every *man* in America was secured in all his rights, we should be ready to sacrifice this substantial good to the phantom of *State* sovereignty: that his feelings were more harrowed & his fears more agitated for his Country than he could express, that he conceived this to be the last opportunity of providing for its liberty & happiness: that he could not therefore but repeat his amazement that when a just Govern! founded on a fair representation of the *people* of America was within our reach, we should renounce the blessing, from an attachment to the ideal freedom & importance of *States:* that should this wonderful illusion continue to prevail, his mind was prepared for every event, rather than to [4] sit down under a Gov! founded in [5] a vicious principle of representation, and which must be as short lived as it would be unjust. He might prevail on himself to accede to some such expedient as had been hinted by M! Wilson: but he never could listen to an equality of votes as proposed in the motion.

M! DAYTON. When assertion is given for proof, and terror substituted for argument, he presumed they would have no effect however eloquently spoken. It should have been shewn that the evils we have experienced have proceeded from the equality now objected to: and that the seeds of dissolution for the State Governments are not sown in the Gen! Government. He considered the system on the table as a novelty, an amphibious monster; and was persuaded that it never would be rec! by the people.

M! MARTIN, w! never confederate if it could not be done on just principles

M! MADISON would acquiesce in the concession hinted by M! Wilson, on condition that a due independence should be given to the Senate. The plan in its present shape makes the Senate absolutely dependent on the States. The Senate therefore is only another edition of Cong! He knew the faults of that Body & had used a bold language ag!t it. Still he w! preserve the State rights, as carefully as the trials by jury.

---

[4] The word "to" is omitted in the transcript.
[5] The word "on" is substituted in the transcript for "in."

Mʳ BEDFORD, contended that there was no middle way between a perfect consolidation and a mere confederacy of the States. The first is out of the question, and in the latter they must continue if not perfectly, yet equally sovereign. If political Societies possess ambition avarice, and all the other passions which render them formidable to each other, ought we not to view them in this light here? Will not the same motives operate in America as elsewhere? If any gentleman doubts it let him look at the votes. Have they not been dictated by interest, by ambition? Are not the large States evidently seeking to aggrandize themselves at the expense of the small? They think no doubt that they have right on their side, but interest had blinded their eyes. Look at Georgia. Though a small State at present, she is actuated by the prospect of soon being a great one. S. Carolina is actuated both by present interest & future prospects. She hopes too to see the other States cut down to her own dimensions. N. Carolina has the same motives of present & future interest. Virgᵃ follows. Maryᵈ is not on that side of the Question. Penᵃ has a direct and future interest. Massᵗˢ has a decided and palpable interest in the part she takes. Can it be expected that the small States will act from pure disinterestedness. Look at G. Britain. Is the Representation there less unequal? But we shall be told again that that is the rotten part of the Constitution. Have not the boroughs however held fast their constitutional rights? and are we to act with greater purity than the rest of mankind. An exact proportion in the Representation is not preserved in any one of the States. Will it be said that an inequality of power will not result from an inequality of votes. Give the opportunity, and ambition will not fail to abuse it. The whole History of mankind proves it. The three large States have a common interest to bind them together in commerce. But whether a combination as we suppose, or a competition as others suppose, shall take place among them, in either case, the smaller [6] States must be ruined. We must like Solon make such a Governᵗ as the people will approve. Will the smaller States ever agree to the proposed degradation of them.

---
[6] The word "small" is substituted in the transcript for "smaller."

It is not true that the people will not agree to enlarge the powers of the present Congs The Language of the people has been that Congs ought to have the power of collecting an impost, and of coercing the States when⁷ it may be necessary. On the first point they have been explicit &, in a manner, unanimous in their declarations. And must they not agree to this & similar measures if they ever mean to discharge their engagements. The little States are willing to observe their engagements, but will meet the large ones on no ground but that of the Confederation. We have been told with a dictatorial air that this is the last moment for a fair trial in favor of a good Governmt It will be the last indeed if the propositions reported from the Committee go forth to the people. He was under no apprehensions. The Large States dare not dissolve the Confederation. If they do the small ones will find some foreign ally of more honor and good faith, who will take them by the hand and do them justice. He did not mean by this to intimidate or alarm. It was a natural consequence; which ought to be avoided by enlarging the federal powers not annihilating the federal system. This is what the people expect. All agree in the necessity of a more efficient Govt and why not make such an one; as they desire.

Mr ELSEWORTH,. Under a National Govt he should participate in the National Security, as remarked by [Mr King] but that was all. What he wanted was domestic happiness. The Natl Govt could not descend to the local objects on which this depended. It could only embrace objects of a general nature. He turned his eyes therefore for the preservation of his rights to the State Govts From these alone he could derive the greatest happiness he expects in this life. His happiness depends on their existence, as much as a new born infant on its mother for nourishment. If this reasoning was not satisfactory, he had nothing to add that could be so.

Mr KING was for preserving the States in a subordinate degree, and as far as they could be necessary for the purposes stated by Mr Elsewth. He did not think a full answer had been given to those who apprehended a dangerous encroachment on their jurisdictions. Expedients might be devised as he conceived that would give them

---

⁷ The word "where" is substituted in the transcript for "when."

all the security the nature of things would admit of. In the establishm.t of Societies the Constitution was to the Legislature what the laws were to individuals. As the fundamental rights of individuals are secured by express provisions in the State Constitutions; why may not a like security be provided for the Rights of States in the National Constitution. The articles of Union between Engl.d & Scotland furnish an example of such a provision in favor of sundry rights of Scotland. When that Union was in agitation, the same language of apprehension which has been heard from the smaller States, was in the mouths of the Scotch patriots. The articles however have not been violated and the Scotch have found an increase of prosperity & happiness. He was aware that this will be called a mere *paper security*. He thought it a sufficient answer to say that if fundamental articles of compact, are no sufficient defence against physical power, neither will there be any safety ag.st it if there be no compact. He could not sit down, without taking some notice of the language of the honorable gentleman from Delaware [M.r Bedford]. It was not he that had uttered a dictatorial language. This intemperance had marked the honorabl gentleman himself. It was not he who with a vehemence unprecedented in that House, had declared himself ready to turn his hopes from our common Country, and court the protection of some foreign hand. This too was the language of the Honbl member himself. He was grieved that such a thought had entered into [8] his heart. He was more grieved that such an expression had dropped from his lips. The gentleman c.d only excuse it to himself on the score of passion. For himself whatever might be his distress, he w.d never court relief from a foreign power.

Adjourned

## Monday July 2.d in Convention

On the question for allowing each State one vote in the second branch as moved by M.r Elseworth,[9] Mass.ts no. Con.t ay. N. Y.

---

[8] The word "into" is omitted in the transcript.

[9] The phrase "it was lost by an equal division of votes," is here inserted in the transcript and the vote reads: "Connecticut, New York, New Jersey, Delaware, Maryland,* aye—5; Massachusetts, Pennsylvania, Virginia, North Carolina, South Carolina, no—5; Georgia, divided [Mr. Baldwin, aye, Mr. Houston, no]." The footnote referring to Maryland reads: "Mr. Jenifer not being present, Mr. Martin alone voted."

ay. N. J. ay. Pᵃ no. Del. ay. Mᵈ ay. Mʳ Jenifer being not present Mʳ Martin alone voted Vᵃ no. N. C. no. S. C. no. Geo. divᵈ Mʳ Houston no. Mʳ Baldwin ay.

Mʳ PINKNEY thought an equality of votes in the 2ᵈ branch inadmissible. At the same time candor obliged him to admit that the large States would feel a partiality for their own Citizens & give them a preference, in appointments: that they might also find some common points in their commercial interests, and promote treaties favorable to them. There is a real distinction [10] the Northern & Southⁿ interests. N. Carolᵃ S. Carol: & Geo. in their Rice & Indigo had a peculiar interest which might be sacrificed. How then shall the larger States be prevented from administering the Genˡ Govᵗ as they please, without being themselves unduly subjected to the will of the smaller? By allowing them some but not a full proportion. He was extremely anxious that something should be done, considering this as the last appeal to a regular experiment. Congˢ have failed in almost every effort for an amendment of the federal System. Nothing has prevented a dissolution of it, but the appointmᵗ of this Convention; & he could not express his alarms for the consequences of such an event He read his motion, to form the States into classes, with an apportionment of Senators among them, [see art. 4, of his plan].

General PINKNEY. was willing the motion might be considered. He did not entirely approve it. He liked better the motion of Docʳ Franklin [which see Saturday June 30]. Some compromise seemed to be necessary: the States being exactly divided on the question for an equality of votes in the 2ᵈ branch. He proposed that a Committee consisting of a member from each State should be appointed to devise & report some compromise.

Mʳ L. MARTIN had no objection to a commitment, but no modifications whatever could reconcile the Smaller States to the least diminution of their equal Sovereignty.

Mʳ SHARMAN. We are now at a full stop, and nobody he supposed meant that we shᵈ break up without doing something. A committee he thought most likely to hit on some expedient.

---

[10] The word "between" is here inserted in the transcript.
See Appendix to Debates, IV, No. 3, p. 600.

*Mr Govr MORRIS. thought a Come adviseable as the Convention had been equally divided. He had a stronger reason also. The mode of appointing the 2d branch tended he was sure to defeat the object of it. What is this object? to check the precipitation, changeableness, and excesses of the first branch. Every man of observation had seen in the democratic branches of the State Legislatures, precipitation—in Congress changeableness, in every department excesses agst personal liberty private property & personal safety. What qualities are necessary to constitute a check in this case? *Abilities* and *virtue,* are equally necessary in both branches. Something more then is now wanted. 1.[13] the checking branch must have a personal interest in checking the other branch, one interest must be opposed to another interest. Vices as they exist, must be turned agst each other. 2.[14] It must have great personal property, it must have the aristocratic spirit; it must love to lord it thro' pride, pride is indeed the great principle that actuates both the poor & the rich. It is this principle which in the former resists, in the latter abuses authority. 3.[15] It should be independent. In Religion the Creature is apt to forget its Creator. That it is otherwise in political affairs, the late debates here are an unhappy proof. The aristocratic body, should be as independent & as firm as the democratic. If the members of it are to revert to a dependence on the democratic choice, the democratic scale will preponderate. All the guards contrived by America have not restrained the Senatorial branches of the Legislatures from a servile complaisance to the democratic. If the 2d branch is to be dependent we are better without it. To make it independent, it should be for life. It will then do wrong, it will be said. He believed so: He hoped so. The Rich will strive to establish their dominion & enslave the rest. They always did. They always will. The proper security agst them is to form them into a separate interest. The two forces will then controul each other. Let the rich mix with the poor and

---

\* Transfer hither the marginal note. [12]

\* He had just returned from N. Y. havg left ye Convention a few days after it commenced business.

[12] Madison's direction concerning the footnote is omitted in the transcript.

[13] The figure "1" is changed to "In the first place" in the transcript.

[14] The figure "2" is changed to "In the second place" in the transcript.

[15] The figure "3" is changed to "In the third place" in the transcript.

in a Commercial Country, they will establish an oligarchy. Take away commerce, and the democracy will triumph. Thus it has been all the world over. So it will be among us. Reason tells us we are but men: and we are not to expect any particular interference of Heaven in our favor. By thus combining & setting apart, the aristocratic interest, the popular interest will be combined ag$^{st}$ it. There will be a mutual check and mutual security. 4.[16] An independence for life, involves the necessary permanency. If we change our measures no body will trust us: and how avoid a change of measures, but by avoiding a change of men. Ask any man if he confides in Cong$^s$ if he confides in the State of Pen$^a$ if he will lend his money or enter into contract? He will tell you no. He sees no stability. He can repose no confidence. If G. B. were to explain her refusal to treat with us, the same reasoning would be employed.—He disliked the exclusion of the 2$^d$ branch from holding offices. It is dangerous. It is like the imprudent exclusion of the military officers during the war, from civil appointments. It deprives the Executive of the principal source of influence. If danger be apprehended from the Executive what a lift-handed way is this of obviating it? If the son, the brother or the friend can be appointed, the danger may be even increased, as the disqualified father &c. can then boast of a disinterestedness which he does not possess. Besides shall the best, the most able, the most virtuous citizens not be permitted to hold offices? Who then are to hold them? He was also ag$^{st}$ paying the Senators. They will pay themselves if they can. If they can not they will be rich and can do without it. Of such the 2$^d$ branch ought to consist; and none but such can compose it if they are not to be paid—He contended that the Executive should appoint the Senate & fill up vacancies. This gets rid of the difficulty in the present question. You may begin with any ratio you please; it will come to the same thing. The members being independ$^t$ & for life, may be taken as well from one place as from another.—It should be considered too how the scheme could be carried through the States. He hoped there was strength of mind eno' in this House to look truth in the face. He did not hesitate therefore to say

---

[16] The figure "4" is changed to "In the fourth place" in the transcript.

MONTICELLO

*The Home of Thomas Jefferson.*

that loaves & fishes must bribe the Demagogues. They must be made to expect higher offices under the general than the State Gov<sup>ts</sup>. A Senate for life will be a noble bait. Without such captivating prospects, the popular leaders will oppose & defeat the plan. He perceived that the 1<sup>st</sup> branch was to be chosen by the people of the States: the 2<sup>d</sup> by those chosen by the people. Is not here a Gov<sup>t</sup> by the States. A Govern<sup>t</sup> by Compact between Virg<sup>a</sup> in the 1<sup>st</sup> & 2<sup>d</sup> branch; Mas<sup>ts</sup> in the 1<sup>st</sup> & 2<sup>d</sup> branch &c. This is going back to mere treaty. It is no Gov<sup>t</sup> at all. It is altogether dependent on the States, and will act over again the part which Cong<sup>s</sup> has acted. A firm Govern<sup>t</sup> alone can protect our liberties. He fears the influence of the rich. They will have the same effect here as elsewhere if we do not by such a Gov<sup>t</sup> keep them within their proper sphere.[17] We should remember that the people never act from reason alone. The Rich will take [18] advantage of their passions & make these the instruments for oppressing them. The Result of the Contest will be a violent aristocracy, or a more violent despotism. The schemes of the Rich will be favored by the extent of the Country. The people in such distant parts can not communicate & act in concert. They will be the dupes of those who have more knowledge & intercourse. The only security ag<sup>st</sup> encroachments will be a select & sagacious body of men, instituted to watch ag<sup>st</sup> them on all sides. He meant only to hint these observations, without grounding any motion on them.

M<sup>r</sup> RANDOLPH favored the commitment though he did not expect much benefit from the expedient. He animadverted on the warm & rash language of M<sup>r</sup> Bedford on Saturday; reminded the small States that if the large States should combine some danger of which he did not deny there would be a check in the revisionary power of the Executive, and intimated that in order to render this still more effectual, he would agree that in the choice of the [19] Executive each State should have an equal vote. He was persuaded that two such opposite bodies as M<sup>r</sup> Morris had planned,

---

[17] The transcript uses the word "sphere" in the plural.
[18] The word "the" is here inserted in the transcript.
[19] The word "an" is substituted in the transcript for "the."

could never long co-exist. Dissentions would arise as has been seen even between the Senate and H. of Delegates in Maryland, appeals would be made to the people; and in a little time, commotions would be the result—He was far from thinking the large States could subsist of themselves any more than the small; an avulsion would involve the whole in ruin, and he was determined to pursue such a scheme of Government as would secure us ag$^{st}$ such a calamity.

M$^r$ STRONG was for the Commitment; and hoped the mode of constituting both branches would be referred. If they should be established on different principles, contentions would prevail, and there would never be a concurrence in necessary measures.

Doc$^r$ WILLIAMSON. If we do not concede on both sides, our business must soon be at an end. He approved of the Commitment, supposing that as the Com$^e$ w$^d$ be a smaller body, a compromise would be pursued with more coolness

M$^r$ WILSON objected to the Committee, because it would decide according to that very rule of voting which was opposed on one side. Experience in Cong$^s$ had also proved the inutility of Committees consisting of members from each State

M$^r$ LANSING w$^d$ not oppose the commitment, though expecting little advantage from it.

M$^r$ MADISON opposed the Commitment. He had rarely seen any other effect than delay from *such* Committees in Cong$^s$ Any scheme of compromise that could be proposed in the Committee might as easily be proposed in the House; and the report of the Committee when [20] it contained merely the *opinion* of the Com$^e$ would neither shorten the discussion, nor influence the decision of the House.

M$^r$ GERRY was for the Commitm$^t$ Something must be done, or we shall disappoint not only America, but the whole world. He suggested a consideration of the State we should be thrown into by the failure of the Union. We should be without an Umpire to decide controversies and must be at the mercy of events. What too is to become of our treaties—what of our foreign debts, what

---

[20] The word "where" is substituted in the transcript for "when."

of our domestic? We must make concessions on both sides. Without these the Constitutions of the several States would never have been formed.

On the question "for committing," generally:

Mass<sup>ts</sup> ay. Con<sup>t</sup> ay. N. Y. ay. N. J. no. P. ay. Del. no. M<sup>d</sup> ay. V<sup>a</sup> ay. N. C. ay. S. C. ay. Geo. ay.[21]

On the question for committing [22] "to a member from each State."

Mass<sup>ts</sup> ay. Con<sup>t</sup> ay. N. Y. ay. N. J. ay. P<sup>a</sup> no. Del. ay. M<sup>d</sup> ay. V<sup>a</sup> ay. N. C. ay. S. C. ay. Geo. ay.[23]

The Committee elected by ballot, were M<sup>r</sup> Gerry, M<sup>r</sup> Elseworth, M<sup>r</sup> Yates, M<sup>r</sup> Patterson, D<sup>r</sup> Franklin, M<sup>r</sup> Bedford, M<sup>r</sup> Martin, M<sup>r</sup> Mason, M<sup>r</sup> Davy, M<sup>r</sup> Rutledge, Mr. Baldwin.

That time might be given to the Committee, and to such as chose to attend to the celebrations on the anniversary of Independence, the Convention adjourned till Thursday.

## Thursday July 5<sup>th</sup> in Convention

M<sup>r</sup> Gerry delivered in from the Committee appointed on Monday last the following Report.

"The Committee to whom was referred the 8<sup>th</sup> Resol. of the Report from the Committee of the whole House, and so much of the 7<sup>th</sup> as has not been decided on, submit the following Report: That the subsequent propositions be recommended to the Convention on condition that both shall be generally adopted. 1. that in the 1<sup>st</sup> branch of the Legislature each of the States now in the Union shall be allowed 1 member for every 40,000 inhabitants of the description reported in the 7<sup>th</sup> Resolution of the Com<sup>e</sup> of the whole House: that each State not containing that number shall be allowed 1 member: that all bills for raising or appropriating money, and for fixing the Salaries of the officers of the Govern<sup>t</sup> of the U. States shall originate in the 1<sup>st</sup> branch of of the Legislature, and shall not be altered or amended by the 2<sup>d</sup> branch: and that no money shall be drawn from the public Treasury. but in pursuance

---

[21] In the transcript the vote reads: "Massachusetts, Connecticut, New York, Pennsylvania, Maryland, Virginia, North Carolina, South Carolina, Georgia, aye—9; New Jersey, Delaware, no—2."

[22] The word "it" is here inserted in the transcript.

[23] In the transcript the vote reads: "Massachusetts, Connecticut, New York, New Jersey, Delaware, Maryland, Virginia, North Carolina, South Carolina, Georgia, aye—10; Pennsylvania, no—1."

of appropriations to be orgininated in the 1ˢᵗ branch" II. That in the 2ᵈ branch each State shall have an equal vote." *

Mʳ GHORUM observed that as the report consisted of propositions mutually conditional he wished to hear some explanations touching the grounds on which the conditions were estimated.

Mʳ GERRY. The Committee were of different opinions as well as the Deputations from which the Comᵉ were taken, and agreed to the Report merely in order that some ground of accomodation might be proposed. Those opposed to the equality of votes have only assented conditionally; and if the other side do not generally agree will not be under any obligation to support the Report.

Mʳ WILSON thought the Committee had exceeded their powers.

Mʳ MARTIN was for taking the question on the whole report.

Mʳ WILSON was for a division of the question: otherwise it wᵈ be a leap in the dark.

Mʳ MADISON. could not regard the exclusive [25] privilege of originating money bills as any concession on the side of the small States. Experience proved that it had no effect. If seven States in the upper branch wished a bill to be originated, they might surely find some member from some of the same States in the lower branch who would originate it. The restriction as to amendments was of as little consequence. Amendments could be handed privately by the Senate to members in the other house. Bills could be negatived that they might be sent up in the desired shape. If the Senate should yield to the obstinacy of the 1ˢᵗ branch the use of that body as a check would be lost. If the 1ˢᵗ branch should yield to that of the Senate, the privilege would be nugatory. Experience had also shewn both in G. B. and the States having a similar regulation that it was a source of frequent & obstinate altercations. These considerations had pro-

---

* This report was founded on a motion in the Committe made by Dʳ Franklin. It was barely acquiesced in by the members from the States opposed to an equality of votes in the 2ᵈ branch and was evidently considered by the members on the other side, as a gaining of their point. A motion was made by Mʳ Sherman [he [24] acted in place of Mʳ Elseworth who was kept away by indisposition.] In the Committee to the following effect "that each State should have an equal vote in the 2ᵈ branch; provided that no decision therein should prevail unless the majority of States concurring should also comprize a majority of the inhabitants of the U. States." This motion was not much deliberated on nor approved in the Committee. A similar proviso had been proposed in the debates on the articles of Confederation in 1777, to the articles giving certain powers to "nine States." See Journals of Congˢ for 1777, p. 462.

[24] The word "who" is substituted in the transcript for "he."

[25] The word "exclusive" is omitted in the transcript.

duced a rejection of a like motion on a former occasion when judged by its own merits. It could not therefore be deemed any concession on the present, and left in force all the objections which had prevailed ag$^{st}$ allowing each State an equal voice. He conceived that the Convention was reduced to the alternative of either departing from justice in order to conciliate the smaller States, and the minority of the people of the U. S. or of displeasing these by justly gratifying the larger States and the majority of the people. He could not himself hesitate as to the option he ought to make. The Convention with justice & the majority of the people on their side, had nothing to fear. With injustice and the minority on their side they had every thing to fear. It was in vain to purchase concord in the Convention on terms which would perpetuate discord among their Constituents. The Convention ought to pursue a plan which would bear the test of examination, which would be espoused & supported by the enlightened and impartial part of America, & which they could themselves vindicate and urge. It should be considered that altho' at first many may judge of the system recommended, by their opinion of the Convention, yet finally all will judge of the Convention by the System. The merits of the System alone can finally & effectually obtain the public suffrage. He was not apprehensive that the people of the small States would obstinately refuse to accede to a Gov$^t$ founded on just principles, and promising them substantial protection. He could not suspect that Delaware would brave the consequences of seeking her fortunes apart from the other States, rather than submit to such a Gov$^t$ much less could he suspect that she would pursue the rash policy of courting foreign support, which the warmth of one of her representatives [M$^r$ Bedford] had suggested, or if she sh$^d$ that any foreign nation w$^d$ be so rash as to hearken to the overture. As little could he suspect that the people of N. Jersey notwithstanding the decided tone of the gentlemen from that State, would choose rather to stand on their own legs, and bid defiance to events, than to acquiesce under an establishment founded on principles the justice of which they could not dispute, and absolutely necessary to redeem them from the exactions levied on them by the commerce of the neighbouring

States. A review of other States would prove that there was as little reason to apprehend an inflexible opposition elsewhere. Harmony in the Convention was no doubt much to be desired. Satisfaction to all the States, in the first instance still more so. But if the principal States comprehending a majority of the people of the U. S. should concur in a just & judicious plan, he had the firmest hopes, that all the other States would by degrees accede to it.

M$^r$ BUTLER said he could not let down his idea of the people, of America so far as to believe they would from mere respect to the Convention adopt a plan evidently unjust. He did not consider the privilege concerning money bills as of any consequence. He urged that the 2$^d$ branch ought to represent the States according to their property.

M$^r$ Gov$^r$ MORRIS. thought the form as well as the matter of the Report objectionable. It seemed in the first place to render amendments impracticable. In the next place, it seemed to involve a pledge to agree to the 2$^d$ part if the 1$^{st}$ sh$^d$ be agreed to. He conceived the whole aspect of it to be wrong. He came here as a Representative of America; he flattered himself he came here in some degree as a Representative of the whole human race; for the whole human race will be affected by the proceedings of this Convention. He wished gentlemen to extend their views beyond the present moment of time; beyond the narrow limits of place from which they derive their political origin. If he were to believe some things which he had heard, he should suppose that we were assembled to truck and bargain for our particular States. He can-not descend to think that any gentlemen are really actuated by these views. We must look forward to the effects of what we do. These alone ought to guide us. Much has been said of the sentiments of the people. They were unknown. They could not be known. All that we can infer is that if the plan we recommend be reasonable & right; all who have reasonable minds and sound intentions will embrace it, notwithstanding what had been said by some gentlemen. Let us suppose that the larger States shall agree; and that the smaller refuse: and let us trace the consequences. The opponents of the syste: in the smaller States will no doubt make a party, and a noise for a time, but the ties of interest, of kindred & of common habits which connect them with the other States will be too strong to be easily broken. In N. Jersey particularly he was sure a great many would follow the sentiments of Pen$^a$ & N. York. This Country must be united. If persuasion does not unite it, the sword will. He begged that [26] this consideration might have its due weight. The scenes of horror attending civil commotion can not be described, and the conclusion of them will be worse than the term of their continuance. The stronger party will then make traytors of the weaker; and the Gallows & Halter will finish the work of the sword. How far foreign powers would be ready to take part in the confusions he would not say. Threats that they will be invited have it seems been thrown out. He drew the melancholy picture of foreign intrusions as exhibited in the History of Germany, & urged it as a standing lesson to other nations. He trusted that the Gentlemen who may have hazarded such expressions, did not entertain them till they reached their own lips. But returning to the Report he could not think it in any respect calculated for the public good. As the 2$^d$ branch is now constituted, there will be constant disputes & appeals to the States which will undermine the Gen$^l$ Government & controul & annihilate the 1$^{st}$ branch. Suppose that the delegates from Mass$^{ts}$ & Rho I. in the Upper House disagree, and that the former are outvoted. What Results? they will immediately declare that their State will not abide by the decision, and make such representations as will produce that effect. The same may happen as to Virg$^a$ & other States. Of what avail then will be what is on paper. State attachments, and State importance have been the bane of this Country. We can not annihilate; but we may perhaps take out the teeth of the serpents. He wished our ideas to be enlarged to the true interest of man, instead of being circumscribed within the narrow compass of a particular Spot. And after all how little can be the motive yielded by selfishness for such a policy. Who can say whether he himself, much less whether his children, will the next year be an inhabitant of this or that State.

---

[26] The word "that" is omitted in the transcript.

Mr BEDFORD. He found that what he had said as to the small States being taken by the hand, had been misunderstood; and he rose to explain. He did not mean that the small States would court the aid & interposition of foreign powers. He meant that they would not consider the federal compact as dissolved untill it should be so by the Acts of the large States. In this case The consequence of the breach of faith on their part, and the readiness of the small States to fulfill their engagements, would be that foreign Nations having demands on this Country would find it their interest to take the small States by the hand, in order to do themselves justice. This was what he meant. But no man can foresee to what extremities the small States may be driven by oppression. He observed also in apology that some allowance ought to be made for the habits of his profession in which warmth was natural & sometimes necessary. But is there not an apology in what was said by [Mr Govr Morris] that the sword is to unite: by Mr Ghorum that Delaware must be annexed to Penna and N. Jersey divided between Pena and N. York. To hear such language without emotion, would be to renounce the feelings of a man and the duty of a Citizen—As to the propositions of the Committee, the lesser States have thought it necessary to have a security somewhere. This has been thought necessary for the Executive Magistrate of the proposed Govt who has a sort of negative on the laws; and is it not of more importance that the States should be protected, than that the Executive branch of the Govt shd be protected. In order to obtain this, the smaller States have conceded as to the constitution of the first branch, and as to money bills. If they be not gratified by correspondent concessions as to the 2d branch is it to be supposed they will ever accede to the plan; and what will be the consequence if nothing should be done! The condition of the U. States requires that something should be immediately done. It will be better that a defective plan should be adopted, than that none should be recommended. He saw no reason why defects might not be supplied by meetings 10, 15, or 20 years hence.

Mr ELSEWORTH said he had not attended the proceedings of the Committee, but was ready to accede to the compromise they had reported. Some compromise was necessary; and he saw none more convenient or reasonable.

Mʳ WILLIAMSON hoped that the expressions of individuals would not be taken for the sense of their colleagues, much less of their States which was not & could not be known. He hoped also that the meaning of those expressions would not be misconstrued or exaggerated. He did not conceive that [Mʳ Govʳ Morris] meant that the sword ought to be drawn agˢᵗ the smaller States. He only pointed out the probable consequences of anarchy in the U. S. A similar exposition ought to be given of the expressions [of Mʳ Ghorum]. He was ready to hear the Report discussed; but thought the propositions contained in it, the most objectionable of any he had yet heard.

Mʳ PATTERSON said that he had when the Report was agreed to in the Comᵉ reserved to himself the right of freely discussing it. He acknowledged that the warmth complained of was improper; but he thought the Sword & the Gallows as [27] little calculated to produce conviction. He complained of the manner in which Mʳ M— & Mʳ Govʳ Morris had treated the small States.

Mʳ GERRY. Tho' he had assented to the Report in the Committee, he had very material objections to it. We were however in a peculiar situation. We were neither the same Nation nor different Nations. We ought not therefore to pursue the one or the other of these ideas too closely. If no compromise should take place what will be the consequence. A secession he foresaw would take place; for some gentlemen seem decided on it; two different plans will be proposed; and the result no man could foresee. If we do not come to some agreement among ourselves some foreign sword will probably do the work for us.

Mʳ MASON. The Report was meant not as specific propositions to be adopted; but merely as a general ground of accomodation. There must be some accomodation on this point, or we shall make little further progress in the work. Accomodation was the object of the House in the appointment of the Committee; and of the Committee in the Report they had made. And however liable the Report might be to objections, he thought it preferable to an appeal to the world by the different sides, as had been talked of by some Gentlemen. It could not be more inconvenient to any

---

[27] The word "as" is crossed out in the transcript.

gentleman to remain absent from his private affairs, than it was for him: but he would bury his bones in this City rather than expose his Country to the Consequences of a dissolution of the Convention without any thing being done.

The 1st proposition in the report for fixing the representation in the 1st branch, one member for every 40,000 inhabitants, being taken up.

M: Gov: MORRIS objected to that scale of apportionment. He thought property ought to be taken into the estimate as well as the number of inhabitants. Life & liberty were generally said to be of more value, than property. An accurate view of the matter would nevertheless prove that property was the main object of Society. The savage State was more favorable to liberty than the Civilized; and sufficiently so to life. It was preferred by all men who had not acquired a taste for property; it was only renounced for the sake of property which could only be secured by the restraints of regular Government. These ideas might appear to some new, but they were nevertheless just. If property then was the main object of Gov: certainly it ought to be one measure of the influence due to those who were to be affected by the Governm: He looked forward also to that range of New States which w<sup>d</sup> soon be formed in the West. He thought the rule of representation ought to be so fixed as to secure to the Atlantic States a prevalence in the National Councils. The new States will know less of the public interest than these, will have an interest in many respects different, in particular will be little scrupulous of involving the Community in wars the burdens & operations of which would fall chiefly on the maritime States. Provision ought therefore to be made to prevent the maritime States from being hereafter outvoted by them. He thought this might be easily done by irrevocably fixing the number of representatives which the Atlantic States should respectively have, and the number which each new State will have. This w<sup>d</sup> not be unjust, as the Western settlers w<sup>d</sup> previously know the conditions on which they were to possess their lands. It would be politic as it would recommend the plan to the present as well as future interest of the States which must decide the fate of it.

Mr. RUTLIDGE. The gentleman last up had spoken some of his sentiments precisely. Property was certainly the principal object of Society. If numbers should be made the rule of representation, the Atlantic States will [28] be subjected to the Western. He moved that the first proposition in the report be postponed in order to take up the following viz "that the suffrages of the several States be regulated and proportioned according to the sums to be paid towards the general revenue by the inhabitants of each State respectively. that an apportionment of suffrages, according to the ratio aforesaid shall be made and regulated at the end of      years from the 1st meeting of the Legislature of the U. S. and at the end of every      years but that for the present, and until the period above mentioned, the suffrages shall be for N. Hampshire      [29] Massachts     &c.—

Col. MASON said the case of new States was not unnoticed in the Committee; but it was thought and he was himself decidedly of opinion that if they made a part of the Union, they ought to be subject to no unfavorable discriminations. Obvious considerations required it.

Mr. RADOLPH concurred with Col.[30] Mason.

On [31] Question on Mr. Rutlidges motion.

Masts no. Cont no. N. Y. no. N. J. no. Pa no. Del. no. Maryd no. Va no. N. C. no. S. C. ay. Geo. not on floor.[32]

Adjd

---

## FRIDAY JULY 6TH IN CONVENTION

Mr. Govr MORRIS moved to commit so much of the Report as relates to "1 member for every 40,000 inhabitants" His view was that they might absolutely fix the number for each State in the first instance; leaving the Legislature at liberty to provide for changes in the relative importance of the States, and for the case of new States.

---

[28] The word "would" is substituted in the transcript for "will."
[29] The word "for" is here inserted in the transcript.
[30] The word "Mr." is substituted in the transcript for "Col."
[31] The word "the" is here inserted in the transcript.
[32] In the transcript the vote reads: "South Carolina, aye—1; Massachusetts, Connecticut, New York, New Jersey, Pennsylvania, Delaware, Maryland, Virginia, North Carolina, no—9; Georgia not on the floor."

Mr WILSON 2ded the motion; but with a view of leaving the Committee under no implied shackles.

Mr GHORUM apprehended great inconveniency [33] from fixing directly the number of Representatives to be allowed to each State. He thought the number of Inhabitants the true guide; tho' perhaps some departure might be expedient from the full proportion. The States also would vary in their relative extent by separations of parts of the largest States. A part of Virga is now on the point of a separation. In the province of Mayne a Convention is at this time deliberating on a separation from Masts In such events the number of representatives ought certainly to be reduced. He hoped to see all the States made small by proper divisions, instead of their becoming formidable as was apprehended, to the Small States. He conceived that let the Genl [34] Government be modified as it might, there would be a constant tendency in the State Governmts to encroach upon it: it was of importance therefore that the extent of the States shd be reduced as much & as fast as possible. The stronger the Govt shall be made in the first instance the more easily will these divisions be effected; as it will be of less consequence in the opinion of the States whether they be of great or small extent.

Mr GERRY did not think with his Colleague that the large States ought to be cut up. This policy has been inculcated by the middling and smaller States, ungenerously & contrary to the spirit of the Confederation. Ambitious men will be apt to solicit needless divisions, till the States be reduced to the size of Counties. If this policy should still actuate the small States, the large ones cou'd not confederate safely with them; but would be obliged to consult their safety by confederating only with one another. He favored the Commitment and thought that Representation ought to be in the Combined ratio of numbers of Inhabitants and of wealth, and not of either singly.

Mr KING wished the clause to be committed chiefly in order to detach it from the Report with which it had no connection. He thought also that the Ratio of Representation proposed could not

---

[33] The word "inconveniency" is changed to "inconvenience" in the transcript.

[34] The word "Genl" is omitted in the transcript.

be safely fixed, since in a century & a half our computed increase of population would carry the number of representatives to an enormous excess; that yᵉ number of inhabitants was not the proper index of ability & wealth; that property was the primary object of Society; and that in fixing a ratio this ought not to[35] be excluded from the estimate. With regard to new States, he observed that there was something peculiar in the business which had not been noticed. The U. S. were now admitted to be proprietors of the Country N. West of the Ohio. Congˢ by one of their ordinances have impoliticly laid it out into ten States, and have made it a fundamental article of compact with those who may become settlers, that as soon as the number in any one State shall equal that of the smallest of the 13 original States, it may claim admission into the union. Delaware does not contain it is computed more than 35,000 souls, and for obvious reasons will not increase much for a considerable time. It is possible then that if this plan be persisted in by Congˢ 10 new votes may be added, without a greater addition of inhabitants than are represented by the single vote of Penᵃ The plan as it respects one of the new States is already irrevocable, the sale of the lands having commenced, and the purchasers & settlers will immediately become entitled to all the privileges of the compact.

Mʳ BUTLER agreed to the Commitment if the Committee were to be left at liberty. He was persuaded that the more the subject was examined, the less it would appear that the number of inhabitants would be a proper rule of proportion. If there were no other objection the changeableness of the standard would be sufficient. He concurred with those who thought some balance was necessary between the old & new States. He contended strenuously that property was the only just measure of representation. This was the great object of Governᵗ: the great cause of war; the great means of carrying it on.

Mʳ PINKNEY saw no good reason for committing. The value of land had been found on full investigation to be an impracticable rule. The contributions of revenue including imports & exports, must be too changeable in their amount; too difficult to be ad-

---

[35] The word "to" is omitted in the transcript.

justed; and too injurious to the non-commercial States. The number of inhabitants appeared to him the only just & practiable rule. He thought the blacks ought to stand on an equality with [36] whites: But w̅d̅ agree to the ratio settled by Cong̅s̅ He contended that Cong̅s̅ had no right under the articles of Confederation to authorize the admission of new States; no such case having been provided for.

M̅r̅ DAVY, was for committing the clause in order to get at the merits of the question arising on the Report. He seemed to think that wealth or property ought to be represented in the 2d branch; and numbers in the 1st branch.

On the Motion for committing as made by M̅r̅ Gov̅r̅ Morris.

Masts ay. Cont ay. N. Y. no. N. J. no. Pa ay. Del. no. Md divd Va ay. N. C. ay. S. C. ay. Geo. ay.[37]

The members appd by Ballot were M̅r̅ Gov̅r̅ Morris, M̅r̅ Gorham, M̅r̅ Randolph, M̅r̅ Rutledge, M̅r̅ King.

M̅r̅ WILSON signified that his view in agreeing to the commitm̅t̅ was that the Com̅e̅ might consider the propriety of adopting a scale similar to that established by the Constitution of Masts which w̅d̅ give an advantage to ye small States without substantially departing from a [38] rule of proportion.

M̅r̅ WILSON & M̅r̅ MASON moved to postpone the clause relating to money bills in order to take up the clause relating to an equality of votes in the second branch.

On the question [39] Masts no. Cont no. N. Y. ay. N. J. ay. Pa ay. Del. ay. Md ay. Va ay. N. C. no. S. C. ay. Geo. ay.

The clause relating to equality of votes being under consideration,

Doc̅r̅ FRANKLIN observed that this question could not be properly put by itself, the Committee having reported several propositions as mutual conditions of each other. He could not vote for it if separately taken, but should vote for the whole together.

---

[36] The word "the" is here inserted in the transcript.
[37] In the transcript the vote reads: "Massachusetts, Connecticut, Pennsylvania, Virginia, North Carolina, South Carolina, Georgia, aye—7; New York, New Jersey, Delaware, no—3; Maryland, divided."
[38] The word "the" is substituted in the transcript for the word "a."
[39] The words "of postponement" are here inserted in the transcript and the vote reads: "New York, New Jersey, Pennsylvania, Delaware, Maryland, Virginia, South Carolina, Georgia, aye—8; Massachusetts, Connecticut, North Carolina, no—3."

Col. MASON perceived the difficulty & suggested a reference of the rest of the Report to yᵉ Committee just appointed, that the whole might be brought into one view.

Mʳ RANDOLPH disliked yᵉ reference to that Committee, as it consisted of members from States opposed to the wishes of the smaller States, and could not therefore be acceptable to the latter.

Mʳ MARTIN & Mʳ JENIFER moved to postpone the clause till the Comᵉ last appointed should report.

Mʳ MADISON observed that if the uncommitted part of the Report was connected with the part just committed, it ought also to be committed; if not connected, it need not be postponed till report should be made.

On the question for postponing moved by Mʳ Martin & Mʳ Jennifer    Conᵗ N. J. Del. Mᵈ Vᵃ Geo., ay [40]
P ᵃ N. C. S. C..............no [41]
Mas. N. Y..........divided

The 1ˢᵗ clause relating to the originating of money bills was then resumed.

Mʳ GOVERNʳ MORRIS was opposed to a restriction of this right in either branch, considered merely in itself and as unconnected with the point of representation in the 2ᵈ branch. It will disable the 2ᵈ branch from proposing its own money plans, and giving the people an opportunity of judging by comparison of the merits of those proposed by the 1ˢᵗ branch.

Mʳ WILSON could see nothing like a concession here on the part of the smaller States. If both branches were to say yes [42] or no, [42] it was of little consequence which should say yes [42] or no [42] first, which last. If either was indiscriminately to have the right of originating, the reverse of the Report, would he thought be most proper; since it was a maxim that the least numerous body was the fittest for deliberation; the most numerous for decision. He observed that this discrimination had been transcribed from the British into several American constitutions. But he was persuaded that on examination of the American experiments it would be found to be a trifle light as air. Nor could he ever discover the

---

[40] The figure "6" is here inserted in the transcript.
[41] The figure "3" is here inserted in the transcript.
[42] The transcript italicizes the words "yes" and "no."

advantage of it in the Parliamentary history of G. Britain. He hoped if there was any advantage in the privilege, that it would be pointed out.

M: WILLIAMSON thought that if the privilege were not common to both branches it ought rather to be confined to the 2ᵈ as the bills in that case would be more narrowly watched, than if they originated with the branch having most of the popular confidence.

M: MASON. The consideration which weighed with the Committee was that the 1ˢᵗ branch would be the immediate representatives of the people, the 2ᵈ would not. Should the latter have the power of giving away the people's money, they might soon forget the source from whence they received it. We might soon have an aristocracy. He had been much concerned at the principles which had been advanced by some gentlemen, but had the satisfaction to find they did not generally prevail. He was a friend to proportional representation in both branches; but supposed that some points must be yielded for the sake of accomodation.

M: WILSON. If he had proposed that the 2ᵈ branch should have an independent disposal of public money, the observations of [Col Mason] would have been a satisfactory answer. But nothing could be farther from what he had said. His question was how is the power of the 1ˢᵗ branch increased or that of the 2ᵈ diminished by giving the proposed privilege to the former? Where is the difference, in which branch it begins if both must concur, in the end?

M: GERRY would not say that the concession was a sufficient one on the part of the small States. But he could not but regard it in the light of a concession. It wᵈ make it a constitutional principle that the 2ᵈ branch were not possessed of the Confidence of the people in money matters, which wᵈ lessen their weight & influence. In the next place if the 2ᵈ branch were dispossessed of the privilege, they wᵈ be deprived of the opportunity which their continuance in office 3 times as long as the 1ˢᵗ branch would give them of makig three successive essays in favor of a particular point.

M: PINKNEY thought it evident that the Concession was wholly on one side, that of the large States, the privilege of originating money bills being of no account.

M: Gov: Morris had waited to hear the good effects of the restriction. As to the alarm sounded, of an aristocracy, his creed was that there never was, nor ever will be a civilized Society without an aristocracy. His endeavor was to keep it as much as possible from doing mischief. The restriction if it has any real operation will deprive us of the services of the 2ᵈ branch in digesting & proposing money bills of which it will be more capable than the 1ˢᵗ branch. It will take away the responsibility of the 2ᵈ branch, the great security for good behavior. It will always leave a plea, as to an obnoxious money bill that it was disliked, but could not be constitutionally amended; nor safely rejected. It will be a dangerous source of disputes between the two Houses. We should either take the British Constitution altogether or make one for ourselves. The Executive there has dissolved two Houses as the only cure for such disputes. Will our Executive be able to apply such a remedy? Every law directly or indirectly takes money out of the pockets of the people. Again What use may be made of such a privilege in case of great emergency? Suppose an Enemy at the door, and money instantly & absolutely necessary for repelling him, may not the popular branch avail itself of this duress, to extort concessions from the Senate destructive of the Constitution itself. He illustrated this danger by the example of the Long Parliament's exped'ᵗˢ for subverting the H. of Lords; concluding on the whole that the restriction would be either useless or pernicious.

Doc: Franklin did not mean to go into a justification of the Report; but as it had been asked what would be the use of restraining the 2ᵈ branch from medling with money bills, he could not but remark that it was always of importance that the people should know who had disposed of their money, & how it had been disposed of. It was a maxim that those who feel, can best judge. This end would, he thought, be best attained, if money affairs were to be confined to the immediate representatives of the people. This was his inducement to concur in the report. As to the danger or difficulty that might arise from a negative in the 2ᵈ [43] where the

---

[43] The word "branch" is here inserted in the transcript.

people w{d} not be proportionally represented, it might easily be got over by declaring that there should be no such Negative: or if that will not do, by declaring that there shall be no such branch at all.

Mr MARTIN said that it was understood in the Committee that the difficulties and disputes which had been apprehended, should be guarded ag{st} in the detailing of the plan.

Mr WILSON. The difficulties & disputes will increase with the attempts to define & obviate them. Queen Anne was obliged to dissolve her Parliam{t} in order to terminate one of these obstinate disputes between the two Houses. Had it not been for the mediation of the Crown, no one can say what the result would have been. The point is still *sub judice* in England. He approved of the principles laid down by the Hon'ble President [44] [Doctr Franklin] his Colleague, as to the expediency of keeping the people informed of their money affairs. But thought they would know as much, and be as well satisfied, in one way as in the other.

Genl PINKNEY was astonished that this point should have been considered as a concession. He remarked that the restriction [45] to money bills had been rejected on the merits singly considered, by 8 States ag{st} 3. and that the very States which now called it a concession, were then ag{st} it as nugatory or improper in itself.

On the Question whether the clause relating to money bills in the Report of the Com{e} consisting of a member from each State, sh{d} stand as part of the Report—

Mass{ts} divid{d} Con{t} ay. N. Y. div{d} N. J. ay. P{a} no. Del. ay. M{d} ay. V{a} no. N. C. ay. S. C. no. Geo. div{d}.[46]

A Question was then raised whether the question was carried in the affirmative: there being but 5 ays out of 11. States present. The words of the rule are [47] (see May 28).[48]

---

[44] In the transcript after the word "President" reference is made to a footnote which reads: "He was at that time President of the State of Pennsylvania."

[45] The word "as" is here inserted in the transcript.

[46] In the transcript the vote reads: "Connecticut, New Jersey, Delaware, Maryland, North Carolina, aye—5; Pennsylvania, Virginia, South Carolina, no—3; Massachusetts, New York, Georgia, divided."

[47] The phrase "For the words of the Rule" is substituted in the transcript for "The words of the rule are."

[48] A House to do business shall consist of the Deputies of not less than seven States; and all questions shall be decided by the greater number of these which shall be fully represented: but a less number than seven may adjourn from day to day.

On the [49] question: Mas. Con[t] N. J. P[a] Del. M[d] N. C. S. C. Geo ay [50]

N. Y. V[a].........................no [51]

[In several preceding instances like votes had *sub silentio* been entered as decided in the affirmative.]

Adjourned

---

SATURDAY, JULY 7.   IN CONVENTION

[52] "Shall the clause allowing each State one vote in the 2[d] branch, stand as part of the Report"? being taken up—

M[r] GERRY. This is the critical question. He had rather agree to it than have no accomodation. A Govern[t] short of a proper national plan, if generally acceptable, would be preferable to a proper one which if it could be carried at all, would operate on discontented States. He thought it would be best to suspend the [53] question till the Comm[e] yesterday appointed,[54] should make report.

M[r] SHERMAN Supposed that it was the wish of every one that some Gen[l] Gov[t] should be established. An equal vote in the 2[d] branch would, he thought, be most likely to give it the necessary vigor. The small States have more vigor in their Gov[ts] than the large ones, the more influence therefore the large ones have, the weaker will be the Gov[t] In the large States it will be most difficult to collect the real & fair sense of the people. Fallacy & undue influence will be practiced with most success: and improper men will most easily get into office. If they vote by States in the 2[d] branch, and each State has an equal vote, there must be always a majority of States as well as a majority of the people on the side of public measures, & the Gov[t] will have decision and efficacy. If this be not the case in the 2[d] branch there may be a majority of the [55] States ag[st] public measures, and the difficulty of compelling them to abide by the public determination, will render the Government feebler than it has ever yet been.

---

[49] The word "this" is substituted in the transcript for "the."
[50] The figure "9" is here added in the transcript.
[51] The figure "2" is here added in the transcript.
[52] The words "The question" are here inserted in the transcript.
[53] The word "this" is substituted in the transcript for "the."
[54] The words "yesterday appointed" are transposed to read "appointed yesterday" in the transcript.
[55] The word "the" is omitted in the transcript.

M.r WILSON was not deficient in a conciliating temper, but firmness was sometimes a duty of higher obligation. Conciliation was also misapplied in this instance. It was pursued here rather among the Representatives, than among the Constituents; and it w.d be of little consequence, if not established among the latter; and there could be little hope of its being established among them if the foundation should not be laid in justice and right.

On [56] Question shall the words stand as part of the Report?

Mass.ts div.d Con.t ay. N. Y. ay. N. J. ay. P.a no. Del. ay. M.d ay. V.a no. N. C. ay. S. C. no. Geo. div.d [57]

[Note. Several votes were given here in the affirmative or were div.d because another final question was to be taken on the whole report.]

M.r GERRY thought it would be proper to proceed to enumerate & define the powers to be vested in the Gen.l Gov.t before a question on the report should be taken, as to the rule of representation in the 2.d branch.

M.r MADISON, observed that it w.d be impossible to say what powers could be safely & properly vested in the Gov.t before it was known, in what manner the States were to be represented in it. He was apprehensive that if a just representation were not the basis of the Gov.t it would happen, as it did when the Articles of Confederation were depending, that every effectual prerogative would be withdrawn or withheld, and the New Gov.t w.d be rendered as impotent and as shortlived as the old.

M.r PATTERSON would not decide whether the privilege concerning money bills were a valuable consideration or not: But he considered the mode & rule of representation in the 1.st branch as fully so. and that after the establishment of that point, the small States would never be able to defend themselves without an equality of votes in the 2.d branch. There was no other ground of accomodation. His resolution was fixt. He would meet the large States on that Ground and no other. For himself he should vote ag.st the Report, because it yielded too much.

---

[56] The word "the" is here inserted in the transcript.
[57] In the transcript the vote reads: "Connecticut, New York, New Jersey, Delaware, Maryland, North Carolina, aye—6; Pennsylvania, Virginia, South Carolina, no—3; Massachusetts, Georgia, divided."

Mr Govr MORRIS. He had no resolution unalterably fixed except to do what should finally appear to him right. He was agst the Report because it maintained the improper Constitution of the 2d branch. It made it another Congress, a mere whisp of straw. It had been sd [by Mr Gerry] that the new Governt would be partly national, partly federal; that it ought in the first quality to protect individuals; in the second, the States. But in what quality was it to protect the aggregate interest of the whole. Among the many provisions which had been urged, he had seen none for supporting the dignity and splendor of the American Empire. It had been one of our greatest misfortunes that the great objects of the nation had been sacrificed constantly to local views; in like manner as the general interests of States had been sacrificed to those of the Counties. What is to be the check in the Senate? none; unless it be to keep the majority of the people from injuring particular States. But particular States ought to be injured for the sake of a majority of the people, in case their conduct should deserve it. Suppose they should insist on claims evidently unjust, and pursue them in a manner detrimental to the whole body. Suppose they should give themselves up to foreign influence. Ought they to be protected in such cases. They were originally nothing more than colonial corporations. On the declaration of Independence, a Governmt was to be formed. The small States aware of the necessity of preventing anarchy, and taking advantage of the moment, extorted from the large ones an equality of votes. Standing now on that ground, they demand under the new system greater rights as men, than their fellow Citizens of the large States. The proper answer to them is that the same necessity of which they formerly took advantage, does not now exist, and that the large States are at liberty now to consider what is right, rather than what may be expedient. We must have an efficient Govt and if there be an efficiency in the local Govts the former is impossible. Germany alone proves it. Notwithstanding their common diet, notwithstanding the great prerogatives of the Emperor as head of the Empire, and his vast resources, as sovereign of his particular dominions, no union is maintained: foreign influence disturbs every internal operation, & there is no energy whatever in the general Governm! Whence does this proceed? From the energy of the local authorities; from its being considered of more consequence to support the Prince of Hesse, than the Happiness of the people of Germany. Do Gentlemen wish this to be yᵉ case here. Good God, Sir, is it possible they can so delude themselves. What if all the Charters & Consitutions of the States were thrown into the fire, and all their demagogues into the ocean. What would it be to the happiness of America. And will not this be the case here if we pursue the train in wᶜʰ the business lies. We shall establish an Aulic Council without an Emperor to execute its decrees. The same circumstances which unite the people here, unite them in Germany. They have there a common language, a common law, common usages and manners, and a common interest in being united; yet their local jurisdictions destroy every tie. The case was the same in the Grecian States. The United Netherlands are at this time torn in factions. With these examples before our eyes shall we form establishments which must necessarily produce the same effects. It is of no consequence from what districts the 2ᵈ branch shall be drawn, if it be so constituted as to yield an asylum agˢᵗ these evils. As it is now constituted he must be agˢᵗ its being drawn from the States in equal portions. But shall he was [58] ready to join in devising such an amendment of the plan, as will be most likely to secure our liberty & happiness.

Mʳ SHERMAN & Mʳ ELSEWORTH moved to postpone the Question on the Report from the Committee of a member from each State, in order to wait for the Report from the Comᵉ of 5 last appointed.

Masᵗˢ ay. Conᵗ ay. N. Y. no. N. J. ay. Pᵃ ay. Del. ay. Maryland ay. Vᵃ no. N. C. no. S. C. no. Geo. no.[59]

Adjᵈ

---

MONDAY JULY 9ᵀᴴ IN CONVENTION

Mʳ Daniel Carroll from Maryland took his Seat.

Mʳ Govʳ MORRIS delivered a report from the Comᵉ of 5 members to whom was committed the clause in the Report of the Comᵉ con-

---

[58] The words "shall be" are substituted in the transcript for "shall he was."

[59] In the transcript the vote reads: Massachusetts, Connecticut, New Jersey, Pennsylvania, Delaware, Maryland, aye—6; New York, Virginia, North Carolina, South Carolina, Georgia, no—5."

sisting of a member from each State, stating the proper ratio of Representatives in the 1st branch, to be as 1 to every 40,000 inhabitants, as follows viz

" The Committee to whom was referred the 1st clause of the 1st proposition reported from the grand Committee, beg leave to report

I.[60] that in the 1st meeting of the Legislature the 1st branch thereof consist of 56. members of which Number, N. Hamshire shall have 2. Mass<sup>ts</sup> 7. R. I<sup>d</sup> 1. Con<sup>t</sup> 4. N. Y. 5. N. J. 3. P<sup>a</sup> 8. Del. 1. M<sup>d</sup> 4. V<sup>a</sup> 9. N. C. 5. S. C. 5. Geo. 2.—

II.[60] But as the present situation of the States may probably alter as well in point of wealth as in the number of their inhabitants, that the Legislature be authorized from time to time to augment y<sup>e</sup> number of Representatives. And in case any of the States shall hereafter be divided, or any two or more States united, or any new States created within the limits of the United States, the Legislature shall possess authority to regulate the number of Representatives in any of the foregoing cases, upon the principles of their wealth and number of inhabitants."

M<sup>r</sup> SHERMAN wished to know on what principles or calculations the Report was founded. It did not appear to correspond with any rule of numbers, or of any requisition hitherto adopted by Cong<sup>s</sup>

M<sup>r</sup> GORHAM. Some provision of this sort was necessary in the outset: The number of blacks & whites with some regard to supposed wealth was the general guide Fractions could not be observed. The Legisl<sup>re</sup> is to make alterations from time to time as justice & propriety may require. Two objections prevailed ag<sup>st</sup> the rate [61] of 1 member for every 40,000. inh<sup>ts</sup> The 1<sup>st</sup> was that the Representation would soon be too numerous: the 2<sup>d</sup> that the West<sup>n</sup> States who may have a different interest, might if admitted on that principle by degrees, outvote the Atlantic. Both these objections are removed. The number will be small in the first instance and may be continued so; and the Atlantic States having y<sup>e</sup> Gov<sup>t</sup> in their own hands, may take care of their own interest, by dealing out the right of Representation in safe proportions to the Western States. These were the views of the Committee.

---

[60] The Roman numerals "I" and "II" are omitted in the transcript.
[61] The word "rule" is substituted in the transcript for "rate."

Mr L. MARTIN wished to know whether the Comᵉ were guided in the ratio, by the wealth or number of inhabitants, of the States, or by [62] both; noting its variations from former apportionments by Congˢ

Mr Govr MORRIS & Mr RUTLIDGE moved to postpone the 1ˢᵗ paragraph relating to the number of members to be allowed each State in the first instance, and to take up the 2ᵈ paragraph authorizing the Leg̣iṣlʳᵉ to alter the number from time to time according to wealth & inhabitants. The motion was agreed to nem. con.

On [63] Question on the 2ᵈ paragʰ taken without any debate

Masᵗˢ ay. Conᵗ ay. N. Y. no. N. J. no. Pᵃ ay. Del. ay. Mᵈ ay. Vᵃ ay. N. C. ay. S. C. ay. Geo. ay.[64]

Mr SHERMAN moved to refer the 1ˢᵗ part apportioning the Representatives, to a Commᵉ of a member from each State.

Mr Govr MORRIS seconded the motion; observing that this was the only case in which such Committees were useful.

Mr WILLIAMSON. thought it would be necessary to return to the rule of numbers, but that the Western States stood on different footing. If their property shall [65] be rated as high as that of the Atlantic States, then their representation ought to hold a like proportion. Otherwise if their property was not to be equally rated.

Mr Govr MORRIS. The Report is little more than a guess. Wealth was not altogether disregarded by the Comᵉ Where it was apparently in favor of one State, whose nᵒˢ were superior to the numbers of another, by a fraction only, a member extraordinary was allowed to the former: and so vice versa. The Committee meant little more than to bring the matter to a point for the consideration of the House.

Mr REED asked why Georgia was allowed 2 members, when her number of inhabitants had stood below that of Delaware.

Mr Govr MORRIS. Such is the rapidity of the population of that State, that before the plan takes effect, it will probably be entitled to 2 Representatives

---

[62] The word "by" is omitted in the transcript.
[63] The word "the" is here inserted in the transcript.
[64] In the transcript the vote reads: "Massachusetts, Connecticut, Pennsylvania, Delaware, Maryland, Virginia, North Carolina, South Carolina, Georgia, aye—9; New York, New Jersey, no—2."
[65] The word "should" is substituted in the transcript for "shall."

Mʳ RANDOLPH. disliked the report of the Comᵉ but had been unwilling to object to it. He was apprehensive that as the number was not to be changed till the Natˡ Legislature should please, a pretext would never be wanting to postpone alterations, and keep the power in the hands of those possessed of it. He was in favor of the commitmᵗ to a member from each State.

Mʳ PATTERSON considered the proposed estimate for the future according to the Combined rule ⁶⁶ of numbers and wealth, as too vague. For this reason N. Jersey was agˢᵗ it. He could regard negroes ⁶⁷ slaves in no light but as property. They are no free agents, have no personal liberty, no faculty of acquiring property, but on the contrary are themselves property, & like other property entirely at the will of the Master. Has a man in Virgᵃ a number of votes in proportion to the number of his slaves? And if Negroes are not represented in the States to which they belong, why should they be represented in the Genˡ Govᵗ What is the true principle of Representation? It is an expedient by which an assembly of certain individˡˢ chosen by the people is substituted in place of the inconvenient meeting of the people themselves. If such a meeting of the people was actually to take place, would the slaves vote? They would not. Why then shᵈ they be represented. He was also agˢᵗ such an indirect encouragemᵗ of the slave trade; observing that Congˢ in their act relating to the change of the 8 art: of Confedⁿ had been ashamed to use the term "slaves" & had substituted a description.

Mʳ MADISON, reminded Mʳ Patterson that his doctrine of Representation which was in its principle the genuine one, must for ever silence the pretensions of the small States to an equality of votes with the large ones. They ought to vote in the same proportion in which their citizens would do, if the people of all the States were collectively met. He suggested as a proper ground of compromise, that in the first branch the States should be represented according to their number of free inhabitants; and in the 2ᵈ which had for one of its primary objects the guardianship of property, according to the whole number, including slaves.

---

[66] The transcript uses the word "rule" in the plural.
[67] The transcript uses the word "negroes" in the singular.

Mr BUTLER urged warmly the justice & necessity of regarding wealth in the apportionment of Representation.

Mr KING had always expected that as the Southern States are the richest, they would not league themselves with the Northr unless some respect were paid to their superior wealth. If the latter expect those preferential distinctions in Commerce & other advantages which they will derive from the connection they must not expect to receive them without allowing some advantages in return. Eleven out of 13 of the States had agreed to consider Slaves in the apportionment of taxation; and taxation and Representation ought to go together.

On the question for committing the first paragraph of the Report to a member from each State.

Masts. ay. Cont. ay. N. Y. no. N. J. ay. Pa. ay. Del. ay. Md ay. Va ay. N. C. ay. S. C. no. Geo. ay.[68]

The Come. appointed were Mr King. Mr Sherman, Mr Yates, Mr Brearly, Mr Govr Morris, Mr Reed, Mr Carrol, Mr Madison, Mr Williamson, Mr Rutledge, Mr Houston.

Adjd

---

TEUSDAY. JULY 10 IN CONVENTION

Mr KING reported from the Come yesterday appointed that the States at the 1st meeting of the General Legislature, should be represented by 65 members in the following proportions, to wit. N. Hamshire by 3. Masts. 8. R. Isd 1. Cont 5. N. Y. 6. N. J. 4. Pa 8. Del. 1. Md 6. Va 10. N. C. 5. S. C. 5. Georgia 3.

Mr RUTLIDGE moved that N. Hampshire be reduced from 3 to 2. members. Her numbers did not entitle her to 3 and it was a poor State.

Genl PINKNEY seconds the motion.

Mr KING. N. Hamshire has probably more than 120,000 Inhabts and has an extensive Country of tolerable fertility. Its inhabts therefore may[69] be expected to increase fast. He remarked that the four Eastern States having 800,000 souls, have

---

[68] In the transcript the vote reads: "Massachusetts, Connecticut, New Jersey, Pennsylvania, Delaware, Maryland, Virgina, North Carolina, Georgia, aye—9; New York, South Carolina, no—2."

[69] The words "therefore may" are transposed to read "may therefore" in the transcript.

⅓ fewer representatives than the four Southern States, having not more than 700,000 souls rating the blacks, as 5 for 3. The Eastern people will advert to these circumstances, and be dissatisfied. He believed them to be very desirous of uniting with their Southern brethren, but did not think it prudent to rely so far on that disposition as to subject them to any gross inequality. He was fully convinced that the question concerning a difference of interests did not lie where it had hitherto been discussed, between the great & small States; but between the Southern & Eastern. For this reason he had been ready to yield something in the proportion of representatives for the security of the Southern. No principle would justify the giving them a majority. They were brought as near an equality as was possible. He was not averse to giving them a still greater security, but did not see how it could be done.

Gen! PINKNEY. The Report before it was committed was more favorable to the S. States than as it now stands. If they are to form so considerable a minority, and the regulation of trade is to be given to the Gen! Government, they will be nothing more than overseers for the Northern States. He did not expect the S. States to be raised to a majority of representatives, but wished them to have something like an equality. At present by the alterations of the Com<sup>e</sup> in favor of the N. States they are removed farther from it than they were before. One member had indeed [70] been added to Virg<sup>a</sup> which he was glad of as he considered her as a Southern State. He was glad also that the members of Georgia were increased.

M<sup>r</sup> WILLIAMSON was not for reducing N. Hamshire from 3 to 2. but for reducing some others. The South<sup>n</sup> Interest must be extremely endangered by the present arrangement. The North<sup>n</sup> States are to have a majority in the first instance and the means of perpetuating it.

M<sup>r</sup> DAYTON observed that the line between the [71] North<sup>n</sup> & Southern interest had been improperly drawn: that P<sup>a</sup> was the dividing State, there being six on each side of her.

---

[70] The words "had indeed" are transposed to read "indeed had" in the transcript.
[71] The word "the" is omitted in the transcript.

348

Gen! PINKNEY urged the reduction, dwelt on the superior wealth of the Southern States, and insisted on its having its due weight in the Government.

M! Gov! MORRIS regretted the turn of the debate. The States he found had many Representatives on the floor. Few he fears [72] were to be deemed the Representatives of America. He thought the Southern States have by the report more than their share of representation. Property ought to have its weight, but not all the weight. If the South? States are to supply money. The North? States are to spill their blood. Besides, the probable Revenue to be expected from the S. States has been greatly overrated. He was ag:t reducing N. Hamshire.

M! RANDOLPH was opposed to a reduction of N. Hamshire, not because she had a full title to three members: but because it was in his contemplation 1.[73] to make it the duty instead of leaving it in [74] the discretion of the Legislature to regulate the representation by a periodical census. 2.[73] to require more than a bare majority of votes in the Legislature in certain cases, & particularly in commercial cases.

On the question for reducing N. Hamshire from 3 to 2 Represent: it passed in the negative

Mas:ts no. Con:t no. N. J. no. P:a no. Del. no. M:d no. V:a no. N. C. ay.* S. C. ay. Geo. no.* [75]

Gen! PINKNEY and M! ALEX! MARTIN moved that 6 Rep:s instead of 5 be allowed to N. Carolina

On the Question, it passed in the negative.

Mas:ts no. Con:t no. N. J. no. P:a no. Del. no. M:d no. V:a no. N. C. ay. S. C. ay. Geo. ay.[76]

Gen! PINKNEY & M! BUTLER made the same motion in favor of S. Carolina.

On the Question it passed in the negative

---

*In the printed Journal N. C. no. Georgia ay

[72] The word "feared" is substituted in the transcript for "fears."

[73] The figures "1" and "2" are changed to "first" and "secondly" in the transcript.

[74] The word "to" is substituted in the transcript for "in."

[75] In the transcript the vote reads: "North Carolina,* South Carolina, aye—2; Massachusetts, Connecticut, New Jersey, Pennsylvania, Delaware, Maryland, Virginia, Georgia,* no—8."

[76] In the transcript the vote reads: "North Carolina, South Carolina, Georgia, aye—3; Massachusetts, Connecticut, New Jersey, Pennsylvania, Delaware, Maryland, Virginia, no—7."

Mas.$^{ts}$ no. Con.$^t$ no. N. Y. no N. J. no. P.$^a$ no. Del. ay. M.$^d$ no. V.$^a$ no. N. C. ay. S. C. ay. Geo. ay.[77]

Gen.$^l$ PINKNEY & M.$^r$ HOUSTON moved that Georgia be allowed 4 instead of 3 Rep.$^s$ urging the unexampled celerity of its population. On the Question, it passed in the Negative

Mas.$^{ts}$ no. Con.$^t$ no. N. Y no N. J. no. P.$^a$ no. Del. no. M.$^d$ no. V.$^a$ ay. N. C. ay. S. C. ay. Geo. ay.[78]

M.$^r$ MADISON, moved that the number allowed to each State be doubled. A *majority* of a *Quorum* of 65 members, was too small a number to to represent the whole inhabitants of the U. States; They would not possess enough of the confidence of the people, and w.$^d$ be too sparsely taken from the people, to bring with them all the local information which would be frequently wanted. Double the number will not be too great, even with the future additions from New States. The additional expence was too inconsiderable to be regarded in so important a case. And as far as the augmentation might be unpopular on that score, the objection was overbalanced by its effect on the hopes of a greater number of the popular Candidates.

M.$^r$ ELSEWORTH urged the objection of expence, & that the greater the number, the more slowly would the business proceed; and the less probably be decided as it ought, at last. He thought the number of Representatives too great in most of the State Legislatures: and that a large number was less necessary in the Gen.$^l$ Legislature than in those of the States,—as its business would relate to a few great, national Objects only.

M.$^r$ SHERMAN would have preferred 50 to 65. The great distance they will have to travel will render their attendance precarious and will make it difficult to prevail on a sufficient number of fit men to undertake the service. He observed that the expected increase from New States also deserved consideration.

M.$^r$ GERRY was for increasing the number beyond 65. The larger the number, the less the danger of their being corrupted. The people are accustomed to & fond of a numerous representation,

---

[77] In the transcript the vote reads: "Delaware, North Carolina, South Carolina, Georgia, aye—4: Massachusetts, Connecticut, New York, New Jersey, Pennsylvania, Maryland, Virginia, no—7."

[78] In the transcript the vote reads: "Virginia, North Carolina, South Carolina, Georgia, aye—4: Massachusetts, Connecticut, New York, New Jersey, Pennsylvania, Delaware, Maryland, no—7."

and will consider their rights as better secured by it. The danger of excess in the number may be guarded ag$^{st}$ by fixing a point within which the number shall always be kept.

Col. MASON admitted that the objection drawn from the consideration of expence, had weight both in itself, and as the people might be affected by it. But he thought it outweighed by the objections ag$^{st}$ the smallness of the number. 38, will he supposes, as being a majority of 65, form a quorum. 20 will be a majority of 38. This was certainly too small a number to make laws for America. They would neither bring with them all the necessary information relative to various local interests, nor possess the necessary confidence of the people. After doubling the number, the laws might still be made by so few as almost to be objectionable on that account.

M$^r$ READ was in favor of the Motion. Two of the States [Del. & R. I.] would have but a single member if the aggregate number should remain at 65. and in case of accident to either of these one State w$^d$ have no representative present to give explanations or informations of its interests or wishes. The people would not place their confidence in so small a number. He hoped the objects of the Gen$^l$ Gov$^t$ would be much more numerous than seemed to be expected by some gentlemen, and that they would become more & more so. As to [79] New States the highest number of Rep$^s$ for the whole might be limited, and all danger of excess thereby prevented.

M$^r$ RUTLIDGE opposed the motion. The Representatives were too numerous in all the States. The full number allotted to the States may be expected to attend & the lowest possible quorum sh$^d$ not therefore be considered. The interests of their Constituents will urge their attendance too strongly for it to be omitted: and he supposed the Gen$^l$ Legislature would not sit more than 6 or 8 weeks in the year.

On the Question for doubling the number, it passed in the negative.

Mas$^{ts}$ no. Con$^t$ no. N. Y. no. N. J. no. P$^a$ no. Del. ay. M$^d$ no. V$^a$ ay. N. C. no. S. C. no. Geo. no.[80]

---

[79] The word "the" is here inserted in the transcript.

[80] In the transcript the vote reads: "Delaware, Virginia, aye—2; Massachusetts, Connecticut, New York, New Jersey, Pennsylvania, Maryland, North Carolina, South Carolina, Georgia, no—9."

On the question for agreeing to the apportionment of Rep: as amended by the last committee, it passed in the affirmative

Mas. ay. Con! ay. N. Y. ay. N. J. ay. P? ay. Del. ay. M? ay. V? ay. N. C. ay. S. C. no. Geo. no.[81]

M: BROOM gave notice to the House that he had concurred with a reserve to himself of an intention to claim for his State an equal voice in the 2? branch: which he thought could not be denied after this concession of the small States as to the first branch.

M: RANDOLPH moved as an amendment to the report of the Comm? of five "that in order to ascertain the alterations in the population & wealth of the several States the Legislature should be required to cause a census, and estimate to be taken within one year after its first meeting; and every      years thereafter— and that the Legisl<sup>re</sup> arrange the Representation accordingly."

M: Gov: MORRIS opposed it as fettering the Legislature too much. Advantage may be taken of it in time of war or the apprehension of it, by new States to extort particular favors. If the mode was to be fixed for taking a census, it might certainly be extremely inconvenient: if unfixt the Legislature may use such a mode as will defeat the object: and perpetuate the inequality. He was always ag?t such Shackles on the Legisl<sup>re</sup> They had been found very pernicious in most of the State Constitutions. He dwelt much on the danger of throwing such a preponderancy [82] into the Western Scale, suggesting that in time the Western people w? outnumber the Atlantic States. He wished therefore to put it in the power of the latter to keep a majority of votes in their own hands. It was objected he said that if the Legisl<sup>re</sup> are left at liberty, they will never readjust the Representation. He admitted that this was possible; but he did not think it probable unless the reasons ag?t a revision of it were very urgent & in this case, it ought not to be done.

It was moved to postpone the proposition of M: Randolph in order to take up the following, viz. "that the Committee of

---

[81] In the transcript the vote reads: "Massachusetts, Connecticut, New York, New Jersey, Pennsylvania. Delaware, Maryland, Virginia, North Carolina, aye—9; South Carolina, Georgia, no—2."

[82] The word "preponderancy" is changed to "preponderance" in the transcript.

Eleven, to whom was referred the report of the Committee of five on the subject of Representation, be requested to furnish the Convention with the principles on which they grounded the Report," which was disagreed to: S. C. only [83] voting in the affirmative.

Adjourned

WEDNESDAY JULY 11. IN CONVENTION

M$^r$ Randolph's motion requiring the Legisl$^{re}$ to take a periodical census for the purpose of redressing inequalities in the Representation, was resumed.

M$^r$ SHERMAN was ag$^{st}$ shackling the Legislature too much. We ought to choose wise & good men, and then confide in them.

M$^r$ MASON. The greater the difficulty we find in fixing a proper rule of Representation, the more unwilling ought we to be, to throw the task from ourselves, on the Gen$^l$ Legisl$^{re}$ He did not object to the conjectural ratio which was to prevail in the outset; but considered a Revision from time to time according to some permanent & precise standard as essential to y$^e$ fair representation required in the 1$^{st}$ branch. According to the present population of America, the North$^n$ part of it had a right to preponderate, and he could not deny it. But he wished it not to preponderate hereafter when the reason no longer continued. From the nature of man we may be sure, that those who have power in their hands will not give it up while they can retain it. On the contrary we know they will always when they can rather increase it. If the S. States therefore should have $\frac{3}{4}$ of the people of America within their limits, the Northern will hold fast the majority of Representatives. $\frac{1}{4}$ will govern the $\frac{3}{4}$. The S. States will complain: but they may complain from generation to generation without redress. Unless some principle therefore which will do justice to them hereafter shall be inserted in the Constitution, disagreeable as the declaration was to him, he must declare he could neither vote for the system here, nor support it, in his State. Strong objections had been drawn from the danger to the Atlantic interests from new Western States. Ought we to sacrifice what we know to be right in itself, lest it

---

[83] The word "alone" is substituted in the transcript for "only."

should prove favorable to States which are not yet in existence. If the Western States are to be admitted into the Union, as they arise, they must, he w{d} repeat, be treated as equals, and subjected to no degrading discriminations. They will have the same pride & other passions which we have, and will either not unite with or will speedily revolt from the Union, if they are not in all respects placed on an equal footing with their brethern. It has been said they will be poor, and unable to make equal contributions to the general Treasury. He did not know but that in time they would be both more numerous & more wealthy than their Atlantic brethren. The extent & fertility of their soil, made this probable; and though Spain might for a time deprive them of the natural outlet for their productions, yet she will, because she must, finally yield to their demands. He urged that numbers of inhabitants; though not always a precise standard of wealth was sufficiently so for every substantial purpose.

Mr WILLIAMSON was for making it the duty of the Legislature to do what was right & not leaving it at liberty to do or not [84] do it. He moved that Mr Randolph's proposition be postpon{d} in order to consider the following "that in order to ascertain the alterations that may happen in the population & wealth of the several States, a census shall be taken of the free white inhabitants and $\frac{3}{5}$ths of those of other descriptions on the 1{st} year after this Government shall have been adopted and every     year thereafter; and that the Representation be regulated accordingly."

Mr RANDOLPH agreed that Mr Williamson's proposition should stand in the place of his. He observed that the ratio fixt for the 1st meeting was a mere conjecture, that it placed the power in the hands of that part of America, which could not always be entitled to it, that this power would not be voluntarily renounced; and that it was consequently the duty of the Convention to secure its renunciation when justice might so require; by some constitutional provisions. If equality between great & small States be inadmissible, because in that case unequal numbers of Constituents w{d} be represented by equal number [85] of votes; was it not equally

---

[84] The word "to" is here inserted in the transcript.
[85] The transcript uses the word "number" in the plural.

inadmissible that a larger & more populous district of America should hereafter have less representation, than a smaller & less populous district. If a fair representation of the people be not secured, the injustice of the Gov.̇ will shake it to its foundations. What relates to suffrage is justly stated by the celebrated Montesquieu, as a fundamental article in Republican Gov.ṭṣ If the danger suggested by M.ṛ Gov.ṛ Morris be real, of advantage being taken of the Legislature in pressing moments, it was an additional reason, for tying their hands in such a manner that they could not sacrifice their trust to momentary considerations. Cong.ṣ have pledged the public faith to New States, that they shall be admitted on equal terms. They never would nor ought to accede on any other. The census must be taken under the direction of the General Legislature. The States will be too much interested to take an impartial one for themselves.

M.ṛ BUTLER & Gen.! PINKNEY insisted that blacks be included in the rule of Representation, *equally* with the Whites: and for that purpose moved that the words "three fifths" be struck out.

M.ṛ GERRY thought that ⅗ of them was to say the least the full proportion that could be admitted.

M.ṛ GHORUM. This ratio was fixed by Cong.ṣ as a rule of taxation. Then it was urged by the Delegates representing the States having slaves that the blacks were still more inferior to freemen. At present when the ratio of representation is to be established, we are assured that they are equal to freemen. The arguments on y.ẹ former occasion had convinced him that ⅗ was pretty near the just proportion and he should vote according to the same opinion now.

M.ṛ BUTLER insisted that the labour of a slave in S. Carol.ạ was as productive & valuable as that of a freeman in Mass.ṭṣ, that as wealth was the great means of defence and utility to the Nation they were equally valuable to it with freemen; and that consequently an equal representation ought to be allowed for them in a Government which was instituted principally for the protection of property, and was itself to be supported by property.

M.ṛ MASON, could not agree to the motion, notwithstand it was favorable to Virg.ạ because he thought it unjust. It was certain that the slaves were valuable, as they raised the value of land, increased the exports & imports, and of course the revenue, would supply the means of feeding & supporting an army, and might in cases of emergency become themselves soldiers. As in these important respects they were useful to the community at large, they ought not to be excluded from the estimate of Representation. He could not however regard them as equal to freemen and could not vote for them as such. He added as worthy of remark, that the Southern States have this peculiar species of property, over & above the other species of property common to all the States.

Mr WILLIAMSON reminded Mr Ghorum that if the South<sup>n</sup> States contended for the inferiority of blacks to whites when taxation was in view, the Eastern States on the same occasion contended for their equality. He did not however either then or now, concur in either extreme, but approved of the ratio of ⅗.

On Mr Butlers motion for considering blacks as equal to Whites in the apportionm<sup>t</sup> of Representation.

Mass<sup>ts</sup> no. Con<sup>t</sup> no. [N. Y. not on floor.] N. J. no. P<sup>a</sup> no. Del. ay. M<sup>d</sup> no. V<sup>a</sup> no N. C. no. S. C. ay. Geo. ay.[86]

Mr Gov<sup>r</sup> MORRIS said he had several objections to the proposition of Mr Williamson. 1.[87] It fettered the Legislature too much. 2.[88] it would exclude some States altogether who would not have a sufficient number to entitle them to a single Representative. 3.[89] it will not consist with the Resolution passed on Saturday last authorising the Legislature to adjust the Representation from time to time on the principles of population & wealth or [90] with the principles of equity. If slaves were to be considered as inhabitants, not as wealth, then the s<sup>d</sup> Resolution would not be pursued: If as wealth, then why is no other wealth but slaves included? These objections may perhaps be removed by amendments. His great objection was that the number of inhabitants was not a proper standard of wealth. The amazing difference between the comparative numbers & wealth of different Countries, rendered all

---

[86] In the transcript the vote reads: "Delaware, South Carolina, Georgia, aye—3; Massachusetts, Connecticut, New Jersey, Pennsylvania, Maryland, Virginia, North Carolina, no—7; New York not on the floor."

[87] The figure "1" is changed to "In the first place" in the transcript.

[88] The figure "2" is changed to "In the second place" in the transcript.

[89] The figure "3" is changed to "In the third place" in the transcript.

[90] The word "or" is changed to "nor" in the transcript.

reasoning superfluous on the subject. Numbers might with greater propriety be deemed a measure of stregth, than of wealth, yet the late defence made by G. Britain, ag:ʷ her numerous enemies proved in the clearest manner, that it is entirely fallacious even in this respect.

M⁥ KING thought there was great force in the objections of M⁥ Gov⁥ Morris: he would however accede to the proposition for the sake of doing something.

M⁥ RUTLIDGE contended for the admission of wealth in the estimate by which Representation should be regulated. The Western States will not be able to contribute in proportion to their numbers; they sh:ᵈ not therefore be represented in that proportion. The Atlantic States will not concur in such a plan. He moved that "at the end of      years after the 1:ˢᵗ meeting of the Legislature, and of every      years thereafter, the Legislature shall proportion the Representation according to the principles of wealth & population"

M⁥ SHERMAN thought the number of people alone the best rule for measuring wealth as well as representation; and that if the Legislature were to be governed by wealth, they would be obliged to estimate it by numbers. He was at first for leaving the matter wholly to the discretion of the Legislature; but he had been convinced by the observations of [M⁥ Randolph & M⁥ Mason,] that the *periods* & the *rule*, of revising the Representation ought to be fixt by the Constitution

M⁥ REID thought the Legislature ought not to be too much shackled. It would make the Constitution like Religious Creeds, embarrassing to those bound to conform to them & more likely to produce dissatisfaction and scism, than harmony and union.

M⁥ MASON objected to M⁥ Rutlidge motion, as requiring of the Legislature something too indefinite & impracticable, and leaving them a pretext for doing nothing.

M⁥ WILSON had himself no objection to leaving the Legislature entirely at liberty. But considered wealth as an impracticable rule.

M⁥ GHORUM. If the Convention who are comparatively so little biassed by local views are so much perplexed, How can it be expected that the Legislature hereafter under the full biass of those views, will be able to settle a standard. He was convinced by the arguments of others & his own reflections, that the Convention ought to fix some standard or other.

Mr Govr MORRIS. The argts of others & his own reflections had led him to a very different conclusion. If we can't agree on a rule that will be just at this time, how can we expect to find one that will be just in all times to come. Surely those who come after us will judge better of things present, than we can of things future. He could not persuade himself that numbers would be a just rule at any time. The remarks of [Mr Mason] relative to the Western Country had not changed his opinion on that head. Among other objections it must be apparent they would not be able to furnish men equally enlightened, to share in the administration of our common interests. The Busy haunts of men not the remote wilderness, was the proper school of political Talents. If the Western people get the power into their hands they will ruin the Atlantic interests. The Back members are always most averse to the best measures. He mentioned the case of Pena formerly. The lower part of the State had ye power in the first instance. They kept it in yr own hands & the Country was ye better for it. Another objection with him agst admitting the blacks into the census, was that the people of Pena would revolt at the idea of being put on a footing with slaves. They would reject any plan that was to have such an effect. Two objections had been raised agst leaving the adjustment of the Representation from time, to time, to the discretion of the Legislature. The 1.[91] was they would be unwilling to revise it at all. The 2.[91] that by referring to *wealth* they would be bound by a rule which if willing, they would be unable to execute. The 1st objn distrusts their fidelity. But if their duty, their honor & their oaths will not bind them, let us not put into their hands our liberty, and all our other great interests: let us have no Govt at all. 2.[92] If these ties will bind them, we need not distrust the practicability of the rule. It was followed in part by the Come in the apportionment of Representa-

---

[91] The figures "1" and "2" are changed to "first" and "second" in the transcript.
[92] The figure "2" is changed to "In the second place" in the transcript.

tives yesterday reported to the House. The best course that could be taken would be to leave the interests of the people to the Representatives of the people.

Mr MADISON, was not a little surprised to hear this implicit confidence urged by a member who on all occasions, had inculcated so strongly, the political depravity of men, and the necessity of checking one vice and interest by opposing to them another vice & interest. If the Representatives of the people would be bound by the ties he had mentioned, what need was there of a Senate? What of a Revisionary power? But his reasoning was not only inconsistent with his former reasoning, but with itself. At the same time that he recommended this implicit confidence to the Southern States in the Northern Majority, he was still more zealous in exhorting all to a jealousy of [93] Western Majority. To reconcile the gentln with himself, it it must be imagined that he determined the human character by the points of the compass. The truth was that all men having power ought to be distrusted to a certain degree. The case of Pena had been mentioned where it was admitted that those who were possessed of the power in the original settlement, never admitted the new settlemts to a due share of it. England was a still more striking example. The power there had long been in the hands of the boroughs, of the minority; who had opposed & defeated every reform which had been attempted. Virga was in a lesser [94] degree another example. With regard to the Western States, he was clear & firm in opinion, that no unfavorable distinctions were admissible either in point of justice or policy. He thought also that the hope of contributions to the Treasy from them had been much underrated. Future contributions it seemed to be understood on all hands would be principally levied on imports & exports. The extent and and fertility of the Western Soil would for a long time give to agriculture a preference over manufactures. Trials would be repeated till some articles could be raised from it that would bear a transportation to places where they could be exchanged for imported manufactures. Whenever the Mississpi should be opened to them, which would

---

[93] The word "a" is here inserted in the transcript.
[94] The word "lesser" is changed to "less" in the transcript.

of necessity be y:̲ case, as soon as their population would subject them to any considerable share of the public burdin, imposts on their trade could be collected with less expence & greater certainty, than on that of the Atlantic States. In the mean time, as their supplies must pass thro' the *Atlantic States*, their contributions would be levied in the same manner with those of the Atlantic States.—He could not agree that any substantial objection lay ag:̲s:̲t fixi:̲g numbers for the perpetual standard of Representation. It was said that Representation & taxation were to go together; that taxation and wealth ought to go together, that population & wealth were not measures of each other. He admitted that in different climates, under different forms of Gov:̲t and in different stages of civilization the inference was perfectly just. He would admit that in no situation, numbers of inhabitants were an accurate measure of wealth. He contended however that in the U. States it was sufficiently so for the object in contemplation. Altho' their climate varied considerably, yet as the Gov:̲t:̲s the laws, and the manners of all were nearly the same, and the intercourse between different parts perfectly free, population, industry, arts, and the value of labour, would constantly tend to equalize themselves. The value of labour, might be considered as the principal criterion of wealth and ability to support taxes; and this would find its level in different places where the intercourse should be easy & free, with as much certainty as the value of money or any other thing. Wherever labour would yield most, people would resort, till the competition should destroy the inequality. Hence it is that the people are constantly swarming from the more to the less populous places—from Europe to Am:̲a from the North:̲n & Middle parts of the U. S. to the Southern & Western. They go where land is cheaper, because there labour is dearer. If it be true that the same quantity of produce raised on the banks of the Ohio is of less value, than on the Delaware, it is also true that the same labor will raise twice or thrice, the quantity in the former, that it will raise in the latter situation.

Col. MASON. Agreed with M:̲r Gov:̲r Morris that we ought to leave the interests of the people to the Representatives of the people: but the objection was that the Legislature would cease to be the Representatives of the people. It would continue so no longer than the States now containing a majority of the people should retain that majority. As soon as the Southern & Western population should predominate, which must happen in a few years, the power w?d be in the hands of the minority, and would never be yielded to the majority, unless provided for by the Constitution

On the Question for postponing M? Williamson's motion, in order to consider that of M? Rutlidge it passed in the negative. Mass?ts ay. Con?t no. N. J. no. P?a ay. Del. ay. M?d no. V?a no. N. C. no. S. C. ay. Geo. ay.[95]

On the question on the first clause of M? Williamson's motion as to taking a census of the *free* inhabitants; it passed in the affirmative Mas?ts ay. Con?t ay. N. J. ay. P?a ay. Del. no. M?d no. V?a ay. N. C. ay. S. C. no. Geo. no.[96]

the next clause as to ⅗ of the negroes [97] considered.

M? KING. being much opposed to fixing numbers as the rule of representation, was particularly so on account of the blacks. He thought the admission of them along with Whites at all, would excite great discontents among the States having no slaves. He had never said as to any particular point that he would in no event acquiesce in & support it; but he w?d say that if in any case such a declaration was to be made by him, it would be in this. He remarked that in the temporary allotment of Representatives made by the Committee, the Southern States had received more than the number of their white & three fifths of their black inhabitants entitled them to.

M? SHERMAN. S. Carol?a had not more beyond her proportion than N. York & N. Hampshire, nor either of them more than was necessary in order to avoid fractions or reducing them below their proportion. Georgia had more; but the rapid growth of that State seemed to justify it. In general the allotment might

---

[95] In the transcript the vote reads: "Massachusetts, Pennsylvania, Delaware, South Carolina, Georgia, aye—5; Connecticut, New Jersey, Maryland, Virginia, North Carolina, no—5."

[96] In the transcript the vote reads: "Massachusetts, Connecticut, New Jersey, Pennsylvania, Virginia, North Carolina, aye—6; Delaware, Maryland, South Carolina, Georgia, no—4."

[97] The word "being" is here inserted in the transcript.

not be just, but considering all circumstances, he was satisfied with it.

Mr GHORUM. supported the propriety of establishing numbers as the rule. He said that in Mass<sup>ts</sup> estimates had been taken in the different towns, and that persons had been curious enough to compare these estimates with the respective numbers of people; and it had been found even including Boston, that the most exact proportion prevailed between numbers & property. He was aware that there might be some weight in what had fallen from his colleague, as to the umbrage which might be taken by the people of the Eastern States. But he recollected that when the proposition of Cong<sup>s</sup> for changing the 8<sup>th</sup> art: of Confed<sup>n</sup> was before the Legislature of Mass<sup>ts</sup> the only difficulty then was to satisfy them that the negroes ought not to have been counted equally with [98] whites instead of being counted in the ratio of three fifths only.*

Mr WILSON did not well see on what principle the admission of blacks in the proportion of three fifths could be explained. Are they admitted as Citizens? then why are they not admitted on an equality with White Citizens? are they admitted as property? then why is not other property admitted into the computation? These were difficulties however which he thought must be overruled by the necessity of compromise. He had some apprehensions also from the tendency of the blending of the blacks with the whites, to give disgust to the people of Pen<sup>a</sup> as had been intimated by his Colleague [Mr Gov<sup>r</sup> Morris]. But he differed from him in thinking numbers of inhab<sup>ts</sup> so incorrect a measure of wealth. He had seen the Western settlem<sup>ts</sup> of P<sup>a</sup> and on a comparison of them with the City of Philad<sup>a</sup> could discover little other difference, than that property was more unequally divided among individuals [99] here than there. Taking the same number in the aggregate in the two situations he believed there would be little difference in their wealth and ability to contribute to the public wants.

Mr Gov<sup>r</sup> MORRIS was compelled to declare himself reduced to the dilemma of doing injustice to the Southern States or to human

---
\* They were then to have been a rule of taxation only.
[98] The word "the" is here inserted in the transcript.
[99] The words "among individuals" are omitted in the transcript.

nature, and he must therefore do it to the former. For he could never agree to give such encouragement to the slave trade as would be given by allowing them a representation for their negroes, and he did not believe those States would ever confederate on terms that would deprive them of that trade.

On [1] Question for agreeing to include ⅗ of the blacks

Mass.ts no. Con.t ay. N. J. no. P.a no. Del. no. Mar.d* no. V.a ay. N. C. ay. S. C. no. Geo. ay [3]

On the question as to taking [1] census "the first year after [1] meeting of the Legislature"

Mas.ts ay. Con.t no. N. J. ay. P.a ay. Del. ay. M.d no. V.a ay. N. C. ay. S. ay. Geo. no [4]

On filling the blank for the periodical census, with 15 years," Agreed to nem. con.

M.r MADISON moved to add after "15 years," the words "at least" that the Legislature might anticipate when circumstances were likely to render a particular year inconvenient.

On this motion for adding "at least," it passed in the negative the States being equally divided.

Mas. ay. Con.t no. N. J. no. P.a no. Del. no. M.d no. V.a ay. N. C. ay. S. C. ay. Geo. ay.[5]

A Change of [6] the phraseology of the other clause so as to read; "and the Legislature shall alter or augment the representation accordingly" was agreed to nem. con.

On the question on the whole resolution of M.r Williamson as amended.

Mas. no. Con.t no. N. J. no. Del. no. M.d no. V.a no. N. C. no. S. C. no. Geo. no.[7,8]

---

[1] The word "the" is here inserted in the transcript.

* [M.r Carrol s.d in explanation of the vote of M.d that he wished the phraseology [2] to be so altered as to obviate if possible the danger which had been expressed of giving umbrage to the Eastern & Middle States.]

[2] The transcript italicizes the word "phraseology."

[3] In the transcript the vote reads: Connecticut, Virginia, North Carolina, Georgia, aye—4; Massachusetts, New Jersey, Pennsylvania, Delaware, Maryland,* South Carolina, no—6."

[4] In the transcript the note reads: "Massachusetts, New Jersey, Pennsylvania, Delaware, Virginia, North Carolina, South Carolina, aye—7; Connecticut, Maryland, Georgia, no—3."

[5] In the transcript the vote reads: "Massachusetts, Virginia, North Carolina, South Carolina, Georgia, aye—5; Connecticut, New Jersey, Pennsylvania, Delaware, Maryland, no—5."

[6] The word "in" is substituted in the transcript for "of."

[7] In the transcript the vote reads: "Massachusetts, Connecticut, New Jersey, Delaware, Maryland, Virginia, North Carolina, South Carolina, Georgia, no—9; so it was rejected unanimously."

[8] The word "Adjourned" is here inserted in the transcript.

## Thursday. July 12. In Convention

Mʳ Govʳ Morris moved to add to the clause empowering the Legislature to vary the Representation according to the principles of wealth & number [9] of inhabᵗˢ a "proviso that taxation shall be in proportion to Representation."

Mʳ Butler contended again that Representation sᵈ be according to the full number of inhabᵗˢ including all the blacks; admitting the justice of Mʳ Govʳ Morris's motion.

Mʳ Mason also admitted the justice of the principle, but was afraid embarrassments might be occasioned to the Legislature by it. It might drive the Legislature to the plan of Requisitions.

Mʳ Govʳ Morris, admitted that some objections lay agˢᵗ his motion, but supposed they would be removed by restraining the rule to *direct* taxation. With regard to indirect taxes on *exports* & imports & on consumption, the rule would be inapplicable. Notwithstanding what had been said to the contrary he was persuaded that the imports & consumption were pretty nearly equal throughout the Union.

General Pinkney liked the idea. He thought it so just that it could not be objected to. But foresaw that if the revision of the census was left to the discretion of the Legislature, it would never be carried into execution. The rule must be fixed, and the execution of it enforced by the Constitution. He was alarmed at what was said yesterday,* concerning the negroes. He was now again alarmed at what had been thrown out concerning the taxing of exports. S. Carolᵃ has in one year exported to the amount of £600,000 Sterling all which was the fruit of the labor of her blacks. Will she be represented in proportion to this amount? She will not. Neither ought she then to be subject to a tax on it. He hoped a clause would be inserted in the system, restraining the Legislature from a [10] taxing Exports.

Mʳ Wilson approved the principle, but could not see how it could be carried into execution; unless restrained to direct taxation.

---

[9] The transcript uses the word "number" in the plural.
* By Mʳ Govʳ Morris.
[10] The word "a" is omitted in the transcript.

M[r] Gov[r] Morris having so varied his Motion by inserting the word "direct." It pass[d] nem. con. as follows—"provided the always that direct taxation ought to be proportioned to representation."

M[r] Davie, said it was high time now to speak out. He saw that it was meant by some gentlemen to deprive the Southern States of any share of Representation for their blacks. He was sure that N. Carol[a] would never confederate on any terms that did not rate them at least as ⅗. If the Eastern States meant therefore to exclude them altogether the business was at an end.

D[r] Johnson, thought that wealth and population were the true, equitable rule [11] of representation; but he conceived that these two principles resolved themselves into one; population being the best measure of wealth. He concluded therefore that ye. number of people ought to be established as the rule, and that all descriptions including blacks *equally* with the whites, ought to fall within the computation. As various opinions had been expressed on the subject, he would move that a Committee might be appointed to take them into consideration and report thereon.

M[r] Gov[r] Morris. It has [12] been said that it is high time to speak out, as one member, he would candidly do so. He came here to form a compact for the good of America. He was ready to do so with all the States. He hoped & believed that all would enter into such a Compact. If they would not he was ready to join with any States that would. But as the Compact was to be voluntary, it is in vain for the Eastern States to insist on what the South[n] States will never agree to. It is equally vain for the latter to require what the other States can never admit; and he verily believed the people of Pen[a] will never agree to a representation of Negroes. What can be desired by these States more than has been already proposed; that the Legislature shall from time to time regulate Representation according to population & wealth.

Gen[l] Pinkney desired that the rule of wealth should be ascertained and not left to the pleasure of the Legislature; and that

---

[11] The transcript uses the word "rule" in the plural.
[12] The word "had" is substituted in the transcript for "has."

property in slaves should not be exposed to danger under a Govt instituted for the protection of property.

The first clause in the Report of the first Grand Committee was postponed.

Mr ELSEWORTH. In order to carry into effect the principle established, moved to add to the last clause adopted by the House the words following "and that the rule of contribution by direct taxation for the support of the Government of the U. States shall be the number of white inhabitants, and three fifths of every other description in the several States, until some other rule that shall more accurately ascertain the wealth of the several States can be devised and adopted by the Legislature."

Mr BUTLER seconded the motion in order that it might be committed.

Mr RANDOLPH was not satisfied with the motion. The danger will be revived that the ingenuity of the Legislature may evade or pervert the rule so as to perpetuate the power where it shall be lodged in the first instance. He proposed in lieu of Mr Elseworth's motion, "that in order to ascertain the alterations in Representation that may be required from time to time by changes in the relative circumstances of the States, a census shall be taken within two years from the 1st meeting of the Genl Legislature of the U. S., and once within the term of every      year afterwards, of all the inhabitants in the manner & according to the ratio recommended by Congress in their resolution of the 18th day of Apl 1783; [rating the blacks at ⅗ of their number] and, that the Legislature of the U. S. shall arrange the Representation accordingly."—He urged strenuously that express security ought to be provided for including slaves in the ratio of Representation. He lamented that such a species of property existed. But as it did exist the holders of it would require this security. It was perceived that the design was entertained by some of excluding slaves altogether; the Legislature therefore ought not to be left at liberty.

Mr ELSEWORTH withdraws his motion & seconds that of Mr Randolph.

Mr WILSON observed that less umbrage would perhaps be taken agst an admission of the slaves into the Rule of representation, if it should be so expressed as to make them indirectly only an ingredient in the rule, by saying that they should enter into the rule of taxation: and as representation was to be according to taxation, the end would be equally attained. He accordingly moved & was 2$^{ded}$ so to alter the last clause adopted by the House, that together with the amendment proposed the whole should read as follows— provided always that the representation ought to be proportioned according to direct taxation, and in order to ascertain the alterations in the direct taxation which may be required from time to time by the changes in the relative circumstances of the States. Resolved that a census be taken within two years from the first meeting of the Legislature of the U. States, and once within the term of every      years afterwards of all the inhabitants of the U. S. in the manner and according to the ratio recommended by Congress in their Resolution of April 18.[13] 1783; and that the Legislature of the U. S. shall proportion the direct taxation accordingly."

M$^r$ KING. Altho' this amendment varies the aspect somewhat, he had still two powerful objections ag$^{st}$ tying down the Legislature to the rule of numbers. 1.[14] they were at this time an uncertain index of the relative wealth of the States. 2.[14] if they were a just index at this time it can not be supposed always to continue so. He was far from wishing to retain any unjust advantage whatever in one part of the Republic. If justice was not the basis of the connection it could not be of long duration. He must be short-sighted indeed who does not foresee that whenever the Southern States shall be more numerous than the Northern, they can & will hold a language that will awe them into justice. If they threaten to separate now in case injury shall be done them, will their threats be less urgent or effectual, when force shall back their demands. Even in the intervening period, there will [15] no point of time at which they will not be able to say, do us justice or we will separate. He urged the necessity of placing confidence to a certain degree in every Gov$^t$ and did not conceive that the proposed confidence as to

---

[13] The date "April 18" is changed to "the eighteenth day of April" in the transcript.
[14] The figures "1" and "2" are changed to "first" and "secondly" in the transcript.
[15] The word "be" is here inserted in the transcript.

a periodical readjustment, of the representation exceeded that degree.

M? PINKNEY moved to amend M? Randolph's motion so as to make "blacks equal to the whites in the ratio of representation." This he urged was nothing more than justice. The blacks are the labourers, the peasants of the Southern States: they are as productive of pecuniary resources as those of the Northern States. They add equally to the wealth, and considering money as the sinew of war, to the strength of the nation. It will also be politic with regard to the Northern States, as taxation is to keep pace with Representation.

Gen! PINKNEY moves to insert 6 years instead of two, as the period computing from [16] 1st meeting of ye Legis– within which the first census should be taken. On this question for inserting six [17] instead of "two" in the proposition of M? Wilson, it passed in the affirmative

Mas$^{ts}$. no. C$^t$ ay. N. J. ay. P$^a$ ay. Del. div$^d$ May$^d$ ay. V$^a$ no. N. C. no. S. C. ay. Geo. no.[18]

On a [19] question for filling the blank for ye periodical census with 20 years, it it passed in the negative.

Mas$^{ts}$ no. C$^t$ ay. N. J. ay. P. ay. Del. no. M$^d$ no. V$^a$ no. N. C. no. S. C. no. Geo. no.[20]

On a [19] question for 10 years, it passed in the affirmative.

Mas. ay. Con$^t$ no. N. J. no. P. ay. Del. ay. M$^d$ ay. V$^a$ ay. N. C. ay. S. C. ay. Geo. ay.[21]

On M? Pinkney's motion for rating blacks as equal to Whites instead of as ⅗—

Mas. no. Con$^t$ no. [D$^r$ Johnson ay] N. J. no. P$^a$ no. [3 ag$^{st}$ 2.] Del. no. M$^d$ no. V$^a$ no. N. C. no. S. C. ay. Geo—ay.[22]

---

[16] The word "the" is here inserted in the transcript.

[17] The word "years" is here inserted in the transcript.

[18] In the transcript the vote reads: "Connecticut, New Jersey, Pennsylvania, Maryland, South Carolina, aye—5; Massachusetts, Virginia, North Carolina, Georgia, no—4; Delaware, divided."

[19] The word "the" is substituted in the transcript for "a."

[20] In the transcript the vote reads: "Connecticut, New Jersey, Pennsylvania, aye—3; Massachusetts, Delaware, Maryland, Virginia, North Carolina, South Carolina, Georgia, no—7."

[21] In the transcript the vote reads: "Massachusetts, Pennsylvania, Delaware, Maryland, Virginia, North Carolina, South Carolina, Georgia, aye—8; Connecticut, New Jersey, no—2."

[22] In the transcript the vote reads: "South Carolina, Georgia, aye—2; Massachusetts, Connecticut, [Doctor Johnson, aye], New Jersey, Pennslyvania, [3 against 2] Delaware, Maryland, Virginia, North Carolina, no—8."

Mr Randolph's proposition as varied by Mr Wilson being read for [23] question on the whole.

Mr GERRY, urged that the principle of it could not be carried into execution as the States were not to be taxed as States. With regard to taxes in[24] imports, he conceived they would be more productive. Where there were no slaves than where there were; the consumption being greater—

Mr ELSEWORTH. In case of a poll tax there wd be no difficulty. But there wd probably be none. The sum allotted to a State may be levied without difficulty according to the plan used by the State in raising its own supplies. On the question on ye whole proposition; as proportioning representation to direct taxation & both to the white & ⅗ of [25] black inhabitants, & requiring a Census within six years—& within every ten years afterwards.

Mas. divd Cont ay. N. J. no. Pa ay. Del. no. Md ay. Va ay. N. C. ay. S. C. divd Geo. ay.[26, 27]

### FRIDAY. JULY 13.   IN CONVENTION

It being moved to postpone the clause in the Report of the Committee of Eleven as to the originating of money bills in *the* [28] *first* branch, in order to take up the following—"that in the 2d branch each State shall have an equal voice."

Mr GERRY, moved to add as an amendment to the last clause agreed to by the House, "that from the first meeting of the Legislature of the U. S. till a census shall be taken all monies to be raised for supplying the public Treasury by direct taxation, shall be assessed on the inhabitants of the several States according to the number of their Representatives respectively in the 1st branch." He said this would be as just before as after the Census: according to the general principle that taxation & Representation ought to go together.

---

[23] The words "taking the" are here inserted in the transcript.

[24] The word "on" is substituted in the transcript for "in."

[25] The word "the" is here inserted in the transcript.

[26] In the transcript the vote reads: "Connecticut, Pennsylvania, Maryland, Virginia, North Carolina, Georgia, aye—6; New Jersey, Delaware, no—2; Massachusetts, South Carolina, divided."

[27] The word "Adjourned" is here inserted in the transcript.

[28] The word "*the*" is not italicized in the transcript.

Mʳ WILLIAMSON feared that N. Hamshire will have reason to complain. 3 members were allotted to her as a liberal allowance, for this reason among others, that she might not suppose any advantage to have been taken of her absence. As she was still absent, and had no opportunity of deciding whether she would chuse to retain the number on the condition, of her being taxed in proportion to it, he thought the number ought to be reduced from three to two, before the question [29] on Mʳ G's motion.

Mʳ READ could not approve of the proposition. He had observed he said in the Committee a backwardness in some of the members from the large States, to take their full proportion of Representatives. He did not then see the motive. He now suspects it was to avoid their due share of taxation. He had no objection to a just & accurate adjustment of Representation & taxation to each other.

Mʳ Govʳ MORRIS & Mʳ MADISON answered that the charge itself involved an acquittal, since notwithstanding the augmentation of the number of members allotted to Masᵗˢ & Vᵃ the motion for proportioning the burdens thereto was made by a member from the former State & was approved by Mʳ– M from the latter who was on the Comᵉ Mʳ Govʳ Morris said that he thought Pᵃ had her due share in 8 members; and he could not in candor ask for more. Mʳ M. said that having always conceived that the difference of interest in the U, States lay not between the large & small, but the N. & Southⁿ States, and finding that the number of members allotted to the N. States was greatly superior, he should have preferred, an addition of two members to the S. States, to wit one to N. & 1 to S. Carlᵃ rather than of one member to Virgᵃ. He liked the present motion, because it tended to moderate the views both of the opponents & advocates for rating very high, the negroes.

Mʳ ELSEWORTH hoped the proposition would be withdrawn. It entered too much into detail. The general principle was already sufficiently settled. As fractions can not be regarded in apportioning the *Nº of representatives*, the rule will be unjust, until an actual census shall be made. after that taxation may be precisely pro-

---

[29] The words "was taken" are here inserted in the transcript.

portioned according to the principle established, to the *number of inhabitants.*

Mr WILSON hoped the motion would not be withdrawn. If it shd it will be made from another quarter. The rule will be as reasonable & just before, as after a Census. As to fractional numbers, the Census will not distroy, but ascertain them. And they will have the same effect after as before the Census: for as he understands the rule, it is to be adjusted not to the number of *inhabitants*, but of *Representatives.*

Mr SHERMAN opposed the motion. He thought the Legislature ought to be left at liberty: in which case they would probably conform to the principles observed by Congs

Mr MASON did not know that Virga would be a loser by the proposed regulation, but had some scruple as to the justice of it. He doubted much whether the conjectural rule which was to precede the Census, would be as just, as it would be rendered by an actual census.

Mr ELSEWORTH & Mr SHERMAN moved to postpone the motion of Mr Gerry, on ye question, it passed in the negative.

Mas. no. Cont ay. 'N. J. ay. Pa no. Del. ay. Md ay. Va no. N. C. no. S. C. no. Geo. no.[30]

[31] Question on Mr Gerry's motion; it passed in the negative, the States being equally divided.

Mas. ay. Cont no. N. J. no. Pa ay. Del. no. Md no. Va no. N. C. ay. S. C. ay. Geo. ay.[32]

Mr GERRY finding that the loss of the question had proceeded from an objection with some, to the proposed assessment of direct taxes on the *inhabitants* of the States, which might restrain the Legislature to a poll tax, moved his proposition again, but so varied as to authorise the assessment on the *States*, which wd leave [33] the mode to the Legislature, at this caret insert the words interlined [34] viz "that from the 1st meeting of the Legislature of the U. S. untill a census shall be taken, all monies for supplying

---

[30] In the transcript the vote reads: "Connecticut, New Jersey, Delaware, Maryland, aye—4; Massachusetts, Pennsylvania, Virginia, North Carolina, South Carolina, Georgia, no—6."

[31] The words "On the" are here inserted in the transcript.

[32] In the transcript the vote reads: "Massachusetts, *Pennsylvania*, North Carolina, South Carolina, Georgia, aye—5; Connecticut, New Jersey, Delaware, Maryland, *Virginia*, no—5."

[33] The word "leaves" is substituted in the transcript for "wd leave."

[34] Madison's direction concerning the interlined words is omitted in the transcript.

the public Treasury by direct taxation shall be raised from the said several States according to the number of their representatives respectively in the 1ˢᵗ branch."

On this varied question, it passed in the affirmative

Mas. ay. Conᵗ no. N. J. no. Pᵃ divᵈ Del. no. Mᵈ no. Vᵃ ay. N. C. ay. S. C. ay. Geo. ay.[35]

On the motion of Mʳ Randolph, the vote of saturday [36] last authorising the Legislʳᵉ to adjust from time to time, the representation upon the principles of *wealth* & numbers of inhabitants was reconsidered by common consent in order to strike out "Wealth"[37] and adjust the resolution to that requiring periodical revisions according to the number of whites & three fifths of the blacks: the motion was in the words following—"But as the present situation of the States may probably alter in the number of their inhabitants, that the Legislature of the U. S. be authorized from time to time to apportion the number of representatives: and in case any of the States shall hereafter be divided or any two or more States united or new States created within the limits of the U. S. the Legislature of [38] U. S. shall possess authority to regulate the number of Representatives in any of the foregoing cases, upon the principle of their number of inhabitants; according to the provisions hereafter mentioned."

Mʳ Govʳ MORRIS opposed the alteration as leaving still an incoherence. If Negroes were to be viewed as inhabitants, and the revision was to proceed on the principle of numbers of inhabᵗˢ they ought to be added in their entire number, and not in the proportion of ⅗. If as property, the word wealth was right, and striking it out, would produce the very inconsistency which it was meant to get rid of.—The train of business & the late turn which it had taken, had led him he said, into deep meditation on it, and He wᵈ candidly state the result. A distinction had been set up & urged, between the Nⁿ & Southⁿ States. He had hitherto considered this doctrine as heretical. He still thought the distinction groundless. He sees however that it is persisted in, and that

---

[35] In the transcript the vote reads: "Massachusetts, *Virginia*, North Carolina, South Carolina, Georgia, aye—5; Connecticut, New Jersey, Delaware, Maryland, no—4; *Pennsylvania*, divided."

[36] The word "saturday" is changed to "Monday" in the transcript.

[37] The transcript italicizes the word "Wealth."

[38] The word "the" is here inserted in the transcript.

the South? Gentlemen will not be satisfied unless they see the way open to their gaining a majority in the public Councils. The consequence of such a transfer of power from the maritime to the interior & landed interest will he foresees be such an oppression of [39] commerce, that he shall be obliged to vote for y<sup>e</sup> vicious principle of equality in the 2<sup>d</sup> branch in order to provide some defence for the N. States ag<sup>st</sup> it. But to come more to the point; either this distinction is fictitious or real; if fictitious let it be dismissed & let us proceed with due confidence. If it be real, instead of attempting to blend incompatible things, let us at once take a friendly leave of each other. There can be no end of demands for security if every particular interest is to be entitled to it. The Eastern States may claim it for their fishery, and for other objects, as the South? States claim it for their peculiar objects. In this struggle between the two ends of the Union, what part ought the middle States in point of policy to take: to join their Eastern brethren according to his ideas. If the South? States get the power into their hands, and be joined as they will be with the interior Country, they will inevitably bring on a war with Spain for the Mississippi. This language is already held. The interior Country having no property nor interest exposed on the sea, will be little affected by such a war. He wished to know what security the North? & middle States will have ag<sup>st</sup> this danger. It has been said that N. C. S. C., and Georgia only will in a little time have a majority of the people of America. They must in that case include the great interior Country, and every thing was to be apprehended from their getting the power into their hands.

M<sup>r</sup> BUTLER. The security the South? States want is that their negroes may not be taken from them, which some gentlemen within or without doors, have a very good mind to do. It was not supposed that N. C. S. C. & Geo. would have more people than all the other States, but many more relatively to the other States than they now have. The people & strength of America are evidently bearing Southwardly & S. westw<sup>dly</sup>

---

[39] The word "to" is substituted in the transcript for "of."

Mr WILSON. If a general declaration would satisfy any gentleman he had no indisposition to declare his sentiments. Conceiving that all men wherever placed have equal rights and are equally entitled to confidence, he viewed without apprehension the period when a few States should contain the superior number of people. The majority of people wherever found ought in all questions to govern the minority. If the interior Country should acquire this majority, it will not only have the right, but will avail themselves [40] of it whether we will or no. This jealousy misled the policy of G. Britain with regard to America. The fatal maxims espoused by her were that the Colonies were growing too fast, and that their growth must be stinted in time. What were the consequences? first. enmity on our part, then actual separation. Like consequences will result on the part of the interior settlements, if like jealousy & policy be pursued on ours. Further, if numbers be not a proper rule, why is not some better rule pointed out. No one has yet ventured to attempt it. Congs have never been able to discover a better. No State as far as he had heard, has suggested any other. In 1783, after elaborate discussion of a measure of wealth all were satisfied then as they are now that the rule of numbers, does not differ much from the combined rule of numbers & wealth. Again he could not agree that property was the sole or the [41] primary object of Govern! & society. The cultivation & improvement of the human mind was the most noble object. With respect to this object, as well as to other *personal* rights, numbers were surely the natural & precise measure of Representation. And with respect to property, they could not vary much from the precise measure. In no point of view however could the establishm! of numbers as the rule of representation in the 1st branch vary his opinion as to the impropriety of letting a vicious principle into the 2d branch.—On the Question to strike out *wealth*, & to make the change as moved by Mr Randolph, it passed in the affirmative—

---

[40] The word "itself" is substituted in the transcript for "themselves."
[41] The word "the" is omitted in the transcript.

Mas. ay. Con.^t ay. N. J. ay. P.^a ay. Del. div.^d M.^d ay. V.^a ay. N. C. ay. S. C. ay. Geo. ay.[42]

M.^r REED moved to insert after the word— "divided," "or enlarged by addition of territory" which was agreed to nem. con. [his object probably was to provide for such cases as an enlargem.^t of Delaware by annexing to it the Peninsula on the East side of [43] Chesapeak]

Adjourned

### SATURDAY. JULY 14. IN CONVENTION

M.^r L. MARTIN called for the question on the whole report, including the parts relating to the origination of money bills, and the equality of votes in the 2.^d branch.

M.^r GERRY. wished before the question should be put, that the attention of the House might be turned to the dangers apprehended from Western States. He was for admitting them on liberal terms, but not for putting ourselves into their hands. They will if they acquire power like all men, abuse it. They will oppress commerce, and drain our wealth into the Western Country. To guard ag.^{st} these consequences, he thought it necessary to limit the number of new States to be admitted into the Union, in such a manner, that they should never be able to outnumber the Atlantic States. He accordingly moved "that in order to secure the liberties of the States already confederated, the number of Representatives in the 1.^{st} branch, of the States which shall hereafter be established, shall never exceed in number, the Representatives from such of the States as shall accede to this confederation.

M.^r KING. seconded the motion.

M.^r SHERMAN, thought there was no probability that the number of future States would exceed that of the Existing States. If the event should ever happen, it was too remote to be taken into consideration at this time. Besides We are providing for our posterity, for our children & our grand Children, who would be as likely to be citizens of new Western States, as of the old States. On this consideration alone, we ought to make no such discrimination as was proposed by the motion.

---

[42] In the transcript the vote reads: "Massachusetts, Connecticut New Jersey, Pennsylvania, Maryland, Virginia, North Carolina, South Carolina, Georgia, aye—9; Delaware, divided."

[43] The word "the" is here inserted in the transcript; and the sentence in brackets is a footnote.

Mʳ GERRY. If some of our children should remove, others will stay behind, and he thought it incumbent on us to provide for their interests. There was a rage for emigration from the Eastern States to the Western Country, and he did not wish those remaining behind to be at the mercy of the Emigrants. Besides foreigners are resorting to that country, and it is uncertain what turn things may take there.—On the question for agreeing to the Motion of Mʳ Gerry, it passed in the negative.

Mas. ay. Conᵗ ay. N. J. no. Pᵃ divᵈ Del: ay. Mᵈ ay. Vᵃ no. N. C. no. S. C. no. Geo. no.[44]

Mʳ RUTLIDGE proposed to reconsider the two propositions touching the originating of money bills in the first & the equality of votes in the second branch.

Mʳ SHERMAN was for the question on the whole at once. It was he said a conciliatory plan, it had been considered in all its parts, a great deal of time had been spent on [45] it, and if any part should now be altered, it would be necessary to go over the whole ground again.

Mʳ L. MARTIN urged the question on the whole. He did not like many parts of it. He did not like having two branches, nor the inequality of votes in the 1ˢᵗ branch. He was willing however to make trial of the plan, rather than do nothing.

Mʳ WILSON traced the progress of the report through its several stages, remarking yᵗ when on the question concerning an equality of votes, the House was divided, our Constituents had they voted as their representatives did, would have stood as ⅔ agˢᵗ the equality, and ⅓ only in favor of it. This fact would ere long be known, and it will [46] appear that this fundamental point has been carried by ⅓ agˢᵗ ⅔. What hopes will our Constituents entertain when they find that the essential principles of justice have been violated in the outset of the Governmᵗ As to the privilege of originating money bills, it was not considered by any as of much moment, and by many as improper in itself. He hoped both clauses wᵈ be reconsidered. The equality of votes was a point of

---
[44] In the transcript the vote reads: "Massachusetts, Connecticut, Delaware, Maryland, aye—4; New Jersey, Virginia, North Carolina, South Carolina, Georgia, no—5; Pennsylvania, divided."
[45] The word "upon" is substituted in the transcript for "on."
[46] The word "would" is substituted in the transcript for "will."

such critical importance, that every opportunity ought to be allowed, for discussing and collecting the mind of the Convention on [47] it.

M! L. MARTIN denies that there were ⅔ ag!! the equality of votes. The States that please to call themselves large, are the weekest in the Union. Look at Mas!! Look at Virg! Are they efficient States? He was for letting a separation take place if they desired it. He had rather there should be two Confederacies, than one founded on any other principle than an equality of votes in the 2ᵈ branch at least.

M! WILSON was not surprised that those who say that a minority is [48] more than the [49] majority should say that [50] the minority is stronger than the majority. He supposed the next assertion will be that they are richer also; though he hardly expected it would be persisted in when the States shall be called on for taxes & troops—

M! GERRY. also animadverted on M! L. Martins remarks on the weakness of Mast! He favored the reconsideration with a view not of destroying the equality of votes; but of providing that the States should vote per capita, which he said would prevent the delays & inconveniences that had been experienced in Cong! and would give a national aspect & Spirit to the management of business. He did not approve of a reconsideration of the clause relating to money bills. It was of great consequence. It was the corner stone of the accomodation. If any member of the Convention had the exclusive privilege of making propositions, would any one say that it would give him no advantage over other members. The Report was not altogether to his mind. But he would agree to it as it stood rather than throw it out altogether.

The reconsideration being tacitly agreed to.

M! PINKNEY moved that instead of an equality of votes, the States should be represented in the 2ᵈ branch as follows: N. H. by. 2. members. Mas. 4. R. I. 1. Con! 3. N. Y. 3. N. J. 2. P! 4. Del 1. Mᵈ 3. Virg! 5. N. C. 3. S. C. 3. Geo. 2. making in the whole 36.

---

[47] The word "upon" is substituted in the transcript for "on."
[48] The word "does" is substituted in the transcript for "is."
[49] The word "a" is substituted in the transcript for "the."
[50] The word "that" is omitted in the transcript.

M! WILSON seconds the motion

M! DAYTON. The smaller States can never give up their equality. For himself he would in no event yield that security for their rights.

M! SHERMAN urged the equality of votes not so much as a security for the small States; as for the State Gov<sup>ts</sup> which could not be preserved unless they were represented & had a negative in the Gen! Government. He had no objection to the members in the 2ᵈ b. voting per capita, as had been suggested by [M! Gerry]

M! MADISON concurred in this motion of M! Pinkney as a reasonable compromise.

M! GERRY said he should like the motion, but could see no hope of success. An accomodation must take place, and it was apparent from what had been seen that it could not do so on the ground of the motion. He was utterly against a partial confederacy, leaving other States to accede or not accede; as had been intimated.

M! KING said it was always with regret that he differed from his colleagues, but it was his duty to differ from [M! Gerry] on this occasion. He considered the proposed Government as substantially and formally, a General and National Government over the people of America. There never will be a case in which it will act as a federal Government on the States and not on the individual Citizens. And is it not a clear principle that in a free Gov! those who are to be the objects of a Gov! ought to influence the operations of it? What reason can be assigned why the same rule of representation s! not prevail in the 2ᵈ branch [51] as in the 1ˢᵗ? He could conceive none. On the contrary, every view of the subject that presented itself, seemed to require it. Two objections had been raised ag<sup>st</sup> it: drawn 1.[52] from the terms of the existing compact 2.[52] from a supposed danger to the smaller States.—As to the first objection he thought it inapplicable. According to the existing confederation, the rule by which the public burdens is to be apportioned is *fixed*, and must be pursued.

---

[51] In the transcript the word "branch" is transposed, making the phrase read: "second, as in the first, branch."

[52] The figures "1" and "2" are changed to "first" and "secondly" in the transcript.

In the proposed Goverm! it can not be fixed, because indirect taxation is to be substituted. The Legislature therefore will have full discretion to impose taxes in such modes & proportions as they may judge expedient. As to the 2ᵈ objection, he thought it of as little weight. The Gen! Govern! can never wish to intrude on the State Govern᪽ There could be no temptation. None had been pointed out. In order to prevent the interference of measures which seemed most likely to happen, he would have no objection to throwing all the State debts into the federal debt, making one aggregate debt of about 70,000,000 of dollars, and leaving it to be discharged by the Gen! Gov!—According to the idea of securing the State Gov᪽ there ought to be three distinct legislative branches. The 2ᵈ was admitted to be necessary, and was actually meant, to check the 1ˢᵗ branch, to give more wisdom, system, & stability to the Gov! and ought clearly as it was to operate on the people to be proportioned to them. For the third purpose of securing the States, there ought then to be a 3ᵈ branch, representing the States as such, and guarding by equal votes their rights & dignities. He would not pretend to be as thoroughly acquainted with his immediate Constituents as his colleagues, but it was his firm belief that Mas᪽ would never be prevailed on to yield to an equality of votes. In N. York (he was sorry to be obliged to say any thing relative to that State in the absence of its representatives, but the occasion required it), in N. York he had seen that the most powerful argument used by the considerate opponents to the grant of the Impost to Congress, was pointed ag᪽ the viccious constitution of Cong᪽ with regard to representation & suffrage. He was sure that no Gov! could [53] last that was not founded on just principles. He prefer'd the doing of nothing, to an allowance of an equal vote to all the States. It would be better he thought to submit to a little more confusion & convulsion, than to submit to such an evil. It was difficult to say what the views of different Gentlemen might be. Perhaps there might be some who thought no Governm! co-extensive with the U. States could be established with a hope of its answering the purpose. Perhaps there might be other fixed

---

[53] The word "would" is substituted in the transcript for "could."

opinions incompatible with the object we were [54] pursuing. If there were, he thought it but candid that Gentlemen would [55] speak out that we might understand one another.

M! STRONG. The Convention had been much divided in opinion. In order to avoid the consequences of it, an accomodation had been proposed. A committee had been appointed: and though some of the members of it were averse to an equality of votes, a Report has [56] been made in favor of it. It is agreed on all hands that Congress are nearly at an end. If no Accomodation takes place, the Union itself must soon be dissolved. It has been suggested that if we can not come to any general agreement, the principal States may form & recommend a scheme of Government. But will the small States in that case ever accede [57] it. Is it probable that the large States themselves will under such circumstances embrace and ratify it. He thought the small States had made a considerable concession in the article of money bills; and that they might naturally expect some concessions on the other side. From this view of the matter he was compelled to give his vote for the Report taken all together.

M! MADISON expressed his apprehensions that if the proper foundation of Govenm!– was destroyed, by substituting an equality in place of a proportional Representation, no proper superstructure would be raised. If the small States really wish for a Government armed with the powers necessary to secure their liberties, and to enforce obedience on the larger members as well as on [58] themselves he could not help thinking them extremely mistaken in their [59] means. He reminded them of the consequences of laying the existing confederation [60] on improper principles. All the principal parties to its compilation, joined immediately in mutilating & fettering the Governm! in such a manner that it has disappointed every hope placed on it. He appealed to the doctrine & arguments used by themselves on a former occasion. It had been very

---

[54] The word "are" is substituted in the transcript for "were."
[55] The word "should" is substituted in the transcript for "would."
[56] The word "had" is substituted in the transcript for "has."
[57] The word "to" is here inserted in the transcript.
[58] The word "on" is omitted in the transcript.
[59] The word "the" is substituted in the transcript for "their."
[60] The transcript italicizes the words "existing confederation."

380

properly observed by [M<sup>r</sup> Patterson] that Representation was an expedient by which the meeting of the people themselves was rendered unnecessary; and that the representatives ought therefore to bear a proportion to the votes which their constituents if convened, would respectively have. Was not this remark as applicable to one branch of the Representation as to the other? But it had been said that the Govern<sup>t</sup> would in its operation be partly federal, partly national; that altho' in the latter respect the Representatives of the people ought to be in proportion to the people: yet in the former it ought to be according to the number of States. If there was any solidity in this distinction he was ready to abide by it, if there was none it ought to be abandoned. In all cases where the Gen<sup>l</sup> Governm<sup>t</sup> is to act on the people, let the people be represented and the votes be proportional. In all cases where the Govern<sup>t</sup> is to act on the States as such, in like manner as Cong<sup>s</sup> now act on them, let the States be represented & the votes be equal. This was the true ground of compromise if there was any ground at all. But he denied that there was any ground. He called for a single instance in which the Gen<sup>l</sup> Gov<sup>t</sup> was not to operate on the people individually. The practicability of making laws, with coercive sanctions, for the States as Political bodies, had been exploded on all hands. He observed that the people of the large States would in some way or other secure to themselves a weight proportioned to the importance accruing from their superior numbers. If they could not effect it by a proportional representation in the Gov<sup>t</sup> they would probably accede to no Gov<sup>t</sup> which did not in[61] great measure depend for its efficacy on their voluntary cooperation; in which case they would indirecty secure their object. The existing confederacy proved that where the Acts of the Gen<sup>l</sup> Gov<sup>t</sup> were to be executed by the particular Gov<sup>ts</sup> the latter had a weight in proportion to their importance. No one would say that either in Cong<sup>s</sup> or out of Cong<sup>s</sup> Delaware had equal weight with Pensylv<sup>a</sup> If the latter was to supply ten times as much money as the former, and no compulsion could be used, it was of ten times more importance, that she should volun-

---

[61] The word "a" is here inserted in the transcript.

tarily furnish the supply. In the Dutch confederacy the votes of the Provinces were equal. But Holland which supplies about half the money, governs[62] the whole republic. He enumerated the objections ag:t an equality of votes in the 2d branch, notwithstanding the proportional representation in the first. 1. the minority could negative the will of the majority of the people. 2. they could extort measures by making them a condition of their assent to other necessary measures. 3. they could obtrude measures on the majority by virtue of the peculiar powers which would be vested in the Senate. 4. the evil instead of being cured by time, would increase with every new State that should be admitted, as they must all be admitted on the principle of equality. 5. the perpetuity it would give to the preponderance of the Northn ag:t the Southn Scale was a serious consideration. It seemed now to be pretty well understood that the real difference of interests lay, not between the large & small but between the N. & Southn States. The institution of slavery & its consequences formed the line of discrimination. There were 5 States on the South,[63] 8 on the Northn side of this line. Should a proport! representation take place it was true, the N. side[64] would still outnumber the other; but not in the same degree, at this time; and every day would tend towards an equilibrium.

Mr WILSON would add a few words only. If equality in the 2d branch was an error that time would correct, he should be less anxious to exclude it being sensible that perfection was unattainable in any plan; but being a fundamental and a perpetual error, it ought by all means to be avoided. A vice in the Representation, like an error in the first concoction, must be followed by disease, convulsions, and finally death itself. The justice of the general principle of proportional representation has not in argument at least been yet contradicted. But it is said that a departure from it so far as to give the States an equal vote in one branch of the Legislature is essential to their preservation. He had considered this position maturely, but could not see its application. That the States ought to be preserved he admitted. But does it follow that

---

[62] The word "governed" is substituted in the transcript for "governs."
[63] The word "Southern" is substituted in the transcript for "South."
[64] The word "side" is omitted in the transcript.

an equality of votes is necessary for the purpose? Is there any reason to suppose that if their preservation should depend more on the large than on the small States the security of the States ag:st the Gen! Government would be diminished? Are the large States less attached to their existence, more likely to commit suicide, than the small? An equal vote then is not necessary as far as he can conceive: and is liable among other objections to this insuperable one: The great fault of the existing confederacy is its inactivity. It has never been a complaint ag:st Cong:s that they governed overmuch. The complaint has been that they have governed too little. To remedy this defect we were sent here. Shall we effect the cure by establishing an equality of votes as is proposed? no: this very equality carries us directly to Congress: to the system which it is our duty to rectify. The small States cannot indeed act, by virtue of this equality, but they may controul the Gov:t as they have done in Cong:s This very measure is here prosecuted by a minority of the people of America. Is then the object of the Convention likely to be accomplished in this way? Will not our Constituents say? we sent you to form an efficient Gov:t and you have given us one more complex indeed, but having all the weakness of the former Govern:t He was anxious for uniting all the States under one Govern:t He knew there were some respectable men who preferred three confederacies, united by offensive & defensive alliances. Many things may be plausibly said, some things may be justly said, in favor of such a project. He could not however concur in it himself; but he thought nothing so pernicious as bad first principles.

M:r ELSEWORTH asked two questions one of M:r Wilson, whether he had ever seen a good measure fail in Cong:s for want of a majority of States in its favor? He had himself never known such an instance: the other of M:r Madison whether a negative lodged with the majority of the States even the smallest, could be more dangerous than the qualified negative proposed to be lodged in a single Executive Magistrate, who must be taken from some one State?

M:r SHERMAN, signified that his expectation was that the Gen! Legislature would in some cases act on the *federal principle*, of requiring quotas. But he thought it ought to be empowered to carry their own plans into execution, if the States should fail to supply their respective quotas.

On the question for agreeing to Mr Pinkney's motion for allowing N. H. 2. Mas. 4. &c—it passed in the negative

Mas. no. Mr King ay. Mr Ghorum absent. Cont no. N. J. no. Pa ay. Del. no. Md ay. Va ay. N. C. no. S. C. ay Geo. no.[65]

Adjourned

---

MONDAY. JULY 16. IN CONVENTION

On the question for agreeing to the whole Report as amended & including the equality of votes in the 2d branch. it passed in the Affirmative.

Mas. divided Mr Gerry, Mr Strong, ay. Mr King Mr Ghorum no. Cont ay. N. J. ay. Pena no. Del. ay. Md ay. Va no. N. C. ay. Mr Spaight no. S. C. no. Geo. no.[66]

[Here enter the whole in the words entered in the Journal July 16][67]

The whole, thus passed is in the words following viz

" Resolved that in the original formation of the Legislature of the U. S. the first branch thereof shall consist of sixty five members, of which number N. Hampshire shall send 3. Massts 8. Rh. I. 1. Connt 5. N. Y. 6. N. J. 4. Pena 8. Del. 1. Maryd 6. Virga 10. N. C. 5. S. C. 5. Geo. 3.—But as the present situation of the States may probably alter in the number of their inhabitants, the Legislature of the U. S. shall be authorized from time to time to apportion the number of Reps; and in case any of the States shall hereafter be divided, or enlarged by, addition of territory, or any two or more States united, or any new States created with [68] the limits of the U. S. the Legislature of the U. S. shall possess authority to regulate the number of Reps in any of the foregoing cases, upon the principle of their number of inhabitants, according

---

[65] In the transcript the vote reads: "Pennsylvania, Maryland, Virginia, South Carolina, aye—4; Massachusetts, [Mr. King, aye, Mr. Gorham, absent], Connecticut, New Jersey, Delaware, North Carolina, Georgia, no—6."
[66] In the transcript the vote reads: "Connecticut, New Jersey, Delaware, Maryland, North Carolina [Mr. Spaight, no], aye—5; Pennsylvania, Virginia, South Carolina, Georgia, no—4; Massachusetts, divided, [Mr. Gerry, Mr. Strong, aye; Mr. King, Mr. Gorham, no.]"
[67] Madison's direction is omitted in the transcript.
[68] The word "within" is substituted in the transcript for the word "with."

to the provisions hereafter mentioned, namely [69]—provided always that representation ought to be proportioned according to direct taxation; and in order to ascertain the alteration in the direct taxation, which may be required from time to time by the changes in the relative circumstances of the States—

Resolved, that a Census be taken within six years from the 1st meeting of the Legislature of the U. S. and once within the term of every 10 years afterwards of all the inhabitants of the U. S. in the manner and according to the ratio recommended by Congress in their Resolution of April 18.[70] 1783, and that the Legislature of the U. S. shall proportion the direct taxation accordingly—

"Resolved, that all bills for raising or appropriating money, and for fixing the salaries of officers of the Govt of the U. S. shall originate in the first branch of the Legislature of the U. S. and shall not be altered or amended in the 2d branch: and that no money shall be drawn from the public Treasury, but in pursuance of appropriations to be originated in the 1st branch.

"Resolvd that in the 2d branch of the Legislature of the U. S. each State shall have an equal vote."

The 6th Resol: in the Report from the Come of the whole House, which had been postponed in order to consider the 7 & 8th Resolns: was now resumed. see the Resoln

The 1st member [71] "That the Natl Legislature ought to possess the Legislative Rights vested in Congs by the Confederation." was agreed to nem. Con.

The next,[72] "And moreover to legislate in all cases to which the separate States are incompetent; or in which the harmony of the U. S. may be interrupted by the exercise of individual legislation," being read for a question

Mr BUTLER calls for some explanation of the extent of this power: particularly of the word *incompetent*. The vagueness of the terms rendered it impossible for any precise judgment to be formed.

Mr GHORUM. The vagueness of the terms constitutes the propriety of them. We are now establishing general principles, to be extended hereafter into details which will be precise & explicit.

---

[69] The word "namely" is omitted in the transcript.
[70] The date "April 18" is changed to "the eighteenth of April" in the transcript.
[71] The words "The 1st member" are omitted in the transcript.
[72] The words "The next" are omitted in the transcript.

385

Mr RUTLIDGE, urged the objection started by Mr Butler and moved that the clause should be committed to the end that a specification of the powers comprised in the general terms, might be reported.

On the question for a[73] commitment, the States[74] were equally divided.

Mas. no. Cont ay. N. J. no. Pa no. Del. no. Md ay. Va ay. N. C. no. S. C. ay. Geo. ay:[75] So it was lost.

Mr RANDOLPH. The vote of this morning [involving an equality of suffrage in 2d branch] had embarrassed the business extremely. All the powers given in the Report from the Come of the whole, were founded on the supposition that a Proportional representation was to prevail in both branches of the Legislature. When he came here this morning his purpose was to have offered some propositions that might if possible have united a great majority of votes, and particularly might provide agst the danger suspected on the part of the smaller States, by enumerating the cases in which it might lie, and allowing an equality of votes in such cases.* But finding from the preceding vote that they persist in demanding an equal vote in all cases, that they have succeeded in obtaining it, and that N. York if present would probably be on the same side, he could not but think we were unprepared to discuss this subject further. It will probably be in vain to come to any final decision with a bare majority on either side. For these reasons he wished the Convention might[78] adjourn, that the large States might consider the steps proper to be taken in the present solemn crisis of the business, and that the small States might also deliberate on the means of conciliation.

Mr PATTERSON, thought with Mr R. that it was high time for the Convention to adjourn that the rule of secrecy ought to be rescinded, and that our Constituents should be consulted. No conciliation could be admissible on the part of the smaller States

---

[73] The word "a" is omitted in the transcript.

[74] The word "votes" is substituted in the transcript for "States."

[75] In the transcript the vote reads: "Connecticut, Maryland, Virginia, South Carolina, Georgia, aye—5; Massachusetts, New Jersey, Pennsylvania, Delaware, North Carolina, no—5."

* See the paper in[76] appendix communicated by Mr R. to J. M. July 10.[77]

[76] The word "the" is here inserted in the transcript.

[77] The transcript here inserts "No.—"

[78] The word "to" is substituted in the transcript for "might."

on any other ground than that of an equality of votes in the 2ᵈ branch. If Mʳ Randolph would reduce to form his motion for an adjounrment sine die, he would second it with all his heart.

Genˡ PINKNEY wished to know of Mʳ R. whether he meant an adjournment sine die, or only an adjournment for the day. If the former was meant, it differed much from his idea. He could not think of going to S. Carolina and returning again to this place. Besides it was chimerical to suppose that the States if consulted would ever accord separately, and beforehand.

Mʳ RANDOLPH, had never entertained an idea of an adjournment sine die; & was sorry that his meaning had been so readily & strangely misinterpreted. He had in view merely an adjournment till tomorrow, in order that some conciliatory experiment might if possible be devised, and that in case the smaller States should continue to hold back, the larger might then take such measures, he would not say what, as might be necessary.

Mʳ PATTERSON seconded the adjournment till tomorrow, as an opportunity seemed to be wished by the larger States to deliberate further on conciliatory expedients.

On the question for adjourning till tomorrow, the States were equally divided.

Mas. no. Conᵗ no. N. J. ay. Pᵃ ay. Del. no. Mᵈ ay. Vᵃ ay. N. C. ay. S. C. no. Geo. no.[79] So it was lost.

Mʳ BROOME thought it his duty to declare his opinion agˢᵗ an adjournment sine die, as had been urged by Mʳ Patterson. Such a measure he thought would be fatal. Something must be done by the Convention, tho' it should be by a bare majority.

Mʳ GERRY observed that Masᵗˢ was opposed to an adjournment, because they saw no new ground of compromise. But as it seemed to be the opinion of so many States that a trial shᵈ— be made, the State would now concur in the adjournmᵗ

Mʳ RUTLIDGE could see no need of an adjournᵗ because he could see no chance of a compromise. The little States were fixt. They had repeatedly & solemnly declared themselves to be so. All that the large States then had to do, was to decide whether

---

[79] In the transcript the vote reads: "New Jersey, Pennsylvania, Maryland, Virginia, North Carolina aye—5; Massachusetts, Connecticut, Delaware, South Carolina, Georgia, no—5."

they would yield or not. For his part he conceived that altho' we could not do what we thought best, in itself, we ought to do something. Had we not better keep the Gov! up a little longer, hoping that another Convention will supply our omissions, than abandon every thing to hazard. Our Constituents will be very little satisfied with us if we take the latter course.

M! RANDOLPH & M! KING renewed the motion to adjourn till tomorrow.

On the question. Mas. ay. Con! no. N. J. ay. P! ay. Del. no. M! ay. V! ay. N. C. ay. S. C. ay. Geo. div! [80]

Adjourned

On the morning following before the hour of the convention a number of the members from the larger States, by common agreement met for the purpose of consulting on the proper steps to be taken in consequence of the vote in favor of an equal Representation in the 2! branch, and the apparent inflexibility of the smaller States on that point. Several members from the latter States also attended. The time was wasted in vague conversation on the subject, without any specific proposition or agreement. It appeared indeed that the opinions of the members who disliked the equality of votes differed so [81] much as to the importance of that point, and as to the policy of risking a failure of any general act of the Convention, by inflexibly opposing it. Several of them supposing that no good Governn! could or would be built on that foundation, and that as a division of the Convention into two opinions was unavoidable; it would be better that the side comprising the principal States, and a majority of the people of America, should propose a scheme of Gov! to the States, than that a scheme should be proposed on the other side, would have concurred in a firm opposition to the smaller States, and in a separate recommendation, if eventually necessary. Others seemed inclined to yield to the smaller States, and to concur in such an act however imperfect & exceptionable, as might be agreed on by the Convention as a body, tho' decided by a bare majority of

---

[80] In the transcript the vote reads: "Massachusetts, New Jersey, Pennsylvania, Maryland, Virginia North Carolina, South Carolina, aye—7; Connecticut, Delaware, no—2; Georgia, divided."

[81] The word "so" is omitted in the transcript.

States and by a minority of the people of the U. States. It is probable that the result of this consultation satisfied the smaller States that they had nothing to apprehend from a union of the larger, in any plan whatever ag$^{st}$ the equality of votes in the 2$^d$ branch.

---

TUESDAY JULY 17.   IN CONVENTION

M$^r$ GOVERN$^r$ MORRIS. moved to reconsider the whole Resolution agreed to yesterday concerning the constitution of the 2 branches of the Legislature. His object was to bring the House to a consideration in the abstract of the powers necessary to be vested in the general Government. It had been said, Let us know how the Gov$^t$ is to be modelled, and then we can determine what powers can be properly given to it. He thought the most eligible course was, first to determine on the necessary powers, and then so to modify the Govern$^t$ as that it might be justly & properly enabled to administer them. He feared if we proceeded to a consideration of the powers, whilst the vote of yesterday including an equality of the States in the 2$^d$ branch, remained in force, a reference to it, either mental or expressed, would mix itself with the merits of every question concerning the powers.— this motion was not seconded. [It was probably approved by several members, who either despaired of success, or were apprehensive that the attempt would inflame the jealousies of the smaller States.]

The 6$^{th}$ Resol$^n$ in the Report of the Com$^e$ of the Whole relating to the powers, which had been postponed in order to consider the 7 & 8$^{th}$ relating to the constitution of the Nat$^l$ Legislature, was now resumed.

M$^r$ SHERMAN observed that it would be difficult to draw the line between the powers of the Gen$^l$ Legislatures, and those to be left with the States; that he did not like the definition contained in the Resolution, and proposed in [82] place of [83] the words "of [84] individual Legislation" line 4.[85] inclusive, to insert "to make laws

---

[82] The word "its" is here inserted in the transcript.
[83] The word "of" is crossed out in the transcript and "to" is written above it.
[84] The word "of" is omitted in the transcript.
[85] The word and figure "line 4" are crossed out in the transcript.

binding on the people of the United States in all cases which may concern the common interests of the Union; but not to interfere with the Government of the individual States in any matters of internal police which respect the Gov! of such States only, and wherein the general welfare of the U. States is not concerned."

M! WILSON 2ded the amendment as better expressing the general principle.

M! Gov! MORRIS opposed it. The internal police, as it would be called & understood by the States ought to be infringed in many cases, as in the case of paper money & other tricks by which Citizens of other States may be affected.

M! SHERMAN, in explanation of his idea read an enumeration of powers, including the power of levying taxes on trade, but not the power of *direct taxation*.

M! Gov! MORRIS remarked the omission, and inferred that for the deficiencies of taxes on consumption, it must have been the meaning of M! Sherman, that the Gen! Gov! should recur to quotas & requisitions, which are subversive of the idea of Gov!

M! SHERMAN acknowledged that his enumeration did not include direct taxation. Some provision he supposed must be made for supplying the deficiency of other taxation, but he had not formed any.

On [86] Question of M! Sherman's motion, it passed in the negative
Mas. no. Con! ay. N. J. no. P? no. Del. no. M? ay. V? no. N. C. no. S. C. no. Geo. no.[87]

M! BEDFORD moved that the 2? member of Resolution 6.[88] be so altered as to read "and moreover to legislate in all cases for the general interests of the Union, and also in those to which the States are separately [89] incompetent," or in which the harmony of the U. States may be interrupted by the exercise of individual Legislation."

M! Gov! MORRIS 2?? the motion

M! RANDOLPH. This is a formidable idea indeed. It involves the power of violating all the laws and constitutions of the States, and of intermeddling with their police. The last member of the sentence is also superfluous, being included in the first.

---

[86] The word "the" is here inserted in the transcript.
[87] In the transcript the vote reads: "Connecticut, Maryland, aye—2; Massachusetts, New Jersey, Pennsylvania, Delaware, Virginia, North Carolina, South Carolina, Georgia, no—8."
[88] The words "the sixth Resolution" are substituted in the transcript for "Resolution 6."
[89] The word "severally" is substituted in the transcript for "separately."

M! BEDFORD. It is not more extensive or formidable than the clause as it stands: *no State* being *separately* competent to legislate for the *general interest* of the Union.

On⁹⁰ question for agreeing to M! Bedford's motion, it passed in the affirmative.

Mas. ay. Con! no. N. J. ay. P? ay. Del. ay. M? ay. V? no. N. C. ay. S. C. no. Geo. no.⁹¹

On the sentence as amended, it passed in the affirmative.

Mas. ay. Con! ay. N. J. ay. P? ay. Del. ay. M? ay. V? ay. N. C. ay. S. C. no. Geo. no.⁹²

The next.⁹³ "To negative all laws passed by the several States contravening in the opinion of the Nat: Legislature the articles of Union, or any treaties subsisting under the authority of y? Union" ⁹⁴

M! Gov! MORRIS opposed this power as likely to be terrible to the States, and not necessary, if sufficient Legislative authority should be given to the Gen! Government.

M! SHERMAN thought it unnecessary, as the Courts of the States would not consider as valid any law contravening the Authority of the Union, and which the legislature would wish to be negatived.

M! L. MARTIN considered the power as improper & inadmissible. Shall all the laws of the States be sent up to the Gen! Legislature before they shall be permitted to operate?

M! MADISON, considered the negative on the laws of the States as essential to the efficacy & security of the Gen! Gov! The necessity of a general Gov! proceeds from the propensity of the States to pursue their particular interests in opposition to the general interest. This propensity will continue to disturb the system, unless effectually controuled. Nothing short of a negative on their laws will controul it. They can⁹⁵ pass laws which will accomplish their injurious objects before they can be repealed by the Gen! Legisl:⁰ or be⁹⁶ set aside by the National Tribunals. Confidence can not be

---

⁹⁰ The word "the" is here inserted in the transcript.

⁹¹ In the transcript the vote reads: "Massachusetts, New Jersey, Pennsylvania, Delaware, Maryland, North Carolina, aye—6; Connecticut, Virginia, South Carolina, Georgia, no—4."

⁹² In the transcript the vote reads: "Massachusetts, Connecticut, New Jersey, Pennsylvania, Delaware, Maryland, Virginia, North Carolina, aye—8; South Carolina, Georgia, no—2."

⁹³ The word "clause" is here inserted in the transcript.

⁹⁴ The phrase "was then taken up" is here inserted in the transcript.

⁹⁵ The word "will" is substituted in the transcript for "can."

⁹⁶ The word "be" is omitted in the transcript.

put in the State Tribunals as guardians of the National authority and interests. In all the States these are more or less depend: on the Legislatures. In Georgia they are appointed annually by the Legislature. In R. Island the Judges who refused to execute an unconstitutional law were displaced, and others substituted, by the Legislature who would be [97] willing instruments of the wicked & arbitrary plans of their masters. A power of negativing the improper laws of the States is at once the most mild & certain means of preserving the harmony of the system. Its utility is sufficiently displayed in the British System. Nothing could maintain the harmony & subordination of the various parts of the empire, but the prerogative by which the Crown, stifles in the birth every Act of every part tending to discord or encroachment. It is true the prerogative is sometimes misapplied thro' ignorance or a partiality to one particular part of y$^e$ empire; but we have not the same reason to fear such misapplications in our System. As to the sending all laws up to the Nat! Legisl: that might be rendered unnecessary by some emanation of the power into the States, so far at least, as to give a temporary effect to laws of immediate necessity.

M$^r$ Gov$^r$ Morris was more & more opposed to the negative. The proposal of it would disgust all the States. A law that ought to be negatived will be set aside in the Judiciary departm$^t$ and if that security should fail; may be repealed by a Nation! law.

M$^r$ Sherman. Such a power involves a wrong principle, to wit, that a law of a State contrary to the articles of the Union, would if not negatived, be valid & operative.

M$^r$ Pinkney urged the necessity of the Negative.

On the question for agreeing to the power of negativing laws of States &c" it passed in the negative.

Mas. ay. C$^t$ no. N. J. no. P$^a$ no. Del. no. M$^d$ no. V$^a$ ay. N. C. ay. S. C. no. Geo. no.[98]

M$^r$ Luther Martin moved the following resolution "that the Legislative acts of the U. S. made by virtue & in pursuance of the

---

[97] The word "the" is here inserted in the transcript.
[98] In the transcript the vote reads: "Massachusetts, Virginia, North Carolina, aye—3; Connecticut, New Jersey, Pennsylvania, Delaware, Maryland, South Carolina, Georgia, no—7."

articles of Union, and all Treaties made & ratified under the authority of the U. S. shall be the supreme law of the respective States, as far as those acts or treaties shall relate to the said States, or their Citizens and inhabitants—& that the Judiciaries of the several States shall be bound thereby in their decisions, any thing in the respective laws of the individual States to the contrary notwithstanding" which was agreed to nem: con:

9th Resol: "that Natl Executive consist of a single person." Agd to nem. con.[99]

[1] "To be chosen by the National Legisl:"[2]

Mr Governr Morris was pointedly agst his being so chosen. He will be the mere creature of the Legisl: if appointed & impeachable by that body. He ought to be elected by the people at large, by the freeholders of the Country. That difficulties attend this mode, he admits. But they have been found superable in N. Y. & in Cont and would he believed be found so, in the case of an Executive for the U. States. If the people should elect, they will never fail to prefer some man of distinguished character, or services; some man, if he might so speak, of continental reputation.—If the Legislature elect, it will be the work of intrigue, of cabal, and of faction; it will be like the election of a pope by a conclave of cardinals; real merit will rarely be the title to the appointment. He moved to strike out "National Legislature" & insert "citizens of [3] U. S."

Mr Sherman thought that the sense of the Nation would be better expressed by the Legislature, than by the people at large. The latter will never be sufficiently informed of characters, and besides will never give a majority of votes to any one man. They will generally vote for some man in their own State, and the largest State will have the best chance for the appointment. If the choice be made by the Legislre A majority of voices may be made necessary to constitute an election.

---

[1] The words "The next clause" are here inserted in the transcript.
[2] The words "being considered" are here inserted in the transcript.
[3] The word "the" is here inserted in the transcript.
[99] In the transcript this sentence reads as follows: "The ninth Resolution being taken up, the first clause, 'That a National Executive be instituted, to consist of a single person,' was agreed to, *nem. con.*"

Mr WILSON. two arguments have been urged agst an election of the Executive Magistrate by the people. 1 [4] the example of Poland where an Election of the supreme Magistrate is attended with the most dangerous commotions. The cases he observed were totally dissimilar. The Polish nobles have resources & dependents which enable them to appear in force, and to threaten the Republic as well as each other. In the next place the electors all assemble in [5] one place: which would not be the case with us. The 2d argt is that a *majority* [6] of the people would never concur. It might be answered that the concurrence of a majority of [7] people is not a necessary principle of election, nor required as such in any of the States. But allowing the objection all its force, it may be obviated by the expedient used in Masts where the Legislature by [8] majority of voices, decide in case a majority of people do not concur in favor of one of the candidates. This would restrain the choice to a good nomination at least, and prevent in a great degree intrigue & cabal. A particular objection with him agst an absolute election by the Legislre was that the Exec: in that case would be too dependent to stand the mediator between the intrigues & sinister views of the Representatives and the general liberties & interests of the people.

Mr PINKNEY did not expect this question would again have been brought forward; An Election by the people being liable to the most obvious & striking objections. They will be led by a few active & designing men. The most populous States by combining in favor of the same individual will be able to carry their points. The Natl Legislature being most immediately interested in the laws made by themselves, will be most attentive to the choice of a fit man to carry them properly into execution.

Mr Govr MORRIS. It is said that in case of an election by the people the populous States will combine & elect whom they please. Just the reverse. The people of such States cannot combine. If their be any combination it must be among their representatives

---

[4] The figure "1" is changed to "The first is" in the transcript.
[5] The word "at" is substituted in the transcript for "in."
[6] The transcript does not italicize the word "*majority.*"
[7] The word "the" is here inserted in the transcript.
[8] The word "a" is here inserted in the transcript.

in the Legislature. It is said the people will be led by a few designing men. This might happen in a small district. It can never happen throughout the continent. In the election of a Gov.r of N. York, it sometimes is the case in particular spots, that the activity & intrigues of little partizans are successful, but the general voice of the State is never influenced by such artifices. It is said the multitude will be uninformed. It is true they would be uninformed of what passed in the Legislative Conclave, if the election were to be made there; but they will not be uninformed of those great & illustrious characters which have merited their esteem & confidence. If the Executive be chosen by the Nat.l Legislature, he will not be independent on [9] it; and if not independent, usurpation & tyranny on the part of the Legislature will be the consequence. This was the case in England in the last Century. It has been the case in Holland, where their Senates have engrossed all power. It has been the case every where. He was surprised that an election by the people at large should ever have been likened to the polish election of the first Magistrate. An election by the Legislature will bear a real likeness to the election by the Diet of Poland. The great must be the electors in both cases, and the corruption & cabal w.ch are known to characterise the one would soon find their way into the other. Appointments made by numerous bodies, are always worse than those made by single responsible individuals, or by the people at large.

Col. MASON. It is curious to remark the different language held at different times. At one moment we are told that the Legislature is entitled to thorough confidence, and to indifinite power. At another, that it will be governed by intrigue & corruption, and cannot be trusted at all. But not to dwell on this inconsistency he would observe that a Government which is to last ought at least to be practicable. Would this be the case if the proposed election should be left to the people at large. He conceived it would be as unnatural to refer the choice of a proper character for chief Magistrate to the people, as it would, to refer a trial of colours to a blind man. The extent of the Country renders it impossible

---

[9] In the transcript the word "on" is crossed out and "of" is written above it.

that the people can have the requisite capacity to judge of the respective pretensions of the Candidates.

Mṛ WILSON. could not see the contrariety stated [by Col. Mason] The Legislṛe might deserve confidence in some respects, and distrust in others. In acts which were to affect them & yṛ Constituents precisely alike confidence was due. In others jealousy was warranted. The appointment to great offices, where the Legislṛe might feel many motives, not common to the public confidence was surely misplaced. This branch of business it was notorious was [10] most corruptly managed of any that had been committed to legislative bodies.

Mṛ WILLIAMSON, conceived that there was the same difference between an election in this case, by the people and by the legislature, as between an appṭ by lot, and by choice. There are at present distinguished characters, who are known perhaps to almost every man. This will not always be the case. The people will be sure to vote for some man in their own State, and the largest State will be sure to succeed. This will not be Virgạ however. Her slaves will have no suffrage. As the Salary of the Executive will be fixed, and he will not be eligible a 2ḍ time, there will not be such a dependence on the Legislature as has been imagined.

[11] Question on an election by the people instead of the Legislature; which [12] passed in the negative.

Mas. no. Conṭ no. N. J. no. Pạ ay. Del. no. Mḍ no. Vạ no. N. C. no. S. C. no. Geo. no.[13]

Mṛ L. MARTIN moved that the Executive be chosen by Electors appointed by the several Legislatures of the individual States.

Mṛ BROOME 2ḍs On the Question, it passed in the negative. Mas. no. Conṭ no. N. J. no. Pạ no. Del. ay. Mḍ ay. Vạ no. N. C. no. S. C. no. Geo. no.[14]

On the question on the words "to be chosen by the Nationḷ Legislature" it passed unanimously in the affirmative.

---

[10] The word "the" is here inserted in the transcript.
[11] The words "On the" are here inserted in the transcript.
[12] The word "which" is crossed out and "it" is written above it in the transcript.
[13] In the transcript the vote reads: "Pennsylvania, aye—1; Massachusetts, Connecticut, New Jersey, Delaware, Maryland, Virginia, North Carolina, South Carolina, Georgia, no—9."
[14] In the transcript the vote reads: "Delaware, Maryland, aye—2; Massachusetts, Connecticut, New Jersey, Pennsylvania, Virginia, North Carolina, South Carolina, Georgia, no—8."

"For the term of seven years"—postponed nem. con. on motion of Mr Houston & [15] Gov. Morris.

"to carry into execution the national laws"—agreed to nem. con.

"to appoint to offices in cases not otherwise provided for."—agreed to nem. con.

"to be ineligible a second time"—Mr HOUSTON moved to strike out this clause.

Mr SHERMAN 2ds the motion.

Mr Govr MORRIS espoused the motion. The ineligibility proposed by the clause as it stood tended to destroy the great motive to good behavior, the hope of being rewarded by a re-appointment. It was saying to him, make hay while the sun shines.

On the question for striking out as moved by Mr Houston, it passed in the affirmative

Mas. ay. Cont ay. N. J. ay. Pa ay. Del. no. Md ay. Va no. N. C. no. S. C. no. Geo. ay.[16]

[17] "For the term of 7 years" [18] resumed

Mr BROOM was for a shorter term since the Executive Magistrate was now to be re-eligible. Had he remained ineligible a 2d time, he should have preferred a longer term.

Docr MCCLURG moved * to strike out 7 years, and insert "during good behavior." By striking out the words declaring him not re-eligible, he was put into a situation that would keep him dependent for ever on the Legislature; and he conceived the independence of the Executive to be equally essential with that of the Judiciary department.

Mr Govr MORRIS 2ded the motion. He expressed great pleasure in hearing it. This was the way to get a good Government. His fear that so valuable an ingredient would not be attained had led him to take the part he had done. He was indifferent how the

---

[15] The word "Mr." is here inserted in the transcript.

[16] In the transcript the vote reads: "Massachusetts, Connecticut, New Jersey, Pennsylvania, Maryland, Georgia, aye—6; Delaware, Virginia, North Carolina, South Carolina, no—4."

[17] The words "The clause" are here inserted in the transcript.

[18] The word "being" is here inserted in the transcript.     z

* The probable object of this motion was merely to enforce the argument against the re-eligibility of the Executive Magistrate, by holding out a tenure during good behaviour as the alternative for keeping him independent of the Legislature.

Executive should be chosen, provided he held his place by this tenure.

Mr BROOME highly approved the motion. It obviated all his difficulties

Mr SHERMAN considered such a tenure as by no means safe or admissible. As the Executive Magistrate is now re-eligible, he will be on good behavior as far as will be necessary. If he behaves well he will be continued; if otherwise, displaced. on a succeeding election.

Mr MADISON † If it be essential to the preservation of liberty that the Legisl: Execut: & Judiciary powers be separate, it is essential to a maintenance of the separation, that they should be independent of each other. The Executive could not be independent of the Legislure, if dependent on the pleasure of that branch for a reappointment. Why was it determined that the Judges should not hold their places by such a tenure? Because they might be tempted to cultivate the Legislature, by an undue complaisance, and thus render the Legislature the virtual expositor, as well [19] the maker of the laws. In like manner a dependence of the Executive on the Legislature, would render it the Executor as well as the maker of laws; & then according to the observation of Montesquieu, tyrannical laws may be made that they may be executed in a tyrannical manner. There was an analogy between the Executive & Judiciary departments in several respects. The latter executed the laws in certain cases as the former did in others. The former expounded & applied them for certain purposes, as the latter did for others. The difference between them seemed to consist chiefly in two circumstances— 1.[20] the collective interest & security were much more in the power belonging to the Executive than to the Judiciary department. 2.[20] in the administration of the former much greater latitude is left to opinion and discretion than in the administration of the latter. But if the 2ᵈ consideration proves that it will

---

† The view here taken of the subject was meant to aid in parrying the animadversions likely to fall on the motion of Dr McClurg, for whom J. M. had a particular regard. The Doctr though possessing talents of the highest order, was modest & unaccustomed to exert them in public debate.

[19] The word "as" is here inserted in the transcript.

[20] The figures "1" and "2" are changed to "first" and "secondly" in the transcript.

be more difficult to establish a rule sufficiently precise for trying the Execut: than the Judges, & forms an objection to the same tenure of office, both considerations prove that it might be more dangerous to suffer a union between the Executive & Legisl: powers, than between the Judiciary & Legislative powers. He conceived it to be absolutely necessary to a well constituted Republic that the two first sh{d} be kept distinct & independent of each other. Whether the plan proposed by the motion was a proper one was another question, as it depended on the practicability of instituting a tribunal for impeachm{ts} as certain & as adequate in the one case as in the other. On the other hand, respect for the mover entitled his proposition to a fair hearing & discussion, until a less objectionable expedient should be applied for guarding ag{st} a dangerous union of the Legislative & Executive departments.

Col. MASON. This motion was made some time ago, & negatived by a very large majority. He trusted that it w{d} be again negatived. It w{d} be impossible to define the misbehaviour in such a manner as to subject it to a proper trial; and perhaps still more impossible to compel so high an offender holding his office by such a tenure to submit to a trial. He considered an Executive during good behavior as a softer name only for an Executive for life. And that the next would be an easy step to hereditary Monarchy. If the motion should finally succeed, he might himself live to see such a Revolution. If he did not it was probable his children or grand children would. He trusted there were few men in that House who wished for it. No state he was sure had so far revolted from Republican principles as to have the least bias in its favor.

Mr MADISON, was not apprehensive of being thought to favor any step towards monarchy. The real object with him was to prevent its introduction. Experience had proved a tendency in our governments to throw all power into the Legislative vortex. The Executives of the States are in general little more than Cyphers; the legislatures omnipotent. If no effectual check be devised for restraining the instability & encroachments of the latter, a revolution of some kind or other would be inevitable. The preservation of Republican Gov.! therefore required some expedient for the purpose, but required evidently at the same time that in devising it, the genuine principles of that form should be kept in view.

M! Gov.! MORRIS was as little a friend to monarchy as any gentleman. He concurred in the opinion that the way to keep out monarchical Gov! was to establish such a Repub. Gov! as w.d make the people happy and prevent a desire of change.

Doc! M.cCLURG was not so much afraid of the shadow of monarchy as to be unwilling to approach it; nor so wedded to Republican Gov! as not to be sensible of the tyrannies that had been & may be exercised under that form. It was an essential object with him to make the Executive independent of the Legislature; and the only mode left for effecting it, after the vote destroying his ineligibility a second time, was to appoint him during good behavior.

On the question for inserting "during good behavior" in place of 7 years [with a re-eligibility] it passed in the negative.

Mas. no. C.t no. N. J. ay. P.a ay. Del. ay. M.d no. V.a ay. N. C. no. S. C. no. Geo. no.* [21]

On the motion "to strike out seven years" it passed in the negative.

Mas. ay. C.t no. N. J. no. P.a ay. Del. ay. M.d no. V.a no. N. C. ay. S. C. no. Geo. no.* [25]

It was now unanimously agreed that the vote which had struck out the words " to be ineligible a second time " should be reconsidered to-morrow.

Adj.d

---

[21] In the transcript the vote reads: "New Jersey, Pennsylvania, Delaware, Virginia, aye—4; Massachusetts, Connecticut, Maryland, North Carolina, South Carolina, Georgia, no—6.*"

* Transfer the above notes hither.[22]

[* This vote is not [23] be considered as any certain index of opinion, as a number in the affirmative probably had it chiefly in view to alarm those attached to a dependence of the Executive on the Legislature, & thereby facilitate some final arrangement of a contrary tendency. The avowed friends of an Executive, "during good behaviour" were not more than three or four, nor is it certain they would finally [24] have adhered to such a tenure. An independence of the three great departments of each other, as far as possible, and the responsibility of all to the will of the community seemed to be generally admitted as the true basis of a well constructed government.]

[22] Madison's direction concerning the footnotes is omitted in the transcript.

[23] The word "to" is here inserted in the transcript.

[24] The word "finally" is omitted in the transcript.

[* There was no debate on this motion, the apparent object of many in the affirmative was to secure the re-eligibility by shortening the term, and of many in the negative to embarrass the plan of referring the appointment & dependence of the Executive to the Legislature.]

[25] In the transcript the vote reads: "Massachusetts, Pennsylvania, Delaware, North Carolina, aye—4; Connecticut, New Jersey, Maryland, Virginia, South Carolina, Georgia, no—6.*"

## Wednesday July 18. in Convention

On motion of M̲r̲ L. Martin to fix tomorrow for reconsidering the vote concerning "eligibility of Exec$^{tive}$ [26] a 2$^d$ time" it passed in the affirmative.

Mas. ay. Con$^t$ ay. N. J. absent. P$^a$ ay. Del. ay. M$^d$ ay. V$^a$ ay. N. C. ay. S. C. ay. Geo. absent.[27]

The residue of Resol. 9 [28] concerning the Executive was postp$^d$ till tomorrow.

Resol. 10.[29] that Executive sh$^l$ have a right to negative legislative acts not afterwards passed by $\frac{2}{3}$ of each branch.[30] Agreed to nem. con.

Resol. 11 [31] "that a Nat$^l$ Judiciary [32] be estab$^d$ to consist of one supreme tribunal." ag$^d$ to nem. con.

[33] "The Judges of which to be appoint$^d$ by the 2$^d$ branch of the Nat$^l$ Legislature."

M̲r̲ GHORUM, w$^d$ prefer an appointment by the 2$^d$ branch to an appointm$^t$ by the whole Legislature; but he thought even that branch too numerous, and too little personally responsible, to ensure a good choice. He suggested that the Judges be appointed by the Execu$^{ve}$ with the advice & consent of the 2$^d$ branch, in the mode prescribed by the constitution of Mas$^{ts}$ This mode had been long practised in that country, & was found to answer perfectly well.

M̲r̲ WILSON, still w$^d$ [34] prefer an appointm$^t$ by the Executive; but if that could not be attained, w$^d$ prefer in the next place, the mode suggested by M̲r̲ Ghorum. He thought it his duty however to move in the first instance "that the Judges be appointed by the Executive." M̲r̲ Gov$^r$ MORRIS 2$^{ded}$ the motion.

M̲r̲ L. MARTIN was strenuous for an app$^t$ by the 2$^d$ branch. Being taken from all the States it w$^d$ be best informed of characters & most capable of making a fit choice.

---

[26] The words "eligibility of Executive" are changed to "the ineligibility of the Eexcutive" in the transcript.

[27] In the transcript the vote reads: "Massachusetts, Connecticut, Pennsylvania, Delaware, Maryland, Virginia, North Carolina, South Carolina, aye—8; New Jersey, Georgia, absent."

[28] The words "the ninth Resolution" are substituted in the transcript for "Resol. 9."

[29] The words "The tenth Resolution" are substituted in the transcript for "Resol. 10."

[30] The word "was" is here inserted in the transcript.

[31] The words "The Eleventh Resolution" are substituted in the transcript for "Resol. 11."

[32] The word "shall" is here inserted in the transcript.

[33] The words "On the clause" are here inserted in the transcript.

[34] The words "still w$^d$" are transposed to read "would still" in the transcript.

*The Home of Patrick Henry*

M.? SHERMAN concurred in the observations of M.? Martin, adding that the Judges ought to be diffused, which would be more likely to be attended to by the 2.ᵈ branch, than by the Executive.

M.? MASON. The mode of appointing the Judges may depend in some degree on the mode of trying impeachments of the Executive. If the Judges were to form a tribunal for that purpose, they surely ought not to be appointed by the Executive. There were insuperable objections besides ag.ˢᵗ referring the appointment to the Executive. He mentioned as one, that as the Seat of Gov.ᵗ must be in some one State, and ³⁵ the Executive would remain in office for a considerable time, for 4, 5, or 6 years at least, he would insensibly form local & personal attachments within the particular State that would deprive equal merit elsewhere, of an equal chance of promotion.

M.? GHORUM. As the Executive will be responsible in point of character at least, for a judicious and faithful discharge of his trust, he will be careful to look through all the States for proper characters. The Senators will be as likely to form their attachments at the seat of Gov.ᵗ where they reside, as the Executive. If they can not get the man of the particular State to which they may respectively belong, they will be indifferent to the rest. Public bodies feel no personal responsibility, and give full play to intrigue & cabal. Rh. Island is a full illustration of the insensibility to character, produced by a participation of numbers, in dishonorable measures, and of the length to which a public body may carry wickedness & cabal.

M.? Gov.ʳ MORRIS supposed it would be improper for an impeachm.ᵗ of the Executive to be tried before the Judges. The latter would in such case be drawn into intrigues with the Legislature and an impartial trial would be frustrated. As they w.ᵈ be much about the Seat of Gov.ᵗ they might even be previously consulted & arrangements might be made for a prosecution of the Executive. He thought therefore that no argument could be drawn from the probability of such a plan of impeachments ag.ˢᵗ the motion before the House.

---

³⁵ The word "as" is here inserted in the transcript.

Mʳ MADISON, suggested that the Judges might be appointed by the Executive with the concurrence of ⅓ at least, of the 2ᵈ branch. This would unite the advantage of responsibility in the Executive with the security afforded in the 2ᵈ branch agˢᵗ any incautious or corrupt nomination by the Executive.

Mʳ SHERMAN, was clearly for an election by the Senate. It would be composed of men nearly equal to the Executive, and would of course have on the whole more wisdom. They would bring into their deliberations a more diffusive knowledge of characters. It would be less easy for candidates to intrigue with them, than with the Executive Magistrate. For these reasons he thought there would be a better security for a proper choice in the Senate than in the Executive.

Mʳ RANDOLPH. It is true that when the appᵗ of the Judges was vested in the 2ᵈ branch an equality of votes had not been given to it. Yet he had rather leave the appointmᵗ there than give it to the Executive. He thought the advantage of personal responsibility might be gained in the Senate by requiring the respective votes of the members to be entered on the Journal. He thought too that the hope of receiving appᵗˢ would be more diffusive if they depended on the Senate, the members of which wᵈ be diffusively known, than if they depended on a single man who could not be personally known to a very great extent; and consequently that opposition to the System, would be so far weakened.

Mʳ BEDFORD thought there were solid reasons agˢᵗ leaving the appointment to the Executive. He must trust more to information than the Senate. It would put it in his power to gain over the larger States, by gratifying them with a preference of their Citizens. The responsibility of the Executive so much talked of was chimerical. He could not be punished for mistakes.

Mʳ GHORUM remarked that the Senate could have no better information than the Executive. They must like him, trust to information from the members belonging to the particular State where the Candidates resided. The Executive would certainly be more answerable for a good appointment, as the whole blame of a bad one would fall on him alone. He did not mean that he would be answerable under any other penalty than that of public censure, which with honorable minds was a sufficient one.

On the question for referring the appointment of the Judges to the Executive, instead of the 2ᵈ branch

Mas. ay. Conᵗ no. Pᵃ ay. Del. no. Mᵈ no. Vᵃ no. N. C. no. S. C. no.—Geo. absent.³⁶

Mʳ GHORUM moved "that the Judges be nominated and appointed by the Executive by & with the advice & consent of the 2ᵈ branch & every such nomination shall be made at least      days prior to such appointment." This mode he said had been ratified by the experience of 140 years in Massachussᵗˢ If the appᵗ should be left to either branch of the Legislature, it will be a mere piece of jobbing.

Mʳ Govʳ MORRIS 2ᵈᵉᵈ & supported the motion.

Mʳ SHERMAN thought it less objectionable than an absolute appointment by the Executive; but disliked it as too much fettering the Senate.

³⁷ Question on Mʳ Ghorum's motion

Mas. ay. Conᵗ no. Pᵃ ay. Del. no. Mᵈ ay. Vᵃ ay. N. C. no. S. C. no. Geo. absent.³⁸

Mʳ MADISON moved that the Judges should be nominated by the Executive, & such nomination should become an appointment if not disagreed to within       days by ⅔ of the 2ᵈ branch Mʳ Govʳ MORRIS 2ᵈᵉᵈ the motion. By common consent the consideration of it was postponed till tomorrow.

"To hold their offices during good behavior" & "to receive fixed salaries" agreed to nem: con:

"In which [salaries of Judges] no increase or diminution shall be made so as to affect the persons at the time in office." ³⁹

Mʳ Govʳ MORRIS moved to strike out "or increase." He thought the Legislature ought to be at liberty to increase salaries as circumstances might require, and that this would not create any improper dependence in the Judges.

---

³⁶ In the transcript the vote reads: "Massachusetts, Pennsylvania, aye—2; Connecticut, Delaware, Maryland, Virginia, North Carolina, South Carolina, no—6; Georgia, absent."

³⁷ The words "On the" are here inserted in the transcript.

³⁸ In the transcript the vote reads: " Massachusetts, Pennsylvania, Maryland, Virginia, aye—4; Connecticut, Delaware, North Carolina, South Carolina, no—4; Georgia, absent."

³⁹ The phrase "actually in office at the time" is substituted in the transcript for "at the time in office."

Doc: FRANKLIN was in favor of the motion. Money may not only become plentier, but the business of the department may increase as the Country becomes more populous.

Mr MADISON. The dependence will be less if the *increase alone* should be permitted, but it will be improper even so far to permit a dependence  Whenever an increase is wished by the Judges, or may be in agitation in the legislature, an undue complaisance in the former may be felt towards the latter.  If at such a crisis there should be in Court suits, to which leading members of the Legislature may be parties, the Judges will be in a situation which ought not to [40] suffered, if it can be prevented.  The variations in the value of money, may be guarded ag:st by taking for a standard wheat or some other thing of permanent value. The increase of business will be provided for by an increase of the number who are to do it.  An increase of salaries may be easily so contrived as not to affect persons in office.

Mr Gov: MORRIS. The value of money may not only alter but the State of Society may alter.  In this event the same quantity of wheat, the same value would not be the same compensation. The Amount of salaries must always be regulated by the manners & the style of living in a Country.  The increase of business can not, be provided for in the supreme tribunal in the way that has been mentioned.  All the business of a certain description whether more or less must be done in that single tribunal. Additional labor alone in the Judges can provide for additional business.  Additional compensation therefore ought not to be prohibited.

On the question for striking out "or increase"

Mas. ay. Con:t ay. Pa. ay. Del. ay. Md ay. Va no. N. C. no. S. C. ay. Geo. absent.[41]

The whole clause as amended was then agreed to nem: con:

12. Resol:[42] "that[43] Nat! Legislature be empowered to appoint inferior tribunals"[44]

---

[40] The word "be" is here inserted in the transcript.
[41] In the transcript the vote reads: "Massachusetts, Connecticut, Pennsylvania, Delaware, Maryland, South Carolina, aye—6; Virginia, North Carolina, no—2; Georgia, absent."
[42] The words "The twelfth Resolution" are substituted in the transcript for "12. Resol."
[43] The word "the" is here inserted in the transcript.
[44] The words "being taken up" are here inserted in the transcript.

Mr. BUTLER could see no necessity for such tribunals. The State Tribunals might do the business.

Mr. L. MARTIN concurred. They will create jealousies & oppositions in the State tribunals, with the jurisdiction of which they will interfere.

Mr. GHORUM. There are in the States already federal Courts with jurisdiction for trial of piracies &c. committed on the Seas. No complaints have been made by the States or the Courts of the States. Inferior tribunals are essential to render the authority of the Natl. Legislature effectual

Mr. RANDOLPH observed that the Courts of the States can not be trusted with the administration of the National laws. The objects of jurisdiction are such as will often place the General & local policy at variance.

Mr. Govr. MORRIS urged also the necessity of such a provision

Mr. SHERMAN was willing to give the power to the Legislature but wished them to make use of the State Tribunals whenever it could be done, with safety to the general interest.

Col. MASON thought many circumstances might arise not now to be foreseen, which might render such a power absolutely necessary.

On [45] question for agreeing to 12. Resol: [46] empowering the National Legislature to appoint "inferior tribunals." [47] Agd. to· nem. con.

[48] 13. Resol: "Impeachments of national officers" were struck out" on motion for the purpose. "The jurisdiction of Natl. Judiciary." Several criticisms having been made on the definition; it was proposed by Mr. Madison so to alter [49] as to read thus— "that the jurisdiction shall extend to all cases arising under the Natl. laws: And to such other questions as may involve the Natl. peace & harmony," which was agreed to nem. con.

---

[45] The word "the" is here inserted in the transcript.
[46] The words "the twelfth Resolution" are substituted in the transcript for "12. Resol."
[47] The words "it was" are here inserted in the transcript.
[48] This paragraph is changed in the transcript to read as follows: "The clause of 'Impeachments of national officers,' was struck out, on motion for the purpose. The thirteenth Resolution, 'The jurisdiction of the National Judiciary, &c.' being then taken up, several . . .'"
[49] The word "it" is here inserted in the transcript.

Resol. 14.[50] providing for the admission of new States [51] Agreed to nem. con.

Resol. 15.[52] that provision ought to be made for the continuance of Cong⁑ &c. & for the completion of their engagements.[53]

Mr Govr MORRIS thought the assumption of their engagements might as well be omitted; and that Cong⁑ ought not to be continued till all the States should adopt the reform; since it may become expedient to give effect to it whenever a certain number of States shall adopt it.

Mr MADISON the clause can mean nothing more than that provision ought to be made for preventing an interregnum; which must exist in the interval between the adoption of the New Govt and the commencement of its operation, if the old Govt should cease on the first of these events.

Mr WILSON did not entirely approve of the manner in which the clause relating to the engagements of Cong⁑ was expressed; but he thought some provision on the subject would be proper in order to prevent any suspicion that the obligations of the Confederacy might be dissolved along with the Govern⁑ under which they were contracted.

On the question on the 1st part—relating to [54] continuance of Cong⁑"

Mas. no. Cont. no. Pa no. Del. no. Md no. Va ay. N. C. ay. S. C.* ay. Geo. no.[55]

The 2d part as to [54] completion of their engagements,[56] disagd to. nem. con.

Resol. 16.[57] "That a Republican Constitution & its existing laws ought to be guarantied to each State by the U. States." [58]

Mr Govr MORRIS—thought the Resol: very objectionable. He should be very unwilling that such laws as exist in R. Island should be guarantied.

---

[50] The words "The fourteenth Resolution" are substituted in the transcript for "Resol. 14."
[51] The word "was" is here inserted in the transcript.
[52] The words "The fifteenth Resolution" are substituted in the transcript for "Resol. 15."
[53] The words "being considered" are here inserted in the transcript.
[54] The word "the" is here inserted in the transcript.
* In the printed Journal, S. Carolina—no.
[55] In the transcript the vote reads: "Virginia, North Carolina, South Carolina,* aye—3; Massachusetts, Connecticut, Pennsylvania, Delaware, Maryland, Georgia, no—6."
[56] The word "was" is here inserted in the transcript.
[57] The words "The sixteenth Resolution" are substituted in the transcript for "Resol. 16."
[58] The words "being considered" are here added in the transcript.

M! WILSON. The object is merely to secure the States ag.ˢᵗ dangerous commotions, insurrections and rebellions.

Col. MASON. If the Gen! Gov! should have no right to suppress rebellions ag.ˢᵗ particular States, it will be in a bad situation indeed. As Rebellions ag.ˢᵗ itself originate in & ag.ˢᵗ individual States, it must remain a passive Spectator of its own subversion.

M! RANDOLPH. The Resol.ⁿ has 2. objects. 1.⁵⁹ to secure Republican Government. 2.⁵⁹ to suppress domestic commotions. He urged the necessity of both these provisions.

M! MADISON moved to substitute "that the Constitutional authority of the States shall be guarantied to them respectively ag.ˢᵗ domestic as well as foreign violence."

Doc! M°CLURG seconded the motion.

M! HOUSTON was afraid of perpetuating the existing Constitutions of the States. That of Georgia was a very bad one, and he hoped would be revised & amended. It may also be difficult for the Gen! Gov! to decide between contending parties each of which claim the sanction of the Constitution.

M! L. MARTIN was for leaving the States to suppress Rebellions themselves.

M! GHORUM thought it strange that a Rebellion should be known to exist in the Empire, and the Gen! Gov! sh.ᵈ be restrained from interposing to subdue it. At this rate an enterprising Citizen might erect the standard of Monarchy in a particular State, might gather together partizans from all quarters, might extend his views from State to State, and threaten to establish a tyranny over the whole & the Gen! Gov! be compelled to remain an inactive witness of its own destruction. With regard to different parties in a State; as long as they confine their disputes to words, they will be harmless to the Gen! Gov! & to each other. If they appeal to the sword, it will then be necessary for the Gen! Gov!, however difficult it may be to decide on the merits of their contest, to interpose & put an end to it.

M! CARROL. Some such provision is essential. Every State ought to wish for it. It has been doubted whether it is a casus federis at present. And no room ought to be left for such a doubt hereafter.

---

[59] The figures "1" and "2" are changed to "first" and "secondly" in the transcript.

Mʳ RANDOLPH moved to add as [60] amendᵗ to the motion; "and that no State be at liberty to form any other than a Republican Govᵗ Mʳ MADISON seconded the motion

Mʳ RUTLIDGE thought it unnecessary to insert any guarantee. No doubt could be entertained but that Congˢ had the authority if they had the means to co-operate with any State in subduing a rebellion. It was & would be involved in the nature of the thing.

Mʳ WILSON moved as a better expression of the idea, "that a Republican form of Governmᵗ shall be guaranteed to each State & that each State shall be protected agˢᵗ foreign & domestic violence.

This seeming to be well received, Mʳ MADISON & Mʳ RANDOLPH withdrew their propositions & on the Question for agreeing to Mʳ Wilson's motion, it passed nem. con.

Adjᵈ

THURSDAY. JULY 19. IN CONVENTION

On reconsideration of the vote rendering the Executive re-eligible a 2ᵈ time, Mʳ MARTIN moved to reinstate the words, "to be ineligible a 2ᵈ time."

Mʳ GOVERNEUR MORRIS. It is necessary to take into one view all that relates to the establishment of the Executive; on the due formation of which must depend the efficacy & utility of the Union among the present and future States. It has been a maxim in Political Science that Republican Government is not adapted to a large extent of Country, because the energy of the Executive Magistracy can not reach the extreme parts of it. Our Country is an extensive one. We must either then renounce the blessings of the Union, or provide an Executive with sufficient vigor to pervade every part of it. This subject was of so much importance that he hoped to be indulged in an extensive view of it. One great object of the Executive is to controul the Legislature. The Legislature will continually seek to aggrandize & perpetuate themselves; and will sieze those critical moments produced by war, invasion or convulsion for that purpose. It is necessary then that the Executive Magistrate should be the guardian of the people,

---

[60] The word "an" is here inserted in the transcript.

even of the lower classes, ag:t Legislative tyranny, against the Great & the wealthy who in the course of things will necessarily compose the Legislative body. Wealth tends to corrupt the mind & [61] to nourish its love of power, and to stimulate it to oppression. History proves this to be the spirit of the opulent. The check provided in the 2d branch was not meant as a check on Legislative usurpations of power, but on the abuse of lawful powers, on the propensity in [62] the 1st branch to legislate too much to run into projects of paper money & similar expedients. It is no check on Legislative tyranny. On the contrary it may favor it, and if the 1st branch can be seduced may find the means of success. The Executive therefore ought to be so constituted as to be the great protector of the Mass of the people.—It is the duty of the Executive to appoint the officers & to command the forces of the Republic: to appoint 1.[63] ministerial officers for the administration of public affairs. 2.[63] officers for the dispensation of Justice. Who will be the best Judges whether these appointments be well made? The people at large, who will know, will see, will feel the effects of them. Again who can judge so well of the discharge of military duties for the protection & security of the people, as the people themselves who are to be protected & secured?—He finds too that the Executive is not to be re-eligible. What effect will this have? 1.[64] it will destroy the great incitement to merit public esteem by taking away the hope of being rewarded with a reappointment. It may give a dangerous turn to one of the strongest passions in the human breast. The love of fame is the great spring to noble & illustrious actions. Shut the Civil road to Glory & he may be compelled to seek it by the sword. 2.[65] It will tempt him to make the most of the short space of time allotted him, to accumulate wealth and provide for his friends. 3.[66] It will produce violations of the very constitution it is meant to secure. In moments of pressing danger the tried abilities and established character of a favorite Magistrate will prevail over respect for the forms of the Constitution. The

---

[61] The word "and" is crossed out in the transcript.
[62] The word "of" is substituted in the transcript for "in."
[63] The figures "1" and "2" are changed to "first" and "secondly" in the transcript.
[64] The figure "1" is changed to "In the first place" in the transcript.
[65] The figure "2" is changed to "In the second place" in the transcript.
[66] The figure "3" is changed to "In the third place" in the transcript.

Executive is also to be impeachable. This is a dangerous part of the plan. It will hold him in such dependence that he will be no check on the Legislature, will not be a firm guardian of the people and of the public interest. He will be the tool of a faction, of some leading demagogue in the Legislature. These then are the faults of the Executive establishment as now proposed. Can no better establishm$^t$ be devised? If he is to be the Guardian of the people let him be appointed by the people? If he is to be a check on the Legislature let him not be impeachable. Let him be of short duration, that he may with propriety be re-eligible. It has been said that the candidates for this office will not be known to the people. If they be known to the Legislature, they must have such a notoriety and eminence of Character, that they can not possibly be unknown to the people at large. It cannot be possible that a man shall have sufficiently distinguished himself to merit this high trust without having his character proclaimed by fame throughout the Empire. As to the danger from an unimpeachable magistrate he could not regard it as formidable. There must be certain great officers of State; a minister of finance, of war, of foreign affairs &c. These he presumes will exercise their functions in subordination to the Executive, and will be amenable by impeachment to the public Justice. Without these ministers the Executive can do nothing of consequence. He suggested a biennial election of the Executive at the time of electing the 1$^{st}$ branch, and the Executive to hold over, so as to prevent any interregnum in the administration. An election by the people at large throughout so great an extent of country could not be influenced, by those little combinations and those momentary lies which often decide popular elections within a narrow sphere. It will probably, be objected that the election will be influenced by the members of the Legislature; particularly of the 1$^{st}$ branch, and that it will be nearly the same thing with an election by the Legislature itself. It could not be denied that such an influence would exist. But it might be answered that as the Legislature or the candidates for it would be divided, the enmity of one part would counteract the friendship of another: that if the administration of the Executive were good, it would be unpopular to oppose his reelection, if bad it ought to be opposed & a reappointm̃ prevented; and lastly that in every view this indirect dependence on the favor of the Legislature could not be so mischievous as a direct dependence for his appointment. He saw no alternative for making the Executive independent of the Legislature but either to give him his office for life, or make him eligible by the people— Again, it might be objected that two years would be too short a duration. But he believes that as long as he should behave himself well, he would be continued in his place. The extent of the Country would secure his re-election agṣt the factions & discontents of particular States. It deserved consideration also that such an ingredient in the plan would render it extremely palatable to the people. These were the general ideas which occurred to him on the subject, and which led him to wish & move that the whole constitution of the Executive might undergo reconsideration.

Mṛ RANDOLPH urged the motion of Mṛ L. Martin for restoring the words making the Executive ineligible a 2ḍ time. If he ought to be independent, he should not be left under a temptation to court a re-appointment. If he should be re-appointable by the Legislature, he will be no check on it. His revisionary power will be of no avail. He had always thought & contended as he still did that the danger apprehended by the little States was chimerical; but those who thought otherwise ought to be peculiarly anxious for the motion. If the Executive be appointed, as has been determined, by the Legislature, he will probably be appointed either by joint ballot of both houses, or be nominated by the 1ṣt and appointed by the 2ḍ branch. In either case the large States will preponderate. If he is to court the same influence for his re-appointment, will he not make his revisionary power, and all the other functions of his administration subservient to the views of the large States. Besides, is there not great reason to apprehend that in case he should be re-eligible, a false complaisance in the Legislature might lead them to continue an unfit man in office in preference to a fit one. It has been said that a constitutional bar to reappointment will inspire unconstitutional endeavours to perpetuate himself. It may be answered that his endeavours can have no effect unless the people be corrupt to such a degree as to render all precautions hopeless: to which may be added that this argument supposes him to be more powerful & dangerous, than other arguments which have been used, admit, and consequently calls for stronger fetters on his authority. He thought an election by the Legislature with an incapacity to be elected a second time would be more acceptable to the people that [67] the plan suggested by M: Gov: Morris.

M: KING. did not like the ineligibility. He thought there was great force in the remark [68] of M: Sherman, that he who has proved himself to be [69] most fit for an Office, ought not to be excluded by the constitution from holding it. He would therefore prefer any other reasonable plan that could be substituted. He was much disposed to think that in such cases the people at large would chuse wisely. There was indeed some difficulty arising from the improbability of a general concurrence of the people in favor of any one man. On the whole he was of opinion that an appointment by electors chosen by the people for the purpose, would be liable to fewest objections.

M: PATTERSON's ideas nearly coincided he said with those of M: King. He proposed that the Executive should be appointed by Electors to be chosen by the States in a ratio that would allow one elector to the smallest and three to the largest States.

M: WILSON. It seems to be the unanimous sense that the Executive should not be appointed by the Legislature, unless he be rendered in-eligible a 2ᵈ time: he perceived with pleasure that the idea was gaining ground, of an election mediately or immediately by the people.

M: MADISON. If it be a fundamental principle of free Gov: that the Legislative, Executive & Judiciary powers should be *separately* exercised, it is equally so that they be *independently* exercised. There is the same & perhaps greater reason why the Executive shᵈ be independent of the Legislature, than why the Judiciary should: A coalition of the two former powers would be

---

[67] The word "that" is changed to "than" in the transcript.
[68] The word "remark" is used in the plural in the transcript.
[69] The words "to be" are omitted in the transcript.

more immediately & certainly dangerous to public liberty. It is essential then that the appointment of the Executive should either be drawn from some source, or held by some tenure, that will give him a free agency with regard to the Legislature. This could not be if he was to be appointable from time to time by the Legislature. It was not clear that an appointment in the 1st instance even with an eligibility afterwards would not establish an improper connection between the two departments. Certain it was that the appointment would be attended with intrigues and contentions that ought not to be unnecessarily admitted. He was disposed for these reasons to refer the appointment to some other source. The people at large was in his opinion the fittest in itself. It would be as likely as any that could be devised to produce an Executive Magistrate of distinguished Character. The people generally could only know & vote for some Citizen whose merits had rendered him an object of general attention & esteem. There was one difficulty however of a serious nature attending an immediate choice by the people. The right of suffrage was much more diffusive in the Northern than the Southern States; and the latter could have no influence in the election on the score of the Negroes. The substitution of electors obviated this difficulty and seemed on the whole to be liable to fewest objections.

Mr GERRY. If the Executive is to be elected by the Legislature he certainly ought not to be re-eligible. This would make him absolutely dependent. He was agst a popular election. The people are uninformed, and would be misled by a few designing men. He urged the expediency of an appointment of the Executive by Electors to be chosen by the State Executives. The people of the States will then choose the 1st branch: The legislatures of the States the 2d branch of the National Legislature, and the Executives of the States, the National Executive. This he thought would form a strong attachnt in the States to the National System. The popular mode of electing the chief Magistrate would certainly be the worst of all. If he should be so elected & should do his duty, he will be turned out for it like Govr Bowdoin in Massts & President Sullivan in N. Hamshire.

On the question on M: Gov: Morris motion to reconsider generally the constitution of the Executive.

Mas. ay.   C: ay.   N. J. ay & all the others ay.[70]

M: ELSEWORTH moved to strike out the appointm: by the Nat! Legislature, and [71] insert " to be chosen by electors appointed, by the Legislatures of the States in the following ratio; towit— one for each State not exceeding 200,000 inhab:: two for each above y: number & not exceeding 300,000. and three for each State exceeding 300,000.—M: BROOME 2ded the motion

M: RUTLIDGE was opposed to all the modes except the appointm: by the Nat! Legislature. He will be sufficiently independent, if he be not re-eligible.

M: GERRY preferred the motion of M: Elseworth to an appointm: by the Nat! Legislature, or by the people; tho' not to an app: by the State Executives. He moved that the electors proposed by M: E. should be 25 in number, and allotted in the following proportion. to N. H. 1. to Mas. 3. to R. I. 1. to Con: 2. to N. Y. 2.[72] N. J. 2. [72] P:ª 3. [72] Del. 1. [72] M:d 2. [72] V:ª 3. [72] N. C. 2. [72] S. C. 2. [72] Geo. 1.

The question as moved by M: Elseworth being divided, on the 1:st part shall y:e Nat! Executive be appointed by Electors?

Mas. div:d Con: ay.   N. J. ay.   P:ª ay.   Del. ay.   M:d ay.   V:ª ay.   N. C. no.   S. C. no.   Geo. no.[73]

On [74] 2:d part shall the Electors be chosen by [74] State Legislatures?

Mas. ay.   Con: ay.   N. J. ay.   P:ª ay.   Del. ay.   M:d ay.   V:ª no.   N. C. ay.   S. C. no.   Geo. ay.[75]

The part relating to the ratio in which the States s:d chuse electors was postponed nem. con.

M: L. MARTIN moved that the Executive be ineligible a 2:d time.

M: WILLIAMSON 2:d: the motion. He had no great confidence in the Electors to be chosen for the special purpose. They would

---

[70] In the transcript the vote reads: "Massachusetts, Connecticut, New Jersey, and all the others, aye."

[71] The word "to" is here inserted in the transcript.

[72] The word "to" is here inserted in the transcript.

[73] In the transcript the vote reads: "Connecticut, New Jersey, Pennsylvania, Delaware, Maryland, Virginia, aye—6; North Carolina, South Carolina, Georgia, no—3; Massachusetts, divided."

[74] The word "the" is here inserted in the transcript.

[75] In the transcript the vote reads: "Massachusetts, Connecticut, New Jersey, Pennsylvania, Delaware, Maryland, North Carolina, Georgia, aye—8; Virginia, South Carolina, no—2."

not be the most respectable citizens; but persons not occupied in the high offices of Gov!. They would be liable to undue influence, which might the more readily be practised as some of them will probably be in appointment 6 or 8 months before the object of it comes on.

M! ELSEWORTH supposed any persons might be appointed Electors, excepting [76] solely, members of the Nat! Legislature.

On the question shall he be ineligible a 2ᵈ time?

Mas. no. C! no. N. J. no. P? no. Del. no. Mᵈ no. Vᵃ no. N. C. ay. S. C. ay. Geo. no.[77]

On the question Shall the Executive continue for 7 years? It passed in the negative

Mas. divᵈ Con! ay.* N. J. no.* P? no. Del. no. Mᵈ no. Vᵃ no. N. C. divᵈ S. C. ay. Geo. ay.[78]

M! KING was afraid we shᵈ shorten the term too much.

M! Gov! MORRIS was for a short term, in order to avoid impeach!? which wᵈ be otherwise necessary.

M! BUTLER was ag?! a [79] frequency of the elections. Geo. & S. C. were too distant to send electors often.

M! ELSEWORTH was for 6. years. If the elections be too frequent, the Executive will not be firm eno'. There must be duties which will make him unpopular for the moment. There will be *outs* as well as *ins*. His administration therefore will be attacked and misrepresented.

M! WILLIAMSON was for 6 years. The expence will be considerable & ought not to be unnecessarily repeated. If the Elections are too frequent, the best men will not undertake the service and those of an inferior character will be liable to be corrupted.

On [80] question for 6 years?

Mas. ay. Con! ay. N. J. ay. Pᵃ ay. Del. no. Mᵈ ay. V? ay. N. C. ay. S. C. ay. Geo. ay.[81]

Adjourned

---

[76] The word "except" is substituted in the transcript for "excepting."

[77] In the transcript the vote reads: "North Carolina, South Carolina, aye—2; Massachusetts, Connecticut, New Jersey, Pennsylvania, Delaware, Maryland, Virginia, Georgia, no—8."

* in the printed Journal Con!, no: N. Jersey ay

[78] In the transcript the vote reads: "Connecticut,* South Carolina, Georgia, aye—3; New Jersey,* Pennsylvania, Delaware, Maryland, Virginia, no—5; Massachusetts, North Carolina, divided."

[79] The word "the" is substituted in the transcript for "a."

[80] The word "the" is here inserted in the transcript.

[81] In the transcript the vote reads: "Massachusetts, Connecticut, New Jersey, Pennsylvania, Maryland, Virginia, North Carolina, South Carolina, Georgia, aye—9; Delaware, no."

## Friday July 20. in Convention

The postponed [82] Ratio of Electors for appointing the Executive; to wit 1 for each State whose inhabitants do not exceed 100,000,[83] &c. being taken up.

Mr. MADISON observed that this would make in time all or nearly all the States equal. Since there were few that would not in time contain the number of inhabitants intitling them to 3 Electors: that this ratio ought either to be made temporary, or so varied as that it would adjust itself to the growing population of the States.

Mr. GERRY moved that in the *1st instance* the Electors should be allotted to the States in the following ratio: to N. H. 1. Mas. 3. R. I. 1. Cont. 2. N. Y. 2. N. J. 2. Pa. 3. Del. 1. Md. 2. Va. 3. N. C. 2. S. C. 2. Geo. 1.

On the question to postpone in order to take up this motion of Mr. Gerry. It passed in the affirmative.

Mas. ay. Cont. no. N. J. no. Pa. ay. Del. no. Md. no. Va. ay. N. C. ay. S. C. ay. Geo. ay.[84]

Mr. ELSEWORTH moved that 2 Electors be allotted to N. H. Some rule ought to be pursued; and N. H. has more than 100,000 inhabitants. He thought it would be proper also to allot 2. to Georgia

Mr. BROOM & Mr. MARTIN moved to postpone Mr. Gerry's allotment of Electors, leaving a fit ratio to be reported by the Committee to be appointed for detailing the Resolutions.

On this motion.

Mas. no. Ct. no. N. J. ay. Pa. no. Del. ay. Md. ay. Va. no. N. C. no. S. C. no. Geo. no.[85]

Mr. HOUSTON 2ded the motion of Mr. Elseworth to add another Elector to N. H. & Georgia. On the Question:

Mas. no. Ct. ay. N. J. no. Pa. no. Del. no. Md. no. Va. no. N. C. no. S. C. ay. Geo. ay.[86]

---

[82] The word "proposed" is substituted in the transcript for "postponed."

[83] In the figure "100,000" the "1" is crossed out and a figure "2" is written above it in the transcript

[84] In the transcript the vote reads: "Massachusetts, Pennsylvania, Virginia, North Carolina, South Carolina, Georgia, aye—6; Connecticut, New Jersey, Delaware, Maryland, no—4."

[85] In the transcript the vote reads: "New Jersey, Delaware, Maryland, aye—3; Massachusetts, Connecticut, Pennsylvania, Virginia, North Carolina, South Carolina, Georgia, no—7."

[86] In the transcript the vote reads: "Connecticut, South Carolina, Georgia, aye—3; Massachusetts, New Jersey, Pennsylvania, Delaware, Maryland, Virginia, North Carolina, no—7."

Mr WILLIAMSON moved as an amendment to Mr Gerry's allotment of Electors in the 1st instance that in future elections of the Natl Executive, the number of Electors to be appointed by the several States shall be regulated by their respective numbers of Representatives in the 1st branch pursuing as nearly as may be the present proportions.

On question on Mr Gerry's ratio of Electors

Mas. ay. Ct ay. N. J. no. Pa ay. Del. no. Md no. Va ay. N. C. ay. S. C. ay. Geo. no.[87]

[88] "to be removeable on impeachment and conviction for mal practice or neglect of duty." see Resol: 9.[89]

Mr PINKNEY & Mr Govr MORRIS moved to strike out this part of the Resolution. Mr P. observd he ought not to be impeachable whilst in office

Mr DAVIE. If he be not impeachable whilst in office, he will spare no efforts or means whatever to get himself re-elected. He considered this as an essential security for the good behaviour of the Executive.

Mr WILSON concurred in the necessity of making the Executive impeachable whilst in office.

Mr Govr MORRIS. He can do no criminal act without Coadjutors who may be punished. In case he should be re-elected, that will be [90] sufficient proof of his innocence. Besides who is to impeach? Is the impeachment to suspend his functions. If it is not the mischief will go on. If it is the impeachment will be nearly equivalent to a displacement, and will render the Executive dependent on those who are to impeach

Col. MASON. No point is of more importance than that the right of impeachment should be continued. Shall any man be above Justice? Above all shall that man be above it, who can commit the most extensive injustice? When great crimes were committed he was for punishing the principal as well as the Coadjutors. There had been much debate & difficulty as to the mode of chusing

---

[87] In the transcript the vote reads: "Massachusetts, Connecticut, Pennsylvania, Virginia, North Carolina, South Carolina, aye—6; New Jersey, Delaware, Maryland, Georgia, no—4."
[88] The words "On the clause" are here inserted in the transcript.
[89] The words "the ninth Resolution" are substituted in the transcript for "Resol: 9."
[90] The word "a" is here inserted in the transcript.

the Executive. He approved of that which had been adopted at first, namely of referring the appointment to the Nat! Legislature. One objection ag:^t Electors was the danger of their being corrupted by the Candidates; & this furnished a peculiar reason in favor of impeachments whilst in office. Shall the man who has practised corruption & by that means procured his appointment in the first instance, be suffered to escape punishment, by repeating his guilt?

Doc:^r FRANKLIN was for retaining the clause as favorable to the Executive. History furnishes one example only of a first Magistrate being formally brought to public Justice. Every body cried out ag:^t this as unconstitutional. What was the practice before this in cases where the chief Magistrate rendered himself obnoxious? Why recourse was had to assassination in w^ch he was not only deprived of his life but of the opportunity of vindicating his character. It w:^d be the best way therefore to provide in the Constitution for the regular punishment of the Executive where his misconduct should deserve it, and for his honorable acquittal when [91] he should be unjustly accused.

M:^r Gov:^r MORRIS admits corruption & some few other offences to be such as ought to be impeachable; but thought the cases ought to be enumerated & defined:

M:^r MADISON thought it indispensable that some provision should be made for defending the Community ag:^t the incapacity, negligence or perfidy of the chief Magistrate. The limitation of the period of his service, was not a sufficient security. He might lose his capacity after his appointment. He might pervert his administration into a scheme of peculation or oppression. He might betray his trust to foreign powers. The case of the Executive Magistracy was very distinguishable, from that of the Legislature or of any other public body, holding offices of limited duration. It could not be presumed that all or even a majority of the members of an Assembly would either lose their capacity for discharging, or be bribed to betray, their trust. Besides the restraints of their personal integrity & honor, the difficulty of acting in concert for purposes of corruption was a security to the

---

[91] The word "where" is substituted in the transcript for "when."

public. And if one or a few members only should be seduced, the soundness of the remaining members, would maintain the integrity and fidelity of the body. In the case of the Executive Magistracy which was to be administered by a single man, loss of capacity or corruption was more within the compass of probable events, and either of them might be fatal to the Republic.

M？ PINKNEY did not see the necessity of impeachments. He was sure they ought not to issue from the Legislature who would in that case hold them as a rod over the Executive and by that means effectually destroy his independence. His revisionary power in particular would be rendered altogether insignificant.

M？ GERRY urged the necessity of impeachments. A good magistrate will not fear them. A bad one ought to be kept in fear of them. He hoped the maxim would never be adopted here that the chief magistrate could do no wrong.

M？ KING expressed his apprehensions that an extreme caution in favor of liberty might enervate the Government we were forming. He wished the House to recur to the primitive axiom that the three great departments of Gov$^{t}$? should be separate & independent: that the Executive & Judiciary should be so as well as the Legislative: that the Executive should be so equally with the Judiciary. Would this be the case, if the Executive should be impeachable? It had been said that the Judiciary would be impeachable. But it should have been remembered at the same time that the Judiciary hold their places not for a limited time, but during good behaviour. It is necessary therefore that a forum should be established for trying misbehaviour. Was the Executive to hold his place during good behaviour? The Executive was to hold his place for a limited term like the members of the Legislature: Like them particularly the Senate whose members would continue in appointm$^{t}$ the same term of 6 years he would periodically be tried for his behaviour by his electors, who would continue or discontinue him in trust according to the manner in which he had discharged it. Like them therefore, he ought to be subject to no intermediate trial, by impeachment. He ought not to be impeachable unless he held his office during good behaviour, a tenure which would be most agreeable to him; provided an independent and effectual forum could be devised. But under no circumstances ought he to be impeachable by the Legislature. This would be destructive of his independence and of the principles of the Constitution. He relied on the vigor of the Executive as a great security for the public liberties.

Mr RANDOLPH. The propriety of impeachments was a favorite principle with him. Guilt wherever found ought to be punished. The Executive will have great opportunitys of abusing his power; particularly in time of war when the military force, and in some respects the public money will be in his hands. Should no regular punishment be provided, it will be irregularly inflicted by tumults & insurrections. He is aware of the necessity of proceeding with a cautious hand, and of excluding as much as possible the influence of the Legislature from the business. He suggested for consideration an idea which had fallen [from Col Hamilton] of composing a forum out of the Judges belonging to the States: and even of requiring some preliminary inquest whether just grounds [92] of impeachment existed.

Doctr FRANKLIN mentioned the case of the Prince of Orange during the late war. An agreement was made between France & Holland; by which their two fleets were to unite at a certain time & place. The Dutch fleet did not appear. Every body began to wonder at it. At length it was suspected that the Statholder was at the bottom of the matter. This suspicion prevailed more & more. Yet as he could not be impeached and no regular examination took place, he remained in his office, and strengthening his own party, as the party opposed to him became formidable, he gave birth to the most violent animosities & contentions. Had he been impeachable, a regular & peaceable enquiry would have taken place and he would if guilty have been duly punished, if innocent restored to the confidence of the public.

Mr KING remarked that the case of the Statholder was not applicable. He held his place for life, and was not periodically elected. In the former case impeachments are proper to secure good behaviour. In the latter they are unnecessary; the periodical responsibility to the electors being an equivalent security.

---

[92] The transcript uses the word "grounds" in the singular.

GEORGE WASHINGTON

Mr WILSON observed that if the idea were to be pursued, the Senators who are to hold their places during the same term with the Executive, ought to be subject to impeachment & removal.

Mr PINKNEY apprehended that some gentlemen reasoned on a supposition that the Executive was to have powers which would not be committed to him: He presumed that his powers would be so circumscribed as to render impeachments unnecessary.

Mr Govr MORRIS's opinion had been changed by the arguments used in the discussion. He was now sensible of the necessity of impeachments, if the Executive was to continue for any [93] time in office. Our Executive was not like a Magistrate having a life interest, much less like one having an hereditary interest in his office. He may be bribed by a greater interest to betray his trust; and no one would say that we ought to expose ourselves to the danger of seeing the first Magistrate in forign pay, without being able to guard agst it by displacing him. One would think the King of England well secured agst bribery. He has as it were a fee simple in the whole Kingdom. Yet Charles II was bribed by Louis XIV. The Executive ought therefore to be impeachable for treachery; Corrupting his electors, and incapacity were other causes of impeachment. For the latter he should be punished not as a man, but as an officer, and punished only by degradation from his office. This Magistrate is not the King but the prime-Minister. The people are the King. When we make him amenable to Justice however we should take care to provide some mode that will not make him dependent on the Legislature.

It was moved & 2ded to postpone the question of impeachments which was negatived. Mas. & S. Carolina only being ay.

On ye Question, Shall the Executive be removeable on impeachments &c.?

Mas. no. Ct ay. N. J. ay. Pa ay. Del ay. Md ay. Va ay. N. C. ay. S. C. no. Geo. ay.[94]

"[95] Executive to receive fixed compensation." Agreed to nem. con.

---

[93] The words "length of" are here inserted in the transcript.
[94] In the transcript the vote reads: "Connecticut, New Jersey, Pennsylvania, Delaware, Maryland, Virginia, North Carolina, Georgia, aye—8; Massachusetts, South Carolina, no—2."
[95] The word "The" is here inserted in the transcript.

"to be paid out of the National Treasury" agreed to, N. Jersey only in the negative.

M! GERRY & [96] Gov! MORRIS moved "that the Electors of the Executive shall not be members of the Nat! Legislature, nor officers of the U. States, nor shall the Electors themselves be eligible to the supreme magistracy." Agreed to nem. con.

Doc! M?CLURG asked whether it would not be necessary, before a Committee for detailing the Constitution should be appointed, to determine on the means by which the Executive is to carry the laws into effect, and to resist combinations ag:t them. Is he to have a military force for the purpose, or to have the command of the Militia, the only existing force that can be applied to that use? As the Resolutions now stand the Committee will have no determinate directions on this great point.

M! WILSON thought that some additional directions to the Committee w? be necessary.

M! KING. The Committee are to provide for the end. Their discretionary power to provide for the means is involved according to an established axiom.

Adjourned

SATURDAY JULY '21 IN CONVENTION

M! WILLIAMSON moved that the Electors of the Executive should be paid out of the National Treasury for the Service to be performed by them." Justice required this: as it was a national service they were to render. The motion was agreed to Nem. Con.

M! WILSON moved as an amendment to Resol? 10.[97] that the supreme Nat! Judiciary should be associated with the Executive in the Revisionary power." This proposition had been before made and failed: but he was so confirmed by reflection in the opinion of its utility, that he thought it incumbent on him to make another effort: The Judiciary ought to have an opportunity of remonstrating ag:t projected encroachments on the people as well as on themselves. It had been said that the Judges, as expositors of the Laws would have an opportunity of defending

---

[96] The word "Mr." is here inserted in the transcript.
[97] The words "the tenth Resolution" are substituted for "Resol? 10."

their constitutional rights. There was weight in this observation; but this power of the Judges did not go far enough. Laws may be unjust, may be unwise, may be dangerous, may be destructive; and yet may not be so unconstitutional as to justify the Judges in refusing to give them effect. Let them have a share in the Revisionary power, and they will have an opportunity of taking notice of these [98] characters of a law, and of counteracting, by the weight of their opinions the improper views of the Legislature.—

M? MADISON 2<sup>d</sup>?<sup>d</sup> the motion

M? GHORUM did not see the advantage of employing the Judges in this way. As Judges they are not to be presumed to possess any peculiar knowledge of the mere policy of public measures. Nor can it be necessary as a security for their consitutional rights. The Judges in England have no such additional provision for their defence, yet their jurisdiction is not invaded. He thought it would be best to let the Executive alone be responsilbe, and at most to authorize him to call on [99] Judges for their opinions.

M? ELSEWORTH approved heartily of the motion. The aid of the Judges will give more wisdom & firmness to the Executive. They will possess a systematic and accurate knowledge of the Laws, which the Executive can not be expected always to possess. The law of Nations also will frequently come into question. Of this the Judges alone will have competent information.

M? MADISON considered the object of the motion as of great importance to the meditated Constitution. It would be useful to the Judiciary departm<sup>t</sup> by giving it an additional opportunity of defending itself ag<sup>st</sup> Legislative encroachments; It would be useful to the Executive, by inspiring additional confidence & firmness in exerting the revisionary power: It would be useful to the Legislature by the valuable assistance it would give in preserving a consistency, conciseness, perspicuity & technical propriety in the laws, qualities peculiarly necessary; & yet shamefully wanting in our republican Codes. It would moreover be useful to the Community at large as an additional check ag<sup>st</sup> a pursuit of those unwise & unjust measures which constituted so great a portion of our calamities. If any solid objection could be urged ag<sup>st</sup> the motion,

---
[98] The word "those" is substituted in the transcript for "these."
[99] The word "the" is here inserted in the transcript.

it must be on the supposition that it tended to give too much strength either to the Executive or Judiciary. He did not think there was the least ground for this apprehension. It was much more to be apprehended that notwithstanding this co-operation of the two departments, the Legislature would still be an overmatch for them. Experience in all the States had evinced a powerful tendency in the Legislature to absorb all power into its vortex. This was the real source of danger to the American Constitutions; & suggested the necessity of giving every defensive authority to the other departments that was consistent with republican principles.

M: MASON said he had always been a friend to this provision. It would give a confidence to the Executive, which he would not otherwise have, and without which the Revisionary power would be of little avail.

M: GERRY did not expect to see this point which had undergone full discussion, again revived. The object he conceived of the Revisionary power was merely to secure the Executive department ag$^{st}$ legislative encroachment. The Executive therefore who will best know and be ready to defend his rights ought alone to have the defence of them. The motion was liable to strong objections. It was combining & mixing together the Legislative & the other departments. It was establishing an improper coalition between the Executive & Judiciary departments. It was making Statesmen of the Judges; and setting them up as the guardians of the Rights of the people. He relied for his part on the Representatives of the people as the guardians of their Rights & interests. It was making the Expositors of the Laws, the Legislators which ought never to be done. A better expedient for correcting the laws, would be to appoint as had been done in Pen$^a$ a person or persons of proper skill, to draw bills for the Legislature.

M: STRONG thought with M: Gerry that the power of making ought to be kept distinct from that of expounding, the laws. No maxim was better established. The Judges in exercising the function of expositors might be influenced by the part they had taken, in framing [1] the laws.

---

[1] The word "passing" is substituted in the transcript for "framing."

Mʳ Govʳ Morris. Some check being necessary on the Legislature, the question is in what hands it should be lodged. On one side it was contended that the Executive alone ought to exercise it. He did not think that an Executive appointed for 6 years, and impeachable whilst in office wᵈ be a very effectual check. On the other side it was urged that he ought to be reinforced by the Judiciary department. Agˢᵗ this it was objected that Expositors of laws ought to have no hand in making them, and arguments in favor of this had been drawn from England. What weight was due to them might be easily determined by an attention to facts. The truth was that the Judges in England had a great share in yᵉ Legislation. They are consulted in difficult & doubtful cases. They may be & some of them are members of the Legislature. They are or may be members of the privy Council, and can there advise the Executive as they will do with us if the motion succeeds. The influence the English Judges may have in the latter capacity in strengthening the Executive check can not be ascertained, as the King by his influence in a manner dictates the laws. There is one difference in the two Cases however which disconcerts all reasoning from the British to our proposed Constitution. The British Executive has so great an interest in his prerogatives and such powerful means of defending them that he will never yield any part of them. The interest of our Executive is so inconsiderable & so transitory, and his means of defending it so feeble, that there is the justest ground to fear his want of firmness in resisting incroachments. He was extremely apprehensive that the auxiliary firmness & weight of the Judiciary would not supply the deficiency. He concurred in thinking the public liberty in greater danger from Legislative usurpations than from any other source. It had been said that the Legislature ought to be relied on as the proper Guardians of liberty. The answer was short and conclusive. Either bad laws will be pushed or not. On the latter supposition no check will be wanted. On the former a strong check will be necessary: And this is the proper supposition. Emissions of paper money, largesses to the people—a remission of debts and similar measures, will at some times be popular, and will be pushed for that reason At other times such measures will coincide with the interests of the Legislature themselves, & that will be a reason not less cogent for pushing them. It may be thought that the people will not be deluded and misled in the latter case. But experience teaches another lesson. The press is indeed a great means of diminishing the evil, yet it is found to be unable to prevent it altogether.

M: L. MARTIN. Considered the association of the Judges with the Executive as a dangerous innovation; as well as one which [2] could not produce the particular advantage expected from it. A knowledge of Mankind, and of Legislative affairs cannot be presumed to belong in a higher deger degree to the Judges than to the Legislature. And as to the Constitutionality of laws, that point will come before the Judges in their proper [3] official character. In this character they have a negative on the laws. Join them with the Executive in the Revision and they will have a double negative. It is necessary that the Supreme Judiciary should have the confidence of the people. This will soon be lost, if they are employed in the task of remonstrating ag$^{st}$ popular measures of the Legislature. Besides in what mode & proportion are they to vote in the Council of Revision?

M: MADISON could not discover in the proposed association of the Judges with the Executive in the Revisionary check on the Legislature any violation of the maxim which requires the great departments of power to be kept separate & distinct. On the contrary he thought it an auxiliary precaution in favor of the maxim. If a Constitutional discrimination of the departments on paper were a sufficient security to each ag$^{st}$ encroachments of the others, all further provisions would indeed be superfluous. But experience had taught us a distrust of that security; and that it is necessary to introduce such a balance of powers and interests, as will guarantee the provisions on paper. Instead therefore of contenting ourselves with laying down the Theory in the Constitution that each department ought to be separate & distinct, it was proposed to add a defensive power to each which should maintain the Theory in practice. In so doing we did not blend the departments

---

[2] The word "that" is substituted in the transcript for "which."
[3] The word "proper" is omitted in the transcript.

together. We erected effectual barriers for keeping them separate. The most regular example of this theory was in the British Constitution. Yet it was not only the practice there to admit the Judges to a seat in the legislature, and in the Executive Councils, and to submit to their previous examination all laws of a certain description, but it was a part of their Constitution that the Executive might negative any law whatever; a part of *their* Constitution which had been universally regarded as calculated for the preservation of the whole. The objection ag$^{st}$ a union of the Judiciary & Executive branches in the revision of the laws, had either no foundation or was not carried far enough. If such a Union was an improper mixture of powers, or such a Judiciary check on the laws, was inconsistent with the Theory of a free Constitution, it was equally so to admit the Executive to any participation in the making of laws; and the revisionary plan ought to be discarded altogether.

Col. MASON Observed that the defence of the Executive was not the sole object of the Revisionary power. He expected even greater advantages from it. Notwithstanding the precautions taken in the Constitution of the Legislature, it would still so much resemble that of the individual States, that it must be expected frequently to pass unjust and pernicious laws. This restraining power was therefore essentially necessary. It would have the effect not only of hindering the final passage of such laws; but would discourage demagogues from attempting to get them passed. It had been said [by M$^r$ L. Martin] that if the Judges were joined in this check on the laws, they would have a double negative, since in their expository capacity of Judges they would have one negative. He would reply that in this capacity they could impede in one case only, the operation of laws. They could declare an unconstitutional law void. But with regard to every law however unjust oppressive or pernicious, which [4] did not come plainly under this description, they would be under the necessity as Judges to give it a free course. He wished the further use to be made of the Judges, of giving aid in preventing every improper

---

[4] The word "that" is substituted in the transcript for "which."

law. Their aid will be the more valuable as they are in the habit and practice of considering laws in their true principles, and in all their consequences.

Mr WILSON. The separation of the departments does not require that they should have separate objects but that they should act separately tho' on the same objects. It is necessary that the two branches of the Legislature should be separate and distinct, yet they are both to act precisely on the same object.

Mr GERRY had rather give the Executive an absolute negative for its own defence than thus to blend together the Judiciary & Executive departments. It will bind them together in an offensive and defensive alliance agst the Legislature, and render the latter unwilling to enter into a contest with them.

Mr Govr MORRIS was surprised that any defensive provision for securing the effectual separation of the departments should be considered as an improper mixture of them. Suppose that the three powers, were to be vested in three persons, by compact among themselves; that one was to have the power of making, another of executing, and a third of judging, the laws. Would it not be very natural for the two latter after having settled the partition on paper, to observe, and would not candor oblige the former to admit, that as a security agst legislative acts of the former which might easily be so framed as to undermine the powers of the two others, the two others ought to be armed with a veto for their own defence, or at least to have an opportunity of stating their objections agst acts of encroachment? And would any one pretend that such a right tended to blend & confound powers that ought to be separately exercised? As well might it be said that If three neighbours had three distinct farms, a right in each to defend his farm agst his neighbours, tended to blend the farms together.

Mr GHORUM. All agree that a check on the Legislature is necessary. But there are two objections agst admitting the Judges to share in it which no observations on the other side seem to obviate. the 1st is that the Judges ought to carry into the exposition of the laws no prepossessions with regard to them.

⁵ 2ᵈ that as the Judges will outnumber the Executive, the revisionary check would be thrown entirely out of the Executive hands, and instead of enabling him to defend himself, would enable the Judges to sacrifice him.

Mʳ WILSON. The proposition is certainly not liable to all the objections which have been urged agˢᵗ it. According [to Mʳ Gerry] it will unite the Executive & Judiciary in an offensive & defensive alliance agˢᵗ the Legislature. According to Mʳ Ghorum it will lead to a subversion of the Executive by the Judiciary influence. To the first gentleman the answer was obvious; that the joint weight of the two departments was necessary to balance the single weight of the Legislature. To the 1ˢᵗ objection stated by the other Gentleman it might be answered that supposing the prepossion to mix itself with the exposition, the evil would be overbalanced by the advantages promised by the expedient. To the 2ᵈ objection, that such a rule of voting might be provided in the detail as would guard agˢᵗ it.

Mʳ RUTLIDGE thought the Judges of all men the most unfit to be concerned in the revisionary Council. The Judges ought never to give their opinion on a law till it comes before them. He thought it equally unnecessary. The Executive could advise with the officers of State, as of war, finance &c. and avail himself of their information & opinions.

On ⁵ Question on Mʳ Wilson's motion for joining the Judiciary in the Revision of laws it passed in the negative—

Mas. no. Conᵗ ay. N. J. not present. Pᵃ divᵈ Del. no. Mᵈ ay. Vᵃ ay. N. C. no. S. C. no. Geo. divᵈ ⁶

Resol. 10, giving the Ex. a qualified veto, without the amendᵗ was then agᵈ to nem. con.⁷

The motion made by Mʳ Madison July 18.⁸ & then postponed, 'that the Judges shᵈ be nominated by the Executive & such nominations become appointments unless disagreed to by ⅔ of the 2ᵈ branch of the Legislature," was now resumed.

---

⁵ The word "the" is here inserted in the transcript.

⁶ In the transcript the vote reads: "Connecticut, Maryland, Virginia, aye—3; Massachusetts, Delaware, North Carolina, South Carolina, no—4; Pennsylvania, Georgia, divided; New Jersey, not present."

⁷ This sentence has been changed in the transcript to read as follows: "The tenth Resolution, giving the Executive a qualified veto, requiring two-thirds of each branch of the Legislature to overrule it was then agreed to *nem. con.*"

⁸ The date "July 18" is changed in the transcript to "on the eighteenth of July."

M̲r̲ MADISON stated as his reasons for the motion. 1.⁹ that it secured the responsibility of the Executive who would in general be more capable & likely to select fit characters than the Legislature, or even the 2ᵈ b. of it, who might hide their selfish motives under the number concerned in the appointment.—2.⁹ that in case of any flagrant partiality or error, in the nomination it might be fairly presumed that ⅔ of the 2ᵈ branch would join in putting a negative on it. 3.⁹ that as the 2ᵈ b. was very differently constituted when the appointment of the Judges was formerly referred to it, and was now to be composed of equal votes from all the States, the principle of compromise which had prevailed in other instances required in this that their shᵈ be a concurrence of two authorities, in one of which the people, in the other the States, should be represented. The Executive Magistrate wᵈ be considered as a national officer, acting for and equally sympathising with every part of the U. States. If the 2ᵈ branch alone should have this power, the Judges might be appointed by a minority of the people, tho' by a majority, of the States, which could not be justified on any principle as their proceedings were to relate to the people, rather than to the States: and as it would moreover throw the appointments entirely into the hands of yᵉ Northern States, a perpetual ground of jealousy & discontent would be furnished to the Southern States.

M̲r̲ PINKNEY was for placing the appointmᵗ in the 2ᵈ b. exclusively. The Executive will possess neither the requisite knowledge of characters, nor confidence of the people for so high a trust.

M̲r̲ RANDOLPH wᵈ have preferred the mode of appointmᵗ proposed formerly by M̲r̲ Ghorum, as adopted in the Constitution of Massᵗˢ but thought the motion depending so great an improvement of the clause as it stands, that he anxiously wished it success. He laid great stress on the responsibility of the Executive as a security for fit appointments. Appointments by the Legislatures have generally resulted from cabal, from personal regard, or some other consideration than a title derived from the proper qualifications. The same inconveniencies will proportionally prevail, if the appointments be be referred to either branch of the Legislature or to any other authority administered by a number of individuals.

---

⁹ The figures "1," "2" and "3" are changed to "first," "Secondly" and "Thirdly" in the transcript.

431

M: ELSEWORTH would prefer a negative in the Executive on a nomination by the 2ᵈ branch, the negative to be overruled by a concurrence of ⅔ of the 2ᵈ b. to the mode proposed by the motion; but preferred an absolute appointment by the 2ᵈ branch to either. The Executive will be regarded by the people with a jealous eye. Every power for augmenting unnecessarily his influence will be disliked. As he will be stationary it was not to be supposed he could have a better knowledge of characters. He will be more open to caresses & intrigues than the Senate. The right to supersede his nomination will be ideal only. A nomination under such circumstances will be equivalent to an appointment.

M: GOV: MORRIS supported the motion. 1.¹⁰ The States in their corporate capacity will frequently have an interest staked on the determination of the Judges. As in the Senate the States are to vote the Judges ought not to be appointed by the Senate. Next to the impropriety of being Judge in one's own cause, is the appointment of the Judge. 2.¹⁰ It had been said the Executive would be uninformed of characters. The reverse was yᵉ truth. The Senate will be so. They must take the character of candidates from the flattering pictures drawn by their friends. The Executive in the necessary intercourse with every part of the U. S. required by the nature of his administration, will or may have the best possible information. 3.¹⁰ It had been said that a jealousy would be entertained of the Executive. If the Executive can be safely trusted with the command of the army, there cannot surely be any reasonable ground of Jealousy in the present case. He added that if the objections agˢᵗ an appointment of the Executive by the Legislature, had the weight that had been allowed there must be some weight in the objection to an appointment of the Judges by the Legislature or by any part of it.

M: GERRY. The appointment of the Judges like every other part of the Constitution shᵈ be so modelled as to give satisfaction both to the people and to the States. The mode under consideration will give satisfaction to neither. He could not conceive that the Executive could be as well informed of characters throughout the Union, as the Senate. It appeared to him also a strong

---
¹⁰ The figures "1," "2" and "3" are changed to "First," "Secondly" and "Thirdly" in the transcript.

objection that ⅔ of the Senate were required to reject a nomination of the Executive. The Senate would be constituted in the same manner as Congress. And the appointments of Congress have been generally good.

Mr MADISON, observed that he was not anxious that ⅔ should be necessary to disagree to a nomination. He had given this form to his motion chiefly to vary it the more clearly from one which had just been rejected. He was content to obviate the objection last made, and accordingly so varied the motion as to let a majority reject.

Col. MASON found it his duty to differ from his colleagues in their opinions & reasonings on this subject. Notwithstanding the form of the proposition by which the appointment seemed to be divided between the Executive & Senate, the appointment was substantially vested in the former alone. The false complaisance which usually prevails in such cases will prevent a disagreement to the first nominations. He considered the appointment by the Executive as a dangerous prerogative. It might even give him an influence over the Judiciary department itself. He did not think the difference of interest between the Northern and Southern States could be properly brought into this argument. It would operate & require some precautions in the case of regulating navigation, commerce & imposts; but he could not see that it had any connection with the Judiciary department.

On the question, the motion now being [11] that the executive should nominate, & such nominations should become appointments unless disagreed to by the Senate"

Mas. ay. Ct no. Pa ay. Del. no. Md no. Va ay. N. C. no. S. C. no. Geo. no.[12]

On [13] question for agreeing to the clause as it stands by which the Judges are to be appointed by [13] 2d branch

Mas. no. Ct ay. Pa no. Del. ay. Md ay. Va no. N. C. ay. S. C. ay. Geo. ay.[14]

Adjourned

---

[11] The words "now being" are transposed to read "being now" in the transcript.

[12] In the transcript the vote reads: "Massachusetts, Pennsylvania, Virginia, aye—3; Connecticut, Delaware, Maryland, North Carolina, South Carolina, Georgia, no—6."

[13] The word "the" is here inserted in the transcript.

[14] In the transcript the vote reads: "Connecticut, Delaware, Maryland, North Carolina, South Carolina, Georgia, aye—6; Massachusetts, Pennsylvania, Virginia, no—3; so it passed in the affirmative."

Monday. July. 23.   in Convention

M.^r John Langdon & M.^r Nicholas Gilman from N. Hampshire, took their seats.

Resol.^n : 17.[15] that provision ought to be made for future amendments of the articles of Union,[16] agreed to, nem. con.

Resol.^n 18.[17] "requiring the Legis: Execut: & Jud.^y of the States to be bound by oath to support the articles of Union,"[16] taken into consideration.

M.^r Williamson suggests that a reciprocal oath should be required from the National officers, to support the Governments of the States.

M.^r Gerry moved to insert as an amendm.^t that the oath of the officers of the National Government also should extend to the support of the Nat.^l Gov.^t which was agreed to nem. con.

M.^r Wilson said he was never fond of oaths, considering them as a left handed security only. A good Gov.^t did not need them, and a bad one could not or ought not to be supported. He was afraid they might too much trammel the members of the Existing Gov.^t— in case future alterations should be necessary; and prove an obstacle to Resol: 17.[15] just ag.^d to.

M.^r Ghorum did not know that oaths would be of much use; but could see no inconsistency between them and the 17. Resol: or any regular amend.^t of the Constitution. The oath could only require fidelity to the existing Constitution. A constitutional alteration of the Constitution, could never be regarded as a breach of the Constitution, or of any oath to support it.

M.^r Gerry thought with M.^r Ghorum there could be no shadow of inconsistency in the case. Nor could he see any other harm that could result from the Resolution. On the other side he thought one good effect would be produced by it. Hitherto the officers of the two Governments had considered them as distinct from,[18] not as parts of the General System, & had in all cases of interference given a preference to the State Gov.^ts. The proposed oaths will cure that error.

---

[15] The words "The seventeenth Resolution" are substituted in the transcript for "Resol.^n 17."
[16] The word "was" is here inserted in the transcript.
[17] The words "The eighteenth Resolution" are substituted in the transcript for "Resol.^n 18."
[18] The word " and " is here inserted in the transcript.

The Resol[n]. [18 [19]] was agreed to nem. con.—

Resol: 19.[20] "referring the new Constitution to Assemblies to be chosen by the people for the express purpose of ratifying it" was next taken into consideration.

M[r] ELSEWORTH moved that it be referred to the Legislatures of the States for ratification. M[r] PATTERSON 2[ded] the motion.

Col. MASON considered a reference of the plan to the authority of the people as one of the most important and essential of the Resolutions. The Legislatures have no power to ratify it. They are the mere creatures of the State Constitutions, and can not be greater than their creators. And he knew of no power in any of the Constitutions, he knew there was no power in some of them, that could be competent to this object. Whither then must we resort? To the people with whom all power remains that has not been given up in the Constitutions derived from them. It was of great moment he observed that this doctrine should be cherished as the basis of free Government. Another strong reason was that admitting the Legislatures to have a competent authority, it would be wrong to refer the plan to them, because succeeding Legislatures having equal authority could undo the acts of their predecessors; and the National Gov[t] would stand in each State on the weak and tottering foundation of an Act of Assembly. There was a remaining consideration of some weight. In some of the States the Gov[ts] were not derived from the clear & undisputed authority of the people. This was the case in Virginia Some of the best & wisest citizens considered the Constitution as established by an assumed authority. A National Constitution derived from such a source would be exposed to the severest criticisms.

M[r] RANDOLPH. One idea has pervaded all our proceedings, to wit, that opposition as well from the States as from individuals, will be made to the System to be proposed. Will it not then be highly imprudent, to furnish any unnecessary pretext by the mode of ratifying it. Added to other objections ag[st] a ratification by Legislative authority only, it may be remarked that there have been

---

[19] The words " the eighteenth " are substituteed in the transcript for " 18."

[20] The words "The nineteenth Resolution" are substituted in the transcript for "Resol: 19."

instances in which the authority of the Common law has been set up in particular States ag$^{st}$ that of the Confederation which has had no higher sanction than Legislative ratification.—Whose opposition will be most likely to be excited ag$^{st}$ the System? That of the local demagogues who will be degraded by it from the importance they now hold. These will spare no efforts to impede that progress in the popular mind which will be necessary to the adoption of the plan, and which every member will find to have taken place in his own, if he will compare his present opinions with those brought with him into the Convention. It is of great importance therefore that the consideration of this subject should be transferred from the Legislatures where this class of men, have their full influence to a field in which their efforts can be less mischeivous. It is moreover worthy of consideration that some of the States are averse to any change in their Constitution, and will not take the requisite steps, unless expressly called upon to refer the question to the people.

M$^{r}$ GERRY. The arguments of Col. Mason & M$^{r}$ Randolph prove too much. they prove an unconstitutionality in the present federal system even in some of the State Gov$^{ts}$ Inferences drawn from such a source must be inadmissible. Both the State Gov$^{ts}$ & the federal Gov$^{t}$ have been too long acquiesced in, to be now shaken. He considered the Confederation to be paramount to any State Constitution. The last article of it authorizing alterations must consequently be so as well as the others, and every thing done in pursuance of the article must have the same high authority with the article.—Great confusion he was confident would result from a recurrence to the people. They would never agree on any thing. He could not see any ground to suppose that the people will do what their rulers will not. The rulers will either conform to, or influence the sense of the people.

M$^{r}$ GHORUM was ag$^{st}$ referring the plan to the Legislatures. 1. Men chosen by the people for the particular purpose, will discuss the subject more candidly than members of the Legislature who are to lose the power which is to be given up to the Gen$^{l}$ Gov$^{t}$ 2. Some of the Legislatures are composed of several branches. It will consequently be more difficult in these cases to get the plan through the Legislatures, than thro' a Convention. 3. in the States many of the ablest men are excluded from the Legislatures, but may be elected into a Convention. Among these may be ranked many of the Clergy who are generally friends to good Government. Their services were found to be valuable in the formation & establishment of the Constitution of Massach$^{ts}$ 4. the Legislatures will be interrupted with a variety of little business, by artfully pressing which, designing men will find means to delay from year to year, if not to frustrate altogether, the national system. 5. If the last art: of the Confederation is to be pursued the unanimous concurrence of the States will be necessary. But will any one say, that all the States are to suffer themselves to be ruined, if Rho. Island should persist in her opposition to general measures. Some other States might also tread in her steps. The present advantage which N. York seems to be so much attached to, of taxing her neighbours by the regulation of her trade, makes it very probable, that she will be of the number. It would therefore deserve serious consideration whether provision ought not to be made for giving effect to the System without waiting for the unanimous concurrence of the States.

M$^r$ ELSEWORTH. If there be any Legislatures who should find themselves incompetent to the ratification, he should be content to let them advise with their constitutents and pursue such a mode as w$^d$ be competent. He thought more was to be expected from the Legislatures than from the people. The prevailing wish of the people in the Eastern States is to get rid of the public debt; and the idea of strengthening the Nat$^l$ Gov$^t$ carries with it that of strengthening the public debt. It was said by Col. Mason 1.[21] that the Legislatures have no authority in this case. 2.[22] that their successors having equal authority could rescind their acts. As to the 2$^d$ point he could not admit it to be well founded. An Act to which the States by their Legislatures, make themselves parties, becomes a compact from which no one of the parties can recede of itself. As to the 1$^{st}$ point, he observed that a new sett of ideas seemed to have crept in since the articles of Confederation were established. Conventions of the people, or with power

---

[21] The figure "1" is changed to "in the first place" in the transcript.
[22] The figure "2" is changed to "and in the second" in the transcript.

derived expressly from the people, were not then thought of. The Legislatures were considered as competent. Their ratification has been acquiesced in without complaint. To whom have Congs applied on subsequent occasions for further powers? To the Legislatures; not to the people. The fact is that we exist at present, and we need not enquire how, as a federal Society, united by a charter one article of which is that alterations therein may be made by the Legislative authority of the States. It has been said that if the confederation is to be observed, the States must *unanimously* concur in the proposed innovations. He would answer that if such were the urgency & necessity of our situation as to warrant a new compact among a part of the States, founded on the consent of the people; the same pleas would be equally valid in favor of a partial compact, founded on the consent of the Legislatures.

Mr WILLIAMSON thought the Resoln: [19 [23]] so expressed as that it might be submitted either to the Legislatures or to Conventions recommended by the Legislatures. He observed that some Legislatures were evidently unauthorized to ratify the system. He thought too that Conventions were to be preferred as more likely to be composed of the ablest men in the States.

Mr Govr MORRIS considered the inference of Mr Elseworth from the plea of necessity as applied to the establishment of a new System on ye consent of the people of a part of the States, in favor of a like establishnt on the consent of a part of the Legislatures as a non sequitur. If the Confederation is to be pursued no alteration can be made without the unanimous consent of the Legislatures: Legislative alterations not conformable to the federal compact, would clearly not be valid. The Judges would consider them as null & void. Whereas in case of an appeal to the people of the U. S., the supreme authority, the federal compact may be altered by a *majority of them;* in like manner as the Constitution of a particular State may be altered by a majority of the people of the State. The amendmt moved by Mr Elseworth erroneously supposes that we are proceeding on the basis of the Confederation. This Convention is unknown to the Confederation.

---

[23] The words "the nineteenth" are substituted in the transcript for "19."

Mr KING thought with Mr Elseworth that the Legislatures had a competent authority, the acquiescence of the people of America in the Confederation, being equivalent to a formal ratification by the people. He thought with Mr E— also that the plea of necessity was as valid in the one case as in [24] the other. At the same time he preferred a reference to the authority of the people expressly delegated to Conventions, as the most certain means of obviating all disputes & doubts concerning the legitimacy of the new Constitution; as well as the most likely means of drawing forth the best men in the States to decide on it. He remarked that among other objections made in the State of N. York to granting powers to Congs one had been that such powers as would operate within the State,[25] could not be reconciled to the Constitution; and therefore were not grantible by the Legislative authority. He considered it as of some consequence also to get rid of the scruples which some members of the State Legislatures might derive from their oaths to support & maintain the existing Constitutions.

Mr MADISON thought it clear that the Legislatures were incompetent to the proposed changes. These changes would make essential inroads on the State Constitutions, and it would be a novel & dangerous doctrine that a Legislature could change the constitution under which it held its existence. There might indeed be some Constitutions within the Union, which had given a power to the Legislature to concur in alterations of the federal Compact. But there were certainly some which had not; and in the case of these, a ratification must of necessity be obtained from the people. He considered the difference between a system founded on the Legislatures only, and one founded on the people, to be the true difference between a *league* or *treaty*, and a *Constitution*. The former in point of *moral obligation* might be as inviolable as the latter. In point of *political operation*, there were two important distinctions in favor of the latter.  1.[26] A law violating a treaty ratified by a pre-existing law, might be respected by the Judges as a law, though an unwise or perfidious

---

[24] The word "in" is omitted in the transcript.
[25] The transcript uses the word "State" in the plural.
[26] The figures "1" and "2" are changed to "First" and "Secondly" in the transcript.

one. A law violating a constitution established by the people themselves, would be considered by the Judges as null & void. 2.[26] The doctrine laid down by the law of Nations in the case of treaties is that a breach of any one article by any of the parties, frees the other parties from their engagements. In the case of a union of people under one Constitution, the nature of the pact has always been understood to exclude such an interpretation. Comparing the two modes in point of expediency he thought all the considerations which recommended this Convention in preference to Congress for proposing the reform were in favor of State Conventions in preference to the Legislatures for examining and adopting it.

On [27] question on Mr Elseworth's motion to refer the plan to the Legislatures of the States

N. H. no. Mas. no. Ct ay. no.[28] Pa no. Del. ay. Md ay. Va no. N. C. no. S. C. no. Geo. no.[29]

Mr Govr MORRIS moved that the reference of the plan be made to one general Convention, chosen & authorized by the people to consider, *amend*, & establish the same.—Not seconded.

On [27] question for agreeing to Resolution 19.[30] touching the mode of Ratification as reported from the Committee of the Whole; viz, to refer the Constn after the approbation of Congs to assemblies chosen by the people:

N. H. ay. Mas. ay. Ct ay. Pa ay. Del. no. Md ay Va ay. N. C. ay. S. C. ay. Geo. ay.[31]

Mr Govr MORRIS & Mr KING moved that the representation in the second branch consist of          members from each State, who shall vote per capita.

Mr ELSEWORTH said he had always approved of voting in that mode.

---

[26] The figures "1" and "2" are charged to "First" and "Secondly" in the transcript.
[27] The word "the" is here inserted in the transcript.
[28] The entry in the notes was originally "N. J. no." Madison struck out "N. J." but inadvertently let "no" remain.
[29] In the transcript the vote reads: "Connecticut, Delaware, Maryland, aye—3; New Hampshire, Massachusetts, Pennsylvania, Virginia, North Carolina, South Carolina, Georgia, no—7."
[30] The words "the nineteenth Resolution" are substituted in the transcript for "Resolution 19."
[31] In the transcript the vote reads: "New Hampshire, Massachusetts, Connecticut, Pennsylvania, Maryland, Virginia, North Carolina, South Carolina, Georgia, aye—9; Delaware, no—1."

Mr Govr Morris moved to fill the *blank* [32] with *three*. He wished the Senate to be a pretty numerous body. If two members only should be allowed to each State, and a majority be made a quorum, the power would be lodged in 14 members, which was too small a number for such a trust.

Mr Ghorum preferred two to three members for the blank. A small number was most convenient for deciding on peace & war &c. which he expected would be vested in the 2d branch. The number of States will also increase. Kentucky, Vermont, the Province of Mayne & Franklin will probably soon be added to the present number. He presumed also that some of the largest States would be divided. The strenghth of the General Govt will lie not in the largeness, but in the smallness of the States.

Col. Mason thought *3* from each State including new States would make the 2d branch too numerous. Besides other objections, the additional expence ought always to form one, where it was not absolutely necessary:

Mr Williamson. If the number be too great, the distant States will not be on an equal footing with the nearer States. The latter can more easily send & support their ablest Citizens. He approved of the voting per capita.

On the question for filling the blank with "*three.*"

N. H. no. Mas. no. Cont no. Pa ay. Del. no. Va no. N. C. no. S. C. no. Geo. no.[33]

On [34] question for filling it with "two." Agreed to nem. con.

Mr L Martin was opposed to voting per Capita, as departing from the idea of the *States* being represented in the 2d branch.

Mr Carrol, was not struck with any particular objection agst the mode; but he did not wish so hastily to make so material an innovation.

On the question on the whole motion viz. the 2d b. to consist of of 2 members from each State and to vote per capita."

N. H. ay. Mas. ay. Ct ay. Pa ay. Del. ay. Md no. Va ay. N. C. ay. S. C. ay. Geo. ay.[35]

---

[32] The transcript does not italicise the word "*blank.*"
[33] In the transcript the vote reads: "Pennsylvania, aye—1; New Hampshire, Massachusetts, Connecticut, Delaware, Virginia, North Carolina, South Carolina, Georgia, no—8."
[34] The word "the" is here inserted in the transcript.
[35] In the transcript the vote reads: "New Hampshire, Massachusetts, Connecticut, Pennsylvania, Delaware, Virginia, North Carolina, South Carolina, Georgia, aye—9; Maryland, no—1."

Mʳ HOUSTON & Mʳ SPAIGHT moved "that the appointment of the Executive by Electors chosen by the Legislatures of the States, be reconsidered." Mʳ Houston urged the extreme inconveniency & the considerable expense, of drawing together men from all the States for the single purpose of electing the Chief Magistrate.

On the question which was put without any [36] debate.

N. H. ay. Mas. ay. Cᵗ ay. Pᵃ no. Del. ay. Mᵈ no. Virgᵃ no. N. C. ay. S. C. ay. Geo. ay.[37]

Ordered that tomorrow be assigned for the reconsideration.

Conᵗ & Penᵃ no—all the rest ay.

Mʳ GERRY moved that the proceedings of the Convention for the establishment of a Natˡ Govᵗ (except the part relating to the Executive), be referred to a Committee to prepare & report a Constitution conformable thereto.

Genˡ PINKNEY reminded the Convention that if the Committee should fail to insert some security to the Southern States agˢᵗ an emancipation of slaves, and taxes on exports, he shᵈ be bound by duty to his State to vote agˢᵗ their Report— The appᵗ of a Comᵉ as moved by Mʳ Gerry.[38] Agᵈ to nem. con.

[39] Shall the Comᵉ consist of 10 members one from each State presᵗ? All the States were *no*, except Delaware *ay*.

Shall it consist of 7. members.

N. H. ay. Mas. ay. Cᵗ ay. Pᵃ no. Del. no. Mᵈ ay. Vᵃ no. N. C. no. S. C. ay. Geo. no.[40] The question being lost by an equal division of Votes.

It was agreed nem- con- that the Comtttee [41] consist of 5 members, to be appointed tomorrow.

Adjourned

---

[36] The word "any" is omitted in the transcript.
[37] In the transcript the vote reads: "New Hampshire, Massachusetts, Connecticut, Delaware, North Carolina, South Carolina, Gerogia, aye—7; Pennsylvania, Maryland, Virginia, no—3."
[38] The word "was" is here inserted in the transcript.
[39] The words "On the question" are here inserted in the transcript.
[40] In the transcript the vote reads: "New Hampshire, Massachusetts, Connecticut, Maryland, South Carolina, aye—5; Pennsylvania, Delaware, Virginia, North Carolina, Georgia, no—5."
[41] The word "should" is here inserted in the transcript.

## Tuesday July 24. in Convention

The appointment of the Executive by Electors [42] reconsidered.

Mʳ Houston moved that he be appointed by the "Natˡ Legislature," instead of "Electors appointed by the State Legislatures" according to the last decision of the mode. He dwelt chiefly on the improbability, that capable men would undertake the service of Electors from the more distant States.

Mʳ Spaight seconded the motion.

Mʳ Gerry opposed it. He thought there was no ground to apprehend the danger urged by Mʳ Houston. The election of the Executive Magistrate will be considered as of vast importance and will excite [43] great earnestness. The best men, the Governours of the States will not hold it derogatory from their character to be the electors. If the motion should be agreed to, it will be necessary to make the Executive ineligible a $2^d$ time, in order to render him independent of the Legislature; which was an idea extremely repugnant to his way of thinking.

Mʳ Strong supposed that there would be no necessity, if the Executive should be appointed by the Legislature, to make him ineligible a $2^d$ time; as new elections of the Legislature will have intervened; and he will not depend for his $2^d$ appointment on the same sett of men as [44] his first was recᵈ from. It had been suggested that *gratitude* for his past appointment wᵈ produce the same effect as dependence for his future appointment. He thought very differently. Besides this objection would lie agˢᵗ the Electors who would be objects of gratitude as well as the Legislature. It was of great importance not to make the Govᵗ too complex which would be the case if a new sett of men like the Electors should be introduced into it. He thought also that the first characters in the States would not feel sufficient motives to undertake the office of Electors.

Mʳ Williamson was for going back to the original ground; to elect the Executive for 7 years and render him ineligible a $2^d$ time. The proposed Electors would certainly not be men of the $1^{st}$ nor even of the $2^d$ grade in the States. These would all prefer a seat

---

[42] The word "being" is here inserted in the transcript.
[43] The word "create" is substituted in the transcript for "excite."
[44] The word "that" is substituted in the transcript for "as."

either [45] in the Senate or the other branch of the Legislature. He did not like the Unity in the Executive. He had wished the Executive power to be lodged in three men taken from three districts into which the States should be divided. As the Executive is to have a kind of veto on the laws, and there is an essential difference of interests between the N. & S. States, particularly in the carrying trade, the power will be dangerous, if the Executive is to be taken from part of the Union, to the part from which he is not taken. The case is different here from what it is in England; where there is a sameness of interests throughout the Kingdom. Another objection ag$^{st}$ a single Magistrate is that he will be an elective King, and will feel the spirit of one. He will spare no pains to keep himself in for life, and will then lay a train for the succession of his children. It was pretty certain he thought that we should at some time or other have a King; but he wished no precaution to be omitted that might postpone the event as long as possible.—Ineligibility a 2$^d$ time appeared to him to be the best precaution. With this precaution he had no objection to a longer term than 7 years. He would go as far as 10 or 12 years.

M$^r$ GERRY moved that the Legislatures of the States should vote by ballot for the Executive in the same proportions as it had been proposed they should chuse electors; and that in case a majority of the votes should not center on the same person, the 1$^{st}$ branch of the Nat$^l$ Legislature should chuse two out of the 4 candidates having most votes, and out of these two, the 2$^d$ branch should chuse the Executive.

M$^r$ KING seconded the motion—and on the Question to postpone in order to take it into consideration. The *noes* were so predominant, that the States were not counted.

[46] Question on M$^r$ Houston's motion that the Executive be app$^d$ by [47] Na$^l$ Legislature

N. H. ay. Mas. ay. C$^t$ no. N. J. ay. P$^a$ no. Del. ay. M$^d$ no. V$^a$ no. N. C. ay. S. C. ay. Geo. ay.[48]

---

[45] The word "either" is omitted in the transcript.
[46] The words "On the" are here inserted in the transcript.
[47] The word "the" is here inserted in the transcript.
[48] In the transcript the vote reads: "New Hampshire, Massachusetts, New Jersey, Delaware, North Carolina, South Carolina, Georgia, aye—7; Connecticut, Pennsylvania, Maryland, Virginia, no—4."

M: L. MARTIN & M: GERRY moved to re-instate the ineligibility of the Executive a 2ᵈ time.

M: ELSEWORTH. With many this appears a natural consequence of his being elected by the Legislature. It was not the case with him. The Executive he thought should be reelected if his conduct proved him worthy of it. And he will be more likely to render himself, worthy of it if he be rewardable with it. The most eminent characters also will be more willing to accept the trust under this condition, than if they foresee a necessary degradation at a fixt period.

M: GERRY. That the Executive shᵈ be independent of the Legislature is a clear point. The longer the duration of his appointment the more will his dependence be diminished. It will be better then for him to continue 10, 15, or even 20, years and be ineligible afterwards.

M: KING was for making him re-eligible. This is too great an advantage to be given up for the small effect it will have on his dependence, if impeachments are to lie. He considered these as rendering the tenure during pleasure.

M: L. MARTIN, suspending his motion as to the ineligibility, moved "that the appointmᵗ of the Executive shall continue for Eleven years.

M: GERRY suggested fifteen years

M: KING twenty years. This is the medium life of princes.*

M: DAVIE Eight years

M: WILSON. The difficulties & perplexities into which the House is thrown proceed from the election by the Legislature which he was sorry had been reinstated. The inconveniency [50] of this mode was such that he would agree to almost any length of time in order to get rid of the dependence which must result from it. He was persuaded that the longest term would not be equivalent to a proper mode of election; unless indeed it should be during good behaviour. It seemed to be supposed that at a certain ad-

---

\* This might possibly be meant as a carricature of the previous motions in order to defeat the object of them.

\* Transfer hither.[49]

[49] Madison's direction concerning the footnote is omitted in the transcript.

[50] The word "inconveniency" is changed to "inconvenience" in the transcript.

vance in life, a continuance in office would cease to be agreeable to the officer, as well as desirable to the public. Experience had shewn in a variety of instances that both a capacity & inclination for public service existed—in very advanced stages. He mentioned the instance of a Doge of Venice who was elected after he was 80 years of age. The popes have generally been elected at very advanced periods, and yet in no case had a more steady or a better concerted policy been pursued than in the Court of Rome. If the Executive should come into office at 35. years of age, which he presumes may happen & his continuance should be fixt at 15 years. at the age of 50. in the very prime of life, and with all the aid of experience, he must be cast aside like a useless hulk. What an irreparable loss would the British Jurisprudence have sustained, had the age of 50. been fixt there as the ultimate limit of capacity or readiness to serve the public. The great luminary [L$^d$ Mansfield] held his seat for thirty years after his arrival at that age. Notwithstanding what had been done he could not but hope that a better mode of election would yet be adopted; and one that would be more agreeable to the general sense of the House. That time might be given for further deliberation he w$^d$ move that the present question be postponed till tomorrow.

M$^r$ BROOM seconded the motion to postpone.

M$^r$ GERRY. We seem to be entirely at a loss on this head. He would suggest whether it would not be adviseable to refer the clause relating to the Executive to the Committee of detail to be appointed. Perhaps they will be able to hit on something that may unite the various opinions which have been thrown out.

M$^r$ WILSON. As the great difficulty seems to spring from the mode of election, he w$^d$ suggest a mode which had not been mentioned. It was that the Executive be elected for 6 years by a small number, not more than 15 of the Nat$^l$ Legislatuie, to be drawn from it, not by ballot, but by lot and who should retire immediately and make the election without separating. By this mode intrigue would be avoided in the first instance, and the dependence would be diminished. This was not he said a digested idea and might be liable to strong objections.

Mʳ Govʳ MORRIS. Of all possible modes of appointment that by the Legislature is the worst. If the Legislature is to appoint, and to impeach or to influence the impeachment, the Executive will be the mere creature of it. He had been opposed to the impeachment but was now convinced that impeachments must be provided for, if the appᵗ was to be of any duration. No man wᵈ say, that an Executive known to be in the pay of an Enemy, should not be removeable in some way or other. He had been charged heretofore [by Col. Mason] with inconsistency in pleading for confidence in the Legislature on some occasions, & urging a distrust on others. The charge was not well founded. The Legislature is worthy of unbounded confidence in some respects, and liable to equal distrust in others. When their interest coincides precisely with that of their Constituents, as happens in many of their Acts, no abuse of trust is to be apprehended. When a strong personal interest happens to be opposed to the general interest, the Legislature can not be too much distrusted. In all public bodies there are two parties. The Executive will necessarily be more connected with one than with the other. There will be a personal interest therefore in one of the parties to oppose as well as in the other to support him. Much had been said of the intrigues that will be practised by the Executive to get into office. Nothing had been said on the other side of the intrigues to get him out of office. Some leader of [51] party will always covet his seat, will perplex his administration, will cabal with the Legislature, till he succeeds in supplanting him. This was the way in which the King of England was got out, he meant the real King, the Minister. This was the way in which Pitt [Lᵈ Chatham] forced himself into place. Fox was for pushing the matter still farther. If he carried his India bill, which he was very near doing, he would have made the Minister, the King in form almost as well as in substance. Our President will be the British Minister, yet we are about to make him appointable by the Legislature. Something had been said of the danger of Monarchy. If a good government should not now be formed, if a good organization of the Execuve should not be provided, he doubted whether we should not have something worse than a limited Monarchy. In

---

[51] The word "a" is here inserted in the transcript.

order to get rid of the dependence of the Executive on the Legislature, the expedient of making him ineligible a 2ᵈ time had been devised. This was as much as to say we shᵈ give him the benefit of experience, and then deprive ourselves of the use of it. But make him ineligible a 2ᵈ time—and prolong his duration even to 15-years, will he by any wonderful interposition of providence at that period cease to be a man? No he will be unwilling to quit his exaltation, the road to his object thro' the Constitution will be shut; he will be in possession of the sword, a civil war will ensue, and the Commander of the victorious army on which ever side, will be the despot of America. This consideration renders him particularly anxious that the Executive should be properly constituted. The vice here would not, as in some other parts of the system be curable. It is the most difficult of all rightly to balance the Executive. Make him too weak: The Legislature will usurp his powers: Make him too strong. He will usurp on the Legislature. He preferred a short period, a re-eligibility, but a different mode of election. A long period would prevent an adoption of the plan: it ought to do so. He shᵈ himself be afraid to trust it. He was not prepared to decide on Mr Wilson's mode of election just hinted by him. He thought it deserved consideration It would be better that chance sᵈ decide than intrigue.

On a [52] question to postpone the consideration of the Resolution on the subject of the Executive

N. H. no. Mas. no. Cᵗ ay. N. J. no. Pᵃ ay. Del. divᵈ Mᵈ ay. Vᵃ ay. N. C. no. S. C. no. Geo. no.[53]

Mr WILSON then moved that the Executive be chosen every     years by     Electors to be taken by lot from the Natˡ Legislature who shall proceed immediately to the choice of the Executive and not separate until it be made."

Mr CARROL 2ᵈˢ the motion

Mr GERRY. this is committing too much to chance. If the lot should fall on a sett of unworthy men, an unworthy Executive must be saddled on the Country. He thought it had been demon-

---

[52] The word "the" is substituted in the transcript for "a."
[53] In the transcript the vote reads: "Connecticut, Pennsylvania, Maryland, Virginia, aye—4; New Hampshire, Massachusetts, New Jersey, North Carolina, South Carolina, Georgia, no—6."

strated that no possible mode of electing by the Legislature could be a good one.

M! KING. The lot might fall on a majority from the same State which w? ensure the election of a man from that State. We ought to be governed by reason, not by chance. As nobody seemed to be satisfied, he wished the matter to be postponed

M! WILSON did not move this as the best mode. His opinion remained unshaken that we ought to resort to the people for the election. He seconded the postponement.

M! Gov! MORRIS observed that the chances were almost infinite ag?t a majority of electors from the same State.

On a question whether the last motion was in order, it was determined in the affirmative; 7. ays. 4 noes.

On the question of postponen! it was agreed to nem. con.

M! CARROL took occasion to observe that he considered the clause declaring that direct taxation on the States should be in proportion to representation, previous to the obtaining an actual census, as very objectionable, and that he reserved to himself the right of opposing it, if the Report of the Committee of detail should leave it in the plan.

M! Gov! MORRIS hoped the Committee would strike out the whole of the clause proportioning direct taxation to representation. He had only meant it as a\* bridge to assist us over a certain gulph; having passed the gulph the bridge may be removed. He thought the principle laid down with so much strictness, liable to strong objections

On a ballot for a Committee to report a Constitution conformable to the Resolutions passed by the Convention, the members chosen were

M! Rutlidge, M! Randolph, M! Ghorum, M! Elseworth, M! Wilson—

On motion to discharge the Com? of the whole from the propositions submitted to the Convention by M! C. Pinkney as the basis

---

\* The object was to lessen the eagerness on one side,[54] & the opposition on the other, to the share of representation claimed by the S. Sothern States on account of the Negroes.

\* The N. B. to be transferred hither without the N. B.[55]

[54] The word "for" is here inserted in the transcript.

[55] Madison's direction concerning the footnote is omitted in the transcript.

of a constitution, and to refer them to the Committee of detail just appointed, it was ag^d to nem: con.

A like motion was then made & agreed to nem: con: with respect to the propositions of M^r Patterson

Adjourned.

WEDNESDAY JULY 25. IN CONVENTION

[56] Clause relating to the Executive [57] again under consideration.

M^r ELSEWORTH moved "that the Executive be appointed by the Legislature," except when the magistrate last chosen shall have continued in office the whole term for which he was chosen, & be reeligible, in which case the choice shall be by Electors appointed by the Legislatures of the States for that purpose." By this means a deserving magistrate may be reelected without making him dependent on the Legislature.[58]

M^r GERRY repeated his remark that an election at all by the Nat^l Legislature was radically and incurably wrong; and moved that the Executive be appointed by the Governours & Presidents of the States, with advice of their Councils, and where there are no Councils by Electors chosen by the Legislatures. The executives to vote in the following proportions: viz—

M^r MADISON. There are objections ag^st every mode that has been, or perhaps can be proposed. The election must be made either by some existing authority under the Nat^l or State Constitutions—or by some special authority derived from the people—or by the people themselves.—The two Existing authorities under the Nat^l Constitution w^d be the Legislative & Judiciary. The latter he presumed was out of the question. The former was in his Judgment liable to insuperable objections. Besides the general influence of that mode on the independence of the Executive, 1.[59] the election of the Chief Magistrate would agitate & divide the legislature so much that the public interest would materially suffer by it. Public bodies are always apt to be thrown into contentions, but into more violent ones by such occasions than by any others.

---

[56] The word "The" is here inserted in the transcript.
[57] The word "being" is here inserted in the transcript.
[58] The transcript italicizes the phrase "making him dependent on the Legislature."
[59] The figure "1" is changed to "In the first place" in the transcript.

2.[60] the candidate would intrigue with the Legislature, would derive his appointment from the predominant faction, and be apt to render his administration subservient to its views. 3.[61] The Ministers of foreign powers would have and [62] make use of, the opportunity to mix their intrigues & influence with the Election. Limited as the powers of the Executive are, it will be an object of great moment with the great rival powers of Europe who have American possessions, to have at the head of our Governm.<sup>t</sup> a man attached to their respective politics & interests. No pains, nor perhaps expence, will be spared, to gain from the Legislature an appointm.<sup>t</sup> favorable to their wishes. Germany & Poland are witnesses of this danger. In the former, the election of the Head of the Empire, till it became in a manner hereditary, interested all Europe, and was much influenced by foreign interference. In the latter, altho' the elective Magistrate has very little real power, his election has at all times produced the most eager interference of forign princes, and has in fact at length slid entirely into foreign hands. The existing authorities in the States are the Legislative, Executive & Judiciary. The appointment of the Nat.<sup>l</sup> Executive by the first, was objectionable in many points of view, some of which had been already mentioned. He would mention one which of itself would decide his opinion. The Legislatures of the States had betrayed a strong propensity to a variety of pernicious measures. One object of the Nat.<sup>l</sup> Legisl.<sup>re</sup> was to controul this propensity. One object of the Nat.<sup>l</sup> Executive, so far as it would have a negative on the laws, was to controul the Nat.<sup>l</sup> Legislature, so far as it might be infected with a similar propensity. Refer the appointm.<sup>t</sup> of the Nat.<sup>l</sup> Executive to the State Legislatures, and this controuling purpose may be defeated. The Legislatures can & will act with some kind of regular plan, and will promote the appointm.<sup>t</sup> of a man who will not oppose himself to a favorite object. Should a majority of the Legislatures at the time of election have the same object, or different objects of the same kind, The Nat.<sup>l</sup> Executive would be rendered subservient to them.—An appointment by the State

---

[60] The figure "2" is changed to "In the second place" in the transcript.
[61] The figure "3" is changed to "In the third place" in the transcript.
[62] The word "would" is here inserted in the transcript.

Executives, was liable among other objections to this insuperable one, that being standing bodies, they could & would be courted, and intrigued with by the Candidates, by their partizans, and by the Ministers of foreign powers. The State Judiciarys had not [63] & he presumed w.d not be proposed as a proper source of appointment. The option before us then lay between an appointment by Electors chosen by the people—and an immediate appointment by the people. He thought the former mode free from many of the objections which had been urged ag.st it, and greatly preferable to an appointment by the Nat.l Legislature. As the electors would be chosen for the occasion, would meet at once, & proceed immediately to an appointment, there would be very little opportunity for cabal, or corruption. As a farther precaution, it might be required that they should meet at some place, distinct from the seat of Gov.t and even that no person within a certain distance of the place at the time sh.d be eligible. This Mode however had been rejected so recently & by so great a majority that it probably would not be proposed anew. The remaining mode was an election by the people or rather by the qualified part of them, at large: With all its imperfections he liked this best. He would not repeat either the general argum.ts for or the objections ag.st this mode. He would only take notice of two difficulties which he admitted to have weight. The first arose from the disposition in the people to prefer a Citizen of their own State, and the disadvantage this w.d throw on the smaller States. Great as this objection might be he did not think it equal to such as lay ag.st every other mode which had been proposed. He thought too that some expedient might be hit upon that would obviate it. The second difficulty arose from the disproportion of qualified voters in the N. & S. States, and the disadvantages which this mode would throw on the latter. The answer to this objection was 1.[64] that this disproportion would be continually decreasing under the influence of the Republican laws introduced in the S. States, and the more rapid increase of their population. 2.[65] That local considerations must give way to the

---

[63] The word "been" is here inserted in the transcript.
[64] The figure "1" is changed to "in the first place" in the transcript.
[65] The figure "2" is changed to "in the second place" in the transcript.

general interest. As an individual from the S. States he was willing to make the sacrifice.

Mʳ ELSEWORTH. The objection drawn from the different sizes of the States, is unanswerable. The Citizens of the largest States would invariably prefer the Candidate within the State; and the largest States wᵈ invariably have the man.

[66] Question on Mʳ Elseworth's motion as above.

N. H. ay. Mas. no. Cᵗ ay. N. J. no. Pᵃ ay. Del. no. Mᵈ ay. Vᵃ no. N. C. no. S. C. no. Geo. no.[67]

Mʳ PINKNEY moved that the election by the Legislature be qualified with a proviso that no person be eligible for more than 6 years in any twelve years. He thought this would have all the advantage & at the same time avoid in some degree the inconveniency,[68] of an absolute ineligibility a 2ᵈ time.

Col. MASON approved the idea. It had the sanction of experience in the instance of Congˢ and some of the Executives of the States. It rendered the Executive as effectually independent, as an ineligibility after his first election, and opened the way at the same time for the advantage of his future services. He preferred on the whole the election by thé Natˡ Legislature: Tho' Candor obliged him to admit, that there was great danger of foreign influence, as had been suggested. This was the most serious objection with him that had been urged.

Mʳ BUTLER. The two great evils to be avoided are cabal at home, & influence from abroad. It will be difficult to avoid either if the Election be made by the Natˡ Legislature. On the other hand: The Govᵗ should not be made so complex & unwieldy as to disgust the States. This would be the case, if the election shᵈ be referred to the people. He liked best an election by Electors chosen by the Legislatures of the States. He was agˢᵗ a re-eligibility at all events. He was also agˢᵗ a ratio of votes in the States. An equality should prevail in this case. The reasons for departing from it do not hold in the case of the Executive as in that of the Legislature.

Mʳ GERRY approved of Mʳ Pinkney's motion as lessening the evil.

---

[66] The words "On the" are here inserted in the transcript.

[67] In the transcript the vote reads: "New Hampshire, Connecticut, Pennsylvania, Maryland, aye—4; Massachusetts, New Jersey, Delaware, Virginia, North Carolina, South Carolina, Georgia, no—7."

[68] The word "inconveniency" is changed to "inconvenience" in the transcript.

Mr Govr MORRIS was agst a rotation in every case. It formed a political School, in wch we were always governed by the scholars, and not by the Masters. The evils to be guarded agst in this case are 1.[69] the undue influence of the Legislature. 2.[69] instability of Councils. 3.[69] misconduct in office. To guard agst the first, we run into the second evil. We adopt a rotation which produces instability of Councils. To avoid Sylla we fall into Charibdis. A change of men is ever followed by a change of measures. We see this fully exemplified in the vicissitudes among ourselves, particularly in the State of Pena. The self-sufficiency of a victorious party scorns to tread in the paths of their predecessors. Rehoboam will not imitate Soloman. 2.[70] the Rotation in office will not prevent intrigue and dependence on the Legislature. The man in office will look forward to the period at which he will become re-eligible. The distance of the period, the improbability of such a protraction of his life will be no obstacle. Such is the nature of man, formed by his benevolent author no doubt for wise ends, that altho' he knows his existence to be limited to a span, he takes his measures as if he were to live for ever. But taking another supposition, the inefficacy of the expedient will be manifest. If the magistrate does not look forward to his re-election to the Executive, he will be pretty sure to keep in view the opportunity of his going into the Legislature itself. He will have little objection then to an extension of power on a theatre where he expects to act a distinguished part; and will be very unwilling to take any step that may endanger his popularity with the Legislature, on his influence over which the figure he is to make will depend. 3.[71] To avoid the third evil, impeachments will be essential, and hence an additional reason agst an election by the Legislature. He considered an election by the people as the best, by the Legislature as the worst, mode. Putting both these aside, he could not but favor the idea of Mr Wilson, of introducing a mixture of lot. It will diminish, if not destroy both cabal & dependence.

Mr WILLIAMSON was sensible that strong objections lay agst an election of the Executive by the Legislature, and that it opened a

---
[69] The figures "1," "2" and "3" are changed to "first," "secondly" and "thirdly" in the transcript.
[70] The figure "2" is changed to "Secondly" in the transcript.
[71] The figure "3" is changed to "Finally" in the transcript.

door for foreign influence. The principal objection ag$^{st}$ an election by the people seemed to be, the disadvantage under which it would place the smaller States. He suggested as a cure for this difficulty, that each man should vote for 3 candidates, One of these [72] he observed would be probably of his own State, the other 2. of some other States; and as probably of a small as a large one.

M$^r$ Gov$^r$ MORRIS liked the idea, suggesting as an amendment that each man should vote for two persons one of whom at least should not be of his own State.

M$^r$ MADISON also thought something valuable might be made of the suggestion with the proposed amendment of it. The second best man in this case would probably be the first, in fact. The only objection which occurred was that each Citizen after hav$^g$ given his vote for his favorite fellow Citizen, w$^d$ throw away his second on some obscure Citizen of another State, in order to ensure the object of his first choice. But it could hardly be supposed that the Citizens of many States would be so sanguine of having their favorite elected, as not to give their second vote with sincerity to the next object of their choice. It might moreover be provided in favor of the smaller States that the Executive should not be eligible more than      times in      years from the same State.

M$^r$ GERRY. A popular election in this case is radically vicious. The ignorance of the people would put it in the power of some one set of men dispersed through the Union & acting in Concert to delude them into any appointment. He observed that such a Society of men existed in the Order of the Cincinnati. They are respectable, United, and influencial. They will in fact elect the chief Magistrate in every instance, if the election be referred to the people. His respect for the characters composing this Society could not blind him to the danger & impropriety of throwing such a power into their hands.

M$^r$ DICKENSON. As far as he could judge from the discussions which had taken place during his attendance, insuperable objections lay ag$^{st}$ an election of the Executive by the Nat$^l$ Legislature; as also by the Legislatures or Executives of the States. He had

---

[72] The word "them" is substituted in the transcript for "these."

long leaned towards an election by the people which he regarded as the best & purest source. Objections he was aware lay ag:t this mode, but not so great he thought as ag:t the other modes. The greatest difficulty in the opinion of the House seemed to arise from the partiality of the States to their respective Citizens. But, might not this very partiality be turned to a useful purpose. Let the people of each State chuse its best Citizen. The people will know the most eminent characters of their own States, and the people of different States will feel an emulation in selecting those of which [73] they will have the greatest reason to be proud. Out of the thirteen names thus selected, an Executive Magistrate may be chosen either by the Nat: Legislature, or by Electors appointed by it.

On a Question which was moved for postponing M:r Pinkney's motion; in order to make way for some such proposition as had been hinted by M:r Williamson & others: it passed in the negative.

N. H. no. Mas. no. C:t ay. N. J. ay. P:a ay. Del. no. M:d ay. V:a ay. N. C. no. S. C. no. Geo. no.[74]

On M:r Pinkney's motion that no person shall serve in the Executive more than 6 years in 12. years, it passed in the negative.

N. H. ay. Mas. ay. C:t no. N. J. no. P:a no. Del. no. M:d no. V:a no. N. C. ay. S. C. ay. Geo. ay.[75]

On a motion that the members of the Committee be furnished with copies of the proceedings it was so determined; S. Carolina alone being in the negative.

It was then moved that the members of the House might take copies of the Resolions which had been agreed to; which passed in the negative. N. H. no. Mas. no. Con: ay. N. J. ay. P:a no. Del. ay. Mary:d no. V:a ay. N. C. ay. S. C. no. Geo. no.[76]

M:r GERRY & M:r BUTLER moved to refer the resolution relating to the Executive (except the clause making it consist of a single person) to the Committee of detail

---

[73] The word "whom" is substituted in the transcript for "which."
[74] In the transcript the vote reads: "Connecticut, New Jersey, Pennsylvania, Maryland, Virginia, aye—5; New Hampshire, Massachusetts, Delaware, North Carolina, South Carolina, Georgia, no—6."
[75] In the transcript the vote reads: "New Hampshire, Massachusetts, North Carolina, South Carolina, Georgia, aye—5; Connecticut, New Jersey, Pennsylvania, Delaware, Maryland, Virginia, no—6."
[76] In the transcript the vote reads: "Connecticut, New Jersey, Delaware, Virginia, North Carolina, aye—5; New Hampshire, Massachusetts, Pennsylvania, Maryland, South Carolina, Georgia, no—6."

456

M! WILSON hoped that so important a branch of the System w⁴ not be committed untill a general principle sh⁴ be fixed by a vote of the House.

M! LANGDON, was for the Commitment—Adj⁴

---

THURSDAY JULY. 26. IN CONVENTION

Col.[77] MASON. In every Stage of the Question relative to the Executive, the difficulty of the subject and the diversity of the opinions concerning it have appeared. Nor have any of the modes of constituting that department been satisfactory. 1.[78] It has been proposed that the election should be made by the people at large; that is that an act which ought to be performed by those who know most of Eminent characters, & qualifications, should be performed by those who know least. 2.[78] that the election should be made by the Legislatures of the States. 3.[78] by the Executives of the States. Ag⁵ᵗ these modes also strong objections have been urged. 4.[78] It has been proposed that the election should be made by Electors chosen by the people for that purpose. This was at first agreed to: But on further consideration has been rejected. 5.[78] Since which, the mode of M! Williamson, requiring each freeholder to vote for several candidates has been proposed. This seemed like many other propositions, to carry a plausible face, but on closer inspection is liable to fatal objections. A popular election in any form, as M! Gerry has observed, would throw the appointment into the hands of the Cincinnati, a Society for the members of which he had a great respect; but which he never wished to have a preponderating influence in the Gov! 6.[79] Another expedient was proposed by M! Dickenson, which is liable to so palpable & material an inconvenience that he had little doubt of its being by this time rejected by himself. It would exclude every man who happened not to be popular within his own State; tho' the causes of his local unpopularity might be of such a nature as to recommend him to the States at large. 7.[79] Among other expedients, a lottery has been introduced. But

---

[77] The word "Mr." is substituted in the transcript for "Col."
[78] The figures "1," "2," "3," "4" and "5" are changed to "First," "Secondly," "Thirdly," etc. in the transcript.
[79] The figures "6" and "7" are changed to "Sixthly" and "Seventhly" in the transcript.

as the tickets do not appear to be in much demand, it will probably, not be carried on, and nothing therefore need be said on that subject. After reviewing all these various modes, he was led to conclude, that an election by the Natl Legislature as originally proposed, was the best. If it was liable to objections, it was liable to fewer than any other. He conceived at the same time that a second election ought to be absolutely prohibited. Having for his primary object, for the pole [80]-star of his political conduct, the preservation of the rights of the people, he held it as an essential point, as the very palladium of Civil liberty, that the great officers of State, and particularly the Executive should at fixed periods return to that mass from which they were at first taken, in order that they may feel & respect those rights & interests, which are again to be personally valuable to them. He concluded with moving that the constitution of the Executive as reported by the Come of the whole be re-instated, viz. "that the Executive be appointed for seven years, & be ineligible a 2d time"

Mr DAVIE seconded the motion

Docr FRANKLIN. It seems to have been imagined by some that the returning to the mass of the people was degrading the magistrate. This he thought was contrary to republican principles. In free Governments the rulers are the servants, and the people their superiors & sovereigns. For the former therefore to return among the latter was not to *degrade* but to *promote* them. And it would be imposing an unreasonable burden on them, to keep them always in a State of servitude, and not allow them to become again one of the Masters.

[81] Question on Col. Masons motion as above; which [82] passed in the affirmative

N. H. ay. Masts not on floor. Ct no. N. J. ay. Pa no. Del. no. Md ay. Va ay. N. C. ay. S. C. ay. Geo. ay.[83]

Mr Govr MORRIS was now agst the whole paragraph. In answer to Col. Mason's position that a periodical return of the great officers

---

[80] The word "polar" is substituted in the transcript for the word "pole."
[81] The words "On the" are here inserted in the transcript.
[82] The word "which" is crossed out in the transcript and "it" is written above it.
[83] In the transcript the vote reads: "New Hampshire, New Jersey, Maryland, Virginia, North Carolina, South Carolina, Georgia, aye—7; Connecticut, Pennsylvania, Delaware, no—3; Massachusetts not on the floor."

of the State into the mass of the people, was the palladium of Civil liberty he w.d observe that on the same principle the Judiciary ought to be periodically degraded; certain it was that the Legislature ought on every principle, yet no one had proposed, or conceived that the members of it should not be re-eligible. In answer to Doc.r Franklin, that a return into the mass of the people would be a promotion, instead of a degradation, he had no doubt that our Executive like most others would have too much patriotism to shrink from the burden of his office, and too much modesty not to be willing to decline the promotion.

On the question on the whole resolution as amended in the words following—"that a National Executive be instituted—to consist of a single person—to be chosen by the Nat.l legislature—for the term of seven years—to be ineligible a 2.d time—with power to carry into execution the nat.l laws—to appoint to offices in cases not otherwise provided for—to be removable on impeachment & conviction of malpractice or neglect of duty—to receive a fixt compensation for the devotion of his time to the public service, to be paid out of the Nat.l treasury"—it passed in the affirmative

N. H. ay. Mas. not on floor. C.t ay. N. J. ay. P.a no. Del. no. M.d no. V.a div.d M.r Blair & Col. Mason ay. Gen.l Washington & M.r Madison no. M.r Randolph happened to be out of the House. N. C. ay. S. C. ay. Geo. ay.[84]

M.r MASON moved "that the Committee of detail be instructed to receive a clause requiring certain qualifications of landed property & citizenship of the U. States in members of the [85] Legislature, and disqualifying persons having unsettled Acc.ts with or being indebted to the U. S. from being members of the Nat.l Legislature"—He observed that persons of the latter descriptions had frequently got into the State Legislatures, in order to promote laws that might shelter their delinquencies; and that this evil had crept into Cong.s if Report was to be regarded.

M.r PINCKNEY seconded the motion

---

[84] In the transcript the vote reads: "New Hampshire, Connecticut, New Jersey, North Carolina, South Carolina, Georgia, aye—6; Pennsylvania, Delaware, Maryland, no—3; Massachusetts not on the floor; Virginia, divided [Mr. Blair and Col. Mason, aye. General Washington and Mr. Madison no, Mr. Randolph happened to be out of the House.]"

[85] The word "National" is here inserted in the transcript.

Mʳ Govʳ MORRIS. If qualifications are proper, he wᵈ prefer them in the electors rather than the elected. As to debtors of the U. S. they are but few. As to persons having unsettled accounts he believed them to pretty many. He thought however that such a discrimination would be both odious & useless, and in many instances unjust & cruel. The delay of settlemᵗ had been more the fault of the public than of the individuals. What will be done with those patriotic Citizens who have lent money, or services or property to their Country, without having been yet able to obtain a liquidation of their claims? Are they to be excluded?

Mʳ GHORUM was for leaving to the Legislature, the providing agˢᵗ such abuses as had been mentioned.

Col. MASON mentioned the parliamentary qualifications adopted in the Reign of Queen Anne, which he said had met with universal approbation

Mʳ MADISON had witnessed the zeal of men having accᵗˢ with the public, to get into the Legislatures for sinister purposes. He thought however that if any precaution were to be [86] taken for excluding them, the one proposed, by Col. Mason ought to be new [87] modelled. It might be well to limit the exclusion to persons who had recᵈ money from the public, and had not accounted for it.

Mʳ Govʳ MORRIS. It was a precept of great antiquity as well as [88] high authority that we should not be righteous overmuch. He thought we ought to be equally on our guard agˢᵗ being wise over much. The proposed regulation would enable the Govenᵗ to exclude particular persons from office as long as they pleased He mentioned the case of the Commander in Chief's presenting his account for secret services, which he said was so moderate that every one was astonished at it; and so simple that no doubt could arise on it. Yet had the Auditor been disposed to delay the settlement, how easily might he [89] have effected it, & how cruel wᵈ it be in such a case to keep a distinguished & meritorious Citizen

---

[86] The words "to be" are omitted in the transcript.
[87] The word "new" is crossed out and the syllable "re" is written above it.
[88] The word "of" is here inserted in the transcript.
[89] The words "might he" are transposed to read "he might" in the transcript.

under a temporary disability & disfranchisement. He mentioned this case merely to illustrate the objectionable nature of the proposition. He was opposed to such minutious regulations in a Constitution. The parliamentary qualifications quoted by Col. Mason, had been disregarded in practice; and was but a scheme of the landed ag:st the monied interest.

M:r PINCKNEY & Gen! PINCKNEY moved to insert by way of amendm:t the words Judiciary & Executive so as to extend the qualifications to those departments which was agreed to nem. con.

M:r GERRY thought the inconveniency [90] of excluding a few worthy individuals who might be public debtors or have unsettled acc:ts ought not to be put in the scale ag:st the public advantages of the regulation, and that the motion did not go far enough.

M:r KING observed that there might be great danger in requiring landed property as a qualification since it would [91] exclude the monied interest, whose aids may be essential in particular emergencies to the public safety.

M:r DICKENSON, was ag:st any recital of qualifications in the Constitution. It was impossible to make a compleat one, and a partial one w:d by implication tie up the hands of the Legislature from supplying the omissions, The best defence lay in the freeholders who were to elect the Legislature. Whilst this Source [92] should remain pure, the public interest would be safe. If it ever should be corrupt, no little expedients would repel the danger. He doubted the policy of interweaving into a Republican constitution a veneration for wealth. He had always understood that a veneration for poverty & virtue, were the objects of republican encouragement. It seemed improper that any man of merit should be subjected to disabilities in a Republic where merit was understood to form the great title to public trust, honors & rewards.

M:r GERRY if property be one object of Government, provisions for securing [93] it cannot be improper.

---

[90] The word "inconveniency" is changed to "inconvenience" in the transcript.
[91] The word "might" is substituted in the transcript for the word "would."
[92] The word "resource" is erroneously substituted in the transcript for the word "source."
[93] The words "to secure" are substituted for "for securing," in the transcript.

Mount Vernon

Mr MADISON moved to strike out the word *landed*, before the word "qualifications." If the proposition sd be agreed to he wished the Committee to be at liberty to report the best criterion they could devise. Landed possessions were no certain evidence of real wealth. Many enjoyed them to a great extent who were more in debt than they were worth. The unjust laws of the States had proceeded more from this class of men, than any others. It had often happened that men who had acquired landed property on credit, got into the Legislatures with a view of promoting an unjust protection agst their Creditors. In the next place, if a small quantity of land should be made the standard, it would be no security; if a large one, it would exclude the proper representatives of those classes of Citizens who were not landholders. It was politic as well as just that the interests & rights of every class should be duly represented & understood in the public Councils. It was a provision every where established that the Country should be divided into districts & representatives taken from each, in order that the Legislative Assembly might equally understand & sympathise, with the rights of the people in every part of the Community. It was not less proper that every class of Citizens should have an opportunity of making their rights be felt & understood in the public Councils. The three principal classes into which our citizens were divisible, were the landed the commercial, & the manufacturing. The 2d & 3d class, bear as yet a small proportion to the first. The proportion however will daily increase. We see in the populous Countries in [94] Europe now, what we shall be hereafter. These classes understand much less of each others interests & affairs, than men of the same class inhabiting different districts. It is particularly requisite therefore that the interests of one or two of them should not be left entirely to the care, or the [95] impartiality of the third. This must be the case if landed qualifications should be required; few of the mercantile, & scarcely any of the manufacturing class, chusing whilst they continue in business to turn any part of their Stock into landed property. For these reasons

---

[94] The word "of" is substituted in the transcript for "in."
[95] The word "the" is omitted in the transcript.

he wished if it were possible that some other criterion than the mere possession of land should be devised. He concurred with M! Gov! Morris in thinking that qualifications in the Electors would be much more effectual than in the elected. The former would discriminate between real & ostensible property in the latter; But he was aware of the difficulty of forming any uniform standard that would suit the different circumstances & opinions prevailing in the different States.

M! Gov! Morris 2<sup>d.ed</sup> the motion.

On the Question for striking out "landed"

N. H. ay. Mas. ay. C! ay. N. J. ay. P! ay. Del. ay. M<sup>d</sup> no. V<sup>a</sup> ay. N. C. ay. S. C. ay. Geo. ay.[96]

On [97] Question on [97] 1<sup>st</sup> part of Col. Masons proposition as to qualification of property & citizenship," as so amended

N. H. ay. Mas<sup>ts</sup> ay. C! no. N. J. ay. P! no. Del. no. M<sup>d</sup> ay. V<sup>a</sup> ay. N. C. ay. S. C. ay. Geo. ay.[98]

"The 2<sup>d</sup> part, for disqualifying debtors, and persons having unsettled accounts," being under consideration

M! Carrol moved to strike out "having unsettled accounts"

M! Ghorum seconded the motion; observing that it would put the commercial & manufacturing part of the people on a worse footing than others as they would be most likely to have dealings with the public.

M! L. Martin. if these words should be struck out, and the remaining words concerning debtors retained, it will be the interest of the latter class to keep their accounts unsettled as long as possible.

M! Wilson was for striking them out. They put too much power in the hands of the Auditors, who might combine with rivals in delaying settlements in order to prolong the disqualifications of particular men. We should consider that we are providing a Constitution for future generations, and not merely for the peculiar circumstances of the moment. The time has been, and will again be, when the public safety may depend on the voluntary aids of

---

[96] In the transcript the vote reads: "New Hampshire, Massachusetts, Connecticut, New Jersey, Pennsylvania, Delaware, Virginia, North Carolina, South Carolina, Georgia, aye—10; Maryland, no."

[97] The word "the" is here inserted in the transcript.

[98] In the transcript the vote reads: "New Hampshire, Massachusetts, New Jersey, Maryland, Virginia, North Carolina, South Carolina, Georgia, aye—8; Connecticut, Pennsylvania, Delaware, no—3."

individuals which will necessarily open acc'.' with the public, and when such acc'.' will be a characteristic of patriotism. Besides a partial enumeration of cases will disable the Legislature from disqualifying odious & dangerous characters.

M: LANGDON was for striking out the whole clause for the reasons given by M: Wilson. So many exclusions he thought too would render the system unacceptable to the people.

M: GERRY. If the argum'.' used to day were to prevail, we might have a Legislature composed of public debtors, pensioners, placemen & contractors. He thought the proposed qualifications would be pleasing to the people. They will be considered as a security ag:' unnecessary or undue burdens being imposed on them. He moved to add "pensioners" to the disqualified characters which was negatived.

N. H. no. Mas. ay. Con. no. N. J. no. P: no. Del. no. Mary⁴ ay. V: no. N. C. divided. S. C. no. Geo. ay.⁹⁹

M: Gov: MORRIS. The last clause, relating to public debtors will exclude every importing merchant. Revenue will be drawn it is foreseen as much as possible, from trade. Duties of course will be bonded, and the Merch'.' will remain debtors to the public. He repeated that it had not been so much the fault of individuals as of the public that transactions between them had not been more generally liquidated & adjusted. At all events to draw from our short & scanty experience rules that are to operate through succeeding ages, does not savour much of real wisdom.

On[1] question for striking out, "persons having unsettled accounts with the U. States."

N. H. ay. Mas. ay. C: ay. N. J. no. P: ay. Del. ay. M⁴ ay. V: ay. N. C. ay. S. C. ay. Geo. no.[2]

M: ELSEWORTH was for disagreeing to the remainder of the clause disqualifying public debtors; and for leaving to the wisdom of the Legislature and the virtue of the Citizens, the task of provid-

---

[99] In the transcript the vote reads: "Massachusetts, Maryland, Georgia, aye—3; New Hampshire, Connecticut, New Jersey, Pennsylvania, Delaware, Virginia, South Carolina, no—7; North Carolina, divided."

[1] The word "the" is here inserted in the transcript.

[2] In the transcript the vote reads: " New Hampshire, Massachusetts, Connecticut, Pennsylvania, Delaware, Maryland, Virginia, North Carolina, South Carolina, aye—9; New Jersey, Georgia, no—2."

ing ag:t such evils. Is the smallest as well³ largest debtor to be excluded? Then every arrear of taxes will disqualify. Besides how is it to be known to the people when they elect who are or are not public debtors. The exclusion of pensioners & placemen in Engld is founded on a consideration not existing here. As persons of that sort are dependent on the Crown, they tend to increase its influence.

M:r PINKNEY s:d he was at first a friend to the proposition, for the sake of the clause relating to qualifications of property; but he disliked the exclusion of public debtors; it went too far. It w:d exclude persons who had purchased confiscated property or should purchase Western territory of the public, and might be some obstacle to the sale of the latter.

On the question for agreeing to the clause disqualifying public debtors

N. H. no. Mas. no. C:t no. N. J. no. P:a no. Del. no. M:d no. V:a no. N. C. ay. S. C. no. Geo. ay.⁴

Col. MASON. observed that it would be proper, as he thought, that some provision should be made in the Constitution ag:st choosing for the seat of the Gen:l Gov:t the City or place at which the seat of any State Gov:t might be fixt. There were 2 objections ag:st having them at the same place, which without mentioning others, required some precaution on the subject. The 1:st was that it tended to produce disputes concerning jurisdiction. The 2:d & principal one was that the intermixture of the two Legislatures tended to give a provincial tincture to y:e Nat:l deliberations. He moved that the Com:e be instructed to receive a clause to prevent the seat of the Nat:l Gov:t being in the same City or town with the Seat of the Gov:t of any State longer than until the necessary public buildings could be erected.

M:r ALEX. MARTIN 2:ded the motion.

M:r Gov:r MORRIS did not dislike the idea, but was apprehensive that such a clause might make enemies of Phild:a & N. York which had expectations of becoming the Seat of the Gen:l Gov:t

---

³ The words "as the" are here inserted in the transcript.

⁴ In the transcript the vote reads: "North Carolina, Georgia, aye—2; New Hampshire, Massachusetts, Connecticut, New Jersey, Pennsylvania, Delaware, Maryland, Virginia, South Carolina, no—9."

Mr LANGDON approved the idea also: but suggested the case of a State moving its seat of Govt to the natl seat after the erection of the public buildings.

Mr GHORUM. The precaution may be evaded by the Natl Legislre by delaying to erect the public buildings.

Mr GERRY conceived it to be the genel sense of America, that neither the Seat of a State Govt nor any large commercial City should be the seat of the Genl Govt.

Mr WILLIAMSON liked the idea, but knowing how much the passions of men were agitated by this matter, was apprehensive of turning them agst the System. He apprehended also that an evasion might be practiced in the way hinted by Mr Ghorum.

Mr PINKNEY thought the seat of a State Govt ought to be avoided; but that a large town or its vicinity would be proper for the Seat of the Genl Govt.

Col. MASON did not mean to press the motion at this time, nor to excite any hostile passions agst the system. He was content to withdraw the motion for the present.

Mr BUTLER was for fixing by the Constitution the place, & a central one, for the seat of the Natl Govt.

The proceedings since Monday last were referred unanimously [5] to the Come of detail, and the Convention then unanimously Adjourned till Monday, Augst 6. that the Come of detail might have time to prepare & report the Constitution. The whole proceedings [6] as referred are as follow: "[here copy them from the Journal p. 207 [7]

| | | |
|---|---|---|
| [June 20.[8] | I. | RESOLVED, That the Government of the United States ought to consist of a supreme legislative, judiciary, and executive. |
| June 21. | II. | RESOLVED, That the legislature consist of two branches. |

---

[5] The words "referred unanimously" are transposed to read "unanimously referred" in the transcript.
[6] The word "proceedings" is crossed out in the transcript and "Resolutions" is written above it.
[7] Madison's direction is omitted in the transcript.
[8] The printed Journal says, page 11, that these 23 Resolutions are "collected from the proceedings of the convention, as they are spread over the journal from June 19th to July 26th." The dates in the margin show when the respective Resolutions were adopted. They are omitted in the transcript.

|  |  |  |
|---|---|---|
| June 22. | III. | RESOLVED, That the members of the first branch of the legislature ought to be elected by the people of the several states for the term of two years; to be paid out of the publick treasury; to receive an adequate compensation for their services; to be of the age of twenty-five years at least; to be ineligible [9] and incapable of holding any office under the authority of the United States (except those peculiarly belonging to the functions of the first branch) during the term of service of the first branch. |
| June 23. | | |
| June 25. | IV. | RESOLVED, That the members of the second branch of the legislature of the United States ought to be chosen by the individual legislatures; to be of the age of thirty years at least; to hold their offices for six years, one third to go out biennally; to receive a compensation for the devotion of their time to the publick service; to be ineligible to and incapable of holding any office, under the authority of the United States (except those peculiarly belonging to the functions of the second branch) during the term for which they are elected, and for one year thereafter. |
| June 26. | | |
|  | V. | RESOLVED, That each branch ought to possess the right of originating acts. |
| Postponed 27. July 16. July 17. | VI. | RESOLVED, That the national legislature ought to possess the legislative rights vested in Congress by the confederation; and moreover, to legislate in all cases for the general interests of the union, and also in those to which the states are separately incompetent, or in which the harmony of the United States may be interrupted by the exercise of individual legislation. |

---

[9] The word "to" is here inserted in the transcript.

VII. RESOLVED, That the legislative acts of the United States, made by virtue and in pursuance of the articles of union, and all treaties made and ratified under the authority of the United States, shall be the supreme law of the respective states, as far as those acts or treaties shall relate to the said states, or their citizens and inhabitants; and that the judiciaries of the several states shall be bound thereby in their decisions, any thing in the respective laws of the individual states to the contrary, notwithstanding.

16.   VIII. RESOLVED, That in the original formation of the legislature of the United States, the first branch thereof shall consist of sixty-five members; of which number

| | |
|---|---|
| New Hampshire shall send | three, |
| Massachusetts | eight, |
| Rhode Island | one, |
| Connecticut | five, |
| New York | six, |
| New Jersey | four, |
| Pennsylvania | eight, |
| Delaware | one, |
| Maryland | six, |
| Virginia | ten, |
| North Carolina | five, |
| South Carolina | five, |
| Georgia | three. |

But as the present situation of the states may probably alter in the number of their inhabitants, the legislature of the United States shall be authorized, from time to time, to apportion the number of representatives; and in case any of the states shall hereafter be divided, or enlarged by addition of territory, or any two or more states united, or any new states created within the limits of the United States, the legislature of the United States shall possess authority to regulate the number of representatives, in any of the foregoing cases, upon the principle of their number of inhabitants according to the provisions hereafter mentioned, namely—Provided always, that representation ought to be proportioned according [10] to direct taxation. And in order to ascertain the alteration in the direct taxation, which may be required from time to time by the changes in the relative circumstances of the states—

IX. RESOLVED, That a census be taken within six years from the first meeting of the legislature of the United States, and once within the term of every ten years afterwards, of all the inhabitants of the United States, in the manner and according to the ratio recommended by Congress in their resolution of April 18, 1783; and that the legislature of the United States shall proportion the direct taxation accordingly.

X. RESOLVED, That all bills for raising or appropriating money, and for fixing the salaries of the officers of the government of the United States, shall originate in the first branch of the legislature of the United States, and shall not be altered or amended by the second branch; and that no money shall be drawn from the publick treasury, but in pursuance of appropriations to be originated by the first branch.

XI. RESOLVED, That in the second branch of the legislature of the United States, each state shall have an equal vote.

---

[10] The word "according" is omitted in the transcript.

July 26.   XII. RESOLVED, That a national executive be instituted, to consist of a single person; to be chosen by the national legislature, for the term of seven years; to be ineligible a second time; with power to carry into execution the national laws; to appoint to offices in cases not otherwise provided for; to be removable on impeachment, and conviction of malpractice or neglect of duty; to receive a fixed compensation for the devotion of his time to [11] publick service; to be paid out of the publick treasury.

July 21.   XIII. RESOLVED, That the national executive shall have a right to negative any legislative act, which shall not be be afterwards passed, unless by two third parts of each branch of the national legislature.

18.
July 21.
18.
XIV. RESOLVED, That a national judiciary be established, to consist of one supreme tribunal, the judges of which shall be appointed by the second branch of the national legislature; to hold their offices during good behaviour; to receive punctually, at stated times, a fixed compensation for their services, in which no diminution shall be made, so as to affect the persons actually in office at the time of such diminution.

XV. RESOLVED, That the national legislature be empowered to appoint inferior tribunals.

XVI. RESOLVED, That the jurisdiction of the national judiciary shall extend to cases arising under laws passed by the general legislature; and to such other questions as involve the national peace and harmony.

---

[11] The word "the" is here inserted in the transcript.

XVII. RESOLVED, That provision ought to be made for the admission of states lawfully arising within the limits of the United States, whether from a voluntary junction of government and territory, or otherwise, with the consent of a number of voices in the national legislature less than the whole.

XVIII. RESOLVED, That a republican form of government shall be guarantied to each state; and that each state shall be protected against foreign and domestick violence.

23.   XIX. RESOLVED, That provision ought to be made for the amendment of the articles of union, whensoever it shall seem necessary.

XX. RESOLVED, That the legislative, executive, and judiciary powers, within the several states, and of the national government, ought to be bound, by oath, to support the articles of union.

XXI. RESOLVED, That the amendments which shall be offered to the confederation by the convention ought, at a proper time or times after the approbation of Congress, to be submitted to an assembly or assemblies of representatives, recommended by the several legislatures, to be expressly chosen by the people to consider and decide thereon.

XXII. RESOLVED, That the representation in the second branch of the legislature of the United States [12] consist of two members from each state, who shall vote per capita.

26.   XXIII. RESOLVED, That it be an instruction to the committee, to whom were referred the proceedings of the convention for the establishment of a national govern-

---

[12] The word "shall" is here inserted in the transcript.

ment, to receive a clause or clauses, requiring certain qualifications of property and citizenship, in the United States, for the executive, the judiciary, and the members of both branches of the legislature of the United States.]

With the above resolutions were referred the propositions offered by Mr C. Pinckney on the 29ᵗʰ of May, & by Mr Patterson on the 15ᵗʰ of June.[13]

MONDAY AUGUST 6ᵀᴴ IN CONVENTION

Mr John Francis Mercer from Maryland took his seat.

Mr RUTLIDGE delivered in the Report of the Committee of detail as follows: a printed copy being at the same time furnished to each member:[14]

"We the people of the States of New Hampshire, Massachussetts, Rhode-Island and Providence Plantations, Connecticut, New-York, New-Jersey, Pennsylvania, Delaware, Maryland, Virginia, North-Carolina, South-Carolina, and Georgia, do ordain, declare, and establish the following Constitution for the Government of Ourselves and our Posterity.

ARTICLE I

The stile of the Government shall be, "The United States of America"

[15] II

The Government shall consist of supreme legislative, executive; and judicial powers.

[15] III

The legislative power shall be vested in a Congress, to consist of two separate and distinct bodies of men, a House of Representatives and a Senate; each of which shall in all cases have a negative

---

[13] The word "Adjourned" is here inserted in the transcript.
[14] Madison's printed copy is marked: "As Reported by Come of Detail viz of five. Aug. 6. 1787." It is a large folio of seven pages. In the enumeration of the Articles by a misprint VI. was repeated, and the alterations in Article VII. and succeeding articles were made by Madison. In Sec. 11 of Article VI., as it was printed, it appeared: "The enacting stile of the laws of the United States shall be. 'Be it enacted, and it is hereby enacted by the House of Representatives, and by the Senate of the United States, in Congress assembled.'" which Madison altered to read: "The enacting stile of the laws of the United States shall be. 'Be it enacted by the Senate & representatives in Congress assembled.'" The printed copy among the Madison papers is a duplicate of the copy filed by General Washington with the papers of the Constitution, and Sec. 11 is there given as actually printed.

Madison accurately transcribed the report for his notes and it is this copy which is used in the text.
[15] The word "Article" is here inserted in the transcript.

on the other. The Legislature shall meet on the first Monday in December [16] every year.

## IV

Sect. 1. The members of the House of Representatives shall be chosen every second year, by the people of the several States comprehended within this Union. The qualifications of the electors shall be the same, from time to time, as those of the electors in the several States, of the most numerous branch of their own legislatures.

Sect. 2. Every member of the House of Representatives shall be of the age of twenty five years at least; shall have been a citizen in the United States for at least three years before his election; and shall be, at the time of his election, a resident of the State in which he shall be chosen.

Sect. 3. The House of Representatives shall, at its first formation, and until the number of citizens and inhabitants shall be taken in the manner herein after described, consist of sixty five Members, of whom three shall be chosen in New-Hampshire, eight in Massachusetts, one in Rhode-Island and Providence Plantations, five in Connecticut, six in New-York, four in New-Jersey, eight in Pennsylvania, one in Delaware, six in Maryland, ten in Virginia, five in North-Carolina, five in South-Carolina, and three in Georgia.

Sect. 4. As the proportions of numbers in different States will alter from time to time; as some of the States may hereafter be divided; as others may be enlarged by addition of territory; as two or more States may be united; as new States will be erected within the limits of the United States, the Legislature shall, in each of these cases, regulate the number of representatives by the number of inhabitants, according to the provisions herein after made, at the rate of one for every forty thousand.

Sect. 5. All bills for raising or appropriating money, and for fixing the salaries of the officers of Government, shall originate in the House of Representatives, and shall not be altered or amended by the Senate. No money shall be drawn from the Public Treasury, but in pursuance of appropriations that shall originate in the House of Representatives.

Sect. 6. The House of Representatives shall have the sole power of impeachment. It shall choose its Speaker and other officers.

---

[16] The word "in" is here inserted in the transcript.

Sect. 7. Vacancies in the House of Representatives shall be supplied by writs of election from the executive authority of the State, in the representation from which it [17] shall happen.

## [15] V

Sect. 1 The Senate of the United States shall be chosen by the Legislatures of the several States. Each Legislature shall chuse two members. Vacancies may be supplied by the Executive until the next meeting of the Legislature. Each member shall have one vote.

Sect. 2. The Senators shall be chosen for six years; but immediately after the first election they shall be divided, by lot, into three classes, as nearly as may be, numbered one, two and three. The seats of the members of the first class shall be vacated at the expiration of the second year, of the second class at the expiration of the fourth year, of the third class at the expiration of the sixth year, so that a third part of the members may be chosen every second year.

Sect. 3. Every member of the Senate shall be of the age of thirty years at least; shall have been a citizen in the United States for at least four years before his election; and shall be, at the time of his election, a resident of the State for which he shall be chosen.

Sect. 4. The Senate shall chuse its own President and other officers.

## [15] VI

Sect. 1. The times and places and manner of holding the elections of the members of each House shall be prescribed by the Legislature of each State; but their provisions concerning them may, at any time be altered by the Legislature of the United States.

Sect. 2. The Legislature of the United States shall have authority to establish such uniform qualifications of the members of each House, with regard to property, as to the said Legislature shall seem expedient.

Sect. 3. In each House a majority of the members shall constitute a quorum to do business; but a smaller number may adjourn from day to day.

Sect. 4. Each House shall be the judge of the elections, returns and qualifications of its own members.

---

[15] The word "Article" is here inserted in the transcript.
[17] The word "it" is crossed out and the word "they" is written above it in the transcript.

Sect. 5. Freedom of speech and debate in the Legislature shall not be impeached or questioned in any Court or place out of the Legislature; and the members of each House shall, in all cases, except treason felony and breach of the peace, be privileged from arrest during their attendance at Congress, and in going to and returning from it.

Sect. 6. Each House may determine the rules of its proceedings; may punish its members for disorderly behaviour; and may expel a member.

Sect. 7. The House of Representatives, and the Senate, when it shall be acting in a legislative capacity, shall keep a journal of their proceedings, and shall, from time to time, publish them: and the yeas and nays of the members of each House, on any question, shall at the desire of one-fifth part of the members present, be entered on the journal.

Sect. 8. Neither House, without the consent of the other, shall adjourn for more than three days, nor to any other place than that at which the two Houses are sitting. But this regulation shall not extend to the Senate, when it shall exercise the powers mentioned in the       article.

Sect. 9. The members of each House shall be ineligible to, and incapable of holding any office under the authority of the United States, during the time for which they shall respectively be elected: and the members of the Senate shall be ineligible to, and incapable of holding any such office for one year afterwards.

Sect. 10. The members of each House shall receive a compensation for their services, to be ascertained and paid by the State, in which they shall be chosen.

[18] Sect. 11. The enacting stile of the laws of the United States shall be. "Be it enacted by the Senate and Representatives in Congress assembled."

Sect. 12. Each House shall possess the right of originating bills, except in the cases beforementioned.

Sect. 13. Every bill, which shall have passed the House of Representatives and the Senate, shall, before it become [19] a law, be presented to the President of the United States for his revision: if, upon such revision, he approve of it, he shall signify his approbation by signing it: But if, upon such revision, it shall appear to him improper for being passed into a law, he shall return it, together with his objections against it, to that House in which it

---

[18] Section 11 is copied in the transcript as originally printed. See footnote [14] on p. 471.

[19] The word "becomes" is substituted in the transcript for "become."

shall have originated, who shall enter the objections at large on their journal and proceed to reconsider the bill. But if after such reconsideration, two thirds of that House shall, notwithstanding the objections of the President, agree to pass it, it shall together with his objections, be sent to the other House, by which it shall likewise be reconsidered, and if approved by two thirds of the other House also, it shall become a law. But in all such cases, the votes of both Houses shall be determined by yeas and nays; and the names of the persons voting for or against the bill shall be entered on the journal of each House respectively. If any bill shall not be returned by the President within seven days after it shall have been presented to him, it shall be a law, unless the legislature, by their adjournment, prevent its return; in which case it shall not be a law.

[15] VII

Sect. 1. The Legislature of the United States shall have the power to lay and collect taxes, duties, imposts and excises;

To regulate commerce with foreign nations, and among the several States;

To establish an uniform rule of naturalization throughout the United States;

To coin money;

To regulate the value of foreign coin;

To fix the standard of weights and measures;

To establish Post-offices;

To borrow money, and emit bills on the credit of the United States;

To appoint a Treasurer by ballot;

To constitute tribunals inferior to the Supreme Court;

To make rules concerning captures on land and water;

To declare the law and punishment of piracies and felonies committed on the high seas, and the punishment of counterfeiting the coin of the United States, and of offenses against the law of nations;

To subdue a rebellion in any State, on the application of its legislature;

To make war;

To raise armies;

To build and equip fleets;

To call forth the aid of the militia, in order to execute the laws of the Union, enforce treaties, suppress insurrections, and repel invasions;

---

[15] The word "Article" is here inserted in the transcript.

And to make all laws that shall be necessary and proper for carrying into execution the foregoing powers, and all other powers vested, by this Constitution, in the government of the United States, or in any department or officer [20] thereof;

Sect. 2. Treason against the United States shall consist only in levying war against the United States, or any of them; and in adhering to the enemies of the United States, or any of them. The Legislature of the United States shall have power to declare the punishment of treason. No person shall be convicted of treason, unless on the testimony of two witnesses. No attainder of treason shall work corruption of blood, nor forfeiture, except during the life of the person attainted.

Sect. 3. The proportions of direct taxation shall be regulated by the whole number of white and other free citizens and inhabitants of every age, sex and condition, including those bound to servitude for a term of years, and three fifths of all other persons not comprehended in the foregoing description, (except Indians not paying taxes) which number shall, within six years after the first meeting of the Legislature, and within the term of every ten years afterwards, be taken in such [21] manner as the said Legislature shall direct.

Sect. 4. No tax or duty shall be laid by the Legislature on articles exported from any State; nor on the migration or importation of such persons as the several States shall think proper to admit; nor shall such migration or importation be prohibited.

Sect. 5. No capitation tax shall be laid, unless in proportion to the Census hereinbefore directed to be taken.

Sect. 6. No navigation act shall be passed without the assent of two thirds of the members present in the each House.

Sect. 7. The United States shall not grant any title of Nobility.

## [15] VIII

The Acts of the Legislature of the United States made in pursuance of this Constitution, and all treaties made under the authority of the United States shall be the supreme law of the several States, and of their citizens and inhabitants; and the judges in the several States shall be bound thereby in their decisions; any thing in the Constitutions or laws of the several States to the contrary notwithstanding.

---

[15] The word "Article" is here inserted in the transcript.

[20] The letter "r" is stricken from the word "officer" in the transcript.

[21] The word "a" is here inserted in the transcript.

[15] IX

Sect 1. The Senate of the United States shall have power to make treaties, and to appoint Ambassadors, and Judges of the Supreme Court.

Sect. 2. In all disputes and controversies now subsisting, or that may hereafter subsist between two or more States, respecting jurisdiction or territory, the Senate shall possess the following powers. Whenever the Legislature, or the Executive authority, or lawful agent of any State, in controversy with another, shall by memorial to the Senate, state the matter in question, and apply for a hearing; notice of such memorial and application shall be given by order of the Senate, to the Legislature or the Executive authority of the other State in Controversy. The Senate shall also assign a day for the appearance of the parties, by their agents, before the [22] House. The Agents shall be directed to appoint, by joint consent, commissioners or judges to constitute a Court for hearing and determining the matter in question. But if the Agents cannot agree, the Senate shall name three persons out of each of the several States; and from the list of such persons each party shall alternately strike out one, until the number shall be reduced to thirteen; and from that number not less than seven nor more than nine names, as the Senate shall direct, shall in their presence, be drawn out by lot; and the persons whose names shall be so drawn, or any five of them shall be commissioners or Judges to hear and finally determine the controversy; provided a majority of the Judges, who shall hear the cause, agree in the determination. If either party shall neglect to attend at the day assigned, without shewing sufficient reasons for not attending, or being present shall refuse to strike, the Senate shall proceed to nominate three persons out of each State, and the Clerk of the Senate shall strike in behalf of the party absent or refusing. If any of the parties shall refuse to submit to the authority of such Court; or shall not appear to prosecute or defend their claim or cause, the Court shall nevertheless proceed to pronounce judgment. The judgment shall be final and conclusive. The proceedings shall be transmitted to the President of the Senate, and shall be lodged among the public records, for the security of the parties concerned. Every Commissioner shall, before he sit in judgment, take an oath, to be administered by one of the Judges of the Supreme or Superior Court of the State where the cause shall be tried, "well

---

[15] The word "Article" is here inserted in the transcript.
[22] The word "the" is changed to "that" in the transcript.

and truly to hear and determine the matter in question according to the best of his judgment, without favor, affection, or hope of reward."

Sect. 3. All controversies concerning lands claimed under different grants of two or more States, whose jurisdictions, as they respect such lands shall have been decided or adjusted subsequent[23] to such grants, or any of them, shall, on application to the Senate, be finally determined, as near as may be, in the same manner as is before prescribed for deciding controversies between different States.

[15] X

Sect. 1. The Executive Power of the United States shall be vested in a single person. His stile shall be, "The President of the United States of America;" and his title shall be, "His Excellency." He shall be elected by ballot by the Legislature. He shall hold his office during the term of seven years; but shall not be elected a second time.

Sect. 2. He shall, from time to time, give information to the Legislature, of the state of the Union: he may recommend to their consideration such measures as he shall judge necessary, and expedient: he may convene them on extraordinary occasions. In case of disagreement between the two Houses, with regard to the time of adjournment, he may adjourn them to such time as he thinks proper: he shall take care that the laws of the United States be duly and faithfully executed: he shall commission all the officers of the United States; and shall appoint officers in all cases not otherwise provided for by this Constitution. He shall receive Ambassadors, and may correspond with the supreme Executives of the several States. He shall have power to grant reprieves and pardons; but his pardon shall not be pleadable in bar of an impeachment. He shall be commander in chief of the Army and Navy of the United States, and of the Militia of the several States. He shall, at stated times, receive for his services, a compensation, which shall neither be increased nor diminished during his continuance in office. Before he shall enter on the duties of his department, he shall take the following oath or affirmation, "I ———— solemnly swear, (or affirm) that that[24] I will faithfully execute the office of President of the United States of America." He shall be removed from his office on impeachment by the House of

---

[15] The word "Article" is here inserted in the transcript.
[23] The syllable "ly" is added in the transcript to the word "subsequent."
[24] The word "that" is omitted in the transcript.

Representatives, and conviction in the supreme Court, of treason, bribery, or corruption. In case of his removal as aforesaid, death, resignation, or disability to discharge the powers and duties of his office, the President of the Senate shall exercise those powers and duties, until another President of the United States be chosen, or until the disability of the President be removed.

## [15] XI

Sect. 1. The Judicial Power of the United States shall be vested in one Supreme Court, and in such inferior Courts as shall, when necessary, from time to time, be constituted by the Legislature of the United States.

Sect. 2. The Judges of the Supreme Court, and of the Inferior Courts, shall hold their offices during good behaviour. They shall, at stated times, receive for their services, a compensation, which shall not be diminished during their continuance in office.

Sect. 3. The Jurisdiction of the Supreme Court shall extend to all cases arising under laws passed by the Legislature of the United States; to all cases affecting Ambassadors, other Public Ministers and Consuls; to the trial of impeachments of officers of the United States; to all cases of Admiralty and maritime jurisdiction; to controversies between two or more States, (except such as shall regard Territory or Jurisdiction) between a State and Citizens of another State, between Citizens of different States, and between a State or the Citizens thereof and foreign States, citizens or subjects. In cases of impeachment, cases affecting Ambassadors, other Public Ministers and Consuls, and those in which a State shall be party, this jurisdiction shall be original. In all the other cases beforementioned, it shall be appellate, with such exceptions and under such regulations as the Legislature shall make. The Legislature may assign any part of the jurisdiction abovementioned (except the trial of the President of the United States) in the manner, and under the limitations which it shall think proper, to such Inferior Courts, as it shall constitute from time to time.

Sect. 4. The trial of all criminal offences (except in cases of impeachments) shall be in the State where they shall be committed; and shall be by Jury.

Sect. 5. Judgment, in cases of Impeachment, shall not extend further than to removal from office, and disqualification to hold and enjoy any office of honour, trust or profit, under the United States. But the party convicted shall, nevertheless be liable and subject to indictment, trial, judgment and punishment according to law.

---

[15] The word "Article" is here inserted in the transcript.

### [15] XII

No State shall coin money; nor grant letters of marque and reprisal; nor enter into any Treaty, alliance, or confederation; nor grant any title of Nobility.

### [15] XIII

No State, without the consent of the Legislature of the United States, shall emit bills of credit, or make any thing but specie a tender in payment of debts; nor lay imposts or duties on imports; nor keep troops or ships of war in time of peace; nor enter into any agreement or compact with another State, or with any foreign power; nor engage in any war, unless it shall be actually invaded by enemies, or the danger of invasion be so imminent, as not to admit of delay, until the Legislature of the United States can be consulted.

### [15] XIV

The Citizens of each State shall be entitled to all privileges and immunities of citizens in the several States.

### [15] XV

Any person charged with treason, felony or high misdemeanor in any State, who shall flee from justice, and shall be found in any other State, shall, on demand of the Executive power of the State from which he fled, be delivered up and removed to the State having jurisdiction of the offence.

### [15] XVI

Full faith shall be given in each State to the acts of the Legislatures, and to the records and judicial proceedings of the Courts and magistrates of every other State.

### [15] XVII

New States lawfully constituted or established within the limits of the United States may be admitted, by the Legislature, into this Government; but to such admission the consent of two thirds of the members present in each House shall be necessary. If a new State shall arise within the limits of any of the present States, the consent of the Legislatures of such States shall be also necessary to its admission. If the admission be consented to, the new States shall be admitted on the same terms with the original States. But

---

[15] The word "Article" is here inserted in the transcript.

WASHINGTON CROSSING THE DELAWARE
*From a painting by Leutze*

481

the Legislature may make conditions with the new States, concerning the public debt which shall be then subsisting.

### [15] XVIII

The United States shall guaranty to each State a Republican form of Government; and shall protect each State against foreign invasions, and, on the application of its Legislature, against domestic violence.

### [15] XIX

On the application of the Legislatures of two thirds of the States in the Union, for an amendment of this Constitution, the Legislature of the United States shall call a Convention for that purpose.

### [15] XX

The members of the Legislatures, and the Executive and Judicial officers of the United States, and of the several States, shall be bound by oath to support this Constitution.

### [15] XXI

The ratifications of the Conventions of        States shall be sufficient for organizing this Constitution.

### [15] XXII

This Constitution shall be laid before the United States in Congress assembled, for their approbation; and it is the opinion of this Convention, that it should be afterwards submitted to a Convention chosen,[25] under the recommendation of its legislature, in order to receive the ratification of such Convention.

### [15] XXIII

To introduce this government, it is the opinion of this Convention, that each assenting Convention should notify its assent and ratification to the United States in Congress assembled; that Congress, after receiving the assent and ratification of the Conventions of        States, should appoint and publish a day, as early as may be, and appoint a place for commencing proceedings under this Constitution; that after such publication, the Legislatures of the several States should elect members of the Senate, and direct the election of members of the House of Representatives; and that the members of the Legislature should meet at the time and place

---

[15] The word "Article" is here inserted in the transcript.
[25] The phrase "in each State" is here inserted in the transcript.

assigned by Congress, and should, as soon as may be, after their meeting, choose the President of the United States, and proceed to execute this Constitution."

A motion was made to adjourn till Wednesday, in order to give leisure to examine the Report; which passed in the negative— N. H. no. Mas. no. Ct no. Pa ay. Md ay. Virg. ay. N. C. no. S. C. no.[26]

The House then adjourned till to morrow [27] 11 OC.

### TEUSDAY AUGUST 7TH. IN CONVENTION

The Report of the Committee of detail being taken up,

Mr PINKNEY moved that it be referred to a Committee of the whole. This was strongly opposed by Mr GHORUM & several others, as likely to produce unnecessary delay; and was negatived. Delaware Maryd & Virga only being in the affirmative.

The preamble of the Report was agreed to nem. con. So were Art: I & II.[28]

Art: III.[29, 30] considered. Col. MASON doubted the propriety of giving each branch a negative on the other "in all cases." There were some cases in which it was he supposed not intended to be given as in the case of balloting for appointments.

Mr GOVr MORRIS moved to insert "legislative acts" instead of "all cases"

Mr WILLIAMSON 2ds him.

Mr SHERMAN. This will restrain the operation of the clause too much. It will particularly exclude a mutual negative in the case of ballots, which he hoped would take place.

Mr GHORUM contended that elections ought to be made by *joint ballot*. If separate ballots should be made for the President, and the two branches should be each attached to a favorite, great delay contention & confusion may ensue. These inconveniences have been felt in Masts in the election of officers of little importance compared with the Executive of the U. States. The only objection

---

[26] In the transcript the vote reads: "Pennsylvania, Maryland, Virginia, aye—3; New Hampshire, Massachusetts, Connecticut, North Carolina, South Carolina, no—5."
[27] The word "at" is here inserted in the transcript.
[28] See *ante*.
[29] See *ante*.
[30] The word "being" is here inserted in the transcript.

ag$^{st}$ a joint ballot is that it may deprive the Senate of their due weight; but this ought not to prevail over the respect due to the public tranquility & welfare.

M$^r$ WILSON was for a joint ballot in several cases at least; particularly in the choice of the President, and was therefore for the amendment. Disputes between the two Houses during & concern$^s$ the vacancy of the Executive might have dangerous consequences.

Col. MASON thought the amendment of M$^r$ Gov$^r$ Morris extended too far. Treaties are in a subsequent part declared to be laws, they will be therefore [31] subjected to a negative; altho' they are to be made as proposed by the Senate alone. He proposed that the mutual negative should be restrained to "cases requiring the distinct assent" of the two Houses.

M$^r$ Gov$^r$ MORRIS thought this but a repetition of the same thing; the mutual negative and distinct assent, being equivalent expressions. Treaties he thought were not laws.

M$^r$ MADISON moved to strike out the words "each of which shall in all cases, have a negative on the other; the idea being sufficiently expressed in the preceding member of the article; vesting the "legislative power" in "distinct bodies," especially as the respective powers and mode of exercising them were fully delineated in a subsequent article.

Gen$^l$ PINKNEY 2$^{ded}$ the motion

On [32] question for inserting legislative Acts as moved by M$^r$ Gov$^r$ Morris.[33]

N. H. ay. Mas. ay. C$^t$ ay. P$^a$ ay. Del. no. M$^d$ no. V$^a$ no. N. C. ay. S. C. no. Geo. no.[34]

On [32] question for agreeing to M$^r$ M's motion to strike out &c.–

N. H. ay. Mas. ay. C$^t$ no. P$^a$ ay. Del. ay. M$^d$ no. V$^a$ ay. N. C. no. S. C. ay. Geo. ay.[35]

M$^r$ MADISON wished to know the reasons of the Com$^e$ for fixing by y$^e$ Constitution the time of Meeting for the Legislature; and sug-

---

[31] The words "be therefore" are changed in the transcript to "therefore be."

[32] The word "the" is here inserted in the transcript.

[33] The phrase "it passed in the negative, the votes being equally divided," is here inserted in the transcript.

[34] In the transcript the vote reads: "New Hampshire, Massachusetts, Connecticut, Pennsylvania, North Carolina, aye—5; Delaware, Maryland, Virginia, South Carolina, Georgia, no—5."

[35] In the transcript the vote reads: "New Hampshire, Massachusetts, Pennsylvania, Delaware, Virginia, South Carolina, Georgia, aye—7; Connecticut, Maryland, North Carolina, no—3."

gested, that it be required only that one meeting at least should be held every year leaving the time to be fixed or varied by law.

Mr Govr Morris moved to strike out the sentence. It was improper to tie down the Legislature to a particular time, or even to require a meeting every year. The public business might not require it.

Mr Pinkney concurred with Mr Madison.

Mr Ghorum. If the time be not fixed by the Constitution, disputes will arise in the Legislature; and the States will be at a loss to adjust thereto, the times of their elections. In the N. England States the annual time of meeting had been long fixed by their Charters & Constitutions, and no inconveniency [36] had resulted. He thought it necessary that there should be one meeting at least every year as a check on the Executive department.

Mr Elseworth was agst striking out the words. The Legislature will not know till they are met whether the public interest required their meeting or not. He could see no impropriety in fixing the day, as the Convention could judge of it as well as the Legislature.

Mr Wilson thought on the whole it would be best to fix the day.

Mr King could not think there would be a necessity for a meeting every year. A great vice in our system was that of legislating too much. The most numerous objects of legislation belong to the States. Those of the Natl Legislature were but few. The chief of them were commerce & revenue. When these should be once settled, alterations would be rarely necessary & easily made.

Mr Madison thought if the time of meeting should be fixed by a law it wd be sufficiently fixed & there would be no difficulty then as had been suggested, on the part of the States in adjusting their elections to it. One consideration appeared to him to militate strongly agst fixing a time by the Constitution. It might happen that the Legislature might be called together by the public exigencies & finish their Session but a short time before the annual period. In this case it would be extremely inconvenient to reassemble so quickly & without the least necessity. He thought one annual meeting ought to be required; but did not wish to make two unavoidable.

---

[36] The word "inconveniency" is changed in the transcript to "inconvenience."

Col. MASON thought the objections against fixing the time insuperable: but that an annual meeting ought to be required as essential to the preservation of the Constitution. The extent of the Country will supply business. And if it should not, the Legislature, besides *legislative,* is to have *inquisitorial* powers, which can not safely be long kept in a state of suspension.

M$^r$ SHERMAN was decided for fixing the time, as well as for frequent meetings of the Legislative body. Disputes and difficulties will arise between the two Houses, & between both & the States, if the time be changeable—frequent meetings of Parliament were required at the Revolution in England as an essential safeguard of liberty. So also are annual meetings in most of the American charters & constitutions. There will be business eno' to require it. The Western Country, and the great extent and varying state of our affairs in general will supply objects.

M$^r$ RANDOLPH was ag$^{st}$ fixing any day irrevocably; but as there was no provision made any where in the Constitution for regulating the periods of meeting, and some precise time must be fixed, untill the Legislature shall make provision, he could not agree to strike out the words altogether. Instead of which he moved to add the words following—"unless a different day shall be appointed by law."

M$^r$ MADISON 2$^{ded}$ the motion, & on the question

N. H. no. Mas. ay. C$^t$ no. P$^a$ ay. Del. ay. M$^d$ ay. V$^a$ ay. N. C. ay. S. C. ay. Geo. ay.[87]

M$^r$ Gov$^r$ MORRIS moved to strike out Dec$^r$ & insert May. It might frequently happen that our measures ought to be influenced by those in Europe, which were generally planned during the Winter and of which intelligence would arrive in the Spring.

M$^r$ MADISON 2$^{ded}$ the motion, he preferred May to Dec$^r$ because the latter would require the travelling to & from the seat of Gov$^t$ in the most inconvenient seasons of the year.

M$^r$ WILSON. The Winter is the most convenient season for business.

---

[87] In the transcript the vote reads: "Massachusetts, Pennsylvania, Delaware, Maryland, Virginia, North Carolina, South Carolina, Georgia, aye—8; New Hampshire, Connecticut, no—2."

Mr. ELSEWORTH. The summer will interfere too much with private business, that of almost all the probable members of the Legislature being more or less connected with agriculture.

Mr. RANDOLPH. The time is of no great moment now, as the Legislature can vary it. On looking into the Constitutions of the States, he found that the times of their elections with which the election [38] of the Natl. Representatives would no doubt be made to co-incide, would suit better with Decr. than May. And it was adviseable to render our innovations as little incommodious as possible.

On [39] question for "May" instead of "Decr."

N. H. no. Mas. no. Ct. no. Pa. no. Del. no. Md. no. Va. no. N. C no. S. C. ay. Geo. ay.[40]

Mr. READ moved to insert after the word "Senate" the words, "subject to the Negative to be hereafter provided." His object was to give an absolute negative to the Executive—He considered this as so essential to the Constitution, to the preservation of liberty, & to the public welfare, that his duty compelled him to make the motion.

Mr. Govr. MORRIS 2ded. him. And on the question

N. H. no. Mas. no. Ct. no. Pa. no. Del. ay. Md. no. Va. no. N. C. no. S. C. no. Geo. no.[41]

Mr. RUTLIDGE. Altho' it is agreed on all hands that an annual meeting of the Legislature should be made necessary, yet that point seems not to be freed from doubt as the clause stands. On this suggestion, "Once at least in every year," were inserted, nem. con.

Art. III with the foregoing alterations was agd. to nem. con. and is as follows "The Legislative power shall be vested in a Congress to consist of 2 separate & distinct bodies of men; a House of Reps. & a Senate The Legislature shall meet at least once in every year, and such meeting shall be on the 1st. monday in Decr. unless a different day shall be appointed by law."

---

[38] The word "election" is used in the plural in the transcript.

[39] The word "the" is here inserted in the transcript.

[40] In the transcript the vote reads: "South Carolina, Georgia, aye—2; New Hampshire, Massachusetts, Connecticut, Pennsylvania, Delaware, Maryland, Virginia, North Carolina, no—8."

[41] In the transcript the vote reads: "Delaware, aye—1; New Hampshire, Massachusetts, Connecticut, Pennsylvania, Maryland, Virginia, North Carolina, South Carolina, Georgia, no—9."

"Art IV. Sect. 1.⁴²,⁴³ taken up."

Mʳ Govʳ Morris moved to strike out the last member of the section beginning with the words "qualifications" of Electors," in order that some other provision might be substituted which wᵈ restrain the right of suffrage to freeholders.

Mʳ Fitzimmons 2ᵈᵉᵈ the motion

Mʳ Williamson was opposed to it.

Mʳ Wilson. This part of the Report was well considered by the Committee, and he did not think it could be changed for the better. It was difficult to form any uniform rule of qualifications for all the States. Unnecessary innovations he thought too should be avoided. It would be very hard & disagreeable for the same persons at the same time, to vote for representatives in the State Legislature and to be excluded from a vote for those in the Natˡ Legislature.

Mʳ Govʳ Morris. Such a hardship would be neither great nor novel. The people are accustomed to it and not dissatisfied with it, in several of the States. In some the qualifications are different for the choice of the Govʳ & ⁴⁴ Representatives; In others for different Houses of the Legislature. Another objection agˢᵗ the clause as it stands is that it makes the qualifications of the Natˡ Legislature depend on the will of the States, which he thought not proper.

Mʳ Elseworth. thought the qualifications of the electors stood on the most proper footing. The right of suffrage was a tender point, and strongly guarded by most of the State Constitutions. The people will not readily subscribe to the Natˡ Constitution if it should subject them to be disfranchised. The States are the best Judges of the circumstances & temper of their own people.

Col. Mason. The force of habit is certainly not attended to by those gentlemen who wish for innovations on this point. Eight or nine States have extended the right of suffrage beyond the freeholders, what will the people there say, if they should be disfranchised. A power to alter the qualifications would be a dangerous power in the hands of the Legislature.

---

[42] See *ante*.
[43] The words "was then" are here inserted in the transcript.
[44] The words "of the" are here inserted in the transcript.

488

Mr BUTLER. There is no right of which the people are more jealous than that of suffrage. Abridgments of it tend to the same revolution as in Holland where they have at length thrown all power into the hands of the Senates, who fill up vacancies themselves, and form a rank aristocracy.

Mr DICKINSON. had a very different idea of the tendency of vesting the right of suffrage in the freeholders of the Country. He considered them as the best guardians of liberty; And the restriction of the right to them as a necessary defence agst the dangerous influence of those multitudes without property & without principle with which our Country like all others, will in time abound. As to the unpopularity of the innovation it was in his opinion chemirical. The great mass of our Citizens is composed at this time of freeholders, and will be pleased with it.

Mr ELSEWORTH. How shall the freehold be defined? Ought not every man who pays a tax, to vote for the representative who is to levy & dispose of his money? Shall the wealthy merchants & manufacturers, who will bear a full share of the public burdens be not allowed a voice in the imposition of them—taxation & representation ought to go together.

Mr Govr MORRIS. He had long learned not to be the dupe of words. The sound of Aristocracy therefore had no effect on [45] him. It was the thing, not the name, to which he was opposed, and one of his principal objections to the Constitution as it is now before us, is that it threatens this [46] Country with an Aristocracy. The aristocracy will grow out of the House of Representatives. Give the votes to people who have no property, and they will sell them to the rich who will be able to buy them. We should not confine our attention to the present moment. The time is not distant when this Country will abound with mechanics & manufacturers [47] who will receive their bread from their employers. Will such men be the secure & faithful Guardians of liberty? Will they be the impregnable barrier agst aristocracy?—He was as little duped by the association of the words "taxation & Representation." The man who does not give his vote freely is not

---

[45] The word "upon" is substituted in the transcript for "on."
[46] The word "the" is substituted in the transcript for "this."
[47] The word "manufacturers" is substituted in the transcript for "manufactures."

represented. It is the man who dictates the vote. Children do not vote. Why? because they want prudence, because they have no will of their own. The ignorant & the dependent can be as little trusted with the public interest. He did not conceive the difficulty of defining "freeholders" to be insuperable. Still less that the restriction could be unpopular. $9/_{10}$ of the people are at present freeholders and these will certainly be pleased with it. As to Merch$^{ts}$ &c. if they have wealth & value the right they can acquire it. If not they don't deserve it.

Col. MASON. We all feel too strongly the remains of antient prejudices, and view things too much through a British medium. A Freehold is the qualification in England, & hence it is imagined to be the only proper one. The true idea in his opinion was that every man having evidence of attachment to & permanent common interest with the Society ought to share in all its rights & privileges. Was this qualification restrained to freeholders? Does no other kind of property but land evidence a common interest in the proprietor? does nothing besides property mark a permanent attachment. Ought the merchant, the monied man, the parent of a number of children whose fortunes are to be pursued in his own Country, to be viewed as suspicious characters, and unworthy to be trusted with the common rights of their fellow Citizens

M$^r$ MADISON. the right of suffrage is certainly one of the fundamental articles of republican Government, and ought not to be left to be regulated by the Legislature. A gradual abridgment of this right has been the mode in which Aristocracies have been built on the ruins of popular forms. Whether the Constitutional qualification ought to be a freehold, would with him depend much on the probable reception such a change would meet with in [48] States where the right was now exercised by every description of people. In several of the States a freehold was now the qualification. Viewing the subject in its merits alone, the freeholders of the Country would be the safest depositories of Republican liberty. In future times a great majority of the people will not only be without landed, but any other sort of, property. These will either combine under the influence of their common situation;

---

[48] The word "the" is here inserted in the transcript.

in which case, the rights of property & the public liberty, will not be secure in their hands: or which [49] is more probable, they will become the tools of opulence & ambition, in which case there will be equal danger on another side. The example of England had been misconceived [by Col Mason]. A very small proportion of the Representatives are there chosen by freeholders. The greatest part are chosen by the Cities & boroughs, in many of which the qualification of suffrage is as low as it is in any one of the U. S. and it was in the boroughs & Cities rather than the Counties, that bribery most prevailed, & the influence of the Crown on elections was most dangerously exerted.[50]

Doc.$^r$ FRANKLIN. It is of great consequence that we sh$^d$ not depress the virtue & public spirit of our common people; of which they displayed a great deal during the war, and which contributed principally to the favorable issue of it. He related the honorable refusal of the American seamen who were carried in great numbers into the British Prisons during the war, to redeem themselves from misery or to seek their fortunes, by entering on board the Ships of the Enemies to their Country; contrasting their patriotism with a contemporary instance in which the British seamen made prisoners by the Americans, readily entered on the ships of the latter on being promised a share of the prizes that might be made out of their own Country. This proceeded he said from the different manner in which the common people were treated in America & G. Britain. He did not think that the elected had any right in any case to narrow the privileges of the electors. He quoted as arbitrary the British Statute setting forth the danger of tumultuous meetings, and under that pretext narrowing the right of suffrage to persons having freeholds of a certain value; observing that this Statute was soon followed by another under the succeeding Parliam$^t$ subjecting the people who had no votes to peculiar labors & hardships. He was persuaded also that such a restriction as was proposed would give great uneasiness in the populous States. The sons of a substantial farmer, not being themselves freeholders, would not be pleased at being disfranchised, and there are a great many persons of that description.

---

[49] The word "which" is crossed out in the transcript and "what" is written above it.

[50] In the transcript the following footnote is here added: "See Appendix No. — for a note of Mr. Madison to this speech."

Mr MERCER. The Constitution is objectionable in many points, but in none more than the present. He objected to the footing on which the qualification was put, but particularly to the *mode of election* by the people. The people can not know & judge of the characters of Candidates. The worse possible choice will be made. He quoted the case of the Senate in Virgª as an example in point. The people in Towns can unite their votes in favor of one favorite; & by that means always prevail over the people of the Country, who being dispersed will scatter their votes among a variety of candidates.

Mr RUTLIDGE thought the idea of restraining the right of suffrage to the freeholders a very unadvised one. It would create division among the people & make enemies of all those who should be excluded.

On the question for striking out as moved by Mr Govr Morris, from the word "qualifications" to the end of the III article.

N. H. no. Mas. no. Cᵗ no. Pª no. Del. ay. Mᵈ divᵈ Vª no. N. C. no. S. C. no. Geo. not presᵗ [51]

Adjourned

---

WEDNESDAY AUGᵗ 8. IN CONVENTION

Art: IV. Sect. 1.[52, 53]—Mr MERCER expressed his dislike of the whole plan, and his opinion that it never could succeed.

Mr GHORUM. he had never seen any inconveniency [54] from allowing such as were not freeholders to vote, though it had long been tried. The elections in Philª N. York & Boston where the Merchants, & Mechanics vote are at least as good as those made by freeholders only. The case in England was not accurately stated yesterday [by Mr Madison] The Cities & large towns are not the seat of Crown influence & corruption. These prevail in the Boroughs, and not on account of the right which those who are not freeholders have to vote, but of the smallness of the number who

---

[51] In the transcript the vote reads: "Delaware, aye—1; New Hampshire, Massachusetts, Connecticut, Pennsylvania, Virginia, North Carolina, South Carolina, no—7; Maryland, divided; Georgia, not present"
[52] See *ante*.
[53] The words "being under consideration" are here inserted in the transcript.
[54] The word "inconveniency" is changed to "inconvenience" in the transcript.

vote. The people have been long accustomed to this right in various parts of America, and will never allow it to be abridged. We must consult their rooted prejudices if we expect their concurrence in our propositions.

M! MERCER did not object so much to an election by the people at large including such as were not freeholders, as to their being left to make their choice without any guidance. He hinted that Candidates ought to be nominated by the State Legislatures.

On [55] question for agreeing to Art: IV– Sect. 1 it pass<sup>d</sup> nem. con.

Art IV. Sect. 2 [52], [56] taken up.

Col. MASON was for opening a wide door for emigrants; but did not chuse to let foreigners and adventurers make laws for us & govern us. Citizenship for three years was not enough for ensuring that local knowledge which ought to be possessed by the Representative. This was the principal ground of his objection to so short a term. It might also happen that a rich foreign Nation, for example Great Britain, might send over her tools who might bribe their way into the Legislature for insidious purposes. He moved that "seven" years instead of "three," be inserted.

M! Gov! MORRIS 2<sup>ded</sup> the Motion, & on the question, all the States agreed to it except Connecticut.

M! SHERMAN moved to strike out the word "resident" and insert "inhabitant," as less liable to miscontruction.

M! MADISON 2<sup>ded</sup> the motion, both were vague, but the latter least so in common acceptation, and would not exclude persons absent occasionally for a considerable time on public or private business. Great disputes had been raised in Virg<sup>a</sup> concerning the meaning of residence as a qualification of Representatives which were determined more according to the affection or dislike to the man in question, than to any fixt interpretation of the word.

M! WILSON preferred "inhabitant."

M! Gov! MORRIS, was opposed to both and for requiring nothing more than a freehold. He quoted great disputes in N. York occasioned by these terms, which were decided by the arbitrary will

---
[52] See *ante*.
[55] The word "the" is here inserted in the transcript.
[56] The words "was then" are here inserted in the transcript.

of the majority. Such a regulation is not necessary. People rarely chuse a nonresident—It is improper as in the 1ˢᵗ branch, *the people at large*, not the *States*, are represented.

Mʳ RUTLIDGE urged & moved that a residence of 7 years shᵈ be required in the State Wherein the Member shᵈ be elected. An emigrant from N. England to S. C. or Georgia would know little of its affairs and could not be supposed to acquire a thorough knowledge in less time.

Mʳ READ reminded him that we were now forming a *Natˡ* Govᵗ and such a regulation would correspond little with the idea that we were one people.

Mʳ WILSON. enforced the same consideration.

Mʳ MADISON suggested the case of new States in the West, which could have perhaps no representation on that plan.

Mʳ MERCER. Such a regulation would present a greater alienship among the States [57] than existed under the old federal system. It would interweave local prejudices & State distinctions in the very Constitution which is meant to cure them. He mentioned instances of violent disputes raised in Maryland concerning the term "residence"

Mʳ ELSEWORTH thought seven years of residence was by far too long a term: but that some fixt term of previous residence would be proper. He thought one year would be sufficient, but seemed to have no objection to three years.

Mʳ DICKENSON proposed that it should read "inhabitant actually resident for          year.[58] This would render the meaning less indeterminate.

Mʳ WILSON. If a short term should be inserted in the blank, so strict an expression might be construed to exclude the members of the Legislature, who could not be said to be actual residents in their States whilst at the Seat of the Genˡ Government.

Mʳ MERCER. It would certainly exclude men, who had once been inhabitants, and returning from residence elsewhere to resettle in their original State; although a want of the necessary knowledge could not in such case [59] be presumed.

---

[57] The phrase "among the States" is omitted in the transcript.
[58] The transcript uses the word "year" in the plural.
[59] The transcript uses the word "case" in the plural.

M! MASON thought 7 years too long, but would never agree to part with the principle. It is a valuable principle. He thought it a defect in the plan that the Representatives would be too few to bring with them all the local knowledge necessary. If residence be not required, Rich men of neighbouring States, may employ with success the means of corruption in some particular district and thereby get into the public Councils after having failed in their own State.[60] This is the practice in the boroughs of England.

On the question for postponing in order to consider M! Dickensons motion.

N. H. no. Mas. no. C! no. N. J. no. P! no. Del. no. M! ay. V! no. N. C. no. S. C. ay. Geo. ay.[61]

On the question for inserting "inhabitant" in place of "resident"—ag! to nem. con.

M! ELSEWORTH & Col. MASON move to insert "one year" for previous inhabitancy

M! WILLIAMSON liked the Report as it stood. He thought "resident" a good eno' term. He was ag!! requiring any period of previous residence. New residents if elected will be most zealous to Conform to the will of their constituents, as their conduct will be watched with a more jealous eye.

M! BUTLER & M! RUTLIDGE moved "three years" instead of "one year" for previous inhabitancy

On the question for 3 years—

N. H. no. Mas. no. C! no. N. J. no. P! no. Del. no. M! no. V! no. N. C. no. S. C. ay. Geo. ay.[62]

On the question for "1 year"

N. H. no—Mas. no. C! no. N. J. ay. P! no. Del. no. M! div! V! no. N. C. ay. S. C. ay. Geo. ay.[63]

Art. IV. Sect. 2. As amended in manner preceding, was agreed to nem. con.

Art: IV. Sect. 3." [64, 65] taken up.

---

[60] The transcript uses the word "State" in the plural.

[61] In the transcript the vote reads: "Maryland, South Carolina, Georgia, aye—3; New Hampshire, Massachusetts, Connecticut, New Jersey, Pennsylvania, Delaware, Virginia, North Carolina, no—8."

[62] In the transcript the vote reads: "South Carolina, Georgia, aye—2; New Hampshire, Massachusetts, Connecticut, New Jersey, Pennsylvania, Delaware, Maryland, Virginia, North Carolina, no—9."

[63] In the transcript the vote reads: "New Jersey, North Carolina, South Carolina, Georgia, aye—4; New Hampshire, Massachusetts, Connecticut, Pennsylvania, Delaware, Virginia, no—6; Maryland, divided."

[64] See *ante*.

[65] The words "was then" are here inserted in the transcript.

Gen! Pinkney & M! Pinkney moved that the number of representatives allotted to S. Carol⍺ be "six" on the question,

N. H. no. Mas. no. C! no. N. J. no. P⍺ no. Delaware ay M⍺ no. V⍺ no. N. C. ay. S. C. ay. Geo. ay.[66]

The 3. Sect. of Art: IV was then agreed to.

Art: IV. Sect. 4 [64, 65] taken up.

M! Williamson moved to strike out "according to the provisions hereinafter after made" and to insert the words "according "to the rule hereafter to be provided for direct taxation"— See Art. VII. sect. 3.[67]

On the question for agreeing to M! Williamson's amendment

N. H. ay. Mas. ay. C! ay. N. J. no. P⍺ ay. Del. no. M⍺ ay. V⍺ ay. N. C. ay. S. C. ay. Geo. ay.[68]

M! King wished to know what influence the vote just passed was meant [69] have on the succeeding part of the Report, concerning the admission of slaves into the rule of Representation. He could not reconcile his mind to the article if it was to prevent objections to the latter part. The admission of slaves was a most grating circumstance to his mind, & he believed would be so to a great part of the people of America. He had not made a strenuous opposition to it heretofore because he had hoped that this concession would have produced a readiness which had not been manifested, to strengthen the Gen! Gov! and to mark a full confidence in it. The Report under consideration had by the tenor of it, put an end to all those hopes. In two great points the hands of the Legislature were absolutely tied. The importation of slaves could not be prohibited—exports could not be taxed. Is this reasonable? What are the great objects of the Gen! System? 1.[70] defence ag!t foreign invasion. 2.[70] ag!t internal sedition. Shall all the States then be bound to defend each; & shall each be at liberty to introduce a weakness which will render defence more difficult? Shall one part of the U. S.

---

[64] See *ante.*

[65] The words "was then" are here inserted in the transcript.

[66] In the transcript the vote reads: "Delaware, North Carolina, South Carolina, Georgia, aye—4; New Hampshire, Massachusetts, Connecticut, New Jersey, Pennsylvania, Maryland, Virginia, no—7."

[67] See *ante.*

[68] In the transcript the vote reads: "New Hampshire, Massachusetts, Connecticut, Pennsylvania, Maryland, Virginia, North Carolina, South Carolina, Georgia, aye—9; New Jersey, Delaware, no—2."

[69] The word "to" is here inserted in the transcript.

[70] The figures "1" and "2" are changed to "First" and "Secondly" in the transcript.

be bound to defend another part, and that other part be at liberty not only to increase its own danger, but to withhold the compensation for the burden? If slaves are to be imported shall not the exports produced by their labor, supply a revenue the better to enable the Gen! Gov! to defend their masters?—There was so much inequality & unreasonableness in all this, that the people of the Northern States could never be reconciled to it. No candid man could undertake to justify it to them. He had hoped that some accomodation w<sup>d</sup> have taken place on this subject; that at least a time w<sup>d</sup> have been limited for the importation of slaves. He never could agree to let them be imported without limitation & then be represented in the Nat! Legislature. Indeed he could so little persuade himself of the rectitude of such a practice, that he was not sure he could assent to it under any circumstances. At all events, either slaves should not be represented, or exports should be taxable.

M<sup>r</sup> SHERMAN regarded the slave trade as iniquitous; but the point of representation having been settled after much difficulty & deliberation, he did not think himself bound to make opposition; especially as the present article as amended did not preclude any arrangement whatever on that point in another place of the Report.

M<sup>r</sup> MADISON objected to 1 for every 40,000, inhabitants as a perpetual rule. The future increase of population if the Union sh<sup>d</sup> be permanent, will render the number of Representatives excessive.

M<sup>r</sup> GHORUM. It is not to be supposed that the Gov! will last so long as to produce this effect. Can it be supposed that this vast Country including the Western territory will 150 years hence remain one nation?

M<sup>r</sup> ELSEWORTH. If the Gov! should continue so long, alterations may be made in the Constitution in the manner proposed in a subsequent article.

M<sup>r</sup> SHERMAN & M<sup>r</sup> MADISON moved to insert the words "not exceeding" before the words "1 for every 40,000, which was agreed to nem. con.

M.̲ Gov.̲ Morris moved to insert "free" before the word inhabitants. Much he said would depend on this point. He never would concur in upholding domestic slavery. It was a nefarious institution. It was the curse of heaven on the States where it prevailed. Compare the free regions of the Middle States, where a rich & noble cultivation marks the prosperity & happiness of the people, with the misery & poverty which overspread the barren wastes of V.ª Mary.ᵈ & the other States having slaves. Travel thro' y.ᵉ whole Continent & you behold the prospect continually varying with the appearance & disappearance of slavery. The moment you leave y.ᵉ E. Sts. & enter N. York, the effects of the institution become visible, passing thro' the Jerseys & entering P.ª every criterion of superior improvement witnesses the change. Proceed southw$^{dly}$ & every step you take thro' y.ᵉ great region of slaves presents a desert increasing, with y.ᵉ increasing proportion of these wretched beings. Upon what principle is it that the slaves shall be computed in the representation? Are they men? Then make them Citizens and let them vote. Are they property? Why then is no other property included? The Houses in this city [Philad.ª] are worth more than all the wretched slaves which cover the rice swamps of South Carolina. The admission of slaves into the Representation when fairly explained comes to this: that the inhabitant of Georgia and S. C. who goes to the Coast of Africa, and in defiance of the most sacred laws of humanity tears away his fellow creatures from their dearest connections & damns them to the most cruel bondages,[71] shall have more votes in a Gov.ᵗ instituted for protection of the rights of mankind, than the Citizen of P.ª or N. Jersey who views with a laudable horror, so nefarious a practice. He would add that Domestic slavery is the most prominent feature in the aristocratic countenance of the proposed Constitution. The vassalage of the poor has ever been the favorite offspring of Aristocracy. And What is the proposed compensation to the Northern States for a sacrifice of every principle of right, of every impulse of humanity. They are to bind themselves to march their militia for the defence of the S. States;

---

[71] The transcript uses the word "bondages" in the singular.

for their defence ag$^{st}$ those very slaves of whom they complain. They must supply vessels & seamen in case of foreign Attack. The Legislature will have indefinite power to tax them by excises, and duties on imports: both of which will fall heavier on them than on the Southern inhabitants; for the bohea tea used by a Northern freeman, will pay more tax than the whole consumption of the miserable slave, which consists of nothing more than his physical subsistence and the rag that covers his nakedness. On the other side the Southern States are not to be restrained from importing fresh supplies of wretched Africans, at once to increase the danger of attack, and the difficulty of defence; nay they are to be encouraged to it by an assurance of having their votes in the Nat$^l$ Gov$^t$ increased in proportion, and are at the same time to have their exports & their slaves exempt from all contributions for the public service. Let it not be said that direct taxation is to be proportioned to representation. It is idle to suppose that the Gen$^l$ Gov$^t$ can stretch its hand directly into the pockets of the people scattered over so vast a Country. They can only do it through the medium of exports imports & excises. For what then are all these sacrifices to be made? He would sooner submit himself to a tax for paying for all the negroes in the U. States, than saddle posterity with such a Constitution.

M$^r$ DAYTON 2$^{ded}$ the motion. He did it he said that his sentiments on the subject might appear whatever might be the fate of the amendment.

M$^r$ SHERMAN. did not regard the admission of the Negroes into the ratio of representation, as liable to such insuperable objections. It was the freemen of the South$^n$ States who were in fact to be represented according to the taxes paid by them, and the Negroes are only included in the Estimate of the taxes. This was his idea of the matter.

M$^r$ PINKNEY, considered the fisheries & the Western frontier as more burdensome to the U. S. than the slaves. He thought this could be demonstrated if the occasion were a proper one.

M$^r$ WILSON. thought the motion premature. An agreement to the clause would be no bar to the object of it.

[72] Question On [73] motion to insert "free" before "inhabitants."

N. H. no. Mas. no. Cͭ no. N. J. ay. Pᵃ no. Del. no. Mᵈ no. Vᵃ no. N. C. no. S. C. no. Geo. no.[74]

On the suggestion of Mʳ DICKENSON the words, "provided that each State shall have one representative at least."—were added nem. con.

Art. IV. Sect. 4. as amended was agreed to nem. con.

Art. IV. Sect. 5.[75, 76] taken up

Mʳ PINKNEY moved to strike out Sect. 5. As giving no peculiar advantage to the House of Representatives, and as clogging the Govͭ If the Senate can be trusted with the many great powers proposed, it surely may be trusted with that of originating money bills.

Mʳ GHORUM. was agˢͭ allowing the Senate to *originate;* but [77] only to *amend*.

Mʳ GOVʳ MORRIS. It is particularly proper that the Senate shᵈ have the right of originating money bills. They will sit constantly, will consist of a smaller number, and will be able to prepare such bills with due correctness; and so as to prevent delay of business in the other House.

COL. MASON was unwilling to travel over this ground again. To strike out the section, was to unhinge the compromise of which it made a part. The duration of the Senate made it improper. He does not object to that duration. On the Contrary he approved of it. But joined with the smallness of the number, it was an argument against adding this to the other great powers vested in that body. His idea of an Aristocracy was that it was the governͭ of the few over the many. An aristocratic body, like the screw in mechanics, workiᵍ its way by slow degrees, and holding fast whatever it gains, should ever be suspected of an encroaching tendency. The purse strings should never be put into its hands.

---

[72] The words "On the" are here inserted in the transcript.

[73] The word "the" is here inserted in the transcript.

[74] In the transcript the vote reads: "New Jersey, aye—1; New Hampshire, Massachusetts, Connecticut, Pennsylvania, Delaware, Maryland, Virginia, North Carolina, South Carolina, Georgia, no—10."

[75] See *ante*.

[76] The words "was then" are here inserted in the transcript.

[77] The words "was for allowing it" are here inserted in the transcript.

M！ MERCER. considered the exclusive power of originating Money bills as so great an advantage, that it rendered the equality of votes in the Senate ideal & of no consequence.

M！ BUTLER was for adhering to the principle which had been settled.

M！ WILSON was opposed to it on its merits without regard to the compromise

M！ ELSEWORTH did not think the clause of any consequence, but as it was thought of consequence by some members from the larger States, he was willing it should stand.

M！ MADISON was for striking it out: considering it as of no advantage to the large States as fettering the Gov！ and as a source of injurious altercations between the two Houses.

On the question for striking out "Sect. 5. Art. IV"

N. H. no. Mas. no. C！ no. N. J. ay. P！ ay. Del. ay. M！ ay. V！ ay. N. C. no. S. C. ay. Geo. ay.[78]

Adj！

## THURSDAY. AUG！ 9. IN CONVENTION

Art: IV. Sect. 6.[79, 80] M！ RANDOLPH expressed his dissatisfaction at the disagreement yesterday to Sect. 5. concerning money bills, as endangering the success of the plan, and extremely objectionable in itself; and gave notice that he should move for a reconsideration of the vote.

M！ WILLIAMSON said he had formed a like intention.

M！ WILSON, gave notice that he sh！ move to reconsider the vote, requiring seven instead of three years of Citizenship as a qualification of candidates for the House of Representatives.

Art. IV. Sect. 6 & 7.[79, 81] Agreed to nem. con.

Art. V. Sect 1.[82, 83] taken up.

M！ WILSON objected to vacancies in the Senate being supplied by the Executives of the States. It was unnecessary as the Legis-

---

[78] In the transcript the vote reads: "New Jersey, Pennsylvania, Delaware, Maryland, Virginia, South Carolina, Georgia, aye—7; New Hampshire, Massachusetts, Connecticut, North Carolina, no—4."
[79] See *ante*.
[80] The words "was taken up" are here inserted in the transcript.
[81] The word "were" is here inserted in the transcript.
[82] See *ante*.
[83] The words "was then" are here inserted in the transcript.

JAMES MONROE

latures will meet so frequently. It removes the appointment too far from the people; the Executives in most of the States being elected by the Legislatures. As he had always thought the appointment of the Executives [84] by the Legislative department wrong: so it was still more so that the Executive should elect into the Legislative department.

Mʳ RANDOLPH thought it necessary in order to prevent inconvenient chasms in the Senate. In some States the Legislatures meet but once a year. As the Senate will have more power & consist of a smaller number than the other House, vacancies there will be of more consequence. The Executives might be safely trusted he thought with the appointment for so short a time.

Mʳ ELSEWORTH. It is only said that the Executive *may* supply the [85] vacancies. When the Legislative meeting happens to be near, the power will not be exerted. As there will be but two members from a State vacancies may be of great moment.

Mʳ WILLIAMSON. Senators may resign or not accept. This provision is therefore absolutely necessary.

On the question for striking out "vacancies shall be supplied by [86] Executives

N. H. no. Mas. no. Cᵗ no. N. J. no. Pᵃ ay. Mᵈ divᵈ Vᵃ no. N. C. no. S. C. no. Geo. no.[87]

Mʳ WILLIAMSON moved to insert after "vacancies shall be supplied by the Executives," the following [88] words "unless other provision shall be made by the Legislature" [of the State].

Mʳ ELSEWORTH. He was willing to trust the Legislature, or the Executive of a State, but not to give the former a discretion to refer appointments for the Senate to whom they pleased.

[89] Question on Mʳ Williamson's motion

N. H. no. Mas. no. Cᵗ no. N. J. no. Pᵃ no. Mᵈ ay. Vᵃ no. N. C. ay. S. C. ay. Geo. ay.[90]

---

[84] The word "Executives" is in the singular in the transcript.
[85] The word "the" is omitted in the transcript.
[86] The word "the" is here inserted in the transcript.
[87] In the transcript the vote reads: "Pennsylvania, aye—1; New Hampshire, Massachusetts, Connecticut, New Jersey, Virginia, North Carolina, South Carolina, Georgia, no—8; Maryland, divided."
[88] The word "following" is omitted in the transcript.
[89] The words "On the" are here inserted in the transcript.
[90] In the transcript the vote reads: "Maryland, North Carolina, South Carolina, Georgia, aye—4; New Hampshire, Massachusetts, Connecticut, New Jersey, Pennsylvania, Virginia, no—6."

Mr MADISON in order to prevent doubts whether resignations, could be made by Senators, or whether they could refuse to accept, moved to strike out the words after "vacancies," & insert the words "happening by refusals to accept, resignations or otherwise may be supplied by the Legislature of the State in the representation of which such vacancies shall happen, or by the Executive thereof until the next meeting of the Legislature"

Mr Govr MORRIS this is absolutely necessary, otherwise, as members chosen into the Senate are disqualified from being appointed to any office by Sect. 9. of this art: it will be in the power of a Legislature by appointing a man a Senator agst his consent to deprive the U. S. of his services.

The motion of Mr Madison was agreed to nem. con.

Mr RANDOLPH called for division of the Section, so as to leave a distinct question on the last words "each member shall have one vote." He wished this last sentence to be postponed until the reconsideration should have taken place on Sect. 5. Art. IV. concerning money bills. If that section should not be reinstated his plan would be to vary the representation in the Senate.

Mr STRONG concurred in Mr Randolphs ideas on this point

Mr READ did not consider the section as to money bills of any advantage to the larger States and had voted for striking it out as being viewed in the same light by the larger States. If it was considered by them as of any value, and as a condition of the equality of votes in the Senate, he had no objection to its being re-instated.

Mr WILSON—Mr ELSEWORTH & Mr MADISON urged that it was of no advantage to the larger States, and that it might be a dangerous source of contention between the two Houses. All the principal powers of the Natl Legislature had some relation to money.

Docr FRANKLIN, considered the two clauses, the originating of money bills, and the equality of votes in the Senate, as essentially connected by the compromise which had been agreed to.

Col. MASON said this was not the time for discussing this point. When the originating of money bills shall be reconsidered, he thought it could be demonstrated that it was of essential importance to restrain the right to the House of Representatives the immediate choice of the people.

M！ WILLIAMSON. The State of N. C. had agreed to an equality in the Senate, merely in consideration that money bills should be confined to the other House: and he was surprised to see the Smaller States forsaking the condition on which they had received their equality.

[91] Question on the Section 1.[92] down to the last sentence

N. H. ay. Mas. no. C！ ay. N. J. ay. P！ no* Del. ay. M！ ay. Virg！ ay N. C. no. S. C. div！ Geo. ay.[93]

M！ RANDOLPH moved that the last sentence "each member shall have one vote." be postponed

It was observed that this could not be necessary; as in case the section as to originating [94] bills should not be reinstated, and a revision of the Constitution should ensue, it w！ still be proper that the members should vote per Capita. A postponement of the preceding sentence allowing to each State 2 members w！ have been more proper

M！ MASON, did not mean to propose a change of this mode of voting per capita in any event. But as there might be other modes proposed, he saw no impropriety in postponing the sentence. Each State may have two members, and yet may have unequal votes. He said that unless the exclusive [95] orginating of money bills should be restored to the House of Representatives, he should, not from obstinacy, but duty and conscience, oppose throughout the equality of Representation in the Senate.

M！ Gov！ MORRIS. Such declarations were he supposed, addressed to the smaller States in order to alarm them for their equality in the Senate, and induce them ag！！ their judgments, to concur in restoring the section concerning money bills. He would declare in his turn that as he saw no prospect of amending the Constitution of the Senate & considered the section relating to money bills as intrinsically bad, he would adhere to the section establishing the equality at all events.

---

\* In the printed Journal Pensylvania. ay.
[91] The words "On the" are here inserted in the transcript.
[92] The words "first section" are substituted for "Section 1" in the transcript.
[93] In the transcript the vote reads: "New Hampshire, Connecticut, New Jersey, Delaware, Maryland, Virginia, Georgia, aye—7; Massachusetts, Pennsylvania,* North Carolina, no—3; South Carolina, divided."
[94] The word "money" is here inserted in the transcript.
[95] The words "right of" are here inserted in the transcript.

Mr WILSON. It seems to have been supposed by some that the section concerning money bills is desirable to the large States. The fact was that two of those States [Pa & Va] had uniformly voted agst it without reference to any other part of the system.

Mr RANDOLPH, urged as Col. Mason had done that the sentence under consideration was connected with that relating to Money bills, and might possibly be affected by the result of the motion for reconsidering the latter. That the postponement was therefore not improper.

[96] Question for postponing "each member shall have one vote."
N. H. divd. Mas. no. Ct. no. N. J. no. Pa. no. Del. no. Md. no. Va. ay. N. C. ay. S. C. no. Geo. no.[97]

The words were then agreed to as part of the section.

Mr RANDOLPH then gave notice that he should move to reconsider this whole Sect: 1. Art. V. as connected with the 5. Sect. art. IV. as to which he had already given such notice.

Art. V. Sect. 2d [98, 99] taken up.

Mr Govr MORRIS moved to insert after the words "immediately after," the following "they shall be assembled in consequence of—" which was agreed to nem. con. as was then the whole Sect. 2.[1]

Art: V. Sect. 3.[98, 2] taken up.

Mr Govr MORRIS moved to insert 14 instead of 4 years citizenship as a qualification for Senators: urging the danger of admitting strangers into our public Councils. Mr PINKNEY 2 ds him

Mr ELSEWORTH. was opposed to the motion as discouraging meritorious aliens from emigrating to this Country.

Mr PINKNEY. As the Senate is to have the power of making treaties & managing our foreign affairs, there is peculiar danger and impropriety in opening its door to those who have foreign attachments. He quoted the jealousy of the Athenians on this subject who made it death for any stranger to intrude his voice into their Legislative proceedings.

---

[96] The words "On the" are here inserted in the transcript.
[97] In the transcript the vote reads: "Virginia, North Carolina, aye—2; Massachusetts, Connecticut, New Jersey, Pennsylvania, Delaware, Maryland, South Carolina, Georgia, no—8; New Hampshire, divided."
[98] See p. —.
[99] The words "was then" are here inserted in the transcript.
[1] The figure "2" is omitted in the transcript.
[2] The words "was then" are here inserted in the transcript.

Col. MASON highly approved of the policy of the motion. Were it not that many not natives of this Country had acquired great merit[3] during the revolution, he should be for restraining the eligibility into the Senate, to natives.

M? MADISON, was not averse to some restrictions on this subject; but could never agree to the proposed amendment. He thought any restriction however in the *Constitution* unnecessary, and improper. unnecessary; because the Nat! Legisl<sup>re</sup> is to have the right of regulating naturalization, and can by virtue thereof fix different periods of residence as conditions of enjoying different privileges of Citizenship: Improper; because it will give a tincture of illiberality to the Constitution: because it will put it out of the power of the Nat¹ Legislature even by special acts of naturalization to confer the full rank of Citizens on meritorious strangers & because it will discourage the most desireable class of people from emigrating to the U. S. Should the proposed Constitution have the intended effect of giving stability & reputation to our Gov<sup>t</sup>: great numbers of respectable Europeans: men who love liberty and wish to partake its blessings, will be ready to transfer their fortunes hither. All such would feel the mortification of being marked with suspicious incapacitations though they s<sup>d</sup> not covet the public honors He was not apprehensive that any dangerous number of strangers would be appointed by the State Legislatures, if they were left at liberty to do so: nor that foreign powers would made use of strangers as instruments for their purposes. Their bribes would be expended on men whose circumstances would rather stifle than excite jealousy & watchfulness in the public.

M? BUTLER was decidely opposed to the admission of foreigners without a long residence in the Country. They bring with them, not only attachments to other Countries; but ideas of Gov! so distinct from ours that in every point of view they are dangerous. He acknowledged that if he himself had been called into public life within a short time after his coming to America, his foreign habits opinions & attachments would have rendered him an improper agent in public affairs. He mentioned the great strictness observed in Great Britain on this subject.

---

[3] The word "credit" is substituted in the transcript for "merit."

Doc.<sup>r</sup> FRANKLIN was not ag.<sup>st</sup> a reasonable time, but should be very sorry to see any thing like illiberality inserted in the Constitution. The people in Europe are friendly to this Country. Even in the Country with which we have been lately at war, we have now & had during the war, a great many friends not only among the people at large but in both houses of Parliament. In every other Country in Europe all the people are our friends. We found in the course of the Revolution that many strangers served us faithfully– and that many natives took part ag.<sup>st</sup> their Country. When foreigners after looking about for some other Country in which they can obtain more happiness, give a preference to ours it is a proof of attachment which ought to excite our confidence & affection.

M.<sup>r</sup> RANDOLPH did not know but it might be problematical whether emigrations to this Country were on the whole useful or not: but he could never agree to the motion for disabling them for 14 years to participate in the public honours. He reminded the Convention of the language held by our patriots during the Revolution, and the principles laid down in all our American Constitutions. Many foreigners may have fixed their fortunes among us under the faith of these invitations. All persons under this description, with all others who would be affected by such a regulation, would enlist themselves under the banners of hostility to the proposed System. He would go as far as seven years, but no farther.

M.<sup>r</sup> WILSON said he rose with feelings which were perhaps peculiar; mentioning the circumstance of his not being a native, and the possibility, if the ideas of some gentlemen should be pursued, of his being incapacitated from holding a place under the very Constitution, which he had shared in the trust of making. He remarked the illiberal complexion which the motion would give to the System, & the effect which a good system would have in inviting meritorious foreigners among us, and the discouragement & mortification they must feel from the degrading discrimination, now proposed. He had himself experienced this mortification. On his removal into Maryland, he found himself, from defect of residence, under certain legal incapacities which never ceased to produce chagrin, though he assuredly did not desire & would not have accepted the offices to which they related. To be appointed to a place may be matter of indifference. To be incapable of being appointed, is a circumstance grating and mortifying.

Mʳ Govʳ Morris. The lesson we are taught is that we should be governed as much by our reason, and as little by our feelings as possible. What is the language of Reason on this subject? That we should not be polite at the expence of prudence. There was a moderation in all things. It is said that some tribes of Indians, carried their hospitality so far as to offer to strangers their wives & daughters. Was this a proper model for us? He would admit them to his house, he would invite them to his table, would provide for them confortable lodgings; but would not carry the complaisance so far as, to bed them with his wife. He would let them worship at the same altar, but did not choose to make Priests of them. He ran over the privileges which emigrants would enjoy among us, though they should be deprived of that of being eligible to the great offices of Government; observing that they exceeded the privileges allowed to foreigners in any part of the world; and that as every Society from a great nation down to a club had the right of declaring the conditions on which new members should be admitted, there could be no room for complaint. As to those philosophical gentlemen, those Citizens of the World as they call themselves, He owned he did not wish to see any of them in our public Councils. He would not trust them. The men who can shake off their attachments to their own Country can never love any other. These attachments are the wholesome prejudices which uphold all Governments, Admit a Frenchman into your Senate, and he will study to increase the commerce of France: an Englishman,[4] he will feel an equal biass in favor of that of England. It has been said that The Legislatures will not chuse foreigners, at least improper ones. There was no knowing what Legislatures would do. Some appointments made by them, proved that every thing ought to be apprehended from

---

[4] The word "and" is here inserted in the transcript.

the cabals practised on such occasions. He mentioned the case of a foreigner who left this State in disgrace, and worked himself into an appointment from another to Congress.

[5] Question on the motion of Mr Govr MORRIS to insert 14 in place of 4 years

N. H. ay. Mas. no. Ct. no. N. J. ay. Pa. no. Del. no. Md. no. Va. no. N. C. no. S. C. ay. Geo. ay.[6]

On 13 years, moved Mr Govr Morris[7]

N. H. ay. Mas. no. Ct. no. N. J. ay. Pa. no. Del. no. Md. no. Va. no. N. C. no. S. C. ay. Geo. ay.

On 10 years moved by Genl PINKNEY[8]

N. H. ay. Mas. no. Ct. no. N. J. ay. Pa. no. Del. no. Md. no. Va. no. N. C. no. S. C. ay. Geo. ay.

Dr FRANKLIN reminded the Convention that it did not follow from an omission to insert the restriction in the Constitution that the persons in question wd be actually chosen into the Legislature.

Mr RUTLIDGE. 7 years of Citizenship have been required for the House of Representatives. Surely a longer term is requisite for the Senate, which will have more power.

Mr WILLIAMSON. It is more necessary to guard the Senate in this case than the other House. Bribery & cabal can be more easily practised in the choice of the Senate which is to be made by the Legislatures composed of a few men, than of the House of Represents who will be chosen by the people.

Mr RANDOLPH will agree to 9 years with the expectation that it will be reduced to seven if Mr Wilson's motion to reconsider the vote fixing 7 years for the House of Representatives should produce a reduction of that period.

On a [9] question for 9 years.

N. H. ay. Mas. no. Ct. no. N. J. ay. Pa. no. Del. ay. Md. no. Va. ay. N. C. divd. S. C. ay. Geo. ay.[10]

---

[5] The words "On the" are here inserted in the transcript.

[6] In the transcript the vote reads: "New Hampshire, New Jersey, South Carolina, Georgia, aye—4; Massachusetts, Connecticut, Pennsylvania, Delaware, Maryland, Virginia, North Carolina, no—7."

[7] In the transcript this sentence reads as follows: "On the question for thirteen years, moved by Mr. Gouverneur Morris, it was negatived, as above." The vote by States is omitted.

[8] The phrase "the votes were the same," is here inserted in the transcript, and the vote by States is omitted.

[9] In the transcript the word "a" is stricken out and "the" is written above it.

[10] In the transcript the vote reads: "New Hampshire, New Jersey, Delaware, Virginia, South Carolina, Georgia, aye—6; Massachusetts, Connecticut, Pennsylvania, Maryland, no—4; North Carolina, divided."

The term "Resident" was struck out, & "inhabitant" inserted nem. con.

Art. V Sect. 3, as amended [11] agreed to nem. con.

Sect. 4.[12] agreed to nem. con.[13]

Art. VI. sect. 1.[12, 14] taken up.

M: MADISON & M: Gov: MORRIS moved to strike out "each House" & to insert "the House of Representatives"; the right of the Legislatures to regulate the times & places &c in the election of Senators being involved in the right of appointing them, which was disagreed to.

[15] Division of the question being called,[16] it was taken on the first part down to "but their provisions concerning &c"

The first part was agreed to nem. con.

M: PINKNEY & M: RUTLIDGE moved to strike out the remaining part viz but their provisions concerning them may at any time be altered by the Legislature of the United States." The States they contended could & must be relied on in such cases.

M: GHORUM. It would be as improper [17] take this power from the Nat¹ Legislature, as to Restrain the British Parliament from regulating the circumstances of elections, leaving this business to the Counties themselves—

M: MADISON. The necessity of a Gen! Gov! supposes that the State Legislatures will sometimes fail or refuse to consult the common interest at the expence of their local conveniency [18] or prejudices. The policy of referring the appointment of the House of Representatives to the people and not to the Legislatures of the States, supposes that the result will be somewhat influenced by the mode. This view of the question seems to decide that the Legislatures of the States ought not to have the uncontrouled right of regulating the times places & manner of holding elections. These were words of great latitude. It was impossible to foresee all the abuses that might be made of the discretionary power. Whether

---

[11] The words "was then" are here inserted in the transcript

[12] See *ante*.

[13] In the transcript this sentence reads as follows: "Article 5, Sect. 4 was agreed to *nem. con.*"

[14] The words "was then" are here inserted in the transcript.

[15] The word "A" is here inserted in the transcript.

[16] The word "for" is here inserted in the transcript.

[17] The word "to" is here inserted in the transcript.

[18] The word "conveniency" is changed to "convenience" in the transcript.

the electors should vote by ballot or viva voce, should assemble at this place or that place; should be divided into districts or all meet at one place, sh? all vote for all the representatives; or all in a district vote for a number allotted to the district; these & many other points would depend on the Legislatures, and might materially affect the appointments. Whenever the State Legislatures had a favorite measure to carry, they would take care so to mould their regulations as to favor the candidates they wished to succeed. Besides, the inequality of the Representation in the Legislatures of particular States, would produce a like inequality in their representation in thc Nat! Legislature, as it was presumable that the Counties having the power in the former case would secure it to themselves in the latter. What danger could there be in giving a controuling power to the Nat! Legislature? Of whom was it to consist? 1.[19] of a Senate to be chosen by the State Legislatures. If the latter therefore could be trusted, their representatives could not be dangerous. 2.[19] of Representatives elected by the same people who elect the State Legislatures; surely then if confidence is due to the latter, it must be due to the former. It seemed as improper in principle, though it might be less inconvenient in practice, to give to the State Legislatures this great authority over the election of the Representatives of the people in the Gen! Legislature, as it would be to give to the latter a like power over the election of their Representatives in the State Legislatures.

M! KING. If this power be not given to the Nat! Legislature, their right of judging of the returns of their members may be frustrated. No probability has been suggested of its being abused by them. Altho this scheme of erecting the Gen! Gov! on the authority of the State Legislatures has been fatal to the federal establishment, it would seem as if many gentlemen, still foster the dangerous idea.

M! Gov! MORRIS– observed that the States might make false returns and then make no provisions for new elections

M! SHERMAN did not know but it might be best to retain the clause, though he had himself sufficient confidence in the State Legislatures. The motion of M! P. and M! R. did not prevail—

---

[19] The figures "1" and "2" are changed to "First" and "Secondly" in the transcript.

The word "respectively" was inserted after the word "State"

On the motion of M⁀ Read the word "their" was struck out, & "regulations in such cases" inserted in place of "provisions concerning them." the clause then reading—"but regulations in each of the foregoing cases may at any time, be made or altered by the Legislature of the U. S" This was meant to give the Nat⁀ Legislature a power not only to alter the provisions of the States, but to make regulations in case the States should fail or refuse altogether.

Art. VI. Sect. 1. as thus amended was agreed to nem. con.

Adjourned.

---

FRIDAY AUG⁀ 10.   IN CONVENTION

Art. VI. Sect. 2.[20, 21] taken up.

M⁀ PINKNEY. The Committee as he had conceived were instructed to report the proper qualifications of property for the members of the Nat⁀ Legislature; instead of which they have referred the task to the Nat⁀ Legislature itself. Should it be left on this footing, the first Legislature will meet without any particular qualifications of property: and if it should happen to consist of rich men they might fix such such qualifications as may be too favorable to the rich; if of poor men, an opposite extreme might be run into. He was opposed to the establishment of an undue aristocratic influence in the Constitution but he thought it essential that the members of the Legislature, the Executive, and the Judges, should be possessed of competent property to make them independent & respectable. It was prudent when such great powers were to be trusted to connect the tie of property with that of reputation in securing a faithful administration. The Legislature would have the fate of the Nation put into their hands. The President would also have a very great influence on it. The Judges would have not only[22] important causes between Citizen & Citizen but also, where foreigners are concerned. They will even be the Umpires between the U. States and individual States

---

[20] See *ante.*
[21] The word "was" is here inserted in the transcript.
[22] The words "have not only" are transposed in the transcript to read "not only have."

as well as between one State & another. Were he to fix the quantum of property which should be required, he should not think of less than one hundred thousand dollars for the President, half of that sum for each of the Judges, and in like proportion for the members of the Nat! Legislature. He would however leave the sums blank. His motion was that the President of the U. S. the Judges, and members of the Legislature should be required to swear that they were respectively possessed of a cleared [23] unincumbered Estate to the amount of       in the case of the President &c &c.

M: RUTLIDGE seconded the motion; observing. that the Committee had reported no qualifications because they could not agree on any among themselves, being embarrassed by the danger on one side of displeasing the people by making them high, and on the other of rendering them nugatory by making them low.

M: ELSEWORTH. The different circumstances of different parts of the U. S. and the probable difference between the present and future circumstances of the whole, render it improper to have either *uniform or fixed* qualifications. Make them so high as to be useful in the S. States, and they will be inapplicable to the E. States. Suit them to the latter, and they will serve no purpose in the former. In like manner what may be accomodated to the existing State of things among us, may be very inconvenient in some future state of them. He thought for these reasons that it was better to leave this matter to the Legislative discretion than to attempt a provision for it in the Constitution.

Doct: FRANKLIN expressed his dislike of [24] every thing that tended to debase the spirit of the common people. If honesty was often the companion of wealth, and if poverty was exposed to peculiar temptation, it was not less true that the possession of property increased the desire of more property. Some of the greatest rogues he was ever acquainted with, were the richest rogues. We should remember the character which the Scripture requires in Rulers, that they should be men hating covetousness. This Constitution will be much read and attended to in Europe,

---

[23] The word "clear" is substituted in the transcript for "cleared."
[24] The word "to" is substituted in the transcript for "of."

and if it should betray a great partiality to the rich, will not only hurt us in the esteem of the most liberal and enlightened men there, but discourage the common people from removing into [25] this Country.

The Motion of M.r Pinkney was rejected by so general a *no*, that the States were not called.

M.r MADISON was opposed to the Section as vesting an improper & dangerous power in the Legislature. The qualifications of electors and elected were fundamental articles in a Republican Gov.t and ought to be fixed by the Constitution. If the Legislature could regulate those of either, it can by degrees subvert the Constitution. A Republic may be converted into an aristocracy or oligarchy as well by limiting the number capable of being elected, as the number authorised to elect. In all cases where the representatives of the people will have a personal interest distinct from that of their Constituents, there was the same reason for being jealous of them, as there was for relying on them with full confidence, when they had a common interest. This was one of the former cases. It was as improper as to allow them to fix their own wages, or their own privileges. It was a power also which might be made subservient to the views of one faction ag:st another. Qualifications founded on artificial distinctions may be devised, by the stronger in order to keep out partizans of a weaker faction.

M.r ELSEWORTH, admitted that the power was not unexceptionable; but he could not view it as dangerous. Such a power with regard to the electors would be dangerous because it would be much more liable to abuse.

M.r GOV.r MORRIS moved to strike out "with regard to property" in order to leave the Legislature entirely at large.

M.r WILLIAMSON. This could [26] surely never be admitted. Should a majority of the Legislature be composed of any particular description of men, of lawyers for example, which is no improbable supposition, the future elections might be secured to their own body.

---

[25] The word "to" is substituted in the transcript for "into."
[26] The word "would" is substituted in the transcript for "could."

M！ MADISON observed that the British Parliam！ possessed the power of regulating the qualifications both of the electors, and the elected; and the abuse they had made of it was a lesson worthy of our attention. They had made the changes in both cases subservient to their own views, or to the views of political or Religious parties.

[27] Question on the motion to strike out with regard to property N. H. no. Mas. no. C！ ay. N. J. ay. P！ ay. Del. no.*  M！ no. V！ no. N. C. no. S. C. no. Geo. ay.[28]

M！ RUTLIDGE was opposed to leaving the power to the Legislature. He proposed that the qualifications should be the same as for members of the State Legislatures.

M！ WILSON thought it would be best on the whole to let the Section go out. A uniform rule would probably be never[29] fixed by the Legislature, and this particular power would constructively exclude every other power of regulating qualifications.

On the question for agreeing to Art. VI. Sect. 2ᵈ—

N. H. ay. Mas. ay. C！ no. N. J. no. P！ no. M！ no. V！ no. N. C. no. S. C. no. Geo. ay.[30]

On Motion of M！ Wilson to reconsider Art: IV. Sect. 2; so as to restore 3 in place of seven years of citizenship as a qualification for being elected into the House of Represent！

N. H. no. Mas. no. C！ ay. N. J. no. P！ ay. Del. ay. M！ ay. V！ ay. N. C. ay. S. C. no. Geo. no.[31]

Monday next was then assigned for the reconsideration: all the States being ay. except Mass！ & Georgia

Art: VI. Sect. 3.[32, 33] taken up.

M！ GHORUM contended that less than a Majority in each House should be made of [34] Quorum, otherwise great delay might hap-

---

[27] The words "On the" are here inserted in the transcript.

*In the printed Journal Delaware did not vote.

[28] In the transcript the vote reads: "Connecticut, New Jersey, Pennsylvania, Georgia, aye—4; New Hampshire, Massachusetts, Delaware,* Maryland, Virginia, North Carolina, South Carolina, no—7."

[29] In the transcript the words "be never" are transposed to read "never be."

[30] In the transcript the vote reads: "New Hampshire, Massachusetts, Georgia, aye—3; Connecticut, New Jersey, Pennsylvania, Maryland, Virginia, North Carolina, South Carolina, no—7."

[31] In the transcript the vote reads: "Connecticut, Pennsylvania, Delaware, Maryland, Virginia, North Carolina, aye—6; New Hampshire, Massachusetts, New Jersey, South Carolina, Georgia, no—5."

[32] See *ante*.

[33] The words "was then" are here inserted in the transcript.

[34] In the transcript the word "of" is crossed out and "a" is written above it.

pen in business, and great inconvenience from the future increase of numbers.

M! MERCER was also for less than a majority. So great a number will put it in the power of a few by seceding at a critical moment to introduce convulsions, and endanger the Governm! Examples of secession have already happened in some of the States. He was for leaving it to the Legislature to fix the Quorum, as in Great Britain, where the requisite number is small & no inconveniency [35] has been experienced.

Col. MASON. This is a valuable & necessary part of the plan. In this extended Country, embracing so great a diversity of interests, it would be dangerous to the distant parts to allow a small number of members of the two Houses to make laws. The Central States could always take care to be on the Spot and by meeting earlier than the distant ones, or wearying their patience, and outstaying them, could carry such measures as they pleased. He admitted that inconveniences might spring from the secession of a small number: But he had also known good produced by an apprehension, of it. He had known a paper emission prevented by that cause in Virginia. He thought the Constitution as now moulded was founded on sound principles, and was disposed to put into it extensive powers. At the same time he wished to guard ag:t abuses as much as possible. If the Legislature should be able to reduce the number at all, it might reduce it as low as it pleased & the U. States might be governed by a Juncto— A majority of the number which had been agreed on, was so few that he feared it would be made an objection ag:t the plan.

M! KING admitted there might be some danger of giving an advantage to the Central States; but was of opinion that the public inconveniency [35] on the other side was more to be dreaded.

M! Gov! MORRIS moved to fix the quorum at 33 members in the H. of Rep: & 14 in the Senate. This is a majority of the present number, and will be a bar to the Legislature: fix the number low and they will generally attend knowing that advantage may be taken of their absence. the Secession of a small number ought not to be suffered to break a quorum. Such events

---

[35] The word "inconveniency" is changed to "inconvenience" in the transcript.

in the States may have been of little consequence. In the national Councils, they may be fatal. Besides other mischiefs, if a few can break up a quorum, they may seize a moment when a particular part of the Continent may be in need of immediate aid, to extort, by threatening a secession, some unjust & selfish measure.

M: MERCER 2$^{ded}$ the motion

M: KING said he had just prepared a motion which instead of fixing the numbers proposed by M: Gov: Morris as Quorums, made those the lowest numbers, leaving the Legislature at liberty to increase them or not. He thought the future increase of members would render a majority of the whole extremely cumbersome.

M: MERCER agreed to substitute M: Kings motion in place of M: Morris's.

M: ELSEWORTH was opposed to it. It would be a pleasing ground of confidence to the people that no law or burden could be imposed on them, by a few men. He reminded the movers that the Constitution proposed to give such a discretion with regard to the number of Representatives that a very incovenient number was not to be apprehended. The inconveniency [36] of secessions may be guarded ag:t by giving to each House an authority to require the attendance of absent members.

M: WILSON concurred in the sentiments of M: Elseworth.

M: GERRY seemed to think that some further precautions than merely fixing the quorum might be necessary. He observed that as 17 w$^d$ be a majority of a quorum of 33, and 8 of 14, questions might by possibility be carried in the H. of Rep: by 2 large States, and in the Senate by the same States with the aid of two small ones.—He proposed that the number for a quorum in the H. of Rep: should not exceed 50 nor be less than 33, leaving the intermediate discretion to the Legislature.

M: KING, as the quorum could not be altered with: the concurrence of the President by less than $\tfrac{2}{3}$ of each House, he thought there could be no danger in trusting the Legislature.

M: CARROL this will be no security ag:t a continuance of the quorums at 33 & 14. when they ought to be increased.

---

[36] The word "inconveniency" is changed to "inconvenience" in the transcript.

On [37] question on Mʳ Kings motion "that not less than 33 in the H. of Repˢ nor less than 14 in the Senate shᵈ constitute a Quorum, which may be increased by a law, on additions to [37] members in either House.

N. H. no. Mas. ay. Cᵗ no. N. J. no. Pᵃ no. Del. ay. Mᵈ no. Vᵃ no. N. C. no. S. C. no. Geo. no.[38]

Mʳ RANDOLPH & Mʳ MADISON moved to add to the end of Art. VI. Sect 3. " and may be authorised to compel the attendance of absent members in such manner & under such penalties as each House may provide." Agreed to by all except Penᵃ which was divided.

Art: VI. Sect. 3.[39] agreed to as amended Nem. con.

Sect. 4.[40]  
Sect. 5.[40] } Agreed to nem. con.[41]

Mʳ MADISON observed that the right of expulsion (Art. VI. Sect. 6.) [40] was too important to be exercised by a bare majority of a quorum: and in emergencies of faction might be dangerously abused. He moved that "with the concurrence of ⅔" might be inserted between may & expel.

Mʳ RANDOLPH & Mʳ MASON approved the idea.

Mʳ Govʳ MORRIS. This power may be safely trusted to a majority. To require more may produce abuses on the side of the minority. A few men from factious motives may keep in a member who ought to be expelled.

Mʳ CARROL thought that the concurrence of ⅔ at least ought to be required.

On the question for [42] requiring ⅔ in cases of expelling a member.[43]

N. H. ay. Mas. ay. Cᵗ ay. N. J. ay. Pᵃ divᵈ Del. ay. Mᵈ ay. Vᵃ ay. N. C. ay. S. C. ay. Geo. ay.[43]

Art. VI. Sect. 6. as thus amended [44] agreed to nem. con.

---

[37] The word "the" is here inserted in the transcript.  
[38] In the transcript the vote reads: "Massachusetts, Delaware, aye—2; New Hampshire, Connecticut, New Jersey, Pennsylvania, Maryland, Virginia, North Carolina, South Carolina, Georgia, no.—9."  
[39] The word "was" is here inserted in the transcript.  
[40] See *ante*.  
[41] In the transcript this reads as follows: "Sections 4 and 5, of Article 6, were then agreed to, *nem. con.*"  
[42] The word "for" is omitted in the transcript.  
[43] In the transcript the vote by States is omitted and the following sentence is inserted: "ten States were in the affirmative, Pennsylvania, divided."  
[44] The words "was then" are here inserted in the transcript.

Art: VI. Sect. 7 ⁴⁴, ⁴⁰ taken up.

M! Gov! Morris urged that if the yeas & nays were proper at all any individual ought to be authorised to call for them: and moved an amendment to that effect.– The small States may otherwise be under a disadvantage, and find it difficult, to get a concurrence of $^1/_5$

M! Randolph 2$^{ded}$ y$^e$ motion.

M! Sherman had rather strike out the yeas & nays altogether. They never have done any good, and have done much mischief. They are not proper as the reasons governing the voter never appear along with them.

M! Elseworth was of the same opinion.

Col. Mason liked the Section as it stood. it was a middle way between the two extremes.

M! Ghorum was opposed to the motion for allowing a single member to call the yeas & nays, and recited the abuses of it, in Mass$^{ts}$ 1 ⁴⁵ in stuffing the journals with them on frivolous occasions. 2 ⁴⁵ in misleading the people who never know the reasons determining the votes.

The motion for allowing a single member to call the yeas & nays was disag$^d$ to nem. con.

M! Carrol. & M! Randolph moved   Here insert the motion at the bottom of page * ⁴⁶

* to strike out the words "each House" and to insert the words "the House of Representatives" in Sect. 7. Art. 6. and to add to the Section the words "and any member of the Senate shall be at liberty to enter his dissent."

M! Gov! Morris & M! Wilson observed that if the minority were to have a right to enter their votes & reasons, the other side would have a right to complain, if it were not extended to them: & to allow it to both, would fill the Journals, like the records of a Court, with replications, rejoinders &c.

⁴⁷Question on M! Carrols motion to allow a member to enter his dissent

---

⁴⁰ See *ante.*
⁴⁴ The words "was then" are here inserted in the transcript.
⁴⁵ The figures "1" and "2" are changed to "first" and "secondly" in the transcript.
⁴⁶ Madison's direction is omitted in the transcript.
⁴⁷ The words "On the" are here inserted in the transcript.

N. H. no. Mas. no. Con͠t no. N. J. no. P͠a no. Del. no. M͠d ay. V͠a ay. N. C. no. S. C. ay. Geo. no.⁴⁸

M͠r GERRY moved to strike out the words "when it shall be acting in its legislative capacity" in order to extend the provision to the Senate when exercising its peculiar authorities and to insert "except such parts thereof as in their judgment require secrecy" after the words "publish them."—[It was thought by others that provision should be made with respect to these when that part came under consideration which proposed to vest those additional authorities in the Senate.]

On this question for striking out the words "when acting in its Legislative capacity"

N. H. div͠d Mas. ay. C͠t no. N. J. no. P͠a no. Del. ay. M͠d ay. V͠a ay. N. C. ay. S. C. ay. Geo. ay.⁴⁹

Adjourned

SATURDAY AUG͠ST 11. IN CONVENTION

M͠r MADISON & M͠r RUTLIDGE moved "that each House shall keep a journal of its proceeding,⁵⁰ & shall publish the same from time to time; except such part of the proceedings of the Senate, when acting not in its Legislative capacity as may be judged by that House to require secrecy."

M͠r MERCER. This implies that other powers than legislative will be given to the Senate which he hoped would not be given.

M͠r Madison & M͠r R's motion. was disag͠d to by all the States except Virg͠a

M͠r GERRY & M͠r SHARMAN moved to insert after the words "publish them" the following "except such as relate to treaties & military operations." Their object was to give each House a discretion in such cases.—On this question

N. H. no. Mas. ay. C͠t ay. N. J. no. P͠a no. Del. no. V͠a no. N. C. no. S. C. no. Geo. no.⁵¹

---

⁴⁸ In the transcript the vote reads: "Maryland, Virginia, South Carolina, aye—3; New Hampshire, Massachusetts, Connecticut, New Jersey, Pennsylvania, Delaware, North Carolina, Georgia, no—8."

⁴⁹ In the transcript the vote reads: "Massachusetts, Delaware, Maryland, Virginia, North Carolina, South Carolina, Georgia, aye—7; Connecticut, New Jersey, Pennsylvania, no—3; New Hampshire, divided."

⁵⁰ The transcript uses the word "proceeding" in the plural.

⁵¹ In the transcript the vote reads: "Massachusetts, Connecticut, aye—2; New Hampshire, New Jersey, Pennsylvania, Delaware, Virginia, North Carolina, South Carolina, Georgia, no—8."

Mr ELSEWORTH. As the clause is objectionable in so many shapes, it may as well be struck out altogether. The Legislature will not fail to publish their proceedings from time to time. The people will call for it if it should be improperly omitted.

Mr WILSON thought the expunging of the clause would be very improper. The people have a right to know what their Agents are doing or have done, and it should not be in the option of the Legislature to conceal their proceedings. Besides as this is a clause in the existing confederation, the not retaining it would furnish the adversaries of the reform with a pretext by which week & suspicious minds may be easily misled.

Mr MASON thought it would give a just alarm to the people, to make a conclave of their Legislature.

Mr SHERMAN thought the Legislature might be trusted in this case if in any.

[52] Question on [53] 1st part of the section down to "*publish them*" inclusive: [54] Agreed to nem. con.

[52] Question on the words to follow, to wit except such parts thereof as may in their Judgment require secrecy." N. H. divd Mas. ay. Ct ay. N. J. ay. Pa no. Del. no. Md no. Va ay. N. C. ay. S. C. no. Geo. ay.[55]

The remaining part as to yeas & nays,—[56] agreed to nem. con.

Art VI. Sect. 8.[57, 58] taken up.

Mr KING remarked that the section authorized the 2 Houses to adjourn to a new place. He thought this inconvenient. The mutability of place had dishonored the federal Govt and would require as strong a cure as we could devise. He thought a law at least should be made necessary to a removal of the Seat of Govt

Mr MADISON, viewed the subject in the same light, and joined with Mr King in a motion requiring a law.

---

[52] The words "On the" are here inserted in the transcript.
[53] The word "the" is here inserted in the transcript.
[54] The words "it was" are here inserted in the transcript.
[55] In the transcript the vote reads: "Massachusetts, Connecticut, New Jersey, Virginia, North Carolina, Georgia, aye—6; Pennsylvania, Delaware, Maryland, South Carolina, no—4; New Hampshire, divided."
[56] The word "was" is here inserted in the transcript.
[57] See *ante*.
[58] The words "was then" are here inserted in the transcript.

*The Home of James Monroe*

Mr. Governr Morris proposed the additional alteration by inserting the words "during the Session" &c."

Mr. Spaight. this will fix the seat of Govt at N. Y. The present Congress will convene them there in the first instance, and they will never be able to remove; especially if the Presidt should be [59] Northern Man.

Mr Govr Morris such a distrust is inconsistent with all Govt

Mr Madison supposed that a central place for the seat of Govt was so just and wd be so must insisted on by the H. of Representatives, that though a law should be made requisite for the purpose, it could & would be obtained. The necessity of a central residence of the Govt wd be much greater under the new than old Govt The members of the new Govt wd be more numerous. They would be taken more from the interior parts of the States; they wd not like members of ye present Congs come so often from the distant States by water. As the powers & objects of the new Govt would be far greater yn heretofore, more private individuals wd have business calling them to the seat of it, and it was more necessary that the Govt should be in that position from which it could contemplate with the most equal eye, and sympathize most equally with, every part of the nation. These considerations he supposed would extort a removal even if a law were made necessary. But in order to quiet suspicions both within & without doors, it might not be amiss to authorize the 2 Houses by a concurrent vote to adjourn at their first meeting to the most proper place, and to require thereafter, the sanction of a law to their removal.

The motion was accordingly moulded into the following form—
"the Legislature shall at their first assembling determine on a place at which their future sessions shall be held; neither House shall afterwards, during the session of the House of Reps without the consent of the other, adjourn for more than three days, nor shall they adjourn to any other place than such as shall have been fixt by law"

Mr Gerry thought it would be wrong to let the Presidt check the will of the 2 Houses on this subject at all

Mr Williamson supported the ideas of Mr Spaight

---

[59] The word "a" is here inserted in the transcript.

M? CARROL was actuated by the same apprehensions

M? MERCER, it will serve no purpose to require the two Houses at their first meeting to fix on a place. They will never agree.

After some further expressions from others denoting an apprehension that the seat of Gov? might be continued at an improper place if a law should be made necessary to a removal, and [60] the motion above stated with another for recommitting the section had been negatived, the section was left in the shape it which it was reported as to this point. The words "during the session of the Legislature were prefixed to the 8th section—and the last sentence "But this regulation shall not extend to the Senate when it shall exercise the powers mention [61] in the article" struck struck out. The 8th section as amended was then agreed to.

M? RANDOLPH moved according to notice to reconsider Art: IV. Sect. 5.[62] concerning money-bills which had been struck out. He argued 1.[63] that he had not wished for this privilege whilst a proportional Representation in the Senate was in contemplation, but since an equality had been fixed in that house, the large States would require this compensation at least. 2.[63] that it would make the plan more acceptable to the people, because they will consider the Senate as the more aristocratic body, and will expect that the usual guards ag?? its influence [64] be provided according to the example in [65] G. Britain. 3.[63] the privilege will give some advantage to the House of Rep? if it extends to the originating only—but still more, if it restrains the Senate from amend? 4.[63] he called on the smaller States to concur in the measure, as the condition by which alone the compromise had entitled them to an equality in the Senate. He signified that he should propose instead of the original Section, a clause specifying that the bills in question should be for the purpose of Revenue, in order to repel y? objection ag?? the extent of the words "*raising money,*" which might happen incidentally, and that the Senate should not so amend or alter as to increase

---

[60] The word "after" is here inserted in the transcript.
[61] The word "mentioned" is substituted in the transcript for "mention."
[62] See *ante*.
[63] The figures "1," "2," "3" and "4" are changed in the transcript to "first," "Secondly" etc.
[64] The word "will" is here inserted in the transcript.
[65] The word "of" is substituted in the transcript for "in."

or diminish the sum; in order to obviate the inconveniences urged ag:st a restriction of the Senate to a simple affirmative or negative.

M: WILLIAMSON 2:ded the motion

M: PINKNEY was sorry to oppose the opportunity gentlemen asked to have the question again opened for discussion, but as he considered it a mere waste of time he could not bring himself to consent to it. He said that notwithstanding what had been said as to the compromise, he always considered this section as making no part of it. The rule of Representation in the 1:st branch was the true condition of that in the 2:d branch.—Several others spoke for & ag:st the reconsideration, but without going into the merits— On the Question to reconsider

N. H. ay. Mas. ay. C:t ay. N. J.* ay. P:a ay. Del. ay. M:d no. V:a ay. N. C. ay. S. C. div:d Geo. ay.—⁶⁶ Monday was then assigned—⁶⁷

Adj:d

---

MONDAY AUG:ST 13. IN CONVENTION.

Art. IV. Sect. 2 ⁶⁸, ⁶⁹ reconsidered—

M: WILSON & M: RANDOLPH moved to strike out "7 years" and insert "4 years," as the requisite term of Citizenship to qualify for the House of Rep:s M: Wilson said it was very proper the electors should govern themselves by this consideration; but unnecessary & improper that the Constitution should chain them down to it.

M: GERRY wished that in future the eligibility might be confined to Natives. Foreign powers will intermeddle in our affairs, and spare no expence to influence them. Persons having foreign attachments will be sent among us & insinuated into our councils, in order to be made instruments for their purposes. Every one knows the vast sums laid out in Europe for secret services. He was not singular in these ideas. A great many of the most influencial men in Mass:ts reasoned in the same manner.

---

\* In the printed Journal N. Jersey—No.

⁶⁶ In the transcript the vote reads: "New Hampshire, Massachusetts, Connecticut, New Jersey,* Pennsylvania, Delaware, Virginia, North Carolina, Georgia, aye—9; Maryland, no—1; South Carolina, divided."

⁶⁷ The words "for the reconsideration" are here inserted in the transcript.

⁶⁸ See *ante*.

⁶⁹ The word "being" is here inserted in the transcript.

Mr WILLIAMSON moved to insert 9 years instead of seven. He wished this Country to acquire as fast as possible national habits. Wealthy emigrants do more harm by their luxurious examples, than good, by the money, they bring with them.

Col. HAMILTON was in general agst embarrassing the Govt with minute restrictions. There was on one side the possible danger that had been suggested. On the other side, the advantage of encouraging foreigners was obvious & admitted. Persons in Europe of moderate fortunes will be fond of coming here where they will be on a level with the first Citizens. He moved that the section be so altered as to require merely citizenship & inhabitancy. The right of determining the rule of naturalization will then leave a discretion to the Legislature on this subject which will answer every purpose.

Mr MADISON seconded the motion. He wished to maintain the character of liberality which had been professed in all the Constitutions & publications of America. He wished to invite foreigners of merit & republican principles among us. America was indebted to emigrations for her settlement & Prosperity. That part of America which had encouraged them most had advanced most rapidly in population, agriculture & the arts. There was a possible danger he admitted that men with foreign predilections might obtain appointments but it was by no means probable that it would happen in any dangerous degree. For the same reason that they would be attached to their native Country, our own people wd prefer natives of this Country to them. Experience proved this to be the case. Instances were rare of a foreigner being elected by the people within any short space after his coming among us. If bribery was to be practised by foreign powers, it would not be attempted among the electors but among the elected; and among natives having full Confidence of the people not among strangers who would be regarded with a jeoulous eye.

Mr WILSON, cited Pennsylva as a proof of the advantage of encouraging emigrations. It was perhaps the youngest [except Georgia] settlemt on the Atlantic; yet it was at least among the foremost in population & prosperity. He remarked that almost all the Gen! officers of the Pen᷉ line of the late army were foreigners. And no complaint had ever been made against their fidelity or merit. Three of her deputies to the Convention [M᷉ R. Morris, M᷉ Fitzimmons & himself] were also not natives. He had no objection to Col. Hamiltons motion & would withdraw the one made by himself.

M᷉ BUTLER was strenuous ag᷉t admitting foreigners into our public Councils.

[70] Question on Col. Hamilton's Motion

N. H. no. Mas. no. C᷉ ay. N. J. no. P᷉ ay. Del. no. M᷉ ay. V᷉ ay. N. C. no. S. C. no. Geo. no.[71]

[70] Question on M᷉ Williamson's moution to insert 9 years instead of seven.

N. H. ay. Mas᷉ no. C᷉ no. N. J. no. P᷉ no. Del. no. M᷉ no. V᷉ no. N. C. no. S. C. ay. Geo. ay.[72]

M᷉ WILSON'S renewed the motion for 4 years instead of 7. & on [73] question

N. H. no. Mas. no. C᷉ ay. N. J. no. P᷉ no Del. no. M᷉ ay. V᷉ ay. N. C. no. S. C. no. Geo. no.[74]

M᷉ Gov᷉ MORRIS moved to add to the end of the section [art IV. S. 2] a proviso that the limitation of seven years should not affect the rights of any person now a Citizen.

M᷉ MERCER 2᷉ed the motion. It was necessary he said to prevent a disfranchisement of persons who had become Citizens under and on [75] the faith & according to the laws & Constitution from being on a [76] level in all respects with natives.

M᷉ RUTLIDGE. It might as well be said that all qualifications are disfranchisem᷉᷉ and that to require the age of 25 years was a disfranchisement. The policy of the precaution was as great with regard to foreigners now Citizens; as to those who are to be naturalized in future.

---

[70] The words "On the" are here inserted in the transcript.
[71] In the transcript the vote reads: "Connecticut, Pennsylvania, Maryland, Virginia, aye—4; New Hampshire, Massachusetts, New Jersey, Delaware, North Carolina, South Carolina, Georgia, no—7."
[72] In the transcript the vote reads: "New Hampshire, South Carolina, Georgia, aye—; Massachusetts, Connecticut, New Jersey, Pennsylvania, Delaware, Maryland, Virginia, North Carolina, no—8."
[73] The word "the" is here inserted in the transcript.
[74] In the transcript the vote reads: "Connecticut, Maryland, Virginia, aye—3; New Hampshire, Massachusetts, New Jersey, Pennsylvania, Delaware, North Carolina, South Carolina, Georgia, no—8."
[75] The words "and on" are omitted in the transcript.
[76] The words "their actual" are substituted in the transcript for "being on a."

M![r] SHERMAN. The U. States have not invited foreigners nor pledged their faith that they should enjoy equal privileges with native Citizens. The Individual States alone have done this. The former therefore are at liberty to make any discriminations they may judge requisite.

M![r] GHORUM. When foreigners are naturalized it w[d] seem as if they stand on an equal footing with natives. He doubted then the propriety of giving a retrospective force to the restriction.

M![r] MADISON animadverted on the peculiarity of the doctrine of M![r] Sharman. It was a subtilty by which every national engagement might be evaded. By parity of reason, wherever our public debts, or foreign treaties become inconvenient nothing more would be necessary to relieve us from them, than to new [77] model the Constitution. It was said that the *U. S.* as such have not pledged their faith to the naturalized foreigners, & therefore are not bound. Be it so, & that the States alone are bound. Who are to form the New Constitution by which the condition of that class of citizens is to be made worse than the other class? Are not the States y[e] Agents? will they not be the members of it? Did they not appoint this Convention? Are not they to ratify its proceedings? Will not the new Constitution be their Act? If the new Constitution then violates the faith pledged to any description of people will not the makers of it, will not the States, be the violators. To justify the doctrine it must be said that the States can get rid of their [78] obligation by revising the Constitution, though they could not do it by repealing the law under which foreigners held their privileges. He considered this a matter of real importance. It woud expose us to the reproaches of all those who should be affected by it, reproaches which w[d] soon be ecchoed from the other side of the Atlantic; and would unnecessarily enlist among the Adversaries of the reform a very considerable body of Citizens: We should moreover reduce every State to the dilemma of rejecting it or of violating the faith pledged to a part of its Citizens.

M![r] Gov[r] MORRIS considered the case of persons under 25 years,[79] as very dfferent from that of foreigners. No faith could be pleaded

---
[77] In the transcript the word "new" is crossed out and the syllable "re" is written above it.
[78] The wod "the" is substituted in the transcript for "their."

by the former in bar of the regulation. No assurance had ever been given that persons under that age should be in all cases on a level with those above it. But with regard to foreigners among us, the faith had been pledged that they should enjoy the privileges of Citizens. If the restriction as to age had been confined to natives, & had left foreigners under 25 years,[79] eligible in this case, the discrimination w$^d$ have been an equal injustice on the other side.

M$^r$ PINKNEY remarked that the laws of the States had varied much the terms of naturalization in different parts of America; and contended that the U. S. could not be bound to respect them on such an occasion as the present. It was a sort of recurrence to first principles.

Col. MASON was struck not like [M$^r$ Madison] with the *peculiarity*, but the *propriety* of the doctrine of M$^r$ Sharman. The States have formed different qualifications themselves, for enjoying different rights of citizenship. Greater caution w$^d$ be necessary in the ouset of the Gov$^t$ than afterwards. All the great objects w$^d$ be then [80] provided for. Everything would be then set in Motion. If persons among us attached to G. B. should work themselves into our Councils, a turn might be given to our affairs & particularly to our Commercial regulations which might have pernicious consequences. The great Houses of British Merchants will spare no pains to insinuate the instruments of their views into the Gov$^t$

M$^r$ WILSON read the clause in the Constitution of Pen$^a$ giving to foreigners after two years residence all the rights whatsoever of citizens, combined it with the article of Confederation making the Citizens of one State Citizens of all, inferred the obligation Pen$^a$ was under to maintain the faith thus pledged to her citizens of foreign birth, and the just complaints which her failure would authorize: He observed likewise that the Princes & States of Europe would avail themselves of such breach of faith to deter their subjects from emigrating to the U. S.

M$^r$ MERCER enforced the same idea of a breach of faith.

---

[79] The words "of age" are here inserted in the transcript.

[80] The words "be then" are transposed in the transcript to read "then be."

Mr BALDWIN could not enter into the force of the arguments agst extending the disqualification to foreigners now Citizens. The discrimination of the place of birth, was not more objectionable than that of age which all had concurred in the propriety of.

[81] Question on the proviso of Mr Govr Morris in favor of foreigners now Citizens

N. H. no. Mas. no. Ct ay. N. J. ay. Pa ay. Del. no. Maryd ay. Va ay. N. C. no. S. C. no. Geo. no.[82]

Mr CARROL moved to insert "5 years" instead "of seven," in Section 2d Art: IV

N. H. no. Mas. no. Ct ay. N. J. no. Pa divd Del. no. Md ay. Va ay. N. C. no. S. C. no. Geo. no.[83]

The Section [Art IV. Sec. 2.] as formerly amended was then agreed to nem. con.

Mr WILSON moved that [in Art: V. Sect. 3.[84]] 9 years be reduced to seven, which was disagd to and the 3d section [Art. V.] confirmed by the following vote.

N. H. ay. Mas. ay. Ct no. N. J. ay. Pa no. Del. ay. Md no. Va ay. N. C. ay. S. C. ay. Geo. ay.[85]

Art. IV. Sec 5[86] being reconsidered.

Mr RANDOLPH moved that the clause be altered so as to read— "Bills for raising money for the *purpose of revenue* or for appropriating the same shall originate in the House of Representatives and shall not be so amended or altered by the Senate as to increase or diminish the sum to be raised, or change the mode of levying it, or the objects of its appropriation."—He would not repeat his reasons, but barely remind the members from the smaller States of the compromise by which the larger States were entitled to this privilege.

Col. MASON. This amendment removes all the objections urged agst the section as it stood at first. By specifying *purposes of*

---

[81] The words 'On the" are here inserted in the transcript.

[82] In the trancript the vote reads: "Connecticut, New Jersey, Pennsylvania, Maryland, Virginia, aye—5; New Hampshire, Massachusetts, Delaware, North Carolina, South Carolina, Georgia, no—6."

[83] In the trapscript the vote reads: "Connecticut, Maryland, Virginia, aye—3; New Hampshire, Massachusetts, New Jersey, Delaware, North Carolina, South Carolina, Georgia, no—7; Pennsylvania, divided."

[84] See *ante*.

[85] In the tanscript the vote reads: "New Hampshire, Massachusetts, New Jersey, Delaware, Virginia, North Carcina, South Carolina, Georgia, aye—8; Connecticut, Pennsylvania, Maryland, no—3."

[86] See *ant*.

*revenue*, it obviated the objection that the Section extended to all bills under which money might incidentally arise. By authorising amendments in the Senate it got rid of the objections that the Senate could not correct errors of any sort, & that it would introduce into the House of Rep<sup>s</sup> the practice of tacking foreign matter to money bills. These objections being removed, the arguments in favor of the proposed restraint on the Senate ought to have their full force. 1.[87] the Senate did not represent the *people*, but the *States* in their political character. It was improper therefore that it should tax the people. The reason was the same ag<sup>st</sup> their doing it; as it had been ag<sup>st</sup> Cong<sup>s</sup> doing it. [88]Nor was it in any respect necessary in order to cure the evils of our Republican system. He admitted that notwithstanding the superiority of the Republican form over every other, it had its evils. The chief ones, were the danger of the majority oppressing the minority, and the mischievous influence of demagogues. The Gen<sup>l</sup> Government of itself will cure these.[89] As the States will not concur at the same time in their unjust & oppressive plans, the General Gov<sup>t</sup> will be able to check & defeat them, whether they result from the wickedness of the majority, or from the misguidance of demagogues. Again, the Senate is not like the H. of Rep<sup>s</sup> chosen frequently and obliged to return frequently among the people. They are to be chosen by the Sts for 6 years, will probably settle themselves at the seat of Gov<sup>t</sup> will pursue schemes for their own aggrandizement—will be able by weary<sup>g</sup> out the H. of Rep<sup>s</sup> and taking advantage of their impatience at the close of a long Session, to extort measures for that purpose. If they should be paid as he expected would be yet determined & wished to be so, out of the Nat<sup>l</sup> Treasury, they will particularly extort an increase of their wages. A bare negative was a very different thing from that of originating bills. The practice in Engl<sup>d</sup> was in point. The House of Lords does not represent nor tax the people, because not elected by the people. If the Senate can originate, they will in the recess of the Legislative Sessions, hatch their mischievous projects, for their own purposes, and have their

---

[87] The figure "1" is changed to "First" in the transcript.
[88] The word "Secondly" is here inserted in the transcript.
[89] The word "them" is substituted in the transcript for "these."

money bills ready [90] cut & dried, (to use a common phrase) for the meeting of the H. of Rep? He compared the case to Poyning's law—and signified that the House of Rep? might be rendered by degrees like the Parliament of Paris, the mere depository of the decrees of the Senate. As to the compromise so much had passed on that subject that he would say nothing about it. He did not mean by what he had said to oppose the permanency of the Senate. On the contrary he had no repugnance to an increase of it—nor to allowing it a negative, though the Senate was not by its present constitution entitled to it. But in all events he would contend that the purse strings should be in the hands of the Representatives of the people.

M? WILSON was himself directly opposed to the equality of votes granted to the Senate by its present Constitution. At the same time he wished not to multiply the vices of the system. He did not mean to enlarge on a subject which had been so much canvassed, but would remark as an insuperable objection ag?t the proposed restriction of money bills to the H. of Rep? that it would be a source of perpetual contentions where there was no mediator to decide them. The Presid? here could not like the Executive Magistrate in England interpose by a prorogation, or dissolution. This restriction had been found pregnant with altercation in every State where the Constitution had established it. The House of Rep? will insert other things in money bills, and by making them conditions of each other, destroy the deliberative liberty of the Senate. He stated the case of a Preamble to a money bill sent up by the House of Commons in the reign of Queen Anne, to the H. of Lords, in which the conduct of the displaced Ministry, who were to be impeached before the Lords, was condemned; the Commons thus extorting a premature judgm? without any hearing of the Parties to be tried, and the H. of Lords being thus reduced to the poor & disgraceful expedient of opposing to the authority of a law, a protest on their Journals ag?t its being drawn into precedent. If there was any thing like Poynings law in the present case, it was in the attempt to vest the exclusive right of originating in the H. of Rep? and so far he was ag?t it.

---

[90] The word "ready" is omitted in the transcript.

He should be equally so if the right were to be exclusively vested in the Senate. With regard to the purse strings, it was to be observed that the purse was to have two strings, one of which was in the hands of the H. of Rep? the other in those of the Senate. Both houses must concur in untying, and of what importance could it be which untied first, which last. He could not conceive it to be any objection to the Senate's preparing the bills, that they would have leisure for that purpose and would be in the habits of ·business. War, Commerce, & Revenue were the great objects of the Gen! Government. All of them are connected with money. The restriction in favor of the H. of Represt? would exclude the Senate from originating any important bills whatever—

M! GERRY considered this as a part of the plan that would be much scrutinized. Taxation & representation are strongly associated in the minds of the people, and they will not agree that any but their immediate representatives shall meddle with their purses. In short the acceptance of the plan will inevitably fail, if the Senate be not restrained from originating Money bills.

M! GOVERN! MORRIS All the arguments suppose the right to originate money [91] & to tax, to be exclusively vested in the Senate.—The effects commented on may be produced by a Negative only in the Senate. They can tire out the other House, and extort their concurrence in favorite measures, as well by withholding their negative, as by adhering to a bill introduced by themselves.

M! MADISON thought If the substitute offered by M! Randolph for the original section is to be adopted it would be proper to allow the Senate at least so to amend as to *diminish* the sum [92] to be raised. Why should they be restrained from checking the extravagance of the other House? One of the greatest evils incident to Republican Gov! was the spirit of contention &.faction. The proposed substitute, which in some respects lessened the objections ag?t the section, had a contrary effect with respect to this particular. It laid a foundation for new difficulties and disputes between the two houses. The word *revenue* was ambiguous. In many acts,

---

[91] The word "money" is omitted in the transcript. In Madison's notes it is written above the words "originate" and "&" without a caret indicating its position. It appears to have been omitted in all previous editions.

[92] The transcript uses the word "sum" in the plural.

particularly in the regulations of trade, the object would be twofold. The raising of revenue would be one of them. How could it be determined which was the primary or predominant one; or whether it was necessary that revenue sh⁀ be the sole object, in exclusion even of other incidental effects. When the Contest was first opened with G. B. their power to regulate trade was admitted. Their power to raise revenue rejected. An accurate investigation of the subject afterward proved that no line could be drawn between the two cases. The words *amend or alter*, form an equal source of doubt & altercation. When an obnoxious paragraph shall be sent down from the Senate to the House of Rep⁀—it will be called an origination under the name of an amendment. The Senate may actually couch extraneous matter under that name. In these cases, the question will turn on the *degree* of connection between the matter & object of the bill and the alteration or amendment offered to it. Can there be a more fruitful source of dispute, or a kind of dispute more difficult to be settled? His apprehensions on this point were not conjectural. Disputes had actually flowed from this source in Virg⁀ where the Senate can originate no bill. The words "so as to *increase or diminish* the sum to be raised," were liable to the same objections. In levying indirect taxes, which it seemed to be understood were to form the principal revenue of the new Gov⁀ the sum to be raised, would be increased or diminished by a variety of collateral circumstances influencing the consumption, in general, the consumption of foreign or of domestic articles—of this or that particular species of articles, and even by the mode of collection which may be closely connected with the productiveness of a tax.—The friends of the section had argued its necessity from the permanency of the Senate. He could not see how this argum⁀ applied. The Senate was not more permanent now than in the form it bore in the original propositions of M⁀ Randolph and at the time when no objection whatever was hinted ag⁀ its originating money bills. Or if in consequence of a loss of the present question, a proportional vote in the Senate should be reinstated as has been urged as the indemnification the permanency of the Senate will remain the same.—If the right to originate be vested exclusively in the House of Rep⁀ either the

Senate must yield ag:t its judgment to that House, in which case the Utility of the check will be lost—or the Senate will be inflexible & the H. of Rep: must adapt its money bill to the views of the Senate, in which case, the exclusive right will be of no avail.—As to the Compromise of which so much had been said, he would make a single observation. There were 5 States which had opposed the equality of votes in the Senate, viz. Mas:ts Penn:a Virg:a N. Carolina & S. Carol:a As a compensation for the sacrifice extorted from them on this head, the exclusive origination of money bills in the other House had been tendered. Of the five States a majority viz. Penn:a Virg:a & S. Carol:a have uniformly voted ag:st the proposed compensation, on its own merits, as rendering the plan of Gov:t still more objectionable. Mass:ts has been divided. N. Carolina alone has set a value on the compensation, and voted on that principle. What obligation then can the small States be under to concur ag:st their judgments in reinstating the section?

M:r DICKENSON. Experience must be our only guide. Reason may mislead us. It was not Reason that discovered the singular & admirable mechanism of the English Constitution. It was not Reason that discovered or ever could have discovered the odd & in the eye of those who are governed by reason, the absurd mode of trial by Jury. Accidents probably produced these discoveries, and experience has give a sanction to them. This is then our guide. And has not experience verified the utility of restraining money bills to the immediate representatives of the people. Whence the effect may have proceeded he could not say; whether from the respect with which this privilege inspired the other branches of Gov:t to the H. of Commons, or from the turn of thinking it gave to the people at large with regard to their rights, but the effect was visible & could not be doubted—Shall we oppose to this long experience, the short experience of 11 years which we had ourselves, on this subject. As to disputes, they could not be avoided any way. If both Houses should originate, each would have a different bill to which it would be attached, and for which it would contend.—He observed that all the prejudices of the people would be offended by refusing this exclusive privilege to the H. of Repres: and these prejudices sh<sup>d</sup> never be disregarded by us when no essential purpose was to be served. When this plan goes forth it will be attacked by the popular leaders. Aristocracy will be the watchword; the Shibboleth among its adversaries. Eight States have inserted in their Constitutions the exclusive right of originating money bills in favor of the popular branch of the Legislature. Most of them however allowed the other branch to amend. This he thought would be proper for us to do.

M<sup>r</sup> RANDOLPH regarded this point as of such consequence, that as he valued the peace of this Country, he would press the adoption of it. We had numerous & monstrous difficulties to combat. Surely we ought not to increase them. When the people behold in the Senate, the countenance of an aristocracy; and in the president, the form at least of a little monarch, will not their alarms be sufficiently raised without taking from their immediate representatives, a right which has been so long appropriated to them.— The Executive will have more influence over the Senate, than over the H. of Rep: Allow the Senate to originate in this case, & that influence will be sure to mix itself in their deliberations & plans. The Declaration of War he conceived ought not to be in the Senate composed of 26 men only, but rather in the other House. In the other House ought to be placed the origination of the means of war. As to Commercial regulations which may involve revenue, the difficulty may be avoided by restraining the definition to bills, for the *mere* or *sole*, purpose of raising revenue. The Senate will be more likely to be corrupt than the H. of Rep: and should therefore have less to do with money matters. His principal object however was to prevent popular objections against the plan, and to secure its adoption.

M<sup>r</sup> RUTLIDGE. The friends of this motion are not consistent in their reasoning. They tell us that we ought to be guided by the long experience of G. B. & not our own experience of 11 years: and yet they themselves propose to depart from it. The *H. of Commons* not only have the exclusive right of originating, but the *Lords* are not allowed to alter or amend a money bill. Will not the people say that this restriction is but a mere tub to the whale.

They cannot but see that it is of no real consequence; and will be more likely to be displeased with it as an attempt to bubble them, than to impute it to a watchfulness over their rights. For his part, he would prefer giving the exclusive right to the Senate, if it was to be given exclusively at all. The Senate being more conversant in business, and having more leisure, will digest the bills much better, and as they are to have no effect, till examined & approved by the H. of Rep: there can be no possible danger. These clauses in the Constitutions of the States had been put in through a blind adherence to the British model. If the work was to be done over now, they would be omitted. The experiment in S. Carolina, where the Senate cannot originate or amend money bills, has shewn that it answers no good purpose; and produces the very bad one of continually dividing & heating the two houses. Sometimes indeed if the matter of the amendment of the Senate is pleasing to the other House they wink at the encroachment; if it be displeasing, then the Constitution is appealed to. Every Session is distracted by altercations on this subject. The practice now becoming frequent is for the Senate not to make formal amendments; but to send down a schedule of the alterations which will procure the bill their assent.

Mr CARROL. The most ingenious men in Maryd are puzzled to define the case of money bills, or explain the Constitution on that point; tho' it seemed to be worded with all possible plainness & precision. It is a source of continual difficulty & squabble between the two houses.

Mr McHenry mentioned an instance of extraordinary subterfuge, to get rid of the apparent force of the Constitution.

On[93] Question on the first part of the motion as to the exclusive originating of Money bills in [93] H. of Rep:

N. H. ay. Mas. ay. Ct no. N. J. no. Pa no. Del. no. Md no. Virga ay. Mr Blair & Mr M. no. Mr R. Col. Mason and * Genl Washington ay N. C. ay. S. C. no. Geo. no.[94]

---

[93] The word "the" is here inserted in the transcript.

* He disapproved & till now voted agst the exclusive privilege, he gave up his judgment he said because it was not of very material weight with him & was made an essential point with others who if disappointed, might be less cordial in other points of real weight.

[94] In the transcript the vote reads: "New Hampshire, Massachusetts, Virginia [Mr. Blair, and Mr. Madison no, Mr. Randolph, Colonel Mason and General Washington,* aye], North Carolina, aye—4; Connecticut, New Jersey, Pennsylvania, Delaware, Maryland, South Carolina, Georgia, no—7."

[95] Question on Originating by [96] H. of Rep: & *amending* by [96] Senate, as reported Art. IV. Sect. 5.

N. H. ay. Mas. ay. C: no. N. J. no. P: no. Del. no. M: no. V:† ay. N. C. ay. S. C. no. Geo. no.[97]

[95] Question on the last clause of Sect: 5—Art. IV—viz " No money shall be drawn from the Public Treasury, but in pursuance of *appropriations* that shall originate in the House of Rep: It passed in the negative

N. H. no. Mas. ay Con. no. N. J. no. P: no Del. no. M: no. V: no. N. C. no. S. C. no. Geo. no.[98]

Adj:

---

TUESDAY AUG. 14. IN CONVENTION

Article VI. Sect. 9.[99], [1] taken up.

M: PINKNEY argued that the making the members ineligible to offices was *degrading* to them, and the more improper as their election into the Legislature implied that they had the confidence of the people; that it was *inconvenient*, because the Senate might be supposed to contain the fittest men. He hoped to see that body become a School of public Ministers, a nursery of Statesmen: that it was *impolitic*, because the Legislature would cease to be a magnet to the first talents and abilities. He moved to postpone the section in order to take up the following proposition viz—" the members of each House shall be incapable of holding any office under the U. S. for which they or any of [2] others for their benefit receive any salary, fees, or emoluments of any kind—and the acceptance of such office shall vacate their seats respectively"

Gen: MIFFLIN 2ded the motion.

Col. MASON ironically proposed to strike out the whole section, as a more effectual expedient for encouraging that exotic corruption which might not otherwise thrive so well in the American

---

[95] The words "On the" are here inserted in the transcript.
[96] The word "the" is here inserted in the transcript.
† In the printed Journ Virg:—no.
[97] In the transcript the vote reads: "New Hampshire, Massachusetts, Virginia,† North Carolina aye—4; Connecticut, New Jersey, Pennsylvania, Delaware, Maryland, South Carolina, Georgia, no—7."
[98] In the transcript the vote reads: "Massachusetts, aye—1; New Hampshire, Connecticut, New Jersey, Pennsylvania, Delaware, Maryland, Virginia, North Carolina, South Carolina, Georgia, no—10."
[99] See *ante*.
[1] The word 'was" is here inserted in the transcript.
[2] The word "of" is omitted in the trancript.

Soil— for compleating that Aristocracy which was probably in the contemplation of some among us, and for inviting into the Legislative Service, those generous & benevolent characters who will do justice to each other's merit, by carving out offices & rewards for it. In the present state of American morals & manners, few friends it may be thought will be lost to the plan, by the opportunity of giving premiums to a mercenary & depraved ambition.

M! MERCER. It is a first principle in political science, that wherever the rights of property are secured, an aristocracy will grow out of it. Elective Governments also necessarily become aristocratic, because the rulers being few can & will draw emoluments for themselves from the many. The Governments of America will become aristocracies. They are so already. The public measures are calculated for the benefit of the Governors, not of the people. The people are dissatisfied & complain. They change their rulers, and the public measures are changed, but it is only a change of one scheme of emolument to the rulers, for another. The people gain nothing by it, but an addition of instability & uncertainty to their other evils.—Governm!ˢ can only be maintained by *force* or *influence*. The Executive has not *force*, deprive him of influence [3] by rendering the members of the Legislature ineligible to Executive offices, and he becomes a mere phantom of authority. The aristocratic part will not even let him in for a share of the plunder. The Legislature must & will be composed of wealth & abilities, and the people will be governed by a Junto. The Executive ought to have a Council, being members of both Houses. Without such an influence, the war will be between the aristocracy & the people. He wished it to be between the Aristocracy & the Executive. Nothing else can protect the people ag!ᵗ those speculating Legislatures which are now plundering them throughout the U. States.

M! GERRY read a resolution of the Legislature of Mass!ˢ passed before the Act of Cong! recommending the Convention, in which her deputies were instructed not to depart from the rotation estab-

---

[3] The transcript italicizes the word "influence."

lished in the 5th art: of [4] Confederation, nor to agree in any case to give to the members of Congs a capacity to hold offices under the Government. This he said was repealed in consequence of the Act of Congs with which the State thought it proper to comply in an unqualified manner. The Sense of the State however was still the same. He could not think with Mr Pinkney that the disqualification was degrading. Confidence is the road to tyranny. As to Ministers & Ambassadors few of them were necessary. It is the opinion of a great many that they ought to be discontinued, on our part; that none may be sent among us, & that source of influence be [5] shut up. If the Senate were to appoint Ambassadors as seemed to be intended, they will multiply embassies for their own sakes. He was not so fond of those productions as to wish to establish nurseries for them. If they are once appointed, the House of Reps will be obliged to provide salaries for them, whether they approve of the measures or not. If men will not serve in the Legislature without a prospect of such offices, our situation is deplorable indeed. If our best Citizens are actuated by such mercenary views, we had better chuse a single despot at once. It will be more easy to satisfy the rapacity of one than of many. According to the idea of one Gentleman [Mr Mercer] our Government it seems is to be a Govt of plunder. In that case it certainly would be prudent to have but one rather than many to be employed in it. We cannot be too circumspect in the formation of this System. It will be examined on all sides and with a very suspicious eye. The People who have been so lately in arms agst G. B. for their liberties, will not easily give them up. He lamented the evils existing at present under our Governments, but imputed them to the faults of those in office, not to the people. The misdeeds of the former will produce a critical attention to the opportunities afforded by the new system to like or greater abuses. As it now stands it is as compleat an aristocracy as ever was framed If great powers should be given to the Senate we shall be governed in reality by a Junto as has been apprehended. He remarked that it would be very differently constituted from Congs – 1.[6] there

---

[4] The word "the" is here inserted in the transcript.
[5] The word "be" is omitted in the transcript.
[6] The figure "1" is changed to "In the first place" in the transcript.

will be but 2 deputies from each State, in Congs there may be 7. and are generally 5.—2.[7] they are chosen for six years, those of Congs annually. 3.[8] they are not subject to recall; those of Congs are. 4. In Congs 9 *States* [9] are necessary for all great purposes—here 8 *persons* will suffice. Is it to be presumed that the people will ever agree to such a system? He moved to render the members of the H. of Reps as well as of the Senate ineligible not only during, but for one year after the expiration of their terms.—If it should be thought that this will injure the Legislature by keeping out of it men of abilities who are willing to serve in other offices it may be required as a qualification for other offices, that the Candidate shall have served a certain time in the Legislature.

Mr Govr Morris. Exclude the officers of the army & navy, and you form a band having a different interest from & opposed to the civil power: you stimulate them to despise & reproach those "talking Lords who dare not face the foe." Let this spirit be roused at the end of a war, before your troops shall have laid down their arms, and though the Civil authority "be intrenched in parchment to the teeth" they will cut their way to it. He was agst rendering the members of the Legislature ineligible to offices. He was for rendering them eligible agn after having vacated their Seats by accepting office. Why should we not avail ourselves of their services if the people chuse to give them their confidence. There can be little danger of corruption either among the people or the Legislatures who are to be the Electors. If they say, we see their merits, we honor the men, we chuse to renew our confidence in them, have they not a right to give them a preference; and can they be properly abridged of it.

Mr Williamson; introduced his opposition to the motion by referring to the question concerning "money bills." That clause he said was dead. Its ghost he was afraid would notwithstanding haunt us. It had been a matter of conscience with him, to insist

[7] The figure "2" is changed to "In the second place" in the transcript.

[8] The figure "3" is changed to "In the third place" in the transcript.

[9] The phrase "And finally, in Congress *nine* States" is substituted in the transcript for "4. In Congs 9 *States*."

upon [10] it as long as there was hope of retaining it. He had swallowed the vote of rejection, with reluctance. He could not digest it. All that was said on the other side was that the restriction was not *convenient*. We have now got a House of Lords which is to originate money-bills.—To avoid another *inconveniency*,[11] we are to have a whole Legislature at liberty to cut out offices for one another. He thought a self-denying ordinance for ourselves would be more proper. Bad as the Constitution has been made by expunging the restriction on the Senate concerning money bills he did not wish to make it worse by expunging the present Section. He had scarcely seen a single corrupt measure in the Legislature of N. Carolina, which could not be traced up to office hunting.

Mr SHERMAN. The Constitution shd lay as few temptations as possible in the way of those in power. Men of abilities will increase as the Country grows more populous and, and [12] the means of education are more diffused.

Mr PINKNEY. No State has rendered the members of the Legislature ineligible to offices. In S. Carolina the Judges are eligible into the Legislature. It can not be supposed then that the motion will be offensive to the people. If the State Constitutions should be revised he believed restrictions of this sort wd be rather diminished than multiplied.

Mr WILSON could not approve of the Section as it stood, and could not give up his judgment to any supposed objections that might arise among the people. He considered himself as acting & responsible for the welfare of millions not immediately represented in this House. He had also asked himself the serious question what he should say to his constituents in case they should call upon him to tell them why he sacrified his own Judgment in a case where they authorised him to exercise it? Were he to own to them that he sacrificed it in order to flatter their prejudices, he should dread the retort: did you suppose the people of Penna had not good sense enough to receive a good Government? Under this impression he should certainly follow his own Judgment which disapproved of the section. He would remark in addition

---

[10] The word "on" is substituted in the transcript for "upon."

[11] The word "*inconveniency*" is changed to "*inconvenience*" in the transcript.

[12] The word "as" is substituted in the transcript for "and."

to the objections urged ag:<sup>st</sup> it, that as one branch of the Legislature was to be appointed by the Legislatures of the States, the other by the people of the States, as both are to be paid by the States, and to be appointable to State offices, nothing seemed to be wanting to prostrate the Nat! Legislature, but to render its members ineligible to Nat! offices, & by that means take away its power of attracting those talents which were necessary to give weight to the Govern! and to render it useful to the people. He was far from thinking the ambition which aspired to Offices of dignity and trust, an ignoble or culpable one. He was sure it was not politic to regard it in that light, or to withold from it the prospect of those rewards, which might engage it in the career of public service. He observed that the State of Penn<sup>a</sup> which had gone as far as any State into the policy of fettering power, had not rendered the members of the Legislature ineligible to offices of Gov!

M! ELSWORTH did not think the mere postponement of the reward would be any material discouragement of merit. Ambitious minds will serve 2 years or 7 years in the Legislature for the sake of qualifying themselves for other offices. This he thought a sufficient security for obtaining the services of the ablest men in the Legislature, although whilst members they should be ineligible to Public offices. Besides, merit will be most encouraged, when most impartially rewarded. If rewards are to circulate only within the Legislature, merit out of it will be discouraged.

M! MERCER was extremely anxious on this point. What led to the appointment of this Convention? The corruption & mutability of the Legislative Councils of the States. If the plan does not remedy these, it will not recommend itself; and we shall not be able in our private capacities to support & enforce it: nor will the best part of our Citizens exert themselves for the purpose.—It is a great mistake to suppose that the paper we are to propose will govern the U. States? It is The men whom it will bring into the Govern! and interest in maintaining it that is [13] to govern them. The paper will only mark out the mode & the form. Men are the

---

[13] The word "are" is substituted in the transcript for "is."

substance and must do the business. All Gov<sup>t</sup> must be by force or influence. It is not the King of France—but 200,000 janisaries of power that govern that Kingdom. There will be no such force here; influence then must be substituted; and he would ask whether this could be done, if the members of the Legislature should be ineligible to offices of State; whether such a disqualification would not determine all the most influencial men to stay at home, and & prefer appointments within their respective States.

M<sup>r</sup> WILSON was by no means satisfied with the answer given by M<sup>r</sup> Elsewoth to the argument as to the discouragement of merit. The members must either go a second time into the Legislature, and disqualify themselves—or say to their Constituents, we served you before only from the mercenary view of qualifying ourselves for offices, and have<sup>g</sup> answered this purpose we do not chuse to be again elected.

M<sup>r</sup> Gov<sup>r</sup> MORRIS put the case of a war, and the Citizen the [14] most capable of conducting it, happening to be a member of the Legislature. What might have been the consequence of such a regulation at the commencement, or even in the Course of the late contest for our liberties?

On [15] question for postponing in order to take up M<sup>r</sup> Pinkneys motion, it was lost.

N. H. ay. Mas. no. C<sup>t</sup> no. N. J. no. P<sup>a</sup> ay. Del. ay. M<sup>d</sup> ay. V<sup>a</sup> ay. N. C. no. S. C. no. Geo. div<sup>d</sup> [16]

M<sup>r</sup> Gov<sup>r</sup> MORRIS moved to insert, after "office," except offices in the army or navy: but in that case their offices shall be vacated.

M<sup>r</sup> BROOM 2<sup>ds</sup> him.

M<sup>r</sup> RANDOLPH had been & should continue uniformly opposed to the striking out of the clause; as opening a door for influence & corruption. No arguments had made any impression on him, but those which related to the case of war, and a co-existing incapacity of the fittest commanders to be employed. He admitted great weight in these, and would agree to the exception proposed by M<sup>r</sup> Gov<sup>r</sup> Morris.

---

[14] The word "the" is omitted in the transcript.

[15] The word "the" is here inserted in the transcript.

[16] In the transcript the vote reads: "New Hampshire, Pennsylvania, Delaware, Maryland, Virginia, aye—5; Massachusetts, Connecticut, New Jersey, North Carolina, South Carolina, no—5; Georgia, divided."

Mr BUTLER & Mr PINKNEY urged a general postponemt of 9 Sect. Art. VI. till it should be seen what powers would be vested in the Senate, when it would be more easy to judge of the expediency of allowing the officers of State to be chosen out of that body. —a general postponement was agreed to nem. con.

Art: VI. sect. 10.[17],[18] taken up—"that members be paid by their respective States."

Mr ELSEWORTH said that in reflecting on this subject he had been satisfied that too much dependence on the States would be produced by this mode of payment. He moved to strike [19] out and insert "that they should" be paid out of the Treasury of the U. S. an allowance not exceeding (blank) dollars per day or the present value thereof.

Mr Govr MORRIS, remarked that if the members were to be paid by the States it would throw an unequal burden on the distant States, which would be unjust as the Legislature was to be a national Assembly. He moved that the payment be out of the Natl Treasury; leaving the quantum to the discretion of the Natl Legislature. There could be no reason to fear that they would overpay themselves.

Mr BUTLER contended for payment by the States; particularly in the case of the Senate, who will be so long out of their respective States, that they will lose sight of their Constituents unless dependent on them for their support.

Mr LANGDON was agst payment by the States. There would be some difficulty in fixing the sum; but it would be unjust to oblige the distant States to bear the expence of their members in travelling to and from the Seat of Govt

Mr MADISON If the H. of Reps is to be chosen *biennially*— and the Senate to be *constantly* dependent on the Legislatures which are chosen *annually*, he could not see any chance for that stability in the Genl Govt the want of which was a principal evil in the State Govts His fear was that the organization of the Govt supposing the Senate to be really independt for six years, would not effect our purpose. It was nothing more than a com-

---
[17] See *ante*.
[18] The words "was then" are here inserted in the transcript.
[19] The word "it" is here inserted in the transcript.

bination of the peculiarities of two of the State Gov$^{ts}$ which separately had been found insufficient. The Senate was formed on the model of that of Maryl$^d$ The Revisionary check, on that of N. York. What the effect of a union of these provisions might be, could not be foreseen. The enlargement of the sphere of the Government was indeed a circumstance which he thought would be favorable as he had on several occasions undertaken to shew. He was however for fixing at least two extremes not to be exceeded by the Nat! Legisl$^{re}$ in the payment of themselves.

M$^r$ GERRY. There are difficulties on both sides. The observation of M$^r$ Butler has weight in it. On the other side, the State Legislatures may turn out the Senators by reducing their salaries. Such things have been practised.

Col. MASON. It has not yet been noticed that the clause as it now stands makes the House of Represent$^s$ also dependent on the State Legislatures; so that both houses will be made the instruments of the politics of the States whatever they may be.

M$^r$ BROOM could see no danger in trusting the Gen! Legislature with the payment of themselves. The State Legislatures had this power, and no complaint had been made of it.

M$^r$ SHERMAN was not afraid that the Legislature would make their own wages too high; but too low, so that men ever so fit could not serve unless they were at the same time rich. He thought the best plan would be to fix a moderate allowance to be paid out of the Nat! Treas$^y$ and let the States make such additions as they might judge fit. He moved that 5 dollars per day be the sum, any further emoluments to be added by the States.

M$^r$ CARROL had been much surprised at seeing this clause in the Report. The dependence of both Houses on the State Legislatures is compleat; especially as the members of the former are eligible to State offices. The States can now say: if you do not comply with our wishes, we will starve you: if you do we will reward you. The new Gov$^t$ in this form was nothing more than a second edition of Congress in two volumes, instead of one, and perhaps with very few amendments—

M$^r$ DICKENSON took it for granted that all were convinced of the necessity of making the Gen! Gov$^t$ independent of the prejudices, passions, and improper views of the State Legislatures. The contrary of This was effected by the section as it stands. On the other hand there were objections ag$^{st}$ taking a permanent standard as wheat which had been suggested on a former occasion, as well as against leaving the matter to the pleasure of the Nat! Legislature. He proposed that an Act should be passed every 12 years by the Nat! Legisl$^{re}$ settling the quantum of their wages. If the Gen! Gov$^t$ should be left dependent on the State Legislatures, it would be happy for us if we had never met in this Room.

M$^r$ ELSEWORTH was not unwilling himself to trust the Legislature with authority to regulate their own wages, but well knew that an unlimited discretion for that purpose would produce strong, tho' perhaps not insuperable objections. He thought changes in the value of money, provided for by his motion in the words, "or the present value thereof."

M$^r$ L. MARTIN. As the Senate is to represent the States, the members of it ought to be paid by the States.

M$^r$ CARROL. The Senate was to represent & manage the affairs of the whole, and not to be the advocates of State interests. They ought then not to be dependent on nor paid by the States.

On the question for paying the Members of the Legislature out of the Nat! Treasury,

N. H. ay. Mas. no. C$^t$ ay. N. J. ay. P$^a$ ay. Del. ay. M$^d$ ay. V$^a$ ay. N. C. ay. S. C. no. Geo. ay.[20]

M$^r$ ELSEWTH moved that the pay be fixed at 5 doll$^{rs}$ or the present value thereof per day during their attendance & for every thirty miles in travelling to & from Congress.

M$^r$ STRONG preferred 4 dollars, leaving the Sts. at liberty to make additions.

On [21] question for fixing the pay at 5 dollars.

N. H. no. Mas. no. C$^t$ ay. N. J. no. P$^a$ no. Del. no. M$^d$ no. V$^a$ ay. N. C. no. S. C. no. Geo. no.[22]

M$^r$ DICKENSON proposed that the wages of the members of both houses s$^d$ be required to be the same.

---

[20] In the transcript the vote reads: "New Hampshire, Connecticut, New Jersey, Pennsylvania, Delaware, Maryland, Virginia, North Carolina, Georgia, aye—9; Massachusetts, South Carolina, no—2."
[21] The word "the" is here inserted in the transcript.
[22] In the transcript the vote reads: "Connecticut, Virginia, aye—2; New Hampshire, Massachusetts, New Jersey, Pennsylvania, Delaware, Maryland, North Carolina, South Carolina, Georgia, no—9."

Mʳ BROOME seconded him.

Mʳ GHORUM. this would be unreasonable. The Senate will be detained longer from home, will be obliged to remove their families, and in time of war perhaps to sit constantly. Their allowance should certainly be higher. The members of the Senates in the States are allowed more, than those of the other house.

Mʳ DICKENSON withdrew his motion

It was moved & agreed to amend the Section by adding—"to be ascertained by law."

The Section [Art VI. Sec. 10] as amended, agreed to nem. con.

Adjᵈ

---

WEDNESDAY AUGUST 15. IN CONVENTION

Art: VI. Sect. 11.²³, ²⁴   Agreed to nem. con.

Art: VI Sect. 12.²³, ²⁵ taken up.

Mʳ STRONG moved to amend the article so as to read—"Each House shall possess the right of originating all bills, except bills for raising money for the purposes of revenue, or for appropriating the same and for fixing the salaries of the officers of the Govᵗ which shall originate in the House of Representatives; but the Senate may propose or concur with amendments as in other cases"

Col. MASON, 2ᵈᵈ the motion. He was extremely earnest to take this power from the Senate, who he said could already sell the whole Country by means of Treaties.

Mʳ GHORUM urged the amendment as of great importance. The Senate will first acquire the habit of preparing money bills, and then the practice will grow into an exclusive right of preparing them.

Mʳ GOVERNʳ MORRIS opposed it as unnecessary and inconvenient.

Mʳ WILLIAMSON. some think this restriction on the Senate essential to liberty, others think it of no importance. Why should not the former be indulged. he was for an efficient and stable Govᵗ but many would not strengthen the Senate if not

---

²³ See *ante.*
²⁴ The word "was" is here inserted in the transcript.
²⁵ The words "was then" are here inserted in the transcript.

restricted in the case of money bills. The friends of the Senate would therefore lose more than they would gain by refusing to gratify the other side. He moved to postpone the subject till the powers of the Senate should be gone over.

M$^r$ RUTLIDGE 2$^{ds}$ the motion.

M$^r$ MERCER should hereafter be ag$^{st}$ returning to a reconsideration of this section. He contended, (alluding to M$^r$ Mason's observations) that the Senate ought not to have the power of treaties. This power belonged to the Executive department; adding that Treaties would not be final so as to alter the laws of the land, till ratified by legislative authority. This was the case of Treaties in Great Britain; particularly the late Treaty of Commerce with France.

Col. MASON. did not say that a Treaty would repeal a law; but that the Senate by means of treaty [26] might alienate territory &c, without legislative sanction. The cessions of the British Islands in [27] W. Indies by Treaty alone were an example. If Spain should possess herself of Georgia therefore the Senate might by treaty dismember the Union. He wished the motion to be decided now, that the friends of it might know how to conduct themselves.

On [27] question for postponing Sec: 12. it passed in the affirmative.

N. H. ay. Mas. ay C$^t$ no. N. J. no Pen$^a$ no. Del. no Mary$^d$ no. V$^a$ ay. N. C. ay. S. C. ay. Geo. ay. —[28]

M$^r$ MADISON moved that all acts before they become laws should be submitted both to the Executive and Supreme Judiciary Departments, that if either of these should object ⅔ of each House, if both should object, ¾ of each House, should be necessary to overrule the objections and give to the acts the force of law—[29]

See the motion at large in the Journal of this date, page 253, & insert it here."[30]

---

[26] The transcript uses the word "treaty" in the plural.
[27] The word "the" is here inserted in the transcript.
[28] In the transcript the vote reads: "New Hampshire, Massachusetts, Virginia, North Carolina, South Carolina, Georgia, aye—6; Connecticut, New Jersey, Pennsylvania, Delaware, Maryland, no—5."
[29] This paragraph is stricken out in the transcript.
[30] Madison's direction concerning the motion is omitted in the transcript and the following sentence is inserted: "M$^r$ Madison moved the following amendment of Article 6, Section 13." [81]
[81] See *ante*.

["Every bill which shall have passed the two houses, shall, before it become a law, be severally presented to the President of the United States, and to the judges of the supreme court for the revision of each. If, upon such revision, they shall approve of it, they shall respectively signify their approbation by signing it; but if, upon such revision, it shall appear improper to either, or both, to be passed into a law, it shall be returned, with the objections against it, to that house, in which it shall have originated, who shall enter the objections at large on their journal, and proceed to reconsider the bill: but if, after such reconsideration, two thirds of that house, when either the President, or a majority of the judges shall object, or three fourths, where both shall object, shall agree to pass it, it shall, together with the objections, be sent to the other house, by which it shall likewise be reconsidered; and, if approved by two thirds, or three fourths of the other house, as the case may be, it shall become a law."]

M.<sup>r</sup> WILSON seconds the motion

M.<sup>r</sup> PINKNEY opposed the interference of the Judges in the Legislative business: it will involve them in parties, and give a previous tincture to their opinions.

M.<sup>r</sup> MERCER heartily approved the motion. It is an axiom that the Judiciary ought to be separate from the Legislative: but equally so that it ought to be independent of that department. The true policy of the axiom is that legislative usurpation and oppression may be obviated. He disapproved of the Doctrine that the Judges as expositors of the Constitution should have authority to declare a law void. He thought laws ought to be well and cautiously made, and then to be uncontroulable.

M.<sup>r</sup> GERRY. This motion comes to the same thing with what has been already negatived.

[32] Question on the motion of M.<sup>r</sup> Madison.

N. H. no. Mass. no. C.<sup>t</sup> no. N. J. no. P.<sup>a</sup> no. Del. ay. Mary.<sup>d</sup> ay. Virg.<sup>a</sup> ay. N. C. no. S. C. no. Geo. no.[33]

M.<sup>r</sup> Gov.<sup>r</sup> MORRIS regretted that something like the proposed check could not be agreed to. He dwelt on the importance of public credit, and the difficulty of supporting it without some

---

[32] The words "On the" are here inserted in the transcript.
[33] In the transcript the vote reads: "Delaware, Maryland, Virginia, aye—3; New Hampshire, Massachusetts, Connecticut, New Jersey, Pennsylvania, North Carolina, South Carolina, Georgia, no—8."

strong barrier against the instability of legislative Assemblies. He suggested the idea of requiring three fourths of each house to *repeal* laws where the President should not concur. He had no great reliance on the revisionary power as the Executive was now to be constituted [elected by the [34] Congress]. The legislature will contrive to soften down the President. He recited the history of paper emissions, and the perseverance of the legislative assemblies in repeating them, with all the distressing effects of such measures before their eyes. Were the National legislature formed, and a war was now to break out, this ruinous expedient would be again resorted to, if not guarded against. The requiring ¾ to repeal would, though not a compleat remedy, prevent the hasty passage of laws, and the frequency of those repeals which destroy faith in the public, and which are among our greatest calamities.–

Mr DICKENSON was strongly impressed with the remark of Mr Mercer as to the power of the Judges to set aside the law. He thought no such power ought to exist. He was at the same time at a loss what expedient to substitute. The Justiciary of Arragon he observed became by degrees, the lawgiver.

Mr Govr MORRIS, suggested the expedient of an absolute negative in the Executive. He could not agree that the Judiciary which was part of the Executive, should be bound to say that a direct violation of the Constitution was law. A controul over the legislature might have its inconveniences. But view the danger on the other side. The most virtuous Citizens will often as members of a legislative body concur in measures which afterwards in their private capacity they will be ashamed of. Encroachments of the popular branch of the Government ought to be guarded agst The Ephori at Sparta became in the end absolute. The Report of the Council of Censors in Pennsylva points out the many invasions of the legislative department on the Executive numerous as the latter* is, within the short term of seven years, and in a State where a strong party is opposed to the Constitution, and watching every occasion of turning the public resentments

---

[34] The word "the" is omitted in the transcript.
*The Executive consists at this time [35] of abt 20 members.
[35] The phrase "consisted at that time" is substituted in the transcript for "consists at this time."

ag$^{st}$ it. If the Executive be overturned by the popular branch, as happened in England, the tyranny of one man will ensue. In Rome where the Aristocracy overturned the throne, the consequence was different. He enlarged on the tendency of the legislative Authority to usurp on the Executive and wished the section to be postponed, in order to consider of some more effectual check than requiring ⅔ only to overrule the negative of the Executive.

M$^r$ SHERMAN. Can one man be trusted better than all the others if they all agree? This was neither wise nor safe. He disapproved of Judges meddling in politics and parties. We have gone far enough in forming the negative as it now stands.

M$^r$ CARROL. when the negative to be overruled by ⅔ only was agreed to, the *quorum* was not fixed. He remarked that as a majority was now to be the quorum, 17. in the larger, and 8 in the smaller house might carry points. The advantage that might be taken of this seemed to call for greater impediments to improper laws. He thought the controuling power however of the Executive could not be well decided, till it was seen how the formation of that department would be finally regulated. He wished the consideration of the matter to be postponed.

M$^r$ GHORUM saw no end to these difficulties and postponements. Some could not agree to the form of Government before the powers were defined. Others could not agree to the powers till it was seen how the Government was to be formed. He thought a majority as large a quorum as was necessary. It was the quorum almost every where fixt in the U. States.

M$^r$ WILSON; after viewing the subject with all the coolness and attention possible was most apprehensive of a dissolution of the Gov$^t$ from the legislature swallowing up all the other powers. He remarked that the prejudices ag$^{st}$ the Executive resulted from a misapplication of the adage that the parliament was the palladium of liberty. Where the Executive was really formidable, *King* and *Tyrant*, were naturally associated in the minds of people; not *legislature* and *tyranny*. But where the Executive was not formidable, the two last were most properly associated. After the destruction of the King in Great Britain, a more pure and unmixed tryanny sprang up in the parliament than had been exercised by the monarch. He insisted that we had not guarded ag:t the danger on this side by a sufficient self-defensive power either to the Executive or Judiciary department.

M: RUTLIDGE was strenuous ag:t postponing; and complained much of the tediousness of the proceedings.

M: ELSEWORTH held the same language. We grow more & more skeptical as we proceed. If we do not decide soon, we shall be unable to come to any decision.

The question for postponement passed in the negative: Del: & Mary:d only being in the affirmative.

M: WILLIAMSON moved to change "⅔ of each House" into "¾" as requisite to overrule the dissent of the President. He saw no danger in this, and preferred giving the power to the Presid:t alone, to admitting the Judges into the business of legislation.

M: WILSON 2:ds the motion; referring to and repeating the ideas of M: Carroll.

On this motion for ¾. instead of two thirds; it passed in the affirmative

N. H. no. Mas. no. C:t ay. N. J. no. Pen:a div:d Del. ay. M:d ay. V:a ay. N. C. ay. S. C. ay. Geo. no.[36]

M: MADISON, observing that if the negative of the President was confined to *bills;* it would be evaded by acts under the form and name of Resolutions, votes &c, proposed that or resolve" should be added after "*bill*" in the beginning of sect 13. with an exception as to votes of adjournment &c.—after a short and rather confused conversation on the subject, the question was put & rejected, the States[37] being as follows,

N. H. no. Mas. ay. C:t no. N. J. no. Pen:a no. Del. ay. M:d no. V:a no. N. C. ay. S. C. no. Geo. no.[38]

"*Ten*[39] days (Sundays excepted)" instead of "*seven*" were allowed to the President for returning bills with his objections N. H. & Mas: only voting ag:st it.

The 13 Sect: of art. VI as amended was then agreed to.

Adjourned

---

[36] In the transcript the vote reads: "Connecticut, Delaware, Maryland, Virginia, North Carolina, South Carolina, aye—6; New Hampshire, Massachusetts, New Jersey, Georgia, no—4; Pennsylvania, divided."

[37] The word "votes" is substituted in the transcript for "States."

[38] In the transcript the vote reads: "Massachusetts, Delaware, North Carolina, aye—3; New Hampshire, Connecticut, New Jersey, Pennsylvania, Maryland, Virginia, South Carolina, Georgia, no—8."

[39] The transcript does not italicize the word "*Ten.*"

## Thursday. August 16. In Convention

Mr RANDOLPH having thrown into a new form the motion, putting votes, Resolutions &c. on a footing with *Bills*, renewed it as follows "Every order resolution or vote, to which the concurrence of the Senate & House of Rep? may be necessary (except on a question of adjournment and in the cases hereinafter mentioned) shall be presented to the President for his revision; and before the same shall have force shall be approved by him, or being disapproved by him shall be repassed by the Senate & House of Rep? according to the rules & limitations prescribed in the case of a Bill."

Mr SHERMAN thought it unnecessary, except as to votes taking money out of the Treasury which might be provided for in another place.

On [40] Question as moved by Mr Randolph [41]

N. H. ay. Mas: not present, Ct ay. N. J. no. Pa ay. Del. ay. Md ay. Va ay. N. C. ay. S. C. ay. Geo. ay.[42]

The Amendment was made a Section 14. of Art VI.

Art: VII. Sect. 1.[43, 44] taken up.

Mr L. MARTIN asked what was meant by the Committee of detail in the expression "*duties*" and "*imposts*." If the meaning were the same, the former was unnecessary; if different, the matter ought to be made clear.

Mr WILSON, *duties* are applicable to many objects to which the word *imposts* does not relate. The latter are appropriated to commerce; the former extend to a variety of objects, as stamp duties &c.

Mr CARROLL reminded the Convention of the great difference of interests among the States, and doubts the propriety in that point of view of letting a majority be a quorum.

Mr MASON urged the necessity of connecting with the power of levying taxes duties &c, the prohibition in Sect 4 of art VI that

---

[40] The word "the" is here inserted in the transcript.
[41] The phrase "it was agreed to" is here inserted in the transcript.
[42] In the transcript the vote reads: "New Hampshire, Connecticut, Pennsylvania, Delaware, Maryland, Virginia, North Carolina, South Carolina, Georgia, aye—9; New Jersey, no—1; Massachusetts, not present."
[43] See *ante*.
[44] The words "was then" are here inserted in the transcript.

no tax should be laid on exports. He was unwilling to trust to its being done in a future article. He hoped the Northn States did not mean to deny the Southern this security. It would hereafter be as desirable to the former when the latter should become the most populous. He professed his jealousy for the productions of the Southern or as he called them, the staple States. He moved to insert the following amendment "provided that no tax duty or imposition shall be laid by the Legislature of the U. States on articles exported from any State"

Mr SHERMAN had no objection to the proviso here, other than [45] it would derange the parts of the report as made by the Committee, to take them in such an order.

Mr RUTLIDGE. It being of no consequence in what order points are decided, he should vote for the clause as it stood, but on condition that the subsequent part relating to negroes should also be agreed to.

Mr GOVERNEUR MORRIS considered such a proviso as inadmissible any where. It was so radically objectionable, that it might cost the whole system the support of some members. He contended that it would not in some cases be equitable to tax imports without taxing exports; and that taxes on exports would be often the most easy and proper of the two.

Mr MADISON   1.[46] the power of taxing [47] exports is proper in itself, and as the States can not with propriety exercise it separately, it ought to be vested in them collectively.   2.[46] it might with particular advantage be exercised with regard to articles in which America was not rivalled in foreign markets, as Tobo. &c. The contract between the French Farmers Genl and Mr Morris stipulating that if taxes sd be laid in America on the export of Tobo. they sd be paid by the Farmers, shewed that it was understood by them, that the price would be thereby raised in America, and consequently the taxes be paid by the European Consumer.   3.[48] it would be unjust to the States whose produce was exported by their neighbours, to leave it subject to be taxed by the latter. This was a grievance

---

[45] The word "that" is here inserted in the transcript.
[46] The figures "1" and "2" are changed in the transcript to "First" and "Secondly."
[47] The words "laying taxes on" are substituted in the transcript for "taxing."
[48] The figures "3" and "4" are changed in the transcript to Thirdly" and "Fourthly."

which had already filled N. H. Con.t N. Jer.y Del: and N. Carolina with loud complaints, as it related to imports, and they would be equally authorised by taxes by the States on exports. 4.[48] The South.n States being most in danger and most needing naval protection, could the less complain if the burden should be somewhat heaviest on them. 5.[49] we are not providing for the present moment only, and time will equalize the situation of the States in this matter. He was for these reasons ag.st the motion

M.r WILLIAMSON considered the clause proposed ag.st taxes on exports as reasonable and necessary.

M.r ELSEWORTH was ag.st Taxing exports; but thought the prohibition stood in the most proper place, and was ag.st deranging the order reported by the Committee

M.r WILSON was decidedly ag.st prohibiting general taxes on exports. He dwelt on the injustice and impolicy of leaving N. Jersey Connecticut &c any longer subject to the exactions of their commercial neighbours.

M.r GERRY thought the legislature could not be trusted with such a power. It might ruin the Country. It might be exercised partially, raising one and depressing another part of it.

M.r Gov.r MORRIS. However the legislative power may be formed, it will if disposed be able to ruin the Country. He considered the taxing of exports to be in many cases highly politic. Virginia has found her account in taxing Tobacco. All Countries having peculiar articles tax the exportation of them; as France her wines and brandies. A tax here on lumber, would fall on the W. Indies & punish their restrictions on our trade. The same is true of live stock and in some degree of flour. In case of a dearth in the West Indies, we may extort what we please. Taxes on exports are a necessary source of revenue. For a long time the people of America will not have money to pay direct taxes. Seize and sell their effects and you push them into Revolts.

M.r MERCER was strenuous against giving Congress power to tax exports. Such taxes were [50] impolitic, as encouraging the raising of articles not meant for exportation. The States had now a

---

[48] The figures "3" and "4" are changed in the transcript to "Thirdly" and "Fourthly."
[49] The figure "5" is changed in the transcript to "And finally."
[50] The word "are" is substituted in the transcript for "were."

right where their situation permitted, to tax both the imports and exports of their uncommercial neighbours. It was enough for them to sacrifice one half of it. It had been said the Southern States had most need of naval protection. The reverse was the case. Were it not for promoting the carrying trade of the Northⁿ States, the Southⁿ States could let their trade go into foreign bottoms, where it would not need our protection. Virginia by taxing her tobacco had given an advantage to that of Maryland.

Mr SHERMAN. To examine and compare the States in relation to imports and exports will be opening a boundless field. He thought the matter had been adjusted, and that imports were to be subject, and exports not, to be taxed. He thought it wrong to tax exports except it might be such articles as ought not to be exported. The complexity of the business in America would render an equal tax on exports impracticable. The oppression of the uncommercial States was guarded agⁿᵗ by the power to regulate trade between the States. As to compelling foreigners, that might be done by regulating trade in general. The Government would not be trusted with such a power. Objections are most likely to be excited by considerations relating to taxes & money. A power to tax exports would shipwreck the whole.

Mr CARROL was surprised that any objection should be made to an exception of exports from the power of taxation.

It was finally agreed that the question concerning exports shᵈ lie over for the place in which the exception stood in the report: Maryᵈ alone voting agⁿᵗ it

Sect: 1. [art. VII][51, 52] agreed to: Mr GERRY alone answering no.

[53] Clause for regulating commerce with foreign nations &c.[54] agreed to nem. con.

[55] for coining money. agᵈ to nem. con.

[55] for regulating foreign coin. dº dº

[55] for fixing the standard of weights & measures. dº dº

---

[51] This phrase was erroneously copied in the transcript as "Article 1, Section 1," but was corrected when printed.

[52] The words "was then" are here inserted in the transcript.

[53] The word "The" is here inserted in the transcript.

[54] The word "was" is here inserted in the transcript.

[55] In the transcript these three lines are changed to read as follows: "Several clauses,—for coining money—for regulating foreign coin,—for fixing the standard of weights and measures,—were agreed to, *nem. con.*"

⁵⁶ "To establish post-offices." Mͬ GERRY moved to add, and post-roads. Mͬ MERCER 2ᵈᵉᵈ & on ⁵⁷ question

N. H. no. Mas. ay. Cᵗ no. N. J. no. Penª no. Del. ay. Mᵈ ay. Vª ay. N. C. no. S. C. ay. Geo. ay.⁵⁸

Mͬ Govʳ MORRIS moved to strike out "and emit bills on the credit of the U. States"—If the United States had credit such bills would be unnecessary: if they had not, unjust & useless.

Mͬ BUTLER, 2ᵈˢ the motion.

Mͬ MADISON, will it not be sufficient to prohibit the making them a *tender?* This will remove the temptation to emit them with unjust views. And promissory notes in that shape may in some emergencies be best.

Mͬ Govʳ MORRIS. striking out the words will leave room still for notes of a *responsible* minister which will do all the good without the mischief. The Monied interest will oppose the plan of Government, if paper emissions be not prohibited.

Mͬ GHORUM was for striking out, without inserting any prohibition. if the words stand they may suggest and lead to the measure.

Col.⁵⁹ MASON had doubts on the subject. Congˢ he thought would not have the power unless it were expressed. Though he had a mortal hatred to paper money, yet as he could not foresee all emergences, he was unwilling to tie the hands of the Legislature. He observed that the late war could not have been carried on, had such a prohibition existed.

Mͬ GHORUM. The power as far as it will be necessary or safe, is involved in that of borrowing.

Mͬ MERCER was a friend to paper money, though in the present state & temper of America, he should neither propose nor approve of such a measure. He was consequently opposed to a prohibition of it altogether. It will stamp suspicion on the Government to deny it a discretion on this point. It was impolitic also to excite the opposition of all those who were friends to paper money. The people of property would be sure to be on the side of the plan, and it was impolitic to purchase their further attachment with the loss of the opposite class of Citizens

---

⁵⁶ The words "The clause" are here inserted in the transcript.
⁵⁷ The word "the" is here inserted in the transcript.
⁵⁸ In the transcript the vote reads: "Massachusetts, Delaware, Maryland, Virginia, South Carolina, Georgia, aye—6; New Hampshire, Connecticut, New Jersey, Pennsylvania, North Carolina, no—5."
⁵⁹ The word "Mr." is substituted in the transcript for "Col."

Mʳ ELSEWORTH thought this a favorable moment to shut and bar the door against paper money. The mischiefs of the various experiments which had been made, were now fresh in the public mind and had excited the disgust of all the respectable part of America. By witholding the power from the new Governᵗ more friends of influence would be gained to it than by almost any thing else. Paper money can in no case be necessary. Give the Government credit, and other resources will offer. The power may do harm, never good.

Mʳ RANDOLPH, notwithstanding his antipathy to paper money, could not agree to strike out the words, as he could not foresee all the occasions which [60] might arise.

Mʳ WILSON. It will have a most salutary influence on the credit of the U. States to remove the possibility of paper money. This expedient can never succeed whilst its mischiefs are remembered, and as long as it can be resorted to, it will be a bar to other resources.

Mʳ BUTLER. remarked that paper was a legal tender in no Country in Europe. He was urgent for disarming the Government of such a power.

Mʳ MASON was still averse to tying the hands of the Legislature *altogether.* If there was no example in Europe as just remarked, it might be observed on the other side, that there was none in which the Government was restrained on this head.

Mʳ READ, thought the words, if not struck out, would be as alarming as the mark of the Beast in Revelations.

Mʳ LANGDON had rather reject the whole plan than retain the three words "(and emit bills")

On the motion for striking out

N. H. ay. Mas. ay. Cᵗ ay. N. J. no. Pᵃ ay. Del. ay. Mᵈ no. Vᵃ ay.* N. C. ay. S. C. ay. Geo. ay.[61]

The clause for borrowing money,[63] agreed to nem. con.

Adjᵈ

---

[60] The word "that" is substituted in the transcript for "which."

[61] In the transcript the vote reads: "New Hampshire, Massachusetts, Connecticut, Pennsylvania, Delaware, Virginia,* North Carolina, South Carolina, Georgia, aye—9; New Jersey, Maryland, no—2."

* This vote in the affirmative [by Virgᵃ was occasioned by the acquiescence of Mʳ Madison who became satisfied that striking out the words would not disable the Govᵗ from the use of public notes as far as they could be safe & proper; & would only cut off the pretext for a paper currency, [63] and particularly for making the bills a tender [62] either for public or private debts.

[62] The transcript italicizes the words "paper currency" and "a tender."

[63] The word "was" is here inserted in the transcript.

## Friday August 17ᵀᴴ   in Convention

Art VII. Sect. 1.[64, 65] resumed. on the clause "to appoint[66] Treasurer by ballot."

Mʳ Ghorum moved to insert "joint" before ballot, as more convenient as well as reasonable, than to require the separate concurrence of the Senate.

Mʳ Pinkney 2ᵈˢ the motion.   Mʳ Sherman opposed it as favoring the larger States.

Mʳ Read moved to strike out the clause, leaving the appointment of the Treasurer as of other officers to the Executive. The Legislature was an improper body for appointments. Those of the State legislatures were a proof of it. The Executive being responsible would make a good choice.

Mʳ Mercer 2ᵈˢ the motion of Mʳ Read.

On the motion for inserting the word "joint" before ballot

N. H. ay.   Mas. ay.   Cᵗ no.   N. J. no.   Pª ay.   Mᵈ no.   Vª ay. N. C. ay.   S. C. ay.   Geo. ay.[67]

Col. Mason in opposition to Mʳ Reads motion desired it might be considered to whom the money would belong; if to the people, the legislature representing the people ought to appoint the keepers of it.

On striking out the clause as amended by inserting "Joint"

N. II. no.   Mas. no.   Cᵗ no   Pª ay.   Del. ay.   Mᵈ ay.   Vª no. N. C. no.   S. C. ay.   Geo. no.[68]

[69] "To constitute inferior tribunals" [70] agreed to nem. con.[71]

"To make rules as to captures on land & water"-dᵒ d [72]

[69] "To declare the law and punishment of piracies and felonies &c" &c [73] considered.

Mʳ Madison moved to strike out "and punishment" &c.[74]

---

[64] See *ante*.
[65] The word "was" is here inserted in the transcript.
[66] The word "a" is here inserted in the transcript.
[67] In the transcript the vote reads: "New Hampshire, Massachusetts, Pennsylvania, Virginia, North Carolina, South Carolina, Georgia, aye—7; Connecticut, New Jersey, Maryland, no—3."
[68] In the transcript the vote reads: "Pennsylvania, Delaware, Maryland, South Carolina, aye—4; New Hampshire, Massachusetts, Connecticut, Virginia, North Carolina, Georgia, no—6."
[69] The words "The clause" are here inserted in the transcript.
[70] The word "was" is here inserted in the transcript.
[71] The phrase "as also the clause" is here inserted in the transcript.
[72] The words "do. do." are omitted in the transcript.
[73] The word "being" is here inserted in the transcript.
[74] In the transcript the following phrase is here added: "after the words, 'To declare the law.'"

M! MASON doubts the safety of it, considering the strict rule of construction in criminal cases. He doubted also the propriety of taking the power in all these cases wholly from the States.

M! GOVERN! MORRIS thought it would be necessary to extend the authority farther, so as to provide for the punishment of counterfeiting in general. Bills of exchange for example might be forged in one State and carried into another:

It was suggested by some other member that *foreign* paper might be counterfeited by Citizens; and that it might be politic to provide by national authority for the punishment of it.

M! RANDOLPH did not conceive that expunging "the punishment" would be a constructive exclusion of the power. He doubted only the efficacy of the word "declare."

M! WILSON was in favor of the motion. Strictness was not necessary in giving authority to enact penal laws; though necessary in enacting & expounding them.

On motion [75] for striking out "and punishment" as moved by M! Madison

N. H. no. Mas. ay. C! no. P? ay. Del. ay. M? no. V? ay. N. C. ay. S. C. ay. Geo. ay.[76]

M! GOV! MORRIS moved to strike out "declare the law" and insert "punish" before "piracies." and on the question

N. H. ay. Mas. ay. C! no. P? ay. Del. ay. M? ay. V? no. N. C. no. S. C. ay. Geo. ay.[77]

M! MADISON, and M! RANDOLPH moved to insert, "define &," before "punish."

M! WILSON, thought "felonies" sufficiently defined by common law.

M! DICKENSON concurred with M! Wilson.

M! MERCER was in favor of the amendment.

M! MADISON. felony at common law is vague. It is also defective. One defect is supplied by Stat: of Anne as to running away with vessels which at common law was a breach of trust only.

---

[75] The words "the question" are substituted in the transcript for "motion."

[76] In the transcript the vote reads: "Massachusetts, Pennsylvania, Delaware, Virginia, North Carolina, South Carolina, Georgia, aye—7; New Hampshire, Connecticut, Maryland, no—3."

[77] In the transcript the vote reads: "New Hampshire, Massachusetts, Pennsylvania, Delaware, Maryland, South Carolina, Georgia, aye—7; Connecticut, Virginia, North Carolina, no—3."

Besides no foreign law should be a standard farther than [78] is expressly adopted—If the laws of the States were to prevail on this subject, the citizens of different States would be subject to different punishments for the same offence at sea. There would be neither uniformity nor stability in the law—The proper remedy for all these difficulties was to vest the power proposed by the term "define" in the Nat! legislature.

M! Gov! Morris would prefer *designate* to *define*, the latter being as he he conceived, limited to the preexisting meaning.—

It was said by others to be applicable to the creating of offences also, and therefore suited the case both of felonies & of piracies. The motion of M! M. & M! R was agreed to.

M! Elseworth enlarged the motion so as to read "to define and punish piracies and felonies committed on the high seas, counterfeiting the securities and current coin of the U. States, and offences ag!t the law of Nations" which was agreed to nem. con.

[79] "To subdue a rebellion in any State, on the application of its legislature." [80]

M! Pinkney moved to strike out "on the application of its legislature"

M! Gov! Morris 2ds

M! L. Martin opposed it as giving a dangerous & unnecessary power. The consent of the State ought to precede the introduction of any extraneous force whatever.

M! Mercer supported the opposition of M! Martin.

M! Elseworth proposed to add after "legislature" "or Executive."

M! Gov! Morris. The Executive may possibly be at the head of the Rebellion. The Gen! Gov! should enforce obedience in all cases where it may be necessary.

M! Elseworth. In many cases The Gen! Gov! ought not to be able to interpose, unless called upon. He was willing to vary his motion so as to read, "or without it when the legislature cannot meet."

---

[78] The word "it" is here inserted in the transcript.
[79] The words "The clause" are here inserted in the transcript.
[80] The phrase "was next considered" is here inserted in the transcript.

Mʳ GERRY was agˢᵗ letting loose the myrmidons of the U. States on a State without its own consent. The States will be the best Judges in such cases. More blood would have been spilt in Massᵗˢ in the late insurrection, if the Genˡ authority had intermeddled.

Mʳ LANGDON was for striking out as moved by Mʳ Pinkney. The apprehension of the national force, will have a salutary effect in preventing insurrections.

Mʳ RANDOLPH. If the Natˡ Legislature is to judge whether the State legislature can or cannot meet, that amendment would make the clause as objectionable as the motion of Mʳ Pinkney.

Mʳ Govʳ MORRIS. We are acting a very strange part. We first form a strong man to protect us, and at the same time wish to tie his hands behind him, The legislature may surely be trusted with such a power to preserve the public tranquility.

On the motion to add "or without it [application] when the legislature cannot meet" [81]

N. H. ay. Mas. no. Cᵗ ay. Pᵃ divᵈ Del. no. Mᵈ no. Vᵃ ay. N. C. divᵈ S. C. ay. Geo. ay.[82] So agreed to—[83]

Mʳ MADISON and Mʳ DICKENSON moved to insert as explanatory, after "State"—"against the Government thereof" There might be a rebellion agˢᵗ the U. States—which [84] was Agreed to nem. con.

On the clause as amended

N. H. ay. Mas * absᵗ Cᵗ ay. Pen. absᵗ Del. no. Mᵈ no. Vᵃ ay. N. C. no. S. C. no. Georg. ay—so it was lost.[85]

[86] "To make war"

Mʳ PINKNEY opposed the vesting this power in the Legislature. Its proceedings were too slow. It wᵈ meet but once a year. The Hˢ of Repˢ would be too numerous for such deliberations. The Senate would be the best depositary, being more acquainted with foreign affairs, and most capable of proper resolutions. If the

---

[81] The phrase "it was agreed to" is here added in the transcript.
[82] In the transcript the vote reads: "New Hampshire, Connecticut, Virginia, South Carolina, Georgia, aye—5; Massachusetts, Delaware, Maryland, no—3; Pennsylvania, North Carolina, divided."
[83] The words "So agreed to" are omitted in the transcript.
[84] The words "The motion" are substituted in the transcript for "which."
* In the printed Journal, Mas. no.
[85] In the transcript the vote reads: "New Hampshire, Connecticut, Virginia, Georgia, aye—4; Delaware, Maryland, North Carolina, South Carolina, no—4; Massachusetts,* Pennsylvania, absent. So it was lost."
[86] The words "The clause" are here inserted in the transcript.

States are equally represented in [87] Senate, so as to give no advantage to [87] large States, the power will notwithstanding be safe, as the small have their all at stake in such cases as well as the large States. It would be singular for one authority to make war, and another peace.

M:̣ BUTLER. The objections ag:̣ᵗ the Legislature lie in [88] great degree ag:̣ᵗ the Senate. He was for vesting the power in the President, who will have all the requisite qualities, and will not make war but when the Nation will support it.

M:̣ MADISON and M:̣ GERRY moved to insert "*declare*," striking out "*make*" war; leaving to the Executive the power to repel sudden attacks.

M:̣ SHARMAN thought it stood very well. The Executive sh:ᵈ be able to repel and not to commence war. "Make" [89] better than "declare" the latter narrowing the power too much.

M:̣ GERRY never expected to hear in a republic a motion to empower the Executive alone to declare war.

M:̣ ELSWORTH. there is a material difference between the cases of making *war* and making *peace*. It sh:ᵈ be more easy to get out of war, than into it. War also is a simple and overt declaration. peace attended with intricate & secret negociations.

M:̣ MASON was ag:ᵗ giving the power of war to the Executive, because not safely to be trusted with it; or to the Senate, because not so constructed as to be entitled to it. He was for clogging rather than facilitating war; but for facilitating peace. He preferred "*declare*" to "*make*."

On the motion to insert *declare*—in place of *make*, it was agreed to.

N. H. no. Mas. abs:ᵗ. Con:ᵗ no.* P:ᵃ ay. Del. ay. M:ᵈ ay. V:ᵃ ay. N. C. ay. S. C. ay. Geo. ay.[92]

---

[57] The word "the" is here inserted in the transcript.
[88] The word "a" is here inserted in the transcript.
[89] The word "is" is here inserted in the transcript.
[90] The transcript here inserts the following: "Connecticut voted in the negative; but."
[91] The words "of Con:ᵗ. are omittd in the transcript.
* On the remark by M:̣ King that "*make*" war might be understood to "conduct" it which was an Executive function, M:̣ Elseworth gave up his objection, and the vote of Con:ᵗ [91] was changed to—ay.
[92] In the transcript the vote reads: "Connecticut,* Pennsylvania, Delaware, Maryland, Virginia, North Carolina, South Carolina, Georgia, aye—8; New Hampshire, no—1; Massachusetts, absent."

M<sup>r</sup> Pinkney's motion to strike out [93] whole clause,[94] disag<sup>d</sup> to without call of States.

M<sup>r</sup> Butler moved to give the Legislature [93] power of peace, as they were to have that of war.

M<sup>r</sup> Gerry 2<sup>ds</sup> him.   8 Senators may possibly exercise the power if vested in that body, and 14 if all should be present; and may consequently give up part of the U. States.  The Senate are more liable to be corrupted by an Enemy than the whole Legislature.

On the motion for adding "and peace" after "war" [95]

N. H. no.   Mas. no.   C<sup>t</sup> no.   P<sup>a</sup> no.   Del. no.   M<sup>d</sup> no.   V<sup>a</sup> no. N. C. no   S. C. no.   Geo. no.[96]

Adjourned

---

Saturday August 18.   in Convention

M<sup>r</sup> Madison submitted in order to be referred to the Committee of detail the following powers as proper to be added to those of the General Legislature

"To dispose of the unappropriated lands of the U. States"

"To institute temporary Governments for New States arising therein"

"To regulate affairs with the Indians as well within as without the limits of the U. States

"To exercise exclusively Legislative authority at the Seat of the General Government, and over a district around the same, not exceeding     square miles; the Consent of the Legislature of the State or States comprizing the same, being first obtained"

"To grant charters of incorporation in cases where the public good may require them, and the authority of a single State may be incompetent"

"To secure to literary authors their copy rights for a limited time"

"To establish an University"

"To encourage by premiums & provisions, the advancement of useful knowledge and discoveries"

"To authorize the Executive to procure and hold for the use of the U. S. landed property for the erection of Forts, Magazines, and other necessary buildings"

---

[93] The word "the" is here inserte in the transcript.
[94] The word "was" is here inserted in the transcript.
[95] The transcript here adds the following: "it was unanimously negatived."
[96] The vote by States is omitted.

These propositions were referred to the Committee of detail which had prepared the Report and at the same time the following which were moved by M̃ Pinkney: in both cases unanimously.

"To fix and permanently establish the seat of Government of the U. S. in which they shall possess the exclusive right of soil & jurisdiction"

"To establish seminaries for the promotion of literature and the arts & sciences"

"To grant charters of incorporation"

"To grant patents for useful inventions"

"To secure to Authors exclusive rights for a certain time"

"To establish public institutions, rewards and immunities for the promotion of agriculture, commerce, trades and manufactures"

"That funds which shall be appropriated for [97] payment of public Creditors, shall not during the time of such appropriation, be diverted or applied to any other purpose and that the Committee prepare a clause or clauses for restraining the Legislature of the U. S. from establishing a perpetual revenue"

"To secure the payment of the public debt"

"To secure all creditors under the New Constitution from a violation of the public faith when pledged by the authority of the Legislature"

"To grant letters of mark and reprisal"

"To regulate Stages on the post roads"

M̃ MASON introduced the subject of regulating the militia. He thought such a power necessary to be given to the Genl Government. He hoped there would be no standing army in time of peace, unless it might be for a few garrisons. The Militia ought therefore to be the more effectually prepared for the public defence. Thirteen States will never concur in any one system, if the displining of the Militia be left in their hands. If they will not give up the power over the whole, they probably will over a part as a select militia. He moved as an addition to the propositions just referred to the Committee of detail, & to be referred in like manner, "a power to regulate the militia."

M̃ GERRY remarked that some provision ought to be made in favor of public Securities, and something inserted concerning letters of marque, which he thought not included in the power of war. He proposed that these subjects should also go to a Committee.

---

[97] The word "the" is here inserted in the transcript.

Mʳ RUTLIDGE moved to refer a clause "that funds appropriated to public creditors should not be diverted to other purposes."

Mʳ MASON was much attached to the principle, but was afraid such a fetter might be dangerous in time of war. He suggested the necessity of preventing the danger of perpetual revenue which must of necessity subvert the liberty of any Country. If it be objected to on the principle of Mʳ Rutlidge's motion that public credit may require perpetual provisions, that case might be excepted: it being declared that in other cases, no taxes should be laid for a longer term than          years. He considered the caution observed in Great Britain on this point as the paladium of the public liberty.

Mʳ RUTLIDGE'S motion was referred—He then moved that a Grand Committee be appointed to consider the necessity and expediency of the U. States assuming all the State debts—A regular settlement between the Union & the several States would never take place. The assumption would be just as the State debts were contracted in the common defence. It was necessary, as the taxes on imports the only sure source of revenue were to be given up to the Union. It was politic, as by disburdening the people of the State debts it would conciliate them to the plan.

Mʳ KING and Mʳ PINKNEY seconded the motion

[Col. MASON interposed a motion that the Committee prepare a clause for restraining perpetual revenue, which was agreed to nem. con.]

Mʳ SHERMAN thought it would be better to authorise the Legislature to assume the State debts, than to say positively it should be done. He considered the measure as just and that it would have a good effect to say something about the Matter.

Mʳ ELSEWORTH differed from Mʳ Sherman- As far as the State debts ought in equity to be assumed, he conceived that they might and would be so.

Mʳ PINKNEY observed that a great part of the State debts were of such a nature that although in point of policy and true equity they ought,[98] yet would they not be viewed in the light of fœderal expenditures.

---

[98] The words "to be" are here inserted in the transcript.

M.<sup>r</sup> KING thought the matter of more consequence tnan M.<sup>r</sup> Elseworth seemed to do; and that it was well worthy of commitment. Besides the considerations of justice and policy which had been mentioned, it might be remarked that the State Creditors an active and formidable party would otherwise be opposed to a plan which transferred to the Union the best resources of the States without transferring the State debts at the same time. The State Creditors had generally been the strongest foes to the impost-plan. The State debts probably were of greater amount than the fœderal. He would not say that it was practicable to consolidate the debts, but he thought it would be prudent to have the subject considered by a Committee.

On M.<sup>r</sup> Rutlidge's motion, that [99] Com.<sup>e</sup> be appointed to consider of the assumption &c [1]

N. H. no. Mas. ay. C.<sup>t</sup> ay. N. J. no. P.<sup>a</sup> div.<sup>d</sup> Del. no. M.<sup>d</sup> no. V.<sup>a</sup> ay. N. C. ay. S. C. ay. Geo. ay.[2]

M.<sup>r</sup> Gerry's motion to provide for public securities, for stages on post-roads, and for letters of marque & reprisal, were [3] committed nem. con.

M.<sup>r</sup> KING suggested that all unlocated lands of particular States ought to be given up if State debts were to be assumed:—M.<sup>r</sup> Williamson concurred in the idea.

A Grand Committee was appointed consisting of* transfer hither the appointment & names of the Committee.[4] [The Com.<sup>e</sup> appointed by ballot were [5] M.<sup>r</sup> Langdon, M.<sup>r</sup> King, M.<sup>r</sup> Sherman, M.<sup>r</sup> Livingston, M.<sup>r</sup> Clymer, M.<sup>r</sup> Dickenson, M.<sup>r</sup> M<sup>c</sup>Henry, M.<sup>r</sup> Mason, M.<sup>r</sup> Williamson, M.<sup>r</sup> C. C. Pinkney,[6] M.<sup>r</sup> Baldwin.]

M.<sup>r</sup> RUTLIDGE remarked on the length of the Session, the probable impatience of the public and the extreme anxiety of many members of the Convention to bring the business to an end; concluding with a motion that the Convention meet henceforward

---

[99] The word "a" is here inserted in the transcript.

[1] The transcript here adds the following: "it was agreed to."

[2] In the transcript the vote reads: "Massachusetts, Connecticut, Virginia, North Carolina, South Carolina, Georgia, aye—6; New Hampshire, New Jersey, Delaware, Maryland, no—4; Pennsylvania, divided."

[3] In the transcript the word "were" is crossed out and "was" is written above it.

[4] Madison's direction is omitted in the transcript.

[5] The phrase "The Com.<sup>e</sup> appointed by ballot were" is omitted in the transcript.

[6] The word "and" is here inserted in the transcript.

precisely at 10 OC. A. M. and that precisely at 4 OC. P. M. the President adjourn the House without motion for the purpose. and that no motion to adjourn sooner be allowed

On this question

N. H. ay. Mas. ay. C! ay. N. J. ay. P? no. Del. ay. M? no. V? ay. N. C. ay. S. C. ay. Geo. ay.[7]

M! ELSEWORTH observed that a Council had not yet been provided for the President. He conceived there ought to be one. His proposition was that it should be composed of the President of the Senate—the Chief-Justice, and the ministers as they might be estab? for the departments of foreign & domestic affairs, war finance and marine, who should advise but not conclude the President.

M! PINKNEY wished the proposition to lie over, as notice had been given for a like purpose by M! Gov! Morris who was not then on the floor. His own idea was that the President sh? be authorised to call for advice or not as he might chuse. Give him an able Council and it will thwart him; a weak one and he will shelter himself under their sanction.

M! GERRY was ag?! letting the heads of the departments, particularly of finance have any thing to do in business connected with legislation. He mentioned the Chief Justice also as particularly exceptionable. These men will also be so taken up with other matters as to neglect their own proper duties.

M! DICKENSON urged that the great appointments should be made by the Legislature, in which case they might properly be consulted by the Executive, but not if made by the Executive himself—This subject by general consent lay over; & the House proceeded to the clause "To raise armies."

M! GHORUM moved to add "and support" after "raise." Agreed to nem. con. and then the clause [8] agreed to nem. con. as amended

M! GERRY took notice that there was no check here ag?! standing armies in time of peace. The existing Cong? is so constructed

---

[7] In the transcript the vote reads: "New Hampshire, Massachusetts, Connecticut, New Jersey, Delaware, Virginia, North Carolina, South Carolina, Georgia, aye—9; Pennsylvania, Maryland, no—2."

[8] The word "was" is here inserted in the transcript.

that it cannot of itself maintain an army. This w? not be the case under the new system. The people were jealous on this head, and great opposition to the plan would spring from such an omission. He suspected that preparations of force were now making ag?! it. [he seemed to allude to the activity of the Gov? of N. York at this crisis in disciplining the militia of that State.] He thought an army dangerous in time of peace & could never consent to a power to keep up an indefinite number. He proposed that there shall [9] not be kept up in time of peace more than thousand troops. His idea was that the blank should be filled with two or three thousand.

Instead of "to build and equip fleets"—"to provide & maintain a navy" [10] agreed to nem. con. as a more convenient definition of the power.

[11] "To make rules for the Government and regulation of the land & naval forces," [10] added from the existing Articles of Confederation.

M? L. MARTIN and M? GERRY now regularly moved "provided that in time of peace the army shall not consist of more than thousand men."

Gen! PINKNEY asked whether no troops were ever to be raised untill an attack should be made on us?

M? GERRY. if there be no restriction, a few Stàtes may establish a military Gov?

M? WILLIAMSON, reminded him of M? Mason's motion for limiting the appropriation of revenue as the best guard in this case.

M? LANGDON saw no room for M? Gerry's distrust of the Representatives of the people.

M? DAYTON. preparations for war are generally made in [12] peace; and a standing force of some sort may, for ought we know, become unavoidable. He should object to no restrictions consistent with these ideas.

The motion of M? Martin & M? Gerry was disagreed to nem. con.

---

[9] The word "should" is substituted in the transcript for "shall."
[10] The word "was" is here inserted in the transcript.
[11] The words "A clause" are here inserted in the transcript.
[12] The words "time of" are here inserted in the transcript.

Mʳ MASON moved as an additional power "to make laws for the regulation and discipline of the militia of the several States reserving to the States the appointment of the officers." He considered uniformity as necessary in the regulation of the Militia throughout the Union.

Genˡ PINKNEY mentioned a case during the war in which a dissimilarity in the militia of different States had produced the most serious mischiefs. Uniformity was essential. The States would never keep up a proper discipline of their militia.

Mʳ ELSEWORTH was for going as far in submitting the militia to the Genˡ Government as might be necessary, but thought the motion of Mʳ Mason went too far. He moved that the militia should have the same arms & exercise and be under rules established by the Genˡ Govᵗ when in actual service of the U. States and when States neglect to provide regulations for militia, it shᵈ be regulated & established by the Legislature of [13] U. S. The whole authority over the Militia ought by no means to be taken away from the States whose consequence would pine away to nothing after such a sacrifice of power. He thought the Genˡ Authority could not sufficiently pervade the Union for such a purpose, nor could it accomodate itself to the local genius of the people. It must be vain to ask the States to give the Militia out of their hands.

Mʳ SHERMAN 2ᵈˢ the motion.

Mʳ DICKENSON. We are come now to a most important matter, that of the sword. His opinion was that the States never would nor ought to give up all authority over the Militia. He proposed to restrain the general power to one fourth part at a time, which by rotation would discipline the whole Militia.

Mʳ BUTLER urged the necessity of submitting the whole Militia to the general Authority, which had the care of the general defence.

Mʳ MASON. had suggested the idea of a select militia. He was led to think that would be in fact as much as the Genˡ Govᵗ could advantageously be charged with. He was afraid of creating insuperable objections to the plan. He withdrew his original motion, and moved a power "to make laws for regulating and disciplining

---

[13] The word "the" is here inserted in the transcript.

the militia, not exceeding one tenth part in any one year, and reserving the appointment of officers to the States."

Gen! PINKNEY, renewed M? Mason's original motion. For a part to be under the Gen! and [14] part under the State Gov!? w? be an incurable evil. he saw no room for such distrust of the Gen! Gov!

M? LANGDON 2^(d?) Gen! Pinkney's renewal. He saw no more reason to be afraid of the Gen! Gov! than of the State Gov!? He was more apprehensive of the confusion of the different authorities on this subject, than of either.

M? MADISON thought the regulation of the Militia naturally appertaining to the authority charged with the public defence. It did not seem in its nature to be divisible between two distinct authorities. If the States would trust the Gen! Gov! with a power over the public treasure, they would from the same consideration of necessity grant it the direction of the public force. Those who had a full view of the public situation w? from a sense of the danger, guard ag?? it: the States would not be separately impressed with the general situation, nor have the due confidence in the concurrent exertions of each other.

M? ELSEWORTH. considered the idea of a select militia as impracticable; & if it were not it would be followed by a ruinous declension of the great body of the Militia. The States will [15] never submit to the same militia laws. Three or four shilling's as a penalty will enforce obedience better in New England, than forty lashes in some other places.

M? PINKNEY thought the power such an one as could not be abused, and that the States would see the necessity of surrendering it. He had however but a scanty faith in Militia. There must be also a real military force. This alone can effectually answer the purpose. The United States had been making an experiment without it, and we see the consequence in their rapid approaches towards anarchy.*

---

[14] The word "a" is here inserted in the transcript.
[15] The word "would" is substituted in the transcript for "will."
* This had reference to the disorders particularly which had occurred in Massach?? which had called for the interposition of the federal troops.

Mr SHERMAN, took notice that the States might want their Militia for defence ag.st invasions and insurrections, and for enforcing obedience to their laws. They will not give up this point. In giving up that of taxation, they retain a concurrent power of raising money for their own use.

Mr GERRY thought this the last point remaining to be surrendered. If it be agreed to by the Convention, the plan will have as black a mark as was set on Cain. He had no such confidence in the Genl Govt as some gentlemen professed, and believed it would be found that the States have not.

Col. MASON. thought there was great weight in the remarks of Mr Sherman, and moved an exception to his motion "of such part of the Militia as might be required by the States for their own use."

Mr READ doubted the propriety of leaving the appointment of the Militia officers in [16] the States. In some States they are elected by the legislatures; in others by the people themselves. He thought at least an appointment by the State Executives ought to be insisted on.

On [17] committing to the grand Committee last appointed, the latter motion of Col. Mason, & the original one revived by Genl Pinkney

N. H. ay. Mas. ay. Ct no. N. J. no. Pa ay. Del. ay. Md divd Va ay. N. C. ay. S. C. ay. Geo. ay.[18]

Adjourned

---

MONDAY AUGUST 20. IN CONVENTION

Mr PINKNEY submitted to the House, in order to be referred to the Committee of detail, the following propositions—

"Each House shall be the Judge of its own privileges, and shall have authority to punish by imprisonment, every person violating the same; or who, in the place where the Legislature may be sitting and during the time of its Session, shall threaten any of

---

[16] The word "in" is crossed out in the transcript and "to" is written above it.
[17] The words "the question for" are here inserted in the transcript.
[18] In the transcript the vote reads: "New Hampshire, Massachusetts, Pennsylvania, Delaware, Virginia, North Carolina, South Carolina, Georgia, aye—8; Connecticut, New Jersey, no—2; Maryland, divided."

its members for any thing said or done on the House—or who shall assault any of them therefor—or who shall assault or arrest any witness or other person ordered to attend either of the Houses in his way going or returning; or who shall rescue any person arrested by their order."

"Each branch of the Legislature, as well as the supreme Executive shall have authority to require the opinions of the supreme Judicial Court upon important questions of law, and upon solemn occasions"

"The privileges and benefit of the Writ of Habeas corpus shall be enjoyed in this Government in the most expeditious and ample manner; and shall not be suspended by the Legislature except upon the most urgent and pressing occasions, and for a limited time not exceeding      months."

"The liberty of the Press shall be inviolably preserved"

"No troops shall be kept up in time of peace, but by consent of the Legislature"

"The military shall always be subordinate to the Civil power, and no grants of money shall be made by the Legislature for supporting military Land forces, for more than one year at a time"

"No soldier shall be quartered in any House in time of peace without consent of the owner."

"No person holding the office of President of the U. S., a Judge of their supreme Court, Secretary for the department of Foreign Affairs, of Finance, of Marine, of War, or of      , shall be capable of holding at the same time any other office of Trust or Emolument under the U. S. or an individual State"

"No religious test or qualification shall ever be annexed to any oath of office under the authority of the U. S."

"The U. S. shall be for ever considered as one Body corporate and politic in law, and entitled to all the rights privileges and immunities, which to Bodies corporate do or ought to appertain"

"The Legislature of the U. S. shall have the power of making the great seal which shall be kept by the President of the U. S. or in his absence by the President of the Senate, to be used by them as the occasion may require.—It shall be called the great Seal of the U. S. and shall be affixed to all laws."

"All Commissions and writs shall run in the name of the U. S."

"The Jurisdiction of the supreme Court shall be extended to all controversies between the U. S. and an individual State, or the U. S. and the Citizens of an individual State"

These propositions were referred to the Committee of detail without debate or consideration of them, by the House.

M$^r$ Gov$^r$ MORRIS 2$^{ded}$ by M$^r$ PINKNEY submitted the following propositions which were in like manner referred to the Committee of Detail.

"To assist the President in conducting the public affairs there shall be a council of State composed of the following officers—

1. The Chief Justice of the Supreme Court, who shall from time to time recommend such alterations of and additions to the laws of the U. S. as may in his opinion, be necessary to the due administration of Justice, and such as may promote useful learning and inculcate sound morality throughout the Union: He shall be President of the Council in the absence of the President

2. The Secretary of Domestic Affairs who shall be appointed by the President and hold his office during pleasure. It shall be his duty to attend to matters of general police, the State of Agriculture and manufactures, the opening of roads and navigations, and the facilitating communications thro' the U. States; and he shall from time to time recommend such measures and establishments as may tend to promote those objects.

3. The Secretary of Commerce and Finance, who shall also be appointed by the President during pleasure. It shall be his duty to superintend all matters relating to the public finances, to prepare & report plans of revenue and for the regulation of expenditures, and also to recommend such things as may in his Judgment promote the commercial interests of the U. S.

4. The Secretary of foreign affairs who shall also be appointed by the President during pleasure. It shall be his duty to correspond with all foreign Ministers, prepare plans of Treaties, & consider such as may be transmitted from abroad; and generally to attend to the interests of the U. S. in their connections with foreign powers.

5. The Secretary of War who shall also be appointed by the President during pleasure. It shall be his duty to superintend every thing relating to the war-Department, such as the raising and equipping of troops, the care of military stores, public fortifications, arsenals & the like—also in time of war to prepare & recommend plans of offence and Defence.

6. The Secretary of the Marine who shall also be appointed during pleasure—It shall be his duty to superintend every thing relating to the Marine-Department, the public Ships, Dock-Yards,

Naval-Stores & arsenals—also in [19] time of war, to prepare and recommend plans of offence and defence.

The President shall also appoint a Secretary of State to hold his office during pleasure; who shall be Secretary to the Council of State, and also public Secretary to the President. It shall be his duty to prepare all public despatches from the President which he shall countersign

The President may from time to time submit any matter to the discussion of the Council of State, and he may require the written opinions of any one or more of the members: But he shall in all cases exercise his own judgment, and either Conform to such opinions or not as he may think proper; and every officer abovementioned shall be responsible for his opinion on the affairs relating to his particular Department.

Each of the officers abovementioned shall be liable to impeachment. & removal from office for neglect of duty malversation, or corruption"

Mr GERRY moved "that the Committee be instructed to report proper qualifications for the President, and [20] mode of trying the Supreme Judges in cases of impeachment.

The clause " to call forth the aid of the Militia &c. was postponed till report should be made as to the power over the Militia referred yesterday to the Grand Committee of eleven.

Mr MASON moved to enable Congress "to enact sumptuary laws." No Government can be maintained unless the manners be made consonant to it. Such a discretionary power may do good and can do no harm. A proper regulation of excises & of trade may do a great deal but it is best to have an express provision. It was objected to sumptuary laws that they were contrary to nature. This was a vulgar error. The love of distinction it is true is natural; but the object of sumptuary laws is not to extinguish this principle but to give it a proper direction.

Mr ELSEWORTH. The best remedy is to enforce taxes & debts. As far as the regulation of eating & drinking can be reasonable, it is provided for in the power of taxation.

Mr Govr MORRIS argued that sumptuary laws tended to create a landed Nobility, by fixing in the great-landholders and their posterity their present possessions.

---

[19] The word "the" is here inserted in the transcript.
[20] The word "a" is here inserted in the transcript.

Mʳ GERRY. the law of necessity is the best sumptuary law.

On [19] Motion of Mʳ Mason "as to Sumptuary laws"

N. H. no. Mas. no. Cᵗ no. N. J. no. Pᵃ no. Del. ay. Mᵈ ay. Vᵃ no. N. C. no. S. C. no. Geo. ay.[21]

[22] "And to make all laws necessary and proper for carrying into execution the foregoing powers, and all other powers vested, by this Constitution, in the Government of the U. S. or any department or officer thereof."

Mʳ MADISON and Mʳ PINKNEY moved to insert between "laws" and "necessary" "and establish all offices," it appearing to them liable to cavil that the latter was not included in the former.

Mʳ Govʳ MORRIS, Mʳ WILSON, Mʳ RUTLIDGE and Mʳ ELSEWORTH urged that the amendment could not be necessary.

On the motion for inserting "and establish all offices"

N. H. no. Mas. ay. Cᵗ no. N. J. no. Pᵃ no. Del. no. Mᵈ ay. Vᵃ no. N. C. no. S. C. no. Geo. no.[23]

The clause as reported was then agreed to nem. con.

Art: VII sect. 2 [24] concerning Treason which see.[25]

Mʳ MADISON, thought the definition too narrow. It did not appear to go as far as the Stat. of Edwᵈ III. He did not see why more latitude might not be left to the Legislature. It wᵈ be as safe as in the hands of State legislatures; and it was inconvenient to bar a discretion which experience might enlighten, and which might be applied to good purposes as well as be abused.

Mʳ MASON was for pursuing the Stat: of Edwᵈ III

Mʳ Govʳ MORRIS was for giving to the Union an exclusive right to declare what shᵈ be treason. In case of a contest between the U. S. and a particular State, the people of the latter must, under the disjunctive terms of the clause, be traitors to one or other authority.

---

[19] The word "the" is here inserted in the transcript.

[21] In the transcript the vote reads: "Delaware, Maryland, Georgia, aye—3; New Hampshire, Massachusetts, Connecticut, New Jersey, Pennsylvania, Virginia, North Carolina, South Carolina, no—8."

[22] The words "On the clause" are here inserted in the transcript.

[23] In the transcript the vote reads: "Massachusetts, Maryland, aye—2; New Hampshire, Connecticut, New Jersey, Pennsylvania, Delaware, Virginia, North Carolina, South Carolina, Georgia, no—9."

[24] See *ante*.

[25] In the transcript the words "which see" are crossed out and the phrase "was then taken up" is written above them.

Mr RANDOLPH thought the clause defective in adopting the words "in adhering" only. The British Stat: adds, "giving them aid and comfort" which had a more extensive meaning.

Mr ELSEWORTH considered the definition as the same in fact with that of the Statute.

Mr Govr MORRIS "adhering" does not go so far as "giving aid and Comfort" or the latter words may be restrictive of "adhering," in either case the Statute is not pursued.

Mr WILSON held "giving aid and comfort" to be explanatory, not operative words; and that it was better to omit them.

Mr DICKENSON, thought the addition of "giving aid & comfort" unnecessary & improper; being too vague and extending too far. He wished to know what was meant by the "testimony of two witnesses" whether they were to be witnesses to the same overt act or to different overt acts. He thought also that proof of an overt-act ought to be expressed as essential in the case.

Docr JOHNSON considered "giving aid & comfort" as explanatory of "adhering" & that something should be inserted in the definition concerning overt-acts. He contended that Treason could not be both agst the U. States—and individual States; being an offence agst the Sovereignty which can be but one in the same community.

Mr MADISON remarked that "and" before "in adhering" should be changed into "or" otherwise both offences viz of levying war, & of adhering to the Enemy might be necessary to constitute Treason. He added that as the definition here was of treason against *the U. S.* it would seem that the individual States wd be left in possession of a concurrent power so far as to define & punish treason particularly agst themselves; which might involve double punishmt

It was moved that the whole clause be recommitted which was lost, the votes being equally divided.

N. H. no. Mas. no. Ct. no. N. J. ay. Pa. ay. Del. no. Md ay. Va ay. N. C. divd. S. C. no. Geo. ay.—[26]

[26] In the transcript the vote reads: "New Jersey, Pennsylvania, Maryland, Virginia, Georgia, aye—5 New Hampshire, Massachusetts, Connecticut, Delaware, South Carolina, no—5; North Carolina, divided."

M⟨r⟩ WILSON & Doc⟨r⟩ JOHNSON moved, that "or any of them" after "United States" be struck out in order to remove the embarrassment: which was agreed to nem. con.

M⟨r⟩ MADISON. This had [27] not removed the embarrassment. The same Act might be treason ag⟨st⟩ the United States as here defined—and ag⟨st⟩ a particular State according to its laws.

M⟨r⟩ ELSEWORTH. There can be no danger to the gen⟨l⟩ authority from this; as the laws of the U. States are to be paramount.

Doc⟨r⟩ JOHNSON was still of opinion there could be no Treason ag⟨st⟩ a particular State. It could not even at present, as the Confederation now stands, the Sovereignty being in the Union; much less can it be under the proposed system.

Col. MASON. The United States will have a qualified sovereignty only. The individual States will retain a part of the Sovereignty. An Act may be treason ag⟨st⟩ a particular State which is not so ag⟨st⟩ the U. States. He cited the Rebellion of Bacon in Virginia as an illustration of the doctrine.

Doc⟨r⟩ JOHNSON: That case would amount to Treason ag⟨st⟩ the Sovereign, the Supreme Sovereign, the United States.

M⟨r⟩ KING observed that the controversy relating to Treason might be of less magnitude than was supposed; as the Legislature might punish capitally under other names than Treason.

M⟨r⟩ Gov⟨r⟩ MORRIS and M⟨r⟩ RANDOLPH wished to substitute the words of the British Statute and moved to postpone Sect 2. art VII in order to consider the following substitute—" Whereas it is essential to the preservation of liberty to define precisely and exclusively what shall constitute the crime of Treason, it is therefore ordained, declared & established, that if a man do levy war ag⟨st⟩ the U. S., within their territories, or be adherent to the enemies of the U. S. within the said territories, giving them aid and comfort within their territories or elsewhere, and thereof be provably attainted of open deed by the people of his condition, he shall be adjudged guilty of Treason."

On this question

N. H. Mas. no. C⟨t⟩ no. N. J. ay. P⟨a⟩ no. Del. no. M⟨d⟩ no. V⟨a⟩ ay. N. C. no. S. C. no. Geo. no.[28]

---

[27] The word "has" is substituted in the transcript for "had."

[28] In the transcript the vote reads: "New Jersey, Virginia, aye—2; Massachusetts, Connecticut, Pennsylvania, Delaware, Maryland, North Carolina, South Carolina, Georgia, no—8."

It was [29] moved to strike out "ag$^{st}$ [30] United States" after "treason" so as to define treason generally, and on this question

Mas. ay. C$^t$ ay. N. J. ay. P$^a$ ay. Del. ay. M$^d$ ay. V$^a$ no. N. C. no. S. C. ay. Geo. ay.[31]

It was then moved to insert after "two witnesses" the words "to the same overt act."

Doc$^r$ FRANKLIN wished this amendment to take place– prosecutions for treason were generally virulent; and perjury too easily made use of against innocence.

M$^r$ WILSON. much may be said on both sides. Treason may sometimes be practised in such a manner, as to render proof extremely difficult—as in a traitorous correspondence with an Enemy.

On the question—as to same overt act

N. H. ay. Mas. ay. C$^t$ ay. N. J. no. P$^a$ ay. Del. ay. M$^d$ ay. V$^a$ no. N. C. no. S. C. ay. Geo. ay.[32]

M$^r$ KING moved to insert before the word "power" the word "sole," giving the U. States the exclusive right to declare the punishment of Treason.

M$^r$ BROOM 2$^{ds}$ the motion.

M$^r$ WILSON in cases of a general nature, treason can only be ag$^{st}$ the U— States. and in such they sh$^d$ have the sole right to declare the punishment—yet in many cases it may be otherwise. The subject was however intricate and he distrusted his present judgment on it.

M$^r$ KING this amendment results from the vote defining, treason generally by striking out ag$^{st}$ the U. States; which excludes any treason ag$^{st}$ particular States. These may however punish offences as high misdemesnors.

On [33] inserting the word "sole." It passed in the negative

N. H. ay. Mas. ay. C$^t$ no. N. J. no. P$^a$ ay. Del. ay. M$^d$ no V$^a$ no. N. C. no. S. C. ay. Geo. no.—[34]

---

[29] The word "then" is here inserted in the transcript.
[30] The word "the" is here inserted in the transcript.
[31] In the transcript the vote reads: "Massachusetts, Connecticut, New Jersey, Pennsylvania, Delaware, Maryland, South Carolina, Georgia, aye—8; Virginia, North Carolina, no—2."
[32] In the transcript the vote reads: "New Hampshire, Massachusetts, Connecticut, Pennsylvania, Delaware, Maryland, South Carolina, Georgia, aye—8; New Jersey, Virginia, North Carolina, no—3."
[33] The words "the question for" are here inserted in the transcript.
[34] In the transcript the vote reads: "New Hampshire, Massachusetts, Pennsylvania, Delaware, South Carolina, aye—5; Connecticut, New Jersey, Maryland, Virginia, North Carolina, Georgia, no—6."

Mr WILSON. the clause is ambiguous now. "Sole" ought either to have been inserted- or "against the U. S." to be re-instated.

Mr KING no line can be drawn between levying war and adhering to [35] enemy- agst the U. States and agst an individual State— Treason agst the latter must be so agst the former.

Mr SHERMAN, resistance agst the laws of the U. States as distinguished from resistance agst the laws of a particular State, forms the line.

Mr ELSEWORTH. the U. S. are sovereign on their [36] side of the line dividing the jurisdictions—the States on the other—each ought to have power to defend their respective Sovereignties.

Mr DICKENSON, war or insurrection agst a member of the Union must be so agst the whole body; but the Constitution should be made clear on this point.

The clause was reconsidered nem. con—& then, Mr WILSON & Mr ELSEWORTH moved to reinstate "agst the U. S." after "Treason"—on which question

N. H. no. Mas. no. Ct ay. N. J. ay. Pa no. Del. no. Md ay. Va ay. N. C. ay. S. C. no. Geo. ay.[37]

Mr MADISON was not satisfied with the footing on which the clause now stood. As Treason agst the U. States involves treason agst particular States, and vice versa, the same act may be twice tried & punished by the different authorities. Mr Govr MORRIS viewed the matter in the same light—

It was moved & 2ded to amend the sentence to read—"Treason agst the U. S. shall consist only in levying war against them, or in adhering to their enemies" which was agreed to.

Col. MASON moved to insert the words "giving them aid [38] com fort," as restrictive of "adhering to their Enemies &c." the latter he thought would be otherwise too indefinite—This motion was agreed to: Cont Del: & Georgia only being in the Negative.

Mr L. MARTIN moved to insert after conviction &c—"or on confession in open court"—and on the question, (the negative States thinking the words superfluous) it was agreed to

---

[35] The word "the" is here inserted in the transcript.
[36] The word "one" is substituted in the transcript for "their."
[37] In the transcript the vote reads: "Connecticut, New Jersey, Maryland, Virginia, North Carolina, Georgia, aye—6; New Hampshire, Massachusetts, Pennsylvania, Delaware, South Carolina, no—5."
[38] The word "and" is here inserted in the transcript.

N. H: ay. Mas. no. C: ay. N. J. ay. P. ay. Del. ay. M.d ay. V.a ay. N. C. div.d S. C. no. Geo. no.³⁹

Art: VII. Sect. 2, as amended was then agreed to nem. con.

⁴⁰ Sect. 3 ⁴¹ taken up "white & other" struck out nem. con. as superfluous.

M.r ELSEWORTH moved to require the first census to be taken within "three" instead of "six" years from the first meeting of the Legislature—and on ⁴² question

N. H. ay. Mas. ay. C.t ay. N. J. ay. P.a ay. Del. ay. M.d ay V.a ay. N. C. ay. S. C. no. Geo. no.⁴³

M.r KING asked what was the precise meaning of *direct* taxation? No one answ.d

M.r GERRY moved to add to the ⁴⁴ 3.d Sect. art. VII, the following clause "That from the first meeting, of the Legislature of the U. S. until a Census shall be taken all monies for supplying the public Treasury by direct taxation shall be raised from the several States according to the number of their Representatives respectively in the first branch"

M.r LANGDON. This would bear unreasonably hard on N· H. and he must be ag.st it.

M.r CARROL. opposed it. The number of Rep.s did not admit of a proportion exact enough for a rule of taxation.

Before any question the House
Adjourned

---

TUESDAY AUGUST 21. IN CONVENTION

Governour LIVINGSTON from the Committee of Eleven to whom was referred the propositions respecting the debts of the several States and also the Militia entered on the 18.th inst: delivered the following report:

---

³⁹ In the transcript the vote reads: "New Hampshire, Connecticut, New Jersey, Pennsylvania, Delaware, Maryland, Virginia, aye—7; Massachusetts, South Carolina, Georgia, no—3; North Carolina, divided."

⁴⁰ In the transcript this sentence reads as follows: "Article 7, Sect. 3 was taken up. The words 'white and others,' were struck out". . .

⁴¹ See *ante*.

⁴² The word "the" is here inserted in the transcript.

⁴³ In the transcript the vote reads: "New Hampshire, Massachusetts, Connecticut, New Jersey, Pennsylvania, Delaware, Maryland, Virginia, North Carolina, aye—9; South Carolina, Georgia, no—2."

⁴⁴ The word "the" is omitted in the transcript.

*The Home of James Madison*

"The Legislature of the U: S. shall have power to fulfil the engagements which have been entered into by Congress, and to discharge as well the debts of the U. S. as the debts incurred by the several States during the late war, for the common defence and general welfare"

"To make laws for organizing arming and disciplining the militia, and for governing such part of them as may be employed in the service of the U. S. reserving to the States respectively, the appointment of the officers, and the authority of training the Militia according to the discipline prescribed by the U. States"

Mr GERRY considered giving the power only, without adopting the obligation, as destroying the security now enjoyed by the public creditors of the U— States. He enlarged on the merit of this class of citizens, and the solemn faith which had been pledged under the existing Confederation. If their situation should be changed as here proposed great opposition would be excited agst the plan. He urged also that as the States had made different degrees of exertion to sink their respective debts, those who had done most would be alarmed, if they were now to be saddled with a share of the debts of States which had done least.

Mr SHERMAN. It means neither more nor less than the confederation as it relates to this subject.

Mr ELSEWORTH moved that the Report delivered in by Govr Livingston should lie on the table.[45] Agreed to nem. con.

Art: VII. Sect. 3.[46] resumed.—Mr DICKENSON moved to postpone this in order to reconsider Art: IV. Sect. 4. and to *limit* the number of representatives to be allowed to the large States. Unless this were done the small States would be reduced to entire insignificancy,[47] and encouragement given to the importation of slaves.

Mr SHERMAN would agree to such a reconsideration, but did not see the necessity of postponing the section before the House.—Mr DICKENSON withdrew his motion.

Art: VII. Sect. 3.[48] then agreed to 10 ays. Delaware alone being [49] no.

---

[45] The words "which was" are here inserted in the transcript.
[46] The words "was then" are here inserted in the transcript.
[47] The word "insignificancy" is changed to "insignificance" in the transcript.
[48] The word "was" is here inserted in the transcript.
[49] The word "being" is omitted in the transcript.

M! SHERMAN moved to add to Sect. 3. the following clause "and all accounts of supplies furnished, services performed, and monies advanced by the several States to the U. States, or by the U. S. to the several States shall be adjusted by the same rule"

M! GOVERN! MORRIS 2ᵈˢ the motion.

M! GHORUM, thought it wrong to insert this in the Constitution. The Legislature will no doubt do what is right. The present Congress have such a power and are now exercising it.

M! SHERMAN unless some rule be expressly given none will exist under the new system.

M! ELSEWORTH. Though The contracts of Congress will be binding, there will be no rule for executing them on the States; and one ought to be provided.

M! SHERMAN withdrew his motion to make way for one of M! WILLIAMSON to add to Sect. 3. "By this rule the several quotas of the States shall be determined in Settling the expences of the late war."

M! CARROL brought into view the difficulty that might arise on this subject from the establishment of the Constitution as intended without the *unanimous* consent of the States

M! Williamson's motion was postponed nem- con-

Art: VI Sect. 12.⁵⁰ which had been postponed Aug: 15.⁵¹ was now called for by Col. MASON, who wished to know how the proposed amendment as to money bills would be decided, before he agreed to any further points.

M! Gerry's motion of yesterday that previous to a census, direct taxation be proportioned on the States according to the number of Representatives, was taken up. He observed that the principal acts of Government would probably take place within that period, and it was but reasonable that the States should pay in proportion to their share in them.

M! ELSEWORTH thought such a rule unjust. there was a great difference between the number of Represent⁸, and the number of inhabitants as a rule in this case. Even if the former were proportioned as nearly as possible to the latter, it would be a very

---

⁵⁰ See *ante*.
⁵¹ The words "on the fifteenth of August" are substituted in the transcript for "Aug: 15."

inaccurate rule. A State might have one Representative only that had inhabitants enough for 1½ or more, if fractions could be applied, &c—. He proposed to amend the motion by adding the words "subject to a final liquidation by the foregoing rule when a census shall have been taken."

Mr MADISON. The last apportionment of Congs, on which the number of Representatives was founded, was conjectural and meant only as a temporary rule till a Census should be established.

Mr READ. The requisitions of Congs had been accomodated to the the impoverishments produced by the war; and to other local and temporary circumstances—

Mr WILLIAMSON opposed Mr Gerry's motion

Mr LANGDON was not here when N. H. was allowed three members. If [52] it was more than her share; he did not wish for them.

Mr BUTLER contended warmly for Mr Gerry's motion as founded in reason and equity.

Mr ELSEWORTH's proviso to Mr Gerry's motion was agreed to nem. con.

Mr KING thought the power of taxation given to the Legislature rendered the motion of Mr Gerry altogether unnecessary.

On Mr Gerry's motion as amended

N. H. no. Mas. ay. Ct no. N. J. no. Pa no. Del. no. Md no. Va no. N. Ci. divd S. C. ay. Geo. no.[53]

On a question, Shall Art: VI Sect. 12. with the amendment to it proposed & entered on the 15 instant, as called for by Col. Mason be now taken up? it passed in the Negative.

N. H. ay. Mas no. Ct ay. N. J. no. Pa no. Del. no. Md ay. Va ay. N. C. ay. S. C. no. Geo. no [54]

Mr L. MARTIN. The power of taxation is most likely to be criticised by the public. Direct taxation should not be used but in case of absolute necessity; and then the States will be best Judges of the mode. He therefore moved the following addition to Sect: 3. Art: VII "And whenever the Legislature of the U: S: shall find it necessary that revenue should be raised by direct taxation, having

---

[52] The word "if" is omitted in the transcript.
[53] In the transcript the vote reads "Massachusetts, South Carolina, aye—2; New Hampshire, Connecticut, New Jersey, Pennsylvania, Delaware, Maryland, Virginia, Georgia, no—8; North Carolina, divided."
[54] In the transcript the vote reads: "New Hampshire, Connecticut, Virginia, Maryland, North Carolina, aye—5; Massachusetts, New Jersey, Pennsylvania, Delaware, South Carolina, Georgia, no—6."

apportioned the same, according to the above rule on the several States, requisitions shall be made of the respective States to pay into the Continental Treasury their respective quotas within a time in the said requisitions specified, and in case of any of the States failing to comply with such requisitions, then and then only to devise and pass acts directing the mode, and authorizing the collection of the same"

M: M⁰HENRY 2ᵈᵉᵈ the motion—there was no debate, and on the question

N. H. no. C: no. N. J. ay. Penᵃ no. Del. no. Mᵈ divᵈ (Jenifer & Carrol no). Vᵃ no. N. C. no. S. C. no. Geo. no.⁵⁵

Art. VII. Sect. 4.⁵⁶, ⁵⁷—M: LANGDON. by this section the States are left at liberty to tax exports. N. H. therefore with other non-exporting States, will be subject to be taxed by the States exporting its produce. This could not be admitted. It seems to be feared that the Northern States will oppress the trade of the Southⁿ This may be guarded agᵗ by requiring the concurrence of ⅔ or ¾ of the legislature in such cases.

M: ELSEWORTH. It is best as it stands. The power of regulating trade between the States will protect them agᵗ each other. Should this not be the case, the attempts of one to tax the produce of another passing through its hands, will force a direct exportation and defeat themselves. There are solid reasons agᵗ Congᵉ taxing exports. 1.⁵⁸ it will discourage industry, as taxes on imports discourage luxury. 2.⁵⁸ The produce of different States is such as to prevent uniformity in such taxes. There are indeed but a few articles that could be taxed at all; as Tobᵒ rice & indigo, and a tax on these alone would be partial & unjust. 3.⁵⁸ The taxing of exports would engender incurable jealousies.

M: WILLIAMSON. Tho' N. C. has been taxed by Virgᵃ by a duty on 12,000 Hhs of her Tobᵒ exported thro' Virgᵃ yet he would never agree to this power. Should it take take place, it would distroy the last hope of an adoption of the plan.

---

⁵⁵ In the transcript the vote reads: "New Jersey, aye—1; New Hampshire, Connecticut, Pennsylvania, Delaware, Virginia, North Carolina, South Carolina, Georgia, no—8; Maryland, divided [Jenifer and Carroll, no]."

⁵⁶ See *ante*.

⁵⁷ The words "was then taken up" are here inserted in the transcript.

⁵⁸ The figures "1," "2" and "3" are changed in the transcript to "First," "Secondly" and "Thirdly."

Mr Govr Morris. These local considerations ought not to impede the general interest. There is great weight in the argument, that the exporting States will tax the produce of their uncommercial neighbours. The power of regulating the trade between Pa & N. Jersey will never prevent the former from taxing the latter. Nor will such a tax force a direct exportation from N. Jersey. The advantages possessed by a large trading City, outweigh the disadvantage of a moderate duty; and will retain the trade in that channel.– If no tax can be laid on exports, an embargo cannot be laid though in time of war such a measure may be of critical importance. Tobacco, lumber and live-stock are three objects belonging to different States, of which great advantage might be made by a power to tax exports. To these may be added Ginseng and Masts for Ships by which a tax might be thrown on other nations. The idea of supplying the West Indies with lumber from Nova Scotia is one of the many follies of lord Sheffield's pamphlets. The State of the Country also will change, and render duties on exports, as skins, beaver & other peculiar raw materials, politic in the view of encouraging American Manufactures.

Mr Butler was strenuously opposed to a power over exports; as unjust and alarming to the Staple-States.

Mr Langdon suggested a prohibition on the States from taxing the produce of other States exported from their harbours.

Mr Dickenson. The power of taxing exports may be inconvenient at present; but it must be of dangerous consequence to prohibit it with respect to all articles and for ever. He thought it would be better to except particular articles from the power.

Mr Sherman. It is best to prohibit the National legislature in all cases. The States will never give up all power over trade. An enumeration of particular articles would be difficult invidious and improper.

Mr Madison As we aught to be governed by national and permanent views, it is a sufficient argument for giving ye power over exports that a tax, tho' it may not be expedient at present, may be so hereafter. A proper regulation of exports may & probably will be necessary hereafter, and for the same purposes as the regulation of imports; viz, for revenue—domestic manufactures—and procuring equitable regulations from other nations. An Embargo may be of absolute necessity, and can alone be effectuated by the Genl authority. The regulation of trade between State and State can not effect more than indirectly to hinder a State from taxing its own exports; by authorizing its Citizens to carry their commodities freely into a neighbouring State which might decline taxing exports in order to draw into its channel the trade of its neighbours. As to the fear of disproportionate burdens on the more exporting States, it might be remarked that it was agreed on all hands that the revenue wd principally be drawn from trade, and as only a given revenue would be needed, it was not material whether all should be drawn wholly from imports—or half from those, and half from exports. The imports and exports must be pretty nearly equal in every State—and relatively the same among the different States.

Mr ELSEWORTH did not conceive an embargo by the Congress interdicted by this section.

Mr McHENRY conceived that power to be included in the power of war.

Mr WILSON. Pennsylvania exports the produce of Maryd N. Jersey, Delaware & will by & by when the River Delaware is opened, export for N- York. In favoring the general power over exports therefore, he opposed the particular interest of his State. He remarked that the power had been attacked by reasoning which could only have held good in case the Genl Govt had been *compelled*, instead of *authorized*, to lay duties on exports. To deny this power is to take from the Common Govt half the regulation of trade. It was his opinion that a power over exports might be more effectual than that over imports in obtaining beneficial treaties of commerce

Mr GERRY was strenuously opposed to the power over exports. It might be made use of to compel the States to comply with the will of the Genl Government, and to grant it any new powers which might be demanded. We have given it more power already than we know how will be exercised. It will enable the Genl Govt to oppress the States as much as Ireland is oppressed by Great Britain.

M.̲ FITZIMMONS would be ag.ˢᵗ a tax on exports to be laid immediately; but was for giving a power of laying the tax when a proper time may call for it. This would certainly be the case when America should become a manufacturing Country. He illustrated his argument by the duties in G. Britain on wool &c.

Col. MASON. If he were for reducing the States to mere corporations as seemed to be the tendency of some arguments, he should be for subjecting their exports as well as imports to a power of general taxation. He went on a principle often advanced & in which he concurred, that "a majority when interested will oppress the minority." This maxim had been verified by our own Legislature [of Virginia]. If we compare the States in this point of view the 8 Northern States have an interest different from the five South.ⁿ States; and have in one branch of the legislature 36 votes ag.ˢᵗ 29. and in the other, in the proportion of 8 ag.ˢᵗ 5. The Southern States had therefore good ground for their suspicions. The case of Exports was not the same with that of imports. The latter were the same throughout the States: The former very different. As to Tobacco other nations do raise it, and are capable of raising it as well as Virg.ᵃ &c. The impolicy of taxing that article had been demonstrated by the experiment of Virginia.

M.̲ CLYMER remarked that every State might reason with regard to its particular productions, in the same manner as the Southern States. The middle States may apprehend an oppression of their wheat flour, provisions &c. and with more reason, as these articles were exposed to a competition in foreign markets not incident to Tob.ᵒ rice &c. They may apprehend also combinations ag.ˢᵗ them between the Eastern & Southern States as much as the latter can apprehend them between the Eastern & middle. He moved as a qualification of the power of taxing Exports that it should be restrained to regulations of trade, by inserting after the word "duty" Sect 4 art VII the words, "for the purpose of revenue."

On [59] Question on M.̲ Clymer's motion

N. H. no. Mas. no. C.ᵗ no. N. J. ay. P.ᵃ ay. Del. ay. M.ᵈ no. V.ᵃ no. N. C. no. S. C. no. Geo. no.[60]

---

[59] The word "the" is here inserted in the transcript.
[60] In the transcript the vote reads: "New Jersey, Pennsylvania, Delaware, aye—3; New Hampshire, Massachusetts, Connecticut, Maryland, Virginia, North Carolina, South Carolina, Georgia, no—8."

Mʳ MADISON. In order to require ⅔ of each House to tax exports—as a lesser evil than a total prohibition moved to insert the words "unless by consent of two thirds of the Legislature."

Mʳ WILSON 2ᵈˢ and on this question, it passed in the Negative.

N. H. ay. Mas. ay. Cᵗ no. N. J. ay. Pᵃ ay. Del. ay. Mᵈ no. Vᵃ no [Col. Mason, Mʳ Randolph, Mʳ Blair no. Genˡ Washington & J. M. ay.] N. C. no. S. C. no. Geo. no.[61]

[62] Question on Sect: 4. art VII. as far as to "no tax shˡ be laid on exports—It passed in the affirmative.

N. H. no. Mas. ay. Cᵗ ay. N. J. no. Pᵃ no. Del. no. Mᵈ ay. Vᵃ ay (Genˡ W. & J. M. no) N. C. ay. S. C. ay. Geo. ay.[63]

Mʳ L. MARTIN, proposed to vary the Sect: 4. art VII. so as to allow a prohibition or tax on the importation of slaves. 1.[64] as five slaves are to be counted as 3 free men in the apportionment of Representatives; such a clause wᵈ leave an encouragement to this trafic. 2.[65] slaves weakened one part of the Union which the other parts were bound to protect: the privilege of importing them was therefore unreasonable. 3.[66] it was inconsistent with the principles of the revolution and dishonorable to the American character to have such a feature in the Constitution.

Mʳ RUTLIDGE did not see how the importation of slaves could be encouraged by this Section. He was not apprehensive of insurrections and would readily exempt the other States from the obligation to protect the Southern against them.— Religion & humanity had nothing to do with this question. Interest alone is the governing principle with nations. The true question at present is whether the Southⁿ States shall or shall not be parties to the Union. If the Northern States consult their interest, they will not oppose the increase of Slaves which will increase the commodities of which they will become the carriers.

---

[61] In the transcript the vote reads: "New Hampshire, Massachusetts, New Jersey, Pennsylvania, Delaware, aye—5; Connecticut, Maryland, Virginia [Col. Mason, Mr. Randolph, Mr. Blair, no; General Washington, Mr. Madison, aye] North Carolina, South Carolina, Georgia, no—6."

[62] The words "On the" are here inserted in the transcript.

[63] In the transcript the vote reads: "Massachusetts, Connecticut, Maryland, Virginia [Genl. Washington and Mr. Madison, no] North Carolina, South Carolina, Georgia, aye—7; New Hampshire, New Jersey, Pennsylvania, Delaware, no—4."

[64] The figure "1" is changed in the transcript to "In the first place."

[65] The figure "2" is changed in the transcript to "In the second place."

[66] The figure "3" is changed in the transcript to "And in the third place."

Mr ELSEWORTH was for leaving the clause as it stands. let every State import what it pleases. The morality or wisdom of slavery are considerations belonging to the States themselves. What enriches a part enriches the whole, and the States are the best judges of their particular interest. The old confederation had not meddled with this point, and he did not see any greater necessity for bringing it within the policy of the new one:

Mr PINKNEY. South Carolina can never receive the plan if it prohibits the slave trade. In every proposed extension of the powers of the Congress, that State has expressly & watchfully excepted that of meddling with the importation of negroes. If the States be all left at liberty on this subject, S. Carolina may perhaps by degrees do of herself what is wished, as Virginia & Maryland have already [67] done.

Adjourned

---

WEDNESDAY AUGUST 22. IN CONVENTION

Art VII sect 4. [68],[69] resumed. Mr SHERMAN was for leaving the clause as it stands. He disapproved of the slave trade; yet as the States were now possessed of the right to import slaves, as the public good did not require it to be taken from them, & as it was expedient to have as few objections as possible to the proposed scheme of Government, he thought it best to leave the matter as we find it. He observed that the abolition of Slavery seemed to be going on in the U. S. & that the good sense of the several States would probably by degrees compleat it. He urged on the Convention the necessity of despatching its business.

Col. MASON. This infernal trafic originated in the avarice of British Merchants. The British Govt constantly checked the attempts of Virginia to put a stop to it. The present question concerns not the importing States alone but the whole Union. The evil of having slaves was experienced during the late war. Had slaves been treated as they might have been by the Enemy, they would have proved dangerous instruments in their hands. But

---

[67] The words "have already" are transposed in the transcript to read "already have."
[68] See *ante*.
[69] The word "was" is here inserted in the transcript.

their folly dealt by the slaves, as it did by the Tories. He mentioned the dangerous insurrections of the slaves in Greece and Sicily; and the instructions given by Cromwell to the Commissioners sent to Virginia, to arm the servants & slaves, in case other means of obtaining its submission should fail. Maryland & Virginia he said had already prohibited the importation of slaves expressly. N. Carolina had done the same in substance. All this would be in vain if S. Carolina & Georgia be at liberty to import. The Western people are already calling out for slaves for their new lands, and will fill that Country with slaves if they can be got thro' S. Carolina & Georgia. Slavery discourages arts & manufactures. The poor despise labor when performed by slaves. They prevent the immigration of Whites, who really enrich & strengthen a Country. They produce the most pernicious effect on manners. Every master of slaves is born a petty tyrant. They bring the judgment of heaven on a Country. As nations can not be rewarded or punished in the next world they must be in this. By an inevitable chain of causes & effects providence punishes national sins, by national calamities. He lamented that some of our Eastern brethren had from a lust of gain embarked in this nefarious traffic. As to the States being in possession of the Right to import, this was the case with many other rights, now to be properly given up. He held it essential in every point of view that the Genl Govt should have power to prevent the increase of slavery.

Mr Elsworth. As he had never owned a slave could not judge of the effects of slavery on character: He said however that if it was to be considered in a moral light we ought to go farther and free those already in the Country.—As slaves also multiply so fast in Virginia & & Maryland that it is cheaper to raise than import them, whilst in the sickly rice swamps foreign supplies are necessary, if we go no farther than is urged, we shall be unjust towards S. Carolina & Georgia. Let us not intermeddle. As population increases poor laborers will be so plenty as to render slaves useless. Slavery in time will not be a speck in our Country. Provision is already made in Connecticut for abolishing it. And the abolition has already taken place in Massachusetts. As to the danger of insurrections from foreign influence, that will become a motive to kind treatment of the slaves.

M! PINKNEY. If slavery be wrong, it is justified by the example of all the world. He cited the case of Greece Rome & other antient States; the sanction given by France England, Holland & other modern States. In all ages one half of mankind have been slaves. If the S. States were let alone they will probably of themselves stop importations. He wd himself as a Citizen of S. Carolina vote for it. An attempt to take away the right as proposed will produce serious objections to the Constitution which he wished to see adopted.

General PINKNEY declared it to be his firm opinion that if himself & all his colleagues were to sign the Constitution & use their personal influence, it would be of no avail towards obtaining the assent of their Constituents. S. Carolina & Georgia cannot do without slaves. As to Virginia she will gain by stopping the importations. Her slaves will rise in value, & she has more than she wants. It would be unequal to require S. C. & Georgia to confederate on such unequal terms. He said the Royal assent before the Revolution had never been refused to S. Carolina as to Virginia. He contended that the importation of slaves would be for the interest of the whole Union. The more slaves, the more produce to employ the carrying trade; The more consumption also, and the more of this, the more of revenue for the common treasury. He admitted it to be reasonable that slaves should be dutied like other imports, but should consider a rejection of the clause as an exclusion of S. Carola from the Union.

M! BALDWIN had conceived national objects alone to be before the Convention, not such as like the present were of a local nature. Georgia was decided on this point. That State has always hitherto supposed a Gen! Governm! to be the pursuit of the central States who wished to have a vortex for every thing—that her distance would preclude her from equal advantage—& that she could not prudently purchase it by yielding national powers. From this it might be understood in what light she would view an attempt to abridge one of her favorite prerogatives. If left to herself, she may probably put a stop to the evil. As one ground for this conjecture, he took notice of the sect of       which he said was a respectable class of people, who carried their ethics beyond the mere *equality of men*, extending their humanity to the claims of the whole animal creation.

Mr WILSON observed that if S. C. & Georgia were themselves disposed to get rid of the importation of slaves in a short time as had been suggested, they would never refuse to Unite because the importation might be prohibited. As the Section now stands all articles imported are to be taxed. Slaves alone are exempt. This is in fact a bounty on that article.

Mr GERRY thought we had nothing to do with the conduct of the States as to Slaves, but ought to be careful not to give any sanction to it.

Mr DICKENSON considered it as inadmissible on every principle of honor & safety that the importation of slaves should be authorised to the States by the Constitution. The true question was whether the national happiness would be promoted or impeded by the importation, and this question ought to be left to the National Govt not to the States particularly interested. If Engd & France permit slavery, slaves are at the same time excluded from both those Kingdoms. Greece and Rome were made unhappy by their slaves. He could not believe that the Southn States would refuse to confederate on the account apprehended; especially as the power was not likely to be immediately exercised by the Genl Government.

Mr WILLIAMSON stated the law of N. Carolina on the subject, to wit that it did not directly prohibit the importation of slaves. It imposed a duty of £5. on each slave imported from Africa. £10 on each from elsewhere, & £50 on each from a State licensing manumission. He thought the S. States could not be members of the Union if the clause shd be rejected, and that it was wrong to force any thing down, not absolutely necessary, and which any State must disagree to.

Mr KING thought the subject should be considered in a political light only. If two States will not agree to the Constitution as stated on one side, he could affirm with equal belief on the other, that great & equal opposition would be experienced from the other

States. He remarked on the exemption of slaves from duty whilst every other import was subjected to it, as an inequality that could not fail to strike the commercial sagacity of the Northⁿ & middle States.

Mʳ LANGDON was strenuous for giving the power to the Genˡ Govᵗ He cᵈ not with a good conscience leave it with the States who could then go on with the traffic, without being restrained by the opinions here given that they will themselves cease to import slaves.

Genˡ PINKNEY thought himself bound to declare candidly that he did not think S. Carolina would stop her importations of slaves in any short time, but only stop them occasionally as she now does. He moved to commit the clause that slaves might be made liable to an equal tax with other imports which he he thought right & wᶜʰ wᵈ remove one difficulty that had been started.

Mʳ RUTLIDGE. If the Convention thinks that N. C. S. C. & Georgia will ever agree to the plan, unless their right to import slaves be untouched, the expectation is vain. The people of those States will never be such fools as to give up so important an interest. He was strenuous agˢᵗ striking out the Section, and seconded the motion of Genˡ Pinkney for a commitment.

Mʳ Govʳ MORRIS wished the whole subject to be committed including the clauses relating to taxes on exports & to a navigation act. These things may form a bargain among the Northern & Southern States.

Mʳ BUTLER declared that he never would agree to the power of taxing exports.

Mʳ SHERMAN said it was better to let the S. States import slaves than to part with them, if they made that a sine qua non. He was opposed to a tax on slaves imported as making the matter worse, because it implied they were *property*. He acknowledged that if the power of prohibiting the importation should be given to the Genˡ Government that it would be exercised. He thought it would be its duty to exercise the power.

Mʳ READ was for the commitment provided the clause concerning taxes on exports should also be committed.

M! SHERMAN observed that that clause had been agreed to & therefore could not [70] committed.

M! RANDOLPH was for committing in order that some middle ground might, if possible, be found. He could never agree to the clause as it stands. He w? sooner risk the constitution. He dwelt on the dilemma to which the Convention was exposed. By agreeing to the clause, it would revolt the Quakers, the Methodists, and many others in the States having no slaves. On the other hand, two States might be lost to the Union. Let us then, he said, try the chance of a commitment.

On the question for committing the remaining part of Sect. 4 & 5.[71] of art: 7. N. H. no. Mas. abs! Con! ay N. J. ay P? no. Del. no Mary? ay. V? ay. N. C. ay. S. C. ay. Geo. ay.[72]

M! PINKNEY & M! LANGDON moved to commit Sect. 6.[71] as to [73] navigation act by two thirds of each House

M! GORHAM did not see the propriety of it. Is it meant to require a greater proportion of votes? He desired it to be remembered that the Eastern States had no motive to Union but a commercial one. They were able to protect themselves. They were not afraid of external danger, and did not need the aid of the South? States.

M! WILSON wished for a commitment in order to reduce the proportion of votes required.

M! ELSWORTH was for taking the plan as it is. This widening of opinions has [74] a threatening aspect. If we do not agree on this middle & moderate ground he was afraid we should lose two States, with such others as may be disposed to stand aloof, should fly into a variety of shapes & directions, and most probably into several confederations and not without bloodshed.

On [75] Question for committing 6 Sect. as to [73] navigation act to a member from each State—N. H. ay. Mas. ay. C! no. N. J. no.

---

[70] The word "be" is here inserted in the transcript.
[71] See *ante*.
[72] In the transcript the vote reads: "Connecticut, New Jersey, Maryland, Virginia, North Carolina, South Carolina, Georgia, aye—7; New Hampshire, Pennyslvania, Delaware, no—3; Massachusetts, absent."
[73] The word "a" is here inserted in the transcript.
[74] The word "had" is substituted in the transcript for "has."
[75] The word "the" is here inserted in the transcript.

Pa. ay. Del. ay. Md ay. Va ay. N. C. ay. S. C. ay. Geo. ay.[76]

The Committee appointed were Mr Langdon, King, Johnson, Livingston, Clymer, Dickenson, L. Martin, Madison, Williamson, C. C. Pinkney, & Baldwin.

To this committee were referred also the two clauses abovementioned, of the 4 & 5. Sect: of Art. 7.

Mr RUTLIDGE, fron the Committee to whom were referred on the 18 & 20th instant the propositions of Mr Madison & Mr Pinkney, made the Report following.—

[Here insert the Report from the Journal of the Convention of this date.] [77]

["The committee report, that in their opinion the following additions should be made to the report now before the convention namely,

"At the end of the first clause of the first section of the seventh article add, 'for payment of the debts and necessary expenses of the United States; provided that no law for raising any branch of revenue, except what may be specially appropriated for the payment of interest on debts or loans, shall continue in force for more than     years.'

"At the end of the second clause, second section, seventh article, add, 'and with Indians, within the limits of any state, not subject to the laws thereof.'

"At the end of the sixteenth clause of the second section, seventh article, add, 'and to provide, as may become necessary, from time to time, for the well managing and securing the common property and general interests and welfare of the United States in such manner as shall not interfere with the governments of individual states, in matters which respect only their internal police, or for which their individual authorities [78] may be competent.'

"At the end of the first section, tenth article, add, 'he shall be of the age of thirty five years, and a citizen of the United States, and shall have been an inhabitant thereof for twenty one years.'

"After the second section of the tenth article, insert the following as a third section:

" 'The President of the United States shall have a privy council, which shall consist of the president of the senate, the speaker of

---

[76] In the transcript the vote reads: "New Hampshire, Massachusetts, Pennsylvania, Delaware, Maryland, Virginia, North Carolina, South Carolina, Georgia, aye—9; Connecticut, New Jersey, no—2."
[77] Madison's direction is omitted in the transcript.
[78] The transcript uses the word "authorities" in the singular.

the house of representatives, the chief justice of the supreme court, and the principal officer in the respective departments of foreign affairs, domestic affairs, war, marine, and finance, as such departments of office shall from time to time be established, whose duty it shall be to advise him in matters respecting the execution of his office, which he shall think proper to lay before them: but their advice shall not conclude him, nor affect his responsibility for the measures which he shall adopt.'

"At the end of the second section of the eleventh article, add, 'the judges of the supreme court shall be triable by the senate, on impeachment by the house of representatives.'

"Between the fourth and fifth lines of the third section of the eleventh article, after the word 'controversies,' insert 'between the United States and an individual state, or the United States and an individual person.' "] [79]

A motion to rescind the order of the House respecting the hours of meeting & adjourning, was negatived:

Mass: P? Del. Mar?..............ay [80]
N. H. Con: N. J. V? N. C. S. C. Geo. no [81]

M? GERRY & M? M?HENRY moved to insert after the 2? sect.[82] Art: 7, the Clause following, to wit, "The Legislature shall pass no bill of attainder nor any ex post facto law." *

M? GERRY urged the necessity of this prohibition, which he said was greater in the National than the State Legislature, because the number of members in the former being fewer [83] were on that account the more to be feared.

M? GOV? MORRIS thought the precaution as to ex post facto laws unnecessary; but essential as to bills of attainder

M? ELSEWORTH contended that there was no lawyer, no civilian who would not say that ex post facto laws were void of themselves. It can not then be necessary to prohibit them.

M? WILSON was against inserting any thing in the Constitution as to ex post facto laws. It will bring reflexions on the Constitu-

[79] *Journal, Acts and Proceedings of the Convention . . . which formed the Constitution of the United States* (1819), p. 277.
   [80] The figure "4" is here inserted in the transcript.
   [81] The figure "7" is here inserted in the transcript.
   [82] The word "of" is here inserted in the transcript.
   *The proceedings on this motion involving the two questions on "attainders & ex post facto laws," are not so fully stated in the Printed Journal.
   [83] The word "they" is here inserted in the transcript.

tion—and proclaim that we are ignorant of the first principles of Legislation, or are constituting a Government which [84] will be so.

The question being divided, The first part of the motion relating to bills of attainder was agreed to nem. contradicente.

On the second part relating to ex post facto laws—

Mr CARROL remarked that experience overruled all other calculations. It had proved that in whatever light they might be viewed by civilians or others, the State Legislatures had passed them, and they had taken effect.

Mr WILSON. If these prohibitions in the State Constitutions have no effect, it will be useless to insert them in this Constitution. Besides, both sides will agree to the principle, & [85] will differ as to its application.

Mr WILLIAMSON. Such a prohibitory clause is in the Constitution of N. Carolina, and tho it has been violated, it has done good there & may do good here, because the Judges can take hold of it.

Docr JOHNSON thought the clause unnecessary, and implying an improper suspicion of the National Legislature.

Mr RUTLIDGE was in favor of the clause.

On the question for inserting the prohibition of ex post facto laws.

N. H. ay. Mas. ay. Cont no. N. J. no. Pa no. Del. ay. Md ay. Virga ay N. C. divd S. C. ay. Geo. ay.[86]

The report of the committee of 5. made by Mr Rutlidge, was taken up & then postponed that each member might furnish himself with a copy.

The Report of the Committee of Eleven delivered in & entered on the Journal of the 21st inst. was then taken up. and the first clause containing the words "The Legislature of the U. S. *shall have power* to fulfil the engagements which have been entered into by Congress" being under consideration,

Mr ELSWORTH argued that they were unnecessary. The U. S. heretofore entered into Engagements by Congs who were their

---

[84] The word "that" is substituted in the transcript for "which."

[85] The word "but" is substituted in the transcript for "&."

[86] In the transcript the vote reads: "New Hampshire, Massachusetts, Delaware, Maryland, Virginia, South Carolina, Georgia, aye—7; Connecticut, New Jersey, Pennsylvania, no—3; North Carolina, divided."

agents. They will hereafter be bound to fulfil them by their new agents.

Mr RANDOLPH thought such a provision necessary: for though the U. States will be bound, the new Govt will have no authority in the case unless it be given to them.

Mr MADISON thought it necessary to give the authority in order to prevent misconstruction. He mentioned the attempts made by the Debtors to British subjects-to shew that contracts under the old Government, were dissolved by the Revolution which destroyed the political identity of the Society.

Mr GERRY thought it essential that some explicit provision should be made on this subject, so that no pretext might remain for getting rid of the public engagements.

Mr Govr MORRIS moved by way of amendment to substitute— "The Legislature *shall* discharge the debts & fulfil the engagements, of the U. States."

It was moved to vary the amendment by striking out "discharge the debts" & to insert "liquidate the claims," which being negatived,

The amendment moved by Mr Govr Morris was agreed to all the States being in the affirmative.

It was moved & 2ded to strike the following words out of the 2d clause of the report "and the authority of training the Militia according to the discipline prescribed by the U. S." Before a question was taken

The House adjourned

IN CONVENTION    THURSDAY AUG: 23. 1787 [87]

The Report of the Committee of Eleven made Aug: 21.[88] being taken up, and the following clause being under consideration to wit "To make laws for organizing, arming & disciplining the Militia, and for governing such part [89] of them as may be employed in the service of the U. S. reserving to the States respectively, the appointment of the officers, and authority of training the militia according to the discipline prescribed—"

---

[87] The year "1787" is omitted in the transcript.
[88] The words "the twenty-first of August" are substituted in the transcript for "Aug: 21."
[89] The transcript uses the word "part" in the plural.

M! SHERMAN moved to strike out the last member— "and authority of training &c. He thought it unnecessary. The States will have this authority of course if not given up.

M! ELSWORTH doubted the propriety of striking out the sentence. The reason assigned applies as well to the other reservation of the appointment to offices. He remarked at the same time that the term discipline was of vast extent and might be so expounded as to include all power on the subject.

M! KING, by way of explanation, said that by *organizing*, the Committee meant, proportioning the officers & men—by *arming*, specifying the kind size & caliber of arms—& by *disciplining* prescribing the manual exercise evolutions &c.

M! SHERMAN withdrew his motion

M! GERRY. This power in the U. S. as explained is making the States drill-sergeants. He had as lief let the Citizens of Massachussets be disarmed, as to take the command from the States, and subject them to the Gen! Legislature. It would be regarded as a system of Despotism.

M! MADISON observed that "*arming*" as explained did not did not extend to furnishing arms; nor the term "disciplining" to penalties & Courts Martial for enforcing them.

M! KING added, to his former explanation that *arming* meant not only to provide for uniformity of arms, but included [90] authority to regulate the modes of furnishing, either by the Militia themselves, the State Governments, or the National Treasury: that *laws* for disciplining, must involve penalties and every thing necessary for enforcing penalties.

M! DAYTON moved to postpone the paragraph, in order to take up the following proposition

"To establish an uniform & general system of discipline for the Militia of these States, and to make laws for organizing, arming, disciplining & governing *such part of them as may be employed in the service of the U. S.*, reserving to the States respectively the appointment of the officers, and all authority over the Militia not herein given to the General Government"

On the question to postpone in favor of this proposition: it passed in the Negative

---

[90] The word "the" is here inserted in the transcript.

N. H. no. Mas no. Cᵗ no. N. J. ay. P. no. Del. no. Maryᵈ ay. Vᵃ no. N. C. no. S. C. no. Geo. ay.[91]

Mʳ Elsworth & Mʳ Sherman moved to postpone the 2ᵈ clause in favor of the following "To establish an uniformity of arms, exercise & organization for the Militia, and to provide for the Government of them when called into the service of the U. States" The object of this proposition was to refer the plan for the Militia to the General Govᵗ but [92] leave the execution of it to the State Govᵗˢ

Mʳ Langdon said He could not understand the jealousy expressed by some Gentleman.[93] The General & State Govᵗˢ were not enemies to each other, but different institutions for the good of the people of America. As one of the people he could say, the National Govᵗ is mine, the State Govᵗ is mine. In transferring power from one to the other, I only take out of my left hand what it can not so well use, and put it into my right hand where it can be better used.

Mʳ Gerry thought it was rather taking out of the right hand & putting it into the left. Will any man say that liberty will be as safe in the hands of eighty or a hundred men taken from the whole continent, as in the hands of two or three hundred taken from a single State.

Mʳ Dayton was against so absolute a uniformity. In some States there ought to be a greater proportion of cavalry than in others. In some places rifles would be most proper, in others muskets &c.

Genˡ Pinkney preferred the clause reported by the Committee, extending the meaning of it to the case of fines &c.

Mʳ Madison. The primary object is to secure an effectual discipline of the Militia. This will no more be done if left to the States separately than the requisitions have been hitherto paid by them. The States neglect their Militia now, and the more they are consolidated into one nation, the less each will rely on its own interior provisions for its safety & the less prepare its Militia for

---

[91] In the transcript the vote reads: "New Jersey, Maryland, Georgia, aye—3; New Hampshire, Massachusetts, Connecticut, Pennsylvania, Delaware, Virginia, North Carolina, South Carolina, no—8."

[92] The word "to" is here inserted in the transcript.

[93] The word "gentleman" is used in the plural in the transcript.

Charles Cotesworth Pinckney

that purpose; in like manner as the militia of a State would have been still more neglected than it has been if each County had been independently charged with the care of its Militia. The Discipline of the Militia is evidently a *National* concern, and ought to be provided for in the *National* Constitution.

M! L. MARTIN was confident that the States would never give up the power over the Militia; and that, if they were to do so the militia would be less attended to by the Gen! than by the State Governments.

M! RANDOLPH asked what danger there could be that the Militia could be brought into the field and made to commit suicide on themselves. This is a power that can not from its nature be abused, unless indeed the whole mass should be corrupted. He was for trammelling the Gen! Gov! wherever there was danger, but here there could be none. He urged this as an essential point; observing that the Militia were every where neglected by the State Legislatures, the members of which courted popularity too much to enforce a proper discipline. Leaving the appointment of officers to the States protects the people ag:t every apprehension that could produce murmur.

On [94] Question on M! Elsworth's Motion

N. H. no. Mas. no. C! ay. N. J. no. P! no. Del. no. M! no. V! no. N. C. no. S. C. no. Geo. no.[95]

A motion was then made to recommit the 2! clause which was negatived.

On the question to agree to the 1!t part of the clause, namely

"To make laws for organizing arming & disciplining the Militia, and for governing such part of them as may be employed in the service of the U. S."

N. H ay. Mas. ay. C!. no. N. J. ay. P! ay. Del. ay. M! no. V! ay. N. C. ay. S. C. ay. Geo. ay.[96]

M! MADISON moved to amend the next part of the clause so as to read "reserving to the States respectively, the appointment of the officers, *under the rank of General officers*"

---

[94] The word "the" is here inserted in the transcript.
[95] In the transcript the vote reads: "Connecticut, aye; the other ten States, no."
[96] In the transcript the vote reads: "New Hampshire, Massachusetts, New Jersey, Pennsylvania, Delaware, Virginia, North Carolina, South Carolina, Georgia, aye—9; Connecticut, Maryland, no—2."

M! SHERMAN considered this as absolutely inadmissible. He said that if the people should be so far asleep as to allow the most influential officers of the militia to be appointed by the Gen! Government, every man of discernment would rouse them by sounding the alarm to them.

M! GERRY. Let us at once destroy the State Gov!ˢ have an Executive for life or hereditary, and a proper Senate, and then there would be some consistency in giving full powers to the Gen! Gov! but as the States are not to be abolished, he wondered at the attempts that were made to give powers inconsistent with their existence. He warned the Convention agᵅᵗ pushing the experiment too far. Some people will support a plan of vigorous Government at every risk. Others of a more democratic cast will oppose it with equal determination, and a Civil war may be produced by the conflict.

M! MADISON. As the greatest danger is that of disunion of the States, it is necessary to guard agᵅᵗ it by sufficient powers to the Common Gov! and as the greatest danger to liberty is from large standing armies, it is best to prevent them, by an effectual provision for a good Militia.

On the Question to agree to M! Madison's motion

N. H. ay. Mas. no. Cᵗ no. N. J. no. Pᵅ no. Del. no. Mᵈ no. Vᵅ no. N. C. no. S. C. ay. Geo.* ay.⁹⁷

On the question to agree to the "reserving to the States the appointment of the officers." It was agreed to nem: contrad:

On the question on the clause "and the authority of training the Militia according to the discipline prescribed by the U. S—"

N. H. ay. Mas. ay. Cᵗ ay. N. J. ay. Pᵅ ay. Del. no. Mᵈ ay. Vᵅ no. N. C. ay. S. C. no. Geo. no.⁹⁸

On the question to agree to Art. VII. Sect. 7.⁹⁹ as reported It passed nem. contrad:

M! PINKNEY urged the necessity of preserving foreign Ministers & other officers of the U. S. independent of external influence and

---

*In the printed Journal, Geo: no.

⁹⁷ In the transcript the vote reads: "New Hampshire, South Carolina, Georgia,* aye—3; Massachusetts, Connecticut, New Jersey, Pennsylvania, Delaware, Maryland, Virginia, North Carolina, no—8."

⁹⁸ In the transcript the vote reads: "New Hampshire, Massachusetts, Connecticut, New Jersey, Pennsylvania, Maryland, North Carolina, aye—7; Delaware, Virginia, South Carolina, Georgia, no—4."

⁹⁹ See *ante*.

moved to insert, after Art VII Sect 7. the clause following—"No person holding any office of profit or trust [1] under the U. S. shall without the consent of the Legislature, accept of any present, emolument, office or title of any kind whatever, from any King, Prince or foreign State which passed nem: contrad.

M⸳ RUTLIDGE moved to amend Art: VIII [99] to read as follows,

"This Constitution & the laws of the U. S. made in pursuance thereof, and all Treaties made under the authority of the U. S. shall be the supreme law of the several States and of their citizens and inhabitants; and the Judges in the several States shall be bound thereby in their decisions, any thing in the Constitutions or laws of the several States, to the contrary notwithstanding."

which was agreed to nem: contrad:

Art: IX [99] being next for consideration,

M⸳ GOV⸳ MORRIS argued ag⸳st the appointment of officers by the Senate. He considered the body as too numerous for the [2] purpose; as subject to cabal; and as devoid of responsibility. If Judges were to be tried by the Senate according to a late report of a Committee it was particularly wrong to let the Senate have the filling of vacancies which its own decrees were to create.

M⸳ WILSON was of the same opinion & for like reasons.

The [3] art IX being waived and art VII. sect 1.[4] resumed,

M⸳ GOV⸳ MORRIS moved to strike the following words out of the 18 clause "enforce treaties" as being superfluous, since treaties were to be "laws"—which was agreed to nem: contrad:

M⸳ GOV⸳ MORRIS moved to alter [5] 1⸳st part. of [5] 18. clause sect. 1. to execute the laws of the Union, suppress insurrections and repel invasions."

art. VII [6] so as to read "to provide for calling forth the Militia
which was agreed to nem: contrad

On the question then to agree to the 18 clause of Sect. 1. art: 7. as amended it passed in the affirmative nem: contradicente.

---

[99] ee *ante.*
[1] The words "profit or trust" are transposed to read "trust or profit" in the transcript.
[2] The word "that" is substituted in the transcript for "the."
[3] The word "the" is crossed out in the transcript.
[4] See *ante.*
[5] The word "the" is here inserted in the transcript.
[6] The transcript omits "sect. 1. art. VII."

Mr C- PINKNEY moved to add as an additional power to be vested in the Legislature of the U. S. "To negative all laws passed by the several States interfering in the opinion of the Legislature with the general interests and harmony of the Union; provided that two thirds of the members of each House assent to the same"

This principle he observed had formerly been agreed to. He considered the precaution as essentially necessary: The objection drawn from the predominance of the large States had been removed by the equality established in the Senate. Mr BROOME 2$^{ded}$ the proposition.

Mr SHERMAN thought it unnecessary; the laws of the General Government being Supreme & paramount to the State laws according to the plan, as it now stands.

Mr MADISON proposed that it should be committed. He had been from the beginning a friend to the principle; but thought the modification might be made better.

Mr MASON wished to know how the power was to be exercised. Are all laws whatever to be brought up? Is no road nor bridge to be established without the Sanction of the General Legislature? Is this to sit constantly in order to receive & revise the State Laws? He did not mean by these remarks to condemn the expedient, but he was apprehensive that great objections would lie ag$^{st}$ it.

Mr WILLIAMSON thought it unnecessary, & having been already decided, a revival of the question was a waste of time.

Mr WILSON considered this as the key-stone wanted to compleat the wide arch of Government, we are raising. The power of self-defence had been urged as necessary for the State Governments. It was equally necessary for the General Government. The firmness of Judges is not of itself sufficient. Something further is requisite. It will be better to prevent the passage of an improper law, than to declare it void when passed.

Mr RUTLIDGE. If nothing else, this alone would damn and ought to damn the Constitution. Will any State ever agree to be bound hand & foot in this manner. It is worse than making mere corporations of them whose bye laws would not be subject to this shackle.

Mʳ ELSEWORTH observed that the power contended for wᵈ require either that all laws of the State Legislatures should previously to their taking effect be transmitted to the Genˡ Legislature, or be repealable by the Latter; or that the State Executives should be appointed by the Genˡ Government, and have a controul over the State laws. If the last was meditated let it be declared.

Mʳ PINKNEY declared that he thought the State Executives ought to be so appointed with such a controul, & that it would be so provided if another Convention should take place.

Mʳ GOVERNʳ MORRIS did not see the utility or practicability of the proposition of Mʳ Pinkney, but wished it to be referred to the consideration of a Committee.

Mʳ LANGDON was in favor of the proposition. He considered it as resolvable into the question whether the extent of the National Constitution was to be judged of by the Genˡ or the State Governments.

On the question for commitment, it passed in the negative.

N. H. ay. Masᵗˢ no. Conᵗ no. N. J. no. Pᵃ ay. Del: ay. Mᵈ ay. Vᵃ ay. N. C. no. S. C. no. Geo. no.[7]

Mʳ PINKNEY then withdrew his proposition.

The 1ˢᵗ sect. of art: VII[8] being so amended as to read "The Legislature *shall* fulfil the engagements and discharge the debts of the U. S. & shall have the power to lay & collect taxes duties imposts & excises," was agreed to.

Mʳ BUTLER expressed his dissatisfaction lest it should compel payment as well to the Blood-suckers who had speculated on the distresses of others, as to those who had fought & bled for their country. He would be ready he said tomorrow to vote for a discrimination between those classes of people, and gave notice that he should [9] move for a reconsideration.

Art IX. sect. 1.[10] being resumed, to wit "The Senate of the U. S. shall have power to make treaties, and to appoint Ambassadors, and Judges of the Supreme Court."

---

[7] In the transcript the vote reads: "New Hampshire, Pennsylvania, Delaware, Maryland, Virginia, aye—5; Massachusetts, Connecticut, New Jersey, North Carolina, South Carolina, Georgia, no—6."

[8] The phrase "The first clause of article 7. section 1" is substituted in the transcript for "The 1ṣt sect of art: VII."

[9] The word "would" is substituted in the transcript for "should."

[10] See p. ——.

Mʳ MADISON observed that the Senate represented the States alone, and that for this as well as other obvious reasons it was proper that the President should be an agent in Treaties.

Mʳ Govʳ MORRIS did not know that he should agree to refer the making of Treaties to the Senate at all, but for the present wᵈ move to add, as an amendment to the section after "Treaties"—[11] "but no Treaty shall be binding on the U. S. which is not ratified by a law."

Mʳ MADISON suggested the inconvenience of requiring a legal *ratification* of treaties of alliance for the purposes of war &c &c

Mʳ GHORUM. Many other disadvantages must be experienced if treaties of peace & all negociations are to be previously ratified— and if not previously, the Ministers would be at a loss how to proceed. What would be the case in G. Britain if the King were to proceed in this manner. American Ministers must go abroad not instructed by the same Authority (as will be the case with other Ministers) which is to ratify their proceedings.

Mʳ Govʳ MORRIS. As to treaties of alliance, they will oblige foreign powers to send their Ministers here, the very thing we should wish for. Such treaties could not be otherwise made, if his amendment shᵈ succeed. In general he was not solicitous to multiply & facilitate Treaties. He wished none to be made with G. Britain, till she should be at war. Then a good bargain might be made with her. So with other foreign powers. The more difficulty in making treaties, the more value will be set on them.

Mʳ WILSON. In the most important Treaties, the King of G. Britain being obliged to resort to Parliament for the execution of them, is under the same fetters as the amendment of Mʳ Morris will impose on the Senate. It was refused yesterday to permit even the Legislature to lay duties on exports. Under the clause, without the amendment, the Senate alone can make a Treaty, requiring all the Rice of S. Carolina to be sent to some one particular port.

Mʳ DICKINSON concurred in the amendment, as most safe and proper, tho' he was sensible it was unfavorable to the little States; wᶜʰ would otherwise have an *equal* share in making Treaties.

---

[11] The words "the following" are here inserted in the transcript.

Doc.r JOHNSON thought there was something of solecism in saying that the acts of a Minister with plenipotentiary powers from one Body, should depend for ratification on another Body. The Example of the King of G. B. was not parallel. Full & compleat power was vested in him. If the Parliament should fail to provide the necessary means of execution, the Treaty would be violated.

M.r GHORUM in answer to M.r Gov.r MORRIS, said that negociations on the spot were not to be desired by us, especially if the whole Legislature is to have any thing to do with Treaties. It will be generally influenced by two or three men, who will be corrupted by the Ambassadors here. In such a Government as ours, it is necessary to guard against the Government itself being seduced.

M.r RANDOLPH observing that almost every Speaker had made objections to the clause as it stood, moved in order to a further consideration of the subject, that the Motion of M.r Gov.r Morris should be postponed, and on this question It was lost the States being equally divided.

Mass.ts no. Con.t no. N. J. ay. Pen.a ay. Del. ay. M.d ay. V.a ay. N. C. no. S. C. no. Geo. no.[12]

On M.r Gov.r Morris Motion

Mas.ts no. Con.t no. N. J. no. P.a ay. Del. no. M.d no. V.a no. N. C. div.d S. C. no. Geo. no.[13]

The several clauses of Sect: 1. Art IX, were then separately postponed after inserting "and other public Ministers" next after "Ambassadors."

M.r MADISON hinted for consideration, whether a distinction might not be made between different sorts of Treaties—Allowing the President & Senate to make Treaties eventual and of Alliance for limited terms—and requiring the concurrence of the whole Legislature in other Treaties.

The 1.st Sect art IX. was finally referred nem: con: to the committee of Five, and the House then

Adjourned

---

[12] In the transcript the vote reads: "New Jersey, Pennsylvania, Delaware, Maryland, Virginia, aye—5; Massachusetts, Connecticut, North Carolina, South Carolina, Georgia, no—5."

[13] In the transcript the vote reads: "Pennsylvania, aye—1; Massachusetts, Connecticut, New Jersey, Delaware, Maryland, Virginia, South Carolina, Georgia, no—8."

## Friday August 24. 1787.[14] In Convention

Governour LIVINGSTON, from the Committee of Eleven, to whom were referred the two remaining clauses of the 4th Sect & the 5 & 6 Sect: of the 7th art:[15] delivered in the following Report:

"Strike out so much of the 4th Sect: as was referred to the Committee and insert—"The migration or importation of such persons as the several States now existing shall think proper to admit, shall not be prohibited by the Legislature prior to the year 1800, but a tax or duty may be imposed on such migration or importation at a rate not exceeding the average of the duties laid on imports."

"The 5 Sect: to remain as in the Report"

"The 6 Sect to be stricken out"

Mr BUTLER, according to notice, moved that clause 1st sect. 1. of Art VII, as to the discharge of debts, be reconsidered tomorrow. He dwelt on the division of opinion concerning the domestic debts, and the different pretensions of the different classes of holders. Genl PINKNEY 2ded him.

Mr RANDOLPH wished for a reconsideration in order to better the expression, and to provide for the case of the State debts as is done by Congress.

On the question for reconsidering

N. H. no. Mas: ay. Cont ay N. J. ay. Pena absent. Del. ay Md no. Va ay. N. C. absent, S. C. ay. Geo. ay.[16]—and tomorrow assigned for the reconsideration.

Sect: 2 & 3 of art: IX[17] being taken up,

Mr RUTLIDGE said this provision for deciding controversies between the States was necessary under the Confederation, but will be rendered unnecessary by the National Judiciary now to be established, and moved to strike it out.

Docr JOHNSON 2ded the Motion

Mr SHERMAN concurred: so did Mr DAYTON.

Mr WILLIAMSON was for postponing instead of striking out, in order to consider whether this might not be a good provision, in

---

[14] The year "1787" is omitted in the transcript.
[15] See *ante*.
[16] In the transcript the vote reads: "Massachusetts, Connecticut, New Jersey, Delaware, Virginia, South Carolina, Georgia, aye—7; New Hampshire ,Maryland, no—2; Pennsylvania, North Carolina, absent."
[17] See *ante*.

cases where the Judiciary were interested or too closely connected with the parties.

Mr GHORUM had doubts as to striking out. The Judges might be connected with the States being parties—He was inclined to think the mode proposed in the clause would be more satisfactory than to refer such cases to the Judiciary.

On the Question for postponing the 2ᵈ & 3ᵈ Section, it passed in the negative

N. H. ay. Masᵗˢ no. Conᵗ no  N. J. no.  Penᵃ absᵗ  Del. no. Mᵈ no.  Vᵃ no.  N. C. ay.  S. C. no.  Geo. ay.[18]

Mr WILSON urged the striking out, the Judiciary being a better provision.

On Question for striking out [19] 2 & 3 Sections [20] Art: IX

N. H. ay.  Mas. ay.  Cᵗ ay.  N. J. ay.  Pᵃ absᵗ  Del. ay. Mᵈ ay.  Vᵃ ay.  N. C. no.  S. C. ay.  Geo. no.[21]

Art. X. sect. 1.[22] "The executive power of the U. S. shall be vested in a single person. His stile shall be "The President of the U. S. of America" and his title shall be "His Excellency." He shall be elected by ballot by the Legislature. He shall hold his office during the term of seven years; but shall not be elected a second time.

On the question for vesting the power in a *single person*. It was agreed to nem: con: So also on the *Stile* and *title*.

Mr RUTLIDGE moved to insert "joint" before the word "ballot," as the most convenient mode of electing.

Mr SHERMAN objected to it as depriving the *States* represented in the *Senate* of the negative intended them in that house.

Mr GHORUM said it was wrong to be considering at every turn whom the Senate would represent. The public good was the true object to be kept in view. Great delay and confusion would ensue if the two Houses shᵈ vote separately, each having a negative on the choice of the other.

---

[18] In the transcript the vote reads: "New Hampshire, North Carolina, Georgia, aye—3; Massachusetts, Connecticut, New Jersey, Delaware, Maryland, Virginia, South Carolina, no—7; Pennsylvania, absent."
[19] The word "the" is here inserted in the transcript.
[20] The word "of" is here inserted in the transcript.
[21] In the transcript the vote reads: "New Hampshire, Massachusetts, Connecticut, New Jersey, Delaware, Maryland, Virginia, South Carolina, aye—8; North Carolina, Georgia, no—2; Pennsylvania, absent."
[22] See *ante*.

M: DAYTON. It might be well for those not to consider how the Senate was constituted, whose interest it was to keep it out of sight.—If the amendment should be agreed to, a *joint* [23] ballot would in fact give the appointment to one House. He could never agree to the clause with such an amendment. There could be no doubt of the two Houses separately concurring in the same person for President. The importance & necessity of the case would ensure a concurrence.

M: CARROL moved to strike out "by the Legislature" and insert "by the people." M: WILSON 2$^{ded}$ him & on the question

N. H. no.   Mass$^{ts}$ no.   Con$^t$ no.   N. J. no.   P$^a$ ay.   Del. ay.   M$^d$ no.   V$^a$ no   N. C. no.   S. C. no.   Geo. no.[24]

M: BREARLY was opposed to the motion for [25] inserting the word "joint." The argument that the small States should not put their hands into the pockets of the large ones did not apply in this case.

M: WILSON urged the reasonableness of giving the larger States a larger share of the appointment, and the danger of delay from a disagreement of the two Houses. He remarked also that the Senate had peculiar powers balancing the advantage given by a joint balot in this case to the other branch of the Legislature.

M: LANGDON. This general officer ought to be elected by the joint & general voice. In N. Hampshire the mode of separate votes by the two Houses was productive of great difficulties. The negative of the Senate would hurt the feelings of the man elected by the votes of the other branch. He was for inserting "joint" tho' unfavorable to N. Hampshire as a small State.

M: WILSON remarked that as the President of the Senate was to be President of the U. S. that Body in cases of vacancy might have an interest in throwing dilatory obstacles in the way, if its separate concurrence should be required.

M: MADISON. If the amendment be agreed to the rule of voting will give to the largest State, compared with the smallest, an influence as 4 to 1 only, altho the population is as 10 to 1. This surely

---

[23] The transcript does not italicize the word "*joint.*"
[24] In the transcript the vote reads: "Pennsylvania, Delaware, aye—2; New Hampshire, Massachusetts, Connecticut, New Jersey, Maryland, Virginia, North Carolina, South Carolina, Georgia, no—9."
[25] The words "the motion for" are omitted in the transcript.

can not be unreasonable as the President is to act for the *people* not for the *States*. The President of the *Senate* also is to be occasionally President of the U. S. and by his negative alone can make ¾ of the other branch necessary to the passage of a law. This is another advantage enjoyed by the Senate.

On the question for inserting "joint," it passed in the affirmative

N. H. ay. Mas<sup>ts</sup> ay. C<sup>t</sup> no N. J. no. P<sup>a</sup> ay. Del. ay. M<sup>d</sup> no V<sup>a</sup> ay. N. C. ay. S. C. ay. Geo. no.[26]

M<sup>r</sup> DAYTON then moved to insert, after the word "Legislatures"[27] the words "each State having one vote" M<sup>r</sup> BREARLEY 2<sup>ded</sup> him, and on the question it passed in the negative

N. H. no. Mas. no. C<sup>t</sup> ay. N. J. ay. P<sup>a</sup> no. Del. ay. M<sup>d</sup> ay. V<sup>a</sup> no. N. C. no. S. C. no. Geo. ay.[28]

M<sup>r</sup> PINKNEY moved to insert after the word "Legislature" the words "to which election a majority of the votes of the members present shall be required" &

On this question, it passed in the affirmative

N. H. ay. Mas. ay. C<sup>t</sup> ay. N. J. no. P<sup>a</sup> ay. Del. ay. M<sup>d</sup> ay. V<sup>a</sup> ay. N. C. ay. S. C. ay. Geo. ay.[29]

M<sup>r</sup> READ moved "that in case the numbers for the two highest in votes should be equal, then the President of the Senate shall have an additional casting vote," which was disagreed to by a general negative.

M<sup>r</sup> Gov<sup>r</sup> MORRIS opposed the election of the President by the Legislature. He dwelt on the danger of rendering the Executive uninterested in maintaining the rights of his Station, as leading to Legislative tyranny. If the Legislature have the Executive depedent on them, they can perpetuate & support their usurpations by the influence of tax-gatherers & other officers, by fleets armies &c. Cabal & corruption are attached to that mode of election: so also [30] is ineligibility a second time. Hence the Executive is interested in Courting popularity in the Legislature by

---

[26] In the transcript the vote reads: "New Hampshire, Massachusetts, Pennsylvania, Delaware, Virginia, North Carolina, South Carolina, aye—7; Connecticut, New Jersey, Maryland, Georgia, no—4."

[27] In the transcript the word "Legislatures" is in the singular.

[28] In the transcript the vote reads: "Connecticut, New Jersey, Delaware, Maryland, Georgia, aye—5; New Hampshire, Massachusetts, Pennsylvania, Virginia, North Carolina, South Carolina, no—6."

[29] In the transcript the vote reads: "New Hampshire, Massachusetts, Connecticut, Pennsylvania, Delaware, Maryland, Virginia, North Carolina, South Carolina, Georgia, aye—10; New Jersey, no—1."

[30] The word "also" is omitted in the transcript.

sacrificing his Executive Rights; & then he can go into that Body, after the expiration of his Executive office, and enjoy there the fruits of his policy. To these considerations he added that rivals would be continually intrigueing to oust the President from his place. To guard against all these evils he moved that the President "shall be chosen by Electors to be chosen by the People of the several States" M. CARROL 2ded him & on the question it passed in the negative.

N. H. no.  Mas. no.  C.t ay.  N. J. ay.  P.a ay.  Del. ay.  M.d no. V.a ay.  N. C. no.  S. C. no.  Geo. no.[31]

M. DAYTON moved to postpone the consideration of the two last clauses of Sect. 1. art. X. which was disagreed to without a count of the States.

M. BROOME moved to refer the two clauses to a Committee of a member from each State, & on the question, it failed the States being equally divided

N. H. no.  Mas. no.  C.t div.d  N. J. ay.  P.a ay.  Del. ay.  M.d ay. V.a ay.  N. C. no.  S. C. no.  Geo. no.[32]

On the question taken on the first part of M. Gov. Morris's Motion towit "shall be chosen by electors" as an abstract question, it failed the States being equally divided.

N. H. no.  Mas. abs.t  C.t div.d  N. Jersey ay.  P.a ay.  Del. ay. M.d div.d  V.a ay.  N. C. no.  S. C. no.  Geo. no.[33]

The consideration of the remaining clauses of Sect 1. art X. was then postponed till tomorrow at the instance of the Deputies of New Jersey.

Sect. 2. Art: X [34] being taken up, the word information was transposed & inserted after "Legislature"

On motion of M. Gov. MORRIS, "he may" was struck out, & "and" inserted before "recommend" in clause 2.d sect 2.d art: X. in order to make it the *duty* of the President to recommend, & thence prevent umbrage or cavil at his doing it.

---

[31] In the transcript the vote reads: "Connecticut, New Jersey, Pennsylvania, Delaware, Virginia, aye—5; New Hampshire, Massachusetts, Maryland, North Carolina, South Carolina, Georgia, no—6."

[32] In the transcript the vote reads: "New Jersey, Pennsylvania, Delaware, Maryland, Virginia, aye—5; New Hampshire, Massachusetts, North Carolina, South Carolina, Georgia, no—5; Connecticut, divided."

[33] In the transcript the vote reads: "New Jersey, Pennsylvania, Delaware, Virginia, aye—4; New Hampshire, North Carolina, South Carolina, Georgia, no—4; Connecticut, Maryland, divided; Massachusetts, absent."

[34] See *ante*.

Mr SHERMAN objected to the sentence "and shall appoint officers in all cases not otherwise provided for by [35] this Constitution." He admitted it to be proper that many officers in the Executive Department should be so appointed—but contended that many ought not, as general officers in the army in time of peace &c. Herein lay the corruption in G. Britain. If the Executive can model the army, he may set up an absolute Government; taking advantage of the close of a war and an army commanded by his creatures. James 2ḍ was not obeyed by his officers because they had been appointed by his predecessors not by himself. He moved to insert "or by law" after the word "Constitution."

On Motion of Mr MADISON "officers" was truck out and "to offices" inserted, in order to obviate doubts that he might appoint officers without a previous creation of the offices by the Legislature.

On the question for inserting "or by law as moved by Mr Sherman

N. H. no. Mas. no. Cṭ ay. N. J. no. Penạ no. Del. no. Mḍ no. Vạ no. N. C. absent. S. C. no. Geo. no.[36]

Mr DICKINSON moved to strike out the words "and shall appoint to offices in all cases not otherwise provided for by this Constitution" and insert—"and shall appoint to all offices established by this Constitution, except in cases herein otherwise provided for, and to all offices which may hereafter be created by law."

Mr RANDOLPH observed that the power of appointments was a formidable one both in the Executive & Legislative hands—and suggested whether the Legislature should not be left at liberty to refer appointments in some cases, to some State authority.

Mr DICKENSON's motion, it [37] passed in the affirmative

N. H. no. Mas. no. Cṭ ay. N. J. ay. Pạ ay. Del. no. Mḍ ay. Vạ ay. N. C. absṭ S. C. no. Geo. ay.[38]

Mr DICKINSON then moved to annex to his last amendment "except where by law the appointment shall be vested in the Legislatures or Executives of the several States." Mr RANDOLPH 2ḍeḍ the motion

---

[35] The word "in" is substituted in the transcript for "by."

[36] In the transcript the vote reads: "Connecticut, aye—1; New Hampshire, Massachusetts, New Jersey, Pennsylvania, Delaware, Maryland, Virginia, South Carolina, Georgia, no—9; North Carolina, absent."

[37] The word "it" is omitted in the transcript.

[38] In the transcript the vote reads: "Connecticut, New Jersey, Pennsylvania, Maryland, Virginia, Georgia, aye—6; New Hampshire, Massachusetts, Delaware, South Carolina, no—4; North Carolina, absent."

Mr WILSON— If this be agreed to it will soon be a standing instruction from the State Legislatures to pass no law creating offices, unless the app$^{ts}$ be referred to them.

Mr SHERMAN objected to "Legislatures" in the motion, which was struck out by consent of the movers.

Mr Govr MORRIS. This would be putting it in the power of the States to say, "You shall be viceroys but we will be viceroys over you"—

The Motion was negatived without a Count of the States—

Ordered unanimously that the order respecting the adjournment at 4 OClock be repealed, & that in future the House assemble at 10 OC. & adjourn at 3 OC.[39]

Adjourned

---

SATURDAY AUGUST. 25. 1787.[40] IN CONVENTION

The 1$^{st}$ clause of 1 Sect. of art: VII [41] being reconsidered

Col. MASON objected to the term "*shall*"—fullfil the engagements & discharge the debts &c as too strong. It may be impossible to comply with it. The Creditors should be kept in the same plight. They will in one respect be necessarily and properly in a better. The Government will be more able to pay them. The use of the term *shall* will beget speculations and increase the pestilent practice of stock-jobbing. There was a great distinction between original creditors & those who purchased fraudulently of the ignorant and distressed. He did not mean to include those who have bought Stock in open market. He was sensible of the difficulty of drawing the line in this case, but He did not wish to preclude the attempt. Even fair purchasers at 4. 5. 6. 8 for 1 did not stand on the same footing with [42] first Holders, supposing them not to be blameable. The interest they receive even in paper is equal to their purchase money. What he particularly wished was to leave the door open for buying up the securities,

---

[39] The letters "OC" are omitted in the transcript.
[40] The year "1787" is omitted in the transcript
[41] See *ante*.
[42] The word "the" is here inserted in the transcript.

which he thought would be precluded by the term "shall" as requiring *nominal payment*, & which was not inconsistent with his ideas of public faith. He was afraid also the word *shall*, might extend to all the old continental paper.

Mr LANGDON wished to do no more than leave the Creditors in statu quo.

Mr GERRY said that for himself he had no interest in the question being not possessed of more of the securities than would, by the interest, pay his taxes. He would observe however that as the public had received the value of the literal amount, they ought to pay that value to some body. The frauds on *the soldiers* ought to have been foreseen. These poor & ignorant people could not but part with their securities. There are other creditors who will part with any thing rather than be cheated of the capital of their advances. The interest of the States he observed was different on this point, some having more, others less than their proportion of the paper. Hence the idea of a scale for reducing its value had arisen. If the public faith would admit, of which he was not clear, he would not object to a revision of the debt so far as to compel restitution to the ignorant & distressed, who have been defrauded. As to Stock-jobbers he saw no reason for the censures thrown on them. They keep up the value of the paper. Without them there would be no market.

Mr BUTLER said he meant neither to increase nor diminish the security of the creditors.

Mr RANDOLPH moved to postpone the clause in favor of the following "All debts contracted & engagements entered into, by or under the authority of Congs shall be as valid agst the U. States under this constitution as under the Confederation."

Docr JOHNSON. The debts are debts of the U- S- of the great Body of America. Changing the Government can not change the obligation of the U- S- which devolves of course on the New Government. Nothing was in his opinion necessary to be said. If any thing, it should be a mere declaration as moved by Mr Randolph.

Mr Govr MORRIS, said he never had become a public Creditor that he might urge with more propriety the compliance with public faith. He had always done so and always would, and preferr'd the term *shall* as most explicit. As to *buying up* the debt, the term *shall* was not inconsistent with it, if provision be first made for paying the interest: if not, such an expedient was a mere evasion. He was content to say nothing as the New Government would be bound of course—but would prefer the clause with the term "*shall*, because it would create many friends to the plan.

On Mr Randolph's Motion -

N. H. ay. Mas. ay. Ct ay. N. J. ay. Pa no Del. ay. Maryd ay Va ay. N. C. ay. S. C. ay. Geo ay.[43]

Mr SHERMAN thought it necessary to connect with the clause for laying taxes duties &c an express provision for the object of the old debts &c—and moved to add to the 1st clause of 1st sect. art VII "for the payment of said debts and for the defraying the expences that shall be incurred for the common defence and general welfare."

The proposition, as being unnecessary was disagreed to, Connecticut alone, being in the affirmative.

The Report of the Committee of eleven [see friday the 24th instant] being taken up,

Genl PINKNEY moved to strike out the words "the year eighteen hundred" as the year limiting the importation of slaves, and to insert the words "the year eighteen hundred and eight"

Mr GHORUM 2ded the motion

Mr MADISON. Twenty years will produce all the mischief that can be apprehended from the liberty to import slaves. So long a term will be more dishonorable to the National [44] character than to say nothing about it in the Constitution.

On the motion; which passed in the affirmative.

N. H. ay. Mas. ay. Ct ay. N. J. no. Pa no. Del. no. Md ay. Va no. N. C. ay. S. C. ay. Geo. ay.[45]

Mr Govr MORRIS was for making the clause read at once, "[46] importation of slaves into N. Carolina, S. Carolina & Georgia

---

[43] In the transcript the vote reads: "New Hampshire, Massachusetts, Connecticut, New Jersey," Delaware, Maryland, Virginia, North Carolina, South Carolina, Georgia, aye—10; Pennsylvania, no—1.

[44] The word "American" is substituted in the transcript for "National."

[45] In the transcript the vote reads: "New Hampshire, Massachusetts, Connecticut, Maryland, North Carolina, South Carolina, Georgia, aye—7; New Jersey, Pennsylvania, Delaware, Virginia, no—4."

[46] The word "the" is here inserted in the transcript.

shall not be prohibited &c." This he said would be most fair and would avoid the ambiguity by which, under the power with regard to naturalization, the liberty reserved to the States might be defeated. He wished it to be known also that this part of the Constitution was a compliance with those States. If the change of language however should be objected to by the members from those States, he should not urge it.

Col: MASON was not against using the term "slaves" but ag$^{st}$ naming N. C. S. C. & Georgia, lest it should give offence to the people of those States.

M$^r$ SHERMAN liked a description better than the terms proposed, which had been declined by the old Cong$^s$ & were not pleasing to some people. M$^r$ CLYMER concurred with M$^r$ Sherman

M$^r$ WILLIAMSON said that both in opinion & practice he was, against slavery; but thought it more in favor of humanity, from a view of all circumstances, to let in S. C. & Georgia on those terms, than to exclude them from the Union.

M$^r$ Gov$^r$ MORRIS withdrew his motion.

M$^r$ DICKENSON wished the clause to be confined to the States which had not themselves prohibited the importation of slaves, and for that purpose moved to amend the clause so as to read " The importation of slaves into such of the States as shall permit the same shall not be prohibited by the Legislature of the U- S- until the year 1808 "—which was disagreed to nem: cont: *

The first part of the report was then agreed to, amended as follows.

"The migration or importation of such persons as the several States now existing shall think proper to admit, shall not be prohibited by the Legislature prior to the year 1808."

   N. H. Mas. Con. M$^d$ N. C. S. C. Geo: ay [47]
   N. J. P$^a$ Del. Virg$^a$.............no [48]

M$^r$ BALDWIN in order to restrain & more explicitly define "the average duty" moved to strike out of the 2$^d$ part the words "average of the duties laid on imports" and insert "common impost on articles not enumerated" which was agreed to nem: cont:

---

\* In the printed Journal, Con$^t$ Virg$^a$ & Georgia voted in the affirmative.
[47] The figure "7" is here inserted in the transcript.
[48] The figure "4" is here inserted in the transcript.

M.^r SHERMAN was ag.^st this 2.^d part, as acknowledging men to be property, by taxing them as such under the character of slaves.

M.^r KING & M.^r LANGDON considered this as the price of the 1.^st part.

Gen.^l PINKNEY admitted that it was so.

Col: MASON. Not to tax, will be equivalent to a bounty on the importation of slaves.

M.^r GHORUM thought that M.^r Sherman should consider the duty, not as implying that slaves are property, but as a discouragement to the importation of them.

M.^r GOV.^r MORRIS remarked that as the clause now stands it implies that the Legislature may tax freemen imported.

M.^r SHERMAN in answer to M.^r Ghorum observed that the smallness of the duty shewed revenue to be the object, not the discouragement of the importation.

M.^r MADISON thought it wrong to admit in the Constitution the idea that there could be property in men. The reason of duties did not hold, as slaves are not like merchandize, consumed, &c

Col. MASON (in answ.^r to Gov.^r Morris) the provision as it stands was necessary for the case of Convicts in order to prevent the introduction of them.

It was finally agreed nem: contrad: to make the clause read "but a tax or duty may be imposed on such importation not exceeding ten dollars for each person," and then the 2.^d part as amended was agreed to.

Sect 5. art. VII was agreed to nem: con: as reported.

Sect. 6. art. VII. in the Report, was postponed.

On motion of M.^r MADISON 2.^ded by M.^r GOV.^r MORRIS Art VIII was reconsidered and after the words "all treaties made," were inserted nem: con: the words "or which shall be made" This insertion was meant to obviate all doubt concerning the force of treaties preexisting, by making the words "all treaties made" to refer to them, as the words inserted would refer to future treaties.

M.^r CARROL & M.^r L. MARTIN expressed their apprehensions, and the probable apprehensions of their constituents, that under the power of regulating trade the General Legislature, might favor the ports of particular States, by requiring vessels destened to or from other States to enter & clear thereat, as vessels belonging or bound to Baltimore, to enter & clear at Norfolk &c They moved the following proposition

"The Legislature of the U: S: shall not oblige vessels belonging to citizens thereof, or to foreigners, to enter or pay duties or imposts in any other State than in that to which they may be bound, or to clear out in any other than the State in which their cargoes may be laden on board; nor shall any privilege or immunity be granted to any vessels on entering or clearing out, or paying duties or imposts in one State in preference to another"

Mr GHORUM thought such a precaution unnecessary; & that the revenue might be defeated, if vessels could run up long rivers, through the jurisdiction of different States without being required to enter, with the opportunity of landing & selling their cargoes by the way.

Mr McHENRY & Genl PINKNEY made the following propositions

"Should it be judged expedient by the Legislature of the U. S. that one or more ports for collecting duties or imposts other than those ports of entrance & clearance already established by the respective States, should be established, the Legislature of the U. S. shall signify the same to the Executives of the respective States, ascertaining the number of such ports judged necessary; to be laid by the said Executives before the Legislatures of the States at their next Session; and the Legislature of the U. S. shall not have the power of fixing or establishing the particular ports for collecting duties or imposts in any State, except the Legislature of such State shall neglect to fix and establish the same during their first session to be held after such notification by the Legislature of the U. S. to the Executive of such State"

"All duties imposts & excises, prohibitions or restraints laid or made by the Legislature of the U. S. shall be uniform & equal throughout the U. S."

These several propositions were referred, nem: con: to a Committee composed of a member from each State. The committee appointed by ballot were Mr Langdon, Mr Ghorum, Mr Sherman,

M̰ Dayton, M̰ Fitzimmons, M̰ Read, M̰ Carrol, M̰ Mason, M̰ Williamson, M̰ Butler, Mr. Few.

On the question now taken on M̰ Dickinson motion of yesterday, allowing appointments to offices, to be referred by the Gen! Legislature to the Executives of the Several States" as a farther amendment to sect. 2, art. X. the votes were,

N. H. no. Mas. no. C̰ ay. P̰ no. Del. no. M̰ divided. V̰ ay. N. C. no. S. C. no. Geo. ay.[50]

In amendment of the same section,[51] "other public Ministers" were inserted after "ambassadors."

M̰ Gov̰ Morris moved to strike out of the section—"and may correspond with the supreme Executives of the several States" as unnecessary and implying that he could not correspond with others. M̰ Broome 2$^{ded}$ him.

On the question

N. H. ay. Mas. ay. C̰ ay. P̰ ay. Del. ay. M̰ no. V̰ ay. N. C. ay. S. C. ay. Geo. ay.[52]

[53] "Shall receive ambassadors & other public Ministers," [54] agreed to, nem. con.

M̰ Sherman moved to amend the "power to grant reprieves & pardon [55]" so as to read "to grant reprieves until the ensuing session of the Senate, and pardons with consent of the Senate."

On the question

N. H. no. Mas. no. C̰ ay. P̰ no M̰ no. V̰ no. N. C. no. S. C. no. Geo. no.[56]

[57] "except in cases of impeachment" [58] inserted nem: con: after "pardon" [55]

On the question to agree to —"but his pardon shall not be pleadable in bar" [59]

---

[49] See *ante*.
[50] In the transcript the vote reads: "Connecticut, Virginia, Georgia, aye—3; New Hampshire, Massachusetts, Pennsylvania, Delaware, North Carolina, South Carolina, no—6; Maryland, divided."
[51] The expression "the words" is here inserted in the transcript.
[52] In the transcript the vote reads: "New Hampshire, Massachusetts, Connecticut, Pennsylvania, Delaware, Virginia, North Carolina, South Carolina, Georgia, aye—9; Maryland, no—1."
[53] The words "The clause" are here inserted in the transcript.
[54] The word "was" is here inserted in the transcript.
[55] The transcript uses the word "pardon" in the plural.
[56] In the transcript the vote reads: "Connecticut, aye—1; New Hampshire, Massachusetts, Pennsylvania, Maryland, Virginia, North Carolina, South Carolina, Georgia, no—8."
[57] The expression "the words" is here inserted in the transcript.
[58] The word "were" is here inserted in the transcript.
[59] The phrase "It passed in the negative" is here inserted in the transcript.

621

N. H. ay. Mas. no. C⟨ no. P⟨ no. Del. no. M⟨ ay. V⟨ no.
N. C. ay. S. C. ay. Geo. no.⁶⁰

Adjourned

---

MONDAY AUG⟨ᵀ 27ᵀᴴ 1787.⁶¹ IN CONVENTION

Art X. Sect. 2.⁶² being resumed.

M⟨ L. MARTIN moved to insert the words "after conviction" after the words "reprieves and pardons"

M⟨ WILSON objected that pardon before conviction might be necessary in order to obtain the testimony of accomplices. He stated the case of forgeries in which this might particularly happen.—M⟨ L. MARTIN withdrew his motion.

M⟨ SHERMAN moved to amend the clause giving the Executive the command of the Militia, so as to read "and of the Militia of the several States, *when called into the actual service of the U. S.*" and on the Question

N. H. ay. Mas. abs⟨ C⟨ ay. N. J. abs⟨ P⟨ ay. Del. no. M⟨ ay. V⟨ ay. N. C. abs⟨ S. C. no. Geo. ay.⁶³

The clause for removing the President on impeachment by the House of Rep⟨ and conviction in the supreme Court, of Treason, Bribery or corruption, was postponed nem: con: at the instance of M⟨ Gov⟨ MORRIS, who thought the Tribunal an improper one, particularly, if the first judge was to be of the privy Council.

M⟨ Gov⟨ MORRIS objected also to the President of the Senate being provisional successor to the President, and suggested a designation of the Chief Justice.

M⟨ MADISON added as a ground of objection that the Senate might retard the appointment of a President in order to carry points whilst the revisionary power was in the President of their own body, but suggested that the Executive powers during a vacancy, be administered by the persons composing the Council to the President.

---

⁶⁰ In the transcript the vote reads: "New Hampshire, Maryland, North Carolina, South Carolina, aye—4; Massachusetts, Connecticut, Pennsylvania, Delaware, Virginia, Georgia, no—6."
⁶¹ The year "1787" is omitted in the transcript.
⁶² See *ante*.
⁶³ In the transcript the vote reads: "New Hampshire, Connecticut, Pennsylvania, Maryland, Virginia, Georgia, aye—6; Delaware, South Carolina, no—2; Massachusetts, New Jersey, North Carolina, absent."

M! WILLIAMSON suggested that the Legislature ought to have power to provide for occasional successors & moved that the last clause [of 2 sect. X art:] relating to a provisional successor to the President be postponed.

M! DICKINSON 2 ded the postponement, remarking that it was too vague. What is the extent of the term "disability" & who is to be the judge of it?

The postponement was agreed to nem: con:

Col: MASON & M! MADISON, moved to add to the oath to be taken by the supreme Executive "and will to the best of my judgment and power preserve protect and defend the Constitution of the U. S."

M! WILSON thought the general provision for oaths of office, in a subsequent place, rendered the amendment unnecessary—

On the question

N. H. ay. Mas. abs! C! ay. P? ay. Del. no. M? ay. V? ay. N. C. abs! S. C. ay. Geo. ay.[64]

Art: XI.[65] being [66] taken up.

Doc! JOHNSON suggested that the judicial power ought to extend to equity as well as law—and moved to insert the words "both in law and equity" after the words "U. S." in the 1st line, of sect. 1.

M! READ objected to vesting these powers in the same Court.

On the question

N. H. ay. Mas absent. C! ay. N. J. abs! P. ay. Del. no. M? no. Virg? ay. N. C. abs! S. C. ay. Geo. ay.[67]

On the question to agree to Sect. 1. art. XI. as amended.[68]

N. H. ay. Mas. abs! C! ay. P? ay. N. J. abs! Del. no. M? no. V? ay. N. C. abs! S. C. ay. Geo. ay.

M! DICKINSON moved as an amendment to sect. 2. art XI [65] after the words "good behavior" the words "provided that they may be removed by the Executive on the application by the Senate and House of Representatives."

M! GERRY 2ded the motion

---

[64] In the transcript the vote reads: "New Hampshire, Connecticut, Pennsylvania, Maryland, Virginia, South Carolina, Georgia, aye—7; Delaware, no, Massachusetts, New Jersey, North Carolina, absent."
[65] See *ante*.
[66] The word "next" is here inserted in the transcript.
[67] In the transcript the vote reads: "New Hampshire, Connecticut, Pennsylvania, Virginia, South Carolina, Georgia, aye—6; Delaware, Maryland, no—2; Massachusetts, New Jersey, North Carolina, absent "
[68] The transcript here inserts the following: "the States were the same as on the preceding question." The vote by States is omitted.

623

M: Gov: Morris thought it a contradiction in terms to say that the Judges should hold their offices during good behavior, and yet be removeable without a trial. Besides it was fundamentally wrong to subject Judges to so arbitrary an authority.

M: Sherman saw no contradiction or impropriety if this were made part of the constitutional regulation of the Judiciary establishment. He observed that a like provision was contained in the British Statutes.

M: Rutlidge. If the Supreme Court is to judge between the U. S. and particular States, this alone is an insuperable objection to the motion.

M: Wilson considered such a provision in the British Government as less dangerous than here, the House of Lords & House of Commons being less likely to concur on the same occasions. Chief Justice Holt, he remarked, had *successively* offended by his independent conduct, both houses of Parliament. Had this happened at the same time, he would have been ousted. The judges would be in a bad situation if made to depend on every [69] gust of faction which might prevail in the two branches of our Gov:

M: Randolph opposed the motion as weakening too much the independence of the Judges.

M: Dickinson was not apprehensive that the Legislature composed of different branches constructed on such different principles, would improperly unite for the purpose of displacing a Judge.

On the question for agreeing to M: Dickinson's Motion [70]

N. H. no. Mas. abs: C: ay. N. J. abs: P: no. Del. no. M: no. V: no. N. C. abs: S. C. no. Geo. no.

On the question on Sect. 2. art: XI as reported. Del & Mary: only no.

M: Madison and M: M:Henry moved to reinstate the words "increased or" before the word "diminished" in the 2: sect. art XI.

M: Gov: Morris opposed it for reasons urged by him on a former occasion—

---

[69] The word "any" is substituted in the transcript for "every."
[70] The transcript here inserts the following: "it was negatived, Connecticut, aye; all the other States present, no." The vote by States is omitted.

Col: MASON contended strenuously for the motion. There was no weight he said in the argument drawn from changes in the value of the metals, because this might be provided for by an increase of salaries so made as not to affect persons in office, and this was the only argument on which much stress seemed to have been laid.

Gen! PINKNEY. The importance of the Judiciary will require men of the first talents: large salaries will therefore be necessary, larger than the U. S. can allow [71] in the first instance. He was not satisfied with the expedient mentioned by Col: Mason. He did not think it would have a good effect or a good appearance, for new Judges to come in with higher salaries than the old ones.

M: Gov: MORRIS said the expedient might be evaded & therefore amounted to nothing. Judges might resign, and then be reappointed to increased salaries.

On the question

N. H. no. C: no. P: no. Del. no. M$^d$ div$^d$ V: ay. S. C. no. Geo. abs: also Mas$^{ts}$ N. J. & N. C. [72]

M: RANDOLPH & M: MADISON then moved to add the following words to sect. 2. art XI. "nor increased by any Act of the Legislature which shall operate before the expiration of three years after the passing thereof"

On this question

N. H. no. C: no. P: no. Del. no. M$^d$ ay. V: ay. S. C. no. Geo. abs: also Mas. N. J. & N. C.[73]

Sect. 3. art. XI [74] being taken up, the following clause was postponed—viz. "to the trial of impeachments of officers of the U. S." by which the jurisdiction of the supreme Court was extended to such cases.

M: MADISON & M: GOV: MORRIS moved to insert after the word "controversies" the words "to which the U. S. shall be a party." which was agreed to nem: con:

Doc: JOHNSON moved to insert the words "this Constitution and the" before the word "laws"

---

[71] The word "afford" is substituted in the transcript for "allow."

[72] In the transcript the vote reads: "Virginia, aye—1; New Hampshire, Connecticut, Pennsylvania, Delaware, South Carolina, no—5; Maryland, divided. Massachusetts, New Jersey, North Carolina, Georgia, absent."

[73] In the transcript the vote reads: "Maryland, Virginia, aye—2; New Hampshire, Connecticut, Pennsylvania, Delaware, South Carolina, no—5; Massachusetts, New Jersey, North Carolina, Georgia, absent."

[74] See *ante*.

625

M: MADISON doubted whether it was not going too far to extend the jurisdiction of the Court generally to cases arising under the Constitution & whether it ought not to be limited to cases of a Judiciary Nature. The right of expounding the Constitution in cases not of this nature ought not to be given to that Department.

The motion of Doc: Johnson was agreed to nem: con: it being generally supposed that the jurisdiction given was constructively limited to cases of a Judiciary nature.

On motion of M: RUTLIDGE the words "passed by the Legislature" were struck out, and after the words "U. S" were inserted nem. con: the words "and treaties made or which shall be made under their authority" conformably to a preceding amendment in another place.

The clause "in cases of impeachment," was postponed.

M: GOV: MORRIS wished to know what was meant by the words "In all the cases before mentioned it [jurisdiction] shall be appellate with such exceptions &c," whether it extended to matters of fact as well as law—and to cases of Common law as well as Civil law.

M: WILSON. The Committee he believed meant facts as well as law & Common as well as Civil law. The jurisdiction of the federal Court of Appeals had he said been so construed.

M: DICKINSON moved to add after the word "appellate" the words both as to law & fact which was agreed to nem: con:

M: MADISON & M: GOV: MORRIS moved to strike out the beginning of the 3ᵈ sect. "The jurisdiction of the supreme Court" & to insert the words "the Judicial power" which was agreed to nem: con:

The following motion was disagreed to, to wit to insert "In all the other cases before mentioned the Judicial power shall be exercised in such manner as the Legislature shall direct"

Del. Virgᵃ ay [75]

N. H Con. P. M. S. C. G no [76]

On a question for striking out the last sentence of sect. 3. "The Legislature may assign &c." [77]

---

[75] The figure "2" is here inserted in the transcript.
[76] The figure "6" is here inserted in the transcript.
[77] The phrase "it passed *nem. con.*" is here added in the transcript.

N. H. ay. C! ay. P? ay. Del. ay. M? ay. V? ay. S. C. ay. Geo. ay.[78]

M? SHERMAN moved to insert after the words "between Citizens of different States" the words, "between Citizens of the same State claiming lands under grants of different States"—according to the provision in the 9th Art: of the Confederation—which was agreed to nem: con:

Adjourned

---

TUESDAY AUGUST 28. 1787.[79] IN CONVENTION

M? SHERMAN from the Committee to whom were referred several propositions on the 25th instant, made the following report—[80]

That there be inserted after the 4 clause of [81] 7th section

"Nor shall any regulation of commerce or revenue give preference to the ports of one State over those of another, or oblige vessels bound to or from any State to enter, clear or pay duties in another and all tonnage, duties, imposts & excises laid by the Legislature shall be uniform throughout the U. S."

Ordered to lie on the table.[82]

Art XI Sect. 3 [83],[84] It was moved to strike out the words "it shall be appellate" & to insert the words "the supreme Court shall have appellate jurisdiction,"—in order to prevent uncertainty whether "it" referred to the *supreme Court*, or to the *Judicial power*.

On the question

N. H ay. Mas. ay. C! ay. N. J. abs! P? ay. Del. ay. M? no. V? ay. N C ay. S. C. ay. Geo. ay.[85]

Sect. 4.[86] was so amended nem: con: as to read "The trial of all crimes (except in cases of impeachment) shall be by jury, and such trial shall be held in the State where the said crimes

---

[78] The vote by States is omitted in the transcript.
[79] The year "1787" is omitted in the transcript.
[80] The phrase "which was ordered to lie on the table" is here added in the transcript.
[81] The word "the" is here inserted in the transcript.
[82] This sentence is omitted in the transcript.
[83] See *ante*.
[84] The words "being considered" are here inserted in the transcript.
[85] In the transcript the vote reads: "New Hampshire, Massachusetts, Connecticut, Pennsylvania, Delaware, Virginia, North Carolina, South Carolina, Georgia, aye—9; Maryland, no—1; New Jersey absent."
[86] See *ante*.

shall have been committed; but when not committed within any State, then the trial shall be at such place or places as the Legislature may direct." The object of this amendment was to provide for trial by jury of offences committed out of any State.

Mr PINKNEY, urging the propriety of securing the benefit of the Habeas corpus in the most ample manner, moved "that it should not be suspended but on the most urgent occasions, & then only for a limited time, not exceeding twelve months"

Mr RUTLIDGE was for declaring the Habeas Corpus inviolable.[87] He did not conceive that a suspension could ever be necessary at the same time through all the States.

Mr Govr MORRIS moved that "The privilege of the writ of Habeas Corpus shall not be suspended; unless where in cases of Rebellion or invasion the public safety may require it."

Mr WILSON doubted whether in any case a suspension could be necessary, as the discretion now exists with Judges, in most important cases to keep in Gaol or admit to Bail.

The first part of Mr Govr Morris' motion, to the word "unless" was agreed to nem: con:—on the remaining part;

N. H. ay. Mas. ay. Ct ay. Pa ay. Del. ay. Md ay. Va ay. N. C. no. S. C. no. Geo. no.:[88]

Sec. 5. of art: XI.[86] was agreed to *nem: con:*\*

Art: XII.[86] being [89] taken up.

Mr WILSON & Mr SHERMAN moved to insert after the words "coin money" the words "nor emit bills of credit, nor make any thing but gold & silver coin a tender in payment of debts" making these prohibitions absolute, instead of making the measures allowable (as in the XIII art:) *with the consent of the Legislature of the U. S.*

Mr GHORUM thought the purpose would be as well secured by the provision of art: XIII which makes the consent of the Genl Legislature necessary, and that in that mode, no opposition would

---

[87] The word "inviolate" is substituted in the transcript for "inviolable."

[88] In the transcript the vote reads: "New Hampshire, Massachusetts, Connecticut, Pennsylvania, Delaware, Maryland, Virginia, aye—7; North Carolina, South Carolina, Georgia, no—3."

\* The vote on this section as stated in the printed Journal is not unanimous; the statement here is probably the right one.

[89] The word "then" is here inserted in the transcript.

be excited; whereas an absolute prohibition of paper money would rouse the most desperate opposition from its partizans.

M[r] SHERMAN thought this a favorable crisis for crushing paper money. If the consent of the Legislature could authorise emissions of it, the friends of paper money, would make every exertion to get into the Legislature in order to licence it.

The question being divided; on the 1[st] part—"nor emit bills of credit"

N. H. ay. Mas. ay. C[t] ay. P[a] ay. Del. ay. M[d] div[d] V[a] no. N. C. ay. S. C. ay. Geo. ay.[90]

The remaining part of M[r] Wilson's & Sherman's motion was agreed to nem: con:

M[r] KING moved to add, in the words used in the Ordinance of Cong[s] establishing new States, a prohibition on the States to interfere in private contracts.

M[r] GOV[r] MORRIS. This would be going too far. There are a thousand laws, relating to bringing actions—limitations of actions &[91] which affect contracts. The Judicial power of the U. S. will be a protection in cases within their jurisdiction; and within the State itself a majority must rule, whatever may be the mischief done among themselves.

M[r] SHERMAN. Why then prohibit bills of credit?

M[r] WILSON was in favor of M[r] King's motion.

M[r] MADISON admitted that inconveniences might arise from such a prohibition but thought on the whole it would be overbalanced by the utility of it. He conceived however that a negative on the State laws could alone secure the effect. Evasions might and would be devised by the ingenuity of [92] Legislatures.

Col: MASON. This is carrying the restraint too far. Cases will happen that can not be foreseen, where some kind of interference will be proper & essential. He mentioned the case of limiting the period for bringing actions on open account—that of bonds after a certain lapse of time—asking whether it was proper to tie the hands of the States from making provision in such cases?

---

[90] In the transcript the vote reads: "New Hampshire, Massachusetts, Connecticut, Pennsylvania, Delaware, North Carolina, South Carolina, Georgia, aye—8; Virginia, no—1; Maryland, divided."
[91] The character "&" is changed in the transcript to "&c."
[92] The word "the" is here inserted in the transcript.

Mr WILSON. The answer to these objections is that *retrospective* [93] interferences [94] only are to be prohibited.

Mr MADISON. Is not that already done by the prohibition of ex post facto laws, which will oblige the Judges to declare such interferences null & void.

Mr RUTLIDGE moved instead of Mr King's Motion to insert— "nor pass bills of attainder nor retrospective * laws" on which motion

N. H. ay. Ct no. N. J. ay. Pa ay. Del. ay. Md no. Virga no. N. C. ay. S. C. ay. Geo. ay.[95]

Mr MADISON moved to insert after the word "reprisal" (art. XII) the words "nor lay embargoes." He urged that such acts by the States would be unnecessary—impolitic—and unjust.

Mr SHERMAN thought the States ought to retain this power in order to prevent suffering & injury to their poor.

Col: MASON thought the amendment would be not only improper but dangerous, as the Genl Legislature would not sit constantly and therefore could not interpose at the necessary moments. He enforced his objection by appealing to the necessity of sudden embargoes during the war, to prevent exports, particularly in the case of a blockade.

Mr Govr MORRIS considered the provision as unnecessary; the power of regulating trade between State & State already vested in the Genl Legislature, being sufficient.

On the question

N. H. no. Mas. ay. Ct no. N. J. no. Pa no. Del. ay. Md no. Va no. N. C. no. S. C. ay. Geo. no.[96]

Mr MADISON moved that the words "nor lay imposts or duties on imports" be transferred from art: XIII where the consent of the Genl Legislature may licence the act—into art: XII which will make the prohibition on the States absolute. He observed that as the States interested in this power by which they could tax the imports of their neighbors passing thro' their markets,

---

[93] The transcript does not italicize the word *"retrospective."*
[94] The transcript italicizes the word "interferences."
* In the printed Journal—"ex post facto."
[95] In the transcript the vote reads: "New Hampshire, New Jersey, Pennsylvania, Delaware, North Carolina, South Carolina, Georgia, aye—7; Connecticut, Maryland, Virginia, no—3."
[96] In the transcript the vote reads: "Massachusetts, Delaware, South Carolina, aye—3; New Hampshire, Connecticut, New Jersey, Pennsylvania, Maryland, Virginia, North Carolina, Georgia, no—8."

were a majority, they could give the consent of the Legislature, to the injury of N. Jersey, N. Carolina &c-

Mr WILLIAMSON 2ded the motion

Mr SHERMAN thought the power might safely be left to the Legislature of the U. States.

Col: MASON, observed that particular States might wish to encourage by import [97] duties certain manufactures for which they enjoyed natural advantages, as Virginia, the manufacture of Hemp &c.

Mr MADISON. The encouragement of Manufactures in that mode requires duties not only on imports directly from foreign Countries, but from the other States in the Union, which would revive all the mischiefs experienced from the want of a Genl Government over commerce.

On the question

N. H. ay. Mas. no. Ct no. N. J. ay. Pa no. Del: ay. Md no. Va no. N. C. ay. S. C. no. Geo. no.[98]

Art: XII as amended [99] agreed to nem: con:

Art: XIII [1] being [2] taken up. Mr KING moved to insert after the word "imports" the words "or exports" so as to prohibit the states from taxing either,—&

On this question it passed in the affirmative.

N. H. ay. Mas. ay. Ct no. N. J. ay. P. ay. Del. ay. Md no. Va no. N. C. ay. S. C. no. Geo. no.[3]

Mr SHERMAN moved to add after the word "exports"—the words "nor with such consent but for the use of the U. S."—so as to carry the proceeds of all State duties on imports & [4] exports, into the common Treasury.

Mr MADISON liked the motion as preventing all State imposts— but lamented the complexity we were giving to the commercial system.

---

[97] The word "impost" is substituted in the transcript for "import."
[98] In the transcript the vote reads: "New Hampshire, New Jersey, Delaware, North Carolina, aye—4; Massachusetts, Connecticut, Pennsylvania, Maryland, Virginia, South Carolina, Georgia, no—7."
[99] The words "was then" are here inserted in the transcript.
[1] See *ante*.
[2] The words "was then" are substituted in the transcript for "being."
[3] In the transcript the vote reads: "New Hampshire, Massachusetts, New Jersey, Pennsylvania, Delaware, North Carolina, aye—6; Connecticut, Maryland, Virginia, South Carolina, Georgia, no—5."
[4] The word "or" is substituted for "&" in the transcript.

M: Gov: Morris thought the regulation necessary to prevent the Atlantic States from endeavoring to tax the Western States— & promote their interest by opposing the navigation of the Mississippi which would drive the Western people into the arms of G. Britain.

M: Clymer thought the encouragement of the Western Country was suicide on [5] the old States. If the States have such different interests that they can not be left to regulate their own manufactures without encountering the interests of other States, it is a proof that they are not fit to compose one nation.

M: King was afraid that the regulation moved by M: Sherman would too much interfere with a policy of States respecting their manufactures, which may be necessary. Revenue he reminded the House was the object of the general Legislature.

On M: Sherman's motion

N. H. ay. Mas. no. C: ay. N. J. ay. P: ay. Del. ay. M: no. V: ay. N. C. ay. S. C. ay. Geo. ay.[6]

Art XIII was then agreed to as amended.

Art. XIV [7] was [8] taken up.

Gen! Pinkney was not satisfied with it. He seemed to wish some provision should be included in favor of property in slaves.

On the question on Art: XIV.

N. H. ay. Mas. ay. C: ay. N. J. ay. P: ay. Del. ay. M: ay. V: ay. N. C. ay. S. C. no. Geo. divided.[9]

Art: XV [7] being taken up, the words "high misdemesnor," were struck out, and [10] "other crime" inserted, in order to comprehend all proper cases: it being doubtful whether "high misdemeanor" had not a technical meaning too limited.

M: Butler and M: Pinkney moved "to require fugitive slaves and servants to be delivered up like criminals."

M: Wilson. This would oblige the Executive of the State to do it at the public expence.

---

[5] The words "the part of" are here inserted in the transcript.

[6] In the transcript the vote reads: "New Hampshire, Connecticut, New Jersey, Pennsylvania, Delaware, Virginia, North Carolina, South Carolina, Georgia, aye—9; Massachusetts, Maryland, no—2."

[7] See ante.

[8] The word "then" is here inserted in the transcript.

[9] In the transcript the vote reads; "New Hampshire, Massachusetts, Connecticut, New Jersey, Pennsylvania, Delaware, Maryland, Virginia, North Carolina, aye—9; South Carolina, no—1; Georgia, divided."

[10] The expression "the words" is here inserted in the transcript.

Mr SHERMAN saw no more propriety in the public seizing and surrendering a slave or servant, than a horse.

Mr BUTLER withdrew his proposition in order that some particular provision might be made apart from this article.

Art XV as amended was then agreed to nem: con:

Adjourned

---

WEDNESDAY AUGUST 29<sup>th</sup> 1787.[11] IN CONVENTION

Art: XVI.[7, 12,] taken up.

Mr WILLIAMSON moved to substitute in place of it, the words of the Articles of Confederation on the same subject. He did not understand precisely the meaning of the article.

Mr WILSON & Docr JOHNSON supposed the meaning to be that Judgments in one State should be the ground of actions in other States, & that acts of the Legislatures should be included, for the sake of Acts of insolvency &c.

Mr PINKNEY moved to commit art XVI, with the following proposition, "To establish uniform laws upon the subject of bankruptcies, and respecting the damages arising on the protest of foreign bills of exchange"

Mr GHORUM was for agreeing to the article, and committing the proposition.

Mr MADISON was for committing both. He wished the Legislature might be authorized to provide for the *execution* of Judgments in other States, under such regulations as might be expedient. He thought that this might be safely done, and was justified by the nature of the Union.

Mr RANDOLPH said there was no instance of one nation executing judgments of the Courts of another nation. He moved the following proposition:

"Whenever the act of any State, whether Legislative, Executive or Judiciary shall be attested & exemplified under the seal thereof, such attestation and exemplification, shall be deemed in other States as full proof of the existence of that act—and its operation

---

[7] See *ante*.
[11] The year "1787" is omitted in the transcript.
[12] The word "being" is here inserted in the transcript.

shall be binding in every other State, in all cases to which it may relate, and which are within the cognizance and jurisdiction of the State, wherein the said act was done."

On the question for committing Art: XVI. with M! Pinkney's motion

N. H. no. Mas. no. C! ay. N. J. ay. P? ay. Del. ay. M? ay. V? ay. N. C. ay. S. C. ay. Geo. ay.[13]

The motion of M! Randolph was also committed nem: con:

M! Gov! MORRIS moved to commit also the following proposition on the same subject.

"Full faith ought to be given in each State to the public acts, records, and judicial proceedings of every other State; and the Legislature shall by general laws, determine the proof and effect of such acts, records, and proceedings," and it was committed nem: contrad:

The committee appointed for these references, were M! Rutlidge, M! Randolph, M! Gorham, M! Wilson, & M! Johnson.

M! DICKENSON mentioned to the House that on examining Blackstone's Commentaries, he found that the terms,[14] "ex post facto" related to criminal cases only; that they would not consequently restrain the States from retrospective laws in civil cases, and that some further provision for this purpose would be requisite.

Art. VII Sect. 6 by y? Committee of eleven reported to be struck out (see the 24 instant) being now taken up,

M! PINKNEY moved to postpone the Report in favor of the following proposition—"That no act of the Legislature for the purpose of regulating the commerce of the U- S. with foreign powers, or among the several States, shall be passed without the assent of two thirds of the members of each House." He remarked that there were five distinct commercial interests. 1. the fisheries & W. India trade, which belonged to the N. England States. 2. the interest of N. York lay in a free trade. 3. Wheat & flour the Staples of the two Middle States (N. J. & Penn?).

[13] In the transcript the vote reads: "Connecticut, New Jersey, Pennsylvania, Delaware, Maryland, Virginia, North Carolina, South Carolina, Georgia, aye—9; New Hampshire, Massachusetts, no—2."
[14] The transcript uses the word "terms" in the singular.

4 Tob? the staple of Mary.d & Virginia & partly of N. Carolina. 5. Rice & Indigo, the staples of S. Carolina & Georgia. These different interests would be a source of oppressive regulations if no check to a bare majority should be provided. States pursue their interests with less scruple than individuals. The power of regulating commerce was a pure concession on the part of the S. States. They did not need the protection of the N. States at present.

M.r MARTIN 2.d.e.d the motion

Gen.l PINKNEY said it was the true interest of the S. States to have no regulation of commerce; but considering the loss brought on the commerce of the Eastern States by the revolution, their liberal conduct towards the views* of South Carolina, and the interest the weak South.n States had in being united with the strong Eastern States, he thought it proper that no fetters should be imposed on the power of making commercial regulations; and that his constituents though prejudiced against the Eastern States, would be reconciled to this liberality. He had himself, he said, prejudices ag.s.t the Eastern States before he came here, but would acknowledge that he had found them as liberal and candid as any men whatever.

M.r CLYMER. The diversity of commercial interests of necessity creates difficulties, which ought not to be increased by unnecessary restrictions. The Northern & middle States will be ruined, if not enabled to defend themselves against foreign regulations.

M.r SHERMAN, alluding to M.r Pinkney's enumeration of particular interests, as requiring a security ag.s.t abuse of the power; observed that the diversity was of itself a security, adding that to require more than a majority to decide a question was always embarrassing as had been experienced in cases requiring the votes of nine States in Congress.

M.r PINKNEY replied that his enumeration meant the five minute interests. It still left the two great divisions of Northern & Southern Interests.

---

*he meant the permission to import slaves. An understanding on the two subjects of *navigation* and *slavery*, had taken place between those parts of the Union, which explains the vote on the motion depending, as well as the language of Gen.l Pinkney & others.

Mr. Govr. MORRIS, opposed the object of the motion as highly injurious. Preferences to American ships will multiply them, till they can carry the Southern produce cheaper than it is now carried.—A navy was essential to security, particularly of the S. States, and can only be had by a navigation act encouraging American bottoms & seamen. In those points of view then alone, it is the interest of the S. States that navigation acts should be facilitated. Shipping he said was the worst & most precarious kind of property, and stood in need of public patronage.

Mr. WILLIAMSON was in favor of making two thirds instead of a majority requisite, as more satisfactory to the Southern people. No useful measure he believed had been lost in Congress for want of nine votes. As to the weakness of the Southern States, he was not alarmed on that account. The sickliness of their climate for invaders would prevent their being made an object. He acknowledged that he did not think the motion requiring ⅔ necessary in itself, because if a majority of [15] Northern States should push their regulations too far, the S. States would build ships for themselves: but he knew the Southern people were apprehensive on this subject and would be pleased with the precaution.

Mr. SPAIGHT was against the motion. The Southern States could at any time save themselves from oppression, by building ships for their own use.

Mr. BUTLER differed from those who considered the rejection of the motion as no concession on the part of the S. States. He considered the interests of these and of the Eastern States, to be as different as the interests of Russia and Turkey. Being notwithstanding desirous of conciliating the affections of the East: States, he should vote agst. requiring ⅔ instead of a majority.

Col. MASON. If the Govt. is to be lasting, it must be founded in the confidence & affections of the people, and must be so constructed as to obtain these. The *Majority* will be governed by their interests. The Southern States are the *minority* in both Houses. Is it to be expected that they will deliver themselves bound hand & foot to the Eastern States, and enable them to

---

[15] The word "the" is here inserted in the transcript.

exclaim, in the words of Cromwell on a certain occasion—"the lord hath delivered them into our hands.

M.<sup>r</sup> WILSON took notice of the several objections and remarked that if every peculiar interest was to be secured, *unanimity* ought to be required. The majority he said would be no more governed by interest than the minority. It was surely better to let the latter be bound hand and foot than the former. Great inconveniences had, he contended, been experienced in Congress from the article of confederation requiring nine votes in certain cases.

M.<sup>r</sup> MADISON, went into a pretty full view of the subject. He observed that the disadvantage to the S. States from a navigation act, lay chiefly in a temporary rise of freight, attended however with an increase of South.<sup>n</sup> as well as Northern Shipping— with the emigration of Northern Seamen & merchants to the Southern States—& with a removal of the existing & injurious retaliations among the States on each other. The power of foreign nations to obstruct our retaliating measures on them by a corrupt influence would also be less if a majority sh.<sup>d</sup> be made competent than if ⅔ of each House sh.<sup>d</sup> be required to Legislative acts in this case. An abuse of the power would be qualified with all these good effects. But he thought an abuse was rendered improbable by the provision of 2 branches—by the independence of the Senate, by the negative of the Executive, by the interest of Connecticut & N: Jersey which were agricultural, not commercial States; by the interior interest which was also agricultural in the most commercial States,[16] by the accession of Western States which w.<sup>d</sup> be altogether agricultural. He added that the Southern States would derive an essential advantage in the general security afforded by the increase of our maritime strength. He stated the vulnerable situation of them all, and of Virginia in particular. The increase of the coasting trade, and of seamen, would also be favorable to the S. States, by increasing, the consumption of their produce. If the Wealth of the Eastern should in a still greater proportion be augmented, that wealth w.<sup>d</sup> contribute the more to the public wants, and be otherwise a national benefit.

---

[16] The word " and " is here inserted in the transcript.

M? RUTLIDGE was ag?! the motion of his colleague. It did not follow from a grant of the power to regulate trade, that it would be abused. At the worst a navigation act could bear hard a little while only on the S. States. As we are laying the foundation for a great empire, we ought to take a permanent view of the subject and not look at the present moment only. He reminded the House of the necessity of securing the West India trade to this country. That was the great object, and a navigation Act was necessary for obtaining it.

M? RANDOLPH said that there were features so odious in the constitution as it now stands, that he doubted whether he should be able to agree to it. A rejection of the motion would compleat the deformity of the system. He took notice of the argument in favor of giving the power over trade to a majority, drawn from the opportunity foreign powers would have of obstructing retaliating [17] measures, if two thirds were made requisite. He did not think there was weight in that consideration. The difference between a majority & two thirds did not afford room for such an opportunity. Foreign influence would also be more likely to be exerted on the President who could require three fourths by his negative. He did not mean however to enter into the merits. What he had in view was merely to pave the way for a declaration which he might be hereafter obliged to make if an accumulation of obnoxious ingredients should take place, that he could not give his assent to the plan.

M? GORHAM. If the Government is to be so fettered as to be unable to relieve the Eastern States what motive can they have to join in it, and thereby tie their own hands from measures which they could otherwise take for themselves. The Eastern States were not led to strengthen the Union by fear for their own safety. He deprecated the consequences of disunion, but if it should take place it was the Southern part of the Continent that had the [18] most reason to dread them. He urged the improbability of a combination against the interest of the Southern States, the different situations of the Northern & Middle States being a security against it. It was moreover certain that foreign ships would never be altogether excluded especially those of Nations in treaty with us.

---

[17] The word "retaliatory" is substituted in the transcript for "retaliating."
[18] The word "the" is omitted in the transcript.

On the question to pospone in order to take up M! Pinkney's Motion

N. H. no. Mas. no. C! no. N. J. no. P? no. Del. no. M? ay. V? ay. N. C. ay. S. C. no. Geo. ay.[19]

The Report of the Committee for striking out sect: 6. requiring two thirds of each House to pass a navigation act was then agreed to, nem: con:

M! BUTLER moved to insert after art: XV. "If any person bound to service or labor in any of the U. States shall escape into another State, he or she shall not be discharged from such service or labor, in consequence of any regulations subsisting in the State to which they escape, but shall be delivered up to the person justly claiming their service or labor," which was agreed to nem: con:

Art: XVII [20] being [21] taken up, M! Gov! MORRIS moved to strike out the two last sentences, to wit "If the admission be consented to, the new States shall be admitted on the same terms with the original States. But the Legislature may make conditions with the new States, concerning the public debt, which shall be then subsisting."—He did not wish to bind down the Legislature to admit Western States on the terms here stated.

M! MADISON opposed the motion, insisting that the Western States neither would nor ought to submit to a union which degraded them from an equal rank with [18] other States.

Col: MASON. If it were possible by just means to prevent emigrations to the Western Country, it might be good policy. But go the people will as they find it for their interest, and the best policy is to treat them with that equality which will make them friends not enemies.

M! Gov! MORRIS, did not mean to discourage the growth of the Western Country. He knew that to be impossible. He did not wish however to throw the power into their hands.

M! SHERMAN, was ag!t the motion, & for fixing an equality of privileges by the Constitution.

---

[18] The word "the" is here inserted in the transcript.
[19] In the transcript the vote reads: "Maryland, Virginia, North Carolina, Georgia, aye—4; New Hampshire, Massachusetts, Connecticut, New Jersey, Pennsylvania, Delaware, South Carolina, no—7."
[20] See p. ——.
[21] The word "then" is here inserted in the transcript.

Mr LANGDON was in favor of the Motion, he did not know but circumstances might arise which would render it inconvenient to admit new States on terms of equality.

Mr WILLIAMSON was for leaving the Legislature free. The existing *small* States enjoy an equality now, and for *that* reason are admitted to it in the Senate. This reason is not applicable to new Western States.

On Mr Govr Morris's motion for striking out.
N. H. ay. Mas. ay. Ct ay. N. J. ay. Pa ay. Del. ay. Md no Va no. N. C. ay. S. C. ay. Geo. ay.[22]

Mr L. MARTIN & Mr Govr MORRIS moved to strike out of art XVII. "but to such admission the consent of two thirds of the members present shall be necessary." Before any question was taken on this motion,

Mr Govr MORRIS moved the following proposition as a substitute for the XVII art:

"New States may be admitted by the Legislature into this Union: but no new State shall be erected within the limits of any of the present States, without the consent of the Legislature of such State, as well as of the Genl Legislature"

The first part to Union inclusive was agreed to nem: con:

Mr L. MARTIN opposed the latter part. Nothing he said would so alarm the limited States as to make the consent of the large States claiming the Western lands, necessary to the establishment of new States within their limits. It is proposed to guarantee the States. Shall Vermont be reduced by force in favor of the States claiming it? Frankland & the Western country of Virginia were in a like situation.

On Mr Govr Morris's motion to substitute &c it was agreed to.
N. H. no. Mas. ay. Ct no. N. J. no. Pa ay. Del. no. Md no. Va ay. N. C. ay. S. C. ay. Geo. ay.[23]

Art: XVII—[24] before the House, as amended.

Mr SHERMAN was against it. He thought it unnecessary. The Union can not dismember a State without its consent.

---

[22] In the transcript the vote reads: "New Hampshire, Massachusetts, Connecticut, New Jersey, Pennsylvania, Delaware, North Carolina, South Carolina, Georgia, aye—9; Maryland, Virginia, no—2."
[23] In the transcript the vote reads: "Massachusetts, Pennsylvania, Virginia, North Carolina, South Carolina, Georgia, aye—6; New Hampshire, Connecticut, New Jersey, Delaware, Maryland, no—5."
[24] The word "being" is here inserted in the transcript.

M.<sup>r</sup> LANGDON thought there was great weight in the argument of M.<sup>r</sup> Luther Martin, and that the proposition substituted by M.<sup>r</sup> Gov.<sup>r</sup> Morris would excite a dangerous opposition to the plan.

M.<sup>r</sup> GOV.<sup>r</sup> MORRIS thought on the contrary that the small States would be pleased with the regulation, as it holds up the idea of dismembering the large States.

M.<sup>r</sup> BUTLER. If new States were to be erected without the consent of the dismembered States, nothing but confusion would ensue. Whenever taxes should press on the people, demagogues would set up their schemes of new States.

Doc.<sup>r</sup> JOHNSON agreed in general with the ideas of M.<sup>r</sup> Sherman, but was afraid that as the clause stood, Vermont would be subjected to N. York, contrary to the faith pledged by Congress. He was of opinion that Vermont ought to be compelled to come into the Union.

M.<sup>r</sup> LANGDON said his objections were connected with the case of Vermont. If they are not taken in, & remain exempt from taxes, it would prove of great injury to N. Hampshire and the other neighbouring States

M.<sup>r</sup> DICKINSON hoped the article would not be agreed to. He dwelt on the impropriety of requiring the small States to secure the large ones in their extensive claims of territory.

M.<sup>r</sup> WILSON. When the *majority* of a State wish to divide they can do so. The aim of those in opposition to the article, he perceived, was that the Gen.<sup>l</sup> Government should abet the *minority*, & by that means divide a State against its own consent.

M.<sup>r</sup> GOV.<sup>r</sup> MORRIS. If the forced division of States is the object of the new System, and is to be pointed ag.<sup>st</sup> one or two States, he expected, the Gentleman [25] from these would pretty quickly leave us.

Adjourned

---

THURSDAY AUGUST 30<sup>TH</sup> 1787.[26] IN CONVENTION

Art XVII [27] resumed for a question on it as amended by M.<sup>r</sup> Gov.<sup>r</sup> Morris's substitutes.[28]

---

[25] The transcript uses the word "Gentleman" in the plural.
[26] The year "1787" is omitted in the transcript.
[27] The word "being" is here inserted in the transcript.
[28] The transcript uses the word "substitutes" in the singular.

Independence Hall, Philadelphia, 1776

Mr CARROL moved to strike out so much of the article as requires the consent of the State to its being divided. He was aware that the object of this prerequisite might be to prevent domestic disturbances, but such was our situation with regard to the Crown lands, and the sentiments of Maryland on that subject, that he perceived we should again be at sea, if no guard was provided for the right of the U. States to the back lands. He suggested that it might be proper to provide that nothing in the Constitution should affect the Right of the U. S. to lands ceded by G. Britain in the Treaty of peace, and proposed a committment to a member from each State. He assured the House that this was a point of a most serious nature. It was desirable above all things that the act of the Convention might be agreed to unanimously. But should this point be disregarded, he believed that all risks would be run by a considerable minority, sooner than give their concurrence.

Mr L. MARTIN 2ded the motion for a committment.

Mr RUTLIDGE is it to be supposed that the States are to be cut up without their own consent. The case of Vermont will probably be particularly provided for. There could be no room to fear, that Virginia or N. Carolina would call on the U. States to maintain their Government over the Mountains.

Mr WILLIAMSON said that N. Carolina was well disposed to give up her western lands, but attempts at compulsion was [29] not the policy of the U. S. He was for doing nothing in the constitution in the present case, and for leaving the whole matter in Statu quo.

Mr WILSON was against the committment. Unanimity was of great importance, but not to be purchased by the majority's yielding to the minority. He should have no objection to leaving the case of [30] new States as heretofore. He knew of [31] nothing that would give greater or juster alarm than the doctrine, that a political society is to be torne asunder without its own consent.

On Mr Carrol's motion for commitment

---

[29] In the transcript the word "was" is crossed out and "were" is written above it.

[30] The word "the" is here inserted in the transcript.

[31] The word "of" is omitted in the transcript.

N. H. no. Mas. no. C⸲ no. N. J. ay. P⸲ no. Del. ay. M⸲ ay. V⸲ no. N. C. no. S. C. no. Geo. no.³²

M⸲ SHERMAN moved to postpone the substitute for art: XVII agreed to yesterday in order to take up the following amendment "The Legislature shall have power to admit other States into the Union, and new States to be formed by the division or junction of States now in the Union, with the consent of the Legislature of such States." [The first part was meant for the case of Vermont to secure its admission.]

On the question, it passed in the negative

N. H. ay. Mas. ay. C⸲ ay. N. J. no. P⸲ ay. Del. no. M⸲ no. V⸲ no. N. C. no. S. C. ay. Geo. no.³³

Doc⸲ JOHNSON moved to insert the words "hereafter formed or" after the words "shall be" in the substitute for art: XVII, [the more clearly to save Vermont as being already formed into a State, from a dependence on the consent of N. York to ³⁴ her admission.] The motion was agreed to Del. & M⸲ only dissenting.

M⸲ GOVERN⸲ MORRIS moved to strike out the word "limits" in the substitute, and insert the word "jurisdiction" [This also ³⁵ meant to guard the case of Vermont, the jurisdiction of N. York not extending over Vermont which was in the exercise of sovereignty, tho' Vermont was within the asserted limits of New York]

On this question

N. H. ay. Mas. ay. C⸲ ay. N. J. no. P⸲ ay. Del. ay. M⸲ ay. V⸲ ay. N. C. no. S. C. no. Geo. no.³⁶

M⸲ L. MARTIN, urged the unreasonableness of forcing & guaranteeing the people of Virginia beyond the Mountains, the Western people, of N. Carolina, & of Georgia, & the people of Maine, to continue under the States now governing them, without the consent of those States to their separation. Even if

---

[32] In the transcript the vote reads: "New Jersey, Delaware, Maryland, aye—3; New Hampshire, Massachusetts, Connecticut, Pennsylvania, Virginia, North Carolina, South Carolina, Georgia, no—8."

[33] In the transcript the vote reads; "New Hampshire, Massachusetts, Connecticut, Pennsylvania, South Carolina, aye—5; New Jersey, Delaware, Maryland, Virginia, North Carolina, Georgia, no—6."

[34] The word "for" is substituted in the transcript for "to."

[35] The word "was" is here inserted in the transcript.

[36] In the transcript the vote reads: "New Hampshire, Massachusetts, Connecticut, Pennsylvania, Delaware, Maryland, Virginia, aye—7; New Jersey, North Carolina, South Carolina, Georgia, no—4."

they should become the *majority*, the majority of *Counties*, as in Virginia may still hold fast the dominion over them. Again the majority may place the seat of Government entirely among themselves & for their own conveniency,[37] and still keep the injured parts of the States in subjection, under the guarantee of the Genl Government agst domestic violence. He wished Mr Wilson had thought a little sooner of the value of *political* bodies. In the beginning, when the rights of the small States were in question, they were phantoms, ideal beings. Now when the Great States were to be affected, political societies were of a sacred nature. He repeated and enlarged on the unreasonableness of requiring the small States to guarantee the Western claims of the large ones.—It was said yesterday by Mr Govr Morris, that if the large States were to be split to pieces without their consent, their representatives here would take their leave. If the Small States are to be required to guarantee them in this manner, it will be found that the Representatives of other States will with equal firmness take their leave of the Constitution on the table.

It was moved by Mr L. MARTIN to postpone the substituted article, in order to take up the following.

"The Legislature of the U. S. shall have power to erect New States within as well as without the territory claimed by the several States or either of them, and admit the same into the Union: provided that nothing in this constitution shall be construed to affect the claim of the U. S. to vacant lands ceded to them by the late treaty of peace. which passed in the negative: N. J. Del. & Md only ay.

On the question to agree to Mr Govr Morris's substituted article as amended in the words following,

"New States may be admitted by the Legislature into the Union: but no new State shall be hereafter formed or erected within the jurisdiction of any of the present States without the consent of the Legislature of such State as well as of the General Legislature"

---

[37] The word "conveniency" is changed to "convenience" in the transcript.

N. H. ay. Mas. ay. C! ay. N. J. no. P? ay. Del. no. M? no. V? ay. N. C. ay. S. C. ay. Geo. ay.[38]

M! DICKINSON moved to add the following clause to the last—
" Nor shall any State be formed by the junction of two or more States or parts thereof, without the consent of the Legislatures of such States, as well as of the Legislature of the U. States." which was agreed to without a count of the votes.

M! CARROL moved to add—" Provided nevertheless that nothing in this Constitution shall be construed to affect the claim of the U. S. to vacant lands ceded to them by the Treaty of peace." This he said might be understood as relating to lands not claimed by any particular States, but he had in view also some of the claims of particular States.

M! WILSON was ag!t the motion. There was nothing in the Constitution affecting one way or the other the claims of the U. S. & it was best to insert nothing leaving every thing on that litigated subject in statu quo.

M! MADISON considered the claim of the U. S. as in fact favored by the jurisdiction of the judicial power of the U. S. over controversies to which they should be parties. He thought it best on the whole to be silent on the subject. He did not view the proviso of M! Carrol as dangerous; but to make it neutral & fair, it ought to go farther & declare that the claims of particular States also should not be affected.

M! SHERMAN thought the proviso harmless, especially with the addition suggested by M! Madison in favor of the claims of particular States.

M! BALDWIN did not wish any undue advantage to be given to Georgia. He thought the proviso proper with the addition proposed. It should be remembered that if Georgia has gained much by the cession in the Treaty of peace, she was in danger during the war, of a Uti possidetis.

M! RUTLIDGE thought it wrong to insert a proviso where there was nothing which it could restrain, or on which it could operate.

M! CARROL withdrew his motion and moved the following.

---

[38] In the transcript the vote reads: "New Hampshire, Massachusetts, Connecticut, Pennsylvania, Virginia, North Carolina, South Carolina, Georgia, aye—8; New Jersey, Delaware, Maryland, no—3."

645

"Nothing in this Constitution shall be construed to alter the claims of the U. S. or of the individual States to the Western territory, but all such claims shall be examined into & decided upon, by the Supreme Court of the U. States."

Mr Govr MORRIS moved to postpone this in order to take up the following.

"The Legislature shall have power to dispose of and make all needful rules and regulations respecting the territory or other property belonging to the U. States; and nothing in this constitution contained, shall be so construed as to prejudice any claims either of the U. S. or of any particular State."—The postponemt agd to nem. con.

Mr L. MARTIN moved to amend the proposition of Mr Govr Morris by adding— "But all such claims may be examined into & decided upon by the supreme Court of the U. States."

Mr Govr MORRIS. this is unnecessary, as all suits to which the U. S. are parties, are already to be decided by the Supreme Court.

Mr L. MARTIN, it is propor in order to remove all doubts on this point.

[39] Question on Mr L. Martin's amendatory motion

N. H. no. Mas. no. Ct no. N. J. ay. Pa no. Del. no. Md ay. Va no—[40] States not farther called the negatives being sufficient & the point [41] given up.

The Motion of Mr Govr Morris was then agreed to, Md alone dissenting.

Art: XVIII [42] being taken up,—the word "foreign" was struck out. nem: con: as superfluous, being implied in the term "invasion."

Mr DICKINSON moved to strike out "on the application of its Legislature, against" He thought it of essential importance to the tranquility of the U. S. that they should in all cases suppress domestic violence, which may proceed from the State Legislature itself, or from disputes between the two branches where such exist

---

[39] The words "On the" are here inserted in the transcript.
[40] In the transcript the vote reads: "New Jersey, Maryland, aye—2; New Hampshire, Massachusetts, Connecticut, Pennsylvania, Delaware, Virginia, no—6."
[41] The word "being" is here inserted in the transcript.
[42] See *ante*.

M.̲ DAYTON mentioned the Conduct of Rho: Island as shewing the necessity of giving latitude to the power of the U. S. on this subject.

On the question

N. H. no. Mas. no. C.̲ no. N. J. ay. P.ᵃ ay. Del. ay. M.ᵈ no. V.ᵃ no. N. C. no. S. C. no. Geo. no.⁴³

On a question for striking out "domestic violence" and inserts "insurrections." It passed in the negative.

N. H. no. Mas. no. C.̲ no. N. J. ay. P.ᵃ no. Del. no. M.ᵈ no. V.ᵃ ay. N. C. ay. S. C. ay. Geo. ay.⁴⁴

M.̲ DICKINSON moved to insert the words, "or Executive" after the words "application of its Legislature"—The occasion itself he remarked might hinder the Legislature from meeting.

On this question

N. H. ay. Mas. no. C.̲ ay. N. J. ay. P.ᵃ ay. Del. ay. M.ᵈ div.ᵈ V.ᵃ no. N. C. ay. S. C. ay. Geo. ay.⁴⁵

M.̲ L. MARTIN moved to subjoin to the last amendment the words "in the recess of the Legislature" On which question ⁴⁶

N. H. no. Mas. no. C.̲ no. P.ᵃ no. Del. no. M.ᵈ ay. V.ᵃ no. N. C. no. S. C. no. Geo. no.

On ⁴⁷ Question on the last clause as amended

N. H. ay. Mas. ay. C.̲ ay. N. J. ay. P.ᵃ ay. Del. no. M.ᵈ no. V.ᵃ ay. N. C. ay. S. C. ay. Geo. ay.⁴⁸

Art: XIX ⁴⁹, ⁵⁰ taken up.

M.̲ GOV.̲ MORRIS suggested that the Legislature should be left at liberty to call a Convention, whenever they please.

The art: was agreed to nem: con:

Art: XX.⁴⁹, ⁵⁰ taken up.—⁵¹ "or affirmation" was ⁵² added after "oath."

---

[43] In the transcript the vote reads: "New Jersey, Pennsylvania, Delaware, aye—3; New Hampshire, Massachusetts, Connecticut, Maryland, Virginia, North Carolina, South Carolina, Georgia, no—8."
[44] In the transcript the vote reads: "New Jersey, Virginia, North Carolina, South Carolina, Georgia, aye—5; New Hampshire, Massachusetts, Connecticut, Pennsylvania, Delaware, Maryland, no—6."
[45] In the transcript the vote reads: "New Hampshire, Connecticut, New Jersey, Pennsylvania, Delaware, North Carolina, South Carolina, Georgia, aye—8; Massachusetts, Virginia, no—2; Maryland, divided."
[46] The transcript here adds the words: "Maryland only, aye," and omits the vote by States.
[47] The word "the" is here inserted in the transcript.
[48] In the transcript the vote reads: "New Hampshire, Massachusetts, Connecticut, New Jersey, Pennsylvania, Virginia, North Carolina, South Carolina, Georgia, aye—9; Delaware, Maryland, no—2."
[49] See *ante*.
[50] The words "was then" are here inserted in the transcript.
[51] The expression "the words" is here inserted in the transcript.
[52] In the transcript the word "was" is crossed out and "were" is written above it.

M! PINKNEY moved to add to the art:—"but no religious test shall ever be required as a qualification to any office or public trust under the authority of the U. States"

M! SHERMAN thought it unnecessary, the prevailing liberality being a sufficient security ag[st] such tests.

M! Gov[r] MORRIS & Gen[l] PINKNEY approved the motion.

The motion was agreed to nem: con: and then the whole Article; N. C. only no—& M[d] divided

Art: XXI.[53, 54] taken up. viz:[55] "The ratifications of the Conventions of           States shall be sufficient for organizing this Constitution."

M! WILSON proposed to fill the blank with "seven" that being a majority of the whole number & sufficient for the commencement of the plan.

M! CARROL moved to postpone the article in order to take up the Report of the Committee of Eleven (see Tuesday Aug[st] 28)[56]— and on the question

N. H. no. Mas. no. C[t] no. N. J. ay. P[a] no. Del. ay. M[d] ay. V[a] no. N. C. no. S. C. no. Geo. no.[57]

M! Gov[r] MORRIS thought the blank ought to be filled in a twofold way, so as to provide for the event of the ratifying States being contiguous which would render a smaller number sufficient, and the event of their being dispersed, which w[d] require a greater number for the introduction of the Government.

M! SHERMAN. observed that the States being now confederated by articles which require unanimity in changes, he thought the ratification in this case of ten States at least ought to be made necessary.

M! RANDOLPH was for filling the blank with "nine" that being a respectable majority of the whole, and being a number made familiar by the constitution of the existing Congress.

M! WILSON mentioned "eight" as preferable.

---

[53] See *ante.*
[54] The words "being then" are here inserted in the transcript.
[55] The word "viz" is omitted in the transcript.
[56] The words "the twenty-eighth of August" are substituted in the transcript for "Tuesday Aug[st] 28."
[57] In the transcript the vote reads: "New Jersey, Delaware, Maryland, aye—3; New Hampshire Massachusetts, Connecticut, Pennsylvania, Virginia, North Carolina, South Carolina, Georgia, no—8."

M! DICKINSON asked whether the concurrence of Congress is to be essential to the establishment of the system, whether the refusing States in the Confederacy could be deserted—and whether Congress could concur in contravening the system under which they acted?

M! MADISON, remarked that if the blank should be filled with "seven" eight, or "nine"—the Constitution as it stands might be put in force over the whole body of the people, tho' less than a majority of them should ratify it.

M! WILSON. As the Constitution stands, the States only which ratify can be bound. We must he said in this case go to the original powers of Society. The House on fire must be extinguished, without a scrupulous regard to ordinary rights.

M! BUTLER was in favor of "nine." He revolted at the idea, that one or two States should restrain the rest from consulting their safety.

M! CARROL moved to fill the blank with "the thirteen," unanimity being necessary to dissolve the existing confederacy which had been unanimously established.

M! KING thought this amend! necessary, otherwise as the Constitution now stands it will operate on the whole though ratified by a part only.

Adjourned

---

FRIDAY AUGUST 31ST 1787.[58] IN CONVENTION

M! KING moved to add to the end of art: XXI the words "between the said States" so as to confine the operation of the Gov! to the States ratifying it.

On the question

N. H. ay. Mas. ay. C! ay. N. J. ay. P$^a$ ay. M$^d$ no. Virg$^a$ ay. N. C. ay. S. C. ay. Geo. ay.[59]

M! MADISON proposed to fill the blank in the article with "any seven or more States entitled to thirty three members at least in the House of Representatives according to the allotment made

---

[58] The year "1787" is omitted in the transcript.
[59] In place of the vote by States the transcript reads: "nine States voted in the affirmative; Maryland, no; Delaware, absent."

in the 3 Sect: of art: 4." This he said would require the concurrence of a majority both of the States and [60] people.

M.<sup>r</sup> SHERMAN doubted the propriety of authorizing less than all the States to execute the Constitution, considering the nature of the existing Confederation. Perhaps all the States may concur, and on that supposition it is needless to hold out a breach of faith.

M.<sup>r</sup> CLYMER and M.<sup>r</sup> CARROL moved to postpone the consideration of Art: XXI in order to take up the Reports of Committees not yet acted on. On this question, the States were equally divided.

N. H. ay. Mas. no. C.<sup>t</sup> div.<sup>d</sup> N. J. no. P.<sup>a</sup> ay. Del. ay. M.<sup>d</sup> ay. V.<sup>a</sup> no. N. C no. S. C. no. G. ay.[61]

M.<sup>r</sup> GOV.<sup>r</sup> MORRIS moved to strike out "Conventions of the" after "ratifications," leaving the States to pursue their own modes of ratification.

M.<sup>r</sup> CARROL mentioned the mode of altering the Constitution of Maryland pointed out therein, and that no other mode could be pursued in that State.

M.<sup>r</sup> KING thought that striking out "Conventions" as the requisite mode was equivalent to giving up the business altogether. Conventions alone, which will avoid all the obstacles from the complicated formation of the Legislatures, will succeed, and if not positively required by the plan, its enemies will oppose that mode.

M.<sup>r</sup> GOV.<sup>r</sup> MORRIS said he meant to facilitate the adoption of the plan, by leaving the modes approved by the several State Constitutions to be followed.

M.<sup>r</sup> MADISON considered it best to require Conventions; among other reasons, for this, that the powers given to the Gen! Gov.<sup>t</sup> being taken from the State Gov.<sup>ts</sup> the Legislatures would be more disinclined than conventions composed in part at least of other men; and if disinclined, they could devise modes apparently promoting, but really, thwarting the ratification. The difficulty

---

[60] The word "the" is here inserted in the transcript.

[61] In the transcript the vote reads: "New Hampshire, Pennsylvania, Delaware, Maryland, Georgia, aye—5; Massachusetts, New Jersey, Virginia, North Carolina, South Carolina, no—5; Connecticut, divided."

in Maryland was no greater than in other States, where no mode of change was pointed out by the Constitution, and all officers were under oath to support it. The people were in fact, the fountain of all power, and by resorting to them, all difficulties were got over. They could alter constitutions as they pleased. It was a principle in the Bills of rights, that first principles might be resorted to.

Mr. McHENRY said that the officers of Govt in Maryland were under oath to support the mode of alteration prescribed by the Constitution.

Mr. GHORUM, urged the expediency of "Conventions" also Mr. PINKNEY, for reasons, formerly urged on a discussion of this question.

Mr. L. MARTIN insisted on a reference to the State Legislatures. He urged the danger of commotions from a resort to the people & to first principles in which the Governments might be on one side & the people on the other. He was apprehensive of no such consequences however in Maryland, whether the Legislature or the people should be appealed to. Both of them would be generally against the Constitution. He repeated also the peculiarity in the Maryland Constitution.

Mr. KING observed that the Constitution of Massachussets was made unalterable till the year 1790, yet this was no difficulty with him. The State must have contemplated a recurrence to first principles before they sent deputies to this Convention.

Mr. SHERMAN moved to postpone art. XXI [62] & [63] take up art: XXII [62] on which question,

N. H. no. Mas. no. Ct ay. N. J. no. P. ay. Del. ay. Md ay. Va ay. N. C. no S. C. no. Geo. no.[64]

On Mr. Govr Morris's motion to strike out "Conventions of the," it was negatived.

N. H. no. Mas. no. Ct ay. N. J. no. Pa ay. Del. no. Md ay. Va no. S. C. no. Geo. ay.[65]

---

[62] See *ante.*
[63] The word "to" is here inserted in the transcript.
[64] In the transcript the vote reads: "Connecticut, Pennsylvania, Delaware, Maryland, Virginia, aye—5; New Hampshire, Massachusetts, New Jersey, North Carolina, South Carolina, Georgia, no—6."
[65] In the transcript the vote reads: "Connecticut, Pennsylvania, Maryland, Georgia, aye—4; New Hampshire, Massachusetts, New Jersey, Delaware, Virginia, South Carolina, no—6."

On [66] filling the blank in Art: XXI with "thirteen" moved by M! CARROL & L. MARTIN

N. H. no. Mas. no. C! no—all no. except Maryland.[87]

M! SHERMAN & M! DAYTON moved to fill the blank with "ten"

M! WILSON supported the motion of M! MADISON, requiring a majority both of the people and of States.

M! CLYMER was also in favor of it.

Col: MASON was for preserving ideas familiar to the people. Nine States had been required in all great cases under the Confederation & that number was on that account preferable

On the question for "ten"

N. H. no. Mas. no. C! ay. N. J. ay. P? no. Del. no. M? ay. V? no. N. C. no. S. C. no. Geo. ay.[68]

On question for "nine"

N. H. ay. Mas. ay. C! ay. N. J. ay. P? ay. Del. ay. M? ay. V? no. N. C. no. S. C. no. Geo. ay [69]

Art: XXI. as amended was then agreed to by all the States, Maryland excepted, & M! Jenifer being, ay.

Art. XXII [62, 70] taken up, to wit, "This Constitution shall be laid before the U. S. in Cong? assembled for their approbation; and it is the opinion of this Convention that it should be afterwards submitted to a Convention chosen, in each State under the recommendation of its Legislature, in order to receive the ratification of such Convention"

M! GOV! MORRIS & M! PINKNEY moved to strike out the words "for their approbation" On this question

N. H. ay. Mas. no. C! ay. N. J. ay.* P? ay. Del. ay. M? no V? ay. N. C. ay. S. C. ay. Geo. no.[71]

---

[62] See *ante*.
[66] The words "the question for" are here inserted in the transcript.
[67] In the transcript the vote reads: "all the States were no, except Maryland."
[68] In the transcript the vote reads: "Connecticut, New Jersey, Maryland, Georgia, aye—4; New Hampshire, Massachusetts, Pennsylvania, Delaware, Virginia, North Carolina, South Carolina, no—7."
[69] In the transcript the vote reads: "New Hampshire, Massachusetts, Connecticut, New Jersey, Pennsylvania, Delaware, Maryland, Georgia, aye—8; Virginia, North Carolina, South Carolina, no—3."
[70] The words "was then" are here inserted in the transcript.
*In the printed Journal N. Jersey—no.
[71] In the transcript the vote reads: "New Hampshire, Connecticut, New Jersey,* Pennsylvania, Delaware, Virginia, North Carolina, South Carolina, aye—8; Massachusetts, Maryland, Georgia, no—3."

M.^r Gov.^r Morris & M.^r Pinkney then moved to amend the art: so as to read

"This Constitution shall be laid before the U. S. in Congress assembled; and it is the opinion of this Convention that it should afterwards be submitted to a Convention chosen in each State, in order to receive the ratification of such Convention: to which end the several Legislatures ought to provide for the calling Conventions within their respective States as speedily as circumstances will permit."—M.^r Gov.^r Morris said his object was to impress in stronger terms the necessity of calling Conventions in order to prevent enemies to the plan, from giving it the go by. When it first appears, with the sanction of this Convention, the people will be favorable to it. By degrees the State officers, & those interested in the State Gov.^ts will intrigue & turn the popular current against it.

M.^r L. Martin believed M.^r Morris to be right, that after a while the people would be ag.^st it, but for a different reason from that alledged. He believed they would not ratify it unless hurried into it by surprize.

M.^r Gerry enlarged on the idea of M.^r L. Martin in which he concurred, represented the system as full of vices, and dwelt on the impropriety of distroying the existing Confederation, without the unanimous consent of the parties to it.

[72] Question on M.^r Gov.^r Morris's & M.^r Pinkney's motion

N. H. ay. Mas. ay. C.^t no. N. J. no. P.^a ay. Del. ay. M.^d no. V.^a no. N. C. no. S. C. no. Geo. no.[73]

M.^r Gerry moved to postpone art: XXII.

Col: Mason 2.^d.^ed the motion, declaring that he would sooner chop off his right hand than put it to the Constitution as it now stands. He wished to see some points not yet decided brought to a decision, before being compelled to give a final opinion on this article. Should these points be improperly settled, his wish would then be to bring the whole subject before another general Convention.

---

[72] The words "On the" are here inserted in the transcript.
[73] In the transcript the vote reads: "New Hampshire, Massachusetts, Pennsylvania, Delaware, aye—4; Connecticut, New Jersey, Maryland, Virginia, North Carolina, South Carolina, Georgia, no—7."

Mr Govr MORRIS was ready for a postponement. He had long wished for another Convention, that will have the firmness to provide a vigorous Government, which we are afraid to do.

Mr RANDOLPH stated his idea to be, in case the final form of the Constitution should not permit him to accede to it, that the State Conventions should be at liberty to propose amendments to be submitted to another General Convention which may reject or incorporate them, as shall [74] be judged proper.

On the question for postponing

N. H. no. Mas. no. Ct no. N. J. ay. Pa no. Del. no. Md ay. Va no. N. C. ay. S. C. no. Geo. no.[75]

On the question on Art: XXII

N. H. ay. Mas. ay. Ct ay. N. J. ay. Pa ay. Del. ay. Md no. Va ay. N. C. ay. S. C. ay. Geo. ay.[76]

Art: XXIII [77] being taken up, as far as the words "assigned by Congress" inclusive, was agreed to nem: con: the blank having been first filled with the word "nine" as of course.

On a motion for postponement the residue of the clause, concerning the choice of the President &c.

N. H. no. Mas. ay. Ct no. N. J. no. Pa no. Del. ay. Md no. Va ay. N. C. ay. S. C. no. Geo. no.[78]

Mr Govr MORRIS then moved to strike out the words "choose the President of the U. S. and"—this point, of choosing the President not being yet finally determined, & on this question

N. H. no. Mas. ay. Ct ay. N. J. ay. Pa ay Del. ay. Md divd Va ay. N. C. ay. S. C. ay.* Geo. ay [79]

Art: XXIII as amended was then agreed to nem: con:

The Report of the Grand Committee of eleven made by Mr SHERMAN was then taken up (see Aug: 28).[80]

---

[74] The word "may" is substituted in the transcript for "shall."
[75] In the transcript the vote reads: "New Jersey, Maryland, North Carolina, aye—3; New Hampshire, Massachusetts, Connecticut, Pennsylvania, Delaware, Virginia, South Carolina, Georgia, no—8."
[76] In the transcript the vote reads: "ten States aye; Maryland no."
[77] See ante.
[78] In the transcript the vote reads: "Massachusetts, Delaware, Virginia, North Carolina, aye—4; New Hampshire, Connecticut, New Jersey, Pennsylvania, Maryland, South Carolina, Georgia, no—.7"
* In printed Journal—S. C.—no.
[79] In the transcript the vote reads: "Massachusetts, Connecticut, New Jersey, Pennsylvania, Delaware, Virginia, North Carolina, South Carolina,* Georgia, aye—9; New Hampshire, no; Maryland, divided."
[80] In the transcript this date reads "the twenty-eighth of August."

On the question to agree to the following clause, to be inserted after Sect. 4. art: VII. "nor shall any regulation of commerce or revenue give preference to the ports of one State over those of another." Agreed to nem: con:

On the clause "or oblige vessels bound to or from any State to enter clear or pay duties in another"

M: MADISON thought the restriction w⟨d⟩ be inconvenient, as in the River Delaware, if a vessel cannot be required to make entry below the jurisdiction of Pennsylvania.

M: FITZIMMONS admitted that it might be inconvenient, but thought it would be a greater inconveniency [81] to require vessels bound to Philad⟨a⟩ to enter below the jurisdiction of the State.

M: GORHAM & M: LANGDON, contended that the Gov⟨t⟩ would be so fettered by this clause, as to defeat the good purpose of the plan. They mentioned the situation of the trade of Mas. & N. Hampshire, the case of Sandy Hook which is in the State of N. Jersey, but where precautions ag⟨st⟩ smuggling into N. York, ought to be established by the Gen⟨l⟩ Government.

M: M⟨c⟩HENRY said the clause would not shreen a vessel from being obliged to take an officer on board as a security for due entry &c.

M: CARROL was anxious that the clause should be agreed to. He assured the House, that this was a tender point in Maryland.

M: JENNIFER urged the necessity of the clause in the same point of view.

On the question for agreeing to it

N. H. no. C⟨t⟩ ay. N. J. ay. P⟨a⟩ ay. Del. ay. M⟨d⟩ ay. V⟨a⟩ ay. N. C. ay. S. C. no. Geo. ay.[82]

The word "tonnage" was struck out, nem: con: as comprehended in "duties"

On [83] question on the clause of the Report "and all duties, imposts & excises, laid by the Legislature shall be uniform throughout the U. S." It was agreed to nem: con: *

---

[81] The word "inconveniency" is changed to "inconvenience" in the transcript.

[82] In the transcript the vote reads: "Connecticut, New Jersey, Pennsylvania, Delaware, Maryland, Virginia, North Carolina, Georgia, aye—8; New Hampshire, South Carolina, no—2."

[83] The word "the" is here inserted in the transcript.

*In printed Journal N. H. and S. C. entered as [84] in the negative.

[84] The word "as" is omitted in the transcript.

On motion of Mr SHERMAN it was agreed to refer such parts of the Constitution as have been postponed, and such parts of Reports as have not been acted on, to a Committee of a member from each State; the Committee appointed by ballot, being—Mr Gilman, Mr King, Mr Sherman, Mr Brearly, Mr Govr Morris, Mr Dickinson, Mr Carrol, Mr Madison, Mr Williamson, Mr Butler & Mr Baldwin.

[The House [85] adjourned]

---

SATURDAY SEPR 1. 1787 [86] IN CONVENTION

Mr BREARLEY from the Comme of eleven to which were referred yesterday, the postponed parts of the Constitution, & parts of Reports not acted upon, made the following partial report.

That in lieu of the 9th Sect: of art: 6. the words following be inserted viz "The members of each House shall be ineligible to any civil office under the authority of the U. S. during the time for which they shall respectively be elected, and no person holding an office under the U. S. shall be a member of either House during his continuance in office."

Mr RUTLIDGE from the Committee to whom were referred sundry propositions (see Aug: 29), together with art: XVI, reported that the following additions be made to the Report—viz

After the word "States" in the last line on the Margin of the 3d page (see the printed Report)—add "to establish uniform laws on the subject of Bankruptcies."

And insert the following as Art: XVI viz

"Full faith and credit ought to be given in each State to the public acts, records, and Judicial proceedings of every other State, and the Legislature shall by general laws prescribe the manner in which such acts, Records, & proceedings shall be proved, and the effect which Judgments obtained in one State, shall have in another."

After receiving these reports

The House adjourned to 10 OC. on Monday next [87]

---

[85] The words "The House" are omitted in the transcript.
[86] The year "1787" is omitted in the transcript.
[87] The phrase "to 10 OC on Monday next" is omitted in the transcript.

MONDAY SEP<sup>R</sup> 3. 1787.[86] IN CONVENTION

M<sup>r</sup> Gov<sup>r</sup> MORRIS moved to amend the Report concerning the respect to be paid to Acts Records &c of one State, in other States (see Sep<sup>r</sup> 1.) by striking out "judgments obtained in one State shall have in another" and to insert the word "thereof" after the word "effect"

Col: MASON favored the motion, particularly if the "effect" was to be restrained to judgments & Judicial proceedings

M<sup>r</sup> WILSON remarked, that if the Legislature were not allowed to *declare the effect* the provision would amount to nothing more than what now takes place among all Independent Nations.

Doc<sup>r</sup> JOHNSON thought the amendment as worded would authorise the Gen<sup>l</sup> Legislature to declare the effect of Legislative acts of one State, in another State.

M<sup>r</sup> RANDOLPH considered it as strengthening the general objection ag<sup>st</sup> the plan, that its definition of the powers of the Government was so loose as to give it opportunities of usurping all the State powers. He was for not going farther than the Report, which enables the Legislature to provide for the effect of *Judgments*.

On the amendment as moved by M<sup>r</sup> Gov<sup>r</sup> Morris

Mas. ay. C<sup>t</sup> ay. N. J. ay. P<sup>a</sup> ay. M<sup>d</sup> no. V<sup>a</sup> no. N. C. ay. S. C. ay. Geo. no.[88]

On motion of M<sup>r</sup> MADISON,[89] "ought to" was [90] struck out, and "shall" inserted; and "shall" between "Legislature" & "by general laws" struck out, and "may" inserted, nem: con:

On the question to agree to the report as amended viz "Full faith & credit shall be given in each State to the public acts, records & judicial proceedings of every other State, and the Legislature may by general laws prescribe the manner in which such acts records & proceedings shall be proved, and the effect thereof" [91] Agreed to with<sup>t</sup> a count of [92] Sts.

---

[86] The year "1787" is omitted in the transcript.
[88] In the transcript the vote reads: "Massachusetts, Connecticut, New Jersey, Pennsylvania, North Carolina, South Carolina, aye—6; Maryland, Virginia, Georgia, no—3."
[89] The expression "the words" is here inserted in the transcript.
[90] The word "was" is crossed out in the transcript and "were" is written above it.
[91] The words "it was" are here inserted in the transcript.
[92] The word "the" is here inserted in the transcript.

The clause in the Report "To establish uniform laws on the subject of Bankruptcies" being taken up.

M.̱ SHERMAN observed that Bankruptcies were in some cases punishable with death by the laws of England, & He did not chuse to grant a power by which that might be done here.

M.̱ Gov.̱ MORRIS said this was an extensive & delicate subject. He would agree to it because he saw no danger of abuse of the power by the Legislature of the U. S.

On the question to agree to the clause

N. H. ay. Mas. ay. C.̱ no. N. J. ay. P.̱ ay. M.̱ ay. V.̱ ay. N. C. ay. S. C. ay. Geo. ay.[93]

M.̱ PINKNEY moved to postpone the Report of the Committee of Eleven (see Sep.̱ 1) in order to take up the following,

"The members of each House shall be incapable of holding any office under the U. S. for which they or any other for their benefit, receive any salary, fees or emoluments of any kind, and the acceptance of such office shall vacate their seats respectively." He was strenuously opposed to an ineligibility of members to office, and therefore wished to restrain the proposition to a mere incompatibility. He considered the eligibility of members of the Legislature to the honorable offices of Government, as resembling the policy of the Romans, in making the temple of virtue the road to the temple of fame.

On this question

N. H. no. Mas. no. C.̱ no. N. J. no. P.̱ ay. M.̱ no. V.̱ no. N. C. ay. S. C. no. Geo. no.[94]

M.̱ KING moved to insert the word "created" before the word "during" in the Report of the Committee. This he said would exclude the members of the first Legislature under the Constitution, as most of the offices w.̱ then be created.

M.̱ WILLIAMSON 2.̱ded the motion. He did not see why members of the Legislature should be ineligible to *vacancies* happening during the term of their election.

M.̱ SHERMAN was for entirely incapacitating members of the Legislature. He thought their eligibility to offices would give too

---

[93] In place of the vote by States the transcript reads: "Connecticut alone was in the negative."
[94] In the transcript the vote reads: "Pennsylvania, North Carolina, aye—2; New Hampshire, Massachusetts, Connecticut, New Jersey, Maryland, Virginia, South Carolina, Georgia, no—8."

much influence to the Executive. He said the incapacity ought at least to be extended to cases where salaries should be *increased* as well as *created*, during the term of the member. He mentioned also the expedient by which the restriction could be evaded to wit: an existing officer might be translated to an office created, and a member of the Legislature be then put into the office vacated.

M!̣ Gov!̣ Morris contended that the eligibility of members to office w.̣d lessen the influence of the Executive. If they cannot be appointed themselves, the Executive will appoint their relations & friends, retaining the service & votes of the members for his purposes in the Legislature. Whereas the appointment of the members deprives him of such an advantage.

M!̣ Gerry. thought the eligibility of members would have the effect of opening batteries ag.̣st good officers, in order to drive them out & make way for members of the Legislature.

M!̣ Gorham was in favor of the amendment. Without it we go further than has been done in any of the States, or indeed any other Country. The experience of the State Governments where there was no such ineligibility, proved that it was not necessary; on the contrary that the eligibility was among the inducements for fit men to enter into the Legislative service

M!̣ Randolph was inflexibly fixed against inviting men into the Legislature by the prospect of being appointed to offices.

M!̣ Baldwin remarked that the example of the States was not applicable. The Legislatures there are so numerous that an exclusion of their members would not leave proper men for offices. The case would be otherwise in the General Government.

Col: Mason. Instead of excluding merit, the ineligibility will keep out corruption, by excluding office-hunters.

M!̣ Wilson considered the exclusion of members of the Legislature, as increasing the influence of the Executive as observed by M!̣ Gov!̣ Morris at the same time that it would diminish, the general energy of the Government. He said that the legal disqualification for office would be odious to those who did not wish for office, but did not wish either to be marked by so degrading a distinction.

Mr PINKNEY. The first Legislature will be composed of the ablest men to be found. The States will select such to put the Government into operation. Should the Report of the Committee or even the amendment be agreed to, The great offices, even those of the Judiciary Department which are to continue for life, must be filled whilst those most capable of filling them will be under a disqualification.

On the question on Mr King's motion

N. H. ay. Mas. ay. Ct no. N. J. no. Pa ay. Md no. Va ay. N. C. ay. S. C. no. Geo. no.[95]

The amendment being thus lost by the equal division of the States, Mr WILLIAMSON moved to insert the words "created or the emoluments whereof shall have been increased" before the word "during" in the Report of the Committee

Mr KING 2ded the motion, &

On the question

N. H. ay. Mas. ay. Ct no. N. J. no. Pa ay. Md no. Va ay N. C. ay. S. C. no. Geo. divided.[96]

The last clause rendering a Seat in the Legislature & an office incompatible was agreed to nem. con:

The Report as amended & agreed to is as follows.

"The members of each House shall be ineligible to any Civil office under the authority of the U. States, created, or the emoluments whereof shall have been increased during the time for which they shall respectively be elected—and no person holding any office under the U. S. shall be a member of either House during his continuance in office."

Adjourned

TUESDAY SEPR 4. 1787.[97] IN CONVENTION

Mr BREARLY from the Committee of eleven made a further partial Report as follows

"The Committee of Eleven to whom sundry resolutions &c were referred on the 31st of August, report that in their opinion

---

[95] In the transcript the vote reads: "New Hampshire, Massachusetts, Pennsylvania, Virginia, North Carolina, aye —5; Connecticut, New Jersey, Maryland, South Carolina, Geogria, no—5."

[96] In the transcript the vote reads: "New Hampshire, Massachusetts, Pennsylvania, Virginia, North Carolina, aye—5; Connecticut, New Jersey, Maryland, South Carolina, aye—4; Georgia, divided."

[97] The year "1787" is omitted in the transcript.

the following additions and alterations should be made to the Report before the Convention, viz

\* (1.) The first clause of sect: 1. art. 7. to read as follow—'The Legislature shall have power to lay and collect taxes duties imposts & excises, to pay the debts and provide for the common defence & general welfare, of the U. S.'

(2). At the end of the 2$^d$ clause of sect. 1. art. 7. add 'and with the Indian Tribes.'

(3) In the place of the 9$^{th}$ art. Sect. 1. to be inserted 'The Senate of the U. S. shall have power to try all impeachments; but no person shall be convicted without the concurrence of two thirds of the members present.'

(4) After the word 'Excellency' in sect. 1. art. 10. to be inserted. 'He shall hold his office during the term of four years, and together with the vice-President, chosen for the same term, be elected in the following manner, viz. Each State shall appoint in such manner as its Legislature may direct, a number of electors equal to the whole number of Senators and members of the House of Representatives to which the State may be entitled in the Legislature. The Electors shall meet in their respective States, and vote by ballot for two persons, of whom one at least shall not be an inhabitant of the same State with themselves; and they shall make a list of all the persons voted for, and of the number of votes for each, which list they shall sign and certify and transmit sealed to the Seat of the Gen$^l$ Government, directed to the President of the Senate—The President of the Senate shall in that House open all the certificates; and the votes shall be then & there counted. The Person having the greatest number of votes shall be the President, if such number be a majority of that of the electors; and if there be more than one who have such majority, and have an equal number of votes, then the Senate shall immediately choose by ballot one of them for President: but if no person have a majority, then from the five highest on the list, the Senate shall choose by ballot the President. And in every case after the choice of the President, the person having the greatest number of votes shall be vice-president: but if there should remain two or more who have equal votes, the Senate shall choose from them the vice-President. The Legislature may determine the time of choosing and assembling the Electors, and the manner of certifying and transmitting their votes.'

---

\* This is an exact copy. The variations in that in the printed Journal are occasioned by its incorporation of subsequent amendments. This remark is applicable to other cases.

(5) 'Sect. 2. No person except a natural born citizen or a Citizen of the U. S. at the time of the adoption of this Constitution shall be eligible to the office of President; nor shall any person be elected to that office, who shall be under the age of thirty five years, and who has not been in the whole, at least fourteen years a resident within the U. S.'

(6) 'Sect. 3. The vice-president shall be ex officio President of the Senate, except when they sit to try the impeachment of the President, in which case the Chief Justice shall preside, and excepting also when he shall exercise the powers and duties of President, in which case & in case of his absence, the Senate shall chuse a President pro tempore—The vice President when acting as President of the Senate shall not have a vote unless the House be equally divided.'

(7) 'Sect. 4. The President by and with the advice and Consent of the Senate, shall have power to make Treaties; and he shall nominate and by and with the advice and consent of the Senate shall appoint ambassadors, and other public Ministers, Judges of the Supreme Court, and all other Officers of the U. S., whose appointments are not otherwise herein provided for. But no Treaty shall be made without the consent of two thirds of the members present.'

(8) After the words—"into the service of the U. S." in sect. 2. art: 10. add 'and may require the opinion in writing of the principal officer in each of the Executive Departments, upon any subject relating to the duties of their respective offices.'

[98] The latter part of Sect. 2. Art: 10. to read as follows.

(9) [98] 'He shall be removed from his office on impeachment by the House of Representatives, and conviction by the Senate, for Treason, or bribery, and in case of his removal as aforesaid, death, absence, resignation or inability to discharge the powers or duties of his office, the vice-president shall exercise those powers and duties until another President be chosen, or until the inability of the President be removed.'

The (1st) clause of the Report was agreed to, nem. con.

The (2) clause was also agreed to nem: con:

The (3) clause was postponed in order to decide previously on the mode of electing the President.

The (4) clause was accordingly taken up.

---

[98] The figure "9" is transposed to precede the sentence beginning "The latter" . . . in the transcript.

M.^r GORHAM disapproved of making the next highest after the President, the vice-President, without referring the decision to the Senate in case the next highest should have less than a majority of votes. as the regulation stands a very obscure man with very few votes may arrive at that appointment

M.^r SHERMAN said the object of this clause of the report of the Committee was to get rid of the ineligibility, which was attached to the mode of election by the Legislature, & to render the Executive independent of the Legislature. As the choice of the President was to be made out of the five highest, obscure characters were sufficiently guarded against in that case; and he had no objection to requiring the vice-President to be chosen in like manner, where the choice was not decided by a majority in the first instance

M.^r MADISON was apprehensive that by requiring both the President & vice President to be chosen out of the five highest candidates, the attention of the electors would be turned too much to making candidates instead of giving their votes in order to a definitive choice. Should this turn be given to the business, the election would, in fact be consigned to the Senate altogether. It would have the effect at the same time, he observed, of giving the nomination of the candidates to the largest States.

M.^r GOV.^r MORRIS concurred in, & enforced the remarks of M.^r Madison.

M.^r RANDOLPH & M.^r PINKNEY wished for a particular explanation & discussion of the reasons for changing the mode of electing the Executive.

M.^r GOV.^r MORRIS said he would give the reasons of the Committee and his own. The 1.^st was the danger of intrigue & faction if the appointm.^t should be made by the Legislature. 2.⁹⁹ the inconveniency ¹ of an ineligibility required by that mode in order to lessen its evils. 3.² The difficulty of establishing a Court of Impeachments, other than the Senate which would not be so proper for the trial nor the other branch for the impeachment of the President, if appointed by the Legislature, 4.³ No body had

---

⁹⁹ The figure "2" is changed in the transcript to "The next was."
¹ The word "inconveniency" is changed in the transcript to "inconvenience."
² The figure "3" is changed in the transcript to "The third was."
³ The figure "4" is changed in the transcript to "In the fourth place."

appeared to be satisfied with an appointment by the Legislature.
5.[4] Many were anxious even for an immediate choice by the people.
6.[5] the indispensible necessity of making the Executive independent of the Legislature.—As the Electors would vote at the same time throughout the U. S. and at so great a distance from each other, the great evil of cabal was avoided. It would be impossible also to corrupt them. A conclusive reason for making the Senate instead of the Supreme Court the Judge of impeachments, was that the latter was to try the President after the trial of the impeachment.

Col: MASON confessed that the plan of the Committee had removed some capital objections, particularly the danger of cabal and corruption. It was liable however to this strong objection, that nineteen times in twenty the President would be chosen by the Senate, an improper body for the purpose

M<sup>r</sup> BUTLER thought the mode not free from objections, but much more so than an election by the Legislature, where as in elective monarchies, cabal faction & violence would be sure to prevail.

M<sup>r</sup> PINKNEY stated as objections to the mode 1.[6] that it threw the whole appointment in fact into the hands of the Senate. 2.[6] The Electors will be strangers to the several candidates and of course unable to decide on their comparative merits. 3.[6] It makes the Executive reeligible which will endanger the public liberty. 4.[6] It makes the same body of men which will in fact elect the President his Judges in case of an impeachment.

M<sup>r</sup> WILLIAMSON had great doubts whether the advantage of re-eligibility would balance the objection to such a dependence of the President on the Senate for his reappointment. He thought at least the Senate ought to be restrained to the *two* highest on the list

M<sup>r</sup> Gov<sup>r</sup> MORRIS said the principal advantage aimed at was that of taking away the opportunity for cabal. The President may be made if thought necessary ineligible on this as well as on any other mode of election. Other inconveniences may be no less redressed on this plan than any other.

---

[4] The figure "5" is changed in the transcript to "In the fifth place."
[5] The figure "6" is changed in the transcript to "And finally, the sixth reason was."
[6] The figures "1," "2," "3" and "4" are changed in the transcript to "first," "Secondly," etc.

Mr BALDWIN thought the plan not so objectionable when well considered, as at first view. The increasing intercourse among the people of the States, would render important characters less & less unknown; and the Senate would consequently be less & less likely to have the eventual appointment thrown into their hands.

Mr WILSON. This subject has greatly divided the House, and will also divide [7] people out of doors. It is in truth the most difficult of all on which we have had to decide. He had never made up an opinion on it entirely to his own satisfaction. He thought the plan on the whole a valuable improvement on the former. It gets rid of one great evil, that of cabal & corruption; & Continental Characters will multiply as we more & more coalesce, so as to enable the electors in every part of the Union to know & judge of them. It clears the way also for a discussion of the question of re-eligibility on its own merits, which the former mode of election seems to forbid. He thought it might be better however to refer the eventual appointment to the Legislature than to the Senate, and to confine it to a smaller number than five of the Candidates. The eventual election by the Legislature wd not open cabal anew, as it would be restrained to certain designated objects of choice, and as these must have had the previous sanction of a number of the States: and if the election be made as it ought as soon as the votes of the electors are opened & it is known that no one has a majority of the whole, there can be little danger of corruption. Another reason for preferring the Legislature to the Senate in this business, was that the House of Reps will be so often changed as to be free from the influence & faction to which the permanence of the Senate may subject that branch.

Mr RANDOLPH preferred the former mode of constituting the Executive, but if the change was to be made, he wished to know why the eventual election was referred to the *Senate* and not to the *Legislature?* He saw no necessity for this and many objections to it. He was apprehensive also that the advantage of the eventual appointment would fall into the hands of the States near the Seat of Government.

---

[7] The word "the" is here inserted in the transcript.

Mr Govr Morris said the *Senate* was preferred because fewer could then, say to the President, you owe your appointment to us. He thought the President would not depend so much on the Senate for his re-appointment as on his general good conduct.

The further consideration of the Report was postponed that each member might take a copy of the remainder of it.

The following motion was referred to the Committee of Eleven— to wit,—"To prepare & report a plan for defraying the expences of the Convention"

\* Mr Pinkney moved a clause declaring "that each House should be judge of the privilege ⁹ of its own members. Mr Govr Morris 2ded the motion

Mr Randolph & Mr Madison expressed doubts as to the propriety of giving such a power, & wished for a postponement.

Mr Govr Morris thought it so plain a case that no postponement could be necessary.

Mr Wilson thought the power involved, and the express insertion of it needless. It might beget doubts as to the power of other public bodies, as Courts &c. Every Court is the judge of its own privileges.

Mr Madison distinguished between the power of Judging of privileges previously & duly established, and the effect of the motion which would give a discretion to each House as to the extent of its own privileges. He suggested that it would be better to make provision for ascertaining by *law*, the privileges of each House, than to allow each House to decide for itself. He suggested also the necessity of considering what privileges ought to be allowed to the Executive.

Adjourned

---

Wednesday Sepr 5. 1787.¹⁰ In Convention

Mr Brearley from the Committee of Eleven made a farther report as follows,

(1) To add to the clause "to declare war" the words "and grant letters of marque and reprisal"

---
\* This motion not inserted ⁸ in the printed Journal.
⁸ The words "is not contained" are substituted in the transcript for "not inserted."
⁹ The transcript uses the word "privilege" in the plural.
¹⁰ The year "1787" is omitted in the transcript.

(2) To add to the clause "to raise and support armies" the words "but no appropriation of money to that use shall be for a longer term than two years"

(3) Instead of sect: 12. art 6. say—"All bills for raising revenue shall originate in the House of Representatives, and shall be subject to alterations and amendments by the Senate: no money shall be drawn from the Treasury, but in consequence of appropriations made by law."

(4) Immediately before the last clause of sect. 1. art. 7. insert "To exercise exclusive legislation in all cases whatsoever over such district (not exceeding ten miles square) as may by Cession of particular States and the acceptance of the Legislature become the seat of the Government of the U. S. and to exercise like authority over all places purchased for the erection of Forts, Magazines, Arsenals, Dock-Yards, and other needful buildings"

(5) "To promote the progress of Science and [11] useful arts by securing for limited times to authors & inventors, the exclusive right to their respective writings and discoveries"

This report being taken up.—The (1) clause was agreed to nem: con:

To the (2) clause Mr GERRY objected that it admitted of appropriations to an army, for two years instead of one, for which he could not conceive a reason. that it implied that[12] there was to be a standing army which he inveighed against as dangerous to liberty, as unnecessary even for so great an extent of Country as this, and if necessary, some restriction on the number & duration ought to be provided: Nor was this a proper time for such an innovation. The people would not bear it.

Mr SHERMAN remarked that the appropriations were permitted only, not required to be for two years. As the Legislature is to be biennially elected, it would be inconvenient to require appropriations to be for one year, as there might be no Session within the time necessary to renew them. He should himself he said like a reasonable restriction on the number and continuance of an army in time of peace.

The clause (2) was [13] agreed to nem: con:

---

[11] The word "the" is here inserted in the transcript.
[12] The word "that" is omitted in the transcript.
[13] The word "then" is here inserted in the transcript.

The (3) clause, M<sup>r</sup> Gov<sup>r</sup> MORRIS moved to postpone. It had been agreed to in the Committee on the ground of compromise, and he should feel himself at liberty to dissent to [14] it, if on the whole he should not be satisfied with certain other parts to be settled.— M<sup>r</sup> PINKNEY 2<sup>ded</sup> the motion

M<sup>r</sup> SHERMAN was for giving immediate ease to those who looked on this clause as of great moment, and for trusting to their concurrence in other proper measures.

On the question for postponing

N. H. ay. Mas. no. C<sup>t</sup> ay. N. J. ay. P<sup>a</sup> ay. Del. ay. M<sup>d</sup> ay. V<sup>a</sup> no. N. C. ay. S. C. ay. Geo. ay.[15]

So much of the (4) clause as related to the seat of Government was agreed to nem: con:

On the residue, to wit, "to exercise like authority over all places purchased for forts &c.

M<sup>r</sup> GERRY contended that this power might be made use of to enslave any particular State by buying up its territory, and that the strongholds proposed would be a means of awing the State into an undue obedience to the Gen<sup>l</sup> Government.

M<sup>r</sup> KING thought himself the provision unnecessary, the power being already involved: but would move to insert after the word "purchased" the words "by the consent of the Legislature of the State" This would certainly make the power safe.

M<sup>r</sup> Gov<sup>r</sup> MORRIS 2<sup>ded</sup> the motion, which was agreed to nem: con: as was then the residue of the clause as amended.

The (5) clause was agreed to nem: con:

The following resolution & order being reported from the Committee of eleven, to wit,

"Resolved that the U. S. in Congress be requested to allow and cause to be paid to the Secretary and other officers of this Convention such sums in proportion to their respective times of service, as are allowed to the Secretary & similar officers of Congress."

---

[14] The word "to" is crossed out in the transcript and "from" is written above it.

[15] In the transcript the vote reads: "New Hampshire, Connecticut, New Jersey, Pennsylvania, Delaware, Maryland, North Carolina, South Carolina, Georgia, aye—9; Massachusetts, Virginia, no—2."

"Ordered that the Secretary make out & transmit to the Treasury office of the U. S. an account for the said Services, & for the incidental expenses of this Convention"

The resolution & order were separately agreed to nem: con:

M.<sup>r</sup> GERRY gave notice that he should move to reconsider articles XIX. XX. XXI. XXII.

M.<sup>r</sup> WILLIAMSON gave like notice as to the Article fixing the number of Representatives, which he thought too small. He wished also to allow Rho: Island more than one, as due to her probable number of people, and as proper to stifle any pretext arising from her absence on the occasion.

The Report made yesterday as to the appointment of the Executive being [16] taken up. M.<sup>r</sup> PINKNEY renewed his opposition to the mode, arguing 1.[17] that the electors will not have sufficient knowledge of the fittest men, & will be swayed by an attachment to the eminent men of their respective States. Hence 2<sup>d.</sup><sup>ly</sup> the dispersion of the votes would leave the appointment with the Senate, and as the President's reappointment will thus depend on the Senate he will be the mere creature of that body. 3.[17] He will combine with the Senate ag.<sup>st</sup> the House of Representatives. 4.[17] This change in the mode of election was meant to get rid of the ineligibility of the President a second time, whereby he will become fixed for life under the auspices of the Senate

M.<sup>r</sup> GERRY did not object to this plan of constituting the Executive in itself, but should be governed in his final vote by the powers that may be given to the President.

M.<sup>r</sup> RUTLIDGE was much opposed to the plan reported by the Committee. It would throw the whole power into the Senate. He was also against a re-eligibility. He moved to postpone the Report under consideration & take up the original plan of appointment by the Legislature, to wit. "He shall be elected by joint ballot by the Legislature to which election a majority of the votes of the members present shall be required: He shall hold his office during the term of seven years; but shall not be elected a second time."

---

[16] The word "then" is here inserted in the transcript.

[17] The figures "1," "3" and "4" are changed to "first," "Thirdly" and "Fourthly" in the transcript.

On this motion to postpone

N. H. div⁴ Mas. no. C⁺ no. N. J. no. Pᵃ no. Del. no. M⁴ no. Vᵃ no. N. C. ay. S. C. ay. Geo. no.[18]

Col. MASON admitted that there were objections to an appointment by the Legislature as originally planned. He had not yet made up his mind, but would state his objections to the mode proposed by the Committee. 1.[19] It puts the appointment in fact into the hands of the Senate, as it will rarely happen that a majority of the whole votes will fall on any one candidate: and as the Existing President will always be one of the 5 highest, his re-appointment will of course depend on the Senate. 2.[19] Considering the powers of the President & those of the Senate, if a coalition should be established between these two branches, they will be able to subvert the Constitution—The great objection with him would be removed by depriving the Senate of the eventual election. He accordingly moved to strike out the words "if such number be a majority of that of the electors."

Mʳ WILLIAMSON 2ᵈᵉᵈ the motion. He could not agree to the clause without some such modification. He preferred making the highest tho' not having a majority of the votes, President, to a reference of the matter to the Senate. Referring the appointment to the Senate lays a certain foundation for corruption & aristocracy.

Mʳ Govʳ MORRIS thought the point of less consequence than it was supposed on both sides. It is probable that a majority of votes will fall on the same man. As each elector is to give two votes, more than ¼ will give a majority. Besides as one vote is to be given to a man out of the State, and as this vote will not be thrown away, ½ the votes will fall on characters eminent & generally known. Again if the President shall have given satisfaction, the votes will turn on him of course, and a majority of them will reappoint him, without resort to the Senate: If he should be disliked, all disliking him, would take care to unite their votes so as to ensure his being supplanted.

---

[18] In the transcript the vote reads: "North Carolina, South Carolina, aye—2; Massachusetts, Connecticut, New Jersey, Pennsylvania, Delaware, Maryland, Virginia, Georgia, no—8; New Hampshire, divided."
[19] The figures "1" and "2" are changed in the transcript to "First" and "Secondly."

Col. MASON those who think there is no danger of there not being a majority for the same person in the first instance, ought to give up the point to those who think otherwise.

Mʳ SHERMAN reminded the opponents of the new mode proposed that if the small states had the advantage in the Senate's deciding among the five highest candidates, the large States would have in fact the nomination of these candidates

On the motion of Col: Mason

N. H. no.   Mas. no.   Cᵗ no.   N. J. no.   Pᵃ no.   Del. no.   Mᵈ ay.*   Vᵃ no.   N. C. ay.   S. C. no.   Geo. no.[20]

Mʳ WILSON moved to strike out "Senate" and insert the word "Legislature"

Mʳ MADISON considered it as[21] a primary object to render an eventual resort to any part of the Legislature improbable. He was apprehensive that the proposed alteration would turn the attention of the large States too much to the appointment of candidates, instead of aiming at an effectual appointment of the officer, as the large States would predominate in the Legislature which would have the final choice out of the Candidates. Whereas if the Senate in which the small States predominate should have this[22] final choice, the concerted effort of the large States would be to make the appointment in the first instance conclusive.

Mʳ RANDOLPH. We have in some revolutions of this plan made a bold stroke for Monarchy. We are now doing the same for an aristocracy. He dwelt on the tendency of such an influence in the Senate over the election of the President in addition to its other powers, to convert that body into a real & dangerous Aristocracy.

Mʳ DICKINSON was in favor of giving the eventual election to the Legislature, instead of the Senate. It was too much influence to be superadded to that body.

On the question moved by Mʳ Wilson

N. H. divᵈ   Mas. no.   Cᵗ no.   N. J. no.   Pᵃ ay.   Del. no.   Mᵈ no.   Vᵃ ay.   N. C. no.   S. C. ay.   Geo. no.[23]

---

* In printed Journal Maryland—no.

[20] In the transcript the vote reads: "Maryland,* North Carolina, aye; the other nine States, no."

[21] The word "as" is stricken out in the transcript.

[22] The word "the" is substituted in the transcript for "this."

[23] In the transcript the vote reads: "Pennsylvania, Virginia, South Carolina, aye—3; Massachusetts, Connecticut, New Jersey, Delaware, Maryland, North Carolina, Georgia, no—7; New Hampshire, divided."

M! MADISON & M! WILLIAMSON moved to strike out the word "majority" and insert "one third" so that the eventual power might not be exercised if less than a majority, but not less than ⅓ of the Electors should vote for the same person.

M! GERRY objected that this would put it in the power of three or four States to put in whom they pleased.

M! WILLIAMSON. There are seven States which do not contain one third of the people. If the Senate are to appoint, less than one sixth of the people will have the power.

On the question

N. H. no. Mas. no. C! no. N. J. no. P!! no. Del. no. M! no. V!! ay. N. C. ay. S. C. no. Geo. no.[24]

M! GERRY suggested that the eventual election should be made by six Senators and seven Representatives chosen by joint ballot of both Houses.

M! KING observed that the influence of the Small States in the Senate was somewhat balanced by the influence of the large States in bringing forward the candidates; * and also by the Concurrence of the small States in the Committee in the clause vesting the exclusive origination of Money bills in the House of Representatives.

Col: MASON moved to strike out the word "five" and insert the word "three" as the highest candidates for the Senate to choose out of.

M! GERRY 2ded the motion

M! SHERMAN would sooner give up the plan. He would prefer seven or thirteen.

On the question moved by Col: Mason & M! Gerry

N. H. no. Mas. no. C! no. N. J. no. P!! no. Delaware M! no. V!! ay. N. C. ay. S. C. no. Geo. no. [26]

---

[24] In the transcript the vote reads: "Virginia, North Carolina, aye; the other nine States, no."

* This explains the compromise mentioned above[25] by M! Gov! Morris. Col. Mason M! Gerry & other members from large States set great value on this privilege of originating money bills. Of this the members from the small States, with some from the large States who wished a high mounted Gov! endeavored to avail themselves, by making that privilege, the price of arrangements in the constitution favorable to the small States, and to the elevation of the Government.

[25] The words "alluded to" are substituted in the transcript for "mentioned above."

[26] In the transcript the vote reads: "Virginia, North Carolina, aye; nine States, no,"

Mr SPAIGHT and Mr RUTLIDGE moved to strike out "five" and insert "thirteen"—to which all the States disagreed—except N. C. & S. C.

Mr MADISON & Mr WILLIAMSON moved to insert after "Electors" the words "who shall have balloted" so that the non voting electors not being counted might not increase the number necessary as a majority of the whole, to decide the choice without the agency of the Senate.

On this question

N. H. no. Mas. no. Ct no. N. J. no. Pa ay. Del. no. Md ay. Va ay. N. C. ay. S. C. no. Geo. no.[27]

Mr DICKINSON moved, in order to remove ambiguity from the intention of the clause as explained by the vote, to add, after the words "if such number be a majority of the whole number of the Electors" the word "appointed"

On this motion

N. H. ay. Mas. ay. Con: ay. N. J. ay. Pa ay. Delaware Md ay. Va no. N. C. no. S. C. ay. Geo. ay.[28]

Col: MASON. As the mode of appointment is now regulated, he could not forbear expressing his opinion that it is utterly inadmissible. He would prefer the Government of Prussia to one which will put all power into the hands of seven or eight men, and fix an Aristocracy worse than absolute monarchy.

The words "and of their giving their votes" being inserted on motion for that purpose, after the words "The Legislature may determine the time of chusing and assembling the Electors."

The House adjourned

---

THURSDAY SEPR 6. 1787.[29] IN CONVENTION

Mr KING and Mr GERRY moved to insert in the (5)[30] clause of the Report (see Sepr 4[31]) after the words "may be entitled in the Legislature" the words following—"But no person shall be ap-

---

[27] In the transcript the vote reads: "Pennsylvania, Maryland, Virginia, North Carolina, aye—4; New Hampshire, Massachusetts, Connecticut, New Jersey, Delaware, South Carolina, Georgia, no—7."
[28] In the transcript the vote reads: "New Hampshire, Massachusetts, Connecticut, New Jersey, Pennsylvania, Delaware, Maryland, South Carolina, Georgia, aye—9; Virginia, North Carolina, no—2."
[29] The year "1787" is omitted in the transcript.
[30] The word "fourth" is substituted in the transcript for "(5)," the latter being an error.
[31] In the transcript the date reads: "the fourth of September."

pointed an elector who is a member of the Legislature of the U. S. or who holds any office of profit or trust under the U. S." which passed nem: con:

M: GERRY proposed, as the President was to be elected by the Senate out of the five highest candidates, that if he should not at the end of his term be re-elected by a majority of the Electors, and no other candidate should have a majority, the eventual election should be made by the Legislature. This he said would relieve the President from his particular dependence on the Senate for his continuance in office.

M: KING liked the idea, as calculated to satisfy particular members & promote unanimity, & as likely to operate but seldom.

M: READ opposed it, remarking that if individual members were to be indulged, alterations would be necessary to satisfy most of them.

M: WILLIAMSON espoused it as a reasonable precaution against the undue influence of the Senate.

M: SHERMAN liked the arrangement as it stood, though he should not be averse to some amendments. He thought he said that if the Legislature were to have the eventual appointment instead of the Senate, it ought to vote in the case by States, in favor of the small States, as the large States would have so great an advantage in nominating the candidates.

M: Gov: MORRIS thought favorably of M: Gerry's proposition. It would free the President from being tempted in naming to Offices, to Conform to the will of the Senate, & thereby virtually give the appointments to office, to the Senate.

M: WILSON said that he had weighed carefully the report of the Committee for remodelling the constitution of the Executive; and on combining it with other parts of the plan, he was obliged to consider the whole as having a dangerous tendency to aristocracy; as throwing a dangerous power into the hands of the Senate. They will have in fact, the appointment of the President, and through his dependence on them, the virtual appointment to offices; among others the offices of the Judiciary Department. They are to make Treaties; and they are to try all impeachments. In allowing them thus to make the Executive & Judiciary appointments, to be the Court of impeachments, and to make Treaties which are to be laws of the land, the Legislative, Executive & Judiciary powers are all blended in one branch of the Government. The power of making Treaties involves the case of subsidies, and here as an additional evil, foreign influence is to be dreaded. According to the plan as it now stands, the President will not be the man of the people as he ought to be, but the Minion of the Senate. He cannot even appoint a tide-waiter without the Senate. He had always thought the Senate too numerous a body for making appointments to office. The Senate, will moreover in all probability be in constant Session. They will have high salaries. And with all those powers, and the President in their interest, they will depress the other branch of the Legislature, and aggrandize themselves in proportion. Add to all this, that the Senate sitting in conclave, can by holding up to their respective States various and improbable candidates, contrive so to scatter their votes, as to bring the appointment of the President ultimately before themselves. Upon the whole, he thought the new mode of appointing the President, with some amendments, a valuable improvement; but he could never agree to purchase it at the price of the ensuing parts of the Report, nor befriend a system of which they make a part.

Mr Govr Morris expressed his wonder at the observations of Mr Wilson so far as they preferred the plan in the printed Report to the new modification of it before the House, and entered into a comparative view of the two, with an eye to the nature of Mr Wilsons objections to the last. By the first the Senate he observed had a voice in appointing the President out of all the Citizens of the U. S: by this they were limited to five candidates previously nominated to them, with a probability of being barred altogether by the successful ballot of the Electors. Here surely was no increase of power. They are now to appoint Judges nominated to them by the President. Before they had the appointment without any agency whatever of the President. Here again was surely no additional power. If they are to make Treaties as the plan now stands, the power was the same in the printed plan. If they are to try impeachments, the Judges must have been triable by them before. Wherein then lay the dangerous tendency of the innovations to establish an aristocracy in the Senate? As to the appointment of officers, the weight of sentiment in the House, was opposed to the exercise of it by the President alone; though it was not the case with himself. If the Senate would act as was suspected, in misleading the States into a fallacious disposition of their votes for a President, they would, if the appointment were withdrawn wholly from them, make such representations in their several States where they have influence, as would favor the object of their partiality.

Mr WILLIAMSON. replying to Mr Morris: observed that the aristocratic complexion proceeds from the change in the mode of appointing the President which makes him dependent on the Senate.

Mr CLYMER said that the aristocratic part to which he could never accede was that in the printed plan, which gave the Senate the power of appointing to offices.

Mr HAMILTON said that he had been restrained from entering into the discussions by his dislike of the Scheme of Govt in General; but as he meant to support the plan to be recommended, as better than nothing, he wished in this place to offer a few remarks. He liked the new modification, on the whole, better than that in the printed Report. In this the President was a Monster elected for seven years, and ineligible afterwards; having great powers, in appointments to office, & continually tempted by this constitutional disqualification to abuse them in order to subvert the Government. Although he should be made re-eligible, still if appointed by the Legislature, he would be tempted to make use of corrupt influence to be continued in office. It seemed peculiarly desireable therefore that some other mode of election should be devised. Considering the different views of different States, & the different districts Northern Middle & Southern, he concurred with those who thought that the votes would not be concentered, and that the appointment would consequently in the present mode devolve on the Senate. The nomination to offices will give great weight to the President. Here then is a mutual connection & influence, that will perpetuate the President, and aggrandize both him & the Senate. What is to be the remedy? He saw none better than to let the highest number of ballots, whether a majority or not, appoint the President. What was the objection to this? Merely that too small a number might appoint. But as the plan stands, the Senate may take the candidate having the smallest number of votes, and make him President.

M̃ʳ SPAIGHT & M̃ʳ WILLIAMSON moved to insert "seven" instead of "four" years for the term of the President—*

On this motion

N. H. ay. Mas. no. Cᵗ no. N. J. no. Pᵃ no. Del. no. Mᵈ no. Vᵃ ay. N. C. ay. S. C. no. Geo. no.³³

M̃ʳ SPAIGHT & M̃ʳ WILLIAMSON, then moved to insert "six" instead of "four."

On which motion

N. H. no. Mas. no. Cᵗ no. N. J. no. Pᵃ no. Del. no. Mᵈ no. Vᵃ no. N. C. ay. S. C. ay. Geo. no³⁴

On the term "four" all the States were ay, except N. Carolina, no.

On the question³⁵ (Clause 4. in the Report) for Appointing³⁶ President by electors—down to the words,—"entitled in the Legislature" inclusive.

N. H. ay. Mas: ay. Conᵗ ay N. J. ay. Pᵃ ay. Del. ay. Mᵈ ay. Vᵃ ay. N. C. no. S. C. no. Geo. ay.³⁷

It was moved that the Electors meet at the seat of the Genˡ Govᵗ which passed in the Negative. N. C. only being ay.

It was ³⁸ moved to insert the words "under the seal of the State" after the word "transmit" in ³⁶ 4ᵗʰ clause of the Report which was disagreed to; as was another motion to insert the words "and who shall have given their votes" after the word "appointed" in

---

* Transfer hither what is brackets.³¹

[* An ineligibility wᵈ have followed (tho' it wᵈ seem from the vote not in the opinion of all) this prolongation of the term.]

³² Madison's direction is omitted in the transcript.

³³ In the transcript the vote reads: "New Hampshire, Virginia, North Carolina, aye—3; Massachusetts, Connecticut, New Jersey, Pennsylvania, Delaware, Maryland, South Carolina, Georgia, no—8."

³⁴ In the transcript the vote reads: "North Carolina, South Carolina, aye—2; New Hampshire, Massachusetts, Connecticut, New Jersey, Pennsylvania, Delaware, Maryland, Virginia, Georgia, no—9."

³⁵ The words "on the" are here inserted in the transcript.

³⁶ The word "the" is here inserted in the transcript.

³⁷ In the transcript the vote reads: "New Hampshire, Massachusetts, Connecticut, New Jersey, Pennsylvania, Delaware, Maryland, Virginia, Georgia, aye—9; North Carolina, South Carolina, no—2."

³⁸ The word "then" is here inserted in the transcript.

the 4th Clause of the Report as added yesterday on motion of Mr Dickinson.

On several motions, the words "in presence of the Senate and House of Representatives" were inserted after the word "counted" and the word "immediately" before the word "choose"; and the words "of the Electors" after the word "votes."

Mr SPAIGHT said if the election by Electors is to be crammed down, he would prefer their meeting altogether and deciding finally without any reference to the Senate and moved " That the Electors meet at the seat of the General Government."

Mr WILLIAMSON 2ded the motion, on which all the States were in the negative except N: Carolina.

On motion the words "But the election shall be on the same day throughout the U. S." were added after the words "transmitting their votes"

N. H. ay. Mas. no. Ct ay. N. J. no. Pa ay. Del. no. Md ay. Va ay. N. C. ay. S. C. ay. Geo—ay.[39]

On a question on the sentence in clause (4). "if such number be a majority of that of the Electors appointed."

N. H. ay. Mas. ay. Ct ay. N. J. ay. Pa no. Del. ay. Md ay. Va no. N. C. no. S. C. ay. Geo. ay.[40]

On a question on the clause referring the eventual appointment of the President to the Senate

N. H. ay. Mas. ay. Ct ay. N. J. ay. Pa ay. Del. ay. Va ay. N. C. no.[41] Here the call ceased.

Mr MADISON made a motion requiring ⅔ at least of the Senate to be present at the choice of a President. Mr PINKNEY 2ded the motion

Mr GORHAM thought it a wrong principle to require more than a majority in any case. In the present case [42] it might prevent for a long time any choice of a President. On the question moved by Mr M. & Mr P.

---

[39] In the transcript the vote reads: "New Hampshire, Connecticut, Pennsylvania, Maryland, Virginia, North Carolina, South Carolina, Georgia, aye—8; Massachusetts, New Jersey, Delaware, no—3."

[40] In the transcript the vote reads: "New Hampshire, Massachusetts, Connecticut, New Jersey, Delaware, Maryland, South Carolina, Georgia, aye—8; Pennsylvania, Virginia, North Carolina, no—3."

[41] In the transcript the vote reads: "New Hampshire, Massachusetts, Connecticut, New Jersey, Pennsylvania, Delaware, Virginia, aye—7; North Carolina, no."

[42] The word "case" is omitted in the transcript.

N. H. ay: Mas. abs? C? no. N. J. no. P? no. Del. no. M? ay. V? ay. N. C. ay. S. C. ay. Geo. ay.⁴³

Mʳ WILLIAMSON suggested as better than an eventual choice by the Senate, that this choice should be made by the Legislature, voting *by States* and not *per capita*.

Mʳ SHERMAN suggested the House of Repˢ as preferable to the Legislature, and moved, accordingly,

To strike out the words "The Senate shall immediately choose &c." and insert "The House of Representatives shall immediately choose by ballot one of them for President, the members from each State having one vote."

Col: MASON liked the latter mode best as lessening the aristocratic influence of the Senate.

On the Motion of Mʳ Sherman

N. H. ay. Mas. ay. C? ay. N. J. ay. P? ay. Del. no. M?. ay. V? ay. N. C. ay. S. C. ay. Geo. ay.⁴⁴

Mʳ Govʳ MORRIS suggested the idea of providing that in all cases, the President in office, should not be one of the five Candidates; but be only re-eligible in case a majority of the electors should vote for him. [This was another expedient for rendering the President independent of the Legislative body for his continuance in office.]

Mʳ MADISON remarked that as a majority of members wᵈ make a quorum in the H. of Repˢ it would follow from the amendment of Mʳ Sherman giving the election to a majority of States, that the President might be elected by two States only, Virgᵃ & Penᵃ which have 18 members, if these States alone should be present

On a motion that the eventual election of Presidᵗ in case of *an equality*⁴⁵ of the votes of the electors be referred to the House of Repˢ

N. H. ay. Mas. ay. N. J. no. P? ay. Del. no. Mᵈ no. V? ay. N. C. ay. S. C. ay. Geo. ay.⁴⁶

Mʳ KING moved to add to the amendment of Mʳ Sherman "But a quorum for this purpose shall consist of a member or members

---

⁴³ In the transcript the vote reads: "New Hampshire, Maryland, Virginia, North Carolina, South Carolina, Georgia, aye—6; Connecticut, New Jersey, Pennsylvania, Delaware, no—4; Massachusetts, absent."

⁴⁴ In the transcript the vote reads: "New Hampshire, Massachusetts, Connecticut, New Jersey, Pennsylvania, Maryland, Virginia, North Carolina, South Carolina, Georgia, aye—10. Delaware, no—1."

⁴⁵ The transcript does not italicize the words "*an equality*."

⁴⁶ In the transcript the vote reads: "New Hampshire, Massachusetts, Pennsylvania, Virginia, North Carolina, South Carolina, Georgia, aye—7; New Jersey, Delaware, Maryland, no—3."

from two thirds of the States," and also of a majority of the whole number of the House of Representatives."

Col: MASON liked it as obviating the remark of M!‍ Madison— The motion as far as "States" inclusive was ag.d to. On the residue to wit, "and also of a majority of the whole number of the House of Rep.s it passed in the Negative.

N. H. no. Mas. ay. C.t ay. N. J. no. P.a ay. Del. no. M.d no. V.a ay. N. C. ay. S. C. no. Geo. no.[47]

The Report relating to the appointment of the Executive stands as amended, as follows,

"He shall hold his office during the term of four years, and together with the vice-President, chosen for the same term, be elected in the following manner.

Each State shall appoint in such manner as its Legislature may direct, a number of electors equal to the whole number of Senators and members of the House of Representatives, to which the State may be entitled in the Legislature:

But no person shall be appointed an Elector who is a member of the Legislature of the U. S. or who holds any office of profit or trust under the U. S.

The Electors shall meet in their respective States and vote by ballot for two persons, of whom one at least shall not be an inhabitant of the same State with themselves; and they shall make a list of all the persons voted for, and of the number of votes for each, which list they shall sign and certify, and transmit sealed to the Seat of the General Government, directed to the President of the Senate.

The President of the Senate shall in the presence of the Senate and House of Representatives open all the certificates & the votes shall then be counted.

The person having the greatest number of votes shall be the President (if such number be a majority of the whole number of electors appointed) and if there be more than one who have such majority, and have an equal number of votes, then the House of Representatives shall immediately choose by ballot one of them for President, the Representation from each State having one vote. But if no person have a majority, then from the five highest on the list, the House of Representatives shall in like manner choose

---

[47] In the transcript the vote reads: "Massachusetts, Connecticut, Pennsylvania, Virginia, North Carolina, aye—5; New Hampshire, New Jersey, Delaware, Maryland, South Carolina, Georgia, no—6."

by ballot the President. In the choice of a President by the House of Representatives, a Quorum shall consist of a member or members from two thirds of the States [\* and the concurrence of a majority of all the States shall be necessary to such choice.]—And in every case after the choice of the President, the person having the greatest number of votes of the Electors shall be the vice-president: But, if there should remain two or more who have equal votes, the Senate shall choose from them the vice-President.

The Legislature may determine the time of choosing the Electors, and of their giving their votes; and the manner of certifying and transmitting their votes—But the election shall be on the same day throughout the U. States."

Adjourned

---

FRIDAY SEP.<sup>R</sup> 7. 1787.<sup>50</sup>  IN CONVENTION

The mode of constituting the Executive being resumed, M.<sup>r</sup> RANDOLPH moved, to insert in the first Section of the report made yesterday <sup>51</sup>

"The Legislature may declare by law what officer of the U. S. shall act as President in case of the death, resignation, or disability of the President and Vice-President; and such officer shall act accordingly until the time of electing a President shall arrive."

M.<sup>r</sup> MADISON observed that this, as worded, would prevent a supply of the vacancy by an intermediate election of the President, and moved to substitute—"until such disability be removed, or a President shall be elected.† M.<sup>r</sup> GOVERN.<sup>r</sup> MORRIS 2<sup>ded</sup> the motion, which was agreed to.

It seemed to be an objection to the provision with some, that according to the process established for chusing the Executive there would be difficulty in effecting it at other than the fixed periods; with others, that the Legislature was restrained in the temporary appointment to "*officers*" of the *U. S:* They wished it to be at liberty to appoint others than such.

---

\* NOTE. This clause was not inserted on this day, but on the 7.<sup>th</sup> <sup>48</sup> Sep.<sup>r</sup> See Friday the 7.<sup>th</sup> <sup>49</sup>
<sup>48</sup> The word "of" is here inserted in the transcript.
<sup>49</sup> The word "inst." is here inserted in the transcript.
<sup>50</sup> The year "1787" is omitted in the transcript.
<sup>51</sup> The words "the following" are here inserted in the transcript.
† In the printed Journal this amendment is put into the original Motion.

*The Home of John Randolph*

On the Motion of Mr Randolph as amended, it passed in the affirmative

N. H. divided. Mas. no. Ct no. N. J. ay. Pa ay. Del. no. Md ay. Va ay. N. C. no. S. C. ay. Geo. ay.[52]

Mr GERRY moved "that in the election of President by the House of Representatives, no State shall vote by less than three members, and where that number may not be allotted to a State, it shall be made up by its Senators; and a concurrence of a majority of all the States shall be necessary to make such choice." Without some such provision five individuals might possibly be competent to an election; these being a majority of two thirds of the existing number of States; and two thirds being a quorum for this business.

Mr MADISON 2ded the motion

Mr READ observed that the States having but one member only in the House of Reps would be in danger of having no vote at all in the election: the sickness or absence either of the Representative or one of the Senators would have that effect.

Mr MADISON replied that, if one member of the House of Representatives should be left capable of voting for the State, the states having one Representative only would still be subject to that danger. He thought it an evil that so small a number at any rate should be authorized, to elect. Corruption would be greatly facilitated by it. The mode itself was liable to this further weighty objection that the representatives of a *Minority* of the people, might reverse the choice of a *majority* of the *States* and of the *people*. He wished some cure for this inconveniency [53] might yet be provided.

Mr GERRY withdrew the first part of his motion; and on the,— Question on the 2d part viz. "and a concurrence of a majority of all the States shall be necessary to make such choice" to follow the words "a member or members from two thirds of the States"—It was agreed to nem: con:

---

[52] In the transcript the vote reads: "New Jersey, Pennsylvania, Maryland, Virginia, South Carolina, Georgia, aye—6; Massachusetts, Connecticut, Delaware, North Carolina, no—4; New Hampshire, divided."

[53] The word "inconveniency" is changed to "inconvenience" in the transcript.

The section 2. (see Sep: 4) requiring that the President should be a natural-born Citizen, &c & have been resident for fourteen years, & be thirty five years of age, was agreed to nem: con:

[54] Section 3. (see Sep: 4). " The vice President shall be ex-officio President of the Senate"

M: GERRY opposed this regulation. We might as well put the President himself at the head of the Legislature. The close intimacy that must subsist between the President & vice-president makes it absolutely improper. He was ag$^{st}$ having any vice President.

M: GOV: MORRIS. The vice president then will be the first heir apparent that ever loved his father. If there should be no vice president, the President of the Senate would be temporary successor, which would amount to the same thing.

M: SHERMAN saw no danger in the case. If the vice-President were not to be President of the Senate, he would be without employment, and some member by being made President must be deprived of his vote, unless when an equal division of votes might happen in the Senate, which would be but seldom.

M: RANDOLPH concurred in the opposition to the clause.

M: WILLIAMSON, observed that such an officer as vice-President was not wanted. He was introduced only for the sake of a valuable mode of election which required two to be chosen at the same time.

Col: MASON, thought the office of vice-President an encroachment on the rights of the Senate; and that it mixed too much the Legislative & Executive, which as well as the Judiciary departments,[55] ought to be kept as separate as possible. He took occasion to express his dislike of any reference whatever of the power to make appointments to either branch of the Legislature. On the other hand he was averse to vest so dangerous a power in the President alone. As a method for avoiding both, he suggested that a privy Council of six members to the president should be established; to be chosen for six years by the Senate, two out of the Eastern two out of the middle, and two out of the Southern quarters of the Union, & to go out in rotation two every second

---

[54] This paragraph is changed in the transcript to read as follows: "The third section, 'The Vice-President shall be *ex-officio* President of the Senate' being then considered."

[55] The letter "s" is striken from the word "departments" in the transcript.

year; the concurrence of the Senate to be required only in the appointment of Ambassadors, and in making treaties, which are more of a legislative nature. This would prevent the constant sitting of the Senate which he thought dangerous, as well as keep the departments separate & distinct. It would also save the expence of constant sessions of the Senate. He had he said always considered the Senate as too unwieldy & expensive for appointing officers, especially the smallest, such as tide waiters &c. He had not reduced his idea to writing, but it could be easily done if it should be found acceptable.

On the question shall the vice President be ex officio President of the Senate?

N. H. ay. Mas. ay. C$^t$ ay. N. J. no. P$^a$ ay. Del ay. Mas no. V$^a$ ay. N. C. abs$^t$ S. C. ay. Geo. ay.[56]

The other parts of the same Section (3)[57] were then agreed to.

The Section 4.—to wit, "The President by & with the advice and consent of the Senate shall have power to make Treaties &c"[58]

M$^r$ WILSON moved to add, after the word "Senate" the words, "and House of Representatives." As treaties he said are to have the operation of laws, they ought to have the sanction of laws also. The circumstance of secrecy in the business of treaties formed the only objection; but this he thought, so far as it was inconsistent with obtaining the Legislative sanction, was outweighed by the necessity of the latter.

M$^r$ SHERMAN thought the only question that could be made was whether the power could be safely trusted to the Senate. He thought it could; and that the necessity of secresy in the case of treaties forbade a reference of them to the whole Legislature.

M$^r$ FITZIMMONS 2$^{ded}$ the motion of M$^r$ Wilson, & on the question N. H. no. Mas. no. C$^t$ no. N. J. no. P$^a$ ay. Del. no. M$^d$ no. V$^a$ no. N. C. no. S. C. no. Geo. no.[59]

---

[56] In the transcript the vote reads: "New Hampshire, Massachusetts, Connecticut, Pennsylvania, Delaware, Virginia, South Carolina, Georgia, aye—8; New Jersey, Maryland, no—2; North Carolina, absent."

[57] The figure "3" is omitted in the transcript.

[58] The phrase "was then taken up" is here added in the transcript.

[59] In the transcript the vote reads: "Pennsylvania, aye—1; New Hampshire, Massachusetts, Connecticut, New Jersey, Delaware, Maryland, Virginia, North Carolina, South Carolina, Georgia, no—10."

The first sentence as to making treaties was then Agreed to: nem: con:

[60] "He shall nominate &c Appoint Ambassadors &c."

Mʳ WILSON objected to the mode of appointing, as blending a branch of the Legislature with the Executive. Good laws are of no effect without a good Executive; and there can be no good Executive without a responsible appointment of officers to execute. Responsibility is in a manner destroyed by such an agency of the Senate. He would prefer the council proposed by Col: Mason, provided its advice should not be made obligatory on the President.

Mʳ PINKNEY was against joining the Senate in these appointments, except in the instance of Ambassadors whom [61] he thought ought not to be appointed by the President.

Mʳ Govʳ MORRIS said that as the President was to nominate, there would be responsibility, and as the Senate was to concur, there would be security. As Congress now make appointments there is no responsibility.

Mʳ GERRY. The idea of responsibility in the nomination to offices is chimerical. The President can not know all characters, and can therefore always plead ignorance.

Mʳ KING. As the idea of a Council proposed by Col. Mason has been supported by Mʳ Wilson, he would remark that most of the inconveniencies charged on the Senate are incident to a Council of Advice. He differed from those who thought the Senate would sit constantly. He did not suppose it was meant that all the minute officers were to be appointed by the Senate, or any other original source, but by the higher officers of the departments to which they belong. He was of opinion also that the people would be alarmed at an unnecessary creation of new Corps which must increase the expence as well as influence of the Government.

On the question on these words in the clause viz—"He shall nominate & by & with the advice and consent of the Senate, shall appoint ambassadors, and other public ministers (and Consuls) [62]

---

[60] The words "On the clause" are here inserted in the transcript.
[61] The word "who" is substituted in the transcript for "whom."
[62] The word "and" is here inserted in the transcript.

Judges of the Supreme Court."[63] Agreed to nem: con: the insertion of "and consuls" having first taken place.

On the question on the following words "And all other officers of [64] U. S."

N. H. ay. Mas. ay. Ct ay. N. J. ay. Pa no. Del. ay. Md ay. Va ay. N. C. ay. S. C. no. Geo. ay.[65]

On motion of Mr SPAIGHT—"that the President shall have power to fill up all vacancies that may happen during the recess of the Senate by granting Commissions which shall expire at the end of the next Session of the Senate" It was agreed to nem: con:

[64] Section 4. "The President by and with the advice and consent of the Senate shall have power to make Treaties"—"*But no treaty shall be made without the consent of two thirds of the members present*"—this last [66] being before the House.

Mr WILSON thought it objectionable to require the concurrence of ⅔ which puts it in [67] the power of a minority to controul the will of a majority.

Mr KING concurred in the objection; remarking that as the Executive was here joined in the business, there was a check which did not exist in Congress where The concurrence of ⅔ was required.

Mr MADISON moved to insert after the word "treaty" the words "except treaties of peace" allowing these to be made with less difficulty than other treaties—It was agreed to nem: con:

Mr MADISON then moved to authorise a concurrence of two thirds of the Senate to make treaties of peace, without the concurrence of the President."—The President he said would necessarily derive so much power and importance from a state of war that he might be tempted, if authorised, to impede a treaty of peace. Mr BUTLER 2ded the motion

Mr GORHAM thought the precaution [68] unnecessary as the means of carrying on the war would not be in the hands of the President, but of the Legislature.

---

[63] The words "it was" are here inserted in the transcript.
[64] The word "the" is here inserted in the transcript.
[65] In the transcript the vote reads: "New Hampshire, Massachusetts, Connecticut, New Jersey, Delaware, Maryland, Virginia, North Carolina, Georgia, aye—9; Pennsylvania, South Carolina, no—2."
[66] The words "being considered, and the last clause" are substituted in the transcript for "this last."
[67] The word "into" is substituted in the transcript for "in."
[68] In the transcript the word "precaution" is stricken out and the word "security" is written above it.

Mr Govr Morris thought the power of the President in this case harmless; and that no peace ought to be made without the concurrence of the President, who was the general Guardian of the National interests.

Mr Butler was strenuous for the motion, as a necessary security against ambitious & corrupt Presidents. He mentioned the late perfidious policy of the Statholder in Holland; and the artifices of the Duke of Marlbro' to prolong the war of which he had the management.

Mr Gerry was of opinion that in treaties of peace a greater rather than less proportion of votes was necessary, than in other treaties. In Treaties of peace the dearest interests will be at stake, as the fisheries, territory &c. In treaties of peace also there is more dander to the extremities of the Continent, of being sacrificed, than on any other occasions.

Mr Williamson thought that Treaties of peace should be guarded at least by requiring the same concurrence as in other Treaties.

On the motion of Mr Madison & Mr Butler

N. H. no. Mas. no. Ct no. N. J. no. Pa no. Del. no. Md ay. Va no. N. C. no. S. C. ay. Geo. ay.[69]

On the part of the clause concerning treaties amended by the exception as to Treaties of peace,

N. H. ay. Mas. ay. Ct ay. N. J. no. Pa no. Del. ay. Md ay. Va ay. N. C. ay. S. C. ay. Geo. no.[70]

[71] "and may require the opinion in writing of the principal officer in each of the Executive Departments, upon any subject relating to the duties of their respective offices," being before the House

Col: Mason * said that in rejecting a Council to the President we were about to try an experiment on which the most despotic Governments had never ventured. The Grand Signor himself

---

[69] In the transcript the vote reads: "Maryland, South Carolina, Georgia, aye—3; New Hampshire, Massachusetts, Connecticut, New Jersey, Pennsylvania, Delaware, Virginia, North Carolina, no—8."

[70] In the transcript the vote reads: "New Hampshire, Massachusetts, Connecticut, Delaware, Maryland, Virginia, North Carolina, South Carolina, aye—8; New Jersey, Pennsylvania, Georgia, no—3."

[71] The words "The clause" are here inserted in the transcript.

* In the printed Journal, Mr Madison is erroneously substituted for Col: Mason.

had his Divan. He moved to postpone the consideration of the clause in order to take up the following

"That it be an instruction to the Committee of the States to prepare a clause or clauses for establishing an Executive Council, as a Council of State, for the President of the U. States, to consist of six members, two of which from the Eastern, two from the middle, and two from the Southern States, with a Rotation and duration of office similar to those of the Senate; such Council to be appointed by the Legislature or by the Senate."

Doctor FRANKLIN 2$^{ded}$ the motion. We seemed he said too much to fear cabals in appointments by a number, and to have too much confidence in those of single persons. Experience shewed that caprice, the intrigues of favorites & mistresses, &c [72] were nevertheless the means most prevalent in monarchies. Among instances of abuse in such modes of appointment, he mentioned the many bad Governors appointed in G. B. for the Colonies. He thought a Council would not only be a check on a bad President but be a relief to a good one.

M$^r$ Gov$^r$ MORRIS. The question of a Council was considered in the Committee, where it was judged that the Presid$^t$ by persuading his Council, to concur in his wrong measures, would acquire their protection for them.

M$^r$ WILSON approved of a Council in preference to making the Senate a party to appointm$^{ts}$

M$^r$ DICKENSON was for a Council. It w$^d$ be a singular thing if the measures of the Executive were not to undergo some previous discussion before the President.

M$^r$ MADISON was in favor of the instruction to the Committee proposed by Col: Mason.

The motion of M$^r$ [73] Mason was negatived. Mary$^d$ ay. S. C. ay. Geo. ay— N. H. no. Mas. no. C$^t$ no. N. J. no P$^a$ no. Del. no. V$^a$ no. N C no.[74]

---

[72] The character "&c" is omitted in the transcript.

[73] The word "Col." is substituted in the transcript for "Mr."

[74] In the transcript the vote reads' "Maryland, South Carolina, Georgia, aye—3; New Hampshire, Massachusetts, Connecticut, New Jersey, Pennsylvania, Delaware, Virginia, North Carolina, no—8."

On the question,[75] "authorising the President to call for the opinions of the Heads of Departments, in writing": it passed in the affirmative, N. H. only being no.*

The clause was then unanimously agreed to—

Mr WILLIAMSON & Mr SPAIGHT moved "that no Treaty of Peace affecting Territorial rights shd; be made without the concurrence of two thirds of the members of the Senate present.

Mr KING. It will be necessary to look out for securities for some other rights, if this principle be established; he moved to extend the motion—"to all present rights of the U. States."

Adjourned

SATURDAY SEPTEMBER 8TH. IN CONVENTION

The last Report of [76] Committee of Eleven (see Sepr 4) was resumed.

Mr KING moved to strike out the "exception of Treaties of peace" from the general clause requiring two thirds of the Senate for making Treaties

Mr WILSON wished the requisition of two thirds to be struck out altogether If the majority cannot be trusted, it was a proof, as observed by Mr Ghorum, that we were not fit for one Society.

A reconsideration of the whole clause was agreed to.

Mr Govr MORRIS was agst striking out the "exception of Treaties of peace" If two thirds of the Senate should be required for peace, the Legislature will be unwilling, to make war for that reason, on account of the Fisheries or the Mississippi, the two great objects of the Union. Besides, if a majority of the Senate be for peace, and are not allowed to make it, they will be apt to effect their purpose in the more disagreeable mode, of negativing the supplies for the war.

Mr WILLIAMSON remarked that Treaties are to be made in the branch of the Govt where there may be a majority of the States without a majority of the people. Eight men may be a majority

---

[75] The word "for" is here inserted in the transcript.

* Not so stated in the Printed Journal; but conformable to the result-afterwards appearing.

[76] The word "the" is here inserted in the transcript.

of a quorum, & should not have the power to decide the conditions of peace. There would be no danger, that the exposed States, as S. Carolina or Georgia, would urge an improper war for the Western Territory.

M⃨ WILSON If two thirds are necessary to make peace, the minority may perpetuate war, against the sense of the majority.

M⃨ GERRY enlarged on the danger of putting the essential rights of the Union in the hands of so small a number as a majority of the Senate, representing, perhaps, not one fifth of the people. The Senate will be corrupted by foreign influence.

M⃨ SHERMAN was ag.⃨ leaving the rights established by the Treaty of peace, to the Senate, & moved to annex a "proviso that no such rights sh.⃨ be ceded without the sanction of the Legislature."

M⃨ Gov⃨ MORRIS seconded the ideas of M⃨ Sherman.

M⃨ MADISON observed that it had been too easy in the present Congress to make Treaties altho' nine States were required for the purpose.

On the question for striking [77] "except Treaties of peace"

N. H. ay. Mas. ay. C.⃨ ay. N. J. no. P.⃨ ay. Del. no. M.⃨ no V.⃨ ay. N. C. ay. S. C. ay. Geo. ay.[78]

M⃨ WILSON & M⃨ DAYTON move to strike out the clause requiring two thirds of the Senate for making Treaties—on which,

N. H. no. Mas. no. C.⃨ div.⃨ N. J. no. P.⃨ no Del. ay. M.⃨ no. V.⃨ no. N. C. no. S. C. no. Geo. no.[79]

M⃨ RUTLIDGE & M⃨ GERRY move that "no Treaty [80] be made without the consent of $\frac{2}{3}$ of all the members of the Senate"— according to the example in the present Cong⃨

M⃨ GHORUM. There is a difference in the case, as the President's consent will also be necessary in the new Gov.⃨

On the question

---

[77] The word "out" is here inserted in the transcript.
[78] In the transcript the vote reads: "New Hampshire, Massachusetts, Connecticut, Pennsylvania, Virginia, North Carolina, South Carolina, Georgia, aye—8; New Jersey, Delaware, Maryland, no—3."
[79] In the transcript the vote reads: "Delaware, aye—1; New Hampshire, Massachusetts, New Jersey, Pennsylvania, Maryland, Virginia, North Carolina, South Carolina, Georgia, no—9; Connecticut, divided."
[80] The word "shall" is here inserted in the transcript.

N. H. no. Mass. no. (M！ Gerry ay) C！ no. N. J. no. P͟a no. Del. no. M͟d no. V͟a no. N. C. ay. S. C. ay. Geo. ay.[81]

M！ SHARMAN mov͟d that no Treaty [82] be made without a Majority of the whole number of the Senate. M！ GERRY seconded him.

M！ WILLIAMSON. This will be less security than ⅔ as now required.

M！ SHERMAN. It will be less embarrassing.

On the question, it passed in the negative.

N. H. no. Mas. ay. C！ ay. N. J. no. P͟a no. Del. ay. M͟d no. V͟a no. N. C. no. S. C. ay. Geo. ay.[83]

M！ MADISON mov͟d that a Quorum of the Senate consist of ⅔ of all the members.

M！ GOV！ MORRIS—This will put it in the power of one man to break up a Quorum.

M！ MADISON, This may happen to any Quorum.

On the Question it passed in the negative

N. H. no. Mas. no. C！ no. N. J. no. P͟a no. Del. no. M͟d ay. V͟a ay. N. C. ay. S. C. ay. Geo. ay.[84]

M！ WILLIAMSON & M！ GERRY, mov͟d "that no Treaty sh͟d be made with͟t previous notice to the members, & a reasonable time for their attending."

On the Question

All the States no, except N. C. S. C. & Geo. ay.

On the question on [85] clause of the Report of the Com！ of Eleven relating to Treaties by ⅔ of the Senate. All the States were ay— except P͟a N. J. & Geo. no.

M！ GERRY mov͟d that no officer [82] be app͟d but to offices created by the Constitution or by law"—This was rejected as unnecessary by six no's & five ays; [86]

---

[81] In the transcript the vote reads: "North Carolina, South Carolina, Georgia, aye—3; New Hampshire, Massachusetts (Mr. Gerry, aye), Connecticut, New Jersey, Pennsylvania, Delaware, Maryland, Virginia, no—8."

[82] The word "shall" is here inserted in the transcript.

[83] In the transcript the vote reads: "Massachusetts, Connecticut, Delaware, South Carolina, Georgia, aye—5; New Hampshire, New Jersey, Pennsylvania, Maryland, Virginia, North Carolina, no—6."

[84] In the transcript the vote reads: "Maryland, Virginia, North Carolina, South Carolina, Georgia, aye—5; New Hampshire, Massachusetts, Connecticut, New Jersey, Pennsylvania, Delaware, no—6."

[85] The word "the" is here inserted in the transcript.

[86] The words "by six no's & five ayes" are stricken out in the transcript.

The Ayes. Mas. Ct N. J. N. C. Geo.—Noes. N. H. Pa: Del. Md Va S. C.[87]

The clause referring to the Senate, the trial of impeachments agst the President, for Treason & bribery, was taken up.

Col. MASON. Why is the provision restrained to Treason & bribery only? Treason as defined in the Constitution will not reach many great and dangerous offences. Hastings is not guilty of Treason. Attempts to subvert the Constitution may not be Treason as above defined. As bills of attainder which have saved the British Constitution are forbidden, it is the more necessary to extend: the power of impeachments. He movd to add after "bribery" "or maladministration." Mr GERRY seconded him.

Mr MADISON So vague a term will be equivalent to a tenure during pleasure of the Senate.

Mr Govr MORRIS, it will not be put in force & can do no harm. An election of every four years will prevent maladministration.

Col. MASON withdrew "maladministration" & substitutes "other high crimes & misdemesnors agst the State"

On the question thus altered

N. H. ay. Mas. ay. Ct ay. N. J. no. Pa no. Del. no. Md ay. Va ay. N. C. ay. S. C. ay.* Geo. ay.[88]

Mr MADISON, objected to a trial of the President by the Senate, especially as he was to be impeached by the other branch of the Legislature, and for any act which might be called a misdemesnor. The President under these circumstances was made improperly dependent. He would prefer the Supreme Court for the trial of impeachments, or rather a tribunal of which that should form a part.

Mr Govr MORRIS thought no other tribunal than the Senate could be trusted. The supreme Court were too few in number and might be warped or corrupted. He was agst a dependence of the Executive on the Legislature, considering the Legislative tyranny the great danger to be apprehended; but there could be

---

[87] In the transcript the vote reads: "Massachusetts, Connecticut, New Jersey, North Carolina, Georgia, aye—5; New Hampshire, Pennsylvania, Delaware, Maryland, Virginia, South Carolina, no—6."

* In the printed Journal, S. Carolina—no.

[88] In the transcript the vote reads' "New Hampshire, Massachusetts, Connecticut, Maryland, Virginia, North Carolina, South Carolina,* Georgia, aye—8; New Jersey, Pennsylvania, Delaware, no—3."

no danger that the Senate would say untruly on their oaths that the President was guilty of crimes or facts, especially as in four years he can be turned out.

M! PINKNEY disapproved of making the Senate the Court of Impeachments, as rendering the President too dependent on the Legislature. If he opposes a favorite law, the two Houses will combine ag$^{st}$ him, and under the influence of heat and faction throw him out of office.

M! WILLIAMSON thought there was more danger of too much lenity than [89] too much rigour towards the President, considering the number of cases in which the Senate was associated with the President.

M! SHERMAN regarded the Supreme Court as improper to try the President, because the Judges would be appointed by him.

On motion by M! MADISON to strike out the words—"by the Senate" after the word "conviction"

N. H. no. Mas. no. C$^t$ no. N. J. no. P$^a$ ay. Del. no. M$^d$ no. V$^a$ ay. N. C. no. S. C. no. Geo. no.[90]

In the amendment of Col: Mason just agreed to, the word "State" after the words "misdemeanors against" was struck out, and the words "United States" inserted unanimously,[91] in order to remove ambiguity.

On the question to agree to [92] clause as amended,

N. H. ay. Mas. ay. Cont ay N. J. ay. P$^a$ no. Del ay M$^d$ ay. V$^a$ ay. N. C. ay. S. C. ay. Geo. ay.[93]

On motion [94] "The vice-President and other Civil officers of the U. S. shall be removed from office on impeachment and conviction as aforesaid" was added to the clause on the subject of impeachments.

The clause of the report made on the 5$^{th}$ [89] Sep$^r$ & postponed was taken up, to wit—"All bills for raising revenue shall originate in the House of Representatives; and shall be subject to altera-

---

[89] The word "of" is here inserted in the transcript.
[90] In the transcript the vote reads: "Pennsylvania, Virginia, aye—2; New Hampshire, Massachusetts, Connecticut, New Jersey, Delaware, Maryland, North Carolina, South Carolina, Georgia, no—9."
[91] The words ' inserted unanimously" are transposed in the transcript to read "unanimously inserted."
[92] The word "the" is here inserted in the transcript.
[93] In the transcript the vote reads: "New Hampshire, Massachusetts, Connecticut, New Jersey, Delaware, Maryland, Virginia, North Carolina, South Carolina, Georgia, aye—10; Pennsylvania, no—1."
[94] The words "the following" are here inserted in the transcript.

tions and amendments by the Senate. No money shall be drawn from the Treasury but in consequence of appropriations made by law."

It was moved to strike out the words "and shall be subject to alterations and amendments by the Senate" and insert the words used in the Constitution of Massachussetts on the same subject—[95] "but the Senate may propose or concur with amendments as in other bills"—which was agreed too nem: con:

On the question On the first part of the clause—"All bills for raising revenue shall originate in the house of Representatives"*

N. H. ay. Mas. ay. C? ay. N. J. ay. P? ay. Del. no. M? no. V? ay. N. C. ay. S. C. ay. Geo. ay.[97]

M? Gov? MORRIS moved to add to clause (3)[98] of the report made on Sep? 4.[99] the words "and every member shall be on oath" which being agreed to, and a question taken on the clause so amended viz—"The Senate of the U. S. shall have power to try all impeachments; but no person shall be convicted without the concurrence of two thirds of the members present; and every member shall be on oath"

N. H. ay. Mas. ay. C? ay. N. J. ay. P? no. Del. ay. M? ay. V? no. N. C. ay. S. C. ay. Geo. ay.[1]

M? GERRY repeated his motion above made on this day, in the form following "The Legislature shall have the sole right of establishing offices not herein [2] provided for," which was again negatived: Mas. Con? & Geo. only being ay.

M? M?HENRY observed that the President had not yet been any where authorised to convene the Senate, and moved to amend Art. X. sect. 2. by striking out the words "he may convene them [the Legislature] on extraordinary occasions" & insert "He may convene both or either of the Houses on extraordinary occasions."

---

[95] The word "viz" is here inserted in the transcript.

* This was a conciliatory vote, the effect of the compromise formerly alluded to. See Note Wednesday Sep? 5.[96]

[96] The words "Wednesday, Sep? 5," are stricken out in the transcript and "page —" is inserted in their place.

[97] In the transcript the vote reads: "New Hampshire, Massachusetts, Connecticut, New Jersey, Pennsylvania, Virginia, North Carolina, South Carolina, Georgia, aye—9; Delaware, Maryland, no—2."

[98] The words "the third clause" are substituted in the transcript for "clause (3)."

[99] The words "the fourth of September" are substituted in the transcript for "Sep? 4."

[1] In the transcript the vote reads: "New Hampshire, Massachusetts, Connecticut, New Jersey, Delaware, Maryland, North Carolina, South Carolina, Georgia, aye—9; Pennsylvania, Virginia, no—2."

[2] The word "heretofore" is substituted in the transcript for "herein."

This he added would also provide for the case of the Senate being in Session at the time of convening the Legislature.

M.[r] WILSON said he should vote ag.[st] the motion, because it implied that the senate might be in Session, when the Legislature was not, which he thought improper.

On the question

N. H. ay. Mas. no. C.[t] ay. N. J. ay. P.[a] no. Del. ay. M.[d] ay. V.[a] no. N. C. ay. S. C. no. Geo. ay.[3]

A Committee was then appointed by Ballot to revise the stile of and arrange the articles which had been agreed to by the House. The committee consisted of M.[r] Johnson, M.[r] Hamilton, M.[r] Gov.[r] Morris, M.[r] Madison and M.[r] King.

M.[r] WILLIAMSON moved that previous to this work of the Committee the clause relating to the number of the House of Representatives sh.[d] be reconsidered for the purpose of increasing the number.

M.[r] MADISON 2.[ded] the Motion

M.[r] SHERMAN opposed it. he thought the provision on that subject amply sufficient.

Col: HAMILTON expressed himself with great earnestness and anxiety in favor of the motion. He avowed himself a friend to a vigorous Government, but would declare at the same time, that[4] he held it essential that the popular branch of it should be on a broad foundation. He was seriously of opinion that the House of Representatives was on so narrow a scale as to be really dangerous, and to warrant a jealousy in the people for their liberties. He remarked that the connection between the President & Senate would tend to perpetuate him, by corrupt influence. It was the more necessary on this account that a numerous representation in the other branch of the Legislature should be established.

On the motion of M.[r] Williamson to reconsider, it was negatived

*N. H. no. Mas. no. C.[t] no. N. J. no. P.[a] ay. Del. ay. M.[d] ay. V.[a] ay. N. C. ay. S. C. no. Geo. no.[5]

Adj.[d]

---

[3] In the transcript the vote reads: "New Hampshire, Connecticut, New Jersey, Delaware, Maryland, North Carolina, Georgia, aye—7; Massachusetts, Pennsylvania, Virginia, South Carolina, no—4."

[4] The word "that" is omitted in the transcript.

* This motion & vote are entered on the Printed journal of the ensuing morning.

[5] In the transcript the vote reads: "Pennsylvania, Delaware, Maryland, Virginia, North Carolina, aye—5; New Hampshire, Massachusetts, Connecticut, New Jersey, South Carolina, Georgia, no—6."

Monday Sep.R 10. 1787 [6]   In Convention

M.R Gerry moved to reconsider Art XIX. viz. "On the application of the Legislatures of two thirds of the States in the Union, for an amendment of this Constitution, the Legislature of the U. S. shall call a Convention for that purpose." [see Aug. 6.] [7]

This Constitution he said is to be paramount to the State Constitutions. It follows, hence, from this article that two thirds of the States may obtain a Convention, a majority of which can bind the Union to innovations that may subvert the State-Constitutions altogether. He asked whether this was a situation proper to be run into.

M.R Hamilton 2.d.ed the motion, but he said with a different view from M.R Gerry. He did not object to the consequence stated by M.R Gerry. There was no greater evil in subjecting the people of the U. S. to the major voice than the people of a particular State. It had been wished by many and was much to have been desired that an easier mode for [8] introducing amendments had been provided by the articles of [9] Confederation. It was equally desireable now that an easy mode should be established for supplying defects which will probably appear in the New System. The mode proposed was not adequate. The State Legislatures will not apply for alterations but with a view to increase their own powers. The National Legislature will be the first to perceive and will be most sensible to the necessity of amendments, and ought also to be empowered, whenever two thirds of each branch should concur to call a Convention. There could be no danger in giving this power, as the people would finally decide in the case.

M.R Madison remarked on the vagueness of the terms, "call a Convention for the purpose," as sufficient reason for reconsidering the article. How was a Convention to be formed? by what rule decide? what the force of its acts?

On the motion of M.R Gerry to reconsider

---

[6] The year "1787" is omitted in the transcript.
[7] In the transcript the date reads: "the sixth of August."
[8] The word "of" is found in the transcript in place of "for."
[9] The word "the" is here inserted in the transcript.

N. H. div$^d$ Mas. ay. C$^t$ ay. N. J. no. P$^a$ ay. Del. ay. M$^d$ ay. V$^a$ ay. N. C. ay. S. C. ay. Geo ay.[10]

M$^r$ Sherman moved to add to the article "or the Legislature may propose amendments to the several States for their approbation, but no amendments shall be binding until consented to by the several States."

M$^r$ Gerry 2$^{ded}$ the motion

M$^r$ Wilson moved to insert "two thirds of" before the words "several States"—on which amendment to the motion of M$^r$ Sherman

N. H. ay. Mas. no. C$^t$ no. N. J. no. P$^a$ ay. Del. ay. M$^d$ ay. V$^a$ ay. N. C. no. S. C. no. Geo. no.[11]

M$^r$ Wilson then moved to insert "three fourths of" before "the several Sts" which was agreed to nem: con:

M$^r$ Madison moved to postpone the consideration of the amended proposition in order to take up the following,

"The Legislature of the U. S. whenever two thirds of both Houses shall deem necessary, or on the application of two thirds of the Legislatures of the several States, shall propose amendments to this Constitution, which shall be valid to all intents and purposes as part thereof, when the same shall have been ratified by three fourths at least of the Legislatures of the several States, or by Conventions in three fourths thereof, as one or the other mode of ratification may be proposed by the Legislature of the U S:"*

M$^r$ Hamilton 2$^{ded}$ the motion.

M$^r$ Rutlidge said he never could agree to give a power by which the articles relating to slaves might be altered by the States not interested in that property and prejudiced against it. In order to obviate this objection, these words were added to the proposition:* "provided that no amendments which may be made prior to the year 1808, shall in any manner affect the 4 & 5 sections of the VII article"—The postponement being agreed to,

---

[10] In the transcript the vote reads: "Massachusetts, Connecticut, Pennsylvania, Delaware, Maryland, Virginia, North Carolina, South Carolina, Georgia, aye—9; New Jersey, no—1; New Hampshire, divided."

[11] In the transcript the vote reads: "New Hampshire, Pennsylvania, Delaware, Maryland, Virginia, aye—5; Massachusetts, Connecticut, New Jersey, North Carolina, South Carolina, Georgia, no—6."

* The Printed Journal makes the succeeding proviso as to sections 4 & 5. of art: VII [12] moved by M$^r$. Rutlidge, part of the proposition of M$^r$. Madison.

[12] The words "the fourth and fifth sections of the seventh article" are substituted in the transcript for "sections 4 & 5. of art: VII."

On the question on the proposition of Mr Madison & Mr Hamilton as amended

N. H. divd Mas. ay. Ct ay. N. J. ay. Pa ay. Del. no. Md ay. Va ay. N. C. ay. S. C. ay. Geo ay.[13]

Mr GERRY moved to reconsider art: XXI and XXII. from the latter of which "for the approbation of Congs" had been struck out. He objected to proceeding to change the Government without the approbation of Congress, as being improper and giving just umbrage to that body. He repeated his objections also to an annulment of the confederation with so little scruple or formality.

Mr HAMILTON concurred with Mr Gerry as to the indecorum of not requiring the approbation of Congress. He considered this as a necessary ingredient in the transaction. He thought it wrong also to allow nine States as provided by art XXI. to institute a new Government on the ruins of the existing one. He wd propose as a better modification of the two articles (XXI & XXII) that the plan should be sent to Congress in order that the same if approved by them, may be communicated to the State Legislatures, to the end that they may refer it to State Conventions; each Legislature declaring that if the Convention of the State should think the plan ought to take effect among nine ratifying States, the same shd take effect accordingly.

Mr GORHAM. Some States will say that nine States shall be sufficient to establish the plan, others will require unanimity for the purpose. And the different and conditional ratifications will defeat the plan altogether.

Mr HAMILTON. No Convention convinced of the necessity of the plan will refuse to give it effect on the adoption by nine States. He thought this mode less exceptionable than the one proposed in the article, and [14] would attain the same end.

Mr FITZIMMONS remarked that the words "for their approbation" had been struck out in order to save Congress from the necessity of an Act inconsistent with the Articles of Confederation under which they held their authority.

---

[13] In the transcript the vote reads: "Massachusetts, Connecticut, New Jersey, Pennsylvania, Maryland, Virginia, North Carolina, South Carolina, Georgia, aye—9; Delaware, no—1; New Hampshire, divided."
[14] The words "while it" are substituted in the transcript for "and."

M.<sup>r</sup> RANDOLPH declared, if no change should be made in the [15] this part of the plan, he should be obliged to dissent from the whole of it. He had from the beginning he said been convinced that radical changes in the system of the Union were necessary. Under this conviction he had brought forward a set of republican propositions as the basis and outline of a reform. These Republican propositions had however, much to his regret, been widely, and in his opinion, irreconcileably departed from. In this state of things it was his idea and he accordingly meant to propose, that the State Conventions sh<sup>d</sup> be at liberty to offer amendments to the plan; and that these should be submitted to a second General Convention, with full power to settle the Constitution finally. He did not expect to succeed in this proposition, but the discharge of his duty in making the attempt, would give quiet to his own mind.

M.<sup>r</sup> WILSON was against a reconsideration for any of the purposes which had been mentioned.

M.<sup>r</sup> KING thought it would be more respectful to Congress to submit the plan generally to them; than in such a form as expressly and necessarily to require their approbation or disapprobation. The assent of nine States be considered as sufficient; and that it was more proper to make this a part of the Constitution itself, than to provide for it by a supplemental or distinct recommendation.

M.<sup>r</sup> GERRY urged the indecency and pernicious tendency of dissolving in so slight a manner, the solemn obligations of the articles of confederation. If nine out of thirteen can dissolve the compact, Six out of nine will be just as able to dissolve the new one hereafter.

M.<sup>r</sup> SHERMAN was in favor of M.<sup>r</sup> King's idea of submitting the plan generally to Congress. He thought nine States ought to be made sufficient: but that it would be best [16] to make it a separate act and in some such form as that intimated by Col: Hamilton, than to make it a particular article of the Constitution.

On the question for reconsidering the two articles, XXI & XXII—

---

[15] The word "the" is omitted in the transcript.
[16] The word "best" is crossed out in the transcript and "better" is written above it.

N. H. div.ᵈ Mas. no. Cᵗ ay. N. J. ay. Pᵃ no. Del. ay. Mᵈ ay. Vᵃ ay. N. C. ay. S. C. no. Geo. ay.[17]

Mʳ HAMILTON then moved to postpone art XXI in order to take up the following, containing the ideas he had above expressed, viz

Resolved that the foregoing plan of a Constitution be transmitted to the U. S. in Congress assembled, in order that if the same shall be agreed to by them, it may be communicated to the Legislatures of the several States, to the end that they may provide for its final ratification by referring the same to the Consideration of a Convention of Deputies in each State to be chosen by the people thereof, and that it be recommended to the said Legislatures in their respective acts for organizing such convention to declare, that if the said Convention shall approve of the said Constitution, such approbation shall be binding and conclusive upon the State, and further that if the said Convention should be of opinion that the same upon the assent of any nine States thereto, ought to take effect between the States so assenting, such opinion shall thereupon be also binding upon such State, and the said Constitution shall take effect between the States assenting thereto"

Mʳ GERRY 2ᵈᵉᵈ the motion.

Mʳ WILSON. This motion being seconded, it is necessary now to speak freely. He expressed in strong terms his disapprobation of the expedient proposed, particularly the suspending the plan of the Convention on the approbation of Congress. He declared it to be worse than folly to rely on the concurrence of the Rhode Island members of Congˢ in the plan. Maryland has voted on this floor; for requiring the unanimous assent of the 13 States to the proposed change in the federal System. N. York has not been represented for a long time past in the Convention. Many individual deputies from other States have spoken much against the plan. Under these circusmtances can it be safe to make the assent of Congress necessary. After spending four or five months in the laborious & arduous task of forming a Government for our Country, we are ourselves at the close throwing insuperable obstacles in the way of its success.

---

[17] In the transcript the vote reads: "Connecticut, New Jersey, Delaware, Maryland, Virginia, North Carolina, Georgia, aye—7; Massachusetts, Pennyslvania, South Carolina, no—3; New Hampshire, divided."

Mr CLYMER thought that the mode proposed by Mr Hamilton would fetter & embarrass Congs as much as the original one, since it equally involved a breach of the articles of Confederation.

Mr KING concurred with Mr Clymer. If Congress can accede to one mode, they can to the other. If the approbation of Congress be made necessary, and they should not approve, the State Legislatures will not propose the plan to Conventions; or if the States themselves are to provide that nine States shall suffice to establish the System, that provision will be omitted, every thing will go into confusion, and all our labor be lost.

Mr RUTLIDGE viewed the matter in the same light with Mr King.

On the question to postpone in order to take up Col: Hamilton's motion

N. H. no. Mas. no. Ct ay. N. J. no. Pa no. Del. no. Md no. Va no. N. C. no. S. C. no. Geo. no.[18]

A Question being then taken on the article XXI. It was agreed to unanimously.

Col: HAMILTON withdrew the remainder of the motion to postpone art XXII, observing that his purpose was defeated by the vote just given;

Mr WILLIAMSON & Mr GERRY moved to re-instate the words "for the approbation of Congress" in art: XXII which was disagreed to nem: con:

Mr RANDOLPH took this opportunity to state his objections to the System. They turned on the Senate's being made the Court of Impeachment for trying the Executive—on the necessity of ¾ instead of ⅔ of each house to overrule the negative of the President—on the smallness of the number of the Representative branch,—on the want of limitation to a standing army—on the general clause concerning necessary and proper laws—on the want of some particular restraint on navigation acts—on the power to lay duties on exports—on the Authority of the General Legislature to interpose on the application of the *Executives* of the States—on the want of a more definite boundary between the General & State Legislatures—and between the General and State

---

[18] In the transcript the vote reads: "Connecticut, aye—1; New Hampshire, Massachusetts, New Jersey, Pennsylvania, Delaware, Maryland, Virginia, North Carolina, South Carolina, Georgia, no—10."

Judiciaries—on the the unqualified power of the President to pardon treasons—on the want of some limit to the power of the Legislature in regulating their own compensations. With these difficulties in his mind, what course he asked was he to pursue? Was he to promote the establishment of a plan which he verily believed would end in Tyranny? He was unwilling he said to impede the wishes and Judgment of the Convention, but he must keep himself free, in case he should be honored with a seat in the Convention of his State, to act according to the dictates of his judgment. The only mode in which his embarrassments could be removed, was that of submitting the plan to Cong$^s$ to go from them to the State Legislatures, and from these to State Conventions having power to adopt reject or amend; the process to close with another General Convention with full power to adopt or reject the alterations proposed by the State Conventions, and to establish finally the Government. He accordingly proposed a Resolution to this effect.

Doc$^r$ FRANKLIN 2$^{ded}$ the motion

Col: MASON urged & obtained that the motion should lie on the table for a day or two to see what steps might be taken with regard to the parts of the system objected to by M$^r$ Randolph.

M$^r$ PINKNEY moved "that it be an instruction to the Committee for revising the stile and arrangement of the articles agreed on, to prepare an Address to the People, to accompany the present Constitution, and to be laid with the same before the U. States in Congress."

\* The motion itself was referred to the Committee, nem: con:

\* M$^r$ RANDOLPH moved to refer to the Committee also a motion relating to pardons in cases of Treason—which was agreed to nem: con:

Adjourned

---

\* These motions [19] not entered in the printed Journal.
[19] The word "are" is here inserted in the transcript.

TUESDAY SEP$^R$ 11. 1787.[20] IN CONVENTION

The Report of the Committee of Stile & arrangement not being made & being waited for,

The House Adjourned

---

WEDNESDAY SEP$^R$ 12. 1787.[20] IN CONVENTION

Doc$^r$ JOHNSON from the Committee of stile &c. reported a digest of the plan, of which printed copies were ordered to be furnished to the members. He also reported a letter to accompany the plan, to Congress. (Here insert a transcript of the former from the annexed sheet as *printed* \* and of the latter from the draft as finally agreed to.[22]

WE, THE PEOPLE OF THE UNITED STATES, IN ORDER TO FORM a more perfect union, to establish justice, insure domestic tranquility, provide for the common defence, promote the general welfare, and secure the blessings of liberty to ourselves and our posterity, do ordain and establish this Constitution for the United States of America.

ARTICLE I

*Sect.* 1. ALL legislative powers herein granted shall be vested in a Congress of the United States, which shall consist of a Senate and House of Representatives.

*Sect.* 2. The House of Representatives shall be composed of members chosen every second year by the people of the several states, and the electors in each state shall have the qualifications requisite for electors of the most numerous branch of the state legislature.

No person shall be a representative who shall not have attained to the age of twenty-five years, and been seven years a citizen of the United States, and who shall not, when elected, be an inhabitant of that state in which he shall be chosen.

Representatives and direct taxes shall be apportioned among the several states which may be included within this Union, according to their respective numbers, which shall be determined by adding to the whole number of free persons, including those

---

[20] The year "1787" is omitted in the transcript.

\* "This is a literal copy of the printed Report. The Copy in the printed Journal contains some of the alterations subsequently made in the House.[21]

[21] No transcript of the report was, however, made by Madison, but it was copied by Payne and inserted in this place in the Payne transcript. The text here printed is a copy of the printed report accompanying Madison's notes.

[22] Madison's direction concerning the report is omitted in the transcript.

bound to servitude for a term of years, and excluding Indians not taxed, three-fifths of all other persons. The actual enumeration shall be made within three years after the first meeting of the Congress of the United States, and within every subsequent term of ten years, in such manner as they shall by law direct. The number of representatives shall not exceed one for every forty thousand, but each state shall have at least one representative: and until such enumeration shall be made, the state of New-Hampshire shall be entitled to chuse three, Massachusetts eight, Rhode-Island and Providence Plantations one, Connecticut five, New-York six, New-Jersey four, Pennsylvania eight, Deleware one, Maryland six, Virginia ten, North-Carolina five, South-Caroline five, and Georgia three.

When vacancies happen in the representation from any state, the Executive authority thereof shall issue writs of election to fill such vacancies.

The House of Representatives shall choose their Speaker and other officers; and they shall have the sole power of impeachment.

*Sect.* 3. The Senate of the United States shall be composed of two senators from each state, chosen by the legislature thereof, for six years: and each senator shall have one vote.

Immediately after they shall be assembled in consequence of the first election, they shall be divided * [by lot] as equally as may be into three classes. The seats of the senators of the first class shall be vacated at the expiration of the second year, of the second class at the expiration of the fourth year, and of the third class at the expiration of the sixth year, so that one-third may be chosen every second year: and if vacancies happen by resignation, or otherwise, during the recess of the Legislature of any state, the Executive thereof may make temporary appointments until the next meeting of the Legislature.

No person shall be a senator who shall not have attained to the age of thirty years, and been nine years a citizen of the United States, and who shall not, when elected, be an inhabitant of that state for which he shall be chosen.

The Vice-President of the United States shall be, ex officio [23] President of the senate, but shall have no vote, unless they be equally divided.

---

* The words, "by lot," were not in the Report as printed; but were inserted in manuscript, as a typografical error, departing from the text of the Report referred to the Committee of Style & arrangment.

[23] The words "ex officio" are omitted in the transcript.

The Senate shall choose their other officers, and also a President pro tempore, in the absence of the Vice-President, or when he shall exercise the office of President of the United States.

The Senate shall have the sole power to try all impeachments. When sitting for that purpose, they shall be on oath. When the President of the United States is tried, the Chief Justice shall preside: And no person shall be convicted without the concurrence of two-thirds of the members present.

Judgment in cases of impeachment shall not extend further than to removal from office, and disqualification to hold and enjoy any office of honor, trust or profit under the United States: but the party convicted shall nevertheless be liable and subject to indictment, trial, judgment and punishment, according to law.

*Sect.* 4. The times, places and manner of holding elections for senators and representatives, shall be prescribed in each state by the legislature thereof: but the Congress may at any time by law make or alter such regulations.

The Congress shall assemble at least once in every year, and such meeting shall be on the first Monday in December, unless they shall by law appoint a different day.

*Sect.* 5. Each house shall be the judge of the elections, returns and qualifications of its own members, and a majority of each shall constitute a quorum to do business: but a smaller number may adjourn from day to day, and may be authorised to compel the attendance of absent members, in such manner, and under such penalties as each house may provide.

Each house may determine the rules of its proceedings; punish its members for disorderly behaviour, and, with the concurrence of two-thirds, expel a member.

Each house shall keep a journal of its proceedings, and from time to time publish the same, excepting such parts as may in their judgment require secrecy; and the yeas and nays of the members of either house on any question shall, at the desire of one-fifth of those present, be entered on the journal.

Neither house, during the session of Congress, shall, without the consent of the other, adjourn for more than three days, nor to any other place than that in which the two houses shall be sitting.

*Sect.* 6. The senators and representatives shall receive a compensation for their services, to be ascertained by law, and paid out of the treasury of the United States. They shall in all cases, except treason, felony and breach of the peace, be privileged from arrest during their attendance at the session of their respective houses, and in going to and returning from the same; and for any speech or debate in either house, they shall not be questioned in any other place.

No senator or representative shall, during the time for which he was elected, be appointed to any civil office under the authority of the United States, which shall have been created, or the emoluments whereof shall have been encreased during such time; and no person holding any office under the United States, shall be a member of either house during his continuance in office.

*Sect.* 7. The enacting stile of the laws shall be, "Be it enacted by the senators and representatives in Congress assembled."

All bills for raising revenue shall originate in the house of representatives: but the senate may propose or concur with amendments as on other bills.

Every bill which shall have passed the house of representatives and the senate, shall, before it become a law, be presented to the president of the United States. If he approve he shall sign it, but if not he shall return it, with his objections to that house in which it shall have originated, who shall enter the objections at large on their journal, and proceed to reconsider it. If after such reconsideration two-thirds of that house shall agree to pass the bill, it shall be sent, together with the objections, to the other house, by which it shall likewise be reconsidered, and if approved by two-thirds of that house, it shall become a law. But in all such cases the votes of both houses shall be determined by yeas and nays, and the names of the persons voting for and against the bill shall be entered on the journal of each house respectively. If any bill shall not be returned by the President within ten days (Sundays excepted) after it shall have been presented to him, the same shall be a law, in like manner as if he had signed it, unless the Congress by their adjournment prevent its return, in which case it shall not be a law.

Every order, resolution, or vote to which the concurrence of the Senate and House of Representatives may be necessary (except on a question of adjournment) shall be presented to the President of the United States; and before the same shall take effect, shall be approved by him, or, being disapproved by him, shall be repassed by * three-fourths of the Senate and House of Representatives, according to the rules and limitations prescribed in the case of a bill.

---

\* In the entry of this Report in the printed Journal "two thirds" are substituted for "three fourths." This change was made after the Report was received.[24]

[24] This is a mistake on Madison's part.

*Sect.* 8. The Congress may by joint ballot appoint a treasurer. They shall have power

To lay and collect taxes, duties, imposts and excises; to pay the debts and provide for the common defence and general welfare of the United States.

To borrow money on the credit of the United States.

To regulate commerce with foreign nations, among the several states, and with the Indian tribes.

To establish an uniform rule of naturalization, and uniform laws on the subject of bankruptcies throughout the United States.

To coin money, regulate the value thereof, and of foreign coin, and fix the standard of weights and measures.

To provide for the punishment of counterfeiting the securities and current coin of the United States.

To establish post offices and post roads.

To promote the progress of science and useful arts, by securing for limited times to authors and inventors the exclusive right to their respective writings and discoveries.

To constitute tribunals inferior to the supreme court.

To define and punish piracies and felonies committed on the high seas, and † [punish] offences against the law of nations.

To declare war, grant letters of marque and reprisal, and make rules concerning captures on land and water.

To raise and support armies: but no appropriation of money to that use shall be for a longer term than two years.

To provide and maintain a navy.

To make rules for the government and regulation of the land and naval forces.

To provide for calling forth the militia to execute the laws of the union, suppress insurrections and repel invasions.

To provide for organizing, arming and disciplining the militia, and for governing such part of them as may be employed in the service of the United States, reserving to the States respectively, the appointment of the officers, and the authority of training the militia according to the discipline prescribed by Congress.

To exercise exclusive legislation in all cases whatsoever, over such district (not exceeding ten miles square) as may, by cession of particular States, and the acceptance of Congress, become the seat of the [26] government of the United States, and to exercise like

---

† [punish] a typographical omission.[25]

[25] The words "in the printed Report" are here added in the transcript.

[26] The word "the" is omitted in the transcript.

authority over all places purchased by the consent of the legislature of the state in which the same shall be, for the erection of forts, magazines, arsenals, dock-yards, and other needful buildings —And

To make all laws which shall be necessary and proper for carrying into execution the foregoing powers, and all other powers vested by this constitution in the government of the United States, or in any department or officer thereof.

Sect. 9. The migration or importation of such persons as the several states now existing shall think proper to admit, shall not be prohibited by the Congress prior to the year one thousand eight hundred and eight, but a tax or duty may be imposed on such importation, not exceeding ten dollars for each person.

The privilege of the writ of habeas corpus shall not be suspended, unless when in cases of rebellion or invasion the public safety may require it.

No bill of attainder shall be passed, nor any ex post facto law.

No capitation tax shall be laid, unless in proportion to the census herein before directed to be taken.

No tax or duty shall be laid on articles exported from any state.

No money shall be drawn from the treasury, but in consequence of appropriations made by law.

No title of nobility shall be granted by the United States. And no person holding any office of profit or trust under them, shall, without the consent of the Congress, accept of any present, emolument, office, or title, of any kind whatever, from any king, prince, or foreign state.

Sect. 10. No state shall coin money, nor [27] emit bills of credit, nor [27] make any thing but gold or silver coin a tender in payment of debts, nor [27] pass any bill of attainder, nor [27] ex post facto laws, nor [27] laws altering or impairing the obligation of contracts; nor [27] grant letters of marque and reprisal, nor [27] enter into any treaty, alliance, or confederation, nor [27] grant any title of nobility.

No state shall, without the consent of Congress, lay imposts or duties on imports or exports, nor [27] with such consent, but to the use of the treasury of the United States. Nor [27] keep troops nor [27] ships of war in time of peace, nor [27] enter into any agreement or compact with another state, nor [27] with any foreign power. Nor [27] engage in any war, unless it shall be actually invaded by enemies, or the danger of invasion be so imminent, as not to admit of delay until the Congress can be consulted.

---

[27] The word "or" is substituted in the transcript for "nor," the letter "n" having been crossed off in Madison's printed copy.

## II

*Sect.* 1. The executive power shall be vested in a president of the United States of America. He shall hold his office during the term of four years, and, together with the vice-president, chosen for the same term, be elected in the following manner:

Each state shall appoint, in such manner as the legislature thereof may direct, a number of electors, equal to the whole number of senators and representatives to which the state may be entitled in Congress: but no senator or representative shall be appointed an elector, nor any person holding an office of trust or profit under the United States.

The electors shall meet in their respective states, and vote by ballot for two persons, of whom one at least shall not be an inhabitant of the same state with themselves. And they shall make a list of all the persons voted for, and of the number of votes for each; which list they shall sign and certify, and transmit sealed to the seat of the general government, directed to the president of the senate. The president of the senate shall in the presence of the senate and house of representatives open all the certificates, and the votes shall then be counted. The person having the greatest number of votes shall be the president, if such number be a majority of the whole number of electors appointed; and if there be more than one who have such majority, and have an equal number of votes, then the house of representatives shall immediately chuse by ballot one of them for president; and if no person have a majority, then from the five highest on the list the said house shall in like manner choose the president. But in choosing the president, the votes shall be taken by states and not per capita, the representation from each state having one vote. A quorum for this purpose shall consist of a member or members from two-thirds of the states, and a majority of all the states shall be necessary to a choice. In every case, after the choice of the president by the representatives, the person having the greatest number of votes of the electors shall be the vice-president. But if there should remain two or more who have equal votes, the senate shall choose from them by ballot the vice-president.

The Congress may determine the time of chusing the electors, and the time in which they shall give their votes; but the election shall be on the same day throughout the United States.

No person except a natural born citizen, or a citizen of the United States, at the time of the adoption of this constitution, shall be eligible to the office of president; neither shall any person be eligible to that office who shall not have attained to the age of thirty-five years, and been fourteen years a resident within the United States.

In case of the removal of the president from office, or of his death, resignation, or inability to discharge the powers and duties of the said office, the same shall devolve on the vice-president, and the Congress may by law provide for the case of removal, death, resignation or inability, both of the president and vice-president, declaring what officer shall then act as president, and such officer shall act accordingly, until the disability be removed, or the period for chusing another president arrive.

The president shall, at stated times, receive a fixed compensation for his services, which shall neither be encreased nor diminished during the period for which he shall have been elected.

Before he enter on the execution of his office, he shall take the following oath or affirmation: "I ———, do solemnly swear (or affirm) that I will faithfully execute the office of president of the United States, and will to the best of my judgment and power, preserve, protect and defend the constitution of the United States."

*Sect.* 2. The president shall be commander in chief of the army and navy of the United States, and of the militia of the several States:[28] he may require the opinion, in writing, of the principal officer in each of the executive departments, upon any subject relating to the duties of their respective offices, when called into the actual service of the United States,[28] and he shall have power to grant reprieves and pardons for offences against the United States, except in cases of impeachment.

He shall have power, by and with the advice and consent of the senate, to make treaties, provided two-thirds of the senators present concur; and he shall nominate, and by and with the advice and consent of the senate, shall appoint ambassadors, other public ministers and consuls, judges of the supreme court, and all other officers of the United States, whose appointments are not herein otherwise provided for.

The president shall have power to fill up all vacancies that may happen during the recess of the senate, by granting commissions which shall expire at the end of their next session.

*Sect.* 3. He shall from time to time give to the Congress information of the state of the union, and recommend to their consideration such measures as he shall judge necessary and

---

[28] The phrase "when called into the actual service of the United States" is transposed in the transcript so that it follows the words "several States."

expedient: he may, on extraordinary occasions, convene both houses, or either of them, and in case of disagreement between them, with respect to the time of adjournment, he may adjourn them to such time as he shall think proper: he shall receive ambassadors and other public ministers: he shall take care that the laws be faithfully executed, and shall commission all the officers of the United States.

Sect. 4. The president, vice-president and all civil officers of the United States, shall be removed from office on impeachment for, and conviction of treason, bribery, or other high crimes and misdemeanors.

## III

Sect. 1. The judicial power of the United States, both in law and equity, shall be vested in one supreme court, and in such inferior courts as the Congress may from time to time ordain and establish. The judges, both of the supreme and inferior courts, shall hold their offices during good behaviour, and shall, at stated times, receive for their services, a compensation, which shall not be diminished during their continuance in office.

Sect. 2. The judicial power shall extend to all cases, both in law and equity, arising under this constitution, the laws of the United States, and treaties made, or which shall be made, under their authority. To all cases affecting ambassadors, other public ministers and consuls. To all cases of admiralty and maritime jurisdiction. To controversies to which the United States shall be a party. To controversies between two or more States; between a state and citizens of another state, between citizens of different States; between citizens of the same state claiming lands under grants of different States, and between a state, or the citizens thereof, and foreign States, citizens or subjects.

In cases affecting ambassadors, other public ministers and consuls, and those in which a state shall be party, the supreme court shall have original jurisdiction. In all the other cases before mentioned, the supreme court shall have appellate jurisdiction, both as to law and fact, with such exceptions, and under such regulations as the Congress shall make.

The trial of all crimes, except in cases of impeachment, shall be by jury; and such trial shall be held in the state where the said crimes shall have been committed; but when not committed within any state, the trial shall be at such place or places as the Congress may by law have directed.

*Sect. 3.* Treason against the United States, shall consist only in levying war against them, or in adhering to their enemies, giving them aid and comfort. No person shall be convicted of treason unless on the testimony of two witnesses to the same overt act, or on confession in open court.

The Congress shall have power to declare the punishment of treason, but no attainder of treason shall work corruption of blood nor forfeiture, except during the life of the person attainted.

### IV

*Sect. 1.* Full faith and credit shall be given in each state to the public acts, records, and judicial proceedings of every other state. And the Congress may by general laws prescribe the manner in which such acts, records and proceedings shall be proved, and the effect thereof.

*Sect. 2.* The citizens of each state shall be entitled to all privileges and immunities of citizens in the several states.

A person charged in any state with treason, felony, or other crime, who shall flee from justice, and be found in another state, shall on demand of the executive authority of the state from which he fled be delivered up, and removed to the state having jurisdiction of the crime.

No person legally held to service or labour in one state, escaping into another, shall in consequence of regulations subsisting therein be discharged from such service or labor, but shall be delivered up on claim of the party to whom such service or labour may be due.

*Sect. 3.* New states may be admitted by the Congress into this union; but no new state shall be formed or erected within the jurisdiction of any other state; nor any state be formed by the junction of two or more states, or parts of states, without the consent of the legislatures of the states concerned as well as of the Congress.

The Congress shall have power to dispose of and make all needful rules and regulations respecting the territory or other property belonging to the United States: and nothing in this Constitution shall be so construed as to prejudice any claims of the United States, or of any particular state.

*Sect. 4.* The United States shall guarantee to every state in this union a Republican form of government, and shall protect each of them against invasion; and on application of the legislature or executive, against domestic violence.

## V

The Congress, whenever two-thirds of both houses shall deem necessary, or on the application of two-thirds of the legislatures of the several states, shall propose amendments to this constitution, which shall be valid to all intents and purposes, as part thereof, when the same shall have been ratified by three-fourths at least of the legislatures of the several states, or by conventions in three-fourths thereof, as the one or the other mode of ratification may be proposed by the Congress: Provided, that no amendment which may be made prior to the year 1808 shall in any manner affect the and section of [29] article

## VI

All debts contracted and engagements entered into before the adoption of this Constitution shall be as valid against the United States under this Constitution as under the confederation.

This constitution, and the laws of the United States which shall be made in pursuance thereof; and all treaties made, or which shall be made, under the authority of the United States, shall be the supreme law of the land; and the judges in every state shall be bound thereby, any thing in the constitution or laws of any state to the contrary notwithstanding.

The senators and representatives beforementioned, and the members of the several state legislatures, and all executive and judicial officers, both of the United States and of the several States, shall be bound by oath or affirmation, to support this constitution; but no religious test shall ever be required as a qualification to any office or public trust under the United States.

## VII

The ratification of the conventions of nine States, shall be sufficient for the establishment of this constitution between the States so ratifying the same.

## LETTER [30]

We have now the honor to submit to the consideration of the United States in Congress assembled, that Constitution which as appeared to us the most adviseable.

---

[29] The word "the" is here inserted in the transcript.

[30] The draft of the letter accompanied the draft of the Constitution reported on this date, but was not printed with it. The Journal says: "The draft of a letter to Congress being at the same time reported was read once throughout; and afterwards agreed to by paragraphs." (See *Journal of the Federal Convention* (1819), page 367.) The letter does not appear to have caused debate. Having been accepted September 12th, it was printed with the final Constitution September 17th. The text here used is that of the final print, which was also copied by Payne for the transcript. The letter is printed in full, *infra*, page 639.

The friends of our country have long seen and desired, that the power of making war, peace and treaties, that of levying money and regulating commerce, and the correspondent executive and judicial authorities should be fully and effectually vested in the general government of the Union: but the impropriety of delegating such extensive trust to one body of men is evident—Hence [31] results the necessity of a different organization.

It is obviously impracticable in the fœderal government of these States to secure all rights of independent sovereignty to each, and yet provide for the interest and safety of all—Individuals entering into society must give up a share of liberty to preserve the rest. The magnitude of the sacrifice must depend as well on situation and circumstance, as on the object to be obtained. It is at all times difficult to draw with precision the line between those rights which must be surrendered, and those which may be reserved; and on the present occasion this difficulty was encreased by a difference among the several States as to their situation, extent, habits, and particular interests.

In all our deliberations on this subject we kept steadily in our view, that which appears [32] to us the greatest interest of every true American, the consolidation of our union, in which is involved our prosperity, felicity, safety, perhaps our national existence. This important consideration, seriously and deeply impressed on our minds, led each State in the Convention to be less rigid on [33] points of inferior magnitude, than might have been otherwise expected; and thus the Constitution, which we now present, is the result of a spirit of amity, and of that mutual deference and concession which the peculiarity of our political situation rendered indispensible.

That it will meet the full and entire approbation of every State is not perhaps to be expected; but each will doubtless consider, that had her interest alone been consulted, the consequences might have been particularly disagreeable or [34] injurious to others; that it is liable to as few exceptions as could reasonably have been expected, we hope and believe; that it may promote the lasting welfare of that country so dear to us all, and secure her freedom and happiness, is our most ardent wish.

Mr WILLIAMSON moved to reconsider the clause requiring three fourths of each House to overrule the negative of the President,

---

[31] The word "Thence" is substituted in the transcript for "Hence."
[32] The word "appeared" is substituted in the transcript for "appears."
[33] The word "in" is substituted in the transcript for "on."
[34] The word "and" is substituted in the transcript for "or."

in order to strike out ¾ and insert ⅔. He had he remarked himself proposed ¾ instead of ⅔, but he had since been convinced that the latter proportion was the best. The former puts too much in the power of the President.

Mr SHERMAN was of the same opinion; adding that the States would not like to see so small a minority and the President, prevailing over the general voice. In making laws regard should be had to the sense of the people, who are to be bound by them, and it was more probable that a single man should mistake or betray this sense than the Legislature

Mr Govr MORRIS. Considering the difference between the two proportions numerically, it amounts in one House to two members only; and in the other to not more than five; according to the numbers of which the Legislature is at first to be composed. It is the interest moreover of the distant States to prefer ¾ as they will be oftenest absent and need the interposing check of the President. The excess rather than the deficiency of laws was to be dreaded. The example of N. York shews that ⅔ is not sufficient to answer the purpose.

Mr HAMILTON added his testimony to the fact that ⅔ in N. York had been ineffectual either where a popular object, or a legislative faction operated; of which he mentioned some instances.

Mr GERRY. It is necessary to consider the danger on the other side also. ⅔ will be a considerable, perhaps a proper security. ¾ puts too much in the power of a few men. The primary object of the revisionary check of the President is not to protect the general interest, but to defend his own department. If ¾ be required, a few Senators having hopes from the nomination of the President to offices, will combine with him and impede proper laws. Making the vice-President Speaker increases the danger.

Mr WILLIAMSON was less afraid of too few than of too many laws. He was most of all afraid that the repeal of bad laws might be rendered too difficult by requiring ¾ to overcome the dissent of the President.

Col: MASON had always considered this as one of the most exceptionable parts of the System. As to the numerical argument of Mr Govr Morris, little arithmetic was necessary to understand that

¾ was more than ⅔, whatever the numbers of the Legislature might be. The example of New York depended on the real merits of the laws. The Gentlemen citing it, had no doubt given their own opinions. But perhaps there were others of opposite opinions who could equally paint the abuses on the other side. His leading view was to guard against too great an impediment to the repeal of laws.

M! Gov! Morris dwelt on the danger to the public interest from the instability of laws, as the most to be guarded against. On the other side there could be little danger. If one man in office will not consent where he ought, every fourth year another can be substituted. This term was not too long for fair experiments. Many good laws are not tried long enough to prove their merit. This is often the case with new laws opposed to old habits. The Inspection laws of Virginia & Maryland to which all are now so much attached were unpopular at first.

M! Pinkney was warmly in opposition to ¾ as putting a dangerous power in the hands of a few Senators headed by the President.

M! Madison. When ¾ was agreed to, the President was to be elected by the Legislature and for seven years. He is now to be elected by the people and for four years. The object of the revisionary power is twofold. 1.[35] to defend the Executive Rights 2.[35] to prevent popular or factious injustice. It was an important principle in this & in the State Constitutions to check legislative injustice and incroachments. The Experience of the States had demonstrated that their checks are insufficient. We must compare the danger from the weakness of ⅔ with the danger from the strength of ¾. He thought on the whole the former was the greater. As to the difficulty of repeals, it was probable that in doubtful cases the policy would soon take place of limiting the duration of laws so as to require renewal instead of repeal.

The reconsideration being agreed to. On the question to insert ⅔ in place of ¾.

N. H. div! Mas. no. C! ay. N. J. ay. P! no. Del. no. M! ay. M! M?Henry no. V! no. Gen! Washington M! Blair,

---

[35] The figures "1" and "2" are changed in the transcript to "first" and "secondly."

Mr Madison no. Col. Mason, Mr Randolph ay. N. C. ay. S. C. ay. Geo. ay.³⁶

Mr WILLIAMSON, observed to the House that no provision was yet made for juries in Civil cases and suggested the necessity of it.

Mr GORHAM. It is not possible to discriminate equity cases from those in which juries are proper. The Representatives of the people may be safely trusted in this matter.

Mr GERRY urged the necessity of Juries to guard ag$^{st}$ corrupt Judges. He proposed that the Committee last appointed should be directed to provide a clause for securing the trial by Juries.

Col: MASON perceived the difficulty mentioned by Mr Gorham. The jury cases can not be specified. A general principle laid down on this and some other points would be sufficient. He wished the plan had been prefaced with a Bill of Rights, & would second a Motion if made for the purpose. It would give great quiet to the people; and with the aid of the State declarations, a bill might be prepared in a few hours.

Mr GERRY concurred in the idea & moved for a Committee to prepare a Bill of Rights. Col: MASON 2$^{ded}$ the motion.

Mr SHERMAN, was for securing the rights of the people where requisite. The State Declarations of Rights are not repealed by this Constitution; and being in force are sufficient. There are many cases where juries are proper which can not be discriminated. The Legislature may be safely trusted.

Col: MASON. The Laws of the U. S. are to be paramount to State Bills of Rights.

On the question for a Com$^e$ to prepare a Bill of Rights

N. H. no. Mas. abs$^t$ C$^t$ no. N. J. no. P$^a$ no. Del no. M$^d$ no. V$^a$ no. N. C. no. S. C. no. Geo. no.³⁷

The Clause relating to exports being reconsidered, at the instance of Col: Mason, who urged that the restriction on the States would prevent the incidental duties necessary for the inspection &

---

³⁶ In the transcript the vote reads: "Connecticut, New Jersey, Maryland [Mr. McHenry, no.], North Carolina, South Carolina, Georgia, aye—6; Massachusetts, Pennsylvania, Delaware, Virginia [General Washington, Mr. Blair, Mr. Madison, no; Col. Mason, Mr. Randolph, aye], no—4; New Hampshire divided."

³⁷ In the transcript the vote reads: "New Hampshire, Connecticut, New Jersey, Pennsylvania, Delaware, aye—5; Maryland, Virginia, North Carolina, South Carolina, Georgia, no—5; Massachusetts, absent." This was the copyist's error as Madison's original notes agree with the Journal, which reads: "Which passed unanimously in the negative."

safe-keeping of their produce, and be ruinous to the Staple States, as he called the five Southern States, he moved as follows—"provided nothing herein contained shall be construed to restrain any State from laying duties upon exports for the sole purpose of defraying the charges of inspecting, packing, storing and indemnifying the losses, in keeping the commodities in the care of public officers, before exportation." In answer to a remark which he anticipated, towit, that the States could provide for these expences, by a tax in some other way, he stated the inconveniency [38] of requiring the Planters to pay a tax before the actual delivery for exportation.

M$^r$ MADISON 2$^{ded}$ the motion. It would at least be harmless; and might have the good effect of restraining the States to bona fide duties for the purpose, as well as of authorising explicitly such duties; tho' perhaps the best guard against an abuse of the power of the States on this subject, was the right in the Gen$^l$ Government to regulate trade between State & State.

M$^r$ Gov$^r$ MORRIS saw no objection to the motion. He did not consider the dollar per Hhd laid on Tob$^o$ in Virg$^a$ as a duty on exportation, as no drawback would be allowed on Tob$^o$ taken out of the Warehouse for internal consumption.

M$^r$ DAYTON was afraid the proviso w$^d$ enable Pennsylv$^a$ to tax N. Jersey under the idea of Inspection duties of which Pen$^a$ would Judge.

M$^r$ GORHAM & M$^r$ LANGDON, thought there would be no security if the proviso sh$^d$ be agreed to, for the States exporting thro' other States, ag$^{st}$ the [39] oppressions of the latter. How was redress to be obtained in case duties should be laid beyond the purpose expressed?

M$^r$ MADISON. There will be the same security as in other cases. The jurisdiction of the supreme Court must be the source of redress. So far only had provision been made by the plan ag$^{st}$ injurious acts of the States. His own opinion was, that this was insufficient. A negative on the State laws alone could meet all the shapes which these could assume. But this had been overruled.

---

[38] The word "inconveniency" is changed in the transcript to "inconvenience."
[39] The word "these" is substituted in the transcript for "the."

Mr Fitzimmons. Incidental duties on Tobo & flour, never have been & never can be considered as duties on exports.

Mr Dickinson. Nothing will save [40] States in the situation of N. Hampshire N Jersey Delaware &c from being oppressed by their neighbors, but requiring the assent of Congs to inspection duties. He moved that this assent shd accordingly be required.

Mr Butler 2ded the motion.

Adjourned

---

Thursday Sepr 13. 1787.[41] In Convention

Col: Mason. He had moved without success for a power to make sumptuary regulations. He had not yet lost sight of his object. After descanting on the extravagance of our manners, the excessive consumption of foreign superfluities, and the necessity of restricting it, as well with œconomical as republican views, he moved that a Committee be appointed to report articles of association for encouraging by the advice the influence and the example of the members of the Convention, œconomy frugality and american manufactures.

Docr Johnson 2ded the motion which was without debate agreed to, nem: con: and a Committee appointed, consisting of Col: Mason, Docr Franklin, Mr Dickenson, Docr Johnson, and Mr Livingston.[*]

Col: Mason renewed his proposition of yesterday on the subject of inspection laws, with an additional clause giving to Congress a controul over them in case of abuse—as follows,

"Provided that no State shall be restrained from imposing the usual duties on produce exported from such State, for the sole purpose of defraying the charges of inspecting, packing, storing, and indemnifying the losses on such produce, while in the custody of public officers: but all such regulations shall in case of abuse, be subject to the revision and controul of Congress."

There was no debate & on the question

---

[40] The word "the" is here inserted in the transcript.
[41] The year "1787" is omitted in the transcript.
[*] This motion & appointment of the Comittee, not [42] in the printed Journal. No report was made by the Come
[42] The words "do not appear" are substituted in the transcript for "not."

N. H. ay. Mas. ay. C! ay. P? no. Del. no. M? ay. V? ay. N. C. ay. S. C. no. Geo. ay.⁴³

The Report from the Committee of stile & arrangement, was taken up, in order to be compared with the articles of the plan as agreed to by the House & referred to the Committee, and to receive the final corrections and sanction of the Convention.

Art. 1. sect. 2. On motion of M? RANDOLPH the word "servitude" was struck out, and "service"* unanimously inserted, the former being thought to express the condition of slaves, & the latter the obligations of free persons.

M? DICKENSON & M? WILSON moved to strike out "and direct taxes," from sect. 2. art. 1. as improperly placed in a clause relating merely to the Constitution of the House of Representatives.

M? Gov? MORRIS. The insertion here was in consequence of what had passed on this point; in order to exclude the appearance of counting the negroes in *the Representation*. The including of them may now be referred to the object of direct taxes, and incidentally only to that of Representation.

On the motion to strike out "and direct taxes" from this place
N. H. no. Mas. no. C! no. N. J. ay. P? no. Del. ay. M? ay. V? no. N. C. no. S. C. no. Geo. no.⁴⁴

Art. 1. sect. 7 "—if any bill shall not be returned by the president within ten days (Sundays excepted) after it shall have been presented to him &c"

M? MADISON, moved to insert between "after" and "it" in Sect. 7. Art. 1 the words "the day on which," in order to prevent a question whether the day on which the bill be presented, ought to be counted or not as one of the ten days.

M? RANDOLPH 2ded the motion.

M? GOVERNU? MORRIS. The amendment is unnecessary. The law knows no fractions of days.

A number of members being very impatient & calling for the question

---

⁴³ In the transcript the vote reads: "New Hampshire, Massachusetts, Connecticut, Maryland, Virginia, North Carolina, Georgia, aye—7; Pennsylvania, Delaware, South Carolina, no—3."

* See page 372 of the printed Journal.

⁴⁴ In the transcript the vote reads: "New Jersey, Delaware, Maryland, aye—3; New Hampshire, Massachusetts, Connecticut, Pennsylvania, Virginia, North Carolina, South Carolina, Georgia, no—8."

N. H. no. Mas. no. Cᵗ no. N. J. no. Pᵃ ay. Del. no. Mᵈ ay. Vᵃ ay. N. C. no S. C. no. Geo. no—⁴⁵

Docʳ JOHNSON made a further report from the Committee of stile &c of the following resolutions to be substituted for 22 & 23 articles

"Resolved that the preceding Constitution be laid before the U. States in Congress assembled, and that it is the opinion of this Convention, that it should afterwards be submitted to a Convention of Delegates chosen in each State by the people thereof, under the recommendation of its Legislature, for their assent & ratification; & that each Convention assenting & ratifying the same should give notice thereof to the U. S. in Congˢ assembled.

"Resolved that it is the opinion of this Convention that as soon as the Conventions of nine States, shall have ratified this Constitution, the U. S. in Congˢ assembled should fix a day on which electors should be appointed by the States which shall have ratified the same; and a day on which the Electors should assemble to vote for the President; and the time and place for commencing proceedings under this Constitution—That after such publication the Electors should be appointed, and the Senators and Representatives elected: That the Electors should meet on the day fixed for the election of the President, and should transmit their votes certified signed, sealed and directed, as the Constitution requires, to the Secretary of the U. States in Congˢ assembled: that the Senators and Representatives should convene at the time & place assigned; that the Senators should appoint a President for the sole purpose of receiving, opening, and counting the votes for President, and that after he shall be chosen, the Congress, together with the President should without delay proceed to execute this Constitution."

Adjourned

---

FRIDAY SEPᴿ 14ᵀᴴ 1787.⁴⁶ IN CONVENTION

The Report of the Committee of Stile & arrangement being resumed,

Mʳ WILLIAMSON moved to reconsider in order to increase the number of Representatives fixed for the first Legislature. His purpose was to make an addition of one half generally to the num-

---

⁴⁵ In the transcript the vote reads: "Pennsylvania, Maryland, Virginia, aye—3; New Hampshire, Massachusetts, Connecticut, New Jersey, Delaware, North Carolina, South Carolina, Georgia, no—8."

⁴⁶ The year "1787" is omitted in the transcript.

ber allotted to the respective States; and to allow two to the smallest States.

On this motion

N. H. no. Mas. no. Cᵗ no. N. J. no. Pᵃ ay. Del. ay. Mᵈ ay. Vᵃ ay. N C. ay. S. C. no. Geo. no.[47]

Art. 1. sect. 3.–the words * "by lot" were struck out nem: con: on motion of Mʳ MADISON, that some rule might prevail in the rotation that would prevent both the members from the same State from going out at the same time.

"Ex officio" struck out of the same section as superfluous: nem: con: and "or affirmation." after "oath" inserted also unanimously.

Mʳ RUTLIDGE and Mʳ Govʳ MORRIS moved "that persons impeached be suspended from their office [49] until they be tried and acquitted"

Mʳ MADISON. The President is made too dependent already on the Legislature, by the power of one branch to try him in consequence of an impeachment by the other. This intermediate suspension, will put him in the power of one branch only. They can at any moment, in order to make way for the functions of another who will be more favorable to their views, vote a temporary removal of the existing Magistrate.

Mʳ KING concurred in the opposition to the amendment

On the question to agree to it

N. H. no. Mas. no. Cᵗ ay. N. J. no. Pᵃ no. Del. no. Mᵈ no. Vᵃ no. N. C. no. S. C. ay. Geo. ay.[50]

Art. 1. sect. 4. "except as to the places of choosing Senators" [51] added nem: con: to the end of the first clause, in order to exempt the seats of Govᵗ in the States from the power of Congress.

---

[47] In the transcript the vote reads: "Pennsylvania, Delaware, Maryland, Virginia, North Carolina, aye—5; New Hampshire, Massachusetts, Connecticut, New Jersey, South Carolina, Georgia, no—6."

* "By lot" had been re-instated from the Report of five made Aug. 6. as a correction of the printed report by the Comᵉ of stile & arrangement.[48]

[48] In the transcript this note reads as follows: "'By lot,' had been reinstated from the Report of the Committee of five made on the sixth of August, as a correction of the printed Report by the Committee of style, &c."

[49] The transcript uses the word "office" in the plural.

[50] In the transcript the vote reads: "Connecticut, South Carolina, Georgia, aye—3; New Hampshire, Massachusetts, New Jersey, Pennsylvania, Delaware, Maryland, Virginia, North Carolina, no—8."

[51] The word "was" is here inserted in the transcript.

Art. 1. Sect. 5. "Each House shall keep a Journal of its proceedings, and from time to time publish the same, excepting such parts as may in their judgment require secresy."

Col: MASON & Mr GERRY moved to insert after the word "parts" the words "of the proceedings of the Senate" so as to require publication of all the proceedings of the House of Representatives.

It was intimated on the other side that cases might arise where secresy might be necessary in both Houses. Measures preparatory to a declaration of war in which the House of Reps was to concur, were instanced.

On the question, it passed in the negative

N. H. no. (Rh. I abs) Mas. no. Con: no. (N. Y. abs) N. J. no. Pen. ay. Del. no. Mary. ay. Virg. no. N. C. ay. S. C. divd. Geor. no.[52]

Mr BALDWIN observed that the clause, Art. 1. Sect 6. declaring that no member of Congs "during the time for which he was elected; shall be appointed to any Civil office under the authority of the U. S. which shall have been created, or the emoluments whereof shall have been increased during such time," would not extend to offices *created by the Constitution;* and the salaries of which would be created, *not increased* by Congs at their first session. The members of the first Congs consequently might evade the disqualification in this instance.—He was neither seconded nor opposed; nor did any thing further pass on the subject.

Art. 1. Sect. 8. The Congress "may by joint ballot appoint a Treasurer"

Mr RUTLIDGE moved to strike out this power, and let the Treasurer be appointed in the same manner with other officers.

Mr GORHAM & Mr KING said that the motion, if agreed, to would have a mischievous tendency. The people are accustomed & attached to that mode of appointing Treasurers, and the innovation will multiply objections to the System.

Mr Govr MORRIS remarked that if the Treasurer be not appointed by the Legislature, he will be more narrowly watched, and more readily impeached.

---

[52] In the transcript the vote reads: "Pennsylvania, Maryland, North Carolina, aye—3; New Hampshire, Massachusetts, Connecticut, New Jersey, Delaware, Virginia, Georgia, no—7."

M̶r̶ SHERMAN. As the two Houses appropriate money, it is best for them to appoint the officer who is to keep it; and to appoint him as they make the appropriation, not by joint but several votes.

Gen! PINKNEY. The Treasurer is appointed by joint ballot in South Carolina. The consequence is that bad appointments are made, and the Legislature will not listen to the faults of their own officer.

On the motion to strike out

N. H. ay. Mas. no. C̶t̶ ay. N. J. ay. P̶a̶ no. Del. ay. M̶d̶ ay. V̶a̶ no. N. C. ay. S. C. ay. Geo. ay.[53]

Art I. sect. 8.[54] "but all such duties imposts & excises, shall be uniform throughout the U. S." was[55] unanimously annexed to the power of taxation.

[56] To define & punish piracies and felonies on the high seas, and "punish" offences against the law of nations.

M̶r̶ Gov̶r̶ MORRIS moved to strike out "punish" before the words "offences ag̶s̶t̶ the law of nations," so as to let these be *definable* as well as punishable, by virtue of the preceding member of the sentence.

M̶r̶ WILSON hoped the alteration would by no means be made. To pretend to *define* the law of nations which depended on the authority of all the civilized nations of the world, would have a look of arrogance, that would make us ridiculous.

M̶r̶ Gov̶r̶ [57] The word *define* is proper when applied to *offences* in this case; the law of nations being often too vague and deficient to be a rule.

On the question to strike out the word "punish" it passed in the affirmative

N. H. ay. Mas. no. C̶t̶ ay. N. J. ay. P̶a̶ no. Del. ay. M̶d̶ no. V̶a̶ no. N. C. ay. S. C. ay. Geo. no.[58]

---

[53] In the transcript the vote reads: "New Hampshire, Connecticut, New Jersey, Delaware, Maryland, North Carolina, South Carolina, Georgia, aye—8; Massachusetts, Pennsylvania, Virginia, no—3."

[54] The expression "the words" is here inserted in the transcript.

[55] The word "was" is changed in the transcript to "were."

[56] The words "On the clause" are here inserted in the transcript.

[57] The name "Morris" is here inserted in the transcript.

[58] In the transcript the vote reads: "New Hampshire, Connecticut, New Jersey, Delaware, North Carolina, South Carolina, aye—6; Massachusetts, Pennsylvania, Maryland, Virginia, Georgia, no—5."

Doc.<sup>r</sup> FRANKLIN moved * to add after the words "post roads" Art I. Sect. 8. "a power to provide for cutting canals where deemed necessary"

M.<sup>r</sup> WILSON 2<sup>ded</sup> the motion

M.<sup>r</sup> SHERMAN objected. The expence in such cases will fall on the U. States, and the benefit accrue to the places where the canals may be cut.

M.<sup>r</sup> WILSON. Instead of being an expence to the U. S. they may be made a source of revenue.

M.<sup>r</sup> MADISON suggested an enlargement of the motion into a power "to grant charters of incorporation where the interest of the U. S. might require & the legislative provisions of individual States may be incompetent." His primary object was however to secure an easy communication between the States which the free intercourse now to be opened, seemed to call for. The political obstacles being removed, a removal of the natural ones as far as possible ought to follow. M.<sup>r</sup> RANDOLPH 2<sup>ded</sup> the proposition

M.<sup>r</sup> KING thought the power unnecessary.

M.<sup>r</sup> WILSON. It is necessary to prevent *a State* from obstructing the *general* welfare.

M.<sup>r</sup> KING. The States will be prejudiced and divided into parties by it. In Philad.<sup>a</sup> & New York, It will be referred to the establishment of a Bank, which has been a subject of contention in those Cities. In other places it will be referred to mercantile monopolies.

M.<sup>r</sup> WILSON mentioned the importance of facilitating by canals, the communication with the Western Settlements. As to Banks he did not think with M.<sup>r</sup> King that the power in that point of view would excite the prejudices & parties apprehended. As to mercantile monopolies they are already included in the power to regulate trade.

Col: MASON was for limiting the power to the single case of Canals. He was afraid of monopolies of every sort, which he did not think were by any means already implied by the Constitution as supposed by M.<sup>r</sup> Wilson.

The motion being so modified as to admit a distinct question specifying & limited to the case of canals,

---

* This motion by D.<sup>r</sup> Franklin not stated in the printed Journal, as are some other motions.

N. H. no. Mas. no. C⸚ no. N. J. no. P⸚ ay. Del. no. M⸚ no. V⸚ ay. N. C. no. S. C no. Geo. ay.⁵⁹

The other part fell of course, as including the power rejected.

M⸚ MADISON & M⸚ PINKNEY then moved to insert in the list of powers vested in Congress a power—"to establish an University, in which no preferences or distinctions should be allowed on account of Religion."

M⸚ WILSON supported the motion

M⸚ Gov⸚ MORRIS. It is not necessary. The exclusive power at the Seat of Government, will reach the object.

On the question

N. H. no. Mas. no. Con⸚ div⸚ D⸚ Johnson ay. M⸚ Sherman no. N. J. no. P⸚ ay. Del. no. M⸚ no. V⸚ ay. N. C. ay. S. C. ay. Geo. no.⁶⁰

Col: MASON, being sensible that an absolute prohibition of standing armies in time of peace might be unsafe, and wishing at the same time to insert something pointing out and guarding against the danger of them, moved to preface the clause (Art I sect. 8) "To provide for organizing, arming and disciplining the Militia &c" with the words" "And that the liberties of the people may be better secured against the danger of standing armies in time of peace" M⸚ RANDOLPH 2ded the motion

M⸚ MADISON was in favor of it. It did not restrain Congress from establishing a military force in time of peace if found necessary; and as armies in time of peace are allowed on all hands to be an evil, it is well to discountenance them by the Constitution, as far as will consist with the essential power of the Gov⸚ on that head.

M⸚ Gov⸚ MORRIS opposed the motion as setting a dishonorable mark of distinction on the military class of Citizens

M⸚ PINKNEY & M⸚ BEDFORD concurred in the opposition.

On the question

---

⁵⁹ In the transcript the vote reads: "Pennsylvania, Virginia, Georgia, aye—3; New Hampshire, Massachusetts, Connecticut, New Jersey, Delaware, Maryland, North Carolina, South Carolina, no—8."

⁶⁰ In the transcript the vote reads: "Pennsylvania, Virginia, North Carolina, South Carolina, aye—4; New Hampshire, Massachusetts, New Jersey, Delaware, Maryland, Georgia, no—6; Connecticut, divided [Dr. Johnson, aye; Mr. Sherman, no].

726

N. H. no. Mas. no. C? no. N. J. no. P? no. Del. no. Mary? no V? ay. N. C. no. S. C. no. Geo. ay.⁶¹

Col: MASON moved to strike out from the clause (art I sect 9.) "No bill of attainder nor any expost facto law shall be passed" the words "nor any ex post facto law." He thought it not sufficiently clear that the prohibition meant by this phrase was limited to cases of a criminal nature, and no Legislature ever did or can altogether avoid them in Civil cases.

Mʳ GERRY 2ᵈᵉᵈ the motion but with a view to extend the prohibition to "Civil cases," which he thought ought to be done.

On the question; all the States were—no

Mʳ PINKNEY & Mʳ GERRY, moved to insert a declaration "that the liberty of the Press should be inviolably observed."

Mʳ SHERMAN. It is unnecessary. The power of Congress does not extend to the Press. On the question, it passed in the negative

N. H. no.* Mas. ay. C? no. N. J. no. P? no. Del. no. M? ay. V? ay. N. C. no. S. C. ay. Geo. no.⁶²

Art. I. Sect. 9. "No capitation tax shall be laid, unless &c"

Mʳ READ moved to insert after "capitation" the words, "or other direct tax" He was afraid that some liberty might otherwise be taken to saddle the States, with a readjustment by this rule, of past requisitions of Congˢ—and that his amendment by giving another cast to the meaning would take away the pretext. Mʳ WILLIAMSON 2ᵈᵉᵈ the motion which was agreed to, On motion of Col: MASON⁶³ "or enumeration"⁶⁴ inserted after, as explanatory of "Census" Con. & S. C. only, no.

*Here insert the amendment added in the lateral margin.⁶⁵

*At the end of the clause "no tax or duty shall be laid on articles exported from any State" was added the following amendment conformably to a vote on the      day of ⁶⁶      viz—no preference shall be given by any regulation of commerce or rev-

---

⁶¹ In the transcript the vote reads: "Virginia, Georgia, aye—2; New Hampshire, Massachusetts, Connecticut, New Jersey, Pennsylvania, Delaware, Maryland, North Carolina, South Carolina, no—9."
*In the printed Journal N. Hampshire ay.
⁶² In the transcript the vote reads: Massachusetts, Maryland, Virginia, South Carolina, aye—4; New Hampshire,* Connecticut, New Jersey, Pennsylvania, Delaware, North Carolina, Georgia, no—7.
⁶³ The expression "the words" is here inserted in the transcript.
⁶⁴ The word "were" is here inserted in the transcript.
⁶⁵ Madison's direction concerning the amendment is omitted in the transcript.
⁶⁶ The date "thirty-first of August" is supplied in the transcript.

enue to the ports of one State over those of another: nor shall vessels bound to or from one State, be obliged to enter, clear or pay duties in another.

Col. MASON moved a clause requiring "that an Account of the public expenditures should be annually published" M$^r$ GERRY 2$^{ded}$ the motion

M$^r$ Gov$^r$ MORRIS urged that this w$^d$ be impossible in many cases.

M$^r$ KING remarked, that the term expenditures went to every minute shilling. This would be impracticable. Cong$^s$ might indeed make a monthly publication, but it would be in such general statements as would afford no satisfactory information.

M$^r$ MADISON proposed to strike out "annually" from the motion & insert "from time to time," which would enjoin the duty of frequent publications and leave enough to the discretion of the Legislature. Require too much and the difficulty will beget a habit of doing nothing. The articles of Confederation require half-yearly publications on this subject. A punctual compliance being often impossible, the practice has ceased altogether.

M$^r$ WILSON 2$^{ded}$ & supported the motion. Many operations of finance can not be properly published at certain times.

M$^r$ PINKNEY was in favor of the motion.

M$^r$ FITZIMMONS. It is absolutely impossible to publish expenditures in the full extent of the term.

M$^r$ SHERMAN thought "from time to time" the best rule to be given.

"Annual" was struck out—& those words—inserted nem: con:

The motion of Col: Mason so amended was then agreed to nem: con: and added after—"appropriations by law as follows—"and a regular statement and account of the receipts & expenditures of all public money shall be published from time to time"

Here insert the Amendment at the foot of the page [67]

\* The first clause of Art. I Sect 10—was altered so as to read— "No State shall enter into any Treaty alliance or confederation; grant letters of marque and reprisal; coin money; emit bills of

---

[67] Madison's direction concerning the amendment is omitted in the transcript.

\* In the printed Journal N. Hampshire ay.

credit; make any thing but gold & silver coin a tender in payment of debts; pass any bill of attainder, ex post [68] law, or law impairing the obligation of contracts, or grant any title of nobility."

M.^r GERRY entered into observations inculcating the importance of public faith, and the propriety of the restraint put on the States from impairing the obligation of contracts, alledging that Congress ought to be laid under the like prohibitions, he made a motion to that effect. He was not 2.^ded

Adjourned

---

SATURDAY SEP.^R 15.^TH 1787.[69] IN CONVENTION

M.^r CARROL reminded the House that no address to the people had yet been prepared. He considered it of great importance that such an one should accompany the Constitution. The people had been accustomed to such on great occasions, and would expect it on this. He moved that a Committee be appointed for the special purpose of preparing an Address.

M.^r RUTLEDGE objected on account of the delay it would produce and the impropriety of addressing the people before it was known whether Congress would approve and support the plan. Congress, if an address be thought proper can prepare as good a one. The members of the Convention can also explain the reasons of what has been done to their respective Constituents.

M.^r SHERMAN concurred in the opinion that an address was both unnecessary and improper.

On the motion of M.^r Carrol

N. H. no. Mas. no. C.^t no. N. J. no. P.^a ay. Del. ay. M.^d ay. V.^a ay. N. C.* ab.^st S. C.* no. Geo. no [70]

M.^r LANGDON. Some gentlemen have been very uneasy that no increase of the number of Representatives has been admitted. It has in particular been thought that one more ought to be allowed to N. Carolina. He was of opinion that an additional one was

---

[68] The word "facto" is here inserted in the transcript.
[69] The year "1787" is omitted in the transcript.
* In the printed Journal N. Carolina—no & S. Carol: omitted.
[70] In the transcript the vote reads: "Pennsylvania, Delaware, Maryland, Virginia, aye—4; New Hampshire, Massachusetts, Connecticut, New Jersey, South Carolina,* Georgia, no—6; North Carolina,* absent."

due both to that State & to Rho: Island, & moved to reconsider for that purpose.

Mʳ SHERMAN. When the Committee of eleven reported the apportionment—five Representatives were thought the proper share of N. Carolina. Subsequent information however seemed to entitle that State to another.

On the motion to reconsider

N. H. ay. Mas. no. Cᵗ ay. N. J. no. Pen. divᵈ Del. ay. Mᵈ ay. Vᵃ ay. N. C. ay. S. C. ay. Geo. ay.[71]

Mʳ LANGDON moved to add 1 member to each of the Representations of N. Carolina & Rho: Island.

Mʳ KING was agˢᵗ any change whatever as opening the door for delays. There had been no official proof that the numbers of N. C. are greater than before estimated, and he never could sign the Constitution if Rho: Island is so be allowed two members that is, one fourth of the number allowed to Massts, which will be known to be unjust.

Mʳ PINKNEY urged the propriety of increasing the number of Repˢ allotted to N. Carolina.

Mʳ BEDFORD contended for an increase in favor of Rho: Island, and of Delaware also

On the question for allowing two Repˢ to Rho: Island, it passed in the negative

N. H. ay. Mas. no. Cᵗ no. N. J. no. Pᵃ no. Del. ay. Mᵈ ay. Vᵃ no. N. C. ay. S. C. no. Geo. ay.[72]

On the question for allowing six to N. Carolina, it passed in the negative.

N. H. no. Mas. no. Cᵗ no. N. J. no. Pᵃ no. Del. no. Mᵈ ay. Vᵃ ay. N. C. ay. S. C. ay. Geo. ay.[73]

Art 1. Sect. 10. (paragraph 2). "No State shall, without the consent of Congress lay imposts or duties on imports or exports; nor with such consent, but to the use of the Treasury of the U. States."

---

[71] In the transcript the vote reads: "New Hampshire, Connecticut, Delaware, Maryland, Virginia, North Carolina, South Carolina, Georgia, aye—8; Massachusetts, New Jersey, no—2; Pennsylvania, divided."

[72] In the transcript the vote reads: "New Hampshire, Delaware, Maryland, North Carolina, Georgia, aye—5; Massachusetts, Connecticut, New Jersey, Pennsylvania, Virginia, South Carolina, no—6."

[73] In the transcript the vote reads: "Maryland, Virginia, North Carolina, South Carolina, Georgia, aye—5; New Hampshire, Massachusetts, Connecticut, New Jersey, Pennsylvania, Delaware, no—6."

In consequence of the proviso moved by Col: Mason: and agreed to on the 13 [74] Sep.<sup>r</sup>, this part of the section was laid aside in favor of the following substitute viz. "No State shall, without the consent of Congress, lay any imposts or duties on imports or exports, except what may be absolutely necessary for executing its Inspection laws; and the nett produce of all duties and imposts, laid by any State on imports or exports, shall be for the use of the Treasury of the U. S; and all such laws shall be subject to the revision and controul of the Congress"

On a motion to strike out the last part "and all such laws shall be subject to the revision and controul of the Congress" it passed in the negative.

N. H. no. Mas. no. C.<sup>t</sup> no. N. J. no. P.<sup>a</sup> div.<sup>d</sup> Del. no. M.<sup>d</sup> no. V.<sup>a</sup> ay. N. C. ay. S. C. no. Geo. ay.[75]

The substitute was then agreed to: Virg.<sup>a</sup> alone being in the negative.

The remainder of the paragraph being under consideration— viz—"nor keep troops nor ships of war in time of peace, nor enter into any agreement or compact with another State, nor with any foreign power. Nor engage in any war, unless it shall be actually invaded by enemies, or the danger of invasion be so imminent as not to admit of delay, until Congress can be consulted"

M.<sup>r</sup> M.<sup>c</sup> HENRY & M.<sup>r</sup> CARROL moved that "no State shall be restrained from laying duties of tonnage for the purpose of clearing harbours and erecting light-houses."

Col. MASON in support of this explained and urged the situation of the Chesapeak which peculiarly required expences of this sort.

M.<sup>r</sup> Gov.<sup>r</sup> MORRIS. The States are not restrained from laying tonnage as the Constitution now Stands. The exception proposed will imply the contrary, and will put the States in a worse condition than the gentleman [Col Mason] wishes.

M.<sup>r</sup> MADISON. Whether the States are now restrained from laying tonnage duties depends on the extent of the power "to regulate commerce." These terms are vague, but seem to exclude this power of the States. They may certainly be restrained by Treaty.

---

[74] The word "of" is here inserted in the transcript.

[75] In the transcript the vote reads: "Virginia, North Carolina, Georgia, aye—3; New Hampshire, Massachusetts, Connecticut, New Jersey, Delaware, Maryland, South Carolina, no—7; Pennsylvania, divided."

He observed that there were other objects for tonnage Duties as the support of Seamen &c. He was more & more convinced that the regulation of Commerce was in its nature indivisible and ought to be wholly under one authority.

Mr SHERMAN. The power of the U. States to regulate trade being supreme can controul interferences of the State regulations when [76] such interferences happen; so that there is no danger to be apprehended from a concurrent jurisdiction.

Mr LANGDON insisted that the regulation of tonnage was an essential part of the regulation of trade, and that the States ought to have nothing to do with it. On motion "that no State shall lay any duty on tonnage without the Consent of Congress"

N. H. ay. Mas. ay. Ct divd N. J. ay. Pa no. Del. ay. Md ay. Va no. N. C. no. S. C. ay. Geo. no.[77]

The remainder of the paragraph was then remoulded and passed as follows viz—" No State shall without the consent of Congress, lay any duty of tonnage, keep troops or ships of war in time of peace, enter into any agreement or compact with another State, or with a foreign power, or engage in war, unless actually invaded, or in such imminent danger as will not admit of delay."

[78] Art II. sect. 1. (paragraph 6) "or the period for chusing another president arrive" was changed into "or a President shall be elected" conformably to a vote of the       day of

Mr RUTLIDGE and Docr FRANKLIN moved to annex to the end of paragraph 7. Sect. 1. art II—"and he [the President] shall not receive, within that period, any other emolument from the U. S. or any of them," on which question

N. H. ay. Mas. ay. Ct no. N. J. no. Pa ay. Del. no. Md ay Va ay. N. C. no. S. C. ay. Geo. ay.[79]

Art: II. Sect. 2. "he shall have power to grant reprieves and pardons for offences against the U. S. &c"

---

[76] In Madison's notes the word "when" is written above "which." The transcript uses "when."

[77] In the transcript the vote reads: "New Hampshire, Massachusetts, New Jersey, Delaware, Maryland, South Carolina, aye—6; Pennsylvania, Virginia, North Carolina, Georgia, no—4; Connecticut, divided."

[78] In the transcript this paragraph reads as follows: "Article 2, sect. 1, (the sixth paragraph) the words 'or the period for choosing another President arrive,' were changed into, 'or a President shall be elected,' conformably to a vote of the seventh of September."

[79] In the transcript the vote reads: "New Hampshire, Massachusetts, Pennsylvania, Maryland, Virginia, South Carolina, Georgia, aye—7; Connecticut, New Jersey, Delaware, North Carolina, no—4."

Mr RANDOLPH moved to "except cases of treason." The prerogative of pardon in these cases was too great a trust. The President may himself be guilty. The Traytors may be his own instruments.

Col: MASON supported the motion.

Mr Govr MORRIS had rather there should be no pardon for treason, than let the power devolve on the Legislature.

Mr WILSON. Pardon is necessary for cases of treason, and is best placed in the hands of the Executive. If he be himself a party to the guilt he can be impeached and prosecuted.

Mr KING thought it would be inconsistent with the Constitutional separation of the Executive & Legislative powers to let the prerogative be exercised by the latter. A Legislative body is utterly unfit for the purpose. They are governed too much by the passions of the moment. In Massachussets, one assembly would have hung all the insurgents in that State: the next was equally disposed to pardon them all. He suggested the expedient of requiring the concurrence of the Senate in Acts of Pardon.

Mr MADISON admitted the force of objections to the Legislature, but the pardon of treasons was so peculiarly improper for the President that he should acquiesce in the transfer of it to the former, rather than leave it altogether in the hands of the latter. He would prefer to either an association of the Senate as a Council of advice, with the President.

Mr RANDOLPH could not admit the Senate into a share of the Power. the great danger to liberty lay in a combination between the President & that body.

Col: MASON. The Senate has already too much power. There can be no danger of too much lenity in legislative pardons, as the Senate must con concur, & the President moreover can require ⅔ of both Houses.

On the motion of Mr Randolph.

N. H. no. Mas. no. Ct divd N. J. no. Pa no. Del. no. Md no. Va ay. N. C. no. S. C. no. Geo. ay.[80]

---

[80] In the transcript the vote reads: "Virginia, Georgia, aye—2; New Hampshire, Massachusetts, New Jersey, Pennsylvania, Delaware, Maryland, North Carolina, South Carolina, no—8; Connecticut, divided."

Art II. Sect. 2. (paragraph 2)  To the end of this, Mr GOVERNr MORRIS moved to annex "but the Congress may by law vest the appointment of such inferior officers as they think proper, in the President alone, in the Courts of law, or in the heads of Departments." Mr SHERMAN 2ded the motion

Mr MADISON.  It does not go far enough if it be necessary at all. Superior officers below Heads of Departments ought in some cases to have the appointment of the lesser offices.

Mr Govr MORRIS  There is no necessity.  Blank commissions can be sent—

On the motion

N. H. ay.  Mas. no.  Ct ay.  N. J. ay.  Pa ay.  Del. no.  Md divd Va. no.  N. C. ay.  S C no.  Geo. no.[81]

The motion being lost by the [82] equal division of votes, It was urged that it be put a second time, some such provision being too necessary to be omitted, and on a second question it was agreed to nem. con.

Art II. Sect. 1.  The words, "and not per capita"—were struck out as superfluous—and the words "by the Representatives" also—as improper, the choice of a [83] President being in another mode as well as eventually by the House of Reps

Art. II. Sect. 2.  After [84] "officers of the U. S. whose appointments are not otherwise provided for." were added the words "and which shall be established by law."

Art III. Sect. 2. parag: 3.  Mr PINKNEY & Mr GERRY moved to annex to the end, "And a trial by jury shall be preserved as usual in civil cases."

Mr GORHAM.  The constitution of Juries is different in different States and the trial itself is *usual* in different cases in different States.

Mr KING urged the same objections

Genl PINKNEY also.  He thought such a clause in the Constitution would be pregnant with embarrassments.

---

[81] In the transcript the vote reads: "New Hampshire, Connecticut, New Jersey, Pennsylvania, North Carolina, aye—5; Massachusetts, Delaware, Virginia, South Carolina, Georgia, no—5; Maryland, divided."
[82] The word "an" is substituted in the transcript for "the."
[83] The word "a" is omitted in the transcript.
[84] The expression "the words" is here inserted in the transcript.

The motion was disagreed to nem: con:

Art. IV. Sect 2. parag: 3. the term "legally" was struck out, and [85] "under the laws thereof" inserted after the word "State," in compliance with the wish of some who thought the term legal [86] equivocal, and favoring the idea that slavery was legal in a moral view.

Art. IV. Sect 3. " New States may be admitted by the Congress into this Union: but no new State shall be formed or erected within the jurisdiction of any other State; nor any State be formed by the junction of two or more States, or parts of States, without the consent of the Legislatures of the States concerned as well as of the Cong⁵ "

Mr GERRY moved to insert after "or parts of States" the words "or a State and part of a State" which was disagreed to by a large majority; it appearing to be supposed that the case was comprehended in the words of the clause as reported by the Committee.

Art. IV. Sect. 4. After the word "Executive" were inserted the words "when the Legislature can not be convened."

Art. V. "The Congress, whenever two thirds of both Houses shall deem necessary, or on the application of two thirds of the Legislatures of the several States shall propose amendments to this Constitution, which shall be valid to all intents and purposes as part thereof, when the same shall have been ratified by three fourths at least of the Legislatures of the several States, or by Conventions in three fourths thereof, as the one or the other mode of ratification may be proposed by the Congress: Provided that no amendment which may be made prior to the year 1808 shall in any manner affect the 1 & 4 clauses in the 9. section of article 1"

Mr SHERMAN expressed his fears that three fourths of the States might be brought to do things fatal to particular States, as abolishing them altogether or depriving them of their equality in the Senate. He thought it reasonable that the proviso in favor of the States importing slaves should be extended so as to provide that no State should be affected in its internal police, or deprived of its equality in the Senate.

---

[85] The expression "the words" is here inserted in the transcript.
[86] The transcript italicizes the word "legal."

Col: MASON thought the plan of amending the Constitution exceptionable & dangerous. As the proposing of amendments is in both the modes to depend, in the first immediately, in the second, ultimately, on Congress, no amendments of the proper kind would ever be obtained by the people, if the Government should become oppressive, as he verily believed would be the case.

Mr Govr MORRIS & Mr GERRY moved to amend the article so as to require a Convention on application of ⅔ of the Sts.

Mr MADISON did not see why Congress would not be as much bound to propose amendments applied for by two thirds of the States as to call a call a Convention on the like application. He saw no objection however against providing for a Convention for the purpose of amendments, except only that difficulties might arise as to the form, the quorum &c. which in Constitutional regulations ought to be as much as possible avoided.

The motion of Mr Govr MORRIS & Mr GERRY was agreed to nem: con: [see the first part of the article as finally past][87]

Mr SHERMAN moved to strike out of art. V. after "legislatures" the words "of three fourths" and so after the word "Conventions" leaving future Conventions to act in this matter, like the present Conventions[88] according to circumstances.

On this motion

N. H. divd. Mas. ay. Ct ay. N. J. ay. Pa no. Del. no. Md no. Va no. N. C. no. S. C. no. Geo. no.[89]

Mr GERRY moved to strike out the words "or by Conventions in three fourths thereof"

On this[90] motion

N. H. no. Mas. no. Ct ay. N. J. no. Pa no. Del. no. Md no. Va no. N. C. no. S. C. no. Geo. no.[91]

Mr SHERMAN moved according to his idea above expressed to annex to the end of the article a further proviso "that no State

---

[87] Madison's direction is omitted in the transcript.
[88] The transcript uses the word "Conventions" in the singular.
[89] In the transcript the vote reads: "Massachusetts, Connecticut, New Jersey, aye—3; Pennsylvania, Delaware, Maryland, Virginia, North Carolina, South Carolina, Georgia, no—7; New Hampshire, divided."
[90] The word "which" is substituted in the transcript for "this."
[91] In the transcript the vote reads: "Connecticut, aye—1; New Hampshire, Massachusetts, New Jersey, Pennsylvania, Delaware, Maryland, Virginia, North Carolina, South Carolina, Georgia, no—10."

shall without its consent be affected in its internal police, or deprived of its equal suffrage in the Senate."

M! MADISON. Begin with these special provisos, and every State will insist on them, for their boundaries, exports &c.

On the motion of M! Sherman

N. H. no. Mas. no. C! ay. N. J. ay. P! no. Del. ay. M! no. V! no. N. C. no. S. C. no. Geo. no.[92]

M! SHERMAN then moved to strike out art V altogether.

M! BREARLEY 2^ded the motion, on which

N. H. no. Mas. no. C! ay. N. J. ay. P! no. Del div! M! no. V! no. N. C. no. S. C. no. Geo. no.[93]

M! Gov! MORRIS moved to annex a further proviso—"that no State, without its consent shall be deprived of its equal suffrage in the Senate"

This motion being dictated by the circulating murmurs of the small States was agreed to without debate, no one opposing it, or on the question, saying no.

Col: MASON expressing his discontent at the power given to Congress by a bare majority to pass navigation acts, which he said would not only enhance the freight, a consequence he did not so much regard—but would enable a few rich merchants in Philad^a N. York & Boston, to monopolize the Staples of the Southern States & reduce their value perhaps 50 Per C!—moved a further proviso "that no law in [94] nature of a navigation act be passed before the year 1808, without the consent of $\frac{2}{3}$ of each branch of the Legislature" On this [95] motion

N. H. no. Mas. no. C! no. N. J. no. P! no. Del. no. M! ay. V! ay. N. C. abs!. S. C. no. Geo. ay.[96]

M! RANDOLPH animadverting on the indefinite and dangerous power given by the Constitution to Congress, expressing the pain he felt at differing from the body of the Convention, on the close of the great & awful subject of their labours, and anxiously wish-

---

[92] In the transcript the vote reads: "Connecticut, New Jersey, Delaware, aye—3; New Hampshire, Massachusetts, Pennsylvania, Maryland, Virginia, North Carolina, South Carolina, Georgia, no—8."

[93] In the transcript the vote reads: "Connecticut, New Jersey, aye—2; New Hampshire, Massachusetts, Pennsylvania, Maryland, Virginia, North Carolina, South Carolina, Georgia, no—8; Delaware, divided."

[94] The word "the" is here inserted in the transcript.

[95] The word "which" is substituted in the transcript for "this."

[96] In the transcript the vote reads: "Maryland, Virginia, Georgia, aye—3; New Hampshire, Massachusetts, Connecticut, New Jersey, Pennsylvania, Delaware, South Carolina, no—7; North Carolina, absent."

ing for some accomodating expedient which would relieve him from his embarrassments, made a motion importing "that amendments to the plan might be offered by the State Conventions, which should be submitted to and finally decided on by another general Convention" Should this proposition be disregarded, it would he said be impossible for him to put his name to the instrument. Whether he should oppose it afterwards he would not then decide but he would not deprive himself of the freedom to do so in his own State, if that course should be prescribed by his final judgment.

Col: MASON 2$^{ded}$ & followed M$^r$ Randolph in animadversions on the dangerous power and structure of the Government, concluding that it would end either in monarchy, or a tyrannical aristocracy; which, he was in doubt, but one or other, he was sure. This Constitution had been formed without the knowledge or idea of the people. A second Convention will know more of the sense of the people, and be able to provide a system more consonant to it. It was improper to say to the people, take this or nothing. As the Constitution now stands, he could neither give it his support or [97] vote in Virginia; and he could not sign here what he could not support there. With the expedient of another Convention as proposed, he could sign.

M$^r$ PINKNEY. These declarations from members so respectable at the close of this important scene, give a peculiar solemnity to the present moment. He descanted on the consequences of calling forth the deliberations & amendments of the different States on the subject of Government at large. Nothing but confusion & contrariety could [98] spring from the experiment. The States will never agree in their plans, and the Deputies to a second Convention coming together under the discordant impressions of their Constituents, will never agree. Conventions are serious things, and ought not to be repeated. He was not without objections as well as others to the plan. He objected to the contemptible weakness & dependence of the Executive. He objected to the power of a majority only of Cong$^s$ over Commerce. But apprehending the danger of a

---

[97] The word "or" is changed in the transcript to "nor."
[98] The word "will" is substituted in the transcript for "could."

general confusion, and an ultimate decision by the sword, he should give the plan his support.

Mr GERRY, stated the objections which determined him to withhold his name from the Constitution. 1. the duration and re-eligibility of the Senate. 2. the power of the House of Representatives to conceal their journals. 3. the power of Congress over the places of election. 4 the unlimited power of Congress over their own compensations. 5.⁹⁹ Massachusetts has not a due share of Representatives allotted to her. 6.⁹⁹ ³/₅ of the Blacks are to be represented as if they were freemen. 7.⁹⁹ Under the power over commerce, monopolies may be established. 8. The vice president being made head of the Senate. He could however he said get over all these, if the rights of the Citizens were not rendered insecure 1.[1] by the general power of the Legislature to make what laws they may please to call necessary and proper. 2.[2] raise armies and money without limit. 3.[3] to establish a tribunal without juries, which will be a Star-chamber as to Civil cases. Under such a view of the Constitution, the best that could be done he conceived was to provide for a second general Convention.

On the question on the proposition of Mr Randolph. All the States answered—no

On the question to agree to the Constitution, as amended. All the States ay.

The Constitution was then ordered to be engrossed.

And the House adjourned.

---

MONDAY SEPR 17. 1787:[4] IN CONVENTION

The engrossed Constitution being read,

Docr FRANKLIN rose with a speech in his hand, which he had reduced to writing for his own conveniency,[5] and which Mr Wilson read in the words following.

---

[99] The word "that" is here inserted in the transcript.
[1] The figure "1" is changed in the transcript to "first."
[2] The figure "2" is changed in the transcript to "secondly, to."
[3] The figure "3" is changed in the transcript to "thirdly."
[4] The year "1787" is omitted in the transcript.
[5] The word "conveniency" is changed in the transcript to "convenience."

Mr President

I confess that there are several parts of this constitution which I do not at present approve, but I am not sure I shall never approve them: For having lived long, I have experienced many instances of being obliged by better information, or fuller consideration, to change opinions even on important subjects, which I once thought right, but found to be otherwise. It is therefore that the older I grow, the more apt I am to doubt my own judgment, and to pay more respect to the judgment of others. Most men indeed as well as most sects in Religion, think themselves in possession of all truth, and that wherever others differ from them it is so far error. Steele a Protestant in a Dedication tells the Pope, that the only difference between our Churches in their opinions of the certainty of their doctrines is, the Church of Rome is infallible and the Church of England is never in the wrong. But though many private persons think almost as highly of their own infallibility as of that of their sect, few express it so naturally as a certain french lady, who in a dispute with her sister, said "I don't know how it happens, Sister but I meet with no body but myself, that's always in the right—*Il n'y a que moi qui a toujours raison.*"

In these sentiments, Sir, I agree to this Constitution with all its faults, if they are such; because I think a general Government necessary for us, and there is no form of Government but what may be a blessing to the people if well administered, and believe farther that this is likely to be well administered for a course of years, and can only end in Despotism, as other forms have done before it, when the people shall become so corrupted as to need despotic Government, being incapable of any other. I doubt too whether any other Convention we can obtain, may be able to make a better Constitution. For when you assemble a number of men to have the advantage of their joint wisdom, you inevitably assemble with those men, all their prejudices, their passions, their errors of opinion, their local interests, and their selfish views. From such an assembly can a perfect production be expected? It therefore astonishes me, Sir, to find this system approaching so near to perfection as it does; and I think it will astonish our enemies, who are waiting with confidence to hear that our councils are confounded like those of the Builders of Babel; and that our States are on the point of separation, only to meet hereafter for the purpose of cutting one another's throats. Thus I consent, Sir, to this Constitution because I expect no better, and because I am not sure, that it is not the best. The opinions I have had of its errors, I sacrifice to the public good. I have never whispered a syllable of them abroad. Within these walls they were born, and here they shall die. If every one of us in returning to our Constituents were to report the objections he has had to it, and endeavor to gain partizans in support of them, we might prevent its being generally received, and thereby lose all the salutary effects & great advantages resulting naturally in our favor among foreign Nations as well as among ourselves, from our real or apparent unanimity. Much of the strength & efficiency of any Government in procuring and securing happiness to the people, depends, on opinion, on the general opinion of the goodness of the Government, as well as well as of the wisdom and integrity of its Governors. I hope therefore that for our own sakes as a part of the people, and for the sake of posterity, we shall act heartily and unanimously in recommending this Constitution (if approved by Congress & confirmed by the Conventions) wherever our influence may extend, and turn our future thoughts & endeavors to the means of having it well administred.

On the whole, Sir, I can not help expressing a wish that every member of the Convention who may still have objections to it, would with me, on this occasion doubt a little of his own infallibility, and to make manifest our unanimity, put his name to this instrument.—

He then moved that the Constitution be signed by the members and offered the following as a convenient form viz. " Done in Convention by the unanimous consent of *the States* present the 17th of Sepr &c—In Witness whereof we have hereunto subscribed our names."

This ambiguous form had been drawn up by Mr G. M. in order to gain the dissenting members, and put into the hands of Docr Franklin that it might have the better chance of success.

*The Home of John Marshall*

Mr GORHAM said if it was not too late he could wish, for the purpose of lessening objections to the Constitution, that the clause declaring "the number of Representatives shall not exceed one for every forty thousand" which had produced so much discussion, might be yet reconsidered, in order to strike out 40,000 & insert "thirty thousand." This would not he remarked establish that as an absolute rule, but only give Congress a greater latitude which could not be thought unreasonable.

Mr KING & Mr CARROL seconded & supported the idea of Mr Gorham.

When the PRESIDENT rose, for the purpose of putting the question, he said that although his situation had hitherto restrained him from offering his sentiments on questions depending in the House, and it might be thought, ought now to impose silence on him, yet he could not forbear expressing his wish that the alteration proposed might take place. It was much to be desired that the objections to the plan recommended might be made as few as possible. The smallness of the proportion of Representatives had been considered by many members of the Convention an insufficient security for the rights & interests of the people. He acknowledged that it had always appeared to himself among the exceptionable parts of the plan, and late as the present moment was for admitting amendments, he thought this of so much consequence that it would give [6] much satisfaction to see it adopted *

No opposition was made to the proposition of Mr Gorham and it was agreed to unanimously.

On the question to agree to the Constitution enrolled in order to be signed. It was agreed to all the States [8] answering ay.

Mr RANDOLPH then rose and with an allusion to the observations of Docr Franklin apologized for his refusing to sign the Constitution notwithstanding the vast majority & venerable names that would give sanction to its wisdom and its worth. He said however that he did not mean by this refusal to decide that he should oppose

---

[6] The word "him" is here inserted in the transcript.

* Transfer the remarks in brackets, to the bottom margin.[7]

*[This was the only occasion on which the President entered at all into the discussions of the Convention].

[7] Madison's direction is omitted in the transcript.

[8] The word "States" is italicized in the transcript.

the Constitution without doors. He meant only to keep himself free to be governed by his duty as it should be prescribed by his future judgment. He refused to sign, because he thought the object of the Convention would be frustrated by the alternative which it presented to the people. Nine States will fail to ratify the plan and confusion must ensue. With such a view of the subject he ought not, he could not, by pledging himself to support the plan, restrain himself from taking such steps as might appear to him most consistent with the public good.

M! Gov! Morris said that he too had objections, but considering the present plan as the best that was to be attained, he should take it with all its faults. The majority had determined in its favor and by that determination he should abide. The moment this plan goes forth all other considerations will be laid aside, and the great question will be, shall there be a national Government or not? and this must take place or a general anarchy will be the alternative. He remarked that the signing in the form proposed related only to the fact that the [9] *States* present were unanimous.

M! Williamson suggested that the signing should be confined to the letter accompanying the Constitution to Congress, which might perhaps do nearly as well, and would he found be [10] satisfactory to some members * who disliked the Constitution. For himself he did not think a better plan was to be expected and had no scruples against putting his name to it.

M! Hamilton expressed his anxiety that every member should sign. A few characters of consequence, by opposing or even refusing to sign the Constitution, might do infinite mischief by kindling the latent sparks which [11] lurk under an enthusiasm in favor of the Convention which may soon subside. No man's ideas were more remote from the plan than his [12] were known to be; but is it possible to deliberate between anarchy and Convulsion on one side, and the chance of good to be expected from the plan on the other.

---

[9] The transcript italicizes the word "the."
[10] The words "be found" are substituted in the transcript for "he found be."
* He alluded to M! Blount for one.
[11] The word "which" is changed in the transcript to "that."
[12] The word "own" is here inserted in the transcript.

Mʳ BLOUNT said he had declared that he would not sign, so as to pledge himself in support of the plan, but he was relieved by the form proposed and would without committing himself attest the fact that the plan was the unanimous act of the States in Convention.

Docʳ FRANKLIN expressed his fears from what Mʳ Randolph had said, that he thought himself alluded to in the remarks offered this morning to the House. He declared that when drawing up that paper he did not know that any particular member would refuse to sign his name to the instrument, and hoped to be so understood. He professed a high sense of obligation to Mʳ Randolph for having brought forward the plan in the first instance, and for the assistance he had given in its progress, and hoped that he would yet lay aside his objections, and by concurring with his brethren, prevent the great mischief which the refusal of his name might produce.

Mʳ RANDOLPH could not but regard the signing in the proposed form, as the same with signing the Constitution. The change of form therefore could make no difference with him. He repeated that in refusing to sign the Constitution, he took a step which might be the most awful of his life, but it was dictated by his conscience, and it was not possible for him to hesitate, much less, to change. He repeated also his persuasion, that the holding out this plan with a final alternative to the people, of accepting or rejecting it in toto, would really produce the anarchy & civil convulsions which were apprehended from the refusal of individuals to sign it.

Mʳ GERRY described the painful feelings of his situation, and the embarrassment [13] under which he rose to offer any further observations on the subject wᶜʰ had been finally decided. Whilst the plan was depending, he had treated it with all the freedom he thought it deserved. He now felt himself bound as he was disposed to treat it with the respect due to the Act of the Convention. He hoped he should not violate that respect in declaring on this occasion his fears that a Civil war may result from the present crisis of the U. S. In Massachussetts, particularly he saw the dan-

---

[13] The transcript uses the word "embarrassment" in the plural.

ger of this calamitous event—In that State there are two parties, one devoted to Democracy, the worst he thought of all political evils, the other as violent in the opposite extreme. From the collision of these in opposing and resisting the Constitution, confusion was greatly to be feared. He had thought it necessary, for this & other reasons that the plan should have been proposed in a more mediating shape, in order to abate the heat and opposition of parties. As it has been passed by the Convention, he was persuaded it would have a contrary effect. He could not therefore by signing the Constitution pledge himself to abide by it at all events. The proposed form made no difference with him. But if it were not otherwise apparent, the refusals to sign should never be known from him. Alluding to the remarks of Doc: Franklin, he could not he said but view them as levelled at himself and the other gentlemen who meant not to sign;

Gen! PINKNEY. We are not likely to gain many converts by the ambiguity of the proposed form of signing. He thought it best to be candid and let the form speak the substance. If the meaning of the signers be left in doubt, his purpose would not be answered. He should sign the Constitution with a view to support it with all his influence, and wished to pledge himself accordingly.

Doc: FRANKLIN. It is too soon to pledge ourselves before Congress and our Constituents shall have approved the plan.

M: INGERSOL did not consider the signing, either as a mere attestation of the fact, or as pledging the signers to support the Constitution at all events; but as a recommendation, of what, all things considered, was the most eligible.

On the motion of Doc: Franklin

N. H. ay. Mas. ay. C: ay. N. J. ay. P.ª ay. Del. ay. M.ᵈ ay. V.ª ay. N. C. ay. S. C. div.ᵈ* Geo. ay.[15]

M: KING suggested that the Journals of the Convention should be either destroyed, or deposited in the custody of the President. He thought if suffered to be made public, a bad use would be

---

\* Gen! Pinkney & M.ʳ Butler disliked the equivocal form of the [14] signing, and on that account voted in the negative.

[14] The word "the" is omitted in the transcript.

[15] In the transcript the vote reads: "New Hampshire, Massachusetts, Connecticut, New Jersey, Pennsylvania, Delaware, Maryland, Virginia, North Carolina, Georgia, aye—10; South Carolina,* divided."

\* To be transferred hither.[16]

[16] Madison's direction concerning his note is omitted in the transcript.

papers, subject to the order of the Ex: [Executive] of [the] U. S. [United] subject to any [future] orders in [Convention]
The members then proceeded to sign the instrument.

Whilst the last members were signing ^it^ Doctr. Franklin looking towards the Presidents Chair, at the back of which a rising sun happened to be painted, observed to a few members near him, that Painters had found it difficult to distinguish in their art a rising from a setting sun. I have said he, often and often in the course of the Session, and the vicissitudes of my hopes and fears as to its ^issue,^ looked at that behind the President without being able to tell whether it was rising or setting: But now at length I have the happiness to know that it is a rising and not a setting Sun. —

^Whilst^ ^the last members were signing it^ ^the Constitution being signed by^ all the members except Mr. Randolph, Mr. Mason, and Mr. Gerry who declined giving it the sanction of their names, the Convention ^dissolved^ itself by an Adjournment sine die. —

^The few alterations and corrections made in these debates which are not in my handwriting, were dictated by me and made in my presence by John C Payne^

made of them by those who would wish to prevent the adoption of the Constitution.

Mr WILSON prefered the second expedient, he had at one time liked the first best; but as false suggestions may be propagated it should not be made impossible to contradict them.

A question was then put on depositing the Journals and other papers of the Convention in the hands of the President, on which,

N. H. ay. Mts ay. Ct ay. N. J. ay. Pena ay. Del. ay. Md* no. Va ay. N. C. ay. S. C. ay. Geo. ay.[18]

The President having asked what the Convention meant should be done with the Journals &c, whether copies were to be allowed to the members if applied for. It was Resolved nem: con "that he retain the Journal and other papers, subject to the order of the [19] Congress, if ever formed under the Constitution.

The members then proceeded to sign the instrument.[20]

[21] Whilst the last members were signing it [22] Doctr FRANKLIN looking towards the Presidents Chair, at the back of which a rising sun happened to be painted, observed to a few members near him, that Painters had found it difficult to distinguish in their art a rising from a setting sun. I have said he, often and often in the course of the Session, and the vicisitudes of my hopes and fears as to its issue, looked at that behind the President without being able to tell whether it was rising or setting: But now at length I have the happiness to know that it is a rising and not a setting Sun.

[21] The Constitution being signed by all the members except Mr Randolph, Mr Mason, and Mr Gerry who declined giving it the sanction of their names, the Convention dissolved itself by an Adjournment sine die—

[23] The few alterations and corrections made in these debates which are not in my hand writing, were dictated by me and made in my presence by John C. Payne.      JAMES MADISON.

* This negative of Maryland was occasioned by the language of the instructions to the Deputies of that State, which required them to report to the State, the *proceedings* of the Convention.

[17] Madison's direction concerning his note is omitted in the transcript.

[18] In the transcript the vote reads; "New Hampshire, Massachusetts, Connecticut, New Jersey, Pennsylvania, Delaware, Virginia, North Carolina, South Carolina, Georgia, aye—10; Maryland,* no—1."

* Transfer.[17]

[19] The word "the" is omitted in the transcript.

[20] In place of the word "instrument," the transcript inserts the following words: "Constitution, as finally amended, as follows." The Constitution is then inserted.

[21] These two final paragraphs of Madison's notes are transposed in the transcript to follow the signatures to the Constitution.

[22] The word "it" is omitted in the transcript.

[23] This statement and Madison's signature are omitted in the transcript.

NOTES OF THE SECRET DEBATES OF THE FEDERAL CONVENTION OF 1787, TAKEN BY THE LATE HON ROBERT YATES, CHIEF JUSTICE OF THE STATE OF NEW YORK, AND ONE OF THE DELEGATES FROM THAT STATE TO THE SAID CONVENTION.[1]

FRIDAY, MAY 25, 1787.

Attended the convention of the States at the state house in Philadelphia, when the following States were represented:

| | |
|---|---|
| NEW YORK, | Alexander Hamilton, |
| | Robert Yates. |
| NEW JERSEY, | David Brearly, |
| | William Churchill Houston, |
| | William Patterson. |
| PENNSYLVANIA, | Robert Morris, |
| | Thomas Fitzsimons, |
| | James Wilson, |
| | Gouverneur Morris. |
| DELAWARE, | George Read, |
| | Richard Bassett, |
| | Jacob Broom. |
| VIRGINIA, | George Washington, |
| | Edmund Randolph, |
| | George Wythe, |
| | George Mason, |
| | James Madison, |
| | John Blair, |
| | James M'Clurg. |
| NORTH CAROLINA, | Alexander Martin, |
| | William Richardson Davie, |
| | Richard Dobbs Spaight, |
| | Hugh Williamson. |
| SOUTH CAROLINA, | John Rutledge, |
| | Charles Cotesworth Pinkney, |
| | Charles Pinckney, |
| | Pierce Butler. |

A motion by R. Morris, and seconded, that General Washington take the chair—unanimously agreed to.

[1] Printed for G. Templeman (Washington, 1836).

When seated, he (General Washington) declared, that as he never had been in such a situation, he felt himself embarrassed; that he hoped his errors, as they would be unintentional, would be excused.

Mr. Hamilton, in behalf of the State of New York, moved that Major Jackson be appointed secretary; the delegates for Pennsylvania, moved for Temple Franklin: by a majority Mr. Jackson carried it—called in and took his seat,

After which, the respective credentials of the seven States were read. N. B. That of Delaware restrained its delegates from assenting to an abolition of the fifth article of the confederation, by which it is declared that each State shall have one vote.

Door keeper and messengers being appointed, the house adjourned to Monday, the 28th day of May, at ten o'clock.

MONDAY, MAY 28, 1787.

Met pursuant to adjournment.

A committee of three members, (whose appointment I omitted in the entry of the proceedings of Friday last,) reported a set of rules for the order of the convention; which being considered by articles, were agreed to, and additional ones proposed and referred to the same committee. The representation was this day increased to nine States—Massachusetts and Connecticut becoming represented. Adjourned to next day.

TUESDAY, MAY 29TH, 1787.

The additional rules agreed to.

His excellency Governor Randolph, a member from Virginia, got up, and in a long and elaborate speech, showed the defects in the system of the present federal government as totally inadequate to the peace, safety, and security of the confederation, and the absolute necessity of a more energetic government.

He closed these remarks with a set of resolutions, fifteen in number, which he proposed to the convention for their adoption, and as leading principles whereon to form a new government. He candidly confessed that they were not intended for a federal government—he meant a strong *consolidated* union, in which the idea of states should be nearly annihilated. [I have taken a copy of these resolutions, which are hereunto annexed.]

He then moved that they should be taken up in committee of the whole house.

Mr. C. Pinkney, a member from South Carolina, then added, that he had reduced his ideas of a new government to a system, which he read, and confessed it was grounded on the same principle as of the above resolutions.

The house then resolved, that they would the next day form themselves into a committee of the whole, to take into consideration *the state of the union.*

Adjourned to next day.

---

### WEDNESDAY, MAY 30TH, 1787.

Convention met pursuant to adjournment.

The convention, pursuant to order, resolved itself into a committee of the whole—Mr. Gorham (a member from Massachusetts) appointed chairman.

Mr. Randolph then moved his first resolve, to wit: "Resolved, that the articles of the confederation ought to be so corrected and enlarged as to accomplish the objects proposed by their institution, namely, common defence, security of liberty, and general welfare."

Mr. G. Morris observed, that it was an unnecessary resolution, as the subsequent resolutions would not agree with it. It was then withdrawn by the proposer, and in lieu thereof the following were proposed, to wit:

1. *Resolved,* That a union of the States merely federal, will not accomplish the objects proposed by the articles of the confederation, namely, common defence, security of liberty, and general welfare.

2. *Resolved,* That no treaty or treaties among any of the States as sovereign, will accomplish or secure their common defence, liberty, or welfare.

3. *Resolved*, That a national government ought to be established, consisting of a supreme judicial, legislative, and executive.

In considering the question on the first resolve, various modifications were proposed, when Mr. Pinkney observed, at last, that if the convention agreed to it, it appeared to him that their business was at an end; for as the powers of the house in general were to revise the present confederation, and to alter or amend it as the case might require; to determine its insufficiency or incapability of amendment or improvement, must end in the dissolution of the powers.

This remark had its weight, and in consequence of it, the 1st and 2d resolve was dropt, and the question agitated on the third.

This last resolve had also its difficulties; the term *supreme* required explanation. It was asked whether it was intended to annihilate State governments? It was answered, only so far as the powers intended to be granted to the new government should clash with the States, when the latter was to yield.

*For the resolution*—Massachusetts, Pennsylvania, Delaware, Virginia, North Carolina, South Carolina.

*Against it*—Connecticut, New York divided, Jersey, and the other States unrepresented.

The next question was on the following resolve:

In substance that the mode of the present representation was unjust—the suffrage ought to be in proportion to number or property.

To this Delaware objected, in consequence of the restrictions in their credentials, and moved to have the consideration thereof postponed, to which the house agreed.

Adjourned to to-morrow.

---

THURSDAY, MAY 31ST, 1787.

Met pursuant to adjournment.

This day the State of Jersey was represented, so that there were now ten States in convention.

The house went again into committee of the whole, Mr. Gorham in the chair.

The 3d resolve, to wit, "That the national legislature ought to consist of two branches," was taken into consideration, and without any debate agreed to. [N. B. As a previous resolution had already been agreed to, to have a supreme legislature, I could not see any objection to its being in two branches.]

The 4th resolve, "That the members of the first branch of the national legislature ought to be elected by the people of the several States," was opposed; and strange to tell, by Massachusetts and Connecticut, who supposed they ought to be chosen by the legislatures; and Virginia supported the resolve, alleging that this ought to be the democratic branch of government, and as such, immediately vested in the people.

This question was carried, but the remaining part of the resolve detailing the powers, was postponed.

The 5th resolve, That the members of the second branch of the national legislature ought to be elected by those of the first out of a proper number of persons nominated by the individual legislatures, and the detail of the mode of election and duration of office, was postponed.

The 6th resolve is taken in detail: "That each branch ought to possess the right of originating acts." Agreed to.

"That the national legislature ought to be empowered to enjoy the legislative rights vested in congress by the confederation."—Agreed to.

"And, moreover, to legislate in all cases to which the separate States are incompetent."—Agreed to.

## Friday, June 1st, 1787.

Met pursuant to adjournment.

The 7th resolve, that a national executive be instituted. Agreed to.

To continue in office for seven years. Agreed to.

A general authority to execute the laws. Agreed to.

To appoint all officers not otherwise provided for. Agreed to.

Adjourned to the next day.

## Saturday, June 2D, 1787.

Met pursuant to adjournment. Present 11 States.

Mr. Pinkney called for the order of the day.

The convention went into committee of the whole.

Mr. Wilson moved that the States should be divided into districts, consisting of one or more States, and each district to elect a number of senators to form the second branch of the national legislature—The senators to be elected, and a certain proportion to be annually dismissed—avowedly on the plan of the New York senate. Question put—rejected.

In the 7th resolve, the words *to be chosen by the national legislature*, were agreed to.

President Franklin moved, that the consideration of that part of the 7th resolve, which had in object the making provision for a compensation for the service of the executive, be postponed for the purpose of considering a motion, *that the executive should receive no salary, stipend, or emolument for the devotion of his time to the public services, but that his expenses should be paid.*

Postponed.

Mr. Dickinson moved that in the seventh resolution, the words, *and removable on impeachment and conviction for mal conduct or neglect in the execution of his office*, should be inserted after the words *ineligible a second time*. Agreed to. The remainder postponed.

Mr. Butler moved to fill the number of which the executive should consist.

Mr. RANDOLPH.—The sentiments of the people ought to be consulted—they will not hear of the semblance of monarchy—He preferred three divisions of the States, and an executive to be taken from each. If a single executive, those remote from him would be neglected—local views would be attributed to him, frequently well founded, often without reason. This would excite disaffection. He was therefore for an executive of three.

Mr. BUTLER.—Delays, divisions, and dissensions arise from an executive consisting of many. Instanced Holland's distracted state, occasioned by her many counsellor's. Further consideration postponed.

Mr. C. Pinkney gave notice for the re-consideration of the mode of election of the first branch.

Adjourned till Monday next.

---

## Monday, June 4th, 1787.

Met pursuant to adjournment.

Mr. Pinkney moved that the blank in the 7th resolve *consisting of* be filled up with an individual.

Mr. Wilson, in support of the motion, asserted, that it would not be obnoxious to the minds of the people, as they in their State governments were accustomed and reconciled to a single executive. Three executives might divide, so that two could not agree in one proposition—the consequence would be anarchy and confusion.

Mr. Sherman thought there ought to be one executive, but that he ought to have a council. Even the king of Great Britain has his privy council.

Mr. Gerry was for one executive—if otherwise, it would be absurd to have it consist of three. Numbers equally in rank would oddly apply to a general or admiral.

Question put—7 States for, and 3 against  New York against it.

The 8th resolve, That the executive and a number of the judicial officers ought to compose a council of revision.

Mr. Gerry objects to the clause—moves its postponement in order to let in a motion—*that the right of revision should be in the executive only.*

Mr. Wilson contends that the executive and judicial ought to have a joint and full negative—they cannot otherwise preserve their importance against the legislature.

Mr. King was against the interference of the judicial—they may be biased in the interpretation—He is therefore to give the executive a complete *negative.*

Carried to be postponed, 6 States against 4—New York for it.

The next question, that the executive have a complete negative; and it was therefore moved to expunge the remaining part of the clause.

Dr. Franklin against the motion—The power dangerous, and would be abused so as to get money for passing bills.

Mr. Madison against it—because of the difficulty of an executive venturing on the exercise of this negative, and is therefore of opinion that the revisional authority is better.

Mr. Bedford is against the whole, either negative or revisional—the two branches are sufficient checks on each other—no danger of subverting the executive, because his powers may by the convention be so well defined that the legislature cannot overleap the bounds.

Mr. Mason against the negative power in the executive, because it will not accord with the genius of the people.

On this the question was put and carried, *nem. con.* against expunging part of the clause so as to establish a complete negative.

Mr. Butler then moved that all acts passed by the legislature be suspended for the space of        days by the executive.

Unanimously in the negative.

It was resolved and agreed, that the blank be filled up with the words *two thirds of the legislature.* Agreed to.

The question was then put on the whole of the resolve as amended and filled up. Carried, 8 states for—2 against. New York for it.

Mr. Wilson then moved for the addition *of a convenient number of the national judicial* to the executive as a council of revision. Ordered to be taken into consideration to-morrow.

Adjourned until to-morrow.

TUESDAY, JUNE 5TH, 1787.

Met pursuant to adjournment.

The 9th resolve, *That a national judicial be established, to consist of one supreme tribunal, and of inferior tribunals, to hold their offices during good behavior, and no augmentation or diminution in the stipends during the time of holding their offices.* Agreed to.

Mr. Wilson moved *that the judicial be appointed by the executive,* instead of *the national legislature.*

Mr. Madison opposed the motion, and inclined to think that the executive ought by no means to make the appointments, but rather that branch of the legislature called the senatorial; and moves that the words, *of the appointment of the legislature,* be expunged.

Carried by 8 states—against it 2.

The remaining part of the resolve postponed.

The 10th resolve read and agreed to

The 11th resolve agreed to be postponed.

The 12th resolve agreed to without debate.

The 13th and 14th resolves postponed.

The 15th or last resolve, *That the amendment which shall be offered to the confederation, ought at a proper time or times, after the approbation of Congress, to be submitted to an assembly or assemblies of representatives, recommended by the several legislatures, to be expressly chosen by the people, to consider and decide thereon,* was taken into consideration.

Mr. Madison endeavored to enforce the necessity of this resolve—because the new national constitution ought to have the highest source of authority, at least paramount to the powers of the respective constitutions of the States—points out the mischiefs that have arisen in the old confederation, which depends upon no higher authority than the confirmation of an ordinary act of a legislature—instances the law operation of treaties, when contravened by any antecedent acts of a particular State.

Mr. King supposes, that as the people have tacitly agreed to a federal government, that therefore the legislature in every State have a right to confirm any alterations or amendments in it—a convention in each State to approve of a new government he supposes however the most eligible.

Mr. Wilson is of opinion that the people by a conventions are the only power that can ratify the proposed system of the new government.

It is possible that not all the States, nay, that not even a majority, will immediately come into the measure; but such as do ratify it will be immediately bound by it, and others as they may from time to time accede to it.

Question put for postponement of this resolve. 7 States for postponement—3 against it.

Question on the 9th resolve to strike out the words, *and of inferior tribunals*.

Carried by 5 States against 4—2 States divided, of which last number New York was one.

Mr. Wilson then moved, *that the national legislature shall have the authority to appoint inferior tribunals*, be added to the resolve.

Carried by 7 States against 3. New York divided. [N. B Mr. Lansing from New York was prevented by sickness from attending this day.]

Adjourned to to-morrow morning.

---

WEDNESDAY, JUNE 6TH, 1787.

Met pursuant to adjournment.

Mr. Pinkney moved (pursuant to a standing order for re-consideration) that in the 4th resolve, the words *by the people*, be expunged, and the words *by the legislature*, be inserted.

Mr. GERRY.—If the national legislature are appointed by the state legislatures, demagogues and corrupt members will creep in.

Mr. Wilson is of opinion that the national legislative powers ought to flow immediately from the people, so as to contain all their understanding, and to be an exact transcript of their minds. He observed that the people had already *parted* with as much of their power as was necessary, to form on its basis a perfect government; and the particular states must part with such a portion of it as to make the present national government, adequate to their peace and the security of their liberties. He admitted that the State governments would probably be rivals and opposers of the national government.

Mr. Mason observed that the national legislature, as to one branch, ought to be elected by the people; because the objects of their legislation will not be on States, but on individual persons.

Mr. Dickinson is for combining the State and national legislatures in the same views and measures, and that this object can only be effected by the national legislature flowing from the State legislatures.

Mr. Read is of opinion, that the State governments must sooner or later be at an end, and that therefore we must make the present national government as perfect as possible.

Mr. Madison is of opinion, that when we agreed to the first resolve of having a national government, consisting of a supreme executive, judicial, and legislative power, it was then intended to operate to the exclusion of a federal government, and the more extensive we made the basis, the greater probability of duration, happiness, and good order.

The question for the amendment was negatived, by 8 States against 3. New York in the majority.

On the 8th resolve, Mr. Wilson moved (in consequence of a vote to re-concider the question on the revisional powers vested in the executive) that there be added these words, *with a convenient number of the national judicial.*

Upon debate, carried in the negative—3 states for and 8 against it. New York for the addition.

---

THURSDAY, JUNE 7TH, 1787.

Met pursuant to adjournment.

Mr. Rutledge moved to take into consideration the mode of electing the second branch of the national legislature.

Mr. Dickinson thereupon moved, *that the second branch of the national legislature be chosen by the legislatures of the individual states.* He observed, that this mode will more intimately connect the State governments with the national legislature—it will also draw forth the first characters either as to family or talent, and that it ought to consist of a considerable number.

Mr. Wilson against the motion, because the two branches thus constituted, cannot agree, they having different views and different sentiments.

Mr. Dickinson is of opinion that the mode by him proposed, like the British house of lords and commons, whose powers flow from different sources, are mutual checks on each other, and will thus promote the real happiness and security of the country—a government thus established would harmonize the whole, and like the planetary system, the national council like the sun, would illumine the whole—the planets revolving round it in perfect order; or like the union of several small streams, would at last form a respectable river, gently flowing to the sea.

Mr. WILSON. The State governments ought to be preserved—the freedom of the people and their internal good police depends on their existence in full vigor—but such a government can only answer local purposes—That it is not possible a general government, as despotic as even that of the Roman emperors, could be adequate to the government of the whole without this distinction. He hoped that the national government would be independent of State governments, in order to make it vigorous, and therefore moved that the above resolution be postponed, and that the convention in its room adopt the following resolve: *That the second branch of the national legislature be chosen by districts, to be formed for that purpose.*

Mr. Sherman supposes the election of the national legislature will be better vested in the State legislatures, than by the people, for by pursuing different objects, persons may be returned who have not one tenth of the votes.

Mr. Gerry observed, that the great mercantile interest and of stockholders, is not provided for in any mode of election—they will however be better represented if the State legislatures choose the second branch.

Question carried against the postponement—10 states against 1.

Mr. Mason then spoke to the general question—observing on the propriety, that the second branch of the national legislature should flow from the legislature of each State, to prevent the encroachments on each other and to harmonize the whole.

The question put on the first motion, and carried unanimously. Adjourned to to-morrow morning.

## Friday, June 8, 1787.

Met pursuant to adjournment—11 states.

Mr. Pinkney moved, *That the national legislature shall have the power of negativing all laws to be passed by the State legislatures which they may judge improper*, in the room of the clause as it stood reported.

He grounds his motion on the necessity of one supreme controlling power, and he considers this as the *corner-stone* of the present system; and hence the necessity of retrenching the State authorities in order to preserve the good government of the national council.

Mr. Williamson against the motion. The national legislature ought to possess the power of negativing such laws only as will encroach on the national government.

Mr. Madison wished that the line of jurisprudence could be drawn—he would be for it—but upon reflection he finds it impossible, and therefore lie is for the amendment. If the clause remains without the amendment it is inefficient—The judges of the State must give the State laws their operation, although the law abridges the rights of the national government—how is it to be repealed? By the power who made it? How shall you compel them? By force? To prevent this disagreeable expedient, the power of negativing is absolutely necessary—this is the only attractive principle which will retain its centrifugal force, and without this the planets will fly from their orbits.

Mr. Gerry supposes that this power ought to extend to all laws already made; but the preferable mode would be to designate the powers of the national legislature, to which the negative ought to apply—he has no objection to restrain the laws which may be made for issuing paper money. Upon the whole he does not choose on this important trust, *to take a leap in the dark*.

Mr. Pinkney supposes that the proposed amendment had no retrospect to the State laws already made. The adoption of the new government must operate as a complete repeal of all the constitutions and State laws, as far as they are inconsistent with the new government.

Mr. Wilson supposes the surrender of the rights of a federal government to be a surrender of sovereignty. True, we may define some of the rights, but when we come near the line it cannot be found. One general excepting clause must therefore apply to the whole. In the beginning of our troubles, congress themselves were as one State—dissentions or State interests were not known—they gradually crept in after the formation of the constitution, and each took to himself a slice. The original draft of confederation was drawn on the first ideas, and the draft concluded on how different!

Mr. Bedford was against the motion, and states the proportion of the intended representation of the number 90: Delaware 1—Pennsylvania and Virginia one third. On this computation where is the weight of the small States when the interest of the one is in competition with the other on trade, manufactures, and agriculture? When he sees this mode of government so strongly advocated by the members of the great States, he must suppose it a question of *interest*.

Mr. Madison confesses it is not without its difficulties on many accounts—some may be removed, others modified, and some are unavoidable. May not this power be vested in the senatorial branch? they will probably be always sitting. Take the question on the other ground, who is to determine the line when drawn in doubtful cases? The State legislatures cannot, for they will be partial in support of their own powers—no tribunal can be found. It is impossible that the articles of confederation can be amended—they are too tottering to be invigorated—nothing but the present system, or something like it, can restore the peace and harmony of the country.

The question put on Mr. Pinkney's motion—7 States against it—Delaware divided—Virginia, Pennsylvania and Massachusetts for it.

Adjourned to to-morrow morning.

## Saturday, June 9th, 1787.

Met pursuant to adjournment.

Motion by Mr. Gerry to reconsider the appointment of the national executive.

*That the national executive be appointed by the State executives.*

He supposed that in the national legislature there will be a great number of bad men of various descriptions—these will make a wrong appointment. Besides, an executive thus appointed, will have his partiality in favor of those who appointed him—that this will not be the case by the effect of his motion, and the executive will by this means be independent of the national legislature, but the appointment by the State executives ought to be made by votes in proportion to their weight in the scale of the representation.

Mr. Randolph opposes the motion. The power vested by it is dangerous—confidence will be wanting—the large States will be masters of the election—an executive ought to have great experience, integrity, and activity. The executives of the States cannot know the persons properly qualified as possessing these. An executive thus appointed will court the officers of his appointment, and will relax him in the duties of commander of the militia—Your single executive is already invested with negativing laws of the State. Will he duly exercise the power? Is there no danger in the combinations of States to appoint such an executive as may be too favorable to local State governments? Add to this the expense and difficulty of bringing the executives to one place to exercise their powers. Can you suppose they will ever cordially raise the great oak, when they must sit as shrubs under its shade?

Carried against the motion, 10 noes, and Delaware divided.

On motion of Mr. Patterson, the consideration of the 2d resolve was taken up, which is as follows: *Resolved, therefore, that the rights of suffrage in the national legislature ought to be apportioned to the quotas of contribution, or to the number of inhabitants, as the one or other rule may seem best in different cases.*

JOHN JAY

Judge BREARLY.—The present question is an important one. On the principle that each State in the Union was sovereign, congress, in the articles of confederation, determined that each State in the public councils had one vote. If the States still remain sovereign, the form of the present resolve is founded on principles of injustice. He then stated the comparative weight of each State—the number of votes 90. Georgia would be 1, Virginia 16, and so of the rest. This vote must defeat itself, or end in despotism. If we must have a national government, what is the remedy? Lay the map of the confederation on the table, and extinguish the present boundary lines of the respective State jurisdictions, and make a new division so that each State is equal—then a government on the present system will be just.

Mr. Patterson opposed the resolve. Let us consider with what powers are we sent here? (moved to have the credentials of Massachusetts read, which was done.) By this and the other credentials we see, that the basis of our present authority is founded on a revision of the articles of the present confederation, and to alter or amend them in such parts where they may appear defective. Can we on this ground form a national government? I fancy not.—Our commissions give a complexion to the business; and can we suppose that when we exceed the bounds of our duty, the people will approve our proceedings?

We are met here as the deputies of 13 independent, sovereign States, for federal purposes. Can we consolidate their sovereignty and form one nation, and annihilate the sovereignties of our States who have sent us here for other purposes?

What, pray, is intended by a proportional representation? Is property to be considered as part of it? Is a man, for example, possessing a property of £4000 to have 40 votes to one possessing only £100? This has been asserted on a former occasion. If State distinctions are still to be held up, shall I submit the welfare of the State of New Jersey, with 5 votes in the national council, opposed to Virginia who has 16 votes? Suppose, as it was in agitation before the war, that America had been represented in the British parliament, and had sent 200 members; what would this number avail against 600? We would have been as much enslaved in that case as when unrepresented; and what is worse, without the prospect of redress. But it is said that this national government is to act on individuals and not on States; and cannot a federal government be so framed as to operate in the same way? It surely may. I therefore declare, that I will never consent to the present system, and I shall make all the interest against it in the State which I represent that I can. Myself or my State will never submit to tyranny or despotism.

Upon the whole, every sovereign State, according to a confederation, must have an equal vote, or there is an end to liberty. As long, therefore, as State distinctions are held up, this rule must invariably apply; and if a consolidated national government must take place, then State distinctions must cease, or the States must be equalized.

Mr. Wilson was in favor of the resolve. He observed that a majority, nay, even a minority of the States, have a right to confederate with each other, and the rest may do as they please. He considered numbers as the best criterion to determine representation. Every citizen of one State possesses the same rights with the citizen of another. Let us see how this rule will apply to the present question. Pennsylvania, from its numbers, has a right to 12 votes, when on the same principle New Jersey is entitled to 5 votes. Shall New Jersey have the same right or influence in the councils of the nation with Pennsylvania? I say no. It is unjust—I never will confederate on this plan. The gentleman from New Jersey is candid in declaring his opinion—I commend him for it—I am equally so. I say again, I never will confederate on his principles. If no State will part with any of its sovereignty, it is in vain to talk of a national government. The State who has five times the number of inhabitants ought, nay must have the same proportion of weight in the representation. If there was a probability of equalizing the States, he would be for it. But we have no such power. If, however, we depart from the principles of representation in proportion to numbers, we will lose the object of our meeting.

The question postponed for farther consideration.

Adjourned to to-morrow morning.

MONDAY, JUNE 11TH, 1787.

Met pursuant to adjournment. Present 11 States.

Mr. Sherman moved *that the first branch of the national legislature be chosen in proportion to the number of the whole inhabitants in each State.* He observed that as the people ought to have the election of one of the branches of the legislature, the legislature of each State ought to have the election of the second branch, in order to preserve the State sovereignty; and that each State ought in this branch to have one vote.

Governor Rutledge moved, as an amendment of the first proposition, *that the proportion of representation ought to be according to, and in proportion to the contribution of each State.*

Mr. Butler supported the motion, by observing that money is strength, and every State ought to have its weight in the national council in proportion to the quantity it possesses. He further observed, that when a boy he read this as one of the remarks of Julius Cæsar, who declared if he had but money he would find soldiers, and every thing necessary to carry on a war.

Mr. King observed, that it would be better first to establish a principle (that is to say) whether we will depart from federal grounds in forming a national government; and therefore, to bring this point to view, he moved, as a previous question, that the sense of the committee be taken on the following question:

*That the right of suffrage in the first branch of the national legislature, ought not to be according to the rule in the articles of confederation, but according to some equitable ratio of representation.*

Gov. Franklin's written remarks on this point were read by Mr. Wilson. In these Gov. Franklin observes, that representation ought to be in proportion to the importance of numbers or wealth in each State—that there can be no danger of undue influence of the greater against the lesser States. This was the apprehension of Scotland when the union with England was proposed, when in parliament they were allowed only 16 peers and 45 commons; yet experience has proved that their liberties and influence were in no danger.

The question on Mr. King's motion was carried in the affirmative—7 ayes—3 noes, and Maryland divided. New York, New Jersey, and Delaware in the negative.

Mr. Dickinson moved as an amendment, to add the words, *according to the taxes and contributions of each State actually collected and paid into the national treasury.*

Mr. Butler was of opinion that the national government will only have the right of making and collecting the taxes, but that the States individually must lay their own taxes.

Mr. Wilson was of opinion, and therefore moved, *that the mode of representation of each of the States ought to be from the number of its free inhabitants, and of every other description three fifths to one free inhabitant.* He supposed that the impost will not be the only revenue—the post office he supposes would be another substantial source of revenue. He observed further, that this mode had already received the approbation of eleven States in their acquiescence to the quota made by congress. He admitted that this resolve would require further restrictions, for where numbers determined the representation a census at different periods of 5, 7 or 10 years, ought to be taken.

Mr. GERRY. The idea of property ought not to be the rule of representation. Blacks are property, and are used to the southward as horses and cattle to the northward: and why should their representation be increased to the southward on account of the number of slaves, than horses or oxen to the north?

Mr. Madison was of opinion at present, to fix the standard of representation, and let the detail be the business of a sub-committee.

Mr. Rutledge's motion was postponed.

Mr. Wilson's motion was then put, and carried by 9 States against 2. New York in the majority.

Mr. Wilson then moved, as an amendment to Mr. Sherman's motion, *That the same proportion be observed in the election of the second branch as the first.*

The question however was first put on Mr. Sherman's motion, and lost—6 States against, and 5 for it.

Then Mr. Wilson's motion was put and carried—6 ayes, 5 noes.

The eleventh resolve was then taken into consideration. Mr. Madison moved to add after the word *junctions*, the words, *or separation*.

Mr. Read against the resolve *in toto*. We must put away State governments, and we will then remove all cause of jealousy. The guarantee will confirm the assumed rights of several States to lands which do belong to the confederation.

Mr. Madison moved an amendment, to add to or alter the resolution as follows: *The republican constitutions and the existing laws of each State, to be guaranteed by the United States.*

Mr. Randolph was for the present amendment, because a republican government must be the basis of our national union; and no State in it ought to have it in their power to change its government into a monarchy.—Agreed to.

13th Resolve—the first part agreed to.

14th Resolve—taken into consideration.

Mr. WILLIAMSON. This resolve will be unnecessary, as the union will become the law of the land.

Governor RANDOLPH. He supposes it to be absolutely necessary. Not a State government, but its officers will infringe on the rights of the national government. If the State judges are not sworn to the observance of the new government, will they not judicially determine in favor of their State laws? We are erecting a supreme national government; ought it not to be supported, and can we give it too many sinews?

Mr. Gerry rather supposes that the national legislators ought to be sworn to preserve the State constitutions, as they will run the greatest risk to be annihilated—and therefore moved it.

For Mr. Gerry's amendment, 7 ayes, 4 noes.

Main question then put on the clause or resolve—6 ayes, 5 noes. New York in the negative.

Adjourned to to-morrow morning.

## Tuesday, June 12th, 1787.

Met pursuant to adjournment. Present 11 States.

The 15th, or last resolve, was taken into consideration. No debate arose on it, and the question was put and carried—5 States for it, 3 against, and 2 divided. New York in the negative.

Having thus gone through with the resolves, it was found necessary to take up such parts of the preceding resolves as had been postponed, or not agreed to. The remaining part of the 4th resolve was taken into consideration.

Mr. Sherman moved that the blank of the duration of the first branch of the national legislature, be filled with *one year*. Mr. Rutledge with *two years*, and Mr. Jenifer with *three years*.

Mr. Madison was for the last amendment—observing that it will give it stability, and induce gentlemen of the first weight to engage in it.

Mr. Gerry is afraid the people will be alarmed, as savoring of despotism.

Mr. MADISON. The people's opinions cannot be known, as to the particular modifications which may be necessary in the new government—In general, they believe there is something wrong in the present system that requires amendment; and he could wish to make the republican system the basis of the change—because if our amendments should fail of securing their happiness, they will despair it can be done in this way, and incline to monarchy.

Mr. Gerry could not be governed by the prejudices of the people—Their good sense will ever have its weight. Perhaps a limited monarchy would be the best government, if we could organize it by creating a house of peers; but that cannot be done.

The question was put on the three years' amendment, and carried—7 ayes—4 noes. New York in the affirmative.

On motion to expunge the clause of the qualification as to age, it was carried, 10 States against one.

On the question for fixed stipends, without augmentation or diminution, to this branch of the legislature, it was moved that the words, *to be paid by the national treasury*, be added—Carried, 8 States for—3 against. New York in the negative.

The question was then put on the clause as amended, and carried, 8 ayes—3 noes. New York in the negative.

On the clause respecting the ineligibility to any other office, it was moved that the words, *by any particular State*, be expunged. 4 States for—5 against, and 2 divided. New York affirmative.

The question was then put on the whole clause, and carried, 10 ayes—1 no.

The last blank was filled up with *one year*, and carried—8 ayes—2 noes, 1 divided.

Mr. Pinkney moved to expunge the clause. Agreed to, *nem. con.*

The question to fill up the blank with 30 *years*. Agreed to—7 States for—4 against.

It was moved to fill the blank, as to the duration, with *seven years*.

Mr. Pierce moved to have it for three years—instanced the danger of too long a continuance, from the evils arising in the British parliaments from their septenual duration, and the clamors against it in that country by its real friends.

Mr. Sherman was against the 7 years, because if they are bad men it is too long, and if good they may be again elected.

Mr. Madison was for 7 years—Considers this branch as a check on the democracy—it cannot therefore be made too strong.

For the motion, 8 ayes—1 no—2 States divided. New York one of the last.

Mr. Butler moved to expunge the clause of the stipends. Lost—7 against—3 for—1 divided.

Agreed that the second branch of the national legislature be paid in the same way as the first branch.

Upon the subject of ineligibility, it was agreed that the same rule should apply as to the first branch.

6th resolve agreed to be postponed, *sine die*.

9th resolve taken into consideration, but postponed to to-morrow. Then adjourned to to-morrow morning.

## WEDNESDAY, JUNE 13TH, 1787.

Met pursuant to adjournment. Present 11 States.

Gov. Randolph observed the difficulty in establishing the powers of the judiciary—the object however at present is to establish this principle, to wit, the security of foreigners where treaties are in their favor, and to preserve the harmony of States and that of the citizens thereof. This being once established, it will be the business of a sub-committee to detail it; and therefore moved to obliterate such parts of the resolve so as only to establish the principle, to wit, *that the jurisdiction of the national judiciary shall extend to all cases of national revenue, impeachment of national officers, and questions which involve the national peace or harmony.* Agreed to unanimously.

It was further agreed, that the judiciary be paid out of the national treasury.

Mr. Pinkney moved that the judiciary be appointed by the national legislature.

Mr. Madison is of opinion that the second branch of the legislature ought to appoint the judiciary, which the convention agreed to.

Mr. Gerry moved that the first branch shall have the only right of originating bills to supply the treasury.

Mr. Butler against the motion. We are constantly running away with the idea of the excellence of the British parliament, and with or without reason copying from them; when in fact there is no similitude in our situations. With us both houses are appointed by the people, and both ought to be equally trusted.

Mr. GERRY. If we dislike the British government for the oppressive measures by them carried on against us, yet he hoped we would not be so far prejudiced as to make ours in every thing opposite to theirs.

Mr. Madison's question carried.

The committee having now gone through the whole of the propositions from Virginia—Resolved, That the committee do report to the convention their proceedings—This was accordingly done. [*See a copy of it hereunto annexed.*]

The house resolved on the report being read, that the consideration thereof be postponed to to-morrow, and that members have leave to take copies thereof.

Adjourned to to-morrow morning.

## Thursday, June 14th, 1787.

Met pursuant to adjournment. Present 11 States.

Mr. Patterson moved that the further consideration of the report be postponed until to-morrow, as he intended to give in principles to form a federal system of government materially different from the system now under consideration. Postponement agreed to.

Adjourned until to-morrow morning.

## Friday, June 15th, 1787.

Met pursuant to adjournment. Present 11 States.

Mr. Patterson, pursuant to his intentions as mentioned yesterday, read a set of resolves as the basis of amendment to the confederation. [*See those resolves annexed.*

He observed that no government could be energetic on paper only, which was no more than straw—that the remark applied to the one as well as to the other system, and is therefore of opinion that there must be a small standing force to give every government weight.

Mr. Madison moved for the report of the committee, and the question may then come on whether the convention will postpone it in order to take into consideration the system now offered.

Mr. Lansing is of opinion that the two systems are fairly contrasted. The one now offered is on the basis of amending the federal government, and the other to be reported as a national government, on propositions which exclude the propriety of amendment. Considering therefore its importance, and that justice may be done to its weighty consideration, he is for postponing it a day.

Col. Hamilton cannot say he is in sentiment with either plan— supposes both might again be considered as federal plans, and by this means they will be fairly in committee, and be contrasted so as to make a comparative estimate of the two.

Thereupon it was agreed, that the report be postponed, and that the house will resolve itself into a committee of the whole, to take into consideration both propositions to-morrow. Then the convention adjourned to to-morrow morning.

---

### SATURDAY, JUNE 16TH, 1787.

Met pursuant to adjournment. Present 11 States.

Mr. Lansing moved to have the first article of the last plan of government read; which being done, he observed, that this system is fairly contrasted with the one ready to be reported—the one federal, and the other national. In the first, the powers are exercised as flowing from the respective State governments—The second, deriving its authority from the people of the respective States—which latter must ultimately destroy or annihilate the State governments. To determine the powers on these grand objects with which we are invested, let us recur to the credentials of the respective States, and see what the views were of those who sent us. The language is there expressive—it is upon the revision of the present confederation, to alter and amend such parts as may appear defective, so as to give additional strength to the union. And he would venture to assert, that had the legislature of the State of New York, apprehended that their powers would have been construed to extend to the formation of a national government, to the extinguishment of their independency, no delegates would have here appeared on the part of that State. This sentiment must have had its weight on a former occasion, even in this house; for when the second resolution of Virginia, which declared, in substance, that a federal government could not be amended for the good of the whole, the remark of an honorable member of South Carolina, that by determining this question in the affirmative their deliberative powers were at an end, induced this house to waive the resolution. It is in vain to adopt a mode of government which we have reason to believe the people gave us no power to recommend—as they will consider themselves on this ground authorized to reject it. See the danger of exceeding your powers by the example which the requisition of congress of 1783 afforded. They required an impost on all imported articles, to which, on federal grounds, they had no right unless voluntarily granted. What was the consequence? Some, who had least to give, granted it; and others, under various restrictions and modifications, so that it could not be systematized. If we form a government, let us do it on principles which are likely to meet the approbation of the States. Great changes can only be gradually introduced. The States will never sacrifice their essential rights to a national government. New plans, annihilating the rights of the States (unless upon evident necessity) can never be approved. I may venture to assert, that the prevalent opinion of America is, that granting additional powers to congress would answer their views; and every power recommended for their approbation exceeding this idea, will be fruitless.

Mr. PATTERSON.—As I had the honor of proposing a new system of government for the union, it will be expected that I should explain its principles.

1st. The plan accords with our own powers.

2d. It accords with the sentiments of the people.

But if the subsisting confederation is so radically defective as not to admit of amendment, let us say so and report its insufficiency, and wait for enlarged powers. We must, in the present case, pursue our powers, if we expect the approbation of the people. I am not here to pursue my own sentiments of government, but of those who have sent me; and I believe that a little practical virtue is to be preferred to the finest theoretical principles, which cannot be carried into effect. Can we, as representatives of independent States, annihilate the essential powers of independency? Are not the votes of this convention taken on every question under the idea of independency? Let us turn to the 5th article of confederation—in this it is mutually agreed, that each State should have one vote—It is a fundamental principle arising from confederated governments. The 13th article provides for amendments; but they must be agreed to by every State—the dissent of one renders every proposal null. The confederation is in the nature of a compact; and can any State, unless by the consent of the whole, either in politics or law, withdraw their powers? Let it be said by Pennsylvania, and the other large States, that they, for the sake of peace, assented to the confederation; can she now resume her original right without the consent of the donee?

And although it is now asserted that the larger States reluctantly agreed to that part of the confederation which secures an equal suffrage to each, yet let it be remembered, that the smaller States were the last who approved the confederation.

On this ground representation must be drawn from the States to maintain their independency, and not from the people composing those States.

The doctrine advanced by a learned gentleman from Pennsylvania, that all power is derived from the people, and that in proportion to their numbers they ought to participate equally in the benefits and rights of government, is right in principle, but unfortunately for him, wrong in the application to the question now in debate.

When independent societies confederate for mutual defence, they do so in their collective capacity; and then each State, for those purposes, must be considered as *one* of the contracting parties. Destroy this balance of equality, and you endanger the rights of the *lesser societies* by the danger of usurpation in the greater.

Let us test the government intended to be made by the Virginia plan on these principles. The representatives in the national legislature are to be in proportion to the number of inhabitants in each State. So far it is right, upon the principles of equality, when State distinctions are done away; but those to certain purposes still exist. Will the government of Pennsylvania admit a participation of their common stock of land to the citizens of New Jersey? I fancy not. It therefore follows, that a national government upon the present plan, is unjust, and destructive of the common principles of reciprocity. Much has been said that this government is to operate on persons, not on States. This, upon examination, will be found equally fallacious; for the fact is, it will, in the quotas of revenue, be proportioned among the States, as States; and in this business Georgia will have one vote, and Virginia sixteen. The truth is, both plans may be considered to compel individuals to a compliance with their requisitions, although the requisition is made on the States.

Much has been said in commendation of two branches in a legislature, and of the advantages resulting from their being checks to each other. This may be true when applied to State governments, but will not equally apply to a national legislature, whose legislative objects are few and simple.

Whatever may be said of congress, or their conduct on particular occasions, the people in general are pleased with such a body, and in general wish an increase of their powers for the good government of the union. Let us now see the plan of the national government on the score of expense. The least the second branch of the legislature can consist of is 90 members— The first branch of at least 270. How are they to be paid in our present improverished situation? Let us, therefore, fairly try whether the confederation cannot be mended, and if it can, we shall do our duty, and I believe the people will be satisfied.

Mr. Wilson first stated the difference between the two plans
Virginia plan proposes two branches in the legislature.
Jersey a single legislative body.
Virginia, the legislative powers derived from the people.
Jersey, from the States.
Virginia, a single executive.
Jersey, more than one.
Virginia, a majority of the legislature can act.
Jersey, a small minority can control.
Virginia, the legislature can legislate on all national concerns.
Jersey, only on limited objects.
Virginia, legislature to negative all State laws.
Jersey, giving power to the executive to compel obedience by force.
Virginia, to remove the executive by impeachment.
Jersey, on application of a majority of the States.
Virginia, for the establishment of inferior judiciary tribunals.
Jersey, no provision.

It is said and insisted on, that the Jersey plan accords with our powers. As for himself, he considers his powers to extend to every thing or nothing; and therefore that he has a right, and is at liberty to agree to either plan or none. The people expect relief from their present embarrassed situation, and look up for it to this national convention; and it follows that they expect a *national government*, and therefore the plan from Virginia has the preference to the other. I would (says he) with a reluctant hand add any powers to congress, because they are not a body chosen by the people, and consist only of one branch, and each State in it has one vote. Inequality in representation poisons every government. The English courts are hitherto pure, just and incorrupt, while their legislature are base and venal. The one arises from unjust representation, the other from their independency of the legislature. Lord Chesterfield remarks that one of the states of the United Netherlands withheld its assent to a proposition until a major of their state was provided for. He needed not to have added (for the conclusion was self evident) that it was one of the lesser states. I mean no reflection, but I leave it to gentlemen to consider whether this has not also been the case in congress? The argument in favor of the Jersey plan goes too far, as it cannot be completed, unless Rhode Island assents. A single legislature is very dangerous.—Despotism may present itself in various shapes. May there not be legislative despotism if in the exercise of their power they are unchecked or unrestrained by another branch? On the contrary an executive to be restrained must be an individual. The first triumvirate of Rome combined, without law, was fatal to its liberties; and the second, by the usurpation of Augustus, ended in despotism.—The two kings of Sparta and the consuls of Rome, by sharing the executive, distracted their governments.

Mr. C. C. Pinkney supposes that if New Jersey was indulged with one vote out of 13, she would have no objection to a national government. He supposes that the convention have already determined, virtually, that the federal government cannot be made efficient. A national government being therefore the object, this plan must be pursued — as our business is not to conclude but to recommend.

Judge Elsworth is of opinion that the first question on the new plan will decide nothing materially on principle, and therefore moved the postponement thereof, in order to bring on the second.

Gov. RANDOLPH.—The question now is which of the two plans is to be preferred. If the vote on the first resolve will determine it, and it is so generally understood, he has no objection that it be put. The resolutions from Virginia must have been adopted on the supposition that a federal government was impracticable— And it is said that power is wanting to institute such a government.—But when our all is at stake, I will consent to any mode that will preserve us. View our present deplorable situation— France, to whom we are indebted in every motive of gratitude and honor, is left unpaid the large sums she has supplied us with in the day of our necessity—Our officers and soldiers, who have successfully fought our battles—and the loaners of money to the public, look up to you for relief.

The bravery of our troops is degraded by the weakness of our government.

It has been contended that the 5th article of the confederation cannot be repealed under the powers to new modify the confederation by the 13th article. This surely is false reasoning, since the whole of the confederation upon revision is subject to amendment and alteration; besides our business consists in recommending a system of government, not to make it. There are great seasons when persons with limited powers are justified in exceeding them, and a person would be contemptible not to risk it. Originally our confederation was founded on the weakness of each State to repel a foreign enemy; and we have found that the powers granted to congress are insufficient. The body of congress is ineffectual to carry the great objects of safety and protection into execution. What would their powers be over the commander of the military, but for the virtue of the commander? As the State assemblies are constantly encroaching on the powers of congress, the Jersey plan would rather encourage such encroachments than be a check to it; and from the nature of the institution, congress would ever be governed by cabal and intrigue—They are besides too numerous for an executive, nor can any additional powers be sufficient to enable them to protect us against foreign invasion. Amongst other things congress was intended to be a body to preserve peace among the States, and in the rebellion of Massachusetts it was found they were not authorized to use the troops of the confederation to quell it. Every one is impressed with the idea of a general regulation of trade and commerce. Can congress do this? when from the nature of their institution they are subject to cabal and intrigue? And would it not be dangerous to entrust such a body with the power, when they are dreaded on these grounds? I am certain that a national government must be established, and this is the only moment when it can be done—And let me conclude by observing, that the best exercise of power is to exert it for the public good.

Then adjourned to Monday morning.

### Monday, June 19th, 1787.

Met pursuant to adjournment. Present 11 States.

Mr. HAMILTON—To deliver my sentiments on so important a subject, when the first characters in the union have gone before me, inspires me with the greatest diffidence, especially when my own ideas are so materially dissimilar to the plans now before the committee—My situation is disagreeable, but it would be criminal not to come forward on a question of such magnitude. I have well considered the subject, and am convinced that no amendment of the confederation can answer the purpose of a good government, so long as State sovereignties do, in any shape, exist; and I have great doubts whether a national government on the Virginia plan can be made effectual. What is federal? An association of several independent States into one. How or in what manner this association is formed, is not so clearly distinguishable. We find the diet of Germany has in some instances the power of legislation on individuals. We find the United States of America have it in an extensive degree in the cases of piracies.

Let us now review the powers with which we are invested. We are appointed for the *sole* and *express* purpose of revising the confederation, and to *alter* or *amend* it, so as to render it effectual for the purpose of a good government. Those who suppose it must be federal, lay great stress on the terms *sole* and *express*, as if these words intended a confinement to a federal government; when the manifest import is no more than that the institution of a good government must be the *sole* and *express* object of your deliberations. Nor can we suppose an annihilation of our powers by forming a national government, as many of the States have made in their constitutions no provision for any alteration; and thus much I can say for the State I have the honor to represent, that when our credentials were under consideration in the senate, some members were for inserting a restriction in the powers, to prevent an encroachment on the constitution: it was answered by others, and thereupon the resolve carried on the credentials, that it might abridge some of the constitutional powers of the State, and that possibly in the formation of a new union it would be found necessary. This appears reasonable, and therefore leaves us at liberty to form such a national government as we think best adapted to the good of the whole. I have therefore no difficulty as to the extent of our powers, nor do I feel myself restrained in the exercise of my judgment under them. We can only propose and recommend—the power of ratifying or rejecting is still in the States. But on this great question I am still greatly embarrassed. I have before observed my apprehension of the inefficacy of either plan, and I have great doubts whether a more energetic government can pervade this wide and extensive country. I shall now show that both plans are materially defective.

1. A good government ought to be constant, and ought to contain an active principle.
2. Utility and necessity.
3. An habitual sense of obligation.
4. Force.
5. Influence.

I hold it, that different societies have all different views and interests to pursue, and always prefer local to general concerns. For example: New York legislature made an external compliance lately to a requisition of congress; but do they not at the same time counteract their compliance by gratifying the local objects of the State so as to defeat their concession? And this will ever be the case. Men always love power, and States will prefer their particular concerns to the general welfare; and as the States become large and important, will they not be less attentive to the general government? What in process of time will Virginia be? She contains now half a million of inhabitants—in twenty-five years she will double the number. Feeling her own weight and importance, must she not become indifferent to the concerns of the union? And where, in such a situation, will be found national attachment to the general government.

By *force*, I mean the *coercion* of law and the coercion of arms. Will this remark apply to the power intended to be vested in the government to be instituted by their plan? A delinquent must be compelled to obedience by force of arms. How is this to be done? If you are unsuccessful, a dissolution of your government must be the consequence; and in that case the individual legislatures will reassume their powers; nay, will not the interest of the States be thrown into the State governments?

By *influence*, I mean the regular weight and support it will receive from those who will find it their interest to support a government intended to preserve the peace and happiness of the community of the whole. The State governments, by either plan will exert the means to counteract it. They have their State judges and militia, all combined to support their State interests; and these will be influenced to oppose a national government. Either plan is therefore precarious. The national government cannot long exist when opposed by such a weighty rival. The experience of ancient and modern confederacies evince this point, and throw considerable light on the subject. The amphyctionic council of Greece had a right to require of its members troops, money, and the force of the country. Were they obeyed in the exercise of those powers? Could they preserve the peace of the greater States and republics? or where were they obeyed? History shows that their decrees were disregarded, and that the stronger states, regardless of their power, gave law to the lesser.

Let us examine the federal institution of Germany. It was instituted upon the laudable principle of securing the independency of the several states of which it was composed, and to protect them against foreign invasion. Has it answered these good intentions? Do we not see that their councils are weak and distracted, and that it cannot prevent the wars and confusion which the respective electors carry on against each other? The Swiss cantons, or the Helvetic union, are equally inefficient.

Such are the lessons which the experience of others affords us, and from whence results the evident conclusion that all federal governments are weak and distracted. To avoid the evils deducible from these observations, we must establish a general and national government, completely sovereign, and annihilate the State distinctions and State operations; and unless we do this, no good purpose can be answered. What does the Jersey plan propose? It surely has not this for its object. By this we grant the regulation of trade and a more effectual collection of the revenue, and some partial duties. These, at five or ten per cent. would only perhaps amount to a fund to discharge the debt of the corporation.

Let us take a review of the variety of important objects which must necessarily engage the attention of a national government. You have to protect your rights against Canada on the north, Spain on the south, and your western frontier against the savages. You have to adopt necessary plans for the settlement of your frontiers, and to institute the mode in which settlements and good government are to be made.

How is the expense of supporting and regulating these important matters to be defrayed? By requisition on the States, according to the Jersey plan? Will this do it? We have already found it ineffectual. Let one State prove delinquent, and it will encourage others to follow the example; and thus the whole will fail. And what is the standard to quota among the States their respective proportions? Can lands be the standard? How would that apply between Russia and Holland? Compare Pennsylvania with North-Carolina, or Connecticut with New York. Does not commerce or industry in the one or other make a great disparity between these different countries, and may not the comparative value of the States from these circumstances, make an unequal disproportion when the data is numbers? I therefore conclude that either system would utimately destroy the confederation, or any other government which is established on such fallacious principles. Perhaps imposts, taxes on specific articles, would produce a more equal system of drawing a revenue.

Another objection against the Jersey plan is, the unequal representation. Can the great States consent to this? If they did it would eventually work its own destruction. How are forces to be raised by the Jersey plan? By quotas? Will the States comply with the requisition? As much as they will with the taxes.

Examine the present confederation, and it is evident they can raise no troops nor equip vessels before war is actually declared. They cannot therefore take any preparatory measure before an enemy is at your door. How unwise and inadequate their powers! and this must ever be the case when you attempt to define powers.—Something will always be wanting. Congress, by being annually elected, and subject to recall, will ever come with the prejudices of their States rather than the good of the union. Add therefore additional powers to a body thus organized, and you establish a *sovereignty* of the worst kind, consisting of a single body. Where are the checks? None. They must either prevail over the State governments, or the prevalence of the State governments must end in their dissolution. This is a conclusive objection to the Jersey plan.

Such are the insuperable objections to both plans: and what is to be done on this occasion? I confess I am at a loss. I foresee the difficulty on a consolidated plan of drawing a representation from so extensive a continent to one place. What can be the inducements for gentlemen to come 600 miles to a national legislature? The expense would at least amount to £100,000. This however can be no conclusive objection if it eventuates in an extinction of State governments. The burthen of the latter would be saved, and the expense then would not be great. State distinctions would be found unnecessary, and yet I confess, to

*The Home of John Jay*

carry government to the extremities, the State governments reduced to corporations, and with very limited powers, might be necessary, and the expense of the national government become less burdensome.

Yet, I confess, I see great difficulty of drawing forth a good representation. What, for example, will be the inducements for gentlemen of fortune and abilities to leave their houses and business to attend annually and long? It cannot be the wages; for these, I presume, must be small. Will not the power, therefore, be thrown into the hands of the demagogue or middling politician, who, for the sake of a small stipend and the hopes of advancement, will offer himself as a candidate, and the real men of weight and influence, by remaining at home, add strength to the State governments? I am at a loss to know what must be done—I despair that a republican form of government can remove the difficulties. Whatever may be my opinion, I would hold it however unwise to change that form of government. I believe the British government forms the best model the world ever produced, and such has been its progress in the minds of the many, that this truth gradually gains ground. This government has for its object *public strength* and *individual security*. It is said with us to be unattainable. If it was once formed it would maintain itself. All communities divide themselves into the few and the many. The first are the rich and well born, the other the mass of the people. The voice of the people has been said to be the voice of God; and however generally this maxim has been quoted and believed, it is not true in fact. The people are turbulent and changing; they seldom judge or determine right. Give therefore to the first class a distinct, permanent share in the government. They will check the unsteadiness of the second, and as they cannot receive any advantage by a change, they therefore will ever maintain good government. Can a democratic assembly, who annually revolve in the mass of the people, be supposed steadily to pursue the public good? Nothing but a permanent body can check the imprudence of democracy. Their turbulent and uncontroling disposition requires checks. The senate of New York, although chosen for four years, we have found to be inefficient. Will, on the Virginia plan, a continuance of seven years do it? It is admitted that you cannot have a good executive upon a democratic plan. See the excellency of the British executive—He is placed above temptation—He can have no distinct interests from the public welfare. Nothing short of such an executive can be efficient. The weak side of a republican government is the danger of foreign influence. This is unavoidable, unless it is so constructed as to bring forward its first characters in its support. I am therefore for a general government, yet would wish to go the full length of republican principles.

Let one body of the legislature be constituted during good behavior or life.

Let one executive be appointed who dares execute his powers.

It may be asked, is this a republican system? It is strictly so, as long as they remain elective.

And let me observe, that an executive is less dangerous to the liberties of the people when in office during life, than for seven years.

It may be said this constitutes an elective monarchy! Pray what is a monarchy? May not the governors of the respective States be considered in that light? But by making the executive subject to impeachment, the term monarchy cannot apply. These elective monarchs have produced tumults in Rome, and are equally dangerous to peace in Poland, but this cannot apply to the mode in which I would propose the election. Let the electors be appointed in each of the States to elect the executive—[*Here Mr. H. produced his plan, a copy whereof is hereunto annexed*]—to consist of two branches—and I would give them the unlimited power of passing *all laws* without exception. The assembly to be elected for three years by the people in districts—the senate to be elected by electors to be chosen for that purpose by the people, and to remain in office during life. The executive to have the power of negativing all laws—to make war or peace, with the advice of the senate—to make treaties with their advice, but to have the sole direction of all military operations, and to send ambassadors and appoint all military officers, and to pardon all offenders, treason excepted, unless by advice of the senate. On his death or removal, the president of the senate to officiate, with the same powers, until another is elected. Supreme judicial officers to be appointed by the executive and the senate. The legislature to appoint courts in each State, so as to make the State governments unnecessary to it.

All State laws to be absolutely void which contravene the general laws. An officer to be appointed in each State to have a negative on all State laws. All the militia and the appointment of officers to be under the national government.

I confess that this plan and that from Virginia are very remote from the idea of the people. Perhaps the Jersey plan is nearest their expectation. But the people are gradually ripening in their opinions of government—they begin to be tired of an excess of democracy—and what even is the Virginia plan, but *pork still, with a little change of the sauce.*

Then adjourned to-morrow.

TUESDAY, JUNE 19TH, 1787.

Met pursuant to adjournment. Present 11 States.

On the consideration of the first resolve of the Jersey plan.

Mr. MADISON. This is an important question—Many persons scruple the powers of the convention. If this remark had any weight, it is equally applicable to the adoption of either plan. The difference of drawing the powers in the one from the people and in the other from the States, does not affect the powers. There are two States in the union where the members of congress are chosen by the people. A new government must be made. Our all is depending on it; and if we have but a clause that the people will adopt, there is then a chance for our preservation. Although all the States have assented to the confederation, an infraction of any one article by one of the States is a dissolution of the whole. This is the doctrine of the civil law on treaties.

Jersey pointedly refused complying with a requisition of congress, and was guilty of this infraction, although she afterwards rescinded her non-complying resolve. What is the object of a confederation? It is two-fold—1st, to maintain the union; 2dly, good government. Will the Jersey plan secure these points? No; it is still in the power of the confederated States to violate treaties—Has not Georgia, in direct violation of the confederation, made war with the Indians, and concluded treaties? Have not Virginia and Maryland entered into a partial compact? Have not Pennsylvania and Jersey regulated the bounds of the Delaware? Has not the State of Massachusetts, at this time, a considerable body of troops in pay? Has not congress been obliged to pass a conciliatory act in support of a decision of their federal court between Connecticut and Pennsylvania, instead of having the power of carrying into effect the judgment of their own court? Nor does the Jersey plan provide for a ratification by the respective States of the powers intended to be vested. It is also defective in the establishment of the judiciary, granting only an appellate jurisdiction, without providing for a second trial; and in case the executive of a State should pardon an offender, how will it effect the definitive judgment on appeal? It is evident, if we do not *radically* depart from a federal plan, we shall share the fate of ancient and modern confederacies. The amphyctionic council, like the American congress, had the power of judging in the *last resort* in war and peace—call out forces—send ambassadors. What was its fate or continuance? Philip of Macedon, with little difficulty, destroyed every appearance of it. The Athenian had nearly the same fate—The Helvetic confederacy is rather a league—In the German confederacy the parts are too strong for the whole—The Dutch are in a most wretched situation—weak in all its parts, and only supported by surrounding contending powers.

The rights of individuals are infringed by many of the State laws—such as issuing paper money, and instituting a mode to discharge debts differing from the form of the contract. Has the Jersey plan any checks to prevent the mischief? Does it in any instance secure internal tranquillity? Right and force, in a system like this, are synonymous terms. When force is employed to support the system, and men obtain military habits, is there no danger they may turn their arms against their employers? Will the Jersey plan prevent foreign influence? Did not Persia and Macedon distract the councils of Greece by acts of corruption? And is not Jersey and Holland at this day subject to the same distractions? Will not the plan be burdensome to the smaller States, if they have an equal representation? But how is military coercion to enforce government? True, a smaller State may be brought to obedience, or crushed; but what if one of the larger States should prove disobedient, are you sure you can by force effect a submission? Suppose we cannot agree on any plan, what will be the condition of the smaller States? Will Delaware and Jersey be safe against Pennsylvania, or Rhode Island against Massachusetts? And how will the smaller States be situated in case of partial confederacies? Will they not be obliged to make larger concessions to the greater States? The point of representation is the great point of difference, and which the greater States cannot give up; and although there was an equalization of States, State distinctions would still exist. But this is totally impracticable; and what would be the effect of the Jersey plan if ten or twelve new States were added?

Mr. King moved that the committee rise and report that the Jersey plan is not admissible, and report the first plan.

Mr. Dickinson supposed that there were good regulations in both. Let us therefore contrast the one with the other, and consolidate such parts of them as the committee approve.

Mr. King's motion was then put—For it 7 States—3 against—one divided. New York in the minority.

The committee rose and reported again the first plan, and the inadmissibility of the Jersey plan.

The convention then proceeded to take the first plan into consideration.

The first resolve was read.

Mr. WILSON. I am (to borrow a sea-phrase) for taking a new departure, and I wish to consider in what direction we sail, and what may be the end of our voyage. I am for a national government, though the idea of federal is, in my view, the same. With me it is not a desirable object to annihilate the State governments, and here I differ from the honorable gentleman from New York. In all extensive empires a subdivision of power is necessary.

Persia, Turkey, and Rome, under its emperors, are examples in point. These, although despots, found it necessary. A general government, over a great extent of territory, must, in a few years, make subordinate jurisdictions.—Alfred the great, that wise legislator, made this gradation, and the last division on his plan amounted only to ten territories. With this explanation, I shall be for the first resolve.

Mr. HAMILTON. I agree to the proposition. I did not intend yesterday a total extinguishment of State governments; but my meaning was, that a national government ought to be able to support itself without the aid or interference of the State governments, and that therefore it was necessary to have full sovereignty. Even with corporate rights the States will be dangerous to the national government, and ought to be extinguished, new modified, or reduced to a smaller scale.

Mr. KING. None of the States are now sovereign or independent—Many of these essential rights are vested in congress. Congress, by the confederation, possesses the rights of the United States. This is a union of the men of those States. None of the States, individually or collectively, but in congress, have the rights of *peace* or *war*. The magistracy in congress possesses the sovereignty—To certain points we are now a united people. Consolidation is already established. The confederation contains an article to make alterations—Congress have the right to propose such alterations. The 8th article respecting the quotas of the States, has been altered, and eleven States have agreed to it. Can it not be altered in other instances? It can, excepting the guarantee of the States.

Mr. MARTIN. When the States threw off their allegiance on Great Britain, they became independent of her, and each other. They united and confederated for mutual defence, and this was done on principles of perfect reciprocity—They will now again meet on the same ground. But when a dissolution takes place, our original rights and sovereignties are resumed.—Our accession to the union has been by States. If any other principle is adopted by this convention, he will give it every opposition.

Mr. WILSON. The declaration of independence preceded the State constitutions. What does this declare? In the name of the people of these States, we are declared to be free and independent. The power of war, peace, alliances and trade, are declared to be vested in congress.

Mr. HAMILTON. I agree to Mr. Wilson's remark.—Establish a weak government and you must at times overleap the bounds. Rome was obliged to create dictators. Cannot you make propositions to the people because we before confederated on other principles?—The people can yield to them, if they will. The three great objects of government, *agriculture, commerce, and revenue*, can only be secured by a general government.

Adjourned to to-morrow morning.

WEDNESDAY, JUNE 20TH, 1787.

Met pursuant to adjournment. Present 11 States.

Judge ELSWORTH. I propose, and therefore move, to expunge the word *national*, in the first resolve, and to place in the room of it, *government of the United States*—which was agreed to, *nem. con.*

Mr Lansing then moved, that the first resolve be postponed, in order to take into consideration the following: *That the powers of legislation ought to be vested in the United States in congress.*

I am clearly of opinion that I am not authorized to accede to a system which will annihilate the State governments and the Virginia plan is declarative of such extinction. It has been asserted that the public mind is not known. To some points it may be true, but we may collect from the fate of the requisition of the impost, what it may be on the principles of a national government.— When many of the States were so tenacious of their rights on this point, can we expect that *thirteen* States will surrender their governments up to a national plan? Rhode Island pointedly refused granting it. Certainly she had a federal right so to do; and I hold it as an undoubted truth, as long as State distinctions remain, let the national government be modified as you please, both branches of your legislature will be impressed with local and State attachments. The Virginia plan proposes a negative on the

State laws where, *in the opinion* of the national legislature, they contravene the national government: and no State Laws can pass unless approved by them.—They will have more than a law in a day to revise; and are they competent to judge of the wants and necessities of remote States?

This national government will, from their power, have great influence in the State governments; and the existence of the latter are only saved in appearance. And has it not been asserted that they expect their extinction? If this be the object, let us say so, and extinguish them at once. But remember, if we devise a system of government which will not meet the approbation of our constituents, we are dissolving the union—but if we act within the limits of our power, it will be approved of; and should it upon experiment prove defective, the people will entrust a future convention again to amend it. Fond as many are of a general government, do any of you believe it can pervade the whole continent so effectually as to secure the peace, harmony, and happiness of the whole? The excellence of the British model of government has been much insisted on; but we are endeavoring to complicate it with State governments, on principles which will gradually destroy the one or the other. You are sowing the seeds of rivalship, which must at last end in ruin.

Mr. MASON. The material difference between the two plans has already been clearly pointed out. The objection to that of Virginia arises from the want of power to institute it, and the want of practicability to carry it into effect. Will the first objection apply to a power merely recommendatory? In certain seasons of public danger it is commendable to exceed power. The treaty of peace, under which we now enjoy the blessings of freedom, was made by persons who exceeded their powers. It met the approbation of the public, and thus deserved the praises of these who sent them. The impracticability of the plan is still less groundless. These measures are supported by one who, at his time of life, has little to hope or expect from any government. Let me ask, will the people entrust their dearest rights and liberties to the determination of one body of men, and those not chosen by them, and who are invested both with the *sword* and *purse?* They never will—

they never can—to a conclave, transacting their business secret from the eye of the public. Do we not discover by their public journals of the years 1778-9, and 1780, that factions and party spirit had guided many of their acts? The people of America, like all other people, are unsettled in their minds, and their principles fixed to no object, except that a republican government is the best, and that the legislature ought to consist of two branches. The constitutions of the respective States, made and approved of by them, evince this principle. Congress, however, from other causes, received a different organization. What, would you use military force to compel the observance of a social compact? It is destructive to the rights of the people. Do you expect the militia will do it, or do you mean a standing army? The first will never, on such an occasion, exert any power; and the latter may turn its arm against the government which employs them. I never will consent to destroy State governments, and will ever be as careful to preserve the one as the other. If we should, in the formation of the latter, have omitted some necessary regulation, I will trust my posterity to amend it. That the one government will be productive of disputes and jealousies against the other, I believe; but it will produce mutual safety, I shall close with observing, that though some gentlemen have expressed much warmth on this and former occasions, I can excuse it, as the result of sudden passion; and hope that although we may differ in some particular points, if we mean the good of the whole, that our good sense upon reflection, will prevent us from spreading our discontent further.

Mr. MARTIN. I know that government must be supported; and if the one was incompatible with the other, I would support the State government at the expense of the union—for I consider the present system as a system of slavery. Impressed with this idea, I made use on a former occasion, of expressions perhaps rather harsh. If gentlemen conceive that the legislative branch is dangerous, divide them into two. They are as much the representatives of the States, as the State assemblies are the representatives of the people. Are not the powers which we here exercise given by the legislatures? [After giving a detail of the revolution and of State governments, Mr. M. continued.] I confess when the confederation was made, congress ought to have been invested with more extensive powers; but when the States saw that congress indirectly aimed at sovereignty, they were jealous, and therefore refused any farther concessions. The time is now come that we can constitutionally grant them not only new powers, but to modify their government, so that the State governments are not endangered. But whatever we have now in our power to grant, the grant is a State grant, and therefore it must be so organized that the State governments are interested in supporting the union. Thus systematized, there can be no danger if a small force is maintained.

Mr. SHERMAN. We have found during the war that though congress consisted of but one branch, it was that body which carried us through the whole war, and we were crowned with success. We closed the war, performing all the functions of a good government, by making a beneficial peace. But the great difficulty now is, how we shall pay the public debt incurred during that war. The unwillingness of the States to comply with the requisitions of congress, has embarrassed us greatly.—But to amend these defects in government I am not fond of speculation. I would rather proceed on experimental ground. We can so modify the powers of congress, that we will all be mutual supporters of one another. The disparity of the States can be no difficulty. We know this by experience—Virginia and Massachusetts were the first who unanimously ratified the old confederation. They then had no claim to more votes in congress than one.—Foreign States have made treaties with us as confederated States, not as a national government. Suppose we put an end to that government under which those treaties were made, will not these treaties be void?

Mr. WILSON. The question before us may admit of the three following considerations:

1. Whether the legislature shall consist of one or two branches.

2. Whether they are to be elected by the State governments or by the people.

3. Whether in proportion to State importance, or States individually.

Confederations are usually of a short date. The amphyctionic council was instituted in the infancy of the Grecian republics—as those grew in strength, the council lost its weight and power. The Achæan league met the same fate—Switzerland and Holland are supported in their confederation, not by its intrinsic merit, but the incumbent pressure of surrounding bodies. Germany is kept together by the house of Austria. True, congress carried us through the war even against its own weakness. That powers were wanting, you Mr. President, must have felt. To other causes, not to congress, must the success be ascribed. That the great States acceded to the confederation, and that they in the hour of danger, made a sacrifice of their interest to the lesser States is true. Like the wisdom of Solomon in adjudging the child to its true mother, from tenderness to it, the greater States well knew that the loss of a limb was fatal to the confederation—they too, through tenderness, sacrificed their dearest rights to preserve the whole. But the time is come, when justice will be done to their claims—Situations are altered.

Congress have frequently made their appeal to the people. I wish they had always done it—the national government would have been sooner extricated.

Question then put on Mr. Lansing's motion and lost.—6 States against 4—one divided. New York in the minority.

Adjourned till to-morrow morning.

THURSDAY, JUNE 21ST, 1787.

Met pursuant to adjournment. Present 11 States.

Dr. JOHNSON—It appears to me that the Jersey plan has for its principal object, the preservation of the State governments. So far it is a departure from the plan of Virginia, which although it concentres in a distinct national government, it is not totally independent of that of the States. A gentleman from New York, with boldness and decision, proposed a system totally different from both; and though he has been praised by every body, he has been supported by none. How can the State governments be secured on the Virginia plan? I could have wished, that the supporters of the Jersey system could have satisfied themselves with the principles of the Virginia plan, and that the individuality of the States could be supported. It is agreed on all hands that a portion of government is to be left to the States. How can this be done? It can be done by joining the States in their legislative capacity with the right of appointing the second branch of the national legislature, to represent the States individually.

Mr. WILSON. If security is necessary to preserve the one, it is equally so to preserve the other. How can the national government be secured against the States? Some regulation is necessary. Suppose the national government had a component number in the State legislature? But where the one government clashed with the other, the State government ought to yield, as the preservation of the general interest must be preferred to a particular. But let us try to designate the powers of each, and then no danger can be apprehended, nor can the general government be possessed of any ambitious views to encroach on the State rights.

Mr. MADISON. I could have wished that the gentleman from Connecticut had more accurately marked his objections to the Virginia plan. I apprehend the greatest danger is from the encroachment of the States on the national government—This apprehension is justly founded on the experience of ancient confederacies, and our own is a proof of it.

The right of negativing in certain instances the State laws, affords one security to the national government. But is the danger well founded? Have any State governments ever encroached on the corporate rights of cities? And if it was the case that the national government usurped the State government, if such usurpation was for the good of the whole, no mischief could arise.—To draw the line between the two, is a difficult task. I believe it cannot be done, and therefore I am inclined for a general government.

If we cannot form a general government, and the States become totally independent of each other, it would afford a melancholy prospect.

The 2d resolve was then put and carried—7 States for—3 against—one divided. New York in the minority.

The 3d resolve was then taken into consideration by the convention.

Mr. PINKNEY. I move *that the members of the first branch be appointed in such manner as the several State legislatures shall direct*, instead of the mode reported. If this motion is not agreed to, the other will operate with great difficulty, if not injustice— If you make district elections and join, as I presume you must, many counties in one district, the largest county will carry the election as its united influence will give a decided majority in its favor.

Mr. MADISON. I oppose the motion—there are difficulties, but they may be obviated in the details connected with the subject.

Mr. HAMILTON. It is essential to the democratic rights of the community, that this branch be directly elected by the people. Let us look forward to probable events—There may be a time when State legislatures may cease, and such an event ought not to embarrass the national government.

Mr. MASON. I am for preserving inviolably the democratic branch of the government—True, we have found inconveniencies from pure democracies; but if we mean to preserve peace and real freedom, they must necessarily become a component part of a national government. Change this necessary principle, and if the government proceeds to taxation, the States will oppose your powers.

Mr. Sherman thought that an amendment to the proposed amendment is necessary.

Gov. RUTLEDGE. It is said that an election by representatives is not an election by the people. This proposition is not correct. What is done by my order is done by myself. I am convinced that the mode of election by legislatures will be more refined, and better men will be sent.

Mr. WILSON. The legislature of the States by the proposed motion will have an uncontrolable sway over the general government. Election is the exercise of *original* sovereignty in the people—but if by representatives, it is only *relative* sovereignty.

Mr. KING. The magistrates of the States will ever pursue schemes of their own, and this, on the proposed motion, will pervade the national government—and we know the State governments will be ever hostile to the general government.

Mr. PINKNEY. All the reasoning of the gentlemen opposed to my motion has not convinced me of its impropriety. There is an *esprit de corps* which has made heretofore every *unfederal* member of congress, after his election, become strictly *federal*, and this I presume will ever be the case in whatever manner they may be elected.

Question put on Mr. Pinkney's motion and carried by 6 States against 4—one divided.

Question then put on the resolve—9 States for—1 against—one divided.

Gov. RANDOLPH. I move that in the resolve for the duration of the first branch of the general legislature, the word *three* be expunged, and the words *two years* be inserted.

Mr. DICKINSON. I am against the amendment. I propose that the word *three* shall remain, but that they shall be removable annually in classes.

Mr. SHERMAN. I am for one year. Our people are accustomed to annual elections. Should the members have a longer duration of service, and remain at the seat of government, they may forget their constituents, and perhaps imbibe the interest of the State in which they reside, or there may be danger of catching the *esprit de corps*.

Mr. MASON. I am for two years. One year is too short.—In extensive States four months may elapse before the returns can be known. Hence the danger of their remaining too long unrepresented.

Mr. HAMILTON. There is a medium in every thing. I confess three years is not too long—A representative ought to have full freedom of deliberation, and ought to exert an opinion of his own. I am convinced that the public mind will adopt a solid plan—The government of New York, although higher toned than that of any other State, still we find great listlessness and indifference in the electors; nor do they in general bring forward the first characters to the legislature. The public mind is perhaps not now ready to receive the best plan of government, but certain circumstances are now progressing which will give a different complexion to it.

*Two years* duration agreed to.

Adjourned till to-morrow morning.

---

### Friday June 22d, 1787.

Met pursuant to adjournment.

The clause of the 3d resolve, respecting *the stipends*, taken into consideration.

Judge Elsworth. I object to this clause. I think the State legislatures ought to provide for the members of the general legislature, and as each State will have a proportionate number, it will not be burdensome to the smaller States. I therefore move to strike out the clause.

Mr. Gorham. If we intend to fix the stipend, it may be an objection against the system, as the States would never adopt it. I join in sentiment to strike out the whole.

Gov. Randolph. I am against the motion. Are the members to be paid? Certainly—We have no sufficient fortunes to induce gentlemen to attend for nothing. If the State legislatures pay the members of the national council, they will control the members, and compel them to pursue State measures. I confess the payment will not operate impartially, but the members must be paid, and be made easy in their circumstances. Will they attend the service of the public without being paid?

Mr. Sherman. The States ought to pay their members; and I judge of the approbation of the people on matters of government by what I suppose they will approve.

Mr. Wilson. I am against going as far as the resolve. If, however, it is intended to throw the national legislature into the hand of the States, I shall be against it. It is possible the States may become unfederal, and they may then shake the national government. The members ought to be paid out of the national treasury.

Mr. Madison. Our attention is too much confined to the present moment, when our regulations are intended to be perpetual. Our national government must operate for the good of the whole, and the people must have a general interest in its support; but if you make its legislators subject to and at the mercy of the State governments, you ruin the fabric—and whatever new States may be added to the general government the expense will be equally borne.

Mr. HAMILTON. I do not think the States ought to pay the members, nor am I for a fixed sum. It is a general remark, that he who pays is the master. If each State pays its own members, the burden would be disproportionate, according to the distance of the States from the seat of government. If a national government can exist, members will make it a desirable object to attend, without accepting any stipend—and it ought to be so organized as to be efficient.

Mr. WILSON. I move *that the stipend be ascertained by the legislature, and paid out of the national treasury.*

Mr. MADISON. I oppose this motion. Members are too much interested in the question. Besides, it is indecent that the legislature should put their hands in the public purse to convey it into their own.

Question put on Mr. Wilson's motion and negatived—7 States against—2 for, and 2 divided.

Mr. Mason moved to change the phraseology of the resolve, that is to say, *to receive an adequate compensation for their services,* and to be paid out of the treasury. This motion was agreed to.

Mr. RUTLEDGE. I move that the question be taken on these words, *to be paid out of the national treasury.*

Mr. HAMILTON. It has been often asserted, that the interests of the general and of the State legislatures are precisely the same. This cannot be true. The views of the governed are often materially different from those who govern. The science of policy is the knowledge of human nature. A State government will ever be the rival power of the general government. It is therefore highly improper that the State legislatures should be the paymasters of the members of the national government. All political bodies love power, and it will often be improperly attained.

Judge ELSWORTH. If we are so exceedingly jealous of State legislatures, will they not have reason to be equally jealous of us? If I return to my State and tell them, we made such and such regulations for a general government, because we dared not trust you with any extensive powers, will they be satisfied? nay, will they adopt your government? and let it ever be remembered, that without their approbation your government is nothing more than a rope of sand.

Mr. WILSON. I am not for submitting the national government to the approbation of the State legislatures. I know that they and the State officers will oppose it. I am for carrying it to the people of each State.

Mr. Rutledge's motion was then put—4 States for the clause—5 against—2 divided. New York divided.

The clause, to be ineligible to any office, &c., came next to be considered.

Mr. Mason moved that after the words, *two years*, be added, *and to be of the age of 25 years*.

Question put and agreed to—7 ayes—3 noes. New York divided.

Mr. GORHAM. I move that after the words, *and under the national government for one year after its expiraton*, be struck out.

Mr. King for the motion. It is impossible to carry the system of exclusion so far; and in this instance we refine too much by going to *utopian* lengths. It is a mere cobweb.

Mr. BUTLER. We have no way of judging of mankind but by experience. Look at the history of the government of Great Britain, where there is a very flimsy exclusion—Does it not ruin their government? A man takes a seat in parliament to get an office for himself or friends, or both; and this is the great source from which flows its great venality and corruption.

Mr. WILSON. I am for striking out the words moved for. Strong reasons must induce me to disqualify a good man from office. If you do, you give an opportunity to the dependent or avaricious man to fill it up, for to them offices are objects of desire. If we admit there may be cabal and intrigue between the executive and legislative bodies, the exclusion of one year will not prevent the effects of it. But we ought to hold forth every honorable inducement for men of abilities to enter the service of the public.—This is truly a republican principle. Shall talents, which entitle a man to public reward, operate as a punishment? While a member of the legislature, he ought to be excluded from any other office, but no longer. Suppose a war breaks out, and a number of your best military characters were members; must we lose the benefit of their services? Had this been the case in the beginning of the war, what would have been our situation?—and what has happened may happen again.

Mr. MADISON. Some gentlemen give too much weight, and others too little to this subject. If you have no exclusive clause, there may be danger of creating officers or augmenting the stipends of those already created, in order to gratify some members if they were not excluded. Such an instance has fallen within my own observation. I am therefore of opinion, that no office ought to be open to a member, which may be created or augmented while he is in the legislature.

Mr. MASON. It seems as if it was taken for granted, that all offices will be filled by the executive, while I think many will remain in the gift of the legislature. In either case, it is necessary to shut the door against corruption. If otherwise, they may make or multiply offices, in order to fill them. Are gentlemen in earnest when they suppose that this exclusion will prevent the first characters from coming forward? Are we not struck at seeing the luxury and venality which has already crept in among us? If not checked, we shall have ambassadors to every petty state in Europe—the little republic of *St. Marino* not excepted. We must, in the present system, remove the temptation. I admire many parts of the British constitution and government, but I detest their corruption.—Why has the power of the crown so remarkably increased the last century? A stranger, by reading their laws, would suppose it considerably diminished; and yet, by the sole power of appointing the increased officers of government, corruption pervades every town and village in the kingdom. If such a restriction should abridge the right of election, it is still necessary, as it will prevent the people from ruining themselves; and will not the same causes here produce the same effects? I consider this clause as the corner-stone on which our liberties depend—and if we strike it out we are erecting a fabric for our destruction.

Mr. GORHAM. The corruption of the English government cannot be applied to America. This evil exists there in the venality of their boroughs: but even this corruption has its advantage, as it gives stability to their government. We do not know what the effect would be if members of parliament were excluded from offices. The great bulwark of our liberty is the frequency of elections, and their great danger is the septennial parliaments.

Mr. HAMILTON. In all general questions which become the subjects of discussion, there are always some truths mixed with falsehoods. I confess there is danger where men are capable of holding two offices. Take mankind in general, they are vicious—their passions may be operated upon. We have been taught to reprobate the danger of influence in the British government, without duly reflecting how far it was necessary to support a good government. We have taken up many ideas upon trust, and at last, pleased with our own opinions, establish them as undoubted truths. Hume's opinion of the British constitution confirms the remark, that there is always a body of firm patriots, who often shake a corrupt administration. Take mankind as they are, and what are they governed by? Their passions. There may be in every government a few choice spirits, who may act from more worthy motives. One great error is that we suppose mankind more honest than they are. Our prevailing passions are ambition and interest; and it will ever be the duty of a wise government to avail itself of those passions, in order to make them subservient to the public good—for these ever induce us to action. Perhaps a few men in a state may, from patriotic motives, or to display their talents, or to reap the advantage of public applause, step forward; but if we adopt the clause we destroy the motive. I am, therefore, against all exclusions and refinements, except only in this case; that when a member takes his seat, he should vacate every other office. It is difficult to put any exclusive regulation into effect. We must, in some degree, submit to the inconvenience.

The question was then put for striking out—4 ayes—4 noes—3 States divided. New York of the number.

Adjourned till to-morrow morning.

---

SATURDAY JUNE 23D, 1787.

Met pursuant to adjournment. Present 11 States.

Mr. GORHAM. I move that the question which was yesterday proposed on the clause, *to be paid out of the national treasury*, be now put.

Question put—5 ayes—5 noes—one State divided. So the clause was lost.

Mr. Pinkney moved that that part of the clause which disqualifies a person from holding an office in the State, be expunged, because the first and best characters in a State may thereby be deprived of a seat in the national council.

Mr. WILSON. I perceive that some gentlemen are of opinion to give a bias in favor of State governments—This question ought to stand on the same footing.

Mr. SHERMAN. By the conduct of some gentlemen, we are erecting a kingdom to act against itself. The legislature ought to be free and unbiassed.

Question put to strike out the words moved for, and carried—8 ayes—3 noes.

Mr. Madison then moved, that after the word *established*, be added, *or the emoluments whereof shall have been augmented by the legislature of the United States, during the time they were members thereof, and for one year thereafter.*

Mr. BUTLER. The proposed amendment does not go far enough. How easily may this be evaded. What was the conduct of George the second to support the pragmatic sanction? To some of the opposers he gave pensions—others offices, and some, to put them out of the house of commons, he made lords. The great Montesquieu says, it is unwise to entrust persons with power, which by being abused operates to the advantage of those entrusted with it.

Governor Rutledge was against the proposed amendment. No person ought to come to the legislature with an eye to his own emolument in any shape.

801

Mr. MASON. I differ from my colleague in his proposed amendment. Let me state the practice in the State where we came from. There, all officers are appointed by the legislature. Need I add, that many of their appointments are most shameful. Nor will the check proposed by this amendment be sufficient. It will soon cease to be any check at all. It is asserted that it will be very difficult to find men sufficiently qualified as legislators without the inducement of emolument. I do believe that men of genius will be deterred unless possessed of great virtues. We may well dispense with the first characters when destitute of virtue—I should wish them never to come forward—But if we do not provide against corruption, our government will soon be at an end: nor would I wish to put a man of virtue in the way of temptation. Evasions and caballing would evade the amendment. Nor would the danger be less, if the executive has the appointment of officers. The first three or four years we might go on well enough; but what would be the case afterwards? I will add, that such a government ought to be refused by the people—and it will be refused.

Mr. MADISON. My wish is that the national legislature be as uncorrupt as possible. I believe all public bodies are inclined, from various motives, to support its members; but it is not always done from the base motives of venality. Friendship, and a knowledge of the abilities of those with whom they associate, may produce it. If you bar the door against such attachments, you deprive the government of its greatest strength and support. Can you always rely on the patriotism of the members? If this be the only inducement, you will find a great indifferency in filling your legislative body. If we expect to call forth useful characters, we must hold out allurements; nor can any great inconveniency arise from such inducements. The legislative body must be the road to public honor; and the advantage will be greater to adopt my motion, than any possible inconvenience.

Mr. KING. The intimate association of offices will produce a vigorous support to your government. To check it would produce no good consequences. Suppose connections are formed? Do they not all tend to strengthen the government under which they are formed? Let therefore preferment be open to all men. We refine otherwise too much—nor is it possible we can eradicate the evil.

Mr. WILSON. I hope the amendment will be adopted.—By the last vote it appears that the convention have no apprehension of danger of State appointments. It is equally imaginary to apprehend any from the national government. That such officers will have influence in the legislature, I readily admit; but I would not therefore exclude them. If any ill effects were to result from it, the bargain can as well be made with the legislature as with the executive. We ought not to shut the door of promotion against the great characters in the public councils, from being rewarded by being promoted. If otherwise, will not these gentlemen be put in the legislatures to prevent them from holding offices, by those who wish to enjoy them themselves?

Mr. SHERMAN. If we agree to this amendment, our good intentions may be prostrated by changing offices to avoid or evade the rule.

Mr. GERRY. This amendment is of great weight, and its consequences ought to be well considered. At the beginning of the war we possessed more than Roman virtue. It appears to me it is now the reverse. We have more land and stock-jobbers than any place on earth.—It appears to me, that we have constantly endeavored to keep distinct the three great branches of government; but if we agree to this motion, it must be destroyed by admitting the legislators to share in the executive, or to be too much influenced by the executive, in looking up to him for offices.

Mr. MADISON. This question is certainly of much moment. There are great advantages in appointing such persons as are known. The choice otherwise will be chance. How will it operate on the members themselves? Will it not be an objection to become members when they are to be excluded from office? For these reasons I am for the amendment.

Mr. BUTLER. These reasons have no force. Characters fit for offices will always be known.

Mr. MASON. It is said it is necessary to open the door to induce gentlemen to come into the legislature. This door is open, but not immediately. A seat in the house will be the field to exert talents, and when to a good purpose, they will in due time be rewarded.

Mr. JENIFER. Our senators are appointed for 5 years and they can hold no other office. This circumstance gives them the greatest confidence of the people.

The question was put on Mr. Madison's amendment, and lost—8 noes—2 ayes—one State divided.

Question on the clause as amended before. Carried—8 ayes—2 noes—one State divided.

The question was next on the latter part of the clause.

Mr. MASON. We must retain this clause, otherwise evasions may be made. The legislature may admit of resignations and thus make members eligible—places may be promised at the close of their duration, and that a dependency may be made.

Mr. GERRY. And this actually has been the case in congress—a member resigned to obtain an appointment, and had it failed he would have resumed it.

Mr. HAMILTON. The clause may be evaded many ways. Offices may be held by proxy—they may be procured by friends, &c.

Mr. RUTLEDGE. I admit, in some cases, it may be evaded; but this is no argument against shutting the door as close as possible.

The question was then put on this clause, to wit: *and for the space of one year after its expiration*—and negatived.

Then adjourned to Monday morning.

## MONDAY, JUNE 25TH, 1787.

Met pursuant to adjournment. Present 11 States.

Mr. C. PINKNEY. On the question upon the second branch of the general legislature, as reported by the committee in the fourth resolve, now under consideration, it will be necessary to inquire into the true situation of the people of this country. Without this we can form no adequate idea what kind of government will secure their rights and liberties. There is more equality of rank and fortune in America than in any other country under the sun; and this is likely to continue as long as the unappropriated western lands remain unsettled. They are equal in rights, nor is extreme of poverty to be seen in any part of the union. If we are thus singularly situated, both as to fortune and rights, it evidently follows, that we cannot draw any useful lessons from the examples of any of the European states or kingdoms; much less can Great Britain afford us any striking institution, which can be adapted to our own situation—unless we indeed intend to establish an hereditary executive, or one for life. Great Britain drew its first rude institutions from the forests of Germany, and with it that of its nobility. These having originally in their hands the property of the State, the crown of Great Britain was obliged to yield to the claims of power which those large possessions enabled them to assert. The commons were then too contemptible to form part of the national councils. Many parliaments were held, without their being represented until in process of time, under the protection of the crown, and forming distinct communities, they obtained some weight in the British government. From such discordant materials brought casually together, those admirable checks and balances, now so much the boast of the British constitution, took their rise.—But will we be able to copy from this original? I do not suppose that in the confederation, there are one hundred gentlemen of sufficient fortunes to establish a nobility; and the equality of others as to rank would never admit of the distinctions of nobility. I lay it therefore down as a settled principle, that equality of condition is a leading axiom in our government. It may be said we must necessarily establish checks, lest one rank of people should usurp the rights of another. Commerce can never interfere with the government, nor give a complexion to its councils. Can we copy from Greece or Rome? Have we their nobles or patricians? With them offices were open to few—The different ranks in the community formed opposite interests and produced unceasing struggles and disputes. Can this apply equally to the free yeomanry of America? We surely differ from the whole. Our situation is unexampled, and it is in our power, on different grounds, to secure civil and religious liberty; and when we secure these we secure every thing that is necessary to establish happiness. We cannot pretend to rival the European nations in their grandeur or power; nor is the situation of any two nations so exactly alike as that the one can adopt the regulations or government of the other. If we have any distinctions thay may be divided into three classes.

1. Professional men.
2. Commercial men.
3. The landed interest.

The latter is the governing power of America, and the other two must ever be dependent on them—Will a national government suit them? No. The three orders have necessarily a mixed interest, and in that view, I repeat it again, the United States of America compose in fact but one order. The clergy and nobility of Great Britain can never be adopted by us. Our government must be made suitable to the people, and we are perhaps the only people in the world who ever had sense enough to appoint delegates to establish a general government. I believe that the propositions from Virginia, with some amendments, will satisfy the people. But a general government must not be made dependent on the State governments.

The United States include a territory of about 1500 miles in length, and in breadth about 400; the whole of which is divided into States and districts. While we were dependent on the crown of Great Britain, it was in contemplation to have formed the whole into one—but it was found impracticable. No legislature could make good laws for the whole, nor can it now be done. It would necessarily place the power in the hands of the few, nearest the seat of government. State governments must therefore remain, if you mean to prevent confusion. The general negative powers will support the general government. Upon these considerations I am led to form the second branch differently from the report. Their powers are important and the number not too large, upon the principle of proportion. I have considered the subject with great attention: and I propose this plan (reads it) and if no better plan is proposed, I will then move its adoption.

Mr. Randolph moved that the 4th resolve be divided, in the same manner as the 3d resolve.

Mr. Gorham moved the question on the first resolve.—Sixteen members from one State will certainly have greater weight, than the same number of members from different States. We must therefore depart from this rule of apportionment in some shape or other—perhaps on the plan Mr. Pinkney has suggested.

Mr. READ. Some gentlemen argue, that the representation must be determined according to the weight of each State—That we have heretofore been partners in trade, in which we all put in our respective proportions of stock—That the articles of our co-partnership were drawn in forming the confederation—And that before we make a new co-partnership, we must first settle the old business. But to drop the allusion—we find that the great States have appropriated to themselves the common lands in their respective States—These lands having been forfeited as heretofore belonging to the king, ought to be applied to the discharge of our public debts.—Let this still be done, and then if you please, proportion the representation, and we shall not be jealous of one another—A jealousy, in a great measure, owing to the public property appropriated by individual States—and which, as it has been gained by the united power of the confederation, ought to be appropriated to the discharge of the public debts.

Mr. GORHAM. This motion has been agitated often in congress; and it was owing to the want of power, rather than inclination, that it was not justly settled. Great surrenders have been made by the great States, for the benefit of the confederation.

Mr. WILSON. The question now before us is, whether the second branch of the general legislature shall or shall not be appointed by the State legislatures. In every point of view it is an important question. The magnitude of the object is indeed embarrassing. The great system of Henry the IV of France, aided by the greatest statesmen, is small when compared to the fabric we are now about to erect—In laying the stone amiss we may injure the superstructure; and what will be the consequence, if the corner-stone should be loosely placed? It is improper that the State legislatures should have the power contemplated to be given them. A citizen of America may be considered in two points of view—as a citizen of the general government, and as a citizen of the particular State in which he may reside. We ought to consider in what character he acts in forming a general government. I am both a citizen of Pennsylvania and of the United States. I must therefore lay aside my State connections and act for the general good of the whole.— We must forget our local habits and attachments. The general government should not depend on the State governments. This ought to be a leading distinction between the one and the other; nor ought the general government to be composed of an assemblage of different State governments—We have unanimously agreed to establish a general government—That the powers of peace, war, treaties, coinage and regulating of *commerce*, ought to reside in that government. And if we reason in this manner, we shall soon see the impropriety of admitting the interference of State governments into the general government. Equality of representation can not be established, if the second branch is elected by the State legislatures. When we are laying the foundation of a building, which is to last for ages, and in which millions are interested, it ought to be well laid. If the national government does not act upon State prejudices, State distinctions will be lost. I therefore move, *that the second branch of the legislature of the national government be elected by electors chosen by the people of the United States.*

Judge ELSWORTH. I think the second branch of the general legislature ought to be elected agreeable to the report. The other way, it is said, will be more the choice of the people—The one mode is as much so as the other. No doubt every citizen of every State is interested in the State governments; and elect him in whatever manner you please, whenever he takes a seat in the general government, it will prevail in some shape or other. The State legislatures are more competent to make a judicious choice, than the people at large. Instability pervades their choice. In the second branch of the general government we want wisdom and firmness. As to balances, where nothing can be balanced, it is a perfect *utopian* scheme. But still greater advantages will result in having a second branch endowed with the qualifications I have mentioned. Their weight and wisdom may check the inconsiderate and hasty proceedings of the first branch.

I cannot see the force of the reasoning in attempting to detach the State governments from the general government. In that case, without a standing army, you cannot support the general government, but on the pillars of the State governments. Are the larger States now more energetic than the smaller? Massachusetts cannot support a government at the distance of one hundred miles from her capital, without an army; and how long Virginia and Pennsylvania will support their governments it is difficult to say. Shall we proceed like unskilful workmen, and make use of timber, which is too weak to build a first rate ship? We know that the people of the States are strongly attached to their own constitutions. If you hold up a system of general government, destructive of their constitutional rights, they will oppose it. Some are of opinion that if we cannot form a general government so as to destroy State governments, we ought at least to balance the one against the other. On the contrary, the only chance we have to support a general government is to graft it on the State governments. I want to proceed on this ground, as the safest, and I believe no other plan is practicable. In this way, and in this way only, can we rely on the confidence and support of the people.

Dr. JOHNSON. The State governments must be preserved: but this motion leaves them at the will and pleasure of the general government.

Mr. MADISON. I find great differences of opinion in this convention on the clause now under consideration. Let us postpone it in order to take up the 8th resolve, that we may previously determine the mode of representation.

Mr. MASON. All agree that a more efficient government is necessary. It is equally necessary to preserve the State governments, as they ought to have the means of self-defence. On the motion of Mr. Wilson, the only means they ought to have would be destroyed.

The question was put for postponing, in order to take into consideration the 8th resolve, and lost—7 noes—4 ayes.

Question on the 1st clause in the 4th resolve—9 States for—2 against it.

The age of the senators (30 years) agreed to.

Mr. GORHAM proposed that the senators be classed, and to remain 4 years in office; otherwise great inconveniences may arise if a dissolution should take place at once.

Governor RANDOLPH. This body must act with firmness. They may possibly always sit—perhaps to aid the executive. The State governments will always attempt to counteract the general government. They ought to go out in classes; therefore I move, *that they go out of office in fixed proportions of time*, instead of the words, *seven years*.

Mr. READ moved (though not seconded) that they ought to continue in office during good behaviour.

Mr. WILLIAMSON moved that they remain in office for six years.

Mr. PINKNEY. I am for four years. Longer time would give them too great attachment to the States where the general government may reside. They may be induced, from the proposed length of time, to sell their estates, and become inhabitants near the seat of government.

Mr. MADISON. We are proceeding in the same manner that was done when the confederation was first formed. Its original draft was excellent, but in its progress and completion it became so insufficient as to give rise to the present convention. By the vote already taken, will not the temper of the State legislatures transfuse itself into the senate? Do we create a free government?

Question on Governor Randolph's motion—7 ayes—3 noes—one divided.

Motion to fix the term of service at six years—5 ayes—5 noes—one divided.

Do. for 5 years—5 ayes—5 noes—one divided.

The question for 4 years was not put; and the convention adjourned till to-morrow morning.

## Tuesday June 26th, 1787.

Met pursuant to adjournment. Present 11 States.

Mr. GORHAM. My motion for 4 years' continuance, was not put yesterday. I am still of opinion that classes will be necessary, but I would alter the time. I therefore move that the senators be elected for 6 years, and that the rotation be triennial.

Mr. PINKNEY. I oppose the time, because of too long a continuance. The members will by this means be too long separated from their constituents, and will imbibe attachments different from that of the State; nor is there any danger that members, by a shorter duration of office, will not support the interest of the union, or that the States will oppose the general interest. The State of South Carolina was never opposed in principle to congress, nor thwarted their views in any case, except in the requisition of money, and then only for want of power to comply—for it was found there was not money enough in the State to pay their requisition.

Mr. Read moved that the term of *nine years* be inserted, in triennial rotation.

Mr. MADISON. We are now to determine whether the republican form shall be the basis of our government.—I admit there is weight in the objection of the gentleman from South Carolina; but no plan can steer clear of objections. That great powers are to be given, there is no doubt; and that those powers may be abused is equally true. It is also probable that members may lose their attachments to the States which sent them—Yet the first branch will control them in many of their abuses. But we are now forming a body on whose wisdom we mean to rely, and their permanency in office secures a proper field in which they may exert their firmness and knowledge. Democratic communities may be unsteady, and be led to action by the impulse of the moment.—Like individuals, they may be sensible of their own weakness, and may desire the counsels and checks of friends to guard them against the turbulency and weakness of unruly passions. Such are the various pursuits of this life, that in all civilized countries, the interest of a community will be divided. There will be debtors and creditors, and an unequal possession of property, and hence arises different views and different objects in government. This indeed is the ground-work of aristocracy; and we find it blended in every government, both ancient and modern. Even where titles have survived property, we discover the noble beggar haughty and assuming.

The man who is possessed of wealth, who lolls on his sofa, or rolls in his carriage, cannot judge of the wants or feelings of the day laborer. The government we mean to erect is intended to last for ages. The landed interest, at present, is prevalent; but in process of time, when we approximate to the states and kingdoms of Europe; when the number of landholders shall be comparatively small, through the various means of trade and manufactures, will not the landed interest be overbalanced in future elections, and unless wisely provided against, what will become of your government? In England, at this day, if elections were open to all classes of people, the property of the landed proprietors would be insecure. An agrarian law would soon take place. If these observations be just, our government ought to secure the permanent interests of the country against innovation. Landholders ought to have a share in the government, to support these invaluable interests, and to balance and check the other. They ought to be so constituted as to protect the minority of the opulent against the majority. The senate, therefore, ought to be this body; and to answer these purposes, they ought to have permanency and stability. Various have been the propositions; but my opinion is, the longer they continue in office, the better will these views be answered.

Mr. SHERMAN. The two objects of this body are permanency and safety to those who are to be governed. A bad government is the worse for being long. Frequent elections give security and even permanency. In Connecticut we have existed 132 years under an annual government; and as long as a man behaves himself well, he is never turned out of office. Four years to the senate is quite sufficient when you add to it the rotation proposed.

Mr. HAMILTON. This question has already been considered in several points of view. We are now forming a republican government. Real liberty is neither found in despotism or the extremes of democracy, but in moderate governments.

Those who mean to form a solid republican government, ought to proceed to the confines of another government. As long as offices are open to all men, and no constitutional rank is established, it is pure republicanism. But if we incline too much to democracy, we shall soon shoot into a monarchy. The difference of property is already great amongst us. Commerce and industry will still increase the disparity. Your government must meet this state of things, or combinations will in process of time, undermine your system. What was the tribunitial power of Rome? It was instituted by the plebeians as a guard against the patricians. But was this a sufficient check? No—The only distinction which remained at Rome was, at last, between the rich and the poor. The gentleman from Connecticut forgets that the democratic body is already secure in a representation.—As to Connecticut, what were the little objects of their government before the revolution? Colonial concerns merely. They ought now to act on a more extended scale, and dare they do this? Dare they collect the taxes and requisitions of congress? Such a government may do well, if they do not tax, and this is precisely their situation.

Mr. GERRY. It appears to me that the American people have the greatest aversion to monarchy, and the nearer our government approaches to it, the less chance have we for their approbation. Can gentlemen suppose that the reported system can be approved of by them? Demagogues are the great pests of our government, and have occasioned most of our distresses. If four years are insufficient, a future convention may lengthen the time.

Mr. WILSON. The motion is now for nine years, and a triennial rotation. Every nation attends to its foreign intercourse—to support its commerce—to prevent foreign contempt, and to make war and peace. Our senate will be possessed of these powers, and therefore ought to be dignified and permanent. What is the reason that Great Britain does not enter into a commercial treaty with us? Because congress has not the power to enforce its observance. But give them those powers, and give them the stability proposed by the motion, and they will have more permanency than a monarchical government. The great objection of many is, that this duration would give birth to views inconsistent with the interests of the union. This can have no weight, if the triennial rotation is adopted; and this plan may possibly tend to conciliate the minds of the members of the convention on this subject, which have varied more than on any other question.

The question was then put on Mr. Read's motion, and lost, 8 noes—3 ayes.

The question on 5 years, and a biennial rotation, was carried— 7 ayes—4 noes. New York in the minority.

Mr. PINKNEY. I move that the clause for granting stipends, be stricken out.

Question put—5 ayes—6 noes.

On the amendment to the question, *to receive a compensation*— 10 ayes—1 no.

Judge ELSWORTH. I move that the words, *out of the national treasury*, be stricken out, and the words, *the respective State legislatures*, be inserted.

If you ask the States what is reasonable, they will comply— but if you ask of them more than is necessary to form a good government, they will grant you nothing.

Capt. DAYTON. The members should be paid from the general treasury, to make them independent.

The question was put on the amendment and lost—5 ayes 6 noes.

Mr. MASON. I make no motion, but throw out for the consideration of the convention, whether a person in the second branch ought not to be qualified as to property?

The question was then put on the clause, and lost—5 ayes—6 noes.

It was moved to strike out the clause, *to be ineligible to any State office*.

Mr. MADISON. Congress heretofore depended on State interests—we are now going to pursue the same plan.

Mr. WILSON. Congress has been ill managed, because particular States controlled the union. In this convention, if a proposal is made promising independency to the general government, before we have done with it, it is so modified and changed as to amount to nothing. In the present case, the States may say, although I appoint you for six years, yet if you are against the State, your table will be unprovided. Is this the way you are to erect an independent government?

Mr. BUTLER. This second branch I consider as the aristocratic part of our government; and they must be controlled by the States, or they will be too independent.

Mr. PINKNEY. The States and general government must stand together. On this plan have I acted throughout the whole of this business. I am therefore for expunging the clause. Suppose a member of this house was qualified to be a State judge, must the State be prevented from making the appointment?

Question put for striking out—8 ayes—3 noes.

The 5th resolve, *that each house have the right of originating bills*, was taken into consideration, and agreed to.

Adjourned till to-morrow morning.

---

WEDNESDAY, JUNE 27TH, 1787.

Met pursuant to adjournment. Present 11 States.

The 6th resolve was postponed, in order to take into consideration the 7th and 8th resolves. The first clause of the 7th was proposed for consideration, which respected the suffrage of each State in the first branch of the legislature.

[Mr. Martin, the attorney general from Maryland, spoke on this subject upwards of three hours. As his arguments were too diffuse, and in many instances desultory, in was not possible to trace him through the whole, or to methodize his ideas into a systematic or argumentative arrangement. I shall therefore only note such points as I conceive merit most particular notice.]

The question is important, (said Mr. Martin,) and I have already expressed my sentiments on the subject.—My opinion is, that the general government ought to protect and secure the State governments—others, however, are of a different sentiment, and reverse the principle.

The present reported system is a perfect medley of confederated and national government, without example and without precedent. Many who wish the general government to protect the State governments, are anxious to have the line of jurisdiction well drawn and defined, so that they may not clash. This suggests the necessity of having this line well detailed—possibly this may be done. If we do this, the people will be convinced that we meant well to the State governments; and should there be any defects, they will trust a future convention with the power of making further amendments.

A general government may operate on individuals in cases of general concern, and still be federal. This distinction is with the States, as States, represented by the people of those States. States will take care of their internal police and local concerns. The general government has no interest but the protection of the whole. Every other government must fail. We are proceeding in forming this government as if there were no State governments at all. The States must approve, or you will have none at all. I have never heard of a confederacy having two legislative branches. Even the celebrated Mr. Adams, who talks so much of checks and balances, does not suppose it necessary in a confederacy. Public and domestic debts are our great distress. The treaty between Virginia and Maryland about the navigation of the Chesapeake and Potomac, is no infraction of the confederacy. The cornerstone of a federal government is *equality* of votes. States may surrender this right; but if they do, their liberties are lost. If I err on this point, it is the error of the head, not of the heart.

The first principle of government is founded on the natural rights of individuals, and in perfect equality. Locke, Vattel, Lord Somers, and Dr. Priestly, all confirm this principle. This principle of equality, when applied to individuals, is lost in some degree, when he becomes a member of a society, to which it is transferred; and this society, by the name of state or kingdom, is, with respect to others, again on a perfect footing of equality—a right to govern themselves as they please. Nor can any other state, of right, deprive them of this equality. If such a state confederates, it is intended for the good of the whole; and if it again confederate, those rights must be well guarded. Nor can any state demand a surrender of any of those rights; if it can, equality is already destroyed. We must treat as free States with each other, upon the same terms of equality that men originally formed themselves into societies. Vattel, Rutherford, and Locke, are united in support of the position, that states, as to each other, are in a state of nature.

Thus, says Mr. Martin, have I travelled with the most respectable authorities in support of principles, all tending to prove the equality of independent states. This is equally applicable to the smallest as well as the largest states, on the true principles of reciprocity and political freedom.

Unequal confederacies can never produce good effects. Apply this to the Virginia plan. Out of the number 90, Virginia has 16 votes, Massachusetts 14, Pennsylvania 12—in all 42. Add to this a State having four votes, and it gives a majority in the general legislature. Consequently, a combination of these States will govern the remaining nine or ten states. Where is the safety and independency of those States? Pursue this subject farther. The executive is to be appointed by the legislature, and becomes the executive in consequence of this undue influence. And hence flows the appointment of all your officers, civil, military, and judicial. The executive is also to have a negative on all laws. Suppose the possibility of a combination of ten States—he negatives a law—it is totally lost, because those States cannot form two-thirds of the legislature. I am willing to give up private interest for the public good—but I must be satisfied first, that it is the public interest—and who can decide this point? A majority only of the union.

The Lacedemonians insisted, in the amphyctionic council, to exclude some of the smaller states from a right to vote, in order that they might tyrannize over them. If the plan now on the table be adopted, three States in the union have the control, and they may make use of their power when they please.

If there exists no separate interests, there is no danger of an equality of votes; and if there be danger, the smaller States cannot yield. If the foundation of the existing confederation is well laid, powers may be added—You may safely add a third story to a house where the foundation is good. Read then the votes and proceedings of congress on forming the confederation—Virginia only was opposed to the principle of equality—The smaller States yielded rights, not the large States—They gave up their claim to the unappropriated lands with the tenderness of the mother recorded by Solomon—they sacrificed affection to the preservation of others. New Jersey and Maryland rendered more essential services during the war than many of the larger States. The partial representation in congress is not the cause of its weakness, but the want of power. I would not trust a government organized upon the reported plan, for all the slaves of Carolina or the horses and oxen of Massachusetts. Price says, that laws made by one man, or a set of men, and not by common consent, is slavery—And it is so when applied to States, if you give them an unequal representation. What are called human feelings in this instance are only the feelings of ambition and the lust of power.

Adjourned till to-morrow morning

### Thursday, June 28th, 1787.

Met pursuant to adjournment.

Mr. Martin in continuation.

On federal grounds, it is said, that a minority will govern a majority—but on the Virginia plan a minority would tax a majority. In a federal government, a majority of states must and ought to tax. In the local government of states, counties may be unequal—still numbers, not property, govern. What is the Government now forming, over States or persons? As to the latter, their rights cannot be the object of a general government—These are already secured by their guardians, the State governments.

The general government is therefore intended only to protect and guard the rights of the States as States.

This general government, I believe, is the first upon earth which gives checks against democracies or aristocracies. The only necessary check in a general government ought to be a restraint to prevent its absorbing the powers of the State governments. Representation on federal principles can only flow from State societies. Representation and taxation are ever inseparable—not according to the quantum of property, but the quantum of freedom.

Will the representatives of a State forget State interests? The mode of election cannot change it. These prejudices cannot be eradicated—Your general government cannot be just or equal upon the Virginia plan, unless you abolish State interests. If this cannot be done, you must go back to principles purely federal.

On this latter ground the State legislatures and their constituents will have no interests to pursue different from the general government, and both will be interested to support each other. Under these ideas can it be expected that the people can approve the Virginia plan? But it is said, the people, not the State legislatures, will be called upon for approbation—with an evident design to separate the interest of the governors from the governed. What must be the consequence? Anarchy and confusion. We lose the idea of the powers with which we are entrusted. The legislatures must approve. By then it must, on your own plan, be laid before the people. How will such a government, over so many great States, operate? Wherever new settlements have been formed in large States, they immediately want to shake off their independency. Why? Because the government is too remote for their good. The people want it nearer home.

The basis of all ancient and modern confederacies is the freedom and the independency of the States composing it. The states forming the amphyctionic council were equal, though Lacedemon, one of the greatest states, attempted the exclusion of three of the lesser States from this right. The plan reported, it is true, only intends to diminish those rights, not to annihilate them— It was the ambition and power of the great Grecian states which at last ruined this respectable council. The States as societies are ever respectful. Has Holland or Switzerland ever complained of the equality of the states which compose their respective confederacies? Bern and Zurich are larger than the remaining eleven cantons—so of many of the states of Germany; and yet their governments are not complained of. Bern alone might usurp the whole power of the Helvetic confederacy, but she is contented still with being equal.

The admission of the larger States into the confederation, on the principles of equality, is dangerous—But on the Virginia system it is ruinous and destructive. Still it is the true interest of all the States to confederate—It is their joint efforts which must protect and secure us from foreign danger, and give us peace and harmony at home.

[Here Mr. Martin entered into a detail of the comparative powers of each State, and stated their probable weakness and strength.]

At the beginning of our troubles with Great Britain, the smaller States were attempted to be cajoled to submit to the views of that nation, lest the larger States should usurp their rights. We then answered them—your present plan is slavery, which, on the remote prospect of a distant evil, we will not submit to.

I would rather confederate with any single State, than submit to the Virginia plan. But we are already confederated, and no power on earth can dissolve it but by the consent of *all* the contracting powers—and four States, on this floor, have already declared their opposition to annihilate it. Is the old confederation dissolved, because some of the States wish a new confederation?

Mr. LANSING. I move that the word *not* be struck out of the resolve, and then the question will stand on its proper ground— and the resolution will read thus: *that the representation of the first branch be according to the articles of the confederation;* and the sense of the convention on this point will determine the question of a federal or national government.

Mr. MADISON. I am against the motion. I confess the necessity of harmonizing, and if it could be shown that the system is unjust or unsafe, I would be against it. There has been much fallacy in the arguments advanced by the gentleman from Maryland. He has, without adverting to many manifest distinctions, considered confederacies and treaties as standing on the same basis. In the one, the powers act collectively, in the other individually. Suppose, for example, that France, Spain, and some of the smaller States in Europe, should treat on war or peace, or on any other general concern, it would be done on principles of equality; but if they were to form a plan of general government, would they give, or are the greater States obliged to give, to the lesser, the same and equal legislative powers? Surely not. They might differ on this point, but no one can say that the large states were wrong in refusing this concession. Nor can the gentleman's reasoning apply to the present powers of congress; for they may and do, in some cases, affect property, and in case of war, the lives of the citizens. Can any of the lesser States be endangered by an adequate representation? Where is the probability of a combination? What the inducements? Where is the similarity of customs, manners, or religion? If there possibly can be a diversity of interest, it is the case of the three large States. Their situation is remote, their trade different. The staple of Massachusetts is fish, and the carrying trade—of Pennsylvania, wheat and flour—of Virginia, tobacco. Can States thus situated in trade, ever form such a combination? Do we find those combinations in the larger counties in the different State governments to produce rivalships? Does not the history of the nations of the earth verify it? Rome rivalled Carthage, and could not be satisfied before she was destroyed. The houses of Austria and Bourbon acted on the same view—and the wars of France and England have been waged through rivalship; and let me add, that we, in a great measure, owe our independency to those national contending passions. France, through this motive, joined us. She might, perhaps, with less expense, have induced England to divide America between them. In Greece the contention was ever between the larger states. Sparta against Athens—and these again, occasionally,

*The Home of Gouverneur Morris*

against Thebes, were ready to devour each other. Germany presents the same prospect—Prussia against Austria. Do the greater provinces in Holland endanger the liberties of the lesser? And let me remark, that the weaker you make your confederation, the greater the danger to the lesser States. They can only be protected by a strong federal government. Those gentlemen who oppose the Virginia plan do not sufficiently analyze the subject. Their remarks, in general, are vague and inconclusive.

Captain DAYTON. On the discussion of this question the fate of the State governments depend.

Mr. WILLIAMSON. If any argument will admit of demonstration, it is that which declares, that all men have an equal right in society. Against this position, I have heard, as yet, no argument, and I could wish to hear what could be said against it. What is tyranny? Representatives of representatives, if you give them the power of taxation. From equals take equals, and the remainder is equal. What process is to annihilate smaller States, I know not. But I know it must be tyranny if the smaller States can tax the greater, in order to ease themselves. A general government cannot exercise direct taxation. Money must be raised by duties and imposts, &c., and this will operate equally. It is impossible to tax according to numbers. Can a man over the mountains, where produce is a drug, pay equal with one near the shore?

Mr. WILSON. I should be glad to hear the gentleman from Maryland explain himself upon the remark of Old Sarum, when compared with the city of London. This he has allowed to be an unjust proportion; as in the one place one man sends two members, and in the other one million are represented by four members. I would be glad to hear how he applies this to the larger and smaller States in America; and whether the borough, as a borough, is represented, or the people of the borough.

Mr. Martin rose to explain. Individuals, as composing a part of the whole of one consolidated government, are there represented.

The further consideration of the question was postponed.

Mr. SHERMAN. In society, the poor are equal to the rich in voting, although one pays more than the other. This arises from an equal distribution of liberty amongst all ranks; and it is, on the same grounds, secured to the States in the confederation—for this would not even trust the important powers to a majority of the States. Congress has too many checks, and their powers are too limited. A gentleman from New York thinks a limited monarchy the best government, and no State distinctions. The plan now before us gives the power to four States to govern nine States. As they will have the purse, they may raise troops, and can also make a king when they please.

Mr. MADISON. There is danger in the idea of the gentleman from Connecticut. Unjust representation will ever produce it. In the United Netherlands, Holland governs the whole, although she has only one vote. The counties in Virginia are exceedingly disproportionate, and yet the smaller has an equal vote with the greater, and no inconvenience arises.

Governor Franklin read some remarks, acknowledging the difficulties of the present subject. Neither ancient or modern history, (said Gov. Franklin,) can give us light. As a sparrow does not fall without Divine permission, can we suppose that governments can be erected without his will? We shall, I am afraid, be disgraced through little party views. I move *that we have prayers every morning.*

Adjourned till to-morrow morning.

---

FRIDAY, JUNE 29TH, 1787.

Met pursuant to adjournment. Present 11 States.

Dr. JOHNSON. As the debates have hitherto been managed, they may be spun out to an endless length; and as gentlemen argue on different grounds, they are equally conclusive on the points they advance, but afford no demonstration either way. States are political societies.—For whom are we to form a government? for the people of America, or for those societies? Undoubtedly for the latter. They must, therefore, have a voice in the second branch of the general government, if you mean to preserve their existence. The people already compose the first branch. This mixture is proper and necessary—For we cannot form a general government on any other ground.

Mr. GORHAM. I perceive no difficulty in supposing a union of interest in the different States. Massachusetts formerly consisted of three distinct provinces—they have been united into one, and we do not find the least trace of party distinctions arising from their former separation. Thus it is that the interest of the smaller States will unite in a general government. It is thus they will be supported. Jersey, in particular, situated between Philadelphia and New York, can never become a commercial State. It would be her interest to be divided, and part annexed to New York and part to Pennsylvania—or otherwise the whole to the general government.—Massachusetts cannot long remain a large State. The province of Maine must soon become independent of her. Pennsylvania can never become a dangerous State—her western country must, at some period, become separated from her, and consequently her power will be diminished. If some States will not confederate on a new plan, I will remain here, if only one State will consent to confederate with us.

Judge ELSWORTH. I do not despair but that we shall be so fortunate as to devise and adopt some good plan of government.

Judge READ. I would have no objection, if the government was more national—but the proposed plan is so great a mixture of both, that it is best to drop it altogether.—A State government is incompatable with a general government. If it was more national, I would be for a representation proportionate to population. The plan of the gentleman from New York is certainly the best—but the great evil is the unjust appropriation of the public lands. If there was but one national government, we would be all equally interested.

Mr. MADISON. Some gentlemen are afraid that the plan is not sufficiently national, while others apprehend that it is too much so. If this point of representation was once well fixed, we would come nearer to one another in sentiment. The necessity would then be discovered of circumscribing more effectually the State governments, and enlarging the bounds of the general government. Some contend that States are sovereign, when, in fact, they are only political societies. There is a gradation of power in all societies, from the lowest corporation to the highest sovereign. The States never possessed the essential rights of sovereignty. These were always vested in congress. Their voting, as States, in congress, is no evidence of sovereignty. The State of Maryland voted by counties—did this make the counties sovereign? The States, at present, are only great corporations, having the power of making by-laws, and these are effectual only if they are not contradictory to the general confederation. The States ought to be placed under the control of the general government—at least as much so as they formerly were under the king and British parliament. The arguments, I observe, have taken a different turn, and I hope may tend to convince all of the necessity of a strong energetic government, which would equally tend to give energy to, and protect the State governments. What was the origin of the military establishments of Europe? It was the jealousy which one State or kingdom entertained of another. This jealousy was ever productive of evil. In Rome the patricians were often obliged to excite a foreign war to divert the attention of the plebeians from encroaching on the senatorial rights.—In England and France, perhaps this jealousy may give energy to their governments, and contribute to their existence. But a state of danger is like a state of war, and it unites the various parts of the government to exertion. May not our distractions, however, invite danger from abroad? If the power is not immediately derived from the people, in proportion to their numbers, we may make a paper confederacy, but that will be all. We know the effects of the old confederation, and without a general government this will be like the former.

Mr. HAMILTON. The course of my experience in human affairs might perhaps restrain me from saying much on this subject. I shall, however, give birth to some of the observations I have made during the course of this debate. The gentleman from Maryland has been at great pains to establish positions which are not denied. Many of them, as drawn from the best writers on government, are become almost self-evident principles.—But I doubt the propriety of his application of those principles in the present discussion. He deduces from them the necessity that States entering into a confederacy must retain the equality of votes—this position cannot be correct—Facts plainly contradict it. The parliament of Great Britain asserted a supremacy over the whole empire, and the celebrated Judge Blackstone labors for the legality of it, although many parts were not represented. This parliamentary power we opposed as contrary to our colonial rights. With that exception, throughout that whole empire, it is submitted to. May not the smaller and greater States so modify their respective rights as to establish the general interest of the whole, without adhering to the right of equality? Strict representation is not observed in any of the State governments. The senate of New York are chosen by persons of certain qualifications, to the exclusion of others. The question, after all is, is it our interest in modifying this general government to sacrifice individual rights to the preservation of the rights of an *artificial* being, called States? There can be no truer principle than this—that every individual of the community at large has an equal right to the protection of government. If therefore three States contain a majority of the inhabitants of America, ought they to be governed by a minority? Would the inhabitants of the great States ever submit to this? If the smaller States maintain this principle, through a love of power, will not the larger, from the same motives, be equally tenacious to preserve their power? They are to surrender their rights—for what? for the preservation of an artificial being. We propose a free government—Can it be so if partial distinctions are maintained? I agree with the gentleman from Delaware, that if the State governments are to act in the general government, it affords the strongest reason for exclusion. In the State of New-York, five counties form a majority of representatives, and yet the government is in no danger, because the laws have a genaral operation. The small States exaggerate their danger, and on this ground contend for an undue proportion of power. But their danger is increased, if the larger States will not submit to it. Where will they form new alliances for their support? Will they do this with foreign powers? Foreigners are jealous of our increasing greatness, and would rejoice in our distractions. Those who have had opportunities of conversing with foreigners respecting sovereigns in Europe, have discovered in them an anxiety for the preservation of our democratic governments, probably for no other reason, but to keep us weak. Unless your government is respectable, foreigners will invade your rights; and to maintain tranquillity it must be respectable—even to observe neutrality you must have a strong government.—I confess our present situation is critical. We have just finished a war which has established our independency, and loaded us with a heavy debt. We have still every motive to unite for our common defence—Our people are disposed to have a good government, but this disposition may not always prevail. It is difficult to amend confederations—it has been attempted in vain, and it is perhaps a miracle that we are now met—We must therefore improve the opportunity, and render the present system as perfect as possible. Their good sense, and above all, the necessity of their affairs, will induce the people to adopt it.

Mr. PIERCE. The great difficulty in congress arose from the mode of voting. Members spoke on the floor as State advocates, and were biassed by local advantages.—What is federal? No more than a compact between States; and the one heretofore formed is insufficient. We are now met to remedy its defects, and our difficulties are great, but not, I hope, insurmountable. State distinctions must be sacrificed so far as the general government shall render it necessary—without, however, destroying them altogether. Although I am here as a representative from a small State, I consider myself as a citizen of the United States, whose general interest I will always support.

Mr. GERRY. It appears to me that the States never were independent—they had only corporate rights. Confederations are a mongrel kind of government, and the world does not afford a precedent to go by. Aristocracy is the worst kind of government, and I would sooner submit to a monarchy. We must have a system that will execute itself.

The question was then put on Mr. Lansing's motion, and lost—4 ayes—6 noes—one State divided.

Question on the clause—6 ayes—4 noes—and one State divided.

Judge ELSWORTH. I move that the consideration of the 8th resolve be postponed. Carried—9 ayes—2 noes.

I now move the following amendment to the resolve—*that in the second branch each State have an equal vote*. I confess that the effect of this motion is, to make the general government *partly federal and partly national*. This will secure tranquility, and still make it efficient; and it will meet the objections of the larger States. In taxes they will have a proportional weight in the first branch of the general legislature—If the great States refuse this plan, we will be forever separated. Even in the executive the larger States have ever had great influence.—The provinces of Holland ever had it. If all the States are to exist they must necessarily have an equal vote in the general government. Small communities when associating with greater, can only be supported by an equality of votes. I have always found in my reading and experience, that in all societies the governors are ever gradually rising into power.

The larger States, although they may not have a common interest for combination, yet they may be partially attached to each other for mutual support and advancement. This can be more easily effected than the union of the remaining small States to check it; and ought we not to regard antecedent plighted faith to the confederation already entered into, and by the terms of it declared to be perpetual? And it is not yet obvious to me that the States will depart from this ground. When in the hour of common danger we united as equals, shall it now be urged by some that we must depart from this principle when the danger is over? Will the world say that this is just? We then associated as free and independent States, and were well satisfied—To perpetuate that independence, I wish to establish a national legislature, executive, and judiciary, for under these we shall I doubt not preserve peace and harmony—nor should I be surprised (although we made the general government the most perfect in our opinion,) that it should hereafter require amendment—But at present this is as far as I possibly can go—If this convention only chalk outlines of a good government we shall do well.

Mr. BALDWIN. It appears to be agreed that the government we should adopt ought to be energetic and formidable, yet I would guard against the danger of becoming too formidable. The second branch ought not to be elected as the first. Suppose we take the example of the constitution of Massachusetts, as it is commended for its goodness: There the first branch represents the people, and the second its property.

Mr. MADISON. I would always exclude inconsistent principles in framing a system of government. The difficulty of getting its defects amended are great, and sometimes insurmountable. The Virginia State government was the first which was made, and though its defects are evident to every person, we cannot get it amended. The Dutch have made four several attempts to amend their system without success. The few alterations made in it were by tumult and faction, and for the worse. If there was real danger, I would give the smaller States the defensive weapons—But there is none from that quarter. The great danger to our general government *is the great southern and northern interests of the continent, being opposed to each other. Look to the votes in congress, and most of them stand divided by the geography of the country, not according to the size of the States.*

Suppose the first branch granted money, may not the second branch, from State views, counteract the first? In congress, the single State of Delaware prevented an embargo, at the time that all the other States thought it absolutely necessary for the support of the army. Other powers, and those very essential, besides the legislative, will be given to the second branch—such as the negativing all State laws. I would compromise on this question, if I could do it on correct principles, but otherwise not—if the old fabric of the confederation must be the ground-work of the new, we must fail.

Adjourned till to-morrow morning.

---

SATURDAY, JUNE 30TH, 1787.

Met pursuant to adjournment. Present 11 States.

Judge Brearsly moved that the president be directed to write to the executive of New Hampshire, requesting the attendance of its delegates.

Negatived—2 ayes—5 noes—one State divided.

The discussion of yesterday resumed.

Mr. WILSON. The question now before us is of so much consequence, that I cannot give it a silent vote—Gentlemen have said, that if this amendment is not agreed to, a separation to the north of Pennsylvania may be the consequence.—This neither staggers me in my sentiments or my duty. If a minority should refuse their assent to the new plan of a general government, and if they will have their own will, and without it, separate the union, let it be done; but we shall stand supported by stronger and better principles. The opposition to this plan is as 22 is to 90, in the general scale—not quite a fourth part of the union—Shall three-fourths of the union surrender their rights for the support of that artificial being, called State interest? If we must join issue I am willing.—I cannot consent that one-fourth shall controul the power of three-fourths.

If the motion is adopted, seven States will controul the whole, and the lesser seven compose 24 out of 90. One third must controul two-thirds—24 overrule 66. For whom do we form a constitution, for men, or for *imaginary beings* called States, a mere metaphysical distinction? Will a regard to *State* rights justify the sacrifice of the rights of *men?* If we proceed on any other foundation than the last, our building will neither be solid nor lasting. *Weight and numbers* is the only true principle—every other is local, confined or imaginary. Much has been said of the danger of the three larger States combining together to give rise to monarchy, or an aristocracy. Let the probability of this combination be explained, and it will be found that a rivalship rather than a confederacy will exist among them. Is there a single point in which this interest coincides? Supposing that the executive should be selected from one of the larger States, can the other two be gratified? Will not this be a source of jealousy amongst them, and will they not separately court the interest of the *smaller States*, to counteract the views of a favorite rival? How can an aristocracy arise from this combination more than amongst the smaller States? On the contrary, the present claims of the smaller States lead directly to the establishment of an aristocracy, which is the government of the few over the many, and the Connecticut proposal removes only a small part of the objection. There are only two kinds of bad governments—the one which does *too much*, and therefore oppressive, and the other which does *too little*, and therefore weak. Congress partakes of the latter, and the motion will leave us in the same situation and as much fettered as ever we were. The people see its weakness, and would be mortified in seeing our inability to correct it.

The gentleman from Georgia has his doubts how to vote on this question, and wishes some qualification of it to be made—I admit there ought to be some difference as to the numbers in the second branch; and perhaps there are other distinctions which could with propriety, be introduced—such, for example, as the qualifications of the elected, &c. However, if there are leading principles in the system which we adopt, much may be done in the detail We all aim at giving the general government more energy. The State governments are necessary and valuable—No liberty can be obtained without them. On this question depends the essential rights of the general government and of the people.

Judge ELSWORTH. I have the greatest respect for the gentleman who spoke last. I respect his abilities, although I differ from him on many points—He asserts that the general government must depend on the equal suffrage of the people. But will not this put it in the power of few States to controul the rest? It is a novel thing in politics that the few controul the many. In the British government, the few, as a guard, have an equal share in the government: The house of lords, although few in number, and sitting in their own right, have an equal share in their legislature. They cannot give away the property of the community, but they can prevent the commons from being too lavish in their gifts. Where is or was a confederation ever formed, where equality of voices was not a fundamental principle? Mankind are apt to go from one extreme to another, and because we have found defects in the confederation, must we therefore pull down the whole fabric, foundation and all, in order to erect a new building totally different from it, without retaining any of its materials? What are its defects? It is said equality of votes has embarrassed us; but how?

Would the real evils of our situation have been cured, had not this been the case? Would the proposed amendment in the Virginia plan, as to representation, have relieved us? I fancy not. Rhode Island has been often quoted as a small State, and by its refusal once defeated the grant of the impost. Whether she was right in so doing is not the question; but was it a federal requisition? And if it was not, she did not, in this instance, defeat a federal measure.

If the larger States seek security, they have it fully in the first branch of the general government. But can we turn the tables and say that the lesser States are equally secure? In *commercial regulations* they will unite. If policy should require free ports, they would be found at Boston, Philadelphia, and Alexandria. In the disposition of *lucrative offices* they would unite. But I ask no surrender of any of the rights of the great States, nor do I plead *duress* in the makers of the old confederation, nor suppose they soothed the danger, in order to resume their rights when the danger was over. No; small States must possess the power of self-defence or be ruined. Will any one say there is no diversity of interests in the States? And if there is, should not those interests be guarded and secured? But if there is none, then the large States have nothing to apprehend from an equality of rights. And let it be remembered, that these remarks are not the result of partial or local views. The State I represent is respectable, and in importance holds a middle rank.

Mr. MADISON. Notwithstanding the admirable and close reasoning of the gentleman who spoke last, I am not yet convinced that my former remarks are not well founded. I apprehend he is mistaken as to the fact on which he builds one of his arguments. He supposes that equality of votes is the principle on which all confederacies are formed—that of Lycia, so justly applauded by the celebrated Montesquieu, was different. He also appeals to our good faith for the observance of the confederacy. We know we have found one inadequate to the purposes for which it was made—Why then adhere to a system which is proved to be so remarkably defective? I have impeached a number of States for the infraction of the confederation, and I have not even spared my own State, nor can I justly spare his. Did not Connecticut refuse her compliance to a federal requisition? Has she paid, for the two last years, any money into the continental treasury? And does this look like government, or the observance of a solemn compact? Experience shows that the confederation is radically defective, and we must, in a new national government, guard against those defects. Although the large States in the first branch have a weight proportionate to their population, yet as the smaller States have an equal vote in the second branch, they will be able to controul and leave the larger without any essential benefit. As peculiar powers are intended to be granted to the second branch, such as the negativing State laws, &c., unless the larger States have a proportionate weight in the representation, they cannot be more secure.

Judge ELSWORTH. My State has always been strictly federal, and I can with confidence appeal to your excellency [the president] for the truth of it, during the war. The muster-rolls will show that she had more troops in the field than even the State of Virginia. We strained every nerve to raise them; and we neither spared money or exertions to complete our quotas. This extraordinary exertion has greatly distressed and impoverished us, and it has accumulated out State debts—We feel the effects of it even to this day. But we defy any gentleman to show that we ever refused a federal requisition. We are constantly exerting ourselves to draw money from the pockets of our citizens, as fast as it comes in; and it is the ardent wish of the State to strengthen the federal government. If she has proved delinquent through inability only, it is not more than others have been, without the same excuse.

Mr. SHERMAN. I acknowledge there have been failures in complying with the federal requisition. Many States have been defective, and the object of our convention is to amend these defects.

Col. DAVIE. I have great objection to the Virginia plan as to the manner the second branch is to be formed. It is impracticable. The number may, in time, amount to two or three hundred. This body is too large for the purposes for which we intend to constitute it. I shall vote for the amendment. Some intend a compromise.—This has been hinted by a member from Pennsylvania, but it still has its difficulties. The members will have their local prejudices. The preservation of the State societies must be the object of the general government. It has been asserted that we were *one* in war, and *one* in peace. Such we were as States; but every treaty must be the law of the land as it affects individuals. The formation of the second branch, as it is intended by the motion, is also objectionable. We are going the same round with the old confederation—No plan yet presents sufficient checks to a tumultuary assembly, and there is none therefore which yet satisfies me.

Mr. WILSON. On the present motion it was not proper to propose another plan. I think the second branch ought not to be numerous. I will propose an expedient—Let there be one member for every 100,000 souls, and the smallest States not less than one member each. This would give about twenty-six members. I make this proposal not because I belong to a large State, but in order to pull down a rotten house, and lay a foundation for a new building. To give *additional* weight to an old building is to hasten its ruin.

Governor FRANKLIN. The smaller States, by this motion, would have the power of giving away the money of the greater States. There ought to be some difference between the first and second branches. Many expedients have been proposed, and I am sorry to remark, without effect. A joiner, when he wants to fit two boards, takes off with his plane the uneven parts from each side, and thus they fit. Let us do the same—we are all met to do something.

I shall propose an expedient: Let the senate be elected by the States equally—in all acts of sovereignty and authority, let the votes be equally taken—the same in the appointment of all officers, and salaries; but in passing of laws, each State shall have a right of suffrage in proportion to the sums they respectively contribute. Amongst merchants, where a ship has many owners, her destination is determined in that proportion. I have been one of the ministers to France from this country during the war, and we should have been very glad, if they would have permitted us a vote in the distribution of the money to carry on the war.

Mr. MARTIN. Mr. Wilson's motion or plan would amount to nearly the same kind of inequality.

Mr. KING. The Connecticut motion contains all the vices of the old confederation. It supposes an imaginary evil—the slavery of State governments. And should this convention adopt the motion, our business here is at an end.

Captain DAYTON. Declamation has been substituted for argument. Have gentlemen shown, or must we believe it, because it is said, that one of the evils of the old confederation was unequal representation? We, as distinct societies, entered into the compact. Will you now undermine the thirteen pillars that support it?

Mr. MARTIN. If we cannot confederate on just principles, I will never confederate in any other manner.

Mr. MADISON. I will not answer for supporting chimerical objects—but has experience evinced any good in the old confederation? I know it never can answer, and I have therefore made use of bold language against it. I do assert, that a national senate, elected and paid by the people, will have no more efficiency than congress; for the States will usurp the general government. I mean, however, to preserve the State rights with the same care as I would trials by jury; and I am willing to go as far as my honorable colleague.

Mr. BEDFORD. That all the States at present are equally sovereign and independent, has been asserted from every quarter of this house. Our deliberations here are a confirmation of the position; and I may add to it, that each of them act from interested, and many from ambitious motives. Look at the votes which have been given on the floor of this house, and it will be found that their numbers, wealth, and local views, have actuated their determinations; and that the larger States proceed as if our eyes were already perfectly blinded. Impartiality, with them, is already out of the question—the reported plan is their political creed, and they support it, right or wrong. Even the diminutive State of Georgia has an eye to her future wealth and greatness—

South Carolina, puffed up with the possession of her wealth and negroes, and North Carolina, are all, from different views, united with the great States. And these latter, although it is said they can never, from interested views, form a coalition, we find closely united in one scheme of interest and ambition, notwithstanding they endeavor to amuse us with the purity of their principles and the rectitude of their intentions, in asserting that the general government must be drawn from an equal representation of the people. Pretences to support ambition are never wanting. Their cry is, where is the danger? and they insist that although the powers of the general government will be increased, yet it will be for the good of the whole; and although the three great States form nearly a majority of the people of America, they never will hurt or injure the lesser States. *I do not, gentlemen, trust you.* If you possess the power, the abuse of it could not be checked; and what then would prevent you from exercising it to our destruction? You gravely allege that there is no danger of combination, and triumphantly ask, how could combinations be effected? "The larger States," you say, "all differ in productions and commerce; and experience shows, that instead of combinations, they would be rivals, and counteract the views of one another." This, I repeat, is language calculated only to amuse us. Yes, sir, the larger States will be rivals, but not against each other—they will be rivals against the *rest of the States*. But it is urged that such a government would suit the people, and that its principles are equitable and just. How often has this argument been refuted, when applied to a *federal* government. The small States never can agree to the Virginia plan; and why then is it still urged? But it is said that it is not expected that the State governments will approve the proposed system, and that this house must directly carry it to THE PEOPLE for their approbation! Is it come to this, then, that *the sword* must decide this controversy, and that the horrors of war must be added to the rest of our misfortunes? But what have the people already said? "We find the confederation defective—go, and give additional powers to the confederation—give to it the imposts, regulation of trade, power to collect taxes, and the means to discharge our foreign and domestic debts." Can we not then, as their delegates, agree upon these points? As their ambassadors, can we not clearly grant those powers? Why then, when we are met, must entire, distinct, and new grounds be taken, and a government, of which the people had no idea, be instituted? And are we to be told, if we wont agree to it, it is the last moment of our deliberations? I say, it is indeed the last moment, if we do agree to this assumption of power. The States will never again be entrapped into a measure like this. The people will say the *small* States would confederate, and grant further powers to congress; but you, the *large* States, would not. Then the fault will be yours, and all the nations of the earth will justify us. But what is to become of our public debts if we dissolve the union? Where is your plighted faith? Will you crush the smaller States, or must they be left unmolested? Sooner than be ruined, there are *foreign powers who will take us by the hand*. I say not this to threaten or intimidate, but that we should reflect seriously before we act. If we once leave this floor, and solemnly renounce your new project, what will be the consequence? You will annihilate your federal government, and ruin must stare you in the face. Let us then do what is in our power— *amend and enlarge the confederation, but not alter the federal system.* The people expect this, and no more. We all agree in the necessity of a more efficient government—and cannot this be done? Although my State is small, I know and respect its rights, as much, at least, as those who have the honor to represent any of the larger States.

Judge ELSWORTH. I am asked by my honorable friend from Massachusetts, whether by entering into a national government, I will not equally participate in national security? I confess I should; but I want domestic happiness, as well as general security. A general government will never grant me this, as it cannot know my wants or relieve my distress. My State is only as one out of thirteen. Can they, the general government, gratify my wishes? My happiness depends as much on the existence of my State government, as a new-born infant depends upon its mother for nourishment. If this is not an answer, I have no other to give.

Mr. KING. I am in sentiment with those who wish the preservation of State governments; but the general government may be so constituted as to effect it. Let the constitution we are about forming be considered as a *commission* under which the general government shall act, and as such it will be the guardian of the State rights. The rights of Scotland are secure from all danger and encroachments, although in the parliament she has a small representation. May not this be done in our general government? Since I am up, I am concerned for what fell from the gentleman from Delaware—"*Take a foreign power by the hand!*" I am sorry he mentioned it, and I hope he is able to excuse it to himself on the score of passion. Whatever may be my distress, I never will court a foreign power to assist in relieving myself from it.

Adjourned till Monday next.

MONDAY, JULY 2D, 1787.

Met pursuant to adjournment. Present 11 States.

The question was then put on Mr. Elsworth's motion.—5 ayes—5 noes—one State divided. So the question, as to the amendment was lost.

Mr. PINKNEY. As a professional man. I might say, that there is no weight in the argument adduced in favor of the motion on which we were divided; but candor obliges me to own, that equality of suffrage in the States is wrong. Prejudices will prevail, and they have an equal weight in the larger as in the smaller States. There is a solid distinction as to interest between the southern and northern States—To destroy the ill effects thereof, I renew the motion which I made in the early stage of this business. [*See the plan of it before mentioned.*

General Pinkney moved for a select committee, to take into consideration both branches of the legislature.

Mr. MARTIN. It is again attempted to compromise.—You must give each State an equal suffrage, or our business is at an end.

Mr. SHERMAN. It seems we have got to a point, that we can not move one way or the other. Such a committee is necessary to set us right.

Mr. MORRIS. The two branches, so equally poised, cannot have their due weight. It is confessed, on all hands, that the second branch ought to be a check on the first—for without its having this effect it is perfectly useless.—The first branch, originating from the people, will ever be subject to *precipitancy, changeability,* and *excess.* Experience evinces the truth of this remark without having recourse to reading. This can only be checked by *ability* and *virtue* in the second branch. On your present system, can you suppose that one branch will possess it more than the others? The second branch ought to be composed of men of great and established property—*an aristocracy.* Men, who from pride will support consistency and permanency; and to make them completely independent, they must be chosen *for life,* or they will be a useless body. Such an aristocratic body will keep down the turbulency of democracy. But if you elect them for a shorter period, they will be only a name, and we had better be without them. Thus constituted, I hope they will show us the weight of aristocracy.

History proves, I admit, that the men of large property will uniformly endeavor to establish tyranny. How then shall we ward off this evil? Give them the second branch, and you secure their weight for the *public good.* They become responsible for their conduct, and this lust of power will ever be checked by the democratic branch, and thus form a stability in your government. But if we continue changing our measures by the breath of democracy, who will confide in our engagements? Who will trust us? Ask any person whether he reposes any confidence in the government of congress, or that of the State of Pennsylvania—he will readily answer you, no. Ask him the reason, and he will tell you, it is because he has no confidence in their stability.

You intend also that the second branch shall be incapable of holding any office in the general government.—It is a dangerous expedient. They ought to have every inducement to be interested in your government. Deprive them of this right, and they will become inattentive to your welfare. The wealthy will ever exist; and you never can be safe unless you gratify them as a body, in the pursuit of honor and profit. Prevent them by positive institutions, and they will proceed in some left-handed way. A son may want a place—you mean to prevent him from promotion —They are not to be paid for their services—they will in some way pay themselves; nor is it in your power to prevent it. It is good policy that men of property be collected in one body, to give them one common influence in your government. Let vacancies be filled up as they happen, by the executive. Besides, it is of little consequence, on this plan, whether the States are equally represented or not. If the State governments have the division of many of the loaves and fishes, and the general government few, it cannot exist. This senate would be one of the *baubles* of the general government. If you choose them for *seven* years, whether chosen by the people or the States; whether by equal suffrage or in any other proportion, how will they be a check? They will still have local and State prejudices.—A government by compact is no government at all. You may as well go back to your congressional federal government, where, in the character of ambassadors, they may form treaties for each state.

I avow myself the advocate of a strong government, still I admit that the influence of the rich must be guarded; and a pure democracy is equally oppressive to the lower orders of the community. This remark is founded on the experience of history. We are a commercial people, and as such will be obliged to engage in European politics. Local government cannot apply to the general government. These latter remarks I throw out only for the consideration of the committee who are to be appointed.

Gov. RANDOLPH. I am in favor of appointing a committee; but considering the warmth exhibited in debate on Saturday, I have, I confess, no great hopes that any good will arise from it. Cannot a remedy be devised? If there is danger to the lesser States, from an unequal representation in the second branch, may not a check be found in the appointment of one executive, by electing him by an equality of State votes? He must have the right of interposing between the two branches, and this might give a reasonable security to the smaller States.—Not one of the lesser States can exist by itself; and a dissolution of the confederation, I confess, would produce conventions, as well in the larger as in the smaller States. The principle of self-preservation induces me to seek for a government that will be stable and secure.

Mr. Strong moved to refer the 7th resolve to the same committee.

Mr. WILSON. I do not approve of the motion for a committee. I also object to the mode of its appointment—a small committee is the best.

Mr. LANSING. I shall not oppose the appointment, but I expect no good from it.

Mr. MADISON. I have observed that committees only delay business; and if you appoint one from each State, we shall have in it the whole force of State prejudices. The great difficulty is to conquer former opinions. The motion of the gentleman from South Carolina can be as well decided here as in committee.

Mr. GERRY. The world at large expect something from us. If we do nothing, it appears to me we must have war and confusion—for the old confederation would be at an end. Let us see if no concession can be made. Accommodation is absolutely necessary, and defects may be amended by a future convention.

The motion was then put to appoint a committee on the 8th resolve, and so much of the 7th as was not agreed to. Carried—9 States against 2.

And, *by ballot*, the following members were appointed:

| | |
|---|---|
| Massachusetts, | Mr. Gerry. |
| Connecticut, | Mr. Elsworth. |
| New York, | Mr. Yates. |
| New Jersey, | Mr. Patterson. |
| Pennsylvania, | Mr. Franklin. |
| Delaware, | Mr. Bedford. |
| Maryland, | Mr. Martin. |
| Virginia, | Mr. Mason. |
| North Carolina, | Mr. Davie. |
| South Carolina, | Mr. Rutledge. |
| Georgia, | Mr. Baldwin. |

The convention then adjourned to Thursday, the 5th of July.

## Tuesday, July 3d, 1787.

The *grand committee* met. Mr. Gerry was chosen chairman.

The committee proceeded to consider in what manner they should discharge the business with which they were entrusted. By the proceedings in the convention they were so equally divided on the important question of *representation in the two branches*, that the idea of a conciliatory adjustment must have been in contemplation of the house in the appointment of this committee. But still how to effect this salutary purpose was the question. Many of the members, impressed with the utility of a general government, connected with it the indispensable necessity of a representation from the States *according to their numbers and wealth;* while others, equally tenacious of the rights of the States, would admit of no other representation but such *as was strictly federal*, or in other words, *equality of suffrage*. This brought on a discussion of the principles on which the house had divided, and in a lengthly recapitulation of the arguments advanced in the house in support of these opposite propositions. As I had not openly explained my sentiments on any former occasion on this question, but constantly in giving my vote, *showed my attachment to the national government on federal principles, I took this occasion to explain my motives*—[*See a copy of my speech hereunto annexed.*[1]]

These remarks gave rise to a motion of Dr. Franklin, which after some modification was agreed to, and made the basis of the following report of the committee.

The committee to whom was referred the eighth resolution, reported from the committee of the whole house, and so much of the seventh as had not been decided on, submit the following report:

That the subsequent propositions be recommended to the convention, on condition that both shall be generally adopted.

That in the first branch of the legislature, each of the States now in the union, be allowed one member for every 40,000 inhabitants, of the description reported in the seventh resolution of the com-

---

[1] It is matter of regret that this document cannot be found: the principles it contained are perhaps embodied in the letter from Mr. Yates and Mr. Lansing to Gov. George Clinton, on their retiring from the convention.

mittee of the whole house—That each State, not containing that number, shall be allowed one member.

That all bills for raising or apportioning money, and for fixing salaries of the officers of government of the United States, shall originate in the first branch of the legislature, and shall not be altered or amended by the second branch; and that no money shall be drawn from the public treasury, but in pursuance of appropriations to be originated in the first branch.

That in the second branch of the legislature, *each State shall have an equal vote.*

## Thursday, July 5th, 1787.

Met pursuant to adjournment.

The report of the committee was read.

Mr. GORHAM. I call for an explanation of the principles on which it is grounded.

Mr. Gerry, the chairman, explained the principles.

Mr. MARTIN. The one representation is proposed as an expedient for the adoption of the other.

Mr. WILSON. The committee has exceeded their powers.

Mr. Martin proposed to take the question on the whole of the report.

Mr. WILSON. I do not choose to take a leap in the dark. I have a right to call for a division of the question on each distinct proposition.

Mr. MADISON. I restrain myself from animadverting on the report, from the respect I bear to the members of the committee. But I must confess I see nothing of concession in it.

The originating money bills is no concession on the part of the smaller States, for if seven States in the second branch should want such a bill, their interest in the first branch will prevail to bring it forward—It is nothing more than a nominal privilege.

The second branch, small in number, and well connected, will ever prevail. The power of regulating trade, imposts, treaties, &c. are more essential to the community than raising money, and no provision is made for those in the report—We are driven to an unhappy dilemma. Two thirds of the inhabitants of the union are to please the remaining one third by sacrificing their essential rights.

When we satisfy the majority of the people in securing their rights, we have *nothing* to fear; in any other way, *every thing*. The smaller States, I hope will at last see their true and real interest.— And I hope that the warmth of the gentleman from Delaware will never induce him to yield to his own suggestion of seeking for foreign aid.

[At this period Messrs. YATES and LANSING left the convention, and the remainder of the session was employed to complete the constitution on the principles already adopted. See the revised draft of the constitution and the constitution of the United States, with all the ratified amendments as at present existing, in the appendix.]

☞ The preceding Notes of the late Chief Justice YATES, contained in two hundred and forty-five pages,[2] of two volumes, were copied by me, literally, from the original manuscript in his hand writing.—The several papers referred to did not accompany his notes.

JOHN LANSING, Jun.

---

[2] The number of pages in the manuscript.

# NOTES OF RUFUS KING IN THE FEDERAL CONVENTION OF 1787[1]

Among the manuscripts in the handwriting of Rufus King is one containing an abstract of a portion of the debates in the Convention for the formation of the Constitution, which appears to have been made as the debate proceeded. The copy was written out, nearly verbatim, by him, somewhere about 1818–21 [2] (for the paper bears the watermark of 1818), from rough notes taken at the time. It will be observed that he does not reproduce his own remarks, except in speeches on the powers of the Convention. There is no new information as to the proceedings, or the opinions of members of the Convention, but the reports previously published in the Madison and Yates papers are corroborated in these.

### THURSDAY, MAY 31.

House of Representatives to be elected by the People.

Gerry opposes. Appointment by the State Legislature preferable, because the People want information.

*Mason, Virginia*—in favor of popular choice, because the first Branch is to represent the People. We must not go too far. A portion of Democracy should be preserved; our own children in a short time will be among the general mass.

*Wilson of Penn.* agrees with Mason. We ought to adopt measures to secure the popular confidence, and to destroy the Rivalry between the Genl. and State Governments; in this way both will proceed immediately from the People.

*Madison* agrees with Wilson. The measure immediately introduces the People, and will naturally inspire the affection for the Genl. Govt. that exists toward our own offspring. A legislative appointment will remove the Govt. too far from the People. In Maryland the Senate is two Removes from the People, and a

---
[1] Reprinted from the Life and Correspondence of Rufus King (N. Y., 1894), Vol. I, pp. 587–619.
[2] Probably at the time of the publication of the Madison report. Both this copy and the original notes are in the possession of the Editor.

Deputy appointed by them would be three Removes off; and if the first Branch appoint the second, the Deputy wd. be four Removes—and if the Legislature of the U. S. appoint the President or Executive, the Executive wd. be five Removes from the People. If the Election be made by the People in large Districts, there will be no danger of Demagogues.

*Measure carried.* That first Br. be elected by People of the several States. Mass. N. Y. Penn. Virginia. N. Car. & Georgia—aye. Con. & Del. divided N. Jersey & S. Carolina,—No.

Friday June 1. Com. of the whole.

Executive power to be in one person.

Motion by Wilson Penn. Seconded by Chs. Pinckney So. Car.

Rutledge in favor of the motion.

Sherman preferred leaving the number to the Legislature.

Wilson. An Executive should possess the Power of secresy, vigour & Dispatch, and so constituted as to be responsible. Executive powers are intended for the execution of the Laws, and the appointment of officers not otherwise appointed: a single Executive may be responsible, but a numerous one cannot be responsible.

Madison agreed with Wilson in the Definition of Executive power. *Ex vi termini.* Executive power does not include the Power of War and Peace. Executive Power shd. be limited and defined. If large, we shall have the Evils of Elective Monarchies. Perhaps the best plan will be a single Executive of long duration, with a Council and with Liberty to dissent on his personal Responsibility.

*Gerry.* I am in favor of a Council to advise the Executive: they will be organs of information respecting Persons qualified for the various offices. Their opinions may be recorded, so as to be liable to be called to account & impeached—in this way, their Responsibility will be certain, and for misconduct their Punishment sure.

*Dickinson.* A limited yet vigorous Executive is not republican, but peculiar to monarchy—the royal Executive has vigour, not only by power, but by popular Attachment & Report—an Equivalent to popular attachment may be derived from the Veto on the

Legislative acts. We cannot have a limited monarchy—our condition does not permit it. Republics are in the beginning and for a time industrious, but they finally destroy themselves because they are badly constituted. I dread the consolidation of the States, & hope for a good national Govt. from the present Division of the States with a feeble Executive.

We are to have a Legislature of two branches, or two Legislatures, as the sovereign of the nation—this will work a change unless you provide that the judiciary shall aid and correct the Executive. The first Branch of the Legislature, the H. of Representatives, must be on another plan. The second Branch or Senate may be on the present scheme of representing *the States*—the Representatives to be apportioned according to the Quotas of the States paid into the general Treasury. The Executive to be removed from office by the national Legislature, on the Petition of seven States.

Randolph—by a single Executive, there will be danger of Monarchy or Tyranny. If the Executive consist of three persons, they may act without danger. If of one, he will be dependent on the Legislatures & cannot be impeached till the Expiration of his Office. A single Executive against the Genius of America.

Wilson—There are two important Points to be considered, the extent of the Country & the Manners of the People of the U. S.—the former requires the Vigour of Monarchy, the latter, are against a Kingly Executive, our manners are purely republican.

Montesquieu is favorable to confederated Republics—I also am in favor of this Scheme, if we can take for its Basis, Liberty, and are able to ensure a vigourous execution of the Laws. A single executive is not so likely so soon to introduce Monarchy or Despotism, as a complex one. The People of America did not oppose the King, but the Parliament—Our opposition was not against a Unity, but a corrupt Multitude.

Williamson—There is no true difference between an Executive composed of a single person, with a Council, and an Executive composed of three or more persons.

The Question postponed.

After debating the Powers, the Committee proceeded to discuss the Duration of the Executive Power.

Wilson proposed three years, without rotation or exclusion.

Madison proposed good behaviour, or Seven years with exclusion for ever afterward.

Mason—In favor of Seven years, and future ineligibility—by this Provision the executive is made independent of the Legislature, who may be his Electors—if re-elected, he will be complaisant to the Legislature to obtain their favor & his own Re-election.

On the Question for Seven years—Mass. Gerry & Strong, no. Gorham & King aye—divided.[3] Cont. N. C., S. C. & G. no. N. Y. N. J. Penn. Del. Virginia aye. 5 ayes, 4. nos—1. divided. So the blank filled.

## June 4.

Unity of Executive-power resumed.

On Question of a single executive carried thus.

Mass. Cont. N. Y. Penn. Virg. N. C., S. Car. Georg.—Ay. N. J. Del. Mard.—No.

Motion by *Gerry seconded by Mr. King*, to postpone the article for a Council of Revision, and to vest a qualified Negative in the Executive.

Affirmative all the States except Cont. & Mard.

Wilson second Hamilton—proposed a complete Negative in the Executive. The natural operation of the Legislature will be to swallow up the Executive power: divided power becomes the object of contest; if the powers are equal, each will preserve its own—otherwise the strongest will acquire the whole.

Butler opposed—because it will become a King.

Franklin opposed—Our former Govt. in Penn. abused this power of a full Negative and extorted money from the Legislature, before he would sign their acts—in one instance he refused his Signature to a Bill to march the Militia agt. the Indians, till the Bill exempted from Taxes the Estate of the Proprietors on account of the expense of the Militia.

---

[3] The vote in Journal is 8 yeas—Mass. Con. N. Y. Del. Virg. N. Car. S. Car. Geor. Nays Penna. & Mar.

One man cannot be believed to possess more wisdom than both Branches of the Legislature—the Royal Negative has not been exercised since the Revolution; he easily does by corruption what could be done with some risk by his negative.

Madison—opposed—No man would dare negative a Bill unanimously passed. It is even doubtful whether the King of England wd have Firmness enough to do so.

Mason—opposed—We have voted that the executive power be vested in one person—it is now proposed to give this person a negative in all cases—you have agreed that he shall appoint all officers, not otherwise to be appointed, and those he has not the sole power to appoint, you propose to grant to him the power to negative—with these powers the Executive may soon corrupt the Legislature—the Executive will become a monarchy. We must regard the Genius of our People, which is Republican, & will not receive a King.

Franklin—The Prince of Orange at first had limited Powers, and his office was for Life—his son raised a faction & caused himself to be declared hereditary—we may meet the same fate.

Unanimous negative, except Wilson, Hamilton, King.

Madison—The judiciary ought to be introduced in the business of Legislation—they will protect their department, and united with the Executive make its negatives more strong. There is weight in the objections to this measure but a check on the Legislature is necessary, Experience proves it to be so, and teaches us that what has been thought a calumny on a republican Govt. is nevertheless true—In all Countries are diversity of Interests, the Rich & the Poor, the Dr. & Cr., the followers of different Demagogues, the Diversity of religious Sects—the Effects of these Divisions in ancient Govts. are well known, and the like causes will now produce like effects. We must therefore introduce in our system Provisions against the measures of an interested majority—a check is not only necessary to protect the Executive power, but the minority in the Legislature. The independence of the Executive, having the Eyes of all upon him will make him an impartial judge—add the Judiciary, and you greatly increase his respectability.

Wilson—Wilson moved and Madison seconds, that the judiciary be added to the Executive in revising the Laws.

Dickinson opposed—you shd. separate the Departments—you have given the Executive a share in Legislation; and it is asked why not give a share to the judicial power. Because the Judges are to interpret the Laws, and therefore shd. have no share in making them—not so with the executive whose causing the Laws to be executed is a ministerial office only. Besides we have experience in the Br. Constitution which confers the Power of a negative on the Executive.

☞ the motion was withdrawn.

### JUDICIARY POWER.

Wilson proposes that the judiciary be appointed by the National Executive, because he will be responsible.

Rutledge opposes, because the States generally appoint by their Legislatures.

Franklin—The 15 Lords of Sessions in Scotland are appointed by the Barristers or Doctors—these elect the most learned of their own order, because he has the most Business, wh. afterwards is divided among themselves.

Madison—in favor of further deliberation. Perhaps the appointment shd. be by the Senate—

Postponed—N. H., Mass, NY, Penn & Md. by the Executive power R. Island by the People—Con. N. J. Del. Virg. N. Car. & So. Car elect Judges by Legislatre.

Rutledge proposes to have a supreme Natl. Tribunal but no subordinate ones, except those established by the States respectively.

Wilson of a different opinion.

Dickinson—the State & Genl. Tribunals will interfere—we must have a National Tribunal—entire and proceeding from the Genl Govt.

Madison—proposed to vest the Genl. Govt. with power to establish an independent Judiciary, to be co-extensive with the nation. Ayes, 5, No, 4, divided 2.

## REPRESENTATIVES.

Chs. Pinckney—proposes that the Representatives shd. be chosen by the Legislatures & not by the People—as the old members of Congress are chosen.

Gerry—proposes that the People shd. elect double the requisite number, and out of them the Legislature to choose the authorized number of each State. The People may be imposed upon by corrupt and unworthy men.

Wilson—Representatives shd. be elected by the People, thereby we shall come nearer to the will or sense of the majority—If you give the Election to the State Legislatures, you give it to the Rivals of the General Govt.—the People having parted with sufficient Powers, it remains only to divide these Powers between the Genl. & State Govts.

The People will love & respect the Genl. Govt., if it is founded on their consent & derived from them—it will acquire rank above the State Govts.

Mason—at Present the Reps. in Congress do not represent the People but the States—It is now proposed to form a Gov. for men, not for States—therefore draw the Reps. from the People—the Representation to be faithful shd. shew the Defects of the People; if not, how are they to be corrected? A Representation proceeding from the Legislatures will not afford this correction.

Suppose a majority of the Legislature to be in favor of Paper money, or some other bad measure, would they not elect Members to Congress, holding the same opinions?

Sherman—If the State Govts. remain, they shd. appoint Representatives to Congress—if they are to be swept away, then the People must elect,—the State Govts. must continue—few objects in this case will be before the Genl. Govt.—for war, treaties & commerce—Let the Genl. Govt. be a collateral Govt. to secure the States in particular Exigencies—for war, or war between the States.

I am opposed to a Genl. Govt. & in favor of the independence & Confederation of the States—give the Genl. Govt. powers to regulate Commerce, drawing therefrom a Revenue.

Dickinson—We cannot form a Genl. Gov. unless we draw a Branch from the People, and a Br. from the Legislatures of the States—in theory this is requisite, and to the success of the scheme, it is also essential—the objection to popular Elections arise from the nature of free Govts. and are slight in comparison with the Excellence of such Govts.—the other Branch or Senate must come from the State Legislatures—they will thereby be more respectable, and for Respectability & Duration resemble the Br. H. of Lords. They can come from Legislatures who are & have been opposed to the general Govt.—they shd. be appointed for 3, 5 or 7 years, not subject to a recall and dependent on the Genl. Gov. for support.

Read—We must come to a consolidation—State Govts. must be swept away—we had better speak out—that the People will disapprove is perhaps a mistake—the State Magistrates may disapprove but the People are with us.

Genl. Pinckney—An election in South Carolina by the people is impracticable—the settlements are so sparse, that four or five thousand cannot be assembled to give their votes. I am in favor of an Election by the Legislatures—in So. Carolina the Legislature is against the issue of Paper Money with a tender, but in my Opinion a majority of the People are in favor thereof.

Wilson—I would preserve the State Govts.—there is no danger of their being swallowed up by the Genl. Govt.—the States have overpowered the Confederated Governments—The Amphictionic Council & the Achæan League were destroyed by the encroachments of the Members.

Madison—The Election may be safely made by the People, if you enlarge the sphere of Election—Experience shows this—if bad Elections be made by the People, it will be found to happen in small Districts.

Butler—Until the Ratio be fixed, I am opposed to settling the mode of Election; if this be established on a principle favorable to Wealth as well as numbers of free Inhabitants, I am content to unite with Delaware (Mr. Read) in abolishing the State Legislatures and becoming one nation instead of a Confederacy of Republics.

On question *to choose Reps. by States* Legislatures—

Con., N. Jersey & S. Car. aye. The Eight other States—no. Motion by Wilson seconded by Madison.

To reconsider the partial Negative by the Pr. to vest this power in him jointly with the Judiciary—

Madison—A check requisite, to prevent legislative encroachment in the Judiciary, the Executive, or on private Rights.

By the judiciary Union, the check is increased in power and respectability—the Ex. alone is too weak—the King of Eng. wd. hesitate to negative a Bill unanimously passed by Parliament.

Gerry—The motion aims to unite Departments wh. ought to be separate—the union destroys Responsibility.

Chs. Pinckney—opposed as it destroys Responsibility.

Mason—The Purse & the sword must not be in the same Hands—if so, and the Legislature are able to raise revenue and make and direct war, I shall agree to a Restriction in the Executive, or in a Council of Revision.

Dickinson—hurry, vigour and Despatch are not properties of a Republic—we cannot have these in a Council—but Responsibility of such immense value, we can have by a single Executive—unite the judiciary and you lose Responsibility—the measure is furthermore bad by uniting Departments which should be separate and independent. It will require as great talents & firmness to discharge the other executive Duties, as to interpose a veto on the Laws, wh. shall require two thirds of both branches of the Legislature to remove.

We have not introduced a plurality in the Executive in the former instance and why should we do so in this case? For Reconsideration Con. N. Y. Virginia, ay. 8 others no.

SENATE.

The proposition that the Senate be chosen by the H. of Reps. out of Persons nominated by the State Legislatures being negatived.

*Dickinson* moved that the Senators be appointed by the State Legislatures—because the mind & body of the several States shd. be represented in the national Legislature; and because these Legislatures would choose men of distinguished Talents as Senators—such men would have a chance to be chosen by the People as national Representatives—failing in such choice, Wealth, family, or Talents may recommend them to be appointed Senators—let the Number of Senators be more than 200—by enlarging their number, their influence and weight will be increased by combining the Families and Wealth of the aristocracy and thereby you will establish a Balance against, and a check of the Democracy.

Wilson—if this amendment succeed, we shall not have a National Government—the Senate will be too numerous, representing neither Property, nor numbers, but States or Societies, whose interests may oppose the General Govt.; the consequence will be unfavorable to the Harmony of the Nation.

Madison—We propose to form a National Government, and therefore must abandon Ideas founded in the Plan of a Confederation.

The Senate shd. come from, and represent, the wealth of the Nation, and this being the Principle, the proposed amendment cannot be adopted—besides the numbers will be too large—History proves this proposition, that delegated power has most weight and consequence in the hands of a few. The Roman tribunes when few, checked the Senate—when numerous, they divided, became weak and ceased to be the Guardians of the People, which was the object of their institution.

*Dickinson*—The objection is, that you attempt to unite distinct Interests: I do not consider this Union to be an objection that we should regard—Safety may flow from these various Interests—this diversity exists in the Constitution of England—we cannot abolish the States, and consolidate the whole into one Government—if we could consolidate, I should oppose our doing so. Let our Government be like that of the solar system—let the Genl. Govt. be the Sun and States the Planets, repelled yet attracted, and the whole moving harmoniously in their several orbits.

The objection from Virginia (Madison) that Power delegated to a few will prove a more weighty and efficient check upon the

Democracy, as in the instance of the roman Tribunes, proves too much; they never exceeded Ten; and no one thinks that the Senate should consist of so small a number, as that of the Tribunes at any Time, much less when their number was only three.

*Wilson*—I am not in favor of the abolition of the States. I revere the theory of the British Government, but we cannot adopt it. We have no Laws in favor of Primogeniture—no Distinction of Families—the partition of States destroys the influence of the few. Yet I well know that all confederations have been destroyed by the growth and ambition of some of their Members, and if the State Legislatures appoint the Senators, the Principle will be received by which the antient Confederacies were ruined. I therefore propose that the Senators be elected by the People, and for this purpose, that the territory be formed into convenient divisions or Districts.

*Dickinson*—Opposes Mr. Wilson's substitute, because it is either impracticable, or unfair—the Districts must be parts of a State, or entire States, or parts of distinct States—if the first, how can you prevent fraudulent & corrupt elections; if the second, How can you establish an intermediate body, from which to elect those who have a majority of voters, and who are not elected; if the third, the small States will never have a Senator, therefore it would be unfair.

On Question to agree to Wilson's substitute, Penn. aye, the other 10 States, no.

*Mason*—It is true that the old Confederacies were ruined by gt. overgrown power and the ambition of some of their Members—but their circumstances differed from ours—*We have agreed that the natl. Govt. shall have a negative on the acts of the State Legislatures.*—the danger now is that the national Legislature will swallow up the Legislatures of the States. The Protection from this Occurrence will be the securing to the State Legislatures, the choice of the Senators of the U. S. *So adopted unanimously.*

## June 8.

Charles Pinckney moved, seconded by Madison, to reconsider the vote, giving to the National Legislature power in certain cases to negative the State Laws, in order to vest in the Nat. Legislature power in all cases to negative State Laws. agreed to reconsider.

*Chas. Pinckney*—the violation of Treaties and ordinances, passed by Congress, by Laws enacted by the States, are known by all. The Harmony of the Union calls for this Measure of a general Negative, and the National independence requires the same.

*Williamson*—the State Legislatures ought to possess independent Powers in purely local cases, relating to their separate internal Policy.

*Madison*—A Reconsideration of the amendment seems necessary. I am of opinion that the general Govt. will not be able to compel the large and important States to rescind a popular Law, passed by their respective Legislatures. *If this power does not vest in the national Legislature*, a check will be wanting against the centrifugal force, operating constantly to force the several States off from the common centre, or national union.

*Gerry*—This Power may enable the Genl. Govt. to depress one State for the advantage of another State. It may prevent the encouragement that some States may be inclined to give to manufacturers, or prevent the States from training the militia, and thereby establish a military force, and so a Despotism.

*Wilson*—In the establishmt of society, every man yields to it a power over his Life, his Liberty, his Character & his Property. There is no such reservation, that the individuals shall be subjected to one, and exempt from another, Law. We have seen the Legislatures in our own Country deprive the Citizen of Life, of Liberty & of Property. We have seen Laws of Attainder, Punishment and Confiscation. It we mean to found a national Govt., States must submit like individuals—the Govt. must be supreme—either the national, or State Govt. *must be* so. We should remember the language with which we began the Revolution—We then united in saying Virginia is no more, Massachusetts is no more, we are one in name, let us be one in truth and fact. Unless this Power is vested in the general Govt., the States will be employed by foreign Powers, against the Union. New States will soon be formed, the Inhabitants may be foreigners, and possess foreign affections—and unless the Genl. Govt. can check the State Laws, the nation may be involved in tumult and confusion.

*Dickinson*—There can be no line of separation, dividing the Legislative power between the Genl. and State Governments. The consequence is inevitable that there must be a supreme & august national Legislature—the objection that the States may be prevented from training their Militia, is obviated by the Plan of choosing the Senate by the State Legislatures and the H. of Reps. by the People.

*Bedford*—opposed to the power to negative State Laws. Now Delaware makes $\frac{1}{13}$ of the whole—on the system of equal Representation, Delaware will be only $\frac{1}{90}$th, Virginia & Pennsylvania will constitute $\frac{28}{90}$th. In case of Rivalry in respect to commerce, or manufactures, what will be the chance of Delaware, opposed by those States? Bounties may be given in Virginia & Pennsylvania, and by their influence denied in Delaware—the State Laws may be allowed in the former, and negatived in the latter case.

On the Question to vest a power of Negative in the Natl. Legislature on all State Laws, it was negatived.

Mass., Penn. & Virginia being ay. Delaware divided, & Con., N. Y., N. J., Mar., S. Car. N. Car. & Georgia, no. 7 no, 3 ay, 1 divided.

## JUNE 9.

THE MANNER OF COMPOSING THE H. OF REPRESENTATIVES. THE RATIO OF THE CENSUS.

*Brearly*—opposes the *Equality of Representatives* [4]—numerically it is equal, but in operation it will be unequal—there will be two divisions, or parties—one composed of Mass. Penn. & Virginia; and the other of the 10 other States. If Georgia sends one Rep., Virginia will send 16—these will be united, but the Reps. of the smaller States will act without a common impulse and be divided;

---

[4] *Id est*—according to the Ratio of the Census.

the Rule of the Confed. is unequal, the large & small States have the same Power—correct this, take the Map, and divide the whole into 13 equal Parts, this done, equality of Representation will be just.

*Paterson*—Our Powers do not extend to the abolition of State Governments in order to establish a national Govt.—we may amend the present system, keeping for our Basis the Confederation, which establishes the equality of votes among the States—I consent to the equal Division of the Territory of the U. S. when this *Equality will* be the Parent, or origin, of an equality in the Representation.

But perhaps the Inequality of the present system is not so obvious—the States *being equal*, have equal votes—so in the respective States individuals have equal votes, tho' they possess unequal Property.

Men with 4000 pounds, and those with 100 pounds have equal votes, tho' one possesses 40 times the Property of the other.

Mr. Galloway early in Congress from Penn., proposed that America should be represented in Parliament, America to have 200 & G. Br. 500 members—but it was quickly foreseen that in this way there would be no security of the Liberties of America. In like manner an inequality in Representation from the several States will not succeed—should the Convention approve thereof, they cannot bind the States. I cannot agree to the Project here, and will employ my influence against it in N. Jersey, which never will approve of the Plan.

*Wilson*—The true Doctrine of Representation is, that the Representative ought to speak the language of his Constituents, and that his voice should have the same influence, as if given by his Constituents—Apply this Theory, and the conclusion is in favor of a Ratio of Representation and against the present system.

QUERE IF PATERSON'S PROJECT.

The Powers of the Convention only authorize the enlargement of the Provisions of the Confederation, viz.

1. To grant Powers to Congress to collect an impost on the importation of foreign Goods, to pass stamp acts & to regulate

the post off., to regulate Commerce for. & domestic, provided the fines & forfeitures be recovered in the course of the common Law.

2. Apportionments on the States to be according to the number of Whites & ⅗ of all others—and in case of arrears by the State, to pass Laws remedied of the Evil.

3. Congress to appoint Persons as an Executive to hold their Offices —— years, with fixed salaries & to be ineligible afterwards—removable by Congress on application of a majority of the State Executives, but no member of this Executive to command in any military Expedition.

4. The national Executive to appoint the supreme Judicial magistrates for good behaviour—with Power to try impeachments of officers of Gen'l. Govt., and questions of appeal from State judiciaries, in the construction of treaties, where the Laws of trade & Revenue are affected, or in cases in wh. foreigners are Parties.

5. The Laws & treaties of U. S. to be paramount over State Laws in case of opposition to treaties or general Laws, the Executive to call out the militia to cause the treaties and Laws to be observed.

6. Naturalization to be the same in every State.

7. A citizen guilty of offence in one State, and belonging to another State to be punished as tho' belonging to the State where the offence was committed.

18 JUNE (? 19).

*Madison*—It is an Error to say that because unanimity was requisite to form the Confederation, that unanimity is also required to dissolve it.—A contract may be dissolved by the breach of a single article—such is the Law of Treaties and the same Law is applicable to analagous Compacts—provisions are sometimes made to preserve the Treaty or Compact, not withstanding the breach of a single article.

Georgia without authority and against the articles of the Confederation, declared & prosecuted war agt. the Indians, and afterwards treated for Peace with them. New Jersey expressly refused to comply with a constitutional Requisition—Virginia and Maryland formed a Compact respecting the River Potomac. Pennsylvania & N. York made an agreement about their boundary Line. Massachusetts has raised an army and is now about to augment their military Establishment.

Do not these violations of the Confederation prove *that a federal* Govt. will not answer. the Amphictions had power to decide controversies between the members of the League, to fine offenders, to send ambassadors, to choose the Commander in Chief, to command the general forces and to employ them agt. the States who did not obey the General Regulations. The Athenean League was similar to that of the Amphictions—this League failed by the overgrown power of some of the members. Helvetic Confederation, loose & weak, and the situation of the Swiss differs from our own. The German Confederacy, unequal among themselves—the strength of some members being greater than that of the Confederacy—The Netherland Union, subject to great Defects—could act only by unanimity which is not attainable in difficult cases, and may be defeated by for. influence in the most important.

Our System must be such as to escape these Defects.

*Wilson.* I do not apprehend that the General Govt. will swallow up that of the States—the States and their separate Governments must be preserved—they will harmonize with the Genl. Govt. The U. S. are too extensive for one & a free Govt. No Despot has governed a Country so extensive. Persia is divided into 20 subordinate Govts. and the Roman Empire & Republic was divided between the Proconsuls. Alfred divided England into societies of 10. persons, 100 persons & into Towns and Counties.[5]

---

[5] Objections to a general or national Govt.
See p. 212, Madison Papers. Elliot's *Debates*, vol. v.
The Convention does not possess authority to propose any reform which is not purely general.
2. If they possessed such power it wd. be inexpedient to exercise it, because the small States wd. lose their State influence or equality, and because the Genius of the people is of that sort that such a Reform wd. be rejected.
Answer (R. King) The States under the confed. are not soverign States they can do no act but such as are of a subordinate nature or such as terminate in themselves—and even these are restrained—coinage, P. office &c they are wholly incompetent to the exercise of any of the gt. & distinguishing acts of sovereignty—They can neither make nor receive (embassies) to or from any other sovereign—they have not the powers of injuring another or of defending themselves from an Injury offered from one another—they are deaf, dumb and impotent—these Faculties are yielded up and the U. S. in C. Assd. hold and possess

*Mason*—The Powers are sufficient—and were they not so, we should imitate the Amer. Ministers who negotiated the Treaty of Peace & did so without full Powers, trusting to the Congress to ratify.

Moreover the proposed System is not impracticable—the public opinion is not opposed to it—the Impost was opposed because the Congress consisted of a single Branch, possessing Legislative, judicial and executive powers. They were unworthy of being entrusted with additional Powers,—the People would not rest satisfied with the secret Journals of a Conclave.

The whole People agree in two points—first, that the Government should be Republican—Second, that the Legialature shd. consist of two Branches.

That two branches shd. be unanimously adopted, must have happened by a miracle, or by a fixed and universal opinion of the People.

The Gentlemen from N. Jersey adhere to the plan of the Confederation, and think that Requisition, after all experience, may be made on the State, and, if requisite, executed by military Force. I think that this cannot be accomplished. We can no

---

them, and they alone can exercise them—they are so far out of the controul of the separate States yt. if every State in the Union was to instruct yr. Deleg., and those Delegates within ye powers of the Arts. of Union shd. do an act in violation of their Instructions it wd. nevertheless be valid. If they declared a war, any giving aid or comfort to the enemy wd. be Treason; if peace, any capture on the high seas wd. be piracy. This remark proves yt. the States are now subordinate corporations or societies and not sovereigns—these imperfect States are the confederates and they are the electors of the magistrates who exercise the national sovereignty. The Articles of Confedr. are perpetual Union, are partly federal & partly of the nature of a constitution or form of Govt. arising from and applying to the Citizens of the U. S. & not from the individual States.

The only criterion of determining what is federal & what is national is this, those acts which are for the government of the States only are purely federal, those which are for the government of the Citizens of the individual States are national and not federal.

If then the articles of Confedr. & perpetual union have this twofold capacity, and if they provide for an alteration in a certain mode, why may not they be so altered as that the federal article may be changed to a national one, and the national to a federal? I see no argument that can be objected to the authority. The 5th article regulates the influence of the several States and makes them equal—does not the confed. authorize this alteration, that instead of this Equality, one state may have double the Influence of another—I conceive it does—and so of every Article except that wh. destroys the Idea of a confedy. I think it may be proved that every article may be totally altered provided you have one guarantying to each State the right of regulating its private & internal affairs in the manner of a subordinate corporation.

But admitting that the Arts. of Confed. & perpet. Union, or the powers of the Legis. did not extend to the proposed Reform; yet the public Deputations & the public Danger require it—the system proposed to be adopted is no scheme of a day, calculated to postpone the hour of Danger, & thus leave it to fall with double ruin on our successors—It is no crude and undigested plan; the child of narrow and unextensive views, brought forward under the Auspices of Cowardice & Irresolution—It is a measure of Decision, it is the foundation of Freedom & of national Glory. It will draw on itself and be able to support the severest scrutiny & Examination. It is no idle experiment, no romantic speculation—the measure forces itself upon wise men, and if they have not firmness to look it in the face and protect it—Farewell to the Freedom of our Government—our military glory will be tarnished and our boasts of Freedom will be the scorn of the Enemies of Liberty.

Rufus King

more execute civil Regulations by the Militia, than we can unite opposite Elements, mingle fire with water—besides military coercion does not distinguish between the innocent and the guilty—and it would therefore be unjust. I will never consent to abolish the State Govts., because no General Govt. can perform their Duties. We may proceed a certain length in favor of the Genl. Govt., but for myself, I will take equal care of the State Govts. We cannot make a perfect System, there will after doing our best be faults in the work and we can trust our successors with further Amendments.

*Martin*—The Confederation was formed for the safety & Protection of the particular States, and not for the safety & protection of the union. I cannot support the Genl. Govt. at the Expence of the State Govts., but will contend for the Safety and Happiness of the particular States at the expense of the U. S.

*Sherman.* Two Branchs not requisite, one is sufficient and most fit for a Confederation. No example can be given of two Branches in a federal Govt.—Increase the powers of Congress—preserve the States and avoid a Consolidation of them. Our Treaties would become void by the abandonment of the Articles of Confederation—these were formed by & with the U. S. of N. H., Mass., &c.

*Wilson.* It is made a question whether the Legislature shall be composed of one of two bodies—whether it shall be elected by the States, or by the People,—and whether the States shall be equally represented, or in proportion to their respective wealth & numbers.—The antient Confederacies were formed in the infancy of Politicks and soon fell victims to the inefficacy of their organization. Because they had only a single body, it is not therefore expedient that we shd. follow their example.

The Dutch & Swiss Confederacies have been preserved by external balances—The German League is kept by the predominance of the imperial House. Our equality of Votes was an occasional Compact, produced in a crisis of our Affairs. The Great States conducted like the true mother in the controversy of the Harlots—they like her, in the claim of her child, gave their sovereignty to the small States, rather than it shd. be destroyed by the British King.

## June 20 (? 21).

*Johnson*—The Gentleman from N. York is praised by all, but supported by no Gentleman. He goes directly to the abolition of the State Governments. All other Gentlemen agree that the Genl. Govt. shd. be made more powerful and the State Govt. less powerful. In the Virginia Plan, Provision is made to increase the general Powers, but it contains no Provision for the security of the States—The Plan of N. Jersey provides for the Security of the Genl. & State Govts. If the advocates for the Virginia Plan can show that it affords to the States security against the Gen. Govt. we may all agree.

*Wilson*—We have agreed that the Legislatures shall appoint one Branch of the national Govt.—give to the National Gov. power reciprocally to appoint one Br. of each State Legislature—How wd. this endanger the States? What Power of the States would the General Govt. desire to have? Would a portion of the State powers, were they acquired, be of considerable importance to the Genl. Govt.? any attempt to acquire the same would excite and the People would not suffer it.

*Madison*—The History of the antient Confederacies proves, that there has never been Danger of the ruin of the State Govts. by Encroachment of the General Govt., but the converse is true, the particular Govts. have overthrown the Genl. Govt. I have therefore been assiduous to guard the general Govt. from the power of the State Govts. These Govt's. regulate the conduct of their Citizens, they punish offenders, cause ordinary Justice to be administered & perform acts which endear the Govt. to the People, who will not suffer the general Govt. to injure the State Govts.

☞ The Convention resolved that the Genl. Legislature shd. consist of two Branches. So. Carolina moved that Representatives shd. be chosen as the several State Legislatures shd. judge proper.

*Madison and Wilson* opposed the Election by State Legislatures and recommended the Election by the People. State Elections will introduce State influence opposed to that of the Genl. Govt. The States will elect to Congress and manage the affairs of the States also—if the State Legislatures elect, they will also instruct and so embarrass the Representatives—otherwise, if elected by the People. There will be no difficulty in popular Elections—the returns may be made to the State Legislatures who may settle contested Elections.

Decided 4 ay, 1 divided—6 no. Motion negatived.

### DURATION OF TERM OF REPRESENTATIVES.

*Dickinson*—Annual Elections are favorites in America—it suits England which is a small country. But annual, biennial or triennial are two short terms for America—I would consent to three years with a classification by wh. one third shd. expire and be renewed annually.

*Strong & Ellsworth*—Except So. Carolina we are all accustomed to annual Elections.

*Wilson* also agrees to annual Elections.

Mason—An annual Election will give an advantage to some over other States—in Virginia & Georgia, from our sparse and remote settlements, we could not ascertain in less than three years who were elected—The States that are most compactly settled will be the first on the floor, and those of extensive settlements will be absent, unless the Elections precede for a long time the time of meeting.

*Hamilton*—I prefer three years to a longer or shorter Term. The Dependence on Constituents is sufficient, & the independence of the members as little as it ought to be.

### JUNE 25.

#### ELECTION OF SENATE.

*Wilson*—Every man will possess a double character. He will be a citizen of a particular State and also of the U. S. The National Legislature will apply to the latter, and should therefore be chosen by the citizens of the U. S., and not by the State

Legislatures—because the Members of the State Legislatures are particularly chosen on account of their State Citizenship and attachments—they have a remote connexion with the Genl. Govt. and a direct and intimate one with that of the several States.

The Distinction indicates the character of the Electors of the Senate, and the Circumstance shd. influence our decision in respect to the choice of the Senators. The General Govt. is separate and distinct from the State Govts.; War, Peace, Commerce, Revenue, are the particular concerns of the Genl. Govt., while inferior and local interests are confided to the State Government. In whatever concerns the Questions confided to the Genl. Govt., we act as Citz. of the U. S., and in relation to the interests intrusted to the State Govts. we act as Citz. of the respective States. We should not then refer ourselves to the Legislatures of the States in appointing the Senators of the U. S., but should proceed on the Basis of the People, and choose the Senators by Electors appointed by the People.

*Ellsworth*—We must build our Genl. Govt. on the strength & vigour of the State Govts. The Genl. Govt. could not proceed without their support, or by the help of a large standing army. Massachusetts is unable to go on with her republican Govt. without an army—Virginia cannot & does not govern Kentucky—Each of these States (Mass. & Virg.) are too large for a Republican System. I am in favor of the old scheme & for proceeding on the continuation of the States, and therefore for electing Senators of the U. S. by the State Legislatures.

*Johnson*—When the Question of State Security or individuality occurred, it was urged by Mr. Wilson & Mr. Madison that the States were secured by the Rights of their Legislatures to appoint the Senators of the U. S. If their security depend on this mode of choice, the proposed plan to elect the Senators by Electors chosen by the people would destroy the promised security of choosing them by the Legislatures of the States.

*Mason*—The national Executive has a negative on the two Branches and each Branch has a negative on the other. The Genl. Govt. moreover has a negative on the several State Legislatures, and this Regulation is necessary on the principle of Self-

Defence, which is an instinctive Principle, or Law of Nature; and in a suitable degree shd. be possessed by natural and artificial bodies—being granted to the Genl. Govt., why withhold it from the State Govt.? What other influence over, or check upon the Genl. Govt. will the States possess, if their Legislatures do not elect the Senate or second Branch of the Natl. Govt. I am unwilling to have the States without a self-protecting Power—as I desire the continuance of the several States, I shall not agree to deprive them of the Faculty of self-Protection.

## JUNE 27.

That the suffrage of the first Branch of the Legislature (the H. of R.) ought not to be equal among the States.

*Martin.* The States are equal and we have agreed in the Equality of votes excepting Virginia & N. Carolina, the latter being divided—By giving more votes to the large than to the small States, the large ones will combine and tyrannize over the small States—these States would have 42 of 90 votes in the first Branch—Now, under the confederation, seven States may combine—but they are the constitutional majority.

(Remarks. The Ratio of taxes is determined by the 8 art. of the Confederation wh. gives equal votes to the States—even the Post office cannot be so regulated as to obtain a Revenue beyond the Expenses of supporting—but under the proposed amendment the Power of taxation is not limited, but may be exercised in such manner as the national Legislature may prefer.)

*Martin—continued—*The amendment of the Confederation must be made in reference to the State Govts. and for their Safety & Protection—all which relates to external, and concerns that are merely national, may be granted to the U. S. while all that is internal and relative to the individuals of the separate States must continue to belong to the particular States—If further Powers to the U. S. become requisite a future Convention may propose them to the States. If we give more than enough now, it can never be retained (resumed). We hear it said, that if the Genl. Govt. makes Laws affecting individuals instead of States the Govt.

ceases to be federal—but if the persons and concerns affected by the laws of the Genl. Govt. be foreign or external, the Govt. would be merely federal as regards everything within the power of the States separately, which would remain wholly subject to State Laws—the States being equal must have equal influence and equal votes.

All men out of Society are by nature equal, in freedom and every other Property of men. Locke, Vattel and all other writers establish this Truth.

## JUNE 28.

*Madison*—The Gentlemen opposed to a Representation founded upon the number of Citizens of the respective States, are somewhat inaccurate in their observations—They speak of Tyranny and of the small States being swallowed up by the large ones—They apprehend combinations between Mass. Penn. & Virginia against the other States. But there is nothing in Religion, manners, modes of thinking or Habits of any sort, manufactures or course of Business, commerce or natural Productions which would create a common interest or Prejudice between these States exclusive of all others. There is no fact in the history of men or nations that authorizes such a Jealousy. England and France might have combined to divide America. The great States of Greece, Athens & Sparta, which were members of the Amphictionic League never combined to oppress their co-estates—instead thereof, they were Rivals and fought each other. The greater Cantons of the Helvetic Union, did not combine against the small Cantons; no such combination has existed in the Union of the Netherlands. Instead of Combination, the great States of Germany have often been at war with each other—These are not only Historical Facts, but they proceed from a Law of Nature that governs men and Nations, which are but aggregates of men. When men or Nations are strong and equal they become Rivals and Jealousy prevents their Union.

*Chas. Pinckney.* The Honors & Offices may become the objects of strong desire and of combination to acquire them. If Representatives be apportioned among the States in the Ratio of numbers, the Citizens will be free and equal but the States will be unequal, and their sovereignty will be degraded.

---

FRIDAY, JUNE 29.

*Johnson.* The two sides of the House reason in such a manner that we can never meet. Those who contend for the equality of votes between the States, define a State to be a mere association of men and affirm these associations to be equal; on the other side, they who contend for the apportionment of votes according to numbers, define a State to be a District, or country with a certain number of Inhabitants, like a parish or county; and these say that these Districts should have an influence in proportion to the number of their Inhabs. Both reason correctly from their Premises. We must compromise and gratify both; let one branch be composed according to the Rule of Equality, and the other by the Rule of Proportion.

*Madison.* We are vague in our language. We speak of the Sovereignty of the States. The States are not sovereign in the full extent of the term. There is a gradation from a simple corporation for limited and specified objects, such as an incorporation of a number of Mechanicks up to a full sovereignty as possessed by independent Nations, whose Powers are not limited. The last only are truly sovereign. The States, who have not such full power, but are deprived of such as by the Confedn. compose the natl. powers are in the true meaning of the word Sovereigns. They are political associations or corporations, possessing certain powers—by these they may make some, but not all, Laws.

*Hamilton.* Men are naturally equal, and societies or States, when fully independent, are also equal. It is as reasonable, and may be as expedient, that States should form Leagues or compacts, and lessen or part with their national Equality, as that men should form the social compact and, in doing so, lessen or surrender the natural Equality of men. This is done in every society; and the grant to the society affects Persons and Property; age, minority & Estates are all affected.

A Man may not become an Elector or Elected, unless of a given age & having a certain Estate. Let the People be represented according to numbers, the People will be free: every Office will be equally open to all and the majority of the People are to make the Laws. Yet it is said that the States will be destroyed & the People will be Slaves—this is not so. The People are free, at the expense of an artificial & ideal Equality of the States.

On this Question for apportionment.

 Cont. N. Yk, N. Jersey & Delaware—No.
 Maryland            divided
 Mass. Penn. Virg. N. Car. S. Car. Georgia—ay.

*Ellsworth* moved that in the second Br., or Senate, each State should have one Vote only. As the first, or Democratic, Br. represents the People, let the second Br., or Senate, represent the States. The People will thus be secured and the States protected. Without we agree in this motion we shall have met in vain. None of the eastern States, except Mass. will consent to abolish the States. If the southern States agree to a popular, instead of a State, Representation we shall produce a separation. The Union must be cut in two at the Delaware. This plan of forming the Senate is to give an equal vote to the States, will secure the small States, and as the numbers of the large States will have more influence, tho' they have the same & an equal vote with the small States, they will receive no injury. Holland has but one Vote in the States, yet her influence is greater than that of any two of the States. There is Danger that the large States may combine to overpower the small States; the danger is not so great by reason of the distance between the large States, still there is danger; they will be able to combine and therefore there is danger. Three or four can more easily enter into Combinations than nine or ten.

*Madison.* One Gentleman from Connecticut has proposed doing as much as is prudent now, leaving future amendments to Posterity,—this is a dangerous doctrine. The Defects of the Amphictionic League were acknowledged, but were never reformed. The Netherlands have four times attempted to make amendments in their Confederation, but have failed in each attempt. The Fear of innovation, the hue & Cry in favour of the Liberty of the People will as they have done prevent the necessary Reforms. If the States have equal Votes & influence in the Senate we shall be in the utmost danger, the minority of the People will govern the majority. Delaware during the late war opposed and defeated an Embargo, to which twelve States had agreed, and continued to supply the enemy with Provisions in time of war.

## 30 June.

### SHALL THE SENATE BE EQUALLY APPD. AMONG THE STATES?

*Wilson.* The proportionate Representation in the H. of R. was opposed by 22 out of 90: the latter number standing for the who. Population. The Equality of votes among the States will subject the majority of the People & Property to be governed by the minority of each—even if the States, being a majority, make $\frac{24}{66}$ths of the whole—and will be able to govern and control $\frac{66}{90}$ths. This is too palpable an error, too great a Defect in the Constitution to permit the expectation of public harmony & Happiness.

The Gentleman from Connecticut (*Ellsworth*) urges that if the Representation in the Senate be in proportion to the numbers of the People, we shall establish an aristocracy or monarchy—three or four large States may combine for monarchy; if not so, for aristocracy. 4 States containing a majority of People will govern 9 other States—but the danger of combination & aristocracy is not greater, nor so great, among the large States as the small ones. Seven States contain only $\frac{24}{90}$ths of the People: if the 24 control the 66, this would in reality be an Aristocracy—and one that could not endure.

## July 5.

### SHALL THE RATIO OF REPRESENTATIVES BE 40,000?

*G. Morris*—Mere numbers should not be the rule: tho' it may be a fit rule at present, it will cease to be so, when the Western Country is settled. We should take care not to establish a Rule, that will enable the poor but numerous Inhabitants of the West to destroy or oppress the Atlantic States. Men do not enter into Society to preserve their Lives or Liberty—the Savages possess both in perfection—they unite in Society for the Protection of Property.

*Genl. Rutledge.* I agree with Mr. Morris. Property is the object of Society. I therefore propose that the Representation should be in proportion to the taxes paid in given Districts—let the property be represented. I do not consider Numbers to be a true index of wealth even now, hereafter it will become less so.

### SATURDAY, JULY 7.

IN THE HOUSE. ON THE REPORT OF GENL. COMEE. SHALL THE STATES HAVE EQUAL VOTES IN THE SENATE?

*Gerry.* I agree to the measure, provided that the first Br. (H. of Reps.) shall originate money bills and money appropriations. The prejudices as well as the interest of our Constituents must be regarded—two or three thousand men are in office in the States—their influence will be in favor of an Equality of votes among the States.

*Madison.* Equality in the Senate will enable a minority to hold a majority, and to oblige them to submit to their interests, or they will withdraw their assent to measures essential and necessary to the general Good. I have known one man, when the State was represented by only two, and they were divided, oppose six States in Congress on an important occasion for three days, and finally compel them to gratify his caprice in order to obtain his suffrage. The Senate will possess certain exclusive Powers, such as the appointments to office, if the States have equal votes; a minority of People will appoint the Great Offices. Besides the small States may be near the Seat of Govt.—a bare Quorum of the H. of R. may be easily assembled, and carry a bill against the sense of a majority if all were present, and the Senate, tho' all were present, might confirm such Bill. Virginia has objected to every addition of the powers of Congress, because she has only $\frac{1}{13}$ of the Power when she ought to have one sixth.

*Paterson.* I hope the question will be taken: if we do not give equal votes in the Senate to the States, the small States agreeing that money Bills and appropriations shall originate in the H. of Reps., elected according to numbers, it must not be expected that the small States will agree to the amendments of the Confederation. Let us decide this question and lose no more time. I think that I shall vote against the provision, because I think that the exclusive originating of money Bills & appropriations by the H. of Reps. is giving up too much on the part of the small States.

*Gov. Morris.* Let us examine what the small States call the consideration which they are to give for the adventure of an equal vote in the Senate. How did it happen that the small States acquired this advantage of an equal vote? When England pressed hard upon us, the small States said go on with your opposition without us, or give us an equal vote; and so they obtained it. And now they call the Confederation, made under these circumstances, a sacred Compact, that cannot be changed. We are met to propose new and further powers for the Genl. Govt. The great States may truly say that the Confederation is defective, it wants more power, especially as respects the levying of Taxes, and the regulation of Trade—we are sensible of this Truth, but we also know the further Defect of the want of a proportionate Representation in Congress, and are unwilling to add to the Powers unless the Representation bear a just Proportion to the power we confer & the interest that we shall have in the Regulations of the General Govt. Unless we can agree with others in establishing a vigourous General Government, we must for our own safety make vigourous State Govts., & not depend on a weak General Govt. Germany has an Emperor and a powerful one, a common Language; her religion, customs, Habits and interests are not dissimilar, yet the glory of her Princes and the Prosperity of her free cities are preferred to those of the Empire, whose honors are less esteemed than those of the subordinate Princess—In our plan we propose an Aulic Council, but we shall have no Emperor to execute its Decrees.

## July 15.

On question to apportion the Senate differently from the Rule of Equality in the votes, as proposed by Ch. Pinckney 4 ayes, 6 noes, 1 divided—Gorham being absent, Massachusetts, Strong & Gerry against King, voted with the noes.

---

MEMORANDUM.

## July 15, '87.

About twelve days since the Convention appointed a Grand Comee, consisting of Gerry, Ellsworth, Yates, Paterson, Franklin, Bedford, Martin, Mason, Rutledge & Baldwin to adjust the Representation in the two Brs. of the Legislature of the U. S. They reported yt. every 40,000 Inhabs. taken agreeably to the Resolution of Cong. of ye 18 Ap. 1783, shd. send one member to the first Br. of the Legislatre, yt. this Br. shd. originate exclusively Money Bills, & also originate ye appropriations of money; and that in ye Senate or upper Br. each State shd. have one vote & no more. The Representation as to the first Br. was twice recommitted altho' not to the same Committee; finally it was agreed yt Taxation of the direct sort & Representation shd. be in direct proportion with each other—that the first Br. shd. consist of 65 members, viz. N. H. 3, M. 8, R. I. 1, C. 5, N. Y. 6, N. J. 4, P. 8, D. 1, M. 6, V. 10, N. C. 5, S. C. 5, G. 3,—and that the origination of money Bills and the Appropriations of money shd. belong in the first instance to yt Br., but yt in the Senate or 2nd Br. each State shd. have an equal Vote. In this situation of the Report it was moved by S. Car. that in the formation of the 2nd Br., instead of an equality of Votes among the States, that N. H. shd. have 2, M. 4, R. I. 1, C. 3, N. Y. 3, N. J. 2, P. 4, D. 1, M. 3, V. 5, N. C. 3, S. C. 3, G. 2 = total 36.

On the question to agree to this apportionment, instead of the equality (Mr. Gorham being absent) Mass., Con., N. Jer., Del., N. Car., & Georg—No. Penn., Mar., Virg. & S. Car. Aye.

This Question was taken and to my mortification by the vote of Mass. lost on the 14th July.

(endorsed "inequality lost by vote of Mass.")

---

### AUG. 7TH.

3rd Article. A negative in *all cases* proposed to be altered to all cases in which Each Branch has concurrent jurisdiction.

*Madison* proposed to strike the clause out, which was done. He also proposed to omit the provision, fixing the time when the Legislature should meet.

*Morris*—in favor of leaving the time of meeting to the Legislature, and observed that if the time be fixed in the Constitution, it would not be observed, as the Legislature wd. not be punctual in assembling.

*Gorham*—in favor of the Legislature's meeting once a year and of fixing the time. They should meet, if for no other Business, to superintend the Conduct of the Executive.

*Mason*—in favor of an annual meeting.—The Legislatures are also inquisitorial and should meet frequently to inspect the conduct of the public Officers.

4 Art. § 1. Electors to be the same as those of the most numerous Branch of the State Legislature.

. *Morris* proposed to strike out the Clause, and to leave it to the State Legislatures to establish the Qualification of the Electors and Elected, or to add a clause giving to the Nat. Legislature powers to alter the qualifications.

*Ellsworth*—If the Legislature can alter the qualifications, they may disqualify three fourths, or a greater portion of the Electors —this would go far to create aristocracy. The clause is safe as it stands—the States have staked their liberties on the Qualifications which we have proposed to confirm.

*Dickinson*—It is urged that to confine the Right of Suffrage to the Free-Holders is a step towards the creation of an aristocracy. This cannot be true. We are all safe by trusting the owners of the soil; and it will not be unpopular to do so, for the Freeholders are the more numerous Class. Not from freeholders, but from those who are not freeholders, free Govts. have been endangered. Freeholds are by our Laws of inheritance divided among the children of the deceased, and will be parcelled out among all the worthy men of the State; the merchants & mechanicks may become freeholders; and without being so, they are Electors of the State Legislatures, who appoint the Senators of the U. S.

*Ellsworth*—Why confine the Right of Suffrage to freeholders? The Rule should be that he who pays and is governed, should be an Elector. Virtue & Talents are not confined to the Freeholders, and we ought not to exclude them.

*Morris.* I disregard sounds and am not alarmed with the word aristocracy, but I dread the thing and will oppose it, and for this reason I think that I shall oppose this Constitution because it will establish an Aristocracy. There cannot be an aristocracy of Freeholders if they all are Electors. But there will be, when a great & rich man can bring his poor Dependents to Vote in our Elections—unless you establish a qualification of Property, we shall have an aristocracy. Limit the Right of suffrage to freeholders, and it will not be unpopular, because nine Tenths of the Inhabitants are freeholders.

*Mason.* Every one who is of full age and can give evidence of his common Interest in the Community should be an Elector. By this Rule, freeholders alone have not this common Interest. The Father of a family, who has no freehold, has this Interest. When he is dead his children will remain. This is a natural interest or bond which binds men to their country—lands are but an artificial tie. The idea of counting freeholders as the true and only persons to whom the Right of Suffrage shd. be confided is an English Prejudice. In England, a Twig and Turf are the Electors.

*Madison.* I am in favor of entrusting the Right of Suffrage to Freeholders only. It is a mistake that we are governed by English attachments. The Knights of the Shires are chosen by freeholders, but the members of the Cities and Boroughs are elected by freemen without freeholds, & who have as small property as the Electors of any other country. Where is the crown influence seen, where is corruption in the Elections practiced—not in the Counties, but in the Cities and Boroughs.

*Franklin.* I am afraid that by depositing the Right of Suffrage in the freeholders exclusively we shall injure the lower Class of freemen. This Class possess hardy Virtues and great Integrity. The revolutionary war is a glorious Testimony in favor of Plebeian Virtue—our military and naval men are sensible of this Truth. I myself know that our Seamen who were Prisoners in England refused all the allurements that were made use of, to draw them from their allegiance to their Country—threatened with ignominious Halters, they still refused. This was not the case with the English Seamen, who, on being made Prisoners entered into the American Service and pointed out where other Prisoners could be made—and this arose from a plain cause. The Americans were all free and equal to any of their fellow citizens—the English Seamen were not so. In antient Times every free man was an Elector, but afterwards England made a Law which required that every Elector should be a freeholder. This Law related to the County Elections—the Consequence was that the Residue of the Inhabitants felt themselves disgraced, and in the next Parliament a law was made, authorizing the Justice of the Peace to fix the Price of Labour and to compel Persons who were not freeholders to labour for those who were, at a stated rate, or to be put in Prison as idle vagabonds. From this Period the common People of England lost a great Portion of attachment to their Country.

---

WEDNESDAY 8. AUGUST.

QUALIFICATIONS OF ELECTORS OF REPS.

*Gorham.* The Qualifications (being such as the several States prescribe for Electors of their most numerous Branch of the Legislature) stand well. Gentlemen are in error, who suppose the Electors of Cities may not be trusted. In England the members chosen in London, Bristol & Liverpool are as independent as the members of the Counties of England. The Crown has little or no influence in City Elections, but has great influence in Boroughs, where the Votes of Freeholders are bought & sold. There is no risk in allowing the merchants & mechanicks to be Electors;

they have been so time immemorial in this Country & in England. We must not disregard the Habits, usages & Prejudices of the People. Propose a window Law in New England and you would offend the People; propose a Poor Tax in Old England, and it would in like manner offend the People. So if you exclude Merchants & Mechanicks from the list of Electors you will offend them.

Question respecting qualification of Elector & between Resident, Inhabitant with residence of 3 years.

*Morris* proposed that Freeholders only shd. be Electors of Reps.

*Rutledge* proposed Residence for 7 years in the State.

*Mason.* I am in fav. of Residence being a qualification of Representation, otherwise a stranger may offer and by corruption obtain an Election. Without this security, we may have a Borough system and Eng. Corruption. After several votes the Question settled as in ye Constitution.

### NATURALIZATION

14 years Residence after naturalization being proposed as requisite to be chosen a Senator of the U. S.—it was said to be illiberal.

*Morris.* Liberal and illiberal are relative and indefinite Terms. The Indians are the most liberal of any People, because when Strangers come among them, they offer their wives and daughters for their carnal amusement. It is recommended that we throw open our Doors, and invite the oppressed of all Nations to come & find an asylum in America. It is true we have invited them to come & worship in our Temple, but we have never proposed that they should become Priests at our Altars. We should cherish the Love of our Country and exalt its honour—these are wholesome Prejudices in its favor. Foreigners cannot learn our Laws or understand our constitution under fourteen years. Seven years are requisite to learn to be a shoemaker, & double this Term will be necessary to learn to be an American Legislator; and it will require at least fourteen years to eradicate native attachment & the affections of Education.

*Franklin* opposed to fourteen years. It will be illiberal. We have many good friends in England and other parts of Europe who ought not to be excluded.

*Wilson*, opposed to fourteen years.

### POWERS OF THE CONVENTION

Endorsed "Federal Constitution Speeches in Genl. Convention 1787"

K. We have power to propose anything, but to conclude nothing.

We may expect the approbation of Congress and hope for that of the Legislatures of the States. It is not so sure as some Gentlemen believe it to be, that the Power of the States is the idol of the People, and that they are unwilling to see established a general or national Govt. A citizen of N. Jersey who may be gratified by being called so, will not feel himself degraded by being called a Citizen of the U. S. The object of our Convention is to increase the power of the general Govt. and that too at the expense of the State Govts.

It is not requisite, nor expedient, that the Rights or power of the People should be diminished—they have already given powers sufficient both for the State & general Govt. and all that we are called upon for, is to make a right Division of these Powers between the General and the State Governments. Whether we regard the Power, which makes the Laws, or that which interprets them, or that by which they are carried into execution, nothing further is necessary then a proper division of each Department between the Genl. and the State Govts.

The organization of the State Govts. will remain, or may be altered by the States respectively. Our business is to organize the General Govt., to divide it into Legislative, executive & judicial bodies; and to do this on safe Principles, neither giving to either too much power, nor too little, beginning with the Legislative and causing the judicial & executive power to be co-extensive. To constitute the Legislature of a free Govt. it must rest upon the Power of the People, and be created by them—not like the Power of Congress, which rests upon the States & is unsound because it rests upon a single unbalanced body. Moreover it is unequally composed, the Equality of Votes is a Vicious Principle that cannot be endured—tho' with the actual Powers of Congress, it has hitherto been borne, the badness of the Principle is such that the large States will not consent to enlarge these Powers—if further Powers be given, the National Legislature must be appointed in Proportion to the numbers & wealth of the several States. It must also be divided into two Branches—by this means it may be balanced, which is impracticable with one Body.

And tho' to restrain and balance the Powers of the Legislature it must be divided, the contrary is true with the Executive. Division of the Executive destroys Responsibility the members contend with each other, or combine for bad purposes—the first Triumvirs at Rome, and afterwards the Consuls prove that this will be the case.

The Judiciary must be independent, and its powers co-extensive with those of the Natl. Govt.

# NOTES OF WILLIAM PATERSON IN THE FEDERAL CONVENTION OF 1787.[1]

## I. NOTES OF THE VIRGINIA PLAN, MAY 29.[2]

Govʳ Randolph—

Propositions founded upon republican Principles.

1. The Articles of the Confᵈⁿ should be so enlarged and corrected as to answer the Purposes of the Instⁿ

2. That the Rights of Suffrage shall be ascertained by the Quantum of Property or Number of Souls—This the Basis upon which the larger States can assent to any Reform.

Objⁿ—Sovereignty is an integral Thing—We ought to be one Nation[3]—

3. That the national Legʳ should consist of two Branches—

4. That the Members of the first Branch should be elected by the People, etc. This the democratick Branch—Perhaps, if inconvenient, may be elected by the several Legʳˢ—

5. Members of the 2ᵈ Branch to be elected out of the first—to continue for a certain Length of Time, etc. To be elected by Electors appointed for that Purpose—

6. The Powers to be vested in the national Legʳ—A negative upon particular acts, etc. contravening the Articles of the Union—Force—

7. A national Executive to be elected by the national Legʳ

    Checks upon the Legʳ and Ex. Powers—

1. A Council of Revision to be selected out of the ex. and judʸ. Departments, etc.[4]

---

[1] Text and notes reprinted from the American Historical Review, Vol. IX (Washington, 1904), pp. 312-340.

[2] Cf. *Documentary History of the Constitution*, III. 17-20. The original of this paper is in the possession of Miss Emily K. Paterson, of Perth Amboy, New Jersey. It is evidently a condensation, perhaps hastily made, of Randolph's plan presented to the convention May 29.

[3] The purport of this interpolated comment is not plain; but it would seem to be the center of what Paterson afterward contended for *viz*. the convention could not divide up the sovereignty of the states; if there was to be one nation, the states must be thrown together.

[4] Beginning with this note the remaining eight resolutions of the fifteen are summed up, though not numbered as in the plan.

879

2. A nat! Judiciary to be elected by the nat! Leg:—To consist of an inferior and superior Tribunal—To determine Piracies, Captures, Disputes between Foreigners and Citizens, and the Citizen of one State and that of another, Revenue-matters, national Officers—

1. Provision for future States—

2. A Guar⟨y⟩ by the United States to each State·of its Territory, etc.

3. Continuation of Congress till a given Day.

4. Provision, that the Articles of national Union should be amended—

5. That the leg. ex. and jud⟨y⟩ Officers should be bound by Oath to observe the Union.

6. That Members be elected by the People of the several States to ratify the Articles of National Union—

## II. REPORT OF THE COMMITTEE OF THE WHOLE, JUNE 13.[5]

Report of the Committee of the whole House

1. Resolved, that [*it is*] the [*opinion of this Committee* of the U. S.

*that a National*] Government ∧ ought to [*be established*] consist [*ing*] of a Supreme Legislative, Judiciary, and Executive.

Agreed—7 A 3.
No. 1 divided.

9A 1 n-Diivided.

2. Resolved, that the [*National*] Legislature ought to consist of two branches.

3. Resolved, that the Members of the first Branch of of the United States

5 A. 5no. 1 divided lost.

the [(*National*)] Legislature ∧ ought to be elected by the People of the several States, for the term of two      to be of the Age of 25 years at least: three years; ∧ [*to receive*

---

[5] This paper is in the handwriting of David Brearley. It is indorsed "Report of Committee 12 June 1787" in Brearley's handwriting. The committee, as a matter of fact, did not report until June 13. The interlineations and erasures as here represented admirably illustrate the subjects under discussion and the changes made in the report. Erasures are bracketed and in italics. Evidently Brearley, using the report of the Committee of the Whole, or more properly his copy of the report, made changes in it in the course of the succeeding debates.

881

*fixed Stipends, by which they may be compensated for the devotion of their time to Public Service—to be paid out of the Public* and incapable of holding, *National Treasury;*] to be ineligible to, ∧ any Office [*established by a particular State, or*] under the authority of the United States (except those peculiarly belonging to the functions of the first Branch) during the term of the first Branch of service, ∧ [*and under the National Government for the space of one year after its expiration.*]

4. Resolved, that the Members of the second Branch of the U. S. of the [*National*] Legislature ∧ ought to be chosen by the individual Legislatures: to be of the Age of 30 years, at least; to hold their Offices for the Term ∧ [*sufficient* of six years, one third of whom to go out of office biennially; *to ensure their independency namely of seven years*]—to compensation for receive ∧ [*fixed Stipends, by which they may be compensated for*] the devotion of their time to public service,—to be paid out of the National Treasury.

To be ineligible to any office established by a particular State, or under the authority of the United States (except those peculiarly belonging to the functions of the second Branch) during the term of service, and under the Nat! Government for the space of one year after its expiration.

5. Resolved, that each Branch ought to possess the right of originating Acts.      possess

agreed to without amendment.

6. Resolved, that the National Leg? ought to [*be empowered to enjoy*] the Legislative Rights vested in Congress by the Confederation; and moreover to Legislate in all cases to which the separate States are incompetent, or in which the harmony of the United States may be interrupted by the exercise of individual Legislation,—to negative all laws passed by the several States contravening, in the opinion of the National Legisla-

50-766 O-65—57

ture, the Articles of Union, or any Treaties subsisting under the Authority of the Union.

<sup>carried 6. ay. 4</sup>
<sup>no 1 divided</sup> 7. Resolved, that the Right of suffrage in the first Branch of the National Legislature ought *not* to be according to the Rule established in the Articles of Confederation, but according to some equitable Ratio of representation, namely, in proportion to the whole number of White and other free Citizens and Inhabitants, of every Age, Sex and Condition, including those bound to servitude for a Term of Years, and three fifths of all other persons, not comprehended in the foregoing discription, except Indians not paying Taxes in each State.

8. Resolved, that the right of suffrage in the second Branch of the National Legislature ought to be according to the rule established for the first.

9. Resolved, that a National Executive be instituted, to consist of a *single person* to be chosen by the National Legislature for the term of seven years, with Power to carry into execution the National Laws—to appoint to Offices in cases not otherwise provided for; to be ineligible a second time; and to be removable on Impeachment and Conviction of Mal-Practice, or neglect of duty. To receive a fixed stipend by which he may be compensated for the Devotion of his time to public service; to be paid out of the National Treasury.

10. Resolved, that the National Executive shall have a right to negative any [*National*] Legislative Act, which shall not be afterwards passed unless by two third parts of each Branch of the National Legislature.

11. Resolved, that a National Judiciary be established, to consist of one Supreme Tribunal,—the Judges of which to be appointed by the second Branch of the National Legislature; to hold their offices during good behaviour and to receive punctually at stated times, a fixed compensation for their services, in which

883

no increase or diminution shall be made, so as to affect the persons actually in office at the time of such increase or diminution.

12. Resolved, that the Nat! Legislatͤ be empowered to appoint inferior Tribunals.

13. Resolved, that the Jurisdiction of the National Judiciary shall extend to cases which respect the collection of the National Revenue;—Impeachments of any National Officers, and questions which involve the Na! peace and harmony.

14. Resolved, that Provision ought to be made for the admission of States, lawfully arising within the limits of the United States; whether from a voluntary Junction of Government and Territory, or otherwise, with the consent of a Number of Voices in the National Legislature less than the whole.

15. Resolved, that provision ought to be made for the continuance of Congress and their Authorities and privileges, until a given day after the reform of the Articles of Union shall be adopted; and for the completion of all their Engagements.

16. Resolved, that a Republican Constitution, and its existing laws, ought to be garraunteed to each State, by the United States

17. Resolved, that provision ought to be made for the amendment of the Articles of Union, whensoever it shall seem necessary.

18. Resolved, that the Legislative, Executive, and Judiciary Powers within the several States, ought to be bound by Oath, to support the Articles of Union.

19. Resolved, that the amendments which shall be offered to the Confederation, by the Convention, ought at a proper time or times, after the Approbation of Congress, to be submitted to an Assembly or Assemblies of Representatives, recommended by the several Legislatures, to be expressly chosen by the People to

Consider and decide thereon. [*Indorsement:* Report of Committee 12 June 1787]

### III. NOTES APPARENTLY USED BY PATERSON IN PREPARING THE NEW JERSEY PLAN, JUNE 13–15

#### A

1. Resolved, That a union of the States merely federal ought to be the sole Object of the Exercise of the Powers vested in this Convention.[6]

2. Resolved, That the Articles of the Confederation ought to be so revised, corrected, and enlarged as to render the federal Constitution adequate to the Exigencies of Government, and the Preservation of the Union [7]—

3. Resolved, That the federal Government of the United States ought to consist of a Supreme Legislative, Executive, and Judiciary—

4. Resolved, That the Powers of Legislation ought to be vested in Congress.[8]

5. Resolved, That in Addition to the Powers vested in the United States in Congress by the present existing Articles of Confederation, they be authorized to pass Acts for levying a Duty or Duties on all Goods and Merchandize of foreign Growth or Manufacture imported into any Part of the United States not exceeding       per Cent. ad Valorem to be applied to such federal Purposes as they shall deem proper and expedient, and to make Rules and Regulations

---

[6] This resolution is partly stricken out in the original. Jameson says these five resolutions may not improperly be attributed to John Lansing, Jr., of New York. He also says that it will be plainly seen that it represents an early stage of the Paterson plan. The fifth resolution is especially noteworthy. "In short," says Jameson, "we have in this document a *Vorschrift* for the New Jersey plan, drawn up by a man or men who were willing to go but little beyond" the schemes earlier proposed. *Ann. Rep. Am. Hist. Assoc.*, 1902, 1. 142.

[7] This resolution is thus given in Madison's notes, *Documentary History*, III, 125. It is the first resolution of Paterson's plan as there given. Jameson argues (p. 137) that this could not have been the first of Paterson's resolutions as finally presented. His evidence is probably conclusive; and yet it should be noticed that the resolution offered by Dickinson, "That the Articles of Confederation ought to be revised and amended, so as to render the Government of the United States adequate to the exigencies, the preservation, and the prosperity of the Union," would not be acceptable to either party. Paterson's supporters would wish to retain the words "federal Constitution." Is not Dickinson's motion characteristic?

[8] See Jameson, *loc. cit.*, 140–141.

for the Collection thereof; and the same from Time to Time to alter and amend in such Manner as they shall think proper. Provided, That all Punishments, Fines, Forfeitures, and Penalties to be incurred for contravening such Rules and Regulations shall be adjudged and decided upon by the Judiciaries of the State in which any Offence contrary to the true Intent and Meaning of such Rules and Regulations shall be committed or perpetrated; subject nevertheless to an Appeal for the Correction of any Errors in rendering Judgment to the Judiciary of the United States.

That the United States in Congress be also authorized to pass Acts for the Regulation of Trade as well with foreign Nations as with each other, and for laying such Prohibitions, and such Imposts and Duties upon Imports as may be necessary for the Purpose; Provided, That the Legislatures of the several States shall not be restrained from laying Embargoes in Times of Scarcity; and provided further that such Imposts and Duties so far forth as the same shall exceed . . . per Centum ad Valorem on the Imports shall accrue to the Use of the State in which the same may be collected.[9]

*Imposts — Excise — Stamps — Post - Office — Poll-Tax —*

B [10]

1. Resolved, That the articles of the confederation ought to be so revised, corrected, and enlarged as to render the federal constitution adequate to the exigencies of government, and the preservation of the union—

2. Resolved, That the alterations, additions, and provisions made in and to the articles of the confederation shall be reported to the united states in congress and to the individual states composing the

---

[9] This resolution is somewhat similar to the second resolution as given in Madison's notes, *Documentary History*, III. 125, and in the Brearley copy, *ibid.*, I. 322. Either no more was written of this paper or Paterson copied no more, Jameson, *loc. cit.*, 142.

[10] This goes farther than A and marks a later stage of the plan.

union, agreeably to the 13<sup>th</sup> article of the confederation—

3. Resolved, That the federal government of the united states ought to consist of a supreme legislative, executive, and judiciary—

4. Resolved, That the powers of legislation be vested in Congress—

<small>See M.<sup>r</sup> Lansing—</small>    5.

<small>See Gov. Randolph's. 7<sup>th</sup> Prop.</small>    6.

<small>Same—, 9<sup>th</sup></small>    7.

Resolved, That every State in the Union as a State possesses an equal Right to, and Share of, Sovereignty, Freedom, and Independance—

Resolved, therefore, that the Representation in the supreme Legislature ought to be by States, otherwise some of the States in the Union will possess a greater Share of Sovereignty, Freedom, and Independance than others—

Whereas it is necessary in Order to form the People of the U. S. of America into a Nation, that the States should be consolidated, by which Means all the Citizens thereof will become equally intitled to and will equally participate in the same Privileges and Rights, and in all waste, uncultivated, and back Territory and Lands; it is therefore resolved, that all the Lands contained within the Limits of each State individually, and of the U. S. generally be considered as constituting one Body or Mass, and be divided into thirteen or more integral Parts.[11]

Resolved, That such Divisions or integral Parts shall be styled Districts.

---

[11] To account for such a proposition as this in connection with the New Jersey plan is a matter of some difficulty. In the original paper this resolution is so written as undoubtedly to be joined with the preceding. Otherwise it might seem to be a mere sporadic note. Reference is evidently made to this in other notes and memoranda below. See also Brearley's speech of June 9, where the erasure of state boundaries is advocated, and Paterson's reference to the same idea, *Doc. Hist.* III, 96, 97. See also especially Madison's speech of June 19. It is apparent that Paterson and Brearley proposed this as the only way of doing justice to the large states and securing the safety of the small states. *Ibid*, III. 161.

## IV. Notes for Speeches [12]

### A. *Notes for Speech of June 9* [13]

1. The Plan.
2. The words national and federal.
3. Collection of Sentiment—Object, to take under Consideration the State of the American Union—

Consider the Nature and Construction of this Assembly. Formed under the act of Congress passed in Conformity with one of the Articles of the Confed?

See the Com? [14] from Mass?

The Com? measures our Power—to revise the Confed? to report to Congress and the several Leg?—must not go beyond our Powers— *Assumption of Power—*

Self-constituted and self-ordained Body.

The Com? give the political Complexion of the several States—not ripe—we must follow the People; the People will not follow us—The Plan must be accommodated to the public Mind—consult the Genius, the Temper, the Habits, the Prejudices of the People.

A little practicable Virtue to be preferred to Theory.

Not to sport Opinions of my own—not to say w? is the best Gov? or what ought to be done—but what can be done—w? can we do consistently with our Powers; w? can we do that will meet with the Approbation of the People—their Will must guide—

Insurrections—So there are in every Gov?—even in England—it may shew, that our particular Systems are wrong—that our Inst?* are too pure—not sufficiently removed from a State of Nature to answer

---

[12] The notes numbered A-E are in the Bancroft copies marked "Notes for speech of 9 June," but it is by no means clear that all these are notes for the speech of that day. Apparently Paterson worked over his argument several times, and the burden of his thought was somewhat consistently the same; the want of power in the Convention; the unreadiness of the people o support a plan for a consolidated government; the maintenance of the equality of the states. In the notes of Madison, Pierce, King, and Yates we find no indication that Gouverneur Morris made a speech on the ninth. The words in A given in connection with the name of Morris appear again in B.

[13] This document is in the possession of Miss Emily K. Paterson.

[14] Commission.

the Purposes of a State of Society—it will not militate ag[t] the democratick Principle when properly regulated and modified—

The democratick Spirit beats high—

Not half wrong enough to have a good Gov[t]—

2. The Plan proposed—The 1[st] Prop[n] withdrawn[15]—it was incompatible with the 2[d] The Principles were gradually unfolded—

W[t] Q[y] of Land— The 1 Prop[n] accords with the Spirit of the Const[n]

Each State is sovereign, free, and independ[t] etc. Sovereignty includes Equality—

If then the States in Union are as States still to continue in Union, they must be considered as Equals—

13 sovereign and independent States can never constitute one Nation, and at the same Time be States—they may by Treaty make one confederated Body—

M[r] Randolph—We ought to be one Nation—etc. The States as States must be cut up, and destroyed—This is the way to form us into a Nation [16]—It has Equality—it will not break in upon the Rights of any Citizen—it will destroy State Politicks and Attachm[ts]. Will it be acceded to, etc.

G. Morris—Every Citizen should enjoy a rateable Proportion of Sovereignty—

Fœtus of a Monarch—[17]

The Mind of Man is fond of Power—

Enlarge his Prospects, you increase his Desires—

An infant Hercules in his cradle—

Proportion of Votes—State-Politicks, State-Attachments, State-Influence, State-Passions—Districts—

Great Britain and America—Suppose Represent[n] from the latter before the Revolut[n] according to the Quantum of Property or Number of Souls—W[t] the Consequence—

---

[15] Evidently referring to Randolph's first proposition as contradicting the second. The first resolution of Randolph is distinctly like the first of Paterson's as the Paterson plan appears in Madison's notes, *Doc. Hist.*, III. 125. Paterson was here contending that Randolph's original first proposition was constitutionally sound, *i. e.* in conformity with the Articles.

[16] Apparently a reference to the ideal later embodied in the resolution in III. B. See above, also Paterson's speech of June 9.

[17] Randolph used this expression June 2. See Pierce's notes, AM. HIST. REV., III. 322.

889

3 Article [18]—Com. Defence, Security of Liberty, mutual and general Welfare.

A national Gov.̱ to operate individually upon the People in the first Instance, and not upon the States—and therefore a Representation from the People at large and not from the States—

Will the Operation of the nat.̱ Gov.̱ depend upon the Mode of Represent.̱—No—it depends upon the Quantum of Power lodged in the leg. ex. and jud.̱ Departments—it will operate individually in the one Case as well as in the other—

Why not operate upon the States—if they are coerced they will in Turn coerce each individual—

Let the People elect the State-Leg.̱—The State-Leg.̱ elect the federal Leg.̱—assign to the State Leg.̱ its Duty—the same to the federal—they will be Checks upon each other, and the best Checks that can be formed—Cong. the Sun of our political System—

Why a Representation from the People at large—to equalize Represent.̱ Maj.̱ Butler—Represent.̱—Property—People—

M.̱ Wilson—Majority of the States sufficient. This in Opposition to M.̱ King—

2 Views. 1. Under the Confed.̱—13.̱ Article—Rhode-Island. 2. As forming an original Combin.̱ or Confederacy—can bind the contracting Parties only—

The large States can agree upon a Reform only upon the Principle of an equal Represent.̱ [19]

11 Prop.̱ [20]

If the lesser States form a Junction of Gov.̱ and Territory, the G.̱ [21] ceases to operate as to them—This will prevent a Consolid.̱ of Gov.̱ and Territory—

---

[18] Referring to the third article of the Articles of the Confederation.

[19] So the original plainly says. Possibly Paterson meant to write unequal; or by "equal" he meant just or proportional.

[20] Referring to the eleventh proposition of the Virginia plan: "Resd., that a Republican Government and the territory of each State, except in the instance of a voluntary injunction of Government and territory, ought to be guaranteed by the United States to each State.

[21] Guaranty.

The People will likewise prevent any new State from being taken from the old—Vermont—Kentucky—several in Embryo—Republicks—Monarchies—large Frontiers.

B. *Notes for Speech of June 9.*

1. The Confederation—its leading Principle. unanimously assented to—

2. The Nature and Construction of this Assembly. Formed under the Confedⁿ Resⁿ of Congress—The Comⁿ measures our Power—it gives the political Complexion of each State—to revise the Confedⁿ

Must not go beyond our Powers—People not ripe—

A little practicable Virtue to be preferred to Theory.

What expected—Regulation of Commerce, Collⁿ of the Revenue, Negative, etc this will draw after it such a Weight of Influence and Power as will answer the Purpose—they will call forth the dormant Powers—

3. The Plan proposed. The 1 Propⁿ withdrawn—it was incompatible with the 2ᵈ ²² Much Dispute about Distⁿ between federal and National Governments. The Principle was gradually unfolded—

<sub>Wᵗ Qʳ of Land etc they approach each other. etc.</sub> The 1 Propⁿ accords with the Spirit of the Confedⁿ Each State is sovereign, free, and independent etc. The Idea of a Supreme, and the Maxim Imperium in Imperio—

If then the States in Union are as States still to continue in Union, they must be considered as Equals, etc.

13 sovereign and independant states can never constitute one Nation; they may by Treaty make one confederated Body—

Mʳ Randolph—we ought to be one Nation—2 Article ²³—5ᵗʰ Article ²³—

G. Morris—Every Individual should enjoy a rateable Proportion of Sovereignty—

---

²² See above, p. 888, note 15.
²³ Evidently a reference to the second, fifth, and third articles of the Articles of Confederation.

Districts—

3 Article [23]—Common Defence, Security of Liberty, mutual and general Welfare—Proportion of Votes.

11 Prop$^n$

If the lesser States form a Junction of Gov$^t$ and Territory, the G$^t$ ceases to operate as to them—This will prevent a Consol$^n$ of Gov$^t$ and Territory—

The Prop$^n$ will likewise prevent any new States from being taken from the old—Vermont, Kentucky—Several in embryo—Republics—Monarchies—large Frontiers—

The large States can agree to a Reform only upon the Principle of an Equality of Represent$^n$

In what we are all agreed—

### C. *Notes for speech of June 9.*

Mass.

"for the sole and express Purpose of revising the Articles of Conf$^{dn}$ and reporting to Congress and the several Leg$^s$ such Alterations and Provisions therein as shall when agreed to in Congress and confirmed by the States render the federal Const$^n$ adequate to the Exigencies of Government and the Preserv$^n$ of the Union."

Connect$^t$ as above—

Jersey, etc

Georgia,

| States.[24] | Quota of Tax. | Delegates. |
|---|---|---|
| Virginia | 512,974 | 16. |
| Massachusetts | 448,854 | 14. |
| Pennsylvania | 410,378 | 12. ¾ . 42¾ |
| Maryland | 283,034 | 8. ¾. |
| Connecticut | 264 182 | 8. |
| New York | 256 486 | 8. |
| North Carolina | 218 012 | 6¾. |
| South Carolina | 192 366 | 6. |

---

[23] Evidently a reference to the second, fifth, and third articles of the Article of Confederation.

[24] This table is printed in *Doc. Hist.*, I. 331, except that the column giving quotas is not footed here. It is there dated "Sep$^r$ 27$^{th}$ 17.$^{85}$" and indorsed "hon. D. Brearly Esq."

New Jersey............166 716......... 5.
New Hampshire........105 416......... 3¼.
Rhode Island.......... 64 636......... 2.
Delaware............. 44 886......... 1¼.
Georgia............... 32 060......... 1.
                                      ———
                                      90.

D. *A Fragment, possibly connected with Paterson's Speech of June 9.*

Ambition goads him on. The Impulse is progressive—enlarge his Prospects, and you enlarge his Desires. As to orders—as to Societies. Mithradates—Com. Defence—Liberty.

Mr Madison—Districts.

Mr King.

Guarranty.

Nature of Govᵗˢ

So corrected and enlarged.

Regulation of Commerce,

the Collection of Revenue.

Negative in particular Cases.

To promote the general Welfare, to protect Liberty and Property.

Cr. Lands.

E. *Notes for Speech of June 9.*

1—Great Britain and America—Representⁿ from the latter before the Revolution according to the Number of Souls—Wᵗ the Consequence.[25]

2. Representation from the People at large and not from the States [26]—

3. National Governmᵗ to operate individually upon the People in the first Instance, and not upon the States [26]—

---

[25] Apparently referring to the argument used in his speech of June 9: "It was once proposed by Galloway and some others that America should be represented in the British Parlᵗ and then be bound by its laws. America could not have been entitled to more than ⅓ of the Nᵒ of Representatives which would fall to the share of G. B. Would American rights and interests have been safe under an authority thus constituted?" Madison's notes, in *Documentary History*, III. 98.

[26] *Ibid.*

*Durability.*

### F. *Notes for Speech of June 16* [27]

1. Because it accords with our Powers. Suppose an Attorney. Who can vote ag$^t$ it— If Confed$^n$ cannot be amended, say so— The Experim$^t$ has not been made.

2. Because it accords with the Sentiments of the People.

   1. Com$^s$
   2. News-papers—Political Barometer. Jersey never would have sent Delegates under the first Plan—

Not to sport Opinions of my own. W$^t$ can be done. A little practicable Virtue preferrable to Theory.

   1. As States—independant of any Treaty or Confed$^n$—

Each State is sovereign, free, and independant— Sovereignty includes Equality. We come here as States and as Equals—Why vote by States in Convention—We will not give up the Right—

M$^r$ Wilson—A Principle given up in the first Confed$^n$ [28]

   2. As under the existing Articles of the Confed$^n$

5$^{th}$ Article—unanimously entered into.

Back Lands—Jersey—Maryland—[29]

A Contract. The Nature of a Contract. Solemnly entered into—Why break it—why not the new or present one be broke in the same Manner—

*Convenience.*

The last Clause in the Confed$^n$—

Some of the States will not consent—

*Self-Destruction.*

Hitherto argued upon Principle—as States—as subsisting Treaties—The Danger to the lesser States— Abolition of the lesser States—

---

[27] This document is in possession of Miss Emily K. Paterson.
[28] Wilson, according to Madison's notes, made use of some such expression in his speech of June 9, *Doc. Hist.*, III. 99.
[29] "It was the small ones that came in reluctantly and slowly. N. Jersey and Maryland were the two last, the former objecting to the want of power in Congress over trade: both of them to the want of power to appropriate the vacant territory to the benefit of the whole." Paterson, June 16, as condensed by Madison, *Ibid.*, 131.

The Natural Progress of Power—Combination of Parts—Orders—States—Proportion of Votes—State-Politicks and Attachments—Great Britain and America—

Objⁿ. The larger States contribute most, and therefore Representⁿ ought to be in Proportion—

No—they have more to protect.

2. For the Sake of preserving the Liberty of the others—

<small>A rich State and poor State in same Relation as a rich Individual and a poor one.</small>

3. Wealth will have its Influence—

Objⁿ—Mr Wilson [30]—first Principles—All Authority derived from the People—The People entitled to exercise Authority in Person. One free Citizen ought to be of equal Importance with another—true—One free State of equal Importance with another—Both true when properly applied. The Beauty of all Knowledge consists in the Application—

One free Citizen ought to be of equal Importance with another—they are Members of the Society, and therefore true—England and Switzerland. Pennsylva and Jersey—they have the same Privileges, partake in the same common Stock, for Instance, in back and unlocated Lands. The Genⁿ soon found out the

<small>A large County and a small County—[81]</small>

Diffe between a Pennsylva and a Jersey Man when we talked of Consolidⁿ then the Pennsyla gave up ⅓—No; no—A Nation, when it is necessary to go by Majority of Votes, a State, when it is necessary to divide the common Stock—

Equalize the States—No Harm—no Hurt. No authority for that Purpose—and then it is impracticable—

*Authority*—Why talk of the first set of Propositions—Impracticable—how does that appear—Make the

---

[30] Reference is made here and in many of the succeeding arguments to Wilson's speech of June 9, *Doc. Hist.*, III. 99.

[81] Perhaps referring to Williamson's speech of June 9, which he made in answer to Paterson, *Doc. Hist.*, III. 100.

Experiment—Propose the Measure to the Consideration of the States—[32]

Obj$^n$—There must be a national Governm$^t$ to operate individually upon the People in the first Instance, and not upon the States—and therefore a Representation from the People at Large and not from the States—

1. Will the Operation and Force of the Gov$^t$ depend upon the mode of Represent$^n$—No—it will depend upon the Quantum of Power lodged in the leg. ex. and jud$^r$ Departments—it will operate individually in the one Case as well as in the other—

2. Congress are empowered to act individually or to carry the Req$^t$ into Exec$^n$ in the same Manner as is set forth in the first Plan—

3. If not, it may be modified to answer the Purpose.

4. If it cannot be done, better than to have some States devoured by others—

Obj$^n$—Congress not sufficient—there must be two Branches—a House of Delegates and a Senate; why, they will be a Check—This not applicable to the supreme Council of the States—The Representatives from the several States are Checks upon each other.

In a single State Party Heat and Spirit may pervade the whole, and a single Branch may of a sudden do a very improper Act—A second Branch gives Time for Reflexion; the Season of Calmness will return, etc. Is this likely to be the Case among the Representatives of 13 States—

---

[32] Paterson's argument in these paragraphs may be this: The gentlemen are desirous of making a nation but when we propose consolidation by a redivision of the states so that the parts may be equal, then it is apparent that Pennsylvania would lose a portion, one-third, of its land. They are for a nation, when it is a question of voting, but they are for the state when a division of the land is proposed, or a division of the common stock. Let us try the plan of equalizing the states. No harm will be done. Gentlemen argue that they have no authority. If they are hesitating because of want of authority, why do they talk of the Randolph plan? They have no authority to propose those measures either. Why is it argued that it is impracticable to throw the land into a common stock and divide the states anew? How does that appear? Make the experiment. Propose the measure to the consideration of the states.

If Paterson and Brearley had this scheme as much in mind as it would appear they had, it is apparent that they were not quite so determined as some to adhere to the principle of the Confederation as the *only* solution. There came out distinctly the old small state jealousy and above all the interminable land question which had agitated the states almost from the beginning of the war.

What is the Fact—Congress has hitherto conducted with great Prudence and Sagacity—the People have been satisfied—Give Congress the same Powers, that you intend to give the two Branches, and I apprehend they will act with as much Propriety and more Energy than the latter.

The Chance for Wisdom greater—Refinement—Secretion—

The Expence will be enormous—

Congress the Sun of our political World.

G. *Notes, probably for a Speech not delivered.*[33]

1. The Equality of the States—Sovereignty and Equality are convertible Terms. Pennsylv<sup>a</sup> a distinct political Being—

2. As under the existing Articles of the Confed<sup>n</sup> A Contract solemnly entered into.

3. The Danger to the lesser States.

4. The Impracticability of the present System.

5. Its Expence—

It must be admitted, that before a Treaty can be binding, each State must consent.

Obj<sup>ns</sup>—

The larger States contribute most—and therefore Represent<sup>n</sup> ought to be in Proport<sup>n</sup>.

1. Ans<sup>r</sup>. They have more to protect. A rich State and a poor State in same Relation as a rich Individual and a poor one.

2. For the Sake of preserving the Liberty of the others—Compromise—Their System.

3. Wealth will have its Influence.

---

[33] This document is in the possession of Miss Emily K. Paterson. These notes are in one document, and it has not seemed wise to separate them. On the Bancroft copies the first portion, *i. e.* to the words "Obj<sup>n</sup> M<sup>r</sup> Wilson—The Minority," is headed "Notes for speech of 16 June"; what follows is headed "Notes of Wilson's of 30 June; Madison's of 19 June; King's of 30 June cf. Elliot V." A comparison with the notes given below in V. E. p. 336, belonging to June 30, seems to show that the remarks of Madison, as well as those of Wilson and King as here given were made on June 30.

Objⁿ Mr Wilson—The Minority will vote away the Property of the Majority.

Ansr This secured by the first Branch—³⁴

The Majority will vote away the Liberties of the Minority ³⁵—Wt is Wealth when put in Competition with Freedom—

The lesser States will destroy the larger—Lamb and Lyon— <sub>Madn Coercion never can be used agt a large State.</sub>

Objⁿ Mr Maddison—The Confedⁿ inadequate to its Purposes. Repeated Violations in every State—Each Violation renders the Confedⁿ a Nullity—³⁶

1 No. The same Power to rescind as to make. It would be in the Power of one Party always to abrogate a Compact.

Objⁿ Mr Maddison—The Confedⁿ obtained by the Necessity of the Times.

Is the Plea of Compulsion set up. Look at the Confedⁿ unanimously assented to—Mr Wilson given up—Not complained of—We come here under that Confedⁿ

Objⁿ Mr King—Equality is the Vice of the present System. How does it appear—

Objectⁿ—Mr King ³⁷—The great Charter of England—Certain constitutional Principles to be observed—Power in the Magy to prevent a Violation of fundamental Principles—

Union of England and Scotland.

1. A Union or Consolidation—this a Confederacy.

2. It was to be sure agreed to—Bribery made use of—

3. A King.

4. The Vicinity of France—

The last Time of Meeting—

---

[34] This would seem to make it plain that this note was made after June 29.

[35] This probably from Ellsworth.

[36] A reference to V. E. below and to *Doc. Hist.*, III. 253, will show that this is a part of Madison's speech of June 30.

[37] *Doc. Hist.*, III. 262.

**H.** *Notes apparently for Speech of July 9.*

## Number of Inhabitants

| | |
|---|---|
| New Hampshire in 1774 | 100,000 |
| Massachusetts in 1774 | 400,000. |

Rhode-Island by a Return to the Legislature in Feb$^r$ 1783..........

$\left.\begin{array}{r}\text{48. 538 Whites.}\\ \text{3. 331 Blacks.}\end{array}\right\}$ 51. 869.

Connecticut in 1774...................

$\left.\begin{array}{r}\text{Whites 192. 000.}\\ \text{Blacks (nearly) 6. 000.}\end{array}\right\}$ 198. 000.

in 1782 nearly....... 220. 000.

New York in 1756.   96.775.
     in 1771.   168.000.
     in 1786.   $\left.\begin{array}{r}\text{Whites 219.996.}\\ \text{Blacks } \underline{18.889}\end{array}\right\}$ 238. 885.

New Jersey in 1783...................... 139. 000.
    about 10,000 Blacks included—

Pennsylvania—

Delaware—

Maryland in 1774 estimated at............. 350. 000.
    Blacks 3/7 ......................... 150. 000.

Virginia in 1774........................ 650. 000.
    Blacks as 10 to 11................... 300. 000.

In the lower States the acc$^{ts}$ are not to be depended on—

## The Proportion of Blacks

In Connecticut as 1. to 33.
The same Ratio will answer for Massachusetts—
In Rhode-Island as 1 to 15½.
In New York as 1 to 12 nearly.
In New Jersey as 1 to 13 nearly.

| | | |
|---|---|---|
| Virginia................ | 9. | 10 |
| Mass$^{ts}$................. | 7. | 8 |
| Pennsylv$^a$............... | 8. | 8 |
| Maryland............... | 4. | 6. |
| Connecticut............. | 4. | 5. |
| New York............... | 5. | 6. |
| N. Carolina............. | 5. | 5. |
| S. Carolina............. | 5. | 5. |
| N. Jersey............... | 3. | 4. |

20.1
40.1
80.1
160.1

| | | |
|---|---|---|
| New Hampshire | 2. | 3. |
| Rh. Island | 1. | 1 |
| Del. | 1. | 1 |
| Georgia | 2. | 3. |
| | 56. | 65 [38] |
| 4 East<sup>n</sup> States | | 17. |
| 5 Middle States | | 25. |
| 4 South<sup>n</sup> States | | 23. |
| | | 65 |

## V. NOTES ON DEBATES

### A. *Notes on Debate of June 9.*[39]

M! Brearley.

unfair; because of the Combination of the Parts. Districts—

Equalize the States—

M! Wilson—

All Authority is derived from the People—the People entitled to exercise Authority in Person—Italy—Roman Citizens—

2 Things necessary—1. That the Representatives express the Sentiments of the represented. 2. That the Sentiments thus expressed should have the same Operation as if expressed by the People themselves—

Numbers the best Estimate of Property. One free Citizen ought to be of equal Importance with another.

One Mass—13—it will be given away $\frac{1}{3}$ of the Territory—

No Authority—it is besides impracticable.

He wishes the Distinction of States might be destroyed.

A Principle given up in the first Confed<sup>n</sup>

It does not appear to him, that the lesser States will be swallowed up.

M! W<sup>m</sup>son

A small County, and a large County; according to Numbers—

---

[38] The first column shows the representation according to Morris's report of July 9; the second that provided for by King's report from committee, July 10.
[39] See *Documentary History*, III. 94 ff.

Mʳ Maddison

B. *Notes on Debate of June 11.*

Resolved, That the Rights of Suffrage in the first Branch of the national Legʳ ought not to be according to the Article of Confedⁿ, but according to some equitable Ratio of Representation—

Rutledge.

Not by the Number of free Inhabitants, but according to the Quotas of Contribution—

Dickinson—

The Terms, "Quotas of Contribution," very indefinite—it ought to be according to the *actual Contribution*—

Wᵐson.

Supposes, that there will not be any Assignment or Quotas to States; the Governmᵗ to operate individually and not on States—

Dickinson

The Power to be in Proportion to actual Contribution—

King—

Suppose an Impost—Connecticut and Jersey do not import—they will have no Representatives—

Butler.

This to be left to the State Legʳˢ—Sum to be proportioned—

Wilson.

Either Rule good—by Numbers best to ascertain the Right of Representⁿ this agreeably to the Sentiments of 11 States—Impost alone will not be sufficient to answer the national Exigencies—Revenues arising from Postage—The present Quota not a lasting Rule—People to be numbered at fixed Periods—A Rule arising from Property and Numbers—

Gerry.

Rule of Taxation not the Rule of Representation—4 might then have more Voices than ten—Slaves not to be put upon the Footing of freemen—Freemen of Massᵗˢ not to be put upon a Footing with the Slaves of other States—Horses and Cattle ought to have the Right of Representⁿ Negroes—Mules—

The Taxes must be drawn by the natˡ Governmt. immediately from the People; otherwise will never be collected—

Leave the particular Rule for the present. A common Standard ought to be provided— *Madison*

### C. *Notes on Debate of June 16.*

Contrasts the Principles of the two Systems— *Lansing—*

The national Plan proposes to draw Represent? from the People.

The federal Plan proposes to draw Represent? from the States.

The first will absorb the State-Governm*ts*

1. The Powers of the Convention.

2. The Probability as to the Adoption of either System—

Publick Acts—particularly the Act respecting the Impost.

Reasoning upon Systems unsupported by Experience generally erroneous—

The Plans do not agree in the following Instances. *Paterson. Wilson* [40]

1. The Gov? consists of 2 Branches.

2. The original Authority of the People at Large is brought forward. to connect them together as States.

3. Representation to be according to the Number and Importance of the Citizens.

4. A single Executive.

5. A Majority of the United States are to control.

6. The national Leg. can operate in all Cases in which the State Leg. cannot.

7. The national Leg. will have a Right to negative all State-Acts contravening Treaties, etc.

8. Ex. Mag. removable on Conviction.

9. The Ex. to have a qualified Negative over Acts of the Leg?—

10. Provision is made for superior Tribunals—

11. The Jurisd? of the national Leg? is to extend to all Cases of a national Nature.

---

[40] We have here a new summary of Wilson's long and able speech of this date.

12. National Peace, all Questions comprehending it, will be the Object of the national Judiciary—

13. Delegates to come from the People.

The relative Merit of the two Plans.

1. Upon Principles.
2. Upon Experience.
3. The joint Result of both.

He can conclude finally Nothing; and to propose every Thing—he may propose any Plan—

Sentiments of the People; those with whom we converse we naturally conclude to be the Sentiments of the People.

States Sovereignments and State Governm.$^{ts}$ not so much an Idol as is apprehended—a national Government to protect Property and promote Happiness, the Wish of the People.

Will a Citizen of New Jersey think himself honoured when addressed as a Citz$^n$ of that State, and degraded when addressed as a Citizen of the U. S.

The People expect Relief from the national Councils; it can be had only from a national Governm$^t$—

*Equalization—* A new Proposal thrown out for the Sentiments of the People.

Ad$^l$ Powers ought not to be given to Congress. Obj$^{ns}$ to that Body.

1. Congress as a legislative Body does not stand upon the Authority of the People.
2. Congress consists of but one Branch.

An equal Represent$^n$ in Proportion to Numbers.

*Answ$^r$ Citizens of the same State.* The Foundation, the Progress, and Principles of Representation—Look at England—Holland—the Vote of every Province necessary. L$^d$ Chesterfield—

Impost opposed and defeated not by one of the large States—

The Consent of Rhode-Island will be necessary on the Jersey-Plan—

A single Legr

Despotism presents itself in several various Shapes—military Despot—ex. Despot—Is there no such Thing as a leg. Despot—The Leg. Authority ought to be restrained—

The Restraints upon the Legr must be such as will operate within itself—No Check in a single Branch—Should have distinct and independant Branches—reciprocal Controul.

A single Executive—Triumvirate of Rome—2 Triumvirate—Augustus rose superior—Sparta—Rome—

If Jersey can have an equal Representⁿ she will come into the Plan from Virginia—     Pinckney—[41]

Views—to amend the Confedⁿ if not amendable, then to propose a new Governmt—

*Solely recommendatory*—Powers sufficient. Division of Territory; not seriously proposed [42]—The due Settlemt of the Importance of the States necessary—this done at present with Respect to Contribution.

*England.*

1 Congress unfortunately fixed on equal Representⁿ—they had not the Means of determining the Quota—If each State must have a Vote, each State must contribute equally—

1. Whether the Articles of the Confedⁿ can be so reformed as to answer the Purposes of a national Governmt—     Elsworth. Randolph.[43]

No Usurpation of Power in this Convention. The Spirit of the People in Favour of the Plan from Virginia—

Powers pursued; if Powers wanting, we should do what is right.

---

[41] This is considerably longer than the condensation of Pinckney's speech given by Madison. It has here also considerably more force and meaning. Cf. *Doc. Hist.*, III. 136.

[42] Once more a reference to Paterson's and Brearley's plan for consolidation.

[43] An outline of Randolph's able speech of June 16. This throws light on some of Randolph's argument as condensed by Madison.

Our Debts remain unpaid while the federal Gov! remains as it is—

*Delaware.*

The 13th Article—provides for the alteration of the Articles, then of course for the Alteration of the 5th Article.

*Annapolis.*

Powers in a deliberate Assembly—ridiculous—We are only to compare Sentiments—Disdain Danger, and do what is necessary to our political Salvation—We must avail ourselves of the present Moment.

His Constituents will applaud, when he has done every Thing in his Power to relieve America—

No Provision ag! foreign Powers or Invasions. no Mony nor Men—Militia not sufficient—

No Provision ag! internal Insurrections. nor for the Maintenance of Treaties—

Coercion two Ways—1. as to Trade—2. as to an Army—

Legislation affecting Individuals the only Remedy. This Power too great to lodge in one Body—

Congress possess both Legislation and Execution—

The Variety of Interests [44] in the several States require a national Legislation; or else there may be a Combination of States—

The Mode of electing Congress an Obj? the Delegates will be under the Influence of its particular States.

Cabal and Intrigue of which such a Body as Congress may be capable. They are too numerous for an Executive.

No Provision under the Confed? for supporting the Harmony of the States—their commercial Interests different

No provision for Congress to settle Disputes—

No Provision made or Power in Congress for the Suppression of Rebellion—no Troops can be raised—

---

[44] That this argument is important in Paterson's mind is indicated by a hand on the margin of his notes pointing to this.

Congress ought not to have the Power of raising Troops.

A Navigation Act may be necessary—Give Power to whom—not to Congress—capable of Intrigue and Cabal; Inadequacy of Representation; Want of Confidence in Congress—

Congress fallen considerably in their Reputation. Doors not open in Congress.

*Divide leg. and ex. Branches and then Doors may be open—*

This the last Moment ever will be offered [45]—

D. *Notes on Debates of June 27, 28, and 29.*[46]

*June 27. 1787.*[47]

Have those who upon the present plan hold $\frac{1}{13}$ part of the Votes, a 13$^{th}$ part of the weight,—certainly not—upon this plan they sink to nothing

The Individual right of Citizens is given up in the State Gov$^{ts}$ they cannot exercize it again in the Gen$^l$ Government.[48]

It has never been complained of in Congress—the complaint there is the want of proper powers.[49]

*June 28$^{th}$*

M$^r$ Martin resumed his argument.

The Gen$^l$ Gov$^t$ is not to regulate the rights of Individuals, but that of States. The Gen$^l$ Gov$^t$ is to Govern Sovereignties. then where the propriety of the several Branches—they cannot exist—there can be no such checks.

Amphictyonick Council of Greece represented by two from each town—who were notwiths$^g$ the disp$^n$ of the Towns equal—Rollins Ancient Hist. 4 Vol. pa. 79.

---

[45] "A Nat$^l$ Gov$^t$ alone, properly constituted, will answer the purpose; and he begged it to be considered that the present is the last moment for establishing one. After this select experiment, the people will yield to despair." *Doc. Hist.*, III. 138.

[46] In the handwriting of David Brearley.

[47] According to Madison's notes, Martin alone spoke on this day, his speech lasting three hours. *Doc. Hist.*, III. 224.

[48] This is undoubtedly the argument Martin based on his notion that the state governments rested on compact.

[49] Here Mr. Brearley has indicated by a hand the importance of the argument.

All the *Ancient* and *Modern* Confed.ⁿˢ and Leagues were as *equals* notwithstanding the *vast* disproportions in size and wealth.

If the large States, who have got a Majority, will adhere to their plan, we cannot help it, but we will publish to the world our plan and our principles, and leave it to judge.

Mr. Madison  Have we seen the Great Powers of Europe combining to oppress the small—[50]

Yes—the division of Poland.

They talk in vague Terms of the great States combining etc.[51]

Mr. Williamson  Wants to know how it is possible that the large States can oppress the small [52]

The rule to tax the States according to their numbers would be cruel and unjust—it would Create a war.

Mr. Madison.  If you form the present Government, the States will be satisfied—and they will divide and sub-divide so as to become nearly equal—

*June 29th*

Doct. Johnson  If the States are represented as States—they must be represented as Individuals.

Mr. Gorham—  New-Jersey ought not to oppose the plan, as she at present pays the Taxes of Penn. and N. York, from which she would be relieved.

Mr. Madison  Will have the States considered as so many great Corporations, and not otherwise.

Col. Hamilton  That States have equal rights to vote, is not true It is estabd by the Law of Nations that they have equal votes—but does it follow that they can not contract upon a different footing—

That the Genl Governmt will act, not only, upon the States, but upon Individuals.

---
[50] A hand on the margin.
[51] In Madison's notes this speech precedes that of Madison. *Doc. Hist.*, III. 227.
[52] A hand on the margin.

As long as the State influence is kept up there will be danger—but the influence will not be as great as is apprehended.

It is a contest for power in the weaker States.⁵³ <small>The small States have had a lesson of State Honesty Mʳ Pierce.</small>

Gentlemen of Congress when they vote always connect with them the State views and politicks—and therefore—

That upon Tryal it has been found that the Articles of Confⁿ are not adequate— <small>Mʳ Gerry.</small>

That the small States have abused their power, and instanced Rho. Island.

### E. *Notes on Debate of June 30.*⁵⁴

Did not expect this Question at this Stage of the Business. <small>Wilson.</small>

Member of Connecticut said, not more than one State to Eastward would accede.

*Sense of Duty.*

22 out of 90—not ¼— <small>This as to Contribⁿ</small>

Artificial Systems of States—

The Voice of the Minority will vote away the Property of the Majority— <small>Easy to correct it.</small>

A Solecism.

7 States can control the 6.

States imaginary Beings abstracted from Men—

No other Foundation will be solid—

The 3 large States combined. Wᵗ He wants the Principles of the Combⁿ—they will be Rivals.

Their Interests are different.

24 out of 90 carry more of an Aristocracy.

2 Kinds of bad Govᵗ—1. That Govᵗ which does not do enough—and 2. that which does too much—Be as we were before we met. <small>Why wish for an Union of the lesser States—</small>

The System of Virginia and the System of Jersey agree as to the Powers— <small>Yes—but then the 2 Systems oppose each other.</small>

---

⁵³ A hand on the margin.
⁵⁴ This document is in the possession of Miss Emily K. Paterson.

Gov̱ by the States necessary. There can be no Difficulty as to this Point.

M̱ Elsworth

Obj̱ A Minority will govern a Majority. You put it in the Power of a few to prevent the Oppression of the many.

Political Societies are to govern—

In the Br. Consṯ the few has a Check upon the many; and one upon both—

The House must be demolished—but it only wants a Shingle—[55]

If Congress had voted by a Majority, all Evils would have been cured—

Rhode-Island—The Power not in Congress.

Are not the large States safe now—

Suppose the large States should agree that 4 free Ports should be established.

Suppose lucrative Offices—

*Self-Preservation.*

M̱ Maddison.

*No Unity of Interests—*

The Confeḏ inadequate to its Purposes.

Resoḻ of Coṉ refusing to comply with a federal Req̱

*Lycia.*

Germanick Body.

Reported Violations in every State.

The Rule of Conf̱ obtained by the Necessity of the Times—

The large States will not be secure by the lower Branch.

2ᵈ Branch may possess a Negative over the Laws of the State-Leg̱

M̱ Elsworth.
M̱ Sherman.

Coṉ has furnished more tẖ her Quota as to Men—

M̱ Wilson asks, why the Interests of the lesser States cannot be as safe in the Hands of the larger States as in their own—

M̱ Davie—

The Resoḻ as reported by the Com̱ is impracticable—is too large—

---

[55] "We are razing the foundations of the building. When we need only repair the roof." *Doc. Hist.*, III. 252.

The 2ᵈ Branch being executive must sit constantly.

Not necessary to sit constantly—     M.ʳ Wilson—

Each State should have one Senator—1 Member in the second for every 100,000 People; and 1 for the smallest State.

This a Compromise on the Part of the large States.

He will not insist upon small Matters—if the great Principles can be established—

Gov.ᵗ placed upon a false Basis.

The lesser States afraid of their Liberties; the larger States afraid of their Money.     Doct.ʳ Franklin

Treaty between France and the U. S. the latter had no Disposition over the Treasury of the former.

Equality is the Vice of the present System.     M.ʳ King.

    Capt.ⁿ Dayton.

The Am.ᵗ [56] is Congress in a new Form; servile to the States.     M.ʳ Maddison

No Dispos.ⁿ in C.ᵗ [57] Rep. or Corporations to swallow up the Rest.

Purity of Principle—     M.ʳ Bedford—

Magna Charta of England. Certain const.ˡ Principles to be observed.     M.ʳ King.

Union of England and Scotland.

Power in the Mag.ʸ to prevent a Violation of fundamental Principles.     This is a Con solid.ⁿ The King Bribed. France— Ireland.

Gov.ᵗ a *progressive Force.*

### F. *Notes on Debate of July 5.*[58]

The Interest of the smaller States to come into the Measure — Delaware — foreign Power — New-Jersey. Single and unconnected.     Maddison.

The People will not agree to it.

    Butler.

---

[56] Amendment probably; if so, it may refer to Wilson's proposition to have one senator in each state "for every 100,000 souls, and let the States not having that n.º of inhabitants be allowed one." *Doc. Hist.*, III. 256. Such would seem to be the connection judging by Madison's notes; but on the other hand it is much more reasonable to suppose that Madison in this speech is referring either to Ellsworth's motion, "that the rule of suffrage in the 2ᵈ branch be the same with that established by the articles of confederation" (*Doc. Hist.*, III. 245), or to Franklin's proposals (*Ibid.*, 257).

[57] Or C.ʸ meaning county.

[58] The subject under discussion was the report of the Committee providing for equal representation in the second branch and the initiation of revenue and appropriation by the first branch.

G. Morris.  Suppose the larger States agree—the smaller States must come in.

Jersey would follow the Opinions of New York and Pennsylv$^a$

The Sword must decide—

The strongest Party will make the weaker Traitors and hang them—foreign Power.

Should be open to Conviction—

—The larger States must prevail—they must decide; they are most powerful.

Not Members of a Synod, or Conventicle—

G. *Notes on Debates of July 7 and 9.*

Gerry.  About 2,000 Men in the smaller States, who compose the Executives, Legislatives, and Judiciaries; all interested in opposing the present Plan, because it tends to annihilate the State-Governments.

Sherman-  If a Majority of the lesser states be ag$^t$ the Laws of the national Governm$^t$; those Laws cannot be executed—There must then be a Branch immediately from the States.

Wilson—  An Agreem$^t$ elsewhere cannot be expected unless the Representation be fair—

Madison.  1. The Upper Branch may put a Veto upon the Acts of the lower Branch.

2. May extort a Concurrence. The smaller States near the Centre; they may compose a Majority of the Quorum.

Gerry—  The larger States will have more Influence; they have in Congress; this from the Nature of Things.

G. Morris—  Great Care will be taken to lessen the Powers of the 2$^d$ Branch—

Corporations to be protected.

Separate colonial Existances—

Corporations—The small States—go on and fight out the Rev$^n$ or give us an equal Vote.

The small States say, that they will have greater Rights as Citizens—

Must have such a Gov! as will give Safety—

State-Policy not a proper Object for a vigorous Governm!

In Proportion to the Vigour and Strength of the State Governm!ᵗˢ will be the Febleness of the general Governm!—

We must have it in View eventually to lessen and destroy the State Limits and Authorities—

The Germanick Const⁰—The Emperor has never been able to collect them—the separate Parts were too independant—

Monday 9ᵗʰ July, 87.

Report of Comᵉᵉ ⁵⁹  *Gorham.*

Necessary, that the Atlantic States should take Care of themselves; the Western States will soon be very numerous.

### H.  *Notes on Debate of July 23.*⁶⁰

1. The Constitutionality of the Measure.

Reasons

1. The People the Source of Power.  Union—

2. The Leg! of To-Morrow may repeal the Act of the Leg! of To-Day.  So as to Convention—

3. Some of the Constⁿˢ not well or authoritatively founded—Acquiesence.

---

⁵⁹ This was the report of the committee stating the representation of each state in the first Congress.

⁶⁰ The heading on the Lenox Library copy is "Notes of Paterson possibly of Madison's speech of 19 June." The notes seem however to cover the debates of July 23, the day on which Paterson seconded Ellsworth's motion that the Constitution be referred to the legislatures for ratification. Down to the first blank line, *i. e.* through the word "Acquiesence," the notes refer to the speech of Mason. Down to the next blank line, *i. e.* from "Expediency" through "Rh. Island," the notes refer to the speech of Gorham. The next line, beginning with "The Debt" and ending with "Idea," refers to Ellsworth's remarks. From the words "The Leg!," through the words "13 States," reference seems to be to the remarks of G. Morris. Possibly "Congress over again" refers to something said by King but perhaps by Morris. The last sentence is doubtless an assertion of Madison's.

Expediency.

2 Branches in some of the States—

Judges, etc excluded—

The very Men that will oppose—Rh. Island—

The Debt will go with the Gov<sup>t</sup>—this a prevailing Idea—

The Leg<sup>r</sup> has no Right to alter the Const<sup>n</sup> or the Confed<sup>n</sup>—

Not acting under the Confed<sup>n</sup>   Nothing but a Compact resting upon the 13 States.

Congress over again.

A Violation of the Compact by one of the Parties, leaves the rest at Large, and exonerated from the Agreem<sup>t</sup>

# NOTES OF ALEXANDER HAMILTON IN THE FEDERAL CONVENTION OF 1787.[1]

## I. NOTES FOR JUNE 1, 1787.

1—The way to prevent a majority from having an interest to oppress the minority is to enlarge the sphere.

2—Elective Monarchies turbulent and unhappy—    Madison

Men unwilling to admit so decided a superiority of merit in an individual as to accede to his appointment to so preeminent a station—

If several are admitted as there will be many competitors of equal merit they may be all included—contention prevented—and the republican genius consulted—

I   Situation of this Country peculiar—    Randolph—

II   Taught the people an ervasion to Monarchy—

III   All their constitutions opposed to it—

IV   Fixed character of the people opposed to it—

V   If proposed twill prevent a fair discussion of the plan.

VI   Why cannot three execute?—Great exertions only requisite on particular occasions.    View [or Voice] of America Safety to liberty the great object—

—Legislature may appoint a dictator when necessary—

—Seeds of destruction—Slaves—[*former Continental army* struck out] might be safely enlisted—

—May appoint men devoted to them—and even bribe the legislature by offices—

—Chief Magistrate must be free from impeachment

---

[1] Text reprinted from the American Historical Review, Vol. X, (Washington, 1905-6) pp. 98—109.

Wilson— extent—manners—

Confederated republic unites advantages and banishes disadvantages of other kinds of governments—

rendering the executive ineligible an infringement of the right of election—

Bedford— peculiar talents requisite for *executive*, therefore ought to be opportunity of ascertaining his talents—therefore frequent change—

Princ 1 The further men are from the ultimate point of importance the readier they will be [to] concur in a change—

2 Civilization approximates the different species of governments—

3—Vigour is the result of several principles—Activity wisdom—confidence—

4—Extent of limits will occasion the non attendance of remote members and tend to throw the government into the hands of the Country near the seat of government—a reason for strengthening the upper branch and multiplying the Inducements to attendance—

## II. NOTES FOR JUNE 6, 7, AND 8, 1787.

Sent:

A free government to be preferred to an absolute monarchy not because of the occasional violations of *liberty* or *property* but because of the tendency of the Free Government to interest the passions of the community in its favour beget public spirit and public confidence—

Re: When public mind is prepared to adopt the present plan they will outgo our proposition—They will never part with Sovereignty of the state till they are tired [?] of the state governments—

Mr Pinkney. If Legislatures do not partake in the appointment of they will be more jealous

Pinckney—Elections by the state legislatures will be better than those by the people—

915

Principle—Danger that the Executive by too frequent communication with the judicial may corrupt it—They may learn to enter into his passions—

Note—At the period which terminates the duration of the Executive there will be always an awful crisis—in the National situation.

Note. The arguments to prove that a negative would not be used would go so far as to prove that the revisionary power would not be exercised.

M.ʳ Mason—The purse and sword will be in the hands of the [*executive* struck out]—legislature.

I One great defect of our Governments are that they do not present objects sufficiently interesting to the human mind.

I—A reason for leaving little or nothing to the state legislatures will be that as their objects are diminished they will be worse composed—Proper men will be less inclined to participate in them—

[June 7, 1787.]

II—He would have the state legislatures elect senators, because he would bring into the general government the sense of the state Governments etc. Dickinson

II—because the most respectable choices would be made—

Note—Separate states may give stronger organs to their governments and engage more the good will of Ind:—while Gen.ˡ gov.ᵗ
☞ Consider the Principle of Rivalship by excluding the state Legislatures—

General government could not know how to make laws for every part—such as respect *agriculture* etc. Mason
= particular governments would have *no defensive* power unless let into the constitution as a Constituent part— — —

[June 8, 1787.]

Pinckney—For general Negative—

Gerry—Is for a negative on paper emissions—

New States will arise which cannot be controuled—and may outweigh and controul—

Wilson—Foreign influence may infect certain corners of confederacy what ought to be restrained—

Union basis of our oppos and Ind[ependence]:

III. Notes for June 6 and 8, 1787.

PRINCIPLES

I—Human mind fond of Compromise—
Maddisons Theory—

Two principles upon which republics ought to be constructed—

I that they have such extent as to render combinations on the ground of Interest difficult—

II By a process of election calculated to refine the representation of the People—

Answer—There is truth in both these principles but they do not conclude so strongly as he supposes—

—The Assembly when chosen will meet in one room if they are drawn from half the globe—and will be liable to all the passions of popular assemblies.

If more *minute links* are wanting others will supply them—Distinctions of Eastern middle and Southern states will come into view; between commercial and non commercial states—Imaginary lines will influence etc. Human mind prone to limit its view by near and local objects—

Paper money is capable of giving a general impulse—It is easy to conceive a popular sentiment pervading the E. states—

Observ: large districts less liable to be influenced by factious demmagogues than small—

Note—This is in some degree true but not so generally as may be supposed—Frequently small portions of the large districts carry elections—An influential demagogue will give an impulse to the whole—Demagogues are not always *inconsiderable* persons—Patricians were frequently demagogues—Characters are less known and a less active interest taken in them—

[June 8, 1787.]

Arithmetical calculation of proportional influence in Bedford— General Government—

*Pensyl.* and *Delaware* may have rivalship in commerce—and influence of Pens—sacrifice *delaware*

If there be a negative in G G—yet if a law can pass through all the forms of S—C it will require force to abrogate it.

Butler—Will a man throw afloat his property and confide it to a government a thousand *miles distant?*

IV. NOTES FOR JUNE 16 AND 19, 1787.

Mr Lansing—N[ew] S[ystem]—proposes to draw representation from the whole body of people, without regard to S[tate] sovereignties—

Subs: proposes to preserve the State Sovereignties—

Powers—Different Legislatures had a different object—

—Revise the Confederation—

Ind. States cannot be supposed to be willing to annihilate the States—

State of New York would not have agreed to send members on this ground—

In vain to devise systems however good which will not be adopted—

If convulsions happen nothing we can do will give them a direction—

Legislatures cannot be expected to make such a sacrifice—

The wisest men in forming a system from theory apt to be mistaken—

The present national government has no precedent or experience to support it—

General opinion that certain additional powers ought to be given to Congress—

M! Patterson—1—plan accords with powers

2—accords with sentiments of the People—

If Confederation radically defective we ought to return to our states and tell them so—

Comes not here to sport sentiments of his own but to speak the sense of his Constituents—

—States treat[ed] as equal—

Present Compact gives one *Vote to* each state.

alterations are to be made by Congress and all the Legislatures—

All parties to a Contract must assent to its dissolution—

States collectively have advantages in which the smaller states do not participate—therefore individual rules do not apply—

—Force of government will not depend on proportion of representation—but on

Quantity of power—

—Check not necessary in a ge[ne]ral government of communities— but

in an individual state spirit of faction is to be checked—

How have Congress hitherto conducted themselves?

The People approve of Congress but think they have not powers enough—

—body constituted like Congress from the *fewness* of their numbers more wisdom and energy—

than the complicated system of Virginia—

—Expence enormous—

180—commons

90—senators

270—

Wilson—Points of Disagreement—

| | V— | N J— |
|---|---|---|
| 1 | 2 or three branches— | One branch— |
| 2 | Derives authority from People— | from states— |
| 3 | Proportion of suffrage— | Equality— |
| 4 | Single Executive— | Plural— |
| 5 | Majority to govern— | Minority to govern— |
| 6 | Legislate in all matters of general Concern— | partial objects— |
| 7 | Negative— | None— |
| 8 | Removeable by impeachment— | on application of majority of Executives. |
| 9 | Qualified Negative by Executive— | None |
| 10 | Inf[erior]. tribunals— | None— |
| 11 | Orig[inal]: Jurisdiction in all cases of Nat: Rev— | None— |
| 12 | National Government to be ratified by People— | to be ratified by Legislatures— |

—Empowered to propose everything to conclude nothing—

—Does not think state governments the idols of the people—

Thinks a competent national government will be a favourite of the people—

Complaints from every part of United States that the purposes of government cannot be answered—

—In constituting a government—not merely necessary to give proper powers—but to give them to proper hands—

Two reasons against giving additional powers to Congress—

—First it does not stand on the authority of the people—

Second—It is a single branch—

Inequality—the poison of all governments—

—Lord Chesterfield speaks of a Commission to be obtained for a member of a small province—

Pinkney—

Mr Elsworth—

M⟨r⟩ Randolp[h]—Spirit of the People in favour of the Virginian scheme—

We have powers; but if we had not we ought not to scruple—

[June 19, 1787.]

Maddison—Breach of compact in one article releases the whole—

Treaties may still be violated by the states under the Jersey plan—

appellate jurisdiction not sufficient because second trial cannot be had under it—

Attempt made by one of the greatest monarchs of Europe to equalize the local peculiarities of their separate provinces—in which the Agent fell a victim

M⟨r⟩ Pinckney is of opinion that the first branch ought to be appointed in such manner as the legislatures shall direct—

Impracticable for general legislature to decide contested elections—

### V. NOTES FOR JUNE 20, 1787.

M⟨r⟩ Lansing—Resolved that the powers of legislation ought to be vested in the United States in Congress— — — — —

—If our plan be not adopted it will produce those mischiefs which we are sent to obviate—

Principles of system—

 Equality of Representation—

 Dependence of members of Congress on States—

So long as state distinctions exist state prejudices will operate whether election be by *states* or *people*—

—If no interest to *oppress* no need of *apportionment*—

—Virginia 16—Delaware 1—

—Will General Government have leisure to examine state laws—?

—Will G Government have the necessary information?

—Will states agree to surrender?

—Let us meet public opinion and hope the progress of sentiment will make future arrangements—

—Would like my [Hamilton's] system if it could be established System without example—

Mr Mason—Objection to granting power to Congress arose from their constitution.

*Sword* and *purse* in one body—

Two principles in which *America* are unanimous
1   attachment to Republican government
2—to two branches of legislature—

—Military *force* and *liberty* incompatible—

—Will people maintain a standing army?—

—Will endeavour to preserve state governments and draw lines—trusting to posterity to amend—

Mr Martin—General Government originally formed for the preservation of state governments—

Objection to giving power to Congress has originated with the legislatures—

10 of the states interested in an equal voice—

Real motive was an opinion that there ought to be distinct governments and not a general government—

If we should form a general government twould break to pieces— — —

—For common safety instituted a General gover[n]ment—

Jealousy of power the motive—

People have delegated all their authority to state governments—

*Caution* necessary to both systems—

Requisitions necessary upon one system as upon another—

In their *system* made requisitions necessary in the first instance but left Congress in the second instance to assess themselves—

Judicial tribunals in the different states would become odious— — —

If we always to make a change shall be always in a state of infancy—

☞ States will not be disposed hereafter to strengthen—the general government.

Mr Sherman—Confederacy carried us through the war— —
*Non* compliances of States owing to various embarrassments.

Why should state legislatures be unfriendly?
State governments will always have the confidence and government of the people; if they cannot be conciliated no efficacious government can be established.
Sense of all states that one *branch is sufficient*—

If consolidated all treaties will be void.
State governments more fit for local legislation customs habits etc.

### VI. NOTES, PROBABLY FOR DEBATE OF JUNE 26, 1787

I  Every government ought to have the means of self preservation

II—Combinations of a few large states might subvert

II—Could not be abused without a revolt

II  Different genius of the states and different composition of the body

NOTE.  Senate could not desire [?] to promote such a class

III  Uniformity in the time of elections—

Objects of a Senate

To afford a double security against Faction in the house of representatives

Duration of the Senate necessary to its Firmness

Information

sense of national character

Responsibility

# PAPERS OF DR. JAMES McHENRY ON THE FEDERAL CONVENTION OF 1787.[1]

PHILADELPHIA *14 May 1787.*

## Convention.

On the 25th seven states being represented viz. New York, New Jersey, Pennsylvania, Delaware, Virginia, North Carolina and South Carolina, George Washington was elected (unanimously) president of the convention.

The convention appoint a committee to prepare and report rules for conducting business which were reported, debated, and in general agreed to on the 28th.

*29.*

Governor Randolph opened the business of the convention.[2] He observed that the confederation fulfilled *none* of the objects for which it was framed. 1st. It does not provide against foreign invasions. 2dly. It does not secure harmony to the States. 3d. It is incapable of producing certain blessings to the States. 4. It cannot defend itself against encroachments. 5th. It is not superior to State constitutions.

1st. *It does not provide against foreign invasion.* If a State acts against a foreign power contrary to the laws of nations or violates a treaty, it cannot punish that State, or compel its obedience to the treaty. It can only leave the offending State to the operations of the offended power. It therefore cannot prevent a war. If the rights of an ambassador be invaded by any citizen it is only in a few States that any laws exist to punish the offender. A State may encroach on foreign possessions in its neighbourhood and Congress cannot prevent it. Disputes that respect naturalization cannot be adjusted. None of the judges

---
[1] Text and notes reprinted from the American Historical Review, Vol. XI (Washington, 1905-6), pp. 596-618.
[2] McHenry's report of this opening speech of Randolph adds much to that which Randolph gave to Madison and which is printed in Gilpin, pp. 728-730, and elsewhere.

in the several States under the obligation of an oath to support the confederation, in which view this writing will be made to yield to State constitutions.

Imbecility of the Confederation equally conspicuous when called upon to support a war. The journals of Congress a history of expedients. The States in arrears to the federal treasury from the              to the

What reason to expect that the treasury will be better filled in future, or that money can be obtained under the present powers of Congress to support a war. *Volunteers* not to be depended on for such a purpose. *Militia* difficult to be collected and almost impossible to be kept in the field. *Draughts* stretch the strings of government too violently to be adopted. Nothing short of a regular military force will answer the end of war, and this only to be created and supported by money.

2. *It does not secure harmony to the States.* It cannot preserve the particular States against seditions within themselves or combinations against each other. What laws in the confederation authorise Congress to intrude troops into a State. What authority to determine which of the citizens of a State is in the right, The supporters or the opposers of the government, Those who wish to change it, or they who wish to preserve it.

No provision to prevent the States breaking out into war. One State may as it were underbid another by duties, and thus keep up a State of war.

3. *Incapable to produce certain blessings.* The benefits of which we are *singly incapable* cannot be produced by the union. The 5 per cent impost not agreed; a blessing congress ought to be enabled to obtain.

Congress ought to posses[s] a power to prevent emissions of bills of credit.

Under this head may be considered the establishment of great national works—the improvement of inland navigation—agriculture—manufactures—a freer intercourse among the citizens.

4. *It cannot defend itself against incroachments.* Not an animated existence which has not the powers of defence. Not a political existence which ought not to possess it. In every

Congress there has been a party opposed to federal measures. In every State assembly there has been a party opposed to federal measures. The States have been therefore delinquent. To What expedient can congress resort, to compel delinquent States to do what is right. If force, this force must be drawn from the States, and the States may or may not furnish it.

5. *Inferior to State constitutions.* State constitutions formed at an early period of the war, and by persons *elected by the people* for that purpose. These in general with one or two exceptions established about 1786 [*sic*]. The *confederation* was formed long after this, and had its ratification not by any *special appointment* from the people, but from the several assemblies. No judge will say that the *confederation* is paramount to a State consti[tu]tion.

Thus we see that the confederation is incompetent to any *one* object for which it was instituted. The framers of it wise and great men; but human rights were the chief knowle[d]ge of the times when it was framed so far as they applied to oppose Great Britain. Requisitions for men and money had never offered their form to our assemblies. None of those vices that have since discovered themselves were apprehended. Its defects therefore no reflextion [*sic*] on its contrivers.

Having pointed out its defects, let us not be affraid to view with a steady eye the perils with which we are surrounded. Look at the public countenance from New Hampshire to Georgia. Are we not on the eve of war, which is only prevented by the hopes from this convention.

Our chief danger arises from the democratic parts of our constitutions. It is a maxim which I hold incontrovertible, that the powers of government exercised by the people swallows [*sic*] up the other branches. None of the constitutions have provided sufficient checks against the democracy. The feeble Senate of Virginia is a phantom. Maryland has a more powerful senate, but the late distractions in that State, have discovered that it is not powerful enough. The check established in the constitution of New York and Massachusets is yet a stronger barrier against democracy, but they all seem insufficient.

He then submitted the following propositions which he read and commented upon seriatim.[3] . . .

The convention resolved that on to-morrow, the convention resolve itself into a committee of the whole, to take into consideration the state of the american union.[4]

It was observed by Mr. Hamilton before adjourning that it struck him as a necessary and preliminary inquiry to the propositions from Virginia whether the united States were susceptible of one government, or required a separate existence connected only by leagues offensive and defensive and treaties of commerce.[5]

*May 30.*

Mr. Randolph wished the house to dissent from the first proposition on the paper delivered in to the convention in order to take up the following

1st. That a union of the States merely federal will not accomplish the object proposed by the articles of confederation, namely "common defence, security of liberty, and general welfare."

2. That no treaty or treaties between the whole or a less number of the States in their sovereign capacities will accomplish their common defence, liberty, or welfare.[6]

3. That therefore a national government ought to be established consisting of a supreme legislature, judi[c]iary and executive.

On a question taken on the last proposition after various attempts to amend it, the same was agreed to. For it, Massachusetts, Pennsylv., Delaware, Virginia, N. Carolina and S. Carolina— against it Connecticut. New York divided.

[The proceedings of May 30, up to this point, are set forth in much more detail in a loose folio sheet, in Dr. McHenry's handwriting, which was found lying in the book containing the main

---

[3] The text of the Virginia plan here presented is that which is designated as A in Jameson's "Studies in the History of the Federal Convention of 1787", *Annual Report of the American Historical Association* for 1902, I. 103-111. It is not necessary to reprint it.

[4] The diarist ignores Charles Pinckney's plan.

[5] These remarks of Hamilton have not been reported hitherto.

[6] This resolution does not, like the other two, appear in the journal of the committee, but appears, with slightly different phraseology in both cases, in Madison's notes, *Documentary History*, III. 21, and in Yates, *Secret Proceedings*, ed. 1821, p. 98.

927

body of his notes. It seems best to insert this paper at this point. It reads as follows:

*May 30th.*

1st resolution from Mr. Randol[ph]

Mr. R. wishes to have that resol. dissented to. The resol. postponed to take up the following:

1st. That a union of the States merely fœderal will not accomplish the object proposed by the articles of confederation, namely, "common defence, security of liberty, and general welfare".

Mr. C. Pinkney wishes to know whether the establishment of this Resolution is intended as a ground for a consolidation of the several States into one.

Mr. Randol[ph] has nothing further in contemplation than what the propositions he has submitted yesterday has [sic] expressed.

2. Resolved that no treaty or treaties between the whole or a less number of the States in their sovereign capacities will accomplish their common defence, liberty or welfare.

3. Resolved therefore that a national governmen[t] ought to be established consisting of a supreme legislature, judiciary and executive.

Mr. Whythe [sic] [7] presumes from the silence of the house that they gentn. are prepared to pass on the resolution and proposes its being put.

Mr. Butler—does not think the house prepared, that he is not. Wishes Mr. Randolph to shew that the existence of the States cannot be preserved by any other mode than a national government.

Gen. Pinkney—Thinks agreeing to the resolve is declaring that the convention does not act under the authority of the recommendation of Congress.

The first resolution postponed to take up the 3d. viz—Resolved that a national government ought to be established consisting of a supreme legislature, judiciary and executive.

1787, 21 Febry. Resolution of Congress.[8]

---
[7] This speech does not appear elsewhere.
[8] M. Henry probably copies this at this point in his notes for reference in connection with the preceding remarks as to the powers of the Convention.

Resolved that in the opinion of Congress it is expedient that on the 2d Monday of May next a convention of delegates who shall have been appointed by the several States to be held at Philada. for the sole and expres[s] purpose of *revising the articles of confederation*, and reporting to Congress and the several legislatures, such alterations and provisions therein as shall when agreeed [*sic*] to in Congress, and confirmed by the States, render the *fœderal constitution*, adequate to the exigencies of government and the preservation of the union."

Mr. Randolph [9] explains the intention of the 3d Resolution. Repeats the substance of his yesterdays observations. It is only meant to give the national government a power to defend and protect itself. To take therefore from the respective legislatures or States, no more sover[e]ignty than is competent to this end.

Mr. Dickinson. Under obligations to the gentlemen who brought forward the systems laid before the house yesterday. Yet differs from the mode of proceeding to which the resolutions or propositions before the Committee lead. Would propose a more simple mode. All agree that the confederation is defective all agree that it ought to be amended. We are a nation altho' consisting of parts or States—we are also confederated, and he hopes we shall always remain confederated. The enquiry should be—

1. What are the legislative powers which we should vest in Congress.
2. What judiciary powers.
3. What executive powers.

We may resolve therefore, in order to let us into the business. That the confederation is defective; and then proceed to the definition of such powers as may be thought adequate to the objects for which it was instituted.

Mr. E. Gerry. Does not rise to speak to the *merits* of the question before the Committee but to the *mode*.

A distinction has been made between a *federal* and *national* government. We ought not to determine that there is this distinction for if we do, it is questionable not only whether this convention can propose an government totally different or whether

---

[9] These remarks of Randolph, and those of Dickinson which follow, seem not to be found in Madison's or any of the other notes hitherto printed.

Congress itself would have a right to pass such a resolution as that before the house. The commission from Massachusets empowers the deputies to proceed agreeably to the recommendation of Congress. This the foundation of the convention. If we have a right to pass this resolution we have a right to annihilate the confederation.

Proposes—In the opinion of this convention, provision should be made for the establishment of a fœderal legislative, judiciary, and executive.

Governeur Morris. Not yet ripe for a decision, because men seem to have affixed different explanations to the terms before the house. 1. We are not now under a fœderal gover[n]ment. 2. There is no such thing. A fœderal government is that which has a right to compel every part to do its duty. The fœderal gov. has no such compelling capacities, whether considered in their legislative, judicial or Executive qualities.

The States in their appointments Congress in their recommendations point directly to the establishment of a *supreme* government capable of "the common defence, security of liberty and general welfare.

Cannot conceive of a government in which there can exist two *supremes*. A federal agreement which each party may violate at pleasure cannot answer the purpose. One government better calculated to prevent wars or render them less expensive or bloody than many.

We had better take a supreme government now, than a despot twenty years hence—for come he must.

Mr. Reed, Genl. [Pinckney] 2dng. proposes—In order to carry into execution the design of the States in      this meeting [10] and to accomplish the *objects* proposed by the confederation resolved that A more effective government consisting of a legislative judiciary and executive ought to be established.

In order to carry into execution.

Mr. R. King [11]—The object of the motion from Virginia, an establishment of a government that is to act upon the whole people of the U. S.

---
[10] "in forming this Convention" (*Journal*).
[11] King's remarks, and those of Madison which follow, seem not to appear in other records of the debates.

The object of the motion from Delaware seems to have application merely to the strengthening the confederation by some additional powers.

Mr. Maddison—The motion does go to bring out the sense of the house—whether the States shall be governed by one power. If agreed to it will decide nothing. The meaning of the States that the confed. is defect. and ought to be amended. In agreeing to the [12] . . . ]

The Committee then proceeded to consider the 2 Resolution in Mr. Randolphs paper viz

That the rights of suffrage in the national legislature ought to be proportioned to the quotas of contribution or to the number of free inhabitants as the one or the other rule may seem best in different cases.

As this gave the large States the most absolute controul over the lesser ones it met with opposition which produced an adjourn ment without any determination.

The Commitee of the whole to sit to-morrow.

*31 May.*

Mr. Randolph motioned to take into consideration, vz. That the national legislature ought to consist of two branches.

agreed to.

Part of the 4 resolution moved, vz. That the members of the first branch ought to be elected by the people of the several States.

6 States aff.   2 neg.   2 divided.

5 Reso. so far as follows taken up vz. That the members of the second branch of the national legislature ought to be elected by those of the first out of a proper number of persons nominated by the individual legislatures.

Neg. 7. affirm 3. aff. Mass. S. C. Virginia.[13]

Motioned vz.

That each branch ought to possess the right of originating acts.

agreed.

---

[12] End of paper. Unfinished.
[13] More correct than the journal. See Madison, *Documentary History*, III. 32.

That the national legislature ought to be empowered to enjoy the *legislative rights vested in Congress by the confedn.* and *moreover* to legislate in all cases to which the *separate States are incompetent.*[14]

                                                                 agreed.

or in which the harmony of the U. S. may be interrupted by the exercise of individual legislation.

                                                                  agreed.

To negative all laws passed by the several States contravening in the opinion of the national legislature the articles of union, (or any treaty subsisting under the authority of the union, added by Dr. Franklin).

                                                                  agreed.

And to call forth the force of the union against any member of the union failing to fulfil its duty under the articles thereof.[15]

                                                               postponed.

Mr. E. Gery thought this clause "ought to be expressed so as the people might not understand it to prevent their being alarmed".

This idea rejected on account of its *artifice*, and because the system without such a declaration gave the government the means to secure itself.

### June 1st

Recd an express from home that my brother lay dangerously sick in consequence of which I set out immediately for Baltimore.

Left Baltimore 2 August

### August 4th

Returned to Philada. The committee of Convention ready to report. Their report in the hands of Dunlop the printer to strike off copies for the members.[16]

### Augt. 6

Convention met. present 8 States. Report delivered in by Mr. Rutledge. read. Convention adjourned till to-morrow to give the members an opportunity to consider the report.

---

[14] See Jameson, *ubi sup.*, 107.
[15] The next two paragraphs seem not to occur in any other report.
[16] See Bancroft, *Constitution*, II. 119, 139; Ford, *Pamphlets on the Constitution*, 390.

Proposed to Mr. D. Carrol, Mr. Jenifer, Mr. Mercer and Mr. Martin,[17] to meet to confer on the report, and to p[r]epare ourselves to act in unison.

Met at Mr. Carrolls lodgings in the afternoon. I repeated the object of our meeting, and proposed that we should take the report up by paragraphs and give our opinions thereon. Mr. Mercer wished to know of me whether I thought Maryland would embrace such a system. I told him I did not know, but I presumed the people would not object to a wise system. He extended this idea to the other gentlemen. Mr. Martin said they would not; That he was against the system, that a compromise only had enabled its abettors to bring it into its present stage— that had Mr. Jenifer voted with him, things would have taken a different turn. Mr. Jenifer said he voted with him till he saw it was in vain to oppose its progress. I begged the gentlemen to observe some order to enable us to do the business we had convened upon. I wished that we could be unanimous—and would make a proposition to effect it. I would join the deputation in bringing on a motion to postpone the report, to try the affections of the house to an amendment of the confederation without altering the sovereignty of suffrage; which failing we should then agree to render the system reported as perfect as we could, in the mean while to consider our motion to fail and proceed to confer upon the report agreeably to the intention of our meeting. I. E. That we should now and at our future meetings alter the report to our own judgement to be able to appear unanimous in case our motion failed.

Mr. Carrol could not agree to this proposition, because he did not think the confederation could be amended to answer its intentions. I thought that it was susceptable of a revision which would sufficiently invigorate it for the exigencies of the times. Mr. Mercer thought otherwise as did Mr. Jenifer. This proposition to conciliate the deputation was rejected.

Mr. Martin in the course of the conversation observed that he was against two branches—that we [sic] was against the people electing the representatives of the national government. That

---

[17] The other members from Maryland. Mercer did not take his seat till this day.

he wished to see the States governments rendered capable of the most vigorous exertions, and so knit together by a confederation as to act together on national emergencies.

Finding that we could come to no conclusions I recommended meeting again to-morrow, for unless we could appear in the convention with some degree of unanimity it would be unneccessary to remain in it, sacrificing time and money without being able to render any service. They agreed to meet to-morrow, except Mr. Martin who said he was going to New York and would not be back till monday following.[18]

It being of importance to know and to fix the opinions of my colleagues on the most consequential articles of the new system, I prepared the following propositions, for that purpose viz.[19]

Art. IV. Sec. 5. Will you use your best endeavours to obtain for the senate an equal authority over money bills with the house of representatives.?

Art. VII. Sect. 6. Will you use your best endeavours to have it made a part of the system that "no navigation act shall be passed without the assent of two thirds of the representation from each State?

In case these alterations cannot be obtained will you give your assent to the 5 sect. of the IV article and 6 sect. of the VII. article as they stand in the report?

Will you also, (in case these alterations are not obtained) agree that the ratification of the conventions of nine States shall be sufficient for organizing the new constitutions?

N. B. Saw Mr. Mercer make out a list of the members names who had attended or were attending in convention with for and against marked opposite most of them—asked carelesly what question occasioned his being so particular upon which he told me laughing that it was no question but that those marked with a for were for a king. I then asked him how he knew that to which he said no matter the thing is so. I took a copy with his

---

[18] Martin in the *Maryland Journal* says that he was absent five days. Ford, *Essays on the Constitution*, 341. Ellsworth ("Landholder") says ten. *Ibid.*, 186. Martin replied, *ibid.*, 346, that he set out for New York on August 7, and returned and took his seat in the Convention on Monday, August 13. But see *post*, August 16.

[19] On the next page are two insertions, marked "N. B." and "+"; and places are indicated for their insertion.

permission, and Mr. Martin seeing me about it asked What it was. I told him, in the words Mr. Mercer had told me, when he begged me to let him copy the list which I did.[20]

### Augt. 7.

+Mr. Martin set out for New York on this day so we were without his concurrence in the propositions.

Shewed these propositions to Mr. Carroll Mr. Jenifer and Mr. Mercer in convention. They said in general terms that they believed they should accord with them. I observed to Mr. Carrol[l] that we would meet again in the evening and talk over the subject.[21]

The business of the Convention proceeded.

The preamble or caption and the 1. and 2. article passed without debate, the 3 article was amended so as to leave it with the legislature to appoint after the first meeting, the day for the succeeding meetings.

The IV article gave rise to a long debate, respecting the *qualifications of the electors*.

Mr. Dickinson contended for confining the rights of election in the first branch to *free holders*. No one could be considered as having an interest in the .government unless he possessed some of the soil.

The fear of an aristocracy was a theoretical fiction. The owners of the soil could have no interest distinct from the country. There was no reason to dread a few men becoming lords of such an extent of territory as to enable them to govern at their pleasure.

Governeur Morris—thought that wise men should not suffer themselves to be misguided by sound. If the suffrage was to be open to all *freemen*—the government would indubitably be an aristocracy. The system was a system of Aristocracy. It put it in the power of opulent men whose business created numerous dependents to rule at all elections. Hence so soon as we erected large manufactories and our towns became more populous— wealthy merchants and manufacturers would elect the house of

---

[20] See *post*, nos. III.–IX., and especially no. VIII.

[21] Crossed out: "that I had my doubt whether the gentlemen had given themselves time to consider the effect of the propositions or the part we ought to take respecting them."

representatives. This was an aristocracy. This could only be avoided by confining the suffrage to *free holders*. Mr. Maddison supported similar sentiments.

The old ideas of taxation and representation were opposed to such reasoning.[22] Dr. Franklin spoke on this occasion. He observed that in time of war a country owed much to the lower class of citizens. Our late war was an instance of what they could suffer and perform. If denied the right of suffrage it would debase their spirit and detatch them from the interest of the country. One thousand of our seamen were confined in English prisons—had bribes offered them to go on board English vessels which they rejected. An English ship was taken by one of our men of war. It was proposed to the English sailors to join ours in a cruise and share alike with th[e]m in the captures. They immediately agreed to the proposal. This difference of behavior arises from [23] the operation of freedom in America, and the laws in England. One British Statute excluded a number of subjects from a suffrage. These immediately became slaves. At th[r]ee o'clock the house adjourned without coming to any issue.

At five o'clock in the evening I went to Mr. Carrolls lodging to confer with my colleagues on the points I had submitted to their consideration. I found Mr. Carroll alone when We entered upon their merits. He agreed with me that the deputation should oppose a resolute face to the 5 sect of the IV article,[24] and that they ought to reject it. He appeared fully sensible of its tendency—That lodging in the house of representatives the sole right of raising and appropriating money, upon which the Senate had only a negative, gave to that branch an inordinate power in the constitution, which must end in its destruction. That without equal powers they were not an equal check upon each other—and that this was the chance that appeared for obtained [*sic.* obtaining?] an equal suffrage, or a suffrage equal to wh[a]t we had in the present confedn.

[22] This is apparently McHenry's comment. What follows, from "Doctor Franklin" to "became slaves" is written on the opposite page of the manuscript, and marked to be inserted.
[23] Crossed out: "this discription of men having a right of suffrage."
[24] To the effect that money-bills should originate in the House of Representatives alone, and that the Senate should have no right to alter or amend them.

We accorded also that the deputation should in no event consent to the 6 sect. of VII article.[25] He saw plainly that as a quorum consisted of a majority of the members of each house—that the dearest interest[s?] of trade were under the controul of four States or of 17 membe[r]s in one branch and 8 in the other branch.[26]

We adverted also to the 1st sect of the VII article which enabled the legislature to lay and collect taxes, duties, imposts and excises, and to regulate commerce among the several States. We almost shuddered at the fate of the commerce of Maryland should we be unable to make any change in this extraordinary power.

We agreed that our deputation ought never to assent to this article in its present form or without obtaining such a provision as I proposed.

I now begged his particular attention to my last proposition.[27] By the XXII article we were called upon to agree that the system should be submitted to a convention chosen in each State under the recommendation of its legislature. And that a less number of conventions than the whole agreeing to the system should be sufficient to organise the constitution.

We had taken an oath to support our constitution and frame of government. We had been empowered by a legislature legally constituted to revise the confederation and fit it for the *exigencies of government*, and *preservation of the union*. Could we do this business in a manner contrary to our constitution? I feared [(Note by McHenry.) This was said first I *thought*—then I *feared*[28]] we could not. If we relinquished any of the rights or powers of our government to the U. S. of America, we could no otherwise agree to that relinquishment than in the mode our constitution prescribed for making changes or alterations in it.

Mr. Carrol[l] said he had felt his doubts respecting the propriety of this article as it respected Maryland; but he hoped we should be able to get over this difficulty.

Mr. Jenifer now came in to whom Mr. Carroll repeated what we had said upon my propositions and our determinations. Mr.

---

[25] "No navigation act shall be passed without the assent of two thirds of the members present in each house."

[26] Marginal note: "33, 17 and 14, 8."

[27] As to ratification by nine states.

[28] The word "feared" is substituted for a word erased.

Jenifer agreed to act in unison with us but seemed to have vague ideas of the mischiefs of the system as it stood in the report.

I wished to impress him with the necessity to support us, and touched upon some popular points.

I suggested to him the unfavorable impression it would make upon the people on account of its expence. An army and navy was [sic] to be raised and supported, expensive courts of judicature to be maintained, and a princely president to be provided for etc. That it was plain that the revenue for these purposes was to be chiefly drawn from commerce. That Maryland in this case would have this resource taken from her, without the expences of her own government being lessened. That what would be raised from her commerce and by indirect taxation would far exceed the proportion she would be called upon to pay under the present confederation.

An increase of taxes, and a decrease in the objects of taxation as they respected a revenue for the State would not prove very palatable to our people, who might think that the whole objects of taxation were hardly sufficient to discharge the States obligations.

Mr. Mercer came in, and said he would go with the deputation on the points in question. He would wish it to be understood however, that he did not like the system, that it was weak—That he would produce a better one since the convention had undertaken to go radically to work, that perhaps he would not be supported by any one, but if he was not, he would go with the stream.

## August 8.

The 2 sect. of the IV. article was amended to read 7 insted of three years. It was proposed to add to the section "at least one year preceding his election". negatived. Maryland divided. M[ess]rs. Mercer and Carrol neg. Mr. Jenifer and myself aff.

The fifth section giving the sole power of raising and appropriating money to the house of representatives expunged.

*August 9.*

6 and 7 sects. agreed to without amendment.

The 1 section of the V article underwent an emendatory alteration. The last clause—"each member shall have one vote"—opposed by Mr. Mason, Randolph and a few others on account of the Senate by the loss of the 5 sect of the IV article having the same powers over money bills as the house of representatives.—The whole however was agreed to.

Sect. 2. agreed to after an emendatory addition.

Sect. 3 agreed to after inserting inhabitant for resident, as being less equivocal, and 9 years for 4 years.[29]

Governeur Morris proposed insted of 4 years 14. He would have confined the members he said to natives—but for its appearance and the effects it might have against the system.

Mr. *Mason* had the same wishes, but he could not think of excluding those foreigners who had taken a part and borne with the country the dangers and burdenths [*sic*] of the war.

Mr. Maddison was against such an invidious distinction. The matter might be safely intrusted to the respective legislatures. Doctor Franklin was of the same opinion. Mr. Willson expressed himself feelingly on the same side. It might happen, he said, that he who had been thought worthy of being trusted with the framing of the Constitution, might be excluded from it. He had not been born in this country. He considered such exclusing as one of the most galling chains which the human mind could experience. It was wrong to deprive the government of the talents virtue and abilities of such foreigners as might chuse to remove to this country. The corrup[t] of other countries would not come here. Those who were tired in opposing such corruptions would be drawn hither, etc. etc.

Sect. 4 agreed to.

### Article VI.

Sect. 1. Agreed to with this amendment insted of "*but their provisions concerning them.*" [30]

adjourned

---

[29] The next three paragraphs marked for insertion. Written on preceding page.

[30] The reference is to the substitution, for the words indicated, of the words "regulations in each of the foregoing cases," etc.

*August 10.*

Sect. 2. dissented to. Sects. 3. 4 5 and 6 agreed to.[31]

*Augt. 11.*

Sect. 7 agreed to after expunging the words "when it shall be acting in a legislative capacity" and inserting after the words "publish them" except such parts as in their judgement require secrecy.

After much debate [32] agreed to reconsider on monday the 5 sect. of the 4 article.

*August 13.*

The 2 sect. of the 4 article and the 3 sect. of the 5 article was reconsidered and lengthily debated. The 7 years however in the first and the 9 years in the latter remained and the articles stood as before reconsideration.

*Augt. 14.*

Sect. 8 agreed to, premising the words "during the session of the legislature".[33]

Sect. 9. postponed.

Sect. 10. altered, that the members of both branches be paid out of the treasury of the United States, their pay to be ascertained by law.

*August 15.*

Sect. 11. agreed to.

Sect. 12 postponed.

Sect. 13. Agreed to with the alteration of ¾ of each house instead of *two thirds*.

*16 Augt.*

Agreed to Article VII from Sec: 1. to the paragraph "borrow money and emit bills on the credit of the united States inclusive, with the addition of the words "and post roads" and the omission of "*and emit bills*".

Mr. Martin appeared in convention.

---
[31] After amendment of sections 3 and 6.
[32] Not much is reported by Madison, the only other reporter for this day.
[33] This was done on August 11, according to the journal and Madison.

### August 17.

Agreed "to appoint a treasurer by joint Ballot; To constitute tribunals inferior to the supreme court; To make rules concerning captures on land and water;

expunged the next section and inserted

To define and punish piracies and felonies committed on the high seas;

To punish counterfeiting the securities and the current coin of the United States.

Struck out the clause "To subdue a rebellion etc.

Debated the difference between a power to declare war, and to make war—amended by substituting declare—adjourned without a question on the clause.[34]

### Augt. 18.

To make war, to raise armies "to build and equip fleets amended to declare war, to raise and support armies, to provide and maintain fleets" to which was added "to make rules for the government and regulation of the land and naval forces.

The next clause postponed.

### August 20.

The following one agreed to.

Sect. 2. Amended to read. Treason against the U. S. shall consist only in levying war against them, or in adhering to their enemies giving them aid and comfort. The legislature shall have power to declare the punishment of treason. No person shall be convicted of treason unless on confession in open court, or the testimony of two witnesses to the same overt act.

Mr. Mason [35] moved to add to the 1 sect of the VII article.

To make sumptuary laws.

Governeur Morris. sump. laws were calculated to continue great landed estates for ever in the same families. If men had no temptation to dispose of their money they would not sell their estates.

Negatived.

---

[34] Not so the journal, *Documentary History*, I. 130.
[35] From "Mr. Mason" to "Negatived" inserted. Written on preceding page. The proper place for the insertion is however a paragraph earlier according to the journal and Madison. *Ibid.*, 137, III. 567, 568.

Amended section 3 by striking out the words in the second line *white and other*, and the word six in the 5 line and substituting the word three—but adjourned without a question on the section.

*Augt. 21.*

passed the 3 sect.

Took up 4 sect. adjourned, after passing the first clause to the word State 2[d] line inclusive.[36]

*August 22.*

Committed the remainder of the 4 sect. with the 5 and 6.

The 4 sect promitting [permitting] the importation of Slaves gave rise to much desultory debate.

Every 5 slaves counted in representation as one elector without being equal in point of strength to one *white* inhabitant. This gave the slave States an advantage in representation over the others. The slaves were moreover exempt from duty on importation. They served to render the representation from such States aristocratical.[37]

It was replied—That the population or increase of slaves in Virginia exceeded their calls for their services—That a prohibition of Slaves into S. Carolina Georgia etc—would be a monopoly in their favor. These States could not do without Slaves. Virginia etc would make their own terms for such as they might sell. Such was the situation of the country that it could not exist without slaves—That they could confederate on no other condition. They had enjoyed the right of importing slaves when colonies. They enjoyed as States under the confederation. And if they could not enjoy it under the proposed government, they could not associate or make a part of it.

Several additions were reported by the committee.

Mr. Martin[38] shewed us some restrictory clauses drawn up for the VII article respecting commerce—which we agreed to bring forward.

---

[36] *I. e.*, "No tax or duty shall be laid by the Legislature on articles exported from any State."
[37] These remarks cannot be identified with any individual speech in Madison's notes. What follows seems to be General C. C. Pinckney's statement. *Documentary History*, III. 587.
[38] This paragraph is inserted from the preceding page.

Moved that the legislature should pass no ex post facto laws or bills of attainder.

G. Morris Willson Dr. Johnson etc thought the first an unnecessary guard as the principles of justice law et[c] were a perpetual bar to such. To say that the legis. shall not pass an ex post facto law is the same as to declare they shall not do a thing contrary to common sense—that they shall not cause that to be crime which is no crime.

Carried in the affirmative.

*August 23.*

7 sect. agreed to.[39]

On motion, on a proposition reported and amended agreed that "*The legislature* shall fulfil the engagements and discharge the debts of the U. S." To make the first clause in the VII article— Amended the first clause in the report of the said article by striking out the words, *the legislature of the U. S.* Added in the said article after the clause "to provide and maintain fleets":

To organize and discipline the militia and govern such part of them as may be employed in the service of the U. S. reserving to the States respectively the appointment of the officers and the authority of training the militia according to the discipline prescribed by the U. S."

Expunged in the VIII article the words *the acts of the legislature of the U. S.* and *of this constitution,* so as that the constitution and laws made in pursuance thereof etc should be the supreme laws of the several States.

The IX article being taken up, It was motioned that no treaty should be binding till it received the sanction of the legislature.

It was said[40] that a minister could not then be instructed by the Senate who were to appoint him, or if instructed there could be no certainty that the house of representatives would agree to confirm what he might agree to under these instructions.

To this it was answered[41] that all treaties which contravene a law of England or require a law to give them operation or effect are inconclusive till agreed to by the legislature of Great Britain.

---

[39] After amendment.
[40] By Mr. Gorham. *Documentary History,* III. 604.
[41] By Dr. Wilson. *Ibid.*

Except in such cases the power of the King without the concurrence of the parliament conclusive.

Mr. Maddison.[42] the Kings power over treaties final and original except in granting subsidies or dismembering the empire. These required parliamentary acts.

Commiteed [sic].

Adjourned.

### Augt. 24.

2 and 3 sect. struck out. The 10 article give rise to various debate. Amended to read that the election of the president of the U. S. be by *joint ballot*. It was moved to add each State having one vote—Conn: Jer. Mar. Georg.[43] ay. N. H. Mass. Penns. Vir. N. C. and S. C. no. It was moved that the president be elected by the people[44] 3 states affirm—7 neg.

On what respects his ineligibility Gov. Morris observed. That in the strength of the Executive would be found the strength of America. Ineligibility operates to weaken or destroy the constitution. The president will have no interest beyond his period of service. He will for peace and emolument to himself and friends agree to acts that will encrease the power and agrandize the bodies which elect him. The legislature will swallow up the whole powers of the constitution; but to do this effectually they must possess the Executive. This will lead them to tempt him, and the shortness of his reign will subject him to be tempted and overcome. The legislature has great and various appointments in their power. This will create them an extensive influence which may be so used as to put it out of the power of the Executive to prevent them from arriving at supremacy. On the other hand give the Executive a chance of being re-chosen and he will hold his prerogatives with all possible tenaciousness.

postponed the question.

Proceeded, and made some amendments to the 2 sect. Adjourned when the question was going to be put whether the legis-

---

[42] Not in his notes. *Ibid.*, 606.

[43] And Delaware. *Ibid.*, I. 233.

[44] According to the journal and Madison, this second vote came first, and stood 2 to 9. *Ibid.*, 151, 152, 232, III. 609.

lature might enable the State Executives or legislatures to appoint officers to certain offices.

*Augt. 25.*

The clause in the 2 sect. X article, "he shall commission all the officers of the U. S. and shall appoint officers in all cases not otherwise provided for by this constitution, was moved to be amended by adding, except where by law the Executive of the several States shall have the power. Amendment negative[d]. Maryland divided—D. C. and J. against Martin and myself affirm.[45]

Moved several propositions [46] to restrict the legislature from giving any preference in duties, or from obliging duties to be collected in a manner injurious to any State, and from establishing new ports of entrance and clerance, unless neglected to be established by the States after application. Opposed by Massachusets. Mr. Gorahm [sic] said it might be very proper to oblige vessels, for example, to stop at Norfolk on account of the better collection of the revenue.

Mr. King thought it improper to deliberate long on such propositions but to take the sense of the house immediately upon them.[47]

I moved to have them committed to a committee consisting of a member from each State. Committed.

Proceeded a little further in the 2 sect.

Mr. C. Pinkney gave notice that he would move that the consent of ¾ of the whole legislature be necessary to the enacting a law respecting the regulation of trade or the formation of a navigation act.[48]

Adjourned to monday.

*Monday 27 Augt.*

Amended the Presidential oath of office—made some other amendments—postponed what follows from the oath to the end.

Agreed to the 1. 2 and 3 sect. of the XI article with amendments.

---

[45] August 24, according to the journal and Madison, who says, *Documentary History*, III, 613, that it was negatived without a call of states, as also appears from the sheets of votes, *ibid.*, I, 233.

[46] Some of them by Dr. McHenry.

[47] This is not in Madison.

[48] This is not in Madison, who however reports Pinckney as proposing this on August 29, but with a two-thirds vote, not three-fourths. *Documentary History*, III, 636.

*Augt. 28.*

4 Sect. amended. 5 sect. agreed to.

XII article amended by adding that no State shall emit bills of credit, nor make any thing but specie a tender in debts.

XIII amended so [th]at all duties laid by a State shall accrue to the use of the U. S.

*Agt. 29*

XIIII and XV agreed to [49] XVI. article committed.

*Augt. 30.*

XVII article debated by Maryland. Obtained an alteration so that the claim of the U. S. to the Crown lands or Western territory may be decided upon by the supreme judiciary.

XVIIII agreed to.[50]

Endeavoured to recall the house to the reported propositions from maryland, to prevent the U. S. from giving prefe[re]nces to one State above another or to the shipping of one State above another, in collecting or laying duties. The house averse to taking any thing up till this system is got through.[51] XXI. adjourned on this article.

Proposed to have a private conference with each other tomorrow before meeting of the convention to take measures for carrying our propositions, etc.

*Augt. 31.*

Filled up the blank in the XXI article with 9: 8 States afirm: 3 Neg. Maryland moved to fill it up with 13 but stood alone on the question. G. W. was for 7.

Struck out *for their approbation* in the 22 Article. filled up the blank in the 23 article with 9, and amended the last clause by striking out *choose the president of the U. S. and.*

The system being thus far agreed to the restrictory propositions from Maryland [52] were taken up—and carried—against them N. Hamp. Massachus.[53] and S. Carolina.

---

[49] August 28, according to the journal and Madison.
[50] The eighteenth, nineteenth, and twentieth articles were all agreed to on this day.
[51] This episode does not appear in Madison.
[52] As to equality of the states in respect to federal regulation of commerce and navigation.
[53] The vote of Massachusetts not given in the journal.

946

Refered to a grand committee all the sections of the system under postponement and a report of a committee of 5 with several motions.

Adjourned.

*Septmbr. 1.*

Adjourned to let the committee *sit*.

Sepr. 3. and 4 Employed chiefly by the committee.

Agreed on report of the com. that the 1 clause of the 1 sect. of the 7 art. read vz.

"The legislature shall have power to lay and collect taxes duties imposts and excises, to pay the debts and provide for the common defence and general welfare of the U. S."

Also to add at the end of the 2 clause of the 1 sect of the 7 art. "and with the Indian tribes."

+ Took [54] up in the report "in the place of the 9 art. 1 sec.— "The senate of the U. S. shall have power to try all impeachments but no person shall be convicted without the concurrence of $\frac{2}{3}$ of the members present. postponed.

The committee report in part as follows [55] . . .

After the words into the service of the U. S. in the 2 sect 10 art add "and may require the opinion in writing of the principal officer in each of the Executive departments upon any subject relating to the duties of their respective offices.

The latter part of the 2 sect. 10 art. to read "he shall be removed from his office on impeachment by the house of representatives and conviction by the Senate, for treason, or bribery, and in case of his removal as aforesaid, death absence resignation or inability to discharge the powers or duties of his office, the vice pres. shall exercise those powers and duties until another pres. be chosen or until the inability of the pres. be removed.

No provision in the above for a new election in case of the death or removal of the President.

Upon looking over the constitution it does not appear that the national legislature can *erect light houses* or *clean out or preserve the*

---

[54] This paragraph inserted. Written on preceding page.

[55] Here follows the familiar report of the committee of eleven on the mode of electing the President, to be found in all prints of the journal, and therefore omitted here. See *Documentary History*, I. 177-179, III, 668-670.

*navigation of harbours.* This expence ought to be borne by commerce—of course by the general treasury into which all the revenue of commerce must come.

Is it proper to declare all the navigable waters or rivers and within the U. S. common high ways? Perhaps a power to restrain any State from demanding tribute from citizens of another State in such cases is comprehended in the power to regulate trade between State and State.

This to be further considered. A motion to be made on the light house etc. to-morrow.

### *Septr. 5.*

The greatest part of the day spent in desultory conversation on that part of the report respecting the mode of chusing the President. Adjourned without coming to a conclusion.

### *Sepr. 6.*

Spoke to Gov Morris Fitzimmons and Mr. Goram to insert a power in the confederation enabling the legislature to erect piers for protection of shipping in winter and to preserve the navigation of harbours. Mr. Gohram against. The other two gentlemen for it. Mr. Gov: [sic] thinks it may be done under the words of the 1 clause 1 sect 7 art. amended—"and provide for the common defence and general welfare. If this comprehends such a power, it goes to authorise the legisl. to grant exclusive privileges to trading companies etc.

Mr. Willson remarked on the report of the committee considered together That it presented to him a most dangerous appearance. He was not affraid of names—but he was of aristocracy. What was the amount of the report.

1. The Senate in certain events, (which by such management as may be expected would always happen—) is to chuse the President.
2. The Senate may make treaties and alliances.
3. They may appoint almost all officers.
4. May try impeachments.

Montesqu says, an officer is the officer of those who appoint him. This power may in a little time render the Senate independent of the people. The different branches should be independent of each other. They are combined and blended in the Senate. The Senate may exercise, the powers of legislation, and Executive and judicial powers. To make treaties legislative, to appoint officers Executive for the Executive has only the nomination, To try impeachments judicial. If this is not ARISTOCRACY I know not what it is.

Gov. Morris observed that the report had lessened not increased the powers of the Senate. That their powers were greater in the printed paper.

Col Hamilton. In general the choice will rest in the Senate—take this choice from them and the report is an improvement on the printed paper. In the printed paper a destroying monster is created. He is not re eligible, he will therefore consider his 7 years as 7 years of lawful plunder. Had he been made re eligible by the legislature, it would not have removed the evil, he would have purchased his re election. At present the people may make a choice—but hereafter it is probable the choice of a president would centre in the Senate. As the report stands—the President will use the power of nominating to attach the Senate to his interest. He will act by this means continually on their hopes till at length they will boeth [*sic*] act as one body. Let the election of the president be confined to electors,[56] and take from the Senate the power to try impeachments, and the report will be much preferable to the printed paper.

He does not agree with those persons who say they will vote against the report because they cannot get all parts of it to please them. He will take any system which promises to save America from the dangers with which she is threatened.

The report amended by placing the choice of the President in the house of representatives, each State having one vote.

Adjourned.

*Sepr. 7.*

Made some further progress in the report.

Mr. Mason [57] moved to postpone the section giving the President power to require the advice of the heads of the great departments

---

[56] *I. e.*, by a provision that the highest number of electoral votes may elect, even though not a majority.

[57] The printed journal, ed. 1819, attributes this motion to Madison. The latter corrects this in his notes. *Documentary History*, III. 701.

to take up a motion—to appoint a council of State, to consist of 6 members—two from the Eastern, two from the middle and two from the Southern States—who should in conjunction with the President make all appointments and be an advisory body—to be elected by the legislature, to be in for 6 years with such succession as provided for the Senate.

3 States for postponing 8 against it—so it was lost.
Adjourned.

*Septr. 8.*

Agreed to the whole report with some amendments—and refered the printed paper etc to a committee of 5 to revise and place the several parts under their proper heads—with an instruction to bring in draught of a letter to Congres.[58]

    Committee  Gov. Morris
            Maddison
            Hamilton
            Dr. Johnson
            King—

Maryland gave notice that she had a proposition of much importance to bring forward—but would delay it till Monday it being near the hour to adjourn.[59]

*Monday Sepr. 10, 11 and 12.*

Spent in attempts to amend several parts of the system. 12—amended the sect  art [60] from ¾ to ⅔, as it stood in the printed report at first.

*13 Sepr.*

Recd. read and compared the new printed report with the first printed amended report. Made some verbal alterations, and inserted the propositions moved by Maryland which had been overlooked.

---

[58] This instruction appears in the journal under September 10, in a form requiring the preparation of an address to the people, to be laid before Congress.
[59] Of this episode there appears to be no record elsewhere.
[60] Section 13 of article vi. of the report of the Committee of Detail, dealing with the President's veto.

## 14 Septr.

Moved by Dr. Franklin seconded by Mr. Willson, to empowe[r] Congress to open and establish canals. This being objected to—moved by Virginia To empower Congress to grant charters of incorporation in cases where the U. S. may require them and where the objects of them cannot be obtained by a State.

Negatived.

Moved To authorize Congress to establish an university to which and the honors and emoluments of which all persons may be admitted without any distinction of religion whatever. Congress enabled to erect such an institution in the place of the general government. Thus Congress to possess exclusive jurisdiction.

Neg. 6 Noes. 3 ay.[61] 1 State divided.

Moved—And the liberty of the press shall be inviolable. 6 noes. 5 ays.[62]

## 15 Sepr.

Maryland moved.[63]

> No State shall be prohibited from laying such duties of tonnage as may be sufficient for improving their harbors and keeping up lights, but all acts laying such duties shall be subject to the approbation or repeal of Congress.

Moved to amend it viz. No State without the consent of Congress shall lay a duty of tonnage. Carried in the affirmative 6 ays 4 Noes, 1 divided.

Made several verbal amendment[s] in the progression on the system.

Added to the V article amended "No State without its consent shall be deprived of its equal suffrage in the Senate.

Mr. Mason moved in substance that no navigation act be passed without the concurrence of ⅔ of the members present in each house.

Negatived.

---

[61] Four noes, according to Madison.
[62] So the printed journal, though Madison has it 4 to 7.
[63] McHenry and Carroll, according to Madison. *Documentary History*, III. 751.

Mr. Randolp[h] moved that it be recommended to appoint a second convention with plenary powers to consider objections to the system and to conclude one binding upon the States.

rejected unanimously.

The question being taken on the system agreed to unanimously.

Ordered to be engrossed and 500 copies struck.[64] Adjourned till monday the 17th.

*Monday 17 Sepr. 1787.*

Read the engrossed constitution. Altered the representation in the house of representatives from 40 to thirty thousand.

Dr. Franklin put a paper into Mr. Willsons hand to read containing his reasons for assenting to the constitution. It was plain, insinuating persuasive—and in any event of the system guarded the Doctors fame.

Mr. Randolp[h] Mr. Mason and Mr. Gerry declined signing. The other members signed.

Being [65] opposed to many parts of the system I make a remark why I signed it and mean to support it.

1s[t]ly I distrust my own judgement, especially as it is opposite to the opinion of a majority of gentlemen whose abilities and patriotism are of the first cast; and as I have had already frequent occasions to be convinced that I have not always judged right.

2dly Alterations may be obtained, it being provided that the concurrence of $\frac{2}{3}$ of the Congress may at any time introduce them.

3dly Comparing the inconveniences and the evils which we labor under and may experience from the present confederation, and the little good we can expect from it—with the possible evils and probable benefits and advantages promised us by the new system, I am clear that I ought to give it all the support in my power.

Philada. 17 Sepr. 1787    JAMES McHENRY.

---

[64] The number is not elsewhere mentioned, I believe.
[65] From here to McHenry's signature is written on the preceding page in different ink.

Major Jackson Secry. to carry it to Congress. Injunction of secrecy taken off. Members to be provided with printed copies. adjourned sine die. Gentn. of Con. dined together at the City Tavern.

*18—*

A lady asked Dr. Franklin Well Doctor what have we got a republic or a monarchy. A republic replied the Doctor if you can keep it. [(Foot-note by McHenry.) The lady here aluded to was Mrs. Powel of Philada.]

Mr. Martin [66] said one day in company with Mr. Jenifer speaking of the system before Convention.

I'll be hanged if ever the people of Maryland agree to it. I advise you said Mr. Jenifer to stay in Philadelphia lest you should be hanged.[67]

---

[66] The anecdote of Martin is an insert written on the preceding page.
[67] End of book.

# VARIANT TEXTS OF THE VIRGINIA PLAN, PRESENTED BY EDMUND RANDOLPH TO THE FEDERAL CONVENTION, MAY 29, 1787.

## TEXT A.

[Quoted from Hunt, Gaillard, and Scott, James B., ed. *Debates in the Federal Convention of 1787 Reported by James Madison.* (New York, 1920), pp. 23-26.]

1. Resolved that the Articles of Confederation ought to be so corrected & enlarged as to accomplish the objects proposed by their institution; namely, "common defence, security of liberty and general welfare."

2. Res<sup>d</sup> therefore that the rights of suffrage in the National Legislature ought to be proportioned to the Quotas of contribution, or to the number of free inhabitants, as the one or the other rule may seem best in different cases.

3. Res<sup>d</sup> that the National Legislature ought to consist of two branches.

4. Res<sup>d</sup> that the members of the first branch of the National Legislature ought to be elected by the people of the several States every        for the term of        ; to be of the age of        years at least, to receive liberal stipends by which they may be compensated for the devotion of their time to [1] public service; to be ineligible to any office established by a particular State, or under the authority of the United States, except those beculiarly belonging to the functions of the first branch, during the term of service, and for the space of        after its expiration; to be incapable of reelection for the space of        after the expiration of their term of service, and to be subject to recall.

5. Resol<sup>d</sup> that the members of the second branch of the National Legislature ought to be elected by those of the first, out of a proper number of persons nominated by the individual Legislatures, to be of the age of        years at least; to hold their offices for a term sufficient to ensure their independency; [2] to receive liberal stipends,

---

[1] The word "the" is here inserted in the transcript.
[2] The word "independency" is changed to "independence" in the transcript.

by which they may be compensated for the devotion of their time to [3] public service; and to be ineligible to any office established by a particular State, or under the authority of the United States, except those peculiarly belonging to the functions of the second branch, during the term of service, and for the space of        after the expiration thereof.

6. Resolved that each branch ought to possess the right of originating Acts; that the National Legislature ought to be impowered to enjoy the Legislative Rights vested in Congress by the Confederation & moreover to legislate in all cases to which the separate States are incompetent, or in which the harmony of the United States may be interrupted by the exercise of individual Legislation; to negative all laws passed by the several States, contravening in the opinion of the National Legislature the articles of Union; [4] and to call forth the force of the Union ag$^{st}$ any member of the Union failing to fulfill its duty under the articles thereof.

7. Res$^d$ that a National Executive be instituted; to be chosen by the National Legislature for the term of        years,[5] to receive punctually at stated times, a fixed compensation for the services rendered, in which no increase or [6] diminution shall be made so as to affect the Magistracy, existing at the time of increase or diminution, and to be ineligible a second time; and that besides a general authority to execute the National laws, it ought to enjoy the Executive rights vested in Congress by the Confederation.

8. Res$^d$ that the Executive and a convenient number of the National Judiciary, ought to compose a Council of revision with authority to examine every act of the National Legislature before it shall operate, & every act of a particular Legislature before a Negative thereon shall be final; and that the dissent of the said Council shall amount to a rejection, unless the Act of the National Legislature be again passed, or that of a particular Legislature be again negatived by        of the members of each branch.

---

[3] The word "the" is here inserted in the transcript.
[4] The phrase "or any treaty subsisting under the authority of the Union" is here added in the transcript.
[5] The word "years" is omitted in the transcript.
[6] The word "or" is changed to "nor" in the transcript.

9. Res? that a National Judiciary be established to consist of one or more supreme tribunals, and of inferior tribunals to be chosen by the National Legislature, to hold their offices during good behaviour; and to receive punctually at stated times fixed compensation for their services, in which no increase or diminution shall be made so as to affect the persons actually in office at the time of such increase or diminution. that the jurisdiction of the inferior tribunals shall be to hear & determine in the first instance, and of the supreme tribunal to hear and determine in the dernier resort, all piracies & felonies on the high seas, captures from an enemy; cases in which foreigners or citizens of other States applying to such jurisdictions may be interested, or which respect the collection of the National revenue; impeachments of any National officers, and questions which may involve the national peace and harmony.

10. Resolv? that provision ought to be made for the admission of States lawfully arising within the limits of the United States, whether from a voluntary junction of Government & Territory or otherwise, with the consent of a number of voices in the National legislature less than the whole.

11. Res? that a Republican Government & the territory of each State, except in the instance of a voluntary junction of Government & territory, ought to be guarantied by the United States to each State

12. Res? that provision ought to be made for the continuance of Congress and their authorities and privileges, until a given day after the reform of the articles of Union shall be adopted, and for the completion of all their engagements.

13. Res? that provision ought to be made for the amendment of the Articles of Union whensoever it shall seem necessary, and that the assent of the National Legislature ought not to be required thereto.

14. Res? that the Legislative Executive & Judiciary powers within the several States ought to be bound by oath to support the articles of Union

15. Res.d that the amendments which shall be offered to the Confederation, by the Convention ought at a proper time, or times, after the approbation of Congress to be submitted to an assembly or assemblies of Representatives, recommended by the several Legislatures to be expressly chosen by the people, to consider & decide thereon.[7]

---

[7] The fifteen resolutions, constituting the "Virginia Plan," are in Madison's handwriting.

## Text B.

[Quoted from Yates, *Secret Debates*, App., pp. 209-212]

1. *Resolved*, That the articles of the confederation ought to be so corrected and enlarged, as to accomplish the objects proposed by their institution, namely, common defence, security of liberty, and general welfare.

2. *Resolved*, therefore, that the right of suffrage, in the national legislature, ought to be proportioned to the quotas of contribution, or to the number of free inhabitants, as the one or the other may seem best, in different cases.

3. *Resolved*, That the national legislature ought to consist of two branches.

4. *Resolved*, That the members of the first branch of the national legislature ought to be elected by the people of the several States, every      for the term of      to be of the age of      years at least; to receive liberal stipends, by which they may be compensated for the devotion of their time to public service; to be ineligible to any office established by a particular State, or under the authority of the United States (except those peculiarly belonging to the functions of the first branch) during the term of service and for the space of      after its expiration; to be incapable of re-election for the space of      after the expiration of their term of service,; and to be subject to recal.

5. *Resolved*, That the members of the second branch of the national legislature ought to be elected by those of the first, out of a proper number of persons nominated by the individual legislatures; to be of the age of      years, at least; to hold their offices for a term sufficient to ensure their independency; to receive liberal stipends, by which they may be compensated for the devotion of their time to the public service; and to be ineligible to any office established by a particular State, or under the authority of the United States, (except those peculiarly belonging to the functions of the second branch) during the term of service; and for the space of      after the expiration thereof.

6. *Resolved,* That each branch ought to possess the right of originating acts; that the national legislature ought to be empowered to enjoy the legislative right vested in congress, by the confederation; and moreover to legislate in all cases to which the separate States are incompetent, or in which the harmony of the United States may be interrupted by the exercise of individual legislation; to negative all laws passed by the several States, contravening in the opinion of the national legislature, the articles of union, or any treaty subsisting under the authority of the union; and to call forth the force of the union against any member of the union failing to fulfil its duty under the articles thereof.

7. *Resolved,* That a national executive be instituted, to be chosen by the national legislature for the term of      years, to receive punctually, at stated times, a fixed compensation for the services rendered, in which no increase or diminution shall be made, so as to affect the magistracy existing at the time of the increase or diminution; to be ineligible a second time; and that, besides a general authority to execute the national laws, it ought to enjoy the executive rights vested in congress by the confederation.

8. *Resolved,* That the executive, and a convenient number of the national judiciary, ought to compose a council of revision, with authority to examine every act of the national legislature, before it shall operate, and every act of a particular legislature before a negative thereon shall be final; and that the dissent of the said council shall amount to a rejection, unless the act of the national legislature be again passed, or that of a particular legislature be again negatived by      of the members of each branch.

9. *Resolved,* That a national judiciary be established to hold their offices during good behavior, and to receive punctually, at stated times, fixed compensations for their services, in which no increase or diminution shall be made, so as to affect the person actually in office at the time of such increase or diminution— That the jurisdiction of the inferior tribunals shall be, to hear and determine, in the first instance, and of the supreme tribunal to hear and determine, in the dernier resort, all piracies and felonies on the high seas; captures from an enemy; cases in which for-

eigners, or citizens of other States, applying to such jurisdictions, may be interested, or which respect the collection of the national revenue; impeachments of any national officer; and questions which involve the national peace or harmony.

10. *Resolved*, That provision ought to be made for the admission of States, lawfully arising within the limits of the United States, whether from a voluntary junction of government and territory, or otherwise, with the consent of a number of voices in the national legislature less than the whole.

11. *Resolved*, That a republican government, and the territory of each State (except in the instance of a voluntary junction of government and territory) ought to be guaranteed by the United States to each State.

12. *Resolved*, That provision ought to be made for the continuance of a congress, and their authorities and privileges, until a given day, after the reform of the articles of union shall be adopted, and for the completion of all their engagements.

13. That provision ought to be made for the amendment of the articles of union whensoever it shall seem necessary; and that the assent of the national legislature ought not to be required thereto.

14. *Resolved*, That the legislative, executive, and judiciary powers within the several States, ought to be bound by oath to support the articles of union.

15. *Resolved*, That the amendments, which shall be offered to the confederation by the convention, ought, at a proper time or times, after the approbation of congress, to be submitted to an assembly or assemblies of representatives, recommended by the several legislatures, to be expressly chosen by the people to consider and decide thereon.

## Text C

[Quoted from *Documentary History of the Constitution of the United States of America*, vol. 1, pp. 332-335]

1. Resolved that the Articles of Confederation ought to be so corrected and enlarged, as to accomplish the objects proposed by their institution, namely *common Defence Security of Liberty* and *general welfare.*

2. Resolved therefore that the right of Suffrage in the National Legislature ought to be, proportioned to the quotas of Contribution, or to the number of free inhabitants, as the one or the other, may serve best in different cases.

3. Resolved that the National Legislature ought to consist of *two branches.*

4. Resolved that the Members of the first Branch of the National Legislature, ought to be elected by the people of the several States every    for the term of three years, to be of the age of    at least. To receive liberal stipends, by which they may be compensated for the ["duration" stricken out] <sup>devotion</sup> of their time to public service—to be ineligible to any office established by a particular State, or under the authority of the United States, (except those peculiarly belonging to the functions of the first Branch) during the term of service, and for the space of one    after the expiration; to be incapable of re-election for the space of    after the expiration of their term of service, and to be subject to recal.

5. Resolved, that the members of the second Branch of the Legislature, ought to be elected by the individual Legislatures: to be of the age of    years at least; to hold their Offices for a term sufficient to ensure their independancy; to receive liberal Stipends by which they may be compensated for the ["devtion" <sup>devotion</sup> stricken out] of their time to the public service; and to be in-eligible to any office established by a particular State, or under the

authority of the United States (except those peculiarly belonging to the functions of the second Branch) during the term of service, and for the space of      after the expiration thereof.

6. Resolved that each Branch aught to possess the right of originating acts, that the National Legislature ought to be empowered to enjoy, the *Legislative rights vested in Congress.* by the Confederation, and moreover to Legislate in all cases to which the Separate States are incompetent; or in which the harmony of the United States may be interrupted, by the exercise of individual Legislation—to negative all Laws passed by the several States, contravening, in the opinion of the National Legislature, The articles of Union; or any Treaty subsisting under the Authority of the Union—and to call forth the force of the Union, against any Member of the Union, failing to fulfil its duties under the articles thereof

7th Resolved that ["the" stricken out] national Executive be ["consti" stricken out] insti tuted to consist of a *single person*, with powers to carry into execution the National Laws, and to appoint to Offices, in cases not otherwise provided for, to be chosen by the National Legislature, for the term of seven years—to receive punctually at stated times a fixed compensation, for the services rendered, in which no increase or diminution shall be made, so as to affect the Magistracy existing at the time of such increase or diminution, and to be in-eligible a second time.

8th Resolved that the Executive and a convenient number of the National Judiciary ought to compose a *Council of revision,* with authority to examine every act of the National Legislature, before it shall operate, and every act of a particular Legislature before a negative thereon shall be final; and that the dissent of the said council shall amount to a rejection, unless the act of the National Legislature, be again passed, or that of a particular Legislature be again negatived by      of the Members of each Branch.

9. Resolved that a National Judiciary be established to Consist of one Supreme Tribunal, to hold their Offices during good behavior, and to receive punctually at stated times fixed compensa-

tion for their services, in which no increase or diminution shall be made, so as to affect the persons actually in office at the time of such increase or diminution.

That the jurisdiction of the inferior Tribunals, shall be to hear and determine in the first instance, and of the Supreme Tribunal to hear and determine in the dernier resort; all piracies and felonies on the high Seas, Captures from an Enemy; cases in which Foreigners, or Citizens of other States applying to such jurisdictions, may be interested, or which respect the collection of the national Revenue, Impeachment of any national officer and questions which may involve, the National peace and harmony.

agreed

10. Resolved that provision ought to be made for the *admission of States* Lawfully arising within the limits of the United States whether from a voluntary junction of Government and Territory or otherwise, with the Consent of a number of Voices in the National Legislatures less than      the whole.

agreed

11. Resolved that a republican Government of each State (except in the Voluntary junction of Government and Territory) ought to be garranteed by the United States to each State.

agreed

12. Resolved that provision ought to be made for the Continuance of a Congress and their authorities, and privileges, ["untill" stricken out, until] a given day, after the reform of the Articles of the Union shall be adopted, and for the Completion of all their engagements.

agreed

13. That provision ought to be made for the amendment of the Articles of the Union, whensoever it shall seem necessary (and that the assent of the National Legislature, ought to be required thereto)

14. Resolved that the Legislative, Executive and judicial powers of the several States, ought to be bound by oath to support the Articles of Union. agreed

15. Resolved that the amendments which shall be offered to the Confederation, by the Convention, ought at a proper time, or times, after the approbation of Congress, to be submitted to an assembly or assemblies of representatives, recommended by the several Legislatures, to be expressly chosen by the people to consider and decide thereon. postponed

# THE PLAN OF CHARLES PINCKNEY (SOUTH CAROLINA), PRESENTED TO THE FEDERAL CONVENTION, MAY 29, 1787.

[Quoted from *American Historical Review*, Vol. IX, pp. 741-747]

## OUTLINE OF THE PLAN.

1. A Confederation between the free and independent States of N. H. etc. is hereby solemnly made uniting them together under one general superintending Government for their common Benefit and for their Defense and Security against all Designs and Leagues that may be injurious to their Interests and against all Forc[e] [?] [1] and Attacks offered to or made upon them or any of them.

2. The Stile

3. Mutual Intercourse—Community of Privileges—Surrender of Criminals—Faith to Proceedings etc.

4. Two Branches of the Legislature—Senate—House of Delegates—together the U. S. in Congress assembled

H. D. to consist of one Member for every thousand Inhabitants ⅗ of Blacks included

Senate to be elected from four Districts—to serve by Rotation of four years—to be elected by the H. D. either from among themselves or the People at large

5. The Senate and H. D. shall by joint Ballot annually chuse the Presid$^t$ U. S. from among themselves or the People at large.—In the Presd$^t$ the executive authority of the U. S. shall be vested.— His Powers and Duties—He shall have a Right to advise with the Heads of the different Departments as his Council

6. Council of Revision, consisting of the Presid$^t$ S. for for. Affairs, S. of War, Heads of the Departments of Treasury and Admiralty or any two of them tog$^r$ w$^t$ the Presid$^t$

7. The Members of S. and H. D. shall each have one Vote, and shall be paid out of the common Treasury.

---

[1] Or Foes.

8. The Time of the Election of the Members of the H. D. and of the Meeting of U. S. in C. assembled.

9. No State to make Treaties—lay interfering Duties—keep a naval or land Force Militia excepted to be disciplined etc. according to the Regulations of the U. S.

10. Each State retains its Rights not expressly delegated—But no Bill of the Legislature of any State shall become a law till it shall have been laid before S. and H. D. in C. assembled and received their Approbation.

11. The exclusive Power of S. and H. D. in C. Assembled.

12. The S. and H. D. in C. ass. shall have exclusive Power of regulating trade and levying Imposts—Each State may lay Embargoes in Times of Scarcity.

13. —of establishing Post-Offices

14. S. and H. D. in C. ass. shall be the last Resort on Appeal in Disputes between two or more States; which Authority shall be exercised in the following Manner etc

15. S. and H. D. in C. ass. shall institute offices and appoint officers for the Departments of for. Affairs, War, Treasury and Admiralty.

They shall have the exclusive Power of declaring what shall be Treason and Misp. of Treason ag$^t$ U. S.—and of instituting a federal judicial Court, to which an Appeal shall be allowed from the judicial Courts of the several States in all Causes wherein Questions shall arise on the Construction of Treaties made by U. S.—or on the Laws of Nations—or on the Regulations of U. S. concerning Trade and Revenue—or wherein U. S. shall be a Party—The Court shall consist of Judges to be appointed during good Behaviour—S and H. D. in C. ass. shall have the exclusive Right of instituting in each State a Court of Admiralty and appointing the Judges etc of the same for all maritime Causes which may arise therein respectively.

16. S. and H. D. in C. Ass shall have the exclusive Right of coining Money—regulating its Alloy and Value—fixing the Standard of Weights and Measures throughout U. S.

17. Points in which the Assent of more than a bare Majority shall be necessary.

18. Impeachments shall be by the H. D. before the Senate and the Judges of the Federeal judicial Court.

19. S. and H. D. in C. ass. shall regulate the Militia thro' the U. S.

20. Means of enforcing and compelling the Payment of the Quota of each State.

21. Manner and Conditions of admitting new States.

22. Power of dividing annexing and consolidating States, on the Consent and Petition of such States.

23. The assent of the Legislature of     States shall be sufficient to invest future additional Powers in U. S. in C. ass. and shall bind the whole Confederacy.

24. The Articles of Confederation shall be inviolably observed, and the Union shall be perpetual: unless altered as before directed

25. The said States of N. H. etc guarrantee mutually each other and their Rights against all other Powers and against all Rebellion etc.

# VARIANT TEXTS OF THE PLAN PRESENTED BY WILLIAM PATTERSON, (N. J.) TO THE FEDERAL CONVENTION, JUNE 15, 1787.

### TEXT A.

[Quoted from Hunt, Gaillard, and Scott, James B., ed. *Debates in the Federal Convention of 1787 Reported by James Madison.* (New York, 1920), pp. 102-104]

1. Res$^d$ that the articles of Confederation ought to be so revised, corrected & enlarged, as to render the federal Constitution adequate to the exigencies of Government, & the preservation of the Union.

2. Res$^d$ that in addition to the powers vested in the U. States in Congress, by the present existing articles of Confederation, they be authorized to pass acts for raising a revenue, by levying a duty or duties on all goods or merchandizes of foreign growth or manufacture, imported into any part of the U. States, by Stamps on paper, vellum or parchment, and by a postage on all letters or packages passing through the general post-office, to be applied to such federal purposes as they shall deem proper & expedient; to make rules & regulations for the collection thereof; and the same from time to time, to alter & amend in such manner as they shall think proper: to pass Acts for the regulation of trade & commerce as well with foreign nations as with each other: provided that all punishments, fines, forfeitures & penalties to be incurred for contravening such acts rules and regulations shall be adjudged by the Common law Judiciaries of the State in which any offence contrary to the true intent & meaning of such Acts rules & regulations shall have been committed or perpetrated, with liberty of commencing in the first instance all suits & prosecutions for that purpose in the superior common law Judiciary in such State, subject nevertheless, for the correction of all errors, both in law & fact in rendering Judgment, to an appeal to the Judiciary of the U. States.

3. Res$^d$ that whenever requisitions shall be necessary, instead of the rule for making requisitions mentioned in the articles of

Confederation, the United States in Cong: be authorized to make such requisitions in proportion to the whole number of white & other free citizens & inhabitants of every age sex and condition including those bound to servitude for a term of years & three fifths of all other persons not comprehended in the foregoing description, except Indians not paying taxes; that if such requisitions be not complied with, in the time specified therein, to direct the collection thereof in the non complying States & for that purpose to devise and pass acts directing & authorizing the same; provided that none of the powers hereby vested in the U. States in Cong: shall be exercised without the consent of at least      States, and in that proportion if the number of Confederated States should hereafter be increased or diminished.

4. Res<sup>d</sup> that the U. States in Cong: be authorized to elect a federal Executive to consist of      persons, to continue in office for the term of      years, to receive punctually at stated times a fixed compensation for their services, in which no increase or diminution shall be made so as to affect the persons composing the Executive at the time of such increase or diminution, to be paid out of the federal treasury; to be incapable of holding any other office or appointment during their time of service and for      years thereafter; to be ineligible a second time, & removeable by Cong: on application by a majority of the Executives of the several States, that the Executives [1] besides their general authority to execute the federal acts ought to appoint all federal officers not otherwise provided for, & to direct all military operations; provided that none of the persons composing the federal Executive shall on any occasion take command of any troops, so as personally to conduct any [2] enterprise as General or in other capacity.

5. Res<sup>d</sup> that a federal Judiciary be established to consist of a supreme Tribunal the Judges of which to be appointed by the Executive, & to hold their offices during good behaviour, to receive

---

[1] The transcript uses the word "Executives" in the singular.
[2] The word "military" is here inserted in the transcript.

punctually at stated times a fixed compensation for their services in which no increase or diminution shall be made, so as to affect the persons actually in office at the time of such increase or diminution; that the Judiciary so established shall have authority to hear & determine in the first instance on all impeachments of federal officers, & by way of appeal in the dernier resort in all cases touching the rights of Ambassadors, in all cases of captures from an enemy, in all cases of piracies & felonies on the high Seas, in all cases in which foreigners may be interested, in the construction of any treaty or treaties, or which may arise on any of the Acts for [3] regulation of trade, or the collection of the federal Revenue: that none of the Judiciary shall during the time they remain in office be capable of receiving or holding any other office or appointment during their time [4] of service, or for thereafter.

6. Res<sup>d</sup> that all Acts of the U. States in Cong<sup>s</sup> made by virtue & in pursuance of the powers hereby & by the articles of Confederation vested in them, and all Treaties made & ratified under the authority of the U. States shall be the supreme law of the respective States so far forth as those Acts or Treaties shall relate to the said States or their Citizens, and that the Judiciary of the several States shall be bound thereby in their decisions, any thing in the respective laws of the Individual States to the contrary notwithstanding; and that if any State, or any body of men in any State shall oppose or prevent y<sup>e</sup> carrying into execution such acts or treaties, the federal Executive shall be authorized to call forth y<sup>e</sup> power of the Confederated States, or so much thereof as may be necessary to enforce and compel an obedience to such Acts, or an observance of such Treaties.

7. Res<sup>d</sup> that provision be made for the admission of new States into the Union.

8. Res<sup>d</sup> [5] the rule for naturalization ought to be the same in every State.

---

[3] The word "the" is here inserted in the transcript.
[4] The word "term" is substituted in the transcript for "time."
[5] The word "that" is here inserted in the transcript.

9. Res{{d}} that a Citizen of one State committing an offence in another State of the Union, shall be deemed guilty of the same offence as if it had been committed by a Citizen of the State in which the offence was committed.*

---

\* This copy of M{{r}} Patterson's propositions varies in a few clauses from that in the printed Journal furnished from the papers of M{{r}} Brearley a Colleague of M{{r}} Patterson. A confidence is felt, notwithstanding, in its accuracy. That the copy in the Journal is not entirely correct is shewn by the ensuing speech of M{{r}} Wilson [June 16] in which he refers to the mode of removing the Executive by impeachment & conviction as a feature in the Virg{{a}} plan forming one of its contrasts to that of M{{r}} Patterson, which proposed a removal on the application of a majority of the Executives of the States. In the copy printed in the Journal, the two modes are combined in the same clause; whether through inadvertence, or as a contemplated amendment does not appear.

## Text B.

[Quoted from *Documentary History of the Constitution*, vol. 1, pp. 322-326]

1. Resolved, that the Articles of Confeder<sup>n</sup> ought to be so revised, corrected, and enlarged as to render the federal Constitution adequate to the exigencies of Government, and the preservation of the Union.

2. Resolved, that in addition to the Powers vested in the United States in Congress by the present existing Articles of Confederation, they be authorized to pass Acts for raising a Revenue by levying a Duty or Duties on all goods and Merchandise of foreign growth or manufacture imported into any part of the United States,—by Stamps on Paper Vellum or Parchment,—and by a Postage on all Letters and Packages passing through the general Post Office. To be applied to such federal purposes as they shall deem proper and expedient; to make rules and regulations for the collection thereof, and the same from time to time to alter and amend, in such manner as they shall think proper. To pass Acts for the regulation of Trade and Commerce, as well with foreign Nations, as with each other. Provided that all punishments, Fines Forfeitures and Penalties to be incurred for contravening such Rules, and regulations shall be adjudged by the common Law Judiciary of the States in which any offence contrary to the true intent and meaning of such Rules and regulations shall be committed or perpetrated; with liberty of commencing in the first instance all suits or prosecutions for that purpose in the Superior Common Law Judiciary of such State; subject Nevertheless to an Appeal for the Correction of all errors, both in Law in Fact, in rendering Judgment, to the Judiciary of the United States.

3. Resolved, that whenever Requisitions shall be necessary, instead of the present Rule, the United States in Congress be authorized to make such Requisitions in proportion to the whole Number of White and other Free Citizens and Inhabitants of every age, sex and condition, including those bound to servitude

for a Term of years, and three fifths of all other persons not comprehended in the foregoing description—(except Indians not paying Taxes): that if such Requisitions be not complied with, in the time to be specified therein, to direct the Collection thereof in the non complying States and for that purpose to devise and pass Acts directing and authorizing the same. Provided that none of the powers hereby vested in the United States in Congress shall be exercized without the Consent of at least      States, and ∧ in that proportion, if the number of confederated States should be hereafter encreased or diminished.

4. Resolved, that the U. S. in Congress be authorized to elect a fœderal Executive to consist of      Persons, to continue in office for the Term of      years; to receive punctually at Stated times a fixed compensation for the services by them rendered, in which no increase or diminution shall be made, so as to affect the persons composing the Executive at the time of such encrease or diminution; to be paid out of the Fœderal Treasury; to be incapable of holding any other Office or appointment during their time of service, and for      years thereafter; to be ineligible a second time, and removable on impeachment and conviction for Mal practice or neglect of duty—by Congress on application by a Majority of the Executives of the several States. That the Executive, besides a general authority to execute the federal Acts, ought to appoint all federal Officers not other wise provided for, and to direct all Military operations; provided that none of the persons composing the federal Executive shall on any occasion take command of any Troops so as personally to conduct any Military enterprise as general ["Officer" stricken out] or in any other capacity.

5. Resolved, that a federal Judiciary be established, to consist of a supreme Tribunal, the Judges of which to be appointed by the Executive, and to hold their Offices during good behavior; to receive punctually at stated times a fixed compensation for their services, in which no increase or diminution shall be made so as to effect the persons actually in Office at the time of such increase or diminution;—That the Judiciary so established shall have au-

thority to hear and determine in the first instance on all impeachments of federal Officers, and by way of Appeal in the dernier resort in all cases touching the Rights and privileges of Embassadors; in all cases of captures from an Enemy; in all cases of Piricies and Felonies on the high Seas; in all cases in which Foreigners may be interested in the construction of any Treaty or Treaties, or which may arise on any Act or Ordinance of Congress for the regulation of Trade, or the collection of the Federal Revenue: that none of the Judiciary Officers shall during the time they remain in Office be capable of receiving or holding any other Office or appointment during their time of service, or for thereafter.

6. Resolved, that the Legislative, Executive, and Judiciary Powers within the several States ought to be bound by Oath to support the Articles of Union.

7. Resolved, that all Acts of the United States in Congress Assembled, made by virtue and pursuance of the Powers hereby vested in them, and by the Articles of the Confederation, and all Treaties made and ratified under the authority of the United States, shall be the supreme Law of the respective States, as far as those Acts or Treaties shall relate to the said States or their ["subjects" stricken out, citizens]; and that the Judiciaries of the several States shall be bound thereby in their decisions, anything in the respective Laws of the Individual States to the Contrary notwithstanding.

And if any State, or any body of Men in any State, shall oppose or prevent the carrying into Execution such Acts or Treaties, the federal Executive shall be authorized to call forth the Powers of the confederated States, or so much thereof as may be necessary to enforce and compel an obedience to such Acts or an observance of such Treaties.

8. Resolved, that provision ought to be made for the admission of New States into the Union

9. Resolved, that Provision ought to be made for hearing and deciding upon all disputes arising between the United States and an Individual State respecting Territory

10. Resolved, that the Rule for Naturalization ought to be the same in every State.

11. Resolved, that a Citizen of one State committing an Offence in an other State, shall be deemed guilty of the same offence, as if it had been committed by a Citizen of the State in which the offence was committed.

## Text C.

[Quoted from *American Museum*, Vol. III, pp. 362-363]

1. Resolved, that an union of the states, merely federal, ought to be the sole object of the exercise of the powers vested in this convention.

2. Resolved, that the articles of the confederation ought to be so revised, corrected, and enlarged, as to render the federal constitution adequate to the exigencies of government, and the preservation of the union.

3. Resolved, that in addition to the powers vested in the united states in congress, by the present existing articles of confederation, they be authorised to pass acts for raising a revenue by laying a duty or duties on all goods and merchandise of foreign growth or manufacture, imported into any part of the united states; by imposing stamps on paper, parchment, and vellum; and by a postage on all letters and packages passing through the general post office, to be applied to such federal purposes, as they shall deem proper and expedient; to make rules and regulations for the collection thereof; and the same from time to time to alter and amend in such manner as they shall think proper: provided that all punishments, fines, forfeitures, and penalties, to be incurred for contravening such rules and regulations, shall be adjudged by the common law judiciaries of the state in which any offence, contrary to the true intent and meaning of such rules or regulations, shall be committed or perpetrated; with liberty of commencing all suits or prosecutions for that purpose, in the first instance, in the supreme common law judiciary of such state—subject, nevertheless, to an appeal in the last resort, for the correction of errors, both of law and fact, in rendering judgment, to the judiciary of the united states; and that the united states shall have authority to pass acts for the regulation of trade and commerce, as well with foreign nations, as with each other.

4. Resolved, that should requisitions be necessary, instead of the present rule, the united states in congress be authorised to make such requisitions in proportion to the whole number of white and other free citizens and inhabitants, of every age, sex, and condition, including those bound to servitude for a term of years, and three-fifths of all other persons, not comprehended in the foregoing descriptions (except Indians not paying taxes.)

5. Resolved, that if such requisitions be not complied with, in the time specified therein, the united states in congress shall have power to direct the collection thereof in the non-complying states; and for that purpose to devise and pass acts directing and authorising the same: provided that none of the powers hereby vested in the united states in congress shall be exercised without the consent of at least     states; and in that proportion, should the number of confederated states hereafter be increased or diminished.

6. Resolved, that the united states in congress, shall be authorised to elect a federal executive, to consist of     person or persons, to continue in office for the term of     years, to receive punctually, at stated times, a fixed compensation for the services by him or them to be rendered, in which no increase or diminution shall be made, so as to affect the executive in office, at the time of such increase or diminution, to be paid out of the federal treasury; to be incapable of holding any other office or appointment during the time of service, and for     years after; to be ineligible a second time, and removable on impeachment and conviction for mal-practice, corrupt conduct, and neglect of duty.

7. Resolved, that the executive, besides a general authority to execute the federal acts, ought to appoint all federal officers, not otherwise provided for, and to direct all military operations; provided that the executive shall not on any occasion take command of any troops, so as personally to conduct any military enterprise as general, or in any other capacity.

8. Resolved, that the legislative acts of the united states, made under and in pursuance to the articles of union, and all treaties made and ratified under the authority of the united states, shall be the supreme law of the respective states, as far as those acts

or treaties shall relate to the said states or their citizens and inhabitants; and that the judiciaries of the several states shall be bound thereby in their decisions; any thing in the respective laws of the individual states to the contrary notwithstanding.

9. Resolved, that if any state or body of men in any state, shall oppose or prevent the carrying into execution such acts or treaties, the federal executive shall be authorised to call forth the powers of the confederated states, or so much thereof as may be necessary to enforce and compel an obedience to such acts, or an observance of such treaties.

10. Resolved, that a federal judiciary be established, to consist of a supreme tribunal; the judges of which to be appointed by the executive, and to hold their offices during good behaviour; to receive punctually, at stated times, a fixed compensation for their services, to be paid out of the federal treasury; in which no increase or diminution shall be made, so as to affect the persons actually in office, at the time of such increase of diminution. That the judiciary so established, shall have authority to hear and determine, in the first instance, on all impeachments of federal officers, and by way of appeal in the dernier resort in all cases touching the rights and privileges of ambassadors; in all cases of captures from the enemy; in all cases of piracies and felonies committed on the high seas; in all cases in which foreigners may be interested in the construction of any treaty or treaties, or which may arise on any act or ordinance of congress for the regulation of trade, or the collection of the federal revenue; that none of the judiciary officers shall be capable of receiving or holding any other office or appointment, during the time they remain in office, or for       years afterwards.

11. Resolved, that the legislative, executive, and judiciary powers within the several states, ought to be bound by oath to support the articles of union.

12. Resolved, that provision ought to be made for hearing and deciding upon all disputes arising between the united states and an individual state, respecting territory.

13. Resolved, that provision ought to be made for the admission of new states into the union.

14. Resolved, that it is necessary to define what offences, committed in any state, shall be deemed high treason against the united states.

15. Resolved, that the rule for naturalization ought to be the same in every state.

16. Resolved, that a citizen of one state, committing an offence in another state, shall be deemed guilty of the same offence, as if it had been committed by a citizen of the state, in which the offence was committed.

# VARIANT TEXTS OF THE PLAN PRESENTED BY ALEXANDER HAMILTON TO THE FEDERAL CONVENTION, JUNE 18, 1787.

## TEXT A.

[Quoted from Hunt, Gaillard, and Scott, James B., ed. *Debates in the Federal Convention of 1787 Reported by James Madison.* (New York, 1920), pp. 118-120]

I. "The Supreme Legislative power of the United States of America to be vested in two different bodies of men; the one to be called the Assembly, the other the Senate who together shall form the Legislature of the United States with power to pass all laws whatsoever subject to the Negative hereafter mentioned.

II. The Assembly to consist of persons elected by the people to serve for three years.

III. The Senate to consist of persons elected to serve during good behaviour; their election to be made by electors chosen for that purpose by the people: in order to this the States to be divided into election districts. On the death, removal or resignation of any Senator his place to be filled out of the district from which he came.

IV. The supreme Executive authority of the United States to be vested in a Governour to be elected to serve during good behaviour—the election to be made by Electors chosen by the people in the Election Districts aforesaid—The authorities & functions of the Executive to be as follows: to have a negative on all laws about to be passed, and the execution of all laws passed; to have the direction of war when authorized or begun; to have with the advice and approbation of the Senate the power of making all treaties; to have the sole appointment of the heads or chief officers of the departments of Finance, War and Foreign Affairs; to have the nomination of all other officers (Ambassadors to foreign Nations included) subject to the approbation or rejection of the Senate; to have the power of pardoning all offences except Treason; which he shall not pardon without the approbation of the Senate.

V. On the death resignation or removal of the Governour his authorities to be exercised by the President of the Senate till a Successor be appointed.

VI. The Senate to have the sole power of declaring war, the power of advising and approving all Treaties, the power of approving or rejecting all appointments of officers except the heads or chiefs of the departments of Finance War and foreign affairs.

VII. The supreme Judicial authority to be vested in Judges to hold their offices during good behaviour with adequate and permanent salaries. This Court to have original jurisdiction in all causes of capture, and an appellative jurisdiction in all causes in which the revenues of the general Government or the Citizens of foreign Nations are concerned.

VIII. The Legislature of the United States to have power to institute Courts in each State for the determination of all matters of general concern.

IX. The Governour Senators and all officers of the United States to be liable to impeachment for mal- and corrupt conduct; and upon conviction to be removed from office, & disqualified for holding any place of trust or profit—All impeachments to be tried by a Court to consist of the Chief or Judge of the superior Court of Law of each State, provided such Judge shall hold his place during good behavior, and have a permanent salary.

X. All laws of the particular States contrary to the Constitution or laws of the United States to be utterly void; and the better to prevent such laws being passed, the Governour or president of each State shall be appointed by the General Government and shall have a negative upon the laws about to be passed in the State of which he is [1] Governour or President.

XI. No State to have any forces land or Naval; and the Militia of all the States to be under the sole and exclusive direction of the United States, the officers of which to be appointed and commissioned by them.

---

[1] The word "the" is here inserted in the transcript.

## Text B.

[Quoted from *The Works of Alexander Hamilton*, edited by Henry Cabot Lodge, (New York and London, 1885), vol. I, pp. 331-333]

I. The supreme legislative power of the United States of America to be vested in two distinct bodies of men: the one to be called the *Assembly*, the other the *Senate;* who together shall form the Legislature of the United States, with power to pass *all laws whatsoever*, subject to the *negative* hereafter mentioned.

II. The Assembly to consist of persons elected *by the people*, to serve for three years.

III. The Senate to consist of persons elected to serve during *good behavior*. Their election to be made by *electors* chosen for that purpose by the people. In order to this, the States to be divided into election districts. On the death, removal, or resignation of any Senator, his place to be filled out of the district from which he came.

IV. The supreme executive authority of the United States to be vested in *a Governor*, to be elected to serve *during good behavior*. His election to be made by *electors* chosen by *electors* chosen by the people, in the election districts aforesaid; or by electors chosen for that purpose by the respective Legislatures—provided that if an election be not made within a limited time, the President of the Senate shall be the Governor. The Governor to have *a negative* upon all laws about to be passed—and (to have) the execution of all laws passed—to be the Commander-in-Chief of the land and naval forces and of the militia of the United States— to have the entire direction of war when authorized or begun—to have, with the *advice* and *approbation* of the Senate, the power of making all treaties—to have the appointment of the *heads* or *chief* officers of the departments of finance, war, and foreign affairs—to have the *nomination* of all other officers (ambassadors to foreign nations included), subject to the approbation or rejection of the Senate—to have the power of pardoning all offences but *treason*, which he shall not pardon without the approbation of the Senate.

V. On the death, resignation, or removal of the Governor, his authorities to be exercised by the President of the Senate (until a successor be appointed).

VI. The Senate to have the sole power of *declaring war*—the power of advising and approving all treaties—the power of approving or rejecting all appointments of officers, except the heads or chiefs of the departments of finance, war, and foreign affairs.

VII. The supreme judicial authority of the United States to be vested in twelve judges, to hold their offices during good behavior, with adequate and permanent salaries. This court to have original jurisdiction in all causes of capture, and an appellate jurisdiction (from the courts of the several States) in all causes in which the revenues of the General Government or the citizens of foreign nations are concerned.

VIII. The Legislature of the United States to have power to institute courts in each State for the determination of all causes of capture and of all matters relating to their revenues, or in which the citizens of foreign nations are concerned.

IX. The Governor, Senators, and all officers of the United States to be liable to impeachment for mal and corrupt conduct, and upon conviction to be removed from office, and disqualified for holding any place of trust or profit. All impeachments to be tried by a court, to consist of the judges of the Supreme Court, chief or senior judge of the Superior Court of law of each State— provided that such judge hold his place during good behavior and have a permanent salary.

X. All laws of the particular States contrary to the Constitution or laws of the United States to be utterly void. And the better to prevent such laws being passed the Governor or President of each State shall *be appointed by the General Government*, and shall have a *negative* upon the laws about to be passed in the State of which he is Governor or President.

XI. No State to have any forces, land or naval—and the *militia* of all the States to be under the sole and *exclusive direction* of the United States, *the officers* of which to be appointed and commissioned by them.

## TEXT C.

[Quoted from *Documentary History of the Constitution of the United States of America*, vol. 1, pp. 327-329]

1st. The Supreme Legislative Power of the United States of America to be vested in two distinct Bodies of Men, the one to be called the *Assembly*, the other the *Senate*, who together shall form the Legislative of the United States, with Power to pass *all Laws whatsoever*, subject to the *negative* hereafter mentioned.

2d. The Assembly to consist of Persons elected *by the People* to serve for three years.

3d. The Senate to consist of persons elected to serve during *good behavior*, their election to be made by *electors* chosen for that purpose by the People. In order to this the States to be divided into election districts. On the death, removal, or resignation of any Senator his place to be filled out of the district from which he came.

4th. The Supreme Executive Authority of the U. States to be vested in a *Governor* to be elected to serve *during good behavior*. His election to be made by *Electors* chosen by *Electors* chosen by the people in the election districts aforesaid. His Authorities and Functions to be as follow.—to have a *negative* upon all Laws about to be passed, and the execution of all laws passed.—To have the *intire direction* of War when authorized or begun.—To have, with the advice and approbation of the Senate, the Power of making all Treaties.—To have the sole appointment of the *Heads* or *Chief-Officers* of the departments of Finance, War, and Foreign Affairs.—To have the nomination of all other Officers (Ambassadors to Foreign Nations included) subject to the approbation or rejection of the Senate.

To have the power of pardoning all offences *except Treason*, which he shall not pardon without the ["consent" stricken out] approbation of the Senate.

5th. On the death, resignation or removal of the Governor, his Authorities to be exercized by the *President of the Senate* until a successor be appointed.

6th. The Senate to have the sole power of *declaring War:* the power of *advising and approving* all Treaties:—the power of *approving or rejecting* all appointments of Officers, except the heads or chiefs of the departments of Finance War and Foreign Affairs.

7th. The Supreme Judicial Authority of the United States to be vested in Judges, to hold their Offices during good behavior, with adequate and permanent Salaries. This Court to have original Jurisdiction in all Causes of Capture, and an ["Appellant" stricken out] Appellative Jurisdiction in all causes in which the Revenues of the General Government, or the Citizens of foreign Nations are concerned.

8th. The Legislature of the United States to have Power to institute Courts in each State["s" stricken out] for the determination of all matters of general concern.

9th. The Governors, Senators, and all Officers of the United States to be liable to impeachment for Mal and corrupt conduct, and upon Conviction to be removed from office and disqualified for holding any place of trust or profit. All impeachments to be tried by a Court to consist of the Chief or Senior Judge of the Superior Court of Law of each State, provided that such Judge hold his place during good behavior and have a permanent Salary.

10th. All Laws of the particular States contrary to the Constitution or laws of the United States to be utterly void. And the better to prevent such Laws being passed; the Governor or President of each State shall be appointed by the *General Government* and shall have a *Negative* upon the Laws about to be passed in the State of which he is Governor or President.

11th. No State to have any Forces, Land or Naval, and the Militia of all the States to be under the sole and exclusive direction of the United States, the Officers of which to be appointed and commissioned by them.

## Text D.

[Quoted from Read, William T. *Life and Correspondence of George Read.* (Philadelphia, 1870), pp. 453-454]

1. The supreme legislative power to be in an Assembly and Senate,—laws passed by them subject to the after-mentioned negative.

2. Senate,—to serve during good behavior,—to be chosen by electors elected by the people in election districts, into which the States will be divided. In case of death of a senator, the vacancy to be filled out of the district whence he came.

3. The supreme executive to be a governor elected, during good behavior, by electors chosen by the people in the election districts; his functions,—to have a negative on all laws about to be passed, and the execution of all passed; the direction of war, when declared; to make, with the advice and approbation of the Senate, all treaties; to have the sole appointments of the heads of the departments of finance and foreign affairs, and the nomination of all other officers (ambassadors included), subject to the approbation or rejection by the Senate; and the sole power of pardon, except in case of treason, in which he shall exercise it, subject to the approval of the Senate. In case of the death, removal, or resignation of the governor, his authority to be exercised by the President of the Senate till his successor is appointed.

4. The Senate shall have the sole power to declare war; the power of advising and approving treaties, and the power of approving or rejecting all appointments of officers except the chiefs of the departments of finance and foreign affairs.

5. The supreme judicial authority to be     in judges, to hold office during good behavior, with adqeuate and permanent salaries; to have original jurisdiction in all cases of capture, and appellate jurisdiction in all cases concerning the revenues of the general government, or the citizens of foreign nations.

6. The United States Legislature to have power to institute courts in each State for the determination of all matters of general concern.

7. All officers of the United States to be liable to impeachment for malconduct, and, on conviction, to removal from office, and to be disqualified for holding any place of trust or profit. Impeachments to be tried by a court to consist of the chief or judges of the superior court of law of each State, provided he hold his place, during good behavior, and have an adequate salary.

8. All laws of particular States, contrary to the Constitution and laws of the United States, to be utterly void; and the better to prevent the passing of such laws the governor or president of each State shall be appointed by the general government, and shall have a negative upon the laws about to be passed in the State, of which he is governor or president.

9. No State to have any land or naval force; and the militia of all the States to be under the sole and exclusive direction of the United States, who shall appoint and commission all the officers thereof.

## Text E.

[Quoted from Yates. *Secret Debates* (Washington, 1836), pp. 225-227].

1. The supreme legislative power of the United States of America to be vested in two distinct bodies of men, the one to be called the assembly, the other the senate, who, together, shall form the legislature of the United States, with power to pass all laws whatsoever, subject to the negative hereafter mentioned.

2. The assembly to consist of persons elected by the people, to serve for three years.

3. The senate to consist of persons elected to serve during good behaviour; their election to be made by electors chosen for that purpose by the people. In order to this, the States to be divided into election districts. On the death, removal, or resignation of any senator, his place to be filled out of the district from which he came.

4. The supreme executive authority of the United States to be vested in a governor, to be elected to serve during good behaviour. His election to be made by electors, chosen by electors, chosen by the people, in the election districts aforesaid. His authorities and functions to be as follows—

To have a negative upon all laws about to be passed, and the execution of all laws passed; to have the entire direction of war, when authorized, or begun; to have, with the advice and approbation of the senate, the power of making all treaties; to have the sole appointment of the heads or chief officers of the departments of finance, war, and foreign affairs; to have the nomination of all other officers, (ambassadors to foreign nations included,) subject to the approbation or rejection of the senate; to have the power of pardoning all offences, except treason, which he shall not pardon, without the approbation of the senate.

5. On the death, resignation, or removal of the governor, his authorities to be exercised by the president of the senate, until a successor be appointed.

6. The senate to have the sole power of declaring war; the power of advising and approving all treaties; the power of approving or rejecting all appointments of officers, except the heads or chiefs of the departments of finance, war, and foreign affairs.

7. The supreme judicial authority of the United States to be vested in        judges, to hold their offices during good behaviour, with adequate and permanent salaries. This court to have original jurisdiction in all causes of capture; and an appellative jurisdiction in all causes, in which the revenues of the general government, or the citizens of foreign nations, are concerned.

8. The legislature of the United States to have power to institute courts in each State, for the determination of all matters of general concern.

9. The governors, senators, and all officers of the United States to be liable to impeachment for mal and corrupt conduct; and, upon conviction, to be removed from office, and disqualified for holding any place of trust, or profit. All impeachments to be tried by a court to consist of the chief, or senior judge of the superior court of law in each State; provided, that such judge hold his place during good behaviour, and have a permanent salary.

10. All laws of the particular States, contrary to the constitution or laws of the United States, to be utterly void. And the better to prevent such laws being passed, the governor or president of each State shall be appointed by the general government, and shall have a negative upon the laws about to be passed in the State of which he is governor, or president.

11. No State to have any forces, land or naval; and the militia of all the States to be under the sole and exclusive direction of the United States; the officers of which to be appointed and commissioned by them.

# THE CONSTITUTION OF THE UNITED STATES[1]

We the People of the United States, in Order to form a more perfect Union, establish Justice, insure domestic Tranquility, provide for the common defence, promote the general Welfare, and secure the Blessings of Liberty to ourselves and our Posterity, do ordain and establish this Constitution for the United States of America.

## Article. I.

Section. 1. All legislative Powers herein granted shall be vested in a Congress of the United States, which shall consist of a Senate and House of Representatives.

Section. 2. The House of Representatives shall be composed of Members chosen every second Year by the People of the several States, and the Electors in each State shall have ∧ the Qualifications requisite for Electors of the most numerous Branch of the State Legislature.

No person shall be a Representative who shall not have attained to the Age of twenty five Years, and been seven Years a Citizen of the United States, and who shall not, when elected, be an Inhabitant of that State in which he shall be chosen.

Representatives and direct Taxes shall be apportioned among the several States which may be included within this Union, according to their respective Numbers, which shall be determined by adding to the whole Number of free Persons, including those bound to Service for a Term of Years, and excluding Indians not taxed, three fifths of all other Persons. The actual Enumeration shall be made within three Years after the first Meeting of the Congress of the United States, and within every subsequent Term of ten Years, in such Manner as they shall by Law direct. The Number of Representatives shall not exceed one for every thirty Thousand,

---

[1] This is a literal copy of the engrossed Constitution as signed. It is in four sheets, with an additional sheet containing the resolutions of transmittal. The note indented at the end is in the original precisely as reproduced here.

but each State shall have at Least one Representative; and until such enumeration shall be made, the State of New Hampshire shall be entitled to chuse three, Massachusetts eight, Rhode-Island and Providence Plantations one, Connecticut five, New-York six, New Jersey four, Pennsylvania eight, Delaware one, Maryland six, Virginia ten, North Carolina five, South Carolina five, and Georgia three.

. When vacancies happen in the Representation from any State, the Executive Authority thereof shall issue Writs of Election to fill such Vacancies.

The House of Representatives shall chuse their Speaker and other Officers; and shall have the sole Power of Impeachment.

Section. 3. The Senate of the United States shall be composed of two Senators from each State, chosen by the Legislature thereof, for six Years; and each Senator shall have one Vote.

Immediately after they shall be assembled in Consequence of the first Election, they shall be divided as equally as may be into three Classes. The Seats of the Senators of the first Class shall be vacated at the Expiration of the second Year, of the second Class at the Expiration of the fourth Year, and of the third Class at the Expiration of the sixth Year, so that one third may be chosen every second Year; and if Vacancies happen by Resignation, or otherwise, during the Recess of the Legislature of any State, the Executive thereof may make temporary Appointments until the next Meeting of the Legislature, which shall then fill such Vacancies.

No Person shall be a Senator who shall not have attained to the Age of thirty Years, and been nine Years a Citizen of the United States, and who shall not, when elected, be an Inhabitant of that State for which he shall be chosen.

The Vice President of the United States shall be President of the Senate, but shall have no Vote, unless they be equally divided.

The Senate shall chuse their other Officers, and also a President pro tempore, in the Absence of the Vice President, or when he shall exercise the Office of President of the United States.

The Senate shall have the sole Power to try all Impeachments. When sitting for that Purpose, they shall be on Oath or Affirmation.

When the President of the United States is tried, the Chief Justice shall preside: And no Person shall be convicted without the Concurrence of two thirds of the Members present.

Judgment in Cases of Impeachment shall not extend further than to removal from Office, and disqualification to hold and enjoy any Office of honor, Trust or Profit under the United States: but the Party convicted shall nevertheless be liable and subject to Indictment, Trial, Judgment and Punishment, according to Law.

Section. 4. The Times, Places and Manner of holding Elections for Senators and Representatives, shall be prescribed in each State by the Legislature thereof; but the Congress may at any time by Law make or alter such Regulations, except as to the Places of chusing Senators.

The Congress shall assemble at least once in every Year, and such Meeting shall be on the first Monday in December, unless they shall by Law appoint a different Day.

Section. 5. Each House shall be the Judge of the Elections, Returns and Qualifications of its own Members, and a Majority of each shall constitute a Quorum to do Business; but a smaller Number may adjourn from day to day, and may be authorized to compel the Attendance of absent Members, in such Manner, and under such Penalties as each House may provide.

Each House may determine the Rules of its Proceedings, punish its Members for disorderly Behaviour, and, with the Concurrence of two thirds, expel a Member.

Each House shall keep a Journal of its Proceedings, and from time to time publish the same, excepting such Parts as may in their Judgment require Secrecy; and the Yeas and Nays of the Members of either House on any question shall, at the Desire of one fifth of those Present, be entered on the Journal.

Neither House, during the Session of Congress, shall, without the Consent of the other, adjourn for more than three days, nor to any other Place than that in which the two Houses shall be sitting.

Section. 6. The Senators and Representatives shall receive a Compensation for their Services, to be ascertained by Law, and paid out of the Treasury of the United States. They shall in all

Cases, except Treason, Felony and Breach of the Peace, be privileged from Arrest during their Attendance at the Session of their respective Houses, and in going to and returning from the same; and for any Speech or Debate in either House, they shall not be questioned in any other Place.

No Senator or Representative shall, during the Time for which he was elected, be appointed to any civil Office under the Authority of the United States, which shall have been created, or the Emoluments whereof shall have been encreased during such time; and no Person holding any Office under the United States, shall be a Member of either House during his Continuance in Office.

Section. 7. All Bills for raising Revenue shall originate in the House of Representatives; but the Senate may propose or concur with Amendments as on other Bills.

Every Bill which shall have passed the House of Representatives and the Senate, shall, before it become a Law, be presented to the President of the United States; If he approve he shall sign it, but if not he shall return it, with his Objections to that House in which it shall have originated, who shall enter the Objections at large on their Journal, and proceed to reconsider it. If after such Reconsideration two thirds of that House shall agree to pass the Bill, it shall be sent, together with the Objections, to the other House, by which it shall likewise be reconsidered, and if approved by two thirds of that House, it shall become a Law. But in all such Cases the Votes of both Houses shall be determined by yeas and Nays, and the Names of the Persons voting for and against the Bill shall be entered on the Journal of each House respectively. If any Bill shall not be returned by the President within ten days (Sundays excepted) after it shall have been presented to him, the Same shall be a Law, in like Manner as if he had signed it, unless the Congress by their Adjournment prevent its Return in which Case it shall not be a Law.

Every Order, Resolution, or Vote to which the Concurrence of the Senate and House of Representatives may be necessary (except on a question of Adjournment) shall be presented to the President of the United States; and before the Same shall take Effect, shall be approved by him, or being disapproved by him, shall be repassed by two thirds of the Senate and House of Representatives, according to the Rules and Limitations prescribed in the Case of a Bill.

Section. 8. The Congress shall have Power To lay and collect Taxes, Duties, Imposts and Excises, to pay the Debts and provide for the common Defence and general Welfare of the United States; but all Duties, Imposts and Excises shall be uniform throughout the United States;

To borrow Money on the credit of the United States;

To regulate Commerce with foreign Nations, and among the several States, and with the Indian Tribes;

To establish an uniform Rule of Naturalization, and uniform Laws on the subject of Bankruptcies throughout the United States;

To coin Money, regulate the Value thereof, and of foreign Coin, and fix the Standard of Weights and Measures;

To provide for the Punishment of counterfeiting the Securities and current Coin of the United States;

To establish Post Offices and post Roads;

To promote the Progress of Science and useful Arts, by securing for limited Times to Authors and Inventors the exclusive Right to their respective Writings and Discoveries;

To constitute Tribunals inferior to the supreme Court;

To define and punish Piracies and Felonies committed on the high Seas, and Offences against the Law of Nations;

To declare War, grant Letters of Marque and Reprisal, and make Rules concerning Captures on Land and Water;

To raise and support Armies, but no Appropriation of Money to that Use shall be for a longer Term than two Years;

To provide and maintain a Navy;

To make Rules for the Government and Regulation of the land and naval Forces;

To provide for calling forth the Militia to execute the Laws of the Union, suppress Insurrections and repel Invasions;

To provide for organizing, arming, and disciplining, the Militia, and for governing such Part of them as may be employed in the Service of the United States, reserving to the States respectively, the Appointment of the Officers, and the Authority of training the Militia according to the discipline prescribed by Congress;

To exercise exclusive Legislation in all Cases whatsoever, over such District (not exceeding ten Miles square) as may, by Cession of particular States, and the Acceptance of Congress, become the Seat of the Government of the United States, and to exercise like Authority over all Places purchased by the Consent of the Legislature of the State in which the Same shall be, for the Erection of Forts, Magazines, Arsenals, dock-Yards, and other needful Buildings;—And

To make all Laws which shall be necessary and proper for carrying into Execution the foregoing Powers, and all other Powers vested by this Constitution in the Government of the United States, or in any Department or Officer thereof.

Section. 9. The Migration or Importation of such Persons as any of the States now existing shall think proper to admit, shall not be prohibited by the Congress prior to the Year one thousand eight hundred and eight, but a Tax or duty may be imposed on such Importation, not exceeding ten dollars for each Person.

The Privilege of the Writ of Habeas Corpus shall not be suspended, unless when in Cases of Rebellion or Invasion the public Safety may require it.

No Bill of Attainder or ex post facto Law shall be passed.

No Capitation, or other direct, Tax shall be laid, unless in Proportion to the Census or Enumeration herein before directed to be taken.

No Tax or Duty shall be laid on Articles exported from any State.

No Preference shall be given by any Regulation of Commerce or Revenue to the Ports of one State over those of another: nor shall Vessels bound to, or from, one State, be obliged to enter, clear, or pay Duties in another.

No Money shall be drawn from the Treasury, but in Consequence of Appropriations made by Law; and a regular Statement and Account of the Receipts and Expenditures of all public Money shall be published from time to time.

No Title of Nobility shall be granted by the United States: And no Person holding any Office of Profit or Trust under them, shall, without the Consent of the Congress, accept of any present, Emolument, Office, or Title, of any kind whatever, from any King, Prince, or foreign State.

Section. 10. No State shall enter into any Treaty, Alliance, or Confederation; grant Letters of Marque and Reprisal; coin Money; emit Bills of Credit; make any Thing but gold and silver Coin a Tender in Payment of Debts; pass any Bill of Attainder, ex post facto Law, or Law impairing the Obligation of Contracts, or grant any Title of Nobility.

No State shall, without the Consent of the ∧ Congress, lay any Imposts or Duties on Imports or Exports, except what may be absolutely necessary for executing it's inspection Laws: and the net Produce of all Duties and Imposts, laid by any State on Imports or Exports, shall be for the Use of the Treasury of the United States; and all such Laws shall be subject to the Revision and Controul of the ∧ Congress.

No State shall, without the Consent of Congress, lay any Duty of Tonnage, keep Troops, or Ships of War in time of Peace, enter into any Agreement or Compact with another State, or with a foreign Power, or engage in War, unless actually invaded, or in such imminent Danger as will not admit of delay.

## Article. II.

Section. 1. The executive Power shall be vested in a President of the United States of America. He shall hold his Office during the Term of four Years, and, together with the Vice President, chosen for the same Term, be elected as follows

Each State shall appoint, in such Manner as the Legislature thereof may direct, a Number of Electors, equal to the whole Number of Senators and Representatives to which the State may be entitled in the Congress: but no Senator or Representative, or Person holding an Office of Trust or Profit under the United States, shall be appointed an Elector.

The Electors shall meet in their respective States, and vote by Ballot for two Persons, of whom one at least shall not be an

Inhabitant of the same State with themselves. And they shall make a List of all the Persons voted for, and of the Number of Votes for each; which List they shall sign and certify, and transmit sealed to the Seat of the Government of the United States, directed to the President of the Senate. The President of the Senate shall, in the Presence of the Senate and House of Representatives, open all the Certificates, and the Votes shall then be counted. The Person having the greatest Number of Votes shall be the President, if such Number be a Majority of the whole Number of Electors appointed; and if there be more than one who have such Majority, and have an equal Number of Votes, then the House of Representatives shall immediately chuse by Ballot one of them for President; and if no Person have a Majority, then from the five highest on the List the said House shall in like Manner chuse the President. But in chusing the President, the Votes shall be taken by States, the Representation from each State having one Vote; A quorum for this Purpose shall consist of a Member or Members from two thirds of the States, and a Majority of all the States shall be necessary to a Choice. In every Case, after the Choice of the President, the Person having the greatest Number of Votes of the Electors shall be the Vice President. But if there should remain two or more who have equal Votes, the Senate shall chuse from them by Ballot the Vice President.

The Congress may determine the Time of chusing the Electors, and the Day on which they shall give their Votes; which Day shall be the same throughout the United States.

No Person except a natural born Citizen, or a Citizen of the United States, at the time of the Adoption of this Constitution, shall be eligible to the Office of President; neither shall any Person be eligible to that Office who shall not have attained to the Age of thirty five Years, and been fourteen Years a Resident within the United States.

In Case of the Removal of the President from Office, or of his Death, Resignation, or Inability to discharge the Powers and Duties of the said Office, the Same shall devolve on the Vice President, and the Congress may by Law provide for the Case of

Removal, Death, Resignation or Inability, both of the President and Vice President, declaring what Officer shall then act as President, and such Officer shall act accordingly, until the Disability be removed, or a President shall be elected.

The President shall, at stated Times, receive for his Services, a Compensation, which shall neither be encreased nor diminished during the Period for which he shall have been elected, and he shall not receive within that Period any other Emolument from the United States, or any of them.

Before he enter on the Execution of his Office, he shall take the following Oath or Affirmation:—"I do solemnly swear (or affirm) that I will faithfully execute the Office of President of the United States, and will to the best of my Ability, preserve, protect and defend the Constitution of the United States."

Section. 2. The President shall be Commander in Chief of the Army and Navy of the United States, and of the Militia of the several States, when called into the actual Service of the United States; he may require the Opinion, in writing, of the principal Officer in each of the executive Departments, upon any Subject relating to the Duties of their respective Offices, and he shall have Power to grant Reprieves and Pardons for Offences against the United States, except in Cases of Impeachment.

He shall have Power, by and with the Advice and Consent of the Senate, to make Treaties, provided two thirds of the Senators present concur; and he shall nominate, and by and with the Advice and Consent of the Senate, shall appoint Ambassadors, other public Ministers and Consuls, Judges of the supreme Court, and all other Officers of the United States, whose Appointments are not herein otherwise provided for, and which shall be established by Law: but the Congress may by Law vest the Appointment of such inferior Officers, as they think proper, in the President alone, in the Courts of Law, or in the Heads of Departments.

The President shall have Power to fill up all Vacancies that may happen during the Recess of the Senate, by granting Commissions which shall expire at the End of their next Session.

Section. 3. He shall from time to time give to the Congress Information of the State of the Union, and recommend to their Consideration such Measures as he shall judge necessary and expedient; he may, on extraordinary Occasions, convene both Houses, or either of them, and in Case of Disagreement between them, with Respect to the Time of Adjournment, he may adjourn them to such Time as he shall think proper; he shall receive Ambassadors and other public Ministers; he shall take Care that the Laws be faithfully executed, and shall Commission all the Officers of the United States.

Section. 4. The President, Vice President and all civil Officers of the United States, shall be removed from Office on Impeachment for, and Conviction of, Treason, Bribery, or other high Crimes and Misdemeanors.

## Article III.

Section. 1. The judicial Power of the United States, shall be vested in one supreme Court, and in such inferior Courts as the Congress may from time to time ordain and establish. The Judges, both of the supreme and inferior Courts, shall hold their Offices during good Behaviour, and shall, at stated Times, receive for their Services, a Compensation, which shall not be diminished during their Continuance in Office.

Section. 2. The judicial Power shall extend to all Cases, in Law and Equity, arising under this Constitution, the Laws of the United States, and Treaties made, or which shall be made, under their Authority;—to all Cases affecting Ambassadors, other public Ministers and Consuls;—to all Cases of admiralty and maritime Jurisdiction;—to Controversies to which the United States shall be a Party;—to Controversies between two or more States;—between a State and Citizens of another State;—between Citizens of different States,—between Citizens of the same State claiming Lands under Grants of different States, and between a State, or the Citizens thereof, and foreign States, Citizens or Subjects.

In all Cases affecting Ambassadors, other public Ministers and Consuls, and those in which a State shall be Party, the supreme Court shall have original Jurisdiction. In all the other Cases before mentioned, the supreme Court shall have appellate Jurisdiction, both as to Law and Fact, with such Exceptions, and under such Regulations as the Congress shall make.

The Trial of all Crimes, except in Cases of Impeachment, shall be by Jury; and such Trial shall be held in the State where the said Crimes shall have been committed; but when not committed within any State, the Trial shall be at such Place or Places as the Congress may by Law have directed.

Section. 3. Treason against the United States, shall consist only in levying War against them, or in adhering to their Enemies, giving them Aid and Comfort. No Person shall be convicted of Treason unless on the Testimony of two Witnesses to the same overt Act, or on Confession in open Court.

The Congress shall have Power to declare the Punishment of Treason, but no Attainder of Treason shall work Corruption of Blood, or Forfeiture except during the Life of the Person attainted.

## Article. IV.

Section. 1. Full Faith and Credit shall be given in each State to the public Acts, Records, and judical Proceedings of every other State. And the Congress may by general Laws prescribe the Manner in which such Acts, Records and Proceedings shall be proved, and the Effect thereof.

Section. 2. The Citizens of each State shall be entitled to all Privileges and Immunities of Citizens in the several States.

A Person charged in any State with Treason, Felony, or other Crime, who shall flee from Justice, and be found in another State, shall on Demand of the executive Authority of the State from which he fled, be delivered up, to be removed to the State having Jurisdiction of the Crime.

No Person held to Service or Labour in one State, under the Laws thereof, escaping into another, shall, in Consequence of any Law or Regulation therein, be discharged from such Service or Labour, but shall be delivered up on Claim of the Party to whom such Service or Labour may be due.

Section. 3. New States may be admitted by the Congress into this Union; but no new State shall be formed or erected within the Jurisdiction of any other State; nor any State be formed by the

Junction of two or more States, or Parts of States, without the Consent of the Legislatures of the States concerned as well as of the Congress.

The Congress shall have Power to dispose of and make all needful Rules and Regulations respecting the Territory or other Property belonging to the United States; and nothing in this Constitution shall be so construed as to Prejudice any Claims of the United States, or of any particular State.

Section. 4. The United States shall guarantee to every State in this Union a Republican Form of Government, and shall protect each of them against Invasion; and on Application of the Legislature, or of the Executive (when the Legislature cannot be convened) against domestic Violence.

## Article. V.

The Congress, whenever two thirds of both Houses shall deem it necessary, shall propose Amendments to this Constitution, or, on the Application of the Legislatures of two thirds of the several States, shall call a Convention for proposing Amendments, which, in either Case, shall be valid to all Intents and Purposes, as Part of this Constitution, when ratified by the Legislatures of three fourths of the several States, or by Conventions in three fourths thereof, as the one or the other Mode of Ratification may be proposed by the Congress; Provided that no Amendment which may be made prior to the Year One thousand eight hundred and eight shall in any Manner affect the first and fourth Clauses in the Ninth Section of the first Article; and that no State, without its Consent, shall be deprived of it's equal Suffrage in the Senate.

## Article. VI.

All Debts contracted and Engagements entered into, before the Adoption of this Constitution, shall be as valid against the United States under this Constitution, as under the Confederation.

This Constitution, and the Laws of the United States which shall be made in Pursuance thereof; and all Treaties made, or which shall be made, under the Authority of the United States, shall be the supreme Law of the Land; and the Judges in every

State shall be bound thereby, any Thing in the Constitution or Laws of any State to the Contrary notwithstanding.

The Senators and Representatives before mentioned, and the Members of the several State Legislatures, and all executive and judicial Officers, both of the United States and of the several States, shall be bound by Oath or Affirmation, to support this Constitution; but no religious Test shall ever be required as a Qualification to any Office or public Trust under the United States.

## Article. VII.

The Ratification of the Conventions of nine States, shall be sufficient for the Establishment of this Constitution between the States so ratifying the Same.

The Word, "the," being interlined between the seventh and eighth Lines of the first Page, The Word "Thirty" being partly written on an Erazure in the fifteenth Line of the first Page, The Words "is tried" being interlined between the thirty second and thirty third Lines of the first Page and the Word "the" being interlined between the forty third and forty fourth Lines of the second Page.

done in Convention by the Unanimous Consent of the States present the Seventeenth Day of September in the Year of our Lord one thousand seven hundred and Eighty seven and of the Independance of the United States of America the Twelfth In witness whereof We have hereunto subscribed our Names,

G?. WASHINGTON—Presid!
and deputy from Virginia

Attest WILLIAM JACKSON Secretary

| | |
|---|---|
| New Hampshire | John Langdon<br>Nicholas Gilman |
| Massachusetts | Nathaniel Gorham<br>Rufus King |
| Connecticut | W<sup>m</sup> Sam<sup>l</sup> Johnson<br>Roger Sherman |
| New York | Alexander Hamilton |
| New Jersey | Wil: Livingston<br>David Brearley.<br>W<sup>m</sup> Paterson.<br>Jona: Dayton |
| Pensylvania | B Franklin<br>Thomas Mifflin<br>Rob<sup>t</sup> Morris<br>Geo. Clymer<br>Tho<sup>s</sup> FitzSimons<br>Jared Ingersoll<br>James Wilson<br>Gouv Morris |
| Delaware | Geo: Read<br>Gunning Bedford jun<br>John Dickinson<br>Richard Bassett<br>Jaco: Broom |
| Maryland | James M<sup>c</sup>Henry<br>Dan of S<sup>t</sup> Tho<sup>s</sup> Jenifer<br>Dan<sup>l</sup> Carroll |
| Virginia | John Blair—<br>James Madison Jr. |
| North Carolina | W<sup>m</sup> Blount<br>Rich<sup>d</sup> Dobbs Spaight.<br>Hu Williamson |
| South Carolina | J. Rutledge<br>Charles Cotesworth Pinckney<br>Charles Pinckney<br>Pierce Butler. |
| Georgia | William Few<br>Abr Baldwin |

LETTER OF THE PRESIDENT OF THE FEDERAL CONVENTION, DATED SEPTEMBER 17, 1787, TO THE PRESIDENT OF CONGRESS, TRANSMITTING THE CONSTITUTION.[1]

IN CONVENTION, SEPTEMBER 17, 1787.[2]

Sir,

We have now the honor to submit to the consideration of the United States in Congress assembled, that Constitution which has appeared to us the most adviseable.

The friends of our country have long seen and desired, that the power of making war, peace, and treaties, that of levying money and regulating commerce, and the correspondent executive and judicial authorities should be fully and effectually vested in the general government of the Union: But the impropriety of delegating such extensive trust to one body of men is evident—Hence results the necessity of a different organization.

It is obviously impracticable in the federal government of these states, to secure all rights of independent sovereignty to each, and yet provide for the interest and safety of all: Individuals entering into society, must give up a share of liberty to preserve the rest. The magnitude of the sacrifice must depend as well on situation and circumstance, as on the object to be obtained. It is at all times difficult to draw with precision the line between those rights which must be surrendered, and those which may be reserved; and on the present occasion this difficulty was encreased by a difference among the several states as to their situation, extent, habits, and particular interests.

In all our deliberations on this subject we kept steadily in our view, that which appears to us the greatest interest of every true American, the consolidation of our Union, in which is involved our prosperity, felicity, safety, perhaps our national existence. This important consideration, seriously and deeply impressed on our minds, led each state in the Convention to be less rigid on

---
[1] Reprinted from *Documentary History of the Constitution*, Vol. II (1894), pp. 1, 2.
[2] From Washington's copy of the Journal of Congress (Vol. XII, p. 164).

points of inferior magnitude, than might have been otherwise expected; and thus the Constitution, which we now present, is the result of a spirit of amity, and of that mutual deference and concession which the peculiarity of our political situation rendered indispensible.

That it will meet the full and entire approbation of every state is not perhaps to be expected; but each will doubtless consider, that had her interest been alone consulted, the consequences might have been particularly disagreeable or injurious to others; that it is liable to as few exceptions as could reasonably have been expected, we hope and believe; that it may promote the lasting welfare of that country so dear to us all, and secure her freedom and happiness, is our most ardent wish.

With great respect, We have the honor to be, Sir,
    Your Excellency's
        most obedient and humble servants,

            GEORGE WASHINGTON, *President.*
            *By unanimous Order of the Convention.*
*His Excellency* the PRESIDENT of CONGRESS.

# RESOLUTION OF THE FEDERAL CONVENTION SUBMITTING THE CONSTITUTION TO CONGRESS, SEPTEMBER 17, 1787.[1]

IN CONVENTION MONDAY SEPTEMBER 17th 1787.

Present

The States of

New Hampshire, Massachusetts, Connecticut, M$^r$ Hamilton from New York, New Jersey, Pennsylvania, Delaware, Maryland, Virginia, North Carolina, South Carolina and Georgia. Resolved,

That the preceeding Constitution be laid before the United States in Congress assembled, and that it is the Opinion of this Convention, that it should afterwards be submitted to a Convention of Delegates, chosen in each State by the People thereof, under the Recommendation of its Legislature, for their Assent and Ratification; and that each Convention assenting to, and ratifying the Same, should give Notice thereof to the United States in Congress assembled.

Resolved, That it is the Opinion of this Convention, that as soon as the Conventions of nine States shall have ratified this Constitution, the United States in Congress assembled should fix a Day on which Electors should be appointed by the States which shall have ratified the same, and a Day on which the Electors should assemble to vote for the President, and the Time and Place for commencing Proceedings under this Constitution. That after such Publication the Electors should be appointed, and the Senators and Representatives elected: That the Electors should meet on the Day fixed for the Election of the President, and should transmit their Votes certified, signed, sealed and directed, as the Constitution requires, to the Secretary of the United States in Congress assembled, that the Senators and Representatives should convene at the Time and Place assigned; that the Senators should appoint a President of

---

[1] Reprinted from *Documentary History of the Constitution*, Vol. II (1894), pp. 20, 21.

the Senate, for the sole Purpose of receiving, opening and counting the Votes for President; and, that after he shall be chosen, the Congress, together with the President, should, without Delay, proceed to execute this Constitution.

By the Unanimous Order of the Convention

G⁰ WASHINGTON Presid$^t$

W. JACKSON Secretary.

# RESOLUTION OF CONGRESS OF SEPTEMBER 28, 1787, SUBMITTING THE CONSTITUTION TO THE SEVERAL STATES.[1]

FRIDAY SEPT 28. 1787.[2]

Congress assembled present Newhampshire Massachusetts Connecticut New York New Jersey Pensylvania. Delaware Virginia North Carolina South Carolina and Georgia and from Maryland Mʳ Ross

Congress having received the report of the Convention lately assembled in Philadelphia

Resolved Unanimously that the said Report with the resolutions and letter accompanying the same be transmitted to the several legislatures in Order to be submitted to a convention of Delegates chosen in each state by the people thereof in conformity to the resolves of the Convention made and provided in that case.

[1] Reprinted from *Documentary History of the Constitution*, Vol. II (1894), p. 22.
[2] From the "Rough" Journal of Congress (No. 1, Vol. 38).

## CIRCULAR LETTER OF THE SECRETARY OF CONGRESS, DATED SEPTEMBER 28, 1787, TRANSMITTING COPY OF THE CONSTITUTION TO THE SEVERAL GOVERNORS.[1]

(Circular)[2]

Office of Secretary of Congress
Sep$^t$ 28$^{th}$ 1787—

Sir

In obedience to an unanimous resolution of the United States in Congress Assembled, a copy of which is annexed, I have the honor to transmit to Your Excellency, the Report of the Convention lately Assembled in Philadelphia, together with the resolutions and letter accompanying the same; And have to request that Your Excellency will be pleased to lay the same before the Legislature, in order that it may be submitted to a Convention of Delegates chosen in Your State by the people of the State in conformity to the resolves of the Convention, made & provided in that case.—

with the greatest respect

I have the honor &c—

C: T—

transmitting the }
Report of the Convention }

---

[1] Reprinted from *Documentary History of the Constitution*, Vol. II (1894), p. 23.
[2] From the recorded letters of the "Office of Secretary of Congress" (No. 18, p. 129).

# RATIFICATION OF THE CONSTITUTION BY THE SEVERAL STATES, ARRANGED IN THE ORDER OF THEIR RATIFICATION.

## STATE OF DELAWARE [1]

We the Deputies of the People of the Delaware State, in Convention met, having taken into our serious consideration the Fœderal Constitution proposed and agreed upon by the Deputies of the United States in a General Convention held at the City of Philadelphia on the seventeenth day of September in the year of our Lord one thousand seven hundred and eighty seven, Have approved, assented to, ratified, and confirmed, and by these Presents, Do, in virtue of the Power and Authority to us given for that purpose, for and in behalf of ourselves and our Constituents, fully, freely, and entirely approve of, assent to, ratify, and confirm the said Constitution.

Done in Convention at Dover this seventh day of December in the year aforesaid, and in the year of the Independence of the United States of America the twelfth. In Testimony whereof we have hereunto subscribed our Names—

| Sussex County | Kent County | New Castle County |
|---|---|---|
| JOHN INGRAM | NICHOLAS RIDGELEY | JAS LATIMER, President |
| JOHN JONES | RICHARD SMITH | JAMES BLACK |
| WILLIAM MOORE | GEORGE TRUITT | JNO JAMES |
| WILLIAM HALL | RICHARD BASSETT | GUNNING BEDFORD Senr |
| THOMAS LAWS | JAMES SYKES | KENSEY JOHNS |
| ISAAC COOPER | ALLEN MCLANE | THOMAS WATSON |
| WOODMAN STORKLY. | DANIEL CUMMINS senr | SOLOMON MAXWELL |
| JOHN LAWS | JOSEPH BARKER | NICHOLAS WAY |
| THOMAS EVANS | EDWARD WHITE | THOMAS DUFF |
| ISRAEL HOLLAND | GEORGE MANLOVE | GUNNG BEDFORD Junr |

To all whom these Presents shall come Greeting, I Thomas Collins President of the Delaware State do hereby certify, that the above instrument of writing is a true copy of the original ratification of the Fœderal Constitution by the Convention of the Delaware State, which original ratification is now in my possession. In Testimony whereof I have caused the seal of the Delaware State to be hereunto an'exed.

[SEAL.]

THOS COLLINS

---

[1] Reprinted from *Documentary History of the Constitution*, Vol. II (1894), pp. 25, 26.

STATE OF PENNSYLVANIA.[2]

*In the Name of the People of Pennsylvania*

Be it Known unto all Men that We the Delegates of the People of the Commonwealth of Pennsylvania in general Convention assembled Have assented to, and ratified, and by these presents Do in the Name and by the authority of the same People, and for ourselves, assent to, and ratify the foregoing Constitution for the United States of America. Done in Convention at Philadelphia the twelfth day of December in the year of our Lord one thousand seven hundred and eighty seven and of the Independence of the United States of America the twelfth. In witness whereof we have hereunto subscribed our names.

FREDERICK AUGUSTUS MUHLENBERG President

| | |
|---|---|
| J$^{NO}$ ALLISON | THOMAS CHEYN. |
| JONATHAN ROBERTS | JOHN HANNUM |
| JOHN RICHARDS | STEPHEN CHAMBERS |
| JAMES MORRIS | ROBERT COLEMAN |
| TIMOTHY PICKERING | SEBASTIAN GRAFF |
| BENJ$^N$ ELLIOT— | JOHN HUBLEY |
| STEPHEN BALLIET | SAMUEL ASHMEAD |
| JOSEPH HORSFIELD | ENOCH EDWARDS |
| DAVID DASHLER | HENRY WYNKOOP |
| WILLIAM WILSON | JOHN BARCLAY |
| JOHN BOYD | THO$^S$ YARDLEY |
| THO SCOTT | ABRAHAM STOUT |
| JOHN NEVILL | THOMAS BULL |
| JASPER YEATES. | ANTHONY WAYNE |
| HEN$^Y$ SLAGLE | GEORGE LATIMER |
| THOMAS CAMPBELL | BENJ$^N$ RUSH |
| THOMAS HARTLEY | HILARY BAKER |
| DAVID GRIER | JAMES WILSON |
| JOHN BLACK | THOMAS M$^C$KEAN |
| BENJAMIN PEDAN | W MACPHERSON |
| JOHN ARNDT | JOHN HUNN |
| WILLIAM GIBBONS | GEORGE GRAY |
| RICHARD DOWNING | |

Attest JAMES CAMPBELL Secretary

---

[2] Reprinted from *Documentary History of the Constitution*, Vol. II (1894), pp. 44, 45.

## STATE OF NEW JERSEY [3]

### *In Convention of the State of New Jersey*

Whereas a convention of Delegates from the following States, Viz$^t$. New Hampshire, Massachusetts, Connecticut, New York, New Jersey, Pennsylvania, Delaware, Maryland, Virginia, North Carolina, South Carolina and Georgia, met at Philadelphia for the purpose of deliberating on, and forming a constitution for the United States of America, finished their Session on the seventeenth day of September last and reported to Congress the form which they had agreed upon, in the words following, Viz$^t$— . . .

And Whereas Congress on the twenty eighth day of September last unanimously did resolve " that the said report with the Resolutions and letter accompanying the same, be transmitted to the several Legislatures, in order to be submitted to a convention of Delegates, chosen in each State by the People thereof, in conformity to the Resolves of the convention made and provided in that case."

And Whereas the Legislature of this State did on the twenty ninth day of October last Resolve in the words following, Viz$^t$— " Resolved unanimously, That it be recommended to such of the Inhabitants of this State as are entitled to vote for Representatives in General Assembly, to meet in their respective counties on the fourth Tuesday in November next, at the several places fixed by law for holding the annual elections, to choose three suitable persons to serve as Delegates from each County in a State Convention, for the purposes herein before-mentioned, and that the same be conducted agreeably to the mode, and conformably with the Rules and Regulations prescribed for conducting such Elections."

Resolved unanimously, That the Persons so Elected to serve in State Convention, do assemble and meet together on the second Tuesday in December next, at Trenton, in the County of Hunterdon, then and there to take into Consideration the aforesaid Constitution; and if approved of by them, finally to Ratify the same in behalf and on the part of this State; and make Report

---

[3] Reprinted from *Documentary History of the Constitution*, Vol. II (1894), pp. 46, 61–64.

thereof to the United States in Congress assembled, in Conformity with the Resolutions thereto annexed."

"Resolved, That the Sheriffs of the respective Counties of this State shall be, and they are hereby required to give as timely Notice as may be, by Advertisements to the People of their Counties of the time, place and Purpose of holding Elections as aforesaid."

And Whereas the Legislature of this State did also on the first day of November last make and pass the following Act, Viz$^t$— "An Act to authorize the People of this State to meet in Convention, deliberate upon, agree to, and ratify the Constitution of the United States, proposed by the late General Convention. Be it Enacted by the Council and General Assembly of this State, and it is hereby enacted by the Authority of the same, That it shall and may be lawful for the People thereof, by their Delegates, to meet in Convention, to deliberate upon, and, if approved of by them, to ratify the Constitution for the United States, proposed by the General Convention, held at Philadelphia, and every Act, matter and clause therein contained, conformably to the Resolutions of the Legislature, passed the twenty-ninth day of October, Seventeen hundred and eighty seven, any Law, Usage or Custom to the contrary in any wise notwithstanding."

Now be it known that we the Delegates of the State of New-Jersey chosen by the People thereof for the purposes aforesaid having maturely deliberated on, and considered the aforesaid proposed Constitution, do hereby for and on the behalf of the People of the said State of New-Jersey agree to, ratify and confirm the same and every part thereof.

Done in Convention by the unanimous consent of the members present, this eighteenth day of December in the year of our Lord one thousand seven hundred and eighty seven, and of the Independence of the United States of America the twelfth.—In Witness whereof we have hereunto subscribed our names.

Note, Before the signing hereof, the following words, viz, "Cession of" were interlined between the fifteenth and sixteenth lines on the second sheet.

JOHN STEVENS President—
and Delegate from the County of Hunterdon

| | |
|---|---|
| County of Bergen | JOHN FELL<br>PETER ZABRISKIE<br>CORNELIUS HENNION |
| Essex | JOHN CHETWOOD<br>SAMUEL HAY<br>DAVID CRANE |
| Middlesex | JOHN NEILSON<br>JOHN BEATTY<br>BENJAMIN MANNING |
| Monmouth | ELISHA LAWRENCE<br>SAMUEL BREESE<br>WILLIAM CRAWFORD |
| Somersett | $J^{NO}$ WITHERSPOON<br>JACOB R HARDENBERGH<br>FRED: FRELINGHUYSEN |
| Burlington | THOMAS REYNOLDS<br>GEO. ANDERSON<br>JOSHUA M. WALLACE |
| Gloucester | $R^D$ HOWELS<br>$AND^W$ HUNTER<br>BENJAMIN WHITALL |
| Salem | WHITTEN CRIPPS<br>EDMUND WETHERBY |
| County of Cape-May | JESSE HAND<br>JEREMIAH ELDREDGE<br>MATTHEW WHILLDIN |
| Hunterdon | DAVID BREARLEY<br>JOSHUA CORSHON |
| Morris | WILLIAM WINDES<br>WILLIAM WOODHULL<br>JOHN JACOB FAESCH |
| Cumberland | $DAV^D$ POTTER<br>JONATHAN BOWEN<br>ELI ELMER |

Sussex ................ { Robert Ogden  
Thom<sup>s</sup> Anderson  
Rob<sup>t</sup> Hoops }

Attest. Sam<sup>l</sup> W. Stockton Sec<sup>y</sup>.

---

## State of Georgia [4]

*In Convention; Wednesday, January the second, one thousand seven hundred and eighty eight:*

*To all to whom these Presents shall come, Greeting.*

Whereas the form of a Constitution for the Government of the United States of America, was, on the seventeenth day of September, one thousand seven hundred and eighty-seven, agreed upon and reported to Congress by the Deputies of the said United States convened in Philadelphia; which said Constitution is written in the words following, to wit; . . .

[SEAL APPENDANT.] And Whereas the United States in Congress assembled did, on the twenty-eighth day of September, one thousand seven hundred and eighty-seven, Resolve, unanimously, That the said Report, with the resolutions and letter accompanying the same, be transmitted to the several Legislatures, in order to be submitted to a Convention of Delegates chosen in each State by the People thereof, in conformity to the Resolves of the Convention made and provided in that case.

And Whereas the Legislature of the State of Georgia did, on the twenty-sixth day of October, one thousand seven hundred and eighty-seven, in pursuance of the above recited resolution of Congress,

Resolve, That a convention be elected on the day of the next General Election, and in the same manner as representatives are elected; and that the said Convention consist of not more than three members from each County. And that the said Convention should meet at Augusta, on the fourth Tuesday in December then next, and as soon thereafter as convenient, proceed to consider the said Report, letter and resolutions, and to adopt or reject any part or the whole thereof.

---

[4] Reprinted from *Documentary History of the Constitution*, Vol. II (1894), pp. 65, 66, 82-84.

Now Know Ye, That We, the Delegates of the People of the State of Georgia in Convention met, pursuant to the Resolutions of the Legislature aforesaid, having taken into our serious consideration the said Constitution, Have assented to, ratified and adopted, and by these presents DO, in virtue of the powers and authority to Us given by the People of the said State for that purpose, for, and in behalf of ourselves and our Constituents, fully and entirely assent to, ratify and adopt the said Constitution.

Done in Convention, at Augusta in the said State, on the second day of January, in the year of our Lord one thousand seven hundred and eighty eight, and of the Independence of the United States the twelfth. In Witness whereof we have hereunto subscribed our names.

JOHN WEREAT. President
and Delegate for the County of Richmond.

Attest. ISAAC BRIGGS, Secretary.

|  |  |
|---|---|
| W: STEPHENS<br>JOSEPH HABERSHAM | Chatham |
| JENKINS DAVIS<br>N BROWNSON | Effingham |
| EDW<sup>D</sup> TELFAIR<br>H. TODD | Burke |
| WILLIAM FEW<br>JAMES M<sup>C</sup>NEIL | Richmond |
| GEO MATHEWS<br>FLOR<sup>CE</sup> SULLIVAN<br>JOHN KING | Wilkes |
| JAMES. POWELL<br>JOHN ELLIOTT<br>JAMES MAXWELL | Liberty |
| GEO: HANDLEY.<br>CHRISTOPHER HILLARY<br>J: MASON. | Glynn |
| HENRY OSBORNE<br>JAMES SEAGROVE<br>JACOB WEED | Camden |
| JARED IRWIN<br>JOHN RUTHERFORD | Washington |
| ROB<sup>T</sup> CHRISTMAS<br>THOMAS DANIELL<br>R MIDDLETON | Greene |

STATE OF CONNECTICUT [5]

*In the Name of the People of the State of Connecticut.*

We the Delegates of the People of s:d State in general Convention assembled, pursuant to an Act of the Legislature in October last, Have assented to and ratified, and by these presents do assent to, ratify and adopt the Constitution, reported by the Convention of Delegates in Philadelphia, on the 17th day of September AD. 1787. for the United States of Ameriea.

Done in Convention this 9th day of January AD. 1788. In witness whereof we have hereunto set our hands.

MATTHEW GRISWOLD President:

| | |
|---|---|
| JERE:H WADSWORTH | SAM:L HUNTINGTON |
| JESSE ROOT | JED HUNTINGTON |
| ISAAC LEE | ISAAC HUNTINGTON |
| SELAH HEART | ROBERT ROBBINS, |
| ZEBULON PECK ju:r | DAN:LE FOOT |
| ELISHA PITKIN | ELI HYDE |
| ERASTUS WOLCOTT | JOSEPH WOODBRIDGE |
| JOHN WATSON | STEPHEN BILLINGS |
| JOHN TREADWELL | ANDREW LEE |
| WILLIAM JUDD | WILLIAM NOYES |
| JOSEPH MOSELY | JOSHUA RAYMOND Jun:r |
| WAIT GOODRICH | JER:H HALSEY |
| JOHN CURTISS | WHEELER COIT |
| ASA BARNS | CHARLES PHELPS |
| STEPHEN MIX MITCHELL | NATHANIEL MINOR |
| JOHN CHESTER | JONATHAN STURGES |
| OLIV ELLSWORTH | THADDEUS BURR |
| ROGER NEWBERRY | ELISHA WHITTELSEY |
| ROGER SHERMAN | JOSEPH MOSS WHITE |
| PIERPONT EDWARDS | AMOS MEAD |
| SAMUEL BEACH | JABEZ FITCH |
| DANIEL HOLBROOK | NEHEMIAH BEARDSLEY |
| JOHN HOLBROOK | JAMES POTTER |
| GIDEON BUCKINGHAM | JOHN CHANDLER |
| LEWIS MALLET J:r | JOHN BEACH |
| JOSEPH HOPKINS | HEZ:H ROGERS |
| JOHN WELTON | LEM:L SANFORD |
| RICH:D LAW | WILLIAM HERON |
| AMASA LEARNED | PHILIP BURR BRADLEY |

---

[5] Reprinted from *Documentary History of the Constitution*, Vol. II (1894), pp. 87–89.

1017

Nathan Dauchy
James Davenport
John Davenport Jun.<sup>r</sup>
W<sup>m</sup> Sam<sup>l</sup> Johnson
Elisha Mills
Eleph<sup>t</sup> Dyer
Jed<sup>a</sup> Elderkin
Simeon Smith
Hendrick Dow
Seth Paine
Asa Witter
Moses Cleaveland
Sampson Howe
Will<sup>m</sup> Danielson
W<sup>m</sup> Williams
James Bradford
Joshua Dunlop
Daniel Learned
Moses Campbell
Benjamin Dow
Oliver Wolcott
Jedediah Strong
Moses Hawley
Charles Burrall
Nathan Hale
Daniel Miles
Asaph Hall
Isaac Burnham
John Wilder
Mark Prindle
Jedidiah Hubbel
Aaron Austin
Samuel Canfield
Daniel Everitt
Hez: Fitch

Joshua Porter
Benj<sup>n</sup> Hinman
Epaphras Sheldon
Eleazer Curtiss
John Whittlesey
Dan<sup>l</sup> Nath<sup>l</sup> Brinsmade
Thomas Fenn
David Smith
Robert M<sup>c</sup>Cane
Daniel Sherman
Samuel Orton
Asher Miller
Sam<sup>l</sup> H. Parsons
Eben<sup>r</sup> White
Hez<sup>h</sup> Goodrich
Dyar Throop
Jabez Chapman
Cornelius Higgins
Hezekiah Brainerd
Theophilus Morgan
Hez<sup>h</sup> Lane
William Hart
Sam<sup>l</sup> Shipman
Jeremiah West
Samuel Chapman
Ichabod Warner
Samuel Carver
Jeremiah Ripley
Ephraim Root
John Phelps
Isaac Foot
Abijah Sessions
Caleb Holt
Seth Crocker

State of Connecticut, ss. Hartford January ninth, Anno Domini one thousand, seven hundred and eighty eight.

The foregoing Ratification was agreed to, and signed as above, by one hundred and twenty eight, and dissented to by forty Delegates in Convention, which is a Majority of eighty eight.

Certified by MATTHEW GRISWOLD President.

Teste JEDIDIAH STRONG Secretary—

### STATE OF MASSACHUSETTS [6]

*In Convention of the delegates of the People of the Commonwealth of Massachusetts February 6th 1788*

The Convention have impartially discussed, & fully considered the Constitution for the United States of America, reported to Congress by the Convention of Delegates from the United States of America, & submitted to us by a resolution of the General Court of the said Commonwealth, passed the twenty fifth day of October last past, & acknowledging with grateful hearts, the goodness of the Supreme Ruler of the Universe in affording the People of the United States in the course of his providence an opportunity deliberately & peaceably without fraud or surprize of entering into an explicit & solemn Compact with each other by assenting to & ratifying a New Constitution in order to form a more perfect Union, establish Justice, insure Domestic tranquillity, provide for the common defence, promote the general welfare & secure the blessings of Liberty to themselves & their posterity; Do in the name & in behalf of the People of the Commonwealth of Massachusetts assent to & ratify the said Constitution for the United States of America.

And as it is the opinion of this Convention that certain amendments & alterations in the said Constitution would remove the fears & quiet the apprehensions of many of the good people of this Commonwealth & more effectually guard against an undue administration of the Federal Government, The Convention do therefore recommend that the following alterations & provisions be introduced into the said Constitution.

*First*, That it be explicitly declared that all Powers not expressly delegated by the aforesaid Consitution are reserved to the several States to be by them exercised.

*Secondly*, That there shall be one representative to every thirty thousand persons according to the Census mentioned in the Constitution until the whole number of the Representatives amounts to Two hundred.

*Thirdly*, That Congress do not exercise the powers vested in them by the fourth Section of the first article, but in cases when a State

---
[6] Reprinted from *Documentary History of the Constitution*, Vol. II (1894), pp. 93–96.

shall neglect or refuse to make the regulations therein mentioned or shall make regulations subversive of the rights of the People to a free & equal representation in Congress agreeably to the Constitution.

*Fourthly*, That Congress do not lay direct Taxes but when the Monies arising from the Impost & Excise are insufficient for the publick exigencies nor then until Congress shall have first made a requisition upon the States to assess levy & pay their respective proportions of such Requisition agreeably to the Census fixed in the said Constitution; in such way & manner as the Legislature of the States shall think best, & in such case if any State shall neglect or refuse to pay its proportion pursuant to such requisition then Congress may assess & levy such State's proportion together with interest thereon at the rate of Six per cent per annum from the time of payment prescribed in such requisition

*Fifthly*, That Congress erect no Company of Merchants with exclusive advantages of commerce.

*Sixthly*, That no person shall be tried for any Crime by which he may incur an infamous punishment or loss of life until he be first indicted by a Grand Jury, except in such cases as may arise in the Government & regulation of the Land & Naval forces.

*Seventhly*, The Supreme Judicial Federal Court shall have no jurisdiction of Causes between Citizens of different States unless the matter in dispute whether it concerns the realty or personalty be of the value of three thousand dollars at the least. nor shall the Federal Judicial Powers extend to any actions between Citizens of different States where the matter in dispute whether it concerns the Realty or personalty is not of the value of Fifteen hundred dollars at the least.

*Eighthly*, In civil actions between Citizens of different States every issue of fact arising in Actions at common law shall be tried by a Jury if the parties or either of them request it.

*Ninthly*, Congress shall at no time consent that any person holding an office of trust or profit under the United States shall accept of a title of Nobility or any other title or office from any King, prince or Foreign State.

And the Convention do in the name & in behalf of the People of this Commonwealth enjoin it upon their Representatives in Congress at all times until the alterations & provisions aforesaid have been considered agreeably to the Fifth article of the said Constitution to exert all their influence & use all reasonable & legal methods to obtain a ratification of the said alterations & provisions in such manner as is provided in the said Article.

And that the United States in Congress Assembled may have due notice of the Assent & Ratification of the said Constitution by this Convention it is, Resolved, that the Assent & Ratification aforesaid be engrossed on Parchment together with the recommendation & injunction aforesaid & with this resolution & that His Excellency John Hancock Esq[r] President & the Hon[ble] William Cushing Esq[r] Vice President, of this Convention transmit the same, counter-signed by the Secretary of the Convention under their hands & seals to the United States in Congress Assembled

       JOHN HANCOCK President
       W[M] CUSHING Vice President

GEORGE RICHARDS MINOT, Secretary.

Pursuant to the Resolution aforesaid WE the President & Vice President abovenamed Do hereby transmit to the United States in Congress Assembled, the same Resolution with the above Assent and Ratification of the Constitution aforesaid for the United States, And the recommendation & injunction above specified.

In Witness whereof We have hereunto set our hands & Seals at Boston in the Commonwealth aforesaid this Seventh day of February Anno Domini, one thousand Seven Hundred & Eighty eight, and in the Twelfth year of the Independence of the United States of America.

      JOHN HANCOCK President   [SEAL.]
      W[M] CUSHING Vice President   [SEAL.]

## STATE OF MARYLAND [7]

*In Convention of the Delegates of the People of the State of Maryland 28 April 1788.*

We the Delegates of the people of the State of Maryland having fully considered the Constitution of the United States of America reported to Congress by the Convention of Deputies from the United States of America held in Philadelphia on the seventeenth Day of September in the Year Seventeen hundred and eighty seven of which the annexed is a Copy and submitted to us by a Resolution of the General Assembly of Maryland in November Session Seventeen hundred and eighty seven do for ourselves and in the Name and on the behalf of the People of this State assent to and ratify the said Constitution.

In Witness whereof we have hereunto subscribed our Names—

| | |
|---|---|
| | GEO: PLATER President— |
| RICH<sup>D</sup> BARNES | DANIEL SULLIVAN |
| CHARLES CHILTON | JAMES SHAW |
| N LEWIS SEWALL | JOS: GILPIN |
| W<sup>M</sup> TILGHMAN. | H HOLLINGSWORTH |
| DONALDSON YEATES | JAMES GORDON HERON |
| ISAAC PERKINS | SAM<sup>L</sup> EVANS |
| WILLIAM GRANGER | FIELDER BOWIE |
| JOSEPH WILKINSON | OSB SPRIGG |
| CHARLES GRAHAME | BENJAMIN HALL |
| J<sup>NO</sup> CHESLEY Jun<sup>r</sup> | GEORGE DIGGES, |
| W. SMITH | NICHOLAS CARROLL. |
| G. R. BROWN | A C. HANSON |
| J PARNHAM | JA. TILGHMAN |
| ZEPH. TURNER | J<sup>NO</sup> SENEY |
| MICHAEL JENEFER STONE | JAMES HOLLYDAY |
| R. GOLDSBOROUGH junr | WILLIAM HEMSLEY |
| EDW<sup>D</sup> LLOYD | PETER CHAILLE |
| JOHN STEVENS | JAMES MARTIN |
| GEORGE GALE | WILLIAM MORRIS |
| HENRY WAGGAMAN | JOHN DONE |
| JOHN STEWART | TH<sup>S</sup> JOHNSON |
| JOHN GALE | THO. S. LEE |
| N<sup>S</sup> HAMMOND | RICHARD POTTS |

---

[7] Reprinted from *Documentary History of the Constitution*, Vol. II (1894), pp. 121, 122.

| | |
|---|---|
| ABRAHAM FAW | THOMAS SPRIGG |
| W<sup>M</sup> PACA | JOHN STULL |
| J RICHARDSON | MOSES RAWLINGS |
| WILLIAM RICHARDSON | HENRY SHRYOCK |
| MATT: DRIVER | THO<sup>S</sup> CRAMPHIN |
| PETER EDMONDSON | RICH<sup>D</sup> THOMAS |
| JAMES M<sup>C</sup>HENRY | WILL DEAKINS Jun[r] |
| JOHN COULTER | BEN: EDWARDS |

Attest—W<sup>M</sup> HARWOOD Clk.

## STATE OF SOUTH CAROLINA [8]

In Convention of the people of the state of South Carolina by their Representatives held in the city of charleston on Monday the twelfth day of May and continued by divers Adjournments to friday the twenty third day of May Anno Domini One thousand seven hundred and eighty eight, and in the twelfth Year of the Independence of the United States of America.

The Convention having maturely considered the constitution or form of Government reported to Congress by the Convention of Delegates from the United states of America and submitted to them by a Resolution of the Legislature of this State passed the seventeenth and eighteenth days of February last in order to form a more perfect Union, establish Justice, ensure Domestic tranquillity, provide for the common defence, promote the general Welfare and secure the blessings of Liberty to the people of the said United States and their posterity DO in the name and behalf of the people of this State hereby assent to and ratify the said Constitution.

> Done in Convention the twenty third day of May in the Year of our Lord One thousand seven hundred and eighty eight, and of the Independence of the United States of America the twelfth.— THOMAS PINCKNEY
>
> President [SEAL.]

Attest

JOHN SANDFORD DART

Secretary [SEAL.]

---

[8] Reprinted from *Documentary History of the Constitution*, Vol. II (1894), pp. 138-140.

And Whereas it is essential to the preservation of the rights reserved to the several states, and the freedom of the people under the operations of a General government that the right of prescribing the manner time and places of holding the Elections to the Federal Legislature, should be for ever inseparably annexed to the sovereignty of the several states. This convention doth declare that the same ought to remain to all posterity a perpetual and fundamental right in the local, exclusive of the interference of the General Government except in cases where the Legislatures of the States, shall refuse or neglect to perform and fulfil the same according to the tenor of the said Constitution.

This Convention doth also declare that no Section or paragraph of the said Constitution warrants a Construction that the states do not retain every power not expressly relinquished by them and vested in the General Government of the Union.

Resolved that the general Government of the United States ought never to impose direct taxes, *but* where the monies arising from the duties, imposts and excise are insufficient for the public exigencies *nor then until* Congress shall have made a requisition upon the states to Assess levy and pay their respective proportions of such requisitions And in case any state shall neglect or refuse to pay its proportion pursuant to such requisition then Congress may assess and levy such state's proportion together with Interest thereon at the rate of six per centum per annum from the time of payment prescribed by such requisition—

Resolved that the third section of the Sixth Article ought to be amended by inserting the word "*other*" between the words "*no*" and "*religious*"

Resolved that it be a standing instruction to all such delegates as may hereafter be elected to represent this State in the general Government to exert their utmost abilities and influence to effect an Alteration of the Constitution conformably to the foregoing Resolutions.

> Done in Convention the twenty third day of May in the year of our Lord One thousand Seven hundred and eighty eight

and of the Independence of the United States of America the twelfth       THOMAS PINCKNEY

President [SEAL.]

Attest

JOHN SANFORD DART

Secretary [SEAL.]

---

STATE OF NEW HAMPSHIRE.[9]

*In Convention of the Delegates of the People of the State of New-Hampshire June the Twenty first 1788.*

[SEAL.]

The Convention haveing Impartially discussed and fully considered the Constitution for the United States of America, reported to Congress by the Convention of Delegates from the United States of America & submitted to us by a Resolution of the General Court of said State passed the fourteenth Day of December last past and acknowledgeing with gratefull Hearts the goodness of the Supreme ruler of the Universe in affording the People of the United States in the Course of his Providence an Opportunity, deliberately & peaceably without fraud or surprize of entering into an Explicit and solemn compact with each other by assenting to & ratifying a new Constitution, in Order to form a more perfect Union, establish Justice, Insure domestick Tranquility, provide for the common defence, promote the general welfare and secure the Blessings of Liberty to themselves & their Posterity—Do In the Name & behalf of the People of the State of New-Hampshire assent to & ratify the said Constitution for the United States of America. And as it is the Opinion of this Convention that certain amendments & alterations in the said Constitution would remove the fears & quiet the apprehensions of many of the good People of this State & more Effectually guard against an undue Administration of the Federal Government— The Convention do therefore recommend that the following alterations & provisions be introduced into the said Constitution.—

---

[9] Reprinted from *Documentary History of the Constitution*, Vol. II (1894), pp. 141-144.

It will be observed that New Hampshire was the ninth State in order of time to ratify the Constitution, which thereupon, in accordance with Article VII thereof, became binding upon the nine States which ratified it—Delaware, Pennsylvania, New Jersey, Georgia, Connecticut, Massachusetts, Maryland, South Carolina, and New Hampshire.

First That it be Explicitly declared that all Powers not expressly & particularly Delegated by the aforesaid Constitution are reserved to the several States to be, by them Exercised.—

Secondly, That there shall be one Representative to every Thirty thousand Persons according to the Census mentioned in the Constitution, untill the whole number of Representatives amount to Two hundred.—

Thirdly That Congress do not Exercise the Powers vested in them, by the fourth Section of the first Article, but in Cases when a State shall neglect or refuse to make the Regulations therein mentioned, or shall make regulations Subversive of the rights of the People to a free and equal Representation in Congress. Nor shall Congress in any Case make regulations contrary to a free and equal Representation.—

Fourthly That Congress do not lay direct Taxes but when the money arising from Impost, Excise and their other resources are insufficient for the Publick Exigencies; nor then, untill Congress shall have first made a Requisition upon the States, to Assess, Levy, & pay their respective proportions, of such requisitions agreeably to the Census fixed in the said Constitution in such way & manner as the Legislature of the State shall think best and in such Case if any State shall neglect, then Congress may Assess & Levy such States proportion together with the Interest thereon at the rate of six per Cent per Annum from the Time of payment prescribed in such requisition—

Fifthly That Congress shall erect no Company of Merchants with exclusive advantages of Commerce.—

Sixthly That no Person shall be Tryed for any Crime by which he may incur an Infamous Punishment, or loss of Life, untill he first be indicted by a Grand Jury except in such Cases as may arise in the Government and regulation of the Land & Naval Forces.—

Seventhly All Common Law Cases between Citizens of different States shall be commenced in the Common Law-Courts of the respective States & no appeal shall be allowed to the Federal Court in such Cases unless the sum or value of the thing in Controversy amount to three Thousand Dollars.—

Eighthly In Civil Actions between Citizens of different States every Issue of Fact arising in Actions at Common Law shall be Tryed by Jury, if the Parties, or either of them request it—

Ninthly—Congress shall at no Time consent that any Person holding an Office of Trust or profit under the United States shall accept any Title of Nobility or any other Title or Office from any King, Prince, or Foreign State.—

Tenth,

That no standing Army shall be Kept up in time of Peace unless with the consent of three fourths of the Members of each branch of Congress, nor shall Soldiers in Time of Peace be quartered upon private Houses without the consent of the Owners.—

Eleventh

Congress shall make no Laws touching Religion, or to infringe the rights of Conscience—

Twelfth

Congress shall never disarm any Citizen unless such as are or have been in Actual Rebellion.—

And the Convention Do. In the Name & behalf of the People of this State enjoin it upon their Representatives in Congress, at all Times untill the alterations and provisions aforesaid have been Considered agreeably to the fifth Article of the said Constitution to exert all their Influence & use all reasonable & Legal methods to obtain a ratification of the said alterations & Provisions, in such manner as is provided in the said article—And That the United States in Congress Assembled may have due notice of the assent & Ratification of the said Constitution by this Convention.—It is resolved that the Assent & Ratification aforesaid be engrossed on Parchment, together with the Recommendation & injunction aforesaid & with this Resolution—And that John Sullivan Esquire President of Convention, & John Langdon Esquire President of the State Transmit the same Countersigned by the Secretary of Convention & the Secretary of the State under their hands & Seals to the United States in Congress Assembled.—

  J$_{N^o}$ SULLIVAN presid$^t$ of the Convention    [SEAL.]
  JOHN LANGDON Presid$^t$ of State       [SEAL.]

By order
  JOHN CALFE Sec$^y$ of Convention
  JOSEPH PEARSON Sec$^y$ of State

### STATE OF VIRGINIA[10]

Virginia to wit

We the Delegates of the People of Virginia duly elected in pursuance of a recommendation from the General Assembly and now met in Convention having fully and freely investigated and discussed the proceedings of the Fœderal Convention and being prepared as well as the most mature deliberation hath enabled us to decide thereon Do in the name and in behalf of the People of Virginia declare and make known that the powers granted under the Constitution being derived from the People of the United States may be resumed by them whensoever the same shall be perverted to their injury or oppression and that every power not granted thereby remains with them and at their will: that therefore no right of any denomination can be cancelled abridged restrained or modified by the Congress by the Senate or House of Representatives acting in any Capacity by the President or any Department or Officer of the United States except in those instances in which power is given by the Constitution for those purposes: & that among other essential rights the liberty of Conscience and of the Press cannot be cancelled abridged restrained or modified by any authority of the United States. With these impressions with a solemn appeal to the Searcher of hearts for the purity of our intentions and under the conviction that whatsoever imperfections may exist in the Constitution ought rather to be examined in the mode prescribed therein than to bring the Union into danger by a delay with a hope of obtaining Amendments previous to the Ratification, We the said Delegates in the name and in behalf of the People of Virginia do by these presents assent to and ratify the Constitution

---

[10] Reprinted from *Documentary History of the Constitution*, Vol. II (1894), pp. 145, 146, 160, 377–385.

recommended on the seventeenth day of September one thousand seven hundred and eighty seven by the Fœderal Convention for the Government of the United States hereby announcing to all those whom it may concern that the said Constitution is binding upon the said People according to an authentic Copy hereto annexed in the Words following; . . .

  Done in Convention this twenty Sixth day of June one thousand seven hundred and eighty eight
  By Order of the Convention
    EDM<sup>D</sup> PENDLETON President [SEAL.] . . .

Virginia towit:

Subsequent Amendments agreed to in Convention as necessary to the proposed Constitution of Government for the United States, recommended to the consideration of the Congress which shall first assemble under the said Constitution to be acted upon according to the mode prescribed in the fifth article thereof:

  Videlicet;

That there be a Declaration or Bill of Rights asserting and securing from encroachment the essential and unalienable Rights of the People in some such manner as the following;

First, That there are certain natural rights of which men, when they form a social compact cannot deprive or divest their posterity, among which are the enjoyment of life and liberty, with the means of acquiring, possessing and protecting property, and pursuing and obtaining happiness and safety. Second. That all power is naturally vested in and consequently derived from the people; that Magistrates, therefore, are their trustees and agents and at all times amenable to them. Third, That Government ought to be instituted for the common benefit, protection and security of the People; and that the doctrine of non-resistance against arbitrary power and oppression is absurd slavish, and destructive of the good and happiness of mankind. Fourth, That no man or set of Men are entitled to exclusive or seperate public emoluments or privileges from the community, but in Consideration of public services; which not being descendible, neither ought the offices of Magistrate, Legislator or Judge, or any other public office to be hereditary. Fifth, That the legislative, executive, and judiciary powers of Government should be seperate and distinct, and that the members of the two first may be restrained from oppression by feeling and participating the public burthens, they should, at fixt periods be reduced to a private station, return into the mass of the people; and the vacancies be supplied by certain and regular elections; in which all or any part of the former members to be elegible or ineligible, as the rules of the Constitution of Government, and the laws shall direct. Sixth, That elections of representatives in the legislature ought to be free and frequent, and all men having sufficient evidence of permanent common interest with and attachment to the Community ought to have the right of suffrage: and no aid, charge, tax or fee can be set, rated, or levied upon the people without their own consent, or that of their representatives so elected, nor can they be bound by any law to which they have not in like manner assented for the public good. Seventh, That all power of suspending laws or the execution of laws by any authority, without the consent of the representatives of the people in the legislature is injurious to their rights, and ought not to be exercised. Eighth, That in all capital and criminal prosecutions, a man hath a right to demand the cause and nature of his accusation, to be confronted with the accusers and witnesses, to call for evidence and be allowed counsel in his favor, and to a fair and speedy trial by an impartial Jury of his vicinage, without whose unanimous consent he cannot be found guilty, (except in the government of the land and naval forces) nor can he be compelled to give evidence against himself. Ninth. That no freeman ought to be taken, imprisoned, or disseised of his freehold, liberties, privileges or franchises, or outlawed or exiled, or in any manner destroyed or deprived of his life, liberty or property but by the law of the land. Tenth. That every freeman restrained of his liberty is entitled. to a remedy to enquire into the lawfulness thereof, and to remove the same, if unlawful, and that such remedy ought not to be denied nor delayed. Eleventh. That in controversies respecting property, and in suits between man and man, the ancient trial by Jury is one of the greatest Securities to the rights of the people, and ought to remain sacred and inviolable. Twelfth. That every freeman ought to find a certain remedy by recourse to the laws for all injuries and wrongs he may receive in his person, property or character. He ought to obtain right and justice freely without sale, compleatly and without denial, promptly and without delay, and that all establishments or regulations contravening these rights, are oppressive and unjust. Thirteenth, That excessive Bail ought not be required, nor excessive fines imposed, nor cruel and unusual punishments inflicted. Fourteenth, That every freeman has a right to be secure from all unreasonable searches and siezures of his person, his papers and his property; all warrants, therefore, to search suspected places, or sieze any freeman, his papers or property, without information upon Oath (or affirmation of a person religiously scrupulous of taking an oath) of legal and sufficient cause, are grievous and oppressive; and all general Warrants to search suspected places, or to apprehend any suspected person, without specially naming or describing the place or person, are dangerous and ought not to be granted. Fifteenth, That the people have a right peaceably to assemble together to consult for the common good, or to instruct their Representatives; and that every freeman has a right to petition or apply to the legislature for redress of grievances. Sixteenth, That the people have a right to freedom of speech, and of writing and publishing their Sentiments; but the freedom of the press is one of the greatest bulwarks of liberty and ought not to be violated. Seventeenth, That the people have a right to keep and bear arms; that a well regulated Militia composed of the body of the people trained to arms is the proper, natural and safe defence of a free State. That standing armies in time of peace are dangerous to liberty, and therefore ought to be avoided, as far as the circumstances and protection of the Community will admit; and that in all cases the military should be under strict subordination to and governed by the Civil power. Eighteenth, That no Soldier in time of peace ought to be quartered in any house without the consent of the owner, and in time of war in such manner only as the laws direct. Nineteenth, That any person religiously scrupulous of bearing arms ought to be exempted upon payment of an equivalent to employ another to bear arms in his stead. Twentieth, That religion or the duty which we owe to our Creator, and the manner of discharging it can be directed only by reason and conviction, not by force or violence, and therefore all men have an equal, natural and unalienable right to the free exercise of religion according to the dictates of conscience, and that no particular religious sect or society ought to be favored or established by Law in preference to others.

### AMENDMENTS TO THE BODY OF THE CONSTITUTION

First, That each State in the Union shall respectively retain every power, jurisdiction and right which is not by this Constitution delegated to the Congress of the United States or to the departments of the Fœderal Government. Second, That there shall be one representative for every thirty thousand, according to the Enumeration or Census mentioned in the Constitution, until the whole number of representatives amounts to two hundred; after which that number shall be continued or encreased as the Congress shall direct, upon the principles fixed by the Constitution by apportioning the Representatives of each State to some greater number of people from time to time as population encreases. Third, When Congress shall lay direct taxes or excises, they shall immediately inform the Executive power of each State of the quota of such state according to the Census herein directed, which is proposed to be thereby raised; And if the Legislature of any State shall pass a law which shall be effectual for raising such quota at the time required by Congress, the taxes and excises laid by Congress shall not be collected, in such State. Fourth, That the members of the Senate and House of Representatives shall be ineligible to, and incapable of holding, any civil office under the authority of the United States, during the time for which they shall respectively be elected. Fifth, That the Journals of the proceedings of the Senate and House of Representatives shall be published at least once in every year, except such parts thereof relating to treaties, alliances or military operations, as in their judgment require secrecy. Sixth, That a regular statement and account of the receipts and expenditures of all public money shall be published at least once in every year. Seventh, That no commercial treaty shall be ratified without the concurrence of two thirds of the whole number of the members of the Senate; and no Treaty ceding, contracting, restraining or suspending the territorial rights or claims of the United States, or any of them or their, or any of their rights or claims to fishing in the American seas, or navigating the American rivers shall be but in cases of the most urgent and extreme necessity, nor shall any such treaty be ratified without the concurrence of three fourths of the whole number of the members of both houses respectively. Eighth, That no navigation law, or law regulating Commerce shall be passed without the consent of two thirds of the Members present in both houses. Ninth, That no standing army or regular troops shall be raised or kept up in time of peace, without the consent of two thirds of the members present in both houses. Tenth, That no soldier shall be inlisted for any longer term than four years, except in time of war, and then for no longer term than the continuance of the war. Eleventh, That each State respectively shall have the power to provide for organizing, arming and disciplining it's own Militia, whensoever Congress shall omit or neglect to provide for the same. That the Militia shall not be subject to Martial law, except when in actual service in time of war, invasion, or rebellion; and when not in the actual service of the United States, shall be subject only to such fines, penalties and punishments as shall be directed or inflicted by the laws of its own State. Twelfth That the exclusive power of legislation given to Congress over the Fœderal Town and its adjacent District and other places purchased or to be purchased by Congress of any of the States shall extend only to such regulations as respect the police and good government thereof. Thirteenth, That no person shall be capable of being President of the United States for more than eight years in any term of sixteen years. Fourteenth That the judicial power of the United States shall be vested in one supreme Court, and in such courts of Admiralty as Congress may from time to time ordain and establish in any of the different States: The Judicial power shall extend to all cases in Law and Equity arising under treaties made, or which shall be made under the authority of the United States; to all cases affecting ambassadors other foreign ministers and consuls;

to all cases of Admiralty and maritime jurisdiction; to controversies to which the United States shall be a party; to controversies between two or States, and between parties claiming lands under the grants of different States. In all cases affecting ambassadors, other foreign ministers and Consuls, and those in which a State shall be a party, the supreme court shall have original jurisdiction; in all other cases before mentioned the supreme Court shall have appellate jurisdiction as to matters of law only: except in cases of equity, and of admiralty and maritime jurisdiction, in which the Supreme Court shall have appellate jurisdiction both as to law and fact, with such exceptions and under such regulations as the Congress shall make. But the judicial power of the United States shall extend to no case where the cause of action shall have originated before the ratification of this Constitution; except in disputes between States about their Territory, disputes between persons claiming lands under the grants of different States, and suits for debts due to the United States. Fifteenth, That in criminal prosecutions no man shall be restrained in the exercise of the usual and accustomed right of challenging or excepting to the Jury. Sixteenth, That Congress shall not alter, modify or interfere in the times, places, or manner of holding elections for Senators and Representatives or either of them, except when the legislature of any State shall neglect, refuse or be disabled by invasion or rebellion to prescribe the same. Seventeenth, That those clauses which declare that Congress shall not exercise certain powers be not interpreted in any manner whatsoever to extend the powers of Congress. But that they may be construed either as making exceptions to the specified powers where this shall be the case, or otherwise as inserted merely for greater caution. Eighteenth, That the laws ascertaining the compensation to Senators and Representatives for their services be postponed in their operation, until after the election of Representatives immediately succeeding the passing thereof; that excepted, which shall first be passed on the Subject. Nineteenth, That some Tribunal other than the Senate be provided for trying impeachments of Senators. Twentieth, That the Salary of a Judge shall not be encreased or diminished during his continuance in

Office, otherwise than by general regulations of Salary which may take place on a revision of the subject at stated periods of not less than seven years to commence from the time such Salaries shall be first ascertained by Congress. And the Convention do, in the name and behalf of the People of this Commonwealth enjoin it upon their Representatives in Congress to exert all their influence and use all reasonable and legal methods to obtain a Ratification of the foregoing alterations and provisions in the manner provided by the fifth article of the said Constitution; and in all Congressional laws to be passed in the mean time, to conform to the spirit of those Amendments as far as the said Constitution will admit.

> Done in Convention this twenty seventh day of June in the year of our Lord one thousand seven hundred and eighty eight.
> By order of the Convention.
> EDM<sup>D</sup> PENDLETON President [SEAL.]

### STATE OF NEW YORK [11]

WE the Delegates of the People of the State of New York, duly elected and Met in Convention, having maturely considered the Constitution for the United States of America, agreed to on the seventeenth day of September, in the year One thousand Seven hundred and Eighty seven, by the Convention then assembled at Philadelphia in the Common-wealth of Pennsylvania (a Copy whereof precedes these presents) and having also seriously and deliberately considered the present situation of the United States, Do declare and make known.

That all Power is originally vested in and consequently derived from the People, and that Government is instituted by them for their common Interest Protection and Security.

That the enjoyment of Life, Liberty and the pursuit of Happiness are essential rights which every Government ought to respect and preserve.

That the Powers of Government may be reassumed by the People, whensoever it shall become necessary to their Happiness;

---

[11] Reprinted from *Documentary History of the Constitution*, Vol. II (1894), pp. 190-203.

that every Power, Jurisdiction and right, which is not by the said Constitution clearly delegated to the Congress of the United States, or the departments of the Government thereof, remains to the People of the several States, or to their respective State Governments to whom they may have granted the same; And that those Clauses in the said Constitution, which declare, that Congress shall not have or exercise certain Powers, do not imply that Congress is entitled to any Powers not given by the said Constitution; but such Clauses are to be construed either as exceptions to certain specified Powers, or as inserted merely for greater Caution.

That the People have an equal, natural and unalienable right, freely and peaceably to Exercise their Religion according to the dictates of Conscience, and that no Religious Sect or Society ought to be favoured or established by Law in preference of others.

That the People have a right to keep and bear Arms; that a well regulated Militia, including the body of the People *capable of bearing Arms*, is the proper, natural and safe defence of a free State;

That the Militia should not be subject to Martial Law except in time of War, Rebellion or Insurrection.

That standing Armies in time of Peace are dangerous to Liberty, and ought not to be kept up, except in Cases of necessity; and that at all times, the Military should be under strict Subordination to the civil Power.

That in time of Peace no Soldier ought to be quartered in any House without the consent of the Owner, and in time of War only by the Civil Magistrate in such manner as the Laws may direct.

That no Person ought to be taken imprisoned or disseised of his freehold, or be exiled or deprived of his Privileges, Franchises, Life, Liberty or Property but by due process of Law.

That no Person ought to be put twice in Jeopardy of Life or Limb for one and the same Offence, nor, unless in case of impeachment, be punished more than once for the same Offence.

That every Person restrained of his Liberty is entitled to an enquiry into the lawfulness of such restraint, and to a removal thereof if unlawful, and that such enquiry and removal ought not to be denied or delayed, except when on account of Public Danger the Congress shall suspend the privilege of the Writ of Habeas Corpus.

That excessive Bail ought not to be required; nor excessive Fines imposed; nor Cruel or unusual Punishments inflicted.

That (except in the Government of the Land and Naval Forces, and of the Militia when in actual Service, and in cases of Impeachment) a Presentment or Indictment by a Grand Jury ought to be observed as a necessary preliminary to the trial of all Crimes cognizable by the Judiciary of the United States, and such Trial should be speedy, public, and by an impartial Jury of the County where the Crime was committed; and that no person can be found Guilty without the unanimous consent of such Jury. But in cases of Crimes not committed within any County of any of the United States, and in Cases of Crimes committed within any County in which a general Insurrection may prevail, or which may be in the possession of a foreign Enemy, the enquiry and trial may be in such County as the Congress shall by Law direct; which County in the two Cases last mentioned should be as near as conveniently may be to that County in which the Crime may have been committed. And that in all Criminal Prosecutions, the Accused ought to be informed of the cause and nature of his Accusation, to be confronted with his accusers and the Witnesses against him, to have the means of producing his Witnesses, and the assistance of Council for his defense, and should not be compelled to give Evidence against himself.

That the trial by Jury in the extent that it obtains by the Common Law of England is one of the greatest securities to the rights of a free People, and ought to remain inviolate.

That every Freeman has a right to be secure from all unreasonable searches and seizures of his person his papers or his property, and therefore, that all Warrants to search suspected places or seize any Freeman his papers or property, without information upon Oath or Affirmation of sufficient cause, are grievous and oppressive; and that all general Warrants (or such in which the place or person suspected are not particularly designated) are dangerous and ought not to be granted.

1037

That the People have a right peaceably to assemble together to consult for their common good, or to instruct their Representatives; and that every person has a right to Petition or apply to the Legislature for redress of Grievances. —— That the Freedom of the Press ought not to be violated or restrained.

That there should be once in four years an Election of the President and Vice President, so that no Officer who may be appointed by the Congress to act as President in case of the removal, death, resignation or inability of the President and Vice President can in any case continue to act beyond the termination of the period for which the last President and Vice President were elected.

That nothing contained in the said Constitution is to be construed to prevent the Legislature of any State from passing Laws at its discretion from time to time to divide such State into convenient Districts, and to apportion its Representatives to and amongst such Districts.

That the Prohibition contained in the said Constitution against *ex post facto* Laws, extends only to Laws concerning Crimes.

That all Appeals in Causes determineable according to the course of the common Law, ought to be by Writ of Error and not otherwise.

That the Judicial Power of the United States in cases in which a State may be a party, does not extend to criminal Prosecutions, or to authorize any Suit by any Person against a State.

That the Judicial Power of the United States as to Controversies between Citizens of the same State claiming Lands under Grants of different States is not to be construed to extend to any other Controversies between them except those which relate to such Lands, so claimed under Grants of different States.

That the Jurisdiction of the Supreme Court of the United States, or of any other Court to be instituted by the Congress, is not in any case to be encreased enlarged or extended by any Fiction Collusion or mere suggestion;—And That no Treaty is to be construed so to operate as to alter the Constitution of any State.

Under these impressions and declaring that the rights aforesaid cannot be abridged or violated, and that the Explanations aforesaid are consistent with the said Constitution, And in confidence that the Amendments which shall have been proposed to the said Constitution will receive an early and mature Consideration: We the said Delegates, in the Name and in the behalf of the People of the State of New York Do by these presents Assent to and Ratify the said Constitution. In full Confidence nevertheless that until a Convention shall be called and convened for proposing Amendments to the said Constitution, the Militia of this State will not be continued in Service out of this State for a longer term than six weeks without the Consent of the Legislature thereof;—that the Congress will not make or alter any Regulation in this State respecting the times places and manner of holding Elections for Senators or Representatives unless the Legislature of this State shall neglect or refuse to make Laws or regulations for the purpose, or from any circumstance be incapable of making the same, and that in those cases such power will only be exercised until the Legislature of this State shall make provision in the Premises;—that no Excise will be imposed on any Article of the Growth production or Manufacture of the United States, or any of them within this State, Ardent Spirits excepted; And that the Congress will not lay direct Taxes within this State, but when the Monies arising from the Impost and Excise shall be insufficient for the public Exigencies, nor then, until Congress shall first have made a Requisition upon this State to assess levy and pay the Amount of such Requisition made agreably to the Census fixed in the said Constitution in such way and manner as the Legislature of this State shall judge best, but that in such case, if the State shall neglect or refuse to pay its proportion pursuant to such Requisition, then the Congress may assess and levy this States proportion together with Interest at the Rate of six per Centum per Annum from the time at which the same was required to be paid.

    Done in Convention at Poughkeepsie in the County of Dutchess in the State of New York the twenty sixth day of July in the year of our Lord One thousand Seven hundred and Eighty eight.

    By Order of the Convention.

                                         Geo: Clinton President

Attested

    John McKesson      } Secretaries—
    Ab<sup>m</sup> B. Bancker

1039

AND the Convention do in the Name and Behalf of the People of the State of New York enjoin it upon their Representatives in the Congress, to Exert all their Influence, and use all reasonable means to Obtain a Ratification of the following Amendments to the said Constitution in the manner prescribed therein; and in all Laws to be passed by the Congress in the meantime to conform to the spirit of the said Amendments as far as the Constitution will admit.

That there shall be one Representative for every thirty thousand Inhabitants, according to the enumeration or Census mentioned in the Constitution, until the whole number of Representatives amounts to two hundred; after which that number shall be continued or encreased but not diminished, as Congress shall direct, and according to such ratio as the Congress shall fix, in conformity to the rule prescribed for the Apportionment of Representatives and direct Taxes.

That the Congress do not impose any Excise on any Article (except Ardent Spirits) of the Growth Production or Manufacture of the United States, or any of them.

That Congress do not lay direct Taxes but when the Monies arising from the Impost and Excise shall be insufficient for the Public Exigencies, nor then until Congress shall first have made a Requisition upon the States to assess levy and pay their respective proportions of such Requisition, agreably to the Census fixed in the said Constitution, in such way and manner as the Legislatures of the respective States shall judge best; and in such Case, if any State shall neglect or refuse to pay its proportion pursuant to such Requisition, then Congress may assess and levy such States proportion, together with Interest at the rate of six per Centum per Annum, from the time of Payment prescribed in such Requisition.

That the Congress shall not make or alter any Regulation in any State respecting the times places and manner of holding Elections for Senators or Representatives, unless the Legislature of such State shall neglect or refuse to make Laws or Regulations for the purpose, or from any circumstance be incapable of making the same; and then only until the Legislature of such State shall make provision in the premises; provided that Congress may prescribe the time for the Election of Representatives.

That no Persons except natural born Citizens, or such as were Citizens on or before the fourth day of July one thousand seven hundred and seventy six, or such as held Commissions under the United States during the War, and have at any time since the fourth day of July one thousand seven hundred and seventy six become Citizens of one or other of the United States, and who shall be Freeholders, shall be eligible to the Places of President, Vice President, or Members of either House of the Congress of the United States.

That the Congress do not grant Monopolies or erect any Company with exclusive Advantages of Commerce.

That no standing Army or regular Troops shall be raised or kept up in time of peace, without the consent of two-thirds of the Senators and Representatives present, in each House.

That no Money be borrowed on the Credit of the United States without the Assent of two-thirds of the Senators and Representatives present in each House.

That the Congress shall not declare War without the concurrence of two-thirds of the Senators and Representatives present in each House.

That the Privilege of the *Habeas Corpus* shall not by any Law be suspended for a longer term than six Months, or until twenty days after the Meeting of the Congress next following the passing of the Act for such suspension.

That the Right of the Congress to exercise exclusive Legislation over such District, not exceeding ten Miles square, as may by cession of a particular State, and the acceptance of Congress, become the Seat of the Government of the United States, shall not be so exercised, as to exempt the Inhabitants of such District from paying the like Taxes Imposts Duties and Excises, as shall be imposed on the other Inhabitants of the State in which such District may be; and that no person shall be privileged within the said District from Arrest for Crimes committed, or Debts contracted out of the said District.

That the Right of exclusive Legislation with respect to such places as may be purchased for the Erection of Forts, Magazines, Arsenals, Dockyards and other needful Buildings, shall not authorize the Congress to make any Law to prevent the Laws of the States respectively in which they may be, from extending to such places in all civil and Criminal Matters except as to such Persons as shall be in the Service of the United States; nor to them with respect to Crimes committed without such Places.

That the Compensation for the Senators and Representatives be ascertained by standing Laws; and that no alteration of the existing rate of Compensation shall operate for the Benefit of the Representatives, until after a subsequent Election shall have been had.

That the Journals of the Congress shall be published at least once a year, with the exception of such parts relating to Treaties or Military operations, as in the Judgment of either House shall require Secrecy; and that both Houses of Congress shall always keep their Doors open during their Sessions, unless the Business may in their Opinion requires Secrecy. That the yeas & nays shall be entered on the Journals whenever two Members in either House may require it.

That no Capitation Tax shall ever be laid by the Congress.

That no Person be eligible as a Senator for more than six years in any term of twelve years; and that the Legislatures of the respective States may recal their Senators or either of them, and elect others in their stead, to serve the remainder of the time for which the Senators so recalled were appointed.

That no Senator or Representative shall during the time for which he was elected be appointed to any Office under the Authority of the United States.

That the Authority given to the Executives of the States to fill the vacancies of Senators be abolished, and that such vacancies be filled by the respective Legislatures.

That the Power of Congress to pass uniform Laws concerning Bankruptcy shall only extend to Merchants and other Traders; and that the States respectively may pass Laws for the relief of other Insolvent Debtors.

That no Person shall be eligible to the Office of President of the United States a third time.

That the Executive shall not grant Pardons for Treason, unless with the Consent of the Congress; but may at his discretion grant Reprieves to persons convicted of Treason, until their Cases, can be laid before the Congress.

That the President or person exercising his Powers for the time being, shall not command an Army in the Field in person, without the previous desire of the Congress.

That all Letters Patent, Commissions, Pardons, Writs and Process of the United States, shall run in the Name of *the People of the United States*, and be tested in the Name of the President of the United States, or the person exercising his powers for the time being, or the first Judge of the Court out of which the same shall issue, as the case may be.

That the Congress shall not constitute ordain or establish any Tribunals or Inferior Courts, with any other than Appellate Jurisdiction, except such as may be necessary for the Tryal of Causes of Admiralty and Maritime Jurisdiction, and for the Trial of Piracies and Felonies committed on the High Seas; and in all other Cases to which the Judicial Power of the United States extends, and in which the Supreme Court of the United States has not original Jurisdiction, the Causes shall be heard tried, and determined in some one of the State Courts, with the right of Appeal to the Supreme Court of the United States, or other proper Tribunal to be established for that purpose by the Congress, with such exceptions, and under such regulations as the Congress shall make.

That the Court for the Trial of Impeachments shall consist of the Senate, the Judges of the Supreme Court of the United States, and the first or Senior Judge for the time being, of the highest Court of general and ordinary common Law Jurisdiction in each State;—that the Congress shall by standing Laws designate the Courts in the respective States answering this Description, and in States having no Courts exactly answering this Description, shall designate some other Court, preferring such if any there be, whose Judge or Judges may hold their places during good Behaviour—

Provided that no more than one Judge, other than Judges of the Supreme Court of the United States, shall come from one State—That the Congress be authorized to pass Laws for compensating the said Judges for such Services and for compelling their Attendance—and that a Majority at least of the said Judges shall be requisite to constitute the said Court—that no person impeached shall sit as a Member thereof. That each Member shall previous to the entering upon any Trial take an Oath or Affirmation, honestly and impartially to hear and determine the Cause—and that a Majority of the Members present shall be necessary to a Conviction.

That persons aggrieved by any Judgment, Sentence or Decree of the Supreme Court of the United States, in any Cause in which that Court has original Jurisdiction, with such exceptions and under such Regulations as the Congress shall make concerning the same, shall upon application, have a Commission to be issued by the President of the United States, to such Men learned in the Law as he shall nominate, and by and with the Advice and consent of the Senate appoint, not less than seven, authorizing such Commissioners, or any seven or more of them, to correct the Errors in such Judgment or to review such Sentence and Decree, as the case may be, and to do Justice to the parties in the Premises.

That no Judge of the Supreme Court of the United States shall hold any other Office under the United States, or any of them.

That the Judicial Power of the United States shall extend to no Controversies respecting Land, unless it relate to Claims of Territory or Jurisdiction between States, or to Claims of Land between Individuals, or between States and Individuals under the Grants of different States.

That the Militia of any State shall not be compelled to serve without the limits of the State for a longer term than six weeks, without the Consent of the Legislature thereof.

That the words *without the Consent of the Congress* in the seventh Clause of the ninth Section of the first Article of the Constitution, be expunged.

That the Senators and Representatives and all Executive and Judicial Officers of the United States shall be bound by Oath or

Affirmation not to infringe or violate the Constitutions or Rights of the respective States.

That the Legislatures of the respective States may make Provision by Law, that the Electors of the Election Districts to be by them appointed shall chuse a Citizen of the United States who shall have been an Inhabitant of such District for the Term of one year immediately preceeding the time of his Election, for one of the Representatives of such State.

> Done in Convention at Poughkeepsie in the County of Dutchess in the State of New York the twenty sixth day of July in the year of our Lord One thousand seven hundred and Eighty eight.
>
> · By Order of the Convention.

Attested—  GEO: CLINTON President
JOHN McKESSON }
ABM B. BANCKER } Secretaries—

---

STATE OF NORTH CAROLINA.[12]

*In Convention, August 1, 1788.*

Resolved, That a Declaration of Rights, asserting and securing from encroachment the great Principles of civil and religious Liberty, and the unalienable Rights of the People, together with Amendments to the most ambiguous and exceptional Parts of the said Constitution of Government, ought to be laid before Congress, and the Convention of the States that shall or may be called for the Purpose of Amending the said Constitution, for their consideration, previous to the Ratification of the Constitution aforesaid, on the part of the State of North Carolina.

DECLARATION OF RIGHTS

1st That there are certain natural rights of which men, when they form a social compact, cannot deprive or divest their posterity, among which are the enjoyment of life, and liberty, with the means of acquiring, possessing, and protecting property, and pursuing and obtaining happiness and safety.

---

[12] Reprinted from *Documentary History of the Constitution*, Vol. II (1894), pp. 266-275, 276, 290.

2d. That all power is naturally vested in, and consequently derived from the people; that magistrates therefore are their trustees, and agents, and at all times amenable to them.

3d. That Government ought to be instituted for the common benefit, protection and security of the people; and that the doctrine of non-resistance against arbitrary power and oppression is absurd, slavish, and destructive to the good and happiness of mankind.

4th That no man or set of men are entitled to exclusive or separate public emoluments or privileges from the community, but in consideration of public services; which not being descendible, neither ought the offices of magistrate, legislator or judge, or any other public office to be hereditary.

5th. That the legislative, executive and judiciary powers of government should be separate and distinct, and that the members of the two first may be restrained from oppression by feeling and participating the public burthens, they should at fixed periods be reduced to a private station, return into the mass of the people; and the vacancies be supplied by certain and regular elections; in which all or any part of the former members to be eligible or ineligible, as the rules of the Constitution of Government, and the laws shall direct.

6th. That elections of Representatives in the legislature ought to be free and frequent, and all men having sufficient evidence of permanent common interest with, and attachment to the community, ought to have the right of suffrage: and no aid, charge, tax or fee can be set, rated, or levied upon the people without their own consent, or that of their representatives, so elected, nor can they be bound by any law, to which they have not in like manner assented for the public good.

7th. That all power of suspending laws, or the execution of laws by any authority without the consent of the representatives, of the people in the Legislature, is injurious to their rights, and ought not to be exercised.

8th. That in all capital and criminal prosecutions, a man hath a right to demand the cause and nature of his accusation, to be confronted with the accusers and witnesses, to call for evidence and be allowed counsel in his favor, and to a fair and speedy trial by an impartial jury of his vicinage, without whose unanimous consent he cannot be found guilty (except in the government of the land and naval forces) nor can he be compelled to give evidence against himself.

9th That no freeman ought to be taken, imprisoned, or disseized of his freehold, liberties, privileges or franchises, or outlawed or exiled, or in any manner destroyed or deprived of his life, liberty, or property but by the law of the land.

10th. That every freeman restrained of his liberty is entitled to a remedy to inquire into the lawfulness thereof, and to remove the same, if unlawful, and that such remedy ought not to be denied nor delayed.

11th. That in controversies respecting property, and in suits between man and man, the ancient trial by jury is one of the greatest securities to the rights of the people, and ought to remain sacred and inviolable.

12th. That every freeman ought to find a certain remedy by recourse to the laws for all injuries and wrongs he may receive in his person, property, or character. He ought to obtain right and justice freely without sale, completely and without denial, promptly and without delay, and that all establishments, or regulations contravening these rights, are oppressive and unjust.

13th. That excessive bail ought not to be required, nor excessive fines imposed, nor cruel and unusual punishments inflicted,

14. That every freeman has a right to be secure from all unreasonable searches, and seizures of his person, his papers, and property: all warrants therefore to search suspected places, or seize any freeman, his papers or property, without information upon oath (or affirmation of a person religiously scrupulous of taking an oath) of legal and sufficient cause, are grievous and oppressive, and all general warrants to search suspected places, or to apprehend any suspected person without specially naming or describing the place or person, are dangerous and ought not to be granted.

15th. That the people have a right peaceably to assemble together to consult for the common good, or to instruct their representatives; and that every freeman has a right to petition or apply to the Legislature for redress of grievances.

16th. That the people have a right to freedom of speech, and of writing and publishing their sentiments; that the freedom of the press is one of the greatest bulwarks of Liberty, and ought not to be violated.

17th. That the people have a right to keep and bear arms; that a well regulated militia composed of the body of the people, trained to arms, is the proper, natural and safe defence of a free state. That standing armies in time of peace are dangerous to Liberty, and therefore ought to be avoided, as far as the circumstances and protection of the community will admit; and that in all cases, the military should be under strict subordination to, and governed by the civil power.

18th. That no soldier in time of peace ought to be quartered in any house without the consent of the owner, and in time of war in such manner only as the Laws direct

19th. That any person religiously scrupulous of bearing arms ought to be exempted upon payment of an equivalent to employ another to bear arms in his stead.

10. That religion, or the duty which we owe to our Creator, and the manner of discharging it, can be directed only by reason and conviction, not by force or violence, and therefore all men have an equal, natural and unalienable right to the free exercise of religion according to the dictates of conscience, and that no particular religious sect or society ought to be favoured or established by law in preference to others.

## AMENDMENTS TO THE CONSTITUTION

I. THAT each state in the union shall, respectively, retain every power, jurisdiction and right, which is not by this constitution delegated to the Congress of the United States, or to the departments of the Federal Government.

II. That there shall be one representative for every 30.000, according to the enumeration or census, mentioned in the constitution, until the whole number of representatives amounts to two hundred; after which, that number shall be continued or increased, as Congress shall direct, upon the principles fixed in the constitution, by apportioning the representatives of each state to some greater number of people from time to time, as population encreases.

III. When Congress shall lay direct taxes or excises, they shall immediately inform the executive power of each state, of the quota of such State, according to the census herein directed, which is proposed to be thereby raised: And if the legislature of any state shall pass a law, which shall be effectual for raising such quota at the time required by Congress, the taxes and excises laid by Congress shall not be collected in such state.

IV. That the members of the senate and house of representatives shall be ineligible to, and incapable of holding any civil office under the authority of the United States, during the time for which they shall, respectively, be elected.

V. That the journals of the proceedings of the senate and house of representatives shall be published at least once in every year, except such parts thereof relating to treaties, alliances, or military operations, as in their judgment require secrecy.

VI. That a regular statement and account of the receipts and expenditures of the public money shall be published at least once in every year.

VII. That no commercial treaty shall be ratified without the concurrence of two-thirds of the whole number of the members of the Senate: And no treaty, ceding, contracting, or restraining or suspending the territorial rights or claims of the United States, or any of them or their, or any of their rights or claims to fishing in the American seas, or navigating the American rivers shall be made, but in cases of the most urgent and extreme necessity; nor shall any such treaty be ratified without the concurrence of three-fourths of the whole number of the members of both houses respectively.

VIII. That no navigation law, or law regulating commerce shall be passed without the consent of two-thirds of the members present in both houses.

IX That no standing army or regular troops shall be raised or kept up in time of peace, without the consent of two thirds of the members present in both houses.

X. That no soldier shall be enlisted for any longer term than four years, except in time of war, and then for no longer term than the continuance of the war

XI. That each state, respectively, shall have the power to provide for organizing, arming and disciplining its own militia whensoever Congress shall omit or neglect to provide for the same. That the militia shall not be subject to martial law, except when in actual service in time of war, invasion or rebellion: And when not in the actual service of the United States, shall be subject only to such fines, penalties, and punishments as shall be directed or inflicted by the laws of its own state.

XII. That Congress shall not declare any state to be in rebellion without the consent of at least two-thirds of all the members present of both houses.

XIII. That the exclusive power of Legislation given to Congress over the federal town and its adjacent district, and other places, purchased or to be purchased by Congress, of any of the states, shall extend only to such regulations as respect the police and good government thereof.

XIV. That no person shall be capable of being president of the United States for more than eight years in any term of sixteen years.

XV. That the judicial power of the United States shall be vested in one supreme court, and in such courts of admiralty as Congress may from time to time ordain and establish in any of the different states. The judicial power shall extend to all cases in law and equity, arising under treaties made, or which shall be made under the authority of the United States; to all cases affecting ambassadors, other foreign ministers and consuls; to all cases of admiralty, and maritime jurisdiction; to controversies to which the United States shall be a party; to controversies between two or more states, and between parties claiming lands under the grants of different states. In all cases affecting ambassadors, other foreign ministers and consuls, and those in which a state shall be a party;

the supreme court shall have original jurisdiction, in all other cases before mentioned; the supreme court shall have appellate jurisdiction as to matters of law only, except in cases of equity, and of admiralty and maritime jurisdiction, in which the supreme court shall have appelate jurisdiction both as to law and fact, with such exceptions, and under such regulations as the Congress shall make. But the judicial power of the United States shall extend to no case where the cause of action shall have originated before the ratification of this constitution, except in disputes between states about their territory; disputes between persons claiming lands under the grants of different states, and suits for debts due to the united states.

XVI That in criminal prosecutions, no man shall be restrained in the exercise of the usual and accustomed right of challenging or excepting to the jury.

XVII. That Congress shall not alter, modify, or interfere in the times, places, or manner of holding elections for senators and representatives, or either of them, except when the legislature of any state shall neglect, refuse or be disabled by invasion or rebellion, to prescribe the same.

XVIII. That those clauses which declare that Congress shall not exercise certain powers, be not interpreted in any manner whatsoever to extend the powers of Congress; but that they be construed either as making exceptions to the specified powers where this shall be the case, or otherwise, as inserted merely for greater caution.

XIX That the laws ascertaining the compensation of senators and representatives for their services be posponed in their operation, until after the election of representatives immediately succeeding the passing thereof, that excepted, which shall first be passed on the subject,

XX. That some tribunal, other than the senate, be provided for trying impeachments of senators.

XXI That the salary of a judge shall not be increased or diminished during his continuance in office, otherwise than by general regulations of salary which may take place, on a revision of the subject at stated periods of not less than seven years, to commence from the time such salaries shall be first ascertained by Congress.

XXII. That Congress erect no company of merchants with exclusive advantages of commerce.

XXIII. That no treaties which shall be directly opposed to the existing laws of the United States in Congress assembled, shall be valid until such laws shall be repealed, or made conformable to such treaty; nor shall any treaty be valid which is contradictory to the constitution of the United States.

XXIV. That the latter part of the fifth paragraph of the 9th section of the first article be altered to read thus,—Nor shall vessels bound to a particular state be obliged to enter or pay duties in any other; nor when bound from any one of the States be obliged to clear in another.

XXV. That Congress shall not directly or indirectly, either by themselves or thro' the judiciary, interfere with any one of the states in the redemption of paper money already emitted and now in circulation, or in liquidating and discharging the public securities of any one of the states: But each and every state shall have the exclusive right of making such laws and regulations for the above purposes as they shall think proper.

XXVI That Congress shall not introduce foreign troops into the United States without the consent of two-thirds of the members present of both houses.

SAM JOHNSTON President,

By order

    J HUNT Secretary . . .

IN CONVENTION Whereas The General Convention which met in Philadelphia in pursuance of a recommendation of Congress, did recommend to the Citizens of the United States a Constitution or form of Government in the following words Viz$^t$. . . .

Resolved, that this Convention in behalf of the freemen, citizens and inhabitants of the State of North Carolina, do adopt and ratify the said Constitution and form of Government. Done in Convention this 21 day of November 1789.

SAM JOHNSTON, President of the<br>Convention

J HUNT<br>
JAMES TAYLOR } Secretaries

## STATE OF RHODE ISLAND [13]

*Ratification of the Constitution, by the Convention of the State of Rhode-Island and Providence Plantations*

We the Delegates of the People of the State of Rhode-Island, and Providence Plantations, duly elected and met in Convention, having maturely considered the Constitution for the United States of America, agreed to on the seventeenth day of September, in the year one thousand seven hundred and eighty seven, by the Convention then assembled at Philadelphia, in the Commonwealth of Pennsylvania (a Copy whereof precedes these presents) and having also seriously and deliberately considered the present situation of this State, do declare and make known

1st That there are certain natural rights, of which men when they form a social compact, cannot deprive or divest their posterity, among which are the enjoyment of Life and Liberty, with the means of acquiring, possessing and protecting Property, and pursuing and obtaining happiness and safety.

2d That all power is naturally vested in, and consequently derived from the People; that magistrates therefore are their trustees and agents, and at all times amenable to them.

3d That the powers of government may be reassumed by the people, whensoever it shall become necessary to their happiness:— That the rights of the States respectively, to nominate and appoint all State Officers, and every other power, jurisdiction and right, which is not by the said constitution clearly delegated to the Congress of the United States or to the departments of government thereof, remain to the people of the several states, or their respective State Governments to whom they may have granted the same; and that those clauses in the said constitution which declare that Congress shall not have or exercise certain powers, do not imply, that Congress is entitled to any powers not given by the said constitution, but such clauses are to be construed as exceptions to certain specified powers, or as inserted merely for greater caution.

---

[13] Reprinted from *Documentary History of the Constitution*, Vol. II (1894), pp. 310–320.

4th That religion, or the duty which we owe to our Creator, and the manner of discharging it, can be directed only by reason and conviction, and not by force or violence, and therefore all men, have an equal, natural and unalienable right to the free exercise of religion, according to the dictates of conscience, and that no particular religious sect or society ought to be favoured, or established by law in preference to others.

5th That the legislative, executive and judiciary powers of government, should be separate and distinct, and that the members of the two first may be restrained from oppression, by feeling and participating the publick burthens, they should at fixed periods be reduced to a private station, return into the mass of the people, and the vacancies be supplied by certain and regular elections, in which all, or any part of the former members, to be eligible or ineligible, as the rules of the constitution of government and the laws shall direct.

6th That elections of representatives in legislature ought to be free and frequent, and all men having sufficient evidence of permanent common interest with, and attachment to the community ought to have the right of suffrage, and no aid, charge tax or fee can be set, rated or levied upon the people, without their own consent or that of their representatives so elected, nor can they be bound by any law, to which they have not in like manner assented for the publick good.

7th That all power of suspending laws or the execution of laws, by any authority without the consent of the representatives of the people in the legislature, is injurious to their rights, and ought not to be exercised.

8th That in all capital and criminal prosecutions, a man hath a right to demand the cause and nature of his accusation, to be confronted with the accusers and witnesses, to call for evidence and be allowed counsel in his favour, and to a fair and speedy trial by an impartial jury of his vicinage, without whose unanimous consent he cannot be found guilty; (except in the government of the land and naval forces) nor can he be compelled to give evidence against himself.

9th That no freeman ought to be taken, imprisoned or disseised of his freehold, liberties, privileges, or franchises, or outlawed, or exiled, or in any manner destroyed or deprived of his life, liberty or property but by the trial by jury, or by the law of the land.

10th That every freeman restrained of his liberty, is intitled to a remedy, to enquire into the lawfulness thereof, and to remove the same if unlawful, and that such remedy ought not to be denied or delayed.

11th That in controversies respecting property, and in suits between man and man the antient trial by jury, as hath been exercised by us and our ancestors, from the time whereof the memory of man is not to the contrary, is one of the greatest securities to the rights of the people, and ought to remain sacred and inviolate.

12th That every freeman ought to obtain right and justice, freely and without sale, completely and without denial, promptly and without delay, and that all establishments or regulations contravening these rights, are oppressive and unjust.

13th That excessive bail ought not to be required, nor excessive fines imposed, nor cruel or unusual punishments inflicted.

14th That every person has a right to be secure from all unreasonable searches and seisures of his person, his papers or his property, and therefore that all warrants to search suspected places or seise any person, his papers or his property, without information upon oath, or affirmation, of sufficient cause, are grievous and oppressive, and that all general warrants (or such in which the place or person suspected, are not particularly designated,) are dangerous, and ought not to be granted.

15th That the people have a right peaceably to assemble together, to consult for their common good, or to instruct their representatives; and that every person has a right to petition or apply to the legislature for redress of grievances.

16th That the people have a right to freedom of speech and of writing, and publishing their sentiments, that freedom of the press is one of the greatest bulwarks of liberty, and ought not to be violated.

17th That the people have a right to keep and bear arms, that a well regulated militia, including the body of the people capable of bearing arms, is the proper, natural and safe defence of a free state; that the militia shall not be subject to martial law except in time of war, rebellion or insurrection; that standing armies in time of peace, are dangerous to liberty, and ought not to be kept up, except in cases of necessity; and that at all times the military should be under strict subordination to the civil power; that in time of peace no soldier ought to be quartered in any house, without the consent of the owner, and in time of war, only by the civil magistrate, in such manner as the law directs.

18th That any person religiously scrupulous of bearing arms, ought to be exempted, upon payment of an equivalent, to employ another to bear arms in his stead.

Under these impressions, and declaring, that the rights aforesaid cannot be abridged or violated, and that the explanations aforesaid, are consistant with the said constitution, and in confidence that the amendments hereafter mentioned, will receive an early and mature consideration, and conformably to the fifth article of said constitution, speedily become a part thereof; We the said delegates, in the name, and in the behalf of the People, of the State of Rhode-Island and Providence-Plantations, do by these Presents, assent to, and ratify the said Constitution. In full confidence nevertheless, that until the amendments hereafter proposed and undermentioned shall be agreed to and ratified, pursuant to the aforesaid fifth article, the militia of this State will not be continued in service out of this State for a longer term than six weeks, without the consent of the legislature thereof; That the Congress will not make or alter any regulation in this State, respecting the times, places and manner of holding elections for senators or representatives, unless the legislature of this state shall neglect, or refuse to make laws or regulations for the purpose, or from any circumstance be incapable of making the same; and that n those cases, such power will only be exercised, until the legislature of this State shall make provision in the Premises, that the Congress will not lay direct taxes within this State, but when the monies arising from the Impost, Tonnage and Excise shall be insufficient for the publick exigencies, nor until the Congress shall have first made a requisition upon this State to assess, levy and pay the amount of such requisition, made agreeable to the census fixed in the said constitution, in such way and manner, as the legislature of this State shall judge best, and that the Congress will not lay any capitation or poll tax.

>Done in Convention, at Newport in the County of Newport, in the State of Rhode-Island and Providence-Plantations, the twenty ninth day of May, in the Year of our Lord one thousand seven hundred and ninety, and in the fourteenth year of the Independence of the United States of America.
>
>By order of the Convention,
>
>DANIEL OWEN President

Attest, DANIEL UPDIKE Sec'y

And the Convention, do in the name and behalf of the People of the State of Rhode-Island and Providence Plantations, enjoin it upon their Senators and Representative or Representatives, which may be elected to represent this State in Congress, to exert all their influence, and use all reasonable means to obtain a ratification of the following Amendments to the said Constitution, in the manner prescribed therein, and in all laws to be passed by the Congress in the mean time, to conform to the spirit of the said amendments, as far as the constitution will admit.

### AMENDMENTS

1st The United States shall guarantee to each State its sovereignty, freedom and independence, and every power, jurisdiction and right, which is not by this constitution expressly delegated to the United States.

2d That Congress shall not alter, modify or interfere in the times, places or manner of holding elections for Senators and Representatives, or either of them, except when the legislature of any state shall neglect, refuse or be disabled by invasion or rebellion to prescribe the same; or in case when the provision made by the states, is so imperfect as that no consequent election is had, and then only until the legislature of such state, shall make provision in the premises.

3ᵈ It is declared by the Convention, that the judicial power of the United States, in cases in which a state may be a party, does not extend to criminal prosecutions, or to authorize any suit by any person against a State; but to remove all doubts or controversies respecting the same, that it be especially expressed as a part of the constitution of the United States, that Congress shall not directly or indirectly, either by themselves or through the judiciary, interfere with any one of the states, in the redemption of paper money already emitted and now in circulation, or in liquidating or discharging the publick securities of any one state: that each and every state shall have the exclusive right of making such laws and regulations for the before mentioned purpose, as they shall think proper.

4ᵗʰ That no amendments to the constitution of the United States hereafter to be made, pursuant to the fifth article, shall take effect, or become a part of the constitution of the United States after the Year one thousand seven hundred and ninety three, without the consent of eleven of the states, heretofore united under one confederation.

5ᵗʰ That the judicial powers of the United States shall extend to no possible case, where the cause of action shall have originated before the ratification of this constitution, except in disputes between states about their territory, disputes between persons claiming lands under grants of different states, and debts due to the United States.

6ᵗʰ That no person shall be compelled to do military duty, otherwise than by voluntary enlistment, except in cases of general invasion; any thing in the second paragraph of the sixth article of the constitution, or any law made under the constitution to the contrary notwithstanding.

7ᵗʰ That no capitation or poll-tax shall ever be laid by Congress.

8ᵗʰ In cases of direct taxes, Congress shall first make requisitions on the several states to assess, levy and pay their respective proportions of such requisitions, in such way and manner, as the legislatures of the several states shall judge best; and in case any state shall neglect or refuse to pay its proportion pursuant to such requisition, then Congress may assess and levy such state's proportion, together with interest at the rate of six per cent. per annum, from the time prescribed in such requisition.

9th That Congress shall lay no direct taxes, without the consent of the legislatures of three fourths of the states in the Union.

10th That the journals of the proceedings of the Senate and house of Representatives shall be published as soon as conveniently may be, at least once in every year, except such parts thereof relating to treaties, alliances or military operations, as in their judgment require secrecy.

11th That regular statements of the receipts and expenditures of all publick monies, shall be published at least once a year.

12th As standing armies in time of peace are dangerous to liberty and ought not to be kept up, except in cases of necessity; and as at all times the military should be under strict subordination to the civil power, that therefore no standing army, or regular toops shall be raised, or kept up in time of peace.

13th That no monies be borrowed on the credit of the United States without the assent of two thirds of the Senators and Representatives present in each house.

14th That the Congress shall not declare war, without the concurrence of two thirds of the Senators and Representatives present in each house.

15th That the words "without the consent of Congress" in the seventh clause in the ninth section of the first article of the constitution be expunged.

16th That no judge of the supreme court of the United States, shall hold any other office under the United States, or any of them; nor shall any officer appointed by Congress, or by the President and Senate of the United States, be permitted to hold any office under the appointment of any of the states.

17th As a traffick tending to establish or continue the slavery of any part of the human species, is disgraceful to the cause of liberty and humanity, that Congress shall, as soon as may be, promote and establish such laws and regulations, as may effectually prevent the importation of slaves of very description into the United States.

18th That the State Legislatures have power to recall, when they think it expedient, their federal senators, and to send others in their stead.

19th That Congress have power to establish a uniform rule of inhabitancy, or settlement of the poor of the different States throughout the United States.

20th That Congress erect no company with exclusive advantages of commerce.

21st That when two members shall move or call for the ayes and nays on any question, they shall be entered on the journals of the houses respectively.

> Done in Convention at Newport, in the County of Newport in the State of Rhode-Island and Providence Plantations, the twenty ninth day of May, in the year of our Lord one thousand seven hundred and ninety, and the fourteenth year of the independence of the United States of America.
> By order of the Convention,

DANIEL OWEN President.

Attest DANIEL UPDIKE. Sect<sup>y</sup>,

# RESOLUTION OF CONGRESS, DATED JULY 2, 1788, SUBMITTING RATIFICATIONS OF THE CONSTITUTION TO A COMMITTEE.[1]

### WEDNESDAY JULY 2, 1788 [2]

Congress assembled present Newhamshire Massachusetts Rhodeisland Connecticut New York New Jersey, Pensylvania Virginia North Carolina South Carolina & Georgia & from Maryland M$^r$ Contee

\* \* \* \* \* \* \*

The State of Newhampshire having ratified the constitution transmitted to them by the Act of the 28 of Sept$^r$ last & transmitted to Congress their ratification & the same being read, the president reminded Congress that this was the ninth ratification transmitted & laid before them.

Whereupon

On Motion of M$^r$ Clarke seconded by M$^r$ Edwards

Ordered That the ratifications of the constitution of the United States transmitted to Congress be referred to a com$^{ee}$ to examine the same and report an Act to Congress for putting the said constitution into operation in pursuance of the resolutions of the late federal Convention.

On the question to agree to this Order the yeas & nays being required by M$^r$ Yates

| | | | |
|---|---|---|---|
| Newhampshire | M$^r$ Gilman | ay | ay |
| | M$^r$ Wingate | ay | |
| Massachusetts | M$^r$ Dane | ay | ay |
| | M$^r$ Otis | ay | |
| Rhodeisland | M$^r$ Arnold | | excused |
| | M$^r$ Hazard | | |
| Connecticut | (M$^r$ Edwards | ay) | ay |
| | (M$^r$ Huntington | ay) | |

---
[1] Reprinted from *Documentary History of the Constitution*, Vol. II (1894), pp. 161-162.
[2] From the "Rough" Journal of Congress (No. 1, Vol. 39.)

| | | |
|---|---|---|
| New York | Mʳ L'Hommedieu | ay⎫<br>no⎭ d |
| | Mʳ Yates | |
| New Jersey | Mʳ Clarke | ay⎫<br>ay⎬ ay<br>ay⎭ |
| | Mʳ Elmer | |
| | Mʳ Dayton | |
| Pensylvania | Mʳ Bingham | ay⎫<br>ay⎭ ay |
| | Mʳ Reid | |
| Maryland | Mʳ Contee | ay} × |
| Virginia | Mʳ Griffin | ay⎫<br>ay⎬ ay<br>ay⎭ |
| | Mʳ Carrington | |
| | Mʳ Brown | |
| South Carolina | Mʳ Huger | ay⎫<br>ay⎬ ay<br>ay⎭ |
| | Mʳ Parker | |
| | Mʳ Tucker | |
| Georgia | Mʳ Few | ay⎫<br>ay⎭ ay |
| | Mʳ Baldwin | |

RESOLUTION OF THE CONGRESS, OF SEPTEMBER 13, 1788, FIXING DATE FOR ELECTION OF A PRESIDENT, AND THE ORGANIZATION OF THE GOVERNMENT UNDER THE CONSTITUTION, IN THE CITY OF NEW YORK.[1]

SATURDAY SEPT 13. 1788 [2]

Congress assembled present New hampshire Massachusetts Connecticut New York New Jersey Pensylvania Virginia North Carolina South Carolina & Georgia & from Rhodeisland M$^r$ Arnold & from Delaware M$^r$ Kearney. . . .

Whereas the Convention assembled in Philadelphia pursuant to the resolution of Congress of the 21$^{st}$ of Feb$^y$ 1787 did on the 17$^{th}$ of Sept in the same year report to the United States in Congress assembled a constitution for the people of the United States, Whereupon Congress on the 28 of the same Sept did resolve unanimously " That the said report with the resolutions & letter accompanying the same be transmitted to the several legislatures in order to be submitted to a convention of Delegates chosen in each state by the people thereof in conformity to the resolves of the convention made and provided in that case" And whereas the constitution so reported by the Convention and by Congress transmitted to the several legislatures has been ratified in the manner therein declared to be sufficient for the establishment of the same and such ratifications duly authenticated have been received by Congress and are filed in the Office of the Secretary therefore Resolved That the first Wednesday in Jan$^y$ next be the day for appointing Electors in the several states, which before the said day shall have ratified the said Constitution; that the first Wednesday in feb$^y$ next be the day for the electors to assemble in their respective states and vote for a president; And that the first Wednesday in March next be the time and the present seat of Congress the place for commencing proceedings under the said constitution—

---
[1] Reprinted from *Documentary History of the Constitution*, Vol. II (1894), pp. 262, 263, 264.
[2] From the "Rough" Journal of Congress (No. 1, Vol. 39.)

# RESOLUTION OF THE FIRST CONGRESS SUBMITTING TWELVE AMENDMENTS TO THE CONSTITUTION.[1]

Congress of the United States,
egun and held at the City of New-York, on
Wednesday the fourth of March, one thousand seven hundred and eighty nine

THE Conventions of a number of the States, having at the time of their adopting the Constitution, expressed a desire, in order to prevent misconstruction or abuse of its powers, that further declaratory and restrictive clauses should be added: And as extending the ground of public confidence in the Government, will best ensure the beneficent ends of its institution:

RESOLVED by the Senate and House of Representatives of the United States of America, in Congress assembled, two thirds of both Houses concurring, that the following Articles be proposed to the Legislatures of the several States, as Amendments to the Constitution of the United States, all or any of which Articles, when ratified by three fourths of the said Legislatures, to be valid to all intents and purposes, as part of the said Constitution; viz$^t$

ARTICLES in addition to, and Amendment of the Constitution of the United States of America, proposed by Congress, and ratified by the Legislatures of the several States, pursuant to the fifth Article of the original Constitution.

Article the first . . . After the first enumeration required by the first Article of the Constitution, there shall be one Representative for every thirty thousand, until the number shall amount to one hundred, after which, the proportion shall be so regulated by Congress, that there shall be not less than one hundred Representatives, nor less than one Representative for every forty thousand persons, until the number of Representatives shall amount to two hundred, after which the proportion shall be so regulated by Congress, that there shall not be less than two hun-

---
[1] Reprinted from *Documentary History of the Constitution*, Vol. II (1894), pp. 321-324.

dred Representatives, nor more than one Representative for every fifty thousand persons.

Article the second . . . No law, varying the compensation for the services of the Senators and Representatives, shall take effect, until an election of Representatives shall have intervened.

Article the third . . . Congress shall make no law respecting an establishment of religion, or prohibiting the free exercise thereof; or abridging the freedom of speech, or of the press; or the right of the people peaceably to assemble, and to petition the Government for a redress of grievances.

Article the fourth . . . A well regulated Militia, being necessary to the security of a free State, the right of the people to keep and bear Arms, shall not be infringed.

Article the fifth . . . No Soldier shall, in time of peace be quartered in any house, without the consent of the Owner, nor in time of war, but in a manner to be prescribed by law.

Article the sixth . . . The right of the people to be secure in their persons, houses, papers, and effects, against unreasonable searches and seizures, shall not be violated, and no Warrants shall issue, but upon probable cause, supported by Oath or affirmation, and particularly describing the place to be searched, and the persons or things to be seized.

Article the seventh . . . No person shall be held to answer for a capital, or otherwise infamous crime, unless on a presentment or indictment of a Grand Jury, except in cases arising in the land or naval forces, or in the Militia, when in actual service in time of War or public danger; nor shall any person be subject for the same offence to be twice put in jeopardy of life or limb; nor shall be compelled in any criminal case to be a witness against himself, nor be deprived of life, liberty, or property, without due process of law; nor shall private property be taken for public use, without just compensation.

Article the eighth . . . In all criminal prosecutions, the accused shall enjoy the right to a speedy and public trial, by an impartial jury of the State and district wherein the crime shall have been committed, which district shall have been previously ascertained by law, and to be informed of the nature and cause of the accusation; to be confronted with the witnesses against him; to have compulsory process for obtaining witnesses in his favor, and to have the Assistance of Counsel for his defence.

Article the ninth . . . In Suits at common law, where the value in controversy shall exceed twenty dollars, the right of trial by jury shall be preserved, and no fact tried by a jury, shall be otherwise re-examined in any Court of the United States, than according to the rules of the common law.

Article the tenth . . . Excessive bail shall not be required, nor excessive fines imposed, nor cruel and unusual punishments inflicted.

Article the eleventh . . . The enumeration in the Constitution, of certain rights, shall not be construed to deny or disparage others retained by the people.

Article the twelfth . . . The powers not delegated to the United States by the Constitution, nor prohibited by it to the States, are reserved to the States respectively, or to the people.

> FREDERICK AUGUSTUS MUHLENBERG Speaker
> of the House of Representatives.
> JOHN ADAMS, Vice-President of the United States,
> and President of the Senate.

ATTEST,
> JOHN BECKLEY, Clerk of the House of Representatives.
> SAM. A. OTIS Secretary of the Senate.[2]

---

[2] The proposed amendments were transmitted to the legislatures of the several States, upon which the following action was taken:
*By the State of New Hampshire.*—Agreed to the whole of the said amendments, except the 2d article.
*By the State of New York.*—Agreed to the whole of the said amendments, except the 2d article.
*By the State of Pennsylvania.*—Agreed to the 3d, 4th, 5th, 6th, 7th, 8th, 9th, 10th, 11th, and 12th articles of the said amendments.
*By the State of Delaware.*—Agreed to the whole of the said amendments, except the 1st article.
*By the State of Maryland.*—Agreed to the whole of the said twelve amendments.
*By the State of South Carolina.*—Agreed to the whole said twelve amendments.
*By the State of North Carolina.*—Agreed to the whole of the said twelve amendments.
*By the State of Rhode Island and Providence Plantations.*—Agreed to the whole of the said twelve articles.
*By the State of New Jersey.*—Agreed to the whole of the said amendments, except the second article.
*By the State of Virginia.*—Agreed to the whole of the said twelve articles (Elliot's *Debates*, Vol. I, pp. 339-340.)
No returns were made by the states of Massachusetts, Connecticut, Georgia, and Kentucky.
The amendments thus proposed became a part of the constitution—the first and second of them excepted; which were not ratified by a sufficient number of the state legislatures. (*Journal of the Federal Convention*, 1819, Supplement, p. 481.)

# THE FIRST TEN AMENDMENTS TO THE CONSTITUTION

### Article I

Congress shall make no law respecting an establishment of religion, or prohibiting the free exercise thereof; or abridging the freedom of speech, or of the press; or the right of the people peaceably to assemble, and to petition the Government for a redress of grievances.

### Article II

A well regulated Militia, being necessary to the security of a free State, the right of the people to keep and bear Arms, shall not be infringed.

### Article III

No Soldier shall, in time of peace be quartered in any house, without the consent of the Owner, nor in time of war, but in a manner to be prescribed by law.

### Article IV

The right of the people to be secure in their persons, houses, papers, and effects, against unreasonable searches and seizures, shall not be violated, and no Warrants shall issue, but upon probable cause, supported by Oath or affirmation, and particularly describing the place to be searched, and the persons or things to be seized.

### Article V

No person shall be held to answer for a capital, or otherwise infamous crime, unless on a presentment or indictment of a Grand Jury, except in cases arising in the land or naval forces, or in the Militia, when in actual service in time of War or public danger; nor shall any person be subject for the same offence to be twice put in jeopardy of life or limb; nor shall be compelled in any criminal case to be a witness against himself, nor be deprived of life, liberty, or property, without due process of law; nor shall private property be taken for public use, without just compensation.

## Article VI

In all criminal prosecutions, the accused shall enjoy the right to a speedy and public trial, by an impartial jury of the State and district wherein the crime shall have been committed, which district shall have been previously ascertained by law, and to be informed of the nature and cause of the accusation; to be confronted with the witnesses against him; to have compulsory process for obtaining witnesses in his favor, and to have the Assistance of Counsel for his defence.

## Article VII

In Suits at common law, where the value in controversy shall exceed twenty dollars, the right of trial by jury shall be preserved, and no fact tried by a jury, shall be otherwise re-examined in any Court of the United States, than according to the rules of the common law.

## Article VIII

Excessive bail shall not be required, nor excessive fines imposed, nor cruel and unusual punishments inflicted.

## Article IX

The enumeration in the Constitution, of certain rights, shall not be construed to deny or disparage others retained by the people.

## Article X

The powers not delegated to the United States by the Constitution, nor prohibited by it to the States, are reserved to the States respectively, or to the people.

# SUBSEQUENT AMENDMENTS TO THE CONSTITUTION

## Article XI [1]

The Judicial power of the United States shall not be construed to extend to any suit in law or equity, commenced or prosecuted against one of the United States by Citizens of another State, or by Citizens or Subjects of any Foreign State.

## Article XII [2]

The Electors shall meet in their respective states, and vote by ballot for President and Vice-President, one of whom, at least, shall not be an inhabitant of the same state with themselves; they shall name in their ballots the person voted for as President, and in distinct ballots the person voted for as Vice-President, and they shall make distinct lists of all persons voted for as President, and of all persons voted for as Vice-President, and of the number of votes for each, which lists they shall sign and certify, and transmit sealed to the seat of the government of the United States, directed to the President of the Senate;—The President of the Senate shall, in the presence of the Senate and House of Representatives, open all the certificates and the votes shall then be counted;—The person having the greatest number of votes for President, shall be the President, if such number be a majority of the whole number of Electors appointed; and if no person have such majority, then from the persons having the highest numbers not exceeding three on the list of those voted for as President, the House of Representatives shall choose immediately, by ballot, the President. But in choosing the President, the votes shall be taken by states, the representation from each state having one vote; a quorum for this purpose shall consist of a member or members from two-thirds

---

[1] The eleventh amendment was declared in a message from the President to Congress, dated the 8th of January, 1798, to have been ratified by the legislatures of three-fourths of the States.

[2] The twelfth amendment, in lieu of the original third paragraph of the first section of the second article, was declared in a proclamation of the Secretary of State, dated the 25th of September, 1804, to have been ratified by the legislatures of three-fourths of the States.

of the states, and a majority of all the states shall be necessary to a choice. And if the House of Representatives shall not choose a President whenever the right of choice shall devolve upon them, before the fourth day of March next following, then the Vice-President shall act as President, as in the case of the death or other constitutional disability of the President. The person having the greatest number of votes as Vice-President, shall be the Vice-President, if such number be a majority of the whole number of Electors appointed, and if no person have a majority, then from the two highest numbers on the list, the Senate shall choose the Vice-President; a quorum for the purpose shall consist of two-thirds of the whole number of Senators, and a majority of the whole number shall be necessary to a choice. But no person constitutionally ineligible to the office of President shall be eligible to that of Vice-President of the United States.

## Article XIII [3]

Section 1. Neither slavery nor involuntary servitude except as a punishment for crime whereof the party shall have been duly convicted, shall exist within the United States, or any place subject to their juridsiction.

Section 2. Congress shall have power to enforce this article by appropriate legislation.

## Article XIV [4]

Section 1. All persons born or naturalized in the United States, and subject to the jurisdiction thereof, are citizens of the United States and of the State wherein they reside. No State shall make or enforce any law which shall abridge the privileges or immunities of citizens of the United States; nor shall any State deprive any person of life, liberty, or property, without due process of law; nor deny to any person within its jurisdiction the equal protection of the laws.

---

[3] The thirteenth amendment was declared, in a proclamation of the Secretary of State, dated the 18th of December, 1865, to have been ratified by the legislatures of twenty-seven of the thirty-six States.

[4] The fourteenth amendment was, in a proclamation of the Secretary of State, dated the 28th of July, 1868, declared to have been ratified by the legislatures of thirty of the thirty-six States.

SECTION 2. Representatives shall be apportioned among the several States according to their respective numbers, counting the whole number of persons in each State, excluding Indians not taxed. But when the right to vote at any election for the choice of electors for President and Vice President of the United States, Representatives in Congress, the Executive and Judicial officers of a State, or the members of the Legislature thereof, is denied to any of the male inhabitants of such State, being twenty-one years of age, and citizens of the United States, or in any way abridged, except for participation in rebellion, or other crime, the basis of representation therein shall be reduced in the proportion which the number of such male citizens shall bear to the whole number of male citizens twenty-one years of age in such State.

SECTION 3. No person shall be a Senator or Representative in Congress, or elector of President and Vice President, or hold any office, civil or military, under the United States, or under any State, who, having previously taken an oath, as a member of Congress, or as an officer of the United States, or as a member of any State legislature, or as an executive or judicial officer of any State, to support the Constitution of the United States, shall have engaged in insurrection or rebellion against the same, or given aid or comfort to the enemies thereof. But Congress may by a vote of two-thirds of each House, remove such disability.

SECTION 4. The validity of the public debt of the United States, authorized by law, including debts incurred for payment of pensions and bounties for services in suppressing insurrection or rebellion, shall not be questioned. But neither the United States nor any State shall assume or pay any debt or obligation incurred in aid of insurrection or rebellion against the United States, or any claim for the loss or emancipation of any slave; but all such debts, obligations and claims shall be held illegal and void.

SECTION 5. The Congress shall have power to enforce, by appropriate legislation, the provisions of this article.

## Article XV [5]

Section 1. The right of citizens of the United States to vote shall not be denied or abridged by the United States or by any State on account of race, color, or previous condition of servitude.

Section 2. The Congress shall have power to enforce this article by appropriate legislation.

## Article XVI [6]

The Congress shall have power to lay and collect taxes on incomes, from whatever source derived, without apportionment among the several States, and without regard to any census or enumeration.

## Article XVII [7]

(1) The Senate of the United States shall be composed of two Senators from each State, elected by the people thereof, for six years; and each Senator shall have one vote. The electors in each State shall have the qualifications requisite for electors of the most numerous branch of the State legislatures.

(2) When vacancies happen in the representation of any State in the Senate, the executive authority of such State shall issue writs of election to fill such vacancies: *Provided*, That the legislature of any State may empower the executive thereof to make temporary appointments until the people fill the vacancies by election as the legislature may direct.

(3) This amendment shall not be so construed as to affect the election or term of any Senator chosen before it becomes valid as part of the Constitution.

## Article XVIII [8]

Section 1. After one year from the ratification of this article the manufacture, sale, or transportation of intoxicating liquors

---

[5] The fifteenth amendment was declared, in a proclamation of the Secretay of State, dated March 30, 1870, to have been ratified by the legislatures of twenty-nine of the thirty-seven States.

[6] The sixteenth amendment was declared in an announcement by the Secretary of State, dated February 25, 1913, to have been ratified by the legislatures of thirty-eight of the forty-eight States.

[7] The seventeenth amendment was declared, in an announcement by the Secretary of State, dated May 31, 1913, to have been ratified by the legislatures of thirty-six of the forth-eight States

[8] The eighteenth amendment was declared, in an announcement by the Acting Secretary of State, dated January 29, 1919, to have been ratified by the legislatures of thirty-six of the forty-eight States.

within, the importation thereof into, or the exportation thereof from the United States and all territory subject to the jurisdiction thereof for beverage purposes is hereby prohibited.

SECTION 2. The Congress and the several States shall have concurrent power to enforce this article by appropriate legislation.

SECTION 3. This article shall be inoperative unless it shall have been ratified as an amendment to the Constitution by the legislatures of the several States, as provided in the Constitution, within seven years from the date of the submission hereof to the States by the Congress.

## ARTICLE XIX

The right of the citizens of the United States to vote shall not be denied or abridged by the United States or by any State on account of sex.

Congress shall have power to enforce this article by appropriate legislation.[9]

---

[9] The nineteenth amendment was declared, in an announcement of the Secretary of State, dated August 26, 1920, to have been ratified by the legislatures of thirty-eight of the forty-eight States.

# INDEX

Acts of States, mutual recognition of, committed, 632.
Adams, Andrew, signs Articles of Confederation, 36.
Adams, John, signs Declaration of Independence, 26; signs resolution submitting 12 amendments to constitution, 1665.
Adams, Samuel, signs Declaration of Independence, 26; signs Articles of Confederation, 36.
Adams, Thomas, signs Articles of Confederation, 37.
Address to people, referred to committee on style, 701; proposed, 728; rejected, 728.
Adjournment of legislature, provision for, 520.
Admission of new States, 155, 734; debated, 638; agreed to, 639; not to be made out of old States, 639; clause agreed to, 644; resolution agreed to, 754.
Admission of States, basis for, 331.
Amendments to Constitution, provision for, postponed, 155; agreed to, 434; method of making, agreed to, 646; convention for, reconsidered, 695; clause agreed to, 697, 734; provision to be made for, postponed, 754; agreed to in part, 765.
Appointments, power to make, 685; motion that none be made to any offices not created by law, lost, 690; to be referred to State executives, rejected, 620; to office, by Senate, 603; may be vested in lower officers, 733.
Armies, power to raise, debated, 567; limit in time of peace, rejected, 568; appropriation for, to be limited, 666; precaution against, rejected, 726.
Baldwin, Abraham, Georgia, appointed delegate from Georgia, 84, 86; character sketch of, 108; attends convention, 184; thinks Senate should represent property, 305; thinks Senate should not be chosen in same manner as lower House, 827; on committee on representation, 323, 840, 872; favors ineligibility of Members of legislature to offices, 658; thinks Members of First Congress may create offices for themselves, 722; would discriminate against foreigners, 528; on Committee on Assumption of State Debts, 566; defends slavery, 591; on Committee on Navigation Acts, 595; moves amendment relative to imposts, 617; on question of western country, 644; on committee on postponed measures, 655; favors mode of election of Executive, 664; signs Constitution, 951, 1002; would refer ratifications to committee, 1061.
Banister, John, signs Articles of Confederation, 37.
Bankruptcies, laws for, 632, 655; clause agreed to, 655.
Bartlett, Josiah, signs Declaration of Independence, 26; signs Articles of Confederation, 36.
Bassett, Richard, Delaware, attends Annapolis convention, 39, 43; appointed delegate from Delaware, 66, 86; character sketch of, 103; attends, 109, 746; signs Constitution, 951, 1002.
Bedford, Gunning, Delaware, appointed delegate from Delaware, 66, 85; character sketch of, 102; attends, 110; advocates three-year term for President, 91; opposes President's veto, 94; favors short term for Executive, 135; favors removal of Executive on petition of State legislatures, 142; discusses qualifications of Executive, 914; estimates influence of Executive in government, 917; opposes negative and revisionary power for Executive, 753; opposes restrictions on legislature, 150; opposes negative on State laws by legislature, 177, 759, 856; insists on rights of small States, 315; on committee on representation, 323, 840, 872; moves definition of power of legislature, 389; favors increase in representation, 729; opposes proportional repre-

sentation in Senate, 834; on representation in Senate, 909; denies desire for foreign help, 328; opposes appointment of judiciary by Executive, 402; opposes amendment against Army, 725; signs Constitution, 951, 1002.

Benson, Egbert, attends Annapolis convention, 39, 43; votes in favor of New York resolution for revising Articles of Confederation, 45.

Bill of Rights, proposed, 716; rejected, 716.

Bills of attainder, 596; forbidden to States, 728.

Bills of credit, 628; forbidden to States, 727.

Bills, to originate in either House, 546; question postponed, 583; for revenue, to originate in lower House, 666; return of, 10 days allowed, 719; amendment to, rejected, 720.

Bingham, William, votes against New York resolution for revising Articles of Confederation, 45.

Blair, John, Virginia, appointed delegate from Virginia, 71, 86; character sketch of, 105; attends, 109, 746; signs Constitution, 951, 1002.

Blount, William, North Carolina, votes against New York resolution for revising Articles of Confederation, 45; appointed delegate from North Carolina, 76, 86; character sketch of, 106; attends, 240; announces he will sign Constitution, 743; signs Constitution, 951; 1002.

Bowdoin, James, Governor of Massachusetts, 56, 57.

Braxton, Carter, signs Declaration of Independence, 26.

Brearley, David, appointed delegate from New Jersey, 61, 62, 85; character sketch of, 99; attends, 17, 746; seconds resumption of clause relating to the rule of suffrage in legislature, 180; moves New Hampshire be requested to send delegates, 305, 828; rejected, 829; opposes election of Executive by joint ballot, 610; on committee on representation, 346; opposes suffrage plan, 761; on question of representation in lower House, 856; on representation in legislature, 899; on Committee on Postponed Measures, 655; makes report on postponed measures, 655; makes report of committee of eleven, 659, 665; would strike out clause for amendments, 736; signs Constitution, 951, 1002.

Broom, Jacob, Delaware, appointed delegate from Delaware, 66, 86; character sketch of, 102, 103; attends, 109, 746; thinks Executive term should last during good behavior, 396; favors election of Executive by electors, 414; moves ratio of electors be committed, 416; would postpone question of ineligibility of Executive for second term, 415; moves to refer term and duties of Executive to committee, 612; thinks Executive may correspond with States, 620; favors nine-year term for Senate, 279; wants equal vote in Senate, 351; thinks legislature may pay itself, 544; favors equal payment for both branches of legislature, 546; seconds motion that legislature is to have sole power over treason, 578; favors power of legislature to negative State laws, 604; opposes adjournment, 386; signs Constitution, 951, 1002.

Brown, John, would refer ratifications to committee, 1061.

Bull, John, votes against New York resolution for revising Articles of Confederation, 45.

Butler, Pierce, South Carolina, appointed delegate from South Carolina, 81, 86; character sketch of, 107; attends, 109, 746; favors single Executive, 92, 93, 144, 751; opposes absolute negative for Executive, 149, 847; moves power of Executive to suspend laws, 152; opposes short term for Executive, 415; favors election of Executive by electors, 452; moves to commit clause relating to Executive, 455; approves method of election of President, 663; moves Executive have power of suspension of laws, rejected, 753; opposes election by people of Members of first branch of legislature, 88, 127; ask ratio of representation in Senate, 168; opposes power of legislature to negative State laws, 178; favors wealth as basis of representation, 184, 333, 346; thinks representation should depend on contribution, 189, 763; moves that Members of Senate serve without salary, rejected, 197; moves national compensation of legislature, 259; moves to consider representation in Senate, 277; thinks Senate must be controlled by States, 814; opposes ineligibility of Senators to State offices, 286; favors ineligibility clause to offices for Members of the first branch, 263, 797; thinks amendment to eligibility clause insufficient, 800; opposes amendment to eligibility clause, 802; proposes three years residence for Members of legislature, 494; would exclude foreigners from Senate, 505; would postpone question of eligibility of Members of legislature, 543; favors payment of legislature by States, 543; thinks treaties of peace ought to be made with majority of Senate, 686; thinks Congress should consent to inspection duties, 718; opposes power of lower House to originate revenue bills, 768; would postpone mode of election of first branch until ratio of representation is fixed, 851; on representation in lower House, 900; insists blacks should count equally with whites, 354; insists slaves equal in labor to freemen, 354; moves addition of clause relative to runaway slaves, 638; thinks negroes should be counted in representation, 363; favors counting negroes three-fifths in representation, 365; insists on security for slaves, 372; opposes inferior tribunals in national judiciary, 159, 405; would allow Senate to originate money bills, 199; opposes power of lower House to originate money bills, 326; would adhere to compromise on revenue bills, 500; opposes power to emit bills of credit, 556; opposes paper money, 557; thinks States must lay own taxes, 764; on protection of property, 917; moves to consider National Government, 120; would postpone vote on National Government, 927; asks to what extent power is to be taken from States, 127; fears powers of States may be destroyed, 130; thinks persons qualified for offices will be found, 265; moves increase in representation from South Carolina, 348; wants definition of power to legislate where States are incompetent, 384; would designate capital in Constitution, 465; opposes restriction of franchise, 488; would keep out foreigners, 525; opposes power to make war for Senate, 563; on militia, 569; favors taxation by representation, 583; opposes power over exports, 585; opposes tax on exports, 593; fears payment of debts to holders of certificates, 605; would preserve value of debts, 615; on committee on imposts, 620; moves fugitive slaves be delivered up, 631; favors enactment of navigation acts by majority, 635; opposes creation of new States from old, 640; thinks nine States should ratify Constitution, 648; favors ratification of Constitution by conventions chosen by people, 95; on committee on postponed measures, 655; signs Constitution, 951, 1002.

Cadwallader, Lambert, votes in favor of New York resolution for revising Articles of Confederation, 45.

Canals, power to cut, proposed, 724; rejected, 725.

Capital. *See* Seat of government.

Capitation tax, referred to committee, 595; to be prohibited, proposed, 726.

Captures on land and water, rules agreed to, 558.

Carrington, Edward, would refer ratifications to committee, 1061.

Carroll, Charles, signs Declaration of Independence, 26.

Carroll, Daniel, Maryland, signs Articles of Confederation, 37; appointed delegate from Maryland, 68, 86; character sketch of, 103–104; attends, 342; favors election of electors of Executive by lot, 448; moves election of President by people, 610; seconds motion for election of the Executive by electors chosen by the people, 612; on committee on representation, 346; questions vote per capita in Senate, 440; favors two-thirds for expulsion of Members of legislature, 517; proposes five years citizenship for Members of lower House, rejected, 528; opposes payment of Members of legislature by States, 544; thinks Senate should not be dependent on States, 545; would increase representation, 741; favors protecting States against violence, 407; would disqualify debtors from office, 462; opposes direct taxation by representation, 448; moves right of dissent in legislature, 518; fears New York will be seat of government, 522; fears money bills will be controversial subject, 535; moves postponement of question of negative on laws, 550; thinks majority not sufficient to lay taxes,

552; favors tax on exports, 555; opposes taxation by representation, 580; thinks provision against ex post facto laws is necessary, 597; wants ports treated impartially, 618; on committee on imposts, 620; thinks new States may be created in old, 641; thinks western country should belong to Nation, 644; moves to postpone ratification clause, 647; thinks unanimous vote necessary to ratify Constitution, 648; insists vessels must clear from own State, 654; on committee on postponed Measures, 655; proposes address to people, 728; moves power of States to lay duties on tonnage, 730; confers with colleagues from Maryland on report of committee of detail, 932, 935; signs Constitution, 951, 1002.

Caswell, Richard, appointed delegate from North Carolina, 73–77, 86.

Census, proposed as basis for representation, 352; periodical discussed, 352; agreed to, 362, 384; of free inhabitants, agreed to, 360; 6 years agreed to, 367; 20 years rejected, 367; 10 years agreed to, 367; first to be taken within three years of first meeting of legislature, 580.

Chase, Samuel, signs Declaration of Independence, 26.

Clark, Abraham, signs Declaration of Independence, 26; attends Annapolis convention, 39, 43; votes against New York resolution for revising Articles of Confederation, 45; appointed delegate from New Jersey, 61, 62, 85; would refer ratifications to committee, 1061.

Clingar, William, signs Articles of Confederation, 36.

Clinton, George, Governor of New York, 58, 59.

Clymer, George, Pennsylvania, signs Declaration of Independence, 26; appointed delegate from Pennsylvania, 63, 64; 85, character sketch of, 100, 101; attends, 18; on committee on assumption of State debts, 566; proposes taxation of exports, 587; on committee on navigation acts, 595; objects to use of word "slaves," 617; opposes development of western country, 631; wants navigation acts, 634; favors ratification by majority, 651; objects to power of Senate, 675; thinks approval of Congress to Constitution not necessary, 700; signs Constitution, 951, 1002.

Coining, power agreed to, 555.

Collins, John, signs Articles of Confederation, 36.

Collins, Thomas, Governor of Delaware, 66, 67.

Commerce, regulation of, agreed to, 555; discussed, 654.

Commissions, to be in name of United States, 572.

Committee of detail, resolutions referred to, 465; report of, 471; report debated, 482; report of, 931.

Committee of eleven, reports on mode of electing President, 946.

Committee on style, appointed, 949; report of, 702, 949; report compared with plan, 719.

Committee of whole, meets, 120; Patterson's notes on report of, 880.

Congress (see also Legislature); provision for continuation, agreed to, 155, 754; continuation of, debated, 406; rejected, 406; authorizes meeting of convention, 927; resolution submitting 12 amendments to Constitution, 1063–1065.

Congress, Continental, resolution submitting Constitution to States, 1007; circular letter of secretary transmitting copy of Constitution to the several governors, 1008; resolution of, fixing date for organization of Federal Government, 1062.

Constitution, provision for amending, discussed, 190; postponed, 191; State officials to take oath to observe, discussed, 191; agreed to, 192; to be referred to people for ratification, agreed to, 192; committee on, 441; committee on detail, 448; referred to committee on detail, 465; to be supreme law, 603, 942; agreed to 603, 951; to be laid before Congress, 651; time for going into effect, 653; mode of ratification, agreed to, 700; reported by committee on style, 702; provision for ratification, 720; engrossed, 738, 951; read, 738, 951; signed, 745, 951; text of, 989–1002.

Constitution, amendments to, first to tenth, 1066–1067; eleventh, 1068; twelfth, 1068–1069; thirteenth, 1069; fourteenth, 1069–1070; fifteenth, 1071; sixteenth, 1071; seventeenth, 1071; eighteenth, 1071; nineteenth, 1072.

Constitution, plans for:
  Virginia plan, variant texts of:
    Text A, 953–956.
    Text B, 957–959.
    Text C, 960–963.
  Plan of Charles Pinckney, 964–966.
  Plan of William Patterson, variant texts of:
    Text A, 967–970.
    Text B, 971–974.
    Text C, 975–978.
  Plan of Alexander Hamilton, variant texts of:
    Text A, 979–980.
    Text B, 981–982.
    Text C, 983–984.
    Text D, 985–986.
    Text E, 987–988.
Contee, Benjamin, would refer ratifications to committee, 1061.
Contracts, impairment of, forbidden to States, 728; to be forbidden to Congress, proposed, 728.
Controversies between States, provision for, considered, 608.
Convention, meets, 109, 746, 923; rules for, 110; goes into committee of whole, 120; longer sessions for, agreed to, 567; the hours of meeting, 596; changed, 614; expenses of, 665, 667; powers of, discussed, 877; second proposed, rejected, 738; adjourned sine die, 745, 952; letter of President to President of Congress, 1003–1004; resolution submitting Constitution to Congress, 1005–1006.
Copyright, power of, 563.
Copyrights and patents, 666; clause agreed to, 667.
Council of revision, proposed, 752; question postponed, 847.
Council of state, proposed, 573, 752, 845, 948; rejected, 949.
Council, privy, for President, provided for, 595.
Counterfeiting, punishment of, 559.
Coxe, Tench, attends Annapolis convention, 39, 43.
Creditors, protection of, 564, 565.
Dana, Francis, signs Articles of Confederation, 36; appointed delegate from Massachusetts, 56, 57, 85.
Dane, Nathan, votes in favor of New York resolution for revising Articles of Confederation, 45; would refer ratifications to committee, 1060.
Davie, William Richardson, North Carolina, appointed delegate from North Carolina, 73, 74, 76, 77, 86; character sketch of, 106; attends, 109, 746; moves impeachability of Executive, 144; favors impeachability of Executive, 417; moves eight-year term for Executive, 444; favors seven-year term for Executive, 457; favors ineligibility of Executive for second term, 457; wants small Senate, 311; favors equality of vote for States in Senate, 832; on representation in Senate, 908; on committee on representation, 323, 840; insists on representation for blacks, 364; would commit clause on representation, 334.
Dayton, Elias, would refer ratifications to committee, 1061.
Dayton, Jonathan, New Jersey, appointed delegate from New Jersey, 62, 85; character sketch of, 99, 100; attends, 249; opposes election of Executive by ballot, 610; favors vote for Executive by States, 611; thinks Senators should be paid from National Treasury, 285, 813; favors equality of vote in Senate, 834; thinks voting in legislature should be by States, 290; opposes proportional representation, 314; opposes slave representation, 498; wants standing army, 568; moves partial national control over militia, 599; opposes uniformity of militia, 600; on com-

mittee on **imposts, 620**; thinks fate of States depends on question of National or Federal Government, 821; opposes two-thirds vote in Senate for treaties, 689; opposes motion to allow States to lay export duties, 717; signs Constitution, 951, 1002.

Debtors, disqualification for office, 458, 462; rejected, 464.

Debts, committee on assumption of State debts appointed, 566; assumption of, agreed to, 581; provision for payment of, 595; discharge of, debated, 608; payment of, 614; validity agreed to, 616; payment of old, rejected, 616.

Delaware, credentials of deputies, powers reserved, 110; delegates from, threatened to withdraw, 123; object to consideration of suffrage based on numbers or property, 749; postponed, 749; forbids delegates changing rule of suffrage, 123; attitude of, discussed, 123, 124.

Departments, heads of, to advise Executive, 687, 688.

Dickinson, John, Delaware, signs Articles of Confederation, 37; attends Annapolis convention, 39, 43; appointed delegate from Delaware, 66, 86; character sketch of, 102; attends, 113; favors definition of powers of Executive, 91; favors removal of Executive upon request of majority of State legislatures, 92, 141; moves removability of Executive by legislature on request of State legislatures, 142; opposes blending of judiciary with Executive in council of revision, 94; favors election of Executive by people, 454; moves to restrict Executive's power of appointment, 613; objects to President of Senate as successor to President, 622; moves impeachability of Executive, agreed to, 751; opposes strong Executive, 845; favors eventual election of Executive by legislature, 670; moves that vote of presidential electors be from all who are appointed, 672; favors executive council, 687; would elect one branch of legislature by people, 163; would retain confederation in amended form, 928; moves election of Senate by State legislatures, 168, 756, 854; agreed to, 757, 854; opposes election of Senators by people, 854; favors large Senate, 170; moves appointment of Senators by State legislatures, 852; supports motion, 853; approves of wealth as basis for representation in first branch, 185; favors election of first branch by State legislatures, 756; favors three-year term for lower House, 254, 794; proposes short residence period for Members of legislature, 493; favors election of Representatives by people and Senators by State legislatures, 851; would have State legislatures elect Senators, 915; on representation in lower House, 900; favors three-year term for Representatives, 863; proposes one Representative for each State at the least, 499; on qualifications of electors of lower House, 934; would fix compensation of Members of legislature at intervals, 544; moves equal compensation for Members of both branches of legislature, 545; proposes limitation of representation, 581; favors national judiciary, 158; opposes association of judiciary in revisionary power, 167, 849; thinks judges should not have power to set aside laws, 549; moves power to remove judges, 622, 623; opposes giving judiciary joint negative with Executive, 852; on judiciary, 849; approves power of legislature to negative State laws, 177, 856; proposes revision of Articles of Confederation, 215; rejected, 226; opposes qualifications for office, 460; would confine right of suffrage to freeholders, 488, 873; would apportion suffrage according to State contributions, 764; would restrict money bills to lower House, 533; thinks definition of felonies unnecessary, 559; on committee on assumption of State debts, 566; thinks legislature should make important appointments, 567; would let States retain power over militia, 569; on definition of treason, 576, 579; favors taxation of exports, 585; opposes slave trade, 592; on committee on navigation acts, 595; favors inclusion of Executive in treaty-making power, 606; would confine slave trade to States already permitting it, 617; discusses ex post facto laws, 633; thinks new States may be created within old, 640; moves that combination to effect new States be forbidden, 644; would protect States from domestic violence, 645; asks if Congress must consent to Constitution, 648; on committee on postponed measures, 655; thinks Congress should allow inspection duties, 718; on committee on sumptuary laws, 718; on direct taxation, 719; would consolidate Virginia and New Jersey plans, 785; signs Constitution, 951, 1002.

Domestic violence, guarantee against, 734.

Drayton, William Henry, signs Articles of Confederation, 37.

Duane, James, signs Articles of Confederation, 36.

Duer, William, signs Articles of Confederation, 36.

Duties, power to lay, 552; to be uniform, 654; on imports or exports, forbidden to States, 730; on tonnage, forbidden to States, 730, 731.

Edwards, Pierpont, would refer ratifications to committee, 1060.

Electors of Executive. *See* Executive, national.

Electors of Representatives, qualifications of, 873; qualifications of, discussed, 934.

Ellery, William, signs Declaration of Independence, 26; signs Articles of Confederation, 36.

Ellsworth, Oliver, Connecticut, appointed delegate from Connecticut, 58, 85; character sketch of, 98; attends, 110; moves election of Executive by electors, 414; favors six-year term for Executive, 415; proposes ratio of electors for Executive, 416; thinks Executive should be allowed second term, 444; favors election of Executive by legislature, 449; opposes election of Executive by electors, 452; thinks each State should have one vote in Senate, 189; moves election of Members of first branch annually, 192, 863; proposes legislative power remain in Congress, 213; moves supreme government instead of national, 240; favors short term for lower House, 255; moves payment of Senators by States, rejected, 813; favors State compensation of legislature, 256, 795; favors election of Senators by State legislatures, 275, 807, 864; proposes State compensation of Senators, 285, 813; moves that each State have equal vote in Senate, 304, 827, 868; supports motion, 830; moves postponement of suffrage right in Senate, agreed to, 826; opposes representation in Senate according to number of people, 869; on representation in Senate, 908; insists Connecticut is federal, 311; defends Connecticut, 832; insists on preservation of States, 316; thinks Government can not exist without approbation of States, 797; thinks domestic happiness depends upon preservation of State governments, 836; moves word "national" be expunged, agreed to, 787; on committee on representation, 323, 840, 872; favors compromise on representation, 328; opposes increase in representation, 349; favors counting blacks as three-fifths for representation, 365; wants legislature to fix basis for representation, 365; favors representation by Members, 369; thinks equal vote in Senate safe, 382; opposes power of States to fix qualifications for electors of Representatives, 873; opposes confining suffrage to freeholders, 874; would fix time for meeting of legislature, 484; opposes summer sessions of legislature, 486; proposes one-year residence for Members of legislature, 494; thinks money bills, may originate in either House, 500; would have Executive fill vacancies in Senate, 501; would not give legislature power to fill vacancies in Senate, 501; opposes provision for money bills, 502; opposes 14 years' citizenship for Senators, 504; opposes fixing property qualification for legislature, 512, 513; opposes fixing quorum, 516; opposes yeas and nays, 518; on journals of legislature, 520; favors exclusion of Members of legislature from other offices during term of service, 541; favors payment of legislature from National Treasury, 543; would fix compensation of legislature, 545; moves $5 per day as payment for Members of legislature, 545; would have judiciary appointed by Senate with consent of Executive, 431; would refer constitution to State legislatures for ratification, 434, 436; on committee of detail, 449; opposes disqualification of debtors, 463; favors franchise based on taxation, 448; approves qualifications of electors, 487; opposes seven-year residence as qualification for legislature, 493; thinks Constitution may be amended, 496; opposes paper money, 557; enlarges clause giving legislature power to punish crimes on the high seas, counterfeiting, and breaches of international law, 560; proposes power to suppress rebellion on application of Executive, 560; thinks State debts will be assumed, 565; favors executive council, 567; would let power over militia remain in States, 569, 570; thinks taxation will cover sumptuary laws, 574; on definition of treason, 576; would let States retain power over treason, 579; moves postponement of question of State debts, 581; would levy contributions by States, 582; opposes taxation by representation, 582; would give Government power to regulate interstate commerce, 584; thinks legislature may lay embargoes, 586; would allow importation of slaves, 589, 590; would retain clause on navigation, 594; thinks ex post facto laws void, 596; thinks new Government bound to fulfill engagements of old, 597; favors State control of militia, 599; favors uniformity of militia, 600; opposes negative on State laws, 605; would postpone part of Patterson plan, 775; thinks some good plan will be devised, 823; on plan for government, 903.

Elmer, Jonathan, would refer ratifications to committee, 1061.

Emit bills of credit, power to, rejected, 557.

Enacting clause for laws, adopted, 546.

Executive, national, proposed and considered, 131, 413, 750; agreed to, 133, 458, 750; qualifications for, committed, 461; establishment of, considered, 927; title 609.
  Age, 661.
  Citizenship, 661.
  Compensation of, discussed, 137, 731; agreed to, 421; to receive no salary, proposed, postponed, 751.
  Correspondence with State, discussed, struck out, 620.
  Council for, considered, 146, 567, 595, 845; question postponed, 846; rejected, 687.
  Election of, discussed, 134, 135, 136, 137, 456, 668, 943, 947, 948; appointment by States, discussed, 174, 179, 760; rejected, 180, 760; to be chosen by legislature, agreed to, 395, 751; to be elected by people, rejected, 395, 943; to be chosen by electors, rejected, 395; to be chosen by electors, proposed, 412, 413; agreed to, 414; to be chosen by legislature, discussed, 392, 414; ratio considered, 416; ratio agreed to, 417; qualifications of electors considered, 422; payment of electors, 422; election by electors reconsidered, 441; debated, 442; by National Legislature agreed to, 443; election of electors by lot, discussed, 447; election question postponed, 448; election by legislature considered, 449; rejected, 452; election by legislature, reconsidered, 609; election by joint ballot agreed to, 611; equality of vote for States, rejected, 611; election by majority, agreed to, 611; to be elected by electors chosen by people, proposed, rejected, 612; mode of election reported, 666; eventual election by legislature rejected, 670; by less than one-third, rejected, 671; election by six Senators and seven Representatives, proposed, rejected, 671; election by electors debated, 672; election limited to three candidates, rejected, 671; to 13 candidates, rejected, 671; electors to meet at seat of government, 676; rules for counting vote, discussed, 677; election by lower House in the event of a tie, agreed to, 678, 948; quorum for voting fixed, 678; mode of election agreed to, 679; vacancy to be filled by legislature, 680; majority of States necessary to elect, proposed, 681.
  Impeachability of, discussed, 143, 401, 417-421, 751; clause agreed to, 421, 751; impeachment of, debated, 946.
  Ineligibility for second term, debated, 144, 396, 399, 400, 408, 414, 444, 943; rejected, 396, 415; agreed to, 457; eligibility for continuous reelection, considered, 454; rejected, 455; eligibility, postponed, 943.
  Negative, power of, debated, 147; to have negative on legislative acts, proposed, 147; to have power of absolute negative, proposed, 152, 752, 847; rejected, 152, 486, 753, 848; to have negative on laws, proposed, 549; power to negative bills, 551; two-thirds vote required to overrule negative, proposed, 713; agreed to, 715; qualified veto power over legislation, agreed to, 939.

Executive, national—Continued.
  Oath of, 622.
  Powers of, 133; council of revision for, considered, 147; revisionary power to be overruled by two-thirds of legislature, agreed to, 152; to have power to suspend laws, discussed, rejected, 152, 753; to be associated with judiciary in revisionary power, considered, 152, 422, 753; rejected, 429; power of appointment discussed, 153; power of appointment, agreed to, 685; to appoint officers not otherwise provided for, agreed to, 750; amendment to appointing power, rejected, 944; association of judiciary in revisionary power, debated, 165; rejected, 167; to execute laws, agreed to, 396, 750; to appoint to office, agreed to, 396; to have sole power of revision, 752; to be associated with judiciary in revisionary power, 848, 849; motion withdrawn, 849; to appoint judiciary, 849; postponed, 849; to have qualified veto, agreed to, 429; power of appointment, 612; restricted, 613; to appoint public ministers, 620; to receive ambassadors, agreed to, 620; power of pardon, agreed to, 620; impeachment excepted, 620; power over militia, 621; impeachment postponed, 621; power to make treaties, 683, 685, 686; to fill vacancies, 685; to require opinions of heads of departments, 686; to pardon, 731; treason cases excepted, rejected, 732; report of committee of whole, 880; report of committee of eleven, 946.
  Removal of, discussed, 143.
  Single, proposed, 133, 144, 751, 847, 913; agreed to, 146, 932, 609, 752, 847; power to be vested in one person, 845.
  Succession, question postponed, 622; President of Senate to succeed, 621.
  Term of, 134; duration of term discussed, 847; seven-year term agreed to, 135, 750, 847; seven-year term, question postponed, 396; discussed, 396; during good behavior, rejected, 399; seven-year term rejected, 415; term discussed, 444; reported, 660; debated, 676.
Export duties, States may levy to pay charges, 716; forbidden, 726; no preference to be given, 726.
Exports, taxes on, 553; question postponed, 555; for revenue, rejected, 587; by two-thirds vote, rejected, 588; prohibited, 588; question referred to committee, 595.
Ex post facto laws, discussed, 596, 633, 726; clause retained, 726; forbidden to States, 728.
Extradition, power of, agreed to, 945.
Few, William, votes in favor of New York resolution for revising Articles of Confederation, 45; appointed delegate from Georgia, 82, 84, 86; character sketch of, 107, 108; attends, 109; on committee on imposts, 620; signs Constitution, 951, 1002; would refer ratifications to committee, 1061.
Fitzsimmons, Thomas, Pennsylvania, appointed delegate from Pennsylvania, 63, 64, 85; character sketch of, 100, 101; attends, 109, 746; favors taxation of exports, 587; on committee on imports, 620; would have vessels clear from own State, 654; opposes publication of expenditure accounts, 727; signs Constitution, 951, 1002.
Floyd, William, signs Declaration of Independence, 26.
Forest, Uriah, votes against New York resolution for revising Articles of Confederation, 45.
Forts, jurisdiction over, 666, 667.
Franklin, Benjamin, Pennsylvania, signs Declaration of Independence, 26; appointed delegate from Pennsylvania, 65, 85; character sketch of, 100; attends, 110; opposes salary for Executive, 137; moves Executive receive no salary but that expenses be paid, postponed, 751; opposes salaries for public officers, 92; opposes negative for Executive on laws, 93, 148; opposes Executive power, 151; favors Executive power to suspend laws, 152; opposes absolute negative for Executive, 753, 847, 848; favors impeachibility of Executive, 418, 420; thinks Executive is servant of people, 457; favors council for Executive, 687; would limit Executive's pay, 731; opposes two

branches of National Legislature, 125; on basis of representation in legislature, 185; would apportion representation according to number or wealth 763; opposes confining right of suffrage to freeholders, 875; would eliminate "liberal" from amendment regarding compensation of legislators, 194; proposes proportion for Senate, 312; on representation in Senate, 909; on committee on representation, 323, 840, 872; proposes compromise on question of suffrage in Senate, 833; opposes property qualifications for legislature, 512; thinks members need not pledge themselves, 744; on qualifications of electors of lower House, 935; opposes long term of citizenship for Senators, 938; on appointment of judiciary, 153, 849; thinks salaries of judges may be increased, 404; thinks money bills may originate in lower House, 337; agrees to clause for money bills, 502; considers originating of money bills and equality of vote in Senate connected under compromise, 502; proposes prayers in convention, 295, 822; wants sermon on Fourth of July, 297; favors compromise, 334; favors free franchise, 490; wants foreigners treated well, 506; would require two witnesses to treason, 578; favors second convention, 701; on committee on sumptuary laws, 718; on power to cut canals, 724; wants unanimous approval, 739; on naturalization, 877; would empower Congress to establish canals, rejected, 950; pleads with Randolph to sign Constitution, 743; utters prophecy, 745, 952; gives reasons for signing, 951; signs Constitution, 951, 1002.

Franklin, William Temple, nominated for secretary of convention, defeated, 110, 747.

Fugitive slaves, clause relative to, amended, 734.

Georgia, representation to be raised, rejected, 349.

Gerry, Elbridge, Massachusetts, signs Declaration of Independence, 26; signs Articles of Confederation, 36; appointed delegate from Massachusetts, 56, 57, 85; character sketch of, 97; attends, 113; disapproves election of Executive by people, 127; favors executive council, 132, 845; favors single Executive, 752; opposes election of Executive by legislature, 136; opposes plural Executive, 146; proposes Executive be given negative on legislation, 147; favors qualified negative for Executive, 148; opposes power of Executive to suspend laws, 152; moves appointment of Executive be reconsidered, 178, 760; moves that Executive be elected by State governors, 179; opposes popular election of Executive, 413, 454; would elect Executive by electors, 414; moves ratio of electors for appointment of Executive, 416; favors impeachability of Executive, 419; on qualification of electors, 422; moves election of Executive by State legislatures, 442; opposes election of presidential electors by State legislatures, 442; opposes eligibility of Executive for second term, 444; moves ineligibility of Executive for second term, 444; favors 15-year term for Executive, 444; suggests eligibility of Executive for second term be committed, 445; opposes selection of Executive electors by lot, 447; moves election of Executive by State governors, 449; thinks Executive should be ineligible for continuous reelection, 452; moves to commit clause relative to Executive, 455; opposes executive council, 567; fears a few States may choose Executive, 671; moves eventual election of Executive by six senators and seven representatives, 671; seconds motion that eventual election of Executives be limited to three candidates, 671; moves clause relative to qualifications of Executive electors, 673; thinks States must have larger representation to vote for Executive, 681; proposes majority of States to elect President, 681; thinks Executive will not be held responsible for appointments, 684; thinks Executive should have sole right of revision, 752; opposes seven-year term for Executive, 847; opposes joint negative for Executive and judiciary, 852; opposes popular election of members of first branch of legislature, 87, 88; favors election to first branch of legislature on nominations by the people, with election by State legislature, 159; favors election of Senate by State legislatures, 170, 757; opposes negative of National Legislature on State laws, 175, 855; moves to exclude blacks from rule of representation, 189; favors annual election of Members of lower House, 192; opposes equal suffrage of States in legislature, 303; would commit question of representation in Senate, 322; on committee on representation, 323, 840, 872; named chairman of committee on representation, 841; explains report on representation, 324, 842; favors compromise on representation, 329; favors numbers and wealth as basis of representation for States, 332; favors increase in representation, 349; would count blacks as three-fifths, 354; proposes vote per capita in Senate, 376; would fix quorum, 516; on journals of legislature, motion concerning, 519; thinks legislature may fix capital, 521; favors ineligibility of members of legislature to office, 537, 658; on compensation of legislature, 544; thinks Senate should not have power to make peace, 563; opposes making Vice President President of Senate, 682; fears treaties of peace may be made too easily, 686; seconds motion that treaties require a majority of whole Senate for ratification, 690; moves that treaties require two-thirds vote in Senate for ratification, 689; moves notice of treaties be sent to Senators, 690; moves legislature have sole power to create officers, 693; thinks Congress must agree to Constitution, 697, 698, 699; would require two-thirds vote to override veto of Executive, 714; thinks Congress should be forbidden to impair validity of contracts, 728; moves to provide for public securities, stages, letters of marque and reprisal, committed, 566; opposes election of lower House by State legislatures, 755; opposes counting slaves in representation, 764; moves national legislators be sworn to preserve State constitutions, agreed to, 765; opposes three-year term for first branch, 766; moves first branch originate revenue bills, 768; opposes amendment to eligibility clause, 802; favors ineligibility of Representatives for one year after expiration of term, 803; opposes election of lower House by people, 844; would leave final election of lower House to State legislatures, 850; will agree to equal vote in Senate if money bills originate in lower House, 870; on representation in lower House, 900; opposes judicial power to revise laws, 147; opposes association of judiciary with Executive in revisionary power, 166; opposes revisionary power for judiciary, 424; thinks judges can be removed, 622; insists on provision for juries, 716; insists on jury trial in civil cases, 733; doubts powers of convention to form National Government, 121, 928; on evils of democracy, 125; favors system to amend Constitution, 155; fears ratification of Constitution by people, 156; thinks that the interests of the commercial and moneyed class more secure with State legislatures than with people, 172; would not require oaths from members of State governments to observe Constitution, 191; would forbid Senate to originate money bills, 199; urges agreement, 282; considers right to originate money bills a concession from the small States, 336; favors originating money bills in first branch of legislature, 531; insists on national plan, 339; moves consideration of general powers, 340; moves to consider basis of taxation, 368; fears western country, 374; would discriminate against western country, 375; insists on concessions, 377; opposes adjournment, 386; favors oath to support National Government, 433; opposes ratification by people, 435; moves commitment of Constitution, 441; opposes exclusion of debtors from office, 460; considers protection of property an object of government, 460; favors qualifications for legislature, 463; would disqualify pensioners, 463; opposes fixing capital at State capital, 465; favors exclusion of foreigners from Government, 523; opposes taxation of exports, 554; opposes taxing power, 555; would establish post roads, 556; opposes power to suppress rebellion without consent of State, 561; on public securities, 564; opposes armies in time of peace, 567; would limit army in time of peace, 568; favors State control of militia, 571, 600; on impeachment, 574; moves taxation according to representation, 580; opposes assumption of State debts, 581; favors taxation by representation, 582, 583; opposes power over exports, 586; opposes slavery, 592; opposes bills of attainder and ex post facto laws, 596; would fulfill engagements of old Government, 598; fears national control of militia, 599, 600; supports State governments, 602; thinks debts should be paid, 615; opposes Constitution, 652; opposes appropriations for Army for two years, 666; objects to authority over forts, 667; would reconsider question of amendments, oaths, and ratifications,

668; moves appointment to offices not created by, law illegal, 690; moves reconsideration of amendments, 695; approves amendments proposed by legislatures to States, 696; favors Bill of Rights, 716; would extend ex post facto laws to civil cases, 726; moves clause to guarantee liberty of the press, 726; favors publication of expenditure accounts, 727; moves amendment for admission of States, 734; favors amendments by convention, 735; thinks Articles of Confederate inadequate, 907; thinks plan annihilates State governments, 910; favors negative on paper emissions, 916; would establish a federal system, 929; thinks people have aversion to monarchy, 812; opposes confederation as form of government, 826; favors concessions on suffrage questions, 840; states why he will not sign, 738; does not sign, 745, 951.

Gibbons, William, signs ordinance for appointment of deputies, 84.

Gilman, Nicholas, New Hampshire, appointed delegate from New Hampshire, 56, 85; character sketch of, 96; attends, 433; on committee on postponed measures, 655; signs Constitution, 951, 1002; would refer ratifications to committee, 1060.

Gorham, Nathaniel, Massachusetts, appointed delegate from Massachusetts, 56, 57, 85; character sketch of, 96; attends, 110; thinks legislature may state time of elections, 509; favors election of Executive by ballot, 609; thinks majority of Senate may elect Executive, 677; favors seven-year term for Executive, 847; opposes State compensation of legislature, 257; would strike out compensation clause, 795; would pay legislators from National Treasury, 800; opposes ineligibility of Members of first branch to office, 260; moves expunction of ineligibility clause for first branch, 797; supports motion, 799; rejected, 800; proposes compromise of representation in Senate, 274; suggests four-year term for Senators, 277; moves six-year term for Senators, 279; would change rule of apportionment for Senate, 806; would divide Senators into classes, 809; moves six-year term for Senators with triennial rotation, 810; calls for explanation of report on representation, 324, 842; opposes fixing representation in lower House, 332; on committee on representation, 334; explains ratio of representation, 343; favors counting slaves as three-fifths, 354; thinks standard of representation must be fixed, 356; favors numbers as basis for representation, 361; on representation, 906; would leave qualifications to legislature, 459; would fix time of meeting of legislature, 484, 873; on qualifications of electors of lower House, 875; thinks Senate can amend money bills, 499; favors less than a majority for quorum, 514; opposes yeas and nays upon request, 518; would pay Senate more than lower House, 546; opposes power in Senate to enact money bills, 546; favors majority for quorum, 550; thinks legislature can fix scale of contributions, 582; would let Senate settle State controversies, 609; would allow Congress to name ports of entry, 619; favors eligibility of legislators to offices, 658; opposes peace treaties concluded by majority of Senate, 685; wants increased representation, 741; favors election of Executive by joint ballot of legislature, 482; approves appointment of judiciary by Executive, 400, 401, 402; favors appointment with consent of Senate, 403; favors inferior judicial tribunals, 405; opposes association of judiciary in revisionary power, 423; opposes revisionary power for judiciary, 428; thinks provision for juries unnecessary, 716; appointed chairman of committee of whole, 120, 748; favors supreme government rather than national, 240; discusses rights of States, 297; thinks it in interest of smaller States to unite in a general government, 823; favors general principles in Constitution, 384; favors guaranteeing republican government, 407; favors oath to support Constitution, 433; opposes ratification by State legislatures, 435; on committee of detail, 448; seconds amendment inserting voting qualifications, 462; opposes franchise for freeholders alone, 491; thinks Nation will not endure, 496; would place naturalized foreigners on equality with citizens, 526; opposes emission of bills of credit, 556; moves appointment of treasurer by joint ballot, 558; moves power to support armies, 567; declares East is commercial, 594; on ratification of treaties, 606, 607; would allow slave trade until 1808, 616;

thinks duty on slaves discourages importation, 618; on committee on imposts, 619; thinks paper money may be necessary, 627; on committee on mutual recognition by States of public acts, 632; favors navigation acts, 637; favors ratification by conventions, 650; thinks vessel need not clear from its own State, 654; opposes mode of appointment of Vice President, 662; favors appointment of treasurer by legislature, 722; opposes restriction of legislature in giving duty preferences, 944; signs Constitution, 951, 1002.

Grand committee on assumption of State debts, 566, 580, 581.

Grayson, William, report of grand committee recommending convention, 44; favors revision of Articles of Confederation, 45.

Great seal, 572.

Griffin, Cyrus, would refer ratifications to committee, 1061.

Gwinnett, Button, signs Declaration of Independence, 26.

Habeas corpus, writ of, 572, 627.

Hall, Lyman, signs Declaration of Independence, 26.

Hamilton, Alexander, New York, attends Annapolis convention, 39, 43; appointed delegate from New York, 59, 60, 85; character sketch of, 98; attends, 109, 746; moves absolute negative for Executive, 147; thinks Executive may be chosen by plurality of electors, 675; favors election of Executive and one branch of legislature for life, 782; favors absolute negative for Executive, 847; would have election of Executive confined to electors, 948; moves representation by population, 123; moves rule of suffrage in Senate should be same as in lower House, agreed to, 190; opposes elections to legislature by State legislatures, 252; favors three-year term for first branch, 256, 794, 863; opposes State compensation of legislature, 258; opposes ineligibility of Members of first branch to office, 261; favors citizenship requirements for legislature, 524; would reconsider representation, 694; favors election of lower House by people, 793; opposes payment of legislators by States, 796; opposes ineligibility clause for Representatives, 799; thinks ineligibility provision may be evaded, 803; favors representation according to number, 867; on representation, 906; nominates Jackson for secretary, 110, 747; on committee on rules, 110; seconds motion against salaries, 141; would appoint judiciary by Executive, subject to Senate approval, 94; supports National Government, 215; introduces plan for Government, 224, 782; favors strong Government, 281, 787; opposes prayers in convention, 296; discusses rights of States, 301; would reduce power of State governments, 786; thinks strict equality of States in new Government is neither necessary nor just, 824; would not sacrifice individual rights for the preservation of States, 825; inquires whether the States are susceptible of one government, 926; on committee on style, 694, 949; favors easier method of amendment, 695; favors clause for amendments, 696; submits plan for ratification, 699; rejected, 700; thinks Congress must agree to Constitution, 697; does not favor either Randolph or Patterson plan, 769; discusses Randolph and Patterson plans, 776; thinks British Government best model, 781; wants moderate government between extremes of despotism or democracy, 812; hopes every member will sign Constitution, 742; signs Constitution, 951, 1002; notes in Federal convention, 913–922; variant texts of plan of, 979–988.

Hancock, John, signs Declaration of Independence, 25; signs Articles of Confederation, 36.

Hanson, John, signs Articles of Confederation, 37.

Harnett, Cornelius, signs Articles of Confederation, 37.

Harrison, Benjamin, signs Declaration of Independence, 26.

Hart, John, signs Declaration of Independence, 26.

Harvie, John, signs Articles of Confederation, 37.

Hawkins, Benjamin, votes against New York resolution for revising Articles of Confederation, 45.

Hazard, Jonathan, does not vote on commitment of ratifications, 1060.

Henry, Patrick, appointed delegate from Virginia, 71, 72, 86.
Hewes, Joseph, signs Declaration of Independence, 26.
Heyward, Thomas, jr., signs Declaration of Independence, 26; signs Articles of Confederation, 37.
Holten, Samuel, signs Articles of Confederation, 36.
Hooper, William, signs Declaration of Independence, 26.
Hopkins, Stephen, signs Declaration of Independence, 26.
Hopkinson, Francis, signs Declaration of Independence, 26.
Hosmer, Titus, signs Articles of Confederation, 36.
House of Representatives. *See* Legislature, House of Representatives.
Houston, William Churchill, New Jersey, attends Annapolis convention, 39, 43; appointed delegate from New Jersey, 61, 62, 85; character sketch of, 99; attends, 109, 746; moves question of election of Executive, 441.
Houstoun, William, Georgia, appointed delegate from Georgia, 83, 84, 86; character sketch of, 108; attends, 131; would postpone question of Executive term, 396; moves eligibility of Executive for second term, 396; favors increase of ratio of electors, 416; moves election of Executive electors by State legislatures, 442; on committee on representation, 346; moves increase in representation of Georgia, 349; would not perpetuate existing State constitutions, 407.
Huger, Daniel, votes against New York resolution for revising Articles of Confederation, 45; would refer ratifications to committee, 1061.
Huntington, Benjamin, would refer ratifications to committee, 1060.
Huntington, Samuel, signs Declaration of Independence, 26; signs Articles of Confederation, 36.
Hutson, Richard, signs Articles of Confederation, 37.
Impeachments, provision struck out, 405; mode of, 574; of judges, 596; of President, postponed, 621; power of, 691; of high crimes and misdemeanors, agreed to, 691; not to try in Senate, rejected, 692; clause agreed to, 693; to include other civil officers, 692; clause for suspension of persons impeached, rejected, 721; restriction on judgment for, 945.
Imports, tax on, 629.
Imposts, power to lay, 552; to be uniform, 619, 723.
Incorporation, power of, 563; charters of, 724.
Indian affairs, 563.
Ingersoll, Jared, appointed delegate from Pennsylvania, 63, 64; character sketch of, 100, 101; attends, 110; does not regard signing Constitution as pledge to support it, 744; signs Constitution, 951, 1002.
Invasion, amendment to article, agreed to, 645.
Inventions, to be encouraged, 564.
Irwine, William, votes against New York resolution for revising Articles of Confederation, 45.
Jackson, William, elected secretary of convention, 110, 747; to carry Constitution to Congress, 952; signs Constitution, 1001; signs resolution submitting Constitution to Congress, 1006.
Jefferson, Thomas, signs Declaration of Independence, 26.
Jenifer, Daniel of St. Thomas, Maryland, appointed delegate from Maryland, 67, 86; character sketch of, 103; attends, 136; moves three-year term for members of first branch, 192, 766; opposes eligibility of Members of legislature to offices, 265; favors amendment to eligibility clause, 803; would postpone question of money bills, 335; insists vessel must clear from own State, 654; confers with colleague from Maryland on report of committee of detail, 932, 936; anecdote, 952; signs Constitution, 951, 1002.
Johnson, William Samuel, Connecticut, votes in favor of New York resolution for revising Articles of Confederation, 45; appointed delegate from Connecticut, 58,

85; character sketch of, 97; attends, 136; favors preservation of States, 249; thinks State governments must be kept, 276; thinks States must be preserved, 297; contrasts Virginia and New Jersey plans, 791; would have States elect Senate, 792; opposes motion to remove election of Senate from power of States, 808; thinks States as States must have voice in Senate, 822; on election of Senators, 864; contrasts Virginia and New Jersey plans, 862; favors numbers and wealth as basis of representation, 364; favors compromise on question of representation, 867; on representation, 906; on definition of treason, 576; insists treason is offense against Nation, 577; on committee on navigation acts, 595; on ex post facto laws, 597, 942; thinks clause for settlement of State controversies unnecessary, 608; insists on validity of debts, 615; wants judicial power to extend to equity, 622; moves jurisdiction of Supreme Court extend to cases involving Constitution, 624; on committee on mutual recognition, 633; thinks Vermont must come into the Union, 640; moves admission of States already formed, 642; on committee on style, 694, 949; submits report of committee on style, 702; on sumptuary laws, 718; on committee on sumptuary laws, 718; reports provision for ratification, 720; signs Constitution, 951, 1002.

Jones, John, speaker of Virginia Senate, 70.

Jones, Walter, appointed delegate to Annapolis convention, 38.

Jones, Willie, appointed delegate from North Carolina, 73, 74, 76, 77, 86.

Journals of convention, disposition of, 744.

Journals of legislature, publication of, 519, 520; to be secret only in Senate, proposed, rejected, 722.

Judiciary, national, agreed to, 153; single court proposed, 153; clause amended, 198; to be bound by national laws, 391; qualifications for, committed, 460; proposed, 749; to be established, agreed to, 753; establishment and general powers, postponed, 767; report of committee of whole, 880; establishment of, considered, 927; establishment, duration, compensation and jurisdiction, agreed to with amendments, 944;

    Appointment of, by legislature, considered, 153, 154, 155, 768; struck out, 754; by Senate, discussed, 198, 400, 432; agreed to, 768; by Executive, proposed, 403, 754, 849; postponed, 849; by Executive with consent of Senate, 403, 429, 430, 431, 432.

    Compensation of, discussed, 155, 403, 623; not to be changed during term of office, 403; may be increased, 404, 624.

    Impeachment of, 596, 625; clause for removal, rejected, 623.

    Inferior tribunals of, considered, 157, 405; provision for, struck out, 158; legislature to have power to establish, 158, 159; agreed to, 405, 558; establishment of, struck out, 755; to be appointed by legislatures, agreed to, 755.

    Juries, crimes to be tried by, 626; in civil cases, 716; to retain trial by, rejected, 733.

    Jurisdiction of, discussed, 198, 405, 596; power to declare laws unconstitutional, debated, 147; power to declare laws void, rejected, 548, 549, 551; to extend to equity, 622; appellate jurisdiction, 625; to extend to cases under Constitution, 624; jurisdiction of, agreed to, 768; provision for trial of criminal offenses, amended, 945.

    Negative of, to possess joint negative power with Executive, proposed, rejected, 852.

    Revisionary power, as council of revision, 147; revisionary power, 429; to be associated with Executive in revisionary power, 147, 152, 165, 167, 422, 752, 753, 756, 848, 849; rejected, 548, 756, 849.

    Supreme tribunal, agreed to, 400; term of office, 154, 403, 623; proposed, 849

Kean, John, votes against New York resolution for revising Articles of Confederation, 45.

King, Rufus, Massachusetts, votes in favor of New York resolution for revising Articles of Confederation, 45; appointed delegate from Massachusetts, 56, 57, 85; character sketch of, 96; attends, 109; favors revisionary power for Executive, 166; moves reconsideration of election of Executive, 178; favors eligibility of Executive for second term, 412, 444; opposes short term for Executive, 415; favors seven-year term for Executive, 847; opposes impeachability of Executive, 419, 420; thinks State legislatures may vote for Executive, 443; suggest 20-year term for Executive, 444; would postpone question of election of Executive, 448; moves ineligibility of electors to office, 672; would amend clause relative to reelection of Executive, 673; thinks Executive should have pardoning power over treason, 732; would give Executive sole negative, 752; on principle of representation, 122; thinks election of Senate by State legislatures impracticable, 128; would grant suffrage in first branch according to some equitable ratio of representative, 185, 763; agreed to, 189, 764; opposes State compensation of legislature, 257; opposes election of lower House as States may direct, 253, 793; favors expunction of ineligibility clause relating to lower House, 261, 263, 797; opposes amendment to eligibility clause, 802; opposes fixing representation, 332; on committee on representation, 334, 346; thinks Southern States entitled to representation for slaves, 346; reports on representation, 346; objects to basis of representation, 356; opposes blacks as three-fifths in representation, 360; would not tie legislatures in fixing representation, 366; favors limiting representation, 374; on representation in the lower House, 900; moves vote per capita in Senate, 439; favors infrequent meeting of legislatures, 484; opposes slave representation, 495; thinks legislature should regulate elections, 510; favors less than a majority for quorum, 515; agrees to number for quorum, 516; moves sole power over treason be vested in legislature, 578; moves ineligibility of legislators to new offices, 657; rejected, 659; favors ineligibility of legislators for new or increased offices, 659; moves legislature consent to purchase forts, 667; thinks influence of small States balance, 671; defends Senate, 684; opposes change in representation, 729; favors increased representation, 741; thinks convention will end if equality of vote in Senate is adopted, 834; opposes inclusion of judiciary in council of revision, 93; opposes negative for judiciary on legislative acts, 147; favors establishment of inferior tribunals, 159; objects to rule for yeas and nays, 111; favors reference of Constitution to State legislatures for ratification, 95; favors ratification of Constitution by conventions, 156, 438, 649, 754; discusses National Government, 238; expects delegates from New Hampshire, 306; opposes State sovereignty, 313; censures Bedford, 316; favors admission of new States, 332; thinks New Hampshire will increase, 346; thinks Government will act on people, 377; opposes property qualification for office, 460; moves seat of government be fixed, 520; favors assumption of State debts, 565; thinks unlocated land should be given up, 566; on committee on assumption of State debts, 566; thinks definition of treason unnecessary, 577; asks definition of direct taxation, 580; opposes taxation by representation, 583; opposes slavery clause, 592; on committee on navigation acts, 595; explains power over militia, 599; thinks slave trade dependent on navigation laws, 618; thinks new States must observe contract, 628; opposes power to tax exports with consent of States, 631; favors ratification by all States, 648; on committee on postponed measures, 655; moves limitation on treaties affecting rights, 688; moves to strike out provision concerning treaties of peace, 688; on committee on style, 694, 949; would submit constitution to Congress, 698; thinks Congress need not approve Constitution, 700; opposes suspension from office of impeached persons, 721; wants treasurer appointed by legislature, 722; thinks power to grant charters of incorporation unnecessary, 724; thinks publication of expenditures impracticable, 727; on disposition of journals, 744; moves rejection of New Jersey plan, 785; agreed to, 785; declares many essential rights already vested in Congress, 786; thinks General Government may be so constituted as to preserve State governments, 837; on Articles of Confederation, 859n; discusses powers and objects of convention, 877; thinks equality is vice of confederation, 909; states object of Virginia plan, 929; notes of, in federal convention, 844–878; signs Constitution, 951, 1002.

Lands, fund from western, 274; power over, 563.

Langdon, John, New Hampshire, appointed delegate from New Hampshire, 56, 85; character sketch of, 96; attends, 433; would commit question of Executive, 456; favors election of Executive by people, 610; opposes disqualification of debtors, 463; thinks seat of government should not be at State capital, 465; opposes State compensation of legislature, 543; opposes paper money, 557; favors power to suppress rebellion, 561; on committee on assumption of State debts, 566; does not fear army, 568; favors power over militia, 570; opposes taxation by representation, 580; would reduce the representation of New Hampshire, 583; opposes taxation of exports, 584, 585; opposes slave trade, 593; on committee on navigation acts, 595; favors Federal control of militia, 600; thinks State executives ought to be appointed by General Government, 605; would pay debts, 615; thinks provision for slave trade dependent on navigation laws, 618; on committee on imposts, 619; favors conditional admission of new States, 639; thinks new States may be created within old, 640; thinks Vermont should come into the Union, 640; thinks vessel need not clear from its own State, 654; moves additional representation, 729; insists States can not lay duties on tonnage, 731; signs Constitution, 951, 1002.

Lansing, John, jr., New York, appointed delegate from New York, 59, 60, 85; character sketch of, 98, 99; attends, 136; supports Paterson plan, 207; opposes National Government, 241; moves single legislature, 241; thinks voting in legislature should be by States, 290; would commit question of representation in Senate, 322; sick, 755; thinks federal and national systems now contrasted, 769; contrasts plans for government, 770, 771, 901; moves that power of legislation be vested in the United States in Congress, 787; rejected, 791; opposes Virginia plan, 787; would determine question of Federal or National Government, 819; consideration postponed, 821; motion lost, 826; expects no good from appointment of committee to consider representation, 840; leaves convention, 843; signs notes of Yates on convention, 843; wants federal system, 917; moves powers of legislation be vested in the United States in Congress, 920.

Laurens, Henry, signs Articles of Confederation, 37.

Laws, general, power to make, 575.

Lee, Francis Lightfoot, signs Declaration of Independence, 26; signs Articles of Confederation, 37.

Lee, Richard Henry, introduces resolution proposing a Declaration of Independence, 21; signs Declaration of Independence, 26; signs Articles of Confederation, 37.

Legislature, National, each branch to possess right of originating acts, 287; agreed to, 750; postponed, 939; rule of suffrage considered, 286; convening clause agreed to, 486; yeas and nays discussed, 518; adjournment of, 520, 939; seat of government, 520, 521; report of committee of whole, 880; establishment of, considered, 927; enacting style, agreed to, 939.

    Attendance of Members, agreed to, 517.

    Compensation of, to be paid from National Treasury, proposed, 194; considered, 256; to be fixed by legislature, rejected, 259; adequate compensation agreed to, 259; national compensation, rejected, 259; by States, proposed, 543; by Nation, agreed to, 545; rate discussed, 545; $5 per day suggested, rejected, 545; $4 per day, rejected, 545; to be equal in both Houses, 545; higher pay for Senate proposed, 546; to be paid from National Treasury, agreed to, 939.

    Disqualifications, Members to be ineligible for State offices, rejected, 195; to be ineligible to office under National Government for one year after termination of term, 195; of Members to offices, debated, 536; ineligibility to offices, postponed, 939.

Legislature, National—Continued.
> Elections, mode of, 249, 509; agreed to, 509; joint ballot favored, 482; election, quorum, and rules, agreed to; 939; provision for, agreed to, 938.
> Expulsion of Members, considered, 517; by two-thirds agreed to, 517.
> Journal of proceedings, debated, 519, 520; publication permitted, 520; to keep journal, 939.
> Money bills, debated, 499, 502; to originate in first branch, defeated, 500; reconsidered, 500; provision for, agreed to, 503; to originate only in first branch, rejected, 535; power of Senate to amend, rejected, 536.
> Negative of, on State laws, discussed, 174, 390, 758, 855, 916, 931; agreed to, 931; rejected, 178, 391, 856; mutual negative of branches considered, 482; clause struck out, 873; on State laws, 604.
> Powers of, debated, 129, 482, 946; general, 388, 389; of confederation, 384, 750; to legislate where States are incompetent, considered, 130, 384, 750; agreed to, 750; to use force against State failing to fulfil its obligations, considered, 130; postponed, 931; to provide for amending constitution, debated, 190; postponed, 191; each House to originate bills, 546, 814; agreed to, 546; to revise acts by association with Executive, proposed, 547; rejected, 548; of taxation, 552; agreed to, 555; to tax exports, discussed, 584; prohibited, 588; to tax by requisition, 583; taxation clause reported, 660; to emit bills, rejected, 557; to borrow money, agreed to, 557; to define piracies, agreed to, 560; to appoint treasurer, 558; struck out, 723; to provide for appointments by lower officers, 733; to suppress rebellion, discussed, 560; agreed to, 561; defined, 561; rejected, 561; of war, considered, 561; agreed to, 562; of peace, rejected, 563; of incorporation, 563; to grant charters of incorporation, proposed, 724; rejected, 725; over seat of government, 563; over copyrights, inventions, forts, public lands, Indians, 563; over militia, 563, 569, 580, 598, 603, 725; to raise armies, 567; to maintain navy, agreed to, 568; over debts, 564, 581, 605, 614; to safeguard creditors, 564; over stages, 564; to grant letters of marque, 564; to require judicial opinions, 572; to judge privileges of Members, 571, 665; to make sumptuary laws, proposed, 574, 718; to define treason, 575; to make laws, 575; to establish offices, rejected, 575; to take census, 580; to make laws where States are incompetent, 595; to fulfil engagements of old Government, 597; to emit bills of credit, 628; to prohibit the taxation of imports by States, 629; rejected, 630; to prohibit States from taxing imports and exports without consent of legislature, agreed to, 630; to prohibit taxation of imports and exports with consent but for use of United States, 630; rejected, 631; to pass navigation acts, 633; agreed to, 638; to admit new States, 638; agreed to, 644; to regulate commerce, 654; over bankruptcy, 655, 657; to make treaties, 660; to convene legislature in special session, agreed to, 693; to dig canals, 724; rejected, 725; to establish university, rejected, 725; forbidden to pass ex post facto laws, 726; forbidden to enact any legislation impairing the validity of contracts, 728; to enact laws over veto by two-thirds vote, agreed to, 753; general powers, postponed, 767; powers of, postponed, 814; to possess legislative rights vested in Congress by confederation and wherever States are incompetent, agreed to, 931; to legislate where the harmony of the United States may be disrupted by individual legislation, agreed to, 931; to pass acts over veto, agreed to, 939; general powers, discussed, amended and agreed to, 939–942; to give no preference in duties, 944; committed, 944; general powers, 946.
> Property qualifications, considered, 511; reconsidered, 939; clause struck out, 514; in representation, discussed, rejected, 331.
> Quorum, discussed, 514, 939; number rejected, 517.
> Qualifications for Members, postponed, 127; discussed, 458; eligibility of Members, postponed, 543; eligibilityo f Members to civil office, 655; Members forbidden to hold other office, rejected, 657; to hold no other Federal office, agreed to, 659; citizenship qualifications, 939.

Legislature, National—Continued.
>Representation, proportional, proposed, 122; discussed, 180–184, 930; agreed to, 189; both branches to have equal representation, agreed to, 190; equal vote of States rejected, 303; question of representation committed, 334; by wealth and numbers, 371; wealth struck out, 374; representation reconsidered, 388.
>Term, duration of, for first branch, considered, 192; triennial election, 193.
>Time of meeting, 483, 873; to fix time for meeting, 485; agreed to, 934; annual meeting, 486; discussed, 508; agreed to, 509.
>To consist of two branches, discussed and agreed to, 124, 241, 252, 750, 792, 862, 930; single chamber rejected, 248.

Legislature, House of Representatives, compensation of, discussed, 193; to be fixed by legislature, agreed to, 194; "liberal" struck out, 194; States to have equal vote in, rejected, 303; representation, 330; ratio of representation, 331, 334; postponed, 334; to be regulated by legislature, 334; representation committed, 346; increase in representation, rejected, 350; apportionment agreed to, 351; question of blacks in representation, 353; equal representation of blacks rejected, 355; representation by wealth, rejected, 360; census for representation approved, 360; blacks to be counted as three-fifths, 360; rejected, 362; census agreed to, 362; equal representation of blacks, rejected, 367; to be counted as three-fifths, agreed to, 383; representation by taxation, agreed to, 495; representation by slaves, 497; representation by free inhabitants, rejected, 499; each State to have at least one representative, agreed to, 499; reconsideration of representation, motion lost, 694, 720; representation reconsidered, 728; representation changed, 741; right of suffrage to be based on some equitable ratio of representation, 814; agreed to, 826; representation in, to be referred to committee, proposed, 840; report of committee on representation, 841; representation in, discussed, 865; representation not to be according to Articles of Confederation, agreed to, 868; ratio of representation in, discussed, 869; representation in, discussed, 900; ratio of representation altered, 951; election to, considered, 125, 157; election to, by people, agreed to, 127, 254; election by State legislatures, 159, 165; clause forbidding reelection for several years, expunged, 195; to be elected by people, agreed to, 750; to be elected by State legislatures, 755; rejected, 756; to be chosen in proportion to number, 763; in proportion to contribution, 763; to be elected as State legislatures may direct, proposed, 793; agreed to, 794; clause agreed to, 794; to be elected by people, agreed to, 845; to be elected by State legislatures, proposed, 850; rejected, 852; to be chosen as State legislatures may direct, proposed, 862; rejected, 863; to be elected by people, agreed to, 930; to be elected as State legislatures may direct 920; qualifications of electors of, 934; must have been citizen for seven years before election, 937; clause on vacancies agreed to, 938; age limit of Members struck out, 193; age of Members discussed, 260; Members to be 25 years of age, agreed to, 260, 797; ineligibility of Members to offices, discussed, 260; rejected, 261; ineligibility during term and for one year thereafter, discussed, 262; rejected, 266; ineligibility clause agreed to, 266; ineligibility during term, agreed to 266; for one year thereafter, rejected, 266; ineligibility for office, agreed to, 767; Members ineligible for reelection for one year after expiration of term, agreed to, 767; clause expunged, reconsidered, 30 years agreed to, 767; ineligibility for two years, agreed to, 797; expunction of ineligibility clause proposed, 797; rejected, 800; ineligibility for State offices, struck out, 800; ineligibility for any office whose emoluments were increased by National Legislature during their term, 800; rejected, 803; eligibility clause, as amended, agreed to, 803; Members to be ineligible for office for one year after expiration of term, rejected, 803; residence of Members debated, 492; seven years proposed, 493, 937; short period rejected, 493; inhabitant submitted for resident, 494; one year proposed, rejected, 494; three years rejected, 494; representation in, 494; three years citizenship to be required, 514; length of citizenship for service in, considered, 523; Hamilton's motion rejected, 525; nine years rejected, 525; four years rejected, 525; eligibility of those now citizens, 525; motion lost, 528; five years proposed, rejected, 528; duration of term discussed, 254; two-year term, agreed to, 256; three-year term, discussed, 766; seven-year term, proposed, 767; three-year term reconsidered, 767; two-year term proposed, 794; agreed to, 795; duration of term, discussed, 863; Members to be paid by National Treasury, 766, 796, 800; rejected, 796, 797, 800; money bills in, 335, 522; money bills reconsidered, 523, 528; to originate revenue bills, 693, 728, 870, 872; amendment relative to direct taxing power, 719; may originate bills, agreed to, 814, 930; qualifications of electors for, to be fixed by States, proposed, 873; discussed, 875; to possess sole power of raising and appropriating money, clause struck out, 937; to have sole power of impeachment, agreed, to, 938; to elect President in event of tie vote, agreed to, 948.

Legislature, Senate, motion to consider, rejected, 136; considered, 274; election to, considered, 127, 168; by State legislatures, rejected, 129; by State legislatures, agreed to, 173; Members to be elected by lower branch, postponed, 750; to be chosen by State legislatures, 756, 757, 809, 852, 854; to be chosen by districts, 757; motion to postpone mode of election, lost, 757; mode of appointment discussed, 806; to be elected by electors chosen by people, proposed, 807; to be chosen by House of Representatives from persons nominated by State legislatures, rejected, 852; to be elected by people, rejected, 854; to be elected by lower House from persons nominated by State legislatures, rejected, 930; age and citizenship agreed to, 195, 528; senators to be 30 years of age, agreed to, 809; qualifications for, agreed to, 938; duration of term agreed to, 197; to serve without salary, rejected, 197; seven year term proposed, agreed to, 197; reconsidered, 278; six-year term, rejected, 278, 809; duration of term discussed, 279, 809; to go out in classes, agreed to, 809; nine-year term, rejected, 284; six-year term, agreed to, 284; five-year term, rejected, 809; duration of term, discussed, 810; nine-year term proposed, 810; rejected, 813; five-year term with biennial rotation, agreed to, 813; to receive fixed stipends, agreed to, 813; to receive a compensation, agreed to, 813; compensation discussed, 197, 277, 284; State compensation, rejected, 285; to be paid from National Treasury, 767, 813; rejected, 813; duration of term, agreed to, 938; eligibility to state offices considered, 286; struck out, 814; ineligibility to be the same as in lower House, 198; ineligibility to national offices, agreed to, 287; to State offices, rejected, 287; term agreed to, 504; citizenship of members, 504; 14 years' citizenship requirement, rejected, 508; 13 years rejected, 508; 10 years rejected, 508; 9 years' citizenship agreed to, 508; clause agreed to, 509; rule of suffrage, discussed, 190, 304; question postponed, 826; vote in, considered 306, 334, 368, 376, 502, 826, 837, 840, 841, 868, 870, 872, 907, 922, 938, 950; equal vote by States, proposed, 317, 826; rejected, 317, 837; equal vote in, agreed to, 340, 938; question of one vote for each State, 339; two votes for each State, agreed to, 440; vote per capita, discussed, 439, 503; agreed to, 440, 504; Members to be chosen by legislatures, agreed to, 277; age, 30 years, agreed to, 277; term of, considered, 277; representation in, considered, 277; postponed, 277; question of representation committed, 323, 837, 840; committee on representation, 323, 840; report of committee on representation, 323, 841; representation proposed, 376; one member from each State, discussed, 440; each State to have one vote in, proposed, 868; discussed, 870; Pinckney's apportionment, rejected, 872; representation in, discussed, 907; object of, discussed, 922; representation in, agreed to, 938; right to enter dissent, 518; rejected, 519; appointments by, 603; power to make treaties, discussed, 605, 942; power over controversies between States, discussed, 608; clause rejected, 943; power of impeachment, 660, 691; to try impeachments, postponed, 946; clause agreed to, 693; to make treaties in association with Executive, clause reported, 661; appointment to office, 661; to participate in treaty making, 685; power to originate money bills, rejected, 200; money bills, considered, 324, 376; money bills, power to amend, 546; postponed, 547; Franklin's plan, 313; Pinckney's plan rejected, 383;

equal vote agreed to, 383; secret journals, 519; vacancies to be filled by State legislatures, rejected, 501; to be filled by legislatures or executives, agreed to, 502; quorum to be two-thirds, rejected, 690; may originate bills agreed to, 814; general powers of, discussed, 947; no State to be deprived of equal suffrage in, agreed to, 950.
Letter to accompany Constitution, 712.
Lewis, Francis, signs Declaration of Independence, 26; signs Articles of Confederation, 36.
L'Hommedieu, Ezra, would refer ratifications to committee, 1061.
Liberty of the press, 572; to be observed, 726; clause rejected, 726.
Livingston, Philip, signs Declaration of Independence, 26.
Livingston, William, New Jersey, appointed delegate from New Jersey, 61, 62, 85; character sketch of, 99; attends, 153; on committee on assumption of State debts, 566; delivers report of committee, 580; on committee on navigation acts, 595; delivers report of committee of eleven, 608; on committee on sumptuary laws, 718; signs Constitution, 951, 1002.
Lovell, James, signs Articles of Confederation, 36.
Lynch, Thomas, jr., signs Declaration of Independence, 26.
Madison, James, Virginia, appointed delegate to Annapolis convention, 38; attends Annapolis convention, 39, 43; votes in favor of New York resolution for revising Articles of Confederation, 45; appointed delegate from Virginia to federal convention, 71, 86; character sketch of, 105; attends, 109, 746; favors single Executive, aided by council, 91; doubts utility of veto power, 93; favors inclusion of judiciary with Executive for council of revision, 94; on powers of Executive, 133; opposes removability of Executive by State legislatures, 142; wants independent Executive, 397, 412; on ratio of electors of Executive, 416; favors impeachability of Executive, 418; favors election of Executive by electors, 449; would vote for two men for Executive, 454; thinks Executive should make treaties, 606; objects to Senate power in selecting Executive, 610; moves Executive only be empowered to fill existing offices, 613; moves modification of presidential oath, 622; objects to President of Senate as successor of Executive, 621; objects to election of Executive by majority vote, 662; opposes eventual election of Executive by Senate, 670; on eventual elections of Executive, 671; moves that electors not voting be not counted 672; moves two-thirds of Senate be present when voting for Executive, 677; would increase representation of States to vote for Executive, 681; favors executive council, 687; opposes impeachment of Executive for maladministration, 691; opposes trial of Executive by Senate, 691; would not allow Executive pardoning power over treason, 732; opposes absolute negative for Executive, 753, 848; favors single Executive with council, 845; proposes seven-year term for Executive, 847; would associate judiciary with Executive in negative power, 848; favors power of negative for Executive and judiciary, 852; favors appointment of members of first branch of National Legislature by people, 87, 89; doubts practicability of defining limits and powers of Federal Legislature, 90; on principle of representation, 122; opposes equal representation, 123; favors election of first branch of legislature by people, 126, 851, 916; on elections to Senate, 128; on definition of powers of National Legislature, 130; considers election of one branch of legislature by people necessary, 161; favors small Senate, 169; opposes election of Senate by State legislatures, 171; would elect members of lower House every three years, 192, 766; moves legislature fix compensation of members, 193; agreed to, 194; favors seven-year term for Senate, 196; opposes annual elections for lower House, 255; favors national compensation of legislature, 258; would fix compensation of legislature in Constitution, 259; moves ineligibility of members of first branch of legislature during term of office and for one year thereafter, 262; opposes absolute ineligibility of members of legislature to offices, 264; on suffrage in Senate, 276; would consider question of representation in Senate, 277; explains object of Senate, 279; opposes State compensation of Senate;

285; objects to equality of vote for States in legislature, 290; wants proportional representation in Senate, 309; insists on proportional representation in Senate, 314; would not commit question of representation in Senate, 322; insists that representation of States be considered, 340; proposes numbers as basis of representation in first branch and wealth in Senate, 345; on committee on representation, 346; moves increase in representation, 349; would fix standard of representation, 358; favors Pinckney's plan for Senate, 377; favors proportional representation, 379; favors continuance of Congress, 406; favors exclusion of debtors from legislature, 459; favors annual meeting of legislature, 483; favors fixing time of meeting of legislature by law, rather than by Constitution, 484; wants legislature to meet in May, 485; seconds motion providing for meeting time in Constitution unless changed by law, 485; favors residents for members of legislature, 492; opposes seven years' residence for legislature, 493; objects to rule of representation, 496; would limit representation, 496; moves that vacancies in Senate be filled by State legislatures or Executives, 502; would leave question of citizenship for Senate to be fixed by legislature, 505; would have lower House name time of meeting, 509; thinks legislature should regulate elections, 509; thinks qualifications for legislature should be fixed, 513, 514; moves legislature compel attendance, 517; moves expulsion of members of legislature only by two-thirds vote, 517; on journals of legislature, 519; favors national compensation of members of legislature, 543; would give legislature power to declare war, 562; on representation, 583; proposes two-thirds of Senate for quorum, 690; favors reconsideration of representation, 694; doubts if legislature should judge privileges of members, 665; thinks Congress can propose amendments, 735; opposes motion for special provisos, 736; opposes election of lower House by State legislatures, 756; would fix standard of representation and commit details, 764; favors seven-year term for first branch, 767; opposes election of lower House by States, 793; would pay legislators from National Treasury, 796; opposes fixing of compensation by legislature, 796; thinks no office open to member which is created during his tenure of office, 798; moves amendment to eligibility clause for lower House, 800; supports motion, 801, 802; rejected, 803; moves postponement of election of Senate, 808; rejected, 809; thinks Senate should protect land holders, 810, 811; favors long term for Senators, 811; on eligibility of Senators for State offices, 814; opposes equality of vote in Senate, 831; thinks confederation defective, 832; thinks States will usurp powers of General Government of equality of vote in Senate is granted, 834; opposes appointment of committee to consider representation, 840; attacks compromise on representation, 842; favors election of first branch by people, 844; opposes election of Senators by State legislatures, 853; opposes election of Representatives by State legislatures, 862; on representation in lower House, 866; opposes equal vote for States in Senate, 868; would omit provision fixing time of meeting for legislature, 873; on representation in lower House, 900; on danger of large States combining, 906; on representation in Senate, 908; on representation compromise, 909, 910; opposes long term of citizenship for Senators, 938; moves revision of acts by Executive and judiciary, 152, 547; moves appointment of judiciary by Senate, 154, 768; agreed to, 768; prefers appointment of judiciary by Senate, 754; favors inferior tribunals in national judiciary, 158; moves legislature be given power to institute inferior tribunals, 158; favors association of judiciary with Executive in revision of laws, 165, 423, 426, 848; moves that judges of national judiciary be appointed by Senate, 198; agreed to, 199; moves that jurisdiction of judiciary extend to cases concerning revenue and impeachment, 198; agreed to, 198; suggests appointment of judiciary by Executive and Senate, 402; moves appointment of judiciary by executive with two-thirds of Senate, 403; favors appointment of judges by Executive with consent of Senate, 430, 432; opposes increase in salaries of judges, 623; doubts if jurisdiction of judiciary should extend to cases under Constitution, 625; favors qualified negative of Executive on laws, 149; favors negative for National Legislature on State laws, 174, 178, 390, 628, 717, 758, 855; on appointment of judiciary, 849; favors amendment to mutual negative clause, 483; moves negative power extend to resolutions; 551; favors commitment of negative on State laws, 604; favors three-fourths vote to set aside Executive's negative, 715; moves expunction of clause giving each House a negative on other, agreed to, 873; suggests negative on State laws be vested in Senate, 759; defends taxation by representation, 369; favors taxation of exports, 553, 585; proposes taxation of exports by two-thirds vote, 588; insists on power of legislature to tax imports, 629; opposes power of States to tax imports, 630; would allow States to levy export duties to pay charges, 717; on control over militia, 570, 599, 600, 602; would have States appoint officers of militia, 601; would allow money bills to originate in Senate, 199; opposes origination of money bills in lower House, 324; opposes provision for money bills, 500, 502; thinks Senate may amend money bills, 531; objects to ratifications of treaties, 606; suggests distinction in power to make treaties, 607; would amend treaty clause, 618; favors treaties of peace by majority of Senate, 685; opposes power to use force against the State, 131; favors ratification of Constitution by conventions, 156, 438, 754; moves amendment to resolution guaranteeing republican government and territory to each State, agreed to, 190; moves amendment to territorial guaranty clause, 765; would guarantee republican constitution and existing laws of each State, agreed to, 765; discusses powers of convention, 226; opposes New Jersey plan, 226, 920; thinks States will increase with National Government, 250; discusses State rights, 299; would guarantee States against violence, 407; favors property qualification for office, 461; favors franchise for freeholders, 489; thinks seat of government must be fixed, 521; favors liberal policy towards foreigners, 524; thinks State obligations are obligations of National Government, 526; thinks bills of credit should not be legal tender, 556; moves to strike out punishment for piracies, 558; would define piracies, 559; proposes additional powers for legislature, 563; moves power to establish offices, 575; favors power to define treason, 575; thinks treason should be confined to Nation, 576; on treason, 579; on committee on navigation acts, 595; thinks provision to fulfill engagements of old Government necessary, 598; opposes slave trade, 616; opposes idea of men as property, 618; would forbid violation of contracts, 629; thinks States should be forbidden to lay embargoes, 629; thinks commercial system too complex, 630; moves legislature provide for execution of judgments, 632; favors navigation acts, 636; favors admission of new States on basis of equality, 638; opposes mention of western country, 644; thinks ratification must come from majority, 648; favors ratification by conventions, 649; thinks vessels may clear from different States, 654; on committee on postponed measures, 655; on committee on style, 694, 949; moves mode of amendment, 696; opposes suspension of impeached persons, 721; proposes university, 725; proposes power to grant charters, 724; on standing army, 725; would publish account of expenditures, 727; thinks commerce ought to be under one authority, 730; discusses powers of convention, 783; opposes New Jersey plan, 784; thinks greatest danger is from encroachment of States on National Government, 792; favors General Government, 792; defends Virginia plan, 820, 822; discusses National Government, 823; declares real danger lies in opposition of northern and southern interests, 828; thinks Federal Government will not suffice, 858; would protect National Government from States, 862; discusses sovereignty of States, 867; would intrust suffrage rights to freeholders only, 874; thinks elective monarchies unhappy, 913; opposes motion for establishment of more effective government, 930; on treaties, 943; journal of proceedings of federal convention, 109–745; signs Constitution, 951, 1002.

Manufactures, encouragement of by imposts, 630.
Marque and reprisal, letters of, 564.
Marchant, Henry, signs Articles of Confederation, 36.

Martin, Alexander, North Carolina, appointed delegate from North Carolina, 73, 74, 76, 77, 86; character sketch of, 106; attends, 109, 746; seconds motion for ineligibility of members of lower House to office during term and for one year thereafter, 263; opposes fixing seat of government at State capital, 464; declares States must meet as equals, 786; would support State governments at expense of Union if two are incompatible, 789.

Martin, Luther, Maryland, appointed delegate from Maryland, 68, 86; character sketch of, 103; attends, 179; moves election of Executive by electors, 395; moves to consider eligibility of Executive to second term, 400; favors ineligibility of Executive for second term, 408; moves ineligibility of Executive for second term, 414, 444; moves ratio of electors be committed, 416; proposes 11-year term for Executive, 444; favors election of legislature by State legislatures, 252; on committee on representation, 323, 840, 872; would vote on whole of report of committee on representation, 324, 842; asks basis of ratio of representation, 344; opposes voting per capita in Senate, 440; favors State compensation for Senate, 545; would have judges appointed by Senate, 402; favors equality of vote in Senate, 834; thinks convention must end unless suffrage equality is granted in Senate, 837; thinks States should have equal vote in lower House, 865; presents restrictive clause on power of legislature over commerce, 941; opposes establishment of inferior judicial tribunals, 405; opposes revisionary power for judiciary, 426; moves supreme court have jurisdiction over land cases, 645; would postpone question of money bills, 335; wishes to consider money bills and vote in Senate together, 375; opposes oath from State officials to observe Constitution, 191; discusses National Government, 239, 814, 905; insists on sovereignty of States, 245; thinks General Government must operate through State government, 287; thinks States equal, 303; insists on equal rights for small States in Senate, 318; favors compromise, 338, 374; moves supremacy of national law, 391; would support States at expense of Union, 861; thinks final authority rests with State governments, 921; thinks States should suppress rebellions, 407; favors disqualification of debtors, 462; asks meaning of duties and imposts, 552; opposes power to suppress rebellion in States, 560; moves to limit army in time of peace, 568; moves confession as ground for conviction for treason, 579; favors requisition, 583; proposes tax on importation of slaves, 588; on committee on navigation acts, 595; favors State control of militia, 601; moves impartial treatment of ports of entry, 619; moves power of pardon after conviction, withdraws motion, 621; moves to admit new States by two-thirds vote, 639; thinks new States may be created within old, 639; would commit question of creation of new States, 641; thinks western country may separate from States, 642; moves power to establish States, 643; insists on ratification by State legislatures, 650; opposes Constitution, 652; confers with colleagues from Maryland on report of committee of detail, 932; leaves for New York, 934; returns to convention, 939; anecdote, 952.

Mason, George, Virginia, appointed delegate to Annapolis convention, 38; appointed delegate from Virginia to federal convention, 71, 86; character sketch of, 104; attends, 109, 746; favors seven-year term for Executive, 135, 847; favors election of Executive by people, 135; opposes dependence of Executive upon legislature, 142; opposes executive power, 150; would protect Executive against legislature, 167; opposes popular election of Executive, 394; opposes Executive term during good behavior, 398; favors impeachability of Executive, 417; favors ineligibility of Executive for continuous reelection, 452; favors election of Executive by legislature, 456; favors seven-year term and ineligibility, 457; moves modification of presidential oath, 622; thinks Executive will be elected by Senate, 663; would deprive Senate of power of eventual election of Executive, 669; moves eventual election of Executive be limited to three candidates, 671; thinks system of electors autocratic, 672; proposes executive council, 686, 948; rejected, 687, 949; thinks Executive should not be given power to pardon treason, 732; opposes negative for Executive, 753, 848; objects to rule for yeas and nays, 111; favors election of larger branch of legislature by people, 125; favors election of Senate by State legislatures, 173; opposes consent of legislature to amend Constitution, 190; postponed, 191; opposes fixing of compensation by legislature, 194; favors election of legislature by people, 253; favors biennial elections for lower House, 256; moves members of first branch be 25 years of age, 260, 797; favors ineligibility of members of lower House to office, 261; thinks fit characters for offices will be found, 265; suggests property qualification for Senate, 286, 813; on committee on representation, 323, 840, 872; insists on compromise on representation, 329; would consider vote in Senate, 334; favors increase in representation, 350; thinks basis of representation should be fixed, 352; would count slaves in representation, 354; opposes wealth as basis for representation, 356; would fix standard of representation, 359; opposes three Senators from each State, 440; on qualifications for legislature, 458, 459; favors annual meeting of legislature, 485, 873; favors seven years' citizenship for members of legislature, 492; thinks members of legislature must be residents of States, 494; proposes one-year residence, 494; favors vote per capita in Senate, 503; favors long term of citizenship for Senators, 505, 938; favors majority for quorum, 515; approves expulsion of legislators, 517; favors yeas and nays at demand of one-fifth, 518; on publicity in legislature, 520; thinks members of legislature should be ineligible to office, 536; would give legislature power over bills of credit, 556; thinks treasurer should be appointed by legislature, 558; opposes power of punishment for piracies, 559; would give legislature power over funds, 565; thinks Senate has too much power, 732; opposes election of lower House by State legislatures, 755; favors popular election of members of first branch of legislature, 87; opposes selection of Senators from first branch, 89; favors election of Senate by State legislatures, 757; opposes election of first branch by States, 793; favors two-year term for first branch, 794; moves members of first branch receive adequate compensation paid from National Treasury, agreed to, 796; moves Members of lower House be ineligible for two years, agreed to, 797; favors ineligibility clause for Representatives, 798; opposes amendment to eligibility clause, 801, 803; thinks Representatives should be ineligible to office for one year after expiration of term, 803; favors election of Senate by State legislatures, 808; favors election of lower House by people, 844, 850, 915; on question of negative, 852. favors election of Senators by State legislatures, 854, 864; opposes annual election of Representatives, 863; thinks people will never consent to granting extensive powers to Congress alone, 921; opposes equality in Senate, 938; moves power of legislature to make sumptuary laws, rejected, 940; moves navigation acts be not valid without approval of two-thirds of legislature, rejected, 950; opposes appointment of judiciary by Executive, 401; thinks inferior judicial tribunals necessary, 405; favors association of judiciary with Executive in revisionary power, 424, 427; opposes Executive appointment of judges, 432; favors fixed compensation for judges, 624; on regulation of militia, 564; moves power over militia, 569, 571; thinks money bills should originate in lower House, 336; thinks Senate may not originate money bills, 499; favors provision for money bills, 502; favors elimination of Senate from all revenue legislation, 528; would allow Senate power to amend money bills, 546; would consider money bills, 582; thinks Government should operate on individuals, 121; new Government to operate on people, 161; sees necessity for provision for amending Constitution, 190; thinks State governments must have power of defense, 276; will never consent to destroy State governments, 789; thinks some power must be left in States, 915; favors admission of new States on equal basis, 331; urges compromise, 335; favors census, 370; would guarantee republican constitution to States, 407; favors ratification by people, 434; opposes fixing seat of government at State capital, 464; withdraws motion, 465; opposes mutual negative of branches of legislature, 483; opposes restriction of franchise, 489; opposes confining suffrage rights to freeholders, 874; on qualifications for suffrage, 876; would be cautious in admitting foreigners, 527; thinks treaties may alienate territory, 547; opposes taxation of exports, 552; thinks Government should have power to issue paper money, 557; on committee on assumption of State debts, 566; moves power to make sumptuary laws, 574, 940; on definition of treason, 575; thinks treason may be against a State, 577; moves restriction on treason, 579; on taxation of exports, 587; opposes slavery, 589; opposes power to negative State laws, 604; thinks legislature will pay debts, 614; opposes confining slave trade to three States, 617; would not encourage slave trade 618; on committee on imposts, 620; thinks States may make contracts, 628; thinks States may lay embargoes, 629; thinks States may tax imports, 630; on navigation acts, 635; favors equality of western country, 638; favors ratification by nine States, 651; opposes Constitution, 652; opposes vice president, 682; on impeachment, 691; would make repeal of laws easy, 714; favors bill of rights, 716; moves power to pass sumptuary laws, 718; on committee on sumptuary laws, 718; would give States power to tax exports for inspection charges, 718; fears monopolies, 724; opposes standing armies in time of peace, 725; would expunge ex post facto, 726; favors annual publication of expenditures, 727; favors power of State to lay duties on tonnage, 730; opposes plan for amendment, 735; favors two-third vote for navigation act, rejected, 736; supports Virginia plan, 788; seconds motion for second convention, 737; does not sign, 745, 751.

Mathews, George, Governor of Georgia, 82, 83, 84.

Mathews, John, signs Articles of Confederation, 37.

McClurg, James, Virginia, appointed delegate from Virginia, 72, 86; character sketch of, 104, 105; attends, 109, 746; moves Executive term during good behavior, 396; insists on independence of Executive, 399; would guarantee States against violence, 407; asks what force Executive is to possess, 422.

McHenry, James, Maryland, appointed delegate from Maryland, 67, 86; character sketch of, 103; attends, 110; leaves convention, 931; returns to convention, 931; on committee on assumption of State debts, 566; favors taxation by requisition, 584; would restrict legislature from giving any preference in duties, committed, 944; thinks embargoes permitted, 586; opposes bills of attainder and ex post facto laws, 596; proposes State consent to ports of entry, 619; opposes changing compensation of judges, 623; moves Executive have power to convene legislature in extraordinary session, 693; moves power of States to lay duties on tonnage, 730; confers with colleagues from Maryland on report of committee of detail, 932, 935; wants legislature to have power to erect piers and to preserve the navigability of harbors, 947; signs Constitution, 951, 1002.

Mecklenburg Resolves, 6-9.

Mercer, John Francis, Maryland, appointed delegate from Maryland, 68, 86; attends, 471; opposes free franchise, 491; opposes franchise plan, 491; thinks candidates for lower House should be nominated by State legislatures, 492; opposes seven years' residence in State for members of legislature, 493; opposes residence qualifications, 493; thinks Senate without power, 500; favors less than a majority for quorum, 515; would fix quorum, 516; hopes Senate will only have legislative power, 519; thinks legislature can not agree on seat of government, 522; moves those already citizens be eligible for legislature, 525; favors liberal treatment for foreigners, 527; favors eligibility of legislators to office, 537, 541; opposes power of Senate over treaties, 547; denies power of judiciary to declare a law void, 548; favors revisionary power for judiciary, 548; opposes taxation of exports, 544; favors establishment of post roads, 556; favors paper money, 556; favors appointment of treasurer by Executive, 558; favors power to define crimes, 559; confers with colleagues from Maryland on report of committee of detail, 932, 937.

Meredith, Samuel, votes in favor of New York resolution for revising Articles of Confederation, 45.

Middleton, Arthur, signs Declaration of Independence, 26.

Mifflin, Thomas, Pennsylvania, appointed delegate from Pennsylvania, 63, 64, 65, 85; character sketch of, 100; attends, 110; favors eligibility of members of legislature to office, 536; signs Constitution, 951, 1002.

Militia, power to regulate, 564; discussed, 569; power over, referred to committee, 571; legislature to control, 581; power over, 598; partial Federal control, rejected, 599; uniformity in regulation of, rejected, 601; clause agreed to, 601; State appointment of lower officers, 601; rejected, 602; appointment of all officers, agreed to, 602; to be trained by United States, agreed to, 602; to be called out, 603; power of Executive over, 621.

Minutes, committee to superintend, rejected, 114.

Mitchell, Nathaniel, votes against New York resolution for revising Articles of Confederation, 45.

Mitchell, Stephen M., votes against New York resolution for revising Articles of Confederation, 45.

M'Kean, Thomas, signs Declaration of Independence, 26; signs Articles of Confederation, 37.

Money bills, originating, 324, 335; in first branch, 338, 384, 870; question postponed, 342; discussed, 499; considered, 502; reconsidered, 522, 523, 528; exclusive control of, in first branch, rejected, 536; Senate to have power to amend, rejected, 536; Senate to have power to amend, 546; question postponed, 547; discussed, 582.

Morris, Gouverneur, Pennsylvania, signs Articles of Confederation, 36; appointed delegate from Pennsylvania, 63, 64, 85; character sketch of, 100, 101; attends, 109, 746; opposes election of Executive by legislature, 392; favors election of Executive by people, 392, 393; favors eligibility of Executive for second term, 396, 943; favors Executive term during good behavior, 396; opposes monarchy, 399; on impeachment of Executive, 401; thinks Executive eligible for second term, 408; favors short term for Executive, 415; opposes impeachability of Executive, 417; discusses impeachability of Executive, 418, 421; moves qualifications of Executive electors, 422; opposes rotation in Executive, 453; favors voting for two persons for Executive, 454; favors long term for Executive, 457; favors absolute negative for Executive, 486; opposes election of Executive by legislature, 611; moves that Executive be required to recommend and report to legislature, 612; on correspondence of Executives with States, 620; objects to President of Senate as successor to Executive, 621; explains mode of election of Executive, 662; objects to election of Executive by majority vote, 662; favors eventual election of Executive by Senate, 665; defends mode of election of Executive, 669; favors separate provision for reelection of Executive, 673; defends system of electors, 674; favors inclusion of Senate in appointing, 684; opposes executive council, 687; thinks election of President will prevent maladministration, 691; thinks negative of Executive may be overruled by majority, 714; favors appointment of treasurer by Executive, 722; wants Senate elected by people, 169; favors independent Senate, 319; discusses Senate, 838; opposes report of committee on representation, 334; reports on ratio of representation, 342; would postpone question of representation, 344; explains representation of Georgia, 344; on committee on representation, 346; thinks Southern States have too much representation, 348; opposes basis of representation, 355; opposes fixing of basis of representation, 357; thinks West should not be represented equally, 357; opposes representation of blacks, 364, 371; moves consideration of representation, 388; opposes quotas, 389; thinks property rather than numbers should be basis of representation in lower House, 869; discusses apportionment of representation, 871; would let time of meeting be fixed by legislature, 873; would let States fix qualifications for electors of representatives, 873; on representation in Senate, 910; on qualifications of electors for lower House, 934; approves definition of powers of legislature, 389; opposes negative on State laws by legislature, 390, 391; thinks Congress ought not to be continued, 406; moves vote per capita in Senate, 439; moves three Senators from each

1100

State, 440; opposes election of Executive by legislature, 446; on qualifications for legislature, 459; opposes exclusion of debtors from legislature, 459; would modify mutual negative of branches of legislature, 483; opposes fixing time of meeting of legislature, 484; moves legislature meet in May, 485; favors seven years' citizenship for members of legislature, 492; opposes inhabitants for members of legislature, 492; opposes slave representation, 497; favors motion that vacancies in Senate be filled by legislature or Executive, 502; proposes 14 years' citizenship for Senators, 504, 938; moves first branch of legislature fix time of meeting, 509; opposes property qualifications for legislature, 513; moves number for quorum, 515; favors expulsion by majority, 517; on rule for yeas and nays, 518; on right of dissent in legislature, 518; moves those already citizens be eligible for citizenship, 525; opposes ineligibility of legislators to office, 539, 542; moves eligibility of legislators to army and navy, 542; opposes State compensation of legislature, 543; opposes appointments by Senate, 603; opposes treaty power of Senate, 606; moves power of legislature over public lands, 645; suggests legislature may call convention to amend Constitution, 646; thinks ineligibility of members of legislature to offices will be evaded, 658; thinks legislature should judge privileges of members, 665; opposes originating revenue measures in first branch, 667; favors Vice President for President of Senate, 682, opposes treaties of peace with majority of Senate, 686; favors impeachment trials by Senate, 691; moves that no State be deprived of equal vote in Senate, agreed to, 736; seconds motion for appointment of judges by Executive, 400; thinks salaries of judiciary may be increased, 403, 404; favors appointment of judges by Executive with concurrence of two-thirds of Senate, 403; favors inferior judicial tribunals, 406; wants appointment of judiciary by Executive, 431; favors permanent tenure of judges, 623; favors increase in judges' salaries, 624; would preserve habeas corpus, 627; thinks money bills may originate in either branch, 335; opposes origination of money bills in lower House, 337; thinks money bills may originate in Senate, 499, 546; opposes provision for money bills, 503; favors participation of Senate in money bills, 531; opposes committee to superintend minutes, 114; moves consideration of national union, 120; would consider National Government, 120; defines terms, 121; proposes National Government, 748, 749; agreed to, 749; opposes Federal Government, 929; thinks large estates must prevail, 910; asks Delaware delegates not to withdraw, 123; urges national considerations, 341; thinks mode of census should not be fixed, 351; declares South will insist on slave trade, 361; moves commitment of question of slave trade, 593; would confine slave trade to Carolinas and Georgia, 616; withdraws motion, 617; favors direct taxation by representation, 363, 364; favors federal power of police, 389; opposes guaranteeing State governments, 406; on separation of powers, 428; thinks legislature should not ratify, 437; moves ratification by one convention, 439; on direct taxation, 448; favors property qualification for office, 462; opposes disqualification of debtors, 463; thinks Philadelphia or New York may be seat of government, 464; favors restricted franchise, 488; thinks freeholders only should vote, 876; would establish property qualifications for suffrage, 874; on naturalization, 507, 876; opposes State regulation of elections, 510; thinks seat of government should be fixed, 521; on question of foreigners, 526; on revisionary power, 548; proposes absolute negative for Executive, 549; favors taxation of exports, 553, 554; opposes power to emit bills of credit, 556; opposes paper emissions, 556; favors punishment for counterfeiting, 559; moves power to punish piracies, 559; favors power to suppress rebellion, 560; proposes council of state, 573; opposes sumptuary laws, 574, 940; thinks treason should be defined, 575; favors British definition of treason, 577; favors restriction on treason, 579; favors contribution of States according to representation, 582; favors taxation of exports, 585; on ex post facto laws, 596, 942; opposes bills of attainder, 596; moves provision requiring new government to fulfill obligations of old, 598; thinks treaties are laws, 603; moves power to call out militia, 603; opposes many treaties, 606; insists on payment of debts, 616; thinks legislature may not tax free men imported, 618; thinks States may regulate contracts, 628; moves for mutual recognition of acts by States, 633; opposes navigation acts, 635; moves that new States be admitted under conditions, 638; moves admission of new States, by two-thirds vote, 639; thinks States not to be created from old States, 639; thinks States can not be divided, 640; motion in favor of Vermont, 642; would forbid religious test, 647; thinks contiguous States may ratify constitution, 647; favors having State select mode of ratification, 649; thinks constitution need not have approval of Congress, 651; favors convention, 652; favors second convention to make another constitution, 653; on committee on postponed measures, 655; moves amendment to clause relating to validity of acts of States, 656; favors bankruptcy laws, 657; on committee on style, 694, 949; wishes laws to be stable, 715; thinks States may tax exports to pay charges, 717; explains direct taxation provision, 719; would suspend impeached persons, 721; would define law of nations, 723; opposes creation of university, 725; opposes discrimination against army, 725; opposes publication of expenditures, 727; would allows States to lay duties on tonnage, 730; moves power of inferior officers to make appointments, 733; favors amendments by convention, 735; wants all States to sign constitution, 742; signs Constitution, 951, 1002.

Morris, Lewis, signs Declaration of Independence, 26.

Morris, Robert, Pennsylvania, signs Declaration of Independence, 26; signs Articles of Confederation, 36; appointed delegate from Pennsylvania, 63, 64, 85; character sketch of, 101; attends, 109, 746; nominates Washington for president of convention, 109, 746; favors life term for Senators, 278; signs Constitution, 951, 1002.

Morton, John, signs Declaration of Independence, 26.

Muhlenberg, Frederich, signs resolution submitting 12 amendments to Constitution, 1065.

Name of Government, agreed to, 482.

National Government, considered, 120, 121, 122, 237, 240; agreed to, 122.

Naturalization, discussed, 876.

Navigation acts, by two-thirds vote, 594; referred to committee, 595; debated, 633; clause agreed to, 638; not to be passed without concurrence of two-thirds of legislature, rejected, 736, 950.

Navy, power to raise, agreed to, 568.

Negative, to extend to resolutions, rejected, 551; on bills, 10 days allowed for, 551; for legislature to negative State laws, proposed, 604, 758, 855, 916; rejected, 605, 759, 856; mutual negative for each House, struck out, 873; for Executive, to be overruled by three-fourths, agreed to, 551; for Executive and judiciary, proposed, 752; postponed, 752; absolute negative for Executive, 753, 847; rejected, 848; to be vested jointly in Executive and judiciary, rejected, 852; on laws, plan, 549; on paper emissions, 916.

Neilson, John, appointed delegate from New Jersey, 61, 85.

Nelson, Thomas, jr., signs Declaration of Independence, 26.

New Hampshire, attendance of delegates requested, 305, 828; rejected, 306, 829; representation of, discussed, 346; not reduced, 348.

New Jersey plan, introduced, 769; discussed, 770; rejected in committee, 785; introduced, 857; notes of Paterson used in preparation of, 884.

New States, government of, 563.

North Carolina, representation of, 729.

Oath of allegiance, provision for, postponed, 156; to support Union, debated, 433; agreed to, 434; to support Constitution, affirmation permitted, 646; to be required of State officials, postponed, 754; discussed, 765; agreed to, 765; national legislators should be sworn to preserve State constitutions, agreed to, 765.

Oath of office, for President, 622; amended, 944.

1102

Otis, Samuel A., would refer ratifications to committee, 1060.
Paca, William, signs Declaration of Independence, 26.
Paine, Robert Treat, signs Declaration of Independence, 26.
Pardons, power to grant, 620; impeachments excepted, 620; power of for President, 731.
Parker, John, votes against New York resolution for revising Articles of Confederation, 45; would refer ratifications to committee, 1061.
Patents, protection of, 666; agreed to, 667.
Paterson, William, New Jersey, appointed delegate from New Jersey, 61, 62, 85; character sketch of, 100; notes of in federal convention, 879–912; variant texts of plan for Constitution, 967–978; attends, 109, 746; moves resumption of clause relating to rule of suffrage in legislature, 180; opposes proportional representation in legislature, 181; moves question of representation be postponed, 184; proposes plan, 203, 204, 769, 857; supports and explains principles of his plan, 205, 771, 772, 773; would urge New Hampshire to send delegates to convention, 306; on committee on representation, 323, 840, 872; thinks small States have been treated badly, 329; favors equal vote for States in Senate, 340; opposes number and wealth as basis of representation, 345; favors adjournment, 386; proposes election of Executive by electors, 412; moves reconsideration of apportionment plan according to quotas of contribution or numbers of inhabitants, 760; opposes suffrage resolution, 761; will present plan for federal system, 769; on question of representation in lower House, 857; opposes power of lower House to originate money bills, 871; notes on Virginia plan, 879; notes on report of committee of whole, 880; notes used in preparation of New Jersey plan, 884; notes for speech of June 9, 887, 890, 891, 892; notes for speech of June 16, 893; notes for speech, 896; notes for speech of July 9, 898; contrasts plan for government, 918; signs Constitution, 951, 1002.
Paterson's plan (*see also* New Jersey plan); text, 204; debated, 207, 226; representation postponed, 234; referred to committee of detail, 449, 471.
Peace, power of, discussed, 562.
Pendleton, Nathaniel, appointed delegate from Georgia, 84, 86.
Penn, John, signs Declaration of Independence, 26; signs Articles of Confederation, 37.
Pickering, John, appointed delegate from New Hampshire, 56, 85.
Pierce, William, Georgia, votes against New York resolution for revising Articles of Confederation, 45; appointed delegate from Georgia, 82, 84, 86; notes of, in federal convention, 87–95; character sketches by, 96–108; character sketch of, 108; attends, 124; favors election of one branch of legislature by people, 164; moves national compensation of legislature, agreed to, 194; moves three-year term for Senate, 196; thinks State distinctions must be sacrificed, 303; moves three-year term for lower House, 767; favors National Government, 826; on representation, 907.
Pinckney, Charles, South Carolina, appointed delegate from South Carolina, 79, 86; character sketch of, 107; plan for Constitution, 964–966; attends, 109, 746; favors election of Executive by national legislature, 91; on powers of Executive, 133; proposes seven-year term for Executive, 134; favors single Executive, 131, 144, 752, 845; thinks Executive may consult heads of departments in revisionary power, 166; favors election of Executive by legislature, 393; opposes impeachability of Executive, 417, 419; would limit executive powers, 421; moves Executive be ineligible for continuous reelection, 452; opposes executive council, 567; moves Executive be elected by majority vote, 611; thinks Senate will elect President, 663; objects to eventual election of Executive by Senate, 668; favors motion that two-thirds of Senate be present when voting for Executive, 677; proposes mode of nomination and election of Senators, 89; favors appointment of members of first branch of legislature by State legislatures, 95; moves to strike out nomination for Senate by State legislatures, 129; opposes power of legislature to pass laws where States are incompetent, 129; proposes election of lower House by State legislatures, 159, 755, 850, 914; rejected, 756, 852; proposes that members of first branch be chosen as State

legislatures may direct, 793, 920; supports motion, 794; agreed to, 794; wants proportional representation in Senate, 173; moves negative of National Legislature on State laws, 174, 758; rejected, 759; moves reconsideration of negative on State laws by National Legislature, 855; agreed to, 855; favors negative on State laws, 855; moves State be divided into classes as basis for representation, 179; moves elimination of clause prohibiting reelection to first branch for number of years, agreed to, 195; opposes elections to legislature by State legislatures, 252; favors four-year term for Senate, 279, 809; opposes six-year term for Senators, 810; opposes equal vote in Senate, 318; thinks suffrage equality for States in Senate is wrong, 837; recommends consideration of his plan as compromise, 837; thinks numbers best basis for representation, 333; thinks Congress has no right to admit new States, 334; favors equality of blacks in representation, 367; proposes plan for representation in Senate, 376, 872; favors negative on State laws by legislature, 391, 916; on qualifications for legislature, 458; moves increase in representation of South Carolina, 495; defends slave representation, 498; favors 14 years' citizenship for Senators, 504; thinks States should fix time of election to legislature, 509; thinks property qualification for legislature should be fixed, 511; opposes ineligibility of members of legislature to offices, 540, 563, 657, 659; moves postponement of question of eligibility of legislators, 543; would strike out ineligibility clause of legislators to State offices, agreed to, 800; opposes war power for legislature, 561; favors power in Senate, 562, rejected, 563; moves sundry powers for Congress, 564; favors power over militia, 570; moves power in legislature to negative State law, 604; would reconsider mode of election of lower branch, 752; opposes apportionment of representatives according to number, 866; moves legislature judge privileges of members, 665; opposes Senate for trial of impeachments, 692; opposes three-fourths vote to overrule Executive veto, 715; favors increase in representation of North Carolina, 729; favors appointment of judiciary by legislature, 154; opposes revisionary power of judiciary, 167; moves appointment of judiciary by legislature, 198; withdrawn, 199; suggests appointment of judges by Senate, 430; opposes judiciary in revisionary power, 548; to require opinions of judges on questions of law, 572; would preserve writ of habeas corpus, 572, 627; insists on jury trial in civil cases, 733; moves appointment of judiciary by legislature, 768; opposes joint negative for judiciary and Executive, 852; thinks originating of money bills is no concession, 336; opposes money bills in first branch of legislature, 523; insists on slave trade, 589; defends slavery, 591; declares South Carolina insists on slave trade, 593; wants slave trade until 1808, 616; moves fugitive slaves be delivered up, 631; on committee on rules, 110; moves committee to superintend minutes, 114; introduces plan for government, 119, 806; asks if State governments are to be abolished, 120; upholds powers of convention, 213; speech, 267; would extend qualifications for office to Executive and judiciary, 460; opposes disqualification of debtors, 464; thinks capital may be in large town, 465; on naturalization laws, 527; favors appointment of treasurer by joint ballot, 558; favors power to suppress rebellion without application of State legislature, 560; favors assumption of State debts, 565; proposes provision for liberty of press, 572, 726; moves power to establish offices, 575; moves acceptance of presents from foreign governments be prohibited, 602; favors appointment of State executives by General Government, 605; moves establishment of bankruptcy laws, 632; moves regulation of commerce by two-thirds vote, 633; favors power to pass navigation acts, 634, 944; moves religious tests be forbidden, 647; thinks Constitution does not need approval of Congress, 651; would exclude Senate from appointing power, 684; moves an address to people, 701; proposes university, 725; opposes provision against army, 725; favors occasional publication of expenditures, 727; opposes second convention, 737; discusses condition of country, 803; discusses plans of government, 903; signs Constitution, 951, 1002.

Pinckney, Charles Cotesworth, South Carolina, appointed delegate from South Carolina, 80, 86; character sketch of, 107; attends, 109, 746; thinks elections to national legislature by people impracticable, 164; favors election of members of lower House by State legislatures, 95; opposes ineligibility of members of first branch of legislature, 262; moves that first branch of legislature be elected as State legislatures may direct, 252; rejected, 254; moves first branch be elected by people but in such mode as the State legislatures may direct, agreed to, 254; moves Senate be paid no salary, 284, 813; rejected, 813; favors State compensation of Senators, 286; proposes compromise on vote in Senate, 318; favors reduction in representation of New Hampshire, 346; would increase representation of Southern States, 347; moves increase in representation of South Carolina, 348; 495; moves increase in representation of Georgia, 349; moves 10 years' citizenship for Members Senate, 508; thinks salaries of judges may be changed, 624; thinks provision for jury trials unnecessary, 733; thinks Senators be eligible for State offices, 814; moves committee be appointed to consider representation in both branches of legislature, 837; favors election of lower House by State legislatures, 851; thinks Senate may originate money bills, 200; thinks originating money bills in lower House is no concession, 338; on slave representation, 354; insists on security for slaves, 441; admits slave trade is price of navigation laws, 618; wishes provision for property in slaves, 631; doubts authority of convention, 121, 927; would establish a more effective government, 121, 929; favors retention of State power, 254; seconds motion for ratio of representation in proportion to all free inhabitants and three-fifths others, agreed to, 189; favors taxation by representation, 303; thinks rule of wealth should be fixed, 364; favors census, 367; opposes adjournment, 386; would extend qualifications for office to Executive and judiciary, 460; on committee on assumption of State debts, 566; favors army, 568; favors power over militia, 569, 600; on committee on navigation acts, 595; would forbid religious test, 647; opposes election of treasurer by legislature, 723; announces support of Constitution, 744; favors revision of Articles of Confederation, 749; favors National Government, 774; signs Constitution, 951, 1002.

Pinckney, Thomas, Governor of South Carolina, 78, 79, 80, 81.

Pinckney plan, text of, 964–966; introduced, 748, 806; referred to committee of detail, 448, 471.

Piracies, law and punishment of, discussed, 558; punishment expunged, 559; agreed to, 559; power to define, 559; clause struck out, 723.

Ports of entry, State consent to, proposed, 619; regulation of, 654.

Post offices, establishment of, power agreed to, 556.

Prayers, in convention, proposed, 295.

Preamble to constitution, agreed to, 482, 934.

Prentis, Joseph, speaker of Virginia House of Delegates, 70.

Presents, from foreign governments, prohibited, 603.

Press, liberty of, to be inviolable, proposed, rejected, 950.

Privileges, for citizens of States, clause agreed to, 631.

Property qualifications for office, clause agreed to, 462.

Public debt, power to regulate, 564.

Quorum, less than a majority proposed, 514; number, rejected, 517; discussed, 550; for Senate, two-thirds rejected, 690.

Randolph, Edmund, Virginia, appointed delegate to Annapolis convention, 38; attends Annapolis convention, 39, 43; appointed delegate from Virginia, 71, 72, 86; introduces plan for Constitution, 87; character sketch of, 105; attends, 109, 746; opening speech, 114; favors plural Executive, 91, 92, 132, 144, 751, 846, 913; opposes appointment of Executive by governors of States, 179, 760; opposes eligibility of Executive for second term, 411; favors restriction of Executive's power of appointment, 613; wants explanation of reasons for changing mode of election of Executive,

662; thinks eventual election of Executive should be in legislature, 664; opposes Executive pardoning power over treason, 732; favors appointment of Senators by members of first branch of National Legislature, 88; remarks upon difficulty of defining powers of National Legislature, 90; favors small Senate, 128; will not give indefinite powers to National Legislature, 130; favors seven-year term for Senate, 196; favors two-year term for first branch, 254, 794; opposes State compensation of legislature, 257; moves Senators go out in classes, 278, 809; agreed to, 809; favors commitment of question of representation, 321, 345; on committee on representation, 334; wants legislature to fix basis of representation, 365; moves reconsideration of representation, 371; favors appointment of committee to consider representation in legislature, 839; opposes police power of legislature, 389; opposes fixing time of meeting of legislature, 485; thinks vacancies in Senate may be filled by Executive, 501; moves to postpone question of vote in Senate, 502; opposes 14 years' citizenship for Senate, 506; agrees to 9 years' citizenship for Senate, 508; moves legislature compel attendance, 517; approves expulsion of members of legislature by two-thirds vote, 517; thinks one member may call for yeas and nays, 518; proposes four years' citizenship for lower House, 523; agrees to allow eligibility of legislators to army or navy, 542; favors ineligibility of members of legislature to office, 658; doubts if legislature should judge privileges of members, 665; opposes Vice President for President of Senate, 682; would exclude Senate from pardoning power, 732; favors payment of legislators from National Treasury, 795; moves that legislature consist of two branches, agreed to, 930; opposes equality in Senate, 938; moves that jurisdiction of judiciary extend to cases involving revenue and impeachment, 198; agreed to, 199; favors appointment of judiciary by Senate, 402; favors inferior judicial tribunals, 405; favors appointment of judiciary by Executive with concurrence of Senate, 430; favors fixed compensation for judiciary, 624; defines jurisdiction of judiciary, 768; would reconsider question of money bills, 500; favors money bills in lower House, 522; opposes amendment of money bills by Senate, 528; would restrict money bills to first branch, 534; moves to extend negative to resolutions, 552; moves to consider clause for National Government, 120, 926; agreed to, 926; pleads for National Government, 775; proposes National Government, 927; opposes consent of legislature in amending Constitution, 191; question postponed, 191; opposes oaths from State officials to observe Constitution, 191; upholds national plan, 213; accepts supreme government instead of national, 241; proposes sermon on Fourth of July, 296; thinks new States should not be discriminated against, 331; opposes referring to committee question of vote in Senate, 335; opposes reduction of representation in New Hampshire, 348; moves census as basis for representation, 351; favors census, 353; explains adjournment proposal, 386; favors preservation of republican constitutions in States, 407, 765; moves that States must have republican government, 408; opposes ratification by legislatures, 434; defines treason, 576; moves power to define piracies, 559; favors power to punish piracies, 559; approves British definition of treason, 577; would commit question of slave trade, 594; insists on provision to fulfil engagements of old Government, 598; favors national control of militia, 601; moves provision for State debts, 608; thinks debts are valid, 615; moves mutual recognition by States of public acts, 632; on committee on mutual recognition of public acts by States, 633; disapproves portions of Constitution, 637; proposes ratification by nine States, 647; favors State conventions to amend Constitution, 653; thinks powers too loosely defined, 656; favors second convention, 698, 701, 736, 951; states objections to Constitution, 700; moves to strike out servitude, 719; favors power to grant charters of incorporation, 724; regards armies as dangerous in time of peace, 725; proposes resolutions for new Government, 747, 879, 926; moves correction of Articles of Confederation, withdraws motion, 748; would require oath of allegiance by State officials, 765; moves fourth resolve be divided, 806; on defects of confederation, 903; thinks people in favor of Virginia plan, 920; cites defects of confederation, 923; thinks a federal union will not suffice, 927; explains third resolution, 928; gives reasons for not signing, 741, 743; does not sign, 745, 952.

Ratification of Constitution, by conventions, proposed and discussed, 156, 754, 755, 911; agreed to, 766; by plurality of States, proposed, 157; by nine States, proposed 157; postponed, 157; agreed to, 651, 945; by legislature, rejected, 439; by conventions, agreed to, 439; method debated, 434, 647, 720; method agreed to, 653.

Ratification of:

Delaware, 1009.
Pennsylvania, 1010.
New Jersey, 1011–1014.
Georgia, 1014–15.
Connecticut, 1016–17.
Massachusetts, 1018–1020.
Maryland, 1021–22.
South Carolina, 1022–1024.
New Hampshire, 1024–1027.
Virginia, 1027–1034.
New York, 1034–1044.
North Carolina, 1044–1051.
Rhode Island, 1052–1059.

Read, George, Delaware, signs Declaration of Independence, 26; attends Annapolis convention, 39, 43; appointed delegate from Delaware, 66, 85; character sketch of, 102–103; attends, 109, 746; favors absolute negative for Executive, 486; moves President of Senate be empowered to vote in case of tie in election of Executive, 611; opposes separate clause for reelection of Executive, 673; fears small States may have no vote for Executive, 681; would postpone question of representation, 123; motion agreed to, 124; favors fair representation in Senate, 274; proposes life term for Senators, 278, 809; moves nine-year term for Senators, 279, 810; rejected, 813; on committee on representation, 346; favors increase in representation, 350; would not shackle legislature, 356; opposes seven years' residence requirement for members of legislature, 493; thinks origination of money bills no concession, 502; objects to extending judiciary power to equity, 622; moves establishment of more effective government, 121, 929; wishes strong National Government, 164; opposes amendment to territorial guaranty clause, 190, 765; wishes to extinguish State attachments, 281; discusses rights of States, 299; thinks State governments will not last, 756; thinks State governments must be demolished, 851; wishes representation of Delaware increased, 344; opposes taxation by representation, 369; opposes paper money, 557; favors appointment of treasurer by Executive, 558; favors appointment of militia officers by State executives, 571; would commit clause on slave trade and tax on exports, 593; opposes direct taxes, 726; on committee on imposts, 620; signs Constitution, 951, 1002.

Read, James, would refer ratifications to committee, 1061.

Rebellion in State, powers to subdue, discussed, 560; amended, 561; rejected, 561.

Recognition of public acts by States, clause agreed to, 656.

Reed, Joseph, signs Articles of Confederation, 36.

Religious test, 572; forbidden, 647.

Representation, national, proportional, discussed, 123, 180, 184; postponed, 124; agreed to, 189; limitation of, proposed, 581; in lower House, considered, 856, 865, 867, 900, 951; in Senate, considered, 868, 870, 907; agreed to, 938; in Senate, Pinckney's motion rejected, 872; in National Legislature, considered, 899, 930; committee on, appointed, 872; report of, 872; no State to be deprived of equal representation in Senate, 950.

Representatives, House of.  See Legislature, House of Representatives.

Republican constitution, guarantee of, discussed, 406.

Republican government for States, postponed, 155.

Revenue bills, clause agreed to, 693.

Revision of acts, by Executive and judiciary, proposed, 548, 752; postponed, 753.

Rhode Island, letter from, 113; representation of, 739.

Roberdeau, Daniel, signs Articles of Confederation, 36.

Rodney, Caesar, signs Declaration of Independence, 26.

1107

Ross, George, signs Declaration of Independence, 26.
Rules for convention, reported, debated, and agreed to, 110, 113, 923.
Rush, Benjamin, signs Declaration of Independence, 26.
Rutledge, Edward, signs Declaration of Independence, 26.
Rutledge, John, South Carolina, appointed delegate from South Carolina, 78, 86; character sketch of, 106–107; attends, 109, 746; seconds nomination of Washington for president of convention, 109; favors single Executive, 131, 845; suggests election of Executive by Senate, 136; moves single Executive, 144; favors election of Executive by electors, 414; favors election of Executive by joint ballot of legislature, 609; favors election of Executive by legislature, 668; moves eventual election of Executive be limited to 13 candidates, 672; would limit emoluments of Executive, 731; opposes powers of legislature to pass laws where State legislatures are incompetent, 129; favors election to lower House by State legislatures, 159; moves States be divided into classes as basis for representation, 179; favors wealth as basis for representation in lower House, 184; moves addition of quotas of contribution to motion relating to representation, postponed, 189; moves two-year term for members of first branch, 192, 766; moves Senators serve without compensation, rejected, 197; favors election to legislature by State legislatures, 253; favors ineligibility of members of first branch to office, 263; moves to consider suffrage in legislature, 287; on committee on representation, 323, 840, 872; favors property qualification for representation, 332; moves postponement of ratio of representation, 334; on committee on representation, 334, 346; moves reduction in representation of New Hampshire, 346; opposes increase in representation, 350; favors wealth as basis for representation, 356; moves reconsideration of money bills and equal vote in Senate, 375; wants powers of legislature defined, 385; favors seven years' residence for members of legislature, 493; proposes three years' residence for members of legislature, 494; favors long term of citizenship for Senate, 508; thinks States must fix time of election to legislature, 509; thinks property qualifications for legislature should be fixed, 512; moves qualifications for legislature be same as for State legislatures, 514; on journals of legislature, 519; thinks Senate should participate in money bills, 534; favors postponement of money bills, 547; moves consideration of mode of election to Senate, 756; thinks representation should depend on contribution, 763; postponed, 764; favors election of lower House as States may direct, 793; moves payment of legislators from National Treasury, 796; rejected, 797; opposes amendment to eligibility clause, 800; thinks representatives should be ineligible to offices for one year after expiration of term, 803; thinks property should be basis of representation in lower House, 870; on representation in lower House, 900; favors appeals from State courts to national judiciary, 94; wants one Supreme Court, 153; opposes inferior tribunals in judiciary, 157; opposes revisionary power for judiciary, 429; objects to power of removal of judges, 623; opposes appointment of judiciary by Executive, 849; proposes supreme tribunal, 849; opposes requesting New Hampshire to send delegates, 306; opposes adjournment, 386; opposes provision against domestic violence, 408; on committee of detail, 448; delivers report of committee of detail, 471, 931; opposes limiting franchise to freeholders, 491; thinks foreigners should be ineligible to office, 525; favors measure to guard funds, 565; moves committee to consider assumption of State debts, 565; moves longer sessions of convention, 566; opposes tax on importation of slaves, 588; insists on slave trade, 593; introduces additions to report, 595; moves Constitution be supreme law, 603; opposes negative on State laws, 604; opposes provision for controversies between States, 608; favors prohibition of retrospective laws, 629; would preserve habeas corpus, 627; on committee of mutual recognition of public acts by States, 633; favors navigation acts, 637; thinks States can not be divided without their consent, 641; proposes bankruptcy laws, 655; moves treaties shall require two-thirds vote in Senate, 689; opposes amendment to slavery clause, 696; thinks

Congress need not approve Constitution, 700; proposes suspension of impeached persons, 721; moves appointment of treasurer by Executive, 722; opposes address to people, 728; favors seven-year residence for suffrage right, 876; signs Constitution, 951, 1002.

Scheurman, James, attends Annapolis convention, 39, 43; votes against New York resolution for revising Articles of Confederation, 45.

Scudder, Nathaniel, signs Articles of Confederation, 36.

Seat of government, provision for, discussed, 464; jurisdiction over, 563, 666; clause agreed to, 667.

Senate. *See* Legislature; Senate.

Sherman, Roger, Connecticut, signs Declaration of Independence, 26; signs Articles of Confederation, 36; appointed delegate from Connecticut, 58, 85; character sketch of, 97; attends, 120; thinks Executive must carry out will of legislature, 132; favors election of Executive by legislature, 134, 392; favors three-year term for Executive, 135; thinks legislature should have power to remove Executive, 142; proposes executive council, 146; favors eligibility of Executive for second term, 396; opposes tenure during good behavior for Executive, 397; opposes election of Executive by joint ballot of legislature, 609; opposes Executive's power of appointment, 613; favors eventual election of Executive from seven candidates, 671; wants single Executive with council, 752; wants greater powers for legislature, 121; opposes election of first branch by people, 125; favors election of one member of Senate by each State legislature, 129; seconds motion to elect Senate by State legislatures, 168; would base proportion of suffrage in first branch on number of free inhabitants, 184; moves each State have one vote in Senate, 189; rejected, 190; opposes requiring oath from State officials to observe constitution, 191; moves members of lower House be elected annually, 192; approves five years for Senate term, 196; favors unicameral legislature, 246; favors election to legislatures by State legislatures 253, 850; accepts biennial election to lower House, 256; favors State compensation for legislature, 258, 795, 800; opposes ineligibility of Members of lower House to offices, 262, 264; favors six-year term for Senators, 278; opposes seven-year term for Senators, 278; wants frequent elections, 281; thinks States have equal rights, 294; thinks Congress needs more power, 311; would commit question of representation in Senate, 318; favors equal vote in Senate, 339; opposes ratio of representation, 343; on committee on representation, 346; opposes increase in representation, 349; would not shackle legislature, 352; favors numbers as basis of representation, 356; is satisfied with clause for representation of negroes, 360; thinks legislature should fix representation, 370; insists on equal vote in Senate, 377; thinks legislature will require quotas from States, 382; wants powers of legislature defined, 388; favors fixing time of meeting of legislature, 485; wishes members of legislature to be inhabitants, 492; moves to limit representation, 496; thinks legislature may regulate elections, 510; opposes yeas and nays, 518; on journals of legislature, 519, 520; favors ineligibility of members of legislature to offices, 540; thinks both Nation and State may pay members of legislature, 544; thinks members of legislature ineligible to offices with increased salaries, 657; thinks legislature should vote by States in electing Executive, 673; favors inclusion of Senate in treaty-making power, 683; moves treaties require majority of Senate, 690; opposes reconsideration of representation question, 694; moves addition to amendment clause, 696; thinks Congress has no power over press, 726; favors appointment of members of first branch of legislature by State legislatures, 87; opposes election of Senators by Members of lower House, 89; opposes unrestricted veto on State legislation, 90; favors election of Senators by State legislatures, 757; moves lower House be chosen in proportion to number, 763; rejected, 764; favors one-year term for members of first branch, 766; opposes seven years, 767; favors election of first branch as States may direct, 793; favors annual election of lower House, 794; opposes amendment to eligibility clause, 802; favors four-year term for Senators, 811; approves appointment of committee to consider representation in legislature, 837; would let legislature determine number of executives, 845; thinks two branches of legislature unnecessary, 861; on representation in Senate, 908, 910; would vest legislative powers in States in Congress, 922; opposes inferior tribunals in national judiciary, 158; wishes power to remain with State governments, 160; moves appointment of judiciary by legislature, 198; withdraws motion, 199; favors appointment of judiciary by Senate, 401; favors appointment of judges by Senate, 402; would use State tribunals whenever possible, 405; favors power to remove judges, 623; would extend judicial powers to land cases, 626; on appellate jurisdiction of Supreme Court, 626; on trial by jury, 626; thinks Supreme Court should not try President, 692; moves postponement of money bills, 342; would consider money bills and vote in Senate together, 375; favors origination of money bills in first branch, 667; defends slave representation, 496, 498; would permit slave trade, 589, 593; objects to use of word "slaves," 617; favors delivering up of fugitive slaves, 632; opposes negative of Executive on laws, 148; on power of legislature to negative State laws, 176; opposes negative on State laws by legislatures, 390, 391; favors mutual negative by both branches of legislature, 482; opposes negative on laws for judiciary, 550; opposes negative on State laws, 604; favors two-third vote to overrule Executive veto, 714; opposes direct taxation, 388; opposes taxation of exports, 555; opposes tax on exports, 585; opposes taxing men as property, 618; thinks slave tax does not discourage importation, 618; would allow States to lay embargoes, 630; would allow legislature to tax imports, 630; opposes ratification by conventions, 156; thinks Constitution can be ratified by State legislatures, 156; favors prayers in convention, 296; would not discriminate against western country, 374; thinks United States under no obligations to foreigners, 526; opposes election of treasurer by joint ballot, 558; favors election of treasurer by legislature, 723; on question of State debts, 565; on committee on assumption of State debts, 566; moves amendment relative to clause on direct taxation, 581; withdraws motion, 581; moves payment of old debts, 616; favors State control of militia, 569, 571, 599; moves uniformity of militia, 600; opposes State appointment of lower militia officers, 602; favors State power over treason, 579; moves contributions of States according to representation, 582; thinks provision for State controversies unnecessary, 608; on committee on imposts, 619; would regulate commerce, 626; would prohibit paper money, 628; thinks States may lay embargoes, 629; favors navigation acts, 484; favors equality of new States, 638; thinks the State can not be dismembered, 639; moves admission and formation of new States, 642; on claims to western country, 644; thinks religious test unnecessary, 647; thinks 10 States may ratify Constitution, 647; discusses Virginia plan, 821; admits failure of Federal requisitions on States, 832; thinks all States must agree to Constitution, 649; moves ratification by 10 States, 651; would proceed to experiment with new government, 790; brings in report on commercial regulations, 653; moves committee to consider postponed propositions, 655; on committee on postponed measures, 655; favors Vice-President for President of Senate, 682; favors limitations on size of Army, 666; would submit Constitution to Congress, 698; thinks State bills of rights still in force, 716; favors occasional publication of Federal expenditures, 727; believes power of Federal Government supreme in regulation of trade, 731; favors appointment of inferior officers by President, by courts of law, and by heads of departments, 733; fears power of amendment, 734; would strike out article 5 with regard to amendments, 736; motion lost, 736; moves no State shall be affected in its internal administration or deprived of equality in Senate, 735; signs Constitution, 951, 1002.

Slave trade, till 1808 proposed, 616; confined to States already permitting it, 617.

Slavery, word "servitude" struck out, 719.

Slaves, importation of, 588, 508; importation tax on, agreed to, 618; delivery of fugitive, moved, 631.
Smith, James, signs Declaration of Independence, 26.
Smith, Jonathan B., signs Articles of Confederation, 36.
Smith, Melancthon, votes in favor of New York resolution for revising Articles of Confederation, 45.
Smith, Meriwether, appointed delegate to Annapolis convention, 38.
South Carolina, representation from, 348, 495.
Spaight, Richard Dobbs, appointed delegate from North Carolina, 73, 74, 76, 77, 86; character sketch of, 106; attends, 109; moves rule allowing revision of questions, 113; moves question of election of Executive, 441; favors election of electors for Executive by State legislatures, 447; moves election of President be limited to 13 candidates, 672; moves seven-year term for Executive, 676; moves six-year term for President, 676; moves electors meet at seat of government, 677; favors representation by population, 123; thinks members of second branch should be chosen by State legislatures, 88, 127; withdraws motion, 127; moves term of Members of Senate be seven years, 196; agreed to, 197; fears seat of government will be in New York, 521; favors navigation acts, 635; proposes limitation on treaties of peace, 688; signs Constitution, 951, 1002.
Sparhawk, John, speaker of the New Hampshire House of Representatives, 56.
Stockton, Richard, signs Declaration of Independence, 26.
Stone, Thomas, signs Declaration of Independence, 26.
Strong, Caleb, Massachusetts, appointed delegate from Massachusetts, 56, 57, 85; character sketch of, 97; attends, 110; favors one-year term for legislature, 255, 863; would commit question of representation in Senate, 327; favors equal vote in Senate and money bills in lower house, 379; thinks Executive may be elected by State legislatures, 442; proposes $4 per day as compensation for members of legislature, 545; moves Senate have power to amend money bills, 546; would refer question of representation in first branch to committee, 840; opposes seven-year term for Executive, 847.
Style and arrangement, committee on, 694.
Suffrage, restraint of, 487; limitation to freeholders, rejected, 491; discussed, 491, 873.
Sumptuary laws, proposed, 574; rejected, 575; committee on, 718.
Surrender of criminals, by States, clause agreed to, 631.
Suspension of acts, by Executive, proposed and rejected, 753.
Taxation, direct, by representation, agreed to, 364; according to representation, rejected, 370, 583; considered, 389; meaning, 580; apportionment considered, 448; proportioned on representation, 582; proportion agreed to, 581; by requisition, proposed, 583; rejected, 584.
Taxation and slave trade, question committed, 594.
Taylor, George, signs Declaration of Independence, 26.
Telfair, Edward, signs Articles of Confederation, 37.
Thornton, Matthew, signs Declaration of Independence, 26.
Tonnage, duties on, not to be levied by States without consent of Congress, agreed to, 950.
Treason, pardon of, referred to committee, 701.
Treasurer, appointment of, 558; appointment by joint ballot, agreed to, 558; to be appointed by legislature, 722; rejected, 723.
Treaties, power of Senate over, 547; to be laws, 603; power to make, 605, 606, 607, 683; power of Senate over, agreed to, 607; question committed, 607; participation of Senate in, 685; of peace, to be made by majority, rejected, 686; reconsidered, 688; two-thirds of Senate to concur if affecting territorial rights, 688; may be made by majority of Senate, 689; do not require two-thirds of Senate, rejected, 689, 690; to require majority of whole Senate, rejected, 690; with consent of two-thirds of Senate

agreed to, 690; forbidden to States, 727; to receive sanction of legislature, proposed, 942; committed, 943.
Tucker, St. George, appointed delegate to Annapolis convention from Virginia, 38; attends Annapolis convention, 39, 43.
Tucker, Thomas T., would refer ratifications to committee, 1061.
University, power to establish, 563; rejected, 725; to be established by Congress, rejected, 950.
Van Dyke, Nicholas, signs Articles of Confederation, 37.
Vermont, admission of, 641–642.
Vice President, powers of, reported, 661; method of choosing, 662; to be President of Senate, discussed, 682; agreed to, 683.
Virginia convention, preamble and resolution proposing independence, 19–20.
Virginia plan, proposed, 114, 747; discussed, 120; committee of whole, report on, 201, 785; favorably reported, 234; committee discussion finished, 768; report prepared, postponed, 769; notes of Paterson on, 879.
Walton, George, signs Declaration of Independence, 26; appointed delegate from Georgia, 84, 86.
Walton, John, signs Articles of Confederation, 37.
War, power to declare, discussed, 561; agreed to, 562; provision to include letters of marque, 665; States forbidden to engage in, 731.
Washington, George, Virginia, appointed delegate to federal convention from Virginia, 71, 86; character sketch of, 104; attends, 109, 746; elected president of convention, 110, 746, 923; apologizes for lack of experience, 747; favors increased representation, 741; signs Constitution, 951, 1001; sends letter to Congress transmitting Constitution, 1004; signs resolution submitting Constitution to Congress, 1006.
Weights and measures, power over, 555.
Wentworth, John, jr., signs Articles of Confederation, 36.
West, Benjamin, appointed delegate from New Hampshire, 56, 85.
Western country, representation of, 371; dangers from, 372; discrimination against, rejected, 375; encouragement of, opposed, 631; claim to, 644.
Western States, admission of, 638.
Whipple, William, signs Declaration of Independence, 26.
Williams, John, signs Articles of Confederation, 37.
Williams, William, signs Declaration of Independence, 26.
Williamson, Hugh, North Carolina, appointed delegate from North Carolina, 77, 86; character sketch of, 106; attends, 109, 746; favors election of Executive by National Legislature, 92; opposes election of Executive by electors, 137; moves impeachability of Executive, 144; favors ineligibility of Executive for second term, 414; favors six-year term for Executive, 415; proposes Executive electors based on number of representatives, 417; proposes seven-year term and ineligibility for reelection for Executive, 442; favors election of Executive by people, 453; would postpone question of successor to Executive, 622; opposes eventual election of Executive by Senate, 663, 669; moves eventual election of Executive when less than one-third vote for same man, 671; moves that electors not voting be not counted, 672; favors separate clause for reelection of Executive, 673; moves six-year term for Executive, 676; moves seven-year term for Executive, 676; seconds motion that electors meet at seat of government, 677; thinks Executive with council is same as plural Executive, 846; proposes two-thirds vote of legislature for effective acts, 167; favors small Senate, 168; approves proportional representation in legislature, 184; favors State compensation of legislature, 257; would preserve State governments, 276; moves six-year term for Senators, 278, 809; favors compensation for Senators, 285; discusses eligibility of Senators to offices, 286; opposes ineligibility of Senators to State offices, 286; contends for equal sovereignty of States, 290; favors compromise on representation in Senate, 322; opposes report of committee on representation, 329;

favors numbers as basis of representation, 344; on committee on representation, 346; thinks southern representation too small, 347; approves counting blacks as three-fifths, 355; thinks representation of New Hampshire too high, 369; on representation in legislature, 899; favors small Senate, 440; opposes requirement of previous residence for members of legislature, 494; moves representation by taxation, 495; thinks Executive may fill vacancies in Senate, 501; proposes vacancies in Senate be arranged by legislatures, 501; favors long term of citizenship for Senate, 508; favors property qualifications for legislature, 513, proposes nine years citizenship for legislature, 524, 525; opposes eligibility of members of legislature to offices, 539; approves prohibition on States to lay imposts or duties on imports, 630; agrees to ineligibility of members of legislature to new offices, 657; moves ineligibility of members of legislature to new offices, 659; rejected, 659; thinks representation too small, 668; moves reconsideration of representation, 694, 720; opposes power of legislature to negative State laws, 175, 758; would modify mutual negative of both branches of legislature, 482; moves three-fourths vote to overrule Executive veto, 551; opposes negative on State laws, 604; moves two-thirds vote to overrule Executive veto, 713; thinks money bills should originate in Senate, 336; moves to reconsider question of money bills, 500; favors provision for money bills, 503; favors money bills in lower House, 523; moves to postpone question of money bills, 547; thinks convention has no funds to pay clergymen, 296; favors census, 353; suggests oath to support State governments, 433; favors ratification by conventions, 437; thinks passions are excited over question of capital, 465; opposes New York as seat of government, 521; opposes taxation of exports, 554, 584; thinks unlocated lands should be given up, 566; on committee on assumption of State debts, 566; would limit appropriations for army, 568; proposes State quotas by representation, 582; opposes taxation by representation, 583; opposes prohibition of slave trade, 592; on committee on navigation acts, 595; favors provision against ex post facto laws, 597; thinks provision for controversies between States necessary, 608; opposed to slavery, 617; on committee on imposts, 620; favors two-thirds vote for navigation acts, 635; says North Carolina is disposed to surrender western lands, 641; on committee on postponed measures, 655; opposes creation of Vice President, 682; proposes limitation on treaties of peace, 688; moves notice of treaties be sent to Senators, 690; fears too many laws, 714; proposes juries in civil cases, 716; suggests that letter be signed, instead of Constitution, 742; thinks oath of allegiance by State officials unnecessary, 765; declares all men have equal right in society, 821; on negative of State laws 855; questions power of large States to oppress the small, 906; signs Constitution, 951, 1002.

Wilson, James, Pennsylvania, signs Declaration of Independence, 26; appointed delegate to convention from Pennsylvania, 63, 64, 85; character sketch of, 101; attends 109, 746; favors single Executive, 91, 93; favors indirect election of Executive, 92; favors equality of Executive, judiciary, and legislature, 95; proposes single Executive, 131, 132, 133, 145, 752, 845; supports motion, 846; postponed, 846; seconds motion on powers of Executive, 133; favors election of Executive by people, 134, 135, 393, 412; proposes three-year term for Executive, 134, 847; opposes executive council, 146; moves revisionary power by Executive and judiciary, 152, 422, 548, 753, 756, 849; postponed, 753; rejected, 756; favors impeachability, 417, 421; favors long term for Executive, 444; suggests electors for Executive be chosen by lot, 445; wishes to postpone question of election of Executive, 448; insists on fixing principles of Executive, 456; favors joint ballot in legislature for Executive, 483; on qualifications for electors, 487; favors election of Executive by people, 610; thinks election of Executive difficult question, 664; would leave eventual election of Executive to legislature, 670; opposes eventual election of Executive by Senate, 673; favors an executive council, 687; would give Executive pardoning power over treason, 732; favors joint negative for Executive and judiciary, 752; proposes absolute negative for Executive, 847; rejected, 848; on Executive, 914; favors election of first branch by people, 126; favors election of both Houses by people, 128; favors popular election of first branch, 160; wants Senate elected by people, 168, 171; favors proportional representation in legislature, 183, 185, 189; moves right of suffrage in lower House should be based on equitable ratio, 185; agreed to, 189; moves ratio of representation be in proportion to all free inhabitants and three-fifths others, agreed to, 189; moves rule of suffrage in Senate be same as in lower House, agreed to, 190; favors two branches for legislature, 247; favors election to first branch by people, 253; favors annual election of lower House, 255; opposes fixed compensation for legislature, 258; favors national control of compensation of legislature, 258; opposes 25 years as minimum age for members of first branch, 260; favors ineligibility of members of first branch to offices, 263; opposes election of Senators by State legislatures, 274; favors six-year term for Senate, 279; on powers of Senate, 283; thinks Senate should be separated from States, 286; opposes equal vote of States in legislature, 294; opposes equal suffrage for States in Senate, 306; proposes porportion for Senate, 312; opposes commitment of question of representation, 322; thinks committee on representation exceeded powers, 324; would commit question of representation, 334; moves to consider vote in Senate, 334; insists on proportional representation, 340; opposes wealth as basis of representation, 356; opposes blacks in representation, 361; insists on proportional representation in Senate, 375, 381; would define powers of legislature, 389; favors continuance of Congress, 406: would fix time of meeting of legislature, 484; favors meeting of legislature in winter, 485; wants inhabitants as members of legislature, 492; opposes seven years' residence for legislators, 493; favors short residence for legislators, 493; moves to reconsider seven-year residence requirement, 500; thinks qualifications for legislature should not be fixed, 514; thinks quorum should not be fixed, 516; on right of dissent in legislature, 518; on journals of legislature, 520; proposes four years' citizenship for members of first branch, 523, 524; proposes seven years' citizenship for Senate, 528; opposes equal vote in Senate, 530; favors eligibility of members of legislature to office, 540, 542; favors revisionary power over acts, 550; opposes appointment by Senate, 603; opposes treaty making by Senate, 606; opposes ineligibility of legislators to office, 658; thinks legislature is judge of privileges of members, 665; wishes council to share in making appointments, 684; would include lower House in treaty power, 683; thinks majority of Senate may agree to treaties, 685; wants treaties approved by majority of Senate, 688; opposes power to convene either house of legislature, 694; proposes amendments be approved by two-thirds of States, 696; moves that Senate be elected from districts comprising several States, rejected, 751; favors popular election of members of first branch of legislature, 87; favors popular election of Senate, 88; thinks it impossible to enumerate powers of legislature, 90; opposes election of lower House by State legislatures, 755; opposes election of Senate by State legislatures, 756, 757; moves election of Senate by districts, 757; favors proportional suffrage, 762; moves representation be fixed according to number of free inhabitants, agreed to, 764; moves amendment to representation motion, 764; agreed to, 765; states considerations with regard to legislature, 790; opposes election of first branch as States may direct, 793; favors payment of legislators from National Treasury, 795; moves payment of legislators from National Treasury with stipends fixed by legislature, rejected, 796; favors expunction of ineligibility clause for representatives, 797, 800; favors amendment to eligibility clause, 802; discusses mode of appointment to Senate, 806; opposes appointment of Senators by State legislatures, 807; moves election of Senators by electors chosen by people, 807; opposes triennial rotation for Senate, 812; on eligibility of Senators to State offices, 814; opposes equal vote for States in Senate, 829; thinks wealth and numbers should determine representation in Senate, 829; proposes compromise on question of representation in Senate, 833; opposes appointment of committee on representation,

840; thinks committee on representation exceeded powers, 842; would vote separately on provisions of representation report, 842; favors popular election of lower House, 844; opposes election of lower House by State legislatures, 850; opposes election of Senators by State legislatures, 853; proposes popular election of Senators, rejected, 854; on representation in lower House, 857; favors two branches of legislature, 861; suggests appointment of one branch of State legislatures by National Government, 862; opposes election of representatives by State legislatures, 862; favors popular election of Senators, 863; opposes equal vote for States in Senate, 869; on representation in legislature, 899; on representation in lower House, 900; discusses representation in Senate, 907, 909, 910; opposes long term of citizenship for Senators, 938; thinks power of Senate too great, 947; favors ratification by a plurality of States, 157; favors absolute negative of Executive, 147, 149; approves power of legislature to negative State laws, 176, 916; thinks three-fourths of legislature can overrule Executive veto, 550; favors negative on State laws, 604; thinks money bills may originate in either branch, 335, 336; favors publicity of money bills, 338; thinks Senate should originate money bills, 500; opposes clause for money bills, 502, 504; thinks seven States may ratify Constitution, 647; thinks majority necessary for ratification, 651; proposes eight States may ratify Constitution, 647; thinks only States which ratify will be bound, 648; favors ratification by conventions, 754; thinks assent of Congress to Constitution not necessary, 699; opposes appointment of judiciary by legislature, 152; moves legislature have power to institute inferior tribunals, 158; would appoint judiciary by Executive, 400, 849; favors revisionary power for judiciary, 429; opposes power of removal of judiciary, 623; on judiciary, 849; proposes joint negative for judiciary and Executive, rejected, 852; moves inferior tribunals be appointed by legislature, agreed to, 755; moves appointment of Executive by judiciary, 754; favors taxation by representation, 365; favors taxation of exports, 554, 586, 588; moves amendment to direct taxation clause, 719; nominates Temple Franklin for secretary of convention, 110; would preserve the States, 164; contrasts Virginia and New Jersey plans, 210, 773, 774, 919; discusses National Government, 237, 239; thinks States will encroach on National Government, 249; opposes sending for delegates from New Hampshire, 306; supports rights of western country, 373; would guarantee republican constitution to States, 407; moves guarantee of republican constitution and against rebellion in States, 408; Government to act separately, 428; opposes oath to support Government, 433; on committee of detail, 448; would disqualify debtors from office, 462; favors liberal policy toward foreigners, 506; favors immigration, 524; on naturalization, 527, 877; defines duties and imposts, 552; opposes paper money, 557, 627; opposes definition of felonies, 559; would strike out punishment for piracies, 559; on definition of treason, 576; thinks proof of treason difficult, 578; favors sole power in legislature, 578; opposes slave trade, 592; favors navigation acts by majority vote, 594, 636; on ex post facto laws, 596, 942; thinks pardon before conviction may sometimes be granted, 621; would not allow new States to violate contracts, 628; opposes giving up fugitive slaves, 631; on committee on mutual recognition of public acts, 633; opposes power to divide a State, 640; thinks States can not be divided, 641; opposes motion on western country, 644; opposes defining law of nations, 723; favors power to cut canals, 724, 950; favors university, 725; favors occasional publication of expenditures, 727; proposes to hand journals to president of convention, 745; opposes negative on State laws, 759; favors National Government, 774; wants National Government, but would not entirely discard State government, 785; declares we are independent in name of the people, 787; favors National Government, 791; would designate powers of both National and State Governments, 792; would submit plan for National Government to people rather than to State legislatures, 797; would preserve State governments, 851; favors negative for legislature on State laws, 855; defends idea of General Government, 859; contrasts plans for Government, 901; signs Constitution, 951, 1002.

Wingate, Paine, would refer ratifications to committee, 1060.

Witherspoon, John, signs Declaration of Independence, 26; signs Articles of Confederation, 36.

Wolcott, Oliver, signs Declaration of Independence, 26; signs Articles of Confederation, 36.

Wythe, George, Virginia, signs Declaration of Independence, 26; appointed delegate to federal convention from Virginia, 71, 86; character sketch of, 104; attends, 109, 746; favors establishment and acceptance of general principles in convention before drafting detailed instrument, 90; on committee on rules, 110; reports rules, 110, 113; would vote on resolution for National Government, 927.

Yates, Abraham, would refer ratifications to committee, 1061.

Yates, Robert, New York, appointed delegate from New York, 59, 60, 85; character sketch of, 99; attends, 109, 746; on committee on representation, 323, 346; 840, 872; secret journal of debates in Federal convention, 746–843; favors two branches of legislature, 750; favors National Government on Federal principles, 841; leaves convention, 843.

Yeas and nays in legislature, considered, 518; on demand of one member, rejected, 518.

O

OF DAV